Encyclopedia of
THE PEOPLES OF ASIA AND OCEANIA

VOLUME I (A TO L)

Encyclopedia of
THE PEOPLES OF ASIA AND OCEANIA

VOLUME I (A TO L)

Barbara A. West

Facts On File
An imprint of Infobase Publishing

Encyclopedia of the Peoples of Asia and Oceania

Copyright © 2009 Barbara A. West

Facts On File, Inc.
An imprint of Infobase Publishing
132 West 31st Street
New York NY 10001

Library of Congress Cataloging-in-Publication Data

West, Barbara A., 1967–
Encyclopedia of the peoples of Asia and Oceania :/ Barbara A. West.
p. cm.
Includes bibliographical references and index.
ISBN-13: 978-0-8160-7109-8
ISBN-10: 0-8160-7109-8
1. Ethnology—Asia—Encyclopedias. 2. Ethnology—Oceania—Encyclopedias. I. Title.
GN625.W47 2009
305.80095—dc22   2008003055

Facts On File books are available at special discounts when purchased in bulk quantities for businesses, associations, institutions, or sales promotions. Please call our Special Sales Department in New York at (212) 967-8800 or (800) 322-8755.

You can find Facts On File on the World Wide Web at http://www.factsonfile.com

Text design by James Scotto-Lavino
Cover design by Salvatore Luongo
Illustrations by Jeremy Eagle and Lucidity Information Design

Printed in the United States of America

MV Hermitage 10 9 8 7 6 5 4 3 2 1

This book is printed on acid-free paper and contains 30 percent postconsumer recycled content.

CONTENTS

LIST OF ENTRIES

LIST OF ILLUSTRATIONS, MAPS, AND GRAPHS

LIST OF ILLUSTRATIONS

MAPS

GRAPHS

Asia and Oceania

PREFACE ❧

Encyclopedia of the Peoples of Asia and Oceania may seem on the surface to be a self-explanatory title; readers open its pages and find entries on people groups who live in these two regions. But this simply begs the questions, What is a people group? Which places are included in "Asia" and "Oceania"? In trying to answer these questions we thought about the intended audience for this set: students, nonspecialist researchers, and perhaps intelligent tourists who want to dig a bit deeper into the worlds they intend to visit. Based on their needs we made thousands of choices of whom to include, whom to leave out, what information to highlight, how to respond when information is contested, and many others that emerged during the research and writing process.

The first choice and probably the most important one concerned the list of peoples that would be included. There are many different ways that a people group can be defined, and creating our initial list of entries meant defining for ourselves what we mean by "a people." There are many different definitions to choose from: Racial groups are generally defined by physical traits, especially those visible to the naked eye. Ethnic groups are people groups defined by a common culture, history, and sense of community such as the Svan and Tu peoples. Language groups are people groups defined by use of a common dialect or language, or even classification within the same language family such as Turkic and Dravidian peoples. Archaeological complexes are ancient people groups who shared a common material culture as seen in their remains, such as the Yangshao and Longshan cultures. Nationalities, at least as used in this encyclopedia, are people groups that share citizenship within a modern political state, such as the Vietnamese nationality. Tribes are people groups that share membership in these kinds of political units, usually defined by kinship, language, geography, and culture, such as the Aeta. Religious and caste groups are peoples who share membership in these socially defined units, such as Jains.

In the creation of our entries list we have drawn from most of these kinds of people groups in order to provide the most comprehensive view of Asia and Oceania that we could in just two volumes. You will find entries for language, ethnic, national, tribal, and religious groups, as well as a number of archaeological complexes. However, because race is an arbitrary categorization not generally used by cultural anthropologists and is certainly not a useful category for defining how a group of people lives, we have not included racial groups here.

A more difficult choice was not to include "caste groups" from India, Nepal, Sri Lanka, or other countries as people groups in their own right. In many ways, castes can be seen as people groups as a result of their endogamy, the requirement that people from the same caste marry each other. However, membership in the widest possible classification of what in English is known as caste or what Indians call the four *varnas*—Brahmin, Kshatriya, Vaishya, Shudra, plus the former category of Untouchables, Harijans, or their preferred name, *Dalits*—tells us relatively little about the person or the group. In the distant past, Brahmins were Hindu priests who oversaw the religious rituals of the warriors and kings, who came from the Kshatriya *varna*. Vaishyas were merchants and Shudras were workers, servants, artisans, and others, who served the other three *varnas*. The first three of these groupings were considered twice-born and thus able to learn the sacred Sanskrit language and read the Vedas; the once-born Shudras were not. Those who were outside these four groups, whether through what was considered an impure occupation such as butchery, cleaning toilets, or dealing with human death, or membership in a non-Hindu tribal group, were likewise barred from learning Sanskrit but also from other forms of social interaction with the once- and twice-born such as eating together. Today membership in these very large groups is less tied to occupation than it once was; most Brahmins are not priests, not all members of the Indian army are Kshatriyas, and there are Dalits who have entered Indian politics, academia, and the professions. There are also a few poor and landless Brahmins and wealthy Dalits, although certainly this is not true of the majority of peoples in these two categories.

Below the level of the varnas are thousands of what we call castes in English or *jatis* in the Indian context and tens of thousands of subcastes, more subtly defined occupational groupings that have somewhat more meaning for understanding Indian social life. However, even castes and subcastes are difficult to assign as people groups because they differ significantly on the basis of the geographic region and language group in which they are found. In southern India and Sri Lanka agricultural castes tend to be considered fairly high caste positions while in northern India these same agricultural castes are quite low in the social hierarchy. In addition,

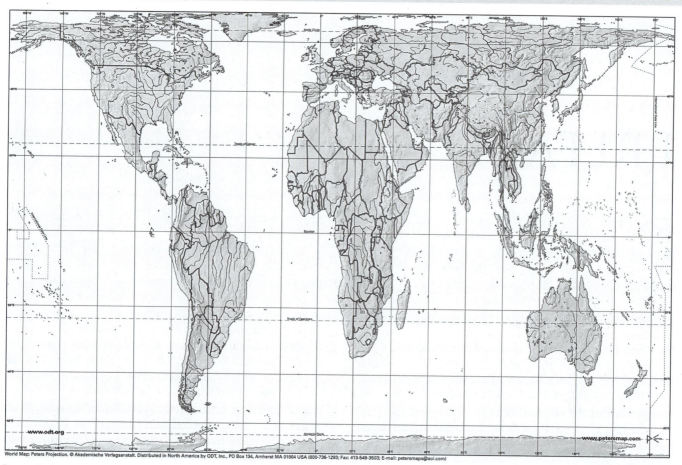

Peters Projection Map of the World

Tamil caste groupings differ from those of the Punjabis, Sinhalese from the Bengalis, and so on, so that while extremely important for Indians, Sri Lankans, and others in choosing a marriage partner, caste is almost impossible to use in defining people groups across geographic space.

Instead of caste in the Indian context we have chosen to follow the Indian government in assigning primacy to language, tribal membership, and schedule in the definition of a people. Following independence from Britain in 1947 India divided its large territory into states largely defined by language family. For example, Tamil Nadu is the southern state largely inhabited by native Tamil speakers, Maharashtra the western state largely inhabited by Marathi speakers, and Punjab the northern state inhabited largely by Punjabi speakers. Although the speakers of these and India's other 12 official languages differ in religion, caste, class, and other categories they constitute a people defined by language, history, a shared notion of caste, and geography.

In addition to language group, India recognizes its large tribal population, both as members of Scheduled Tribes that provide access to certain social and economic benefits set aside for them as disadvantaged members of society, and as members of their individual tribal communities. Tribes generally share a common language but also kinship system, usually with emphasis on lineage and clan membership, indigenous religion, shared subsistence system, and other

cultural traits. Finally, in addition to the category of Scheduled Tribes, India has listed several thousand disadvantaged castes as Scheduled Castes. While we have not singled out any specific Scheduled Caste because of the difficulties already addressed, we have provided an entry on this people group because their recognition by the Indian government has made them a unique people within Indian society.

Outside India the definition of people groups, at least for contemporary peoples, was somewhat easier. For example, in China the central government has created 56 different national groups or ethnicities, the dominant Han plus 55 separate minority groups; the Vietnamese government has created 54 such categories. While both of these governments have grouped together peoples who differ in dialect or even language, history, culture, ethnicity, and religion, their assignment to a common national category has made them into a contemporary people group. However, even the local assignment to a national or ethnic category did not eliminate the need for us to make choices when considering inclusion or exclusion of specific groups. We decided that as a result of the 21st-century importance of China, which is slated to become the world's second largest economy long before midcentury, as well as its importance in Asian and world history, we would include all of China's 56 recognized nationalities as separate people groups. Many of these groups overlap with the national and ethnic groups recognized by China's neighbors in Vietnam, Myanmar, Cambodia, Laos, Thailand, Mongolia, and Russia. That fact plus the relative marginality of these countries in relation to China and the impossibility of including the vast majority of Asia's approximately 10,000 contemporary and historical peoples meant that we did not include every recognized group in the region. Instead, we made decisions based on size, historical relevance to contemporary contexts, and likelihood that students would encounter the group in their high school or university textbooks for social studies, history, or anthropology courses.

In addition to several hundred contemporary people groups we have included a large number of historical groups and archaeological complexes that have disappeared either through migration, integration into other peoples, or death. As we did with contemporary groups, we tried to cover groups that students are most likely to see during the course of their studies and those that left the greatest mark on the contemporary world despite not surviving to see their legacy. In choosing these groups we also tried to cover the flow of major ideas and religions throughout the region, for example, the movement of Buddhism out of India, across Central Asia, and into China and Japan or the movement of Hinduism out of India and into both island and mainland Southeast Asia. Perhaps the most surprising of the historical peoples included in this volume on Asia and Oceania are the Greeks, a thoroughly European people in terms of both language and culture. However, Alexander the Great actually spent much of his time engaged in empire building in Central Asia and for several hundred years after his death in 323 B.C.E. Greeks were the central figures in the politics and economy of the entire region.

In addition to defining "a people" we had to think carefully about what Asia and Oceania mean as geographic regions of the world. As traditionally defined, the border between Asia and Europe runs from the Kara Sea in the north along the Ural Mountains and Ural River, to the Caspian Sea, then west along the Caucasus Mountains to the Black Sea and through the Dardanelles to the Aegean and Mediterranean Seas. The first and most important decision in this matter concerned those western Asian regions commonly referred to as the Middle East: the countries of Turkey, Iran, Iraq, Syria, Lebanon, Jordan, Israel, Saudi Arabia, Yemen, Oman, Kuwait, Bahrain, and the United Arab Emirates. We chose not to cover these peoples because of their greater cultural and historical affiliation with the countries of North Africa and, in the case of Israel, Europe. However, it was impossible for us to ignore the great historical presence of the various Persian empires in Central Asia. So while contemporary Iranians are excluded, their linguistic ancestors of the Achaemenid, Sassanid, and Parthian empires are included because their territory and cultural influence stretched into Central Asia. The same is true of contemporary Turks and the Turkish nationality and the ancient Turkic-speaking peoples. We excluded the first two and included the third because their homeland was the steppe of northern Asia; we also included many of their descendants who live today in the states of Central Asia. On the basis of the standard demarcation described, the countries of the southern Caucasus are located within Asia, so we have included their territory in this encyclopedia. As with other countries that lie along the European-Asian divide, this region has strong historical and cultural ties to both Europe and Asia.

Oceania provided its own challenges, which are due to geography, political boundaries, and other factors. There are tens of thousands of individual islands that make up the world region commonly known as Oceania. Even by excluding those that are uninhabited or only occasionally inhabited, we are still left with thousands of islands, many of which contain small ethnolinguistic groups that identify as a separate people from even their closest neighbors. In making decisions about inclusion and exclusion in this region we were largely guided by historical relevance and the interests of prolific ethnographers and other researchers. For example, it was impossible to ignore such small peoples as the Trobriand Islanders and Rapanui because of the plethora of works written about them by anthropologists, historians, and environmentalists. We also had to include peoples who are actually citizens of countries with governments and dominant societies located far from their island home. Native Hawaiians have been citizens of the United States since their islands were annexed by the United States in 1900 and Kanak have been French citizens as residents of Territoire des Nouvelle-Calédonie et Dépendances or the French overseas territory of New Caledonia since 1946, but both are historically and culturally Oceanic peoples and are included here.

One of the decisions we made in order to cover as many of the Oceanic peoples as possible, at least at a general level, was to include large entries for the three groupings into which Oceanic peoples are generally categorized: Polynesian, Micronesian, and Melanesian. As "people" groups these large categories are defined generally by language family and cultural traits. Language is the overarching criterion defining Polynesians, although they are also known for having developed large seafaring chiefdoms in the precolonial era and for having carried domesticated plants and animals with them from their original homeland in southern China. Micronesians are in some ways quite similar to their distant Polynesian cousins in speaking Oceanic languages and having descended from an original Austronesian population, but they were much less likely to have developed large chiefdoms. The category Melanesian seems at first to be a racial category rather than a cultural one since the name means "black islander"; however, it is much more accurate to point to such cultural features as men's houses, elaborate male initiation rites, and the lack of any formal political structure in defining the Melanesian people. The centrality of pigs to the traditional prestige system is another important cultural trait in defining membership in this large people group.

The decisions we made with regard to people and geography will not suit everybody. Occasionally students will find that the groups they are interested in were not covered here; the inclusion of ancient Persians and Turks but not contemporary ones may also frustrate a few readers. We also had to make decisions about how to spell each group's name and which name to choose; you will find each group's alternative names listed next to their primary one as well as in an appendix. Deciding which name was "primary" was certainly a challenge in many cases: should we use the name the people themselves prefer, the best known in English, or the least controversial? Usually we chose the best-known name in English except in a few cases when we believed that providing an alternative name was more appropriate for the sake of historical accuracy or cultural sensitivity. We made the same choices when faced with the decision of choosing one translation of foreign terms and concepts over another.

There is yet another area in which not everybody's agenda could be met by a single work, no matter how encyclopedic, and that concerns the choices we made with regard to topics, sources, points of view, and the presentation of contested information. Every entry included in this work left out far more information about the people than it included; not every historical detail could be covered nor every cultural trait. We made choices to cover the most important dates and events that we believe contributed to each group's contemporary position or ultimate demise, but in so doing we left out dates and events that others might find more important or interesting. We covered what we believe are the core aspects of each people's culture, as well, usually their economic base, family and social structures, and religion. In making these choices we usually were not able to address fully such topics as art, music, literature, or clothing, which specialists or interested students may have found fascinating. Sadly, without creating something 10 times as long as this set, we could not include much of this kind of detail and focused on what we believe are the material and conceptual cores of each people group.

We also had to make choices when it came to which sources to use in our research, which point of view to highlight, and how to present contested points of view. This was one of the most difficult aspects of producing a work of this size and scope because differences in points of view are inherent in every aspect of what we covered. The most obvious situations were those in which contested sources and points of view clearly had a contemporary political agenda. For example, the history of the South Ossetians is hotly contested by the Ossetians and their neighbors the Georgians. The key difference between their views on history is the period in which the Ossetian peoples moved from their home north of the Caucasus into the region of South Ossetia: 2,000 years or 200 years ago. Those who favor the former date tend to subscribe to the legitimacy of a separate Ossetian state while those who favor the latter tend to desire a unified Georgia with its present boundaries. In cases like these, where the archaeology and history are inconclusive, we chose not to recognize either hypothesis as factual but merely present them both with their accompanying political agendas.

Other decisions had to do with how to label events—such as the entrance of Indo-Aryans into the Indian subcontinent, which some call an "invasion" and others a "migration"—or how to interpret archaeological or other data, as in the case of the migration of Aboriginal Australians, which different sources date to 60,000, 45,000, or 30,000 B.C.E. Many times when we found such divergent points of view in the primary and secondary literature we chose the most accepted version of history at the present time while stating that others may have a different view. There were also many times when we simply presented two competing points of view since neither one of them had yet achieved the status of a dominant position; we hope that later editions or future discoveries will resolve some of these debates, but differences will always remain and it is imperative for students to recognize this in their own further research.

One of the reasons we chose to present contested information in this manner is to remind readers of the difference between facts and knowledge, which is always a work in progress, and to encourage them to seek the latter. Facts are, of course, very important! For example, the dates of a battle, its location, who took part and who won, statistics on loss of life and materiel are all important factors in understanding the event. However, just compiling these bits of information does little to provide knowledge about it, which requires an understanding of the actors' motivations, analysis of these important dates and statistics, and the political, economic, social, and historical contexts in which it took place. Readers will find an enormous number of facts in these two volumes, but at the same time we have also tried to arrange these facts, analyze them in context, and present them as part of a knowledge base about the peoples of Asia and Oceania. As a result, we have been satisfied with presenting these entries as works in progress and encourage readers to use the further reading section as well as other trusted sources to continue to seek knowledge.

This last point, that readers should turn to other trusted sources to continue to develop their own knowledge, is an important one in this era of instant information via the Internet. No doubt if you have picked up this encyclopedia and are reading the preface you already know that much of what you find on the Internet is not compiled by trusted sources but by people with a political agenda, or an economic one, or with relatively little knowledge about their subject. Tourism and many government sites want to present as pretty a picture as possible to attract visitors and tourists while the free access to Wikipedia means that any and every point of view can be presented as the truth with little regard for factual accuracy. Free access also means that entries can change from moment to moment; accurate, well-written entries are just as likely to be replaced as false, misleading, or poorly written ones. There are certainly useful Web sites available and we looked at thousands of them in writing these entries, but we also double and triple checked what we found in order to make sure we were getting correct information; in so doing we found innumerable mistakes and misleading statements that were much more accessible to the nonspecialist, Internet-using public than many of the accurate ones.

On the whole we believe most readers will be more than satisfied with the choices we have made and will find everything they need to continue the research process on their own. We encourage them to go to the sources listed in the further reading sections and to follow the trail of knowledge and information available in the bibliographies of those sources. And when they do so, we want them to remember that Asia and Oceania are broad and dynamic regions that encompass the two largest countries on Earth by population, China and India, and the largest by territory, Russia. They contain peoples who have lived under recognizably modern political states for several thousand years in Indonesia, China, India, mainland Southeast Asia, and elsewhere and tribal peoples who have yet to reconcile themselves to the centralizing power of the modern nation-state, whether it be Indonesian, Papua New Guinean, or something else. There is tremendous wealth in Asia and Oceania as well as great poverty, ancient written histories and people whose languages remain unwritten, people who lived under the yoke of European colonialism for centuries and even a few who still do and those who have never done so. In other words, there is no unity, uniformity, or general Asian or Oceanic people; there is diversity and dynamism that can change from day to day, as we discovered in trying to produce this text. From day to day we had to revise entries as monks were killed protesting in Myanmar, exiled politicians returned to Pakistan and then were assassinated, and coups were staged in Fiji. Indeed, by the time readers have access to this text I have no doubt that some of what we have written is already out of date or in need of further revision. But we also have no doubt that the careful reader will find that out for him- or herself and will build on the knowledge base we have tried to lay down here.

HOW TO USE THIS SET

ENTRIES AND CROSS-REFERENCES

Encyclopedia of the Peoples of Asia and Oceania is organized around people groups, all of which are listed alphabetically in the master list of entries at the beginning and then within the larger body of the two-volume set. There are also quite a number of "blind entries," which are relatively well-known alternative spellings or names of people groups that appear under a different headword in this set; peoples who do not have their own entry but are described in other entries also appear as blind entries: for example, **Shompen** *See* Nicoba-rese. If you are looking for a people and only know what country they live in, you will find a list of peoples by country listed alphabetically in Appendix I. Within many of the entries there are cross-references to other people groups that may provide more information or context for that entry. The first time a cross-referenced people appears in each entry it is printed in capital and small capital letters, such as Mela-nesians. There are also cross-references listed within or at the end of some entries that will direct you to peoples not necessarily discussed in the entry but are still helpful in understanding them with greater depth or context; such cross-references look like this: *See also* Aboriginal Australians.

Entries of different lengths have been treated differently to accommodate the needs of readers and to provide as useful a set as possible. We have utilized three broad categories of entries: short, long, and nationality. Both the short and long entries contain a separate textbox with summaries of important information regarding the group's name, location, period, ancestry, and language. They differ in that the short entries are merely free-standing essays of between 200 and 1,000 words while the long entries contain many separate units, usually including a timeline, a paragraph on geography that describes the location in which the people live or lived, another on their origins, followed by separate essays on their history and culture, and ending with a list of further readings. Occasionally short entries of 500 or 1,000 words also contain a further readings list or are subdivided into history and culture sections, but this is relatively rare. Long entries range from just over 1,000 words to about 8,000 and cover the most central people in each region and period; for example, the Han, Vietnamese, Bengalis, and Parthians are all long entries.

Nationality entries are treated somewhat differently from those for other people groups because they are defined by citizenship rather than by language, ethnicity, or some other cultural trait. Each of the 63 nationality entries from the countries of Asia and Oceania, excluding those in the Middle East but including the southern Caucasus, contains a separate textbox with summaries of important information regarding the group's name, nation or name of their country, derivation of name, government, capital, language, religion, earlier inhabitants, and demographics. As do long entries, nationality entries contain separate sections for a time line, a description of their geographic setting or geography, a description of the inception of the nation, their cultural identity, and a further readings list.

In addition to the text box(es) located at the beginning of all entries with a summary of various demographic and geographic information about them, many entries contain a sidebar with additional biographical information on one of the individuals mentioned in the text. Readers will find that many of the people covered are well known historical figures about whom they already knew a small amount of information, such as Mao Zedong, Genghis Khan, and Benazir Bhutto. Others, however, are much less well known but in their own way have made significant contributions to the lives of others, such as Queen Tamara, who ruled during the Georgian "golden age," and Kamla Jaan, the first Hijra elected to public office in independent India.

OTHER MATERIALS

In recognition that some people learn best through seeing visual images this set also contains 136 pictures and 44 maps and graphs to support readers in their quest for knowledge about the peoples of Asia and Oceania. The pictures were chosen specifically for each of the entries they accompany to assist readers in gaining a visual image of the peoples, places, and events described in the text. The maps were also created specifically for the entries they accompany and serve to clarify information about migrations, locations, and the geographic context for certain dates and events.

We also chose a map to accompany the preface to this work to highlight the point made in that essay: that research and writing are about making choices about sources, inclusion, and points of view. In making each of the choices in the creation of this encyclopedia, whether concerning peoples to include, sources to utilize, or data to present, we had to pick one perspective and reject others. Even as we made these choices we recognized that some of the rejected perspectives were no more right or wrong than those we drew up: they were just different. The map we included with that essay, a Peters projection map, provides a clear visual image of this point. Most maps that students are familiar with use a Mercator projection rather than the Peters, and so this one seems to distort the world, almost as if it were showing Asia and Oceania through the lens of a fun house mirror. However, the Peters map, while strangely shaped, is actually a much more accurate representation of the relative size of the world's landmasses than Mercator maps are, since the latter exaggerate the size of the Northern Hemisphere greatly: Mercator maps show Greenland and Africa to be about the same size while the truth is that Africa is 13 times larger. The cartographer Arno Peters (1916–2002) and others both before and after him believed that the perspective of the world provided by Mercator maps, created originally for sailors, tends to amplify the importance of the rich, developed northern countries over the poorer, developing southern ones. In the end, neither map provides a more accurate representation of the world—Mercator is better if you want to sail from one continent to another; Peters is better if you want to know the relative sizes of India and Australia. But in choosing one of them to present an image of the world we had to reject an equally valid but different one, just as we did in the research and writing of every entry in this set.

Finally, in order to assist readers in finding the information they want we have also provided seven appendices. The first one organizes the contemporary people groups included in the set by country while the second provides a list of all the historical peoples included in the set that are thus not included in the first appendix. The third appendix provides a list of the sidebars for historical personages as well as the entries in which they can be found. The final four appendices are essays that provide readers with further information on the religious, kinship, and subsistence systems described briefly in many of the entries, and a chronology of events. A general bibliography for all the entries covered in the two volumes and a comprehensive index round out the set.

ACKNOWLEDGMENTS

I would like to thank everybody who made the production of this encyclopedia possible. To begin, without Professor Michael Leigh and the rest of the faculty and staff of the Sidney Myer Asia Centre at the University of Melbourne I could not have completed this work. They generously provided me with an honorary fellow position, including office, library, and database access; consultations on difficult material; and much other advice and assistance over the course of the entire project. All of the contributors gave of their time to find obscure data, write up difficult passages, and provide a much-needed new perspective on the material at the most crucial moments. While all of them helped in significant ways, I have to single out Frances Murphy, Faith Merino, Celine Reyes, Katherine Dixon, and Emily Liedel for their significant effort. I am also infinitely grateful to Frances Murphy, who pushed me to accept this project and then provided all of the research and other information necessary to create the maps, which were done by the cartographic team at Facts On File and based on her work; she also compiled the bibliography located in the back matter and assisted with the creation of the blind entries. Without her efforts on this project and extra work in managing the rest of Culture Works, this encyclopedia could not have been completed on time.

I would also like to thank Claudia Schaab for offering this project to me and then helping me to see it through to completion.

Finally, I want to thank all of my friends and family for their patience over the past 15 months, when they saw little of me and heard from me far less often than I wanted. I promise to improve on this front in the upcoming months and years!

CONTRIBUTORS

The following people contributed research, text, or both toward the completion of the entries listed below their names. We would like to acknowledge their assistance here and recognize that without their hard work this set would not be as useful, complete, or up to date as it currently is.

Sara Ahlstedt
    Bangladeshis: nationality
Amy E. Baird
    Warlpiris

Lynsey L. Bourke
    Acehnese
Estee Catti
    Uzbekistanis: nationality
Imma di Biase
    Bai
    Blang
Katherine Dixon
    Kadazan Dusun
    Malaysian Chinese
    Malaysian Indians
    Malaysians: nationality
    Melayu Asli
    Murut
    Orang Asli
    Semang
    Senoi
Rufaro Gwarada
    Derung
    Dong
    Kalingas
    Magars
Morgan Tara Innes
    Afghanistanis: nationality
    Sea Gypsies
    Sherpas
    Sidebars for Ahmad Khan Abdali, Benazir Bhutto,
      Tenzing Norgay
D. E. Kralj
    Sri Lankans: nationality
Jennifer Laedlein
    Dai
    Hani
    Manchus
    Naxi
    Singaporeans: nationality
Kristine Leach
    Fijians: nationality
Emily Liedel
    Altai
    Azerbaijanis: nationality
    Chinese: nationality
    Chukchis
    Russians: nationality
    Turkmenistanis: nationality

ENTRIES A TO L

Abdalis   *See* DURRANIS.

Abkhazians (Abkhaz, Apswa)

The Abkhazians are a Northwest Caucasian people who reside in Abkhazia, an autonomous republic within Georgia, as well as throughout Georgia, Turkey, and Russia. They are culturally and linguistically distinct from the other GEORGIANS, who are primarily South Caucasian speakers. Since the early 1990s and their civil war with Georgia the Abkhazians have had de facto autonomy in their region; however, no country or international organization recognizes their sovereignty.

GEOGRAPHY

Abkhazia is a 3,300-square-mile territory located within the country of Georgia. It is bounded by the Black Sea to the southwest, Russia to the north, and contiguous regions of Georgia to the southeast. About 74 percent of the territory is covered by the Greater Caucasus Mountain Range, with the highest peaks (about 12,120 feet above sea level) covered in glacier and permafrost while the coastal valleys are subtropical. The region's capital city is Sukhumi, or Sukhum as the Abkhazian nationalists call it, while Tkwarchal is its industrial center.

The region is a well-known agricultural center, producing wine, tea, tobacco, and even citrus fruit in the coastal areas. The irrigation water for these crops is taken the many rivers that run from the mountains to the coast, including the Kodori, Bzyb, and Gumista. The Psou River forms the northern boundary with Russia, while the Inguri River divides Abkhazia from the rest of Georgia.

ORIGINS

Abkhazian origins have been the source of many nationalist and intellectual debates over the past 100 years. Georgian nationalists tend to argue for a relatively new Abkhazian presence in the region, going back only about 200 years and the migration of these northwest Caucasian people from their cultural and linguistic homeland in the north. Abkhazian nationalists write of their primordial ties to the land of Abkhazia and use the work of travelers such as Al Massoudi, a Moroccan who, in the middle of the 10th century, traveled in the Caucasus and wrote about his experiences with the Christian Abkhazians, to justify their claims of an ancient connection to their land. One of the places used as fuel in this historical debate is Anacopia, a second- to third-century town that Abkhazian nationalists claim was built by their ancestors as a capital, while Georgians claim that the multiethnic nature of the region precludes any one group's claiming the site as its own. In the absence of good written documents, archaeologists have had difficulty supporting or refuting most of these claims.

HISTORY

The early history of the region of Abkhazia points to colonization by the GREEKS in the sixth cen-

ABKHAZIANS

location:
Abkhazia, an autonomous republic in northern Georgia. Many Abkhazians fled Georgia in the 19th century, and their descendants still live in Turkey.

time period:
Though unknown, many sources point to the eighth century C.E. as the time at which the Abkhazian people became aware of their common identity to the present.

ancestry:
Possibly Apsilae or Abasgoi, but this is disputed by many scholars

language:
Abkhazian, a Northwest Caucasian language

Abkhazians time line

C.E.

mid-sixth century Abkhazians, along with other Caucasians, adopt Christianity while ruled by the Byzantine Empire.

eighth century Georgian texts are the first to use the term *Abkhazeti* to refer to the region of the Abkhazians.

mid-eighth century Leon II unifies the western Georgian kingdoms and names them the Kingdom of Abkhazes-Egrisi.

1008 The Kingdom of the Georgians absorbs the Abkhazes kingdom.

1549–78 Abkhazia is invaded by the Ottomans and subjugated to their empire.

1810 Abkhazia is incorporated into the Russian Empire; many Abkhazians immigrate to Turkey.

1864 Abkhazia is officially annexed by Russia.

1991 Georgia attains independence from the disintegrating USSR.

1992 The Abkhazians declare their independence from Georgia, sparking a civil war.

1994 A cease-fire is reached in the civil war; a UN-monitored peace-keeping mission is established, made up of forces from the other Commonwealth of Independent States countries.

1994 Vladislav Ardzinba is elected the first president of the de facto independent Republic of Abkhazia.

2005 Sergei Vasilyevich Bagapsh is elected the second president of the Republic of Abkhazia; he had served as prime minister from 1997 to 1999.

tury B.C.E., when the settlement of Dioscurias was founded. This was also the period in which the COLCHIANS ruled much of the eastern shores of the Black Sea. By the fourth century C.E., Egrisi or Lazica was the name the Romans were using to refer to much of the territory of today's western Georgia. In the sixth century the entire region was under Byzantine rule, which introduced Christianity to the people of the area.

In the eighth through the 10th centuries Abkhazia was joined with Lazica and other areas of western Georgia into the first unified state in the area with its capital at Kutaisi. This period is of particular interest to both Abkhazian and Georgian nationalists and historians, with people from both groups claiming the kingdom as their own. It remains unclear whether Leon, the figure who began the process of bringing the various peoples together, was Abkhazian, Georgian, LAZ, or some other nationality entirely. It is somewhat clearer that during this amalgamation process the Abkhazians began to differentiate themselves from the South Caucasians among whom they were living in terms of culture and identity, not just language. It is also fairly clear that by the last quarter of the 10th century the Abkhazians were a constituent part of Georgia; whether they were the founders of the state or its subjects remains up for debate.

The Abkhazians and other peoples of the south Caucasus were invaded by the Ottoman Turks in the 16th century and a series of wars was fought between the two peoples, with the Ottomans ultimately taking control of the region. The Abkhazian capital, Sukhumi, became a slave market in the early Ottoman period, serving much of eastern Anatolia and the Caucasus. Over the course of the next three centuries many people converted to Islam, including most Abkhazians; the Georgians retained their Orthodox Christian faith.

The Ottoman status quo continued until the end of the 18th century, when the RUSSIANS began their march south into the Caucasus. In 1768–74 Russia took the north coast of the Black Sea. By 1801 the Russians held eastern Georgia, to which they added western Georgia, including Abkhazia, by mid-century. Abkhazia was officially annexed by Russia in 1864, at which time about 60 percent of the Abkhazian people fled the country for Turkey. This mass migration opened up large amounts of fertile land that was quickly taken over by Russians, Georgians, MINGRELIANS, and ARMENIANS, leaving the Abkhazians as a minority group in their own territory. The dominant Russians quickly moved to *russify* the region by divesting the Georgian Orthodox Church of its autonomy and institutionalizing the use of the Russian language in the public sphere. Christian missionaries tried to reconvert the population to the Orthodox Church as well.

At the time of the Russian Revolution the Abkhazians were granted the same degree of cultural and political autonomy as other national groups, but during Stalin's leadership of the Communist Party (1922–53) Abkhazia was incorporated into his home state of Georgia as an autonomous republic. The Abkhazian and Russian languages were replaced in schools and other public institutions with Georgian and hundreds of place-names were changed to accommodate a Georgian point of view on history. Abkhazians experienced frequent bouts of state terror, and emigration from the region decreased their percentage of the population to about 17 percent by 1989.

The relief experienced by many national groups upon the collapse of the USSR in 1991 was not evident in Abkhazia, for its independence was curtailed because it was merely a territory within the independent state of Georgia. As a result nationalist Abkhazians took up arms in 1992 and fought a deadly war of secession against the Georgians until 1993. By most accounts, the Georgians were defeated in the civil war, and about 200,000 Georgians, mainly ethnic Mingrelians, fled Abkhazia and took up residence in other parts of Georgia. A cease-fire was brokered and signed in 1994 and the United Nations has continued to monitor the situation along with Commonwealth of Independent States troops, but the issue remains unresolved today. Abkhazia is still an official territory within the state of Georgia but yet has held presidential elections in 1994 and 2005 and maintains all the institutional apparatus of an independent country. No country officially recognizes this government apparatus; however, Russia has provided significant support to the Sukhumi-based separatist government, despite its links to Russia's enemies in Chechnya and elsewhere in the north Caucasus. There is also a Georgian-backed legal authority over the district, which works out of the Kodori Valley, but it controls only about 17 percent of Abkhazia's territory.

CULTURE

For hundreds, if not thousands of years the primary economic activities of most Abkhazians were agriculture and the rearing of cattle. In the warm, moist climate of the Black Sea coast they produced grapes, citrus fruit, tobacco, tea, and some wheat. Abkhazians were also well known, from antiquity up to the last century, for their fine metalwork. One of the most important gods in the pre-Christian Abkhazian pantheon was Sessu, god of the forge, whose representatives on earth were the blacksmiths. Sessu himself struck down individuals for making false oaths within earshot of the forge, causing sicknesses that could be cured only by a ritual intervention by a blacksmith.

In addition to blacksmiths the other important mediator between the human and spirit worlds in traditional Abkhazian society were the *acaajus,* women who could read oracles, cure supernatural illnesses, and engage in prophecy. *Acaajus* were similar to shamans in other societies in that their primary role was diagnosing illnesses and then curing them; they also had high status, as did most shamans. Diagnosis often involved going into a trance, during which the name of the offended spirit would be communicated to the *acaaju.* In addition to spiritual causes of illness, *acaajus* were also competent to determine whether illnesses were caused by

social complaints, such as envy or anger, or whether the afflicted person had a more prosaic physical disease. In cases where the cause was seen as more physical than spiritual or social, *acaajus* employed medicine women to enact the cure rather than doing it themselves.

Early in Abkhazian history—many sources say the sixth century or earlier—the Abkhazians adopted Christianity; later, under Ottoman rule, many converted to Sunni Islam. However, a number of traditional ideas about sickness and health continued to inform the Abkhazian worldview. For example the Water Mother, *Dzidlan* in Abkhazian, continued to provide a source of strength and hope to new mothers; Dzidlan was also seen as helpful in fighting off ailments that included a fever. Blacksmiths and *acaajus* also retained their important social positions even after the introduction of Christianity and Islam.

Many who have commented on Abkhazian religion have generally found that their Christian or Islamic conversions have been far from complete. Well into the 18th and 19th centuries, traditional, pre-Christian beliefs and practices survived next to the Bible and Quran. During the earliest period of russification, from the 1860s until the early 20th century, more than 20,000 Abkhazian Muslims converted to Christianity, and Russian Orthodox missionaries reported that even most Muslim Abkhazians celebrated Christmas, Easter, and many Orthodox saints' days. At the same time, Abkhazians fasted for Ramadan, circumcised their sons, and were married and buried in ceremonies presided over by mullahs. These same missionaries complained in numerous letters to their parent organizations in Russia that Christian and Muslim Abkhazians often intermarried and that social status was usually much more important than religion in determining marriage suitability. During the Soviet era, little was done to curtail religion in Abkhazia because, according to the Communist Party first secretary for Abkhazia in the 1920s and 1930s, Nestor Lakoba, religion was meaningless there anyway. Following the fall of the USSR and the establishment of the autonomous Republic of Abkhazia in 1994, there may be some evidence of an upturn in Islamic activity, but this remains largely conjecture based on the links that have been made between the separatist government in Sukhumi and those in the other North Caucasus breakaway states, such as Chechnya. Lack of research makes it difficult to confirm this hypothesis.

See also GEORGIANS: NATIONALITY.

FURTHER READING

Jonathan Cohen, ed. *A Question of Sovereignty: The Georgia-Abkhazia Peace Process* (London: Accord, 1997).
George Hewitt, ed. *The Abkhazians* (Richmond, Surrey: Curzon Press, 1999).

Abor   *See* ADI.

Aboriginal Australians (Anangu, Australian Aborigines, Indigenous Australians, Koori, Koorie, Murri, Native Australians, Nunga, Palawah, Pallawah, Yamatji, Yapa)

Aboriginal Australians are the descendants of the original human inhabitants of the land that today makes up mainland Australia and Tasmania. In the present day the political and cultural group known as Aboriginal Australians often also includes TORRES STRAIT ISLANDERS, people of the island chain located between mainland Australia and New Guinea. Some NEW GUINEA HIGHLANDERS are also genetically related to this population and would have been part of the original settlement of the then much larger landmass of Sahul. The chronology of the Aboriginal Australian population is divided into a very long prehistorical period, including the 45,000 or so years during which the people lived on the continent alone, and a much shorter historical period, dating from 1606 when the Dutch sailor Willem Janszoon first spotted and named the Terra Australis Incognita, the unknown southern land. The prehistorical period is known to us largely through archaeology, genetic testing, and the Dreamtime stories of the present-day Aboriginal population, while the historical period is relatively well documented, at least from the European and white Australian point of view.

GEOGRAPHY

After having island-hopped and then sailed across at least 35 miles of open sea from Sunda, the ancient Aboriginal Australians settled on the giant landmass of Sahul, which made up what is today New Guinea, mainland Australia, and Tasmania. Sunda was itself a much larger landmass than is evident today north of Australia and New Guinea because relatively low sea levels in this part of the world joined together much of today's island Southeast Asia. Sahul was about the size of contemporary Europe until about 11,000 B.C.E., when rising sea levels due to the melting polar ice cut Tasmania

off from the rest of the landmass. Australia and New Guinea were separated 1,000 years later when a giant inland sea became inundated and formed the Torres Strait, Gulf of Carpenteria, and Arafura Sea. Because of this relatively extreme change in the size and shape of the ancient Aboriginal population's homeland, the archaeological record is extremely incomplete, with the earliest sites having been under water for tens of thousands of years.

ORIGINS

The origins of the Aboriginal Australian population are very ancient, dating back to at least 45,000 B.C.E. and possibly as early as 75,000 B.C.E. (For comparison purposes, England's Stonehenge monument was begun in only 3000 B.C.E.; the building of the great Egyptian pyramids at Giza occurred around 2500 B.C.E., when the Aboriginal population had already been in Sahul/Australia for a minimum of 42,500 years!)

The continent upon which these first settlers landed would have looked very different from the Australia of today because of the changes in sea levels since the end of the last ice age. As today, however, Sahul encompassed a variety of climates, including tropical forests, temperate forests and savannahs, and arid deserts, all of which were home to populations of Aboriginal Australians. Some scientific evidence in the form of pollen studies shows that the desert area was significantly smaller than it is today and that central Australia was fairly tree covered. This is a controversial area of study, however, in part because the Aboriginal Australians are often blamed for destroying the trees and increasing desertification. Another difference that these earliest settlers would have seen was the existence of a range of massive animals, called megafauna, including 10-foot-tall kangaroos and rhinoceros-sized marsupials known as *diprotodontids*. The best estimate for the extinction of this group of at least 23 animals is about 20,000 years ago. Whether Aboriginal hunting and burning of the land contributed to this extinction or whether it was caused by climate change is still unknown.

We have little information about the earliest Aboriginal populations, except that they were anatomically modern, lived by hunting and gathering, worked with stone tools, and were able to cross the open seas, probably on bamboo rafts. Genetic testing on both skeletal remains and present-day populations has yet to determine whether just one group of people arrived and then later subdivided into the various

ABORIGINAL AUSTRALIANS

location:
Australia

time period:
Perhaps as early as 60,000 B.C.E., definitely no later than 45,000 B.C.E. to the present

ancestry:
Asian origins but so long ago that the exact ancestry is unknown; some genetic markers indicate an ancient connection to New Guinea Highlanders.

language:
Before European contact, about 250 different languages divided into 600 dialects were spoken; today about 200 languages remain, but only 20 will be viable beyond the next decade, including Pitjantjatjara, Warlpiri, and Arrernte or Arunta. The distinction between separate languages and dialects is unclear because of lack of research and extinction of many languages; thus the number of languages and dialects that existed prior to the 18th century is still under debate.

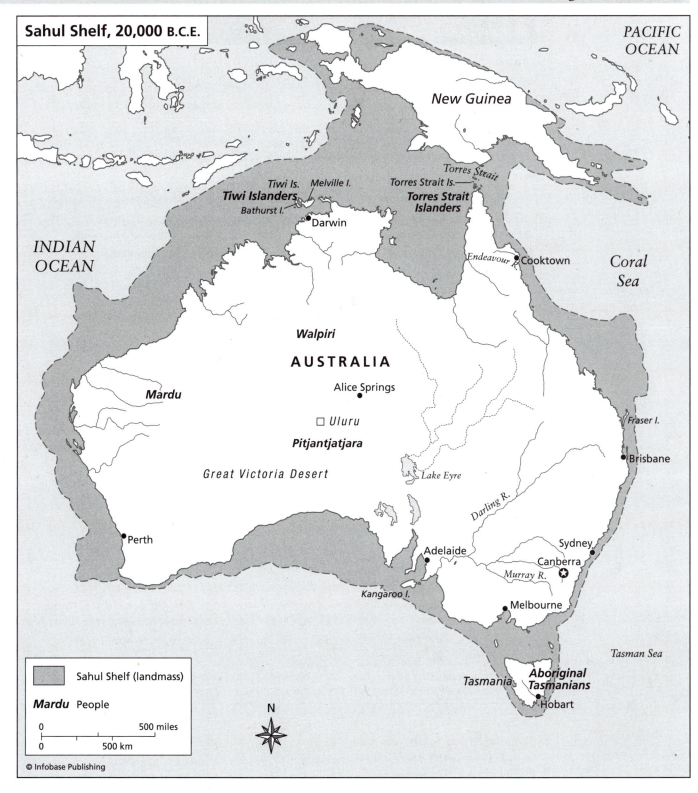

Sahul Shelf, 20,000 B.C.E.

PACIFIC OCEAN

New Guinea

Torres Strait

Tiwi Is. *Melville I.*
Tiwi Islanders Torres Strait Is.
Bathurst I. **Torres Strait Islanders**
• Darwin

INDIAN OCEAN

Endeavour R. • Cooktown

Coral Sea

Walpiri

AUSTRALIA

Alice Springs •

□ *Uluru*

Mardu

Pitjantjatjara

Great Victoria Desert

Lake Eyre

Fraser I.

• Brisbane

Darling R.

• Perth

Adelaide •

Sydney •
Canberra ✪

Murray R.

Kangaroo I.

• Melbourne

Tasman Sea

Tasmania **Aboriginal Tasmanians**

• Hobart

Sahul Shelf (landmass)

Mardu People

0 _____ 500 miles
0 _____ 500 km

N

© Infobase Publishing

New Guinea, mainland Australian, and Tasmanian populations of today or whether several waves of settlement occurred over time. The exact route that this population or populations took out of Africa is also unclear, with some studies using the existence of dark-skinned populations in southern India and Southeast Asia as evidence that the Melanesian and Aboriginal Australian populations arrived via that route. Others trace the path north through Southeast Asia, China, and the Levant. The fact that Aboriginal Australians are genetically only

Aboriginal Australians time line

B.C.E.

68,000–56,000 Contested dating of some archaeological sites in Arnhem Land.

45,000 Date used by more conservative archaeologists to mark the establishment of Aboriginal culture in Australia/Sahul.

20,000 The Aboriginal population has established itself throughout the entire area of today's mainland Australia and Tasmania, and population growth expands at a much faster rate than previously.

Best estimate for the extinction of Sahul's megafauna.

The date of the Last Glacial Maximal, which marks a distinct change in Aboriginal prehistoric culture.

11,000 Rising sea levels separate the Aboriginal population of Tasmania from the mainland.

10,000 Australia and New Guinea are separated by rising sea levels, creating the Torres Straits Islands.

3000 The dingo arrives from Asia and establishes itself in Australia.

C.E.

1606 Willem Janszoon is the first European to see and name what is today Australia.

1770 Captain Cook arrives in Australia.

1788 The First Fleet settles Sydney and within months epidemics of influenza, measles, typhus, and other European diseases kill thousands of Aboriginal Australians.

1900 Government policy of removing Aboriginal children from their families and placing them in foster families or institutions far from their families results in the Stolen Generations. This practice continues until almost 1970 so that today thousands of Aboriginal Australians do not know their origins.

1902 The Commonwealth Franchise Act denies the vote to Aboriginal Australians, who had been able to vote in New South Wales and South Australia since the mid-19th century.

1957 Albert and Robina Namatjira are made special citizens of Australia to recognize Albert's international career as a well-known artist. They are followed one year later by the actor Robert Tudawali.

1962 The Commonwealth Electoral Act 1962 overturns the 1902 act, allowing Aboriginal Australians the right to vote without providing the other rights and privileges of citizenship.

1967 Commonwealth referendum, passed by more than 90 percent of voting Australians, makes Aboriginal Australians citizens of the country for the first time since its inception in 1901.

1992 The *Mabo and Others v. Queensland* case determines that Native Title is a valid part of Australian law.

2006 The federal court rules in favor of the Noongar people in their Native Title claim to portions of the city of Perth in Western Australia; the federal government vows to fight the decision.

distantly related to any other human group tends to confuse the issue rather than clarify it. Finally while it is assumed that Australia specifically, and Sahul more generally, was settled first from the north end, it is difficult to test this hypothesis with archaeological evidence because of the difficulty of obtaining exact dates. In addition, some of the earliest archaeological sites are not in the far north of the continent but in today's New South Wales and Tasmania, in the far south.

LANGUAGES

The first Europeans to record words from Aboriginal Australian languages were Captain James Cook and Sir Joseph Banks when they arrived in Australia in 1770. They wrote down words, including *kangooroo*, provided to them by the Guugu-Yimidhirr people from what is today the Endeavour River area in northeast Queensland. About a generation later, when the First Fleet (*see* AUSTRALIANS: NATIONALITY) arrived to establish a penal colony at today's

Sydney harbor, Arthur Philip was unable to find any local people who could understand the words recorded 18 years earlier in Queensland. Other European explorers discovered even more linguistic diversity in the region, and thus the evidence for the existence of a great many Aboriginal languages became indisputable. However, in 1841 a British explorer, George Grey, found that this great diversity actually masked similarities in pronoun use and a few lexical features. He was the first to posit that all Aboriginal languages are from a single language family, a theory that did not face any theoretical or empirical challenge for a full century. Finally, in 1956 a professional linguist discovered one important division within the Aboriginal language family, between languages that use both prefixes and suffixes and are located primarily in the far northern regions of the country and those in the rest of the country that use only suffixes. These divisions have since been labeled the *non-Pama-Nyungan* language family for the former and the *Pama-Nyungan* for the latter. Nonetheless, most linguists believe that both of these families derive from the same proto-Australian language and thus are genetically related, with just two possible exceptions: TIWI and Djingili. The dating of the development of proto-Australian has been much more difficult, with some experts believing that it arrived with the first Aboriginal settlers at least 45,000 years ago and others arguing that it developed in situ closer to 10,000 years ago. Even if this latter date is more accurate, proto-Australian is still at least twice as ancient as proto-Indo-European, the forebear of English and all European and many South Asian languages.

One common feature of many Aboriginal Australian languages is the use of avoidance speech or what is sometimes called mother-in-law language. This special language usually includes restricted vocabulary that is used when speaking with certain relatives, such as in-laws. Another common feature is the practice of speech taboos during certain ritually prescribed times, such as mourning; many languages also forbid mention of the names of the dead. A third common feature is that many of these languages use only three vowel sounds, *a, i,* and *u,* in long and short forms, with some non-Pama-Nyungan languages having developed two more.

HISTORY

The prehistoric period of Aboriginal Australian settlement is often subdivided into two distinct periods, the pre–Last Glacial Maximal (LGM) and post-LGM periods, with the division occurring in about 20,000 B.C.E. or 22,000 years ago. While both eras are known primarily through the archaeological record, the pre-LGM era is fairly sparse with only eight sites containing materials that have been confirmed as being from the period 40,000–45,000 B.C.E., although nearly 100 sites have been studied and confirmed as being from the pre-LGM period more generally. From these middens, prehistoric garbage dumps, we know that the bulk of the diet of the pre-LGM populations was made up of fish, seafoods, and a few small mammals. Because of the relatively small size of these earliest middens we also know that their related settlement sites were not used for more than a season or two at the most. The people who lived in Australia prior to 20,000 B.C.E. probably also ate a variety of seeds, vegetables, and fruits they gathered locally, but the fact that these products disintegrate very quickly makes the possibility difficult to verify through archaeology. Other products that have been found in archaeological sites older than 22,000 years are stone ax heads, flaked chert (a kind of stone) tools, stones that were probably used for grinding seeds and grains, and a very small number of tools made from animal bones. Generally, the record points to small, mobile groups of people with extremely low population densities living throughout the entire Sahul area.

Beginning around 22,000 years ago with the slow rising of sea levels and change in climate throughout Sahul and later Australia, the people residing in these areas experienced some distinct cultural changes. The key factor in this change seems to have been a rise in population density caused by habitat loss to rising sea levels and increased aridity. Post-LGM archaeological sites, unlike those of the earlier period, show extensive evidence of trade, creation of art and body decoration, management of the land through burning, and in later periods digging of channels for trapping eels and fish. Post-LGM Aboriginal Australians also carried plants from place to place and fostered their growth in new habitats; they did the same with small mammals. The rock art for which Aboriginal Australians have become well known throughout the world seems to be dated almost entirely from the post-LGM period as well, with two possible exceptions whose dates are still under debate.

The history of the Aboriginal Australians since their first interactions with Europeans

Aboriginal rock art from the Kakadu region of Australia's Northern Territory, depicting an ancestral figure from the local community's Dreamtime. *(Shutterstock/Neale Cousland)*

and later white Australians has been tragic. While we will never know the size of the Aboriginal population prior to contact with Europeans, the best estimate is about 750,000, with figures ranging from 250,000 to 1 million. In a period of just 130 years, from Cook's landing in 1770 to federation in 1901, a people who had prospered in Australia for tens of thousands of years had diminished in population to almost nothing. Experts agree that by the time of Australian federation the combination of European diseases, such as measles, typhus, smallpox, syphilis, and influenza; displacement from the most productive lands; violence; and other social disruption led to the elimination of at least 90 percent of the Aboriginal Australian population. Today's Aboriginal population makes up between 2 and 2.5 percent of Australia's total population of around 20 million.

One common misperception that results from this tragic history is that the Aboriginal Australians are thought to have traditionally lived in the desert. While some populations did reside primarily in Australia's desert regions, the areas with the most people prior to European colonization were the same ones with the highest populations today: the temperate southeast and southwest regions and the east coast. As a result of their high population densities as well as the desirability of their lands, these people suffered the greatest population losses early in the colonial period. The Aboriginal groups around today's Sydney began dying of European diseases within weeks of the arrival of the First Fleet, with the same pattern occurring in every area that experienced the arrival of significant numbers of Europeans. Those people who did not die of introduced diseases soon found themselves hunted down or, at best, merely chased from their territories by freed convicts and free settlers who wanted to make a go at farming or raising sheep and cattle. At the same time, Aboriginal populations who lived in Australia's central and far north regions remained relatively undisturbed for decades because the hot and arid climate, as well as local diseases, prevented large numbers of Europeans from settling there. As a result, today it seems as though all the Aboriginal Australians always lived primarily in the hottest, driest regions of the country.

A second common misperception about the Aboriginal Australians that arises from their history of tragic interactions with Europeans is that their culture and way of life did not change, that they were somehow relics of time left over from the Stone Age. One of the justifications that Europeans used in their displacement of Aboriginal populations from the most productive lands was that the land was essentially empty when the Europeans arrived there, the principle of *terra nullius*. The complex relationship that the Aboriginal Australians had developed with the land, which they transformed throughout the post-LGM period, was entirely unrecognized by Europeans, for whom land management meant private ownership and farming. The Aboriginal Australians' extensive developments in terms of linguistic complexity, with many languages containing two sets of vocabulary and grammar rules depending on the relationship of the people speaking with one another, and symbolic thought, best represented by Dreamtime stories and visual arts, were also totally incomprehensible to the European populations. Unfortunately, more than 235 years after Captain Cook's landing, these false perceptions continue to prevent many white Australians from seeing the rich and complex history of the Aboriginal population.

Postcolonial Australian history has not been much kinder to Aboriginal Australians than was the colonial era. In 1902, the new federal government of Australia banned indigenous people from voting, a policy that was to remain in effect for 60 years; they were also denied the other rights and responsibilities of citizenship until 1967. This same period also saw the beginnings of the practice of taking Aboriginal children, especially those who were not considered "full-blooded Aborigines," a term that is no longer used because of its history as part of the Stolen Generations, away from their parents. This policy continued until 1969 so that today many thousands of Aboriginal people have not seen their parents since early childhood and cannot trace their roots. The term for these people is the *Stolen Generation,* and their story is movingly depicted in the 2002 film *Rabbit Proof Fence.*

Contemporary Aboriginal history continues to point to great inequality and struggle for recognition. In 2006 the life expectancy of Aboriginal Australians was 17 years less than for other Australians, the unemployment rate is almost triple the rate for the rest of the country, and the rate of homelessness is three and a half times that of other Australians. Generations of institutionalized racism, in addition to the disruption of indigenous languages, beliefs, and ways of life; the stealing of generations of children; and the creation of Aboriginal reserves in the most barren and underserviced areas of the country have led to a situation in which survival itself is often a struggle. Nonetheless, there are bright spots in this historical record. The 1967 referendum showed that a huge majority of Australians favor reconciliation with the Aboriginal people. Several court cases recognizing the rights associated with Native Title, most recently in Perth in 2006, point to a judicial system ready to tackle hundreds of years of discrimination and theft. A decade-and-a-half-long struggle for reconciliation between Aboriginal and other Australians is also gaining momentum, especially because 2007 was the 40-year anniversary of the 1967 referendum. Late 2007 also saw the federal election of a Labor government in Australia, the first in more than 11½ years, which promised to make reconciliation and even a national apology part of its first-term agenda.

CULTURE

Economy and Society

Traditional Aboriginal Australian societies were all kinship based; all social regulations and laws, taboos, residential patterns, and other aspects of the community were regulated by the laws of kinship. These rules continue to define the social world of many Aboriginal Australians today as well. How Aboriginal people are related to others by blood, marriage, or totemic affiliation defines their rights and responsibilities toward others, and vice versa. Residential groups in the past were made up of people related by blood and by affiliation with a particular totem, usually an animal that represented the identity of a kinship group. With the urbanization of many Aboriginal Australians as well as the forced relocation of many others, this residential pattern does not usually occur nowadays, but all the other aspects of kinship continue to be central to many Aboriginal Australians' understanding of themselves and their social worlds.

The specific kinship systems of Aboriginal Australians were (and continue to be) classificatory: every person in a community is classified in terms of his or her kin relationship and is referred to by a specific kin term, such as *brother, mother,* or *grandfather.* In addition, this classification is determined by age, sex, and lineality so that father and father's brothers are all referred to as *father*; mother and mother's sisters are all *mother*. But mother's brothers are different from father's brothers and father's sisters from mother's sisters because they are cross-sex siblings. Extending down one generational level, all the people English speakers would call cousins are not considered the same in Aboriginal kinship systems. The children of father's brothers and mother's sisters are referred to and treated as siblings, while the children of father's sisters and mother's brothers are cross-cousins and treated differently from siblings since they are potential marriage partners.

In addition to these close relatives, Aboriginal kinship systems recognize the importance of lineages, with both patrilineal and matrilineal societies represented throughout the country. Lineages are groups of people related to one another through one line of descent, reckoned through either men (patrilineal) or women (matrilineal). This is different from the bilateral kinship that most Westerners are familiar with, in which people are equally related to their mother's and to their father's families. For many Aboriginal Australians, the ties to one of these groups are more significant in terms of marriage, avoidance, rights, and responsibilities than the ties to the other.

In addition to lineages these complex kinship systems also recognize membership in clans, which are groups of lineages that have the same common mythical ancestor. Clans are almost always exogamous: people are forbidden to marry someone who belongs to their clan. Clans are also the groups with which individuals take part in major religious rituals and events. Most Aboriginal societies also further divide their populations into moities, which are clanlike groups that act as clans in being exogamous. Finally in addition to these kinship groupings before the disruptions of colonialism and urbanization the final group whom any individual Aboriginal Australian recognized was the band. Bands were residential units consisting of a segment of a lineage plus spouses and occasionally a more distant clan member. These were the primary units in which individuals would eat, sleep, migrate, and participate in regular daily activities including some less important ritual events.

In addition to being kin based these societies were traditionally relatively egalitarian; there were no inherited differences in prestige or wealth. Instead, age, gender, and experience or knowledge served as markers of status with elders, men, and people who were especially clever holding more exalted positions than others. Certain individuals also gained recognition through their shamanic skills, as discussed later. Aside from these part-time religious roles, the only divisions of labor recognized in Aboriginal societies were those based on sex and age. Men typically hunted such animals as kangaroos, goannas (large lizards), birds, turtles, and a variety of other land and sea animals, while women gathered a significant amount of the food eaten on any given day in the form of roots, berries, and grains, and took care of the children.

Religion

The religion of the Aboriginal Australians is based on the Dreaming, a series of stories that explain the nature of the world and everything in it, including creation and proper functioning. The period of prehistory in which the events that created the world happened is called the Dreamtime. But unlike for Westerners for Aboriginal Australians this period of prehistory continues to be active in the present time. The ancestor spirits whose activities formed mountains, rivers, valleys, and other features of the Australian landscape continue to have power in the present. Their songlines or footprints continue to inform contemporary Aboriginal understandings of the world, with the places where the spirits entered and exited this world having particular ritual importance. Humans, animals, ancestor spirits, and the

This Aboriginal painting depicts aspects of its creators' local landscapes including waterholes, a river, and kangaroo tracks, all of which are integral to the Dreamtime stories of their people. *(Shutterstock/Jenny Solomon)*

land itself are all intertwined in this cosmology or worldview, which has been handed down in stories, songs, and rituals for many thousands of years. Aboriginal art, with its well-known dot images of animals and abstract geometric shapes, is also usually a depiction of the stories of the Dreaming and the landscape in which a story occurred.

Another important aspect of Aboriginal religion that is from the Dreaming is totemism. Each Aboriginal clan has its own totemic or special relationship with a specific animal, plant, or even feature of the landscape or cosmos, such as the moon. These totems are said to be the ancestors of both the members of the clans that bear their names as well as of the plant, animal, or feature. For example, the witchety grub clan as well as witchety grubs themselves are said to have emerged from the same ancestor, and as a result members of this clan must not eat this particular delicacy.

While the Dreaming stories provide the underlying ideas and concepts that guide all spirituality in these communities, rituals are the regular enactment of these ideas and concepts. Through initiation, other rites of passage, and Dreaming rituals, the stories from the Dreamtime come to life in the present day. For example, initiation rituals serve as the mechanism through which children learn all the ceremonial and (at least in the past) practical information necessary to live as adults in their community. Both men's and women's initiation ceremonies entail learning secret clan information from the Dreaming, performing dances and songs marking the change in the individual's community status, and a host of symbolic activities such as painting the skin; dressing up; permanently altering the body in some way by knocking out a tooth, scarification, or piercing; and, for boys, circumcision or subincision of the penis. Initiations are not the only rites of passage celebrated by Aboriginal communities. Marriages, funerals, postfuneral bereavement rituals, and others, are all events that transform the status of individuals, marking their passage from one kind of person to another. Dreaming rituals are those that enact specific Dreaming stories through dance, chanting, sand painting, and other symbolic events.

The individuals who are responsible for leading these rituals, as well as generally protecting their people from negative forces from the spirit and human worlds, are the most important people in their bands and, depending on their power, even within their larger clan group. These people are often called shamans or medicine men in English, while each Aboriginal language has its own name for them. These are people whose souls are said to travel into the spirit world in order to carry information between the world of humans and that of spirits. They are also believed to be able to reproduce the actions of the ancestor spirits by flying to heaven, entering the earth's surface, and exiting again, often in a new location; speaking with the ancestors; disappearing; and returning into their own bodies. Only certain elders are able to attain this position through years of work, learning Dreaming stories and practicing their arts, as well as undergoing a long series of initiation rituals held by other shamans. From a biological point of view, they must also be able to attain a trance or ecstatic state with relative ease. Aboriginal religion today remains central to most Aboriginal Australians' identities as Indigenous, although not all rituals and rites of passage continue to be practiced as frequently as in the past. Mentioning and seeing images of the dead remain important taboos, and even among urban Aboriginal communities, learning at least a few sacred songs and myths remains an important marker of community belonging.

See also ABORIGINAL TASMANIANS; MARDU; PITJANTJATJARA; TIWI; TORRES STRAIT ISLANDERS; WARLPIRIS.

FURTHER READING

Diane Bell. *Daughters of the Dreaming* (Minneapolis: University of Minnesota Press, 1993).

James G. Cowan. *The Elements of the Aborigine Tradition* (Rockport, Mass.: Element, 1992).

Stephen Davis. *Above Capricorn: Aboriginal Biographies from Northern Australia* (Sydney, New South Wales: Angus & Robertson, 1994).

Jean A. Ellis. *Aboriginal Australia: The Dreaming, Traditional Lifestyle, Traditional Art, Language Groups* (Penrith, New South Wales: Kaliarna Productions, 2001).

Norman C. Habel. *Reconciliation: Searching for Australia's Soul* (North Blackburn, Victoria: HarperCollins, 1999).

Mudrooro Narogin. *Aboriginal Mythology: An A–Z Spanning the History of the Australian Aboriginal People from the Earliest Legends to the Present Day* (London: Aquarian, 1994).

John Ramsland and Christopher Mooney. *Remembering Aboriginal Heroes: Struggle, Identity and the Media* (Melbourne, Victoria: Brolga, 2006).

Percy Trezise. *Dream Road: A Journey of Discovery* (St. Leonards, New South Wales: Allen & Unwin, 1997).

**ABORIGINAL
TAIWANESE**

location:
Taiwan and Fujian
Province, China

time period:
5000 B.C.E. to the present

ancestry:
Austronesian

language:
There are 10 different
aboriginal languages
spoken on Taiwan, all in
the Austronesian lan-
guage family.

Aboriginal Malay   *See* MELAYU ASLI.

Aboriginal Taiwanese (Gaoshan, Yuanzhumin)

The Aboriginal Taiwanese are the indigenous
peoples of Taiwan and its surrounding islands.
Today they are a population of about 400,000
or around 2 percent of the island's people and
live in conditions similar to those of the Aboriginal peoples of the United States, Canada,
Australia, South Africa, and other places where
state-sponsored colonialism disrupted tribal
social organizations. On the whole they tend to
be poorer, less well educated, and less healthy
and to live shorter lives than the dominant Chinese inhabitants of Taiwan. A few thousand of
these Austronesian-language speakers also live
in Fujian Province, China, where they are considered the Gaoshan minority.

GEOGRAPHY

Taiwan is a subtropical island located about 95
miles from the coast of southeastern China. The
main island, Taiwan proper, is 244 miles long
and 89 miles wide and borders the South China
Sea, East China Sea, Philippine Sea, and Pacific
Ocean. The entire Taiwanese archipelago also
includes 79 other islands, such as Lanyu (Orchid) and the Pescadores, as well as the islets of
Green Island and Liuchiu.

Taiwan itself is divided by the Central
Range, a group of mountains rising as high as
12,966 feet above sea level. On the eastern side
of these mountains elevations fall gradually
into foothills and then a wide plateau before
climbing back to heights of 4,221 feet in the
Coastal Range. On the western side the rise is
much more acute, making for fast-running rivers and steeper climbs.

Taiwan's climate, volcanic soils, and copious rainfall mean that it is ideal for agriculture.
Taiwanese farmers produce sugarcane, fruit,
tea, and rice. The country also produces more
than 70 percent of the world's camphor from the
camphor laurel evergreen trees that grow on the
island. In fact about 55 percent of Taiwan today
remains under forest cover, particularly in the
mountains, where most of the nonurbanized
Aboriginal people live. The islands also have
rich offshore fishing grounds, which have been
exploited by humans for thousands of years.

ORIGINS

The origins of Taiwan's Aboriginal people remain uncertain today because of the great
amount of time that has elapsed since their initial arrival. However, the most likely scenario
is that they arrived from south China in about
6000 B.C.E. bearing some of the hallmarks of
later Austronesian societies, including Austronesian languages, domesticated plants, and possibly chickens and dogs. There is some debate
about these origins, however, because the Aboriginal people did not seem to have another of
the characteristic features of some later Austronesian societies, namely, LAPITA CULTURE pottery. There is also archaeological evidence that
Taiwan had been inhabited prior to this Austronesian arrival, perhaps from as early as 30,000
B.C.E., when the archipelago was still part of the
larger Asian mainland. What happened to these
people to cause their disappearance and when it
occurred both remain mysteries to this day.

HISTORY

The history of Taiwan's Aboriginal people before the arrival of a Chinese army in the third
century C.E. is difficult to tease out of the patchy
and inconclusive archaeological record. Their
earliest culture was probably marked by the
influx of several different Austronesian groups
and the establishment of small-scale horti-
cultural societies with kinship as the primary
organizing principle behind them; chiefs or
headmen may have overseen each group's internal and external affairs.

In 230 C.E. several thousand indigenous
people were carried back to the mainland by
the invading army of the Kingdom of Wu, but
few other consequences of the invasion were felt
on the islands. Further invasions occurred between the 10th and 14th centuries, and Chinese
administrative control was nominally extended
during this period. In the 16th century a somewhat more significant HAN colonial presence
began to be felt throughout the entire Taiwanese Archipelago as more and more mainland-
ers moved to Taiwan and began developing the
west coast of the main island. Chinese sources
claim that indigenous peoples worked with the
colonizers to develop the island's agricultural
capacity and to expel JAPANESE attempts at
colonization, but this version of history hides
decades of exploitation, persecution, and mistreatment of the Aboriginal peoples at the
hands of the Chinese invaders.

The 17th century introduced a new colonial
presence to Taiwan when the Dutch established
a fort and trading post on the main island's
southwest coast and later a capital city at Fort
Provintia, today's Tainan City. As had the Chinese the Dutch colonizers had little respect for
the way of life of the islands' indigenous peo-

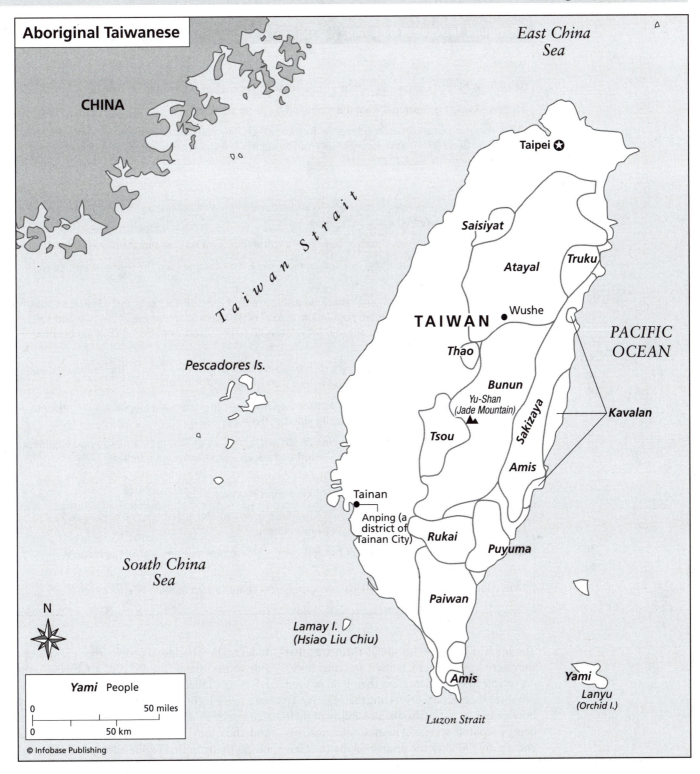

Aboriginal Taiwanese

CHINA

East China
Sea

Taipei ✪

Taiwan Strait

Saisiyat

Atayal

Truku

TAIWAN • Wushe

PACIFIC
OCEAN

Thao

Bunun

Yu-Shan
(Jade Mountain)
▲▲

Sakizaya

Kavalan

Pescadores Is.

Tsou

Amis

Tainan •

Anping (a
district of
Tainan City)

Rukai

Puyuma

South China
Sea

Paiwan

N

Lamay I. ◔
(Hsiao Liu Chiu)

Amis

Yami

Lanyu
(Orchid I.)

Luzon Strait

Yami People

0 ────────── 50 miles

0 ────────── 50 km

© Infobase Publishing

ples. In 1636 hundreds of Aboriginal people were deported and then killed in response to their attack of a Dutch ship off Lamay Island, present-day Hsiao Liu Chiu. Some individual Aboriginal people wound up as slaves living as far from home as Batavia, contemporary Jakarta, Indonesia, the seat of the Dutch East Indies colony. During the Dutch period the Chinese presence in the islands became more evident as well, and finally in 1661–62 a mainland Chinese army drove out the last Dutch administrators and soldiers and began its own long colonial period.

During the more than 200 years of Chinese colonialism the Aboriginal people were seen in a variety of different lights, but none of them respected their autonomy or right to live in Taiwan as they had been doing for thousands of years.

Aboriginal Taiwanese time line

B.C.E.

30,000 A human community settles in Taiwan, then connected to the Chinese mainland.

15,000 Taiwan is separated from the mainland by rising sea levels.

6000 Austronesians take up residence in Taiwan, which they call Pakan. This date is contested and may be 1500–1000 years more recent. The settlers may have been followed by others over the course of the next 4,000 years.

C.E.

1100 The Han Chinese begin migrating to and settling in the Pescadores, an archipelago off the western coast of Taiwan.

1544 Portuguese explorers discover Taiwan and call it Ilha Formosa, meaning "Beautiful Island."

1624 The Dutch begin building Fort Zeelandia in the town of Anping, on the southwestern coast of Taiwan.

1636 In response to an Aboriginal attack on a shipwrecked crew off Lamay Island (Hsiao LiuChiu), the Dutch deport the entire population. A total of 327 people are trapped in a cave and suffocated with smoke; men are sold into slavery in Batavia, and women and children become servants for Dutch officers.

1650 The Dutch build Fort Provintia, which becomes the colony's new capital. The Chinese come to refer to it as "edifice of the red-haired barbarians."

1652 Resentful Chinese farmers rebel against the Dutch administrators after a poll tax is instituted; 6,000 Chinese peasants are brutally killed in the suppression.

1662 After 38 years of administration, the Dutch are driven out of Taiwan. Cheng Cheng-kung introduces Chinese ways of life to the island and constructs a Confucian temple.

1683 China attacks Taiwan and the Cheng family surrenders to the Manchu Qing dynasty. Taiwan consequently becomes a part of China's Fujian Province.

1874 The Japanese attack the Aboriginal Taiwanese in Mutan She; 30 Aboriginal people and 543 Japanese die (12 in battle and 531 from illness).

1887 Taiwan is granted the status of being its own Chinese province and Liu Ming-chu'an is appointed governor.

1895 Upon losing the first Sino-Japanese War, China cedes Taiwan and the Pescadores to Japan.

The initial Chinese belief about them was that they were less than fully human and thus it was acceptable to drive them from their land or even kill them if necessary. Over time their humanity became less an issue than the possibility of their being a separate species of human, although this change did not alter the disgust felt by the Chinese administration. By the 19th century this attitude had been revised somewhat to one that saw "civilization," meaning Chinese civilization, and assimilation into Chinese society as the only logical policy toward the Aboriginal people. The goal by the time of the Qing loss of the first Sino-Japanese War in 1895 was still conquest but conquest followed by transformation rather than conquest followed by extermination. Interestingly, despite these official policies and attitudes many Aboriginal people from the western side of the island, the Pingpu, a Chinese term referring to their residence on the plains of Taiwan, were incorporated into Chinese life. Many Chinese men arrived on Taiwan without wives and thus took Pingpu women as wives while others living in that region adopted Chinese agricultural methods and largely assimilated into Chinese society. The eastern tribes, who lived in more mountainous regions less suitable to Chinese agriculture, called Gaoshan by the Chinese, maintained their independence and continued to struggle against assimilation throughout the entire period.

With the Qing loss to the Japanese in 1895 the Chinese colony of Taiwan was ceded to Japan, beginning a half-century of colonialism at

1930 Anger among the Atayal Aboriginal peoples flares over their mistreatment by the Japanese administrators in the Wushe Uprising, which results in the killing and beheading of 150 Japanese officials. Two thousand to 3,000 Japanese troops are brought in to crush the rebellion; the Wushe Uprising is the last Aboriginal rebellion.

1942 As the United States goes to war with Japan the Chinese government renounces all treaties made with Japan and seeks to reclaim Taiwan as a Chinese territory.

1945 Japan cedes Taiwan to China and the Republic of China declares October 25 "Taiwan Retrocession Day."

1949 In reaction to the 228 incident martial law is enacted. During the period of the White Terror, 140,000 Taiwanese citizens are imprisoned or executed for their proven or imagined opposition to the Kuomintang government.

Chinese Communists take over China and establish the People's Republic. Two million refugees from the previous government and business sectors flee to Taiwan. The United Nations and many Western nations refuse to recognize the People's Republic and see the Republic of China as the legitimate ruler of Taiwan and all of China.

1967 The "concrete housing incident" occurs; public housing is built on Lanyu (Orchid) Island for the resident Yami tribe, who largely reject the homes because they are culturally inappropriate. Most of the housing is occupied by Yami today after open-air pavilions were added to make them more comfortable and appropriate.

1984 Taiwan Yuanzhumin Shehui Yundong, a political organization dedicated to Taiwan's Aboriginal peoples, is formed; it does not begin to make any substantial contributions to public debate and policymaking until 1990.

1987 Martial law is lifted and Aboriginal identity becomes an important tool to differentiate Taiwan from mainland China.

The Taiwanese government creates the Taiwan Aboriginal Culture Park. The park contains houses representing the culture of nine of Taiwan's surviving Aboriginal groups and stages presentations and displays of Aboriginal culture.

2004 The Truku become the 12th Aboriginal group to gain official recognition in Taiwan.

2005 The Taiwanese Aboriginal soap opera *Hunter,* about Aboriginal peoples living in the city, is broadcast in Taiwan on the Indigenous Television Network, said to be the first 24-hour indigenous television station in Asia.

2007 The Sakizaya become the 13th Aboriginal group to gain official recognition by the Council of Indigenous Peoples of Taiwan; they had formerly been a subgroup of the Ami.

the hands of the Japanese. During this period the local Chinese population suffered almost as much as the Aboriginal people from Japanese policies that robbed them of their land and required them to use Japanese names and language. It was also under the Japanese in 1930 that Taiwan's Aboriginal people staged their last uprising against colonialism, the Wushe Uprising or Paran Incident. The incident was the result of Japanese policies that cheated the Aboriginal people of their land and led to their enslavement in Japanese industries and farms. On October 27, 1930, about 300 people from the Atayal and other tribes attacked Japanese soldiers and killed about 150 of them; some reports go on to claim that 4,000 more Japanese colonists were killed over the subsequent two months. In response the

Japanese sent several thousand troops, who over the course of these two months put down all indigenous movements and massacred at least 216 and as many as 1,200 Aboriginal people. This incident has often been used by the Nationalist government established in Taiwan in 1949 to indicate the severity of Japanese colonial policy and to legitimate its own rule; recent interpretations by Aboriginal people dismiss claims that the Nationalists have been any more humane or more supportive of Aboriginal land claims or ways of life than the Japanese had been.

Following Japan's loss in World War II Taiwan was returned to China and the new Kuomintang (KMT) government quickly moved to try to integrate the remaining Aboriginal people into a colonial state. The Aboriginal people were given the communal ethnonym *Gaoshan* in 1945, which they continue to bear under the official national terminology of the People's Republic of China (PRC). At the same time the KMT also tried to create the illusion of national unity on Taiwan following the Japanese departure. Indigenous culture was strictly proscribed and Chinese language and lifestyles became mandatory for all. Assimilation was the only possibility, and many individuals and communities have suffered along the way; alcoholism, prostitution, unemployment, homelessness, and general dissociation with the dominant Chinese society were the results. When the Chinese Communists won the civil war in that country in 1949 and about 2 million Nationalist refugees arrived on Taiwan and established the Republic of China, nothing significant changed for the indigenous people.

The first real cultural transformation in the Taiwanese attitude toward, and treatment of, the Aboriginal population occurred in 1987 when martial law, which had been imposed at the founding of the Republic of China in response to Taiwanese attacks on Chinese colonizers in the "2–28 massacre" of 1947, was lifted. One year later the first leader of the Republic of China to have been born on Taiwan, Lee Teng-hui, took office upon the death of President Chiang Ching-kuo. This initiated a period in which Taiwanese identity began to flower and the idea of a Republic of China as a separate country from the People's Republic of China began to gain more acceptance on the island. Toward these ends the utility of Taiwan's indigenous people was obvious to many as they represented an ancient historical past entirely separate from that of mainland China. In 1987 their heritage began to be resuscitated with the creation of a historical park, which, while incomplete and stereotypical in many ways, was somewhat better than a policy of assimilation and ignorance. Local and national governments made other efforts as well to begin the long process of recognition of, and reconciliation with, the indigenous people.

Throughout the 1990s community revitalization projects to support the growth and development of ethnospecific activities, heritage projects, and teaching sprang up all over Taiwan. Both different communities of Chinese and the 13 officially recognized Aboriginal groups (AMI, Atayal, BUNUN, Kavalan, Paiwan, Puyuma, Rukai, Saisiyat, Sakizaya, Thao, Truku, Tsou, and YAMI) began to reenact rituals, to write their myths and histories for both popular and academic audiences, and to disseminate this information as widely as possible throughout Taiwan and the world. Such Aboriginal practices as tattooing and even headhunting began to be talked about as cultural features to be preserved in writing and pictures rather than buried and ignored. Nonetheless many in the Aboriginal community think that Taiwan's multicultural policies have not gone far enough to compensate their people for the centuries of persecution and even genocide they have experienced. At less than 2 percent of Taiwan's contemporary population and among the country's poorest citizens, these indigenous people can scarcely exert the kind of political clout necessary to bring about real change from below, but Taiwan Yuanzhumin Shehui Yundong and other similar organizations dedicated to the country's indigenous peoples are continuing to push for recognition of land claims and cultural rights long denied by the Chinese majority.

CULTURE

Prior to Taiwan's various colonial periods the indigenous people were shifting horticulturalists who used slash-and-burn techniques to prepare their fields for growing rice, millet, yams, taro, and various vegetables. After a season or two they would then allow the field to lie fallow for many years to regenerate the soil's nutrients and move on to other sections of forest. All of the indigenous peoples used a back strap loom for weaving cloth and stone tools for beating bark into materials for rope and clothing. Most protein was obtained from hunting deer, boar, and other wild animals; fish and other seafood; and domesticated pigs. Kinship was very important in every group but the systems differed, with some groups, such as the Bunun, having a patrilineal descent pattern in which only fathers pass their lineage membership to their children; other groups, such as the Ami, having a matrilineal system in which only mothers pass their lineage membership to their children; and still others, such as the Paiwan, having an ambilineal system in which each individual is able to choose membership in his or her mother's or father's lineage. Animist and shamanistic religious practices were also evident among all the indigenous peoples, with nature spirits and spirits of the dead being central to all indigenous cosmologies.

Much of the culture of the Pingpu of Taiwan's western plains disintegrated and was killed off with the assimilation of these peoples between the 10th and 17th centuries so that today much of our knowledge about them is gained through archaeology rather than ethnography. However, this official version of Pingpu history is disputed by a number of indigenous Taiwanese themselves who claim descent from, and a continuous cultural heritage with, the island's western tribes. The 13 officially recognized Gaoshan tribes, who resided in the more marginal mountainous regions of Taiwan's east and on some of the outer islands, were able to maintain some semblance of their indigenous way of being until well into the 20th century. For example, Ayatal elders in their 80s today still bear the facial tattooing that was common among many indigenous groups until outlawed by the Japanese.

Today there are still several hundred thousand people living on Taiwan and Orchid Island who consider themselves Aboriginal. Some continue to work as farmers, although now in much the same way as their Han Chinese neighbors, utilizing modern tools, fertilizers, and land use patterns. A few smaller communities in the mountains continue to rely on hunting for most of their protein sources and those on the coast and smaller islands rely heavily on fish. A substantial number of Gaoshan have also learned Chinese, gained an education, and moved to the cities of both Taiwan and mainland China, where they work in all sectors of the economy. It is from this population that the small cadre of Aboriginal intellectuals has emerged; since 1987, this group has been pushing for further recognition and compensation for their people.

Another interesting cultural development within Taiwanese indigenous communities is the widespread popularity of baseball. The Japanese introduced the sport to Taiwan prior to their expulsion in 1945, and, despite the Chinese attempts at removing all traces of the Japanese colonial era, baseball has remained popular throughout Taiwanese society. For indigenous boys it provides one access to success and for a very few even international fame; two indigenous players have been drafted to play baseball in the United States.

See also AUSTRONESIANS; TAIWANESE: NATIONALITY.

FURTHER READING

David Blundell, ed. *Austronesian Taiwan: Linguistics, History, Ethnology, Prehistory* (Taipei: SMC Publishing, 2000).

Josiane Cauquelin, *Aborigines of Taiwan: The Puyuma: From Headhunting to the Modern World.* Translated by Caroline Charras-Wheeler (London: RoutledgeCurzon, 2004).

Kwang-chih Chang. *Fengpitou, Tapenking, and the Prehistory of Taiwan.* Yale University Publications in Anthropology, no. 73 (New Haven, Conn.: Yale University, Department of Anthropology, 1969).

David Faure, ed. *In Search of the Hunters and Their Tribes: Studies in the History and Culture of the Taiwan Indigenous People* (Taipei: SMC, 2002).

Raleigh Ferrell. *Taiwan Aboriginal Groups: Problems in Cultural and Linguistic Classification* (Taipei: Academia Sinica, 1969).

A-chin Hsiau. *Contemporary Taiwanese Cultural Nationalism* (London: Routledge, 2000).

Jolan Hsieh. *Collective Rights of Indigenous Peoples: Identity-Based Movement of Plain Indigenous in Taiwan* (New York: Routledge, 2006).

Mutsu Hsu. *Culture, Self, and Adaptation: The Psychological Anthropology of Two Malayo-Polynesian Groups in Taiwan* (Taipei: Institute of Ethnology, Academia Sinica, 1991).

Janet B. Montgomery-McGovern. *Among the Head-Hunters of Formosa* (Boston: Small, Maynard, 1922).

Emma Jinhua Teng. *Taiwan's Imagined Geography: Chinese Colonial Travel Writing and Pictures, 1683–1895* (Cambridge, Mass.: Harvard University Asia Center, 2004).

Aboriginal Tasmanians (Indigenous Tasmanians, Palawah, Pallawah)

The first humans to occupy Tasmania arrived when lower sea levels meant that the small island was actually connected to the Australian mainland, 23,000–25,000 years ago. Then, about 11,000 years ago, rising seas due to global warming stranded this population, and they remained alone until Europeans arrived in 1772.

The Aboriginal Tasmanians practiced a hunter-gatherer mode of subsistence and consumed animals like wombats and kangaroos, fish, and a variety of roots and berries. Their kinship-based political organization was based on individual homestead groups that were linked to others within the same region in what are called bands. Each tribe, a group sharing the same language, culture, and approximate geographic space, was made up of a number of bands. As did other ABORIGINAL AUSTRALIANS, the Tasmanians had a relatively simple technological base, relying on bark and grass building materials for their temporary shelters and using bone, wood, and stone for their toolkit. Also similar to that of the mainland, Aboriginal Tasmanians' religious life centered on Dreamtime stories and observance of the taboos associated with their totemic plants and animals.

**ABORIGINAL
TASMANIANS**

location:
Tasmania

time period:
Probably 21,000–23,000
B.C.E. to the present

ancestry:
Asian origins but so old
that their exact ances-
try is unknown. Some
genetic markers indicate
an ancient connection
to mainland Aboriginal
people and New Guinea
Highlanders.

language:
English is the official
language of Australia.
Before colonization there
were between eight and
16 different Tasmanian
languages. Today,
Palawa kani is taught
to Palawah children
through the Tasmanian
Aboriginal Centre.

This lifestyle came to an abrupt end in Tasmania in 1803 when the first European settlers arrived with their diseases, weapons, and ideology of racial superiority; several earlier explorers had seen or met the Aboriginal people but did not settle on the island and thus had little effect. In 1828 the colonial government granted Europeans the right to kill Aboriginal people during a period of martial law in the state. European diseases took a further toll on the population so that by 1830 only 350 Aboriginal people were reported, of a population that previously may have approached 7,000. In May 1876 the European press reported that the last Aboriginal Tasmanian, Truganini, died.

The report, however, was inaccurate and was based on a combination of 19th-century racial categories that are no longer used and government rhetoric created to deny land rights and other recognition to the remaining population. Since the 1960s Tasmania's Aboriginal population has worked hard to gain recognition not only of its existence as a modern community but also of its rights as the indigenous people of the island. In 2001, 15,773 people identified themselves as Aboriginal Tasmanians.

For a population that has been denied its history for the past 200 years many Aboriginal Tasmanian organizations today are dedicated to the process of cultural recovery. Children are being taught a form of Aboriginal language, Palawa kani, and art, music, stories, and such traditional activities as mutton-bird hunting have all been revived to some extent. Another priority is the repatriation of ancestral remains from museum collections around the world. The state government of Tasmania has made it illegal for museums to hold bones and other specimens that were taken, often by force, in the 18th and 19th centuries. Samples of Truganini's hair and skin have been returned from Great Britain, as have many other bones and biological samples from anonymous Aboriginal Tasmanians. All of them have received a proper burial on ancestral land.

See also ABORIGINAL AUSTRALIANS; AUSTRALIANS: NATIONALITY.

Acehnese (Ache(h)nese, Achinese, Atchinese, Atjehnese, Ureung Aceh, Ureung Baroh, Ureung Tunong)

Nanggröe Aceh Darussalam, more commonly known as Aceh, is a territory of Indonesia and is the northernmost province of the island of Sumatra. The people of Aceh were the first in the archipelago to convert to Islam and even today are generally considered to practice a more orthodox form of the religion than is evident in the rest of the country. Throughout their long history, the Acehnese have fought for their autonomy and beliefs and have resisted opposition and control by outsiders.

Chinese records of Aceh date to about 500 C.E., when it was called the Buddhist state of Poli or Po-Li. In the following centuries Indian mercenaries and traders also introduced Hinduism, which blended with Buddhism to transform both the state and the local religion of the people. Most Acehnese today, however, consider the start of their own history to be about 804, the founding date of the Islamic kingdom of Perlak. By the time of Marco Polo's visit to Aceh in 1292 Islam had spread to a second Acehnese trading port as well, Samudra, from which the modern name of Sumatra is taken. The first sultanate to consolidate power and Islam in the region, however, did not emerge until the 1600s under Sultan Iskandar Muda. At that time the Acehnese were the dominant power in the region and as such engaged in many battles with the Portuguese at Malacca, in which the Acehnese were frequently victorious. By the 1800s as the port of Aceh became particularly attractive to European interests, especially the Dutch, for its control of gold, pepper, and other spices, the Acehnese were increasingly determined to remain independent.

In 1811 in an effort to maintain independence from the encroaching Dutch East India Company or VOC, the Acehnese signed a friendship treaty with England, certifying that each party would defend the other against attack. Although this treaty has never been enforced, the obligation has never been rescinded and still stands to this day. In 1824 although the British had treated Aceh as an independent nation, a second treaty effectively transferred all British possessions on the island of Sumatra to Dutch control. A clause in this treaty stated that Aceh would remain independent, but this agreement was later breached by the British when the Sumatra Treaty of 1871 transferred Aceh to the Netherlands in exchange for lucrative Dutch concessions.

During the Dutch period the colonizers largely allied themselves with the traditional nobility in the province, an arrangement that allowed them to govern at the highest levels. However, the region's religious leaders or *ulama* were zealously anticolonial and led their people in the ensuing fight for independence. The rivalry between these two centers of power in the region quickly escalated into the Aceh War, which continued from 1873 until 1903 and then intermittently until the JAPANESE occupation in 1942. With the use of guerrilla tactics, this was a vicious war that cost more than 10,000 Dutch and 100,000 Acehnese lives.

During World War II the Japanese briefly occupied Indonesia, including Aceh, which they ruled in conjunction with the local nobility in the same way the Dutch had done. The archipelago was never liberated as such, but after the Allies defeated the Japanese the Republic of Indonesia claimed its independence. Soon thereafter the Dutch returned to the region to regain their political and economic interests, setting off a war of independence that ultimately saw the Dutch withdraw. In Aceh the war sparked the same political rivalry between the nobility and religious leaders that had characterized much of the previous century, and victory by the religious leaders made them the legitimate power in Acehnese political life. Despite earlier calls for complete independence with the promise of relative autonomy Indonesia's first president, Sukarno, persuaded the new Acehnese leadership to join the republic and even fund the purchase of its first aircraft and overseas diplomatic posts.

Rather than gaining autonomy, however, Aceh was made a part of North Sumatra Province and secularism was promoted over Islamic law throughout the republic. By 1953 the new Acehnese governor had had enough of Sukarno's empty promises and declared his region an Islamic state, independent of Indonesia. The war that ensued was brutal and took many lives on both sides. The war ended only in the late 1950s when Sukarno granted the province a special status, which allowed the people a certain level of independence, especially over religious and educational matters. Yet this concession ignored two of the most important complaints: Indonesian and foreign control of the region's oil and gas wealth and the repressive military presence. By 1976 the Acehnese were frustrated with the central Indonesian government for two reasons, the practice of transmigration, or the relocation of relatively secular JAVANESE, BALINESE, MÁDURESE, and others into the Aceh region, and the exploitation of Acehnese natural resources. The Acehnese argued that they were culturally different from these migrants and were being exploited by the Javanese for their oil and gas, spurring the Aceh Merdeka (Free Aceh) movement. The Indonesian government made mass indiscriminate arrests of Acehnese, citing terrorist acts by members of Aceh Merdeka as grounds for incarceration, and during the 1980s Indonesia seemed to be winning the war. In 1989, however, Free Aceh reemerged as a strong military factor in the province, prompting the movement of more than 12,000 Indonesian troops into the region. Aceh became a Military Operations Area (MOA), akin to East Timor, in which about 1,000 people were killed, twice that many disappeared, and three times that number tortured.

Finally in 1998 President Suharto was replaced by his vice president, Jusuf Habibie, and the MOA status was lifted from Aceh. But at the same time, violence on the day of primary troop withdrawal, increasing activity by Free Aceh due to Suharto's removal, and increased popular support within Aceh for independence led to even greater military oppression than had been the case during the MOA period. In 2001, as part of the government's attempts at rapprochement with the Acehnese leadership, the province was granted the right officially to implement sharia law. However, Acehnese resentment toward the government prevailed as a result of the exploitation of Aceh's resource-rich environment, since the majority of the revenue from such resources continued to flow into the central purse rather than into the region.

In 2005 as a result of the tsunami that devastated the entire south Asian region the need to reconstruct Aceh led to peace talks. The agreement implemented Acehnese self-rule and the eventual right to establish a political party. The rebels had to agree to give up the struggle for independence. In turn, the Indonesian government agreed to release captured political prisoners and to offer farmland to former Acehnese fighters. It remains to be seen whether these actions will lead to peace and prosperity in Aceh.

The traditional Acehnese economy was based on subsistence rice farming and fishing. Both wet or paddy rice and dry upland rice varieties were grown, depending on geography, and supplemented by sugar, peanuts, coconuts, corn, pepper, tobacco, rubber, and, in the higher elevations, coffee. Many families kept a few cattle or water buffaloes for meat and labor, but most people did not own their own land and worked as tenants or sharecroppers. Today much subsistence land has been damaged through warfare and the tsunami, and it is the commercial farming and mining industries that have become the most lucrative. Unfortunately skill levels in terms of human resources

ACEHNESE

location:
Aceh Province, Sumatra, Indonesia

time period:
At least fifth century C.E. to the present

ancestry:
Blend of many races, Austronesian, Indian, Arab

language:
Aceh or Achinese, a Chamic language in the larger Austronesian language family

are yet to be developed fully and unemployment is high; estimates in 2006 ranged between 26 and more than 50 percent.

Kinship among the Acehnese is a complicated system based on several principles. Generally society recognizes the centrality of bilateral descent, in which each individual is seen as an equal member of both the mother's and father's descent groups, similarly to most Western societies. However, the Acehnese also recognize four distinct patrilineal descent groups, called *kawom,* which once provided each family with its primary associations and alliances during times of conflict. They also recognize matrilineal descent groups, called *karong,* which serve primarily as residential units as part of their matrilocal residence pattern. Thus at marriage it is the husband who moves into his wife's homestead and the house that his wife will eventually inherit. Nonetheless, as it is a Muslim society, inheritance generally follows the pattern that for every share received by a daughter, a son receives two shares, usually in the form of land, animals, or other wealth. The need to have a man's farmland, inherited from his father, near his wife's home, inherited from hers, means that most villages or prayer houses are functionally endogamous, with most people, at least in the past, marrying into their own villages but outside their own matrilineal and patrilineal kinship groups, both of which are exogamous.

Religion among the Acehnese is less syncretic than in much of the rest of Indonesia and reflects the Buddhist, Hindu, and animist past to a lesser degree. The Acehnese consider themselves strict Sunni Muslims, more akin to Arabs than to fellow Indonesians; the region is sometimes called Mecca's Veranda because of its strict interpretation of Islamic texts. Gamblers as well as women not wearing a *hijab* or seen alone in the company of unrelated men are publicly caned for their sins against Islam. Hajj, or pilgrimage to Mecca, and tithing, fasting for Ramadan, abstaining from alcohol, and many other aspects of Muslim society are observed far more strictly in Aceh than throughout Indonesia, and this strictness sets them apart culturally from their secular and syncretic neighbors.

Achang (Daisa, Hansa, Maingtha, Mengsa, Mengsa-shan, Nga Ang, Ochang)

The Achang are one of China's recognized 55 national minority groups; the small population lives in several counties within Yunnan Prov-

ince. A few Achang also live across the border in Kachin State, Myanmar (Burma), but in that country they are called the Maingtha. As a result of their small numbers in both countries, the Achang have largely been integrated into the surrounding populations of DAI, KACHIN (known as Jingpo in China), HAN in China, and SHANS in Myanmar.

Many scholars of China believe that the Achang descend from the ancient QIANG people, who lived in the region of present-day Gansu and Qinghai Provinces prior to the common era. Then throughout much of the first millennium C.E. this population was driven out of its original homeland and into parts of southern China. Both Chinese records and legends from the Achang themselves point to an original settlement a bit farther north and east from where most live today in western Yunnan and eastern Myanmar, particularly along the Lancang River, the Chinese name for the Mekong. By the 12th or 13th century this ancient population, which was known as Xunchuan during the Tang period (618–907), had moved again, this time into the region in which most currently live, the Dehong prefecture in the far west of Yunnan Province. Through the course of this 1,000 years or more of history the Achang both integrated cultural traits from the Han, Dai, and others into their way of life and became more and more differentiated from the original Qiang population, remnants of which remain today in Sichuan Province. By the 16th century there was a clear population of Achang who differed from their closest cultural and linguistic relatives, the Jingpo.

During the Ming and Qing dynasties (1368–1644 and 1644–1911, respectively), the Achang were ruled largely by headmen and chiefs from their own ethnic group who had attained power and prestige through their connections to the Chinese bureaucracy. They and their lineages had the power to collect taxes and tribute, enforce labor requirements, and rule in an essentially feudal manner over their fellow Achang. This system remained largely in place until the communist revolution succeeded in China in 1949, whereupon a major program of land reform and then collectivization threw the local economy into chaos. As did much of China, the Achang experienced great hardship during the so-called Great Leap Forward of 1958, which focused on the economy, industrialization, and collectivization of agricultural land and labor. The Cultural Revolution, during the decade from 1967 to 1977, created even greater trauma

ACHANG

location:
Yunnan Province, China, and Kachin State, Myanmar

time period:
16th century to the present

ancestry:
Probably Qiang

language:
Achang, a Tibeto-Burman language with two recognized dialects, Fusa and Lianghe

for many Achang as all religious symbols, artifacts, and celebrations were banned along with many other symbolic and material aspects of traditional culture. Thousands of individuals were persecuted during these decades, especially those who had owned property prior to 1949, but not only that small group.

Since the 1980s China has relaxed its policies regarding traditional religion and belief systems as well as its economic policies, and many Achang have revived their traditional religion. Most today continue to farm, growing wet rice in paddies watered by monsoon rains. Sugar, tobacco, and a variety of vegetable oil crops, such as rape seed, are also grown for the market. Prior to liberalization in the past decades, these crops were sold to the government at a set price, in payment for use of land and farm implements, but more recently, with the introduction of capitalist strategies, some farmers have joined together to negotiate prices and conditions with both domestic and international buyers.

In addition to farming, the Achang are recognized for their ironwork; Achang blacksmiths are known throughout Yunnan Province. Achang legend states that this knowledge was handed down from the 14th century, when their ancestors provided weapons and armor to the Chinese army garrisoned in Yunnan. Other private handicraft industries that are currently flourishing in China's booming economy include textiles, woodcarving, and silversmithing.

Achang society, whether in China or Myanmar, is similar to that of the Han and many other Chinese ethnic groups in recognizing the primacy of the patrilineal principle in the creation of large kin-based groups. Membership in one's lineage and clan is always inherited from the father, and membership in these groups joins each individual to a large web of relatives who can trace their ancestry back to a common male ancestor. Each individual must marry outside his or her own patrilineal grouping as well. These marriages were largely arranged in the past to unite two family groups, but today some degree of personal choice can be exercised in this matter. Although sons inherit their father's property, it was generally only the youngest son who remained in the family home, taking his wife into the household to help care for his elderly parents. Other sons usually established their own households at marriage, a situation preferable for most women.

The traditional religion of most of the Achang was Theravada Buddhism, which they adopted from the Dai during the centuries immediately after the first millennium. In China this religious tradition, along with aspects of Taoism and traditional ancestor and spirit worship that remained after conversion to Buddhism, was interrupted by the actions of the Communist Party, while in Myanmar this tradition has continued unabated. Today most families in both countries have an altar in the home for domestic worship, and in Myanmar it remains a great honor for a family when a son becomes a monk.

A'chik (Garo)

The A'chik are a tribal people of northeastern India and Bangladesh. Anthropologists believe they originated in what is today northwestern China's Chinghai Province and migrated into Tibet and Bhutan between 3,000 and 5,000 years ago. Subsequently they moved again into Assam and Bengal and settled in what are today called the Garo Hills, a 3,000-square-mile block of territory that encompasses portions of the Indian states of Assam and Meghalaya and part of Bangladesh.

During the British colonial period many A'chik converted to Christianity as a way to bypass the deleterious effects of the Hindu caste system, which classified tribal peoples at the lowest rungs of the hierarchy, and to gain the material benefits of participating in the colonizers' religion. For example baptized Christians were often given tracts of land. As a result by the 1970s nearly 80 percent of Bangladesh's A'chik were Christians, and the number is believed to be even higher today both in Bangladesh and among India's A'chik population.

With colonialism materialist culture and transformation in other areas of A'chik culture arrived as well. Clothing that was traditionally made from tree bark was made instead from plain cotton cloth that men wrapped around their waists and women around their torsos in the form of a dress. Traditionally land was held by matrilineal clans and worked collectively, but in the colonial period landownership became more individual. Nonetheless the need for extensive amounts of land due to the swidden, *jhum*, or slash-and-burn style of agriculture practiced by the A'chik has meant that collective ownership has remained important for many segments of A'chik society.

Despite these widespread changes, many aspects of A'chik society have survived the colonial and the postcolonial eras of nation building in both India and Bangladesh. The traditional

A'CHIK

location:
India and Bangladesh

time period:
3000–1000 B.C.E. to the present

ancestry:
Northwestern Chinese

language:
Garo, a Tibeto-Burman language with about eight separate dialects

A'chik matrilineal kinship system, in which children inherit membership in their mothers' clans instead of their fathers', has persisted into the present despite the prevalence of patrilineal systems in both India and Bangladesh. The postmarriage matrilocal residence pattern, in which new husbands moved into their wives' homes and worked on their in-laws' land, has likewise survived into the 21st century. Many aspects of the A'chik indigenous religious system, called Sangshareq, have also survived despite their nominal conversion to Christianity. Sangshareq is an animistic belief system that recognizes the power of spirits, ancestors, and nature. Snakes and tigers are both believed to be particularly potent spirits of the dead, and some men are believed to turn into these animals at night. Cats generally are also important totemic animals and are the only animal forbidden to A'chik as a food item. Certain hills, trees, and rocks in their locale are also believed to house spirits and are thus avoided as dangerous to humans. Religious specialists, called *khamal,* who organize and supervise festivals, vows, healing ceremonies, and other ritual events, are thought to be extremely strong and potentially dangerous and thus enjoy significant respect in their communities.

Adi (Abor, Abuit, Tani)

The Adi, who were called the Abor until the 1960s, are a group of hill tribes living in the southern Himalayan area of the Indian state of Arunachal Pradesh; smaller groups also live in Tibet and other regions of China. There are about 15 related tribal groups classified together as Adi, all of which are believed to have migrated from southern China in the 16th century. They were well known to the British colonial powers in India during the 19th and early 20th centuries because of their frequent skirmishes with and raids on the property of other tribes and the colonials themselves. The British ultimately failed to conquer the area and in 1866 signed a treaty that recognized Adi sovereignty in the area and allowed the British uninhibited trade, travel, and communication. This action did not settle the region, and in 1912 the Adi killed two British administrators, setting off further military action against them. The entire region was divided into three separate colonial tracts that have undergone a variety of name and boundary changes since that time. In the 21st century the Adi have once again become well known to the British public as well as others in the English-speaking world through the television documentary series *Tribes*. The documentary host Bruce Parry spent a month living with the Adi, claiming to be the first European to visit them in living memory; he ate roasted rat cake and walked across their 250-foot bamboo suspension bridge.

The primary subsistence activities of the traditional Adi were hunting, fishing, gathering wild food products, and swidden or slash-and-burn agriculture. They also engaged in trade with other tribal communities for products they were unable to make or obtain themselves; in the past metal tools, utensils, containers, and adornments were the most valued products obtained through outside trade. In their Himalayan foothills home slash-and-burn agriculture allows for the same field or plot of land to be used from one to three years, depending on the amount of prior vegetation to be burned, the steepness of the hill, and the crops planted on it. The most important crops were rice, millet, corn, vegetables, beans, gourds, oranges, jackfruit, papayas, chilies, ginger, and sugarcane. Cotton and tobacco were also grown, for both local use and trade. In the 21st century agriculture continues to dominate in most Adi villages with many people also depending on forest products to supplement their rice, beans, vegetable, and fruit crops. Unfortunately, in 2006 an economic development project in the area found that about 40 percent of Adi people were living below the poverty line, and the tribe as a whole is considered economically vulnerable.

The division of labor among the Adi is dictated largely by gender and age, with young women helping their mothers and other female relatives and young boys helping the men. Men's primary responsibilities are cutting and burning primary vegetation to open up new agricultural land, hunting, fishing, and building, while women do most domestic chores, maintain animals, gather forest products, and plant, weed, and harvest fields. Occasionally men assist with child care and cooking, but generally these fall within the purview of women; women may also kill small animals during the course of their gathering activities.

The primary social organization in Adi society is based on the dual principles of kinship and residence. Kinship is reckoned patrilineally among these tribes: children inherit membership in their father's lineage, subclan, clan, and tribe. In the past, clans (groups of lineages that can trace their ancestry back to a common, usually mythological ancestor through

ADI

location:
Along the banks of the Siang and Yamne Rivers, central Arunachal Pradesh, India

time period:
Unknown to the present

ancestry:
Tibeto-Burman

language:
Adi, sometimes referred to as Miri, Abor, or Mishing, a Tibeto-Burman language

lines of male descent) were strictly exogamous: a man and a woman could not marry if both were from the same clan. Today this rule has relaxed somewhat; however, subclans continue to be strictly exogamous and membership is inherited from fathers only. Membership in these kinship units beyond the nuclear family provides rules for not only marriage partners but also inheritance, rights of access to agricultural land, responsibilities for mutual assistance, and regulations regarding conflict and warfare.

In addition to kinship residence patterns provide the second principle upon which Adi social organization is based. The nuclear family is the basic unit of production and consumption in Adi society because of its common household. Beyond the household Adi villages are built along rivers and at the tops of hills wherever possible. They each have a council, called a Kebang in the local language, which is made up of clan representatives and organizes local political and economic activity and the mediation of disputes. In the past villages also had decision makers who led them in times of warfare, a frequent occurrence both before and during the British colonial era. Villages are also the primary landowners in Adi society, at least at the theoretical level. In practice, however, individual families have divided up most village land and use it as their own; among the Minyong, one of the subgroups of Adi, it is clans that own land rather than villages or families.

Although many of the tribal communities in Arunachal Pradesh are predominantly Buddhist, the Adi and many of the other communities in the state's central region continue to practice their own indigenous religion, a form of animism with beliefs in spirits, ancestors, and seven gods or eternal beings who are far removed from any human interaction. Two kinds of religious specialists predominate in Adi villages: diviners, who discern information about which spirits are causing problems and what to do about them, and healers or medicine men. Diviners are also the masters of ceremonies at most Adi life cycle rituals. Both specialists communicate with the spirit world in order to go about their specialized activities, but otherwise they are not outside the regular Adi life. In addition to traditional beliefs, many Adi subgroups today have converted to Christianity. In part they did so to gain the material benefits offered to them by the colonial-era missionaries. Another motivation for many of these conversions was to escape the stigma of inclusion in the Hindu worldview with its emphasis on caste; as tribal people the Adi would be incorporated into this system at the very bottom.

Adivasi   *See* Scheduled Tribes.

Aeta (Agta, Ata, Ati, Atta, Ayta, Ita, Negritos)

Aeta is a collective term for the descendants of the first people to have migrated to the Philippines, possibly from Borneo about 30,000 to 20,000 years ago. Today there are 29 different ethnolinguistic groups of Aeta, including 10 groups of Aeta living on the island of Luzon. They are all small in stature, dark skinned, with curly dark hair and dark eyes. Although they resemble some African communities, genetic research shows that they are as removed from African gene pools as the rest of the population of the Philippines.

Aeta time line

B.C.E.

30,000–20,000 Possible period when the Aeta migrate from Borneo, using a land bridge that was submerged by rising sea levels at least 5,000 years ago.

3000 Austronesian speakers arrive in the Philippines from Taiwan and ultimately southern China.

C.E.

1565 The Spanish begin the process of colonizing the entire archipelago.

1898 Spain sells the Philippines to the United States for $20 million; the U.S. colonial period begins.

1960s–70s Some Aeta men work for the U.S. military, training infantrymen and others headed to Vietnam in jungle survival, tracking, and other necessary skills.

1964 End of the forager period of Aeta history and start of the transitional phase.

1980 End of the transitional phase of Aeta history and start of the peasant phase, which continues to this day.

1991 Mount Pinatubo erupts and displaces several thousand Aeta who have lived in that region for thousands of years. Most communities will never be able to return to their homelands.

1997 The Philippines passes the Indigenous Peoples' Rights Act, which seeks to protect the people and ways of life of the country's 18 percent indigenous population, including the Aeta.

2001 Some Aeta are granted ownership of their land through a Certificate of Ancestral Domain Title, which is based on their having continuously occupied the land since before the colonial era.

2006 Ancestral Domain Titles are used to fight the development of a golf course on Aeta land in Bataan.

AETA

location:
The mountainous regions of Luzon, Palawan, Panay, Negros, and Mindanao, the Philippines

time period:
30,000–20,000 years ago to the present

ancestry:
Possibly Bornean

language:
There are 29 separate Aeta languages, all Austronesian languages that were probably adopted and adapted from the incoming Malay community within the past 5,000 years

GEOGRAPHY

The Aeta generally live in mountainous, forested areas of the islands of Luzon, Palawan, Panay, Negros, and Mindanao. Those along the eastern coast of Luzon live in the Sierra Madre Mountain range, the country's longest at about 210 miles, while those in the Pinatubo region live in the Zambales Mountains. Mount Pinatubo itself, while not the most active volcano in the world or even in the Philippines, was the site of one of the largest volcanic eruptions of the 20th century when it exploded in June 1991, in a blast 10 times larger than that of Mount St. Helens, Washington, in 1980. Regardless of which island is their home, the mountainous territory of the Aeta is generally cooler than the tropical lowlands and receives significant rainfall, especially from May until October.

ORIGINS

The origins of the Aeta remain somewhat hazy since definitive proof of events that occurred so far back in history is difficult to find; however, most anthropologists and historians believe that they are the remnants of a population that migrated onto Luzon from Borneo when the two islands were part of the same large landmass. The general consensus is that this migration took place between 30,000 and 20,000 years ago.

HISTORY

Archaeological evidence indicates that prior to the arrival of the AUSTRONESIANS, who entered the Philippines bearing domesticated plants and animals, the Aeta occupied all ecological niches in the region. They hunted and fished along the coasts and lowland rivers and took advantage of the forest products available in the mountains. With the arrival of the agriculturalists the hunting-and-gathering Aeta were forced into the region's higher elevations and more marginal territories. The arrival of the Austronesians produced numerous other changes as well. Linguistic evidence points to a large-scale replacement of indigenous Aeta languages with various elements from Austronesian vocabulary, grammar, and sounds. Today the Aeta likewise speak Austronesian languages, which developed in situ over the past 5,000 years. Many Aeta groups also adopted some rudimentary forms of slash-and-burn agriculture, which served to supplement their diet over the past several millennia.

The arrival of the Spanish in the Philippines in the 16th century set the stage for fur-ther change among the Aeta, although they proved to be highly resilient in the face of European colonialism. The Spanish attempted two widespread forms of cultural change with the Aeta: to settle their seminomadic hunting-and-gathering communities into reservations set aside for them in the highlands and to convert them to Roman Catholicism. At the time, neither of these projects came to much, and for the most part the Aeta themselves chose where, when, and how they would participate in the political, social, and economic world of the colonizers. As a result there were two kinds of Aeta communities evident during this period. The first, the *nonconquestados,* were Aeta who remained hostile to outsiders; moved farther into the mountains and forests whenever approached by lowland MALAYS, Mestizos, or Spaniards; and even organized themselves into small bands of guerrillas to fight back against external encroachment. The other Aeta were known at the time as *conquestados* and were groups who engaged in trade with lowlanders and colonizers and generally maintained more friendly relations with these outsiders.

With the start of the 20th century and the replacement of the Spanish regime with one from the United States the Aeta began to experience greater influences from the outside world. Most important in the early years was the influx of refugees and land-poor peasants from the lowlands. These lowland migrants often established government-like institutions such as police and paramilitary organizations that considerably disrupted the lives of the resident Aeta. At this time the *nonconquestados* continued to fight back against these migrants and their ways of life while the *conquestados* were pulled further into the colonial economy as laborers.

The second half of the 20th century created even greater change for the Aeta, most of whom had been settled and pacified by this time. For example, during the Vietnam War the U.S. military drew upon the skills of a number of Aeta men from the village of Pastolan near the large U.S. military base at Subic Bay to assist in training their soldiers in jungle survival, tracking, and warfare. The 20th century also accelerated the problems brought about by the loss of traditional hunting-and-gathering grounds at the hands of agriculturalists, deforestation, and poor access to governmental resources. In the 1960s it was estimated that more than 80 percent of the Sierra Madre Mountains was covered with old-growth forest, providing ample game and resources for the several thousand Aeta who lived there. Today experts believe that in the country generally 97 percent of old-growth forests have been felled, including those in the Sierra Madre. As a result, Aeta communities have seen significant population decreases over the past half-century and significant change in their traditional culture. One ethnographer who has spent considerable time with the Aeta over the past few decades says that prior to the 1970s all Aeta men and boys over the age of four were skilled archers while today it is almost impossible to find even a single bow and set of arrows in any Aeta community; basketball has replaced hunting as the favorite activity of Aeta boys.

Prior to 1964 the Aeta were considered to have been living in the forager period of their history, during which only minor changes had been introduced to the communities' ways of life since before the Spanish colonial period. The time from 1965 to 1979 is often considered a transitional period in Aeta history, when communities began losing access to their land and its resources and outside political forces began to be felt at all levels of Aeta society. The years 1980 to the present are considered a peasant phase of Aeta history, when most people have entirely lost the ability to survive on traditional hunting-and-gathering activities; work for lowlanders has become the norm, and such problems as poverty, alcoholism, low birth weight, high mortality rates, lack of education, and alienation are threatening the very existence of the Aeta people.

In 1991 the Aeta of the Pinatubo region suffered even further damage to their way of life when this mountain erupted after 600 years of dormancy. The eruption was the second-largest on Earth in the 20th century and killed as many as 800 people. The simultaneous arrival of a tropical storm over the Philippines led to the widespread dispersal of volcanic ash and horrendous mudslides. More than 56,000 Aeta became homeless as a result of the eruptions, mudslides, and other damage caused by earthquakes that accompanied the eruption; most of those will never be able to return to their homes and sacred grounds and today live as internal refugees in other areas of Luzon. Alcoholism, a problem within many Aeta communities, is particularly serious among these refugees and has been estimated to affect more than half of all Aeta adults within this population.

CULTURE

Traditional Aeta culture was based on the economic practices of hunting, fishing, and gathering. Meat was shared among all hunters in a collective hunting party, with the person who made the kill and pregnant women getting two portions and all others getting one. Gathered foods and fish were not shared as frequently and tended to be eaten by the household alone. In addition many Aeta communities had adopted a form of shifting agriculture, growing root crops, some fruits and vegetables, and even tobacco on temporary fields cut out of the forest and used for a season or two before shifting to a new field. Today these traditional activities have largely been replaced by work on other people's farms, some personal cultivation, and trade in forest products. Fishing remains important in some regions, but hunting has largely disappeared because of deforestation and lack of skill among young Aeta.

Aeta society was typical of small-scale band societies that do not recognize formal authority figures. Instead they rely on the expertise and opinions of all adults in the group to form a consensus about when and where to migrate, hunting decisions, social control,

An Aeta headman during the peasant period of their history, serving rice that has been cooked in bamboo tubes. *(OnAsia/Andy Maluche)*

AFGHANISTANIS: NATIONALITY

nation:
Islamic Republic of Afghanistan, Afghanistan

derivation of name:
Afghanistan, "land of the Afghans," was first used officially in the 1801 Anglo-Persian peace treaty. The Pashtun tribes began using the term *Afghan* after the Arabs conquered the area, but it first appears in historical records in a 10th-century book of geography written by authors unknown.

government:
Islamic republic

capital:
Kabul

language:
The official languages are Afghan Persian, also known as Dari (50 percent), and Pashtu (35 percent); other major languages include Pashtu Uzbek, Turkmen, Balochi, and Pashai

religion:
80 percent Sunni Muslim, 19 percent Shia Muslim, and 1 percent other religions

earlier inhabitants:
Bactrians, Sogdians, Scythians, Persians and other Iranians, Greeks, Pashtun, Hazara, and other tribes

demographics:
42 percent Pashtun, 27 percent Tajik, 9 percent Hazara, 9 percent Uzbek, 4 percent Aimak, 3 percent Turkmen, 2 percent Baloch, 4 percent other ethnicities

and everything else. In recent times the Malay practice of assigning a village chief has been imposed on the Aeta and local governments try to choose a person, usually an older male, who has the respect of his own community to serve in this position. It entails some prestige and governmental authority but no monetary compensation; chiefs without the backing of their community have very little local power.

Aeta religious beliefs prior to the introduction of Roman Catholicism, which has only recently been adopted by more than a handful of Aeta, seem to have recognized a dominant creator god as well as numerous lesser gods, spirits, ancestors, and others with supernatural powers. The creator god is called by many different names in different Aeta communities, including Magbabaya among the Mamanua and Apo Namalyari among the Pinatubo Aeta. Gods with power over hunting, forests, the sea, winds, sky, and other natural phenomena are also commonly recognized. Many of these lesser gods and spirits are believed to inhabit special trees in the forests that surround Aeta villages; as a result, forests are seen as ambiguous characters, both the giver of life and the cause of numerous ailments and misfortunes. Good spirits are categorized by the Aeta as *anito* while negative or evil ones as *kamana*. In order to pacify the kamana and to prevent the *anito* from acting like *kamana*, the Aeta perform dances before hunting or gathering shellfish and give compensatory gifts to the spirits when misfortune or illness points to an angry spirit. For the Aeta of Mount Pinatubo, the mountain itself is seen as extremely sacred and many believe that the actions of miners and loggers caused the fatal eruption in 1991.

FURTHER READING

J. D. Early and T. N. Headland. *Population Dynamics of a Philippine Rain Forest People: The San Ildefonso Agta* (Gainesville: University Press of Florida, 1998).

P. Bion Griffin and Agnes Estioko-Griffin, eds. *The Agta of Northeastern Luzon: Recent Studies* (Cebu City, Philippines: San Carlos Publications, 1985).

Navin K. Rai. *Living in a Lean-to: Philippine Negrito Foragers in Transition* (Ann Arbor: Museum of Anthropology, University of Michigan, 1990).

Afghanistanis: nationality
(Afghanis, people of Afghanistan)

The history of Afghanistan and the development of a unique national identity are tied to the history and development of an ethnic identity among the country's PASHTUN majority, who constitute about 42 percent of the population. Even the name *Afghan* was originally synonymous with *Pashtun* and began to refer to citizens of the state only after the formation of the Kingdom of Afghanistan in 1747, although today other ethnic groups in the country may also use the term to refer to their citizenship.

GEOGRAPHY

Afghanistan is a landlocked country in Central Asia covering about 402,500 square miles and bordering on Iran, Pakistan, Tajikistan, Turkmenistan, Uzbekistan, and China. The country is divided by the Hindu Kush Mountains running northeast to southwest and is made up of 34 provinces. The capital city, Kabul, is located in the east, relatively close to the Pakistan border. Other major cities include Kandahar, Herat, Mazar-e-Sharif, Jalalabad, and Konduz. The country has mostly mountainous and desert terrain with 12 percent arable land.

INCEPTION AS A NATION

Ahmad Shah Durrani, known as the father of Afghanistan, was born in modern-day Pakistan in the early 18th century. He was the second son of a powerful clan chief and an excellent soldier who quickly distinguished himself in battle under the Persian king Nadir Shah, who had ruled the region after capturing Kandahar and Kabul in 1738. After Nadir's assassination in 1747 Durrani was responsible for unifying the Pashtun tribes and declaring Afghanistan independent of Persia. A Loya Jirga or Grand Council was called and Durrani was named king of the newly founded Afghanistan. Durrani oversaw a council of tribal chiefs, largely allowing each chief to continue ruling his own tribe. This system of governance stayed in place until the end of the monarchy in 1973, despite the internal conflicts that plagued the kingdom following Durrani's death (*see* DURRANIS).

Unfortunately for the stability of his kingdom Durrani never named an heir and thus left his 23 sons to compete for the Afghan throne. The empire declined as a result, and by 1818 only Kabul and a 99.5-mile radius around the city remained under his successor's control. Civil war broke out in the following years among various tribal powers vying for the throne, and Afghanistan's identity as a single nation dis-

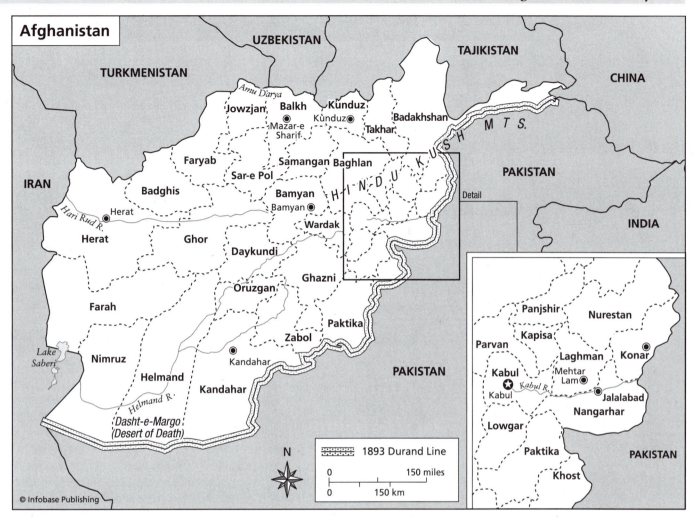

Afghanistan

UZBEKISTAN

TURKMENISTAN

TAJIKISTAN

CHINA

Amu D'arya

Jowzjan   Balkh   Kunduz

Kunduz   Badakhshan

Mazar-e Sharif   Takhar

Faryab   Samangan   Baghlan

PAKISTAN

Sar-e Pol

Detail

IRAN

Badghis   Bamyan

Bamyan

Hari Rud R.   Herat

INDIA

Wardak

Herat   Ghor

Daykundi

Ghazni

Farah   Oruzgan

Paktika

Zabol

Lake Saberi   Nimruz   Kandahar

PAKISTAN

Helmand   Kandahar

Helmand R.

Dasht-e-Margo (Desert of Death)

© Infobase Publishing

N

1893 Durand Line

0   150 miles

0   150 km

Panjshir   Nurestan

Kapisa

Parvan   Laghman   Konar

Kabul   Mehtar Lam

Kabul   *Kabul R.*   Jalalabad

Lowgar   Nangarhar

Paktika   PAKISTAN

Khost

integrated until Dost Mohammad Khan took control in 1826.

As power struggles continued between Dost Mohammad Khan's successors, Afghanistan became trapped between the Czarist Russian Empire and the British Indian empire in the "Great Game." Finding itself caught between the expansive interests of Russia and British India, Afghanistan repeatedly repelled the powers that hoped to use the country for their strategic advantage. A series of three Anglo-Afghan Wars raged between 1839 and 1919, with the British never able to conquer the fierce Afghans. Instead they drew a line nearly 750 miles long, the Durand Line, to separate their own territories in India (which later became Pakistan) from the Afghan kingdom, which they held in a much looser, indirect way. Afghanistan declared its independence in 1919, extricating itself from Britain entirely by 1921. Afghans celebrate their independence day on

August 19 in commemoration of the Rawalpindi agreement, which ended British control of Afghanistan.

The 20th-century development of Afghan national identity follows much of the pattern established in the previous two centuries. In the early decades of the century after independence in 1921 internal conflicts between modernizers and Muslim traditionalists led to only a patchy adoption of modern educational methods and national identities. Later in the century the same pattern emerged with internal conflicts between Leftists and the Islamic mujahideen in the 1970s and the Taliban and the Northern Alliance in the 1990s. The invasions of the country in 1979 by the Soviet Union and in 2001 by the United States–led coalition of forces further eroded the ability of Afghanistanis to unite behind a common national identity. By now, local identities, such as tribe, clan, region, and religion, are more important to many Afghans

Afghanistanis: nationality time line

B.C.E.

3000–2000 Urban civilization begins in the area including present-day Afghanistan.

500 The area of Afghanistan (Bactria) includes several provinces (satrapies) of the Persian Achaemenid empire.

330–327 Alexander the Great subdues Bactria in only three years, leaving behind a lasting Hellenic influence.

293 Parts of present-day Afghanistan fall under the control of the Mauryan empire, introducing elements of Indian culture, including Buddhism.

150 B.C.E.–652 C.E. Several waves of nomadic Indo-European peoples from the north settle in the area, including Yuezhi/Kushans, establishing control, Mahayana Buddhism, and a widespread empire that was a center for art and literature.

C.E.

1st century The Kushan empire is established in Bactria and Gandhara.

652–709 The Arab empire annexes and then conquers the region of present-day Afghanistan, converting most of the area to Islam.

1219 Genghis Khan leads a Mongol invasion, conquering the region.

1227 Genghis Khan's death causes a succession of minor leaders until a descendant of Genghis Khan, Tamerlane (Timur Leng), absorbs the area into his Asian empire.

1504 A supposed descendant of both previous conquerors, Timur Leng (Tamerlane) and Genghis Khan, Babur establishes the largely Indian Mughal Empire, which includes Afghanistan.

1738 The Persian king Nadir Shah conquers Kandahar and Kabul. He is later assassinated, leaving behind a power vacuum and bickering hopefuls for the throne.

1747 Ahmad Shah Durrani (who adopts the name *Durr-i-Durrani,* "pearl of pearls," as his first act of leadership) declares Afghanistan independent of Persia and calls a great council (Loya Jirga) among the newly unified Pashtun tribes, where he is chosen as king of the new nation of Afghanistan.

1772 Timur Shah Durrani, son of Ahmad Shah Durrani, moves the capital of Afghanistan from Kandahar to Kabul.

1839–42 The first Anglo-Afghan War starts over "The Great Game," a rivalry between imperial Russia and the British Indian empire, placing Afghanistan geographically and strategically on center stage.

1878–81 The second Anglo-Afghan War takes place; Afghanistan relinquishes control of its foreign affairs and many frontier areas to the British, who maintain some power even after the war concludes.

1880–1901 King Abdur Rahman's ethnocidal nationalizing processes strengthen the dominant Pashtuns at the expense of the country's many minority groups.

1893 The Durand Line, drawn by Sir Mortimer Durand, marks the almost 750-mile boundary between British India and the Kingdom of Afghanistan, which was held informally by the British. The line is never formally ratified by Afghanistan.

1919 Amanullah Khan declares full independence from Britain and sparks the third Anglo-Afghan War. The British-Afghan Rawalpindi agreement in 1919 is a weak declaration of self-determination; however, by the time the negotiations are concluded in 1921 Afghanistan has reclaimed most of its diplomatic independence.

1947 Pakistan gains independence from Great Britain and retains territory believed by Afghanistanis to be rightfully theirs because it was granted to the British in 1893; the border continues to cause trouble between these two countries today.

1967 Natural gas resources are first accessed in Afghanistan.

1973 Sardar Mohammed Daoud launches a bloodless coup while his ruling brother, Zahir Shah, is in Italy for an eye operation. Daoud declares himself president of an Afghan republic with the support of Leftists, crushing an emerging Islamist movement.

1978 The Saur, or April revolution, launched by the Communist People's Democratic Party of Afghanistan, begins a series of Communist governments in Afghanistan.

1979 The United States begins covertly funding and training anti-Communist mujahideen forces through the Pakistani secret service agency, drawing largely on discontented Muslim populations who oppose Marxist atheism.

1979 To support the vulnerable Afghan Communist government the Soviet Union invades, assassinating the prime minister, replacing him, and causing widespread violence as the Red Army tries to gain control for its imposed government. More than 5 million Afghanistanis flee to refugee camps in Pakistan and Iran.

1989 After Soviet withdrawal an absence of clear leadership and security gives rise to warlordism and a lack of elites and intellectuals, who had primarily relocated abroad for safety.

1992 After the fall of the Communist regime a civil war begins among several mujahideen factions.

1994 A major civil conflict among mujahideen factions in Kabul kills 10,000 people. The Taliban, mostly religious scholars and former mujahideen, emerge from southern Afghanistan, calling for the removal of the other warring mujahideen groups.

1996 The Taliban take Kabul, garnering major international attention for the first time. Heavy criticism is made of the Taliban's extreme Islamic policies and imposition of sharia (Islamic) law, particularly as regards the role of women in society. The Taliban are largely successful in eradicating much of the opium trade in Afghan poppies.

1999 The Afghanistan Museum in Exile is established in Switzerland to house cultural artifacts in danger from the Taliban. These artifacts are returned to the Kabul Museum in 2006.

2000 By the end of 2000 the Taliban control 95 percent of the country, excluding a small territory in the northeast occupied by the Afghan Northern Alliance, which is still recognized by the United Nations as the official government of Afghanistan.

2001 In a campaign to remove images that they claim are offensive to Islam, the Taliban destroy two giant Buddhas carved, in the first to sixth centuries, into the sandstone cliffs of Bamiyan. Before their destruction the monuments are the tallest standing Buddhas in the world.

Following attacks on the United States on September 11 by al-Qaeda, the United States begins air attacks on Afghanistan, allowing opponents of the Taliban to take control of Kabul. These factions meet at a UN-sponsored conference in Bonn, Germany, creating an interim government and establishing Hamid Karzai as chairman.

2002 Karzai is chosen by a national council (Loya Jirga) as president of Afghanistan. The council of 2,000 participants is selected through a complex electoral and appointment process, which includes allotted seats for political leaders, women, academicians, religious scholars, refugees, and trade groups.

2004–05 Following the creation of a new constitution, Karzai is elected president in a nationwide election. Legislative elections (including women as voters, candidates, and elected members) are held in September 2005 and the winning candidates are inaugurated in December.

2005 Afghanistan begins implementing a series of counternarcotics programs to fight the upsurge of opium production from Afghan poppies, which rises dramatically after the fall of the Taliban in 2001.

2006 Afghanistan supplies a record 91 percent of the world's opium.

The Afghanistan Compact is established at a London conference where 60 countries and many international development organizations pledge more than $10.5 billion in U.S. dollars in aid over the next five years. The compact sets forth plans for the security, economic and social development, and governmental system in the country. The presence of local warlords continues to be a problem, and estimates of casualties and refugees are wide-ranging and unreliable.

2007 Zahir Shah, former king of Aghanistan, dies.

Fighting on the border between Afghanistan and Pakistan escalates, and violence throughout the countries continues unabated, including Afghanistan's most devastating suicide bombing in November.

than any abstract conception of a larger Afghan nation, despite widespread voter participation in the 2004 election.

CULTURAL IDENTITY

I come to you and my heart finds rest.
Away from you, grief clings to my heart
   like a snake.
I forget the throne of Delhi
when I remember the mountain tops of
   my Afghan land.
If I must choose between the world and you,
I shall not hesitate to claim your barren
   deserts as my own.

               Ahmad Shah Durrani

An early conception of Afghan identity was formed as Ahmad Shah Durrani unified the Pashtun tribes. After invading India six times and sacking Delhi Durrani chose to focus his kingdom on the landlocked Afghan region, unlike previous leaders who had centered their empires in India. After this brief unification melted back into tribal warfare, a second united Afghan identity formed in opposition to imperialist pressures from Russia and Britain. The influx of other cultures and religions, such as Hellenic influence, Buddhism, and most important, Islam, has created a rich tapestry of cultural roots. Yet this diverse background can also be divisive, and even unifying elements, such as Muslim predominance, are fractured into Sunni and Shia factions.

Of the strongest cultural elements family and clan loyalty trump most other interests, and a man is required to answer a call to arms issued by his clan. Hospitality is also central to the Afghan culture, although socialization is limited to same-gendered groups. Poetry is a major national pursuit, featured in small competitive events and throughout the educational system. As a result of low literacy rates, particularly outside urban areas, poetry is appealing because rhyme and rhythm facilitate memorization.

The horse has played a prominent role in Afghanistan, whether providing mounts for tribal warriors or entertainment in the national game of Buzkashi, which resembles a chaotic version of polo, substituting a calf or goat carcass for a ball. Buzkashi is not only a competitive sport but also an additional arena for Afghan power politics. Leadership figures host and sponsor the games, fielding horsemen and inviting guests, with winners consolidating additional power. President Karzai fielded his first selection of horsemen in 2006, attempting to ingratiate himself with the Afghan people and move away from his reputation as a "Western" leader.

Afghanistan's central location has been a double-edged sword. On the one hand it has enriched the culture of the area with influences from both East and West. On the other hand near-constant conflict has also eradicated many cultures and identities over the years. A tendency toward interclan warfare and independence has caused much destruction, but it has also aided in unseating foreign invaders. While both reconstruction and violence continue today, the future of Afghanistan remains unsure.

See also PASHTUNS.

FURTHER READING

Steve Coll. *Ghost Wars: The Secret History of the CIA, Afghanistan, and Bin Laden, from the Soviet Invasion to September 10, 2001* (New York: Penguin Press, 2004).

Hafizulla Emadi. *Culture and Customs of Afghanistan* (Westport, Conn.: Greenwood Press, 2005).

Larry P. Goodson. *Afghanistan's Endless War: State Failure, Regional Politics, and the Rise of the Taliban* (Seattle: University of Washington Press, 2001).

John C. Griffiths. *Afghanistan: A History of Conflict* (London: Andre Deutsch, 2002).

A 174-foot-tall Buddha statue at Bamiyan, Afghanistan, destroyed by the Taliban in March 2001. *(Scala/Art Resource, NY)*

Ahmed Rashid. *Taliban: Militant Islam, Oil, and Fundamentalism in Central Asia* (New Haven, Conn.: Yale University Press, 2000).

Willem Vogelsang. *The Afghans* (Oxford: Blackwell Publishers, 2002).

Afghans   *See* PASHTUNS.

Afridi (Apridi)

The Afridi are a subgroup of the PASHTUNS, the dominant tribal group in Afghanistan, with significant numbers living in Pakistan as well. There are eight clans within the Afridi: Adam Khel, Aka Khel, Kamar Khel, Kambar Khel, Kuki Khel, Malikdin Khel, Zakka Khel, and Sipah, each of which has its own territory within the larger Afridi region. This region is the southern and western portions of the Peshawar Valley in the Khyber Pass area of the Sufed Koh Range.

The majority of references to the Afridi are related to their military prowess. Early references to the Afridi date from the 16th and 17th centuries, when Afridi soldiers fought against Mughal domination in the region. In the late 19th and early 20th centuries the Afridi were famous among the British for serving as auxiliaries in the Indian army. The Khyber Rifles, one of the many paramilitary forces maintained by the British in the North-West Frontier region of India (today's Pakistan), was an Afridi unit. While many of these units continued to serve from the 1880s until Indian and Pakistani independence in 1947, the Khyber Rifles were broken up twice. The first disbandment occurred when Afridi rebels took the pass in 1897, and 30,000 regular British forces battled to regain it eventually. The second breakup was at the hands of the British in 1919 when Afridi loyalty was seriously questioned during the Third Anglo-Afghan War. For its almost 40 years of existence the Khyber Rifles included British officers from the Indian army who commanded the unit with all subordinate officers and regular soldiers coming from the Afridi. The unit's primary task was to control the pass. Afridi control of the pass on both an official and an unofficial basis meant that they controlled the flow from the northwest of arms and other goods both into and out of India. As a result the two groups reached an unwritten agreement: the British left the Afridi alone to control the passage of goods and the Afridi let the British travel without harassment.

After World War II a new Khyber Rifles unit was created; it was transferred to Pakistani control at the time of that country's independence in 1947. The unit remains active today, having served in Kashmir and in tracking down Afghanistani fugitives. As was the case under the British present-day Afridi are largely left to their own devices in the North-West Frontier Province, where they control the enormous gun trade. The Afridi are also known for smuggling and banditry more generally, though their reputation is probably exaggerated as a result of strategic importance of their location.

In addition to gun trading and crime the Afridi are famous in the 21st century for having produced Shahid Afridi, a cricket player on the Pakistani national team known for his power hitting.

See also AFGHANISTANIS: NATIONALITY; DURRANIS; GHILZAI; PASHTUNS.

Ahom (Asam, Tai)

The Ahom people were a Tai-speaking population who migrated to the region of present-day Assam starting in about the eighth century C.E. The Tai migrations actually began in the first centuries of the common era, when they left what is today Yunnan Province, China, and entered mainland Southeast Asia, but the most important migratory period for the Ahom began in 1228 under the leadership of Siu-Ka-Pha. Their name for themselves, *Asam,* is linguistically related to the name of the SHANS, a related population of Myanmar (Burma), and Siam, the kingdom of the THAIS in the south; it is also the basis for the contemporary Indian state over which they ruled for about 600 years, Assam.

Siu-Ka-Pha is believed to have entered Assam from the northeast, where he crossed the Patkai Mountain range, which today divides Assam from Myanmar. He is said to have had an army of 9,000 soldiers who easily overran the NAGAS, KACHARIS, and other tribal groups with whom they had contact. Eventually the party crossed the Dihing River and entered the Brahmaputra valley, where in 1229 the group settled down to form the first Tai polity in the region. However, this first site was unsuitable because of frequent flooding of the Brahmaputra River, which destroyed crops and homes. For 20 years Siu-Ka-Pha explored his territory and tried to settle in several different locations. Finally in 1252 he found what he was looking for in the Sibsagar division of upper Assam and there he built his capital as the first king or *swargadeo.*

Although the Ahom soldiers were very powerful and able to establish their own dynasty in the region, they arrived without any Tai-speaking women. Instead, on their travels

AFRIDI

location:
Pakistan's North-West Frontier Province and Afghanistan

time period:
About 500 C.E. to the present

ancestry:
Iranian

language:
Pashto, an eastern Iranian language

AHOM

location:
India

time period:
1228 to 1826

ancestry:
Tai

language:
Ahom, an extinct Tai-Kadai language

across Southeast Asia the Tai soldiers and princes married local women whom they encountered. As a result, the Ahom ethnic group very early on was made up of people with a wide variety of different ethnic and tribal backgrounds. Their Tai language, while the official language of the kings and governance of the state, was often spoken by only a minority of inhabitants; today it exists only in historical documents. Therefore although the descendants of the Ahom rulers of Assam are alive today, they are not considered Ahom people but rather Assamese.

The Ahom defeat of the local tribal population and the establishment of a powerful dynasty were challenges to the other established polities in the region, particularly the Mughal rulers in India. Between 1527 and 1682 the Mughal kings tried and failed 17 times to conquer the Ahom kingdom. Their last major attempt in 1671 at the Battle of Saraighat made a hero of the most famous Ahom military leader, Lachit Barphukan, who, legend states, had his own uncle killed for neglecting his military duties.

The final defeat of the Mughals in Assam led to a brief period of internal chaos that was brought to an end by the dynasty's most famous king, Rudra Singha, who ruled from 1696 until 1714. This era is considered a golden age of Ahom power in Assam when numerous civil engineering projects, social reforms, and military exploits expanded and improved the kingdom immeasurably. Unfortunately from the period of his death in 1714 until the final conquest of the kingdom by, first, the Burmese in 1817 and then the British in 1826, the Ahom kingdom experienced an almost continual disintegration. Internal dissent over religion, when followers of the Hindu god Vishnu were harassed and fought back against the centralizing state, combined with various palace intrigues over succession, led to a gradual weakening of the kingdom. In 1817 the Ahom army could no longer hold back the invading armies of the BURMANS and the Ahom dynasty came to an end. About a decade later, the entire region was conquered by the British in the first Anglo-Burmese War.

Aimaq (Aimak, Aymak, Eimak, Chahar Eimak, Char Aimaq)

The Aimaq make up one of the recognized ethnic groups in contemporary Afghanistan, though they are more of a tribe than an ethnic group, having PERSIAN, MONGOL, and TURKIC ancestors. They constitute about 4 percent of the country's total and live primarily in the northwest. Their language is classified as a Persian language; however, the name *Aimaq* actually means "tribe" in Mongolian, indicating the importance of their Mongolian ancestry. The Aimaq are also said to look more Mongolian than Persian, though there is great variation within the population. They are often referred to as *Chahar Eimak,* which means "four tribes," and refers to the number of tribes that make up the Aimaq as a whole. The four separate tribes are Taimani, Ferozkhoi, Temuri, and Jamshidi.

Consistent with about 80 percent of the population of Afghanistan, the dominant religion among the Aimaq is Islam of the Sunni variety. This is one of the features that most distinguish the Aimaq from their closest relatives, the Shiite HAZARAS. Another distinction emerged in 1929 when a number of tribal groups in Afghanistan's northwest region rose up against subjugation at the hands of the PASHTUNS, the majority. At that time the Hazaras continued to support their Pashtun overlords, while the Aimaq joined with the UZBEKS and TAJIKS under the leadership of the Tajik leader Bacha-i-Saqau, who had seized power in Kabul. When the DURRANIS' Pashtun leadership retook the throne, the Aimaq were punished along with the other conspirators.

Already in the early 1880s the Aimaq had the reputation of being fierce warriors. People from one tribe, the Jamshidi, were chosen by the emir of the Herat district to colonize the northern sections of this region as a defense against the incursions of TURKMENISTANIS and RUSSIANS. They were soon joined by many others seeking an opportunity in the relatively virgin grazing lands of the northwest. By 1885 between 1,000 and 2,000 families, including a significant number of Jamshidi and Ferozkhoi Aimaq, were residing in the region of Bala Murghab. Unfortunately the Afghan government soon withdrew its support, and at least some Aimaq elements turned their support to the Russians. As a result the Aimaq suffered at the hands of the nationalizing regime of Abdur Rahman (see AFGHANISTANIS: NATIONALITY; DURRANIS). In the most recent wars in Afghanistan some Aimaq once again turned their support away from those factions dominated by the Durranis, like the Taliban, and toward organizations like the Northern Alliance, dominated largely by ethnic Tajiks.

Most Aimaq are nomadic or seminomadic pastoralists, living primarily off the products and proceeds of their herds of cattle, sheep, and

AIMAQ

location:
Northwestern
Afghanistan

time period:
16th century to the
present day

ancestry:
Persian and Mongolian,
probably some Turkic
ancestry as well

language:
Aimaq, a dialect of Dari
or Afghan Persian

goats. They are skilled horsemen who use these animals in both herding and transport. Their homes are similar to the yurts or tents used in Mongolia; they are made of wool felt and can be dismantled, moved, and reconstructed as weather, grazing conditions, and political expediency necessitate. A few Aimaq have also moved to the cities of the western regions, such as Herat City in Herat Province and Chaghcharan in Ghowr Province.

Ainu (Aino, Emishi, Ezo)

The Ainu are an indigenous people of northern Japan, the Sakhalin Islands, and mainland Russia; their ancestors may have controlled all of Japan in the distant past as well. Into the 20th century there were still three main subgroups, the Kurile, Sakhalin, and Hokkaido Ainu, who spoke somewhat different languages and differed culturally. Today all but a handful of Ainu reside on Japan's northernmost island, Hokkaido, and speak JAPANESE as their first language.

The Ainu differ physically from the rest of the Japanese population in having far more body hair and otherwise more Caucasian features; however, genetic testing has shown the two populations to be much more closely related than expected on the basis of these physical differences. The Ainus' earliest ancestors probably migrated from Siberia during the height of the last ice age around 12,000 B.C.E., while the majority of the Japanese population are descended primarily from migrants who entered the archipelago from Korea and China about 400 B.C.E.

GEOGRAPHY

Prior to the expansion of the Russian and Japanese societies the Ainu homeland or *Ainu-moshir* (tranquil land of human beings) encompassed an area from the Amur River valley in Russia to Honshu, Japan's main island. In the past century only the Sakhalin and Kuril Islands and Hokkaido branches of the Ainu family survived and these branches have been even further limited in recent decades. Today's small Ainu population of fewer than 20,000 people lives primarily on the northern Japanese island of Hokkaido. Hokkaido is about 32,000 square miles large and makes up about one-fifth of Japan's landmass. Two major mountain ranges cover Hokkaido, Kitami in the island's north and Hidaka in the south. The island was heavily forested prior to the industrial era and continues to support many large tracts of old-growth

trees; it also contains many lakes, rivers, and lush valleys. Hokkaido's climate is varied, with many microclimates caused by differences in elevation, distance from the coast, and prevailing currents. Generally, it is dry and warm in summer and extremely cold and snowy in winter. The western coast on the Sea of Japan gets the most snow while the eastern, Pacific coast is cool and foggy in the summer and enjoys its best weather during the bright, sunny winter. Inland, temperature changes can be as much as 60°C, from a very warm 30°C or more in the summer to an extremely cold -30°C or lower in the winter.

ORIGINS

Until recently many archaeologists, anthropologists, and historians considered the immediate ancestors of the Ainu to be Japan's ancient JOMON culture. The Jomon were primarily hunting, fishing, and gathering peoples who started to engage in a small degree of agriculture only at the end of their historic period around 300 B.C.E. They were subsequently displaced by migrants from Korea and China, the Yayoi peoples, who introduced irrigated rice agriculture in addition to several other crops, different forms of pottery, and other technological advancements. On Hokkaido, however, the climate was not conducive to irrigated rice and the Jomon were believed to have survived into the present in the form of the Ainu.

This version of history has in recent decades been challenged by archaeological evidence indicating that the peoples of Hokkaido had adopted advanced agriculture by around 600 C.E. and were not living in a continuation of the Jomon era. These people are called the Ezo by some archaeologists working in this region. While the Ezos' climate was too cold for the Yayois' irrigated rice, they were able to grow the other important Yayoi-era crops: barley, wheat, hemp, and two kinds of millet. They also had a distinctive form of pottery that replaced the earlier Jomon pottery with its rope markings, and they built rectangular pit houses that differed from those of the Jomon, which were round. This new culture has been labeled *Satsumon* after the pottery that characterizes it and serves as the immediate predecessor of the Ainu culture, which developed out of the Satsumon in around 1200.

HISTORY

The Ainu and their predecessors were never isolated communities of indigenous peoples

AINU

location:
Hokkaido, Japan, and formerly on Sakhalin and the Kuril Islands and on the Russian mainland

time period:
1200 C.E. to the present

ancestry:
Satsumon peoples, who are probably Jomon peoples who adopted agriculture from the Yayoi

language:
Ainu, a language isolate that in the past had 19 different dialects; most Ainu in Japan now speak solely Japanese

Ainu time line

B.C.E.

18,000 The first evidence of inhabitation on Hokkaido is from this period, although some contested chronologies place this date as far back as 30,000 B.C.E. These original humans may have migrated from the south or entered Hokkaido from Sakhalin Island to the north.

12,000 The start of the Jomon period in Japanese history. The Ainu were once considered the direct descendants of the hunting, fishing, and gathering Jomon, but the discovery of Ainu agriculture has revised this hypothesis in recent decades.

400 The Jomon culture begins disappearing with the migration of farmers from mainland Asia, usually called Yayoi.

C.E.

0 The approximate period in which iron is introduced on Hokkaido. At this time images of bears also begin to appear on pottery in Hokkaido.

300 Yayoi culture has fully established itself on all of Japan's southern islands; Hokkaido is too cold for Yayoi irrigated rice agriculture and remains in the hands of the Jomon era peoples.

600–700 Satsumon pottery begins to appear on Hokkaido, indicating a shift in cultural form from the previous Jomon period. People in the Satsumon period, sometimes called Ezo, also practice agriculture, which indicates they may be Jomon-era people who adopted farming techniques from the Yayoi but were not replaced by them.

659 The Japanese establish an outpost on Hokkaido.

1200 Satsumon culture begins to disappear and is replaced by Ainu.

1500 Japanese assimilation policy begins to take effect in southern Hokkaido.

1669 The Ainu revolt against the Japanese; the result is even tighter Japanese control over the resources and people of Hokkaido.

1799 The Japanese emperor in Edo or Tokyo assumes direct control over Hokkaido, ending several hundred years of indirect control through local soldiers, merchants, and nobility.

1800s Political and social pressure in Russia drives most of the Ainu out of the mainland and Sakhalin and Kuril Islands and into Hokkaido.

1869 The Japanese government establishes a Colonization Office to regulate affairs on Hokkaido.

1871 Japan bans tattooing, formerly an important cultural marker and rite of passage for the Ainu.

1899 The Hokkaido Former Aborigines Protection Law is enacted and many Ainu are forced to assimilate to the dominant Japanese language and culture. This law remains in effect until 1997.

1946 The Ainu Association of Hokkaido is formed; in the early 21st century this group remains the largest Ainu association in Japan.

1984 The Ainu Museum is opened in Shiraoi, Hokkaido.

1994 Kayano Shigeru, an Ainu, is elected to Japan's parliament, the Diet.

1997 The Sapporo District Court declares the Ainu a recognized indigenous people of Japan.

The Law for the Promotion of the Ainu Culture and Dissemination and Advocacy for the Traditions of the Ainu and the Ainu Culture (Culture Promotion Law) is enacted, replacing the despised Aborigines Protection Law of 1899.

who were left alone to develop their social, economic, and political structures independently of others. This is clearly evident in the adoption of agriculture from the south prior to 600 C.E. In addition from the seventh century onward the early Japanese were familiar with their neighbors to the northeast and referred to them as Emishi; in 659 they built a government post at Shiribishi on the island of Hokkaido. Government notes on the post say that its raison d'être was to keep an eye on the Tungus peoples who lived across the water in Siberia, but certainly its location on Hokkaido also meant that the local population was familiar to them. The predecessors of the Ainu, sometimes called Ezo, also delivered tribute to the Japanese capital of Kyoto in the eighth century, which indicates their relative familiarity with Japanese political life. Evidence of Japanese-Ainu relations prior to the 17th century also shows that the two groups did not always coexist peacefully. The Japanese did not limit the expansion of their growing kingdoms in the Middle Ages voluntarily; rather, the Ainu successfully fought off numerous attempts by the Japanese to colonize Hokkaido.

The Ainu world included the peoples who lived to their north on Sakhalin Island and the Siberian mainland as well as those on the southern Japanese islands. The Okhotsk culture, which existed in these northern reaches, contributed many important cultural traits to the Ainu; these point to a great degree of interrelations between the two peoples. The most important of these shared traits is the centrality of the sacred bear in their religious life. The Ainu also rebuffed the MONGOLS in the 13th century and fought the Chinese Ming dynasty in the Amur River region in the 17th century.

In the transition from Ezo or Satsumon to Ainu culture one of the most important features is the abandonment of pottery altogether. For most utensils the Ainu turned to iron, although trade with Japan, China, and Siberia also imported ceramics from other regions as well as other useful products to replace their own pots. Iron had first been introduced on Hokkaido at the turn of the common era, but it took about 1,200 years for this material to be available in sufficient quantity and quality to replace pottery. As with agriculture and the bear cult, iron was introduced to the Ezo and Ainu peoples from outside their own homeland and required extensive trading networks with both their northern and southern neighbors.

A second important feature of this transition to Ainu culture is a diminished importance of agriculture and its widespread replacement by hunting, fishing, and food collecting. While most Ainu villages remained sedentary, a pattern that usually coincides with an agricultural subsistence pattern, only small-scale gardening of barley, wheat, and millet survived into the Ainu period. Instead, most Ainu families relied on salmon fishing, deer and other game hunting, and gathering of wild foods. It was this pattern that was noted by most outside commentators on Ainu life from the 17th through the 20th

century and led historians and others to assume that the Ainu were the direct descendants of the hunting and gathering Jomon peoples. More cynical explanations for these accounts, which largely overlooked the overwhelming evidence of gardening, state that it was easier to displace the Ainu from their territory if they were depicted as primitive and unfamiliar with modern land-use patterns that emphasize agricultural practices. In this way the Ainu could be treated as the Native Americans in the New World or the Aboriginal peoples in Australia were: pushed off their land, forced to assimilate to the colonizers' way of life, or killed if they did not comply with these agendas.

A variety of other important cultural traits also distinguish the Ainu from the prior Satsumon culture. One of these was the replacement of the Satsumon rectangular pit houses with above-ground homes built from wood and thatch. Another is spiraled clothing decoration for both men and women.

The transition from Ainu independence on Hokkaido to Japanese colonization of the island was relatively slow and gradual. In the 15th and 16th centuries Japanese efforts in northern Honshu and Hokkaido intensified and resulted in the granting of significant power and control to the local feudal nobility, Japanese landowners who moved north to take advantage of the new lands. The Ainu fought back and raids and massacres on both sides were frequent events for many centuries. Gradually, however, Japanese power proved to be greater and a policy of assimilation was put into place. This was done primarily through trade relations that forced the Ainu to provide local forest and animal products at specified trading posts on the island. Eventually the Japanese encroached on the island's hinterland, and the feudal-type trade relations took on a greater marketlike atmosphere. The Ainu staged an armed rebellion against these developments in 1669 but were put down when their leader, Shakushine, attending peace talks with the Japanese, was poisoned. After these events the Japanese redoubled their efforts to assimilate the indigenous Ainu into the Japanese social and political systems, using a one-sided treaty signed by the Ainu after Shakushine's death to provide political legitimacy for their actions.

From the start all Japanese control over Hokkaido had been fairly indirect rather than with the central governments at Kyoto and later Edo or Tokyo; local nobles, soldiers, and merchants controlled the interactions on the

Japanese side. In 1799 the central authorities in Edo, the *bakufu*, took control of Hokkaido, but little actually changed for the Ainu or the local nobility, who continued to serve as local enforcers, regulators of trade, and middlemen for the delivery of tribute to the capital. Until the later half of the 19th century Japanese migration into Hokkaido was generally discouraged, but the Japanese language, monetary system, political and social structures, and material culture were forced upon an unwilling population of Ainu. In 1869 a Colonization Office was established to formulate and direct this policy of assimilation and significant financial and social pressure was exerted on the Ainu for the next three decades. Japanese migration also increased at that time but remained relatively unimportant in the transformation of Ainu society since the Japanese tended to remain on the Oshima Peninsula and southern coastal regions. Most Japanese realized that utilizing Ainu expertise to exploit local fishing grounds and forests vastly outweighed the benefits gained by displacing them entirely from their lands or killing them outright. Instead, they were drawn into the Japanese sphere of influence as laborers, hunters, and traders and in other capacities.

From the Ainu point of view, however, the Japanese were always outside invaders who sought to control their labor, time, and resources. While many Ainu succumbed to Japanese power and largely adopted their agrarian way of life, especially those who lived on the coasts and near the larger Japanese settlements, the loss for all of native fishing grounds and access to forests, in addition to language and other aspects of their way of life, led to significant social disruption, identity crises, and alienation. Japanese government policies tried to mitigate the worst of these effects, but all they ever managed to do was increase the japanification of Hokkaido in the face of increased Japanese migration. Free public education after the World War I period, which was beneficial for the Ainu in working within Japanese society, simultaneously yielded the final destruction of most aspects of Ainu culture.

Nonetheless Ainu identity remains salient for several thousand individuals in Hokkaido today. Various cultural and political organizations operate on the island, pushing for further recognition of Ainu rights and fostering the growth of Ainu identity among the younger generation. In 1997 the Ainu won a significant victory when the Sapporo Supreme Court recognized them as an indigenous people with spe-cial rights appropriate to that status; this ruling finally replaced the assimilationist policy of 1899 and initiated a new era in Ainu-Japanese relations. In response to this ruling, the national government passed a law for the promotion of Ainu culture. Nevertheless one of the purposes of the original case brought before the supreme court had been to protect Ainu land, including several archaeological and sacred sites, from inundation caused by the building of the Nibutani dam, but before the case had been fully heard, the dam was completed and all sites were lost.

CULTURE

The most important social unit in traditional Ainu society was the nuclear family, with a minority of households containing extended families of three or more generations; a small number of Ainu men were also polygynous or had more than one wife, an arrangement that affected their households as well. Kinship generally was bilateral with both mothers' and fathers' lines of descent contributing to people's close kinship relations; however, there were some local norms that favored one side or the other. For example, most hunting and fishing grounds were held by groups of men related to one another through their fathers and paternal grandfathers, but on Hokkaido's Saru River women related to one another through their mothers and maternal grandmothers formed the dominant corporate groups. Among the Saru River Ainu maternal cousins were also forbidden marriage partners, while among other Ainu they were allowed or even encouraged.

Beyond the nuclear family the second most important social unit among traditional Ainu was the settlement or hamlet (*kotan*), usually made up of just five families, with a limited number of small villages uniting to form larger settlements than was the norm. Settlements in the Saru River region, because of the richness of its fish and other resources, occasionally grew to 30 families; however, half the villages even in this rich area contained fewer than five families. Many Ainu villages were settled all year long, but families residing in more difficult climatic regions were forced to migrate between separate summer and winter residences; those on the Kuril Islands migrated even more frequently to take advantage of migrating sea mammals and other resources. All male elders in the village participated in decision-making processes.

Traditional Ainu subsistence consisted of fishing, especially salmon; hunting deer and other land and sea mammals; gathering; and some small-scale gardening. Women were responsible for gardening, gathering wild foods, and food storage and preparation, while men hunted and fished. Women could also fish but were generally prohibited from participating in hunting activities.

With the destruction of most aspects of Ainu society during the Japanese colonial era few features have remained to serve as rallying points for contemporary Ainu identity. The most important of these features is the attachment to specific sacred lands on Hokkaido. Another important cultural trait is religion. Traditional Ainu religion was polytheistic, recognizing the existence of many different gods; in addition, every living thing was believed to contain a soul. The god of the mountains was thought to live in the mountains while the god of the water could be found in rivers and the ocean. In the home, the goddess of fire was believed to control the fate of the family. Animals were generally believed to be gods; the striped owl, killer whale, and bear were the most important. The *I-omante* ceremony, which required the sacrifice and consumption of a bear cub, was one of the most important community rituals. After three days of singing, dancing, and reverence, the cub was killed with arrows, the head placed on an altar, and the meat shared among the community. With its spirit having been released from its temporary bear host, the bear god was believed to return to the spirit world with goodwill toward the village that released it. Unlike other positions of power in Ainu society, religious specialists such as shamans could be women; women also received greater attention as they came of age, with sacred tattoos marking their faces and forearms, until the practice was banned by the Japanese in 1871.

FURTHER READING

William W. Fitzhugh and Chisato O. Dubreuil. *Ainu: Spirit of a Northern People* (Seattle: University of Washington Press, 2000).

Mary Inez Higler. *Together with the Ainu* (Norman: University of Oklahoma Press, 1971).

Shigeru Kayano. *Our Land Was a Forest: An Ainu Memoir.* Translated by Kyoko Selden and Lili Selden (Boulder: Westview Press, 1994).

Neil Gordon Munro. *Ainu Creed and Cult* (New York: Columbia University Press, 1963).

Emiko Ohnuki-Tierney. *The Ainu of the Northwest Coast of Southern Sakhalin* (Prospect Heights, Ill.: Waveland Press, 1984).

Donald L. Philippi. *Songs of Gods, Songs of Humans: The Epic Tradition of the Ainu* (Princeton, N.J.: Princeton University Press, 1979).

Hitoshi Watanabe. *The Ainu Ecosystem* (Seattle: University of Washington Press, 1973).

Akha (Ahka, Aini, Aka, Ak'a, Akka, Edaw, Ekaw, Hani, Houni, Ikaw, Ikho, Kaw, Kha Kho, Kha Ko, Kho, Ko, Woni)

The Akha are a Tibeto-Burman-speaking people who were originally from the border region between Myanmar and Yunnan Province, China. In the past century or so tens of thousands of Akha have migrated southeast into northern Thailand, Laos, and Vietnam, where they now constitute relatively large minority groups. In Thailand, the Akha began arriving in 1911, and today they make up one of the seven large tribal communities of the HILL TRIBES OF THAILAND; in China and Vietnam they are classified along with the HANI into a single ethnic category.

The Akha were among the original inhabitants of Yunnan Province, and their ancestors were probably among those who controlled the Nanzhao kingdom, which ruled the area from the eighth to the 13th century. Groups like the Tai, MONGOLS, and HAN, who all dominated the region after the fall of Nanzhao, were relative newcomers who either subsumed peoples like the Akha and Hani or drove them into the highlands. These in-migrations of non-Tibeto-Burman peoples also set off waves of out-migrations by peoples like the Akha, some of which continued into the 20th century, when the first Akha groups entered Thailand.

In the highlands the Akha continued to live largely as agriculturalists, practicing swidden or slash-and-burn farming techniques to grow rice, corn, and a variety of other fruit and vegetable crops on impermanent fields. Swidden farming allows a family or primary production unit to use a field for only a season or two before the nutrients generated by burning off the primary vegetation have been depleted. Therefore, each year a new plot of land would have to be cut from the jungle, allowed to dry, and then burned off to provide an ash fertilizer. The Thai government in past decades has been working with various Hill Tribe groups, including the Akha, to limit the use of this extensive farming method because of the diminishing forest resources in the country and to encourage the use of more intensive agricultural forms, in which plots of land are artificially fertilized and used a number of times before lying fallow.

Another important crop among some Akha subgroups is opium, which has been used

AKHA

location:
The highlands of Yunnan Province, China; western Vietnam; eastern Myanmar (Burma); and northern Thailand and Laos; in China, the Akha are classified with the Hani though they are separate ethnolinguistic groups

time period:
Unknown to the present

language:
Akha, a Tibeto-Burman language

An Akha woman in traditional garb; note the coins hanging off the decorative headpiece and the heavy shell necklaces. *(Shutterstock/Simone van den Berg)*

for centuries for both medicinal and religious purposes. In the past century opium has also been used recreationally in some communities, leading to significant drug problems. In Thailand, the government has made progress toward limiting both production and consumption of this drug through training programs and, especially, programs designed to increase income from other agricultural products. Despite these programs, however, the Akha are still considered one of the poorest ethnic communities in Thailand and one of the most difficult to integrate into the larger Thai national community.

The other cultural features that make the Akha stand out from the other tribal communities who reside in the highlands of northern Southeast Asia are the colorful clothes and coin-covered headgear worn by Akha women, the ceremonial gates that stand over the entrances to Akha villages, and the giant swing in each village, where each August a "swing festival" takes place. The gates are particularly interesting to outsiders, covered as they are with carvings of aspects of human life, from actual human figures to such contemporary images as cars and airplanes. To touch or otherwise be disrespectful of one of these gates, or the many statues of copulating couples located outside each village, is to draw great shame on both the individual and his or her family. To rectify the situation the family must either pay a fine or donate animals to the community for sacrifice.

Akha society is organized around a patrilineal kinship system, which designates each clan and lineal group into a binary pair of wife givers and wife takers. In this system, women must marry into clans that are classified as wife takers in relation to their own and men must marry into clans that are classified as wife givers in relation to their own. As a result, each individual is constrained in his or her choice of marriage partner on the basis of not only the rules of exogamy, which state that marriage within a lineage or clan is forbidden, but also the complex rules of asymmetric alliance designating each kin unit as a wife giver or taker in relation to all others.

Another important marker of Akha identity is the particular blend of indigenous beliefs, taboos, rituals, and other practices that make up the local religious system. This system among the Akha was more complex and more all-encompassing than the systems of many other Hill Tribes of Southeast Asia, and as a result the Akha were much slower than many others to convert to Christianity, even partially. The first contact between the Akha and Christian missionaries in what was then Burma occurred in 1869, but it took another 40 years before any converts were made and another 27 after that before a local Akha Baptist church was opened in 1936. Conversion in Thailand was even slower; it was 1962 when the first Akha became Christian there. Nonetheless, conversion became more common in both countries in the 1980s and 1990s, not because Christian missionaries were more active but because large numbers of Akha did not have access to the financial and cultural resources needed to participate in traditional Akha religion. They were left without family members or elders to explain the myths and without a community of believers with whom to perform the rituals. In short, conversion occurred not because of the perceived rewards of doing so but because the rewards of not doing so had been stripped away by poverty, war, migration, and other ramifications of political discord.

FURTHER READING

Paul W. Lewis. *Akha Oral Literature* (Bangkok, Thailand: White Lotus, 2002).

Altai (Altaians, Altaic People, Altay, White Mountain Tatars)

The Altai are a group of various TURKIC PEOPLES living in southern Siberia in the region bordering western Mongolia to the south. They are usually divided into two groups, the Northern Altai and the Southern Altai, who speak different languages and have had different cultural influences. Southern Altai have been influenced by MONGOLIANS significantly more than Northern Altai, and they resemble Mongolians physically. Although these tribes had resided in more or less the same area for centuries, there was little indication of an Altai identity prior to a religious revival in 1904, which included promises to unite all of the Altai and lead them out of Russian control.

GEOGRAPHY

The Altai live in the Altai Republic of the Russian Federation, located along the border with western Mongolia; some Altai also live in western Mongolia. Historically the Altai have also lived in the Altai Krai, another region in Russia adjacent to the Altai Republic, but today very few Altai remain in that area. The defining feature of the area is the Altai Mountain Range, in portions of present-day Russia, China, Mongolia, and Kazakhstan, where all four countries meet. The Altai Republic is mountainous and marked by high ridges with deep river valleys. The region contains glaciers and mountain lakes; mineral springs in the area are considered to have medicinal properties.

ORIGINS

The Altai Mountain Range area is considered the birthplace of the Turkic peoples, who later migrated in all directions. It is widely believed that the ancestors of the Altai have been living in the same area for thousands of years; however, prior to the beginning of the 20th century they did not have a sense of ethnic identity. Modern Altai are the descendants of about nine different tribes who inhabited the Altai Mountain region, spoke different languages, and had different lifestyles.

LANGUAGES

The languages spoken by the Altai can be divided into two groups, Northern and Southern. These dialects are distinct enough to impede mutual comprehension; they belong to different subgroups of the Turkic languages. The Northern languages are part of the Uighur-Oguz group and the Southern are part of the Kyrgyz-Kipchack group. Both the Northern and Southern dialects have a number of varieties, generally named after a specific tribe. From 1922 to 1938 written Altai used a Latin alphabet; since 1938 the Latin alphabet has been replaced by a modified Cyrillic alphabet. The Altai language, sometimes referred to as Altaic, should not be confused with the Altaic languages, a language family that includes Turkic, Mongolic, and Tungusic languages, as well as JAPANESE and Korean.

HISTORY

Although the Altai had inhabited the Altai Mountain area for thousands of years, the first historical development to play a significant role in the emergence of a common identity occurred between the 15th and 18th centuries, during which time the Altai were ruled by western Mongolian khans, also known as the Oirat federation or Dzhungaria. The historical records show that the Altai were conquered, subjugated, and required to pay tribute, although these facts were forgotten by the 19th century, when the Altai began to believe the Oirat federation had once unified the Altai tribes and ushered in a golden age.

When Dzhungaria disintegrated in the 18th century, Russia and China each claimed the territory, reaching an agreement by which the Altai tribes had to pay tribute to both countries. During this time Orthodox Christian and Buddhist missionaries began proselytizing among the Altai, who had remained shamanist during their domination by the Oirat federation. Russian influence gradually increased, and Orthodox missionaries began to confiscate land, often legally under Russian laws, from Altai who refused to convert.

In the 1850s Buddhist missionaries from Mongolia also entered the Altai region to encourage the Altai to unite against the RUSSIANS and join Mongolia. The Russians quickly suppressed the movement and became increasingly suspicious of Mongolian missionaries. However, shortly after the official Russian annexation of the Altai region in the 1880s, new influxes of Mongolian missionaries traveled to the Altai region with the same intention and again were quickly suppressed.

In 1904 the Altai tribes again were influenced by Mongolian missionaries, but this time much more profoundly. Chot Chelpan, a native Altai, announced that he had had a vision of a white horse and rider, who announced the return of Oirot Khan, who would unite the Altai,

ALTAI

location:
The Altai Mountains, Russian Altai Republic, and Altai Krai, as well as western Mongolia

time period:
Unknown to the present

ancestry:
This people and region are thought to be the original homeland of the Turkic peoples in Central and Western Asia, although the original population was not Turkic.

language:
About eight different Turkic languages divided into two groups: Northern Altai and Southern Altai

Altai time line

B.C.E.

3000–2000 First evidence of agricultural societies in area inhabited currently by the Altai.

500–400 Evidence of a Mongol culture in the Altai area.

C.E.

500–1000 The Altai region is controlled by various Turkic khanates.

1635–1758 The people of the Altai region are ruled by and pay tribute to the Zunghar khanate, a confederation of Mongol tribes who also referred to themselves as *oirat* (allies).

1758 The Zunghar khanate finally disintegrates after a long conflict with the Manchu (Qing dynasty) in China. The Chinese subsequently claim the right to control all the peoples previously controlled by the Zunghar.

Czarist Russia claims control of the Altai region, placing the Russians in direct conflict with the Chinese over the area. The dispute is resolved by an agreement whereby the Altai pay tribute to both Russia and China.

1800s Missionaries from various religions attempt to convert the Altai. Most significantly, Buddhist lamas from Mongolia and Russian Orthodox missionaries seek to convert the population from their shamanistic religion, with varying success.

1850s Buddhist missionaries from western Mongolia try to unify the Altai people under the leadership of the mythical Oirot Khan.

1866 Russia annexes the Altai territory.

1880s Buddhist missionaries make a second attempt to unify the Altai people.

1900 A Mongolian lama announces himself the returning Oirot Khan but is quickly expelled from the Altai region by Russian forces.

1904 Chot Chelpan, an Altai, claims to have received a vision of the returning Oirot Khan, who promises to unite all of the people but who also hands down 18 commandments that are to become the replacement religion, Burkhanism, for the previously practiced shamanism.

free them from Russian rule, and reestablish the Oirat federation. The Altai had by this time forgotten that under the Oirat federation they had no more rights than under the Russians and had begun to believe the legend that all the Altai had once been unified. There had never been an Oirot Khan; the name was derived from that of the Oirat federation, with a vowel change. In the vision Chot claimed to have seen Oirot Khan, who gave Chot 18 commandments that the Altai were to follow, thereby founding the new religion of Burkhanism. The Altai were quick to react and held many secret meetings planning their secession from the Russian Empire. However, the Russian authorities soon heard of Chot's vision and the supposed return of Oirot Khan, presumably from Mongolia, and they quickly sealed the border with Mongolia and arrested Chot.

Although Oirot Khan never arrived, Burkhanism and the hope of his arrival were enough to unite the Altai tribes, who began to refer to themselves as Oirotia. When the Russian civil war broke out in 1918, the Altai attempted to secede from Russia and form their own country, which would be known as Oirotia. They failed and were under Soviet control by the 1920s. Soviet collectivization starting in the 1930s destroyed many Altai villages and forced the people to abandon their seminomadic lifestyle for a permanently settled one, a process that had started with the first Russian missionaries to the area.

During and after World War II the Altai were accused of being pro-Japanese. As a result, all of the native Altai members of the Communist Party were purged. The word *Oirot* was also declared counterrevolutionary and deleted wherever it was mentioned. This action included changing the name of the Altai territory to *Mountain Altai Autonomous Oblast*. However, there is little evidence that this situation related directly to particularly harsh treatment of the native Altai by Soviet authorities.

1904 The Altai gather from May to July in great numbers in mountain meeting places kept secret from Russians and Christianized Altai, to discuss the new religion and prepare for the return of Oirot Khan, who promised to free them of Russian domination.

By autumn, the Russians begin to fear this movement and close the borders with Mongolia, limiting both trade and the movement of lamas.

Russian forces decide to arrest Chot and his family but arrive at his yurt to find 3,000 followers praying and Chot and his family gone.

1906 Chot is turned over to Russian authorities by a Christian Altai. He is tried in 1906 and although no documents remain from the trial it is believed that he was freed by the end of 1906.

1917–20 Many Altai side with the Mensheviks during the Russian Revolution in the hope that they will be granted their own state.

1920 The Altai territory falls under Soviet control.

1922 The Altai territory is named Oirot (Oyrot) Autonomous Oblast, in reference to the mythical figure of Oirot.

1920s–50s Industrial projects in the region produce an unprecedented influx of Russian migrants, reducing the Altai percentage of the population of the Oirot Autonomous Oblast.

1933 The Soviet government denounces Burkhanism and talk of "Greater Oirotia" as anti-Communist.

1939–45 The Altai are accused of being pro-Japanese.

1948 The Oirot Autonomous Oblast is renamed the Gorno-Altaisk Autonomous Oblast, and the word *Oirot* is declared counterrevolutionary.

1991 The Soviet Union collapses, and the Gorno-Altaisk Autonomous Oblast becomes the Gorno-Altaisk Republic.

1992 The Gorno-Altaisk Republic is renamed the Altai Republic.

1997 The Altai Republic adopts a constitution as a member of the Russian Federation.

After the fall of the Soviet Union there was another, weaker surge of Altai nationalism. Although the people were unable to secede, this time they managed to upgrade their status in the Russian Federation to that of a republic, forming the Altai Republic in 1992. The leaders of the republic have established two official languages, Russian and Altai, and the Altai now have considerably more say in their own government than previously. However, influxes of Russians and other migrants have reduced the Altai percentage of the population to 31 percent, relegating the Altai to minority status even in their native territory.

CULTURE

Prior to the influences of Orthodox missionaries it seems that the Altai were at least seminomadic, although the fact that they had established villages and towns suggests that they returned to settlements for at least some part of the year on a regular basis. The Altai bred cattle, hunted, and cultivated crops, activities that have largely survived the collectivization efforts of the Soviet Union. Modern Altai tribes continue to breed cattle and use the same subsistence patterns as their ancestors. As early as 2000 B.C.E. the peoples of the area were famous for metalwork, including hunting gear, tools, and decorative objects, which they often used to pay tribute to foreign rulers.

The Altai practiced shamanism and were spirit worshipers before the arrival of Orthodox Christian missionaries in the 18th century, particularly revering the mountains among which they lived. When the Orthodox missionaries arrived, some of the Altai converted to Orthodox Christianity, although they usually kept aspects of their shamanistic religion. Around the same time as the Orthodox missionaries Buddhist lamas from Mongolia entered the Altai region to proselytize. While the Altai did not usually convert to Buddhism altogether, many Buddhist principles found their way into Altai religious thought.

Burkhanism, also referred to as the White Religion, is the name given to the religion introduced in 1904 by Chot Chelpan; it speaks of the return of Oirot Khan and the end of Altai subjugation by the Russians. This religion, the rules of which were delivered to Chot in a dream, consists of 18 commandments, which have both anti-Russian and antishamanistic characteristics, such as instructions to burn all of the drums used in shamanistic rituals and not to associate with Russians. Burkhanism was obviously significantly influenced by both Christianity and Buddhism; in fact, *Burkhan* is the Mongolian word for "Buddha" and the existence of commandments is reminiscent of Christianity. Although Burkhanism does not continue to be widely practiced, it has had a lasting impact on Altai society. Among the commandments are prohibitions against smoking and owning cats, as well as a rule regarding the way the Altai should greet each other. These commandments are still generally followed by the Altai, although most are now nominally Orthodox Christian, while retaining some aspects of shamanism and Buddhism.

Further Reading

A. P. Derevianko et al. *Istoriia Respubliki Altai (History of the Altai Republic)* (Gorno-Altaisk: In-t altaiskiki im. S. S. Surazokova: 2002).

Mirra Ginsburg. *Little Rystu: Adapted from an Altai Folktale* (New York: Greenwillow Books, 1978).

L. P. Potapov. *Ocherk Istorii Oirotii (A Study of the History of Oirotia)* (Novosibirsk: OGIZ 1933).

Andrzej Rozwadowski with Maria M. Kośko. *Spirits and Stones: Shamanism and Rock Art in Central Asia and Siberia* (Poznań, Poland: Instytut Wschodni UAM, 2002).

Ambonese (Central Moluccans, Alifuru, Amboynese, Moluccans, Orang Ambon)

Ambon was one of the first areas of contemporary Indonesia to have been contacted and settled by Europeans, when the Portuguese arrived in 1521 and established an export market in cloves, which were native to the region. About a century later the Dutch arrived and expelled the Portuguese; they were followed by the British in 1796, who were then defeated yet again by the Dutch in 1814. In the 20th century the Japanese occupied the island during World War II and Indonesia claimed the island as its own after gaining its independence from the Dutch at the end of the war. As was the case on many Indonesian islands, the local population was not interested in becoming Indonesians and proclaimed

the independent state of the South Moluccan Republic in 1950. The Indonesian military was swift in its reprisals against this movement and Ambon and the other South Moluccan islands have been a part of Indonesia ever since, despite sporadic guerrilla fighting in Seram in the early years. A large number of refugees also fled the region and moved to the Netherlands; they live there today as South Moluccans.

The Ambonese are a mixture of Malay and Melanesian; the former heritage has given them their Austronesian language while the latter has given most of their physical traits. In the past the Ambonese also had a men's secret society, called *kakehan,* into which every adolescent male had to be initiated in order to be considered a man. This society resembled those of many other societies throughout Melanesia but was the only one of its kind in Indonesia. Today most Ambonese are either Muslim, particularly those who live in the north, or Protestant Christian, mainly those in the south. In the 1950s it was largely this Christian population, who had been educated in Dutch schools and the Dutch Reformed Church, who rebelled against the imposition of the Indonesian state; these people feared more for their economic well-being than for their religion but the two factors were interconnected in the minds of many.

Within Ambon society there are two distinct subcultures, the Alifuru of the interior and the Pasisir of the coast. The former group were largely slash-and-burn horticulturalists prior to the Dutch era; they also engaged in frequent intra- and intergroup warfare and headhunting before pacification in the first two decades of the 20th century. The latter had been contacted and acculturated by the Dutch about 400 years before the Alifuru; they converted to Christianity and engaged in trade and intensive agriculture on permanent plots and were closely allied with the Dutch as members of the colonial army and bureaucracy. Interestingly, it is in the coastal Pasisir communities with their long history of interactions with Europeans where many traditional beliefs and practices concerning spirits and ancestors have survived and in the more-recently contacted Alifuru communities where these have been eliminated.

Ami (Amis, Pangcah)

The Ami are the largest of the 13 recognized indigenous groups living on Taiwan and its surrounding islands, where they made up about 37.5 percent of the total of all Aboriginal

AMBONESE

location:
Ambon Island in the South Moluccas, Maluku, Indonesia

time period:
Unknown to the present

ancestry:
Melanesian and Malay

language:
There are three separate Ambon languages, all in the Austronesian phylum, and Ambonese Malay, also an Austronesian language, derived from the Malay spoken throughout Sumatra.

TAIWANESE in 2000. The people call themselves Amis; *Ami,* their more recognized ethnonym, is their name in Chinese.

The origins of all Taiwanese aboriginal peoples are somewhat uncertain but probably stretch back to about 5000 B.C.E. and the migration of proto-AUSTRONESIANS from southern China to Taiwan. During the course of the subsequent 4,000 years other Austronesian populations migrated to the island chain and differentiation along both linguistic and cultural lines occurred to create a variety of different ethnolinguistic groups. All carried out swidden or slash-and-burn agriculture, stressed kinship in their social structures, and practiced animistic or spirit-based religions.

Genetically the Ami are somewhat different from the other Aboriginal Taiwanese peoples in being more heterogeneous and more closely related to the NEW GUINEA HIGHLANDERS and ABORIGINAL AUSTRALIANS. Some scholars hypothesize that the Ami arrived on Taiwan in a migration separate from the other Taiwanese Aboriginal groups and maintained long-term connections with peoples from the Philippines.

The Ami are divided into at least five different subgroups according to location and other principles. One particular subgroup, the Sakizaya, became in January 2007 a 13th recognized aboriginal group, separate from the Ami. The misclassification had resulted from an uprising of Sakizaya people in 1878, known as the Takobowan Incident. In retaliation for the uprising the colonial Qing armies tried to kill off the Sakizaya; as a result the survivors took refuge among the larger and more powerful Ami. For the next 120 years both the Ami and the Sakizaya conspired to keep the rebels' identity secret from the Chinese and Japanese authorities, and the Sakizaya were always spoken of as a subgroup of the Ami people. Starting in 2004, however, a movement began to allow a separate Sakizaya identity to emerge, much as had happened for the Kavalan, another Ami subgroup, who gained official recognition in 2002. After three years of campaigning, paperwork, letter writing by people who consider themselves Sakizaya, cultural revival, and investigations by the Taiwanese Council for Indigenous People, the Sakizaya were recognized in a ceremony in early 2007 as a separate tribe with its own language, culture, and identity.

The traditional Ami homeland lies along the east coast of Taiwan in Hualien and Taitung; the Ami occupy both coastal plains and foothill regions. Fishing and swidden or slash-and-burn agriculture made up the basis of their subsistence system; today fishing continues while more intensive agricultural strategies have replaced swidden. Their kinship system is matrilineal: membership in the lineage is passed down through the mother's family and thus fathers remain outsiders to their children's descent group; maternal uncles are the dominant males for children in matrilineal societies. Groups of lineages are also organized into matrilineal clans in which leadership positions in the past were held by senior males who made decisions about warfare, judicial matters, politics, land, and religion. Post-marriage residence among the Ami is matrilocal, requiring a new husband to move into his wife's family's home. Nonetheless, despite being the householders, women must defer to their maternal uncles for financial and other important decisions.

In the past the most important ceremony held by the Ami was the Harvest Festival, Ilisin, which was a New Year's celebration held to thank the spirit world for providing food and resources to the Ami. It was held sometime between July and September, with more northern regions celebrating later in the year to coincide with their major harvest time. At the end of this ceremony, as is the case with most Ami rituals including initiations, weddings, and funerals, the marker for returning to daily life is either fishing or eating fish; fish represent the mundane or material world as separate from the spiritual world brought to life during the ritual.

While the traditional religion of the Ami was animism, which recognized a wide variety of gods, spirits, and ancestors as important religious figures, some Ami converted to Buddhism after interactions with HAN Chinese migrants to Taiwan. Today many Ami have converted to Christianity and are less likely to celebrate traditional events or to engage in either animistic or Buddhist rituals. Some Ami have also moved to urban areas, and thus their strongest connection to their cultural heritage is to music and dance troupes that perform throughout Taiwan.

Unfortunately the fame some of these groups have achieved has led to exploitation. The most grievous example is of the Ami couple Difag and Igay, whose Chinese names are *Kuo Ying-nan* and *Kuo Hsiu-chu,* respectively; the pair toured Europe in 1988 as part of a larger Taiwanese Aboriginal performance. They were illegally recorded during a concert in France;

AMI

location:
The eastern coast of Taiwan with a few individuals residing in the island's main cities

time period:
5000 B.C.E. to the present

ancestry:
Austronesian

language:
Ami, an East Formosan Austronesian language

Kuo Hsiu-chu and Kuo Ying-nan ⚹⚹⚹

Kuo Hsiu-chu and her husband, Kuo Ying-nan, both members of the indigenous Ami tribe of Taiwan, are best known for their vocal contributions to the 1994 chart-topping song "Return to Innocence," by the musical group Enigma. Part of an aboriginal performance group, their distinctive voices were recorded during a 1988 world-cultures concert in France and later sampled by Michael Cretu, German producer of Enigma, for the song "Return to Innocence." Kuo Hsiu-chu and Kuo Ying-nan were never made aware of this recording and were given neither credit nor royalties. The Aboriginal Taiwanese song that Kuo Hsiu-chu and Kuo Ying-nan were recorded singing was the "Jubilant Drinking Song." At the time of "Return to Innocences'" success the Kuos were farmers in the mountains of southeast Taiwan, growing leaves for wrapping betel nuts. Hsiu-chu and Ying-nan, born in 1923 and 1921, respectively, were of a generation that had grown up singing the traditional Ami songs while working in the fields. After the court settlement with Virgin Records, the two dedicated their time to teaching the songs to younger generations of Ami.

their music was eventually taken up by the group Enigma and incorporated into its song "Return to Innocence," the theme song of the Atlanta summer Olympics in 1996. The Chinese Folk Arts Foundation has received a nominal fee from the French recording company for use of the music clip, but the Ami couple has yet to see a penny for their work.

Amis   *See* AMI.

A-nan   *See* MAONAN.

Andamanese (Andaman Islander, Mincopie)

GEOGRAPHY

The Andaman Islands are located in the Andaman Sea, part of the Bay of Bengal. They are made up of 576 separate islands, the main five of which together are called Great Andaman. North Sentinel Island, located about 18 miles west of South Andaman Island, one of the five that make up Great Andaman, is important as the home of the most undisturbed population of hunter-gatherer peoples left on earth. During the 2004 Sumatra-Andaman earthquake, which caused the massive tsunami to hit the region on December 26 of that year, the Andaman Island chain was greatly affected, with the islands shifting more than four yards to the southwest and sinking more than three feet (*see* NICOBARESE). The Andamans contain the only active volcano in South Asia, on Barren Island

east of Great Andaman, with recent activity in 1991, 1994–95, and 2005.

ORIGINS

The origins of the Andaman Islanders are completely unknown. They resemble populations of so-called pygmies in Central Africa with their short stature (men stand about four feet, 10 inches; women about four feet, six inches), dark skin, and frizzy hair; however, genetically the Andamanese are more closely related to Southeast Asians than to Africans. They were probably part of the first exodus of humans from Africa who went on to colonize Asia, Melanesia, and Australia. They may also be related to other so-called Negrito populations, the Malaysian SEMANG and the Filipino AETA; however, this relationship will be difficult to prove since these other groups have lost all trace of their aboriginal languages and today speak Austronesian languages adopted from more powerful neighbors.

HISTORY

Although their island homelands sit in the middle of a busy shipping lane, a combination of fierce independence and lack of resources allowed the Andaman Islanders to remain fairly isolated until the middle of the 19th century. Even as early as the 13th century Marco Polo wrote about the Andamanese, indicating that their presence was not unknown to the outside world. However, it was the British who finally ended the Andaman isolation in 1857, when they opened a penal colony at what is today the municipal capital of the region, Port Blair, for captives from the Indian mutiny of that year. In 1857 there were probably about 5,000 people living on the islands, divided into at least 12 different tribal groups. As in so many cases of first contact, these first interactions were devastating for the Andaman population. By 1895 their population had shrunk to about 400, mostly as a result of diseases such as measles and influenza.

During the course of the British administration of the islands a number of ethnographic and linguistic studies were carried out with a few of the more willing tribal groups, but interest in these isolated hunter-gatherers waned and much of what we know about their traditional culture was written early in the 20th century. During World War II the JAPANESE occupied the islands, which were liberated by British forces in 1945, and then they were handed over to independent India in 1947. Since that time the Andamanese have been administered

---

ANDAMANESE

location:
The Andaman Islands in the Andaman Sea south of the Bay of Bengal.

time period:
Unknown to the present.

ancestry:
Unknown.

language:
The various languages spoken in the archipelago are all members of a proposed Andaman language family, subdivided into Greater Andamanese and South Andamanese or Onge-Jarawa. Sentinelese is probably related to these other languages, but the resistance of this population to outsiders means that nobody has been able to record any of it, much less study it.

under India's Tribal Policy, which requires all outsiders to have a permit to enter their region or study them; no non-Indian has received such permission (*see* SCHEDULED TRIBES).

Although the Andamanese had a reputation for fierce aggression against all outsiders, the actual responses of the different Andaman groups to outsiders differed. In the early days the Onge on Little Andaman Island, south of Great Andaman, were extremely isolationist. They wounded and even killed several visiting British officers in the late 19th century and refused all interactions with outsiders until the 1950s. At the same time several groups on Great Andaman colluded with the British and served as guards and bush police watching over the Indian prisoners at Port Blair. Today most of the 400–500 indigenous people on Great Andaman, as well as the Onge, are settled and living as a tribal minority under the administration of the Indian government.

One group, however, continues actively to resist most advances by the modern world, the Sentinelese of North Sentinel Island. These people are so isolated that no outsider knows what they call themselves or anything at all about their language. In 1974 National Geographic sent a team to try to win the trust of the Sentinelese in order to film and photograph them; the entire team was met with a volley of arrows, one of which wounded the film director in the thigh. Indeed, there is only one recorded friendly meeting between the Sentinelese and outsiders, an Indian team whose gifts of coconuts were received without incident in 1991. The one Sentinelese man who pointed his drawn arrow at the approaching boat was convinced by a woman to put down his weapon; he buried it and the bow in the sand and accepted the coconuts. The Jarawa of Great Andaman Island are also somewhat more isolated and separate from the modern world than the rest of the Andamanese; however, since the building of a road through their territory in the late 1990s, they too have begun to trade and interact with outsiders, with some young Jarawa even learning HINDI.

On December 26, 2004, the Andaman Islands were at the center of the force that caused a tsunami carrying death to hundreds of thousands of people in India, Indonesia, Malaysia, Maldives, Myanmar, Sri Lanka, Thailand, and Somalia. The Andamans themselves lost more than 3,000 people, but very few of those were indigenous since the islands are also home to some descendants of the original Indian convicts plus other migrants from the Indian

Andamanese time line

B.C.E.

200 Oldest date obtained through carbon-14 (^{14}C) dating of Andaman kitchen middens. Genetic data point to a much more ancient settlement time, possibly as early as 75,000 B.C.E.

C.E.

1296 Marco Polo describes the Andaman Islanders as brutish and savage, probably on the basis of hearsay, as there is no evidence of his having visited the islands.

1771 The British East India Company records sighting lights on the shore of North Sentinel Island, the first written record of the island, which lies to the west of the main Andaman Archipelago.

1789 The British secure the Andaman Islands to protect themselves from pirates, who used the islands as shelter, and from the natives.

1796 The British abandon the post as a result of sickness.

1857–58 British settlement and establishment of a penal colony for Indian rebels finally succeed, at Port Blair on South Andaman Island.

1877 First measles epidemic kills about one-quarter of the Andamanese population.

1942 The Japanese occupy the Andaman Islands.

1945 The Andaman Islands are liberated from the Japanese by Lord Mountbatten and two years later join independent India.

1974 A National Geographic film crew attempts to win over the Sentinelese with gifts, most of which are speared and buried; the Sentinelese also shoot several volleys of arrows at the crew, hitting the director in the thigh.

1991 First recorded friendly meeting between outsiders and Sentinelese, who accept bags of coconuts from a contingent of Indian officials.

1999 An outbreak of measles among the Jarawa kills about 10 percent of the population and indicates the relative failure of Indian tribal policy to prevent outside interference with this isolated community.

2004 A massive earthquake and tsunami kill thousands and cause extensive damage to the islands; the effects on many indigenous Andamanese are unknown because of their hostility to outside contact.

mainland. The Sentinelese have also probably been greatly affected because aerial photographs show that the rich coral reef that surrounded their island and provided a habitat for many species of fish was totally destroyed. Indeed, it was originally thought that the whole population might have been killed by the earthquake and resulting tsunami, but these same aerial photographs showed significant signs of life. It should be noted that a Sentinelese man fired arrows at the hovering helicopter as the photographer snapped pictures. As of late 2006 no outsider had been able to make contact with them to clarify what has happened to them or their way of life in the aftermath.

Andamanese girls from the Jarawa tribe; both probably stand less than four feet tall. *(OnAsia/ Thierry Falise)*

CULTURE

When first contacted by the British, all the Andamanese lived in small villages of 30–50 people, located either along the coast or in the inland jungles. They all lived by hunting and gathering, with some trade between those who hunted turtles on the coast and those who hunted wild Andaman pigs in the jungles. Individual households were made up of strictly monogamous married couples and their children with a fairly simple kinship system that recognized only local family groupings, not larger corporate bodies like lineages or clans. The plethora of kinship terms common in many societies that use kinship as their primary organizing principle was largely absent in all Andamanese languages that have been studied, with most recognizing only the relative ages of the people involved. The one relative who stands out in at least a few Andamanese languages is the mother's brother because of a common practice of naming children after him.

The Andamanese material culture was made up of a fairly limited array of wood, bone, and a few stone tools; simple dugout canoes; bows and arrows, which today are often tipped with iron from waste that washes up on the shoreline; baskets; and a simple form of reddish or black coil pottery that appears in middens but was not in use when the British arrived in the 1850s. All Andamanese went naked, with men wearing a belt to hold their arrows, both practices the Sentinelese continue to this day. Many Andamanese also practiced a form of tattooing, but this practice has been lost over the past century as a result of integration into Indian society. The cultural feature that stood out most for all the early researchers who wrote about the Andamanese is that they were unable to make fire on their own, instead having to wait for lightning to strike and then saving the burning embers for as long as possible. This fact seems to make the Andamanese the technologically most simple society ever discovered by literate Europeans.

Andaman religion seems to be animistic, based on the belief that many or most beings and even natural forces in the world have a spirit. The two most important spirits for the Andamanese were Puluga or Biliku and Deria or Tarai. These two were married, usually with Puluga/Biliku being described as female, and correspond to the northeast and southwest monsoonal winds, respectively. Angering Puluga/Biluka by burning or melting beeswax, digging up some plants, disturbing a cicada's song, or killing the insect results in tremendous storms of wind and rain; when Puluga/Biliku throws her spear it is seen by humans as lightning. There are also myths about the founding ancestors of the Andamanese, many of which bear the names of plants and animals, making it difficult for the few researchers who have studied them to tell whether an informant was talking about an ancestor or an actual plant or animal. Finally, the Andamanese believe that the spirit of a dead person stays with his or her bones. As a result, dead enemies are hacked apart and their torso and limbs are cremated immediately in order to get rid of the enemy spirit. The same belief leads many Andamanese to wear the jawbones of their dead relatives as a necklace, in order to be protected by their spirit, and to cut up turtles and pigs when they are still alive in order to provide a more energizing food.

FURTHER READING

A. R. Radcliffe-Brown. *The Andaman Islanders* (New York: Cambridge University Press, 1933).

Anangu   *See* PITJANTJATJARA.

Ankalyn   *See* CHUKCHIS.

Arleng   *See* KARBIS.

Armenians   (Armyanin, Hay, Somekhi)

GEOGRAPHY

The Armenian people originated in the land of the Lesser Caucasus Mountains in Southwest Asia. Historic Armenia, or the Armenian highland, refers to a vast area of land, about 249,000 square miles, that constitutes the continuation of the Caucasus Mountains. Today most of the Armenian highland is in eastern Turkey, with some parts in Iran and the western part of Azerbaijan.

The kingdom of Armenia, at its peak in 95–66 B.C.E. under Tigranes the Great, extended over an area that is now Turkey, Syria, and Lebanon, with access to both the Caspian and Mediterranean Seas. Today the Armenian Republic is a landlocked nation located in the Lesser Caucasus Mountains. It is bordered on the west by Turkey, the east by Azerbaijan, the north by Georgia, and the south by Iran.

In response to ongoing territorial border changes and subsequent minority status in hostile lands, particularly after the 1915 genocide of Armenians in Turkey, large numbers of Armenians have dispersed throughout the world. Of the total Armenian population living worldwide (in 2004 estimated to be 9 million), only about 3 million live in Armenia and about 130,000 in Nagorno-Karabakh.

The contested land of Nagorno-Karabakh, which lies within the borders of Azerbaijan, is populated primarily by Armenians, who in 1991 declared the region an independent republic. Neither Azerbaijan nor the international community has officially recognized the Nagorno-Karabakh Republic.

ORIGINS

Armenian history may be as old as the Sumerian story of Gilgamesh from the fourth millennium B.C.E., in which the land of Arata is placed in a geographic space that could be describing the Armenian plateau. The name *Arata*, linked also to a city of the third millennium B.C.E., which has not yet been identified by contemporary archaeologists, resembles the sacred mountain of the Armenians, Ararat, closely enough for many scholars to posit a connection between this ancient place and the Armenian people. On more solid archaeological and historical ground, the land of Greater Armenia hosted the Hittite empire (1800–1100 B.C.E.), the Mittani (1500 B.C.E.), and the Nairi (1300 B.C.E.), all of whom must have left behind genetic, material, and cultural traits that have contributed to the development of the Armenians. Armenia's location between two continents has historically left its people vulnerable to invasion by many others, including the Assyrians, Persians, GREEKS, PARTHIANS, Romans, Byzantines, Arabs, MONGOLS, Ottoman Turks, and RUSSIANS. Each of these groups has also contributed to the development of the contemporary Armenian people.

HISTORY

Besides the Gilgamesh stories, the first known account of Armenia appears in the *Anabasis*, written by Xenophon, a Greek historian, in approximately 400 B.C.E. This famous work told the story of an army of Greek mercenaries who left their service for a Persian prince to return overland to Greece. Xenophon wrote in great detail about Armenian village life and the underground dwellings of the inhabitants in certain regions. Access to these subterranean houses was by a ladder via the entrance referred to as *yerdik*. This building feature probably had a defensive purpose but may also have protected the occupants from harsh winter weather.

Armenia's long history is largely as a pawn among the great empires of the day, early Persian, Roman, Arab, Byzantine, Russian, Ottoman, and later Persian. In ancient times, Armenia's history is connected in many ways

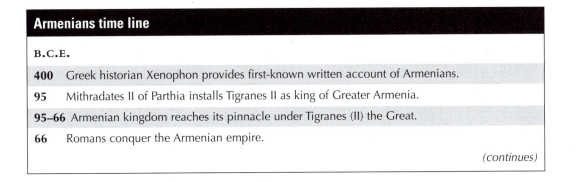

Armenians time line

B.C.E.	
400	Greek historian Xenophon provides first-known written account of Armenians.
95	Mithradates II of Parthia installs Tigranes II as king of Greater Armenia.
95–66	Armenian kingdom reaches its pinnacle under Tigranes (II) the Great.
66	Romans conquer the Armenian empire.

(continues)

Armenians time line (continued)

C.E.

100   The first Christian Armenian Church is founded by Bartholomew and Thaddaeus.

301–30 National conversion to Christianity under Armenian King Trdat III after his meeting with Saint Gregory the Illuminator. This is possibly the first national conversion to Christianity in the world.

500   The Armenian alphabet is devised by Mesrop Mashtots in order to translate biblical texts and other Christian materials.

653   Arabs obtain Armenia from the Byzantine Empire.

900   Brief period of Armenian independence.

990   Armenian architect Trdat is summoned to Constantinople by Byzantine officials to direct earthquake repairs to the Hagia Sophia Basilica, in recognition of the highly innovative Armenian architectural tradition.

1080 Cilicia, an independent Armenian kingdom, emerges on the Mediterranean coast.

1100–1400 Armenia is invaded from the west by Byzantine Greeks and from the east by Seljuk Turks.

1375 Cilicia is conquered by outside forces.

1500 Ottoman Empire and Safavid Persia divide western and eastern Armenia between them, respectively. This marks the origin of the cultural and linguistic division of Armenians between east and west.

1828 Russia replaces Persia as the dominant force in eastern Armenia and makes it a province.

1894 The Hamidian massacre of 300,000 Armenian subjects by Ottoman Turks, so named after Abdul Hamid II.

1915 Young Turks massacre an estimated 600,000–2 million Armenians living in Turkey. This has been referred to as the first genocide of the 20th century.

1918 The Democratic Republic of Armenia is officially established with Armenian Revolutionary Federation (ARF) leader R. I. Kachazuni as prime minister. May 28 is still celebrated annually in Armenia as Republic Day.

1920 The Armenian government is forced to accept a Communist-dominated coalition with Soviet Russia.

1921 Treaty of Kars, between the Soviet Union and Turkey, places Mount Ararat, national symbol of Armenia, in Turkish territory.

1988 Surge in Armenian nationalist movement.

Government of the autonomous Nagorno-Karabakh region of Azerbaijan votes to unify with Armenia.

Earthquake kills 25,000 in northern Armenia.

1989 Unification of Nagorno-Karabakh region with Armenia declared by Nagorno-Karabakh National Council.

1990–91 Moscow sends troops to invade Azerbaijan, ostensibly to stop pogroms against Armenians.

National independence approved by Armenian voters.

Fighting continues as Armenians in Nagorno-Karabakh declare an independent state.

Soviet Union officially dissolved.

1992 Lachin corridor linking Nagorno-Karabakh to Armenia is seized by Armenians.

1994 Russian-brokered cease-fire in Karabakh conflict put in place; however, ongoing international negotiations by Organization for Security and Cooperation in Europe (OSCE) to stop fighting and blockades have so far failed to resolve this issue.

2006 Index of Economic Freedom (Heritage Foundation and *The Wall Street Journal*) rates Armenia the most economically free state in the Commonwealth of Independent States (CIS, 11 former Soviet republics).

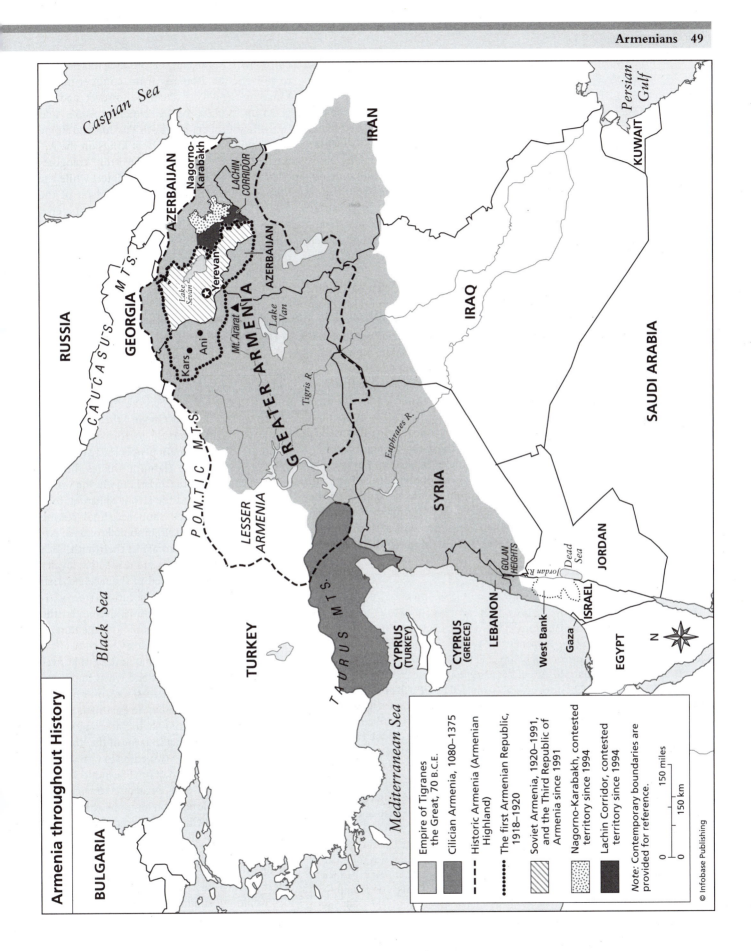

Armenia throughout History

Empire of Tigranes
the Great, 70 B.C.E.

Cilician Armenia, 1080–1375

Historic Armenia (Armenian
Highland)

The first Armenian Republic,
1918–1920

Soviet Armenia, 1920–1991,
and the Third Republic of
Armenia since 1991

Nagorno-Karabakh, contested
territory since 1994

Lachin Corridor, contested
territory since 1994

Note: Contemporary boundaries are
provided for reference.

150 miles

150 km

© Infobase Publishing

to the fate of the various Persian dynasties and empires that ruled much of the Iranian plateau and surrounding regions. As early as 550 B.C.E., Armenia was drawn into the Persian sphere of influence as the 13th satrapy of the greater PERSIANS', ACHAEMENIDS', empire. Armenia's royal dynasty the Orontids ruled in the lands of Greater Armenia as a semiautonomous nobility with tax and military responsibilities to the larger empire. Most Armenians at this time also adopted the Persian religion, Zoroastrianism. This kind of relationship continued as well under the Seleucids, the Greek successors to the Achaemenids in the region.

Only after the fall of the Seleucid Empire was the first independent Armenian kingdom established, in 190 B.C.E. However, this period of complete independence did not last long before a similar subordinate relationship with the mostly Persian PARTHIANS was established in 95 B.C.E., when Mithridates II of Parthia installed Tigranes II as king of Armenia. Under Tigranes II or the Great (95–66 B.C.E.) the Armenian nobles were eventually able to exert themselves as almost equal to those of Parthia proper by extending their rule over eastern Turkey and thus taking over a good portion of the Parthian empire. Tigranes himself was recognized by the Parthians as the "king of kings" in the eastern portion of their lands. Armenia at this time was also allied with the Parthians in their frequent battles with Rome, but this alliance was not able to prevent the Romans from conquering the kingdom in 66 B.C.E. Parthia, however, had not given up its claim to the Armenian lands, and in the first century C.E. both Parthia and Rome tried to place their own client kings on the Armenian throne. The Parthian king Vologeses tried to install his brother Tiridates, while the Romans supported the great-grandson of the great Herod himself, Tigranes VI. In the end, Rome won this challenge, but persistent strife between the two empires for domination in Armenia continued for several hundred years.

Despite these challenges this period of Roman vassalage saw the adoption of many Western social, political, and religious sensibilities in an otherwise Eastern society. For example, in the first century of the common era the first Christian Armenian church, the Armenian Apostolic Church, was founded by Bartholomew and Thaddaeus. By 301 to 330 C.E. the appeal of Christianity had reached the Armenian king Tiridates (Trdat) III via Gregory the Illuminator and a national conversion to Christianity was instituted. The Armenian people today continue to take great pride in claiming this as the first national conversion to Christianity in the world. This early history and the strong spiritual links to Mount Ararat, the supposed final resting place of Noah's ark, have combined to make Armenians extremely steadfast in their faith. As a powerful symbol of their unique identity, loyalty to the church has prevailed in the face of harsh religious restrictions and persecutions from various occupiers over the millennia. Even today the church remains independent of both the Roman Catholic and Eastern Orthodox Churches.

The strife between Rome and Parthia over control of Armenia did not end when the Sassanids (see PERSIANS, SASSANIDS) took over most of the land previously held by the Parthians in 224 C.E. In 296 the Sassanid shah Narses agreed to withdraw from Armenia in favor of the Romans, but within 40 years the two empires were at war again. Eventually, in 361, a final Sassanid victory gave them control over most of Armenia. This was not a favorable position for many Armenians, who had adopted Christianity in the fourth century, because the state religion of the Sassanids was Zoroastrianism. In 451 the Armenians rose up against their Persian overlords and though defeated sent a clear message to the Persians that they would not submit to religious reconversion. In 485 the Treaty of Nvarsag between the Armenians and Persians guaranteed the former the right of religious freedom within the empire.

King Trdat III 〰️

King Trdat III of Armenia, also known as Trdat the Great, is a pivotal figure in Armenian history as well as Christian history as he was responsible for making Armenia one of the first countries to adopt Christianity as the sole national religion.

Trdat III was born into the Arsacid dynasty in the year 250. Shortly after his birth Trdat's father, Chosroes I, was assassinated by a Parthian agent, who was promptly captured and executed. Trdat III was quickly spirited away to Rome, where he was educated in Roman law, language, and military strategy. In 287 he returned to Armenia, raised an army to drive out the Parthian occupation, and took his rightful place as king. Around this time he had contact with the man who would later come to be known as Saint Gregory the Illuminator. Gregory, a Christian convert, was one of the surviving sons of Anak, the assassin who had killed King Chosroes I. Gregory attracted King Trdat's attention when he refused to participate in a pagan ritual, and when his identity as the son of Anak was revealed to King Trdat, he was tortured and imprisoned for 13 years. Toward the end of the third century King Trdat III fell gravely ill and his sister had a dream in which she was told that Gregory was the only person who could cure the king. In 301 Trdat III met with Gregory and was cured instantly; as a result Christianity was promptly declared the official religion of Armenia. Trdat III aggressively took up the task of wiping out all traces of paganism from Armenia by destroying temples, texts, and artwork until his death in 330.

Armenia's history as a pawn among great empires continued in the seventh century with Arab invasion, but in the ninth century Armenia experienced a rare period of independence. At that point the capital, Ani, was a large city of more than 100,000 people and, it is said, 1,001 churches. Unfortunately, as often occurred in Armenian history, this period did not last long before the Byzantines and Turks in succession conquered areas of Armenian territory. In 1080 Cilicia, an independent Armenian kingdom, arose on the Mediterranean, but it too was conquered by outside forces in 1375. During that time Greater Armenia was conquered by the Mongols and then later divided between the Persian and Ottoman Empires, giving rise to the division between east and west that continues today among the Armenian people. In 1828 the Persian half of Armenia was annexed by Russia, while the Ottomans continued to persecute the Armenian Christian minority within their empire.

Beginning in the late 19th century the Armenian people began to be affected by the same concept of nationalism that was sweeping across Europe at that time: the idea that each ethnolinguistic group deserved a state of its own. For more information, see ARMENIANS: NATIONALITY in this volume.

CULTURE

Subsistence

Prior to the industrialization of the economy and of food production, Armenian subsistence consisted mostly of grains and cereals such as bulgur, pilaf, porridge, and flat bread. Additionally, dairy products such as yogurt, butter, milk, and cheese were regularly eaten. A drink that continues to be popular today was a mixture of soured yogurt and water called *tan*. Dried fruits such as apricots and figs were also enjoyed with nuts. Other forms of preserving were also used; for example, berries were canned and vegetables were pickled. Eastern Armenia has a long history of wine production from its many grape-producing regions. Until the present in Eastern Armenia very little meat was consumed because animals were kept primarily for dairy products. Cattle, sheep, and goats were so precious to Armenians that in the winter they cohabited with the family. Men were primarily responsible for the crops but women helped out in the busy harvest season.

Under the central control of the Soviet Union Armenia developed a modern industrial sector. However, along with the rest of the Soviet Union much of this industrial sector collapsed in the late 1980s and early 1990s, and economic activity has returned to subsistence farming and small-scale agriculture for some Armenians today. At the same time, by 2000, 70 percent of the Republic of Armenia's population resided in urban areas and relied on the other 30 percent for most of their foodstuffs.

Social Structure

Many of the traditional cultural practices of Armenians remained intact until the devastating effects of a 1915 genocide at the hands of the Ottoman Turks and the subsequent relocation of Armenians from eastern Anatolia (see ARMENIANS: NATIONALITY). However, some rural villages maintained elements of traditional life during the Soviet period, and this is true in some regions even today.

The largest unit of Armenian kinship was the nonresidential clan (*gerdastan*), although some clans could occupy a certain territory within a village. This was a patriarchal, patrilineal system that included ancestors in the male line, which could extend as far back as six to eight generations. Maintaining clan honor was a serious business administered by the head of the clan, who gave consent for all marriages, organized burials of deceased clan members, and avenged blood feuds.

Traditional village structure was separate from clan structure in that the patriarchal headman was usually a representative of the wealthiest family in the village. His responsibilities included mediation of conflicts within the home and within the village, tax collection, and enforcement of customs. A village was traditionally made up of 200 to 3,000 interdependent households or 20 to 30 in mountainous regions. The barter system was used during times of need to supplement shortfalls in food supplies or other essential materials. Village design maximized the use of communal areas, with households arranged around a shared courtyard where fruit trees grew.

Marriage and Family

Armenian marriages were an important feature of the social fabric of traditional village life and involved the whole community. They were arranged by the parents of the bride and groom or by a matchmaker hired by the groom's family. Marriages were patrilocal, requiring the bride to move in with the groom's family. The bride's average age was between 14 and 16 years and the groom was generally between 15 and 20 years.

Several rituals were performed throughout the celebrations, including a pre-Christian practice of jumping over a fire three times to promote fertility. Also, to ward off evil spirits, both bride and groom wore *lavash* (traditional Armenian flat bread) over their shoulders upon entry to their home for the first time. Marriage was a time of celebration for the groom, but the bride was expected to remain respectfully sorrowful at the prospect of leaving her family home permanently. The day after the wedding her in-laws sent a red apple to her family to signify her virginity, and a week later her family could visit her with symbolic gifts, a practice known as "head washing." The new wife was often unable to visit her family until after the birth of the first child or until her mother-in-law gave her permission 40 days after the wedding.

The life of a young bride was one of subservience to her in-laws, whom she waited on in silence for at least the first year of marriage. The new wife was responsible for the menial tasks of the household such as cleaning everyone's shoes, and given that there could be between 15 and 50 extended family members living together, these jobs were time consuming and laborious. Higher-status tasks, such as cooking, were reserved for the mother-in-law. Additionally, the young bride's face was veiled in public or in some cases tightly bound, a custom known as *mounj*. She could not sleep if her father-in-law was still awake and was expected to help him dress and undress. The often-humiliating tasks required of her during this time can be characterized as a kind of initiation or rite of passage. Some of these practices still occur in some remote rural regions of the Republic of Armenia today.

As a sign of the closeness of Armenian family life, even after the death of a family member the body is kept at home until the burial three days later. The lid of the coffin is placed by the front door in an upright position to indicate publicly that a death has occurred. The grave is visited on the seventh and 14th days after death, at which time the male relatives are permitted to shave for the first time since the person died. Offerings to the deceased of flowers, food, and alcohol are made on the anniversary and in the new year.

Material Culture

Cultural influences run both ways during times of occupation and Armenia is no exception, particularly with regard to the distinctive architectural style of its churches. The Armenian

architect Trdat is said to have influenced the restructuring of the Hagia Sophia Basilica in Constantinople (Istanbul) after an earthquake damaged it in 990. In fact Trdat is often credited with the revolutionary design that supports the circular dome; small archlike structures, or squinches, provide transitional support from the four walls to a circular dome. He also supervised the building of the 10th-century domed cathedral in the medieval Armenian capital of Ani.

Rug weaving; elaborate metalwork, particularly belts in regional styles; woodwork; and literature are all notable among the Armenian folk arts. Over their 3,000 years of traumatic history of occupation one of the features that has bound Armenians together is a strong tradition of poetry and storytelling, a tradition extending even into the Armenians of the diaspora.

FURTHER READING

Levon Abrahamian, Nancy Sweezy, and Sam Sweezy. *Armenian Folk Arts, Culture, and Identity* (Bloomington: Indiana University Press, 2001).

Diana Agabeg Apcar. *From The Book of 1000 Tales: Stories of Armenia and Its People, 1892–1922* (Bloomington, Ind.: AuthorHouse, 2004).

Mack Chahin. *The Kingdom of Armenia* (New York: RoutledgeCurzon, 2001).

C. Maranci. *The Architect Trdat: Building Practices and Cross-Cultural Exchange in Byzantium and Armenia* (New York: Routledge, 2003).

Philip Marsden. *The Crossing Place: A Journey among the Armenians* (London: Flamingo, 1994).

Adriano Alpago Novello. *The Armenians.* Translated by Bryan Fleming (New York: Rizzoli, 1986).

A. E. Redgate. *The Armenians* (Ames, Iowa: Blackwell Publishing Professional, 2000).

Armenians: nationality (Armenians, Hay, people of Armenia, people of Hayasdan)

GEOGRAPHY

The Armenian Republic is a landlocked nation located in the Lesser Caucasus Mountains in Southwest Asia. It shares a border on the west with Turkey, the east with Azerbaijan, the north with Georgia, and the south with Iran. It is composed of 11 *marzes* (provinces): Aragatsotn, Ararat, Armavir, Geghark'unik', Kotaykr', Lorri, Shirak, Syunik', Tavush, Nayots'Dzor, and Yerevan, the country's capital. A largely mountainous terrain, its territory covers 18,500 square miles. Historic Armenia, or the Armenian highland, refers to a vast area of land constituting the continuation of the Caucasus Mountains. Today most of the Armenian high-

---

ARMENIANS: NATIONALITY

nation:
Republic of Armenia; Armenia

derivation of name:
According to legend, a term derived from the Armen tribe of the historic traditional lands of Armenia

government:
Presidential representative democratic republic

land is in eastern Turkey, with some parts in Iran and western Azerbaijan.

INCEPTION AS A NATION

The Armenians are an ancient people who pride themselves on being the first nation to convert to Christianity, which they did in the fourth century. Though periods of autonomy were known over the centuries, political and economic fate has swayed back and forth among various empires including the Roman, Persian, Ottoman, Arab, and Russian.

Despite this long history the real quest for Armenian nationhood did not begin until the late 19th century. The Armenian national movement revolved around three main parties; Social Democrat Hunchakian Party, Armenakan, and Armenian Revolutionary Federation, whose leaders later formed Armenia's first independent government in 1918. The first Armenian revolutionary organization, the Social Democrat Hunchakian Party, was founded in 1887 by a group of Armenian university students in Geneva to awaken national, social, and democratic awareness in the Armenian people and to create an independent Armenian state. From 1887 to 1914 the party newspaper, *Hunchak* (Bell), called for independence, free speech, and freedom from the injustices imposed on the Armenian people by their oppressors, especially the Turks. This period, particularly 1894–96, also saw brutal reprisals against the Armenian nationalist stirrings. As a result, an estimated 300,000 Armenians were massacred within the Ottoman Empire under Sultan Abdul-Hamid. During World War I the Turkish government continued its harsh policies and practices against the Armenians, including forced resettlement, which together resulted in the death of an estimated 600,000–2 million Armenians in what has been called the first genocide of the 20th century.

Finally the end of World War I produced a short-lived promise of Armenian independence with the establishment of the Democratic Republic of Armenia in 1918. However, by 1920 the fledgling state was engaged in the disastrous Turkish-Armenian War, which ended in the treaty of Alexanderpol in which Armenians lost most of their land. Taking advantage of Armenia's weakened state the Soviet Red Army invaded and again took control of the areas of Armenia that had been a Russian province between 1828 and 1917, thus beginning 70 years of Soviet rule. Also in 1920 the Treaty of Sèvres between the Turks and the World War I Allies

awarded some disputed territory in what had been the Ottoman Empire to Armenia; however, most of western Armenia remained in Turkish hands. A final blow was dealt to Armenia in 1921 when the Treaty of Kars (superseding the Treaty of Alexanderpol) was signed between the Soviet Union and Turkey, placing Mount Ararat, the symbol of Armenian national identity, in Turkish territory.

After 70 years of Soviet domination 1988 proved to be a pivotal year in Armenia's long history. With the restructuring of the Soviet Union under Gorbachev's policies of *glasnost* and *perestroika*, Armenians, along with the peoples of the other Soviet-controlled republics, began to reassert long-held claims for independence. Mass demonstrations and strikes in support of withdrawal from the Soviet Union were organized in both Armenia and the Nagorno-Karabakh region of Soviet Azerbaijan, an area with a primarily ethnic Armenian majority. The Karabakh Committee was established initially to represent Armenians who formed the majority in the Nagorno-Karabakh region. Eventually this group became the Armenian Pan-National Movement (APNM), representing the interests of all Armenians in the region.

Regardless of the ethnic makeup of Karabakh the government of Azerbaijan rejected any claims for Armenian independence and responded to Armenian demands with force. The ensuing fighting and blockades by Azerbaijan and Turkey, coupled with a devastating earthquake in northern Armenia in 1988 that left 25,000 people dead and 500,000 homeless, provided a bleak and debilitating backdrop to the Armenian struggle for independence. During this time Moscow arrested the four Karabakh Committee members in an effort to put an end to the movement. However, six months later amid protests and demonstrations they were released from prison and returned to Armenia to form the Armenian Pan-National Movement (APNM). By summer 1989 this party won the parliamentary elections in the Soviet Republic of Armenia. At the end of the year Armenians in Armenia and in Nagorno-Karabakh voted in their respective parliaments to reunify, sparking a severe resurgence of military reprisals from Azerbaijan.

In August 1991 the Soviet Union collapsed and one month later the Armenian people voted overwhelmingly to secede from the USSR, ending 70 years of Soviet rule. Levon Ter-Petrossian, former Karabakh Committee member and leader of the APNM, became the first popularly elected president in Armenian history. At the

capital:
Yerevan
language:
Armenian is the official language. There are two dialects: western and eastern. The western dialect is spoken primarily in the Armenian diaspora of Turkey, Lebanon, and Syria—largely those displaced by the 1915 genocide of Armenians in Turkey. The eastern dialect is spoken primarily by those in the current Armenian Republic.

religion:
Christianity is the official state religion. Of the population, 94.7 percent belong to the Armenian Apostolic Church. Other Christian churches, including Roman Catholic, evangelical Protestant, and Russian Orthodox, make up 4 percent. Another 1.3 percent of the population, mostly ethnic Kurds, follow the ancient Yezidi religion (monotheist with elements of nature worship) but have faced increasing oppression.

earlier inhabitants:
Situated between two continents, Armenia has historically been vulnerable to invasion by many peoples, including the Assyrians, Greeks, Romans, Byzantines, Arabs, Mongols, Persians, Ottoman Turks, and Russians,

demographics:
Ethnic Armenians 97.9 percent, Yezidis 1.3 percent, Russians 0.5 percent, and smaller numbers of Assyrians, Ukrainians, Kurds, Greeks, and others

Armenians: nationality time line

B.C.E.

400   Greek historian Xenophon provides the first-known written account of Armenians.

95–55   Armenian empire reaches its greatest height under Tigranes the Great.

30   Romans conquer Armenian empire.

C.E.

301–30   National conversion to Christianity under Armenian king Trdat III.

653   Arabs receive Armenia from Byzantine Empire.

900   Brief period of Armenian independence.

1080   Cilicia, an independent Armenian kingdom, emerges on the Mediterranean coast.

1100–1400   Armenia is invaded from the west by Byzantine Greeks and from the east by Seljuk Turks.

1375   Cilicia is conquered by outside forces.

1500   Ottoman Empire and Safavid Persia divide western and eastern Armenia between them, respectively.

1700   Russia begins moving into neighboring areas as Persian Empire weakens.

1828   Russia replaces Persia as the dominant force in eastern Armenia and makes it a province.

1878   Congress of Berlin raises the question of rights of Christian Armenians in the Ottoman Empire as an ongoing European issue.

1887   First Armenian revolutionary organization, Social Democrat Hunchakian Party, founded in Geneva, Switzerland.

1894   Massacre of 300,000 Armenian subjects by Ottoman Turks, named the Hamidian massacres after Abdul Hamid II.

1915   Young Turks massacre an estimated 600,000–2 million Armenians living in Turkey.

1917   Bolshevik victory in Russia; Russian troops leave the Caucasus.

1919   Democratic Republic of Armenia is officially established with Armenian Revolutionary Federation (ARF) leader R. I. Kachazuni as prime minister. May 28 is still celebrated in Armenia as Republic Day.

1920   Treaty of Sèvres between the Turks and the Allies awards some disputed territory in what had been the Ottoman Empire to Armenia.

Treaty of Alexanderpol ending the short-lived Turkish-Armenian War in which territory gained in treaty of Sèvres is lost again to Turkey.

Armenian government forced to accept Communist-dominated coalition with Soviet Russia.

1921   Treaty of Kars, between the Soviet Union and Turkey, supersedes Alexanderpol and places Mount Ararat, national symbol of Armenia, in Turkish territory.

1922   Transcaucasian Soviet Federated Socialist Republic (SFSR) combines Armenia, Azerbaijan, and Georgia as a single republic in the Soviet Union.

1936   Soviet Union disbands the Transcaucasian SFSR and establishes separate republics for Armenia, Azerbaijan, and Georgia.

1936–37   Purges under Joseph Stalin reach their peak in Armenia, Azerbaijan, and Georgia.

1974   Karen Demirjiian installed by Moscow to end party corruption in Armenia; later removed for corruption.

1985 Mikhail S. Gorbachev's election as general secretary of the Communist Party ushers in era of *perestroika* (reconstruction) and *glasnost* (openness) in Soviet Union.

1988 Surge in Armenian nationalist movement.

Government of the autonomous Nagorno-Karabakh region of Azerbaijan votes to unify with Armenia.

Earthquake kills 25,000 in northern Armenia.

1989 Karabakh Committee released by the Soviet Union after mass demonstrations against Soviet attempts to stem nationalist movement.

Blockade of Armenian fuel and supplies by Azerbaijan over Karabakh issue.

Unification of Nagorno-Karabakh region with Armenia declared by Nagorno-Karabakh National Council.

1990 Soviet troops sent to Azerbaijan to quell violence against Armenians over Karabakh.

Armenian Supreme Soviet elects Levon Ter-Petrossian of Armenian Pan-National Movement as chairman.

1991 Moscow sends troops to invade Azerbaijan, ostensibly to stop pogroms against Armenians.

National independence approved by Armenian voters.

Ter-Petrossian elected president of Armenia.

Fighting continues as Armenians in Nagorno-Karabakh declare independent state.

Soviet Union officially dissolved.

Armenia switches from large-scale Soviet-style agroindustry to small-scale agriculture.

1992 Lachin corridor linking Nagorno-Karabakh to Armenia seized by Armenians.

1993 Armenia joins World Trade Organization (WTO).

The *dram* (*tram*), the national currency, is introduced and suffers hyperinflation for several years.

1994 Russian-brokered cease-fire in Karabakh conflict put in place; however, ongoing international negotiations by Organization for Security and Cooperation in Europe (OSCE) to stop fighting and blockades have so far failed to resolve this issue.

International Monetary Fund (IMF) sponsors economic liberalization program.

1997 Robert Kocharian, president of Nagorno-Karabakh, appointed prime minister of Armenia by President Ter-Petrossian.

Privatization law and state program on property privatization adopted.

1998 L. Ter-Petrossian resigns presidency over disagreement concerning Nagorno-Karabakh.

Robert Kocharian elected president of Armenia.

1999 Prime Minister Vasken Sarkissian and Parliament Speaker Karen Demirjian assassinated in Armenian parliament building in Yerevan.

2002 Electricity distribution system privatized.

2003 Reporters without Borders places Armenia 90th out of 107 countries in enjoyment of freedom of speech.

2006 Index of Economic Freedom (Heritage Foundation and *The Wall Street Journal*) rates Armenia the most economically free state in the Commonwealth of Independent States (CIS, 11 former Soviet republics).

2007 Scheduled national elections are held in May and Serge Sargsyan retains the position of prime minister, which he took up in April following the death of Prime Minister Andranik Margaryan.

end of the year residents of Nagorno-Karabakh voted in favor of an independent republic (NKR) rather than unification with Armenia, as this was thought to ensure greater security for the population. Nevertheless Azerbaijan responded with a large-scale offensive against Nagorno-Karabakh and Armenian border villages.

Fighting continued until a 1994 cease-fire, brokered by Russia, which is still in effect today; however, the two sides have made little progress in resolving the problem that forms the backdrop to Armenian independence. Strong links with Nagorno-Karabakh continued to shape the face of Armenian politics throughout the late 1990s. For example, in 1997 Levon Ter-Petrossian appointed Robert Kocharian, president of NKR, prime minister of Armenia. Then in 1998 Ter-Petrossian resigned his presidency because he was considered too conciliatory toward Azerbaijan concerning Karabakh. With a far less appeasing attitude Robert Kocharian was elected president of Armenia in both 1998 and 2003 and was to retire in 2008.

The first decade of Armenia's fledgling democracy gave rise to a culture of political violence legitimized by the rhetoric of national survival. Additionally increasing poverty and endemic corruption have contributed to heightened despair for the Armenian people. As a result in October 2006 the international community through the Council of Europe called for election law reform before the next Armenian election in 2007. The reforms were largely carried out and elections held in May 2007 were deemed fair by outside observers, the first since independence to receive this accreditation, and returned Serge Sargsyan as prime minister.

CULTURAL IDENTITY

While political independence and economic well-being were the reasons the original Armenian independence parties came into existence in the late 19th century, the cultural identity that pushed them into this phase of political development is similar to the nationalist movements in many European nations of the same period. A combination of common language and religion, shared struggle against foreign oppressors, and historical attachment to the geographic homeland forms the backbone of the Armenian nation's cultural identity, even into the 21st century.

Although the Armenian language is a subgroup of the Indo-European language family, many Armenians see it as unique because of its lack of shared vocabulary with other languages; most Armenian words are not connected to any existing languages. At the same time Armenian does share some phonetic and grammatical features with Georgian and has borrowed many words from Iranian languages. The Armenian alphabet, too, while derived from the Greek alphabet, has its own unique list of 38 letters, which were invented by Mesrob Mashdots in the early fifth century in order to translate biblical texts. During the Soviet era in the 20th century changes were made to improve the phonetic relationship between the written and spoken languages. Today only the Armenian Apostolic Church uses classical Armenian (*grabar*) as a liturgical language, providing a valuable link between language and religion in Armenian cultural identity.

Armenians pride themselves on the legend that they were the first nation to convert to Christianity, between the years 301 and 330. According to this legend, the Armenian king Trdat III imprisoned Saint Gregory the Illuminator, a PARTHIAN missionary, when he refused to participate in pagan rituals and declared his Christian faith. During the time of Gregory's imprisonment the king is said to have been struck by a malaise of the mind that left him wandering aimlessly in the forest. Gregory had been locked away in a dungeon for 13 years when the king's sister had a dream that only he could save the king from his condition. King Trdat III was taken to Gregory, who miraculously cured him, and the king immediately proclaimed Christianity the official religion of the state.

Prior even to this legendary national conversion to Christianity, the first Christian Armenian church was founded in the first century by Saints Bartholomew and Thaddaeus. Despite pressure over the centuries of foreign occupation, including imprisonment of clergy and confiscation of church property, the Armenian Apostolic Church has managed to survive to this day as a key element in Armenian national identity. Religion is also a defining feature that distinguishes the people from their Muslim neighbors in Turkey, Iran, and Azerbaijan.

Armenians have a long history of territorial integrity in their region, and land is seen as one of the links that hold the nation together. Unfortunately, much of the territory is now located outside the country. Lying between vast empires—first the Roman and Persian Empires and then the Byzantine and Muslim empires—Armenia by the 16th century had been split into distinct eastern and western cultural and linguistic regions. Much of what was historically western Armenia is currently located in the Anatolia region of Turkey, including Armenia's national symbol, Mount Ararat. The eastern region of historical Armenia experienced a further split in the 20th century between the Republic of Armenia and the Republic of Azerbaijan, including the controversial Nagorno-Karabakh region. Though predominantly populated by Armenians, Nagorno-Karabakh had its current borders established during Soviet times within Azerbaijan. Because Armenians had no say in many of the territorial agreements made by the Soviets, particularly the 1921 Treaty of Kars, Armenia does not recognize these agreements' legitimacy and still holds claim to those provinces today.

See also ARMENIANS.

FURTHER READING

Agathangelos; translation and commentary by R. W. Thomson. *History of the Armenians* (Albany: State University of New York Press, 1976).

Philip Marsden. *The Crossing Place: A Journey among the Armenians* (London: Flamingo, 1994).

David Marshall Lang. *Armenia: Cradle of Civilization* (Boston: Allen & Unwin, 1980).

Razmik Panossian. *The Armenians: From Kings and Priests to Merchants and Commissars* (London: Hurst & Co., 2006).

A. E. Redgate. *The Armenians* (Malden, Mass.: Blackwell Publishers, 1998).

Yuri Rost. *Armenian Tragedy: An Eye Witness Account of Human Conflict and Natural Disaster in Armenia and Azerbaijan* (London: Weidenfeld and Nicolson, 1990).

Aryans   *See* INDO-ARYANS.

Ashvaka   *See* KAMBOJA.

Asmat   (Asmat-ow, As-amat, Samot)

The Asmat are an indigenous community of hunters and gatherers living along the rivers of the southeastern region of West Papua, Indonesia. They were first spotted by the Dutch explorer Jan Carstenz in 1623 and then first contacted by Cook's crew in 1770. Asmat ferocity caused Cook's men and several later Dutch explorers to retreat, leaving the Asmat free of European interference until well after 1900. To quell the southeastern New Guinea region's endemic warfare the Dutch established their first police station in Merauke in 1902, about 300 miles to the east of the Asmats' territory around Agats, on the southern coast of the island. But Agats itself remained free of any resident Europeans until 1938, when the Dutch set up a government post, which they closed just four years later in response to World War II. That post was replaced in 1953 by another one, which introduced

An example of a Bis pole carved in the 20th century by an Asmat *wow-ipit,* or carver. *(Metropolitan Museum of Art/Art Resource, NY)*

Roman Catholic and Protestant missionaries to the Asmat. However, despite the Dutch and missionary activities, most Asmat maintained their indigenous way of life until the Indonesian takeover of their territory in 1962.

The coastal region of New Guinea where the Asmat live limits their choice of subsistence strategies largely to hunting, fishing, and gathering. The alluvial swamps and river deltas on which they live, with their constant threat of severe flooding, do not allow for significant agricultural development, at least not at the subsistence level. The starchy pulp of the sago palm is their primary source of calories, which they supplement with bananas, coconuts, fish, wild boar, and an occasional crocodile, bird, or large lizard. Rats and sago beetles or capricorn beetles are also considered important food sources at some times of the year. In addition to lacking food sources the Asmat lack freshwater sources, relying on brackish rivers and coconut milk for hydration.

Prior to the pacification of the region by the Indonesians the twin practices of warfare and headhunting were the fastest routes to male prestige among the Asmat. Taking an enemy head was not a prerequisite for marriage, but any man who had not yet taken one was derided

ASMAT

location:
The southeastern coast of Papua Province, Indonesia

time period:
Unknown to the present

ancestry:
Melanesian

language:
Asmat, a Papuan language

as weak, childish, and effeminate. His wife would not obey him and his peers would not let him speak at public gatherings in the men's house. Enemy heads were symbolically important as symbols of power and regeneration and were used at all major Asmat rituals, including initiating males, sanctifying ancestor poles, and building new men's houses; they were also believed to help sago and banana trees grow. Skulls were also prominently displayed outside the huts of prolific headhunters, to show their status, and outside the men's hut, to ward off enemy spirits because it was believed that spirits did not like to look at their own bodies.

Since the early 20th century when Asmat carvings were first transported back to Europe by the Dutch the Asmat have been well known throughout the art-collecting world for their large sculptures, especially ancestor (*bis*) poles and masks. Traditionally all Asmat men were headhunters and carvers, with great skill in both providing a pathway to prestige, and today being a successful carver or *wow-ipit* is still seen as extremely important. Since the late 1960s with the establishment of a UN project, wood carving has been one of the only sources of cash available to the Asmat.

See also MELANESIANS.

Aspasio   *See* KAMBOJA.

Atoni (Atoni Meto, Atoni Pa Meto, Dawan, Vaikenu)

The Atoni are one of the three major ethnolinguistic groups of West Timor, a province of Indonesia; at the start of the 21st century they numbered about 750,000 people. They speak an Austronesian language, the ancient speakers of which arrived on the island around 3000 B.C.E. These ancient inhabitants introduced agriculture, which probably began in southern China as long ago as 5000 B.C.E. To this day, most Atoni continue to engage in subsistence agriculture as their primary economic activity. They grow corn and rice on small, shifting plots of land cut out of the jungle, allowed to dry, and then burned to provide fertilizer. Each year or two a family must move to a new plot because of the relatively poor soil.

Prior to the dawn of the European colonial era on Timor, which began in the early 16th century with the arrival of the Portuguese, the island was already dotted with small indigenous kingdoms and principalities, as noted by Chinese sailors who went to the island seeking sandalwood. The Atoni kingdom of Sonbai, with its 16 constituent principalities, was just one of these small groups. In the 16th and 17th centuries as a result of their interactions with Portuguese and then Dutch colonizers, the Atoni emerged as the dominant local kingdom on the western half of the island. From the Portuguese the Atoni received muskets and other iron tools, which put them at a distinct advantage over their local rivals for political power. From the Dutch they received corn, a crop that allowed their population to expand at a faster rate than their rivals. With these advantages the Atoni emerged from under the rule of the previously larger and stronger TETUN kingdom of Liurai, with its 46 separate principalities, and then subjugated or assimilated most of the other ethnolingustic groups in their region. The kingdom of Sonbai, however, was not able to maintain its dominant position, and by the 19th century other Atoni subgroups, such as the Amanuban, had emerged as even more powerful than this early centralized kingdom.

Today the Atoni continue to recognize approximately 400 different origin groups, each bearing a name that points to its mythological common ancestor. These origin groups are mapped onto the territory of the Atoni in ways that ritually bind each group and by extension each individual to a particular parcel of land. Most origin-group ancestors are associated with unusual rock formations; however, these same ancestors are described by a botanical metaphor rather than a geological one. Each origin group is said to be like a tree with the trunk representing the ancestor and each limb, twig, and leaf representing the segments of the group. Despite the importance of particular places, origin groups tend not to live in centralized clusters but rather in scattered groups throughout all of West Timor. In fact this settlement pattern is one of the important factors that led to Atoni expansion throughout the island. Each Atoni settlement is believed to have been started by a single origin group at some point in history. When members of a new origin group wished to settle in another group's location, they became wife receivers from the first group; in turn, their own daughters married into the next origin group to move into the locality, and so forth. This system allowed for origin-group exogamy to be maintained since ideally each individual must marry outside his or her own origin group; it also strengthened these residential units at the expense of people's crosscutting ties of kinship. As a result, although kinship is an important local marker for people's identity,

---

ATONI

location:
The western side of Timor, a province of Indonesia

time period:
Possibly 3000 B.C.E. to the present

ancestry:
Austronesian

language:
Uab Meto, an Austronesian language

it has not over time disrupted the alliances and solidarity of villages and other regions.

Australians: nationality (Aussies, people of Australia)

GEOGRAPHY

Australia, the world's smallest continent at just under 3 million square miles, is located between the Indian and South Pacific Oceans. It is composed of six states; Victoria, New South Wales, Queensland, South Australia, Western Australia, and Tasmania, plus the huge mainland Northern Territory and a large number of offshore islands, including the Torres Strait Islands, Kangaroo Island, and King Island. The majority of the inland region of Australia is a desert with very few inhabitants; two-thirds of the entire country is sparsely populated or not populated at all. Approximately 83 percent of the population lives within about 32 miles of a seacoast, with the majority residing in the southeast.

INCEPTION AS A NATION

The Australian continent has been inhabited by the ABORIGINAL AUSTRALIANS for at least 40,000 years, with some experts claiming that the Aboriginal population arrived as early as

Eureka Flag

The Eureka flag, powerful symbol of antiauthoritarianism from 1854 to the present

60,000 years ago. However, as small-scale nomadic to seminomadic groups, the Aboriginal population never established towns or cities or formed a nation. Hundreds of tribes maintained their independence from one another, with some meeting together occasionally to trade, engage in ritual or warfare, or seek marriage

Australians: nationality time line
B.C.E.
60,000–40,000 Aboriginal Australians enter the giant landmass called Sahul (today's New Guinea, Australia, and Tasmania) and spread out, adapting to a variety of different geographic and climatic regions.
C.E.
1770 Captain James Cook takes possession of Australia in the name of Great Britain.
1788 Captain Arthur Phillip arrives with the First Fleet, made up of 11 ships and around 780 convicts, and establishes a settlement at Port Jackson in the new Crown colony of New South Wales.
1803 Matthew Flinders is the first European to circumnavigate Australia.
Van Diemen's Land (Tasmania) is first settled by Europeans.
1825 Van Diemen's Land becomes its own colony.
1829 The western region of Australia is formally claimed by the United Kingdom.
1836 South Australia is founded as a free province, separate from the New South Wales penal colony.
1851 Victoria is created as a free province from the greater New South Wales territory; unlike South Australia, Victoria does accept convicts as well as free settlers.
The Victorian gold rush begins.

(continues)

AUSTRALIANS: NATIONALITY

nation:
Commonwealth of Australia; Australia

derivation of name:
Latin term *australis,* meaning "south"

government:
Constitutional monarchy with a parliamentary system of governance

capital:
Canberra

language:
English is the official language but 20 percent of the population speak one of more than 200 different languages at home, including various Chinese languages, Greek, Italian, Polish, and Vietnamese.

religion:
No state religion; Catholic 26.4 percent, Anglican 20.5 percent; other Christian 20.5 percent; Buddhist 1.9 percent; Muslim 1.5 percent; other 1.2 percent; unspecified 12.7 percent; none 15.3 percent

earlier inhabitants:
Aboriginal Australians

demographics:
Caucasian 88.8 percent; Asian 6.5 percent; Aboriginal 2.2 percent; African, Middle Eastern, and other 2.5 percent; 23.1 percent overseas born, representing more than 150 different countries of origin, including United Kingdom (24 percent), New Zealand (9 percent), Italy (5 percent), and China and Vietnam (4 percent each)

Australians: nationality time line *(continued)*

1854 Eureka Stockade miners' rebellion against British taxation and mistreatment occurs in Ballarat, Victoria. This event is sometimes referred to as the birth of Australian democracy. The Eureka flag continues to be useful for some unions and others on the political Left to depict their struggle against authority.

1859 Queensland is carved out as a separate territory from New South Wales.

1863 The Northern Territory is founded as a region within the province of South Australia.

1840–64 Transportation of convicts to Australia is phased out in all Australian colonies.

1880 Bushranger Ned Kelly and his gang are captured at Glenrowan, Victoria. Kelly is tried and hanged in Melbourne.

1882 Australia defeats England in test cricket for the first time, initiating the Ashes series, a fierce rivalry that continues to this day. The name *Ashes* is taken from an article in an English newspaper following Australia's victory, which stated that English cricket had died and the ashes had been shipped to Australia. The following year, when England beat Australia, the winning team was presented with a small urn that reputedly contained the ashes of the bails used in the 1882 series.

1895 Banjo Paterson writes the words to "Waltzing Matilda."

1897 The Victorian Football League (VFL) begins operating with eight clubs of Australian-rules football teams, expanded to 10 teams in 1908.

1899 Australia's worst natural disaster, Cyclone Mahina, hits Bathurst Bay, Queensland, and leaves more than 400 people dead and 100 ships destroyed.

1901 The six Australian colonies federate to become the Commonwealth of Australia.

The Immigration Restriction Act is signed, restricting immigration to whites only and making white Australia official government policy.

1908 Dorothea Mackellar publishes "My Country," one of the best known Australian poems, written while she was a homesick 19-year-old in England.

1911 The Australian Capital Territory is carved out of New South Wales territory to provide the land for the nation's capital, Canberra.

Control over the Northern Territory is handed from South Australia to the federal government.

1915 Australians serving at Gallipoli suffer defeat at the hands of the Ottoman Turks while trying to take the Dardanelles during World War I.

1927 The capital is officially moved from Melbourne, which had held this position since 1901, to Canberra.

1931 The Statute of Westminster establishes formal equality between the British and Australian governments; adopted by Australia in 1942.

1932 The Sydney Harbor Bridge is officially opened; building began in 1924.

1942 The British defeat in Asia leads Australia to turn toward the United States as its primary foreign relationship.

The Kokoda Track Campaign sees around 1,000 Australian soldiers and their Papuan porters, guides, and assistants defeat a Japanese force at least five times larger during the course of seven months of extreme hardship in the Owen Stanley Ranges of New Guinea.

1947 Immigration Minister Arthur Calwell signs an agreement with the International Refugee Organization (IRO), the successor to the United Nations Relief and Rehabilitation Administration (UNRRA), to accept displaced persons from Europe, changing the face of Australia forever from a largely Anglo-Celtic nation to a multicultural one.

1951 The ANZUS Treaty, signed by Australia, New Zealand, and the United States, formally binds all three countries together in defense of one another's interests in the Pacific. The pact between New Zealand and the United States falls apart in 1984 over nuclear issues but remains active between Australia and the United States as well as between Australia and New Zealand.

1956 Melbourne hosts Australia's first summer Olympic games.

The birth of Australian television in New South Wales and Victoria. Bruce Gyngell ushers in the television age with the words "Good evening and welcome to television."

1967 Prime Minister Harold Holt disappears while swimming off the coast of Victoria.

1973 The aspects of the Migration Act restricting immigration to whites only are finally overturned, ending decades of both de facto and de jure whites-only policy.

The Sydney Opera House opens and holds its first performance, Prokofiev's *War and Peace,* by the Australian Opera Company.

1974 Cyclone Tracy flattens most of the city of Darwin and leaves 64 dead in its wake.

1975 Gough Whitlam's Labor government is fired by the governor-general, the queen's representative in Australia, partly in response to action requested by the Central Intelligence Agency of the United States.

1976 Tasmanian Wilderness Society is formed at the home of Bob Brown, later senator for Tasmania from the Greens Party.

1981 The Great Barrier Reef, off Queensland, is declared a World Heritage Site by UNESCO.

1982 The South Melbourne Swans Victorian Football League team moves to Sydney.

1983 Ash Wednesday bushfires destroy huge amounts of bushland in Victoria and South Australia. The fire conditions are at an extreme level due to the four years of drought that preceded the fires.

The Franklin River dam project is finally halted by the high court of Australia after seven years of struggle by the Tasmanian Wilderness Society and others to save it. The Franklin-Gordon River basins had been named a World Heritage Site by UNESCO a year earlier.

1989 The commonwealth government endorses the principles of the National Agenda for a Multicultural Australia.

1990 In recognition of the three VFL teams with homes outside Victoria (Sydney, West Coast, and Brisbane) the VFL officially changes its name to the Australian Football League. Three other non-Victorian teams join the league over the next seven years, from Adelaide, Port Adelaide, and Fremantle, making the total 16.

1992 The high court overturns 205 years of the *terra nullius* (empty land) doctrine, which had maintained that Australian land had no owner before it became a British colony, in the *Mabo v. State of Queensland* land-rights case.

Eddie Mabo is named Australian of the Year by the newspaper *The Australian*.

1996 John Howard is elected prime minister for the first of his four successful electoral campaigns, which usher in more than 11 years of Liberal Party rule at the federal level.

1999 Referendum to make Australia a republic with an elected head of state to replace the queen is defeated.

2000 Sydney hosts Australia's second summer Olympic games.

2004 The Liberal Party extends its majority in Australia's lower house and becomes the first sitting government for 20 years to gain a majority in the senate. The Liberals initiate sweeping changes to Australia's industrial relations laws, weakening unions and giving employers more leeway in hiring, firing, and negotiations decisions.

2006 One of the most famous Australian entertainers in the world, the Crocodile Hunter, Steve Irwin, is killed by a sting ray while filming off the coast of Queensland.

2007 Kevin Rudd and the Labor Party defeat John Howard and the Liberal/National coalition in a landslide federal election. After holding his seat for 33 years, John Howard becomes the first sitting prime minister since 1929 to lose his seat when he is defeated by the former journalist Maxine McKew.

Eddie Mabo

Eddie Mabo, born Eddie Koiki Sambo, is most famous for his instrumental role in overturning Australia's erroneous *terra nullius* claim to indigenous land in 1992. Before the landmark court decision in 1992, *terra nullius,* Latin for "no-man's land," was an invented term used to justify British colonization of Australia on the grounds that it was previously uninhabited. The Aboriginal Australians were not considered to have a "civilized culture," and thus their inhabitation of the territory did not count.

Born in 1936, Mabo was a member of an indigenous culture of the Torres Strait Islands that is distinct from the other Aboriginal peoples of Australia as it has a stronger cultural relation to the people of Papua New Guinea. While working as a gardener at James Cook University in 1974, Mabo befriended Henry Reynolds, a prominent Australian historian, who informed Mabo that the land he thought he owned on Murray Island was in fact British land. Outraged, Mabo began campaigning for indigenous land rights, and in 1981 he gave a speech in which he outlined landownership and inheritance among the Torres Strait Island people. His speech made perfect legal sense as an argument for native land rights and he soon entered into a 10-year legal battle with the Australian court system to overturn the *terra nullius* claim. In January 1992, Eddie Mabo died of cancer at age 56. Five months later the Australian high court overturned *terra nullius,* thereby recognizing native title and enabling Aboriginal peoples throughout Australia to reclaim territory lost to British colonization. Mabo was posthumously awarded the Human Rights Medal in the Human Rights and Equal Opportunity Commission Awards in 1992.

partners. Therefore although Australia is host to the oldest existing culture in the world, to talk of a social, political, and economic unit known as the Australian nation, we must look only as far back as the continent's colonization by the British beginning in 1770.

The early colonial project in Australia was very different from British colonialism in North America. While the earliest settlers in North America were families in search of religious freedom plus a few soldiers, convicts, and trappers, the earliest European settlers in Australia were almost entirely convicts, who had been sentenced to transport to Australia as punishment for various crimes, from stealing a loaf of bread to murder. In addition to convicts, who were 80 percent male, there was also a population of male British soldiers sent to oversee the convicts; a few of these soldiers also took their wives. In the earliest days of the New South Wales and Tasmanian penal colonies the convicts had to live in the hulls of the ships that had taken them to Australia while they built their own prisons. Later convicts also engaged in a wide variety of other labor, from record keeping to construction and agriculture. In the 1820s and 1830s convicts were also as-

signed to work for private citizens as servants and laborers.

Eventually some convicts earned their freedom or served out their sentences and a population of free women and men attempted to reestablish their lives on a continent whose geography and climate differed immensely from the homes they had known in England, Scotland, and Ireland. They were also joined by free settlers who immigrated to Australia to begin a new life away from the hardships in Great Britain; a few also arrived from Europe and even China. Many of these people quickly realized that Australia was not at all suitable for the kind of agriculture that was familiar to them but that sheep and cattle could be raised on large farms, called stations, in some parts of the country. From these earliest days wool has been one of Australia's most important exports; sheep and, later, agriculture more generally, with the development of the sugar and cotton industries in Queensland and wheat in Western Australia, have become the center of some Australians' understanding of their national character. Even in the face of extensive drought and environmental degradation, agriculture continues to provide significant export earnings for Australia, though only a small number of jobs.

The transport of convicts to Australia was phased out in the first half of the 1860s when the population of the continent stood at about 1 million people. With this number, the Australian colonies had a large enough population to sustain themselves as a flourishing segment of the British Empire throughout the rest of the 19th century. Then, in 1901, the six separate Australian colonies formed the Commonwealth of Australia, retaining the English monarch as the head of state but with an independent federal government headed by a prime minister.

Although 1901 is the official date of the founding of the Australian federation, the birth of Australian national identity is usually seen as the Battle of Gallipoli on April 25, 1915, when the Australian-New Zealand Army Corps (ANZACs), fighting on the side of the Allies during World War I, attempted to take the Dardanelles in eastern Turkey from the Ottoman Turks. The ANZACs evacuated on December 19, after seven months of being dug into the trenches on the coast and having gained nothing toward the eventual Allied victory in the war. Thousands of men lost their lives in the battle, a loss that was seen as entirely in vain.

In 1981, Australian film director Peter Weir's *Gallipoli*, costarring Mel Gibson, received criticism, especially in Great Britain, for conforming to the Australian myth of Gallipoli rather than to the historical facts by depicting the British commanders as sitting safely in their ships offshore while the ANZACs were sent to the slaughter. In actual fact, a significant number of British soldiers also died at Gallipoli. In all about 61,522 Australians lost their lives during World War I. Signifying the enormous impact that these events had on the Australian national identity, all Australian cities and even most large towns today contain a war memorial commemorating the local representatives of those lost in the war.

Another key event in the development of contemporary national identity in Australia was the Kokoda Track Expedition in World War II, when about 1,000 Australian soldiers with their New Guinea allies turned back a Japanese thrust that could have resulted in an invasion of Australia itself. This is the first and only time Australia has had to defend its own territory from imminent attack and led to considerable social and political changes in the postwar era.

As a reaction to the fear of foreign attack fostered by the Kokoda Track events, in the postwar era the concept of "Populate or Perish" emerged as an important principle of government policy. Australian leaders saw the sparse population of the country as a security threat and devised a variety of policies to encourage population growth, including a change in immigration policy that had until then restricted most Australian immigration to Anglo-Celtic migrants from Great Britain and New Zealand. In this postwar era more than 5.3 million people migrated to Australia, including more than 600,000 displaced persons and refugees. The waves of migration began with boatloads of displaced peoples from the Baltic states, Italy, Greece, Yugoslavia, Poland, and other European countries in the late 1940s and early 1950s; continuing in the 1970s and 1980s with refugees from the wars in Southeast Asia; and today with a large flow of people from East Africa and the Middle East. Throughout all of these periods, migration from Great Britain has continued so that British citizens still make up almost a quarter of the migrant population.

With this change in the demographic makeup of the Australian population, national identity has changed as well. In 1972, Australia was the first country to declare multiculturalism the official policy of the state, which contributed to the development of a wide array of services assisting migrants with integrating into Australian society while continuing to foster respect for and engagement with the languages and cultures the newcomers introduced with them. While this policy has not always been as fully supported at the federal and state levels as some would like, it remains today a key concept in the definition of Australian national identity.

CULTURAL IDENTITY

One concept that emerged after the First World War and to some extent remains today as central to Australian cultural identity is a respect for the "Aussie battler," a regular person who refuses to accept defeat despite great difficulties. The soldiers at Gallipoli are often thought to epitomize the battler, and ANZAC Day is celebrated every April 25 as an Australian national holiday. Former Prime Minister John Howard, who emerged from the depths of his political career in the mid-1990s to lead the Liberal Party to an unprecedented four terms in office, is often depicted as an Aussie battler. Respect for the battler or the underdog, as well as a general discomfort with authority figures, seems to be related to Australia's convict past. Even Australians without convict ancestors tend to use humor to defuse authority figures and cheer for the underdog in a competition.

A second key concept in Australian cultural identity is egalitarianism, sometimes depicted colloquially as "giving everyone a fair go." While this belief, like that in the events at Gallipoli, is based on mythology as much as actual fact, as the experiences of many women, Aboriginal people, and Asian Australians attest, it remains central to what it means to be Australian. Indeed some historians (Thompson, 1994) have even claimed that egalitarianism is at the root of Australia's racist immigration policies of the first three-quarters of the 20th century: non-whites had to be excluded because they could not be made equal to whites and thus would destroy the egalitarian nature of the country. A present-day belief in the concept of egalitarianism, despite all evidence to the contrary, has resulted in what Australians refer to as "the tall poppy syndrome": the tallest poppy in the field gets its head knocked off first. That is, Australians (and others in Australia) who try to show off their accomplishments are brought down to size with irony or sardonic humor.

As at every stage of Australian history, contemporary national identity is once again being contested at many levels of society. The current battle lines have been drawn between those who would like to turn back the clock somewhat on Australian multiculturalism and those who want to see it expanded and developed. The former tend to support detention or immediate deportation of illegal migrants, including refugees; assimilation of legal migrants; and testing of potential citizens in English, Australian culture, and values. They tend to view Australian national identity as descended from an earlier British identity with strong agricultural roots and a strong connection to the United States, Great Britain, and, to a lesser extent, Europe. The latter tend to support more liberal immigration laws, more respect for cultural differences, and a continuation of the relaxed citizenship laws of the second half of the 20th century. They tend to view Australian national identity as arising from the multicultural policies of the 1970s and 1980s, with a multilingual heritage and an ability to integrate beliefs and practices from Asia and Africa in addition to Great Britain and Europe. This group also tends to support reconciliation with Australia's Aboriginal population and at least the possibility of a treaty to recognize prior Aboriginal ownership of the land. It remains to be seen which side of this debate will emerge with a dominant voice in Australian politics and society.

See also ABORIGINAL AUSTRALIANS.

FURTHER READING

Tony Bennett, Michael Emmison, and John Frow. *Accounting for Tastes: Australian Everyday Cultures* (New York: Cambridge University Press, 1999).

James Jupp, ed. *The Australian People* (Melbourne: Cambridge University Press, 2001).

Judith Kapferer. *Being All Equal: Identity, Difference, and Australian Cultural Practice* (Washington, D.C.: Berg, 1996).

Peter Read. *Belonging: Australians, Place, and Aboriginal Ownership* (New York: Cambridge University Press, 2000).

Elaine Thompson. *Fair Enough: Egalitarianism in Australia* (Sydney: University of New South Wales Press, 1994).

Austronesians

Austronesian is not the name that a group of people would have used to refer to themselves but rather a reference to several ancient cultures whose descendants today can be classified in three separate groupings: ABORIGINAL TAIWANESE, Malay, and Oceanic, which include both POLYNESIANS and MICRONESIANS. Today the term *Austronesian* is used solely to refer to the language family, which includes about 1,200 different languages spoken by about 300 million people, the largest language group in the world.

The origins of the Austronesian people are probably in south China, from which they sailed in double-outrigger dugout canoes to Taiwan, and then later to the Philippines, Indonesia, and eventually as far west as Madagascar and as far east as RAPANUI. The oldest forms of Austronesian languages are spoken on Taiwan, and thus many sources cite this island as the origin of the Austronesian people; however, archaeological evidence points to south China as these people's ultimate homeland. This evidence includes pottery decorated with cord marks; similarities in stone tools including sinkers, points, bark beaters, and adzes; and domesticated plants and animals, including pigs and dogs, and millet, rice, and sugarcane. Why this population left south China is uncertain, but archaeologists have suggested a combination of population pressure, increased commerce from the Yangtze (Chang) River region of China and moving southward down the river and its tributaries, a growing demand for marine and tropical forest goods, and climate change.

Contemporary Austronesian languages can be subdivided into two distinctive groups that separate the languages of Austronesian Taiwan from those of the remainder of the family, which include all Malay and Oceanic languages. This linguistic division, in addition to several anomalies in the archaeological record, such as a lack of rice in the earliest Austronesian sites in Taiwan, indicates that the origins of the Austronesian people may have been two separate exoduses from southeast China. If these did occur, the first exodus was probably from Fujian Province in China to Taiwan, which saw the rise of TA-P'EN-K'ENG CULTURE, with its distinctively marked pottery and stone tools, but without archaeological evidence of domesticated rice. The descendants of this first wave would be the contemporary speakers of Taiwan's Austronesian languages, the Aboriginal Taiwanese people. The second exodus may have occurred around 3000 B.C.E., taking a second wave of Austronesian speakers from southeastern China to Taiwan and then almost immediately to Luzon in the Philippines around the same period. This second migration pattern continued southward into Borneo, Celebes, and Timor between 2500 to 2000 B.C.E.; then north

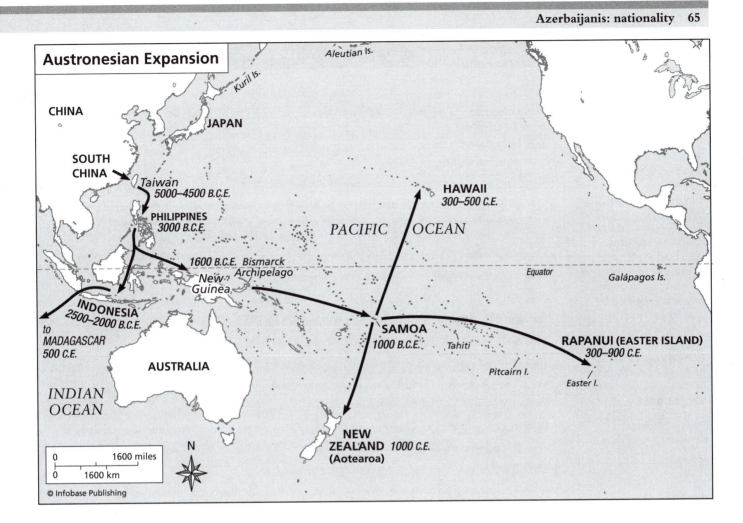

Austronesian Expansion

and east into the Bismarck Archipelago and New Guinea around 1600 B.C.E.; and eventually west to Madagascar in 500 C.E., north to Hawaii from 300 to 500 C.E., east to Rapanui from 300 to 900 C.E., and finally south to New Zealand around 1000 C.E. This second wave, with its red-slipped pottery, may also have been the ultimate source of the LAPITA CULTURE.

Azerbaijanis: nationality (Azeri, Azerbaijani, Azerbaycan, people of Azerbaijan)

GEOGRAPHY

The main geographic features of Azerbaijan are the Caspian Sea to the east and the Caucasus Mountains to the north. In addition, the western border with Armenia is marked by the Lesser Caucasus Mountain range and mountains also line the southern border with Iran. The rest of the country is extensive flatland. Baku, the capital city, is located on the Caspian Sea. Azerbaijan is made up of two separate territories: the main body of the country, which

borders on the Caspian Sea, and the Nakhichevan Autonomous Republic, which is separated from the rest of the country by Armenia.

INCEPTION AS A NATION

The CAUCASIAN ALBANIANS, an ancient population who lived in the area of present-day Azerbaijan, are the first of the many influences that have shaped the Azerbaijani nation. Azerbaijan has been invaded numerous times as well, but only some of the invaders have left significant marks on the society.

The first important invasion was that led by the Achaemenids (*see* PERSIANS, ACHAEMENIDS) under Cyrus the Great. Cyrus had overthrown the empire of the MEDES, which had included some Azerbaijani territory. During the time of Cyrus, Zoroastrianism, a monotheistic religion focused on the battle between a supreme god and an evil spirit, became widespread throughout Azerbaijan, and the Caucasian Albanians adopted many Persian cultural traits. Some Persian influences can still be seen in the Persian place-names in Azerbaijan, the use of the Persian language in early Azerbaijani

AZERBAIJANIS: NATIONALITY

nation:
Republic of Azerbaijan; Azerbaijan

derivation of name:
There are two legends regarding the origins of the name *Azerbaijan*. The first is that Atropates, a Persian governor under Alexander the Great who ruled the area of Azerbaijan, gave his name to the area. The second is that the name is from the Persian words for "land of fire," a reference either to the natural burning of surface oil or to the oil-burning temples of the once-predominant Zoroastrian religion.

government:
Republic

capital:
Baku

language:
Azerbaijani is the official language, Russian is spoken as a first language by 3 percent, and Armenian by 2 percent of the population; another 6 percent of the population speak other languages as a first language. Most of the population speaks Russian as a second language.

religion:
Muslim 93.4 percent, Russian Orthodox 2.5 percent, Armenian Orthodox 2.3 percent, other 1.8 percent

earlier inhabitants:
Azerbaijan has been inhabited since the Palaeolithic age; some of the earliest evidence of cave-dwelling humans and of cave art has been found in Azerbaijan. However, the first people considered indigenous to the region were the Caucasian Albanians.

Azerbaijanis time line

B.C.E.

900s A nomadic population from Central Asia, possibly Scythians, appear in the area that is now Azerbaijan.

800s The Medes, who are related to the Persians, establish an empire including the south of what is now Azerbaijan.

600s The Achaemenid Persians incorporate the western part of Azerbaijan into their empire.

The prophet Zarathustra may have been born in what is now Azerbaijan; he founds Zoroastrianism, which becomes the dominant religion in Azerbaijan. Both the time and place of his birth are strongly contested; he may have been born much earlier, in the region of present-day Afghanistan.

330 Alexander the Great conquers the entire Persian Empire and takes over the area of Azerbaijan.

100s Caucasian Albanians establish their own state.

C.E.

100–300 The Romans annex the entire area of present-day Azerbaijan and call it Albania.

300s–642 Azerbaijan falls under the control of the Persian Sassanid dynasty.

300s The ruler of Caucasian Albania, King Umayr, officially adopts Christianity.

642 The Sassanids are defeated by the Arabs, who take power in Azerbaijan.

642–1050 Arabs, who introduce Islam to the area, control Azerbaijan.

1050 Invading Turkic tribes overcome the Arabs and assert political domination over Azerbaijan.

They introduce Turkic customs and language, both of which survive today in Azerbaijan.

1200 Azerbaijan is invaded by Mongols under Hulegu Khan.

1400 Azerbaijan is ruled by the Azerbaijani Shirvan dynasty. Azerbaijan is invaded by new Mongol forces but remains a tribute state for only a brief time.

1494–1556 Lifetime of Fusuli, an Azerbaijani poet who wrote poetry and prose in Turkish. His most famous works include *Laila and Majnun* and *The Book of Complaints*. These works are still read today in their original form.

1500 The Safavid dynasty, with origins in an Azerbaijani sect of Shiism, takes control of Azerbaijan and much of Persia and converts the area to Shiism. The first shah, Ismail I, is also an important Azerbaijani poet.

1700 The Russian Empire begins to exert influence over northern Azerbaijan, while Persian forces retain control of southern Azerbaijan. The difference between the two regions becomes increasingly pronounced in the following years.

1813 Treaty of Gulistan establishes the Russian-Persian border along the Aras River.

1812–78 Lifetime of Mirza Fath Ali Akhundazade, a playwright and philosopher, who was one of the first to write plays in the Azerbaijani vernacular. His plays remain popular today.

1828 The Treaty of Turkmanchay further extends the territory of Russia in Azerbaijan and divides ethnic Azeris between Russia and Persia.

1848 The first oil well at Absheron is installed and begins working.

1880 Baku's first theater is built by a local philanthropist.

1885–1948 Lifetime of Uzeir Hajibeyli, a composer and poet, whose compositions often use traditional instruments and whose operas are among the first in the Islamic world.

literature, as well as in the widespread Persian belief in Zoroastrianism, which may have originated in Azerbaijan.

Two centuries later, the area of present-day Azerbaijan was conquered by Alexander the Great and became part of Hellenic culture, although this conquest left notably less of a mark on the continued development of an Azerbaijani nation. Much later, in the fourth century C.E., a Caucasian Albanian king converted from

1903–04 The Leftist political party Himmat is formed to protect and champion Azerbaijani culture and language against Russian and other foreign influences.

1918–20 Short period of Azerbaijani independence following the fall of the Russian Empire and before Azerbaijan is occupied by the Soviet Union in 1920.

1920 Azerbaijan is occupied by the Soviet Union. Azerbaijan signs a treaty uniting military, economy, and foreign trade with Russia.

1924 Soviet officials force Azerbaijan to adopt a modified Roman alphabet to replace the Arabic alphabet that had been used for written Azerbaijani.

1930 The Sheki rebellion—about 10,000 protesters against the Communist regime—take to the streets of Sheki in three days of rioting finally quelled by the Red Army. This is just one of 508 protests in 1930 throughout the entire Caucasus region.

1940 Stalin reverses the Soviet decision regarding the Azerbaijani alphabet, now requiring Azerbaijani to be written in a Cyrillic alphabet.

1960 Hostilities between Azerbaijanis and Armenians begin in Nagorno-Karabakh.

1989 Azerbaijan is one of the first Soviet republics to declare independence. This pronouncement is declared illegal by the Soviet Union, and the political party behind the independence movement is declared illegal.

1990 Riots in Baku protesting the lack of sovereignty and the separation of Azerbaijanis in Iran and Russia. During these riots Armenians living in Baku are attacked. The riots are brutally suppressed by the Soviet military.

1991 Azerbaijan gains independence as the Soviet Union falls. Nagorno-Karabakh declares independence, setting off a protracted crisis between Armenia and Azerbaijan.

The Azerbaijani legislature dictates a return to a modified Roman alphabet for written Azerbaijani.

1993 Armenia invades Azerbaijan over the contested status of Nagorno-Karabakh, an area of Azerbaijan inhabited primarily by Armenians. Armenia occupies Nagorno-Karabakh and the surrounding area.

1994 Armenia and Azerbaijan reach a cease-fire regarding Nagorno-Karabakh, but Armenians remain in control of the area and the surrounding territory.

Azerbaijan signs the so-called Contract of a Century with a consortium of oil companies for exploration and exploitation of offshore oilfields.

1998 Protesters against President Heydar Aliyev's reelection are arrested; international observers note several irregularities in the election process.

2001 Azerbaijan becomes a full member of the Council of Europe, though its human rights record is criticized.

2002 Construction begins on a multimillion-dollar pipeline from Azerbaijan to Turkey for oil shipments from the Caspian region.

2003 President Heydar Aliyev names his son, Ilham, prime minister. Ilham Aliyev wins a landslide victory in the presidential elections the same year. Protesters are arrested and international observers again note several irregularities.

2006 Pipeline from Azerbaijan to Turkey is formally opened in July as the first oil from the Caspian Sea starts flowing through it.

demographics:
Azeris account for 90.6 percent of the population, followed by Dagestanis 2.2 percent, Russians 1.8 percent, Armenians 1.5 percent, and other ethnic groups 3.9 percent. Of these groups, most significant are the Armenians, who live primarily in the area of Nagorno-Karabakh and whose secessionist goals have been the source of conflict between Azerbaijan and Armenia.

Zoroastrianism to Christianity, and the population, following, became Christian.

In the seventh century, Azerbaijan was invaded by Arabs who converted the population to Islam, often with significant resistance. Arab rule, more than prior invasions, was met with significant resentment and resistance, and although the Arabs ruled through the 11th century, they did not make many lasting impressions on Azerbaijani society aside from introducing their religion.

The invasion of the tribe of the Oghuz Turks in the mid-11th century left one of the most significant marks on Azerbaijani society. The Oghuz introduced their Turkic language and many Turkic customs to the Azerbaijanis and are the basis for Azeri identity as a Turkic people. During the Seljuk dynasty established by the Oghuz, the first Azerbaijani literature was written by Nizami Ganjavi; advances were made in the sciences and great architectural works were constructed. Azerbaijanis began to see themselves as a nation.

The next important development in Azerbaijani history was the beginning of the Safavid dynasty in Iran and Azerbaijan, led by Ismail I, an Azerbaijani belonging to the Shia Sufi sect known as the Safavids. Ismail I conquered most of Iran and Azerbaijan in the beginning of the 16th century and initiated a brutal policy, forcing the population to convert from the previously predominant Sunni Islam to Shiism. This policy, coupled with numerous defeats by the Ottoman Empire on Azerbaijani territory, was disastrous to Azerbaijan. Although the capital city of the Safavids was originally located in Azerbaijan, it was moved after repeatedly being sacked during Ottoman raids.

Shortly after the fall of the Safavids in the early 18th century Azerbaijan was invaded and changed hands a number of times before being incorporated into the Russian Empire in 1813. At this time the fates of northern Azerbaijanis, who today live in the Republic of Azerbaijan, and southern Azerbaijanis, who live in northern Iran, separated. The Russians, who were largely interested in the region's oil wealth, did not significantly interfere with either local politics or culture until the Soviet Union was established and Azerbaijan incorporated as a Soviet republic. Prior to incorporation in the Soviet Union, Azerbaijan enjoyed two years of independence from 1918 to 1920. This brief period of independence was an inspiration for Azerbaijani nationalists throughout the Soviet period.

During Soviet domination the Azerbaijanis were forced to change their written alphabet from Arabic to Roman, and then from Roman to Cyrillic, in an attempt to isolate the Azerbaijanis from fellow Muslims and Turks. Expressions of Azerbaijani national pride were punished, particularly nationalistic literature, as were expressions of religion. After independence in 1991, Azerbaijan began to reclaim its own history and to encourage study of ancient Azerbaijani literature and arts. (*See also* ARMENIANS: NATIONALITY; AZERIS.)

CULTURAL IDENTITY

The origins of the Azerbaijanis, who speak a Turkic language and have many Persian customs, have long been a topic of speculation. They probably originated as a Caucasian people who were assimilated by numerous conquerors and adopted many foreign customs: in the case of Turkic invaders, their language. Present-day Azerbaijanis in Azerbaijan generally see themselves as a Turkic people, regardless of their closer religious ties with Persians (about 70 percent of Azerbaijani Muslims are Shia, the branch of Islam practiced in Iran). This affiliation is especially apparent in Azerbaijan's close political relations with Turkey and is also reflected in the eight-pin star flag of Azerbaijan, which represents the eight Turkic tribes who had controlled Azerbaijan at one time.

Azerbaijan has been left with many legacies from the Soviet Union as well, one of which is a high degree of secularism. Religion, for Muslim Azerbaijanis, is not very important and is viewed as mainly the by-product of an ethnic affiliation. In urban areas, women are considered equal to men and frequently attend universities and work outside the home, while in rural areas there are still large differences in the treatment of women and men. However, even in urban areas marriages are often arranged, and in rural areas it is still fairly common to kidnap brides.

Under the rule of the Soviet Union Azerbaijani history, national literature, and art forms were repressed, and Soviet officials were especially afraid of any signs of "Pan-Turkism." Instead, the Soviets strongly encouraged the brotherhood of the Caucasian peoples. Azerbaijani historians have been trying to discover the truth about the origins of their people since then. Azerbaijani literature has become especially important in building a post-Soviet identity, as neither modern nor ancient Azerbaijani literature was allowed during Soviet times. The most influential literature in the Azerbaijani language is poetry dating from the 16th century by the poets Fusuli and Ismail I. Part of this search for identity has included seeking greater ties with Iranian Azeris, with whom they continue to have much in common despite two centuries of separation.

Although Iranians, Saudi Arabians, and other foreigners have tried to create fundamentalist movements in Azerbaijan, secularism seems to be solidly entrenched in the population, which is largely dedicated to following Western-style development and Turkish, rather than Iranian, example. While Azerbaijanis identify most closely with other Turkic peoples and follow Turkish models of development, they remain aware of Persian influences, as well as their ties to their neighbors in the Caucasus.

As has been the case since the establishment of the first oil well in Absheron in the mid-19th century Azerbaijan's oil reserves today continue to provide both economic opportunities and foreign interference. For a small number of Azerbaijanis, then as now, oil wealth has meant entrance into the wider world of market consumerism and bourgeois values. For the vast majority, however, oil has been more of a curse than a blessing for it has generated significant outside interference in their political and economic systems, environmental degradation, and greater inequality.

FURTHER READING

John F. Baddeley. *The Russian Conquest of the Caucasus* (Richmond, England: Curzon Press, 1999).

Charles van der Leeuw. *Azerbaijan: A Quest for Identity: A Short History* (New York: St. Martin's Press, 2000).

Ronald Grigor Suny, ed. *Transcaucasia, Nationalism, and Social Change: Essays in the History of Armenia, Azerbaijan, and Georgia* (Ann Arbor: University of Michigan Press, 1996).

Tadeusz Swietochowksi and Brian C. Collins. *Historical Dictionary of Azerbaijan* (Lanham, Md.: Scarecrow Press, 1999).

Thomas de Waal. *Black Garden: Armenia and Azerbaijan through Peace and War* (New York: New York University Press, 2003).

Arif Yunusov. *Islam in Azerbaijan.* Translated by Zhala Mammadova and Murad Gassanty (Baku: Zaman, 2004).

Jahangir Zeynaloglu. *A Concise History of Azerbaijan* (Winthrop, Mass.: F. P. Abasov, 1997).

Azeris (Azerbaijanis, Azeri Turks, Iranian Azeris, Torks)

The Azeris are a Turkish-speaking people, 7 million to 8 million of whom reside in Azerbaijan, and 16 million to 20 million in northwestern Iran, forming the country's largest minority group. These two populations speak the same language and are ethnically the same, but almost 200 years of national separation have created some significant cultural differences. The most pronounced difference is in the sphere of religious belief, with Iranian Azeris being much more likely to profess Islam than their more secular Azerbaijani cousins. The Azerbaijani population has also tended to retain more pre-Islamic beliefs and practices (*see* AZERBAIJANIS: NATIONALITY). Iranian Azeris

are well integrated into the Islamic Republic and do not seem to have aspirations either for independence or for uniting with Azerbaijan.

GEOGRAPHY

Azerbaijan is a small country in the southern Caucasus region with the Caspian Sea making up its eastern border. The country is traversed by the Kura River and surrounded by the Caucasus Mountain ranges to the north and the Lesser Caucasus to the west. The Caspian region and the Kura River valley are both fairly low in elevation and have a temperate climate, while the mountainous regions of Azerbaijan and the Azeri region of Iran are extremely rugged with elevations of more than 6,600 feet and some peaks as high as 16,400 feet. Agriculture is difficult in these areas, where more people live as pastoralists, with some even continuing to practice a seminomadic way of life, moving seasonally.

ORIGINS

The region of contemporary Azerbaijan has been the home of many different ethnic groups in the past four and a half millennia. MEDES, Assyrians, CAUCASIAN ALBANIANS, ARMENIANS, Persians, Khazars, Arabs, MONGOLS, and a host of smaller groups all invaded or made their home there at some point. The region was also conquered by the ancient GREEKS and by Rome centuries later, both of whom no doubt left some genetic and cultural traits in the present-day population.

The contemporary Azeris, however, trace their roots to the invasion by Oghuz Turks in the 11th century. The 24 tribes of the Oghuz were all part of the Seljuk confederation, which originated in Central Asia and had its own empire in the 10th–12th centuries. The Azeris' Turkish language originates with this invasion and thus marks the beginning of the Azeri people as a unique ethnic group.

HISTORY

(*See* AZERBAIJANIS: NATIONALITY for a summary of Azeri history prior to 1991.) Since independence in 1991 Azeris in Azerbaijan have experienced social transformation on a massive scale. Seventy years of Soviet socialism in Azerbaijan created a population that was accustomed to free education, health care, and housing, and in which about 80 percent were considered middle class. Since 1991 the economic and social changes instituted by the privatization of most industries and services have created vast

---

AZERIS

location:
Azerbaijan, throughout the Caucasus, and northwestern Iran

time period:
11th century to the present

ancestry:
Caucasian Albanian, Khazar, Arab, Persian, and Turkish

language:
Azerbaijani, a Turkish language mutually intelligible to Turkmen and Turkish speakers; it is called Torki in Iran

Azeris time line

C.E.

11th century Oghuz Turks migrate from Central Asia into the Caucasus and mix with local populations.

1494–1556 Lifetime of Fusuli, an Azerbaijani poet who wrote poetry and prose in Turkish. His most famous works include *Laila and Majnun* and *The Book of Complaints*. These works are still read today in their original form.

1500 The Safavid dynasty, with origins in an Azerbaijani sect of Shiism, takes control of Azerbaijan and much of Persia and converts the area under its control to Shiism. The first shah, Ismail I, is also an important Azerbaijani poet.

1700 The Russian Empire begins to exert influence over northern Azerbaijan while Persian forces retain control of southern Azerbaijan. The difference between the two regions becomes increasingly pronounced in the following years.

1813 Treaty of Gulistan establishes the Russian-Persian border along the Aras River.

1812–78 Lifetime of Mirza Fath Ali Akhundazade, a playwright and philosopher who was one of the first to write plays in the Azerbaijani vernacular. His plays remain popular today.

1828 The Treaty of Turkmanchay further extends the territory of Russia in Azerbaijan and divides ethnic Azeris between Russia and Persia.

1885–1948 Lifetime of Uzeir Hajibeyli, a composer and poet whose compositions often used traditional instruments and whose operas were among the first in the Islamic world.

1918–20 Short period of Azerbaijani independence, after the fall of the Russian Empire and before Azerbaijan is occupied by the Soviet Union in 1920.

1920 Azerbaijan is occupied by the Soviet Union and signs a treaty uniting military, economy, and foreign trade with Russia.

1920–89 Period of increasing secularization of Soviet Azeris and divergence from their more traditional and religious cousins residing in Iran.

1989 Azerbaijan is one of the first Soviet republics to declare independence. This declaration is contested by the Soviet Union, and the political party behind the independence movement is declared illegal.

1990 Riots in Baku protesting the lack of sovereignty and the separation of Azerbaijanis in Iran and in the USSR. During these riots Armenians living in Baku are attacked. The riots are brutally suppressed by the Soviet military.

1991 Azerbaijan gains independence as the Soviet Union falls. Nagorno-Karabakh declares independence, setting off a protracted crisis between Armenia and Azerbaijan.

1991–the present The large Azeri middle class in Azerbaijan disappears in the course of privatization, corruption, and kleptocracy. The gulf between rich and poor becomes one of the widest in the world.

1993 Armenia invades Azerbaijan over the contested status of Nagorno-Karabakh, an area of Azerbaijan inhabited primarily by Armenians. Armenia occupies Nagorno-Karabakh and the surrounding area.

1994 Armenia and Azerbaijan reach a cease-fire regarding Nagorno-Karabakh, but Armenians remain in control of the area and the surrounding territory. Hundreds of thousands of Azeris leave and live in camps in other areas of the country; many others flee to Russia and other former Soviet republics.

2006 An Iranian newspaper publishes a cartoon of a cockroach speaking Azeri, which sets off riots among Iranian Azeris, the Islamic Republic's largest minority group. Four protesters are killed in Naghadeh.

extremes of wealth and poverty. The very few but highly visible "New Azeris," as the wealthy are called, spend millions of American dollars and euros for cars, household items, vacations, clothing, and everything else a consumer culture tells them they need and want. At the same time, many others are being forced to sell off their family belongings and scavenge the municipal garbage dumps to supplement a meager pension or government wage. About a third of Azerbaijani children no longer attend school because they are needed to help earn enough for the family to live on. In 2004, the World Bank believed that 78 percent of the population was living on a dollar per day or less. As a result, the population has diminished by about half from its 1991 level, with people leaving for Russia, Turkey, and elsewhere.

A culture of corruption has taken over in this economic context where the only paths to success are paying bribes and buying positions of influence. Vast wealth can be made from the country's oil reserves, but it is going into the hands of a few individuals. One of those individuals is Heydar Alieyev, who led the country from 1969 to 2003, with just a brief interlude from 1987 to 1993. He was succeeded by his son, who maintained the culture of corruption.

In addition to the fall of the socialist Soviet regime, the other event that has had a significant effect upon Azerbaijanis is the 1991–94 conflict with Armenia over the contested Nagorno-Karabakh region. In 1991 Nagorno-Karabakh, a largely Armenian region of Azerbaijan, declared its independence, which set off a protracted crisis. Two years later, Armenia invaded the region, displacing about 750,000 Azeris and killing perhaps 35,000 more before fighting ended in 1994. Even with the end of the war, the region remained in the hands of the Armenian military; continued displacement of the Azeri population resulted. Many of the displaced are living in desperate conditions in camps in the Azeri desert; the camps are dominated by elderly people, women, and children who were left behind when the younger men departed from the region or the country to find work. This has had a significant effect on gender roles and other aspects of a culture traditionally dominated by male breadwinners. In the camps women are busy raising children, doing household tasks, and even working in cottage industries while the few men who remain sit idle and traumatized by their loss of status and authority.

Most commentators on Azeri culture are concerned about this volatile mix of poverty in the midst of new wealth and idleness, among a population for whom rebellion is seen as a defining character trait. Whether it was against Russian, Persian, or Soviet domination, the Azeris, especially rural Azeris from the moun- tainous regions of Azerbaijan, believed that rebellion identified them as a people. If this remains true in the present, Azerbaijan may eventually crumble under the pressure of economic disparity, male frustration, and government corruption.

CULTURE

The Azeris are traditionally an agricultural people although in both Azerbaijan and Iran significant numbers live in cities and have joined the industrial economy. The Azeri region of Iran, along with Tehran, is the most industrialized region of the country and Azeris there are active participants in both government and industry, though education and broadcasting in the Azeri language are forbidden. The current supreme leader of the country, Ayatollah Ali Khamenei, is actually of ethnic Azeri origin. In Azerbaijan about half the population is urban in such cities as Baku, Ganca, and Sumqayit. In both countries, urban neighborhoods and rural villages tend to be ethnically homogeneous.

Since the end of the Soviet era and the collapse of collectivization, most rural Azeris in Azerbaijan have gone back to small-scale farming and horticulture. They produce tea, pomegranates, vegetables, honey, hazelnuts, walnuts, cherries, and sheep, goats, and cattle products as well as the illegal *tut aragi,* a mulberry vodka. Azeris are also known for their silk production and carpets, an important tradition throughout the Caucasus region.

Regardless of country of residence, Azeris have a patrilineal kinship system and many live in extended family households, even in cities. Many marriages in rural areas are still arranged and even in cities families expect children to marry in their birth order and to marry someone known to the family. There is more interethnic group marriage in Iran with the Muslim Persians than in Azerbaijan. It is expected that the first child will be born during the first year of marriage.

Azeris, as other TURKIC PEOPLES, have a long tradition of folklore songs, including historical songs called *dastans.* These stories memorialize the lives of Azeri heroes, both male and female, usually people who performed crucial tasks in a fight for independence. These songs are often sung to tunes played on a traditional lutelike musical instrument called a *kopuz.* The oldest of the Azeri folklore songs are those that accompany different tasks, so-called labor songs, such as the famous cattle-breeding songs and those sung while planting.

Ceremonial songs, based on pre-Islamic nature worship, are commonly performed at rituals dedicated to the Sun, Moon, rain, and fire, especially in Azerbaijan.

The sphere of religion is one of the most important aspects of Azeri identity, but in different ways for different people. During the Soviet era in Azerbaijan, being Muslim was synonymous with being Azeri, even for the most secular of people, and being Shiite, as more than three-quarters of the population were, was an important distinction between Azeris and other Soviet Muslims. Despite this use of Islam as an important ethnic marker, however, Azeris in Azerbaijan are largely secularists as a result of 70 years of Soviet socialist education. Even with the religious reawakening since 1991, Azeris in Azerbaijan are not as religious as the Iranian Azeris. In that country, Azeris have been strong supporters of the Islamic government because it has fostered a Shiite-focused nationalism rather than a strictly Persian one, as had been done under the previous secularizing monarchical regime.

In addition to Islam, many pre-Islamic beliefs, especially about nature worship, survive in Azerbaijan, though fewer are preserved in Iran. Su Jeddim, the practice of communing with ancestors through immersing oneself in a sacred river or stream, has reemerged in the post-Soviet era, as has the holiday Novruz Bayram, which is a lunar new year celebration occurring on the vernal equinox. In everyday life, the bark from iron trees is used as a charm or amulet to ward off the evil eye, especially to protect infants, and both fire, the most sacred element, and a kind of black rock believed to cure some ailments have cultic practices around them that some Azeris continue to this day. People hammer a nail into a tree as revenge against others who have done them harm; it is a last resort when other kinds of revenge are not available. In addition to nail trees, the Azerbaijani landscape is dotted with *pirs*, holy places, where people leave money, tie cloths to trees, or simply ask for assistance. Religious leaders' graves, homes, and other significant places are important sites for these activities as well.

As this last category of *pirs* shows, there has been significant syncretism or blending of Islamic and pre-Islamic, especially Zoroastrian, beliefs among many Azeris, especially in Azerbaijan. Another example of this is the strong supernatural power attributed to some *mollas* (mullahs) or religious leaders. One *molla* who participated in one of the many uprisings that took place against the Soviets in 1930 is said to have been protected by his dead father; another religious leader supposedly sent a tremendous rainstorm that prevented the RUSSIANS and their Azeri informants from capturing a fugitive. Dead religious leaders can also appear in the dreams of the living to give advice or rebuke for failing to perform sacrifices for them or for other transgressions. Other religious figures are believed to be able to disappear from one place, especially from prison, and reappear elsewhere.

Both Islam and Azeri traditional culture create relatively strong divisions between men and women and keep them fairly separate. These divisions were largely broken down for urban Azeris in Soviet Azerbaijan, who benefited from state education, employment opportunities, and ideologies about the equality of women and men. For rural Azeri women in Azerbaijan and most of the Iranian Azeri population, however, traditional ideas about the separation of the sexes remain fairly important. Women are responsible for the household's economy and honor, which keep most close to home, while men are able to travel and mix with outsiders. This has resulted in a great gender disparity in rural Azerbaijan with more than a million men having left since 1991 to seek employment in Russia and the other former Soviet republics.

See also AZERBAIJANIS: NATIONALITY; ARMENIANS: NATIONALITY.

FURTHER READING

Farideh Heyat. *Azeri Women in Transition: Women in Soviet and Post-Soviet Azerbaijan* (New York: Routledge Curzon, 2002).

Tadeusz Swietochowski. *Russian Azerbaijan, 1905–1920: The Shaping of National Identity in a Muslim Community* (New York: Cambridge University Press, 1985).

B

Ba (Pa)

The Ba people were an ancient tribal community who lived in what is today southwestern China. The first hint of their existence is from the 11th century B.C.E., when they were under the domination of the Western Zhou, or Chou, dynasty (1040–256 B.C.E.) and may have assisted in that dynasty's overthrow of its predecessor, the Shang. At that time they lived in the Chia-ling valley of central Sichuan although later they dispersed toward the east. A more definitive written account of the existence of the Ba is from 703 B.C.E., when they were recorded in China's first narrative history, the *Zuo Zhuan*, as having assisted the Shu Kingdom, with whom they later intermingled to form a solitary cultural group today called Ba-Shu, against their rivals, the Deng. By the fifth century B.C.E. this intermingling with the Shu had been completed and the new group had formed its own culture and society. Together the Ba-Shu were conquered by the first Chinese imperial dynasty, the short-lived Qin or Chin, in about 316 B.C.E.

The historical evidence about the Ba people and their long-lasting tribal confederacy is liberally interspersed in even the most academic texts with legend and mythology. For example, the possibly legendary first king of the Ba, Lin Jun, is the subject of an extensive mythology that highlights his transformation into a white tiger upon his death. Lin Jun, or Wuxiang as he is also known, probably ruled his people from the town of Changyang in contemporary Hubei Province. This region is watered by the Qing Jiang, or River, which winds through Changyang before finally joining the Yangtze and is surrounded by high, rugged mountains. This river today is still sacred to the Tujia people, who, as the direct descendants of the ancient Ba, consider it their "mother river." However, the Ba have also been connected to the Sichuan city of Chongqing and some sources cite that city as their capital.

The culture of the Ba is known to us only through fragments; it seems to have been built upon a subsistence base of hunting and fishing with only minimal input from slash-and-burn agriculture. They had not yet developed the technology for irrigation and thus lacked the ability to use the same field for more than a season or two. They also seem to have been engaged in frequent wars, both within their own tribal confederacy and with their neighbors, which precipitated their eventual unification with the Shu of the central Yangtze valley.

Perhaps related to this constant threat of violence in Ba society, they may have engaged in a variety of sacrificial activities using human beings. The mythohistorical record of the Ba describes instances whereby they "watered" the soul of their dead king Lin Jun with human blood and offered up human bodies to their king-turned-tiger. Prior to the inundation of the Three Gorges area of the Yangtze, archaeologists found tombs from the Ba era and in the Ba style that contained two separate human skulls at the foot of a third set of remains. The most common interpretation of these findings is that two people were sacrificed to accompany the third, probably a warrior, on his way to the afterlife. In a second tomb archaeologists found bodies that had been dismembered, possibly with the different parts used as separate sacrifices.

Bactrians (Zariaspans)

GEOGRAPHY

Bactria was located in what is today part of Uzbekistan, Tajikistan, and northern Afghanistan, north of Kabul, east of the Arius River, south of the Oxus River, today's Amu Darya, and west of the Hindu Kush Mountains. During the Greek period, Bactria and its sister region Sogdiana were the most remote eastern outposts of the Hellenic world. The region was well watered with its various river systems and was very fertile, at least in the valleys and plains. The Hindu Kush Mountains on the borderlands, however, with their peaks of up to 17,000 feet, were extremely rugged and difficult to cross at most places. The capital of Bactria, Bactra, was located on the Bactrus River; the city exists today as Balkh, the oldest city in Afghanistan. According to both later Islamic myth and local legend, Bactra is the mother of cities and was founded by the first Aryan king, a descendent of the biblical Noah.

ORIGINS

From about 2200 to 1700 B.C.E. a sedentary population of Bronze Age farmers lived in the region of the Oxus River, today's Amu Darya. This culture has been labeled by archaeologists as the Oxus civilization or the Bactria-Margiana Archaeological Complex (BMAC) and probably forms the basis for later Bactrian societies. As the Bactrians, these people relied on crops of wheat and barley for subsistence, lived in settled villages and towns, and traded with other ancient peoples in their region. However, scholars are unsure about the exact origins of the Bactrians since the artifacts that denote BMAC disappear from the record just a few centuries after they appear. By the time of the Persian invasion in the sixth century B.C.E., Bactria is already a settled community with its nobles and merchants living in towns and cities and being supported by a surplus-producing community of farmers in the countryside.

HISTORY

The ancient history of the Bactrians is steeped in legend and is still a relative mystery to historians. Stories abound that place the birth of Zarathustra, the founder of Zoroastrianism, in Bactra, the capital of Bactria, between 1400 and 1300 B.C.E.; however, there is no definitive proof of this event. The Zoroastrian shrine of Anahita, goddess of fertility and water, certainly stood by the banks of the Bactrus River, which ran through the capital Bactra, but other Zoroastrian cities would likewise have contained holy sites of various sorts.

The first definitive mention of Bactria is that of the Achaemenids (*see* PERSIANS, ACHAEMENIDS) of the sixth century B.C.E., when Cyrus the Great first conquered the entire Transoxiana region. Unfortunately the Persian literature is relatively silent on the nature of Bactrian society, beyond mere mention of Bactrian court-

---

Bactrians time line

B.C.E.

1400–1300 Perhaps the century in which Zarathustra, founder of Zoroastrianism, was born, legend has it, in the Bactrian capital of Bactra. The periods around 1100 B.C.E. and 700 B.C.E. have also been posited as dates for Zarathustra's life.

sixth century Bactrians are conquered by Persians and incorporated into the Achaemenid empire.

329–327 Macedonian invasion led by Alexander the Great, who moves a number of Greek soldiers into the region, much to the dismay of both the Greeks and the Bactrians.

323 Alexander the Great dies at Babylon and Bactria falls into chaos until the emergence of his successor generals, the Seleucids, as rulers of Alexander's domains.

235 Greco-Bactrian kingdom established in Transoxiana by the descendants of Alexander the Great's soldiers. Diodotus II is the first Greco-Bactrian king, though his father, Diodotus I, a Seleucid satrap, started the decades-long process of breaking free from Seleucid rule.

230 Euthydemus I deposes Diodotus II.

170 The Greco-Bactrian kingdom splits into eastern and western portions or the houses of Antimachos and Eukradites, respectively.

146 The Greco-Bactrian city of Ai Khanoum is sacked and destroyed by nomads.

135 The Yuezhi invasion from the eastern steppes pushes Scythians and Parthians into Bactria.

130 Heliocles I, the last Greek king of western Bactria, falls to nomadic invaders.

10 The rule of Strato II, the last king of eastern Bactria, ends at the hands of the Kushans.

C.E.

eighth century The Arab invasion eliminates the last traces of a separate Bactrian culture.

iers and subjects. We do know that Bactria was a key eastern outpost for the Achaemenids; controlled their trade with the east, especially China; and was ruled by them for nearly 300 years, until 330 B.C.E., when a Persian nobleman named Bessus had the Achaemenid king, Darius III, murdered. As King Artaxerxes V, Bessus ruled the region for just a few months before Alexander the Great arrived in Central Asia to avenge his father's death.

The Persians and GREEKS had been rival empires in the ancient world for several centuries before Alexander's time, and Alexander himself sought to tip the scales finally toward the Greek side. The two armies fought a number of battles during the years 336–331 B.C.E., with both Alexander and Darius participating in hand-to-hand combat at such battle sites as Issus and Gaza. The final battle in which Alexander overthrew his foe was at Gaugamala, in today's Iraq, in 331 B.C.E. After that Darius and his army retreated toward Bactria to hide out in the rugged terrain and regroup for subsequent battles; it was there that Darius lost his life in Bessus's challenge for leadership and thus denied Alexander the ability to vanquish his rival. The coup also destabilized an already decentralized political situation and made it all the more difficult for Alexander to claim the ultimate victory over the Persians, Bactrians, and their neighbors, the SOGDIANS.

The accounts of Bactria provided by those who traveled with Alexander tell of a population that was more alien to the Greeks and Macedonians than any they had ever encountered. In Egypt, India, and throughout the Middle East, the Greek armies allowed the conquered people to continue worshiping in their accustomed manner and practicing their own funerary rituals. But in Bactria this was not to be the case. The Bactrians were Zoroastrians and rather than bury or cremate their dead they left them in the open to be devoured by sacred dogs and birds of prey. Alexander's men described seeing packs of dogs ripping apart dead and dying Bactrians, sun-bleached human bones littering the streets, and decaying human flesh everywhere. These soldiers were accustomed to similar scenes on battlefields, but when it came to the deaths of ordinary citizens, they could not condone such barbarism. The Bactrians were forbidden to continue practicing their religion, setting the stage for decades and even centuries of unrest. Alexander's troops also pillaged and burned the cities and towns of Bactria, only later to rebuild them on the Greek model.

Alexander died in Babylon just four years after finally conquering the Bactrian area, and the region was thrown into turmoil. The Greek soldiers who had been left there rebelled and the local population refused to adopt Greek ways. Three decades after Alexander's death the armies of Seleucus I finally achieved some degree of order, gave up Greek aspirations to rule India, and eventually incorporated Bactria into the Seleucid Empire. Under the Greek Seleucids Bactria was at least partially transformed into a Hellenistic culture. From agricultural products like grapes and olives to the building of Greek theaters, mansions, and even the entirely new city of Ai Khanoum, Bactria, at least on the surface, was transformed into a Greek outpost for its Greek inhabitants. For the region's Bactrian and other inhabitants, the archaeological evidence is less clear about their ability to live and worship as they pleased.

After less than 100 years of Seleucid building in Bactria, a local satrap or governor, Diodotus I, began accumulating power, a process that eventually led him and his son to mint their own coins and break free of foreign rule. Unfortunately these events are known to us only through their coinage, as the written records have either disappeared entirely or not yet been found in the sands of Afghanistan. The archaeological evidence indicates that this local rule was no less Greek than that of Seleucus or his successors, Antiochus I and Antiochus II. Bactria continued to trade with the rest of the Hellenic world and to adopt building styles from Mediterranean lands. At the same time trade and relations with India that had begun earlier continued unabated during this period, at least from what we can learn from the sites that have been excavated.

The transformation from Seleucid to Greco-Bactrian kingdoms between 250 and 235 B.C.E. was apparently relatively peaceful. It was only a generation later, between 212 and 205 B.C.E., that the Seleucid ruler Antiochus III attempted to take back this eastern portion of his empire by force. By that time the Bactrian kingdom was being ruled by Euthydemus I, who was determined to hold on to the kingdom he had wrested from Diodotus II. After an early defeat the Greco-Bactrians under Euthydemus I retreated to their capital at Bactra and were held there for two years but were not overrun by the Seleucid armies. Eventually Antiochus III sent an emissary, who settled the grievances between the two kings and ratified the legitimacy of Euthydemus I's rule in Bactria.

BACTRIANS

location:
Today's Afghanistan north of the city of Kabul to the Amu Darya (Oxus River), sometimes called Transoxiana or simply Bactria

time period:
Probably eighth century B.C.E. to eighth century C.E.

ancestry:
Iranian

language:
Bactrian, an Eastern Iranian language

As is the case in so much of the Bactrians' history, very little beyond the names of some of the Greco-Bactrian kings can be read in the archaeological record. We know from the coins that a split occurred in about 170 B.C.E. between those Greco-Bactrians who continued to rule in Transoxiana, the so-called house of Eukradites, and those who ruled in the eastern portion of the kingdom in Indo-Bactria, the so-called house of Antimachos. But what the policies of any of these kings were has been lost to history. The same is also true of the daily lives of the people in both regions. Certainly, however, these kings were continually under pressure from bands of nomadic soldiers and looters from the north and from the Indian leaders to the south. Eventually it was the northern KUSHANS who overran the Bactrians and established their own kingdoms in this land. While some aspects of the Bactrian language and religion survived these centuries, the Arab invasion of the eighth century C.E. was the beginning of the end. A few Zoroastrians fled to India and live there today as the minority PARSEES, but whether these people were from Bactria or from more westerly Iranian lands is impossible to tell. In any case all traces of the Bactrians disappeared for centuries until archaeologists began to unearth their coins and other artifacts in the past two centuries.

CULTURE

For as far back as we have historical records, Bactria was a settled community of farmers, merchants, and nobles. There is ample archaeological evidence that the region was well irrigated and able to produce a food surplus that allowed an elaborate division of labor. Urban merchants traded in semiprecious stones and metals as well as in food and other daily necessities. At least as far back as Alexander's time, the region was also highly monetized, with the wealthy dealing in gold and silver coins and daily interactions taking place in bronze. Because of their durability, these coins are often the sole remains of entire cities and historical epochs and thus the basis for our information about rulers and their people.

The religious life of all Bactrians prior to Alexander, and of the non-Hellenic Bactrian population for many centuries after him as well, was dominated by the beliefs and practices of Zoroastrianism. In this system dogs were considered sacred; prayer was conducted at a fire altar, and, as mentioned, funerary practices meant allowing dogs and birds of prey to feast on the bodies of the dead. In addition to these practices that both the ancient Greek invaders as well as modern readers find foreign, other aspects of this religion are much more familiar. Zoroastrians were, and the small number who remain today are, monotheists; they believe in one supreme god, Ahura Mazda. This god revealed himself to Zarathustra, a Persian who may have lived in Bactria between 1400 and 1300 B.C.E. and then went on to write one of the sacred texts of this religion, the Gathas. Zoroastrians, as do Jews and Christians, believe in the coming of a savior who will wage a final battle between good and evil, vanquishing evil once and for all; this savior will also be born of a virgin. Indeed there has been much speculation among historians of religion that these concepts in the Judeo-Christian cosmology originated in Zoroastrianism and were merely borrowed by the founders of these religious systems.

FURTHER READING

Frank L. Holt. *Alexander the Great and Bactria* (New York: E. J. Brill, 1989).

Frank L. Holt. *Into the Land of Bones: Alexander the Great in Afghanistan* (Berkeley and Los Angeles: University of California Press, 2005).

Frank L. Holt. *Thundering Zeus: The Making of Hellenistic Bactria* (Berkeley and Los Angeles: University of California Press, 1999).

Bahnar (Alakong, Ba-Na, Bonom, Ho Drong, Jo Long, Kon Ko De, Kontum, Krem, Tolo, To Sung)

The Bahnar are one of many ethnic groups who reside in the mountains of central Vietnam, sometimes called as a group Montagnards or DEGA. They speak an Austro-Asiatic language in the Eastern Mon-Khmer family and may have moved to the highlands from the coast during the VIETNAMESE migrations south after the 10th century. Today they number about 140,000 people.

HISTORY

The Bahnar, or Ba Na as they are often referred to in Vietnamese sources, have traditionally been horticulturalists and hunters, using slash-and-burn techniques to grow corn, sweet potatoes, and millet for their own consumption and hemp, tobacco, or indigo to sell or trade. They have a long history of trade relations with the other mountain people in the region, the CHAMS, who dominated the central region of Vietnam until the late 15th century, and then with the Vietnamese. One of their most valued trade goods are elephants, captured in the wild and then tamed for local agricultural use or export.

During the French colonial period the Bahnar tended to ally themselves with the French against the Vietnamese, who had been trying to assimilate them by force for hundreds of years. Many Bahnar converted to Christianity during this period and some attended Bahnar-language schools created by the French administration. Some experts point to these schools as the source of a distinct Bahnar identity, distinct from other mountain people and the Vietnamese, with attendant claims for their own land, schools, and cultural traditions. In 1955 the Hanoi government opened its own school for the Southern Bahnar as well as some schools for several other groups in reaction to these calls for ethnic identification.

During the long period of conflict between North and South Vietnam, 1954–76, many Bahnar initially supported the National Liberation Front (NLF), which was fighting the government of South Vietnam in order to reunite the country with Communist North Vietnam. For many years the NLF produced a regular radio broadcast in the Bahnar language and even offered them and other Montagnard groups an autonomous state of their own in exchange for their support in the war. In 1955 a number of Bahnar, Jarai, Rhade, and Koho leaders in South Vietnam formed the group BAJARKA, an acronym using the first letters of each ethnonym, to fight against the repressive South Vietnamese regime. They were actively repressed by the South Vietnamese government under Ngo Dinh Diem, who ruled from 1955 to 1963, but reasserted their claims in the 1960s as part of FULRO, the Front Unifié de Lutte des Races Opprimées, or United Front for the Struggle of Oppressed Races. When the U.S. army began to play a greater part in the war, many soldiers sympathized with the Bahnar and other groups' claims to a separate identity, and thus some FULRO units assisted the Americans. As a result a number of Bahnar families were resettled in the United States as American allies at the end of the war.

After the war the Vietnamese government engaged largely in a policy of assimilation with regard to its minority groups, banning their slash-and-burn agricultural practices, moving Vietnamese families into the highlands, and suppressing both indigenous and Christian religious practices. After 25 years of this policy many mountain peoples staged a protest in February 2001, which accomplished little.

CULTURE

The Bahnar differ from the dominant Vietnamese community in having a matrilineal kinship system, in which family relationships are traced through women rather than men. The postmarital residence pattern is also matrilocal: young husbands usually spend a period living and working with their in-laws right after marriage. Many other Montagnard communities share these kinship and marriage patterns, and there has always been a degree of intermarriage between the Bahnar and other groups, especially the nearby Jarai and Rhade. Today both matrilineal and matrilocal patterns are less common in the face of the diminishing importance of kinship in the country.

Each Bahnar village in the past was ruled by a village headman, and all men in the village participated in political decision making through events held in the *rong* or communal men's house. These houses, built on stilts with an extremely tall, curved thatched roof, continue to serve as a center for male village life. Adolescent boys reside in them prior to marriage in order to learn Bahnar history, mythology, and skills. Women may participate in the building of these houses, especially in gathering thatch for the roof, which can be as tall as 90 feet high, but they must never enter the building. Today many communal houses are simple brick structures with tile roofs, but the Vietnamese government has supported the

The Bahnar *rong,* or men's house, from Kon Tum, Vietnam. *(OnAsia/Luke Duggleby)*

BAHNAR

location:
Central highlands of Vietnam, especially Lai-Cong Turn Province

time period:
Unknown to the present

ancestry:
Mon-Khmer

language:
Bahnar, an Austro-Asiatic language in the Eastern Mon-Khmer family

building of more traditional ones both for tourists and for the Bahnar themselves. Each village also had a local judiciary system to try both civil and criminal cases.

Traditionally the Bahnar were animists who worshipped a variety of natural spirits, including those of the banyan and ficus trees, as well as their own ancestors; buffalo were also considered sacred and were sacrificed at the most important family or communal events. Young children were believed to receive their soul a month or so after their birth in a ceremony that included having the soul blown into the child's ear and having the ears pierced. Those who died prior to this ceremony were not considered fully human and were believed to be taken to the land of the monkeys; those who died after receiving their souls were buried in coffins that resembled canoes. The Bahnar also told of an origin myth that resembles the Noah's ark story, in which a great flood destroys the earth except for Mr. and Madam Drum, so named because they hid in a drum and survived the flood. Upon the arrival of Christian missionaries in the 18th century many Bahnar converted to both Catholicism and Protestant sects, perhaps in part because they already shared an important feature of their religious cosmology.

A final important aspect of Bahnar culture is the centrality of music in both ceremonial and everyday life. Every Bahnar village owns at least one set of *H'onh*, or gongs, to be used during weddings, buffalo sacrifices, or sanctification of a new men's house. These gongs are made from brass; each set has at least 10 gongs of varying sizes and shapes. The gongs are played by men only and may be accompanied by drums and cymbals as well. Other important instruments include the *ala*, a type of flute used by men while courting; the *pruh*, the gong used at the new rice festival; and the *ting ning*, a three-string instrument played by men for leisure. Another important musical event is the *H'mol*, which combines poetry, prose, music, and singing to tell stories from the Bahnar past and Bahnar mythology. These events take place in the men's house and so typically exclude women.

FURTHER READING

Gerald Cannon Hickey. *Sons of the Mountains: Ethnohistory of the Vietnamese Central Highlands to 1954* (New Haven, Conn.: Yale University Press, 1982).

Bai (Baihu, Baihuo, Baini, Baizi, Bozi, Minchia, Pai)

About 2 million Bai people live in the Dali Bai Autonomous Prefecture of the western region of Yunnan Province. Small Bai communities can also be found in neighboring Sichuan, Guizhou, and Hunan Provinces. Some experts suggest that around 50 million people of Bai origin live all over Asia, principally in Myanmar (Burma) and Thailand but also in Cambodia, Laos, and Vietnam, as well as in the other provinces of China. As an ethnic minority the Bai are allowed to have two children instead of the one child prescribed for the HAN majority of the Chinese population.

GEOGRAPHY

The Bai region covers the Yunnan-Guizhou Plateau and is crossed by many rivers, the most important of which are the Lancang, Nujiang, and Jinsha. Green river valleys, lush forests, and majestic mountains create a spectacular landscape, particularly in the area around Erhai Lake, where most of the Bai people are concentrated.

ORIGINS

Archaeological finds indicate that the Erhai area was inhabited as early as the Neolithic Age (from 7000 to 3000 years B.C.E.). Stone implements from that period provide evidence that people had agricultural skills and practiced small-scale farming to supplement fishing and hunting. After this period the exact origins of the Bai remain unclear. During some eras they have been assumed to be of Tai descent while their language points to Tibeto-Burman origins; however, the great number of Chinese features also point to a lengthy Sinitic past.

HISTORY

The ancient history of the Bai is a contested domain for historians and ethnologists both inside and outside China. Some attribute Bai origins to the ancient Diqiang people of Yunnan, who are also the ancestors of the contemporary NAXI. Others claim the Bai may have started developing an identity of their own toward the end of the third century B.C.E. when their Kunming tribal ancestors, who inhabited the Lake Erhai region, came into contact with the Han people from the neighboring regions of China. Gradually the Kunming mixed with the Han and evolved into the Bai ethnic group.

In 109 B.C.E. the Han dynasty sent imperial administrators to the city of Dali on Erhai Lake and a substantial number of Han people settled in this area.

Despite China's political interference, the Bai were able to maintain their independence and in 729 C.E. the Kingdom of Nanzhao was formed by the unification of six small Bai kingdoms. The leader of one of these small kingdoms, Pi-lo-ko (also called Piluoge or Pileguo), invaded and conquered the five neighboring kingdoms with the acquiescence of China, which needed a buffer state to secure itself against hostile TIBETANS. He named himself Nan Zhao, or prince of the south, and his kingdom retained that name. Unfortunately it did not take long for China to feel the new kingdom to be as great a threat as the Tibetans had been and the Chinese attacked in 751 and again three years later. The choice of Dali as the capital of Nanzhao was providential, for natural barriers protected the city from being taken over by force and both Chinese attacks were defeated.

The Nanzhao kingdom was able to control the east-west trade routes from China to India. As a result of this trade, as well as the sale of woven silk and cotton, the kingdom grew in economic prosperity. Salt and gold mines also provided extensive incomes for the state, while slaves were used for hard labor and farmers paid high taxes and were forced to perform various duties, including compulsory military service. Nanzhao adopted an expansionist policy and in 829 conquered the city of Chengdu, taking control of the Sichuan region. The kingdom also expanded temporarily into contemporary Myanmar in 832 and Vietnam in 862. The kingdom reached its peak in that decade and then was forced to retreat back to Yunnan in 873.

In 902 the Nanzhao kingdom was brought to an end by slave rebellions and uprisings, which led to the creation of a smaller kingdom, called the Kingdom of Dali. This kingdom lasted for more than 300 years (937–1253) until it was conquered by the MONGOLS in 1253 and fell under the rule of the Yuan dynasty. In order to strengthen their control over Dali, the Yuan rulers established a feudal system whereby the land was mainly concentrated in the hands of the local aristocracy.

The Ming dynasty (1368–1644) took power from the Yuan rulers in 1381 and appointed court officials to rule the Bai territories. This reform weakened the political and economic privileges of the local lords, freed the slaves, and gave the peasants incentives for farming the land. In addition to the continuation of the Ming policy the subsequent Qing dynasty (1644–1911) also appointed local officials and chieftains as public administrators. This system of government led to the reintroduction of feudal privileges and to the exploitation and oppression of many Bai people until the establishment in 1956 of the Dali Bai Autonomous Prefecture as part of the People's Republic of China.

CULTURE

Economy and Society

Most Bai people are subsistence farmers and herders living off what they grow and raise themselves. The cultivation of rice is central to most agricultural activity, but wheat, vegetables, tobacco, and fruit are also significant crops that together with rice provide the economic basis for many families. Groups of families work together in all agricultural activity and had done so long before the imposition of Communist Party doctrines about communal labor. The Bai, unlike the Han or most other Chinese minority groups, also make two kinds of cheese, from the milk of cows and goats. Both kinds are seen as special ceremonial foods to be prepared and eaten for special occasions. The Bai serve the leftover whey from the cheese-making process to their pigs. Those who live around Erhai Lake, which is about 25 miles long and five miles wide, are also excellent fishermen.

Marble mining and tombstone carving are other sources of income for many Bai men. Dali marble is famous throughout Asia and among collectors of gemstones all over the world. For a few square inches of Shuimohuashi, a particularly precious type of marble, dealers in Hong Kong or Shanghai can charge up to $20,000. For more than 1,000 years Dali has been known as the town of marble; indeed, the Chinese word *dali* means "marble." Some traditional Bai villages are also known for their exquisite blue-dyed cloth, which is created in family-operated workshops by women and men alike. Finally some Bai living in the Cangshan Mountains, adjacent to their lakeside territory, also make money by cutting wood and making charcoal.

The Bai social structure recognizes two important units, the extended family, usually consisting of a couple and their married sons and their children, and the village. Village members work together to farm the land, mine the marble, and fish in the lake. Villagers also tend to

BAI

location:
Dali Bai Autonomous Prefecture in the western region of Yunnan Province

time period:
Possibly third century B.C.E. to the present

ancestry:
Bai origins are heavily contested. Some believe that Bai ancestors were called Kunming during the Qin and Han dynasties (third century B.C.E.) and later became known as Heman, Baiman, and Bairen. Others claim the Bai are the descendants of the Diqiang tribes of Yunnan. Significant mixing with the Han has also occurred throughout time.

language:
Bai, a language belonging to the Tibeto-Burman branch of the Sino-Tibetan language group. Chinese is also widely spoken among the Bai people today.

Bai time line

B.C.E.

third century A tribal community called Kunming may have developed ties with the Han people and gradually evolved into the Bai ethnic group.

109 The Han dynasty set up a county administration and many Han people move into the Bai territories.

C.E.

729 The Nanzhao kingdom is formed. Pi-lo-ko, the leader of one small tribal kingdom, extends his control over five neighboring kingdoms with the support of the Tang dynasty of China.

750 The Nanzhao kingdom rebels against the Tang.

751 The Tang sends an army against the Nanzhao kingdom and is soundly defeated at Xiaguan.

754 The Tang sends another army and is defeated again.

829 Nanzhao conquers the city of Chengdu and takes control of the Sichuan region.

873 Nanzhao is expelled from Sichuan and retreats back to Yunnan.

902 Slave rebellions and uprisings bring the Nanzhao kingdom to an end.

937 A new regime known as the Kingdom of Dali is established.

1253 The Mongols conquer the Kingdom of Dali and establish the Yuan dynasty.

1381 The Ming dynasty takes power from the Yuan rulers.

1644 The Qing dynasty replaces the Ming and appoints local officials to rule over the Bai.

1956 The Dali Bai Autonomous Prefecture is founded as part of the People's Republic of China.

eat together, at least during the day, making the village an important unit of both production and consumption. Family groups constitute the primary units of reproduction and of some activities, such as cloth dying and some cooking; they can also function as units of production and consumption in some contexts. Unlike in most other Chinese ethnic groups, women in Bai culture are not treated as second-class citizens and it is not considered a family tragedy to have daughters and no sons.

As this example of gender illustrates, the Bai people have created a rich culture of their own within the Chinese context. A central symbol for this culture is the color white. Many like to wear white cloths and use the color in their design schemes. *Bai* actually means "white" in Chinese, and possibly the Bai drew their name from this word. Another plausible source of this name is the white sheepskin many Bai women wear over their shoulder as a symbol of their chastity and industriousness.

The Bai are also known for their singing and dancing, particularly during the many festive events they hold each year. Their major festivals are the Raosanlin (Walking Around Three Souls), which is celebrated in spring and is an occasion for men and women of all ages to show off their singing and dancing skills; the Torch Festival at the end of June, when torches are lit everywhere to usher in an abundant harvest; the Shibaoshan Mountain Song Festival; and, above all, the Third Month Fair, which takes place each mid-March at the foot of Diancang Hill to the west of Dali City. For centuries this celebration has been an exhibition of livestock and in more recent times has grown into a big community festival attracting tens of thousands of people to its horse races and other events.

Religion

The spiritual doctrines of Buddhism and Taoism as well as the Confucian philosophical system have all deeply affected the religious outlook and practices of the Bai people. Buddhism has been especially important since the seventh century, and many Buddhist monasteries and temples are located in the Bai region, particularly in the Dali area, such as the convent of Hai Yanan and the Chongsheng Temple in Dali with its three pagodas. The three ancient pagodas of Chongsheng Temple are emblematic of the great architectural skills of the Bai people. Built more than 1,000 years ago, the 16-story main tower is 197 feet high and still stands in its majestic beauty. The Buddhist goddess of mercy, Guanyin, also plays a special role in many Bai myths. She is believed to have killed a demon that put out people's eyes and then ate them. This deed is celebrated at the Bai Third Month Fair.

Despite this attachment to Buddhism the Bai also have their own indigenous religion, worship of a divinity called Benzhu (village god, local lord, or master of the area). Each community has its own Benzhu god, usually a local figure from history such as a warrior, hero, or learned philosopher. These gods are believed to confer good fortune on the Bai by protecting crops and animals, preventing injury and illness, and fostering peace and prosperity. Every community performs regular rituals at its Benzhu shrine, honoring the local god before every major event, at the New Year, and on the village's particular Benzhu's birthday.

FURTHER READING

C. P. Fitzgerald. *The Tower of Five Glories: A Study of the Min Chia of Ta Li, Yunnan* (London: Cresset Press, 1941).

Baiyue (Hundred Yue, Viet, Wu-Yue, Yue)

There are two possibly related usages of the term *Yue* in ancient Chinese history. The first was the Yue kingdom, which was located in what is today northern Zhejiang and southern Anhui Provinces and existed from sometime before 510 B.C.E. until it was defeated by the Chu in about 333 B.C.E. From about 482 B.C.E. to 473 B.C.E. Yue was also under the sovereignty of the rival Wu kingdom but reasserted its autonomy in a three-year war against Wu, during which Yue became the dominant power in the region with Wu as its vassal. The second use of *Yue* was as a collective term in the period of Chinese history after 333 B.C.E. and lasting to the end of the HAN dynasty in 220 C.E., to refer to the "barbarians" who lived to the south of the empire's territory in China's central plains region; a comparable term, HU, referred to northerners. The use of *Baiyue* or "Hundred Yue" in this period has indicated to many scholars that it originally designated the many small principalities established throughout the south by former Yue nobles who were driven out by the invading Chu armies. However, the extensive use of the term for peoples in geographic regions well beyond that of the original Yue kingdom, such as in Guangdong, Guizhou, and Guangxi Provinces, has meant for many historians that by the start of the Han dynasty in 206 B.C.E. *Yue* had lost its original connotation and was simply a collective noun for "southerners." As such the Baiyue did not share a language or culture but were simply related in terms of geography and marginality with regard to imperial Chinese culture of the time.

Although they differed in terms of language and culture, one similarity that does link the various Baiyue cultures is the centrality of wet rice agriculture for their subsistence and state economies. Even as early as the Yue kingdom, wet rice agriculture created the food surplus that allowed for the raising of an army, class differentiation, and occupational specialization. Similar pottery patterns, which were stamped with geometric shapes; stone axes; and other material remains also link some of these small groups.

This history of state-based social organization continued throughout the entire Baiyue period, when a multitude of small states emerged, dominated a region for a period, and then disintegrated without a trace. All were defeated by the Han emperor Wu or Wudi in his southern campaign starting in about 112 B.C.E.,

but the peoples and societies that bore the name *Baiyue* continued to be referred to as such for the remainder of the Han period.

Three of the larger Yue states prior to Han Wudi's conquest were Nam Yue, which emerged in what is today northern Vietnam; Min Yue in Fuzhou; and Nan Yue in Guangdong and Guangxi Provinces. The last of these groups was largely mythological in China until 1983, when excavations in Guangdong revealed the enormous tomb of the state's second king and verified its existence. Since that period several local and national exhibits of Baiyue artifacts have been collected, chronicled, and displayed in museums from Hong Kong to Beijing. They have served to reinforce strong local identities and histories of the many contemporary national minorities that count the Yue as among their ancestors, including the MAONAN and DONG.

Bajau *See* SEA GYPSIES.

Bali Aga (Bali Mula, Old Balinese)

The Bali Aga are the remnants of Bali's original AUSTRONESIANS who escaped into the hills when the island came under direct Majapahit JAVANESE control in the mid-14th century; their name means "original Balinese" or "Old Balinese." This conquest produced tremendous changes for the local people, many of which are still evident today in BALINESE society, such as cremation, the caste system, and other aspects of social hierarchy. Sometimes the Bali Aga are depicted as the descendants of Bali's original Austronesian population before it had any interactions with the Hindu Javanese; however, this does not seem to be quite accurate. The Bali Aga are nominally Hindu but apparently withdrew into the hills when the Majapahit dynasty took over Bali in 1343. Since that time the Bali Aga have eschewed most interactions with outsiders as a way of maintaining their traditional way of life. Today they make up a very small percentage of the island's population, living primarily in two main villages, Trunyan near the shores of Lake Batur, and Tenganan near the Dasa temple in eastern Bali.

One of the most commented-upon aspects of Bali Aga society is their death ritual. Rather than cremating their dead, as is the case throughout the rest of the Hindu world, the Bali Aga weather the corpses of married people in bamboo cages under a sacred banyan tree; those who die prior to marriage are buried. Once the weathered corpse has been reduced

BAIYUE

location:
South China and Vietnam

time period:
Before 510 B.C.E. to 220 C.E.

ancestry:
Non-Han southerners

language:
Probably a variety of Austro-Asiatic, Tai-Kadai, Tibeto-Burman, and Hmong-Mien languages

BALI AGA

location:
A few small villages on Bali, Indonesia

time period:
About 1343 to the present

ancestry:
Balinese

language:
Highland Balinese, a dialect of the Austronesian Balinese language

A Bali Aga cemetery in Kuban, Indonesia, near Trunyan, where skulls of the deceased are displayed following the weathering of the corpse under the fragrant banyan tree. *(Getty Images/Dimas Ardian/ Stringer)*

BALINESE

location:
Bali, Indonesia, as well as other islands in the archipelago

time period:
About 2500 B.C.E. to the present

language:
Balinese, an Austronesian language

to a skeleton, the skull and other bones are removed and put onto a village altar for display. Despite the presence of several corpses at a time in Bali's hot and humid climate, outsiders have frequently commented that the weathering place does not smell bad, because of the powerful aroma of the surrounding banyan tree.

In addition to their unique funereal practice, the Bali Aga are known for their cloth making and ritual of blood sacrifice, *mekare kare*. This event requires villagers to fight each other ritually with bundles of leaves. Two people square off against each other and scratch at each other's skin with the bundles until one begins to bleed. Then a mediator steps in and stops the fight, usually after five to ten minutes, and the vanquished person's wounds are treated. Once the entire village has participated in this event, they all partake in an elaborate feast with food, music, and rice or palm wine; this communal festival must follow the shedding of the blood.

The Bali Aga of Tenganan are also renowned weavers who produce *geringsing*, a double-ikat cloth, that is, one in which the fibers are all dyed before weaving so that when woven together they bleed into one another to make new and unique designs. The technique is very difficult and can take months; as a result the fabric is very expensive and a good source of external income to contemporary villagers, who are less exclusive than their ancestors, who would have nothing to do with outsiders. Most families possess *geringsing* heirlooms, usually in black-and-white check patterns believed to protect their owners from evil spirits and thus used to shroud important familial statues or altars.

Balinese

The Balinese are the dominant population on the Indonesian island of Bali. Because their island is a popular tourist destination their culture and economy have been affected in significant ways.

GEOGRAPHY

Bali, an island of about 2,240 square miles, is located east of Java and about 8° south of the equator in the Indonesian Archipelago. It enjoys a tropical climate with average temperatures in the 80s. The period from April to September is less humid and receives less rainfall than the remainder of the year, which is significantly wetter and more humid.

The main geographic features of the small island are its mountainous western region and the string of volcanoes that runs from east to west through the center of the island. The volcanos are a blessing to the island for the fertile soils and beautiful black sands they have left behind, but they have also caused significant tragedy, as in 1963, when Gunung Agung erupted and killed about 1,000 people.

ORIGINS

The origins of the Balinese, as of all AUSTRONESIANS in Indonesia, are probably in south China, from which they sailed in double-outrigger dugout canoes about 5,000 years ago to Taiwan, and then later to the Philippines, Indonesia, and Polynesia. They probably entered the various islands of Indonesia between 2500 and 2000 B.C.E. This second wave, with its red slipped pottery, may also have been the ultimate source of the LAPITA CULTURE. In addition to pottery, the Austronesians took agriculture with

them; the most important crop then as now was wet rice.

HISTORY

The Austronesian population on Bali probably lived in small-scale, kinship-based societies on their island until after the fifth century C.E. They established extensive irrigation networks throughout the island's plains region, which are still used today, and fished in the island's surrounding coral reefs. In the fifth century travelers from Java began to affect Balinese society greatly. They introduced Hindu-Buddhist-style religions and political structures, language, and Indianized script and began to transform Bali into the society we know today. This period of transformation took many centuries to accomplish but came to fruition in about 1010, when

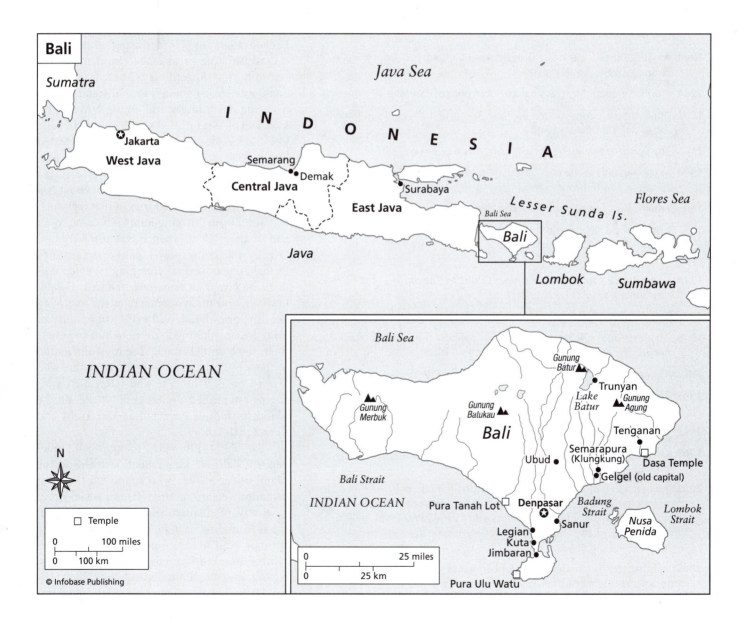

© Infobase Publishing

Airlangga, heir of the Balinese king and a JA-VANESE queen, united his people with those of east Java. In this period the Balinese language began to take on significant aspects of Javanese and both the arts and politics became more Javanese in character; it was in this period that the heavy emphasis on etiquette and hierarchy was adopted on Bali, and these remain central to the culture today.

Balinese time line

B.C.E.

2500 Period in which the Austronesian people first land on Bali.

C.E.

fifth–seventh centuries Javanese travelers begin to transform Balinese society by means of their religion and social order.

1010 Airlangga unites Bali and east Java, setting the stage for further cultural syncretism.

1049 Airlangga dies; a period of struggle to remain independent from the Javanese begins on the island.

1284 Bali is conquered by the Singhasari kingdom of east Java.

1292 Approximate year when the Balinese Pejeng dynasty of Ubud liberates the island from the Javanese.

1343 The Javanese Majapahit dynasty conquers Bali once again.

1500 Majapahit falls to the Muslim sultanate of Demak and many of Java's Hindu nobles relocate to Bali.

16th century Batu Renggong unifies Bali under the Gelgel kingdom.

1597 Cornelius de Houtman is the first European to land on Bali; two of his Dutch sailors refuse to leave with their ship because of the island's beauty.

1710 The Balinese capital is moved from Gelgel to Klungkung, or contemporary Semarapura.

1846 The Dutch conquer the northern, lesser Balinese kingdoms.

1908 After the ritual suicide of thousands of Balinese princes and other nobles, the Dutch finally conquer the entire island.

1942–45 Japanese occupation of Bali during World War II.

1945 The Dutch return, sparking a civil war between those who support independence and those who support their return.

1949 Indonesian independence.

1963 Gunung Agung erupts, killing about 1,000 people but sparing an important religious shrine, the temple of Besakih.

2002 A nightclub frequented by Western tourists in Kuta, Bali, is bombed by Islamic radicals and places Indonesia at the forefront of the so-called war on terror, especially from the point of view of Australia, which lost 88 citizens in the bombing. Altogether more than 200 people are killed.

2005 Another series of bombings, in Jimbaran and Kuta, kills about 20 more people, including Australians, other tourists, and locals.

Airlangga died in 1049, and for several hundred years afterward the rulers of the Balinese kingdoms struggled to remain independent from the larger and stronger kingdoms of east and central Java. Often they were successful, but in 1284 Bali was conquered by the east Javanese kingdom of Singhasari, which held it for only about eight years. The Balinese freed themselves again under kings of the Pejeng dynasty of Ubud, the greatest of whom was Dalem Bedaulu. In Balinese artwork Bedaulu is often depicted with a pig's head, for which there are several legendary explanations. According to one story, Bedaulu showed such stubbornness toward Majapahit that he was nicknamed pig head; according to another, Bedaulu was simply grandstanding, cutting off his own head and replacing it to display his supernatural powers. Eventually the Hindu god Siva became annoyed with Bedaulu's activities and pushed his severed head into a river. As a replacement Bedaulu's servant provided a pig's head, which caused the king great embarrassment for the rest of his life. Regardless of these legends Bedaulu was strong enough to withstand attacks from the much larger and stronger Majapahit kingdom of Java for several years but did finally lose his kingdom when Gajah Mada defeated him in 1343. At the end of the century the Majapahit kings moved their capital from east Java to Gelgel on Bali, setting the stage for about 200 years of strong Balinese kings in that region.

The Majapahit kingdom itself came to an end in about 1500, when it was conquered on Java by the rising power of the sultanate of Demak, one of several emerging Islamic kingdoms on Java. Bali remained staunchly Hindu, however, and many members of the surviving nobility, priesthood, and artist community of Java's Majapahit kingdom fled to Bali and made their home on the island. The most influential of these refugees was the priest Nirartha, who arrived on Bali in 1546 and is credited with having established a number of temples on the island, including Pura Luhur Ulu Watu and Pura Tanah Lot.

For about 100 years many small, independent Balinese kingdoms flourished on the island under leaders who supported the most orthodox version of their Hindu social order as a way of distinguishing themselves from the surrounding islands, which largely became strongly Muslim in this period. The most powerful of these kings was Batu Renggong or Dewa Agung, who rose to power in about 1550 in Gelgel. He briefly reunited these small kingdoms under his own rule and held territory on several surrounding islands, including Lombok and Sumbawa. Batu Renggong's grandson, however, was not the powerful force that his grandfather had been and lost all of the dynasty's territory outside Bali. He subsequently lost his entire kingdom when his more powerful chief minister supplanted him in 1650. But the minister was not able to consolidate his power into a ruling dynasty, and by 1686 the Gelgel dynasty was back on the throne in the person of Dewa Agung Jambe, Batu Renggong's great-grandson. He moved the kingdom's capital to Klungkung, which today bears the name of Jambe's own palace, *Semarapura* or House of the God of Love. The move did not strengthen the kingdom in the face of many lesser kingdoms and set the stage for European colonization in the 19th and 20th centuries.

Europeans landed on Bali in 1597 when the first Dutch explorer in the region, de Houtman, landed there during the course of his first mission to the archipelago. Despite Bali's climatic and geographic delights, which caused two of the original Dutch sailors to abandon their ship to remain on the island, the Dutch took little interest in the small island because it was not a source of great wealth in spices, gold, or other resources. Eventually, however, the Dutch added the island to their large East Indies colony through a long period of conquest over the small kingdoms that ruled each locality. They began in the north in 1846 and by 1908 had conquered the entire island. Rather than accept defeat or exile, many of the local kings, princes, and other nobility committed ritual suicide, called *puputan,* either by turning their ritual daggers on themselves or by marching directly into the line of fire of the modern weapons wielded by the Dutch. Despite their victories, however, the Dutch continued to ignore their new island paradise in favor of the more lucrative regions on Java, Lombok, and elsewhere. As a result of this colonial neglect ordinary Balinese would have noticed few differences from the precolonial era. Most continued to work their subsistence rice farms, pray to their Hindu gods, and maintain strict separation of classes and other aspects of the rigid etiquette system.

The Dutch remained the direct rulers of Bali for the first half of the 20th century, until the island was conquered by the JAPANESE in 1942 as part of their Pacific strategy during World War II. After the war the Balinese population was split between those who supported Indo-

Tanah Lot Temple, probably built by Nirartha, a Hindu priest who fled to Bali from Java in the mid-16th century. *(Shutterstock/Thomas Pozzo di Borgo)*

nesian independence as it had been declared in 1945 and those who supported a return by the Dutch. The ensuing civil war throughout the archipelago was won by the forces for independence and Indonesia was declared a free country in late 1949.

Throughout the late 20th century Bali gained an image as a popular tourist destination and many outsiders' view of Indonesia is based entirely on time spent on the beaches at Kuta, Legian, Sanur, and many other places, all easily reached from the capital at Denpasar. The money provided by these tourists has made the island one of the wealthiest in the country, but it has also produced significant cultural change, ecological damage, and, in the early 21st century, unwanted attention from Islamic radicals from other regions of Indonesia. Bombings in Kuta and elsewhere on the island in 2002 and 2005 killed hundreds of people, injured many more, and made many Westerners reluctant to visit the so-called island paradise. Many Balinese strongly resent this turn of events, especially since they themselves tend to be Hindu and fairly secular in background rather than Muslim, as is the case throughout most of the rest of the country.

An outpouring of grief and sympathy at a prayer service in Kuta, Bali, following the October 2002 bombing of the Sari nightclub. *(AP/John Stanmeyer/VII)*

CULTURE

For the better part of 4,500 years the economic base upon which Balinese culture has developed has been wet rice agriculture. This crop and its attendant technology were imported to Indonesia with the migrations of Austronesians and have remained central to many people's lives ever since. Vast irrigation networks were established in the centuries before the common era, and many are still in use today. The slopes of Bali's many mountains were terraced and formed into paddies in the centuries that followed to expand greatly the amount of land available to farmers. Today double cropping is common, and even triple cropping is possible in some areas with the use of new seeds and fertilizers. Despite these advancements, however, most farming on Bali remains traditional since tractors and other technology are available only in level areas; water buffaloes and human labor continue to be the only ways to work the many hillside and steep terraced farms. In addition to rice western Bali has become a producer of coffee for the international market, and other subsistence and cash products include tea, tobacco, cocoa, corn, cloves, tamarind, vanilla, soybeans, coconuts, chilies, fruits, and vegetables. Most households also keep water buffaloes for their labor, pigs and chickens for food, and a cock or two for fighting, a common male activity.

Although many Balinese still work primarily in agriculture, tourism and its related craft, service, and trade employment are also very important to most families. Woodcarving, goldsmithing, and textile production make up some of the more traditional crafts that are produced and sold to tourists through private shops or large cooperatives, while the many hotels and resorts all hire local women and men as maids, gardeners, cooks, and other service personnel.

The Balinese social structure is made up of four separate castes, Brahmanas, Satrias, Wesias, and Shudras. Originally as in Hindu India these castes reflected different occupational groups; priests were from the first group and farmers the last while political leaders and merchants made up the middle levels. The Shudras are by far the largest of these castes with about 90 percent of the population, but it is no longer the case that all Shudras are farmers. Nonetheless during important village rituals each caste is responsible for certain events and activities, and thus both the classification and its hierarchical underpinnings have not been lost in the present day. Lower-caste individuals still bow to their superiors and many other aspects of social hierarchy remain central to being a good Balinese person.

The Balinese language is one area where these status differences are strongly articulated. Balinese is an Austronesian language, closely related to that of the SASAK of Lombok Island and to Javanese, and has at least three different politeness levels that are reflected in both vocabulary and grammar structure. The highest level, *tinggi*, is used only with Brahmana priests; the middle or refined level, *halus*, is used with higher-caste-status individuals, parents, or those who are older than one; and the low or ordinary level, *biasa*, is for speaking with peers, younger people, or caste inferiors. The Balinese naming system is a form of teknonymy that is also indicative of relative status. Many children are given names indicating their birth order within the family, and then at adulthood most people's names change to indicate their generation; parents are called Father or Mother of the name of their first child and grandparents are called Grandfather or Grandmother of the name of their first grandchild. In addition to refraining from expressing strong emotions, especially negative ones like anger, frustration, or fear, maintaining proper language and etiquette within the hierarchical system is extremely important for Balinese adults; not to do these things draws great shame on both individuals and their families.

In addition to caste Balinese society is divided into many different kinship groups determined through the principle of patrilineal descent, where membership in the group is inherited from one's father, father's father, and so on. Nonetheless one's mother's relatives are also important during one's lifetime, and most people participate in household and even more extensive ritual events with their immediate relatives from both sides. Twice yearly larger kinship groups meet together to perform ritual events for their ancestors, both to thank them for their contributions to the contemporary generations and to prevent their anger, which can lead to illness or other forms of misfortune.

At marriage most Balinese women move out of their natal homes and into those of their husbands. Ideally at least in the past women did not marry men from lower caste or class groupings; that system led to a form of temple group endogamy in some villages where distant cousins married each other to guarantee that they were from the same caste and class. In the few situations where women married men of a higher caste, they became members of their husband's caste at marriage. Today intercaste marriages are much more common, especially in urban areas, but the guidelines about

women's marrying up instead of down have remained important for some families.

Generally Balinese households are made up of several generations and are defined strictly on the basis of sharing food; living in the same home is not necessary. The traditional pattern was that all sons inherited land from their father, while one of them remained behind in the family home, took care of his parents in their old age, and then inherited the house as well. In families without a son fathers could nominate one of their daughters to be the family heir, in which case she and her husband would remain in the house and care for her parents into their old age. Otherwise the man's brothers would divide his estate upon his death.

As some of these rules indicate, Balinese women were traditionally seen as inferior to men but not severely so and this remains the case today. Men and women share many agricultural tasks and women are important for the proper undertaking of all religious rituals, although never as priests. Menstruating women are considered ritually impure and are banned from temples, but women are extremely important to the household economy as agricultural workers, marketers, and, today, employees. Women care for children and the elderly, cook, prepare ritual offerings, tend pigs and chickens, and often are responsible for the household budget.

Balinese households are located within larger residential units or villages, defined not by geography but by membership in the village temple. These are Hindu temples where individuals and households pray that the good and evil forces in the world remain in balanced harmony. Village temples as well as household shrines are sites for offerings to gods and demons, ancestral spirits, and natural spirits, such as the rice goddess. Other supernatural beings in the Balinese cosmology include *leyak* or witches, who are believed to be human by day but disembodied spirits by night and can inhabit the bodies of monkeys, birds, or even just a ghostly light or sound. They are extremely frightening, and both amulets and mantras can be purchased from priests and shamans to combat the human or animal illness, crop failure, or other misfortunes they cause when angry.

FURTHER READING

Clifford Geertz. *Negara: The Theatre State in Nineteenth Century Bali* (Princeton, N.J.: Princeton University Press, 1980).

Clifford Geertz and Hildred Geertz. *Kinship in Bali* (Chicago: University of Chicago Press, 1975).

Robert Pringle. *A Short History of Bali: Indonesia's Hindu Realm* (New York: Allen & Unwin, 2004).
J. L. Swellengrebel et al. *Bali: Further Studies in Life, Thought, and Ritual* (The Hague: W. van Hoeve, 1969).

Balochi   See BALUCHI.

Baluchi (Baloc, Balochi)

The Baluchi are an Iranian-speaking people who live in a territory they call Baluchistan or Balochistan, which straddles Pakistan, Afghanistan, and Iran; there is also a Baluchi community in Turkmenistan. More than 70 percent of the Baluchi community resides in Pakistan, and it is largely in that country where the Baluchi have been struggling for autonomy or independence, although Iran's government has cracked down on Baluchi nationalist activities as well. Baluchi nationalism and claims for independence look back nine centuries to Mir Jalal Khan's confederation of 44 separate Baluchi tribes in the 12th century. Other important historical events often cited by the Baluchi nationalists are the 15th-century league united by Rind Laskhari, the 17th-century khanate of Baluchistan, and the independence that local Baluchi *sardars* or chieftains maintained during the era of British colonialism. Indeed during that period it was the British who paid tribute to the Baluchii chiefs in exchange for free passage into Afghanistan; therefore it came as a great surprise to these same chiefs that their independence had been denied to them in 1947 with the creation of Pakistan.

Surprise quickly turned into rebellion among the Baluchi, who began their first insurgency against the government of Pakistan in 1948. This was followed by four more attempts at freeing themselves from what they considered outside rule, in 1958, 1962, 1973–77, and recently in 2004. The most bloody and protracted of these insurgencies was in the mid-1970s, which began with the election of a Baluchi legislative body in 1972. The refusal of the Pakistani prime minister Zulfikar Ali Bhutto to recognize this body then led to about five years of fighting that killed at least 3,000 government soldiers, 5,000 insurgents, and many more civilians. This action came to an end only once General Muhammad Zia-ul-Haq ousted Bhutto and granted amnesty to the Baluchi fighters.

Since the events in 2004, which killed several hundred more fighters on both sides, the Pakistani government has used all of its international connections to the supposed "war on terror" to crack down on the people of Baluchistan. Six government army brigades and about 25,000 paramilitary soldiers have been deployed in the province, and about 450 local activists, politicians, and other leaders have been killed or have disappeared. One of those killed was Nawab Akbar Bugti, a 79-year-old tribal chief and former governor of the province. In addition locals claim that more than 4,000 civilians are being held in detention camps without being charged or tried, and close to 85,000 Baluchi have been displaced by the fighting in their territory. In reaction to these events, particularly the death of Bugti, current *sardar* or chieftain Mir Suleiman Dawood Khan called a *kirga* or tribal conference in 2006, the first kirga to take place in Baluchistan for 136 years. The tribal, community, and military leaders who attended decided to take their case for independence to the International Court of Justice at the Hague; there they would lay out the treaties signed with the British as well as the documentation of persecution and genocide in Pakistan in their bid for independence. Given the British Home Office's designation of the Balochistan Liberation Army as a terrorist organization because of its activities against the Pakistani government, this group's chances at the Hague seem slim at best. However, the group has expressed its confidence in the International Court to right decades of injustice and its willingness to work within the boundaries of international law, provided Pakistan's government is held to the same standards.

In addition to Baluchi nationalism, the other driving force behind the push for independence is the wealth in minerals and resources located in the province, which currently funnels wealth into the central government in Islamabad rather than into the hands of the local population, the poorest in Pakistan. Baluchistan is sparsely populated, with just 4 percent of Pakistan's population, but it has 36 percent of its gas reserves and more than 40 percent of its total energy in gas, coal, and electricity. Since 1953, however, when gas was first discovered, the Baluchi people have benefited very little from any of these resources or from the wealth they generate. Outsiders play key roles in all industry and the Baluchi people fear becoming poor minorities within their own land. The other major issue is that the region is important strategically as it has two-thirds of Pakistan's naval bases and it is where most of the U.S.-led attacks on the Taliban in Afghanistan were launched.

Bangladeshis: nationality   89

Culturally the Baluchi are Sunni Muslims who engage in both irrigated agriculture and pastoralism, the herding of animals, for economic gain. Dates and cereals such as wheat are the two main crops while goats, sheep, and cattle dominate the herders' way of life. Kinship is considered bilateral so that neither mother's nor father's relatives provide all ancestors and kin ties. However, there are different terms to refer to relatives on these two sides, with those from the father's side being related to the "back" and those from the mother's side related to the "belly." In the past it was also the father's relatives, *patrikin* as they are called, who provided the primary assistance in farming, herding, or warfare, while mother's relatives, *matrikin,* were described as providing more affection than assistance.

Ba Na   *See* BAHNAR.

Bangladeshis: nationality (people of Bangladesh)

GEOGRAPHY

Bangladesh borders India and Myanmar (Burma) and is bounded to the south by the Bay of Bengal. It covers an area roughly the same size as England and Wales combined. The country consists mainly of a delta created by the great rivers Ganges and Brahmaputra, which divide the country into six regions. The country is very flat, the only two exceptions being the hills around Sylhet in the northeast and the Chittagong Hills in the southeast. The river plains never rise more than 33 feet above sea level, making the country vulnerable to floods and cyclones that whip up the ocean, sending waves crashing onto coastal plains and islands. Its density of 1,585 people per square mile makes Bangladesh one of the most densely populated countries in the world.

INCEPTION AS A NATION

From 300 B.C.E. the Bengal region, today divided between Bangladesh and India, was part of the Mauryan empire, which spread over most of present-day India, Pakistan, and Bangladesh. The empire was ruled by Buddhist and, later, Hindu leaders. By 1000 C.E. Bengal had developed its own language and literature. Bengal was invaded and conquered by Turkish Muslims in 1202, and while Sufi religious teachers had previously succeeded in converting many Bengalis to Islam, the invasion of the Turks encouraged conversion and Islam became the dominant religion.

The Portuguese were the first European traders to land in Bengal, in the late 1500s, and they were closely followed by other Europeans. From the mid-1600s British influence over the region increased, and by 1760 all of Bengal was controlled by the British. Bengal was populated by both Hindu and Muslim communities, between which there was animosity. The fact that the British handed much of the administration of the colony to the Hindu ruling class increased the tension between Hindus and Muslims. In 1905 the colonial power divided Bengal into a Hindu-dominated province in the west and a Muslim-dominated province in the east. West Bengal, the Hindu-dominated province, was openly critical of the division, which led in 1906 to the creation of the All-India Muslim League to protect the interests of Muslims. When the British reunited the two provinces in 1912, the Muslims saw this act as a concession to the Hindus.

After Great Britain left India, including Bengal, in 1947, the country was divided along religious lines again. The new nation of Pakistan was created. East Bengal became East Pakistan (present-day Bangladesh), separated by nearly 950 miles of Indian territory from West Pakistan. The two Pakistans did not have a common culture or a common language and were inhabited by different ethnic groups; only Islam united the two. Furthermore Bangla, the language of East Pakistan, was not recognized by West Pakistan, which established its language, Urdu, as the official language. East Pakistanis felt increasingly neglected and exploited by the central government, which was located in the west, and in 1949 the Awami League was established to campaign for East Pakistan's autonomy. Anti–West Pakistani demonstrations were organized during the 1950s, and during the 1960s calls for independence were common.

In the 1970 elections the Awami League, led by Sheikh Mujib Rahman, won 167 of the 169 East Pakistan seats in the Pakistan national assembly. While this was enough to make the party the largest in the assembly, the West Pakistani military junta in power refused to recognize the election results. Talks began between Mujib and the junta, but while the talks were held, West Pakistan moved troops into East Pakistan. On March 26, 1971, Sheikh Mujib Rahman was taken prisoner by the West Pakistani army. The same day East Pakistan proclaimed its independence from West Pakistan, taking the name *Bangladesh.*

BANGLADESHIS: NATIONALITY

nation:
People's Republic of Bangladesh; Bangladesh

derivation of name:
From tribal names of the groups (Vanga, Banga, Bangala, Bangal, and Bengal) that settled in present-day Bangladesh in 1000 B.C.E.

government:
Republic with parliamentary democracy

capital:
Dhaka

language:
Bangla (also known as Bengali) 95 percent, tribal languages 5 percent

religion:
Muslim 88 percent; Hindu 11 percent; Buddhist 0.6 percent; Christian 0.3 percent

earlier inhabitants:
Dravidian-speaking people later known as the Bang settled the area in 1000 B.C.E.

demographics:
Bengali 98 percent, tribal groups and non-Bengali Muslims 2 percent

Bangladeshis: nationality time line

B.C.E.

1000 Dravidian-speaking peoples, who were later known as the Bang, settle the area.

320–180 The Mauryan empire is spread over most of present-day India, Pakistan, and Bangladesh.

C.E.

750 Gopala, a Buddhist chief, seizes power as the first ruler of the Pala dynasty. During the dynasty Bengal is united and Buddhism is spread throughout the state and into neighboring territories.

1202 Turkish Muslims invade and conquer Bengal and the Islamization of Bengal begins.

1341 Bengal becomes independent of Delhi, and Dhaka is established as the seat of the governors of independent Bengal.

1576 Dhaka is conquered by Mughal emperor Akbar the Great (1556–1605) and Bengal becomes a Mughal province.

1650 The British East India Company establishes a factory in Bengal.

1757 The British win Bengal from the Mughals.

1764 The British East India Company is granted the title of *diwan* (collector of revenues) in Bengal, making it the supreme governing power.

1857 Indian soldiers of the British army, mainly Muslim Bengalis, start a year-long insurrection against the British and offer their services to the Mughal emperor.

1858 The Muslim Bengali soldiers surrender and the Mughal Empire is formally ended.

The British East India Company is dissolved and the British assume direct control of India, including Bengal.

1905 The British governor-general, George, Lord Curzon, divides Bengal into a Muslim sector in the east and a Hindu sector in the west. The eastern sector has its capital at Dhaka while the western sector has its capital at Calcutta in present-day India.

1912 The British reunite the two sectors, a decision perceived by Muslims as a British concession to Hindu pressure.

1947 British colonial rule over India, and in extension over Bengal, ends.

The western part of Bengal becomes part of India, today the Indian state of West Bengal.

A largely Muslim state made up of East and West Pakistan is established on each side of India.

1949 The Awami League is organized to campaign for East Pakistan's autonomy from West Pakistan.

1970 The Awami League wins an overwhelming election victory in East Pakistan. The victory is not recognized by West Pakistan, leading to riots.

1971 The leader of the Awami League, Sheikh Mujib Rahman, is incarcerated in West Pakistan.

East Pakistan proclaims its independence on March 26, taking the name *Bangladesh* and sparking a war of independence. Ten million East Pakistanis, the majority Hindu, flee to India and more than 1 million people die during the war. West Pakistani troops are defeated in December with Indian assistance.

1972 Sheikh Mujib Rahman returns as Bangladesh's first prime minister, and a new constitution modeled on the Indian constitution is adopted. Bangladesh is to be founded on the four pillars of nationalism, secularism, socialism, and democracy.

1973 First national elections are held. The Awami League wins 282 of 289 seats.

1974 Pakistan officially recognizes Bangladesh.

1975 Prime Minister Mujib establishes himself as president and proclaims Bangladesh a one-party state, abolishing the parliamentary system. Bangladesh is transformed into a personal dictatorship. A series of coups follow, ending when General Zia Rahman assumes various governmental portfolios.

1976 Dr. Muhammad Yunus begins his microfinance program and founds the Grameen Bank, through which small loans are made available to groups of five women who guarantee one another's loans.

The military bans trade unions and General Zia Rahman makes himself chief martial-law administrator and postpones presidental and parliamentary elections.

1977 The constitution is altered to emphasize Bangladesh as a Muslim country.

1981 President Zia is assassinated during an unsuccessful military coup. Justice Abdul Sattar wins presidential elections.

1983 Prime Minister Ershad becomes president and limited political activity is allowed.

1988 Islam is established as Bangladesh's state religion.

1991 Bangladesh's constitution is changed to render the position of president cermonial and to give executive power to the prime minister.

Begum Khaleda Zia, widow of President Zia and leader of the Bangladesh National Party (BNP), becomes prime minister.

1992 Bangladeshi Muslim mobs attack Bangladeshi Hindus after Indian Hindu fundamentalists destroy a mosque in India.

1993 Author Taslima Nasreen publishes her novel *Shame* (in Bangla *Lajja*), in which she criticizes the 1992 Muslim attacks on Bangladeshi Hindus. Islamic fundamentalists impose a death sentence on the author, who is forced to flee the country.

1996 More than 100,000 Bangladeshi women rally to protest Islamic clerics' attack on female education and employment.

2000 The strained relationship with Pakistan is worsened when Prime Minister Hasina criticizes military regimes in a UN speech, prompting Pakistani president General Musharraf to cancel talks with her. Bangladesh expels a Pakistani diplomat for commenting that the number of dead during the 1971 war of independence was 26,000. According to Bangladesh nearly 3 million people were killed, and Bangladesh wants a Pakistani apology for what Bangladesh calls wartime genocide.

2001 Indian and Bangladeshi border soldiers clash, killing 16 Indians and three Bangladeshis.

Prime Minister Hasina becomes the first prime minister in the country's history to complete a five-year term. She steps down in July and hands over power to the caretaker authority that administers the country at the end of an outgoing government's term until the new government takes over.

Khaleda Zia and the Bangladesh National Party (BNP) win the elections together with three smaller coalition parties.

2002 Pakistani President General Musharraf visits Bangladesh and expresses regret over the atrocities carried out by Pakistan during the indpendence war of 1971.

2004 The Bangladeshi parliament amends the constitution to reserve 45 seats for female members.

2005 On August 17, 350 small bombs explode simultaneously across the country. A banned Islamic group claims responsibility for the attacks, which kill two and injure more than 100.

2006 The opposition party, the Awami League, ends its year-long parliamentary boycott.

The Awami League protests the government's choice of caretaker administration, which is to take over when President Zia completes her term at the end of October. Violent rallies occur and the opposition calls several strikes that halt traffic and close shops in all major towns and cities.

Dr. Muhammad Yunus receives the Nobel Prize in peace for his work with the Grameen Bank, which has given hundreds of thousands of poor Bangladeshis, the majority of whom are women, the opportunity to access small loans to improve their lives.

Muhammad Yunus in 2007 speaking about the Grameen Bank, the micro-credit scheme for which he won a Nobel Prize in 2006. *(AP/Koji Sasahara)*

Muhammed Ali Jinnah

Muhammed Ali Jinnah, a prominent Muslim politician, is best known as the founder of Pakistan and today is remembered by Pakistanis as "Father of the Nation." Prior to Bangladeshi independence in 1971, it was governed as part of Pakistan, formally known as East Pakistan.

Born on December 25, 1876, into a prominent Shia Muslim family in British India, Jinnah received his education in India. Following the receipt of his law degree Jinnah moved to London to practice his profession; there he became acutely aware of racist attitudes toward Indians among the English. In 1913 Jinnah joined the All India Muslim League and was instrumental in negotiating the Lucknow Pact between the league and the Indian National Congress, which stipulated an agreement to pressure the British government to step back and allow home rule in India. In 1918 Jinnah entered into direct conflict with another British-educated Indian lawyer named Mohandas Gandhi, who encouraged civil disobedience as the most efficient means of obtaining independence. Gandhi rejected Western norms, wearing the traditional Indian dhoti and shawl and avoiding the use of the English language when possible, and Jinnah feared that Gandhi's religious devotion would widen the rift between Indian Hindus and Indian Muslims. In 1929 Jinnah drafted the "Fourteen Points of Jinnah," a proposition for constitutional reform that would protect Muslims' political rights, but the proposition was rejected by the congress. In the 1930s Jinnah began to espouse the belief that Muslims and Hindus could not coexist within the same state as any attempt to do so would alienate and repress Muslims; he proposed the Two Nation Theory, which pushed for an autonomous Muslim state to be carved out of the Muslim-populated areas of British India. Jinnah's hopes were realized in 1946, when the British Cabinet Mission to India called for the partitioning of India among religious groups. The plan was met with violent dissent among Indians, but in 1947 Muhammed Ali Jinnah became governor-general of Pakistan, which he governed until his death of tuberculosis the following year.

The independence proclamation sparked a brutal war. The Pakistani army expelled foreign journalists from the country, and on the first day of the war the army systematically killed several hundred people in Dhaka, concentrating its operations in the University of Dhaka and the Hindu area of the old town. By March 28 only two days after the independence proclamation, 15,000 Bangladeshis are estimated to have been killed. The army also carried out systematic rapes of Bangladeshi women. In December 1971 India deployed troops to stop the war, and within two weeks the Pakistani army was forced to surrender. However, during the nine months of the war 10 million Bangladeshis, the majority of them Hindu, fled to India and more than a million people died.

Bangladeshi expectations after the war were enormous and many spoke about Sonar Bangla (the Golden Bengal), which could now be established, but problems soon arose. The new regime was unable to keep corruption at bay and by 1975 a one-party state had been established.

Sheikh Mujib Rahman, Bangladesh's first prime minister and later president, was assassinated in a military coup the same year. Political violence has always been widespread in the region, and Bangladeshis have experienced the assassinations of two presidents as well as three successful military coups and 18 coup attempts.

CULTURAL IDENTITY

Religion, particularly Islam, plays a major role in Bangladeshi cultural identity. The country has one of the largest concentrations of Muslims in the world, and a Bangladeshi not uncommonly starts a conversation with a foreigner by asking what religion he or she is. Everyone is expected to have a religion and to practice it actively. Many Bangladeshis find it next to impossible to grasp the concept of atheism. This cultural feature has become more important politically since independence. In the 1970s and 1980s the secular Bangladeshi constitution was amended several times to include a commitment to an Islamic way of life, despite the country's sizable Hindu minority. Although orthodox Islam and Islamic fundamentalism are uncommon and Muslim Bangladeshis mix their religion with pre-Islamic culture, most follow the Islamic rule of near-total separation of nonrelated women and men, which has a profound impact on Bangladeshi life and behavior. In 1992 religion was again at the forefront, when Hindu fundamentalists destroyed a mosque in India and Bangladeshi Muslims then attacked Hindus. Taslima Nasreen described the attacks in her 1993 book *Shame* (in Bangla, *Lajja*), about a Bangladeshi Hindu family's experience of the attacks. Islamic fundamentalists imposed a death sentence on Nasreen, who was forced to flee the country.

Other key concepts in Bangladeshi cultural identity are nature and rural life, as most Bangladeshis live in rural areas, with 54 percent of the population deriving their income from agriculture. Even those who have migrated to the cities for one reason or another have strong connections to the villages they or their families once lived in; being able to return to the home village is of great importance to most Bangladeshis.

While Bangladesh does not have a long history of independence, the Bengali culture goes back thousands of years, and Bangladeshis identify themselves with their Bengali past and are proud of Bengali poetry, music, literature, and fine arts. These aspects of the Bangladeshi culture unite them as a people. At the same time Bangladesh is a poor country, and poverty, inequality, and other differences between rich and poor also play a large role in the Bangladeshi cultural identity. While a minority of Bangladeshis are wealthy and can afford large houses, servants, and holidays overseas, half the population lives in poverty; in 2006 the average yearly income was only $456 per person. Despite this situation most people accept conditions as they are and think that the Bengali past unites all Bangladeshis, rich or poor.

See also BENGALIS.

FURTHER READING

Betsy Hartmann and James Boyce. *A Quiet Violence: View from a Bangladesh Village* (London: Zed Press, 1983).

Akbar Ali Khan. *Discovery of Bangladesh: Explorations into Dynamics of a Hidden Nation* (Dhaka, Bangladesh: University Press, 1996).

James J. Novak. *Bangladesh: Reflection on the Water* (Bloomington: Indiana University Press, 1993).

Aminur Rahman. *Women and Microcredit in Rural Bangladesh: An Anthropological Study of Grameen Bank Lending* (Boulder, Colo.: Westview Press, 1999).

Jeremy Seabrook. *Freedom Unfinished: Fundamentalism and Popular Resistance in Bangladesh Today* (London: Zed Books, 2001).

Bataks (Batta, Battak)

The Bataks are a loose confederation of related ethnolinguistic groups in central and northern Sumatra, Indonesia; they are not related to the significantly smaller Batak community of the Philippines, which is an AETA subgroup living on the island of Palawan. The Indonesian Bataks are divided into seven different subgroups, with their own languages and slightly different cultures; many of these subgroups do not use the ethnonym *Batak*, and some even see it as pejorative since it was a designation used by lowland Muslims to indicate Batak "primitiveness" in relation to them.

Although the highlands of northern Sumatra are relatively isolated in relation to Indonesia's central JAVANESE region, the Bataks were heavily influenced by a variety of cultural features from the Hindu and Buddhist kingdoms that ruled Java from the first century C.E. until about 1500. Batak astrology, divination systems, in which information from the spirit world is passed to this world in a variety of natural signs and then read by a diviner, and even political concepts reflect this influence from pre-Islamic Java. However, while the Javanese

rapidly adopted Islam after about 1500, Batak society remained relatively isolated from the political and religious structures that emerged following this widespread conversion. Islam did finally spread to the Bataks in the 19th century, from the MINANGKABAU in the 1820s. Even the Portuguese and Dutch, whose colonial systems were well established in much of Indonesia by the mid-18th century, did not reach the Bataks until the mid-19th century, when the Dutch began a 60-year campaign to pacify and control all Batak territory.

Dutch success in the Batak highlands, which was finally consolidated in about 1910, generated considerable change in the region. State schools began teaching in the areas of the Angkola, Mandailing, and Toba subgroups, and Christian missionaries worked hard among the Toba. Just a decade and a half later much of the Batak population had attained literacy and both Medan and Sibolga, on the northeast and northwest coasts, respectively, had attained the status of cities, with all the attendant newspapers, book publishing, and political culture. From the 1920s until independence in 1949 some Batak writers took up the cause of anticolonialism and contributed a great deal of writing on the subject. Since independence the Batak community has remained one of the most literate and cosmopolitan of all the outer islands' populations, more similar to the Javanese than to some of the other small ethnic communities.

The traditional Batak economy was based on the cultivation of both dry and wet rice, the latter in large terraced paddies to take advantage of all fertile land, even on the steep hillsides. Most regions are able to produce only one crop per year, especially in the dry fields of the highlands, but since the green revolution introduced new fertilizers and seed varieties in the 1970s a few valleys can produce two harvests. The commoditization of the Batak economy in the Dutch period also introduced such cash crops as cinnamon, coffee, cloves, and tobacco as well as smaller-scale market production of a number of vegetables including tomatoes and cabbage. To supplement farming many rural Bataks continue to sell wild rubber, camphor, and other forest products; keep domestic animals such as water buffaloes, goats, and fowl; and work for wages in transport, marketing, or agricultural labor.

Since the early 20th century many Bataks have moved into the region's towns and cities and taken up nonagricultural work as mechanics, tailors, builders, and weavers and in a variety of other trades. The relatively long history

---

BATAKS

location:
Sumatra, Indonesia, especially around Lake Toba, and many other Indonesian islands

time period:
No earlier than 2500 B.C.E. to the present

ancestry:
Austronesian

language:
There are seven different Batak languages spoken on Sumatra, all in the Austronesian-language phylum.

of literacy in the region has also produced a fair number of writers, teachers, and other professionals, some of whom work in the region, while others have migrated to Jakarta, Surabaya, and the country's other large cities.

Batak society, like many throughout Indonesia, is relatively hierarchical and recognizes the status of different patrilineal descent groups in relation to one another. In the past the highest-status chiefly lineages even kept slaves from among the lowest groups and non-Batak communities. Today clan or *marga* membership remains important, even for Batak families living far from their ancestral homes, and their status is linked to that of their clan. The Bataks continue to have intermarriage relationships with other clans in which those clans that provide wives to another are superior to those who receive them. For example, Lineage 1 always provides wives to Lineage 2 from a different clan and thus is superior to Lineage 2 in all areas. At the same time Lineage 2 provides wives to Lineage 3 from a third clan and thus is superior to it. These relationships cannot be turned around so that a wife giver becomes a wife receiver, and such ties are maintained through many generations. Because clan groups are so large, sometimes include members from different subgroups of Bataks, and are geographically spread over many miles, they are not face-to-face groups. While lineages and subclans may get together for ceremonial activities such as honoring the ancestors or thanking them for providing assistance in spiritual matters, entire clans never meet.

Although the ideal is for marriages always to take place between these linked and ranked lineages, particularly for a man to marry his mother's brother's daughter, in the present day this is not always possible. Today there is much more toleration of young women and men choosing their own partners, provided they are not from the "wrong" lineage in terms of wife giving or receiving. Despite this change gift exchange at the time of betrothal and marriage remains very important in most Batak subgroups. The wife's family gives food, textiles, and other domestic gifts while the husband's gives livestock, jewelry, and even cash. Ideally the new couple lives in or near the husband's natal home in patrilocal residence for at least a few years before establishing neolocal residence. When Batak men nowadays marry a woman from another ethnic group, as often happens in urban situations, the new wife may be ritually adopted into her husband's mother's brother's household as a daughter so as to create an "ideal" marriage situation. Since patrilineal descent is the accepted pattern for inheritance and the creation of large kin groups, there is no parallel ceremony for non-Batak men marrying into the Bataks.

Although Islam predated Christianity by about 30 years among the Bataks, the latter was adopted by a large percentage, especially among the Toba subgroup, about 90 percent of whom consider themselves Christian, largely Protestant. Very few Bataks today would consider themselves outside either the Islamic or the Christian world; however, most actually engage in a syncretic blend of indigenous beliefs and practices about spirits and ancestors with Islam or Christianity. Events celebrating the latter are often described as being about *adat* or custom rather than religion but do serve to connect contemporary Bataks with the religious beliefs of their pre-19th-century ancestors in times of marriage, birth, coming of age, and death.

FURTHER READING

Achim Sibeth. *The Batak: Peoples of the Island of Sumatra: Living with Ancestors* (New York: Thames & Hudson, 1991).

Bengalis (Baboo, Bangali, Bangli, Bengalee)

The Bengalis are Bangla speakers who reside in Bangladesh and West Bengal, a state in India; there is also a large diaspora both within South Asia and throughout the world.

GEOGRAPHY

The Bengali region of South Asia is a horseshoe-shaped land that incorporates both Indian and Bangladeshi territory and consists largely of the delta region where the Ganges, Meghna, and Brahmaputra Rivers run into the Bay of Bengal. It is bounded by mountains on three sides, with the mountainous states of Nepal, Bhutan, and Sikkim to the north and the bay to the south. The region is low lying and affected by a monsoonal rainy season from April to November, which often results in floods in the lowest regions. The area's rivers and their tributaries have allowed ideas, people, and products to travel in and out easily. They have also carried tons of silt, which has extended the land into what used to be a

BENGALIS

location:
Bangladesh, India

time period:
About 1000 c.e. to the present.

ancestry:
Indo-European

language:
Bangla or Bengali, an Indo-Iranian language

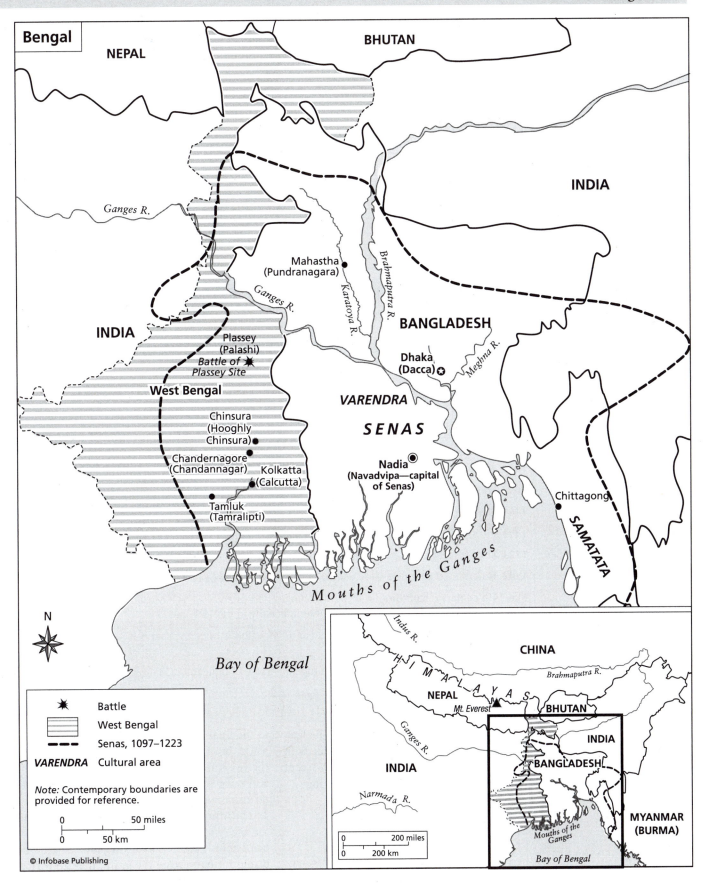

Bengal

NEPAL

BHUTAN

INDIA

Ganges R.

Mahastha
(Pundranagara)

Karatoya R.

Brahmaputra R.

BANGLADESH

Dhaka
(Dacca)

Meghna R.

INDIA

Ganges R.

Plassey
(Palashi)
Battle of
Plassey Site

VARENDRA

West Bengal

SENAS

Chinsura
(Hooghly
Chinsura)

Chandernagore
(Chandannagar)   Kolkatta
(Calcutta)

Nadia
(Navadvipa—capital
of Senas)

Chittagong

Tamluk
(Tamralipti)

SAMATATA

Mouths of the Ganges

N

Bay of Bengal

✶	Battle
▥	West Bengal
– – –	Senas, 1097–1223
VARENDRA	Cultural area

Note: Contemporary boundaries are
provided for reference.

0   50 miles
0   50 km

© Infobase Publishing

Indus R.

CHINA

HIMALAYAS

NEPAL

Brahmaputra R.

Mt. Everest   BHUTAN

INDIA

Ganges R.

BANGLADESH

INDIA

Narmada R.

Mouths of the
Ganges

MYANMAR
(BURMA)

0   200 miles
0   200 km

Bay of Bengal

Bengalis time line

B.C.E.

1800–1500 Probable period that the Indo-Aryans moved into South Asia.

1500 Shifting agriculture already dominates the region's economic system.

1000 Iron and copper tools, weapons, and other implements become common in Bengal.

600–400 Transition from shifting or swidden to intensive, wet rice agriculture in Bengal.

fourth century Pundranagara, the region's first city, is founded by non-Indo-Aryan peoples, probably of the Pundra tribe.

third century Asoka, the great Mauryan king, rules most of the territory that becomes northern India and Bangladesh.

second century Buddhism is introduced in Bengal.

C.E.

second century Buddhism is a major force in the kingdoms of Bengal.

seventh century Hinduism begins to replace Buddhism as the major state religion in the kingdoms of Bengal.

eighth century Founding of the Pala empire by Gopala, a Buddhist warrior.

825 Founding of the Buddhist Chandra empire.

956 Masudi, an Arab geographer who first writes of a Muslim population in Bengal, dies.

1000 Period in which the Old Bengali language is said to have come into being and along with it the ethnolinguistic group, the Bengalis.

1035 Disintegration of the Chandra empire.

1075 The Varman dynasty centralizes the worship of Siva and Vishnu instead of Buddhist practice.

1097 Founding of the Hindu Sena dynasty.

1161 Disintegration of the Pala empire.

1204–05 Muhammad Bakhtiyar conquers Bengal and initiates the Muslim era in the region.

1223 Final disintegration of the Sena empire.

1282 Start of a 60-year period of relative independence in Bengal.

Mid-14th century Shams-ud-din Iliyas Shah unites Bengal and begins a Muslim dynasty that rules the region until 1487, with a brief interlude early in the 15th century.

1576 The Mughal Empire conquers Bengal and the region is ruled by a series of governors or nawabs until the mid-18th century.

1590 The Portuguese establish the first European factory in Bengal, in Chittagong, followed soon after by the Dutch at Chinsura.

much farther inland-reaching Bay of Bengal. Temperatures in the region are tropical, with hot, humid conditions much of the year, except in higher elevations, which are cool and foggy.

ORIGINS

Ancient Times

The prehistoric period of Bengal is still somewhat unclear since archaeological and textual evidence does not always agree. Agriculture probably arrived in the region sometime prior to the final arrival of the Indo-Aryans in 1500 B.C.E., but it was not the intensive agriculture that we know today. Instead swidden or slash-and-burn agriculture, which required cutting down new patches of forest every year or two and burning the vegetation to prepare the land for use, was the norm. The people used small hand tools rather than iron plows and stone blades for harvesting the grain; they grew rice, millet, and a variety of beans and vegetables.

It is difficult to say with certainty the linguistic or ethnic background of these early

17th century The British East India Company establishes itself as the largest and most important European organization on the subcontinent.

1673 The French establish a long-lasting colonial presence in Chandernagore, which they hold off and on until 1952. Its current name is Chandannagar.

1756 The Bengalis capture Fort William, the main British military garrison in Calcutta, and imprison nearly 150 British soldiers in what has come to be known as the Black Hole of Calcutta.

1757 The British under Robert Clive conquer Bengal at the Battle of Plassey.

1769–73 The Bengal famine kills about 10 million people.

1772 The British move their colonial capital to the Bengali city of Calcutta.

1835 The British introduce English as the primary language of higher education in India generally, including Bengal.

1857 A rebellion in Bengal forces the British to transfer power from the East India Company directly to the British Crown, represented locally by the viceroy of India. This initiates the period of Indian history known as the British Raj.

1905 The British attempt to divide Bengal into eastern and western districts; the attempt fails, and the status quo is restored in 1911–12.

1906 The Muslim League is formed in Dhaka and pushes for separate Hindu and Muslim states for postcolonial India.

1947 India and the predominantly Muslim country of East and West Pakistan attain independence from the British; the partition process leads to significant bloodshed on both sides.

1952 Pakistan makes Urdu the national language, causing Bengali speakers in East Pakistan (now Bangladesh) to riot against the reforms.

1960s Strikes, power shortages, and communist agitation in West Bengal (now a state in India) lead to economic stagnation that continues through much of the 1970s as well.

1971 Bangladesh, formerly East Pakistan, achieves independence from Pakistan in a war that kills at least 1 million and sees about 10 million Hindus flee from the newly independent Bangladesh, a primarily Muslim state.

1991 Bangladesh becomes a parliamentary democracy after two decades of military rule and frequent coups.

Muslims and Hindus clash over the destruction of a mosque in India.

1999 Calcutta's name is changed to the less colonial name *Kolkata*.

2006–07 Maoist rebels in West Bengal engage in terrorist activities in the state over increased industrial acquisition of agricultural land.

agriculturalists in Bengal, but they have been labeled proto-MUNDA by some scholars, who believe they were the ancestors of the present-day Munda people. Some of the tribal affiliations believed to dominate the region prior to the INDO-ARYANS' appearance between 1800 and 1500 B.C.E. were the Vangas, Sumahs, Pulindas, and Pundras. The Vedic or Sanskrit literature of these Aryans does not mention most of these groups by name; the Pundras are one exception. Vedic texts generally refer to the native inhabitants as *Mlechchas* or untouchables; *dasyus,* "robbers" is also used occasionally. Eventually these tribal groups were incorporated into the Aryan Hindu social order dominated by the caste system, which classifies people on the basis of the ritual purity of their inherited occupations and requires endogamy or marrying into one's own caste; children always inherit the caste position of their parents. The highest position in this system is the Brahmin or priestly caste, followed by the Kshatriyas or warriors, the caste position assigned to most of the pre-Aryan tribal communities of Bengal.

However, this process took many centuries and it was not before 500 C.E. that the Bengal region was even partially incorporated into the Hindu social order; the Hindu political order with its notion of a divine king at the top of the hierarchy was adopted even later.

The process of Hinduization in this region coincided with the development of more intensive forms of agriculture than occurred earlier; however, linguistic analysis of current Bengali terms for many complex agricultural processes indicates that it was not the Aryans who introduced advanced agriculture to the region. Rather the migrants adopted it upon their arrival from the indigenous people. The introduction of advanced metalworking in the form of iron weapons and tools as well as some copper items took place sometime around 1000 B.C.E. Then in the centuries from 600 to 400 B.C.E. swidden or shifting agriculture, so named because it obliged families to shift their fields yearly, was replaced by more intensively worked wet rice fields. These fields required irrigation systems as well as inputs of animal or human fertilizers so that the land could be used again and again. This process is often called intensive agriculture because the addition of water and fertilizers allows the field to be used for many years rather than being shifted from year to year. The production of wet rice in this manner also requires more intensive labor because rice seedlings must be transplanted after having been first established in a drier field. While shifting agriculture is easily managed by single households working as the primary units of production and consumption, wet rice agriculture as it developed in Bengal required draft animals and the cooperation of many adults and children in the preparation, planting, transplanting, weeding, and harvesting stages.

The transition from shifting to intensive agriculture initiated the first period of state development in Bengal, as has happened throughout the world. The first recorded city in the region, Pundranagara, probably appeared in the fourth century B.C.E. and rose to prominence in the Mauryan period, 321–181 B.C.E., when the Mauryan kingdom ruled the territory to the west of Bengal. Pundranagara was subsequently adopted by the Mauryans as the capital of their eastern province.

Another cultural transformation in Bengal occurred with the introduction of Buddhism. The first real evidence that this religious tradition, with its egalitarian worldview, had been introduced in Bengal is a second-century B.C.E.

monument or stupa in Madhya Pradesh, which lists Bengalis among its supporters. By the second or third century C.E., according to a Buddhist inscription in Andhra Pradesh, Bengal was an important Buddhist territory. In the early fifth century a Chinese author claimed that Tamralipti, a city in southwestern Bengal called Tamluk today, had 22 working Buddhist monasteries. In the eighth century the powerful Pala empire, which was founded by the Buddhist warrior Gopala in the Varendra region, today northern Bangladesh, fostered the development of Buddhism in northern Bengal until the empire's dissolution in 1161. In the southeastern Samatata region the Chandra empire did much the same from about 825 to 1035. Both of these empires had extensive interactions with their Indian and Southeast Asian neighbors as well as with traders, merchants, and explorers from Persia and Arabia. Buddhism spread from their shores to Tibet, Myanmar (Burma), Cambodia, and Java, where Buddhist monuments similar in style and age to those of these Bengali kingdoms have been found. The region's international flavor can also be seen in the work of the Arab geographer Masudi (died in 956), who recorded the first mention of Muslims in Bengal when he wrote of traders who lived in the Chandra territory of Samatata.

Despite the importance of Buddhism to the development of Bengali culture, politics, and even trade relations, Hinduism with its Brahmin priests and hierarchical worldview was to dominate the region and its people in place of the more egalitarian Buddhism. Starting in the seventh century some Bengali dynasties began to turn to Hindu ritual specialists rather than Buddhist ones, with even the powerful Palas doing so in the 11th century. The Pala were followed by the Varmans (1075–1150) and Senas (1097–1223), who both favored the worship of the powerful Hindu gods Siva and Vishnu over Buddhist ritual practices. Brahmin priests, who had always served as the primary religious specialists for ordinary Bengalis during times of life-cycle change such as marriages and funerals, gained even greater status as ritual specialists for the kings, looking after the great religious cults upon which each king had based his own rule.

HISTORY

Medieval Period

While the transition from Buddhist to Hindu, pre-Aryan to Aryan, in Bengal took many centuries and was not complete by about 1000 C.E., that date is often marked as the founding date for the formation of a separate Bengali language and ethnicity; however, some sources claim that it is a bit earlier, around 700 C.E. The earliest Bengali texts, from the Pala kingdom, date from this period. In the 10th–12th centuries the various kingdoms that dominated Bengal became bureaucratic, hierarchical, and, especially in the west, dominated by Brahmins, who received significant grants of land from the kings whose powerful religious cults they oversaw. In this worldview the line between king and god became somewhat blurred, and through their gifts and sacrifices kings were seen as much more powerful than any mere mortal. For this power to be activated, however, required the work of Brahmin ritual specialists who served as mediators between the human and supernatural worlds.

The consolidation of Hindu rule in Bengal was interrupted in 1204–05 when the northwestern region was captured by a Turkish cavalry unit under Muhammad Bakhtiyar, who was employed by Qut buddin Aibak, the sultan of Delhi. Bakhtiyar's forces conquered Bihar in India late in the 12th century; then he turned his attention toward Bengal and the wealth that had been amassed by the Sena trading empire. Legend has it that Bakhtiyar rode so swiftly into the Sena capital of Nadia that only 18 other horsemen could keep up with him. They arrived under the guise of horse traders and took the last Sena king, Lakshman Sen, by surprise, forcing him to flee his castle barefoot just after he had sat down to a meal. The king as well as many of his retainers fled to the eastern regions of Bengal, which, with their Hindu worldview and peasant way of life, had never been fully incorporated into the Aryan-held territories but were instead held by a variety of tribal groups practicing swidden agriculture. Bakhtiyar is himself considered the first Muslim ruler of Bengal and founder of the Khilji dynasty, which marks the transition from ancient to medieval history in the region; he died just a year later while on a military campaign in Tibet.

Under both Pala and Sena rule much of the region of contemporary Bengal was known as Gaura and the kings of both dynasties were called kings of Gaura. Under the Muslims, however, the region took on the old name of *Vanga* or *Banga,* which had been despised by the Aryans. After 1205 the entire region was called *Banga,* although *Gaura* was not completely abandoned and appears in some texts from that time. In the 16th century during the reign of the Mughal emperor Akbar, the region became known as *Subah Bangla,* which was shortened to *Bengala* by the Europeans who arrived a short time later.

Bengal's early Muslim history was intimately connected to the Muslim leadership of north India more generally, with the Sultanate of Bangala largely dominated by the powerful Sultanate of Delhi. Between 1282 and 1342 the Bengalis were able to gain some independence, but no one ruler could unite the region into a single kingdom. This occurred only in the mid-14th century under Shams-ud-din Iliyas Shah, whose dynasty united the region and ruled until 1487, with a brief interlude in the first quarter of the century. This dynasty was followed by the Hussain-Shahi dynasty, which held power until it was overthrown by the Afghan Sher Shah in 1538 and then by the Karranis from the present-day region of Kurram in Afghanistan in the 1560s. Finally in 1576 the Mughal dynasty conquered Bengal and a series of governors ruled the territory until approximately 1757, when the British gained control over the region through the British East India Company.

During the early Muslim period many ordinary Bengalis adopted the religion of their rulers and the Bengali language incorporated a significant number of words from the literary traditions of the Arabs, Turks, and Persians. The reasons for this widespread conversion to Islam in Bengal, especially in eastern Bengal, while much of the rest of India remained thoroughly Hindu despite being ruled by Muslim kings, have interested scholars for generations. Most experts believe that by the time of the Muslim conquest the Hindu worldview had not yet fully replaced the Buddhist one in Bengal, despite the adoption there of the caste system and the model of the divine king. Bengal had been a Hindu frontier region and was considered ritually impure and difficult to conquer, so it was largely left to the non-Indo-Aryan tribal groups to continue their way of life. While the last Hindu kingdom in Bengal, that of the Deva family, ruled from the east until the mid-14th century, Hinduism had arrived only a short time earlier and remained a religion of the king rather than a worldview of the people. In addition as a frontier region Bengal was also the last point in the widespread Muslim conquest that, beginning in the 7th century, spread from the Middle East until it was stopped by the Himalayan barrier. Even today eastern Bengal, which is now the independent country of Bangladesh, is more Muslim than the west, with about 88 percent of the population claiming to be Muslim and 11 percent Hindu; West Bengal, a state within India, is about 72.5 percent Hindu and 25 percent Muslim.

As had the Buddhists and Hindus before them, the Muslim rulers built religious structures and other institutions of learning. Unlike these prior rulers, however, most Muslim rulers learned Bengali and commissioned Bengali-language native works and translations, such as the Aryan *Mahabharata* and significant works from Persian and Arab literature. At the same time as translation of the *Mahabharata* shows, the Muslim rulers and their intelligentsia did not abandon the past entirely. A new folk culture based on the Bengali language and elements from Buddhism, Hinduism, Islam, and even Jainism developed in the region. Among Bengalis generally, both Muslims and Hindus, this folk culture unites them across religious and national boundaries to this day.

Modern Era

Although the British were the longest-lasting colonial power in Bengal, they were not the first. Prior to their takeover in the 18th century the Portuguese, Dutch, and French had all established trading ports and even factories in the region in the 16th and 17th centuries. The Portuguese arrived first and set up factories in the Chittagong region by 1590 at the latest; they were followed by the Dutch in Chinsura, which they held until 1825, and the French at Chandernagore or Chandannagar, starting around 1673 and lasting, off and on, until 1952.

British rule in Bengal, which began in 1757 at the Battle of Plassey and extended until India's independence in 1947, produced change that rivals that generated by the Muslim invasion 550 years earlier. Perhaps the most profound was the introduction of English as the language of higher education in 1835. In addition nationalism in this region, both of the religious variety, which divided primarily Hindu India from mostly Muslim East and West Pakistan in 1947, and of the linguistic variety, which saw the eventual partition of East and West Pakistan into primarily Urdu Pakistan and Bengali Bangladesh in 1971, was also at least in part the child of the colonial era. Parliamentary democracy and a love of cricket are just two more contributions to Bengali culture made by the British.

From the beginning of the British era in India Bengal was central to the colonizing mission, with Calcutta, one of the region's largest

As the capitol of the British Indian colony, Calcutta's Government House was an opulent symbol of the colony's vast wealth, as seen in the throne room shown here. *(Library of Congress Prints and Photographs Division)*

cities, becoming the colonial capital in 1772. This proximity to the seat of colonial power affected Bengalis in many, sometimes contradictory ways. In the early years of British rule the East India Company's policies with regard to land taxes, which they raised, and a prohibition on families' saving rice for use during difficult times resulted in a famine that killed close to 10 million people or about one-third of the region's entire population between 1769 and 1773. Subsequently living in and around the colonial capital both gave Bengalis access to education and minor positions of power within the colonial regime and pushed them to struggle against British rule. In 1756 the governor or nawab of Bengal captured the British Fort William at Calcutta and held almost 150 British prisoners in a small underground cell that has come to be known as the Black Hole of Calcutta because of the number of prisoners who died of asphyxiation or of being crushed in the small space. In 1857 a failed rebellion in Bengal forced the British to transfer the colony from the East India Company directly to the British Crown and the viceroy of India. The region was so volatile and unwieldy for the British that in 1905 an attempt was made to divide Bengal into eastern and western halves for administrative ease; the attempt was rejected by Bengalis and the policy aborted in 1911–12.

The more violent side of the Indian independence movement also had its roots in Bengal in the person of Subhash Chandra Bose. Bose began his career with a high position in the Indian civil service but soon quit in order to pursue the goal of Indian independence. He served as leader of the political party the Indian National Congress for several years before his own views clashed with the nonviolent approach to independence favored by Mohandas Gandhi. Subsequently he formed a new political party, the All India Forward Bloc, and organized mass protests against Britain's entering India into World War II without consulting the Indian population. He was arrested by the British but was released after a short hunger strike and then escaped the country. During his period in exile he tried to work with the Germans and then the JAPANESE to oust the British from his homeland; he did not live to see Indian independence, having died in an airplane crash two years before the British turned over India to the Indians.

In addition to anticolonial sentiment Muslim religious nationalism developed in Bengal as well. In 1906 the Muslim League formed in eastern Bengal's largest city, Dhaka, in reaction to the belief that the Indian National Congress favored the rights of Hindus. After Pakistan's independence in 1947, activists in East Bengal, or East Pakistan as it came to be known, continued their push for separation, this time based not on religion but language. They thought that Pakistan's governance in the western part of the country favored the language (Urdu) and culture of the people of that region over that of the Bengalis of the east. The Bengalis rioted in 1952 following the adoption of Urdu as the country's national language, and the rebellious Awami League in East Bengal continued to agitate for Bengali rights through the 1960s. In 1971 an important Bengali leader, Sheikh Mujibur Rahman, was arrested and West Pakistani forces launched an attack on the eastern region of the country. They were defeated in December 1971 by forces that included Bengali guerrillas, Bengali members of the army, and some from the Indian army as well. During the war about 10 million east Bengalis, mostly Hindus, fled to India and about 1 million were killed.

Throughout the 1970s and 1980s Bangladesh struggled with natural disasters and military coups that kept the country unstable. In 1991 parliamentary democracy finally returned to the country, but so did Muslim-Hindu violence when the destruction of a mosque in India rekindled old animosities in Bengal as well. Similar issues flared between Pakistan and Bangladesh in 2000 and between India and Bangladesh in 2001.

India's state of West Bengal, the most densely populated state in India with almost 8 percent of the country's population housed in less than 3 percent of its territory, has also seen significant discord and agitation for greater autonomy since India's independence in 1947. In the 1960s and 1970s left-wing political movements, strikes, and power shortages contributed to damaging much of the region's infrastructure and helped produce a severe economic downturn. The million refugees who entered the region during and after the Bangladesh Liberation War also flooded the state's social service capabilities and affected the region's economy. The state finally began to recover economically in the 1990s as a result of India's general reforms and the widespread land reform program that made its way into the largely agricultural economy. In 1999 the state's largest city, Calcutta, abandoned its British colonial-era name for the more local *Kolkata,* and there was a push for the state to change its name from *West Bengal* to *Bangla*. In the new millennium communist agitators continue to be active in the state and have organized several attacks on the administration over the process of industrial land acquisition.

CULTURE

Despite half a century of urbanization the Bengal region generally remains fairly rural. In the Indian state of West Bengal about 28 percent of the population is urban, a higher proportion than the 27 percent average in India, while in Bangladesh it is about 23 percent; the world average at the turn of the 21st century when these figures were compiled was about 46.7 percent. In West Bengal more than half of the urban population, about 14 million, live in the Kolkata metropolitan area, while in Bangladesh the number living in the capital and largest city, Dhaka, is slightly lower, only 12 million. The rest of the population in both countries lives in villages of between 100 and 1,000 people. During the British colonial era village boundaries were established for taxation and administrative purposes, but the units, called *mauza*s locally, did not always coincide with the socially defined hamlets and villages of the region. Because of flooding, entire hamlets, which are subunits of villages, are often established on land that has been built up above sea level by a few feet or yards, and in regions that often experience monsoon flooding homesteads are dispersed rather than clumped together or strung out in a linear fashion along a river or canal. Multivillage markets unite the hamlets and villages of each region and draw their populations together for regular trading and social activities.

Households in these rural regions tend to be made up of nuclear families: couples and their unmarried children. These households are the primary units of both agricultural production as the owners or workers of small family farms and consumption. Land has traditionally been privately owned throughout Bengal, and since before the colonial era much of the land has been tied up in large holdings, leaving most people either landless or owning just a hectare or two. Since Bangladesh's independence in 1971 every national government has introduced a form of land reform law, but on the ground very little has changed since the early 1980s, when 80 percent of farmland was owned by just 35 percent of the population and 30 percent of the population was entirely landless. However, the situation in West Bengal is very different.

Since independence in 1947 successive land reform projects in the state have been successful in redistributing millions of acres of land to millions of landless sharecroppers and tenants.

Nuclear-family households in Bengal tend to be grouped together into homesteads made up of extended families and connected to one another through patrilineal kinship ties and patrilocal residence patterns that require wives to move into their husbands' homes. While households engage in most productive and consumptive activities, homesteads join larger projects, such as breaking new ground and building homes and celebrating religious and life-cycle rituals. Each homestead will also generally have a number of shared fruit trees, animal shelters, and possibly a fish pond that also supplies water for personal use. Rural buildings are usually constructed from mud and local brick with thatch roofs or, in the case of wealthier families, corrugated iron. The very poorest families have homes made from bamboo, which need to be reconstructed on a regular basis.

Most rural families throughout the Bengal region focus the bulk of their energy on producing wet rice; jute, used in making rope and string, is also a major commercial crop. The spring season for rice and jute begins with the monsoon rains in April and lasts until about mid-July. This is followed by the year's largest rice-growing season, which extends from July until November, and then comes the dry season, in which certain strains of rice can be grown until the end of March by using irrigated fields. During this drier period legumes and oil seeds are also grown and, in recent decades, some wheat and potatoes. Added to these crops some families, depending on their wealth, also own a few animals, with cows, oxen, goats, and water buffaloes the most common. In addition the region has some members of the Hindu caste specializing in fishing, who make their living primarily through this activity even today.

The division of labor in Bengal as throughout most of South Asia is highly gendered, with men's and women's separate activities strictly demarcated. In general men's activities are those that require movement outside the homestead: trading and commercial activities, plowing, planting, weeding, harvesting, fishing. Women's activities are those that take place within the home: child care, food preparation, other domestic chores, threshing, drying, and husking rice. However, this ideal division is modified in the case of very poor families that require women to work in the households of wealthier families or even to engage in agricultural work and in middle-class and wealthy urban families where women may be highly educated and work in the bureaucracy, as teachers, nurses, and gynecologists and in other professions. The Bengali inheritance system parallels the division of labor in that sons generally inherit all of their father's property along with the proviso that they must provide for their mother and sisters as long as they reside in the family homestead. Islamic law states that sons and daughters are both allowed to inherit property; however, in practice a daughter's dowry is often seen as her inheritance rather than any piece of her father's land. Daughters in Muslim Bengali families are also able to return to their natal homes and receive proper maintenance from their brothers in cases of divorce or widowhood.

The other aspect of the Bengali division of labor is dictated by the constraints of the occupational specialization of the Hindu caste system. Among Hindu Bengalis the caste system divides families into agricultural workers; artisans working in leather, silver, iron, textiles, and other materials; fishermen; merchants and traders; barbers; butchers; priests; and a large number of other tasks. These groups are endogamous, requiring members to marry one another, and both the status of the caste group and its occupation are passed down from parent to child. Even among Muslim families some aspects of the caste system, including the division of labor, have been maintained over time, and in the modern, professional sector of the economy caste remains visible, with high-status professionals tending to be from high-status castes, and vice versa. As a result most of Bengal is affected by this occupational hierarchy that has been handed down from the earliest years of the Indo-Aryan presence thousands of years ago.

Kinship in Bengal is patrilineal although large lineage groupings tend to be neglected in favor of smaller units housed in a single homestead. Marriage rules among both Hindu and Muslim Bengalis forbid marrying within one's own patrilineage but differ in that Hindus may also not marry matrilateral cousins or mother's siblings' children, while Muslims are not prohibited from doing so. Hindu marriages require caste endogamy with the allowance for a small degree of hypergamy for women, which lets women marry men of a slightly higher caste than they. The opposite, women's marrying below their own caste, however, is discouraged and almost never occurs. Caste is a less impor-

tant consideration among Muslim Bengalis, except those of the lowest-ranking occupational groups who are endogamous by necessity; however, social rank is strongly considered in the process of arranging marriages, a practice that still predominates in rural areas among both Hindu and Muslim families. Other differences between Hindus and Muslims regard the ability of a man to have more than one wife, the practice of polygyny, and divorce. Hindus forbid polygyny entirely while Muslims do not; nonetheless, it is not very common in either West Bengal or Bangladesh. Divorce causes great stigma among Hindus, especially those of the higher castes, and thus it is not common in this population, while Muslims see it as less damaging to their social capital and have traditionally had higher rates in both regions of Bengal. The last important distinction with regard to marriage is the ability of widows to remarry. Despite Indian legislation allowing this practice, it is still rare among Hindus in both countries, especially among higher-caste families, while Muslims not only allow but encourage the practice, at least among young widows.

FURTHER READING

Marvin Davis. *Rank and Rivalry: The Politics of Inequality in Rural West Bengal* (Cambridge: Cambridge University Press, 1983).

Ronald B. Inden and Ralph W. Nicholas. *Kinship in Bengali Culture* (Chicago: University of Chicago Press, 1977).

A. K. M. Aminul Islam. *A Bangladesh Village: Political Conflict and Cohesion* (Prospect Heights, Ill.: Waveland Press, 1990).

Ákos Östör. *The Play of the Gods: Locality, Ideology, Structure, and Time in the Festivals of a Bengali Town* (Chicago: University of Chicago Press, 1980).

Tarak C. Raychaudhuri and Bikash Raychaudhuri. *The Brahmins of Bengal* (Calcutta: Anthropological Survey of India, 1981).

Manisha Roy. *Bengali Women* (Chicago: University of Chicago Press, 1972).

Nitish Sengupta. *History of the Bengali-Speaking People* (New Delhi: UBS, 2001).

Benglong   See DE'ANG.

Betawis   (Betawi Asli, Orang Betawi)

The Betawis are the descendants of those who resided in colonial Batavia, the Dutch name for the current Indonesian capital of Jakarta. Today they are an entirely urban population in Jakarta who speak their own creole language combining elements from Malay, JAVANESE, Chinese,

BETAWIS

location:
Jakarta, Indonesia.

time period:
19th century to the
present.

ancestry:
Malay, Javanese,
Balinese, Chinese, and
many others.

language:
Betawi, a Malay-creole
language based in and
around Jakarta.

Ondel Ondel dancers participating in a carnival and parade in Jakarta, 1997, introducing fellow Indonesians to the multicultural aspects of Betawi heritage. *(AP/Muchtar Zakaria)*

BALINESE, and even Dutch and English. It is not mutually intelligible with Bahasa Indonesia, the country's national language, or with any other language spoken in the country. Despite its limited use or perhaps because of it, modern Betawi is considered a trendy language for young Betawis in the city while its older forms are still in use among the senior generations.

The ancestry of this population is as diverse as the elements that have gone into its language; it includes large numbers of Javanese and Balinese people plus representatives from most of the country's other ethnic groups, both indigenous to the archipelago and migrant populations of Chinese, Dutch, and others. From these diverse origins has developed a unique ethnic group, one of the city's largest, which still maintains some of its traditional cuisine, music, dance, and festivals. The most visible of these features are the annual parades in which *ondel ondel* or tall Betawi mascots move around the city to celebrate Batavia's history and its people. The traditional Betawi neighborhood of Condet is another place where this people's unique cultural blend remains visible despite the modernization and urban renewal that have dispersed much of the rest of Betawi culture and people throughout the urban sprawl of Jakarta. Within this neighborhood gardens

and orchards survive in the city and traditional market stalls still sell fish, textiles, and other local products.

Bhils (Bheel)

The Bhils are the third-largest tribal community in India; the majority reside in the central region traditionally called by the RAJASTHANI term *Rewakantha,* where the states of Andhra Pradesh, Gujarat, Madhya Pradesh, Maharashtra, and Rajasthan all meet. They speak INDO-ARYAN languages but are believed to have DRAVIDIAN origins because *villu* or *billu* is the Dravidian root word for "bow" and the Bhil weapons of choice have long been the bow and arrow. The Bhils were probably the aboriginal peoples of this region of India.

The Bhils themselves claim divine origin as the banished and unattractive son of Siva and his human consort. After killing his father's bull this least good-looking son was banished to the mountains, where he and his Bhil descendants have made their home ever since. The more likely scenario is that the Bhils were the aboriginal peoples of central India and were driven into the hills, forests, and later the deserts by waves of invasions from Indo-Aryan Rajputs, Muslims, and finally British.

In the 10th century Bhil and KOL chieftains dominated most of the territory of Rewakantha, but they were pushed out in the subsequent four centuries by invasions of Indo-Aryans of the warrior Rajput caste. In recognition of the prior sovereignty of the Bhils in the region, these Rajput kings could not rule legitimately without first having been anointed in blood by a representative of the Bhil chief. In the 15th century around 1480 the region was conquered by the Muslim Mughal dynasty and most Bhils succumbed to Muslim rule without significant struggle. Indeed some Bhils converted to the new religion and became known as Tadyi Bhils; a second group of Muslim Bhils are the Nirle. By the 16th century the once fairly unified Bhils had fragmented into many subgroups and tribes and had been driven into some of the marginal lands of central India. Today some of the divisions that remain are those between Ujwala, central or pure Bhils, and Kotra Bhomat and Kalia, or Rajput Bhils, those of mixed descent and thus considered impure. Another important division is between Bhils residing on the plains and deserts, who consider themselves superior, and those in the hills. Linguistic divisions also remain today with at least 19 different dialects of Bhil spoken throughout India.

This period of dispersal from their land also changed the Bhil social and economic structures. Traditionally the Bhils survived largely by hunting, fishing, and gathering, using their bows and arrows in addition to bamboo traps, nets, and even poisons. They killed rabbits, deer, bears, foxes, pigs, birds, wildcats, lizards, and even rodents and gathered wild plants, roots, fruits, and honey. Once they had been pushed off their land, however, they turned to other activities, including banditry, looting, and pillaging, which put them at odds with the invading MARATHIS and British. They were pushed even farther into the highlands, resulting in greater independence among each subgroup as well as greater emphasis on self-reliance. During the period of the pax Britannia in India some Bhils were lured back to the lowlands and began to engage in both agriculture and animal husbandry, but others remained scattered. Today the Bhils are the most widely distributed tribal group in India. The British tried to conquer them twice in the 19th century, in 1818 and 1825, but failed both times and later put the Bhil military know how to work by organizing the Bhil Corps. This was successful in controlling the activities of other Bhils, and many settled down by midcentury onto the semiautonomous Bhil territory,

negotiated between a British agent and Kumar Vasava of Sagbara, a dominant Bhil chieftain.

As a result of this history many Bhils today make their living through agriculture. Initially the style of agriculture favored by the Bhils and other tribal communities who were settled at about the same time was swidden or slash-and-burn agriculture, in which tracts of land were cut, burned, and then plowed under to provide fertilizer for a growing season or two. This practice was outlawed in the 20th century as a result of destruction of forest land and now settled agriculture is the norm. However, the lands that the Bhils were granted during the British era tended to lack sufficient water, and irrigation and landlessness have become important economic problems. Crops that continue to be planted are corn, millet, cucumbers, eggplants, wheat, chickpeas, barley, peanuts, and both cotton and tobacco. They use bullocks as draft animals and most families keep cows for milk, never for food; the Bhils are not generally vegetarian, however, and do keep pigs, goats, and chickens to consume. Most also continue to gather wild food products when they are available.

Although many Bhils today live as agriculturalists, there are still some desert-dwelling communities in Rajasthan who continue to engage in hunting antelopes, birds, rabbits, and lizards; they also gather firewood and other forest products and do limited herding of cattle. This group is largely descended from mercenary soldiers who had worked for various chiefs and Marathi kings in the region. Once the area was entirely settled in the early 20th century they

BHILS

location:
Central India

time period:
Unknown to the present

ancestry:
Contested but possibly Dravidian

language:
There are many dialects of Bhil, an Indo-Aryan language family that has been strongly affected by Rajasthani and Gujurati.

Bhils time line

C.E.

10th century Bhil chieftains rule much of central India.

11th–14th centuries Indo-Aryan Rajputs invade the Bhils' central territory and displace many people.

1480 The Mughal dynasty conquers the Bhils' territory, and some individuals convert to Islam.

16th century The Bhil community fragments into many subgroups and tribes.

17th century The Bhils are chased farther into the highlands by the Marathis because of their practices of looting and banditry.

1818 The British try to conquer the Bhils; they try again seven years later and fail both times.

1837 The Bhil Corps, which had been created earlier in the century to control the Bhil bandits, is revised and begins to utilize local Bhils working under British officers. It is much more successful than the original British force.

relocated into scattered villages and reverted to a subsistence economy based on hunting and gathering. Their closest neighbors in this region, the agricultural Bishnoi, are greatly offended at the Bhil hunting of their sacred antelopes and cutting of their sacred trees; however, the two groups have cooperated in trade, in herding, and more recently in water projects to combat the region's drought. Unfortunately this lack of water has also meant that the two peoples' villages have moved closer together and conflict has emerged over their vast cultural differences. Both international and local nongovernmental organization (NGO) activities have tried to address the dual problems of drought and ethnic conflict, so far with limited success.

For both agricultural and desert-dwelling Bhils, trade remains an important economic activity because these people have no tradition of their own with regard to weaving, metalworking, or making pottery or other manufactured items. In exchange for clothing, tools, farm implements, baskets, pots, and other items, the Bhils offer either agricultural goods, including grain, vegetables, cotton, and tobacco, or wild products such as honey. In recent years some Bhils have found it necessary to seek the assistance of moneylenders as well, and some have consequently found themselves in a situation of indentured servitude.

The primary social units in Bhil society are constructed around the dual principles of residence and kinship. For example each tribal community, which speaks a single dialect, occupies a territory with a 20- to 25-mile radius. Within this portion of land all of that tribe's villages are located, each with a population of between three and 40 families. At the same time membership in a village community is largely dictated by kinship. The Bhils generally are patrilineal, tracing membership in lineages, clans, and tribes through men only. The Bhils also have a relatively uncommon patrilineal system: women, who must marry exogamously or outside their own patrilineages, actually become members of their husbands' lineages on marriage. As a result each village contains either members of a single lineage or members of related lineages that are all part of the same subclan. The subclan level of relationship is about the most extensive within which individuals can expect assistance and mutual cooperation, and dominant lineages own most agricultural land. Clans tend not to act in conjunction at any time, although each one does have a chief who controls much of the members' political activity; in the past clans may have been important units during times of war. Today, however, clans serve primarily as the largest exogamous group among the Bhils; both men and women are required to marry outside their own natal clan.

Marriage among all Bhil peoples is exogamous at the clan level, but there are many other marriage rules that differ from subgroup to subgroup. Most groups permit polygyny, the ability to have more than one wife, but its prevalence differs by region, with those who own land in more fertile and wet regions having a greater financial capacity to engage in the practice. In some areas sororal polygyny, where a man married a number of sisters, occurred frequently. In some regions cross-cousin marriage, between a man and his father's sister's daughter, is the preferred marriage type, while in others this marriage is considered incestuous and is strictly forbidden. Traditionally the Bhils married very young, as young as 11 years for girls and 14 years for boys, but the couple was not permitted to live together until the girl men-

A young Bhil woman at the Bhagoria fair in central India, where she may meet her future husband. This practice differs significantly from the traditional one, where young girls are married according to the wishes of their parents and only begin cohabitating at maturity. *(AP/Prakash Hatvalne)*

struated for the first time. When both spouses came of age, the woman generally moved into her husband's village, in a house specially built for the new couple very near the man's parents. At that time the man received some farmland from his father if the family was landed, and the young couple began to exist relatively independently of their parents. Mutual assistance is still offered at times of plowing, planting, and harvesting, but the new nuclear family is expected to be an autonomous unit for production and consumption. For polygynous Bhils husbands are required to establish separate households for all of their wives, a requirement that limits the ability to engage in the practice to the wealthiest.

Prior to the 20th century most Bhils were classified as animists, who believed in spirits and ancestors that interact with humans and other beings here on earth. In 1901 only about 2.75 percent of Bhils identified themselves as Hindu. A century later the religious landscape has changed somewhat, or at least the perspective on Bhil religion has changed. Today the Bhil are seen to practice their own religion, sometimes called Sonatan, which combines elements from their animistic past with a form of Hinduism outside the Vedic tradition. Siva is the most important god in their cosmology, although Hanuman, the monkey god, has also been identified as of central importance to them, and cows are considered sacred as well, as in Hinduism. In addition the prophet Bapuji, a 15th-century warrior, is an important semidivine figure, whom the men worship in a monthly overnight drumming ceremony. The tiger god, Wagh deo, and the god of agriculture, Nandervo, also receive significant attention; the latter is honored specifically when the onset of the rainy season brings forth new growth. Prior to the eradication of smallpox the goddess believed to bring on that disease, Sitala, was also greatly feared for the damage she could cause for an individual and a community. Today the Bhils worship their own ancestors and have shamans who communicate with the spirit world, offer sacrifices to the gods and ancestors, and practice divination to discover the source of illness or other troubles.

FURTHER READING

Robert Deliége. *The Bhils of Western India: Some Empirical and Theoretical Issues in Anthropology in India* (New Delhi, India: National, 1985).

S. L. Doshi. *Processes of Tribal Unification and Integration: A Case Study of the Bhils* (Delhi: Concept, 1978).

Bhuiya (Bhui, Bhuihar, Bhuiyar, Bhumia, Bhumiya, Bui)

The Bhuiya are one of the SCHEDULED TRIBES of India, where they live in the north-central, northeast, and southeastern states of Orissa, Bihar, West Bengal, Assam, Uttar Pradesh, Madhya Pradesh, and Tamil Nadu. They are divided into many subgroups, from the generalized division between northern and southern to more specific geographic and cultural divisions that recognize differences in subsistence practice, mythical origins, and place within the larger Indian social structure.

Because of these widespread geographic and cultural differences within the larger Bhuiya community it is difficult to speak of the group's history or culture. But it is instructive that their name derives from the Sanskrit term *bhumi*, "land," and many communities believe they are descended from Mother Earth since most make their living through some form of agricultural activity. The least economically developed subgroup, the Hill Bhuiya or Pauri, used slash-and-burn or swidden techniques until the past few decades to grow cereals, legumes, and vegetables. They also grew rice in more permanent paddies, the dominant agricultural form of many other subgroups, such as the Paik and Rajkoli. Some groups of Bhuiya were significantly wealthier than others and were landowners in their regions, such as the Ghatwar and Tikait, while the Parja were among the poorest and had to rely on agricultural labor on the land of either their wealthier linguistic cousins or other groups.

In addition to agricultural work of various kinds, many Bhuiya communities, especially the Hill Bhuiya, engaged in food collecting, hunting, fishing, and the sale of forest products such as resin, honey, and firewood. Some groups also kept livestock, including cows, buffaloes, goats, sheep, chickens, and ducks, while others specialized in such crafts as basket making and other bamboo and rattan crafts. Today most of these economic strategies continue with the possible exception of widespread food collecting.

Bhuiya social structure begins with the principle of patrilineal descent, in which each individual is a member of his or her father's sublineage, lineage, and clan. All of these groups are exogamous and thus require that people marry outside the group. Despite the centrality of patrilineal descent, however, in-laws or affines are also important members of one's kin group and can be turned to for assistance in

BHUIYA

location:
India

time period:
Unknown to the present

ancestry:
Indo-Aryan

language:
Bhuiya and Oriya, both Indo-Aryan languages

times of need. As with all kin, this assistance is fully reciprocal.

In addition to kin ties the Bhuiya recognize the importance of residence in a particular village for the creation of lasting alliances. Generally it is villages that control virgin forest lands, and if a family requires a plot for swidden it must request permission for its use from the village council. All members of the village community, however, have access to the community's forest land for use in hunting and gathering. Villages differ widely in size depending on their location; those in valleys or lowlands tend to be larger while those in higher elevations or more marginal lands are smaller. Most villages, regardless of size, have several communal buildings, including a council house and men's dormitory. This latter structure housed adolescent boys who were learning the skills, rituals, and myths necessary to survive as an adult Bhuiya. Today school has replaced village training for most boys and the dormitories have fallen into disuse.

Bhuiya religion can be classified as animism since it recognizes a wide variety of ancestral and natural spirits as well as many deities borrowed from the Hindu pantheon. As is the case in Hinduism, all of these gods and spirits are organized into a hierarchical structure, with the sun and earth gods as supreme beings, and natural and village gods and ancestral spirits below them. The priesthood is an inherited position handed down to a son from the senior family within each village. The role is only part time and entails officiating at village rituals and life cycle events such as marriage, birth, and funerals.

Bhutanese: nationality (people of Bhutan, Drukpa)

GEOGRAPHY

Bhutan is located between China, specifically Tibet, and India in the eastern Himalayas. It is a small, landlocked country of slightly more than 18,000 square miles. The kingdom is mostly mountainous with its highest peak, Kula Kangri, soaring to 24,780 feet above sea level; however, some of the fertile valleys are relatively low with Drangme Chhu lying at just 318 feet. The southern region of the country also contains savannas that are cool in winter and extremely hot in summer, in contrast with the higher elevations, where it is cool in summer and extremely cold and snowy in the winter.

INCEPTION OF NATION

Bhutan's earliest history remains somewhat mysterious for outsiders and for those who would like to separate mythology from "real" history. Many origin stories of Bhutan begin in 747 C.E. with Guru Rinpoche's flight out of Tibet on the back of a female tiger. He is said to have settled in Bhutan's Paro Valley in Taktsang Lhakhang or Tiger's Nest and founded a new school of Buddhist thought; many also consider him to be a second Buddha. Although parts of this story are obviously mythological the foundational aspects of Buddhism in the kingdom are extremely important to this day.

Following this foundation various localities within the mountainous realm seem to have been ruled by a series of Tibetan religious and secular rulers. The historical founding of the state known today in English as Bhutan is usually considered to be the year 1616, when a Tibetan monk named Ngawang Namgyal fled to the region seeking to free himself from control by the Dalai Lama and his Gelugpa sect of Buddhism. Ngawang Namgyal subsequently fought a number of battles against local rivals, TIBETANS, and even invading MONGOLS and upon his ultimate victory took the title of *Shabdrung,* "At Whose Feet One Submits." The new country founded by the Shabdrung was called *Drukyul,* which is the name still used by the Bhutanese today.

The administration established by the Shabdrung and codified in the *Tsa Yig* was maintained in Bhutan for the next 300 years; the *Tsa Yig* remained in place until the 1960s. The governmental structure, with the Shabdrung as the ultimate religious and secular authority, had two important leaders representing these separate realms just below him. The religious leader was titled Je Khenpo or Dharma Raja and the secular one, Druk Desi or Deb Raja. The secular leader could also be a monk but was always selected to serve a three-year term; the selection committee in the early decades was a monastic organization but by the 19th century at the latest had become a state council. The majority of the state's revenue in these early years was generated from taxes levied on the large number of goods traded between India and Tibet across the Shabdrung's territory.

The 18th century produced greater external influence to the small, mountain kingdom in the form of Chinese domination of Bhutan's external affairs and then the actions of the British as they sought domination of south Asia. The first British mission arrived in Bhutan in 1774 seek-

---

BHUTANESE: NATIONALITY

nation:
Bhutan or Kingdom of Bhutan

derivation of name:
There are two theories: *Bhu-uttan* meaning "high land" and *Bhotant* meaning "end of Tibet."

government:
Monarchy with the cabinet head of the national assembly serving as the head of government

capital:
Thimphu; in the past the capital moved to Punakha in the winter

language:
Dzongkha (official), several Tibetan and Nepalese dialects

religion:
Buddhism 75 percent, Hinduism 25 percent

earlier inhabitants:
There has been very little archaeological work done in Bhutan but inhabitation is known to extend back at least 4,000 years; the ethnicity of this early population remains unknown but is assumed to be related to the aboriginal Monpa peoples.

demographics:
Bhote or Bhutia 50 percent; Nepalese, including several ethnic groups, 35 percent; indigenous or migrant tribes 15 percent

ing trade with its Indian colony and peaceful border relations, but the British absorption of Assam in 1826 led to a disintegration of border relations and increased raids from the Bhutanese side. The British and Bhutanese also fought a minor war in the mid-1860s over Bhutan's occupation of several strategic mountain passes in Assam and Bengal. The British defeated the poorly armed Bhutanese, reoccupied the passes taken by Bhutan, and even annexed some land in Bhutan itself; as spelled out in the Treaty of Sinchula the Bhutanese received 50,000 rupees annually in exchange.

Just prior to the British-Bhutan War, the internal organization of Bhutan itself was rocked by a power struggle between the governor of Punakha and the Shabdrung and his ally, the governor of Tongsa. The matter was not settled until the conclusion of the war with Britain, which saw the ascendancy of Ugyen Wangchuk, governor of Tongsa. Wangchuk had his power further challenged in the 1880s but weathered the political storm. Nonetheless he did not have the backing of the entire country until 1907, when, with British assistance, he finally unified all of the local governors and districts into a solitary kingdom. His lineage continues to rule the small monarchy to this day, although the promise of a constitution in 2008 may lead to a greater division of power with the national assembly, first formed in 1953.

Since India's independence in the late 1940s Bhutan has been largely dependent on its large neighbor for defense, foreign affairs, and development of infrastructure. The last of these became extremely important in the 1950s to both Indian and Bhutanese security in the face of Chinese claims to Bhutan as part of the historical territory of Tibet. These claims have subsequently been dropped, and in the 1980s relations between the small kingdom and China improved.

The 20th century also introduced other changes to Bhutan when the third Wangchuk king, Jigme Dorji, began to modernize his country. He emancipated slaves and women, initiated a land reform project, and introduced a secular educational system. These social changes were followed during the reign of the fourth Wangchuk king, Jigme Singye, with political changes that granted more power to the country's national assembly. However, none of these changes has been enough to suit the country's Nepalese and other minorities, some of whom have rebelled against the assimilationist policies of the regime. The semirepressive

Bhutanese: nationality time line	
B.C.E.	
2000	Evidence of the first human inhabitation points to this period.
C.E.	
747	Guru Padsambhava, or Guru Rinpoche as he is sometimes known, flies from Tibet on the back of a tiger and settles in Taktsang Lhakhang, "Tiger's Nest."
1616	Ngawang Namgyal, a Drukpa monk, flees to the eastern Himalayas from Tibet and unites the people into the first incarnation of the Bhutanese state.
1629	First war between the newly founded Bhutan or Drukyul and Tibet. This year also marks the first recorded presence of Europeans, two Portuguese missionaries, in the region.
1631	Second war between Bhutan and Tibet, followed by a third in 1639.
1643	A combined Tibetan-Mongol army marches on Bhutan and neighboring Sikkim and Nepal.
1647	A fifth attempt by the Tibetans to conquer the new state is once again defeated.
1720	Bhutan becomes a vassal state to the Chinese, who also invade Tibet.
1774	The British arrive in Bhutan seeking trade and other relations.
1864–65	Two rivals for power in Bhutan engage in a civil war, which is immediately followed by the British-Bhutanese War, ending with the Treaty of Sinchula in 1865.
1882–85	Further civil strife in Bhutan is eventually put down by the former governor of Tongsa, Ugyen Wangchuk.
1907	Unification of the kingdom and establishment of the current Wangchuk dynasty.
1926	Sir Ugyen Wangchuk is succeeded by his son, King Jigme Wangchuk.
1949	Newly independent India returns the Bhutanese lands annexed by the British in 1865.
1952	The third Wangchuk king ascends to the throne as King Jigme Dorji Wangchuk.
1953	Creation of the national assembly, which in 2008 may become democratically elected.
1971	Bhutan becomes a member of the United Nations.
1972	The fourth Wangchuk king, Druk Gyalpo Jigme Singye Wangchuk, takes the throne at age 17.
1988–94	At least 100,000 people of Nepali descent are driven out of Bhutan and into refugee camps in Nepal.
2006	The fourth Wangchuk king abdicates in favor of his son, King Jigme Khesar Namgyal Wangchuk, two years earlier than expected.

Bhutanese government also blames prodemocracy activism in the kingdom on the Nepalese minority and between 1988 and 1994 forced about 100,000 of them out; most ended up in UN refugee camps in Nepal where they remain to this day.

BHUTIA

location:
Bhutan, Nepal, India, especially Sikkim and West Bengal

time period:
Possibly ninth century to the present

ancestry:
Tibetan

language:
Dzongkha, a Tibeto-Burman language with several dialects

CULTURAL IDENTITY

An important aspect of Bhutan's national identity is the centrality of Buddhism in religious and secular life. The country's origins, both mythological and historical, point to this centrality and it remains to this day. A significant number of Bhutanese continue to reside in the country's many monasteries and the people's name for the country, *Drukyul*, points to the dominant Buddhist sect among them, Drukpa Kagyu, which is also the state religion.

A second important focus for Bhutanese identity is the Wangchuk dynasty, which united the kingdom in the early 20th century and has taken the country into the contemporary world with social and political reforms that have slowly introduced modernization to many people's daily lives. Nonetheless the fact that 85 percent of the population continues to engage in subsistence agriculture while many construction and other jobs go to Indians and Nepalese points to the significant strides yet to be made toward a fully modern realm. Outside observers indicate that the expected adoption of a new constitution in 2008 may begin to produce these necessary changes.

The last important feature of Bhutanese identity are the internal divisions that continue to shake the country at its very core. Approximately one-third of Bhutan's population are from one of several Nepali ethnic groups who speak a language other than Dzongkha and practice Hinduism rather than Drukpa Kagyu Buddhism. These cultural differences have been used to scapegoat this large population for many of the country's social and economic problems, driving thousands into refugee camps in Nepal. Without the creation of a suitable modern national identity that incorporates both ethnic groups and balances cultural integration and political power sharing, the political changes expected in 2008 may not be enough to move the country into the 21st century.

Further Reading

Michael Aris. *Bhutan: The Early History of a Himalayan Kingdom* (Warminster, England: Aris & Phillips, 1979).

Russ Carpenter and Blyth Carpenter. *The Blessings of Bhutan* (Honolulu: University of Hawaii Press, 2002).

Barbara Crossette. *So Close to Heaven: The Vanishing Buddhist Kingdoms of the Himalayas* (New York: A. A. Knopf, distributed by Random House, 1995).

Nari Rustomji. *Bhutan: The Dragon Kingdom in Crisis* (New York: Oxford University Press, 1978).

Jamie Zeppa. *Beyond the Sky and the Earth: A Journey into Bhutan* (London: Macmillan, 1999).

Bhutanese Nepalis   *See* LHOTSHAMPA.

Bhutia (Bhote, Bhotia, Bhotiya, Denzongpa, Drukpa, Lachenpa, Lachungpa, Ngalop)

The Bhutia are the dominant ethnic group in the small Himalayan country of Bhutan; significant numbers also live in Nepal and the Indian regions of Sikkim and West Bengal.

GEOGRAPHY

The Bhutia homeland was originally Tibet, but since at least the 17th century most have made their home in the mountainous territories of Bhutan, Nepal, Sikkim, and West Bengal.

Bhutan is located between China, specifically Tibet, and India in the eastern Himalayas. The kingdom is mostly mountainous with its highest peak, Kula Kangri, soaring to 24,780 feet above sea level; however, some of the fertile valleys are relatively low with Drangme Chhu lying at just 318 feet. Sikkim has a similar geography but at slightly higher altitudes with a low of just 984 feet and a high at Mount Khangchendzonga of 28,166 feet above sea level. Nepal is similarly situated with lows below 1,000 feet above sea level on the Tarai Plain in the south and a high of about 29,000 on Mount Everest, or Sagarmatha as it is known in Nepali. This terrain means that the entire Bhutia region encompasses almost every climate on Earth from the hot, humid tropics of the lowlands to the permanent glaciers on the Himalayan peaks.

ORIGINS

The Bhutia are TIBETANS who began moving away from that region perhaps as early as the ninth century C.E.; however, Bhutanese mythology states that the first monk to flee his homeland, on the back of a female tiger, did so in 747 C.E., whereupon he established the first monastery in the territory that later became Bhutan.

HISTORY

The first historically accurate date for Bhutia activity is 1616, when Ngawang Namgyal, a monk from the Red Hat school of Buddhism,

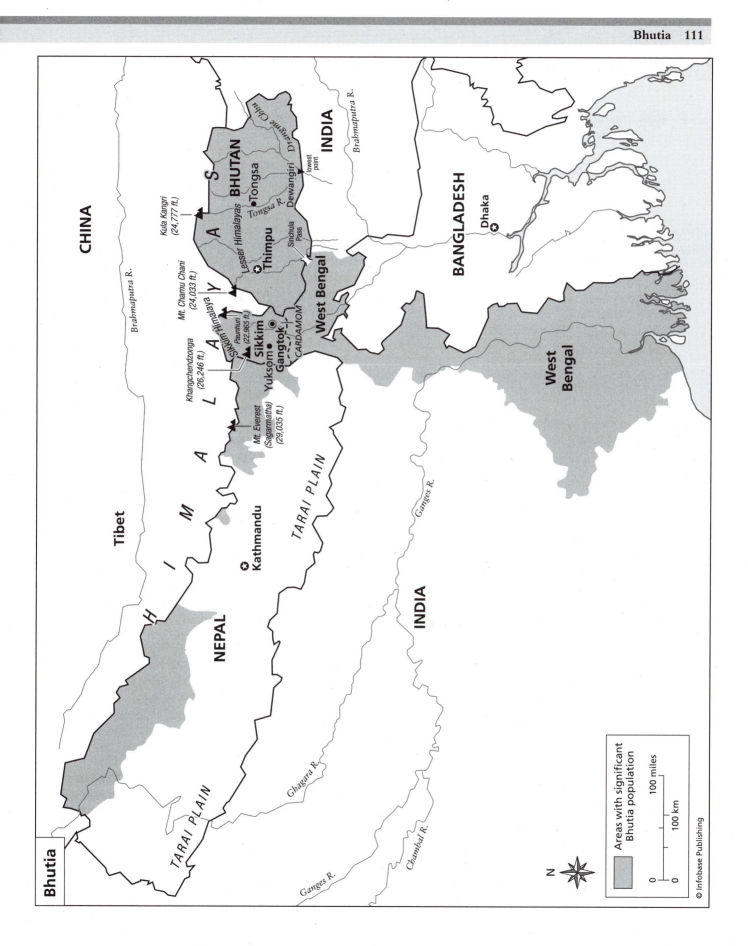

Bhutia

CHINA

Tibet

Brahmaputra R.

BHUTAN

Tongsa

Kula Kangri
(24,777 ft.)

Drangme Chhu

lowest
point

INDIA

Brahmaputra R.

Tongsa R.

Dewangiri

Lesser Himalayas

Thimpu

Sinchula
Pass

Mt. Chamu Chani
(24,033 ft.)

BANGLADESH

Dhaka

Sikkim Himalaya

Paunhuri
(22,965 ft.)

West Bengal

CARDAMOM

BANGLADESH

Khangchendzonga
(26,246 ft.)

Gangtok

Sikkim

Yuksom

West
Bengal

Mt. Everest
(Sagarmatha)
(29,035 ft.)

H I M A L A Y A S

TARAI PLAIN

Ganges R.

Tibet

Kathmandu

NEPAL

Ghagara R.

INDIA

Chambal R.

TARAI PLAIN

Ganges R.

N

Areas with significant
Bhutia population

0   100 miles

0   100 km

© Infobase Publishing

Bhutia time line

C.E.

ninth century Possible point at which the Bhutia begin migrating from Tibet into the Himalayas.

1616 Ngawang Namgyal, a Drukpa monk, flees to the eastern Himalayas from Tibet and unites the people into the first incarnation of the Bhutanese state.

1629 First war between the newly founded Bhutan or Drukyul and Tibet.

1631 Second war between Bhutan and Tibet, followed by a third in 1639.

1642 Phuntsog Namgyal becomes Chogyal or king in Sikkim at his capital of Yuksom.

1643 A combined Tibetan-Mongol army marches on Bhutan, neighboring Sikkim, and Nepal, trying to drive out followers of the Nyingmapa school of Buddhism.

1647 A fifth attempt by the Tibetans to conquer the new Bhutanese state is once again defeated.

1864–65 Two rivals for power in Bhutan engage in a civil war, which is immediately followed by the British-Bhutanese War, ending with the Treaty of Sinchula in 1865.

1882–85 Further civil strife in Bhutan is eventually put down by the former governor of Tongsa, Ugyen Wangchuk.

1907 Unification of the kingdom of Bhutan and establishment of the current Wangchuk dynasty.

1949 Newly independent India returns the Bhutanese lands annexed by the British in 1865.

1974 The Bhutia king of Sikkim is removed from power by a referendum, making the small region India's 22nd state.

fled Tibet after persecution by the dominant Yellow Hat or Gelugpa sect, which is still led by the Dalai Lama today. Ngawang Namgyal went on to establish a new kingdom in Bhutan, land he and his people called Drukyul after the name of their religion. He formalized the relationship between the religious and secular leadership of his people, fought several wars against invading Tibetans and MONGOLS, and codified the new kingdom's political and judicial system in a code called the *Tsa Yig*, parts of which remained in effect until the 1960s.

Ngawang Namgyal's kingdom survived the colonial era in south Asia relatively intact, although the British did capture and later annex a portion of southern Bhutan following a short war in 1864–65. The Bhutanese were granted 50,000 rupees annually for the land as spelled out in the Treaty of Sinchula; India subsequently returned the territory in 1949. Perhaps because of the difficulty of establishing infrastructure or any viable economic pursuit other than subsistence farming and conveyance across the mountains, the British allowed Bhutanese officials to remain relatively sovereign in their local domains. In 1907 they then assisted one of these local officials, Ugyen Wangchuk, governor of Tongsa, to unify all regions of Bhutan, inhabited largely by fellow Bhutia people, into a single kingdom. The Wangchuk dynasty continues to rule Bhutan to this day although the population of the small kingdom is only just over half Bhutia.

The Bhutia in Sikkim are of the same migrant stock as those in Bhutan, having likewise fled Tibet sometime in the early 15th century. As occurred in Bhutan, the Bhutia migrants to Sikkim quickly established monasteries and an autonomous kingdom headed by Phuntsog Namgyal. He took the title of *Chogyal*, "king," and settled his people in the higher altitudes of the region, driving the indigenous LEPCHA community into the forests and river valleys at lower elevations.

Early Bhutia society, wherever it existed, in Tibet, Bhutan, Sikkim, and elsewhere, was made up of three separate socioeconomic classes: royalty; *kazis*, who were landowners and generally participated in local leadership wherever they lived; and commoners. In Sikkim these distinctions have disappeared since the dismantling of the royal family in the 1970s, when the small kingdom became India's 22nd state, but in Bhutan they retain much of their prior importance. Elsewhere they have generally dissipated as well.

Even with the dismantling of the royal family of Sikkim the Bhutia there have retained some of the importance they garnered from having ruled the kingdom for several hundred years, although today they make up just about 15 percent of the state's population. Bhutia tend to be wealthier and better educated than other Sikkimese because of the control they exert over the lucrative cardamom crop; many former kazi also own other productive agricultural land in the mountainous region. In Sikkimese elections since 1974 garnering the vote of the Bhutia remains extremely important since no party has ever been able to form a state government without their support.

CULTURE

The most important cultural feature characterizing the Bhutia is their religion because it was this feature that created the ethnic group. In terms of culture and language more generally, prior to their exodus from Tibet, the Bhutia would not have differed significantly from other Tibetans;

it was only upon settling outside their traditional homeland that they took on their ethnonym or name. It was disagreements between their branch of Buddhism, sometimes called Red Hat for the color of their headgear but also Drukpa as a more specific term, and the larger Gelugpa or Yellow Hat Buddhists, most famously represented by the Dalai Lama, that drove the Bhutia into Bhutan originally. In Sikkim the most important Bhutia families, including the former king and his lineage, were more associated with Nyingma Buddhism, another Tibetan sect that differs slightly from the Gelugpas.

The Drukpa form of Buddhism began in 12th-century Tibet. A young master, Tsangpa Gyare, who subsequently took the title of *terton,* discovered an ancient text, *Six Equal Tastes,* which had been hidden by an earlier Buddhist master. Later he and his followers saw nine dragons emerge from the earth and take to the skies while flowers fell from the heavens. On the basis of this incident their school of religious thought was named Drukpa or Dragon People.

Today Buddhism retains its central position in the life of most Bhutia and most villages have a *gompa* or temple with both monks and nuns who participate in all local rituals and rites of passage, including marriages, birth ceremonies, death rites, agricultural events, and others. Most households have a small shrine with a Buddhist image in the corner of a main room and rituals at these shrines generally incorporate chanting or other participation by local religious specialists. When entering a Bhutia region monasteries are located within a short distance of one another and prayer flags and wheels and other Buddhist material culture become evident almost immediately. Generally speaking monasteries are the leading institutions of Bhutia society, while in Bhutan Drukpa Kagyu has been elevated to a state religion and thus even at the highest political and bureaucratic levels of society it is recognized as central to the Bhutanese identity. In the past every Bhutia family expected that at least one son would enter monastic life; gain an education, which was only available through monasteries; and thus bring honor upon them all.

As is the case with their religion and language, many other aspects of Bhutia life also resemble those of the Tibetans. The calendar used by the Bhutia is the same as that of the Tibetan Buddhists, with 12-year cycles named after animals and 60-year cycles that combine the 12 animal cycles with a cycle of five elements: wood, fire, iron, water, and earth. Prior to the modern era Bhutia dress, decoration, and other aspects of material culture likewise resembled their Tibetan cousins. The Bhutia also shared with the Tibetans the rarest marriage pattern on earth, polyandry, or the ability of a woman to have more than one husband. This pattern is not indicative of women's high status among the Bhutia or Tibetans; both societies are patriarchal and men are always the heads of households; rather, it was an economic strategy for landowning families to prevent the division of their holdings. In both societies the most common form of polyandry was fraternal polyandry, where a group of brothers all married the same woman. As a result the brothers continued to live together, farm the same land, and tend the same herds; thus their small parcel of land did not have to be divided. This marriage pattern is also an effective form of population control since each family could produce only the number of children possible for a single woman to bear and rear, rather than each brother's having his own wife and children. This practice has been outlawed in Bhutan since modernization efforts began in the 1970s but remains common in practice both inside and outside that country; its close cousin, polygyny, the ability to have more than one wife, continues as well. In Bhutan each man is able to have just three wives and only with the permission of the first wife.

Many aspects of Bhutia culture, from subsistence to housing, are dictated by the high altitude and cold terrains in which they live. In Sikkim the dominant subsistence practice among the Bhutia in the past was pastoralism, the rearing of herds of goats, yak, sheep, and horses. In winter families would move with their herds into the low, protected valleys, where grass and water were available in the tropical and subtropical environments, while in the summer they would move up into the mountains, out of the summer heat and humidity of the lowlands. While animal husbandry continues to be important in the north, trade has emerged in the south as an important occupation among Bhutia men. Where the climate allows it Bhutia families also grow barley, millet, potatoes, and other vegetables, while in Sikkim they control the lucrative cardamom crop.

Bhutia houses are made from wood and stone and generally have very thick mud walls that insulate the inhabitants from the cold and snow outside. These two-story structures are designed for animals to be stabled on the ground floor and for humans to live above, thus benefiting from the heat that rises off the backs of their herds. The famous Bhutia woven carpets and woolen clothing, made from sheep or yak wool, are likewise necessary for warmth in the cold Himalayan winters.

See also BHUTANESE: NATIONALITY.

FURTHER READING

Veena Bhasin. *Transhumants of Himalayas: Changspas of Ladakh, Gaddis of Himachal Pradesh, and Bhutias of Sikkim* (Delhi: Kamla-Raj Enterprises, 1996).

Chittaranjan Dash. *Social Ecology and Demographic Structure of Bhotias: Narratives and Discourses* (New Delhi: Concept, 2006).

Anandamayee Ghosh. *The Bhotias in Indian Himalayas: A Socio-Linguistic Approach* (Delhi: B. R., 2007).

Vineeta Hoon. *Living on the Move: Bhotiyas of the Kumaon Himalaya* (Thousand Oaks, Calif.: Sage, 1996).

R. R. Prasad. *Bhotia Tribals of India: Dynamics of Economic Transform[a]tion* (New Delhi: Gian Publishing House, 1989).

Bicolanos (Bicols)

The Bicolanos are lowland Filipinos who reside in the Bicol region of southern Luzon, one of the main islands of the Philippines. Just before the start of the 21st century they made up the fifth largest linguistic group in the country.

GEOGRAPHY

The Bicol region, or Bicolandia as it is sometimes called, is southeast of Manila, surrounded by the Pacific to the east, the Samar Sea to the southeast, the Sibuyan Sea to the southwest, and Quezon Province to the north. The area's six provinces, including the two separate island provinces of Catanduanes and Masbate, contain several volcanic mountains, including Mount Bulusan, Mount Isarog, and the iconic Mount Mayon, but most Bicolanos live in the lowland valleys around these mountains, leaving the hillsides and summits to other ethnic groups. The western and southern provinces of Bicol, Camarines Sur, Camarines Norte, and Albay differ from much of the rest of the country in not having distinct wet and dry seasons, while the eastern and northern regions of Sorsogon, Catanduanes, and Masbate are more typical in receiving extremely heavy rains between November and January; the remainder of the year is also fairly wet in these regions.

ORIGINS

The origins of the Bicolanos, as of all lowlander AUSTRONESIANS in the Philippines, are probably in south China, from which they sailed in double-outrigger dugout canoes about 5,000 years ago to Taiwan, and then later to the Philippines and Polynesia. There is no certainty as to why this population left south China; however, archaeologists have hypothesized that it was a combination of population pressure, increased commerce from the Yangtze River region of China and moving southward down the river and its tributaries, a growing demand for marine and tropical forest goods, and climate change.

Contemporary Austronesian languages can be subdivided into two distinctive groups that separate the languages of Austronesian Taiwan from those of the remainder of the family, which include all Malay and Oceanic languages. This linguistic division, in addition to several anomalies in the archaeological record, such as an absence of rice in the earliest Austronesian sites in Taiwan, indicates that the origins of the Austronesian people may have been two separate exoduses from southeast China. If these did occur in this manner, the first exodus was probably from Fujian Province in China to Taiwan, which saw the rise of TA-P'EN-K'ENG CULTURE, with its distinctively marked pottery and stone tools, but without archaeological evidence of domesticated rice. The descendants of this first wave would be the contemporary speakers of Taiwan's Austronesian languages, the ABORIGINAL TAIWANESE people. The second exodus may have occurred around 3000 B.C.E., taking a second wave of Austronesian speakers from southeastern China to Taiwan and then almost immediately to Luzon in the Philippines around the same period. This second wave, with its red slipped pottery, may also have been the ultimate source of the LAPITA CULTURE.

HISTORY

When they arrived in the Philippines about 3000 B.C.E. the Austronesian speakers would probably have met small bands of people who had already been residing on the islands for approximately 20,000 years. The hunting and gathering AETA peoples, as they are now called, probably lived in the most productive areas of the country, the coastlines, valleys, and lower hills, in very small, impermanent settlements. With the ability to grow their own crops the incoming Austronesians could maintain significantly higher population densities than the Aeta and thus pushed the hunter-gatherers into the more marginal highland forests and mountaintops, where they still live today. The nu-

---

BICOLANOS

location:
The Bicol region of the southeastern peninsula of Luzon, the Philippines

time period:
3000 B.C.E. to the present

ancestry:
Austronesian

language:
There are five different Bicolano dialects, divided by region; all are Austronesian languages.

merically and technologically stronger agriculturalists also seem to have lent their language to the Aeta, all of whom today speak Austronesian languages rather than the more ancient languages they would have carried with them in their much earlier migrations.

There is no distinct Bicol history, as separate from that of the other Austronesian lowlanders, until the arrival of the Spanish in the 16th century. The first dealings were described in 1569, when two events involving the Bicolanos were mentioned. In that year Luis Enriques de Guzman arrived in the Bicol region, then called Ibalon after the village in which he landed and the origin myth of the same name, and the Spanish Augustinian priest Father Alonzo Jimenez learned Bicol, wrote a catechism in this language, and began the process of converting the locals to Catholicism. In these early colonial days the Spanish also built a shipyard in the region, which sent ships out on the trade run between Manila and Acapulco, Mexico.

The region's later colonial period was less peaceful than the early days, and Spanish descriptions of the people tended to focus on the Bicolanos' ferocity; their name appears in the histories of several anticolonial rebellions. The first rebellion with a specific mention of Bicolanos was in 1649, when the people of Sorsogon participated in the largely Waray Samar's Sumuroy Revolt. The people of the Camarines rose up in minor rebellions at the same time as these larger activities as well; they also revolted against the British several times during Britain's occupation of Manila between 1762 and 1764. During this period the Moros, or FILIPINO MUSLIMS, from the southern regions of the archipelago, also frequently raided the Bicol region and left behind a legacy of vocabulary terms from the south, love of spicy food, and fear of these southerners. As late as the 1940s Bicolanos remembered being told to beware of the Moros, a threat that was used by parents to keep their children in line. The Moro Wars against the United States, from 1901 to 1913, likewise took contingents of Moros north to Luzon, where they were joined by many local people, including Bicolanos, in their fight against the country's newest colonial power.

In addition to these anticolonial events, Bicol was also known as a center for the production of Manila hemp or abaca. In the 17th century a Spanish missionary, Father Pedro Espellargas, invented a stripping machine that ultimately made the production of this crop

---

Bicolanos time line

B.C.E.

3000 The initial migration of the Austronesian speakers, including the ancestors of the Bicolanos, to the Philippines.

C.E.

1569 Luis Enriques de Guzman names the Bicol region Ibalon.

Father Alonzo Jimenez learns Bicol, writes a catechism in this language, and begins the process of converting the locals to Catholicism.

1649 Samar's Sumuroy Revolt sees the participation of Bicolanos from Sorsogon; at the same time the residents of the Camarines also rise up against the Spanish.

1669 Spanish missionary Father Pedro Espellargas of Bacon invents a knife that allows abaca or Manila hemp to be harvested and stripped much more easily, leading to a new product for the colonial economy.

1754 Bacon and Bulan are destroyed by the Moros and the townspeople are captured. Moro raids in Bicol continue for more than 100 years.

1762–64 The British occupy Manila and the people of the Camarines rise up against them several times.

1898 Governor Zaidin surrenders in Naga City and Bicol attains independence from Spain.

1900–01 Many Bicolanos participate in the war against the United States.

1901–13 The Moro Wars against the United States move more Moros north into Bicol.

1941 The Japanese occupy the Philippines during World War II.

1944 The United States retakes the Philippines.

1945 The Philippines attain independence from the United States.

---

central to the colonial economy, especially in the 19th century. Although today the uses of abaca in the making of rope and other products have diminished with the invention of artificial fibers, it remains an important part of the local Bicolano economy.

The first phase of Bicol's colonial experience came to an end in September 1898 when the Spanish governor Zaidin surrendered his territory to the local Bicolanos' *guardia civil* after they laid siege to the governor and his retinue at church. After surrounding the church the leaders of the raid, Elias Angeles and Felix Plazo, rounded up the women and children and turned them over to the nuns of the Colegio de Santa Isabel. For two days they held the men inside while the governor's secretary negotiated with the civil guards and an agreement was reached. The governor signed the agreement on September 19, ending about 300 years of Spanish rule in the territory. Today a bell tower at the San Francisco church in Naga City marks the spot of Bicol independence from the Spanish.

The end of Spanish rule in Bicol did not bring about the long-lasting independence envisioned by Angeles, Plazo, and many others. Almost immediately the Philippines were thrown into further conflict against the United States, whose warships arrived in 1899. As they had during the Spanish colonial period, the Bicolanos did not capitulate to the Americans without a fight when they arrived in Bicol in 1900. During the war the Bicolanos of Camarines Sur declared themselves independent, and on March 10, 1900, all chiefs and officials who had submitted to the Americans were dismissed in favor of Ludovico Arejola, who already had significant experience as a resistance fighter. Approximately 10,000 Bicolanos participated in the events of March 10 in the Bicol towns of Taban, Minalabac, and Camarines Sur, including an eight-woman unit from the last-named town called Damas Benemeritas de la Patria who served as nurses, aids, and provisioners. The Bicolanos continued to fight against the much more heavily armed and trained Americans for almost two years, from February 1900 until late 1901; they experienced atrocities such as rape, the pillaging and burning of villages, and having the inhabitants of entire villages tied up with wire and rope and dragged behind horses. Despite the overpowering evidence of these events as described in numerous diaries and local accounts, many American versions of this war's history describe the Bicolanos as willing collaborators with American power, a fact that has continued to cause bitterness in the region ever since.

Complete independence was gained in Bicol in 1945 following the expulsion of the Japanese forces who occupied the country during World War II. Since independence Bicol has attracted international mining companies that extract a significant amount of gold from the region, as well as tourists, who arrive for the surfing and whale watching, and for views of one of the most perfect cone-shaped volcanoes in the world on Mount Mayon.

CULTURE

The Austronesian migrants to the Philippines arrived from Taiwan bearing several domesticated plants, including rice, the contemporary staple crop in the Bicol region; domesticated pigs, dogs, and chickens; and a lifestyle built around the agricultural calendar. Contemporary Bicolanos continue to be largely agricultural people, with that sector of the economy providing about 60 percent of the regional gross domestic product (GDP). In addition to rice, corn, sweet potatoes, cassava, and coconuts are grown both for subsistence and for sale. Other cash crops include abaca or Manila hemp, coffee, cocoa, and *calamansi*, a form of citrus fruit. With its extensive coastlines, Bicol also provides fish for both domestic consumption and sale on the local and national markets. Thirty percent of the regional GDP is derived from the service industry, mostly catering to the many tourists who travel to Bicol for the coastlines and mountains; a small industrial sector contributes about 10 percent. Several abaca industries dominate this sector of the economy.

One of the most important legacies of the Spanish colonial period in Bicol is Roman Catholicism; the Christian Trinity has replaced the local creator god Gugurang and church attendance remains very high to this day. However, this is not to say that some indigenous beliefs and practices have not survived into the 21st century. Infants continue to be named according to the conditions at the time of their birth, and divination and agricultural rituals from the precolonial period continue to serve as important events in many Bicol villages. In addition many evil spirits, witches, and supernatural monsters continue to haunt the imagination of many Bicolanos, even the well educated, and ancestor worship retains its place in most families through the offering of food and other gifts at important times of the year.

Another important cultural feature from the precolonial days that has survived into the present is the centrality of the origin myth of Ibalon, Bicol's prior name. The myth describes a warrior named Handiong who saved Ibalon by slaying various monsters and other evil beings. Handiong also introduced laws, rice, sailboats, plows, pottery, and even writing to the people of his region and thus is basically the founding father of the Bicolanos and their culture. According to the myth the legacy of Handiong was handed down to Bantong, who killed the last monster to reside in Ibalon, Rabot, and after that the humans were able to survive on their own with the products and skills given to them by their warrior ancestor.

FURTHER READING

Domingo Abella. *Bikol Annals: A Collection of Vignettes of Philippine History.* Vol. 1 (Manila: See of Nueva Caceres, 1954).

Fenella Cannell. *Power and Intimacy in the Christian Philippines* (New York: Cambridge University Press, 1999).

Francisco A. Mallari and S. J. Ibalon. *Vignettes of Bicol History* (Quezon City. Philippines: New Day, 1999).

James J. O'Brien, ed. *The Historical and Cultural Heritage of the Bicol People.* 2d ed. (Naga, Philippines: Ateneo de Naga, 1968).

Norman G. Owen. *The Bikol Blend: Bikolanos and Their History* (Quezon City, Philippines: New Day, 1999).

Maria Lilia F. Realubit. *Bikols of the Philippines.* (Naga City, Philippines: AMS Press, 1983).

Biharis (Behari)

The term *Bihari people* can refer to three different groups of people with an affiliation to the Indian state of Bihar. The first and largest group of Biharis are the current residents of the state of Bihar, a multiethnic, multilingual state in northeastern India. A second group of people sometimes called Biharis are the approximately 1 million Urdu speakers who had been residents of the Indian state of Bihar prior to the violence that ensued in 1947 when the former British colony of India was divided into the two independent states of India and Pakistan. At partition a large number of this group fled to what was then East Pakistan. Nearly 25 years later when East Pakistan with its Bengali majority broke free from Pakistan and became the independent country of Bangladesh, these Urdu-speaking people, known locally as Biharis because of their state of origin, became the victims of persecution and reprisals. They had not supported the war of independence because linguistically they were closely related to the Urdu-speaking population of West Pakistan; as a result thousands were killed and many others lost their homes, businesses, bank accounts, jobs, and landholdings. At that time about half a million of these Urdu-speaking Biharis fled Bangladesh, but the new Pakistan only took in about one-third of that number; thousands of others entered the country illegally, and today about 100,000 live in Pakistan as stateless peoples called Biharis or Stateless Pakistanis. In addition about 250,000 more of these Urdu-speaking stateless Biharis live in 66 squalid urban refugee camps located in Bangladesh. The third reference to the Biharis is to the approximately 80 million members of the Bihari ethnolinguistic groups, that is, people who speak one of the 12 recognized Indo-Aryan languages classified as Bihari; this entry is about this particular group of Biharis.

The history of the Bihari people is as ancient as the first Indo-Aryans who carried their dialects and cultures when they moved into the Indian subcontinent from Central Asia in about 1800 B.C.E. Since that time the Biharis have participated in some of the most important events in Indian history. They were the founders of several great Indian empires, the Magadha in the seventh–fourth centuries B.C.E. and the Mauryan in the fourth–second centuries B.C.E. Asoka, the greatest Mauryan king, probably spoke an ancient form of Magahi, or Magadhi, as it is sometimes written, one of the 12 Bihari languages recognized today. Two Indian religions were also centered on the region and people of Bihar, Buddhism and Jainism. Prince Gautama achieved his enlightenment in 509 B.C.E. in the Bihari town of Bodh Gaya and gave birth to the Buddhist tradition, while five of the 24 ancient founders of Jain communities were natives of Bihar, including the most influential, 24th Tirthankar, Lord Mahavira, who was born and achieved nirvana in Bihar. Bihari also established two of India's ancient universities, Nalanda and Vikramshila.

Since the seventh and eighth centuries C.E. Biharis have played a much less influential role in the history of India. During this medieval period the indigenous Gupta dynasty fell and Bihar became a distant outpost of the ruling sultans of Delhi of the Mughal dynasty. During the subsequent British colonial period Biharis were ruled under the presidency of Bengal, and thus all important posts were held and decisions made by BENGALIS rather than local Biharis. However, Mohandas K. Gandhi chose Bihar as the spot from which to launch his anticolonial activism in 1917 because he received a letter from a local indigo farmer, Raj Kumar Shukla, illustrating the hardships suffered at the hands of the British. Gandhi was jailed in Bihar for refusing to leave the state at the behest of the colonial administration and thus began a 30-year process of decolonization in the jewel of the British colonial crown. In the present day the people of Bihar suffer with a nearly 50 percent poverty rate and one of the lowest literacy rates in the country. Of course not all individuals in the state are Bihari, with Hindi and Urdu among the most dominant languages, but the state's profile does provide a glimpse into the world of some Bihari people.

Despite their long history it was only in the early 20th century that George Grierson, an Anglo-Irish linguist serving in the Indian civil service, classified and named the language family known today as Bihari. The family includes Maithili and Bhojpuri, the most common Bihari

BIHARIS

location:
Northern India, especially the state of Bihar, as well as Bangladesh and Nepal

time period:
Approximately 1800 B.C.E. to the present

ancestry:
Indo-Aryan and Munda

language:
Twelve different Bihari languages are spoken by people from this ethnic group; all are Indo-Aryan languages.

languages with almost 50 million speakers between them in the early 21st century, as well as smaller language groups from Nepal, such as Musasa, with only 50,000 speakers. Altogether 12 different languages are classified in the Bihari group: Angika, Bhojpuri, Kudmali, Magahi, Maithili, Panchpargania, Sadri, and Surajpuri primarily in India; Majhi and Musasa primarily in Nepal; Oraon Sadri in Bangladesh; and Hindustani in the Caribbean state of Suriname. Many speakers of these languages also speak and, if literate, read Hindi as well; Nepali, Bengali, Oriya, English, and other Bihari languages are also common second languages. As Indo-Aryan languages, the Bihari languages share a significant number of vocabulary and grammatical structures with Hindi and Bengali. For example Sadri, with its 2.1 million speakers, shares between 58 and 71 percent of its vocabulary with Hindi and between 45 and 65 percent with Bengali. However, even within each language there are sometimes significant dialectical differences based on either region or caste. Among the more than 25 million Bhojpuri speakers in India and Nepal, region is generally more important than caste or class in determining dialect. However, among the nearly 25 million Maithili speakers in India and Nepal, caste produces the widest variation in the version of the language that is spoken, although all dialects are mutually intelligible; the major division is that between the Brahmin caste and others with the two dialects differing by about 10 percent. The Brahmin dialect is viewed as superior by most speakers.

Culturally the speakers of these languages differ significantly in terms of their country and region of residence, religion, caste, and class. Urban and rural differences play a large role in determining the culture of Biharis, probably even more than country of residence. Most rural Biharis are agriculturalists, growing rice and other crops, many as tenant farmers or sharecroppers. Urban Biharis engage in a wide variety of economic activities, from the professions to unskilled labor. Biharis also practice a wide variety of religions, including Hinduism, Islam, Jainism, and traditional religions that place natural and ancestral spirits at the center of their worldviews; among Muslim Bihari most are Sunnis, but a few Shiites can also be found in this group. With regard to caste there are many Brahmin Biharis who occupy the highest hierarchical level in the Indian caste system, that of priests and teachers, especially among Maithili speakers. In the contemporary world not all Brahmins actually engage in these

occupations and there are certainly poor Brahmins throughout India; however, it is also the case that many Brahmins are well-educated urban professionals, including among Biharis. At the other end of the hierarchical spectrum, in Nepal the Musasa people are primarily landless, unskilled laborers and are considered among the lowest of the category that used to be known as the Untouchables. These people are outside the Hindu *varna* system entirely because they are not believed to have sprung from the body of the original human as created by Brahma; in India they would be members of the group SCHEDULED CASTES.

See also INDO-ARYANS.

Blang (Bulang, Bùlǎng Zú, Bulong)

The Blang, along with the DEANG, are believed to be the descendants of an ancient tribe called Pu who were the earliest inhabitants of the Lancang and Nujiang River valleys. At the end of the third century B.C.E. the Pu people and their lands fell under the control of the HAN (Chinese) Empire. Sometime after the 14th century C.E., when the Pu are recorded as having paid tribute to the ruling Yuan dynasty in the form of iron hoes, the blend of Han people and the Pu became its own unique ethnic group, the Blang.

According to the latest survey the Blang have a population of about 92,000 scattered across a mountainous region covered by dense vegetation. With an altitude range of 4,900–7,545 feet above sea level the area has a mild climate, plentiful rainfall, fertile soil, and abundant natural resources.

The Blang draw their living from agriculture, and their main crops include cotton, sugarcane, and the world famous Pu'er tea, a fermented large-leaf tea that is usually sold in compressed cakes of tea leaves. They live in bamboo houses located within small villages of about 100 households representing a variety of different clans. Their culture and traditions are preserved through a rich oral literature that includes legends, folktales, stories, poems, and ballads as well as a body of ritual that brings these stories to life.

The Blang both worship their ancestors and practice animism, reflecting their close relationship with nature. They interpret the signs of nature as good or bad omens. For instance if they see a bamboo rat or toad, they believe they must keep away from it in order to prevent the death of a relative. In addition while

BLANG

location:
Xishuangbanna Dai Autonomous Prefecture in Yunnan Province, China, and the Simao and Lincang regions. Most live in Menghai and Shuangjiang Counties

time period:
Sometime after 1368 to the present

ancestry:
An ancient tribe called Pu

language:
A number of dialects belonging to the Austro-Asiatic Mon-Khmer language group. The two main dialects are Bulang (Blang proper) and Awa (Aerwa). Two different scripts are used: Totham and Tolek. Dai, Wa, and Chinese languages are also in common use.

most Blang are buried at the time of their death, those who die a violent death are cremated, to prevent their misfortune from affecting others. In the Xishuangbanna area some Blang people also practice Buddhism as a result of their close interactions with the DAI people.

Blang festive celebrations are usually accompanied by singing and dancing. Following the rhythm of gongs and drums, girls form a circle and are joined by boys, who jump into the circle and dance with the girls. Boys and girls are initiated into adult life in a special ceremony that is held when they turn 14. Girls light special branches and dye their teeth black by chewing betel nut; blackened teeth or teeth covered with gold are considered much more attractive than those that are left their natural color. After this ceremony they become young adults and are ready for marriage. On full-moon evenings young men dress in new clothes and go to sing at the girls' bamboo houses. Girls open their doors and express their admiration by presenting tea and blowing smoke at their visitors.

Blang patrilineal clans are exogamous: individuals must marry outside their own clan. Present-day Blangs are usually free to choose their own marriage partners with only occasional family pressure to reconsider their choices.

Bonan (Baonan, Bao'an, Baonuo, Paoan, Pao-an, Paongan)

With a population of roughly 16,000 people according to the year 2000 census, the Bonan are one of China's smaller national minority groups. The group was formed through intermarriage with other minorities including the HUI and the HAN. The Bonan minority is thought to have begun to form during the empire of the MONGOLS, when many inhabitants of Central Asia were taken to China to serve as soldiers and administrators. The Bonan were Mongol troops who were ordered to help protect the empire against the TIBETANS. Bonan live in various areas including some villages in Jishishan County. The name *Bonan* can be translated as "I protect you," reflecting the people's history as guardians of their area.

In the early 1800s there was conflict between the Bonans who had adopted Islam and those who retained their Tibetan Buddhist religion, adopted when they moved into Tibet during the Mongol period. Religious quarrels and an argument over water rights split the two groups. The Muslim Bonan moved east to Gansu; at first they resided for a few years in Xunhua before moving to various places including Gansu Province, Dahejia, and Liuji in Linxia County near the Jishi Mountain. At the same time the small Buddhist community remained in Tibet. Nowadays the two communities do not consider themselves a common people, although they are classified together by the Chinese government.

The Bonan are known throughout China for their craftsmanship, specifically the Bonan knife, of high quality and artfully made with ox horn handles. In many places in China the Bonan knife is considered a prized possession. Some Bonan make a living from the profits of selling this knife, along with farming and logging. Those who work as farmers grow corn, barley, and peas.

The Bonan speak a language belonging to the Mongolian branch of the Altaic family, but now, because of daily contacts with the Han, they mostly use Chinese for communication. They are culturally similar to the Hui. The color of clothing that the women wear signifies marital status. Married women wear black veils; unmarried ones wear green veils; old women wear white ones. The Bonan women who reside in Gansu generally wear bright-colored clothing. The men wear black or white round-topped caps and white jackets.

Some sources mention that Bonan are fond of wrestling, horseback riding, and impromptu singing. They have a variety of festivals, including the Almsgiving Festival and the Kaizhai Festival, which ends the Muslim month of Ramadan, when food and drink cannot be taken during the daylight hours.

Bontoc (Bontok)

The Bontoc are a subdivision of the larger IGOROT group, which is made up of 10 Austronesian peoples in and around the Cordillera region of central Luzon, the Philippines. The term *Bontoc* refers to mountains in their own language and points to their residence in the highlands of central Luzon. More specifically the Bontoc live along the Chico River, one of many that had been slated by the Marcos regime in the 1970s for damming for hydroelectric power. The project was scrapped in the 1980s after the World Bank withdrew and both KALINGA and Bontoc activism made the project politically and economically unviable.

The Bontoc, like many of their Igorot neighbors, are wet rice farmers who grow their

BONAN

location:
Southwest Gansu, Qinghai, and Tibet

time period:
The Yuan and Ming dynasties (1271–1644 to the present)

ancestry:
Mongolian

language:
Bonan, a Mongolian language in the larger Altaic language family. There are two dialects of Bonan, Jishishan and Tongren, with several subdialects each. Han Chinese is used for written communication.

BONTOC

location:
Central Mountain Province, Luzon, the Philippines

time period:
3000 B.C.E. to the present

ancestry:
Austronesian

language:
Bontok, a Northern Luzon language in the larger Austronesian language family

BOUYEI

location:
Guizhou (namely, Bjie, Zunyi, Tongren areas), Guiyang, Bouyei-Miao autonomous counties in Xingyi and Anshun Prefectures, Yunnan, and Sichuan Provinces. Some Bouyei also live in Vietnam as one of the 54 minorities of that country.

time period:
900 C.E. to the present

ancestry:
The Bouyei probably share ancestry with the Zhuang; if they do, their ancestors would be the ancient Yue people

language:
Bouyei, a Sino-Tibetan language; some also speak Mandarin. With help from the government in 1956 the Bouyei created their own writing system derived from the Latin alphabet.

staple crop on extensive terraces that their ancestors carved out of the mountains almost 2,000 years ago. Today the terraces of both the Bontoc and related IFUGAO are major tourist attractions that draw in substantial amounts of foreign currency to the local and national economies. In addition to wet rice the Bontoc grow a number of other crops, including millet, beans, maize, and *camotes,* a kind of sweet potato. Whether they are engaged in cutting terraces, sowing, harvesting, weeding, or any other agricultural activity, the Bontoc accompany all practical tasks with religious rituals that thank the gods and spirits, request assistance, or merely acknowledge ownership of the land by ancestors and other spirits.

Although some Bontoc and other Igorot have converted to Christianity since American missionaries began their work in the area in the early 20th century, many aspects of their local religion beyond these agricultural rites have survived. Their religious system is a hierarchical one that recognizes a supreme creator god named Lumawig at the top of the system; he symbolizes the power of nature and is believed to have taught the Bontoc how to live in their mountain home. Priests, who are born into their position, hold monthly rituals to acknowledge Lumawig's power over their crops, the weather, sickness, health, and life itself. Below Lumawig in their religious pantheon the Bontoc also acknowledge the abilities of *anito,* ancestral spirits, who act as elders in family matters and must be consulted about all major decisions. Evil spirits are also part of the Bontoc cosmology, and when a Bontoc person dies he or she is left propped up underneath the house for 10 to 24 days while various rituals and events take place in order to cast out these evil spirits prior to the body's interment.

Bontoc social life in the past was centered around village subsections, called *ato,* in which 15 to 50 interrelated families made their home. Each *ato* was only loosely connected to the others and displayed a considerable degree of local autonomy. On the whole households could be either nuclear or extended families, but prior to the Christian era the most important aspect of the household was that young women and men did not live in them. Instead each *ato* would have female and male dormitories where young people went to learn the skills and knowledge necessary to survive as an adult Bontoc, to interact with other young people, and to find marriage partners among the residents of the other dormitory.

Bouyei (Bafan, Bo-I, Bouyi, Bo-y, Bui, Burao, Buyei, Buyi, Buyui, Chung-Chia, Dioi, Dujunman, Dunjun barbarians, Pui, Pu-I, Pujai, Pu-jui, Puyi, Puyoi, Shuihu, Zhongjia, Zhongmiao)

The roughly 3 million Bouyei alive today are believed by many to have the same ancestry as the ZHUANG people because of their similar language, habits, and traditions. This makes them the descendents of the ancient Yue peoples. Both the Zhuang and Bouyei are categorized as speakers of Zhuang-Dong or Kam-Tai languages.

The Bouyei, who reside in southern China and northern Vietnam, have traditionally been farmers, working the land held by large kin groups or, after reforms made in the Tang dynasty (618–907), on land held by feudal lords who were appointed by local governments. This feudal system of land tenure survived for about 1,000 years until late in the Qing dynasty, which fell in 1911, when rich landlords replaced this landed nobility. Little changed for the Bouyei peasants, who continued to work in the fields and paddies of others. Even today the Bouyei are primarily farmers growing rice, wheat, millet, sorghum, corn, and various vegetables for personal use. The region's fertile soils and mild climate also support fields of cotton, ramie, tobacco, tea, and sugarcane, all grown as cash crops to sell on the local, domestic, and international markets. In addition to these crops many Bouyei keep chickens or a pig or two for domestic consumption. Both pork and chicken have symbolic attributes that go beyond their importance for subsistence, pork signifying a good harvest and various parts of the chicken symbolizing good luck, accomplishment, and relaxation.

In the past century the Bouyei have experienced tremendous change with the various political transformations that have rocked China more generally (*see* CHINESE: NATIONALITY). Landlords and kin groups were replaced as landowners by large, state-run collectives and cooperatives for which the rural peasants continued to work. As a result of these changes productivity in grain output increased with an increase in land under irrigation. Many industries have also arisen in the Bouyei region, including iron, steel, and electronic products, especially since changes in Chinese Communist Party ideology have led to the glorification of wealth. There has also been an increase in roads and in education and medical care infrastructure.

The average yearly income for the Bouyei today is around 2,500 yuan (roughly 300 dollars), five times greater than a decade ago. In addition to improved agricultural output and the introduction of various industries, this increase was caused in part by an enlargement of the tourism industry in Bouyei locations. In the early years of this century tourism began to add roughly $121 million to Bouyei income. Tourist infrastructure built to accommodate this influx includes a museum in Zhenshan Village, Guizhou Province, where costumes from Bouyei history can be observed and visitors can listen to traditional folktales told by Bouyei docents. In addition Bouyei arts and crafts draw tourists to their region. For example their *nuo* dramas, which double as ceremonies to dispel evil spirits and to treat disease, are performed for paying audiences today rather than for their traditional purposes. One of the crafts the Bouyei are particularly known for is batik. According to Bouyei legend batik was a gift to them from a passing stranger who taught them the art during a bad harvest season. From the batik the villagers began to make garments that they could exchange in the market for food. The Bouyei also make a variety of embroidery, mats, and hats that are sold in China and in foreign markets.

Tourists are also drawn to the Bouyei region by the continued use of traditional stone buildings, especially in mountainous areas. In these traditional villages the largest of which has about 220 families or 1,200 people, every structure is built of solid rock. Bouyei men take great pride in their stonemasonry skills, working with tile and stone to create elaborate patterned roofs on solid stone buildings. A few Bouyei villages also contain structures of wood or bamboo, as well as modern brick and tile.

Bouyei practice ancestor worship and believe in gods associated with various mountains, trees, lakes, rivers, thunder, and other forces of nature. The Bouyei worship these gods during festivals, like the Spring and Zhongyuan Festivals, where they make sacrifices to the gods and pray for peace. If a festival is not directed to these gods, it is usually in remembrance of ancestors or leaders of uprisings. One of these festivals is celebrated on April 8 and is called the Ox King Festival. To celebrate an offering is made to ancestors in the form of cakes and dyed glutinous rice. Cattle are given half of the offerings after the ceremony, along with a day of rest as reward for their work.

Bouyei clothing is often dark colored and edged with bright colored lace. Married women are distinguished through a symbol on their headcloths. In the past most women married between the ages of 12 and 16 years. For the most part young people are given the choice of whom they are to marry. Courtship usually begins when a young woman throws an embroidered silk ball to the man she would like to court her. If he consents, they usually go for a walk. During courtship young couples sing to each other to get to know the other person better and to express their love. They sing mainly *langshao* songs. For the Bouyei singing is so popular in courtship that some say that it would be impossible to find a lover without singing.

Although the vast majority of Bouyei people live in China, the 1,500 or so Bouyei living in northern Vietnam are recognized as one of that country's official minority groups. They live in Lao Cai and Ha Giang Provinces, with only those in the latter region retaining their own language. The Lao Cai Bouyei, who speak Mandarin, probably fled to Vietnam during the Nanlong Rebellion in 1797.

Brahui (Brohi)

The Brahui are a Dravidian-speaking people who live much farther north than the majority of speakers in that family, the largest groups of which are TAMILS, MALAYALIS, and TELUGUS. They reside primarily in Baluchistan, northwest Pakistan, and neighboring Afghanistan; a small number of Brahui also live in Iran but are outside the scope of this work.

Because of this geographic separation from fellow DRAVIDIANS, the origins of the Brahui remain of interest to many linguists, historians, and other scholars. Two theories have emerged to explain their location far from the Deccan of India: first, they are a last vestige of a period when Dravidian speakers dominated all of south Asia; second, they migrated north between 880 and 1100 C.E. as a result of political and land pressures in the south. Some scholars who adhere to the former hypothesis also claim the Brahui are the descendants of India's most ancient civilization, the HARAPPANS, but this is a minority view and solid evidence is lacking. Most linguists favor the second hypothesis, that the Brahui are relatively new migrants in the northern reaches of south Asia, having traveled through Gujarat and Sindh until they settled in the Kalat highlands of Baluchistan. The most substantial evidence for this hypothesis is that the vast majority of Indo-Aryan loanwords in Brahui are from Baluchi, the speakers

BRAHUI

location:
Baluchistan in northwest Pakistan and Afghanistan

time period:
Unknown to the present

ancestry:
Dravidian.

language:
Brahui, a northern Dravidian language

BRAO

location:
Northern Cambodia,
southern Laos, and west-
ern Vietnam

time period:
After the 13th century to
the present

ancestry:
Mon-Khmer

language:
Brao or Lave, a Mon-
Khmer language

of which arrived in Baluchistan only in the 13th century. If the Brahui had been in that region significantly earlier, we would expect to find loanwords from many other, more ancient languages from that region, such as Sindhi or Pashto.

Most Brahui in the past lived as nomadic herders, moving up and down the hilly terrain with their herds of goats, sheep, and cattle. Those who live in Afghanistan have largely continued this way of life while some of the majority who live in Pakistan have settled to become tenant farmers. When the Brahui were nomadic they lived in goat hair tents that were easily erected, dismantled, and moved with them on their seasonal migrations. Most of their food items were from their herds but from March to October some families did grow fruit, vegetables, and even some cereal grains such as wheat. In the past century more and more families have begun to rely on these agricultural products and small Brahui villages have sprung up throughout the Kalat highlands of Pakistan.

Brahui society is still largely tribal and there are 29 different tribal divisions still recognized among the community. Each individual inherits membership in his or her lineage, clan, and tribe through the father in a system of patrilineal descent, and the position of *sadar* or tribal chief is likewise handed down from father to son. The *sadar* today is largely a ceremonial position, but in some communities it retains its role as mediator between the local population and the central government. This has been the political situation among the Brahui since about 1700 when they were first ruled by a branch of the GHILZAI tribe, themselves a subgroup of PASHTUNS.

Most Brahui are Sunni Muslims as are the majority of their neighbors in both Pakistan and Afghanistan. However, prior to the 1980s many Brahui women did not experience the separation or purdah of some of their neighbors since their work in fields and with herds was necessary for the family to survive; wearing a veil was also not strictly enforced in many families. Nonetheless polygyny, the ability to have more than one wife, was allowed for those few who could afford it, and divorce was rare. Since the 1980s Brahui women have experienced some loss of independence, especially in Afghanistan, where rule by the Taliban in the 1990s enforced total separation and covering for all women. In Pakistan as well there has been a greater cultural emphasis on controlling

women, and many have chosen or are forced to wear a scarf or full *hijab* when outside their family home.

Brao (Lave, Love, Khmer Loeu)

The Brao are a small Mon-Khmer–speaking ethnic group who live in the region of southern Laos and northern Cambodia; a very small number of Brao also live in the adjacent region of Vietnam. They are usually classified together with the Lun, Kravet, and Kreung because the four groups speak mutually intelligible Mon-Khmer languages and are culturally similar.

The history of the Brao remains somewhat unclear, but some scholars believe that their ancestors were members of the Khmer empire, which ruled Cambodia and adjacent areas of Southeast Asia from the ninth to the 13th century. This belief is based on the Brao Mon-Khmer linguistic heritage as well as on their residence in the Boloven Plateau of southern Laos, which was the center of the Khmer kingdom of Angkor. This region's high elevation of about 3,500 feet, tropical climate, and high rainfall made it extremely productive in the past; that was why Angkor prospered for as long as it did. However, war, disease, and poor infrastructure for transporting products out of the region have conspired to destroy recent experiments in such cash crops as coffee, tobacco, and cotton. Today the border regions of southern Laos and northeastern Cambodia are considered marginal in both countries and remain impoverished; the fact that the dominant population in both regions is tribal rather than the dominant LAO LOUM and Khmers in Laos and Cambodia, respectively, also means that fewer resources have been dedicated to improving infrastructure, land, or people's lives than in the lowlands of both countries.

More recent Brao history is clearer than their origins and is largely one of violence and dislocation. In 1968 the Brao of Cambodia began to protest against state incursions into their highland homelands. They were met by a disproportionate show of force from the government that included tanks and soldiers destroying both fields and villages. During the wars that took place throughout Southeast Asia in the 1970s and 1980s the Brao again suffered. After the fall of the Khmer Rouge in Cambodia in 1979 propaganda teams from the deposed regime continued to pursue their agenda in the remote northeastern provinces inhabited by the Brao and other tribal minorities. However, the Brao had largely allied themselves with the new People's Republic of Kampuchea (PRK) government, even sending four provincial chiefs, from Mondulkiri, Tatanakiri, Stung Treng, and Preah Vihear, to the capital to participate in governance at the national level. By the mid-1980s the PRK had developed their Policy toward Ethnic Minorities, which promoted equal development, participation in collectivization, and literacy for minorities in both Khmer and their own tongues, with the intention of helping minorities become equal to other Cambodian citizens. These efforts have been less than successful in most cases, and in the 1990s and 2000s large numbers of Brao were forced to relocate to lower elevations to engage in wet rice farming and to be closer to schools and clinics as part of the effort toward national inclusion of minorities. Unfortunately instead of inclusion these relocations have led to alienation, loss of tradition, and serious land exploitation since the Brao had no tradition of farming in this manner.

Traditional Brao subsistence activities included fishing and swidden or slash-and-burn agriculture on the hillsides. They grew dry upland rice, sweet potatoes, cassava, bananas, and gourds, symbols of a good harvest. Their land was fertile enough to allow three or four seasons' use of each plot, but once a garden plot had been exhausted it had to remain fallow for at least a dozen years before being used again. Prior to their incorporation into Laos and Cambodia the Brao land tenure system did not require individuals to seek permission to clear forest land for farming, but older men with experience were consulted on the proper time for burning off the dried vegetation to prevent forest fires. In addition to this kind of extensive farming the Brao engaged in market activities, trading or selling a variety of forest products including bamboo, tropical hardwoods like mahogany and teak, and rubber. The Brao population in Laos has been able to maintain this way of life somewhat better than in Cambodia, where so many have been moved to the lowlands, although even in Laos struggles against the government have meant that some Brao have moved into northeastern Thailand.

Brao traditional culture included Buddhist beliefs and practices as well as indigenous beliefs in spirits and many local gods and the power of ancestors. Each village was relatively independent of all others and was ruled by a headman or elder; in Laos some of these head-men have been incorporated into the bureaucratic structure, while in Cambodia in the past several local chiefs have risen to national prominence. Kinship is determined by a bilateral descent system similar to that of most Westerners in which both mother's and father's families are considered equal contributors of an individual's ancestors; as such, clans and other extensive kinship structures are not in evidence, and residence is more important for determining rights and responsibilities than is kinship beyond the scope of about second cousins. Within both families and wider society men were considered to have more power and authority than women and could have multiple wives, a practice called polygyny, and elders were thought superior to younger people.

Bruneians: nationality (people of Brunei)

GEOGRAPHY

Located on the northwestern corner of the island of Borneo in Southeast Asia and nestled between the South China Sea and the Malaysian states of Sarawak and Sabah lies Negara Brunei Darussalam. Brunei shares the island of Borneo, the third largest in the world, with Malaysia and Indonesia; around 16 million people live on the island, only about 380,000 of them in Brunei. Covering an area of only 3,582 square miles, Brunei is one of the smallest countries in the world. It is split into two areas and made up of four administrative districts named Belait, Brunei-Muara, Temburong, and Tutong. Its larger populous western division is home to around 97 percent of the country's population, while the mountainous east, Temburong, has only around 10,000 inhabitants.

Brunei attracts a sizable number of nature lovers as more than 70 percent primary rain forest covers Brunei. Fortunately it is relatively well protected, with timber cutting only for local use. The country has also made concerted efforts to conserve sizable chunks of rain forest land, which is earmarked and developed for nature reserves and national parks. *Ecotourism* is the new catchphrase, and visitors can take a long boat trip through the mangrove swamps to try to spot a rare proboscis monkey, which is indigenous to Borneo; visit nature reserves and pristine rain forests; walk along nature-trail boardwalks and forest-canopy walkways; as well as visit the 55,000-hectare Ulu Temburong National Park.

BRUNEIANS: NATIONALITY

nation:
Brunei; Sultanate of Brunei; official Malay name is Negara Brunei Darussalam

derivation of name:
The translation of its official Malay name is "State of Brunei, the Abode of Peace." *Darussalam* means "Abode of Peace" in Arabic, while *Negara* means "State" in Malay. *Negara* derives from the Dravidian *nagara*, "city."

government:
Constitutional sultanate

capital:
Bandar Seri Begawan

language:
Malay is the official language; however English is widely spoken in the country. A number of other languages such as Mandarin, other Chinese dialects, and native languages of Borneo are spoken by some groups.

religion:
Islam 67 percent, Buddhism 13 percent, Christianity 10 percent, other 10 percent

earlier inhabitants:
Malays. Prior to the current Brunei sultanate, another kingdom existed at the mouth of the Brunei River in the seventh or eighth century C.E. Called Po-ni by the Chinese, it was overthrown by the Sumatran Hindu empire of Srivijaya in the early ninth century and subsequently defeated by the Java-based Majapahit empire before regaining its independence.

(continues)

Bruneians: nationality time line

C.E.

1405 The first sultan, Muhammad Shah, ascends the throne and introduces Islam to Brunei.

1473–1521 The golden era commences for Brunei with the reign of Sultan Bolkiah.

1839 Arrival of the White Rajah of Sarawak, James Brooke.

1847 Brunei signs trade relations treaty with Great Britain.

1888 Brunei becomes a protectorate of the British government.

1906 Residential system is established in Brunei Darussalam.

1929 Oil is discovered at Seria.

1941 Japanese occupation of Brunei during World War II.

1950 Sultan Haji Omar Ali Saifuddin III, known as the architect of modern Brunei, ascends the throne.

1959 A new constitution is established to enable Brunei to govern itself, although security, foreign affairs, and defense are still controlled by the British.

1962 Politician-turned-rebel Yassin Affandi and his fellow rebels lead the Brunei Revolt   in opposition to Brunei's proposed membership in the Federation of Malaysia; the revolt is quelled with the help of British forces.

Brunei opts out of joining the Federation of Malaysia.

1967 The 29th sultan, His Majesty Haji Hassanal Bolkiah Muizzaddin Waddaulah, ascends the throne after the abdication of his father, Sultan Haji Omar Ali Saifuddin III, who remains as defense minister and adopts the royal title of *Seri Begawan*.

Brunei issues its own currency, the Brunei dollar.

1970 The capital, known as Brunei Town, is renamed *Bandar Seri Begawan* in Sultan Omar Ali Saifuddin's honor.

1971 Self-government agreement is amended to allow full internal independence except for defense and external affairs.

1974 Brunei International Airport is opened.

1975 Royal Brunei Airlines, the national airline, is formed.

1979 Brunei and Great Britain sign a fresh treaty of friendship and cooperation.

1984 On January 1 Brunei gains full independence from Great Britain. The legislative council is suspended. Brunei celebrates its first National Day.

1985 The University of Brunei Darussalam opens its doors.

1991 Sale and public consumption of alcohol are banned; however, non-Muslims and foreigners are permitted to take in two bottles of spirits and 12 cans of beer each time they enter the country.

1994 Jerudong Park and Playground, the world's only free theme park, opens.

1998 Crown Prince Haji Al-Muhtadee Billah, the sultan's eldest son, is named heir to the throne.

1999 Brunei hosts Southeast Asian Games.

2004 In September the sultan reconvenes the legislative council, which has not met since independence in 1984.

Crown Prince Pengiran Muda Haji Al-Muhtadee Billah marries Pengiran Anak Isteri Pengiran Anak Sarah.

2005 After a cabinet reshuffle a new ministry is formed, the ministry of energy, and the crown prince is named senior minister of the prime minister's office.

2005 Inaugural Brunei Golf Open is staged at the Empire Hotel and Country Club.

INCEPTION AS A NATION

While there is archaeological evidence that the island of Borneo was inhabited 40,000 years ago, as well as proof that trade activity was occurring with China and India as early as the sixth century, it was in the 15th and 16th centuries that Brunei's golden era occurred. During this time Brunei came into its own, in particular under the reigns of the fifth sultan, Bolkiah (1473–1521), who expanded the sultanate to encompass Borneo and the Philippines (briefly capturing Manila), and the ninth sultan Hassan (1605–19), who developed the royal court. Unfortunately by the 19th century the empire diminished somewhat with the arrival of the White Rajahs of Sarawak, a dynasty that founded and ruled over the Kingdom of Sarawak from 1841 to 1946. Sarawak belonged to Brunei until James Brooke, who was to become the first White Rajah, received a large piece of land from the sultan and greatly expanded Sarawak under British control, creating his own dynasty of White Rajahs who ruled until World War II.

The formation of the modern nation began with the decolonization of British Southeast Asia after World War II. The creation of the Federation of Malaya in 1948, with the inclusion of largely Malay Brunei in order to offset the inclusion of largely Chinese Singapore, was a compromise made between the British and Malaya's local leaders, including the support of Brunei's royal family. However, other factions of Bruneian society vigorously opposed this unification. The left-wing Brunei People's Party (BPP) refused most adamantly, taking up arms in December 1962 under rebel leader Yassin Affandi. His army, the Tentera Nasional Kalimantan Utara or North Kalimantan National Army (TNKU), attacked the oil-producing infrastructure at Seria as well as government buildings and police stations throughout the state. The Brunei revolt or Brunei rebellion ended five months later when Affandi was shot and captured by British troops. In part as the result of these activities, and of the potential diffusion of local oil wealth, the government decided not to join Sabah and Sarawak in the newly formed Malaya and chose to remain an independent state. However, the BPP remains an outlawed organization because of its Leftist politics (*see* MALAYSIANS: NATIONALITY).

The development of modern Brunei owes a great debt to the country's reserves of oil and natural gas, which provide most foreign income. Brunei is the third-largest oil producer in Southeast Asia; its oil production peaked in 1979 with a daily output of 240,000 barrels. It was subsequently cut back to prolong the life of the oil reserves and in 2005 was estimated to be around 200,000 barrels per day. Brunei's liquefied natural gas plant, which opened in 1972, is one of the largest in the world; however, Brunei's gas reserves are expected to last for only another 40 years. The outlook for oil is even more limited, with reserves for another 25 years. As a result the sultan is planning to develop alternative nonoil economies, focusing on foreign investments, small and medium industries, offshore banking, information technology, and tourism, although as yet with limited success. Nowadays however, the people of Brunei enjoy a high standard of living because of the wealth from oil exports. They have a tax-free lifestyle with relatively high wages, free education and sporting facilities, a token B$1 health care system, and subsidized food, oil, and housing.

CULTURAL IDENTITY

Religion is an extremely important part of Brunei's cultural identity, with a population that is 67 percent Muslim, 13 percent Buddhist, 10 percent Christian, and other religions representing about 10 percent. Islam entered the country six centuries ago when a Malay Muslim became head of state. Since that time Islam has grown to dominate much of Bruneian society through a top-down approach to conversion and cultural domination. This trend has continued since Brunei achieved full independence from the British in 1984. At that time Brunei adopted the national philosophy of the Malay Islamic Monarchy (Melayu Islam Beraja), which believes in strong Malay cultural influences as well as the importance of Islam in daily life and governance. The country's constitution states that the Shafeite sect of Islam is the state religion and others "may be practiced in peace and harmony," at least in private. The law also dictates that non-Muslims may not proselytize or teach their religion in schools; in fact all schools, including the eight Chinese and four Christian ones, must provide Islamic instruction to every student. The government also uses its great oil wealth to promote Islam through subsidizing hajj, or pilgrimage to Mecca; building mosques; and expanding social-welfare programs. Because of this government subsidy many Bruneians have undertaken the hajj, and upon their return they utilize the honorific titles *haji* for men and *hajah* for women.

The royal family, which has ruled for six centuries since its introduction in 1405, is revered in Brunei as a source of traditional iden-

Brunei's Sultan Omar Ali Saifuddin Mosque was built in 1958 and named after the country's ruler in the post-World War II era. It is an important symbol of the centrality of Islam in the country. *(Shutterstock/Kenny Goh Wei Kiat)*

tity and unity. The current sultan maintains this symbolic position as well as serving as the supreme executive authority in the country. However, the royal family has occasionally been the subject of unwelcome headlines and scrutiny, especially when the current sultan's brother, the extravagant, disgraced Prince Jefri, was said to have misappropriated an estimated $15 billion from the Brunei Investment Agency in 2000 when holding the position of finance minister. Sultan Hassanal Bolkiah subsequently sued his brother in court and reached an out-of-court settlement, with Prince Jefri's vast assets returned to the state.

FURTHER READING

Michael Cable and Rodney Tyler. *Brunei Darussalam: The Country, the Sultan, the People* (London: AMD Brand Evolution, 2000).
A. G. J. Chalfont. *By God's Will: A Portrait of the Sultan of Brunei* (New Delhi: Penguin Books, 1989).
Graham Saunders. *A History of Brunei* (New York: Routledge Curzon, 2002).

Buginese (Bugis)

The Buginese or Bugis are the dominant ethnic group on Sulawesi, a large island of the Indonesian Archipelago. The group has a long, literate history that goes back to at least about 1400 and probably much earlier. The first texts to have been produced in the language used an Indian script and covered a wide array of topics including religion, politics, and poetry. The best known of these texts is *I La Galigo*, an epic poem written in old Buginese about events that took place before the 14th century.

That period of Buginese history was also important for its political activities since several Buginese communities emerged as relatively strong kingdoms, including Bone, Wajo, and Soppeng. Bone was formed in about 1350 when Mata Selompu united seven smaller Hindu states into the Bone confederacy. In about 1582 Bone joined with these two other Buginese states, Soppeng and Wajo, to form the even larger Tallumpocco alliance to fight off incursions by MAKASSARESE, JAVANESE, and others. The early 17th century saw this Buginese alliance dominated by rulers from the Makassarese Gowa kingdom, but in the early 1660s Arung Palakka allied his forces with the Dutch and conquered both Makassar itself and other islands in the region; this established about 100 years of Buginese domination in this region of the archipelago. At this time Buginese states also developed in Selangor and Riau from migrating sailors and others who carried their language and alliances with them.

By the time of this important Buginese expansion much of the population had already

---

BUGINESE

location:
Sulawesi and other regions of Indonesia and Malaysia

time period:
About 2500 B.C.E. to the present

ancestry:
Austronesian

language:
Bugis or Basa Ugi, an Austronesian language

converted to Islam. This process began in about 1608 in the state of Bone, when the leader or *arumponi* converted to the new religion. Many scholars believe that it was the Buginese who transported Islam to Kalimantan or Borneo and began the process of converting the local population to their religion.

While the Dutch would have preferred to be converting the peoples of the more remote Indonesian islands to Protestantism, they did not stand in the way of the Buginese, and the two peoples had relatively friendly relations until the start of the 20th century, by which time the Buginese were a fairly marginal people in the archipelago. In 1905, however, the Dutch sent an army to pacify the jungles of the island they called Celebes, contemporary Sulawesi, which forced the Bone king, or *arumponi*, to flee. Eventually the Dutch captured him, exiled him to Java, and imposed a council of nobles as the ruling body over the kingdom. The kingdom was restored in 1931 under La Mappanjuki Karaeng Silayar, grandson of the deposed *arumponi*, who later sided with the Indonesian republicans against the Dutch following World War II.

Buginese culture has undergone a variety of changes over the course of the past 600 years or so. For example the earliest records of these people indicate that they were heavily influenced by both Hinduism and Buddhism prior to the arrival of Islam in the 17th century. One characteristic that has remained relatively constant, however, is the centrality of rice cultivation and trade in their economy. While many Buginese live in urban areas, speak Bahasa Indonesia, are fully integrated into the cosmopolitan world economy, and have been for several hundred years, the majority are still rural cultivators who make their living growing rice in irrigated paddies. Their region of southern Sulawesi is mountainous but crossed by many rivers and lakes from which water is available for producing two to three crops of rice, coffee, coconut, cocoa, corn, maniac, cloves, fruit, and vegetables per year. Coastal Buginese supplement these agricultural products, and the income gained by selling cash crops, with fish and interisland trade. They are known for the elaborate silk sarongs woven by Buginese women and then sold in the market or to a middleman trader by the men.

As are those of the Javanese and BALINESE, Buginese society is highly structured and hierarchical. In general the Buginese as a whole see themselves as superior to others because of their long and glorious history as a seafaring kingdom; Buginese pirates were greatly feared in their day. Internally as well the Buginese are

The Buginese established and maintained control of their kingdoms through control of the archipelago's shipping lanes; ideas, products, and people also came and went in ships such as these. *(OnAsia/ Ben Davies)*

ranked according to a variety of different criteria, including wealth, religious faith, and kinship. Many Buginese men migrate away from their homes to work in Java, Kalimantan, and even Malaysia to earn money that can assist in improving their social status at home; high status also results from allowing one's wife and daughters to stay out of the paid workforce. Marriage is still often a family affair, organized by parents to unite two powerful families into one as a front against social climbing by others; another marriage strategy is for relatively close cousins to marry and thus maintain the family's status through endogamy. As is the case in Java and Bali, the Buginese language is a central strategy for maintaining order and hierarchy with its many degrees of formality and ritual for communicating with people of different social strata.

FURTHER READING

Christian Pelras. *The Bugis* (Cambridge, Mass.: Blackwell, 1996).

Bugis   *See* BUGINESE.

Bunun   (the Red Head Tribe)

The Bunun are the third largest of the 13 recognized ABORIGINAL TAIWANESE peoples and the second largest in terms of recognized territory; their name means "people" in their own language.

The origins of all Aboriginal Taiwanese peoples are somewhat uncertain but probably stretch back to about 5000 B.C.E. and the migration of proto-AUSTRONESIANS from southern China to Taiwan. During the course of the subsequent 4,000 years other Austronesian populations migrated to the island chain, and differentiation along both linguistic and cultural lines occurred to create a variety of ethnolinguistic groups. They were all similar in their practice of swidden or slash-and-burn agriculture, the importance of kinship in their social structures, and animistic or spirit-based religions.

The traditional diet of the Bunun consisted of sweet potatoes and millet grown on shifting fields in their mountainous homelands. During the JAPANESE colonial period, 1895–1945, the Bunun were forced to farm rice for the Japanese, a practice that was abandoned in the 1970s when other cash crops became more common. The traditional division of labor entailed women's performing most agricultural tasks such as planting, weeding, and harvesting, in addition to caring for children, tending to household needs, and caring for the old and sick. Men cleared garden plots, helped with the harvest, hunted, went to war against other tribes and both Chinese and Japanese colonists, and held all important community leadership positions from clan headman to shaman.

Despite the similarities between the Bunun and other Aboriginal Taiwanese groups, the Bunun were more nomadic in their residential pattern than the other groups. Most believe Yu-shan or Jade Mountain, the highest mountain in Far East Asia, is their ancestors' traditional homeland, but an 18th-century Bunun migration dispersed much of the population to this area from the eastern plains of the island. Today significant Bunun settlements can be found in the mountainous regions of four different counties, Nantou, Hualien, Taichung, and Kaohsiung. The northern settlements of Taichung County tend to be larger than the others and to be based on patrilineal clan membership, though still generally smaller than settlements of other aboriginal people. Those in Nantou and Hualien Counties in the center and east, respectively, tend to be smaller and more remote, while the southern settlements in Kaohsiung County are even more scattered and lack clear-cut boundaries. Bunun villages also tend to be located in higher elevations than other people's, averaging more than 3,281 feet, a location that perhaps explains their relatively small size since agriculture at these higher elevations is more marginal than at lower sites and can support fewer people. This occupation pattern may also explain their nomadism since fields at these elevations require much longer fallow periods than those in lower elevations with their moister, warmer climates.

The social structure of the Bunun is based on the ties created by patrilineal descent patterns, in which membership in each lineage is inherited from one's father, father's father, and so on. Groups of patrilineages are united through descent from a common male ancestor into patrilineal subclans, which are organized hierarchically within the clan on the basis of the birth order of the founding male ancestors. Today most Bunun use their subclan name as their surname, and thus these connections have remained important markers of social belonging into the present day, even among urbanized Bunun. Groups of clans are connected at the level of the *gavian,* another patrilineal descent grouping. The Bunun traditionally had six different tribal or *gavian* subdivisions, Isbu-

BUNUN

location:
Rural Taiwan, with a few individuals residing in the island's main cities

time period:
5000 B.C.E. to the present

ancestry:
Austronesian.

language:
Bunun, an Austronesian language unrelated to any other still in existence today

kun, which is the largest, and Takebaka, Takebanuan, Taketodo, Takevatan, and Takepulan; however, the last group has disappeared, and its members been integrated into other tribes.

There are also five different residential groupings or communes that are sometimes discussed as social units comparable to tribes in that they also entail both rights and responsibilities of their members. The Chuo and Luan are located in the Yu-shan region of Nantou County, the Ka to the east of them, the Dan on the border between Nantou and Hualien Counties, and the Yu and Lan, both small communes, reside in Nantou's central mountain area. Some sources claim the Lan have disappeared; others state that they remain in remote, high elevations. These residential units are all patrilocal, requiring women to move into their husbands' family's home at the time of their marriage; however, this was not very difficult for many women because of the preference for village endogamy, or marrying within one's own village. Nonetheless some women did have to move out of their own village or commune because the rules of strict clan exogamy or having to marry outside one's own clan could not be observed in small villages or communes.

The traditional Bunun religion was animistic; each person, animal, plant, and even natural object such as distinctive rocks was believed to have a spirit or *hanido* that leaves the person or object when it dies. Humans are unique in this cosmology in having two *hanido*s, a good one residing on the person's right side and a bad one on the left. This pair was in constant competition, and each person's life course was believed to stem from the actions and powers of their spirits. In addition to this plethora of spirits the world was believed to contain a sky deity, *dehanin,* which was thought to have power over the wind, rain, sun, and other climatic features. While *hanido*s were important actors in Bunun everyday life, affecting everything from an individual's mood to the harvest, *dehanin* was important only during times of crisis. Rituals appeasing or thanking *dehanin* were uncommon but extremely important. Today *dehanin* has been incorporated into Christian theology as God, while *hanido* is used to refer to an evil power or even Satan.

In the past the Bunun were known for their resistance to outsiders and for their prowess as headhunters. Today's Bunun are more famous for their baseball players, with their Little League team Hongye or Red Leaf having won several international games, including a famous 7-0 victory over Japan's all-star team in 1968. The Bunun are also famous on the world music scene for their eight-part harmonic system. In the early 1950s a Japanese scholar doing research on aboriginal music in Taiwan recorded a Bunun millet-harvesting song and sent it to UNESCO for archiving and analysis. The complexity of the Bunun harmonic system challenged the dominant theory of the time about the development of music generally and so has become well known throughout the world.

Burakumin (Eta, hinin, Hisabetsu buraku, Kokonotsu)

The Burakumin are a class of JAPANESE people who in the past were treated as outcasts. The word *Burakumin* is a 19th-century invention, meaning "people of the hamlet," because they were forced to live outside towns and villages rather than mixing with other Japanese. The term was meant to be an improvement over such names as *eta,* "outcaste"; *hinin,* "nonhuman"; or *kokonotsu,* "nine," which indicated imperfection when compared with the perfect number, 10. Regardless of the term used, the group of people so labeled has experienced tremendous disadvantage in Japanese society, based on the idea that the pollution of their ancestors' ways of life was inherited by succeeding generations. Other Japanese refused to marry them, making the Burakumin a functionally endogamous group, or to mix with them socially. Even today they can still be considered a separate people group, despite being ethnically and linguistically Japanese, because their outsider status within Japan leads them often to be compared to other outsiders, such as the AINU, KOREANS, or Filipino populations.

Historically the ideas associated with the status of the Burakumin entered Japanese society with the Buddhist belief about the evil inherent in killing animals. This notion combined with the ideas of the indigenous religion, Shinto, about impurity, *kegare* in Japanese, and about avoidance of things connected to blood, dirt, and death, *imi* in Japanese. Until about the 16th century the Eta were peoples whose occupations put them in contact with the world of impurity, such as butchers, leather workers, temple sweepers, and even landscape architects, who got their hands dirty. In some cases such as temple sweepers and landscape architects the tasks they performed gave them a privileged position in society despite the inherent pollution involved in their work. In the 16th century,

BURAKUMIN

location:
Japan, especially Kyushu, Kobe, Osaka, Kyoto, and the coasts of the Inland Sea; Hyogo Prefecture has the highest concentration of Burakumin in the country

time period:
At least the 12th century to the present

ancestry:
Japanese butchers, tanners, leather workers, executioners, and holders of other polluting jobs

language:
Japanese

however, the position of these special-status people in Japan changed. The occupational categories became stricter, and the people involved in polluting activities came to be seen as polluting themselves. In addition their personal pollution was believed to be inherited from one generation to the next, forcing children to follow in their parents' footsteps occupationally and to marry others from the same category. The result was the emergence of endogamous, castelike groups similar to the Dalits or SCHEDULED CASTES of India.

Following from these social changes, Japanese law during the Tokugawa or Edo period (1600–1868) was reformed to institutionalize the place of the Eta in society. They were forced to live in segregated villages or hamlets outside main villages and either to step aside or to prostrate themselves in public when passing other Japanese people. Temples, shrines, festivals, and other public events for non-Eta were usually off limits to those considered polluting to the dominant majority; the Eta also were forbidden to wear silk clothing. Individual localities sometimes enacted even more restrictive laws, such as those of Tosa, where from 1820 until 1871 the Burakumin were banned from city streets after eight o'clock at night.

The year 1871 introduced official relief to the Burakumin population: all legal restrictions on movement, clothing, and social mixing were lifted by the new Meiji government. However, even at the government level discrimination did not stop. An 1880 publication by the Japanese ministry of justice described Burakumin as "almost like animals," and in 1919 an entire Burakumin hamlet was forced to relocate because it was situated too close to an area of Nara Prefecture considered sacred by the dominant majority. World War II finally put an end to the banning of Burakumin from temples used by the majority, but restrictions against their use of hot springs and bathhouses continued until Article 14 of the Constitution of 1947 guaranteed equality to all, including those discriminated against on the basis of social status or family origin.

Today discrimination against Burakumin is illegal, but the 2–3 million or so people classified as such continue to experience difficulty in housing, employment, education, and other areas because of the traditional Japanese taboos about mixing with them. These taboos are based on a fear of pollution that has survived even long after the religious prohibitions against eating meat or slaughtering animals have disappeared. As a result today's Burakumin are more likely than other Japanese people to experience extensive periods of unemployment, to be poorer and less well educated, and to have higher crime rates than the rest of the Japanese population.

In the mid-1970s a famous case of Burakumin action put the position of these people at the forefront of most Japanese people's minds. In November 1974, 52 teachers at a senior high school in Tajima, Hyogo Prefecture, went on strike because they claimed the conditions in their school prevented them from teaching. The conditions they were referring to were actions by the student branch of Buraku Kaiho Domei, the Buraku Liberation League, agitating to have the group's status as an underclass group recognized in the school and beyond; one of their tactics was to participate in a hunger strike. On the day the 52 teachers walked out of the school they were met by a large gathering of Liberation League members. For the next 13 hours the two sides struggled until about 60 people, primarily teachers, were injured, forcing 48 of them into the hospital.

In addition to the Buraku Liberation League, which was formed in the interwar period for the advancement of Burakumin causes, there is a rival organization as well, the National Liaison Council for Buraku Liberation League Normalization, organized in 1969. These two groups are allied with different political parties, allegiances that have increased the rivalry between them; the former is allied with the Japan Socialist Party, while the latter has connections to the more revolutionary Japan Communist Party. The work done by these organizations to raise the national consciousness, combined with increased legal protections and educational programs, has improved the position of many Burakumin in the 21st century. A study published in 2005 states that, according to polls, nearly two-thirds of Burakumin claim never to have experienced discrimination and that almost three-fourths have married or intend to marry a non-Burakumin. Nonetheless the group remains a traditional scapegoat in Japanese society and there are still significant health, education, and wealth markers that divide them from the dominant majority of Japanese.

Burghers

The Burghers are a Sri Lankan ethnic group made up of individuals who can trace at least part of their ancestry back to the Portuguese and Dutch colonizers of the island from the 16th to the early 20th century.

During the initial phase of Portuguese colonization in Sri Lanka, called Ceylon at the time, Portuguese men were encouraged to marry local women and to raise their children as Europeans, speaking Portuguese, practicing Roman Catholicism, and taking up the many midlevel bureaucratic positions available in the new colony. For more than a century the Portuguese controlled the small island and its trade in cinnamon and other spices and successfully practiced intermarrying colonization.

In the first half of the 17th century the Dutch were attracted to Ceylon's trade goods and began to harass the Portuguese settlements. In 1638 the indigenous Kingdom of Kandy signed a treaty with the Dutch agreeing to help them remove the Portuguese, which they accomplished by 1640. The Dutch tried to people their new colony with settlers from the Netherlands but were never very successful; by the 1670s there were never more than 500 Dutch citizens, called Burghers, in residence on the island. By the 18th century the term *Burgher* referred not to Dutch citizens but to anyone in Ceylon who could claim either Dutch or Portuguese ancestry, although the two descent groups tended to make up separate Burgher communities, a phenomenon that has continued until the present day. All Burghers dressed in European-style clothing; belonged to Christian churches, either Dutch Reformed or Roman Catholic; and spoke either Dutch or Portuguese. Dutch groups tended to have lighter skin color and could document descent from Europeans on the father's side; they also spoke Dutch and were members of the Dutch Reformed Church. The Portuguese Burghers, sometimes called Mechanics, tended to have darker skin color and claimed but could not necessarily prove European descent; they spoke Creole Portuguese and were members of the Roman Catholic Church.

By the time of the British takeover of Ceylon in 1796 there were about 900 Dutch Burgher families living in Colombo, Galle, Matara, and Jaffna; the number of Portuguese Burghers is less well documented. During this period most of the Dutch Burgher community quickly learned English and adapted themselves to the new colonial bureaucracy; Dutch disappeared as a first language on the island by about 1860. Burghers filled the ranks of much of the upper middle class, serving as clerks, lawyers, doctors, and soldiers. At the same time the Portuguese Burgher community, generally living outside the capital of Colombo, maintained the Creole language and mixed Portuguese-indigenous way of life. The Portuguese Burghers tended to work in manual labor, in such areas as carpentry, mechanics, and transport, more than their English-speaking counterparts did, and to keep largely to themselves. Today many socioeconomic statuses are represented among the Portuguese Burgher community, from wealthy doctors and lawyers to laborers, carpenters, and welders, but until late 2004 they were still generally looked down upon by their English-speaking, professional-class counterparts living in Columbo. During the early period of the British colonial period, which came to an end in 1970, the Burgher community achieved an all-time high of more than 100,000 members. From 1908 until 1968 the Dutch Burgher community published the *Journal of the Dutch Burgher Union of Ceylon,* and the community thrived. In 1927 the Creole Portuguese Burgher community of Batticaloa created the Burgher Union as an organization similar to Colombo's Burgher Association for its own community. The two Burgher communities were essentially separate and had little contact with each other, but both were successful in the British colony. In 1961, however, the emerging state of Ceylon, which was finally renamed Sri Lanka in 1972, made Sinhalese the only official language of state, and many Burghers began to emigrate, settling in Australia, Canada, and the United Kingdom. Today only about 34,000 Burghers call Sri Lanka home while large communities live in diaspora outside the country. These small numbers, however, do not point to an imminent demise of the community. In 1981 the *Journal of the Dutch Burgher Union* began publication again, and there are still 24 congregations of the Dutch Reformed Church, today called the Presbytery of Ceylon.

Another sign of the resilience of this community is the response to the 2004 Boxing Day tsunami that struck Sri Lanka particularly hard. About 4,000 Portuguese Burghers living in the town of Batticaloa on the island's east coast were affected; between 120 and 150 individuals were killed and between 200 and 290 families lost their homes. When news of their plight spread to the Colombo Burgher community, they immediately raised money and essential goods for the affected families and delivered them to Batticaloa; they also spread word to Burgher associations in Australia, Canada, and the United Kingdom, whose members provided even more resources. Even though the two Burgher com-

BURGHERS

location:
Sri Lanka

time period:
1505 to the present

ancestry:
Dutch, Portuguese, Tamil, and Sinhalese

language:
English, Sinhalese, Tamil, and Portuguese Creole

BURIATS

location:
The Buryat Republic in Russia, northeastern Mongolia, and Inner Mongolia within China

time period:
13th century to the present

ancestry:
Xiongnu, Mongolian, Evenki, and Turkic

language:
Buriat, an eastern Mongolian language related to Khalkha

munities had had no contact for decades and saw themselves as essentially different groups, the tragedy of the tsunami has drawn them together in a new spirit of cooperation and identity building. The tsunami disrupted plans in Batticaloa to celebrate the 500th anniversary of the Portuguese arrival on the island, but future joint celebrations are desired on both sides to link the two communities more closely, on the basis of their European heritage and common experience as both insiders and outsiders in this South Asian country.

Buriats (Bargu, Briat, Buriat-Mongolians, Buriyat, Buryat, Northeastern Mongolians, Northern Mongolians)

The Buriats are MONGOLS, most of whom reside in the Republic of Buryatia in Siberia, Russia, where they make up about a quarter of the population, with smaller groups of about 50,000 living in Mongolia and at least 65,000 living in China. The Chinese Buriats arrived in 1917 from Siberia, having fled the Russian Revolution, and they currently exhibit some cultural differences from their Siberian and Mongo-lian relatives, such as in language and religion. Their numbers remain unknown today because after the 1982 census the Chinese administration combined them with other Mongolians; the 65,000 figure is from that 1982 census.

Within the almost half-million-strong population of Buriats in Russia there are also differences between groups living on the eastern and western sides of Lake Baikal, known as Transbaikal Buriats and Irkutsk Buriats, respectively. On the eastern side the Transbaikal Buriats economy is still largely focused on raising cattle and horses with some families residing in portable yurts and engaging in seminomadic pastoralism. A drink made from fermented mares' or cows' milk is the traditional beverage, prepared by women and often kept in the yurt. This population practices mostly Tibetan-style lamaist Buddhism and is generally less russified than its western counterparts. The Irkutsk Buriats, living on the western side of Lake Baikal, largely became sedentary and raised cereal crops along with their Russian neighbors; they participated in the great collectivization schemes of the Soviet government throughout the 20th century and today continue to raise crops on small plots. They tend to practice a shamanistic religion rather than Buddhism, and some are also Orthodox Christians. In the western region the portable felt yurt or *ger* was transformed into a log home with a sod roof, but it maintained the characteristic round shape of the traditional Mongolian tent.

The Buriat homeland in Siberia was originally largely Mongolian, with small numbers of EVENKIS and TUVANS living there as well, until the 1620s, when Russian Cossacks began arriving in significant numbers. The Buriats resisted this influx for many years but were finally annexed by the Russian Empire in treaties signed in 1689 and 1728; these allowed even greater numbers of Russian and Ukrainian colonists to enter the region. Within a few years of the Russian revolution in 1917 the Buryat-Mongol Autonomous Soviet Socialist Republic was created, dropping the *Mongol* from the name in 1958. With the breakup of the USSR, the Buryat ASSR became a republic within the larger Russian Federation, taking the name *Republic of Buryatia* in 1992.

The pre-Russian history of the Buriats was essentially the history of the Mongolian people more generally. The Buriats trace their ancestry to Genghis Khan's mother, who was from Barguzinsky on the eastern shore of Lake Baikal, and see this as an important source of historical identity. They were first mentioned as a separate

Buriats time line

C.E.

ca. 1240 First mention of the Buriats in *The Secret History of the Mongols*.

17th century The Mongol people generally convert to Tibetan Buddhism, including most Buriats.

1620s Russians begin moving into the Buriat homeland around Lake Baikal.

1689, 1728 Treaties between Russia and Mongolia establish the current borders and attach the Buriat region to Russia. This process marks the real beginning of Russian colonization in the area.

1741 Buddhism is recognized as an official religion within the Russian Empire.

1917 Some Buriats flee Russia during the revolution and take up residence in China, where they reside today as a somewhat separate group from the Russian and Mongolian Buriat populations.

1923 Creation of the Buryat-Mongol Autonomous Soviet Socialist Republic (ASSR).

1939 The Buriat language begins to be written with the Russian Cyrillic script.

1958 The Buryat-Mongol ASSR drops the word *Mongol* from its title.

1990 The Buryat ASSR declares its sovereignty and adopts the name *Republic of Buryatia* in 1992.

1995 The Republic of Buryatia signs a bilateral treaty with the Russian Federation.

people within the larger Mongolian empire in *The Secret History of the Mongols*, a book that outlines not only the life of Genghis Khan but also the creation of his empire. This period marks the creation of the Buriat people as a larger identity encompassing individual tribal membership in such groups as Bugalat, Khora, Ekhirit, and Khongodor. As did other Mongols, many Buriats adopted Tibetan Buddhism in the 17th century; their religion was recognized in Russia in 1741. At the time of the revolution, there were 46 large monasteries or *datsangs* and 150 Buddhist temples in the Buriat region, some dating from the 1740s.

While religious practices were persecuted within both Russia and Mongolia until 1990–91, this persecution was not consistent throughout the entire period. In Mongolia the worst period was between 1920 and 1941; however, mass graves filled with murdered lamas and monks dating between the 1930s and 1960s have been uncovered in the past decade and a half. The extent of persecution is still relatively unknown outside Mongolia. In Russia religious persecution generally began in 1925 and by the late 1930s Buddhism was considered extinct in the Buryat-Mongol ASSR; the religion reemerged during World War II and was officially reborn in 1946, with few adherents. By the 1980s many young Buriats in Mongolia and Russia had begun to practice the religion of their ancestors, and by 1995 Buddhism was thriving in both Mongolia and Russia. At least a dozen lamaist institutions have opened within the Buryat Republic since 1990. Within China religion remains largely taboo.

FURTHER READING

Robert W. Montgomery. *Late Tsarist and Early Soviet Nationality and Cultural Policy: The Buryats and Their Language* (Lewiston, N.Y.: Edwin Mellen Press, 2005).

V. I. Pomus. *Buriat Mongolia, A Brief Survey of Political, Economic, and Social Progress.* Abridged and translated from the Russian work *Buriat Mongol A.S.S.R.* by Rose Maurer and Olga Lang (New York: International Secretariat, Institute of Pacific Relations, 1943).

Burmans (Bamar, Burmese, Mranma, Myanmar)

The Burmans are the largest and politically dominant ethnic group in Myanmar, known as Burma until 1989.

GEOGRAPHY

Myanmar shares borders with Thailand, China, India, Laos, and Bangladesh; it also has an extensive coastline along the Bay of Bengal. The main Burman region is the central plains, which lie between the Irrawaddy and Salween Rivers, while the highlands surrounding the plains are primarily inhabited by minority groups like the SHANS, KACHIN, KAREN, and CHIN, who have been fighting for independence or at least some degree of autonomy from the Burman state for nearly 60 years.

The lowland plains of Myanmar are dominated by a monsoon climate of rain from June to October, a cool interlude for a month or two, and then a hot, dry period lasting till the rains return.

BURMANS

location:
Myanmar, especially in the central plains region between the Irrawaddy and Salween Rivers

time period:
Probably ninth century to the present

language:
Burman, a southern Burmish language in the larger Tibeto-Burman language family, Sino-Tibetan phylum

Burmans time line	
B.C.E.	
600	Possible date for the initial migrations of the Burmans south out of northwestern China.
C.E.	
ninth century	Another possible date for the initial migrations of the Burmans south from China, considered more likely by many sources.
850	Archaeological evidence indicates that the town of Pagan was already a thriving agricultural center by this point.
1044	Founding of the Kingdom of Pagan.
1056	Theravada Buddhism arrives in Pagan from the Mon court of Thaton and King Anawrahta converts right away.
1057	King Anawrahta of Pagan is said to have defeated the Mon.
1287	The Pagan kingdom falls to the Mongols.

(continues)

Burmans time line *(continued)*

1486 King Minkyinyo of Toungoo founds the second Burmese empire by conquering the Mon and Shan.

1569 Toungoo under King Bayinnaung conquers the Thai kingdom at Ayutthaya.

1752 Toungoo falls to the rival Konbaung dynasty under King Alaungpaya, founder of the third Burmese empire.

1766–69 The Chinese attack Konbaung four times and are repelled each time.

1767 The Burmans sack Ayutthaya and in reaction the Thai king moves his capital to Bangkok.

1824–26 The first Anglo-Burmese War sees the British defeat the Kongbaung dynasty for the first time.

1852–53 The second Anglo-Burmese War expands the British territory.

1883–85 The third Anglo-Burmese War sees the final defeat of the Burmans and the annexation of all their territory along with that of their neighboring minority groups such as the Kachin, Karen, Chin, and Shan. All these territories are ruled as part of British India.

1930–31 Saya San's Burmese Rebellion against the British.

1941 The Karen fight with the British against the Burmans and Japanese.

1942 The British are expelled from Burma by the Japanese-Burman alliance.

1945 The British retake Burma with significant military assistance from the Karen.

1947 Aung San is assassinated and the hopes for a multiethnic leadership in an independent Burma are extinguished.

1948 Burma becomes independent of Britain in January and the dominant Burmans consolidate their hold on state power at the expense of all the other ethnic groups in the country.

1958 The military under Ne Win is invited to take over the government to quell rebellion and set the stage for elections in 1960.

1960 Elections are held and the military withdraws from governing.

1962 A military coup puts Ne Win back in control of the state.

1970s General Ne Win formulates and puts into action the Four Cuts Policy, which leads to attempts at cutting off food, money, recruits, and intelligence to the non-Burman rebels.

1975 A massive earthquake in the area around Pagan destroys many structures from the first Burman kingdom but also opens many sealed tombs and reveals art and sculpture not seen since the 11th century.

1989 Burma under Ne Win is renamed *Myanmar*; the capital Rangoon becomes *Yangon*.

1989 Aung San Suu Kyi is put under house arrest for the first time.

1990 The election won by Suu Kyi's National League for Democracy is annulled by the military. In the next couple of years Myanmar becomes one of the 10 poorest countries in the world.

1991 Aung San Suu Kyi wins the Nobel Prize in peace but cannot leave her home to accept it; her son accepts on her behalf.

1995 Aung San Suu Kyi is released from house arrest but told that if she leaves the country she will not be allowed to return.

1997 The State Law and Order Restoration Council is renamed the State Peace and Development Council (SPDC); the new name does not decrease the atrocities committed by national forces.

2000 Suu Kyi is rearrested and held until May 2002, when she is freed again for just one year before being reimprisoned.

2007 Riots in Rangoon lead to the death and disappearance of hundreds of monks and democracy activists.

2008 Cyclone Nargis hits the Irrawaddy River delta, leaving about 100,000 people dead and affecting a population of about 2 million.

ORIGINS

Burman origins, as is the case for all Tibeto-Burman peoples, are in the northwestern region of China and even as far north as Mongolia. However, the date of the Burman migration into Southeast Asia is highly contested. Some evidence points to about 2,600 years ago as the time when the ancestors of today's Burmans began migrating southward while other sources indicate that the Burmans were relative late-comers to Southeast Asia, having arrived only in the ninth century C.E. Certainly they arrived in the area of contemporary Burma/Myanmar later than the MON, fellow north Asians who migrated south and settled the plains of this region.

HISTORY

The first important Burman polity established in the new homeland was centered on the city of Pagan, located on the banks of the Irrawaddy River near Mount Popa, the Burmans' spiritual home prior to the arrival of Buddhism in 1056. The most frequently cited date for the kingdom's founding is 1044, the start of the Pagan dynasty, although 1057, when King Anawrahta is said by the Burmans to have defeated the Mon, is also sometimes listed. An alternative reading of the history of this region states that the Mon actually colonized Pagan with their Buddhist culture and that the Burman "conquest" may have been devised long after the fact to legitimate their domination of the region. Archaeological evidence indicates that a thriving agricultural town was located at Pagan from as early as about 850 C.E., but its ethnic origins are unknown.

The Pagan kings, who ruled until 1287, unified the many dispersed Burman localities into a powerful Burman state that was to be rebuilt in different capitals two more times before the annexation of Burman territory in the 19th century by the British. The Pagan period specifically is considered a golden age for Buddhist Burman culture as each king tried to outdo his predecessors in the building of massive pagodas and monasteries, sponsorship of Buddhist scholarship, and collection of Buddhist relics. Literally thousands of enormous temple structures were erected in the city and along the banks of the Irrawaddy River over the course of two centuries, to house great libraries and the monks who produced and read the libraries' texts. The kingdom's nickname, Land of Four Million Pagodas, certainly overstates the number of such structures but points to the great importance of building at this time. The great wealth that allowed for this cultural flourishing entered the kingdom from tribute and

Even today the land of the Burmans continues to host thousands of Buddhist temples and pagodas. *(Shutterstock/TALOMOR)*

taxes paid for by agriculture. The Burman territory was extremely fertile and various kings improved the land by building reservoirs and canals to facilitate irrigation for wet rice and transportation into and out of the capital.

Following the fall of Pagan to the MONGOLS in 1287, it was not the Burmans who were able to reestablish a powerful political force in the area of contemporary Myanmar, but the Shans. Rather than a centralized kingdom, the Shans maintained a number of loosely allied kingdoms, the strongest of which ruled their territory from Ava. In 1486, however, the Burman king Minkyinyo of Toungoo or Taungu founded the second Burmese empire, also called the Toungoo dynasty. He and his son and heir, Tabinshwehti, conquered both an independent Mon kingdom in the south of Myanmar and the various Shan domains in the north to consolidate Burman power in the plains. These two kings, who ruled from 1486 until 1550, set the stage for later military success against the kingdom of the THAIS at Ayutthaya and much of the LAO territory as well. This expansion took place under Tabinshwehti's son-in-law and heir, King Bayinnaung, who ruled until his death in 1581. After that time the kingdom never regained its former glory, losing Ayutthaya around 1600 and much of the rest of its conquered territory after that. Nonetheless the dynasty remained strong in the Burmese central plains until 1752, when the rival Konbaung dynasty emerged and founded the third Burmese empire under King Alaungpaya.

As did the early Toungoo kings, the rulers of the Konbaung dynasty also used their military power to expand their territory, resource base, and labor pool. They waged war against their closest neighbors, the Mon, Arakenese, and Shans, as well as with the Thais. Against the latter Hsinbyushin, son of the founder Alaungpaya, was able to pillage the capital of Ayutthaya in 1767, forcing a move to Bangkok for the beleaguered Siamese kingdom. Commentators write that Hsinbyushin was driven by the dual motivations of avenging his father's death in 1760 while retreating from the Thais and securing Burman access to the coastal trading ports in Tenasserim and southern Burma more generally. During this period Konbaung also had to reckon with the power of the Chinese, who feared the rise of a powerful, centralizing state to their south and thus attempted to invade on four separate occasions between 1766 and 1769. All four attempts were thwarted and the Burmans were able to consolidate their agricultural and seafaring trade bases over the following decades.

Despite their enormous local power, the Burmans could not maintain their independence in the face of the British army when the two faced off in the first Anglo-Burmese War in 1824–26, following Burmese incursions into Indian territory. The two fought two more wars in 1852–53 and then 1883–85, both of which saw the British expand their territory at the expense of the Burmans; their final victory produced the annexation of Burma and its attachment to the British Indian colony. During the British period, which lasted until independence in 1948, Burma became a world leader in rubies, rice production, and teak; other tropical hardwoods likewise expanded the coffers of the British. The Burman population remained second-class citizens in their own country, working in the lowest levels of the bureaucracy at best and as forced laborers at worst. The majority of the population continued farming rice and practicing both personal and communal Buddhist prayers and ceremonies.

Throughout the course of the colonial era the Burmans frequently tried to rise up against the British, who often worked in conjunction with the territory's many minority groups to put down the Burman majority. This tactic of divide and conquer saw a policy of direct rule used on the Burmans, mostly using Indian bureaucrats, while the Karen, Kachin, Shans, Chin, and other minorities experienced indirect rule in their highland homes, in which local chiefs served as middlemen between the British and the local populace. The largest of the Burman rebellions occurred in 1930–31, at the start of the depression that hit the Burmese export economy very hard. Saya San, a peasant and Burmese commoner, wished to rid his country of the British but had very little political or military know how to carry out his plans. Nonetheless, his use of mythological imagery and so-called traditional values gained him widespread support among the Burmese, eventually even among the small educated elite who at first eschewed the movement because of its rural character and primitive means. While the rebellion ultimately failed, today it is often pointed to as the birth of modern nationalism among the Burmans.

A few years later the inheritor of this movement was Aung San, a Rangoon University student who went on to join with the JAPANESE to form the Burmese Independence Army to expel the British; they succeeded in 1942. He later recanted his ties to the Japanese in founding the Anti-Fascist Organization and as such was able to serve as the head negotiator with the British when they returned to the country in 1945. He is often considered the father of independent Burma and is the actual father of the contemporary politician and peace activist Aung San Suu Kyi. His image for the country was of a multiethnic state that would allow for significant autonomy for minority groups within the framework of a federal system. His assassination in 1947, just prior to independence a year later, was a tremendous blow to the multiethnic movement and led to the Burmans' being able to consolidate almost complete control over the country.

The years between 1948 and 1962 in Burma were marred by significant communist and ethnic violence between the dominant Burmans and other ethnic groups, but politically the government was able to maintain most of its democratic ideals. The military was invited to rule the country briefly in 1958 but was removed in 1960 through relatively free elections. In 1962 however, a military coup toppled the elected government and the Burma Socialist Program Party began its one-party rule over the state. At this time democratically minded Burmans became as anathema to the national government as communists and rebellious ethnic groups had been until that time. The military regime's failed economic policies also drove landowners, capitalists, and other urban elites into the arms of the opposition as well while the country's economy foundered and left it one of the 10 poorest countries in the world by the 1990s. The military rulers also changed the country's name in 1989 from *Burma* to *Myanmar* and that of the capital from *Rangoon* to *Yangon*.

Today Aung San Suu Kyi remains under house arrest, where she has been off and on since 1989. In 1990 her National League for Democracy overwhelmingly won a national election that the military government allowed to be held, but in the period since those results have been ignored in the country and the military has continued to hold power. Suu Kyi has been released and retaken a number of times over the past 18 years but today she remains a prisoner of conscience in her home in Rangoon. She was awarded the Nobel Prize in peace in 1991 for her work toward peace but was unable to travel to Stockholm to receive it; she also could not see her husband in London before he died of prostate cancer in 2000. In late 2007 a widespread democracy movement was brutally repressed by the military government and thousands of

Aung San ✍✍✍

Aung San, born Htain Lin, was born in central Burma on February 13, 1915, to parents who were vocally proresistance. Aung San became a resistance leader when he entered Rangoon University in 1933 and in 1938 he was elected president of the Rangoon University Students' Union as well as the All-Burma Students' Union. Shortly after leaving school, he joined Our Burma Union and assumed the title of Thakin, or "Master," a title that was used to characterize the Burmese people as the rightful rulers of their homeland. He orchestrated a number of nationwide protests against the British imperialists and united with other resistance groups to form the Freedom Bloc. In 1939 Aung San founded the Communist Party of Burma and became its first secretary-general. In 1940 he traveled to Japan, where he received military training and support from the Japanese government, and in 1941 he returned to Burma and established the Burma Independence Army. The Japanese took Burma in 1942 as part of their Asian strategy during World War II and declared Burma's independence in 1943, but independence was never realized under the Japanese administration. In reaction to this betrayal in 1945 Aung San organized a revolt to drive the Japanese out of Burma. Although he had first sided with the Japanese, Aung San's later reversal led the allies to consider him a friend, although he remained on tense terms with Winston Churchill, who called him a "traitor rebel leader."

Although Aung San acted as Burma's prime minister, he nevertheless remained subject to British rule, which changed in 1947, when he signed a treaty in London with the British prime minister Clement Attlee to declare Burma's independence within one year. However, six months before Burma's independence occurred, Aung San was assassinated along with six of his cabinet members, allegedly by U Saw, a political rival. Many political commentators on postcolonial Burma/Myanmar cite this event as one of the factors contributing to the continued instability in that country today. While Aung San had favored a federal state that was to grant significant autonomy to the country's many minority groups, the civilian and military governments that have ruled since his death have tended to favor Burman interests over those of the Karen, Kachin, and others, leading these groups to engage in the country's long-standing civil war. Aung San's daughter, Aung San Suu Kyi, is probably the best known Burman outside her own country for her decades-long struggle for democracy and human rights in her country. She received the Nobel Prize in peace in 1991 but has been under house arrest for so many years that she was unable to travel to Stockholm to receive her prize.

Burman monks and other activists were killed, detained, or disappeared.

CULTURE

During the colonial era and first decades of independence Burman economic activity was focused on the production of wet rice for sale and export. Rubies, teak, and dried shrimp and fish were also important for raising foreign capital and made the country relatively prosperous by global postcolonial standards. Since 1962's military coup and the initiation of centralized control of the economy, most agricultural activity in the central plains has been turned inward for subsistence purposes; almost no rice remains for export. Most Burmans today live as small-scale cultivators growing rice as well as cotton, peanuts, onions, and corn. On the coasts and rivers fishing is also important but generally at a low level and for domestic consumption only.

Burman society, while bilateral in reckoning descent through both mothers and fathers, does not highlight kinship connections beyond those of the family. Instead hierarchical relations classified by age, gender, generation, seniority, and respect mark most social relations, create most alliances, and are indicated by terms of address that organize all of Burman society. Buddhist monks and village priests and headmen hold the highest hierarchical positions in Burman society while the young, especially young women, hold the lowest position. Nonetheless bilateral kinship and a generally neolocal postmarriage residence pattern, in which the new couple makes its home independently of either family, mean that women are not outsiders in their own home or village. They do not experience the dislocation of women in a patrilineal system, where their children and husband are not in the same line of descent, nor of women in patrilocal residences, who must leave the security of their natal home to live as near-servants in their husband's extended family household. There is also no strongly maintained division of labor that bars women from productive work, although Buddhist monks, the most prestigious individuals in the society, are men; serving in the Burmese army, the most lucrative position in the country since the 1960s, is also the prerogative of men.

At the local level the only social organization beyond the household is the village. The vast majority of Burmans remain rural, village dwellers with only Mandalay and Yangon having any large, urban populations. Burmese villages can have one of three separate designs: linear and clustered with or without a fence or palisade. The first variety is found where a river or road allows for the dwellings and other buildings to be built along the side with fields adjacent to the village proper. The second variety is a cluster of houses surrounded by a fence with entry and exit only through a manned gate; fields and monasteries are located outside the walls but within walking distance of them. This type predominates in the northern reaches of Burman territory, adjacent to areas inhabited by the various hill tribes that have been fighting the Burmese state since 1948. The third type of village reproduces the structure of the second but without a fence separating the village from the outside world. None of the three types in the past would have any kind of public building, but today an occasional school or medical facility might be located inside the village; public wells are also available in some villages.

Besides their long, imperial history and common language the most important cultural feature of Burman identity is Buddhism. Technically the form of Buddhism practiced by Burmans can be classified as Theravada, which originated in the oldest Buddhist texts available, written in the Indo-Aryan Pali language, and which recognizes important distinctions between the practice of laypeople and that of monks. Only the latter have a real chance of achieving nirvana while laypeople can only hope to return to earth as monks in the future. In practice however, most Burmans would not know the distinction between Theravada and Hinayana Buddhism, a later variant dominant in Japan, Korea, and China, and would describe their religion as the *boda hatha* or way of the Buddha. Certainly most Burman boys spend some time living in a monastery as a coming-of-age ritual, and having a son or other relative who is a monk is an important source of familial prestige. Supporting local monasteries, temples, and pagodas is important to even the poorest of the Burman people, but historical and canonical distinctions remain outside the purview of most individuals.

In addition most Burmans also believe in a wide variety of *nats* or spirits who exist primarily to cause harm to humans and must be pacified with offerings and gifts. Most also believe in a number of other supernatural beings, including ghosts, goblins, and demons, that live in the forests, mountains, or caves and can cause illness or other misfortunes if treated with disrespect. Village priests and healers are able to communicate with these beings to ask for forgiveness or to find out what the afflicted human must do to appease them; astrologers and others who are able to read horoscopes also make money by assisting in choosing auspicious times for marriages, festivals, and other religious events.

FURTHER READING

Khin Myo Chit. *A Wonderland of Burmese Legends* (Bangkok: Tamarind Press, 1984).

Manning Nash. *The Golden Road to Modernity: Village Life in Contemporary Burma* (Chicago: University of Chicago Press, 1973).

Martin Smith. *Burma: Insurgency and the Politics of Ethnicity* (London: Zed Books, 1999).

Melford E. Spiro. *Buddhism and Society: A Great Tradition and Its Burmese Vicissitudes* (New York: Harper & Row, 1970).

Burusho (Burusha, Burushaski, Hunzakot, Hunzukut, Hunzus)

The Burusho are a small hill tribe who live in the Hunza, Nagar, and Yasin valleys of northern Pakistan. Their ancestry is largely unknown but one legend states that they are the descendants of three soldiers in the army of Alexander the Great, who settled in the mountainous area of northern Pakistan around 300 B.C.E. Another, more likely origin story, given the uniqueness of their language, proclaims that they were indigenous to northwestern India and were pushed into their present homeland by the movements of the INDO-ARYANS, who traveled southward sometime around 1800 B.C.E.

Burusho history states that for many years their territories were governed by a *mir* or prince. He had authority in all matters but was assisted by the grand vizier. Mirs served justice and made sure the local customs remained intact. Each village also had a chief, termed *arbob*, and a sergeant at arms, *chowdikar*.

In 1892 Burusho territory was conquered by the British, who used some of the mirs as indirect rulers in their rugged mountainous territory. In 1947 when India attained its independence from Britain and was split into separate Indian and Pakistani states, the Burusho found themselves living in newly independent Pakistan. For about a generation until 1974 local mirs gained control of their territory, but in that year Pakistan claimed complete control of the Burusho lands.

Most Burusho are farmers but they also maintain flocks of sheep, goats, and cattle. From these animals they mainly get milk and wool. Meat is not a priority because the Burusho diet usually consists primarily of vegetables, fruits, and grains. The main crops Burusho cultivate are barley, millet, and rice. A small number of Burusho make a living through trade or military work as well.

Traditionally there were five classes in the Burusho hierarchy: Thamo were the aristocracy while the Uyongko/Akabirting were those who worked in the state bureaucracy. Land cultivators were of the Bar/Bare/Sis class while the Shadarsho were servants. The final class, Baladakuyo/Tsilgalasho, served the Thamo and Uyongko. Some authors do not include the Shadarsho but have the Bericho, ethnic Indians, as the fifth group. Today the remnants of these divisions remain and intermarriage between the groups is not common.

Each household is generally made up of at least two and sometimes four generations of patrilineal family members and their in-marrying wives, who almost always are from the same Burusho subgroup as their husbands. A few wealthier men are able to maintain more than one wife since polygyny is allowed but it is not the norm. At marriage the wishes of both men and women are taken into consideration in the drawing up of contracts and generally parents will not carry through with an arrangement without their child's consent. Each year on December 21 a large communal wedding is held for all new couples in the community, usually presided over by a *khalifa*, a literate man in the community.

Despite the relative freedom for Burusho women, they do not inherit any property from their family of origin, although some experts point to the practice of giving dowry to a daughter at marriage as parallel to the inheritance of the sons at the father's death. Often daughters receive use rights in the family's trees, especially apricot trees and their fruit. In most cases the eldest son will receive the best part of the land, unless the father has made the divisions before he died that state otherwise.

For at least 300 years most Burusho have been Muslims, largely of the Ismaili sect, which is sometimes described as a form of Shiism, but there is also a small minority of actual Shiites. Through the years, however, many changes have been made in the beliefs and practices of the religion so that it is more practical for the Burusho way of life; many pre-Islamic beliefs and practices also remain, particularly with regard to beliefs in spirits. Some Burusho practice traditional Muslim fasting and ritual prayer, but it is not as common as among many other Muslim peoples.

An interesting fact about Burusho culture is that rivalries between villages are settled through polo matches. Armed conflict is rare even though the Burusho do not have the best relationship with their neighbors. In recent years the Burusho have undergone political unrest. Many also suffer from health problems including eye and dental problems, which stem from poor water quality.

BURUSHO

location:
Hunza, Nagar, and Yasin valleys in northern Pakistan

time period:
Unknown to the present

ancestry:
Unknown but probably indigenous to northwestern India; legend connects them to the army of Alexander the Great

language:
Burushaski, a language isolate, is the primary language, but Hunza, Nagar, and Yasin peoples each have their own dialect; the most significant secondary language is Urdu.

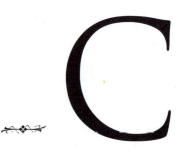

Cambodians: nationality (people of Cambodia)

GEOGRAPHY

The Cambodians occupy the mainland Southeast Asian country of Cambodia. Bordering the Gulf of Thailand, Cambodia sits among Vietnam, Laos, and Thailand, with a total landmass of 112,493 square miles. The Mekong River runs down the middle of the country and flows through Vietnam to the South China Sea.

With a monsoonal climate Cambodia is hot and humid throughout the year and is marked by equally severe wet and dry seasons. In the summer the southwest monsoon draws in moisture from the Indian Ocean and in the winter the northeast monsoon carries in dry air. During the rainy season an enormous amount of water flows into the Tonle Sap (Great Lake), which increases the size of the lake from 1,609 square miles to 15,288 square miles. When the water is carried out of the lake via the Tonle Sap River and the water level decreases, a new layer of sediment is deposited on the surrounding area and turns the area around the lake into unusable marshlands.

INCEPTION AS A NATION

Cambodia has long remained in an unstable position between Vietnam and Thailand, both of which made claims to the country that ultimately prompted King Norodom to sign an agreement in 1863 making Cambodia a French protectorate. Despite both parties' agreement that internal control of the country would remain in the hands of Cambodian royalty, the king was soon made a mere figurehead and French administrators began instituting heavy taxes and forced labor among the Cambodian peasants. Bitterness toward the French administrators was rife and small rebellions cropped up from time to time, with little success. In 1916 thousands of Cambodian peasants marched on the capital to voice their anger to the king and more than 500 were arrested and imprisoned.

Over the following years tensions and uprisings forced the French government to cede more power to the king, little by little. In 1946 Cambodia was made an autonomous kingdom within the French Union. Though this measure temporarily quelled Cambodian frustration, increasing violence eventually forced France to grant complete independence to Cambodia in 1953.

The mid-20th century was a precarious time, however, as Communist forces were gaining a stronghold in Vietnam and some Viet Minh troops were filtering into Cambodia to set up military bases (*see* Vietnamese: nationality). King Sihanouk began rooting out Viet Minh troops with financial backing from the U.S. government, which as part of its Cold War policy supported Cambodia, Laos, and Vietnam in stamping out Communism. U.S. troops had moved into South Vietnam to fight against the Viet Minh and North Vietnamese armies, but when the United States began

Cambodians: nationality time line

B.C.E.

5000 Much of Cambodia is under water.

4200 Cave dwellers become the first inhabitants of Cambodia but are probably unrelated to the modern Khmer people.

1000 A Neolithic tribe travels from southeast China into the Indochinese Peninsula, where the people construct houses on stilts and subsist on a diet of fish and rice.

100 The Khmer, a people heavily influenced by Indian culture, establish the Funan kingdom. The political, architectural, and religious systems of the Funan kingdom have obvious echoes of India.

C.E.

200 The Kingdom of Funan reaches its height during the rule of Fan Shih-Man, extending from contemporary Malaysia to Burma.

500 Funan collapses and is replaced by the Chenla kingdom, which also encompasses large parts of modern-day Laos and Vietnam.

800 Jayarvarman II, a Khmer prince, declares himself ruler of the Kingdom of Kambuja by founding a cult honoring the Hindu god Siva and linking himself with the divine by declaring himself a *devaraja*, or god-king. He is later regarded as an accomplished ruler who made great strides in architecture.

1181–1218 Kambuja flourishes under Jayarvarman VII. A highly developed irrigation system creates an overabundance of rice, and Jayarvarman wages a number of successful battles against Champa and Vietnam, which result in great territorial expansion.

1200–1400 After the death of Jayarvarman VII, Kambuja begins to decline through wars with Siam and the deterioration of the irrigation system. Some believe that the introduction of Theravada Buddhism during this period is what ultimately catalyzes the decline of the Kingdom of Kambuja, as it opposes Cambodian social structure.

1400–1800 Known as the Dark Ages of Cambodia, this is a period in which Cambodia suffers great economic and territorial loss.

1500 Cambodia experiences temporary success when the Cambodian kings initiate trade with other Asian countries. Spanish and Portuguese explorers discover Cambodia at this time as well.

1594 Thai attacks on the capital of Lovek end Cambodia's period of peace and the country soon becomes the center of a power struggle between Siam and Vietnam.

1600 Vietnam annexes the territory surrounding the Mekong Delta and Cambodia loses vital territory.

1862 Vietnamese aggression forces Cambodian prince Norodom to sign an agreement with France that establishes a French protectorate over the kingdom.

1864 Prince Norodom is crowned king.

1867 Siam forfeits claims to Cambodia but France allows Siam to keep Battambang and Siem Riep Provinces.

1884 Despite the agreement made in the protectorate to allow King Norodom to maintain control and authority over Cambodia, France takes administrative, financial, and judicial control, stripping King Norodom of the right to make national decisions.

1912 A Cambodian penal code is instituted.

1916 Thousands of Cambodian peasants march to the capital to protest the heavy taxes and forced labor that have been imposed upon them; 500 are arrested and imprisoned.

1925 The French governor Bardez is attacked and killed by bitter peasants in Kampong Chhang.

1936 The first newspaper in the Khmer language is printed and distributed.

1939 Siam is renamed *Thailand*.

(continues)

CAMBODIANS: NATIONALITY

nation:
Cambodia; Kingdom of Cambodia, Kampuchea

derivation of name:
Kambuja, referring to a north Indian tribe called the Kabojas, which was named after its founder, Kambu Svayambhuva

government:
Democracy within a constitutional monarchy

capital:
Phnom Penh

language:
Khmer 95 percent, French, English

religion:
Theravada Buddhist 95 percent, other 5 percent

earlier inhabitants:
Cham, other Mon-Khmer tribal groups

demographics:
Khmer 90 percent, Vietnamese 5 percent, Chinese 1 percent, other 4 percent

Cambodians: nationality time line *(continued)*

1940 The Franco-Japanese Treaty is signed, agreeing that France will recognize Japan's "Special Rights" in Asia, and in turn, Japan will recognize France's interests in Indochina. Later that same year, however, French officials in Indochina refuse to allow the passage of Japanese troops on their way to China as well as Japanese access to military bases in Tonkin (northern Vietnam).

Thailand's prime minister, General Luang Bipul Songgram, demands that France return Cambodia and parts of Laos to Thailand. Upon France's refusal to cede Cambodia, Thailand attacks and defeats French troops stationed in Cambodia.

1941 Thailand continues to attack French bases in Cambodia and Laos and gains more territory. In exchange for rice, rubber, and coal from Indochina, Japan establishes an armistice and goes to Indochina's defense. A peace conference between French Indochina and Thailand is held in Tokyo, in which France agrees to cede parts of Laos and northern Cambodia to Thailand.

1945 The United States bombs Phnom Penh.

In March Japan stages a coup, imprisoning French officials throughout Indochina and requesting that the rulers of Vietnam, Laos, and Cambodia declare independence.

Cambodia declares independence.

1946 France recognizes Cambodia as an autonomous kingdom within the French Union.

1947 Cambodia's first constitution is drawn up.

1950 The United States and the United Kingdom officially recognize Cambodia under King Sihanouk as an autonomous kingdom within the French Union.

1951 The French commissioner in Cambodia, Jean de Raymond, is assassinated by the Viet Minh.

1953 France hands over internal control to Cambodian authorities, marking the end of France's colonial presence in Cambodia.

King Sihanouk struggles to combat Viet Minh forces in Cambodia.

1954 France signs an agreement granting Cambodia, Vietnam, and Laos full independence.

The United States declares its intentions to support financially the recognized governments of Cambodia, Laos, and Vietnam to help fend off the looming threat of Communism.

1958 Cambodia officially recognizes Communist China.

1959 A gift box sent to the Cambodian royal family from an American military base in South Vietnam turns out to be a plastic bomb. Prince Vakrivan is killed.

bombing areas of Cambodia believed to hold Communist forces, King Sihanouk expressed dismay. The bombing continued and relations between Cambodia and the United States became tense. King Sihanouk threatened the United States with a complete severance of diplomatic relations and the U.S. and British embassies in Cambodia were attacked by locals, who threw objects and destroyed the buildings. When the bombing continued unabated, King Sihanouk refused further financial assistance from the United States, cut off all relations, and sought support from an alliance with Communist China.

In 1970 while out of the country King Sihanouk was stripped of power and was replaced by General Lon Nol, who mended Cambodia's alliance with the United States, renamed the country the *Khmer Republic*, and abolished the monarchy. North Vietnamese troops had begun to infiltrate Cambodia, and Hanoi ignored Lon Nol's request to withdraw them. The Communist Party of Cambodia was also gaining strength. In 1970 President Nixon announced the movement of U.S. and South Vietnamese troops into Cambodia to destroy North Vietnamese bases, but the intruders proved difficult to catch as they moved deeper into Cambodia. Communist forces gained momentum in Cambodia, and in 1975, the Communist Party of Kampuchea launched an offensive that destroyed Lon Nol's regime. U.S. troops evacuated the country and Lon Nol and the rest of his administration surrendered.

With the Communist Party now in power General Secretary Saloth Sar, or Pol Pot, was able to put into action his plans for a reformed Cambodian society. Former Prince Sihanouk

1960 The Khmer Communist Party holds secret meetings at the Phnom Penh railway station. The party renames itself the *Workers' Party of Kampuchea* and Saloth Sar (otherwise known as Pol Pot) becomes a member of the central committee.

1962 Advancing Vietnamese Communists prompt the United States to bomb the border area of Cambodia, an action that strains Cambodia's relations with the United States.

1963 Pol Pot becomes the Cambodian Communist Party's general secretary after his predecessor, Tou Samouth, mysteriously disappears.

Cambodia ceases to accept U.S. military and economic assistance and instead begins receiving assistance from the People's Republic of China.

1970 While away for health reasons, Prince Sihanouk is deposed in a coup d'état. General Lon Nol assumes power, renames the country the *Khmer Republic,* and allies the nation with the United States. President Nixon sends troops into Cambodia to destroy the North Vietnamese Army's bases in Cambodia.

1973 The Cambodian Communist Party, now the Communist Party of Kampuchea, controls 60 percent of Cambodian territory and is supported by 25 percent of the population.

1975 Communist troops launch an offensive that successfully destroys the Khmer Republic. U.S. troops evacuate the country and five days later the Lon Nol government surrenders.

Shortly after its victory the Communist Party of Kampuchea calls for the evacuation of all cities and sends the displaced urban population into the countryside to farm.

1975–79 The U.S. Central Intelligence Agency estimates that approximately 50,000–100,000 Cambodians are executed under the Khmer Rouge, and another 1.2 million die of starvation and illness.

1978 Vietnamese troops invade Cambodia and drive out the Communist regime. The nation is renamed the *People's Republic of Kampuchea* and Heng Samrin is installed as head of state.

1980–82 UNICEF and the World Food Program respond to Cambodia's decimated population by sending roughly $400 million in food and aid to the country.

1993 UN-sponsored elections result in the reinstatement of Norodom Sihanouk as king and a level of stability is restored in Cambodia.

1998 The last remaining members of the Khmer Rouge regime surrender.

was placed under house arrest and all urban Cambodians were forcibly evacuated from their homes and sent to the countryside to farm. Many had no familiarity with farming and thousands died of starvation and illness as they were relocated to newly created villages that lacked food and medical care. But Pol Pot's plan called for more than just relocation; he and his 15-member cabinet sought to abolish completely the former Cambodian society and restructure a new Cambodian people. Religion was abolished, particularly Buddhism and Catholicism; industrial enterprises were seized and destroyed or taken over by the government; and even the banking system was dismantled. Cambodia was plunged into a whirlpool of chaos and Pol Pot's regime soon proved to be a cruel and tyrannical one. As the Communist Party, or Khmer Rouge, sought to rebuild the nation into the country of their political dreams, anyone who posed any threat to the plan was considered a counterrevolutionary. The accusation of being a "counterrevolutionary" was deadly, and one could be charged and executed for the simple crime of wearing glasses, scavenging for food, speaking a foreign language, or even crying over dead relatives. Even Communist officials could be tried and executed as counterrevolutionaries for failing to gather up enough counterrevolutionaries to execute.

Between 1975 and 1979 an estimated 50,000–100,000 people were executed and another 1.2 million died of starvation or illness. Hundreds of thousands more were displaced from their homes. As Pol Pot's regime grew in strength and confidence, Communist troops began pushing into Vietnamese territory,

Cambodia

THAILAND

LAOS

Kong R.

San R.

Srepok R.

Angkor Watt ●

Siem Riep ●

Sen R.

Mekong R.

Battambang ●

Tonle Sap Lake

CAMBODIA

Tonle Sap R.

Kampong Chhang ●

Phnum Adral ▲▲

Lovek (former capital) ●

VIETNAM

Phnom Penh ✪

Mekong R.

N

Gulf of Thailand

CHINA

MYANMAR

LAOS

THAILAND

VIETNAM

CAMBODIA

Andaman Sea

South China Sea

0   100 miles

0   100 km

© Infobase Publishing

0   350 miles

0   350 km

igniting outrage from the Vietnamese government, which had long wished to reclaim parts of Cambodia. Pol Pot's taunting moves provided justification for Vietnamese troops to invade in 1978. The next year the Vietnamese seized the Cambodian capital of Phnom Penh and Pol Pot's Khmer Rouge regime was driven out. The Vietnamese installed Heng Samrin, a defector from the Khmer Rouge, as head of state of the newly renamed People's Republic of Kampuchea. By the time Vietnam began rebuilding Cambodia, 600,000 people were displaced.

UNICEF and the World Food Programme donated more than $400 million to help rebuild Cambodia, but political violence remained a problem for years afterward. Civilians were often attacked by Khmer Rouge guerrillas, and in one instance, a crowded bus was attacked, leaving more than 120 dead and 200 more injured.

In 1993 elections were held and Prince Sihanouk was reinstated as king, affecting a much-needed level of stability in Cambodian culture. In 1998 the last remnants of the Khmer Rouge forces surrendered and the process of rebuilding the country could begin in earnest.

CULTURAL IDENTITY

Perhaps more than countries without the recent tragic history that Cambodia has had, in Cambodia national identity is built largely on symbols and cultural traits from the people's distant past. As part of the nation's effort to revitalize its identity and people, in the mid-1990s the king and government passed and signed a new law for the protection of cultural heritage with the express aim of fostering a new national identity based on the people's glorious past. The three most important principles of the Cambodian state remain "Nation, Religion, King," and most symbols and institutions point to at least one of these three intertwined national institutions. For example Angkor Wat, a temple structure built over the course of about 300 years from the ninth to the 12th century, graces the country's flag, currency, passports, police badges, and even such consumer items as beer cans, newspapers, and cigarette packaging. The temple complex symbolizes the great urban nation developed by the early Khmers, the blend of religious and political values and structures that is still current in today's society, and the strength of cultural heritage in developing a viable contemporary national identity. Other symbols from the Khmer past have also been revived recently, such as the use on the national crest of Raja Simha and Gaja Simha, representing the king's royal power and hospitality, respectively.

The importance of the past in Cambodia can be seen to be at work in most areas of national life. Cambodian culture has its deepest roots in India, as is apparent in ancient works of art and architecture. Politics, society, and religion were also heavily influenced by Indian culture. Part of this Indian influence can be seen in the hierarchical nature of Cambodian society and the rich customs and rituals that are based on respect and honor. Age determines one's level of respectability, and titles are given to mark an individual's place within the hierarchy. The elderly are considered to have the highest level of respectability and are often referred to by family titles even though they are not one's actual relatives. Referring to an individual by the wrong title is considered to be disrespectful.

In the current period 95 percent of the population of Cambodia claims adherence to Theravada Buddhism, a school of Buddhism that originated in India and has since penetrated

---

Pol Pot

Reviled as one of the most ruthless dictators in modern history, Pol Pot, or Saloth Sar, is best known as the Communist leader of the Khmer Rouge movement in Cambodia. Born in the Kampong Thom Province in 1925, Pol Pot had an education that was marred by below-average performance and repeatedly failed exams. He studied in France from 1949 to 1953 and was drawn to the French Communists, joining the Cercle Marxiste in 1951. Upon his return home he quickly ascended the ranks to become the leader of the Cambodian Communist Party. Under his leadership this party in the early 1960s moved away from Marxism to develop the ideals of the Khmer Rouge, which considered the peasant farmer to be the true proletariat. In 1966 peasant revolts over the exorbitant price of rice prompted Pol Pot to organize an uprising against the Cambodian government, and the first raid was launched in January 1968. But the struggles between the government and the Communists were soon eclipsed by the struggles between Cambodia and North Vietnam. During this time the Khmer Rouge seized power and China agreed to support their fight against the Vietnamese with $5 million a year worth of weaponry. As Pol Pot gained increasing stability in the war, he established new guidelines of uniformity by forcing minority populations to dress in the mainstream Cambodian fashion and attempting to reform landholdings to make them all one size. In 1973 Pol Pot ordered a number of purges, focusing on former government officials and the academic elite. That same year Pol Pot ordered the evacuation of the urban areas, the populations of which were forcibly sent out to work in the country's rural areas. One-third of the Cambodian population died under the Khmer Rouge regime of starvation, disease, exhaustion, and execution. The Khmer Rouge was finally overthrown by Vietnamese invasion in 1978, but the party survived in Thailand and Pol Pot was never truly brought to justice for his crimes. In 1997 the Khmer Rouge party placed Pol Pot under house arrest for ordering the execution of a senior party member and his family, and a year later Pol Pot died of heart failure.

---

many other Southeast Asian countries. However, Cambodians have a unique belief system that fuses together Theravada Buddhism with elements from Hinduism as well as indigenous animistic beliefs. This syncretic blend means that religion in Cambodia is unique even among Buddhist nations and is often pointed to as a national religion rather than as an orthodox form of Buddhism.

FURTHER READING

Elizabeth Becker. *When the War Was Over: Cambodia and the Khmer Rouge Revolution* (New York: Public Affairs, 1986).

David P. Chandler. *History of Cambodia* (Boulder, Colo.: Westview Press, 2000).

Karen J. Coates. *Cambodia Now: Life in the Wake of War* (Jefferson, N.C.: McFarland & Company, 1971).

Henry Kamm. *Cambodia: Reports from a Stricken Land* (New York: Arcade, 1999).

Ben Kiernan. *The Pol Pot Regime: Race, Power, and Genocide in Cambodia under the Khmer Rouge, 1975–79* (New Haven, Conn.: Yale University Press, 2002).

CANTONESE

location:
Southern China, Macau, and Hong Kong as well as a large diaspora throughout Asia and beyond

time period:
Possibly around 221 B.C.E. to the present

language:
Yue or Cantonese, a Sino-Tibetan language in the large Chinese language family

John Marston and Elizabeth Guthrie, eds. *History, Buddhism, and New Religious Movements in Cambodia* (Honolulu: University of Hawaii Press, 2004).
Haing Ngor and Roger Warner. *Survival in the Killing Fields* (New York: Carroll and Graf, 1987).
Loung Ung. *First They Killed My Father: A Daughter of Cambodia Remembers* (New York: HarperCollins Publishers, 2000).

Canaque   *See* KANAK.

Cantonese (Yue)

The Cantonese are speakers of the Yue or Cantonese dialect of Chinese. Most live in China's Guangdong and Guangxi Provinces, Hong Kong, and Macao. There is also an extremely large overseas Cantonese population in the United States, Canada, Australia, and elsewhere, since the Chinese migrants to these countries have been largely from Hong Kong and Guangdong.

The exact origins of the Cantonese as distinct from other Chinese-language speakers are difficult to trace because written forms of the language are nearly identical to Mandarin and other dialects. However, most linguists and historians believe that Cantonese as a language and culture began to break away from proto-Chinese during the Qin dynasty (221–206 B.C.E.). During that period HAN settlers began moving into southern China from their original homeland in the central China plains. They brought their language and cultural forms with them, but through interactions with the non-Han Yue populations the Cantonese began to diverge from more northern Han populations. The best estimate for when Cantonese began to diverge from Mandarin is before or during the Tang dynasty or between the seventh and 10th centuries. For about 1,600 years these southerners were called Yue or BAIYUE by their northern cousins; it was only during the European colonial era that *Cantonese* came to be used, referring to the anglicized version of the local pronunciation of *Guangdong*, "Kwangtung." Today even most English-language texts use the proper Chinese name for the city of Guangzhou but continue to use *Cantonese* for the language and people of the region.

Although Cantonese has achieved the status of one of China's major languages with nearly 50 million speakers, it has official language status only in Hong Kong. The language is also divisible into four separate dialects: Yuehai, Siyi, Gaoyang, and Guinan.

The region inhabited by most Cantonese people, Guangdong Province, is largely subtropical with a small portion located in the Tropics. Temperatures are warm and the region receives ample rainfall throughout the year, although there is a distinct rainy season from April through September. Numerous rivers cross the low hills and coastal plains including the Pearl River, the mouth of which is where Guangzhou is located, and its many tributaries. The region was under the control of the Nan Yue kingdom until about 214 B.C.E., when the Qin dynasty conquered it and began moving sections of the Han population south. The region attained provincial status only in 1370 C.E., at the very start of the Ming dynasty (1368–1644), when Guangzhou became the capital.

Since that period the Cantonese have been active in many of the pivotal events that have shaped contemporary China. The Portuguese and later the English both focused their trade, missionary, and colonial activities in the region's ports, thus introducing Western ideas, products, and religions to the Cantonese long before they had any effect upon other Chinese populations. In the 19th century Guangzhou was the main port utilized by the British to import opium and other products to China to trade for tea. In retaliation for this blatant disregard for Chinese law the Chinese government in the late 1830s destroyed thousands of pounds of opium and detained the entire foreign population of Guangzhou, setting off the first Opium War, in which the British soundly

China's defeat by Britain in the First Opium War continued the process of opening up the Cantonese territories of southern China to external trade and relations. *(Library of Congress Prints and Photographs Division)*

defeated the Chinese and began what many consider to be China's modern era. In a strikingly parallel situation when China began to open its markets and industries to the rest of the world in the late 1970s, it was Guangdong and the Cantonese who were the first to experience the transformations resulting from the creation of special economic zones that provided tax incentives and other assistance to foreign businesses. Because of this combination of external investment, local handicraft industries, and a climate and geography conducive to extremely productive agricultural and fishing industries, Guangdong's Cantonese today are among China's richest people. When Hong Kong and Macao's large Cantonese populations are added to the mix, the Cantonese must be seen as China's most Westernized people as well. For example, larger numbers of Cantonese are practitioners of Christianity than elsewhere in China, where religion remains a somewhat taboo subject.

FURTHER READING

Brian Hook, ed. *Guangdong: China's Promised Land* (New York: Oxford University Press, 1996).
Janice E. Stockard. *Daughters of the Canton Delta: Marriage Patterns and Economic Strategies in South China, 1860–1930* (Stanford, Calif.: Stanford University Press, 1989).

Cao Lan   *See* SAN CHAY.

Caucasian Albanians (Aghbanians, Aghvanians, Ałuanki)

The Caucasian Albanians are an ancient people who resided in the territory of present-day Azerbaijan and Russian Dagestan. They are not related to nor should they be confused with contemporary Albanians who live in Eastern Europe. Their descendants are probably the Udi or Udin, one of the few Christian communities in present-day Azerbaijan and eastern Georgia. Caucasian Albanians also contributed to the makeup of contemporary ARMENIANS, AZERIS, and GEORGIANS.

GEOGRAPHY

The Caucasian Albanians' territory largely coincided with present-day Azerbaijan, plus a bit of land from southern Dagestan in Russia. Unlike the rest of the Caucasus region the territory held by the Caucasian Albanians included large plains suitable for agriculture. In the fertile Kura River valley region wheat, grapes, and fruit could be grown with little difficulty.

ORIGINS

According to local legend the kingdom of Caucasian Albania was established in the fourth century B.C.E. by King Aran or Arhan, who is sometimes said to be the grandson of Noah through his son Japheth. Another legend has it that Zarathustra, prophet and founder of the Zoroastrian religion, was a Caucasian Albanian, but this idea is also found in a variety of other regions that came under Zoroastrian influence (*see* BACTRIANS).

In slightly less mythological historiography several ancient Greek and Roman authors also mentioned Caucasian Albania, such as Strabo writing around the time of Jesus, Pliny and Plutarch in the first century C.E., and Ptolemy in the second. Pliny locates the Albanian capital in Gabala, while Strabo and Ptolemy join him in placing the border between Albania and Armenia on the Kura River. Strabo also writes that the Albanians were composed of 26 different tribes, all of them tall and blond with gray eyes. One of these tribes he names as the Udi, perhaps strengthening the hypothesis that the contemporary Udi are the descendants of these ancient people. Another important tribe are the Gagarians, who occupied a region now known as the Mugan Steppe in Azerbaijan.

HISTORY

Most of Caucasian Albania's known history is one of subordination to outside forces. Although the Albanian monarchy remained in existence for most of Caucasian Albania's history until the Arab conquest, these kings were largely vassals to other, more powerful rulers. Locally the Armenian kingdom was often able to control events in Albania. More globally both Persia (Parthian and Sassanid empires) and Rome/Byzantium often held hegemony over Albanian political, economic, and even religious affairs (*see also* PARTHIANS and PERSIANS, SASSANIDS).

The first confirmed reference to the Caucasian Albanians occurs in 331 B.C.E., when they are mentioned as part of the Median forces fighting with Darius III of Achaemenid Persia against Alexander the Great of Macedon (*see* PERSIANS, ACHAEMENIDS). They fought under the leadership of the satrap or governor of Media so the assumption is that they had already been incorporated into that political unit in the decades before (*see* MEDES). They were also listed among the soldiers who served as Darius III's personal guards. However, Iranian sources indicate that the Caucasian Albanians at this time would not have been a unified people but

CAUCASIAN ALBANIANS

location:
Contemporary Azerbaijan and Russian Dagestan, from the Kura River in the south to Derbent in the north

time period:
Possibly fourth century B.C.E. but more likely first century B.C.E. to 700 C.E.

ancestry:
Unknown

language:
Aluan or Caucasian Albanian

Caucasian Albanians time line

B.C.E.

fourth century Legendary founding of the Kingdom of Caucasian Albania by King Aran.

331 Caucasian Albanians participate in the Battle of Gaugamela, when Alexander the Great defeats the forces of Darius III of Persia.

End second century Estimated period of unification of the Albanian tribes under one ruler.

66 Roman legions under Pompeius Magnus defeat 40,000–60,000 Albanian soldiers led by Orois.

C.E.

36 Caucasian Albanians rebel against the Romans, but the revolt fails and the area remains a protectorate of Rome under King Zober.

100–200 The first written Aluan words are recorded in the Oxyrhynchis Papyri; they constitute a partial word list written by Heracleides.

252–253 Caucasian Albania comes under the protection of the Sassanid empire.

third–fifth centuries Feudalism and Christianity spread throughout the region of Caucasian Albania.

fourth century King Urnayr adopts Christianity at the hands of St. Gregory.

At the end of this century the capital of Albania is moved from Gabala to Partaw, contemporary Barda.

451 Albanians, allied with Armenians and other Caucasian Christians, are defeated by the Persian Sassanid empire.

703– Arabs conquer the region and convert many to Islam. Despite the survival of an Albanian church as a diocese within the greater Armenian Church, the Caucasian Albanian people cease to exist as a separate ethnic group.

10th century Movses Dasxuranci puts together his book *The History of the Caucasian Albanians*.

1836 The Albanian Church is abolished by the czar's authorities; it is reestablished in 2003.

rather a disparate group of 26 different tribes, speaking languages that were only partially mutually intelligible. Near the end of the second century B.C.E. is the best estimate for the period of unification.

The next solid historical reference is by the Roman writer Theophanes of Mitylene, who accompanied the general Pompey on his conquests of the Caucasus. In 66 or 65 B.C.E. Roman forces led by Pompeius Magnus attacked the Caucasus region. This area had long been considered the very edge of the world from the perspective of the Mediterranean peoples; Jason's quest for the Golden Fleece is often believed to have taken him to the Caucasus. Caucasian Albania's 40,000–60,000 forces were led by King

Orois or Oroezes, who, despite fighting bravely, was defeated by the Romans. This battle began a long history of contact between the Caucasian Albanians and the Romans, both of the Western Roman and Eastern Byzantine Empires.

Theophanes writes at that time of the Caucasian Albanians as seminomadic shepherds who also practiced hunting rather than agriculture and employed a barter system rather than coins or money. At that time they continued to be divided into 26 different tribal units speaking different dialects, despite being unified under one king. They were able to field both regular soldiers and cavalry in the failed defense of their territory, and both sorts of troops wore iron armor, a practice that Theophanes assumed they had acquired from the Medes.

Writing after Theophanes, Strabo also fails to find any evidence of urbanization among the Albanians, supporting the claim of seminomadism from the period 65 B.C.E. However, archaeological evidence has emerged showing that if not cities, at least towns were beginning to develop in the century before the common era. There is also significant evidence of interaction with the Iranian world in the form of coins and unbaked bricks of the Parthian variety.

Despite their defeat at the hands of the Romans, the Caucasian Albanians did not settle into their subordinate position. In 36 C.E. they rose up against the Romans under King Zober but were defeated once again and were forced to accept the position of protectorate. This did not stop the significant cultural and economic interactions between them and the Parthian rulers in Asia, with archaeological evidence pointing to a continuing strong economic relationship. This connection between Iranian-speaking peoples and Caucasian Albanians becomes even stronger once the Sassanids supplant the Parthians and in 252–53 Albania comes under the protection of the Sassanid king Shapur I.

In the fourth century this Iranian-Albanian connection weakens somewhat when the Albanian king Urnayr joins his Armenian neighbors in converting to Christianity under St. Gregory; however, religious differences did not stop the Albanian king from participating with the Sassanids under Shapur II against the Romans at Amida in Mesopotamia in 359 or with Armenia in 372. However, in the middle of the fifth century the Sassanid king, Yazdegerd II, made conversion to Zoroastrianism mandatory in all parts of the empire, including Albania. The Albanians sought the help of their Christian neighbors, the Armenians, who expelled the Persians from Albania's cities, if only temporarily. The alliance later failed and the Sassanids reasserted themselves in the Caucasus.

Although Albania remained under Sassanid protection, the differences in their religions continued to affect the relationship. At the end of the fifth century between 484 and 488 Albania's leaders took a hard line against individuals who had converted to Zoroastrianism, as well as against other non-Christian beliefs and practices, at their church conference at Aghuen. Almost a century later some Albanian nobles requested protection for their country from the Christian Byzantine ruler Justinian II but were rejected. The beginning of the seventh century saw yet another Christian uprising in Albania against the Zoroastrian Sassanid king Khosrow II; however, the Albanians did not free themselves from the Persians until the Persians themselves had been defeated on Albanian soil by Heraclius, the Byzantine emperor, in 624. But the power vacuum that emerged in the Caucasus allowed the Khazars, a Turkic tribe, to establish themselves and start taxing Albanian fishermen and merchants. This condition seemed to continue until about 703, when Arab conquest of the region finally ended any semblance of Albanian independence.

CULTURE

We do not know very much about Caucasian Albanian social structure, except that it resembled that of Armenia of the same period. Sometime after the earliest Roman reference the Caucasian Albanians adopted agriculture since later authors note wheat fields, vineyards, and orchards. Feudal relationships between landowners and serfs predominated, while a class of royalty allied itself alternately with Rome/Byzantium and Persia.

Some sources state that prior to the adoption of Christianity in the fourth century Albanians worshipped the Moon, stars, and planets. Gabala, which served as the capital for the early centuries of the kingdom, had a temple dedicated to the Moon. How this worship manifested itself remains unclear. Other sources connect the Caucasian Albanians with fire worship, which probably provides evidence of their having adopted Zoroastrianism at some point during their subjugation by the Medes and Persians. Once the people had converted from Zoroastrianism to Christianity, the cultural links between Albanians and Armenians strengthened and soon after the capital was moved to Partaw. If there are any connections between their religious conversion and the movement of their capital, historians have yet to make them.

See also ARMENIANS: NATIONALITY; AZERBAIJANIS: NATIONALITY.

FURTHER READING

Movses Dasxuranci. *The History of the Caucasian Albanians.* Translated and with commentary by C. J. F. Dowsett (London: Oxford University Press, 1961).

Cebuanos (Cebuan, Sugbuhanon)

The Cebuanos, "natives of the island of Cebu" in Spanish, are a linguistic subgroup of the VISAYANS or Bisayan peoples, who number about 20 million. They originate from the island of Cebu but today occupy several of the Visayan islands of the Philippines and portions of the large southern island of Mindanao. They are the second largest linguistic group in the country after TAGALOG speakers.

GEOGRAPHY

Cebu differs from much of the rest of the Philippines in being almost totally protected from volcanoes, earthquakes, typhoons, and monsoons. Rather than being volcanic in origin, Cebu is made of coral, is located away from all major fault lines, and is surrounded by other islands, which protect it from typhoons and monsoons. There is no pronounced rainy season; instead the island receives regular rain throughout the year and vast amounts of sunshine. The island's natural deep seaport has provided safe access to ships for many hundreds of years and has left a legacy of great diversity; it has the largest population density in the Philippines today.

Bohol and Negros, where large numbers of Cebuanos live, are also well known for their geographic features. Bohol is important as a tourist attraction; thousands of international tourists flock to the island each year to view the Chocolate Hills, a grouping of several hundred cone-shaped hills covered with plant life that turns brown in the hot summer months. By contrast Negros is more agroindustrial, having been the center of the country's sugar industry since the mid-19th century.

ORIGINS

The origins of the Cebuanos, as of all Austronesian speakers in the Philippines, are probably in south China, from which they sailed in double-outrigger dugout canoes about 5,000 years ago to Taiwan, and then later to the Philippines and

---

CEBUANOS

location:
The Visayan Islands, especially Cebu, Negros, and Bohol, and parts of Mindanao, the Philippines; originally just the island of Cebu

time period:
3000 B.C.E. to the present

ancestry:
Austronesian

language:
Cebuano, a Meso-Philippine language within the larger Austronesian language family; there are five separate dialects

Cebuanos time line

B.C.E.

3000 The initial migration of Austronesian speakers to the Philippines, including the ancestors of the Cebuanos.

C.E.

fourth century Chinese traders make contact with the Cebuanos and begin centuries of trade between the two peoples.

1400 Arab traders arrive in the Visayan Islands, bringing Islam with them.

1521 Ferdinand Magellan lands on Cebu and converts the local ruler to Catholicism. He is killed a few days later in a battle on the island of Mactan.

1565 Don Miguel Lopez de Legaspi and Fray Andrés de Urdaneta are successful in their Christianization project in the Visayas. They also build Fort San Pedro, the oldest Spanish fort in the archipelago.

1575 Legaspi and others establish the first Spanish settlement in the archipelago, Villa del Santisimo Nombre de Jesus, on the site of contemporary Cebu.

1898 General Leon Kilat leads a band of Cebuanos against the Spanish at Fort San Pedro; he is murdered after five days of battle.

1899 The Spanish cede the Philippines to the United States and a local war of independence breaks out.

1902 A civil U.S. administration replaces military rule upon the pacification of the independence fighters.

1941 The Japanese occupy the Philippines during World War II and use Cebu as their headquarters.

1944 The United States retakes the Philippines.

1945 The Philippines attains independence from the United States.

1965 Cebu celebrates 400 years of Christianity on the island with the conferring of a new basilica, creation of a new missionary organization, and numerous parades and festivals.

1986 Corazon Aquino comes to power in the Philippines

the rest of Polynesia. There is no certainty as to why this population left south China; however, archaeologists have hypothesized that it was a combination of population pressure, increased commerce from the Yangtze River region of China and moving southward down the river and its tributaries, a growing demand for marine and tropical forest goods, and climate change.

Contemporary Austronesian languages can be subdivided into two distinctive groups that separate the languages of Austronesian Taiwan from those of the remainder of the family, which include all Malay and Oceanic languages. This linguistic division, in addition to several anomalies in the archaeological record, such as a lack of rice in the earliest Austronesian sites in Taiwan, indicates that the origins

of the Austronesian people may have been two separate exoduses from southeast China. If these did occur, the first exodus was probably from Fujian Province in China to Taiwan, which saw the rise of TA-P'EN-K'ENG CULTURE, with its distinctively marked pottery and stone tools, but without archaeological evidence of domesticated rice. The descendants of this first wave would be the contemporary speakers of Taiwan's Austronesian languages, the ABORIGINAL TAIWANESE. The second exodus may have occurred around 3000 B.C.E., taking a second wave of Austronesian speakers from southeastern China to Taiwan and then almost immediately to Luzon in the Philippines around the same period. This second wave, with its red slipped pottery, may also have been the ultimate source of the LAPITA CULTURE.

HISTORY

As speakers of a Malayo-Polynesian language, the Cebuanos were fairly integrated into the seafaring kingdoms of both island and mainland Southeast Asia from the early centuries of the common era. Trade with China may have begun by the fourth century C.E. and certainly was a regular occurrence by the eighth. Influence from India, including Sanskrit vocabulary and grammar structures, is also evident in Cebuano language and culture today, as are features from the Muslim Arab trading cultures that made contact with Cebu in about 1400. Elements from Khmer and Thai can also be seen in the region's music and ritual life. The early Cebuanos called their homeland *Zebu* or *Sugbu,* which became *Cebu* in later centuries.

European contact with the Cebuanos began in April 1521 when Ferdinand Magellan landed on the island of Cebu. Some descriptions of Magellan's force of five ships and more than 200 men claim that one of them was himself a Cebuano, who somehow had traveled from his homeland, across Asia, and into Spain. If the story is accurate, that sailor would be the first documented person to have traveled completely around the world. Another important milestone reached by this first European expedition to the archipelago was the baptism of the first Filipinos, two rulers named Datu Humabon and his wife, Juana. Descriptions of the event vary, with some listing just these two individuals as converts; others claim that 400 other Cebuanos joined them. Regardless this initial baptism did not lead to the widespread acceptance of Christianity immediately. Not long after the event Magellan himself was killed by Datu Lapulapu, ruler on the small island of Mactan adjacent to Cebu, and it was another 44 years before Christianity began to take hold in the region, with the missionary activities of Don Miguel Lopez de Legaspi and Fray Andrés de Urdaneta in 1565.

Legaspi is also remembered on Cebu and throughout the Philippines for his military actions in the region. He and his soldiers built the oldest Spanish fort in the archipelago, Fort San Pedro, in 1565, for protection against the Cebuanos, whose attacks on the Spanish grew more intense in the first years of colonization. Nonetheless by the start of the second century of Spanish domination in the Philippines the vast majority of Cebuanos had converted to Roman Catholicism and adopted many other cultural aspects of Spanish and Mestizo cultures. Many Cebuanos continued to chafe against colonialism on an individual basis, rebelling in the sugar fields of Negros or the towns of Cebu, but it was not until the Philippine revolution in 1898 that the Cebuanos fought back with organized military precision. The bloodiest battle between Cebuanos and Spanish forces took place in April 1898 on the site of Fort San Pedro. Cebuano Pantaleon Villegas de Solde, who fought under the name General Leon Kilat, besieged the fort for three days with the help of many of his fellow Cebuanos before being betrayed by a group of Mestizos, who had him murdered.

Despite their failure in April 1898 the Cebuanos were able to take over Fort San Pedro eight months later when the Spanish were defeated by the Americans in the Battle of Manila Bay. Later the fort became a military barracks for American soldiers stationed in the Philippines and then classrooms of a Cebuano school from 1937 to 1941; subsequently it was a prison camp, a hospital, offices, and most recently a zoo and today a historical monument. During this period the town in which the fort was located, Villa del Santisimo Nombre de Jesus, was incorporated as a municipality in 1901 and finally as the city of Cebu in 1937.

During the JAPANESE period, 1941–44, the Cebuanos suffered more than many of the archipelago's other residents because Cebu itself served as the Japanese headquarters. Filipino independence extended to the Cebuanos and the rest of the country in 1945, following liberation from the three-year occupation of the archipelago by the Japanese. Sergio Osmeña, a Cebuano of mixed Mestizo and Chinese ancestry, served as vice president of the Common-wealth of the Philippines under the first president, Manuel L. Quezon, and succeeded him as second president.

In 1965 the Christianity of the Cebuanos was put on display for the entire world to see in a giant celebration of the 400th anniversary of Filipino Christianity in Cebu. In addition to numerous festivals, parades, and other events, the Philippines Bishops' Conference chose that year to initiate a missionary program from the Philippines to send members to Asia, Oceania, Europe, and South America. In the 21st century the missionary program has been extremely busy in Japan, especially in Okinawa, with both local Catholics and English-speaking expatriots residing in the region. In 1965 Cebu's San Agustin Church was also transformed into the Basilica Minore del Santo Niño by the papal legate, His Eminence Ildefonso Cardinal Antonuitte.

CULTURE

The Austronesian migrants to the Philippines arrived from Taiwan bearing several domesticated plants, including rice; domesticated pigs, dogs, and chickens; and a lifestyle built around the agricultural calendar. Throughout most of their history the Cebuanos remained agriculturalists, but in the present day Cebu is almost devoid of primary food production in favor of the industrial, mining, and service industries. Cebuanos on other islands may continue to grow rice, corn, beans, and other crops on permanent fields.

One of the features that Magellan's men first noted about the Cebuanos was their striking

---

Leon Kilat

Leon Kilat (Lightning Leon), born Pantaleon Villegas, was a Filipino revolutionary in the late 19th century. Born in 1873 in Bacong, Negros Oriental, Kilat first worked as an errand boy for a pharmacy before joining a circus troupe, at which point he befriended a member of the Katipunan, a revolutionary group seeking to overthrow the Spanish occupation of the Philippine Islands. Kilat soon joined the Katipunan and secured a position of power within its ranks. In 1898 Kilat was sent to Cebu to lead the Cebuano revolutionaries and on April 7, 1898, Holy Thursday, Kilat devised a plan to attack the Spaniards in Carcar on Easter Sunday, when they would all be assembled in town to celebrate the holy day. A Spanish friar, Father Francisco Blanco, feared the violence of a Spanish backlash and conspired with one of Kilat's men to have Kilat murdered, and on the night of Holy Thursday, Kilat and his men were invited to dinner at the house of Tiyoy Barcenilla. After dinner Kilat went to bed, where his men ambushed him and stabbed him to death. On the morning of Good Friday Kilat's corpse was displayed in town and today he is remembered as a martyr for the revolution.

The Cebuanos, like most lowland Filipinos, are ardent Catholics who celebrate the life of Jesus with numerous parades, spectacles, and festivals. This Sinulog procession in 1998 drew vast crowds of locals and tourists alike. *(APVic Kintanar)*

material culture. Most people were adorned with gold jewelry on their bodies and clothes and wore turbans and blouses made from silk. Men remained naked from the waist up and were often covered with tattoos while upper-class women wore blouses called *chambaras*. Many women also wore lipstick and hair decorations of flowers, gold, and other precious and semiprecious metals and stones. Porcelain jars and utensils were also important enough to be noted in the writings of Magellan's chronicler, Antonio Pigafetta. He commented upon the many ships in Cebu's harbor from Thailand, China, and Arabia and often pointed out that particular aspects of Cebuano material culture originated in these parts of the world.

In contemporary times Cebuanos continue to be a multicultural group with people, products, and ideas from all over the world. Individuals with indigenous, Spanish, Mestizo, Chinese, German, American, and other backgrounds all live as Cebuanos in the central Philippines. Most of them speak Tagalog, Spanish, and/or English in addition to Cebuano, especially in urban areas, and most are Roman Catholic. The most important event in the region is the nine-day Sinulog celebration of the baby Jesus marked by

a parade, religious procession, pilgrimages to Cebu, and dancing by candlelight.

Despite the centrality of Catholicism in the lives of more than 80 percent of all Cebuanos, by the late 1960s many indigenous ritual beliefs and practices had not yet died out and many continue today. One important indigenous practice is the system of folk healing done by *mananambal*s or healers to counteract the effects of sorcery and witchcraft. Both rural and urban Cebuano sorcerers engage in two different malevolent practices: introducing insects into people's vital organs and secretly poisoning them. They may also use sympathetic and contagious magic by putting nails into a wooden doll representing the victim or creating a potion from the victim's saliva, hair, or urine. These activities are believed to cause a wide variety of illnesses and other misfortunes in people who are guilty of some social infraction; nonguilty people are not affected by sorcery and the magic actually bounces back and affects the sorcerer. As in most traditional societies sorcery and witchcraft are considered among the Cebuanos effective forms of social control when shame and the legal system are both ineffective. One reason these practices have survived to this day is the relative weakness of traditional social control in urban and semiurban environments combined with the relative weakness of bureaucratic and governmental control in the poorest barrios.

See also FILIPINOS: NATIONALITY; VISAYANS.

FURTHER READING

Jean-Paul Dumont. *Visayan Vignettes: Ethnographic Traces of a Philippine Island* (Chicago: University of Chicago Press, 1992).

Richard W. Lieban. *Cebuano Sorcery: Malign Magic in the Philippines* (Berkeley and Los Angeles: University of California Press, 1967).

Chakma (Changma, Sawngma)

One explanation given regarding the origin of the Chakma peoples is a myth that the Chakma are connected to the ancient kingdom of Champoknagar (also spelled *Champaknagar*). According to this myth, a prince from Champoknagar and his army traveled east with the goal of attaining new lands. They settled in Burma and intermarried with the local population to form the earliest ancestors of the Chakma. When Sher Daulat, one of the Chakma rulers, was killed for his tyranny, those responsible for his death fled the area and settled in the Chittagong Hills. Most Chakma reside there today.

From about 1650 onward the Chakma began to be influenced by the Muslim Mughals. Through trade with the BENGALIS Chakma chiefs received items like dried fish and salt, which were not available in Chakma villages. For the trade Chakma chiefs promised payment to the administrators of the Mughals. There was conflict in 1724 when this payment was not delivered by the Chakma chief Jalal Khan. He eventually fled the country after being attacked by the Mughal state minister. By 1737 the Chakma surrendered to the Mughals, whose power in the Chittagong region inhabited by the Chakma lasted only until 1760, when it was taken over by the British East India Company.

Despite the British takeover the political structure of Chakma society did not undergo significant colonial transformation until 1900, when the Chittagong Hill Tracts (CHT) Regulation of 1900 was enforced on the Chakma. According to this regulation the hill tracts were divided into Chakma, Mong, and Bohmang circles, and each group was then divided into *mouzas* (or *mawzas*, depending on the source), or collections of villages. The leader of the *mouza* was responsible for such tasks as revenue collection and dispute settlement.

In the postcolonial era the Chakma region was first part of East Pakistan, from 1947 to 1971, and then part of the independent country of Bangladesh from 1971 onward. Under both administrations the Chakma and other hill tribes of the region have experienced tremendous change. For example in the 1960s the building of the Kaptai Dam forced at least 100,000 hill tribespeople from their homes; many of these remain in India today, unable to return to their homeland after it was inundated. Further change has come about from the influx of Bengali peoples from the lowland regions of Bangladesh and West Bengal, India.

The Chakma make their living mostly through agriculture. They grow a variety of crops including rice, taro, and ginger. Recently the Bangladeshi government has been trying to direct the Chakma and other hill tribes to grow fruit so as to steer them away from *jhum* or swidden agriculture, the practice of clearing and burning new lands each season, usually before the rainy season. The Chakma also participate in trading in the marketplace, hunting, fishing, and gathering of wild foods.

The primary organizing principle in the lives of most individual Chakma remains kinship. Generally they are considered patrilineal and trace descent through men only; families are patrilocal, requiring women to leave their natal homes at marriage and move into the homes of their new husbands. These homes can be made up of extended families but generally consist of a couple and their unmarried children; in the case of polygyny, a man's having more than one wife, each wife is allowed her own home; the homes of the various wives may all be located in the same larger homestead.

Chakma peoples are mainly Theravada Buddhists, and there are temples in most villages. However, they also worship a number of Hindu deities, and both local and ancestral spirits are believed to play a role in individual and group fortunes. Buddhist monks, exorcists, and other indigenous healers are held in high esteem in Chakma villages for their specialized religious and ritual knowledge and skills.

Chambri (Tchamberi, Tchambuli)

The Chambri are best known to Westerners as the Tchambuli, the society that anthropologist Margaret Mead claimed exhibited female dominance. Most researchers today, however, dispute this claim, and although Chambri women do engage in far more productive labor

---

CHAKMA

location:
Southeastern Bangladesh in the Chittagong Hill Tracts; Indian states of Tripura, Mizoram, Assam, and Arunachal Pradesh; and Myanmar

time period:
Unknown to the present

ancestry:
Sino-Tibetan

language:
Chakma, an Indo-European language, linked with Pali, Sanskrit, and especially Bengali

CHAMBRI

location:
Three villages on an island in Chambri Lake along the Sepik River

time period:
Unknown to the present

ancestry:
Melanesian

language:
Chambri, a Papuan or non-Austronesian language in the Lower Sepik–Ramu family

than men in terms of fishing, trading, and gardening, in the domain of great importance to the Chambri, ritual knowledge, women remain complete outsiders.

As is the case with most peoples of the Sepik basin of New Guinea, the Chambri are patrilineal and patrilocal, and they allow polygyny if a man can afford the bride wealth for more than one wife. Their society is divided into a number of patrilineal clans, which are the largest sociopolitical units the Chambri recognize. Prior to the 1980s the Chambri did not have any positions of leadership except for "Big Men," who were powerful because of their personalities rather than because of any inherited position. But in 1983 one Chambri clan made the claim that its Big Man was actually a Chambri "chief," and none of the other clans disputed the claim. This was an innovation in Chambri society, which had been characterized by a high degree of male competition and no acceptance of leadership outside the clan. According to the anthropologists who witnessed this transformation, the Chambri themselves actively sought the innovation as a way to deal with the changes that had been introduced to them from the outside world, including environmental degradation and economic disruption. The Chambri believed that having a chief would provide them with the power necessary to fight off the destruction wrought by people of European descent.

The specific environmental problem that contributed to this sociopolitical change was the accidental introduction in the 1970s of an invasive species of fern that choked off Chambri lakes and waterways, disrupting access to fish. As a result of this species and its destruction of the native flora and fauna, half the Chambri population had moved away from the three traditional villages by the mid-1980s. The Papua New Guinea town of Wewak was the primary recipient of this itinerant Chambri population.

As is the case throughout the Sepik, and indeed New Guinea generally, the most important focus for traditional Chambri spirituality was their ancestors. The Chambri place particular weight on their ancestral names, which they believe have great power, but only if they remain hidden from the general population. Older men are extremely careful to reveal these sacred names only to a select group of men, sometimes to only one of their sons. They also try to wait as long as possible before revealing names to the younger generation since the names lose power with every new person who learns them. Often these older men die before they are able to

hand down their sacred knowledge, leaving the younger generation scrambling to compete with other clans in terms of ritual and mythological power. One strategy employed by Chambri men in this position is to steal the sacred names of their rivals, by eavesdropping on sacred rituals, and thus diminishing the ancestral power of their rivals in other clans.

See also MELANESIANS; NEW GUINEA SEPIK BASIN PEOPLE.

FURTHER READING

Deborah B. Gewertz and Frederick K. Errington. *Twisted Histories, Altered Contexts: Representing the Chambri in a World System* (New York: Cambridge University Press, 1991).

Margaret Mead. *Sex and Temperament in Three Primitive Societies* (New York: William Morrow, 1935).

Chamorro

The Chamorro are the native people of the Micronesian islands of Guam, Saipan, Tinian, Rota, and the smaller islands of Maug and Pagan. Not much is known with certainty about their society or culture prior to the arrival of the Spanish in 1521, when Magellan landed on Guam; however, some facts about their subsistence, social structure, and belief system have been pieced together by using a combination of archaeological and ethnographic methods.

As were almost all descendants of the early AUSTRONESIANS, the Chamorro were horticulturalists who lived primarily on foods they grew themselves. According to Spanish accounts the staple crop was taro, with coconuts, breadfruit, bananas, and pandanus also providing a significant amount of calories. To these gardened foods, Chamorro added fish and other seafood and a few species of birds and bats; no other animal was available to hunt or eat. Some rice was grown on Guam as well, for exchange purposes, but very little of that was eaten.

Prior to Spanish colonization the Chamorro lived in small villages, primarily along the coast, with a few communities having developed in southern Guam along its various rivers. These villages tended to be the centers of activity for a particular matrilineal, matrilocal group, which traced descent through women and lived in the wife's family's village after marriage. Chamorro society was ranked with higher-status people living in wooden structures that were supported by *latte* stones. The Chamorro had no political unit larger than the village to regulate social relations and experienced frequent intervillage warfare, primar-

CHAMORRO

location:
Micronesian islands of Guam, Saipan, Tinian, Rota, Maug, and Pagan

time period:
1500 B.C.E. to the present

ancestry:
Austronesian

language:
Chamorro

ily of a ritualized nature, in order to display wealth, status, and prestige.

The *latte* stones are the most visible remains of traditional Chamorro society, indicating the importance of rank as well as the Chamorro connection to other megalith-building societies in the Pacific, like the RAPANUI. The years between 1000 and 1100 C.E. saw the beginning of a period of intensive building of *latte* in the Marianas. Most *latte* sites are made up of paired sets of three to six upright columns of limestone, basalt, or coral, which stand in rows three to four yards apart, with the taller columns indicating the high rank of the builder or owner. Originally many of these posts had a capstone as well but most are gone now. *Latte* were still being built when the Spanish arrived in the 16th century, and the custom continued for another 150–200 years. The exact meaning and function of the *latte* have been lost over time, but archaeological excavations have shown that they were associated with daily living: food preparation, housing, making of tools, and disposing of waste. They also supported wooden housing units with high-ranking people living on top and the bodies of dead adults buried beneath. Their connection to mortuary rituals is still unknown.

While present-day Chamorro are largely Roman Catholic as a result of their earliest experiences with Spanish missionaries, a few aspects of their traditional religion have remained. The most important is a belief in the power of ancestral spirits who cause illness and other kinds of misfortune if not treated with respect. One specific ancestor spirit, the *taotaomono*, actually arises directly out of the Chamorro experience with colonialism. These supernatural beings, or "people from before time," are believed to be the spirits of the thousands of people who died at the hands of the Spanish or from the diseases they carried. The *taotaomono* live in jungles and dislike civilized people, getting particularly angry if people urinate in their territory without asking permission. The diseases they cause can be treated only by witch doctors. While most contemporary Chamorro know many *taotaomono* stories, few believe strongly enough to engage the services of a witch doctor. Yet the positions of *suruhano*, male witch doctor, and *suruhana*, female witch doctor, continue to exist throughout the Marianas for those few who still believe in the power of the *taotaomono*.

Magellan landed on Guam in 1521, but the real age of Spanish colonialism did not begin until 1668, when the first permanent missionaries and soldiers arrived with Father Diego Luis de Sanvitores. The Spanish era lasted until 1898, when Spain sold Saipan and Tinian to Germany to fund the Spanish-American War. The Spanish loss in that war resulted in the United States' taking control of Guam. The Spanish era was extremely difficult for most Chamorro. From a high estimated at 150,000 people the Chamorro population was reduced to only 4,000 after about 50 years of colonialism. The primary culprit in this devastation was disease; however, Chamorro resistance to the Spanish also resulted in a tremendous loss of life at the hands of Spanish soldiers. The Spanish policy of centralization, in which the people of Saipan and Tinian were forcibly removed to Guam, also caused many fatalities. Saipan and Tinian remained uninhabited until 1815, when a mixed population of Chamorro and people from the Carolina Islands were allowed to move back.

On the islands of Saipan and Tinian this mixed population of Chamorro and Carolinians has resulted in a number of difficulties. The Chamorro, perhaps because of their early experience with Spanish colonialism, embraced Western material culture and ways of life earlier than did the Carolinians and looked down on their poorer neighbors. The Chamorro also allied themselves with the German colonists who took control after the Spanish in 1899, the JAPANESE who took over in 1914, and then with the Americans who captured the islands in 1945 and joined them to their colony on Guam. These alliances allowed the Chamorro to reap the financial and status rewards of power, leading them to push harder for independence for the Marianas than did other peoples, who thought that association with larger countries would protect them from the numerically, financially, and politically stronger Chamorro population.

FURTHER READING

Laura Thompson. *The Native Culture of the Marianas Islands* (New York: Kraus, 1971).

Chams (Cam Jva, Chvea, Jahed, Khmer Islam, people of Champa)

The Chams are an ethnic group of Cambodia and Vietnam. For about 1,600 years starting in 192 C.E. they ruled over territory in central Vietnam as the multiethnic Champa kingdom. With the VIETNAMESE expansion to the south,

CHAMS

location:
Cambodia, Vietnam, Thailand

time period:
0 C.E. to the present

ancestry:
Austronesian

language:
Two dialects of Cham, an Austronesian language: Western Cham, spoken in Cambodia, and Eastern Cham, spoken in Vietnam. Western Cham is usually written in Arabic, while Eastern Cham has retained its own writing system, derived from Sanskrit.

Chams time line

C.E.

0   Approximate date for the arrival of the Chamic peoples from Indonesia.

192   Founding date of the kingdom of Champa by Cri Mara, according to Chinese sources.

220   The first Champa diplomatic mission is sent to China.

248   Champa invades northern Vietnam and even pushes into southern China.

third–fourth centuries China retakes its territory around the Red River and the rest of northern Vietnam.

mid-fourth century A stone inscription, written half in Cham and half in Sanskrit, found in Trakieu, is the first recording of any Austronesian language.

543   Champa invades Vietnam but is repelled.

950   The Khmer kingdom of Cambodia attacks Champa from the west.

979   The Chams send their first military mission against Vietnam, which retaliates three years later and takes the Cham capital at Indrapura.

1069 The Vietnamese take more Cham territory.

1074–1080 Champa invades Cambodia and captures the stronghold of Sambor.

1145–1149 The Khmers attack Champa, capturing the capital of Vijaya.

1177 Champa troops sail up the Mekong River and capture Angkor.

1190 Khmer king Jayavarman VII recaptures Vijaya.

1203 The Khmers invade again, this time temporarily annexing Champa as part of Cambodia.

1220 A newly independent Champa becomes the Khmer ally.

1307 The marriage of the Champa king and a Vietnamese princess sees the loss of even more Cham territory, around the Vietnamese city of Hue.

14th–15th centuries Almost constant warfare between Champa and Vietnam.

1470 Defeat of Champa by the Vietnamese, though remnants of the kingdom survive for about 350 years.

1578 The Vietnamese continue their march south and take the Phu Yen region.

17th century Estimated date of the conversion of many Chams to Islam, especially those living in Cambodia.

1653 The Vietnamese take the Cam Ranh region.

1692 The Vietnamese take the Tran Thuan Than region, leaving a dependent Cham ruler in Panduranga with the permission of the Vietnamese emperor.

1832 Official date for the end of Champa when the Vietnamese emperor refuses to recognize Champa nominal sovereignty in Panduranga.

1964 The Champa Liberation Front combines with other Montagnard groups to form FULRO, an organization allied to the United States and dedicated to fighting Communism in Vietnam. FULRO remains active in Vietnam to this day.

1975–79 Close to 100,000 Chams die in Cambodia during the Khmer Rouge reign of terror.

however, most Chams left the country to take refuge in Cambodia and elsewhere. This process began in 1470 and continued until the last of the Champa kingdom was dissolved in 1832. Today the Chams are one of the smaller ethnic groups in Vietnam because of this history.

GEOGRAPHY

Chinese texts chronicling the Champa kingdom place it between the Ngang Pass in Quang Binh Province in the north and the Dong Nai River in the south, territory that includes ocean shores, coastal plains, foothills, and mountains.

However, the exact extent of the kingdom was shifting because of the nature of the federation of smaller kingdoms that constituted Champa. The current cities of Hue and Danang were certainly part of the central region of Champa, but how long the kingdom held on to its frontiers as far south as the Mekong River is uncertain.

Today the Chams occupy a wide variety of geographic spaces in mainland Southeast Asia, from the shores of the Mekong and Tonle Sap Rivers of Cambodia to the Vietnamese highlands. In Cambodia many Chams also live in and around the country's major cities, including Phnom Penh and Kampong Cham.

ORIGINS

Between 5000 and 4500 b.c.e. the predecessors of today's POLYNESIANS and MALAYS left southeastern China and established themselves on Taiwan as the first Austronesian people After an expansion that covered almost half the globe, from Madagascar to Rapa Nui or Easter Island, at the beginning of the common era one branch of the Austronesian family left Indonesia, probably the island of Borneo, and returned to the Asian mainland. This branch settled in what is today central Vietnam, around the area of the Gianh River, and became the Chams. Some experts argue that the Chams and Lin-Yi ethnic groups were one and the same; the Chinese may have first called them *Lin-Yi* and then switched to *Cham*. Others argue that these were two different groups and that the Chams probably defeated and assimilated the Lin-Yi upon their entry into central Vietnam. There is not yet enough evidence to determine which group of scholars is correct.

HISTORY

Champa

By 192 c.e. the Chams had established a series of small kingdoms that together are called Champa, which included several other ethnic and linguistic groups. In the earliest period the Chams engaged in trade and diplomatic relations with the Chinese to the north. Buddhist monks, artistic styles, and a variety of products flowed south from China, while Cham fish and agricultural products flowed north. Champa also engaged with China militarily, taking some Chinese territory in northern Vietnam and even stretching the kingdom into southern China for a brief period after 248. China soon battled back and retook this land, which Champa tried to retake, unsuccessfully, in 543.

At the same time that Champa was looking north toward China, its people also interacted consistently with the FUNANESE, the Hindu Mon-Khmer kingdom located in the southern reaches of what is today Vietnam and Cambodia. Although the Chams would also have had links directly to India through their coastal trading ports and strong seafaring skills, it is believed that the dominant force in the indianization of Champa was Funan. The Cham cosmology or concept of the universe, ruling system, social structure, religion, and alphabet, a derivation of Sanskrit, all reflected the Hindu worldview.

Drawing on the wealth derived from its extensive trading networks, the Champa kingdom was at its most powerful between the sixth and 11th centuries, when the newly independent state of Vietnam began its march to the south. The first Champa military campaign against the Vietnamese occurred as early as 979, just 40 years after the Vietnamese obtained their independence from China. The mission did not change the borders between the two states very much, but it established a pattern of bellicose relations between them that lasted until the decisive defeat of Champa in 1470. The first loss of Champa territory to the Vietnamese occurred in 982, when their border was pushed south to Hoanh Son (Thanh Hoa); still more territory was conceded after 1069 when the Vietnamese were able to sack the capital of Vijaya and take King Pudravarman III prisoner. In 1307 Champa gave up even more land around the city of Hue upon the marriage of the Cham king Jaya Sinhavarman III to the Vietnamese princess Huyen Tran. Succeeding Cham kings tried to reclaim these lands through military action, but the almost endless fighting between the two states did little to change their geopolitical positions. The decisive period emerged in 1470–71, when Vietnam finally captured and then destroyed the Cham capital at Vijaya. Although remnants of the Cham kingdom survived until the 19th century, 1470 is often cited as the kingdom's end date because of this loss and the consequent influx of Vietnamese peasants into the region.

During the same four centuries in which Champa and Vietnam competed for control of the northern and central reaches of today's Vietnam, the Chams also faced enemies from the west. The Khmer kingdom of Cambodia first attacked Champa in about 950 and received retaliatory hits in 1074 and 1080. The region around Sambor in Cambodia suffered the worst of these reprisals: its religious sanctuaries were destroyed and much of its population captured. However, the Khmer were not finished, and between 1145 and 1149 they attacked Champa several times, even capturing Vijaya. At this point, however, Champa was still extremely powerful and within 30 years had regrouped and sent a large military force up the Mekong River to capture Angkor. This back-and-forth movement of troops and plundered booty continued until 1220, when both states were so weakened that peaceful relations between them became the last resort. Indeed the ties between the two indianized states were so strong that it was the Khmer kingdom that accepted most Cham refugees after their greatest defeat at the hands of the Vietnamese in 1470.

Even after the decisive victory of the Vietnamese in 1470 small sections of the Cham kingdom remained as sovereign states until each was individually vanquished by the southward march of the Vietnamese people and their armies. The region around Phu Yen was lost in 1578, Cam Ranh in 1653, and Tran Thuan Than in 1692. The last segment of the Cham kingdom was allowed to persist in Panduranga from the 1690s until 1832, but only with the blessing of the Vietnamese emperor, to whom the Chams owed allegiance and tribute.

Diaspora

The first waves of refugees to flee Champa or Vietnam and settle in Cambodia did so following the decisive Vietnamese victory in 1471. These refugees were made up of commoners, usually peasants, as well as members of the Cham royal family. They were joined by other refugees throughout the subsequent 350 years of Vietnamese military victories, but the heaviest waves occurred in 1692 and 1835. Many of these refugees settled along Cambodia's major rivers, the Tonle Sap and Mekong, and in the provinces of Battambang, Pouthisat, Takey, Kampot, Kampong Cham, Kampong Thum, and Kampong Chhnang; today many Chams live in and around Cambodia's major cities.

After this move the Cham people began to interact with a community of Muslim MA-LAYS, who had moved to the Southeast Asian mainland from Indonesia and the Malay Peninsula in the 14th and 15th centuries. The two groups shared a similar Austronesian language as well as other similar cultural features such as music and rituals. The two communities began to intermarry fairly quickly and many Chams converted to Islam, which distinguished them from the dominant Khmer population, most of whom were Buddhist. In fact in many Khmer texts the two communities became indistinguishable and were referred to as *Cam Jva,* meaning "Cham and Malay." Today there are three categories of Cham people in Cambodia made up of the descendants of these early Cham and Malay migrants: Khmer Islam, Chams, and Jahed peoples.

The Cambodian history of these people was relatively peaceful with generations of fishermen, peasants, scholars, and others living much as the Khmers of Cambodia did until the 1975 emergence of the Khmer Rouge. The Chams were singled out by this regime, along with so many other groups, because their religion and language distinguished them from the majority of the Khmer population. In the four years that the Khmer Rouge reign of terror dominated Cambodia, almost 40 percent of the country's quarter-million Cham population was killed outright or died of hunger or disease. Cham children were forcibly removed from their parents and raised as Khmers. The Cham language was forbidden, as was Muslim prayer, and Chams were forced to eat pork, forbidden by Islamic law. The Khmer Rouge statement on the Chams posited: "The Cham nation no longer exists on Kampuchean soil belonging to the Khmer. Accordingly the Cham nationality, language, customs and religious beliefs must be immediately abolished. Those who fail to obey this order will suffer all the consequences for their acts of opposition to Angkar [the Khmer Rouge high command]." A few Chams fled to Malaysia, the United States, Europe, and Canada at that time, but the vast majority had no escape from the massacre. Experts on the genocide believe that the Chams residing in Cambodia today owe their life to the 1978 invasion of Cambodia by Vietnam, which ended the Khmer Rouge's reign of terror.

Although a large percentage of the Cham people fled Vietnam between 1471 and 1835, today almost 100,000 Chams live in Vietnam as the descendants of the founders of the Champa kingdom. Many had fled to the Vietnamese highlands to escape the ravages of the migrating Vietnamese, while others moved to Hainan Island, currently a Chinese possession. Sometime after Champa's initial defeat in 1471, some of Vietnam's remaining Chams converted to Islam; they were also joined by Chams who returned to Vietnam in the 1850s to try to retake their territory in central Vietnam. Other Chams remained practitioners of the syncretic Hindu-animistic religion of the Champa kingdom. Today Eastern Cham, the language of

Vietnam's Cham population, is still written in its original Sanskritic alphabet, while Western Cham in Cambodia is written in Arabic, denoting the relative importance of Islam among the latter.

During the wars that ravaged Vietnam in the mid-20th century, some Chams participated as part of the Champa Liberation Front and then after 1964 as part of FULRO, the Front Unifié de Lutte des Races Opprimées or United Front for the Struggle of Oppressed Races, an umbrella organization of Vietnamese mountain peoples or Montagnards, which worked with the U.S. and South Vietnamese armies against the National Liberation Front (*see also* VIETNAMESE: NATIONALITY). FULRO continues its work today, resisting Communism in Vietnam and the subjugation of the country's minority groups to the cultural domination of the Vietnamese.

CULTURE

The culture of the Cham who dominated the Champa kingdom was a fusion of Austronesian features taken with them during their migration from Indonesia just before the start of the common era, Buddhism introduced from China, and Hinduism introduced from Funan and by Indian traders. The most important Austronesian cultural feature are the Chamic languages, today divided into Eastern and Western dialects, which are most closely related to ACEHNESE, spoken in Indonesia. The blend of Buddhist and Hindu features in the Cham religious system and cosmology or worldview is evident in the many brick temples that remain in central Vietnam, along with statues and other artwork and to a lesser extent Cham music.

The other notable aspect of this ancient Cham culture is its orientation to the sea. While Champa's territory encompassed coastal plains and both foothills and mountains, many experts believe that the residents of the mountains were some of the other ethnic groups who lived in the multiethnic kingdom, such as the JARAI, M'NONG, and RHADE, while the Chams themselves primarily stayed close to the sea and rivers. They engaged in long-distance trade with Indians, Chinese, Arabs, and others, and looked to the sea for much of their food as well.

In about the 17th century the greatest change was introduced into Cham culture with the conversion of many to Islam. This change affected the migrant communities who had fled Vietnam more than those who remained in Vietnam; however, a portion of Vietnam's Cham population today is Muslim as well.

The syncretic nature of Cham religion, blending Buddhist and Hindu elements together, is an important aspect of the imagery carved onto Cham brick temples such as this one. *(Shutterstock/Trin Le Nguyen)*

Nonetheless contemporary ethnographers who have studied Cambodia and Vietnam's Cham populations cite the existence of at least two and perhaps three separate communities of Cham Muslims. The first group are the Jahed, who adhere to the most heterodox or least orthodox version of Islam, combining it with ancient features from Hinduism and Buddhism. They do not use Arabic but continue to read and write in the Cham alphabet and tend to use recitations of Quranic verse in translation rather than passages of the Quran itself, which is an Arabic text. Some scholars also believe the Jahed pray only once per week, rather than five times per day, and ascribe tremendous force to people's internal power or Chai. This group has been the least likely to join mosques built or even attended by non-Chams in Cambodia and for the most part rejects any outside interference with their religious practice or way of life.

There are also two other Muslim Cham communities in Cambodia and Vietnam. Those that continue to use the name *Cham* and live in Cambodia consider themselves to be the descendents of the Champa kingdom but emphasize their religion rather than their origins in their contemporary identity. They tend to speak Cham but also to be fluent in Khmer and to read the Quran in Arabic. Those who

CHENLA

location:
Laos, Cambodia, and parts of southern Thailand and Myanmar

time period:
600 to 800 C.E.

ancestry:
Mon-Khmer

language:
Old Khmer

consider themselves Chams and live in Vietnam tend to emphasize their historical origins and may or may not be practicing Muslims; they also speak Cham, and some can communicate in Vietnamese. A third group of Cambodian Chams are known today as Chvea, Khmer Islam, or Cam Jva. They tend to be made up of communities that reckon their origins were the mixtures of Indonesian Malays and Chams who intermarried soon after the Cham migrations to Cambodia began in the 15th century. The words *Chvea* and *Cam Jva* both include a reference to Java in them. Both the Chams and Cam Jvas in Cambodia accept aid and religious teaching from outside their community, especially from Saudi Arabia and Malaysia, which strongly distinguishes them from the Jahed, who refuse such offers.

Another important aspect of Cham society, one that sets them apart from many of their patrilineal neighbors, is their matrilineal pattern of descent, in which children are seen primarily as the descendants of their mother, mother's mother, and so forth. This means that children do not inherit property or their name from their father but rather from their mother's brother, who is the key figure in any matrilineal system. The Chams are also matrilocal; that means that at marriage it is the groom who moves into the new bride's family rather than having her move into his home. Women inherit houses from their mothers and are considered extremely important in Cham society. Some sources even indicate that the Chams are matriarchal, but this is a misuse of the term. Matriarchal societies, if any have ever existed, would grant most positions of power and authority to women. This is not currently, nor seemingly ever was, the case for the Chams. Cham religious statues from the days of Champa tend to emphasize male fertility rather than female, and today mother's brothers tend to control much of a family's property and wealth.

FURTHER READING

Emmanuel Guillon. *Cham Art* (London: Thames and Hudson, 2001).

Jean-Francois Hubert. *The Art of Champa* (London: Parkstone Press, 2005).

R. C. Majumdar. *Champa: History and Culture of an Indian Colonial Kingdom in the Far East, 2nd Century A.D.* (Columbia, Mo.: South Asia Books, 1985).

Graham Thurgood. *From Ancient Cham to Modern Dialectics: Two Thousand Years of Language Contact and Change* (Honolulu: University of Hawaii Press, 1999).

Chahar Eimak   *See* AIMAQ.

Chaoxian   *See* KOREANS.

Chavchu   *See* CHUKCHIS.

Chenla (Kambuja, Zhenla)

HISTORY

The people of Chenla are often considered to be KHMERS, as they were probably speakers of the oldest form of that language, but it is more accurate to speak of them as combining features transported during their migrations from southern China in the decades before 200 B.C.E. with Hindu and MON-Khmer elements adopted when they overran the FUNANESE in about 550 C.E.

Chenla emerged from obscurity in about 550 when the people are mentioned in a Chinese text as having obtained their independence from Funan. From their northern base in contemporary Champassak Province, Laos, the people of Chenla had moved along the rivers and conquered most of the Mekong Delta from southern Thailand to southern Vietnam, including much of Cambodia. By about 600 they had conquered Funan and established their capital city at Isanapura, probably the contemporary city of Sambor, Cambodia. The oldest Khmer inscription, found at Angkor Borei, a former Funan stronghold south of Phnom Penh, is also from this period and is dated to 611.

The first rulers of a united and powerful Chenla were related to the royal family of Funan, with the founder, Bhavavarman, being the grandson of King Rudravarman of Funan. Bhavavarman united the two kingdoms and eventually subsumed Funan under his own rule. He was succeeded by his brother Mahendravarman and then the latter's son, Isanavarman, who used their connections and knowledge of Funan to complete the integration process. By 635 and the accession of Bhavavarman II some of the influence of Funan's Indian religion and artistic forms had begun to be replaced by Mahayana Buddhism. Buddhism had always existed side by side with Hinduism in Funan, but the mid-seventh century shows evidence of Buddhism's supplanting Hinduism throughout Chenla society.

In the early eighth century Chenla's royal family experienced a divisive factional dispute that led to the creation of two separate Chenla kingdoms, known from Chinese sources as Land or Upper Chenla and Water or Lower Chenla. The former was centered on contemporary Champassak Province in Laos, while the latter controlled the lower Mekong River. Land Chenla was able to sustain its power base in the region by using its strength in agricultural production and by gathering tribute from the multitude of other, smaller kingdoms in the region. Water Chenla, however, had a more difficult time because of piracy and the emergence of other, more powerful kingdoms in territory that is today Malaysia and Indonesia. This period also saw the waning and eventual cessation of direct contact between Chenla and India as the Indians began utilizing new trade routes to and from China.

In about 790 the king of Water Chenla was murdered by the JAVANESE king of Sailendra; his death put an end to that portion of the kingdom. The southern portion of mainland Southeast Asia was ruled briefly by this Javanese kingdom, which used as legitimacy an origin myth that connected its royal family to the kings of Funan. This period marks the formal end of Chenla. However, by 802 a small Khmer kingdom in what is now southern Cambodia had emerged as powerful enough to expel the Javanese and unite all of the former Chenla territory under the rule of Jayavarman II, considered the first king of Khmers and the founder of the great Khmer state of Kambuja, famous for the building of the temple at Angkor Wat.

Wat Phu Temple is one of the most iconic of the structures that remain from the Chenla kingdom, with its mixture of Hindu and Buddhist statues and images. *(Shutterstock/Juha Sompinmäki)*

CULTURE

The early culture of Chenla reflected the vast importance of Indian cultural forms in Southeast Asia from the start of the common era. Hinduism was the predominant religion and both architecture and statues from the early period reflect the Hindu worldview inherited from Funan's intimate connections with the kingdoms of India. The important temple site of Wat Phu, located today in Laos, shows the importance of the Hindu gods Vishnu, Brahma, and Siva in the worldview of Chenla. Another indicator of the importance of Indian culture is the large number of inscriptions in Sanskrit found in Southeast Asia and dated to the Chenla period.

In contrast with Funan, however, Chenla was generally not a country of trading ports that was open to ongoing influence from India. The people of Chenla, especially Land Chenla after the eighth-century split, tended to look inward rather than outward for cultural features, and soon Indian cultural traits were being replaced with Buddhist and indigenous innovations. This period also coincided with a marked decline in trade from India, caused by a change in preferred trade routes that kept Indian sailors away from the shoreline dominated by Chenla. Hindu traits did not disappear entirely from later Chenla culture, and the Hindu god Siva was important in the unified Khmer kingdom of Jayavarman II, but Buddhism emerged as at least as important. Again the temple site at Wat Phu is a good example of this period; beside the obvious Hindu gods there are three large Buddha statues on the mountaintop complex, a Buddha in a tree on the road to the temple, and a number of depictions of the cobra, seen by many peoples in Southeast Asia from at least the fifth century B.C.E. as the god of the earth. In addition the seventh century also saw the emergence of inscriptions in Khmer, such as the one from Angkor Borei, dated 611 and considered the oldest in the world.

Rather than international trade Chenla was dominated by agricultural production. The river valleys they controlled provided the perfect setting for the production of wet rice. However,

CHHATTISGARHIS

location:
India, primarily in the state of Chhattisgarh but also in adjoining regions

time period:
Unknown to the present

ancestry:
Indo-Aryan

language:
Chhattisgarhi, an Indo-Aryan language with many dialects

this economic system required large inputs of human labor on relatively small parcels of land. Therefore rather than control of territory, the kings of Chenla and all the smaller and weaker states that were vassals to Chenla had a much greater need to control labor. Many of the small wars that eventually saw the division of Land and Water Chenla were based on the need of each sovereign for large numbers of people to work the rice paddies. In addition to rice the people of Chenla raised pigs and chickens, fished, and grew a variety of fruits and vegetables.

Chhattisgarhis

The Chhattisgarhis are the approximately 12 million speakers of that language who reside in the Indian state of Chhattisgarh and the adjoining states of Bihar, Orissa, Maharashtra, Uttar Pradesh, Madhya Pradesh, and Tripura. The state was created only in 2000 and the name itself came into use in only 1795; before that the region in which the language was spoken was called Dakshin Kosala. The first political movement in India pushing for a separate state of Chhattisgarh emerged in the 1920s but the movement's request for official recognition in 1954 was rejected and the region was included in the state of Madhya Pradesh. It took another 46 years of political pressure both in and out of Madhya Pradesh for the movement to gain ground, but on November 1, 2000, 16 districts from the original state were carved out and made into the newly autonomous state of Chhattisgarh.

Besides their Indo-Aryan language and state of residence there is very little that unifies the Chhattisgarhi people. They are crosscut by differences in dialect, caste, class, occupation, kinship structure, and even religion. Indeed it is somewhat difficult to speak of them as a distinct group at all because of these vast differences; however, because India does not define ethnic groups as such and relies on linguistics to categorize people, we have done the same.

See also INDO-ARYANS.

Chin ('kKxou, Kuki, Lushai, Mizo, Zo, Zomi)

The Chin are a Tibeto-Burman ethnic group who live in the borderlands between Myanmar (Burma) and India. *Chin* is an anglicized version of their Burmese name, which means "a people," while they call themselves *Zo*, which means "marginal people." They are closely related to the MIZO, who live in India, and the Plains Chin or Asho, who live to the east of Chin State in Myanmar.

The first reference to the Chin is in a 12th-century Burmese stone inscription that indicates that the people lived around the Chindwin River in what is today northwestern Myanmar. Not long after that period the Tai-speaking SHANS began migrating into this region and drove the Tibeto-Burman Chin into the highlands. In the 17th century more Chin and related Tibeto-Burman peoples migrated into the hills to get away from the Burmese wars with the Shans and other peoples in the lowlands. By about the middle of the 18th century the current ethnic divisions in the hills had been established during these various migrations and the Chin had settled into the region of Burma/Myanmar now known as the Chin State, located in the far western district of the central region. Those few Chin who remained around the Chindwin River area are today known as the Kuki.

Prior to the annexation of the region by the British in the 1890s Chin chiefs and princes ruled over their own people in relatively autonomous small states. The British maintained the local power of these Chin chiefs and used them in a form of indirect rule; Chin and other local chiefs gathered tribute from their people and paid taxes to the British. They also served as go-betweens in the recruitment of laborers and soldiers and for judicial purposes. Because they had been independent prior to the British era, Chin leaders believed that freedom from colonialism in 1948 would also mean independence. However, the assassination of the Burmese political leader Aung San and many other members of his constitutional committee in 1947 led to a situation in which the Burman majority was able to impose its will upon the region's many minority groups, including the Chin, KACHIN, KAREN, and others. The Chin State, much as the Kachin and Shan States, became part of the larger independent country of Burma; almost 60 years of civil war resulted as these minority groups have struggled for either autonomy within the larger framework of Burma/Myanmar or outright independence. In the 21st century the Chin people are continuing to work both inside Myanmar, in such agencies as the United Nationalities League for Democracy, and outside it, in the Unrepresented Nations and Peoples Organization among others, for peace, democracy, and a degree of autonomy over their state. In January 2007 the Chin activist Dr. Lian Hmung Sakhong was awarded the Martin Luther King Prize in Sweden for his significant work toward peace in his country. (See also BURMANS.)

Traditionally the Chin were shifting cultivators who used fire to clear plots of land and to provide ash for fertilizer. They focused their effort on dry, upland rice where possible and in higher elevations supplemented that with millet, corn, or sorghum, the latter used primarily for making beer. In addition to these grains they produced many vegetables and fruits, including beans, peas, pumpkins, chilies, ginger, and melons; they also grew tobacco. Cotton was commonly produced both for local use and for trade or sale. Today some Chin focus on apples, oranges, coffee, and tea for sale in the markets of the lower plains, but transportation costs and difficulties make this a risky venture for most Chin farmers. In addition to farming most Chin families kept pigs, chickens, dogs, and occasionally a goat, cow, or water buffalo; the most important animal, however, was the *gayal*, a kind of ox, used for sacrifice. In the past domestic animals were supplemented by meat from hunting, but today very few wild animals are left in Chin State.

Chin society is ranked and hierarchical with prestige derived largely from wealth in land, animals, and unique or specialized goods from the outside world. During a man's lifetime prestige is gained and validated by holding "merit feasts" for one's village; it is at this time that gayals are sacrificed along with many other animals, and vast amounts of other foods and beer are served to show how wealthy the person is. At an important man's death his worldly goods are displayed for all to see; images of all his past goods are carved into memorial posts and songs about his wealth are composed and sung. The concept behind these ritualized displays of wealth is not that the objects themselves are a sign of importance but that wealth is a sign of favor from the Land of the Dead and thus signifies importance in this lifetime as well. The worst crimes in Chin society were related to the illegitimate passing of these signs of favor from one person to another through theft, having a child out of wedlock, or using the evil eye to gain access to wealth through supernatural means. Women did not have access to this world of rank and prestige, but widows could hold feasts in the name of their dead husbands. Women could also earn position in their village through working as spirit mediums, raising many sons, or, in the case of a very few, serving as a chief in the place of a dead husband.

In addition to prestige and rank earned through the attainment of wealth Chin society recognizes the position of various patrilineal clans in relation to one another. Aristocratic clans tend to have more cases of polygyny, whereby men have more than one wife, while in commoner clans this practice is quite rare. In both cases membership in the clan is inherited from one's father and it is forbidden to marry someone from the same clan; similarly because all clans are defined in relation to one another as wife takers or wife givers, it is also forbidden for a man to marry into any clan that has taken a wife from his own clan.

After marriage the new couple usually live with the husband's parents for a number of years; in the case of the inheriting son the couple will remain in the household and the son will ultimately inherit the house and farm. In some lineages it is the oldest son who so inherits and in others it is the youngest; the same is true for the inheritance of the position of village priest or chief. After a year or two noninheriting sons will move into their own households with their young families, usually in the same village.

In the present many Chin communities are at least nominally Christian, but in the past the Chin worshipped a number of major and minor gods, spirits, and other supernatural beings. Male village priests held recitations and other rituals dedicated to the greater of these deities and spirits, usually those connected to the village as a whole, while female spirit mediums were in communication with the other world to aid in healing, giving thanks, and making requests. Even today some women continue to use trance to communicate with the spirit world, despite the widespread conversion to Christianity since the American Baptist missions began work among the Chin in 1899.

FURTHER READING

F. K. Lehman. *The Structure of Chin Society* (Urbana: University of Illinois Press, 1963).

Chinese   *See* HAN.

Chinese: nationality   (people of China)

GEOGRAPHY

China is the third-largest country in the world after Russia and Canada and spans several types of climate, ranging from tropical on many southeastern islands to Siberia-like cold in the north. China is often described as a land of mountains because about two-thirds of China's area is covered by mountains and plateaus.

CHIN

location:
Chin State, Myanmar (Burma)

time period:
12th century at the latest to the present

ancestry:
Tibeto-Burman

language:
Chin, a Tibeto-Burman language

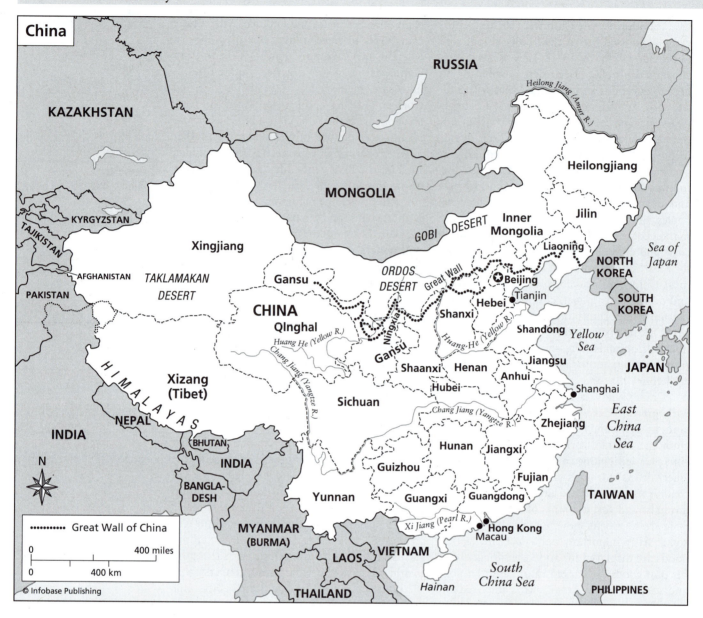

China

RUSSIA

KAZAKHSTAN

KYRGYZSTAN

TAJIKISTAN

AFGHANISTAN

PAKISTAN

MONGOLIA

Heilong Jiang (Amur R.)

Heilongjiang

Jilin

Xingjiang

GOBI DESERT

Inner Mongolia

Liaoning

NORTH KOREA

Sea of Japan

ORDOS DESERT

Great Wall

⊛ Beijing

SOUTH KOREA

Gansu

TAKLAMAKAN DESERT

Hebei ● Tianjin

CHINA

Qinghal

Ningxia

Shanxi

Huang He (Yellow R.)

Shandong

Yellow Sea

Huang He (Yellow R.)

Gansu

Huang He (Yellow R.)

Chang Jiang (Yangtze R.)

Shaanxi

Henan

Jiangsu

JAPAN

H I M A L A Y A S

Xizang (Tibet)

Hubei

Anhui

● Shanghai

NEPAL

Sichuan

Chang Jiang (Yangtze R.)

Zhejiang

East China Sea

BHUTAN

INDIA

Hunan

Jiangxi

Guizhou

Fujian

INDIA

Yunnan

Guangxi

Guangdong

TAIWAN

BANGLA-DESH

Xi Jiang (Pearl R.)

● Hong Kong

N

Macau

MYANMAR (BURMA)

VIETNAM

South China Sea

•••••••• Great Wall of China

LAOS

0 — 400 miles

0 — 400 km

THAILAND

Hainan

PHILIPPINES

© Infobase Publishing

About one-quarter of China's area is made up of the Qinghai-Tibet plateau, in the southwest provinces of Tibet, Qinghai, and western Sichuan, which is the highest region in the country, averaging 13,123 feet above sea level. All of China's great rivers begin here, including the Huang (Yellow) River and the Chang (Yangtze). Both flow toward the east, and population centers have historically been located along the rivers. Only about 14.3 percent of China's land is arable, and only a small percentage of that is used for permanent crops.

INCEPTION AS A NATION

The Xia dynasty, while considered the first Chinese dynasty according to oral histories, was long thought to be a mythic period until archaeological evidence of what was probably the capital city of the Xia dynasty was found in 1959 near Yanshi in central China. The Xia was an agricultural society that used bronze weapons and pottery. The ruling families apparently enacted elaborate rituals that called on the spirits to give legitimacy to their rule.

During the Shang dynasty the first dynasty about which there are written records, writing was developed. Shang scholars created extensive records of the origins of the Chinese people. These histories of both the historical and mythological origins of the Chinese make it clear that as early as 1750 B.C.E. the ancestors of the present-day Chinese had a sense of national identity that would be transformed throughout the following millennia. When the Zhou overthrew the Shang dynasty in

Chinese: nationality time line

B.C.E.

12,000–2200 The Neolithic period in China is marked by the spread of agricultural communities and increased reliance on agriculture, although hunting and gathering are still practiced. Silk production and pottery have already been developed; the two main types of pottery are black and painted. Clothing is made from hemp; pigs and dogs have been domesticated.

2200–1750 The Xia dynasty, which marks the transition between the Neolithic and Bronze Ages.

1750–1040 Shang dynasty; the population becomes more urbanized and cities become the center of intellectual life, especially the Shang capitals and the king's court. The first evidence of writing is found during the Shang dynasty.

1040–256 Zhou dynasty. Chinese history has always asserted that the Zhou were able to overthrow the Shang because the Shang had degenerated morally and were no longer fit to rule. This explanation illustrates the idea of the Mandate of Heaven, which is attributed to the Zhou and had an important effect on subsequent dynasties.

770–476 Period of Spring and Autumn. During this time the Zhou emperor steadily loses power.

604–517 Lifetime of Loazi, the founder of Taoism (Daoism).

551–479 Lifetime of Confucius, founder of Confucianism.

475–221 Period of Warring States. This period marks the end of the Zhou dynasty, in which feudal lords fought for power over the empire. This is also the time of the great Chinese philosophers and is sometimes referred to as the One Hundred Schools Period. The first of many walls in northern China, the precursors to the Great Wall, is built during this time.

221–206 Qin dynasty. Writing systems are first standardized and China is unified.

206 B.C.E.–220 C.E. Han dynasty. Confucianism becomes more influential with the emperors and trade flourishes along the Silk Road to Central Asia and Europe.

C.E.

220–65 The Three Kingdoms. After the fall of the Han dynasty civil war breaks out, and China is divided into three kingdoms, the Wei (to the north), the Shu (to the southwest), and the Wu (to the southeast). Buddhism spreads throughout China.

265–89 Jin dynasty. The Chin emperor reunifies China, but the empire is short-lived, largely because of the emperor's decision to disband the army entirely after the unification, leaving the government vulnerable to outside invasion and internal revolt.

317–589 Northern and Southern dynasties. China is broken into several empires and is plagued by internal wars. Buddhism spreads on a large scale.

580–618 Sui dynasty. The Sui reunite China and the nobles begin to regain their importance, leading to a resurgence in the popularity of Confucianism.

618–907 Tang (T'ang) dynasty. In southern China rice becomes more easily produced as new technologies are introduced in rice cultivation and population centers begin to shift from the wheat-growing north.

701–62 Lifetime of Li Bai, an influential poet, whose work remains popular today. His poems are full of Taoist imagery. More than 1,000 of his poems have survived to the present time.

712–70 Lifetime of Du Fu, a second influential Chinese poet. In contrast to those of Li Bai his poems are most influenced by Confucianism and often describe historical events. Many of his poems survive to this day.

860 Beginning of peasant uprising against the Tang.

874 Peasant uprising against the Tang succeeds, becoming the first successful peasant uprising in Chinese history.

885 The Tang dynasty is restored after members of the government appeal to foreign forces for help in restoring the emperor to the throne. Although the emperor is restored, he loses most of his power and the Tang dynasty collapses soon after.

(continues)

Confucius (551–479 B.C.E.), the Chinese philosopher whose ideas about ethics, obedience, and proper social structure more generally continue to inform the societies of most East Asian nations, particularly China *(Shutterstock/ TAOLMOR)*

CHINESE: NATIONALITY

nation:
People's Republic of China (Zhonghua Renmin Gonghe Guo); short form, China (Zhongguo)

derivation of name:
The name in Chinese (Zhongguo), which has been used since the early dynasties, means "Middle Kingdom" or "Central Nation" and is a reflection of the fact that the Chinese consider their civilization to be the center of the universe. The name *China* in Indo-European languages probably is derived from the Qin dynasty, often considered the origin of a unified China (*Qi*, in pinyin, a transcription system of Chinese into Latin letters, is pronounced *chi*)

government:
The Chinese government is a one-party Communist state, with power being concentrated in the hands of the Chinese Communist Party (CCP).

capital:
Beijing

language:
Mandarin Chinese (Beijing dialect) is the official language in China. Other major dialects of Chinese include Cantonese, Shanghaiese, and Fuzhuo. All of the Chinese dialects have a standard writing system that uses characters that represent whole words instead of sounds. Other minority languages are spoken by about 8 percent of the population.

religion:
Officially atheist. Taoism and Buddhism have historic roots in China,

Chinese: nationality time line *(continued)*

907–60 Five Dynasties. The Five Dynasties are a period of warfare and chaos, especially in northern China. The actual five dynasties are five officially recognized dynasties of the north, while the south is divided into 10 kingdoms. In spite of the chaotic situation a number of advances are made and have a lasting effect on Chinese society. Trade, especially in tea and porcelain, becomes more important. Translucent porcelain develops and is used widely in China and exported. Printing is introduced and the Chinese classics are first printed about 940. Paper money is used for the first time, largely because metal is scarce and the copper coins used for currency are difficult to transport.

950 The first evidence of the practice of binding women's feet. It is not clear why this practice is adopted, but it is practiced by all layers of society and continues until the beginning of the 20th century.

960–1279 Song dynasty. The Song have a technologically advanced fleet of ships, perform autopsies of humans, and are scientifically sophisticated, but they have a weak military, a fact attributed to the low status of the military in Confucianism. Kunqu, or Chinese opera, is developed.

1279–1368 Yuan dynasty. The Yuan dynasty represents the first of two times in Chinese history that non-Chinese rule the entire area of China. The Mongols, led by Genghis Khan, defeat the Chinese and create the Yuan dynasty. Poetry and opera flourish.

1368–1644 Ming dynasty. The novel becomes a popular type of fiction, whereas previously poetry had been most popular and highly regarded. Encyclopedias are written on numerous subjects, as are dictionaries of the Chinese language. Most of the Great Wall of China that stands today is built by the Ming emperors. Xu Guangqi (b. 1562), a civil servant working with the Italian Jesuit Matteo Ricci, translates part of Euclid's *Elements* into Chinese, which introduces knowledge of planar geometry and other aspects of higher mathematics into China.

1644–1911 Qing dynasty is founded by Manchu invaders, the second group of foreigners to rule all of China.

1839 Opium is outlawed by the Qing emporer, beginning the Opium Wars with Great Britain.

1842 China is forced to make a number of concessions to Great Britain in a treaty ending the Opium Wars, including giving Britain Hong Kong and opening up Chinese borders for trade.

1857 Fighting breaks out between Great Britain and China again; China is defeated a second time and forced to make even more concessions to the British.

1894–95 First Sino-Japanese War, in which China is defeated.

1900 Boxer Rebellion, led by the Boxers or "the Righteous and Harmonious Fists," a secret society that had previously rebelled against Qing imperial power, primarily protesting against the excessive influence of foreigners in the government

1911 The revolutionary forces led by Sun Yat-sen topple the emperor and endeavor to establish a democracy. Sun Yat-sen creates the Nationalist Party but is unable to establish a government because of the actions of the warlords who vie for control; he is forced to retreat to southern China.

1919 The May Fourth Movement, which calls for the study of science and democracy, begins.

1921 The Chinese Communist Party (CCP) is founded by Mao Zedong in Shanghai.

1925 Sun Yat-sen dies and is succeeded by Chiang Kai-shek.

1927 The Nationalist Party, led by Chiang Kai-shek, unifies China under its rule.

1040 B.C.E., the former justified its right to rule over China by citing the concept of the Mandate of Heaven. According to this ideal heaven places the mandate to rule on a morally worthy family, and when the ruling family is overthrown, the mandate has been removed. The victors are then assumed to have been given the mandate. This idea became deeply entrenched in Chinese society and was used to justify the sometimes-brutal policies of the rulers and their overarching powers. The Mandate of Heaven also shaped how China viewed its relationship with the outside world.

1927 The Red Army is founded, with the Communist Party remaining in the province of Jiangxi and engaging in brutal campaigns with the Nationalist Party.

1928–37 The Nanjing Decade, referring to the economic progress made during this time, in which Chiang Kai-shek and the Nationalists rule China and the capital city is in Nanjing.

1931 Japan invades Manchuria and establishes a puppet government, known as Manchukuo, in 1932.

1934–35 The Red Army embarks on the Long March, leaving the province of Jiangxi for a new stronghold province, Shaanxi, in the north, some 7,770 miles away.

1935 Mao becomes chairman of the CCP, a position he holds until his death.

1937 China and Japan officially go to war as a result of Japan's attempts to capture Beijing.

December 1937–January 1938 The Nanjing Massacre; approximately 340,000 Chinese are killed in Nanjing by Japanese troops.

1945 The Second World War ends and Japan is expelled from China.

1946 Civil war breaks out between the Nationalist Party and the Chinese Communist Party.

1949 The CCP wins the civil war and pushes the Nationalist Party and its followers to the island of Taiwan. The CCP establishes the new capital in Beijing.

1950 Chinese troops invade Korea to expel American forces.

1957 The Hundred Flowers Campaign, in which intellectuals are undermined and often executed as enemies of the Communist Party.

1958–69 The Great Leap Forward.

1966–76 The Great Cultural Revolution.

1976 Mao Zedong dies and a struggle for political power ensues.

1980 Deng Xiaoping becomes the leader of the CCP and begins a number of economic reforms.

1989 Tiananmen Square massacre. Students protesting for democracy in Tiananmen Square in Beijing are attacked by the military and many are killed, an act that draws world criticism. This is largely ignored by the Chinese government.

Jiang Zenmin assumes control of the CCP.

1997 Britain returns Hong Kong to Chinese sovereignty.

Asian financial crisis. China remains relatively unaffected by the drop in currency values of its neighbors.

1999 Portugal returns Macao to Chinese sovereignty.

2001 China joins the World Trade Organization.

Beijing is selected as the site of the 2008 summer Olympics.

2002 Hu Jintao becomes leader of the CCP.

2002–03 Sudden acute respiratory syndrome (SARS) outbreak in China.

2005 Protesters in Hong Kong take to the streets to protest the Chinese central government's insistence on appointing the president of Hong Kong and members of the legislature instead of allowing elections.

Christian 4 percent, Muslim 2 percent.

earlier inhabitants:
Evidence of hominid activity in China has been found dating from 1 million years ago, although hominid activity in the area is believed to date from 4 to 5 million years ago. Thousands of archaeological sites throughout northern and southeastern China have been identified as settlements from as early as 9000 B.C.E.; the remains of the earliest city in China were found in Henan Province and are believed to be between 4,800 and 5,300 years old. "Modern" Chinese history is considered to begin with the Xia dynasty, 2200–1750 B.C.E.

demographics:
The majority ethnic group of Han Chinese make up about 91.5 percent of the population (1.1 billion) of China, according to a census conducted in 2000. Other ethnic groups include the Zhuang (16.2 million, or 1.3 percent), the Manchu (10.6 million, or 0.8 percent), the Hui (9.8 million, or 0.8 percent), the Hmong (8.9 million, or 0.7 percent), the Uighur (8.3 million, or 0.7 percent), the Tujia (8 million, or 0.7 percent), the Yi (7.7 million, or 0.6 percent), the Mongol (5.8 million, or 0.5 percent), the Tibetans (5.4 million, or 0.4 percent), and several other smaller ethnic groups. The Chinese government officially recognizes 56 ethnic groups living in China, including the majority Han Chinese.

The Chinese, considering their society greater than all others, saw themselves as the guardians of superior moral principles that other societies could choose to accept or not.

The Qin, who were the strongest of the warring states that followed the Zhou, are considered the first to have unified the core of China. Under the Qin writing was standardized throughout the empire because speakers of different dialects needed to be able to understand communications from other regions. In addition currency and measurements, including axle width of chariots, were standardized to facilitate commerce and travel between different regions. The Qin had a legalist form of rule, the most important aspect of which was that the government had absolute control over the people.

While popular Chinese legend says that the HAN governed in a benevolent and intelligent manner from the very beginning, the historical record shows that when this dynasty first overthrew the Qin, it maintained many of the totalitarian systems already in place. However, with the rise of noble families and the weakening of the government's hold on the peasantry, Confucian ideals were gradually adopted by the Han emperors; eventually they decided that force alone was not enough. Emperors needed the moral guidance of Confucius's teaching. During the period of Three Kingdoms the Wei kingdom in the north began the military practice of incorporating non-Chinese into the armed forces. This allowed non-Chinese to assimilate into Chinese society with unprecedented ease and speed; being Chinese became less an "ethnic" or physical characteristic and more a matter of belief in Chinese ideals and adherence to Chinese traditions.

Mao Zedong

Decades after his death Mao Zedong remains a controversial and pivotal figure in modern history. Born in Hunan Province on December 26, 1893, Mao became aware of communist theory while studying at Peking University. In 1921 Mao became involved with the burgeoning National Congress of the Communist Party in Shanghai and two years later was elected as one of the five commissars of the Central Committee of the Party. Mao differed from other Communist leaders in that his focus was on the rural proletariat rather than the urban proletariat, and throughout the 1920s he instigated a number of peasant uprisings, none of which were successful. In 1920 Mao cultivated his theory on violent revolution, inspired by the Russian Revolution. In 1931 he cofounded the Soviet Republic of China, of which he was elected chairman. When Mao's authority was challenged by those who disagreed with his ideas on land policy and military reform, he responded with brutal retaliation that resulted in the deaths of an estimated 186,000 people through revolutionary terrorism. He became the official chairman of the Communist Party of China in 1945, and his legacy is scarred by such controversial sociopolitical programs as the Great Leap Forward, the Hundred Flowers Campaign, and the Cultural Revolution, during which millions of lives were lost. The most notorious of these programs was the Great Leap Forward, under which an estimated 20–70 million people are believed to have died between the years of 1958 and 1961. Under Mao's Great Leap Forward program peasants made to live in communes were forced to work on collective farms and produce grain and other goods for state use, but poor planning and the use of experimental agricultural techniques resulted in a 25 percent drop in production, resulting in the largest famine known to date. Mao Zedong died on September 9, 1976, of amyotrophic lateral sclerosis (ALS, or Lou Gehrig's disease); he was 82.

Under the Song dynasty there was a renaissance of Confucianism, known as neo-Confucianism, which reemphasized following the correct path, education, and unselfish behavior, especially for nobles. Under the Song coveted government jobs were assigned not on the basis of birth but of official examinations. Education and individual achievement became extremely important to the Chinese as the only ways to secure a good life; now birth in a wealthy family was often not enough to ensure comfort. Education and personal achievement remain an important part of Chinese culture.

Toward the end of the Qing dynasty in the wake of embarrassing defeats in the two opium wars with Britain, China was forced to reevaluate many deeply held beliefs. Prior to that time everything foreign had been looked down upon as barbaric. However, it became increasingly clear that these foreign barbarians were stronger militarily and must be taken seriously. When the last emperor was overthrown in 1911, Chinese leaders had already started to look at Western philosophies for ways to govern the people.

By this time women, who had been subordinated to fathers, husbands, and sons for most of recorded Chinese history, began to gain rights in urban republican China, and by the 1920s it was widely accepted in urban settings that women should be the equal of men. Foot binding, practiced throughout the country until the early 1900s, declined.

When the Communists under Mao took over in 1949, they coopted some Chinese philosophies that had been in place for thousands of years but also tried to institute important changes. The Communists believed that women should be equal members of society and they were encouraged to find work outside the home, although often the work they found was lower paying and less desirable than that of men. The Communists also took advantage of the Confucian ideals of subordination to authority, fulfilling one's role in society, and education, replacing the Confucian education with Communist indoctrination programs. On the other hand programs such as the Hundred Flowers Campaign and the Great Cultural Revolution sought to discredit intellectuals and authority figures, and to denounce friends and family members. These far-reaching campaigns, forcibly introduced by Mao, also destroyed many other aspects of Chinese cultural life, such as ancient shrines, and discouraged ancestor worship, Buddhism, and Taoism.

Shanghai is the heart of the massive Chinese economy, and the city's government hopes that by the year 2020 it will be the heart of the global economy as well. *(Shutterstock/Amy Nichole Harris)*

As the Communist Party's official policy has changed, so have the priorities of many Chinese people. The government has been relaxing restrictions on free enterprises, so that becoming rich through enterprise and obtaining material goods have become honorable and desirable.

CULTURAL IDENTITY

To be Chinese is to consider oneself a descendent of the Han dynasty. Although approximately 91 percent of the Chinese population consider themselves Han Chinese, the Han Chinese are diverse and do not have a definition of identity based on physical or ethnic characteristics. Instead to be Han Chinese is to subscribe to the ideas followed by other Chinese. In fact most "Han Chinese" are descendants of outsiders who were assimilated into the Chinese Empire at some time in history. The physical environment usually determined whether an ethnic group would be assimilated. If Han-style agriculture was possible, the group would be assimilated, sometimes by force but often voluntarily. Most non-Chinese live in the rural regions of western China, in environments not suitable for the Han way of life, and generally have a much lower standard of living.

Although there are great regional differences among the Han Chinese, they have considered themselves one group since the early dynastic years. The Han Chinese speak eight or nine mutually unintelligible dialects, but since the Qin dynasty they have shared a written language, based on characters that represent ideas, not pronunciation. The effect of this writing system on Han unity has been great. There is no regional literature, poetry, or song; instead all written heritage is considered to be Han. As a result Han Chinese do not see themselves as divided by region or other factors; instead they view themselves as one nation.

Confucian teaching continues to have a lasting effect on Chinese society, and in some ways the Communist Party has coopted Confucian philosophy, making many parts of modern China resemble eras when Confucianism was dominant. In modern China education is the most secure way to social advancement, just as Confucian scholars advocated, and the most important knowledge is that about a philosophy (Confucianism in earlier times, communism in the present), rather than technical knowledge. Confucianism and communism also share a distrust of religion, leading to very low status for

CHUKCHIS

location:
Chukotka Peninsula of
far northeastern Russia,
across the Bering Strait
from Alaska

time period:
Unknown to the present

ancestry:
North Asian

language:
Chukchi-Kamchatkan
group of Paleo-Asiatic
languages

monks and priests and a low level of religious belief among the Chinese. A third important similarity is the subordination of individual needs in favor of the societal goals. But as China has more contact with the outside world, the Chinese have become more interested in personal advancement and material gain.

In traditional China (imperial China, or China before 1911, is often referred to as "traditional China"), the family was always the most important social unit and demanded the most loyalty from each member. Parents were expected to provide their children with the best possible preparation and assistance to make a living, and children were expected to take care of their parents in their old age. All social interactions took place in the framework of the family. While the family as the most important social unit has remained in rural China, in urban China the family has lost much of its importance; family units have become smaller and parents dictate fewer aspects of the lives of their offspring.

FURTHER READING

Geremie R. Barme. *In the Red: On Contemporary Chinese Culture* (New York: Columbia University Press, 1999).

Zhang Dainian. *Key Concepts in Chinese Philosophy* Translated and edited by Edmund Ryden (New Haven, Conn.: Yale University Press, 2002).

Edward L. Davis. *Encyclopedia of Contemporary Chinese Culture* (New York: Routledge, 2005).

Joseph W. Esherick, Wen-hsin Yeh, and Madeleine Zelin. *Empire, Nation, and Beyond: Chinese History in Late Imperial and Modern Times: A Festschrift in Honor of Frederic Wakeman* (Berkeley, Calif.: Institute of East Asian Studies, 2006).

Theodore Huters, R. Bin Wong, and Pauline Yu. *Culture and State in Chinese History: Conventions, Accommodations, and Critiques* (Stanford, Calif.: Stanford Unversity Press, 1997).

Joseph R. Levenson. *Confucian China and Its Modern Fate: The Problem of Intellectual Continuity* (Berkeley and Los Angeles: University of California Press, 1958).

Hazel Mary Martell. *The Ancient Chinese* (New York: New Discovery Books, 1993).

R. Keith Schoppa. *Revolution and Its Past: Identities and Change in Modern Chinese History* (Upper Saddle River, N.J.: Pearson Prentice Hall, 2006).

Sinolingua. *The Ins and Outs of Chinese Culture* (Beijing: Sinolingu, distributed by China International Book Trading Corp., 1993).

Endymion Wilkinson. *Chinese History: A Manual* (Cambridge, Mass.: Harvard University Press, 2000).

Chinese Malaysians   See MALAYSIAN CHINESE.

Chinese Muslims   *See* HUI.

Chukchis (Luorawetlan)

The Chukchis were historically divided into two subgroups, the reindeer-hunting tundra dwellers, who called themselves Chavchu, "reindeer man," and the coastal seal hunters, who called themselves Ankalyn, "coastal man." The name *Chukchi,* which is the Russian adaptation of the former, has been used since the 17th century, and its use has been reinforced by many geographical names derived from Chukchi.

Although the Chukota Peninsula has been inhabited for around 7,000 years, the Chukchis were not one of the original ethnic groups to settle the area. The Chukchis invaded this region at a period as yet undetermined by archaeologists. The newcomers assimilated many of the former inhabitants and expanded their territory at the expense of other ethnic groups, most notably the YUPIKS or Asiatic Eskimos.

The RUSSIANS first encountered the Chukchis in 1642 C.E., when they began construction of a fortified outpost called Anadyr in 1649 and started to subdue the Chukchis. Although most of the Russian conquests in the East met little resistance, the Chukchis proved to be one of the most difficult groups to subdue. Finally in 1778 the Russians and the Chukchis signed a peace treaty that allowed Russia to claim the area but did not oblige the Chukchis to pay tribute or otherwise compromise their free lifestyle. The Russians subsequently changed tactics and began trading with the Chukchis, often paying them with vodka. Alcoholism became a serious problem for the Chukchis by the early 18th century, and the introduction of new diseases further weakened their society and resistance to Russian rule. During this original time of colonization Russian Orthodoxy spread among the Chukchis, who had previously practiced a shamanistic religion.

Life remained relatively unchanged for the Chukchis until forced collectivization began in 1929. The Chukchis put up armed resistance but were quickly subdued by Soviet military and the KGB (secret police). Collectivization forced the Chukchis to abandon their nomadic life; other efforts to russify the population included opening cultural centers and schools using only the Russian language. With the influx of industry to the Russian Far East during and following World War II many Chukchis took jobs in factories and the area saw an influx of Russians and other foreigners seeking economic opportunities. With the fall of the Soviet Union most of these foreigners have left as the economic opportunities of Soviet times have disappeared.

Prior to Soviet collectivization the inland Chukchis lived in small groups of two to 10 tents that were moved frequently. They herded and hunted reindeer and made tools, sleds, and clothing from their skin, bone, and other parts. The coastal Chukchis had semipermanent seasonal settlements on the coast, traveled by boat or dogsled, and survived primarily by hunting seals. Both had a similar societal structure in which all group decisions were based on consensus and differences in wealth did not amount to differences in authority. Lineages were traced bilaterally, through both the mother and father, and although new couples most frequently settled in a camp with the groom's family, it was not uncommon to settle with the wife's family.

Chukchi society today has been damaged by alcoholism, and the nuclear tests in the Russian Far North during the Soviet period have contaminated the food chain and caused the Chukchis to have extremely high rates of many types of diseases. Intermarriage between Russians and Chukchis has been common since the 1960s, often because Russians are considered healthier and more likely to produce healthy children. Unfortunately the Chukchi language and customs have suffered significantly.

Recently there have been local movements to revive Chukchi language and culture along with sobriety movements to fight the widespread alcoholism. It remains to be seen how the Chukchis will adapt to the 21st century.

See also RUSSIANS: NATIONALITY.

Colchians (Colchoi, Kolchians, Kolkhians)

The Colchians may have been the indigenous inhabitants of the eastern shores of the Black Sea with a Bronze Age culture that resembled the neighboring KOBAN CULTURE in the Caucasus. Possibly the Colchians were a remnant of an Egyptian army that had invaded the Caucasus in the 19th century B.C.E. Their name is well known to us because of the ancient Greek legend of Jason and the Golden Fleece. It was the king of Colchis, Aeetes, from whom Jason stole the fleece, with the assistance of Aeetes' daughter, Medea.

GEOGRAPHY

Colchis was a triangular land on the eastern shore of the Black Sea surrounded by the Caucasus and Meskhetian Mountains to the north and south and the Surami Range to the east. The fertile Phasis River valley, known today as the Rion or Rioni, ran through this territory and provided the basis for the agricultural economy.

ORIGINS

The origins of the Colchian tribes remain a mystery to this day. The fifth-century B.C.E. Greek historian Herodotus claimed that the Colchians had black skin and woolly hair, which some scholars have interpreted to mean that the Colchians were Africans, possibly Bantus. Others have interpreted Herodotus's text to indicate that the Colchians were Egyptians, possibly a community that remained from an Egyptian expedition to the Caucasus sent by Pharaoh Sesostris, who ruled in the 19th century B.C.E. No evidence of this event has been found, although there is some archaeological and textual evidence for a black population in the Caucasus in the fourth century C.E. Apollonius of Rhodes wrote that the Colchians, along with the Egyptians and Ethiopians, invented the notion of circumcision, and Herodotus described their fine linen products, made in the unique Egyptian style, which further supports the East African origins claim.

Although we do not know what the Colchians called themselves, the geographic term *Colchis* first appears in the tragedy *Prometheus Bound,* by Aeschylus, a Greek soldier and dramatist who lived from 525 to 456 B.C.E.

COLCHIANS

location:
The eastern shores of the Black Sea and the Rioni River valley

time period:
15th–13th centuries B.C.E. to 63 B.C.E.

ancestry:
Unknown, though there is some conjecture that they were Africans

language:
Unknown but possibly Zan, the ancient form of the Laz and Mingrelian languages

Colchians time line

B.C.E.

15th–13th centuries Probable era for the founding of the Colchian community on the Black Sea, according to Greek tales describing events in this era.

sixth century The region that includes Colchis is under Achaemenid Persian rule.

fifth century First mention of Colchis, in Aeschylus's tragedy *Prometheus Bound.*

fourth–third centuries Greek influence in the eastern Black Sea increases, and Milesian Greek colonization of the area begins.

320s Alexander the Great enters the region but dies before consolidating power there.

120–75 Mithridates VI Eupator, king of Pontus, conquers the region at some point between these two dates.

75–63 The Third Mithridatic War ends in a Roman victory over the Pontic Greeks. The Romans rename Colchis Lazica after the dominant tribe in the area.

HISTORY

The history of the Colchian people is almost as unclear as their origins, steeped as it is in myth and conjecture. Because of this lack of clear textual or archaeological evidence, Colchis and the Colchians have been used by nationalists from many competing groups in Georgia: GEORGIANS, MINGRELIANS, and LAZ people all assert either linguistic or ethnic inheritance from the Colchians in their nationalistic claims to be the most ancient people in the region. According to some of these Georgian sources, which cite evidence from Greek inscriptions of the Mycenaean period, there has been a state of Colchis or Qolha in existence since at least 1500 B.C.E.

While there were certainly people residing in this region in 1500 B.C.E., it is still unclear whether they had formed a unified political state or were merely a group of tribes that differed linguistically from their Koban neighbors. What is clear from archaeological remains is that extensive trade networks between GREEKS and people in the Colchis region existed from ancient times. Greece received slaves, animal hides, linen, gold, and other products from Asia, and the Colchians received salt, pottery, beads, and other finished products. In the mid-sixth century B.C.E. Greeks from Miletus in present-day Turkey established a colony in the region to facilitate this trade; their main city was called Dioscuras and was located in the region of present-day Sukhumi, the ABKHAZIANS' capital. Georgian sources claim the Greeks never fully colonized the Colchian peoples, but the data remain unclear about the political status of these tribes during the Greek period.

In addition to the Greeks, the Achaemenid Persians (*see* PERSIANS, ALCHAEMENIDS) also established themselves in the eastern Black Sea region in the sixth century B.C.E. The degree of control maintained by the Persians is not certain since trade with the Mediterranean region seems not to have diminished at all at this time. Alexander the Great of Macedonia also invaded the territory of the Colchians but died without establishing a permanent record of his time there. From this period, around 325 B.C.E., until the Mithridatic Wars of the first century B.C.E. between Rome and Pontus, a Greek kingdom in northeast Anatolia, almost nothing is known about the Colchians. Archaeological sites continue to point to an agricultural people who traded with the Mediterranean states, and at some point between 120 and 75 B.C.E. Mithridates VI Eupator, king of Pontus, incorporated the region into his Anatolia-based empire.

In the third Mithridatic War, 75–63 B.C.E., Colchis passed into the hands of the victorious Romans, who renamed the region Lazica after the dominant tribe in the region, the Laz or Lazi. After this period it probably is not accurate to speak of a Colchian people, although some sources continue to use this ethnonym instead of *Laz, Mingrelian,* or *Georgian* in order to justify the primordial ties of these people to their land.

CULTURE

There are several sources of information about the culture of the Colchian people, including the stories and legends told by the Greeks about them; the texts of Herodotus, Apollonius of Rhodes, Strabo, and other ancient writers; and archaeological finds of the past 100 years.

Jason and the Golden Fleece or Jason and the Argonauts is one of the oldest and best known of the Greek tales. It was probably already in existence in Mycenaean times, 15th–14th centuries B.C.E., since inscriptions have been found on pottery from that period. It was well known by the time of Homer in the eighth century B.C.E., since he made reference to the tale several times throughout his works. The best known of the written versions of the story is that of Apollonius of Rhodes, who wrote *Argonautica* in the third century B.C.E.

The story tells of Jason, who traveled from Thessaly in Greece to Colchis, or Aia as it is sometimes called in these tales, to retrieve the famed Golden Fleece. The fleece had been a gift to King Aeetes from Phrixus, prince of Boeotia, who had flown to Colchis on the back of a magical golden ram to escape the murderous intent of his stepmother, Ino. Upon his safe landing in Colchis Phrixus sacrificed the ram and hung its golden fleece on the branches of a huge oak tree, with a dragon at its base to keep the fleece safe. The Colchians believed that as long as they had the fleece they would be blessed with good luck. According to the story rather than steal the fleece outright Jason entered Colchis and asked Aeetes to give it to him. Aeetes agreed but only if Jason accomplished a variety of seemingly impossible tasks: use fire-breathing bulls to plow a field, sow it with a set of dragon's teeth, and then slay all the soldiers that sprouted from the teeth. Jason was able to accomplish all of the required tasks with the help of Aeetes' daughter, Medea, who had magical powers. Some versions of the story claim these powers were from the goddess Hera; others say that Medea herself was a sorcerer, something for which the Colchi-

The ancient Greek myth of Jason and the Argonauts may be based on actual ethnographic information the Greeks had about their distant neighbors, the Colchians. *(British Museum/Art Resource, NY)*

ans were famous among the Greeks. Medea also warned Jason that her father had no intention of giving up the fleece despite Jason's having accomplished all of the necessary tasks; the two of them therefore stole the fleece, again relying on Medea's magical powers to put the dragon to sleep. They escaped Colchis with Jason's band of 50 Greek warriors and experienced many other adventures on their way back to Thessaly.

Although this story cannot be read as historical fact, some of the details of the Colchians that are present in it have subsequently been seen in the archaeological and ethnographic record. For example it is possible that "golden fleece" existed and was used for trade by the Colchians. Even as late as the 20th century people residing in what was Colchis in ancient times used sheep skins to retrieve small flakes and nuggets of gold from the rivers that flowed from the Caucasus to the Black Sea. After lying in the riverbed for a time, the skins were retrieved and dried and the gold then shaken out of the wool. In addition some scholars have conjectured that the Golden Fleece of the Colchians was meant to indicate not just gold but also other forms of wealth that the Greeks obtained from them in trade and plunder, including animal products,

linen, wood, and metals and metal products. Another aspect of the story that has been confirmed by archaeology is the uniqueness of Colchian burial practices. According to the Greek myth the Colchians hanged their dead in trees until all that remained was skeletal material; they then buried just the skulls and arm and leg bones, burning the rest. Archaeological evidence from the eighth century B.C.E. has confirmed that some Colchian burial pits contain only skulls and arm and leg bones.

Archaeological finds also show that the Colchians were among the first people in the Black Sea region to master the art of smelting metal and casting objects from molten ores. They made jewelry and other personal adornments in addition to complex farming implements, indicating the importance of agriculture to their way of life. After the eighth century B.C.E. many Colchians were buried in wooden coffins, held together with iron or brass nails, and a coin was placed in the mouth of the dead. Many burial pits contain amphorae and other pottery beside the dead person's hands.

Some of the most intriguing information about the Colchians appears in the writings of Herodotus, Apollonius, Strabo, and others.

Herodotus's insistence that the Colchians were black skinned is interesting, especially since 1,000 years later other writers confirmed that a population of black people resided in the west Caucasus region. Whether they entered from Egypt on a long-forgotten raid on Caucasian territory remains up for debate. Georgian nationalists fail to mention this aspect of the Colchians in their insistence that they are the direct descendants of this ancient population, perhaps not surprisingly in light of European racial hierarchies that elevate light-skinned populations over dark-skinned ones. These same sources also fail to cite Strabo's information from the first few years of the common era that the Colchians lived as pirates, looting small ships on the Black Sea.

FURTHER READING

David Braund. *Georgia in Antiquity: A History of Colchis and Transcaucasian Iberia, 550 BC–AD 562* (New York: Oxford University Press, 1994).

Otar Lordkipanidze. *Phasis: The River and City in Colchis* (Stuttgart: Steiner, 2000).

D

Dahae *See* PARTHIANS.

Dai (Baiyi, Beiyi, Bitso, Boyi, Chinese Shan, Daide, Daija, Daila, Dailian, Dailu, Dailü, Daina, Dainyue, Daipeng, Dehong Dai, Han Baiyi, Han Dai, La Sam, Mitro, Pudai, Shui Baiyi, Shui Dai, Siam, Tai, Tai Lue, Tai Mao, Taily, Taiyi, Xishuangbanna Dai)

Dai is the official Chinese name for several ethnic groups in southern Yunnan Province who speak a Tai dialect. Roughly two-thirds of the Dai (more than 1.2 million) live in China, where they constitute one of the largest minority groups in Yunnan Province. The Dai people are closely related to other groups in Southeast Asia including the SHANS of Myanmar, the THAIS of Thailand, and the LAO of Laos. For the most part the Dai and related groups in neighboring countries share similar dialects and some common Buddhist practices, but social structures differ over distance.

GEOGRAPHY

Most of the Dai people live in southern China and northern Southeast Asia within a few degrees of the tropic of Cancer. The terrain is a combination of fertile river valleys, foothills, and mountains. The Dai have traditionally inhabited the hills and valleys and have been successful farmers. As early as 1,400 years ago the Dai were also some of the first in the area to develop irrigation techniques necessary for growing rice. In fact, Xishuangbanna, where many Chinese Dai live today, is a Chinese transliteration of *Sipsongbanna,* which means "12,000 rice fields." The geography and tropical climate are also conducive to other Dai crops, which include tea, tobacco, bananas, pineapples, and rubber trees.

ORIGINS

Written Chinese records from the first century B.C.E. refer to the Dai as Dainyue or Shan. This group appears to have originated on territory closer to what is now central China and gradually migrated south over several centuries. Eventually most of the people who are now considered Dai settled along the fertile valleys of the Mekong River and its tributaries in southern China, while other groups diverged southeast and southwest into Laos, Thailand, Myanmar, and Vietnam.

According to Chinese records the Dai made contact with the Chinese emperor and sent tribute to his imperial court. He in turn bestowed gold seals and the title of *Great Chieftain* on the declared Dai leader. This account, however, paints an incomplete picture of the complex relationship between the Dai peoples and surrounding polities. The Dai, similarly to other Southeast Asian peoples, did not observe strict or singular sovereignty. They often paid tribute to more than one neighboring ruler and observed flexible spheres of influence within their own territory as well.

Dai individuals were tightly bound to their villages and kinship networks but not to the

DAI

location:
Primarily the southern Chinese Yunnan Province, also northern Myanmar, Thailand, Laos, and Vietnam

time period:
At least first century B.C.E. to the present

ancestors:
Unknown

language:
Tai-Kadai language family

Dai Migration

Dai pay tribute to court in Luoyang 109 B.C.E.

Huang He (Yellow R.)

Huang He (Yellow R.)

Yellow Sea

Luoyang

Henan

Chang Jiang (Yangtze R.)

INDIA

MYANMAR

Nanchao Kingdom 700 C.E.

Dali

Kunming

CHINA

East China Sea

Yunnan

Dehong

Mong Mao & Kocambi Kingdoms 10th–11th Centuries

Jinglong Golden Hall Kingdom 12th Century

Jinglong

Xi Jiang (Pearl R.)

Kublai Khan & Mongols invade and push Dai farther south 1300 C.E.

Xishuangbanna (Sipsongbanna) Yonaga Kingdom 10th–11th Centuries

LAOS

Mekong R.

Ping R.

VIETNAM

South China Sea

THAILAND

Chao Phraya R.

Dai attack Angkor 1369

PHILIPPINES

Bangkok

Angkor

CAMBODIA

Mekong R.

Ayutthaya (Siam) Tai Kingdom Est. 1351

Phnom Penh

N

Dai migration

0   200 miles

0   200 km

© Infobase Publishing

land itself. If a local ruler exceeded his powers or was found unworthy by his villagers, they would relocate. In fact the word *dai* can be translated as "freedom." Dai traders, monks, and villagers traveled frequently between towns, a pattern that continues today in spite of contemporary national borders. This movement, combined with competing historical narratives, can make it difficult to trace the history of specific communities now collectively referred to as the Dai.

LANGUAGES

The Dai in China and most of their cousin groups in Thailand, Myanmar, Vietnam, and Laos speak some variation of Tai, a large subgroup of the Tai-Kadai language family. There is still some dispute among linguists as to whether this family is Sino-Tibetan or Austronesian in origin. The tonal Tai subgroup includes the national languages of Thailand and Laos and several smaller languages ranging across southern China, northern Vietnam, Myanmar, and northeastern India.

Within China the Tai dialects range from mutually unintelligible to relatively similar, with enough common words to allow easy communication. For example two of the largest Dai communities in China speak mutually unintelligible dialects: Dehong Dai who border Myanmar speak Tai Nüa, while the Xishuangbanna Dai who border both Myanmar and Laos speak Tai Lü (or Tai Lue). Separate local television and radio broadcasts in each dialect are available. The dialects are similar enough to their respective counterparts in Southeast Asia, however, to facilitate a brisk cross-border trade in Tai-language media from Thailand.

Written Tai exhibits as many variations as the spoken dialects. The roughly six traditional Tai scripts present in China appear to derive from Thai and Burmese writing, and they bear no resemblance to Chinese characters. Over the last 50 years literacy in traditional Tai writing among the Chinese Dai population has significantly diminished. In part this is because in the mid-1950s the government worked with select representatives from the larger Dai communities in Dehong and Xishuangbanna to create reformed Tai alphabets. The reformed systems encountered some resistance, especially among Xishuangbanna Dai communities where the traditional script was strongly linked with Buddhist institutions. In the 1980s this Dai community elected to reinstate the traditional system, but the legacy of a generational literacy gap remains.

The spread of Mandarin Chinese as the national language has also eroded Dai literacy. Traditionally male children spent a portion of their childhood in the village temple learning to read and write from the monks. Since the 1950s the responsibility for educating young Dai has shifted from village temples to local schools, where the primary language of instruction is Mandarin. Dai community leaders are working with social organizations to preserve living

Dai time line

B.C.E.

109   The Dai and Han first establish contact with each other; the Dai begin to pay tribute to the court at Luoyang, and their chief is named Great Captain.

1   Earliest records of Dai, then named *Dianyue* or *Shan,* in the historical books of the Han.

C.E.

500–700   The Dai adopt southern Buddhism.

700   The Lao people, the primary ethnic group of present-day Laos and a branch of the Tai-speaking people, establish the kingdom of Nanzhao (Nanchao) in southwestern China, over time moving even farther south into the Indochinese Peninsula.

900   The Chinese document the well-developed agriculture of the Dai with its use of irrigation as well as oxen and elephants as draft animals.

900–1000   The Dai, the dominant political power in Xishuangbanna (then called Sipsongbanna), establish the Yonaga kingdom, and in Dehong the Mong Mao and later the Kocambi kingdoms.

1000   The current Dai language emerges as Buddhism grows in importance. The written language is passed on for 1,000 years in the form of scriptures transcribed onto leaves of the Beiye tree.

12th century   Dai warrior Ba Zhen unifies all Dai tribes under the nearly 1-million-strong Jinglong Golden Hall kingdom. Ba Zhen recognizes the Chinese imperial court as his sovereign and in return receives an official seal and title from the emperor.

1271–1368   The Dai area is made subordinate to Yunnan Province, and the Chinese establish a form of indirect rule by appointing headmen from among the Dai; this practice continues throughout the Ming dynasty (1368–1644) as well.

1300   Mongol invasions of Mong Mao kingdom under Kublai Khan accelerate Dai migration to the Mae Nam Chao Phraya Valley, where the Dai establish kingdoms that eventually become Siam (Thailand) and Laos.

1351   A Tai kingdom, whose court is modeled on Angkor, is founded at Ayutthaya (Ayudhya, or Siam), near modern-day Bangkok.

1369   The first of three Dai attacks on Angkor, which eventually lead to the abandonment of the Khmer capital.

1800   Successive Chinese dynasties extending their reach in south China, challenging local Sipsongbanna authority, and imposing new taxes drive residents to rebel. Chinese Qing troops enlist nonrebel locals to maintain control. Small waves of refugees flee south in a pattern that persists until the 20th century Communist victory and subsequent border closures.

1949   The Chinese Communist Party defeats its rivals for control over China.

1956   The local political system of hereditary chiefs, *tusi,* is dismantled after 500 years.

knowledge of traditional Tai script by reviving temple education programs.

HISTORY

Over the last 1,000 years as the Dai people migrated along the river valleys and into neighboring territories, they spread the Tai language and Buddhist practices. Where they settled they integrated and became the Shans of Myanmar, northern Thais in Thailand, and northern Lao in Laos. Robust trading networks along the rivers and through the intervening forests allowed the disparate communities to remain in relatively close contact with one another.

By the 10th and 11th centuries the Dai communities in both Xishuangbanna (then called Sipsongbanna) and Dehong were dominant political powers in their respective areas. In Dehong the Dai established the Mong Mao and later Kocambi kingdoms, and in Xishuangbanna, one kingdom was called Yonaga. According to local history Ba Zhen was a Dai warrior who unified the valleys and drove other groups such as the Hani up into the mountains in the 12th century. The Chinese considered several other minorities in southern Yunnan (such as the Atsang) to be subject to the Dai. Dai rulers paid tribute to the Han court and in return were given formal titles and administrative authority over smaller minority groups.

As successive Chinese dynasties extended their reach south in search of territory and resources, the Dai model of overlapping sovereignty crumbled. Sipsongpanna's golden age, enhanced by robust trading networks with Tai kingdoms to the south, stretched through the 16th century. By the 18th century the Chinese court's efforts to coopt local rulers and impose new taxes drove some Sipsongbanna residents to rebel. Although they were impaired to some degree by local conditions including malaria, the Chinese Qing troops were able to maintain control, and elites who had not joined the rebellion were rewarded with new titles and authority. During the unrest some residents fled south in small waves that would persist until the 20th-century Chinese Communist victory and subsequent border closures.

The Dai, as have all people in China since 1949, have experienced tremendous changes with the rule of the Communist Party. One important change was the dismantling of the local political system after 1956. Until that year local hereditary chiefs, called *tusi*, received power and authority from the central government to enact legislation, administer justice, and conscript a military force. In exchange they provided tribute, taxes, and laborers to the government. As in any hierarchical system there were different ranks of *tusis*, with some controlling just a small region while others controlled all the lesser *tusis* of a large region; the entire structure resembled a pyramid of power with the Chinese imperial court at the top. This political system was about 500 years old, the oldest *tusi* system in China, when it was abolished in the mid-20th century and replaced with the geographical authority system seen today, with districts as the lowest level of state authority, followed by counties, prefectures, provinces, and states. Districts are made up of administrative villages, which themselves are made up of natural villages.

CULTURE

Economy and Society

Dai societies in China generally share several distinctive features: they are primarily agricultural and share common foods, building designs, and forms of entertainment.

The Dai have traditionally been farmers. In addition to developing early irrigation techniques for growing rice, the Dai have been using oxen to till farmland for more than 1,000 years according to Chinese records. In recent decades more Dai have turned from traditional agriculture to growing cash crops like rubber trees, specialty teas, and cotton or have sought urban employment. Nonetheless most Dai families still rely on rice as their staple food. Locally grown glutinous rice is sometimes steamed and dipped into communal bowls of spicy or sour sauces. It can also be pounded into a sticky dough, rolled out onto countertops or banana leaves, and lightly toasted. Dai cooking frequently uses bamboo tubes and pineapples to steam, boil, and flavor rice, fish, and other foods.

Traditional Dai society was made up of ascribed classes of aristocracy and commoners based on kinship, and it was nearly impossible to change the class into which individuals were born. Each of these larger classes was frequently subdivided; for example in Xinshuangbanna there were three subclasses of aristocracy and three of commoners. Regardless of subdivisions only aristocrats were allowed to own land or hold public office, and all commoners were essentially landless serfs, working as sharecroppers or servants for their aristocratic neighbors. Of course the 1949 takeover by the Chinese Communist Party eliminated all of these classes and caused great suffering for the formerly privileged aristocracy.

The kinship system that determined membership in these separate classes was traditionally patrilineal, and today children receive their father's last name. Nonetheless even in the past members of one's mother's and spouse's patrilines were considered relatives, unlike more strict patrilineal systems that considered only people related through common male ancestors as relatives. Some Dai communities were also matrilocal: young husbands lived and worked with their wives' families for a while after the marriage. This marriage pattern in many families was actually more important than strictly defined kinship ties because for most Dai location was more important than kinship in creating ties of reciprocity and association.

Religion and Expressive Culture

The Dai nominally practice Theravada Buddhism. Buddhism was introduced as early as the seventh century but really spread by the 15th century via trading networks with Tai-speaking communities in modern-day Myanmar and Thailand. Buddhism in Dai areas often coexists with older, more animistic religious practices that recognize gods and spirits in the land and water. In the past many Dai also believed that some of the hills surrounding their river valleys were holy and were inhabited by sacred plants and animals and spirits of notable past leaders. Villages protected their holy hills from tree cutting, hunting, and other human activities, but as Dai and non-Dai communities have expanded and as cash crops like rubber trees have become more popular, some of these protected areas have shrunk.

The Dai have also traditionally had a close relationship with water, which they regard as the source of life. One of the three main Dai festivals is Songkran, a spring celebration that is most commonly known for water splashing. Originally a celebration of the birth of Buddha and the Buddhist new year, this festival includes washing Buddha statues and an activity in which participants splash water at one another to wash away earthly dust and bad fortune. In southern Chinese Dai areas as in northern Thailand and Myanmar some communities also have festivals intended to attract rain gods in which homemade or, in recent years, store-bought bamboo rockets are fired into the skies. Two of the other main festivals initiate and conclude three months of religious activity, between the mid-June Door-Closing Festival and the mid-September Door-Opening Festival. Activities include public chanting of Buddhist scriptures.

Almost every Dai village has its own Buddhist temple, which may include a garden or larger plot of land managed by the monks. In the past the temples were responsible for educating male children, primarily through reading Buddhist sutra inscribed on palm leaves. Although only a few of the children would go on to become full monks, many young men spent years living in the temple before returning to civilian life. The temple authorities were also responsible for conducting ceremonies at important events such as festivals and funerals.

Many Dai temples and religious practices were damaged or repressed just after the Chinese revolution in 1949 and then again during the Cultural Revolution in the 1970s, but they have been undergoing a revival since the 1980s. Elder Dai community members have been critical to this process of remembering and preserving traditional practices. Dai temples have also benefited from cross-border contact with Dai and non-Dai monks from temples in Thailand, who have supplied religious texts and icons.

The Dai people also have a strong oral tradition. Songs, tales, and poems are not just memorized and recited but are often improvised by performers to challenge or otherwise involve the audience. Similarly some traditional Dai dances solicit "replies" from other groups in the audience. In most communities Dai men and women perform separate dances that demonstrate daily activities, martial feats, or romantic ideals. Dai women have become well known for donning especially colorful costumes and wearing flowers in their hair during dances, but this custom (as well as river bathing) is often exaggerated for tourist consumption.

FURTHER READING

Sarah Leila Margaret Davis. *Song and Silence: Ethnic Revival on China's Southern Borders* (New York: Columbia University Press, 2005).

C. Patterson Giersch. *Asian Borderlands: The Transformation of Qing China's Yunnan Frontier* (Boston: Harvard University Press, 2006).

Shih-chung Hsieh. "On the Dynamics of the Tai/Dai-Lue Ethnicity," in *Cultural Encounters on China's Ethnic Frontiers,* edited by Stevan Harrell (Seattle: University of Washington Press, 1995).

Sandra Hyde. *Eating Spring Rice: The Cultural Politics of AIDS in Southwest China* (Berkeley and Los Angeles: University of California Press, 2006).

Zhu Liangwen. *The Dai or the Tai and Their Architecture and Customs in South China* (Bangkok: D D Books, 1992).

Andrew Turton. *Civility and Savagery: Social Identity in Tai States* (New York: Routledge, 2000).

Dalits   *See* Scheduled Castes.

Dangxiang (Tangut)

The Dangxiang or Tangut were a nomadic people in the northwest of China who eventually formed the Xixia or Western Xia dynasty in about 1038 C.E. *Western Xia* is the name given to it by Chinese scholars to refer to its position relative to the Song dynasty; the Dangxiang referred to their dynasty as Da Xia or Great Xia. The first mention of a Dangxiang branch of the Qiang peoples precedes the period of the Northern and Southern dynasties (317–589), when the Dangxiang lived in inner Tibet, just to the south of the Tuyuhun people. Dangxiang legend also points to origins farther south in Sichuan Province, especially the border region with Gansu and Qinghai Provinces, and to intermarriage with Tibetan women. By the early decades of the Tang dynasty (618–970) about 1,000 of their members had sought protection from the Chinese state against other nomadic peoples and had been settled along the Yellow River while Xifeng Bulai, a Dangxiang leader, had been named governor of a region in Guizhou Province. However, other Dangxiang did not ally themselves with the Chinese but rather with the Xianbei, Tuyuhun, and others against Tang domination.

As the Tang dynasty disintegrated over the course of several centuries the Dangxiang alliance strengthened, and in 1038, during the Song dynasty in the south, the Dangxiang formed their own dynastic kingdom, the Western Xia, under Emperor Jingzong. Over the course of almost 200 years 10 successive Dangxiang kings dominated territory in what are today Shaanxi, Ningxia, Gansu, and Inner Mongolia Provinces. The empire's most important city was the Central Asian oasis and trade center of Khara-Khoto, as it is known in Mongolian, where in the early 20th century Russian archaeologists found thousands of Dangxiang cultural materials including walls, fortresses, books, and trade goods. This city, however, was not the empire's capital, which was located in what is today Yinchuan, Ningxia Province. Nothing survives of the city from Dangxiang times because of the destruction wrought by the Mongols in 1227, but the nearby tombs

of the Da Xia kings have presented archaeologists with a wealth of remains. Legend has it that Genghis Khan's dying wish was to see the complete destruction of the Xia capital after its armies defeated his own six times on the way to ultimate defeat in 1227. In addition all of the royal family was killed, all records were destroyed, and most of the population was dispersed. Ethnic identification as Dangxiang disappeared over the next few generations.

Altogether nine major Dangxiang tombs and 208 minor ones have been found, all facing south at the base of Helan Shan, or mountain, Ningxia Province; they were first recorded by Westerners in 1938. The plethora of burial and other sites in the region is noted by many outsiders as resembling a Chinese version of the pyramids at Giza, Egypt, for each one is marked by a large mound of earth. The assumption of most scholars is that the nine major tombs hold many of the rulers of the Western Xia, but confirmation of that fact remains difficult. To date only three inhabitants of the tombs have been identified, the grandfather and son of the first emperor, Li Yuanhao, who changed his name to Jingzong, and Emperor Shenzong, who ruled in the early 13th century just before the Mongol conquest. All nine of the royal tombs are alike in structure, each containing 11 separate elements including the tomb itself, three pavilions, two gate towers, stones inscribed with the ruler's history and achievements, and an offering hall. Other, smaller tomb sites from the Dangxiang period have also been found in Gansu Province, but these contained ashes rather than bodies and inscriptions of Buddhist mantras. Several cave sites with Dangxiang architecture likewise contain Buddhist artifacts, including a Buddha statue in an important site in Gansu. Indeed the assumption of at least some archaeologists is that the mounds at the royal tombs of Yinchuan are likewise of Buddhist origin and served as stupas or domed monuments.

Dangxiang culture was based on animal husbandry, especially of sheep, with the later addition of agriculture in some regions. Trade was also extremely important and Dangxiang control of Khara-Khoto and other oasis centers in the Central Asian desert allowed them to emerge as an independent state among the powerful Song dynasty, Tibetan kingdoms, and Khitan or Liao dynasty. The Dangxiang were also devout tantric Buddhists similar to their Tibetan neighbors; their view of the world, or cosmology, resembled an octagonal mandala, which they reproduced in their tomb mounds. Interestingly while the Dangxiang royalty had

---

DANGXIANG

location:
Northwestern China

time period:
Sometime before 317 C.E. to 1227

ancestry:
Qiang

language:
Dangxiang, a Tibeto-Burman language that has become extinct

adopted the Chinese practice of burial instead of cremation, they held steadfastly to many other aspects of Buddhist culture and outside the royal family cremation seems to have remained central to funereal rites.

See also KHITANS; TIBETANS.

Dani (Ndani)

The Dani are a relatively large sociolinguistic group residing in the highlands of Papua Province, Indonesia. They are one of the best known of the highlands groups because of a documentary film, *Dead Birds,* which records their ritual warfare practices; a number of anthropologists have also published books and articles providing many details of Dani culture and society.

In addition to their ritualized warfare, which resembles that of the ENGA in being primarily about display rather than destruction, the Dani engage in warfare not unfamiliar to Western audiences. Their ritualized warfare entails lines of men shooting arrows at one another and results in minimal injury and loss of life. This activity is meant to placate the ghosts of their ancestors. In contrast secular warfare entails midnight raids of hamlets; murder of men, women, and children; confiscation or destruction of property; and transfer of land from losers to winners. The motivation for this kind of warfare is population pressure and need for land rather than the desire to placate ghosts.

Many aspects of Dani life resemble those of other NEW GUINEA HIGHLANDERS. The societies are patrilineal and polygynous: that is, men can take more than one wife. The people subsist primarily on sweet potatoes and pork, reside in patrilineal hamlets made up of a men's house and one or more other residences for women, children, and pigs; and give great spiritual importance to the ghosts of their ancestors. However, the Dani are also unique in a number of ways. First the various dialects of the Dani language all contain only two color words. While some authors gloss these words as "light" and "dark" in English, or even less accurately as "white" and "black," the Dani words do not have an exact equivalent in English. The colors that we would describe in English as dark blue or dark green are the best representatives of what the Dani know as *mili,* while both dark red and light pink best represent what the Dani know as *mola.*

A second aspect of Dani society, especially the Dani of the Grand Valley, that has been of great interest to Westerners is the relative lack of interest in sex and sexuality. This disinter-est is based on cultural norms and expectations rather than on biological dysfunction, according to the anthropologists who have studied this phenomenon. While such personal information may have been difficult for researchers to study, there is plenty of evidence for this cultural trait. Many societies around the world prohibit sexual relations between a husband and wife for a certain period after childbirth, from a few weeks to a year, but the Dani are almost unique in practicing a four- to six-year period of abstinence after childbirth. In addition rather than complaining, having affairs, or taking another spouse, both Dani men and women seem to accept this rule without much thought. There are no grave punishments meted out by the Dani for breaking this rule because, as they explain, nobody does break it, though the ghosts of the ancestors are thought to punish transgressors in some way. Another piece of evidence for a relative indifference to sex is that the incidence of premarital or extramarital sexual relations is very low.

See also MELANESIANS.

Dariganga

The Dariganga are an Eastern Mongol group who are closely related to the numerically dominant Khalkha Mongols, who make up about 90 percent of the population of Mongolia, and the BURIATS. They live primarily in the hills and on the volcanic plateau of Sukhbaatar Province, near the Gobi Desert in southeastern Mongolia, where the rolling grasslands of the steppes meet the harsh Gobi Desert. The spectacular Dariganga Volcano is made up of more than 200 separate lava and cinder cones from eruptions in the Pleistocene and Holocene Eras.

While the Mongol language has been spoken for possibly thousands of years, the typical starting date for most subgroups of MONGOLS is the 13th century, when Genghis Khan first united the Mongols and provided an overarching identity to both the dominant Khalkha and also the smaller western Mongol or OIRAT groups such as the DURBETS. The documented history of the Mongols, *The Secret History of the Mongols,* while largely focused on the life and times of Genghis Khan, also speaks of the existence of numerous other Mongolian peoples, most of whom participated in the military and political exploits of the larger Mongol Empire.

Many Dariganga today continue to live a nomadic or seminomadic lifestyle, packing up their tents or yurts either seasonally or when their herds of cattle, horses, camels, sheep, and

DASA

location:
India

time period:
The period in which the Rig Veda was written, starting about 1500 B.C.E.

ancestry:
Unknown

language:
Unknown

DAUR

location:
Mainly Heilongjiang and Inner Mongolia Provinces, but some also in the Xinjiang Uighur municipality and Nei Mongol Autonomous Regions

time period:
Early 17th century to the present

ancestry:
Probably Khitan

language:
Daur is a Mongolian language that consists of three dialects: Buteha (Bataxan), Haila'er (Hailar), and Qiqiha'er (Qiqihar, Tsitsikhar); there is no written form of this language so the Daur people use Han, Mongol, and Kazakh for written communication.

goats have exhausted the supplies of grass and water in one area. Most families move about six times per year. Their yurts are round felt tents laid over a wooden latticework that can be built and rebuilt many times; the yurts also have a wooden door, brightly painted according to the family's tastes. Dariganga who have abandoned this nomadic lifestyle work either on collective farms or in industry, mining, or transport. The Dariganga region is renowned in Mongolia for its metalworkers, especially silversmiths. The diet of the Dariganga is very similar to that of other Mongolians, emphasizing meat and fat in the winter and dairy products in the summer. Fermented mares' milk remains a favorite drink, even in settled towns. (*See also* MONGOLIANS: NATIONALITY.)

Although Tibetan Buddhism, the dominant religion in Mongolia, was persecuted throughout most of the 20th century, it has experienced a bit of a revival since 1990. In that year a Buddhist stupa or monument was rebuilt atop the Altan Ovoo, a volcanic crater, on the site of a 19th-century stupa that had been destroyed in 1937. Only men are allowed to visit the stupa to this day; the same is true of the climb to the top of Shiliin Bogd Mountain, made at sunrise, which revives the spirits of male climbers. Statues of gods, known as *balbals*, are also in evidence in the Dariganga region, often accompanied by food offerings left by the local inhabitants in the statues' left hands.

Dasa

In the Rig Veda, the religious text of the Hindus, which was first composed about 1500 B.C.E., codified about 900 years later, and written down probably after 300 B.C.E., the Aryans are depicted as fighting off their enemies, the Dasa or Dasyu. European scholars in the 19th century who attributed racial differences to all human communities read this text as depicting a battle between light-skinned Aryan migrants into India and indigenous dark-skinned enemies. However, present-day analyses have indicated that this was probably a misreading of the Sanskrit text. Dasa are used throughout the Vedas as representatives of disorder, chaos, and the dark side of human nature while Aryans are symbols of order, purity, goodness, and light. The composers of the text are believed today to have thought themselves superior to the Dasa or Dasyu not because of skin color, which was irrelevant, but because of the latter's lack of religion or at least religion in a form understand-able to the authors, as well as their "primitive" language. Certainly the dark skin of the Hindu god Vishnu should be clear enough evidence that this physical trait was not seen in a negative light at the time these texts were composed.

The identity of the Dasa remains in question today. Some scholars assume they were fellow Aryans who had not adopted the religion of their fellow nomads as of about 1500 B.C.E. and thus were enemies from a religious and social order viewpoint. Other scholars believe the Dasa were the indigenous inhabitants of the northern subcontinent, perhaps the descendants of the HARAPPANS. A third group of scholars believe the Dasa were an entirely mythological creation of the Aryans used to represent the larger battle between good and evil that is depicted throughout the religious text; they give as evidence of this hypothesis the number of nonhuman demons in the text, such as Urana with his 99 arms.

See also INDO-ARYANS.

Daur (Dawoerzu)

Though a very small population of roughly 132,000, the Daur people are historically and culturally unique enough to be recognized by the Chinese government as one of the official 55 minority groups. The origins of this ethnic minority have been traced back to the early 17th century, but their direct ancestry is unknown. Most believe, however, that they were descendants of the KHITANS in the Liao dynasty. According to this theory the Daur ethnic group was formed when groups of Khitans migrated from the lower Heilong River to the western region of China. Between 1644 and 1664 when Emperor Shun Zhi ruled, the Daur migrated south near the Nenjiang River. During 1643 and 1651 they aided in fending off Cossack invaders from Russia. In 1931 Daur fought against the JAPANESE when the latter occupied northeastern China.

The main religion of the Daur people is shamanism, in which shamans act as intermediaries between the physical and spiritual worlds and employ their powers to influence spiritual forces. The Daur live in communities along with other groups including HAN and MONGOLS. Most Daur live by farming, herding, hunting, and fishing; the name *Daur* itself means "cultivator" or "explorer," depending on which source one uses. The farmers' main crops are wheat, soybeans, sorghum, maize, and rice; they also raise oxen and horses. In mountainous regions the Daur are known for making carts and wooden pipes. Some Daur have modernized and built factories for the manufacturing of chemical fertilizers and electronics such as motors and transformers.

The Daur have many festivals: the Spring Festival, Black Ash Festival, Butong Festival (regarded as their New Year's Eve), and many more. The five-day (minimum) Spring Festival is regarded as the most important. To prepare for the event women make various foods including dumplings and steamed cakes and girls make gifts to give to their boyfriends. The Daur also sacrifice oxen and pigs at this time, to set the stage for a prosperous coming year.

The Daur are distinct from the Han in terms of kinship. They practice matrilocal marriages, so that a new husband moves into his wife's home, and they have matrilineal inheritance, so that a man generally inherits his wealth and position from his mother's brother instead of his own father. According to one Daur custom women are not to marry at an even-numbered age as this is thought to cause bad luck.

The Daur peoples may also have been the first to play field hockey (*beikuo*): hockey is mentioned in *The History of the Liao Dynasty*, which was written more than 1,000 years ago.

Dawenkou culture (Ta-wen-k'ou culture)

Dawenkou culture is one of many Neolithic societies in territory that is today China; it was primarily located on the lower Yellow River in what is present-day Shandong Province. It coincided with the Yangshao culture of the Yellow River valley and may have been one of the groups to have developed into the Longshan culture. All that we know about Dawenkou culture has been gained from archaeological excavations, mostly of the more than 100 tombs that have been found, more than 30 of those in Juxian County of Shandong Province. All of these gravesites are rectangular pit graves; in most of them the body is located with the head toward the east and a set of deer teeth held in one hand. A large amount of red and black pottery, most decorated with geometric shapes, has also been found along with jade and stone jewelry and adornments, ivory combs and other items, and tools made from bone and stone. The people of Dawenkou culture also buried their dead with pigs' heads and jawbones and a variety of other animal parts, especially teeth.

One of the most important innovations that marks Dawenkou culture from those that preceded it is the creation of wheel-made pottery, often very delicate and ornate. Other important features are the building of fortified villages or other settlements, settled agricultural society based largely on millet and paddy or wet rice, and differentiations in the number and kind of burial goods, indicating the division of society into different classes. As had Yangshao culture, the people of Dawenkou had developed a form of writing by about 4,800 years ago. Archaeologists have identified 14 separate characters that represent words, including those for *fan*, *south*, and *enjoy*.

Dayaks (Bidayuh, Dajaks, Dyaks, Land Dayaks)

Dayak is a generic term that refers to the non-Muslim tribes of the interior of Kalimantan, the Indonesian region of the island of Borneo. Dayaks share a language family, which includes 16 separate languages, as well as a general cultural orientation that distinguishes them from their Muslim coastal neighbors. Within the larger classification as Dayak the main division is that between Land Dayaks, who reside inland and are the subject of this entry, and Sea Dayaks or IBAN, who live primarily on the coast of Sarawak, Malaysia.

Most Land Dayaks live along the rivers of inland Kalimantan in villages of about 600 people. One of the most noteworthy features of Land Dayak villages are their residential units, between one and five longhouses per village that are built like Western apartments or condominiums. The residents of each longhouse share a covered verandah and courtyard but have entirely separate "apartments" or residences within the structure. Whenever a young couple marries and starts a household, usually in the village of the new bride, a new section is added to an existing longhouse. Today this pattern is less evident than in the past, and far more independent structures are being built, but they remain close to one another in the village.

The economic bases of Dayak culture are subsistence farming and fishing. Most families have their own swidden or slash-and-burn field on the hillsides where they grow dry rice and a few vegetables. This diet is supplemented by hunting, fishing, and gathering of wild products such as fruit, sago, medicinal herbs, and roots. The Dayaks have long had exchange relationships with other peoples, including the Muslim Malay-speaking peoples of the coast, the PENAN, and even the Dutch and Chinese,

---

DAWENKOU CULTURE

location:
Shandong Province, China

time period:
Approximately 4300 to 2500 B.C.E.

ancestry:
Unknown

language:
A Sino-Tibetan or proto-Chinese language

Dayak farmers often work together to bring in the harvest at the end of the season. *(Shutterstock/Hubert)*

DAYAKS

location:
Kalimantan, Indonesia,
with a few in Sarawak,
Malaysia

time period:
Unknown to the present

language:
Land Dayak, a language
grouping of 16 separate
Austronesian languages,
including Dayak itself

who provided finished consumer items in exchange for lumber, medicinal herbs, and other forest products.

Traditionally most Dayaks did not consider themselves members of any social unit larger than the village and a common Dayak identity was lacking in most regions. Bilateral kinship systems, in which relatives from both sides are equally weighted in the creation of alliances and in the prohibition against marriage of close relatives, mean that large kinship structures characteristic of lineages and clans do not exist. Indeed social stratification of any kind is relatively absent, with differences in age and sex providing the only distinctions within any Dayak village. Within those differences men are generally considered more socially and politically active as members of a village council and as participants in rituals and other events in the men's house or headhouse as it is often called, because enemy heads are stored there.

Despite this traditional social organization that did not recognize units larger than villages, today Dayaks have united in a variety of political and social actions, mostly to oppose the relocation into their territory of large numbers of MADURESE migrants. Since Indonesian independence in 1949 but especially in the 1970s and 1980s, the central government has engaged in a policy of relocating peoples from the heavily populated islands of Java, Bali, and Madura to the less populated outer islands. In central Kalimantan the Madurese have been seen by the local populations of both Dayaks and MALAYS as particularly difficult because of their lack of respect for and integration into the local communities and their connection to logging and other ecologically destructive activities. In the 1990s and the 21st century some Dayak communities have begun to use more traditional forms of social control, such as headhunting, to try to threaten the Madurese and force them out of their region. Headhunting had been eliminated by government forces by the mid-1960s, and domestic animal heads, such as those of cows or pigs, had been used in ceremonies and sacrifices. In recent years, however, Dayaks wielding machetes, blowguns, and other traditional weapons have waged a form of guerrilla war on these Madurese migrants. Dayaks also participated in violence in 1999 when about 3,000 people were killed in struggles between Madurese and locals, including both Dayaks and Malays.

FURTHER READING

Judith M. Heimann. *The Airmen and the Headhunters: A True Story of Lost Soldiers, Heroic Tribesmen, and the Unlikeliest Rescue of World War II* (Orlando, Fla.: Harcourt, 2007).

William O. Krohn. *In Borneo Jungles: Among the Dyak Headhunters* (New York: Oxford University Press, 1991).

De'ang (Ang, Benlong, Black Benglong, Liang, Niang, Red Benglong)

The De'ang are one of China's recognized 55 national minority groups. In 1949 they were recognized nationally as the Benglong but gained official recognition of their name for themselves, *De'ang*, in 1985. They are now a very small population in Yunnan Province and across the borders in Thailand and Myanmar (Burma) but once constituted a large and powerful force in Yunnan.

The De'ang are considered one of the oldest communities in Yunnan Province, where they are believed to have descended from the Pu of the Nujiang River basin in the second century. They were conquered by the HAN in their march south under Emperor Wu near the start of the common era but in the eighth century were under the DAI in the Nanzhou and Dali kingdoms. During this period they were among the peoples called Mangman or Mang barbarians by Chinese chroniclers in the Sui and Tang dynasties (581–907); it was during the Qing (1644–1911) that the Chinese named them Benglong. Finally the De'ang and others in Yunnan emerged from under the yoke of the Dai in the 12th century, when they became the dominant kingdom of the south, which lasted until about the 15th century, when other groups moved into Yunnan and De'ang nobles were subjected to taxation and tribute from the outside. Since that time their numbers have declined to just a few more than 15,000 at the start of the 21st century and their power has been usurped by the central government.

De'ang economic activities differ somewhat on the basis of region. Those living in the area of Dehong, Yunnan, grow wet rice in permanent paddies irrigated and fertilized so as to produce a crop each year for several years with only an occasional fallow period. Those in the Lincang region however, grow mostly dry rice, corn, and a variety of root crops. In both regions tea has been the main cash crop since the 19th century. De'ang craftsmen also work in bamboo, silver, and cotton to produce wares they sell in Dai or Han markets; the De'ang themselves do not have any local markets of their own.

The De'ang envision their society as made up of a web of intersecting patrilineal groups. Each lineage has between 30 and 40 families who all recognize a common male ancestor and are related to one another through the principle of male descent. Women always marry out of their natal group but usually remain within their village; the preferred marriage pattern is for a man to marry his mother's brother's daughter, who then moves into her new husband's household in patrilocal residence. Occasionally, however, poor men who cannot pay the standard bride price, which legitimates his children as his own and acknowledges the labor and resources that went into raising his wife, take up matrilocal residence: they move into the household of their new bride, work her father's land, and then inherit the land upon the father-in-law's death. This would occur only in a family that had no sons of its own to inherit the land and property and did not need the daughter's bride price in order to obtain a wife for the son. In the 20th and 21st centuries most De'ang households are relatively small, made up of a nuclear family or at most a youngest son's family and his parents. Prior to this period, however, De'ang households in the Lincang region were large, extended family groups that could contain as many as 90 people from three or four generations.

Since their initial interactions with the in-migrating Dai peoples before the eighth century the De'ang have been Theravada Buddhists. Prior to 1949 most villages contained a Buddhist temple and many families sent at least one son to become a monk; in addition all De'ang believed it was their responsibility to feed and support the monks with donations. De'ang religious literature was written in Dai and all monks could read and write in this language. Since the Communist revolution in 1949 religion has been greatly persecuted in China and much of this tradition ceased, especially from the 1950s until the 1980s. Since that time China has relaxed its rules somewhat; a few temples and monasteries have come back into operation and both personal and communal rituals have become important events in the lives of most De'ang, marking marriage, birth, death, and other important events.

Dega (Degar, Moi [derogatory], Montagnards, Nguoi dan toc thieu so, Thuong, Yard)

Dega or *Degar* is the collective self-designation for the approximately 30 different indigenous groups of Vietnam's highland region. They live in the mountainous center of the country, called *Tay Nguyen* in Vietnamese. Dega peoples have struggled for more than 10 centuries against physical, political, and economic incursions by the country's dominant majority, the VIETNAMESE, who referred to them as *moi*,

---

DE'ANG

location:
Yunnan Province, China; Thailand; and Myanmar

time period:
12th century to the present

ancestry:
Mon-Khmer

language:
There are three separate Palaung languages, Pale, Shwe, and Rumai, and speakers of all three are classified as De'ang in China; 50 percent of China's De'ang speak Pale.

DEGA

location:
The highlands of Vietnam

time period:
Unknown to the present

ancestry:
Mixed

language:
All three Southeast Asian language families are represented among the Dega: Austronesian, mostly from the Malayo-Polynesian subgroup; Austro-Asiatic, mostly from the Mon-Khmer subgroup; and Tai-Kadai, mostly from the Tai subgroup.

meaning "savages," until recent times. During the French colonial period they acquired the name *Montagnard,* meaning "mountaineer," which was shortened by U.S. soldiers during the Vietnam War to "Yard."

The collective history of the Dega is one of struggle. Since the early stages of the Vietnamese push to colonize the entire region that is today Vietnam, a process that began soon after the northern Vietnamese Ngo dynasty attained its independence from China in 939 C.E., the Dega have been trying to maintain their own ways of life. Some groups were pushed away from the coastal plains and into the mountains, while others retreated onto even higher ground to escape. Traditionally the Dega engaged in both hunting and gathering activities as well as some slash-and-burn horticulture on shifting or temporary garden plots. As the Vietnamese moved farther south, taking their intensive agricultural practices with them, these more extensive subsistence activities requiring low population densities and large amounts of land became more and more marginalized. Today the few Dega communities that have been able to maintain their traditional subsistence practices are under intense pressure to move into Vietnamese villages and take up rice farming; protests in both 2001 and 2004 resulted in numerous arrests and even deaths at the hands of the Vietnamese authorities. During the French period coffee was also introduced to the highlands, and its cultivation has allowed some Dega communities to remain in the mountains, maintaining their culture and language but at the same time engaging in Vietnam's export economy.

During the Vietnam War the long-standing struggle of the Dega against the Vietnamese led them to ally themselves largely with the U.S. soldiers. The Americans formed and trained a number of Dega fighting forces, both for defense of Dega villages against the Communists and as an offensive force to assist the Americans in reconnaissance, tracking, and other activities for which local knowledge was invaluable. At the end of the war many Dega individuals and even entire villages faced severe recriminations at the hands of the victorious Vietnamese. Thousands were evacuated and allowed to resettle in the United States, while many others were forced from their lands and into Vietnamese villages; many Vietnamese also moved into the highlands. By 1989 only about 30 percent of the prewar Dega total remained within the highlands.

Each of the separate groups that are contained within the larger Dega community has its own social structure, laws, customs, religion, and other facets of traditional culture. However, there are some similarities among many of them. Among the most important are the reckoning of kinship through matrilines, people who are related to one another through common female ancestors, and a matrilocal residence pattern that requires men to move in with their wives at the time of their marriage. The adoption of evangelical Protestantism, a process that has occurred largely since 1975, is also much more common among the Dega than among the Vietnamese and is one of the causes of the crackdowns on Dega communities by the Vietnamese authorities in 2001 and 2004. Prior to their conversion most Dega were animists rather than Buddhists, and the worship of local gods and spirits remains the second most important religion in Dega communities to this day.

See also BAHNAR; M'NONG; MUONG; RHADE; SEDANG; VIETNAMESE: NATIONALITY.

Degar   *See* DEGA.

Derung   (Drung, Dulong, Dulongzu, Dulonh, Qui, Tulong, Tulung)

The Derung are one of the smallest ethnic groups of the 55 national minority groups recognized by the People's Republic of China (PRC). The majority inhabit the Dulong River valley in northwestern Yunnan Province near the border with Myanmar, while a smaller population lives along the Nu Jiang or Salween River. They speak Derung, which is an unwritten Sino-Tibetan language. In lieu of a formal written script in the past records were created and messages were transmitted by etching notches in wood and by tying knots.

Before the founding of the PRC in 1949 the Derung were under the control of a variety of different political entities. The first records of the Derung are from the Tang dynasty (618–907) when they were already present in their current territory and were under the domination of the Nanzhao kingdom of the DAI people and then the Dali kingdom of the BAI. From the Song through the late Qing dynasties (960–1911), they were largely ruled by headmen from the NAXI under the *tusi* system whereby regional chiefs and headmen were granted a degree of autonomy over their people in exchange for loyalty and tribute to the centralized Chinese government.

Near the end of the Qing period, however, the Naxi chiefs were replaced in the Dulong River region by a Tibetan monastery, which acted as the feudal lord and master. Some Derung during these periods were also held in bondage by LISU landowners who used them as slaves. Evidence of all these political and economic relationships can be found in some of the vocabulary in the Derung language even today.

The Derung economy has been based on swidden or slash-and-burn agriculture for as long as there have been records about them. Corn, wheat, and beans are the most important crops today. In addition to agriculture the Derung engage in fishing and hunting, and they also supplement their diets with foraging for wild plants such as mushrooms, bamboo shoots, and various herbs and roots. With the founding of the PRC the Derung were encouraged to cultivate rice paddies, which was possible with the institution of irrigation projects. By the end of the 1950s the Derung were selling surplus grain to the state. Despite the economic gains generated by rice cultivation most Derung have maintained their traditional farming practices. Another activity the Derung engage in is weaving, which produces distinctive striped flax cloth worn by both sexes in the form of cloaks and skirts during the day and used as blankets at night.

The Derung have traditionally been organized into 15 exogamous patrilineal clans called *nile,* membership in which is inherited from fathers only. A *nile* is divided into villages called *ke'eng* in which families live in multigenerational common longhouses. However, in recent times the younger generations have been less inclined to maintain this way of life. Members of a *ke'eng* believe themselves to be descendants of a common ancestor and each *ke'eng* is headed by a *kashan* whose duties are both administrative and ceremonial. In the past *ke'engs* were separate political entities, which allied temporarily in the face of danger posed by outsiders.

Marriages are typically arranged by parents according to the rules of exogamy, which require each individual to marry outside his or her own patrilineal clan. The family of the new husband must pay a bride price at marriage in cattle, iron items, and cloth, which both legitimates any children the couple may have and compensates the new wife's family for the loss of her domestic labor. In the event that payment of bride price is not fulfilled, it can be substituted with bride service where a man provides services to the family whose daughter he has married. Women generally move into the household or village of

their new husband in patrilocal residence, but unlike within the dominant HAN society, Derung women customarily have high status in their marital homes, contributing to economic decisions, overseeing resource distribution, and participating in agricultural activities.

Until 50 years ago Derung women were known for traditional facial tattooing with patterns that indicated their clan membership. Facial tattooing took place with the onset of womanhood when girls were around 12 or 13 years of age. By some estimates as of 2004 there were fewer than 100 living Derung women with facial tattoos. As far as religion is concerned the Derung are animists, who believe all natural objects and phenomena are inhabited by spirits. The shaman plays a central role in rituals and ceremonies, serving as a communicator between the spirit world and the physical world. Sometimes *kashans* may perform certain rites as well.

Dingling (Chile, Gaoche, and Tiele sometimes used but seemingly inaccurately)

There is significant confusion in the historical record about the Dingling, their ancestors, and the possibility of their being the ancestors of other known groups. The problem is that the Dingling themselves did not have writing, and thus all accounts of them are from Chinese sources, many of which are contradictory or unclear because they knew the Dingling only from a distance.

The Dingling seem to have inhabited the northern reaches of the Chinese world between the Altai Mountains and Lake Baikal in ancient times. They are listed as a Turkic-speaking people in most sources available today in English and are often grouped with other TURKIC PEOPLES in having been defeated by Modu, leader of the XIONGNU, between 208 and 203 B.C.E. Another reference to their Turkic background lists the Dingling as among the forebears of the contemporary UIGHUR, who speak a Turkic language. However, one scholar on ancient China speculates that the Dingling were themselves a Chinese population that had been driven north across the Tien Shan Mountains and toward the Altai. This seems unlikely but not impossible.

After about 120 years of subjugation to the Xiongnu the Dingling, along with other conquered peoples, rebelled against their overlords and vanquished the weakened Xiongnu in 85 B.C.E. Subsequently they split into western and

DERUNG

location:
Northwestern Yunnan Province, China

time period:
Unknown to the present

ancestry:
Tibeto-Burman

language:
Derung, a Tibeto-Burman language in the Sino-Tibetan phylum

DINGLING

location:
Siberia, west of Lake Baikal, and northern Mongolia

time period:
At least third century B.C.E. to before seventh century C.E.

ancestry:
Uncertain; possibly Turkic or Chinese

language:
Uncertain

DIVEHI

location:
Republic of Maldives or Dhivehi Raajji, a group of 1,920 islands in the Indian Ocean, 460 miles south-west of Sri Lanka

time period:
Probably 90 B.C.E. to the present

ancestry:
Thought to be Dravidian and Sinhalese from south India and Sri Lanka

language:
Dhivehi, an ancient form of Sinhala, containing Arabic, Hindi, Portuguese, and English words. The script, Thaana, is read right to left.

northern Dingling, with the former being reconquered by the western Xiongnu in 51 B.C.E. and eventually assimilating into the dominant HAN population that conquered the western Xiongnu in the last decades before the common era. After the division of the Dingling the northern section joined the XIANBEI and Han to defeat the north Xiongnu around 90 C.E. Some sources also consider the northern Dingling as the ancestors of the TIELE, but this theory is contested.

The historical record for the Dingling after these victories becomes extremely thin and nothing can be asserted with any certainty. Nonetheless most sources name the seventh century C.E. as the end date of the Dingling, perhaps because that is the first century in which information about the Tiele, the presumed descendants of the Dingling, becomes available.

Next to nothing is known about the culture of the Dingling except that they were great warriors who did not accept Xiongnu subjugation with equanimity. However, one author suggests that the use of the term *Dingling* to refer to an ethnic group may mean that they were known for their metallurgy since the term means "master of the hearth." The Altai region in which they lived is known for early metalworkers, including Mongol shamans who used molten metals in their ritual techniques, so it is not difficult to imagine the Dingling were famed for their ability to forge metal into tools, weapons, and other items.

Divehi (Dhivehin, Maldivian)

From archaeological records Buddhists and to a lesser extent Hindus migrated to the Maldives Archipelago before it was converted to Islam, possibly some 2,500 years ago (*see* MALDIVEANES: NATIONALITY). Although historians have argued that Divehi are a mixture of DRAVIDIANS from southern India and Sinhalese from Sri Lanka, recent evidence suggests that there may well be links with the NAGA and WANNIYALA-AETTO people who developed the pre-Buddhist civilization in Sri Lanka. Whatever the exact pattern of settlement may have been, the great variety of physical characteristics found in the Maldives suggests that independent groups of people reached these islands in prehistoric times. Later Indonesians, MALAYS, Arabs, and Africans all added to the racial and cultural melting pot.

The Maldives is a small Islamic country of about 350,000 people with a history, language, and culture all of its own. Traditionally fishing and trading people, the inhabitants of this country, the Divehi, have been able to maintain their independence for centuries. They live in relative harmony with the ever-present maritime environment. As with all seafarers the Divehi carefully adapt to the weather, which determines when they go fishing, plant crops, and travel by sailboat. For this they use their own complex calendar based on certain stars that are aligned with the Sun or Moon. *Nakaiy* (heavenly body) refers to any one of 28 seasonal divisions of the year and the clusters of stars that represent them. The calendar helps to determine the seasons for fishing and farming and is also used as an astrological system to predict the future, making it a blend of scientific observation and indigenous religion.

The social structure of the Divehi is largely centered around the nuclear family. However, marriage and divorce have always been casual, and until recently women could be divorced on the whim of their husbands, without reason or compensation. Women retain their own names after marriage, a practical arrangement, considering that they marry frequently. Under Islamic law men are allowed to take four wives, and in the past it was considered a mark of esteem and piety to have so many. Polygyny is still legal today; however, men rarely marry more than one wife at a time. In an effort to strengthen the family and lower the high divorce rate, the first-ever codified Family Law came into force in July 2001, raising the minimal age of marriage to 18 and making unilateral divorce illegal. Women can now register prenuptial contracts to strengthen their position within the marriage. According to UN statistics the Maldives has the highest divorce rate of any country in the world. In fact, eight of 10 people divorce at least once, and the average number of marriages per person is between four and 10. Because of the closeness of the extended family on many of the islands, divorce is not considered to be traumatic for either the partners or the children.

Outside the family Divehi do not have a strict caste system, but there are important social divisions. The upper class is largely made up of close friends and relatives of the ruling sultan and his family. In the past it was considered unacceptable to eat with a member of an inferior class or for an inferior person to sit with a superior except on a low stool. Nowadays these distinctions are breaking down and advancement is based more on merit than on birth. Education is often considered less important than wealth. Wealthy persons are more likely to command respect from others than are highly educated people. The number of islands a person leases or the number of boats he owns remains crucial to social standing.

Islam is central to the lives of the Divehi in many ways. Not only is it their religion, but as with many Islamic people, social control is also exercised through this belief system. An Islamic judge (*gazi*) deals with judicial matters by interpreting and applying the principles of sharia law to individual cases. Any misbehavior is reported by the island chief to the atoll chief and in turn to the department of justice in Malè, the capital. Misbehavior can include theft, drinking liquor, not attending mosque or observing Ramadan (spelled *Ramazan* in the Maldives), adultery, and even masturbation. In applying sharia law the Maldives' courts are lenient and usually fines are imposed for petty crimes. Only once in the last century have thieves had their hands amputated for theft; however, people are still flogged with a *durra*, a taut leather strap with flat copper studs down the sides. Adulterers are not stoned to death but do undergo flogging on their thighs. The most common and traditional punishment is house arrest or banishment to an island far away from family and friends. If a banished person works hard and improves his behavior, he can become a respected member of the local community and it is extremely rare that he commits a crime again. Recently prisons have been established for serious criminals and political detainees.

In addition to their strong Islamic faith the Divehi have a vibrant belief, called *fandita*, which refers to special powers or spells possessed by certain men and women. This belief system encompasses ideas about spirits, ghosts, winds, and lights on the sea, and it allows people to control their health, enemies, boats, fishing catch, and destiny. Evil spirits, or *jinnis,* said to be made of fire and possessing superhuman powers, are still much feared by the islanders and are blamed for everything that cannot be explained in terms of religion or education. To ward off these evil spirits, the *hakeem* or medicine man may cast a curing spell by engraving charms with verses from the Quran, to be tied around the neck as is done in South India and Sri Lanka.

With the Maldives being well in excess of 95 percent water, boats are central to the Divehi way of life, essential for earning a living from fishing, collecting wood and coconuts from other islands, and travel. Most families own at least one small boat while richer families may have several. Carpenters build these boats from coconut planking for the carvel hull and local hardwoods for the frame. In the past the hull was sewn together with coir, rope from coconut husks, which made the boats flexible when passing over coral reefs, but the planks are now secured with copper nails. A team of four or five carpenters can carve a standard 32-foot fishing boat with simple tools in 40 days. The traditional fishing boat sails were originally square and made from thatched palm leaves, although the common lateen sail is now woven from cotton strips. Not surprisingly sails have been superseded by diesel engines. The basic boat design has not changed in centuries and the master carpenter knows it so well that he does not need to use plans.

Further Reading

Mohamed Amin, Duncan Willetts, Peter Marshall. *Journey through Maldives* (Nairobi: Camerapix Publishers International, 1992).

Clarence Maloney. *People of the Maldives Islands* (Mumbai: Orient Longman, 1980).

Paul A. Webb. *Maldives, People and Environment* (Bangkok: Media Transasia, 1988).

Dong   (Gam, Gaml, Kam, Tong, Tung)

The Dong are one of China's 55 recognized national minority groups. Most live in Hunan, Guizhou, and Guangxi Provinces, with a smaller number living in Xizang Autonomous Region or Tibet. Those in the north of Guizhou Province have largely been acculturated into the dominant HAN society while those in the south of Guizhou and in Hunan and Guangxi remain more traditional. Their languages were nonwritten prior to 1949, when the new Communist central government helped put the Dong language into script based on the Latin alphabet. Most literate Dong today, however, use Chinese characters as opposed to the post-1949 script.

The Dong people are believed by some to be descendants of BAIYUE tribes who lived in present-day Guangdong and Guangxi during the Qin and Han dynasties (221 B.C.E.–220 C.E.). They are thought to have migrated to their present home during the Tang period; this was the same period when the closely related DAI people were migrating southward to become the contemporary LAO, THAIS, and others. Chinese political literature about them

DONG

location:
Human, Guizhou, Guangxi Provinces and the Xizang Autonomous Region (Tibet), China

time period:
Third century B.C.E. to the present

ancestry:
Unknown, possibly Baiyue

language:
Northern and Southern Dong, Tai-Kadai languages in the Sino-Tibetan phylum

assigns the Dong to the early phases of Marx's dialectic of social development, slave society, for the Qin and Han periods, and then states that they passed into the era of feudalism during the Tang dynasty (61–907). A more likely scenario is that the Dong during all periods of history prior to 1949 were dominated by larger and stronger ethnic groups; some were held as slaves and others worked as tenants or sharecroppers on the lands of others.

More recent Dong history is clearer. During the Long March led by Mao Zedong in the 1930s some Dong families and communities guided and provided grain for the Chinese Red Army when it passed through the Dong region. Later the Communist agrarian reform ended the traditional landlord–tenant relationships that had kept many Dong impoverished for centuries. Nonetheless the Great Leap Forward of the 1950s and the Cultural Revolution of 1967–77 were periods of great difficulty for the Dong, with many dying of starvation during the former period and losing their lives while defending their religion and culture in the latter.

The Dong today are mostly farmers who grow rice, wheat, millet, corn, and sweet potatoes. They also grow cash crops, the most important of which are cotton, tobacco, rape seed, and soybeans. The Dong are also known to grow trees for logging and selling as timber at market. In addition the Dong produce tung oil, lacquer, and oil-tea camellia trees for their edible oil and varnish. Of the timber trees firs play an important role in Dong society. When a child is born the Dong plant fir saplings and when the child marries the saplings, now fully grown trees, are cut down and used to build the newlyweds a house.

Prior to 1949 the patriarchal nuclear family formed the basic social unit. In line with the dominant Han culture traditionally women were at the bottom of the social hierarchy to the extent that they were prohibited from handling sacrificial objects and could not inherit family property. Unlike among the Han, however, upon marriage women did not have to take up patrilocal residence in their husbands' family homes but continued to live with their parents until the birth of the first child. Only then were they required to live permanently with their husbands and to work in his family's household.

Presently the Dong live in villages of 20–30 households near streams. One prominent feature of Dong villages are the drum towers where meetings and celebrations are held. A drum tower of note stands 13 stories high and is located in Gaozhen village in Guizhou. It is adorned with ornate decorations of carved dragons, phoenixes, flowers, and birds. The Dong are also known for their unique and beautiful "wind and rain" bridges, which are made of wood, stone arches, stone slabs, and bamboo.

Dong religion centers on the worship of local, natural, and ancestral spirits in a syncretic blend of animism and ancestor worship; they also revere a number of major and minor gods including a saint mother for whom they have erected altars and temples in their villages. They believe that all natural objects and phenomena have spirits that can be appeased and thanked through rituals specific to each one. Numerous festivals are celebrated in Dong communities, including but not limited to New Year's Day, Mid-Autumn Day, Sisters' Festival, and the New Rice Tasting festival. Much of this religious activity was banned by the Communist state from the 1950s until about 1979, but recently it has started to flourish once again, especially in the southern Dong regions.

A beautiful example of a "wind and rain" bridge in Sanjiang, Guangxi. (OnAsia/Luke Duggleby)

Donghu (Eastern Hu, Tung hu)

The Donghu, or Eastern Hu, were a nomadic people who lived during the last half-millennium before the common era in territory that is today northeastern China and Mongolia. The name *Donghu* or *Tung hu* means "eastern nomads" or, alternatively, "eastern barbarians" in Chinese, a term used to distinguish these people from the XIONGNU or "northern slaves." We do not know what they called themselves. They were most active during China's Warring States period, 475–221 B.C.E. The Donghu are mentioned most often in relation to their battles with the Yan state at that time. According to ancient Chinese record, the Yan general Qin Kai's defeat of the Donghu, perhaps in 300 B.C.E., garnered the Yan an extra thousand *li* of territory, or about 311 miles. It was also against the Donghu that the Yan state built the Wall of the North in 254 B.C.E. This section of the Great Wall was the last portion constructed during the Warring States period; it crosses Hebei and Liaoning Provinces and Inner Mongolia. The Yan also built the original Houcheng fortress against the Donghu; the fortress was expanded during the HAN dynasty between 206 B.C.E. and 220 C.E. and became a small city.

In around 200 B.C.E. the Donghu became one of the first victims of Xiongnu expansion in the region of contemporary Mongolia. Despite Xiongnu superiority the Donghu continued to rebel against their overlords and during times of Xiongnu weakness were able to exert their independence. By the first century C.E. the Donghu had split into two separate groups based largely on locality: the northern Donghu became the XIANBEI and the southern Donghu became the Wuhuan.

Donghu culture was similar to that of other steppe-dwelling nomads in that it relied on herds of animals for most subsistence. As was true throughout their region most families kept goats, sheep, horses, and even camels to be able to take advantage of the different kinds of grasses that grew in small patches in the arid climate. The Donghu also ate pork when available and grew a limited amount of fruits and vegetables, where possible. They lived in felt yurts that could be dismantled, moved, and reassembled fairly quickly as climate, pastureland, and political conditions dictated. Their religion was dominated by spirit worship and shamanism, in which religious leaders fell into a trance to travel to the spirit world and carry messages about healing, success in warfare, and other daily activities back and forth.

Although the Donghu people disappeared when they divided into the Xianbei and Wuhuan in the first century, the name has emerged again today with an entirely new meaning. In the late 1990s the Western media began reporting on the Donghu people as the residents of the village of Donghu in Henan Province and made them into a symbol of the Chinese government's disregard for human rights. The contemporary Donghu have an HIV/AIDS infection rate among adults that approaches at least half the population, with some reports claiming up to 95 percent. Their infections have been almost entirely caused by the mishandling of the blood and needles of blood donors. The *New York Times* has reported that poor villagers in China are paid around five dollars per pint of blood, which is then pooled with the pints of thousands of other donors, the plasma withdrawn, and then the remainder transfused back into volunteers to prevent anemia. In addition to HIV/AIDS hepatitis and many other blood-borne viruses have been spread to large numbers of adults throughout China's central provinces in this manner.

Dong Son culture

The Bronze Age Dong Son culture probably emerged between 1000 and 700 B.C.E. in the Song-koi delta of contemporary northern Vietnam; subsequently this culture encompassed all of Southeast Asia and the Indo-Malaya Archipelago. However, some VIETNAMESE archaeologists date Dong Son somewhat later, beginning after 500 B.C.E. and following the Go Mun phase of cultural development in the region. The name *Dong Son* is from one of the best-explored archaeological sites of the period, first discovered by the French in 1924. In addition to the use of bronze the period covered by the Dong Son culture also introduced the development of iron tools and weapons to the region, as attested in many late Dong Son burials. The people of Dong Son, who may not have made up a single culture area at all, traded with the Chinese as both goods and coins from China have been found extensively in grave sites. Objects from India and Indonesia also appear in Dong Son era burials throughout mainland Southeast Asia, attesting to the wide trade network enjoyed by the wealthy elite of the time.

Some of the important traits of Dong Son culture are intensive rice agriculture and domestication of buffalo for transport and other heavy work; the people also had domesticated

---

DONGHU

location:
Northeastern China and Mongolia

time period:
Fifth century B.C.E. to first century C.E.

ancestry:
Unknown

language:
Unknown, possibly a Tungusic language

DONG SON CULTURE

location:
Mainland Southeast Asia and the Indo-Malaya Archipelago

time period:
Possibly 1000 to about 1 B.C.E.

ancestry:
Indigenous Neolithic cultures of Southeast Asia

language:
Probably an Austro-Asiatic language

pigs for food. They used long dugout canoes for fishing and traveling throughout the region for trade. Their fine bronze work, typified in the so-called Dong Son drums, may have originated in a skill imported from China or from the region of present-day Thailand. Many of the drums and other fine bronze work found in burial sites are decorated with elaborate images of human beings, animals, plants, and scenes from daily life. Some of this artwork shows houses that were built close to rivers and coastlines and elevated on stilts to prevent flood damage.

Scenes on a variety of bronze drums also tell us something about the Dong Son religious and ritual life. A large number of animal images are depicted, especially frogs and seabirds, which are believed to have been important religious symbols. Herons and egrets specifically have been interpreted by some as reflecting either fertility or funerary rites. The sun and water in the form of rain, rivers, and oceans were also important in the religion, which seems to have been a form of nature worship. Images of people playing panpipes, drums, and slit gongs appear on many drums, leading most experts to believe that music played an important role in both the ritual and the daily lives of Dong Son era people. There are also scenes of individuals in elaborate costumes and feathered headdresses, perhaps in procession or dancing in some pattern that may have been part of their ritual life as well. Both boats and rice, the two elements necessary for survival at the time, appear with great regularity and have led some archaeologists to postulate that there were religious events surrounding both rice processing and the building and launching of new boats.

On the basis of the wealthy and elaborate tombs of some Dong Son people and the modest burials of others, most specialists believe that this society had probably developed into a hierarchical form with a king at the apex by the time of its incorporation into the newly emerging Sino-Vietnamese culture around 1 B.C.E. The poorest people tended to be buried with no artifacts or only a simple piece of pottery or set of stone earrings. The middle range of burials have revealed up to four bronze objects, some pottery, a bracelet or two, and possibly an iron piece. The richest sites contain many bronze items including weapons and at least one drum, three or more iron implements, and some pieces that blend bronze and iron. There is also evidence that residence near the larger Dong Son settlements, such as the 600-hectare site at Co Loa, allowed people to have

a wider number and array of goods in their burial sites. Further evidence for the development of class differences during the Dong Son era are to be found at Co Loa. The settlement was surrounded by fortified walls that would have required the labor of hundreds of individuals, probably unpaid or slave labor recruited from the surrounding countryside. Overall the Dong Son society must have been well on its way to becoming the first organized state in mainland Southeast Asia; all it needed was the development of a written script for formalizing the bureaucratic structure and recording both historical and administrative details. In the absence of any apparent writing system most experts consider that Dong Son was probably a large chiefdom ruled autocratically by a politicoreligious hierarchy rather than an actual state.

Dongxiang (Sa'erta, Sarta)

The Dongxiang are one of China's recognized 55 national minority groups. Their name for themselves is *Sarta* while the name *Dongxiang* comes from the geographic term "East Village, Dong Xiang," which was a subdivision of Linxia where many Sarta lived in 1950. Today most live in what has come to be known as Dongxiang Autonomous County, a subsection of Linxia Huizu Autonomous Prefecture, Gansu Province. Smaller numbers of this group live in Xinjiang, Lanzhou, Qinghai, and other regions of Gansu Province. Prior to the mid-20th century the Sarta or Dongxiang were not recognized as a separate ethnic group or nationality but rather as a subsection of the Muslim Hui-huizu or HUI. They achieved nationality status in China in 1949, one year prior to the creation of Dongxiang Autonomous Region, which was reclassified as an Autonomous County in 1955.

The origins of the Dongxiang remain uncertain, but the most likely hypothesis is that they are the descendants of soldiers who accompanied the MONGOLS into western China in the 13th century. They were called Se Mu people and were garrisoned throughout the region inhabited by the Dongxiang today.

The Dongxiang language belongs to the Mongol language family and can be divided into three mutually intelligible dialects; Suonaba or Xiaonan is the dominant dialect, spoken by between 50 and 80 percent of the population. All three dialects have borrowed about 30 percent of their vocabulary from Chinese and have some intelligibility with BONAN. There is

DONGXIANG

location:
Gansu, China

time period:
Possibly 13th century to the present

ancestry:
Mongol

language:
Dongxiang, a Mongol language

no written version of Dongxiang and the small number of literate Dongxiang have learned to read and write in Chinese or UIGHUR.

Most Dongxiang families make a living as farmers growing potatoes, barley, and yams and raising sheep. Many families also raise chickens for eggs as well as for food. Eggs are their primary trade commodity, for which they get salt, cooking oil, and other necessities. Most families are extremely poor, in part because their land is perennially short of rain. Some particularly dry villages are located as far as six miles away from the nearest water source, from which women have to carry their water home; lucky families have a donkey to carry the water while the poorest have to carry it themselves. These drought conditions have meant that the region has been largely ignored by China's centralizing development agencies and no agricultural or industrial development is evident. The one positive sign for the people of Dongxiang is that since 1999 three new schools have been built by donations given to the *China Daily* newspaper and China Youth Development Foundation. The two organizations together formed a charity plan called "Caring for Dropouts; Donate to a Hope School." They have raised several hundred thousand yuan, which by 2003 had been used to build three new schools.

The Dongxiang are Muslims who are divided by the form of worship they favor. Some sources list just two sects among the Dongxiang, the so-called old religion and new religion, while others list three, new, old, and emerging sects. Regardless of the form of Islam practiced, the Dongxiang prior to the onset of the Communist system in 1949 were extremely devout. There were 595 mosques in their region, one for every 30 households. A dozen active imams and 2,000 other full-time religious specialists were also at work in Dongxiang, leading marriages, funerals, and other religious services; presiding at festivals; and assisting with other sacred events in the community.

Dravidians (Dravida)

The origins of the Dravidian people remain a mystery to this day. Many scholars and Dravidian political activists have connected the ancient Dravidians with the HARAPPANS and the people of the Mohenjo-Daro culture, sometimes called Indus Valley culture, but for many others this connection remains speculative at best. While the evidence is strong that it was not Indo-Aryan languages that were spoken in these early cultures there is less definitive proof that they were Dravidian. The writing left behind in these urban societies has yet to be translated, and many features of Harappan culture, including language, remain unknown to us today. Nonetheless there is significant evidence that Dravidian languages are ancient and were in the Indian subcontinent prior to the in-migration of the INDO-ARYANS in about 1800 B.C.E.

The modern concept of a Dravidian people emerged in the early 19th century when Francis W. Ellis, an employee in the British civil service in India, recognized the Dravidian languages as a separate language family; he did not, however, use this term to refer to the language. After this recognition in 1816 it took another 40 years for the term *Dravidian* to emerge; Robert A. Caldwell, a British linguist, first used the term in 1856 in a book entitled *Comparative Grammar of the Dravidian or South Indian Family of Languages.* Although it was meant to classify a language family separate from those of north India that derive from Sanskrit, Caldwell used the Sanskrit term *dravida*, which was used by Indo-Aryan speakers at the time to refer specifically to the Tamil language, as the basis of his term *Dravidian.* Today there are about 200 million speakers of approximately 75 different Dravidian languages spread throughout southern India and Sri Lanka, with smaller numbers in central India, Nepal, and even Pakistan, where the outlier BRAHUI reside. The contemporary existence of this group of Dravidian speakers in the region where Harappan culture existed about 5,000 years ago has been proof enough for some people that the Brahui are a vestigial community of this ancient civilization; however, the more accepted view is that they are migrants from the south who entered their land in only about 1100 C.E.

The category Dravidian has been used in social science to refer not only to this language family but also to a specific form of kinship that some anthropologists believe characterized the ancient Dravidian peoples as a whole. The so-called Dravidian kinship system is characterized by four principles: Kinship terms are distinguished by generation, sex, age, and the equivalence of some blood relatives with in-laws. With regard to the latter, this means that the term for father's sister is the same as that for wife's mother, for mother's brother the same as for wife's father. Dravidian kinship systems are also notable for the normative requirement for bilateral cross-cousin marriages. This does

DRAVIDIANS

location:
Southern and central India, Nepal, Pakistan, and Sri Lanka

time period:
Unknown to the present

language:
Dravidian is a large language family that includes about 75 different languages, the largest of which are Tamil, Malayalam, Kannada, and Telugu.

DUNGANS

location:
Russia and the Central Asian republics of Kyrgyzstan, Kazakhstan, and Uzbekistan

time period:
1871 to the present

ancestry:
Hui and Uighur, part of the Muslim minority in China

language:
Dungan, a Chinese language that has been written in the Dungan version of Cyrillic script since 1955 and has many Arabic, Persian, and Turkish words

not mean that all men marry their mother's brother's daughter or father's sister's daughter, but this is the general preference in Dravidian systems and the basis for the use of the same kinship term for both these relatives and in-laws. As has the assumption by many people that Dravidians were the creators of Harappan culture, the assumption that this kinship form characterized all ancient Dravidian peoples has also come under considerable attack. Today's Dravidian people have a wide variety of different kinship systems, many outside this classical definition.

The main trait that has led to any kind of unity among contemporary Dravidians is their opposition to the size and power of the Indo-Aryan population in India. Since Indian independence in 1947 Dravidian speakers have consistently struggled against the status of Hindi, the largest Indo-Aryan language group in the country, as the sole national language. Dravidian speakers were also among those activists who pressured the Indian government to create separate states for different ethnolinguistic groups; for example, Tamil Nadu, then called Madras, was created for Tamils in 1956.

Another facet of some Dravidian political culture in the past century has been a rejection of Brahminism, or those aspects of the caste and *varna* systems that mean that some people are treated as less human than others. One of the most important of these activists was E. V. Ramasamy Naiker, whose nickname was *Periyar*; he worked first with Gandhi and then apart from him to promote equality and independence in India. Caste inequality remains an important issue for some Dravidian activists because in the dominant Indo-Aryan varna system most Dravidian peoples were assigned positions of relatively low standing, Shudras or agriculturalists and servants, whose lot in life was to serve the needs of higher, born Brahmins, Ksatriyas, and Vaisyas. Today caste in southern India is somewhat different from that in the north and allows for more flexibility and movement within the system. In addition agriculture, which was being practiced by the Dravidian people before the migration of the nomadic Indo-Aryans into south Asia, is seen as a relatively high-caste occupation unlike in the north.

See also Kannadigas; Malayalis; Telugus; Yanadis.

Further Reading

Thomas R. Trautmann. *Dravidian Kinship* (Cambridge: Cambridge University Press, 1981).

Dungans (Chinese Muslims, Huizus, Xueitdzu)

From 1867 to 1881 about 10,000 Chinese Muslims, mostly from the Hui minority group, left their homes in Gansu and Shaanxi Provinces after the failure of the Hui Minority Wars. The migrations occurred in two separate waves, both taking the Hui over the Tien Shan Mountains separating China from Russia. In 1877 the Manchu victory in Xinjiang led about 5,500 Muslims to flee into Russia. Again in 1881 the Treaty of St. Petersburg returned territory to China after 10 years of Russian occupation, and for the following three years many small groups of Hui and Uighur left their homes, adding nearly 5,000 more Chinese Muslims to the already-established communities. The Russian government granted the refugees nearly 5,000 hectares of land and allowed them a tax-free status for 10 years. This initial population of more than 10,000 grew to more than 120,000 by 2004, with more than 80 percent in the Chu Valley of Kyrgyzstan and the Kurdai area of Kazakhstan. Smaller numbers also live in Russia and Uzbekistan.

As they were 120 years ago, the Dungans are still primarily farmers who live in relatively closed, endogamous communities. They have a very high birth rate of between six and eight children per family, and low rates of urbanization. The slight linguistic and cultural differences between those originally from Gansu Province and those from Shaanxi Province continue to be evident today; however, from the perspective of the surrounding Kyrgyz, Kazakhs, and Uzbeks, the Dungans all appear Chinese. They speak Russian and their own national languages in public and learn them in school, except for two hours per week, but the mother tongue of all Dungans remains Chinese. They still eat Chinese food in the Chinese manner and design and decorate their homes in a 19th-century Chinese style.

During the Soviet era visitors to the region did not see many signs of overt religious belief or practice. Rituals at weddings, funerals, and circumcisions seemed to these observers to reflect cultural tradition rather than religious adherence. Many Dungan scholars were Communists, while the majority of the population were successful farmers who lived much better than the rest of the population. Following the fall of the USSR in 1991 the Dungans experienced a tremendous religious revival. Prayers were said before every meal and many young Dungans made a point of speaking to outsiders about their religious faith. In 1991 two mosques were being built in one Dungan community and all young children were taking religious instructions. At this time the Dungans continued to live better than others in Central Asia, with large houses, cars, television sets, and more economic security than the rest of the population. Their small farms, rented from the government once the collective farms had been broken up, were the source of most of the produce available in markets throughout the region. They produce nearly half of all the vegetables and grain for the entire country of Kazakhstan.

As in many migrant communities, the Dungans have preserved aspects of their home culture that have not survived in the original context. For example their Chinese vocabulary has not been modernized and changed so that it sounds strange to contemporary speakers of the Gansu and Shaanxi dialects. Also in contrast to present-day China Dungan marriages are still often arranged through a matchmaker and involve the payment of both dowry, gifts to a bride from her own family, and bride price, gifts to the bride's parents from the husband and his family. The two-week-long ceremony itself also resembles those of 19th-century China; the women's hair is styled in the Qing dynasty manner, and the bride wears a red silk dress and matching embroidered shoes.

Durbets

The Durbets are a subgroup of the larger OIRAT or Western MONGOLS and share most of their history and cultural traits (*see also* ZUNG-HARS). As were other Oirat, and indeed other Mongols, the Durbets were traditionally primarily pastoralists who raised goats, sheep, cattle, camels, and, most important, horses. Community events tended to be dominated by horse racing and other activities related to the breeding, training, and selling of horses. They lived in portable felt tents or yurts that can be dismantled, moved, and reassembled to accommodate their frequent travels in search of grasslands and water. Nomadic or seminomadic Durbets lived primarily on milk and milk products, meat, and a special drink, koumiss or fermented mares' milk, a beverage of great antiquity among Eurasian nomads. They also traded milk and milk products, hides, and meat products with more settled populations in exchange for grains, especially millet, vegetables, and, in the present day, consumer goods. Even today significant numbers of rural Durbets continue to live this kind of nomadic

life, supported by their herds of animals. However a few rural families in Mongolia, including some Durbets, have settled down to engage in agriculture, growing such crops as corn, millet, melons, mustard seed, and sunflowers. About half the population of Mongolia lives either in the capital city, Ulaanbaatar, or in other towns and cities. These Durbets are largely assimilated into the wider Mongolian society and are indistinguishable from their Eastern Mongol neighbors, with the possible exception of accent or dialect differences in their speech (*see* MONGOLIANS: NATIONALITY).

Nomadic and seminomadic Durbets tend to live in nuclear family households, although married sons usually do not move far from their fathers and brothers, in order to share herds and labor. Agricultural families tend to live in more extended families with several generations residing together and working the same plots of land. Upon marriage in either situation young women move into their husband's household, a practice known as patrilocal residency. Prior to the 20th century most of these marriages would have been arranged by the parents in consultation with an astrologer and perhaps a Buddhist lama, to make sure the couple was compatible and the time of marriage auspicious. Today both rural and urban couples generally consult their parents but make these decisions on their own when they are in their 20s.

Despite the Mongolian persecution of Buddhists and Buddhism in the early 20th century, today many families maintain their beliefs and practices in a variety of Buddhist and pre-Buddhist traditions. Both shamans and lamas remain important to daily life and historic poetry continues to serve as an important feature of cultural life. Sites where local spirits are believed to reside, *obo,* continue to be maintained by the Durbets and to host a variety of religious rituals. The pre-Buddhist practice of "sky burial," in which the dead were left out to be devoured by wild animals, has been replaced by burial in the ground.

Durranis (Abdalis)

The Durranis are one of the tribal subgroups of the PASHTUNS of Afghanistan and Pakistan. Prior to 1747 and the election of Ahmad Khan Abdali as king of all the Pashtun people and the newly formed Kingdom of Afghanistan, the Durrani tribespeople were known as the Abdali. Upon his election Ahmad Khan took the title *Durr-i-Durran* (Pearl of Pearls) and became known as Ahmad Shah Durrani.

DURBETS

location:
Mongolia, China, Russia, and Kazakhstan

time period:
13th century to the present

ancestry:
Mongol

language:
Western Mongolian

DURRANIS

location:
Afghanistan and Pakistan with a few communities in Iran and India as well

time period:
About 500 C.E. to the present

ancestry:
Iranian

language:
Pashto, an eastern Iranian language, as well as Dari, sometimes called Afghan Persian

His own tribal group, the Abdali, likewise took the name *Durrani,* which they continue to use to the present day. There are four major clans within the Durrani tribe, Sadowzais, Popalzais, Achekzais, and Barakzais.

The Durranis are one of the largest Pashtun tribes and the one most urbanized and influenced by Persian. Many Durranis are bilingual in Pashto and Dari, sometimes called Afghan Persian. The Durranis see themselves as superior to other peoples, both Pashtuns and non-Pashtuns, because of their long association with the political leadership of Afghanistan. From 1747 to Muhammed Zahir Shah's overthrow in 1973 Afghanistan was ruled by a succession of Durrani kings who provided the sole basis for legitimate political authority over a people with an extremely strong egalitarian ideology. During much of the subsequent 35 years of conflict groups without a Durrani leader tended to be seen as illegitimate or weak by the Durranis and failed to win their support. For example during the struggle between Leftists and mujahideen fighters in the 1980s and early 1990s, many mujahideen groups received little support from the Durranis because they refused to include the former king in any transitional governing body. One exception to this trend was the Taliban, who allowed the Durranis to lay claim to their traditional leadership position. Another sign of the superiority they believe characterizes them is their marriage pattern. Durrani women are strictly forbidden to marry outside the tribe because of the high status of the Durranis in relation to other Pashtuns.

Rural Durranis live very much as other Pashtuns as well as the other tribal groups in Afghanistan and northeastern Pakistan, Persian-speaking AIMAQ and HAZARAS as well as UZBEKS and TURKMEN, do. They make their living by subsistence agriculture and herding and exist largely on a diet of bread made from wheat flour, dairy products, some seasonal vegetables, and occasionally meat.

Because of their long association with political power, many Durranis are also city dwellers who speak Dari, the language of power in the country. Kabul and Kandahar are both Pashtun-dominated cities with a significant number of Durranis living in them. Some urban Durranis may have only limited connections to their traditional tribal lands and customs, while others remain very much connected to their family's tribal roots. One example of this kind of relationship is the first post-Taliban president of Afghanistan, Hamid Karzai, a member of the Popalzai clan of the Durrani tribe. Karzai's father had been the chief of the Popalzais and thus combined his tribal responsibilities, mostly judging land claims and resolving other disputes within his tribe, with his high-ranking government position; he served the king Muhammad Zahir Shah until his deposition in 1973.

See also AFGHANISTANIS: NATIONALITY; AFRIDI; GHILZAI; PASHTUNS.

Dusun   *See* KADAZAN, DUSAN.

Dzhukhurs   *See* TATS AND MOUNTAIN JEWS.

E

Eastern Hu   *See* DONGHU.

East Timorese: nationality (East Timorese, people of East Timor, people of Timor-Leste)

The people of East Timor live in Asia's newest country, established in 1999.

GEOGRAPHY

East Timor is located on the eastern half of the island of Timor within the Malay Archipelago in Southeast Asia. It also includes the Oecussi region of the western half of the island and the islands of Pulau Atauro and Pulau Jaco. It is surrounded by bodies of water including the Timor Sea to the south and Ombai and Wetar Straits to the north.

Except on the country's mountain peaks, the highest of which is Mount Ramelau at 9,721 feet above sea level, the climate is generally hot and humid, characteristic of the tropical location. The rainy season, which begins in October, is usually a time for rejoicing on the island as it initiates a new agricultural season; recently, however, deforestation and the results of years of conflict have meant that rains generate mudslides, flooding, and other disasters.

INCEPTION OF NATION

The Portuguese arrived in the Malay Archipelago in the 16th century as the first European power to establish a base in the region. They focused most of their efforts on the export of sandalwood and other tropical products, such as spices and other hardwoods. In the following century the Dutch joined the Portuguese in the region, and in the mid-18th century the two European powers divided the island of Timor into two separate colonial spheres. The Dutch half in the west was administered from the capital of the Dutch East Indies in Batavia, now known as Jakarta, Indonesia, while the Portuguese administered their small colony from Dili in East Timor. The Dutch half of the island, as a remote province far from the seat of colonial power, was far less influenced by Dutch language and culture than the Portuguese half, where some of the population converted to Roman Catholicism and a few were educated in Portuguese schools and spoke the language. The history of Portuguese colonialism is often depicted as exploitative, neglectful, or both, a characterization that is not entirely inaccurate; however, there is also a strong connection in the country to the Portuguese past, which distinguishes the East Timorese from their Indonesian neighbors in West Timor.

The colonial situation in Timor continued relatively unabated until the mid-20th century when World War II brought it to an end. In 1941 the Dutch and Australians occupied the small island as part of the strategy to fight the JAPANESE in the Pacific. They were unsuccessful and one year later the Japanese occupied Timor, initiating three years of guerrilla warfare by the Timorese and Australians to expel the Japanese forces. In 1945 Japan withdrew and set the stage for independence throughout the former Dutch

**EAST TIMORESE:
NATIONALITY**

nation:
Democratic Republic of
Timor-Leste; East Timor

derivation of name:
Malay and Indonesian
term *timor* or *timur*,
meaning "east"

government:
Parliamentary democ-
racy with an elected
president, a power-shar-
ing arrangement that has
contributed to significant
instability in the new
country

capital:
Dili

language:
Official languages are
Tetum and Portuguese,
but 16 indigenous
languages as well as
Indonesian and English
are spoken.

religion:
No official state religion;
Roman Catholic 90 per-
cent, Muslim 4 percent,
Protestant 3 percent,
Hindu 0.5 percent, other

earlier inhabitants:
Melanesians

demographics:
Timorese including
Austronesian subgroups,
Papuan subgroups, and
Mestizos 78 percent;
Indonesian 19 percent;
Chinese 2 percent;
Portuguese 1 percent

East Timorese: nationality time line

C.E.

1515 Portuguese explorers reach the coast of Timor on what is now the enclave of Oecussi. They export sandalwood and make large profits until the tree becomes nearly extinct.

1613 The Dutch take control of the western part of the island.

1702 The arrival of the first Portuguese governor begins the official colonial period in the region.

1749 Timor is split between the Dutch and Portuguese with the Portuguese taking the eastern half.

1815 Coffee, sugarcane, and cotton plantations are created by the Portuguese.

1859 The Treaty of Lisbon formally gives West Timor to the Netherlands.

1915 The Portuguese and Dutch sign the Arbitrary Sentence, which ends violent clashes between the two countries. It also creates the borders that divide the island today.

1941 Timor's important strategic location in World War II leads to Dutch and Australian troops' occupying Dili over the protests of the Portuguese.

1942 The Japanese invade using the Australians' presence as justification.

1945 Japanese invasion ends. It is estimated that between 40,000 and 70,000 Timorese died during the occupation as they voluntarily sided with the Australians and fought against the Japanese. Portuguese control is reestablished after the Japanese leave.

1949 The Netherlands gives up its colonies in the East Indies, including West Timor, and the inde-pendent country of Indonesia is created.

1974 Portugal moves to the Left and a strong antifascist movement emerges.

1975 Portugal abruptly leaves East Timor. Fretilin (Revolutionary Front for an Independent East Timor) declares independence on November 28, following a short civil war. Few countries recognize the newly independent nation and nine days later Indonesian troops invade. Falintil (Armed Forces of National Liberation of East Timor), a guerrilla force and the armed wing of Fretilin, violently opposes the Indonesian occupation; at least 200,000 people die over the next two decades.

East Timor becomes Indonesia's 27th province.

1981 Xanana Gusmao becomes Falintil's new leader.

1991 More than 100 people are killed at the Santa Cruz Massacre when they march to the funeral of Sebastião Gomes, a young student and Fretilin supporter who was killed by Indonesian troops.

colonial territories; in 1949 Indonesia was cre-ated from these territories. The Portuguese, however, did not give up their overseas colonies for another quarter-century and East Timor re-mained a small Portuguese holding on the mar-gins of Indonesia.

Finally political change in Portugal in 1974, when the fascist government of Marcello Caetano was overthrown, led to the withdrawal of the entire Portuguese colonial apparatus throughout the world, including East Timor. Over the next year the small half-island nation achieved independence for a period of nine days before Indonesian troops occupied and then an-nexed the territory into the larger island nation. The United Nations denounced Indonesia's in-vasion and later annexation of the territory, but

no outside power was willing to protect East Timor's right to self-determination. Over the next quarter-century at least 200,000 East Ti-morese were killed and thousands more impris-oned in Indonesia's heavy-handed attempts to integrate the region into the country. Napalm, aerial bombing, and the creation of resettlement centers, all tactics that the United States had tried and that had failed in Vietnam, were em-ployed throughout the 1970s, 1980s, and early 1990s to try to bring East Timor under control. These tactics have been seen by experts on In-donesia as indicative of an attitude that the East Timorese were a colonial people to be conquered rather than Indonesians to be drawn into the fold of the larger nation. The populations of nei-ther Aceh nor West Papua, two other breakaway

1992 Gusmao is captured, convicted of subversion, and given a life sentence.

1996 Bishop Ximenes Belo and José Ramos-Horta are jointly awarded the Nobel Peace Prize for their work for peaceful freedom. The award raises international awareness of East Timor's struggle for independence.

1998 Indonesian President Suharto resigns amid economic crisis and calls for political change.

He is replaced by Vice President Dr. B. J. Habibie.

1999 In a referendum on independence 78 percent of East Timorese vote to support independence. Indonesia's military steps in and kills at least 1,000 civilians.

The UN Transitional Authority in East Timor (UNTAET) governs the newly independent nation.

2001 On August 30 free elections for the representatives who will write the constitution are held.

2002 A truth and reconciliation commission is established and an Indonesian human rights court is created to call to account military officials for killings and violence following the 1999 referendum outcome.

April 14 Xanana Gusmão becomes the first elected president.

May 20 East Timor declares independence and four months later becomes a member of the United Nations.

2005 The truth and reconciliation commission holds its first meeting.

2006 Australia and East Timor reach an agreement to split evenly profits from oil- and gasfields in the Timor Sea. They decide to wait 50 years to negotiate redrawing the border.

In May and April pandemonium in Dili occurs after fired soldiers striking over low wages and discrimination clash with soldiers who are loyal to Prime Minister Mari Alkatiri. Peacekeeping forces from Australia are necessary to restore order. Alkatiri resigns and Nobel laureate José Ramos-Horta takes over.

2007 Parliamentary and presidential elections once again pit Ramos-Horta and Akatiri supporters against each other in a bid to create lasting peace and stability in the new country. Few regional experts expect the elections to settle the country's divisions, and there are increasing fears that East Timor will become a failed state.

2008 Ramos-Horta is shot and seriously wounded by a rebel soldier; shots are also fired at Gusmão.

territories, have been treated in a similarly vicious manner (*see* ACEHNESE).

As was the case in the 1970s a change in government of East Timor's oppressor, this time the 1998 resignation of Indonesian President Suharto and his replacement by Vice President Habibie, produced change in East Timor. One year later East Timor held a referendum on independence in which 78 percent of the population voted to withdraw from Indonesia. The Indonesian military reacted with violence and killed at least 1,000 individuals before the United Nations stepped in with the UN Transitional Authority in East Timor (UNTAET) to guide the new country to a peaceful independence.

Unfortunately the path to independence has not been smooth in East Timor and the country

In 1996 East Timor's struggle for independence from Indonesia burst onto the world stage with the joint award of the Nobel Peace Prize to two of the region's most important activists, José Ramos-Horta (on the left) and Bishop Belo (on the right). *(AP/ Bjoern Sigurdsoen)*

José Ramos-Horta

José Ramos Horta was born in Dili, East Timor, to a Timorese mother and a Portuguese father on December 26, 1949. When he was a child, Ramos-Horta's village was invaded by the Indonesian military, which killed four of his 11 siblings. In 1983 Ramos-Horta graduated from the Hague Academy of International Law with a degree in public international law before going on to obtain a master's degree in peace studies at Antioch University in 1984. Prior to his studies Horta was actively involved in proindependence political campaigns, prompting the Portuguese government to exile him to Portuguese East Africa for two years in 1970. When he returned, proindependence parties elected Ramos-Horta foreign minister, and under the threat of an impending Indonesian invasion, Ramos-Horta left for New York in 1975 to implore the United Nations to take action on behalf of East Timor. The subsequent Indonesian invasion resulted in 200,000 deaths in East Timor between 1976 and 1981. Ramos-Horta became the permanent representative of Fretilin (Revolutionary Front for an Independent East Timor) in the UN council, and he spent the next several years traveling the world to incite global awareness of the plight of East Timor. In 1996, he was awarded the Nobel Peace Prize with fellow East Timorese citizen Bishop Carlos Filipe Ximines Belo for their "sustained efforts to hinder the oppression of a small people." In 2006 Ramos-Horta resigned as foreign minister and minister of defense amid disagreements with the government, particularly Prime Minister Alkatiri. Alkatiri resigned the next day and Ramos-Horta was appointed prime minister. In May 2007 Ramos-Horta was elected president of East Timor.

is still at risk of becoming a failed state. Part of the blame lies at the feet of the Indonesian military's harassment campaign of those responsible for independence in the 1990s; the country's lack of economic development and endemic poverty are also to blame. However, the greatest problem to date has been the rivalry between different political groups and factions over the right to establish a new governing structure. In 2006 this rivalry came to a head when supporters of President Xanana Gusmão and those of Prime Minister Mari Alkatiri clashed in the capital, Dili, and forced Alkatiri's resignation. Since May 2006 the country has turned out three times for different rounds of the federal election process, none of which has given one party a clear majority to set up a stable government.

CULTURAL IDENTITY

The creation of an East Timorese identity out of the 30 or so local indigenous groups, Mestizos, Portuguese, and others who reside there is almost entirely a reaction against Indonesian colonialism on the half-island. The Indonesian government and media rarely if ever referred to the people as anything other than East Timorese, ignoring all of the local linguistic, cultural, and political diversity. Indonesian schools, political processes, and of course the long reign of terror imposed by the military

also contributed greatly to the new identity. From these outside pressures and institutions a deep sense of common purpose emerged in East Timor in opposition to the Indonesian regime. Interestingly this kind of oppositional identity never formed in reaction to the much longer Portuguese colonial period because of the relative lack of interaction between most local people and the distant colonizers.

In addition the impetus within Indonesian-held East Timor from 1975 to 1998 for people to "develop" and adopt a world religion rather than local animistic beliefs drove thousands into the fold of the Catholic Church, the dominant world religion in the region. The church's subsequent decision to adopt Tetun as the lingua franca of the local Mass has since created a national language. These two cultural features, religion and language, have contributed further to the development of a national cultural identity where prior to the mid-1970s there was very little.

See also INDONESIANS: NATIONALITY; TETUNS.

FURTHER READING

Desmond Ball and Hamish McDonald, eds. *Masters of Terror: Indonesia's Military and Violence in East Timor in 1999* (Canberra: Australian National University Strategic & Defence Studies, 2002).

Hal Hill and João M. Saldanha, eds. *East Timor: Development Challenges for the World's Newest Nation* (Canberra: Australian National University, 2001).

Clement John, ed. *East Timor: Prospects for Peace* (Geneva: Unit on Justice, Peace, and Creation, World Council of Churches, 1995).

Jill Jolliffe. *East Timor: Nationalism and Colonialism* (St. Lucia, Queensland: University of Queensland Press, 1978).

Damien Kingsbury, ed. *Guns and Ballot Boxes: East Timor's Vote for Independence* (Melbourne: Monash Asia Institute, 2000).

John Martinkus. *A Dirty Little War* (New York: Random House, 2001).

Enga

The Enga are the largest indigenous group in Papua New Guinea, with a population of more than 200,000 in 2002. The best known subgroup are the Mae Enga, as a result of the prolific writing of the anthropologist Mervyn Meggitt, but there are about 100 different Enga tribes, including the Tombema, Laiapu, Taro, Tayato, Maramuni, Wage, Kandep, and Western and Central Enga. These last two are not groups recognized by the Enga themselves but are terms often used by outsiders to distinguish segments of the Enga population. Like much of the highlands population, the Enga are a patrilineal society: descent is reckoned only through men, with clans, subclans, lineages, and larger groups of clans known as phratries. The Enga are also patrilocal; at the time of her marriage a new wife must move into the hamlet of her new husband and his patrilineal group. To repay a new wife's family for having raised her as well as to make up for the loss of her household labor, an Enga man pays what is called bridewealth, usually in the form of pigs, to the father of his new wife. This payment serves to validate the marriage and legitimate any children who result from the pairing. Traditionally men and women lived in separate houses within the hamlet, but today nuclear families more commonly live together. Nonetheless because of the fear of women's pollution, husbands and wives tend to sleep in separate rooms, meeting together only occasionally for purposes of procreation.

The main subsistence activity for the Enga is gardening, and the primary food item for the last 250–400 years has been sweet potatoes, although the Enga also rely on taro, bananas, beans, and vegetables. The land on which the Enga reside is marked by granite peaks as well as dense forest and, unfortunately, is relatively low in wild game, leaving the population protein-hungry most of the time. The Enga dedicate a significant amount of time, effort, and food resources toward raising pigs, but there is rarely enough meat to satisfy the entire population. In part this is because raising pigs is much more associated with ritual and exchange than it is with subsistence. As is the case in much of the highlands, pigs are the primary source of wealth among the Enga. Marriage, proper death rites, and most other major events in a person's life are marked by an exchange of pigs and occasionally a ritual pork feast as well.

The most important ritual associated with the exchange of pigs is called the *tee,* an enormous event that takes place about every four years, the time necessary for enough pigs to be produced to make a suitable gift. This exchange is primarily one between two different clans with men within each clan participating both as individuals and as representatives of their clan. The *tee* is competitive; each clan tries to outdo the other in terms of the size of its gift of pigs and other wealth, including shells, and in recent times, cash and other material gifts. Internally the *tee* also provides an opportunity for men within each clan to compete with their relatives for the status of Big Man, a position that confers great respect and prestige but no actual leadership or power. The ability to get others to contribute toward one's own exchange and the capacity

to convince others to allow one to name the date of a large-scale exchange are two areas in which clan members compete with one another.

Another central feature of Enga society, at least prior to pacification by the Australians in the 20th century, was the frequent warfare between different clans or tribes. Rather than war as Westerners understand the concept, with its high rates of death and destruction, Enga warfare was more ceremonial. Certainly a few individuals might have been injured or killed during the clash between men, but Enga warfare was more about displaying relative strength and redistributing land than about vanquishing enemies. These wars usually took place between two tribes or clans over the course of many generations. There were not constant battles, but every few years two groups would meet together to display their relative strength through warfare. This practice was a mechanism for ensuring that the larger and stronger of the two groups got more land when they needed it as well as being a stage for a *tee* exchange, which usually followed the actual war.

As is the case throughout Melanesia, Enga religion centers on the words and deeds of their ancestors (*see* MELANESIANS). As part of this system, men traditionally spent many long hours in the men's houses repeating and analyzing the prophetic messages handed down by their distant ancestors. There is a long history of trying to connect contemporary events both with these prophecies and with mythological stories, or *tindi*. This cultural tradition was the ideal foundation for Christian missionaries, who arrived among the Enga in the middle of the 20th century and introduced their own set of prophecies and stories. As a result today the Enga tend to be very interested in connecting their own histories to biblical events like the flood and plagues, which have local equivalents as seen in their own mythological stories. This combination of local and Christian beliefs has resulted in the development of many small cults during the past 60 to 70 years, some of which are traditional cargo cults while others are unconcerned with an expectation of a large delivery of Western goods.

See also NEW GUINEA HIGHLANDERS.

FURTHER READING

Mervyn Meggitt. *Blood Is Their Argument: Warfare among the Mae Enga Tribesmen of the New Guinea Highlands* (Palo Alto, Calif.: Mayfield Publishing, 1977).

Polly Wiessner and Akii Tumu. *Historical Vines: Enga Networks of Exchange, Ritual, and Warfare in Papua New Guinea* (Washington, D.C.: Smithsonian, 1998).

ENGA

location:
Enga Province in western highlands of Papua New Guinea

time period:
Unknown to the present

ancestry:
Melanesian

language:
Enga

ETORO

location:
The northeast corner of the Strickland-Bosavi area of the highlands of Papua New Guinea, which is bounded by the Strickland River and Mount Bosavi

time period:
Unknown to the present

ancestry:
Melanesian

language:
Edolo

Eta *See* BURAKUMIN.

Etoro (Edolo, Etolo)

The Etoro are a small community of people residing in the northeast corner of the Strickland-Bosavi region of the highlands of Papua New Guinea. Despite their size only a few hundred in number, the Etoro are well known throughout the world because their belief system differs so greatly from that of most Westerners. As do most other groups in the Strickland-Bosavi region, the Etoro believe that semen is the source of all male strength and power. Furthermore, they believe that semen is a limited good that cannot be produced by men but only passed down from older men to pubescent boys. As a result of these ideas, men are reluctant to share their precious semen with women and do so only for purposes of procreation and only on certain ritual days, of which there are about 100 per year. In addition, ritualized homosexual male initiation rites require younger men to swallow the semen of their elders so that they in turn gain adult status and the ability to inseminate younger boys and women.

The Etoro are also interesting because they differ from many other NEW GUINEA HIGHLANDERS, who place pigs at the center of their prestige and subsistence systems. Rather than the ability to exchange pigs, prestige for Etoro men is gained through acts of generosity: as a provider of semen to boys, hunted meat, and, today, trade goods. A man's work as a spirit medium, providing protection against witchcraft, is also central to his standing in society. Etoro women are seen as inferior to men because they cannot do these things. With regard to subsistence rather than the usual highland combination of sweet potatoes and pigs, the Etoro rely on sago as their primary starch, shifting horticulture for vegetables and greens, and both hunting and fishing. Semidomesticated pigs are also available occasionally as a food source. Today a few Etoro also have access to consumer products, which have contributed processed foods to their diet as well.

Kinship is also central to the Etoro conception of the world. As is common in the New Guinea highlands, the Etoro are patrilineal, so that descent is passed down from fathers to their children. They also practice bride service: new husbands must work in the gardens of their inlaws for a number of seasons in order to legitimate both their own marriage and any resulting children. Although today they largely live in nuclear family households, traditionally the Etoro lived primarily in communal longhouses, with men at one end and women and children at the other. One house usually contained a number of brothers and their wives and children, but other members of the brothers' patrilineal clan might also have resided there.

While all women and men participate in gardening activities and in the processing of sago, only men are able to become spirit mediums. This is a tremendously important position in a society such as the Etoro where fear of witchcraft dominates people's thinking, even today. Witchcraft is so feared that people whose families suffer considerable hardship, such as the death of a healthy spouse or child, or who seem to disregard the advice or opinions of their elders may actually be executed by their family members as witches. The anthropologist Raymond Kelly, who has studied the Etoro since the 1960s, has written of a woman who was executed as a witch by her closest male kinsman; he slit her throat during the night following a long period of misfortune and the woman's failure to heed the warnings of her female elders.

See also MELANESIANS.

FURTHER READING

Raymond C. Kelly. *Constructing Inequality: The Fabrication of a Hierarchy of Virtue among the Etoro* (Ann Arbor: University of Michigan Press, 1993).

Evenkis (Ewenkis, Evenks, Tungus)

The Evenkis are one of the indigenous peoples of Siberia; they also live in Mongolia and are one of the 55 recognized minority groups in China. In the past the Evenkis were referred to as the Tungus and were categorized together with several other related groups, including the EVENS and Negidal people. They have been known as Evenkis since 1931.

The original home of all the Tungusic people was the region around Lake Baikal in southern Siberia. From there the Evenkis migrated eastward, toward the Amur River and the coast of the Okhotsk Sea, and northward to the tundra and as far as the Arctic Ocean. This migration probably happened at the beginning of the first millennium when pressure from the TURKIC PEOPLES forced other peoples either to assimilate or to move.

Those Evenkis who migrated to the north traditionally engaged in nomadic hunting and reindeer herding as their primary subsistence activities. The key to the development of Evenki culture in these areas was the domestication

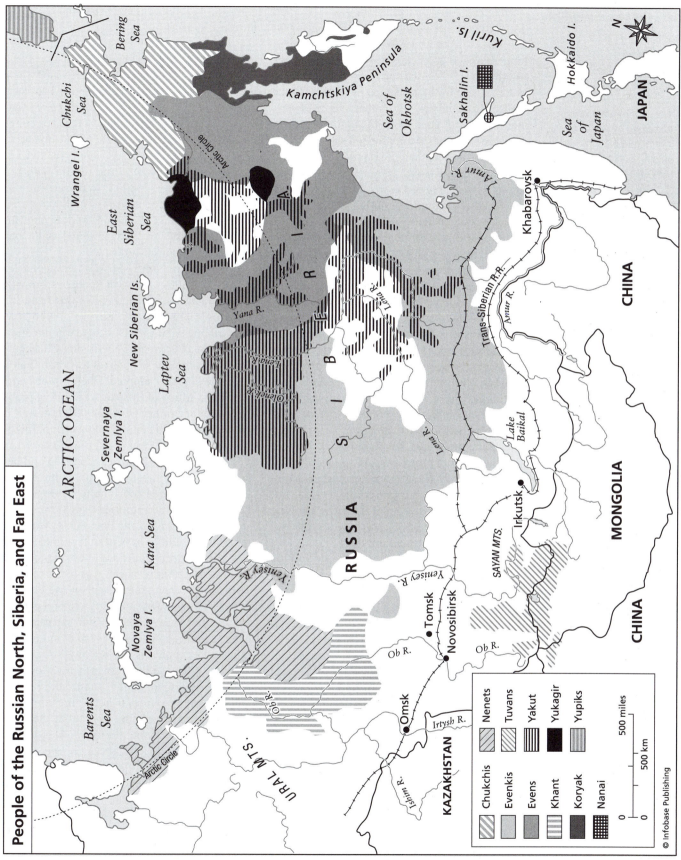

People of the Russian North, Siberia, and Far East

JAPAN

CHINA

MONGOLIA

KAZAKHSTAN

RUSSIA

CHINA

ARCTIC OCEAN

Kamchtskiya Peninsula

Bering Sea

Chukchi Sea

Wrangel I.

East Siberian Sea

New Siberian Is.

Laptev Sea

Severnaya Zemlya I.

Kara Sea

Novaya Zemlya I.

Barents Sea

Sea of Okhotsk

Sakhalin I.

Kuril Is.

Hokkaido I.

Sea of Japan

Amur R.

Khabarovsk

Trans-Siberian R.R.

Lake Baikal

Irkutsk

SAYAN MTS.

Lena R.

Yenisey R.

Tomsk

Novosibirsk

Ob R.

Ob R.

Omsk

Irtysh R.

Ishim R.

URAL MTS.

Arctic Circle

Yana R.

Lena R.

Olenek R.

Yenisey R.

S I B E R I A

Arctic Circle

Legend:

Chukchis

Evenkis

Evens

Khant

Koryak

Nanai

Nenets

Tuvans

Yakut

Yukagir

Yupiks

500 miles

500 km

0

0

© Infobase Publishing

EVENKIS

location:
Siberia's vast territory from the river Ob in the west to the Okhotsk Sea in the east, from the Arctic Ocean in the north to Manchuria in the south; also in Mongolia and China.

time period:
Unknown to the present

ancestry:
Tungusic

language:
Evenk, a Tungusic language within the larger Altaic language family

of reindeer, used for pack animals and even for riding. Without these animals hunting in the vast, cold tundra would have been almost impossible. Those Evenkis who stayed farther south and east around the area of Lake Baikal were subject to the influence of the MONGOLS and utilized horses and camels for transport and bred cattle and sheep for food. They also engaged in some farming of tobacco and vegetables. As among their northern cousins, however, hunting remained extremely important in these southern regions as well. All Evenkis also fished in the summer months when the seas and rivers of Siberia were not frozen.

Starting in 1606 the Evenkis began to interact with the RUSSIANS, beginning with a taxation system that required the Evenkis to pay in furs, which ultimately changed their lives and culture forever. In the 17th and 18th centuries Russian Orthodox missionaries also began their work in Siberia. A degree of conversion took place among the Evenkis, but indigenous shamanism also continued well into the 20th century. The Evenkis avoided the worst excesses of this period of Russian colonization by virtue of their mobility. When disease or onerous tax burdens threatened their way of life, they packed up their tents, belongings, and reindeer and moved out of the Russians' sphere of influence. Generally these moves necessitated giving up access to the region's larger rivers. But not all Evenkis moved out of the pathway of the early Russian pioneers. Trade between the two groups increased throughout the 17th and 18th centuries, and some Evenkis even served in the Cossack regiments that guarded the settlements in the region.

The first decades of the 20th century produced even more change with the onslaught of Soviet ideology and social restructuring of all peoples within the sphere of the USSR. For the Evenkis this meant the creation of tribal councils and executive committees, which instituted a centralized authority system for the Evenkis for the first time in their history, replacing the relatively egalitarian rule by consensus that had dominated their band-based society for millennia. In 1927 the Evenkis were reorganized yet again, this time on the basis of geography and residence with the creation of councils at the village, district, and territory levels. Just three years later the Evenkis were granted a national territory of their own, but since only about one-tenth of the Evenki population resided within it, and its population was only about one-fifth Evenki, the territorial creation was and remains essentially meaningless for most Evenkis.

Even more than these political restructurings the economic restructuring of the Evenkis' nomadic subsistence pattern came their lives forever. Collectivization entered to eastern Siberia in the 1930s along with permanent homes, schools, hospitals, and other trappings of Russian village life. At the same time reindeer breeding and herding were collectivized; brigades of men lived on the tundra with the herds while their families were settled into these villages. The results of this policy were increased loneliness, alienation, and alcoholism among men and loss of traditional skills and knowledge among children.

Interactions with Russian missionaries in the 17th, 18th, and 19th centuries brought about a conversion of many Evenkis from indigenous shamanism to Russian Orthodoxy. Even among China's 21st-century population of about 36,000 Evenkis, Orthodox Christianity is the dominant religion, at least nominally; some Evenkis also adopted Tibetan Mahayana Buddhism. Much of this conversion was probably voluntary rather than coerced; however, it was generally not a complete conversion. Indigenous shamanistic ideas about the spirit world's causing harm or assistance and curing and beliefs about thanking the spirits of hunted or slaughtered animals continue to be important in rural Evenki communities even today.

Some Evenkis in the post-Soviet world of the 1990s and 2000s have been trying to recapture some of the traditional subsistence and cultural practices of their people by making claims to the new government of the Russian Federation for unfettered access to and ownership of their land. As both their spiritual and material home, land for the Evenkis, as for most indigenous peoples, is the key to their cultural survival. With the push for privatization that has occurred throughout Russia since 1991, land and the resources it holds, including oil, gas, and mineral wealth, are among the most important issues facing the Evenkis and other indigenous peoples of Siberia. In one case of land tenure the Evenkis have even fought to stop archaeological excavation of mammoth remains on their land, with the claim that such an excavation goes against their belief that animals can be taken only when they present themselves for such a purpose, and even then gifts must be given in exchange. Despite being able to exert greater pressure on the Russian government than ever before, the Evenkis today remain on the margins of Russian political and economic life. As are most of the indigenous peoples of the Far North, they are on average poorer and less well educated and have higher morbidity and mortality rates than other Russian citizens.

FURTHER READING

David G. Anderson. *Identity and Ecology in Arctic Siberia: The Number One Reindeer Brigade* (New York: Oxford University Press, 2000).

Gail A. Fondahl. *Gaining Ground? Evenkis, Land, and Reform in Southeastern Siberia* (Boston: Allyn & Bacon, 1998).

Juha Janhunen. *Material on Manchurian Khamnigan Evenki* (Helsinki: Finno-Ugrian Society, 1991).

Evens (Eben, Erpe, Eveny, Evesil, Inkan Bey, Koraramkyn, Koyayakyn, Lamu, Lamut, Omuk, Orach)

The Evens are one of the indigenous peoples of Siberia and the Far East of Russia. They are related to the EVENKI people, and prior to 1931 the two groups, along with the Negidals, were all classified together as Tungus people. This classification ignored significant linguistic and cultural differences among the groups and was changed to be more ethnographically and linguistically accurate.

The Evens constitute most of the Tungus-language speakers who migrated to eastern Yakutia, along the Kolyma River, and north of the Okhotsk Sea. Their divergence from the Evenki people occurred about 1,500 years ago, according to linguists who have studied their two Tungusic languages, probably when TURKIC PEOPLES began moving and displaced the Evens and Evenki from their homeland around Lake Baikal. The Evens' migration to the northeast of Siberia was not without its conflicts. The sedentary KORYAK who already occupied the area around the Sea of Okhotsk fiercely resisted the entry of the nomadic hunting and reindeer-herding Evens. The YUKAGIRS also put up resistance to the Evens in the 15th and 16th centuries prior to the pacification of the area by the RUSSIANS in the following centuries. All of these people used spears and bows and arrows in the preliminary stage of conflict and then followed up with hand-to-hand combat, using long-handled knives.

With the arrival of the Russians in Siberia's Far East the relationships among the region's indigenous people changed. The Evens finally consolidated their territory as far east as the Kamchatka Peninsula with Russian assistance; in exchange for their territorial integrity the Evens imposed the Russian taxation system on the other indigenous peoples. Diseases introduced by the Russian traders, missionaries, and government officials significantly reduced the populations of all these indigenous groups at this time, though perhaps more so among the settled Koryaks than the nomadic Evens. Despite the deleterious effects of the Russians' policies, taxation, and disease on the region's native peoples, the interactions among the Evens, Yukagirs, Koryak, CHUKCHIS, and other peoples in the region were peaceful from the later years of the 18th century forward. These centuries of peace have allowed for considerable cultural blending among all the Siberian indigenous peoples so that today the Evens are still a Tungusic-speaking people but with a highly syncretic culture that blends elements from their own and other people's traditions. For example they began to herd reindeer in large groups and to use sleighs for transport after these were introduced by the Koryak and to build conical tents that combine features of their own tepees and the tents of the Chukchis.

Until the 1930s much of this syncretic indigenous culture remained relatively intact, with Even families migrating seasonally between the summer pastures in the mountains and the winter hunting grounds on the taiga. The specific routes that each family took and the places where they settled were strictly dictated by clan "ownership" of the land, which provided the ability to use the land and its resources rather than ownership as capitalism defines the term. Hunting was controlled by clan tradition as well as by Even spiritual beliefs, which taught that killing more animals than was absolutely necessary or killing without thanking the animal's spirit with a gift was prohibited; ignoring these beliefs and traditions would cause the spirit of hunting to turn against the transgressor as punishment. The native shamanistic religion and the large rituals that drew together Evens from many different clans also occurred regularly through the 1930s. The largest celebration was held on June 21, considered the Evens' New Year, and was marked by singing, dancing, and feasting.

With the formation of the Soviet Union after the 1917 revolution "the small peoples of the North" began to see changes in the policy toward them. These policies, which included settling them into villages, introducing Russian education and health care systems, and eliminating the last vestiges of the indigenous religious systems, were not necessarily less

EVENS

location:
Siberia, west of the Sea of Okhotsk

time period:
Unknown to the present

ancestry:
Tungusic

language:
Even, a Siberian language within the Manchu-Tungus branch of the Altaic language family

destructive culturally than those of the Russian Empire, but they did allow for population expansion. In addition to "civilization" as the Russians thought of it, Soviet policy after 1928 included collectivization of hunting, fishing, and reindeer breeding to replace the subsistence activities of the Evens. World War II and the decades that followed also produced great economic change in the region with the Soviet push for industrialization east of the Ural Mountains. This was done originally to keep these industries out of the hands of the Germans but continued after the war when oil and gas were exploited in the region. This industrialization drew huge numbers, relatively speaking, of ethnic Russians into territory that had formerly had just a handful of nonindigenous people. It also generated jobs in construction and mining and work on oil and gas wells for the native peoples, many of whom abandoned traditional subsistence patterns in favor of the cash economy. The end results are a damaged environment, increased morbidity and mortality rates, and near-destruction of the indigenous way of life. In the years since the fall of the Soviet Union in 1991 the Evens have joined other indigenous northern peoples in the Russian Association of Indigenous Peoples of the North, Siberia and Far East (RAIPON), in the fight to maintain their linguistic, cultural, and ecological integrity in the face of increasing industrialization in their region.

F

Farsiwan (Dehgans, Fars, Parsis, Parsibans, Parsiwans)

The Farsiwan are a half-million-strong subgroup of TAJIKS living in Afghanistan. They differ from the majority of Tajiks in their adherence to Shiite Islam, whereas Tajiks are generally Sunni. Culturally and linguistically they are similar to the Persians of Iran, differing largely in their accent, which is closer to Dari, the Persian spoken in Afghanistan, than to Iranian Persian.

Farsiwan identity is less important to many members of this community than is their affiliation with a region or city. Many Farsiwan reside in cities, especially Herat and Kandahar, and make a living as craftsmen or as bureaucrats. Especially for Farsiwan living in Herat the identification of Herati is often more important than this linguistic identification. Rural Farsiwan are more likely to be sedentary farmers of wheat and corn than nomadic pastoralists moving seasonally with their herds of animals.

As have many minority groups in Afghanistan, especially the HAZARAS, the Farsiwan have a long history of being subjugated and attempts at ethnic cleansing at the hands of the Afghan government. In the 19th century Abdur Rahman, the Iron Emir, moved many PASHTUNS, especially from the dominant DURRANIS, into the border region inhabited by the Farsiwan in an attempt to dilute their power. In the 1990s and early 2000s the Taliban again tried to rid the country of a population it saw as anathema in the areas of language, culture, and religion. Those years, however, were not all bleak for this minority. Between 1992 and 1994 when most of the fighting in Afghanistan centered around Kabul, the Farsiwan in the western region of the country attained some stability under the leadership of Ismail Khan in Herat. The Farsiwan community was able to organize itself around

Ismail Khan in 2003 after returning to Afghanistan from Iran; forces loyal to him retook his home city of Herat on March 22, 2004, after an extended battle the day before in which his own son was killed. *(AP/Amir Shah)*

FARSIWAN

location:
Afghanistan

time period:
Unknown to the present

ancestry:
Persian

language:
In Persian the name *Farsiwan* means "Persian speaker."

INDIGENOUS FIJIANS

location:
Fiji, an archipelago of 844 islands in the South Pacific, about 2,775 miles southwest of Hawaii and 1,100 miles north of New Zealand

time period:
1500 B.C.E. to the present

ancestry:
Polynesian and Melanesian

language:
Fijian, in the Melanesian branch of the larger Austronesian language family

a local legal system, begin to disarm, and reopen schools, all while the Pashtuns, Tajiks, and others in and around Kabul fought bitterly over that city. Unfortunately in 1995 Pakistani forces working for the Taliban attacked Herat and quickly took the city away from its largely disarmed Farsiwan leaders. Khan escaped to Iran, and the Taliban, strengthened by its easy victory, went on to capture most of the rest of the country and impose its own views.

As Shiite Muslims the Farsiwan differ from Afghanistan's Sunni majority in some important ways. The first is in the recognition of the proper succession to Muhammad's authority. Sunnis recognize Abu Bakr as the first caliph or leader after the death of Muhammad in 632 C.E., followed by Umar, Uthman, and Ali. Shiites believe that Ali should have been first because of his kinship with the Prophet. The term *Shiite* is derived from the Arabic phrase *Shiat Ali,* partisans of Ali. Another difference is the interpretation of sections of the Quran in which God the person is mentioned. For Shiites references to God's limbs and hands are merely metaphors; God does not have a visible body. Sunnis, on the other hand, take these passages literally as references to the hands of god.

While many *druas* are extremely large, this ceremonial version was made in 1927 merely to illustrate for visiting British royalty—in this case the duchess of York, the future Queen Mother—the style and shape of these canoes. *(Photo by British Combine/British Combine/Time & Life Pictures/Getty Images)*

Fijian Indians   *See* INDO-FIJIANS.

Fijians, Indigenous

The word *Fiji* is a Tongan derivation of the indigenous name *Viti,* still used for the country's largest island, Viti Levu. The first indigenous peoples to settle the Fiji Islands in 1500 B.C.E. were probably POLYNESIANS who left the Bismarck Archipelago bearing their distinctive LAPITA CULTURE pottery; ultimately these people would have come from Taiwan and southern China in the initial Austronesian exoduses. MELANESIANS from Vanuatu, New Caledonia, and the Soloman Islands probably arrived somewhat later, though the archaeological evidence is still unclear about the exact chronology of these arrivals.

Subsistence farming, fishing, and forestry are the central components of life for most Indigenous Fijians on remote and isolated islands, but even on the larger islands semisubsistence production and consumption are important economic activities. Cassava, taro, yams, sweet potatoes, and *yagona,* from which the national drink, kava, is made, are the preferred subsistence crops of Fijian farmers. In addition sugarcane and coconuts as well as a number of different tropical fruits are produced for sale.

Trade has traditionally been an important part of the Indigenous Fijian economy, especially long-distance trade with neighboring islands such as Tonga. This activity was made possible by the renowned and expert ship builders of Fiji. Ship making was the exclusive realm of the men and the most impressive were the gigantic double-hulled *drua.* Capable of carrying well over 100 warriors on their quarter-acre decks, the drua took as long as seven years to construct and required the resources of the entire community. Today the art of shipbuilding has been reduced to a very small scale, with modern powerboats the preferred method of travel.

Indigenous Fijian culture is shaped by both Melanesian and Polynesian influences. For example the Polynesian system for selecting chiefs based on kinship, which is almost unheard of in Melanesia, is used in Fiji. Additionally it is quite common for Indigenous Fijians of the Lau Islands of eastern Fiji and Polynesians of neighboring Tonga to intermarry. At the same time the family unit, village, and land (*vanua*), which are central in both Melanesian and Polynesian societies, are cornerstones of the highly communal Fijian society. The primary social unit is a segment of the larger patrilineal group, an exogamous kinship unit, membership in which each person inherits from his or her father. The smaller family unit, which is usually the primary unit for both production and consumption, generally includes a senior couple, their unmarried children, and the family of a married son or two; in rural areas it is common for a new bride to move into the household of her husband, a practice called patrilocal residence, and assume the domestic duties of that household. It is also not uncommon for extended family members such as a sister of the head of the household and/or a widowed parent or grandchildren to be included in the one residence. As a result Fijian households can be quite large and can include many generations,

Polynesian and Melanesian influences are also evident in the arts and crafts of Fiji, which are separated by gender and dictated by strict rituals. For example the strictly male activities of carving and launching the drua required the ritual sacrifice of many men, whose bodies were used as roller logs to launch the drua into a literal sea of blood for its first voyage. Pottery making also has a long history in the region and remains a vibrant art form for women today, particularly in Nadronga and Rewa Provinces and in the village of Nalotu on Kadavu Island. Also associated with women is the making of *masi* or barkcloth, from the bark of mulberry trees and colored with distinctive Fijian motifs of black on brown. Masi are used for various celebrations throughout the life cycle, from wrapping a newborn baby for its first journey from the hospital to draping a coffin and covering the grave in preparation for the afterlife.

Much of the Indigenous Fijian tradition of elaborate body art, face painting, and hairdressing was widespread throughout the islands from precontact up to the 1940s. Used in everyday casual wear, in festive or war ceremonies, and as an indicator of social status in the community, the special designs were banned by missionaries, who saw them as disgraceful symbols of paganism. Indigenous colors were black, red, white, and yellow. Men usually wore the colors of war, black and red, on their faces and chests and women decorated their eyes with fine black circles. The spidery web tattoo on the elbows and arms, originally used symbolically to let out bad blood, is the one remaining pattern still seen today and has been adopted as part of a global trend in body art. Today temporary face paint is used only during performances of traditional Fijian dances such as the ceremonial Meke, or in the presentation of a Tabua (whale tooth) on significant occasions.

See also AUSTRONESIANS; MELANESIANS.

FURTHER READING

Andrew Arno. *The World of Talk on a Fijian Island: An Ethnography of Law and Communicative Causation* (Norwood, N.J.: Ablex, 1993).

Anne E. Becker. *Body, Self, and Society: The View from Fiji* (Philadelphia: University of Pennsylvania Press, 1995).

Semi B. Seruvakula. *Bula Vakavanua* (Suva: Institute of Pacific Studies, University of the South Pacific, 2000).

Fijians: nationality (people of Fiji)

GEOGRAPHY

Fiji consists of 332 islands in the southwest Pacific Ocean, about one-third of which are inhabited. The two largest are Viti Levu and Vanua Levu; 90 percent of the population lives on these two islands. Most of the islands are of volcanic origin and are mountainous and surrounded by coral reefs. Dense tropical forests cover 65 percent of the islands, but there are fertile plains along the coasts. Flatland is found where rivers form deltas.

INCEPTION AS A NATION

The first inhabitants of the Fiji Islands were probably representatives of the LAPITA CULTURE, essentially POLYNESIANS, who settled there at least 3,500 years ago. A second population also settled in Fiji in prehistoric times, MELANESIANS from the Solomon Islands and Vanuatu, who probably arrived several centuries after the initial Polynesian settlement. In most regions these two waves of settlers generally intermixed and lived in small communities. In the fertile delta regions of southwest Viti Levu, the largest of the Fijian islands, however, larger communities developed. Traditional INDIGENOUS FIJIAN society was hierarchical and warfare was common, as tribal chiefs attempted to consolidate larger areas under their control by forming of alliances or by conquest.

Following thousands of years of independent development as well as 150 years of off-and-on contact with European explorers, during the 1830s Methodist missionaries, traders, whalers, and escaped Australian convicts arrived in the islands seeking souls and fortunes. In the early 19th century some of these traders discovered Fiji's sandalwood forests and began exporting large quantities of the material. This trade gained wealth and power for some indigenous chiefs, but it also introduced the musket. This combination led to increased rivalries

---

FIJIANS: NATIONALITY

nation:
Republic of the Fiji Islands, Fiji

derivation of name:
Tongan version of the indigenous name *Viti,* still used in the name of the country's largest island, Viti Levu

government:
Parliamentary democracy, with a president, who is head of state, and a prime minister, who is the head of the government

capital:
Suva

language:
English is the official language, but Fijian and Hindi are taught in the schools.

religion:
No state religion; Christian 52 percent (Methodist 37 percent, Roman Catholic 9 percent), Hindu 38 percent, Muslim 8 percent, other 2 percent

earlier inhabitants:
Polynesians, Melanesians

demographics:
Indigenous Fijian 51 percent (predominantly Melanesian with a Polynesian admixture); Indian 44 percent; European, other Pacific Islanders, Chinese, and other 5 percent

Fijians: nationality time line

B.C.E.

1500 First indigenous peoples, probably Polynesians, settle the Fiji Islands. Melanesians probably arrive somewhat later, though the archaeological evidence is still somewhat unclear about who arrived first.

C.E.

1643 Dutch explorer Abel Tasman is the first European to sight the islands.

1792 Captain William Bligh arrives in Fiji on H.M.S. *Providence.*

1820s The first European settlement is established on the island of Ovalau.

1830s The London Missionary Society arrives.

1840 The United States Exploring Expedition, led by Commodore Charles Wilkes, creates the first reliable maps of Fiji.

1854 Ratu Seru Cakobau, a regional leader, accepts Christianity and most Fijians follow his lead.

1865 Fiji's first constitution is drawn up and signed by seven independent chiefs.

Cakobau is elected president.

1871 European settlers form a national government and name Cakobau king of Fiji.

1874 At the request of Cakobau and other chiefs Fiji is annexed by Great Britain.

1875 Fiji's first governor, Sir Arthur Gordon, arrives.

Measles is introduced by a local chief who had been to Australia, and more than 40,000 people, about a quarter of the population, die.

1879 The *Leonidas* arrives, carrying the first group of indentured laborers from India. By 1916 more than 60,000 Indians will be taken to Fiji.

1916 The British government halts the recruitment of indentured laborers.

1940 Native Lands Trust Board is established to serve as the custodian of lands owned by Indigenous Fijians.

1942 A force of 6,500, which does not include Indo-Fijians, is recruited to fight with the Allies in World War II.

1963 The first general elections, which give Fijians total franchise, are held. These elections also see the first Indian-dominated political party.

1970 Fiji becomes an independent state and a member of the United Nations.

Ratu Sir Kamisese Mara becomes prime minister.

---

between Fijian groups and ultimately to a new confederation led by Ratu Seru Cakobau, a regional leader. In 1854 Cakobau accepted Christianity, placing many Indigenous Fijians, under the influence of Methodist missionaries.

By the 1860s European settlers were arriving in Fiji, hoping to build cotton plantations and capitalize on the soaring price of cotton caused by a worldwide shortage owing to the American Civil War. As they were to do again and again through the present day, disputes over land and power in Fiji's disparate ethnic communities contributed to general mistrust and instability in the islands. European attempts at government failed and the ongoing chaos, caused by

the struggle for power among the leading chiefs and between the Fijians and the colonizers, led the chiefs to cede Fiji to Great Britain on October 10, 1874, in the hope that this would produce peace and order. This act has been seen in subsequent years as one of the unique features that set Fiji apart from the other postcolonial Pacific nations: Fiji was not colonized against the wishes of the local leadership and Fijians never gave up title to their land.

In an effort to jump-start the new colony's economy, Sir Arthur Gordon, the first governor, promoted the immigration of indentured Indian laborers and urged the Colonial Sugar Refining Company to invest in Fiji. When the indenture

1973 Ratu Sir George Cakobau is appointed governor general.

1983 Ratu Sir Penaia Ganilau becomes governor general.

1987 Lieutenant Colonel Sitiveni Ligamamada Rabuka of the Royal Fiji Military Forces leads a bloodless coup after an election that puts in power a new government that is widely perceived as being dominated by Indo-Fijians.

Rabuka leads a second coup and declares Fiji a republic and appoints Governor General Ratu Sir Penaia Ganilau as president. Ganilau then appoints Mara as prime minister for a second time. Ties are severed with the British monarchy, though not with the Commonwealth of Nations.

1990 A new constitution is written.

1994 Rabuka becomes prime minister.

Mara is chosen by the Great Council of Chiefs to be president.

1997 A new constitution increases the rights of ethnic Indians, encourages multiculturalism, and makes multiparty government mandatory.

1999 Mahenda Chaudhry becomes the first ethnic Indian prime minister.

2000 Nationalist gunmen storm parliament, taking Chaudhry and his ministers hostage. They demand Chaudhry's resignation and suspension of the 1997 constitution. The military takes control, imposes martial law, and installs Laisenia Qarase, an Indigenous Fijian, as prime minister.

Fijian hereditary chief Ratu Josefa Iloilo is named the new president.

2001 Elections put Qarase's Fijian United Party in power and Qarase becomes prime minister.

Qarase's government is ruled illegal by the courts. New elections lead to a coalition government and Qarase again becomes prime minister.

2003 Qarase's government is ruled unconstitutional because it does not include members of the opposition Labour Party. The Labour Party refuses to join the government when Qarase excludes Chaudhry.

2004 Chaudhry agrees to lead the Labour Party, resolving the standoff.

2006 Prime Minister Qarase is reelected. The opposition Labour Party, led by Chaudhry, accepts seven of the 17 seats in the cabinet. This is the first time an opposition party has been part of the cabinet.

In December military leader Frank Bainimarama stages a military coup that leads to the suspension of Fiji from the British Commonwealth.

2007 Bainimarama gives executive power to President Iloilo, schedules elections for 2010, and fires the Great Council of Chiefs.

system ended in 1920, INDO-FIJIANS challenged the commercial and political domination of the small European community, creating one of the many power conflicts that would continue to plague Fiji into the present day.

During World War II Fiji was occupied by Allied forces and 6,500 Fijians fought alongside the Allies. Indians refused to serve in the military because they were not offered the same wages and conditions as Europeans, and accusations of disloyalty resulted. The army, which remained intact after the war, was exclusively Indigenous Fijian except for a handful of European officers, a fact that contributed to the military coups in both 1987 and 2000.

In the 1960s the complex and diverse Fijian community began the process of creating a constitution. The process was a compromise between the principles of parliamentary democracy and the racial divisions within the country. Suffrage, previously enjoyed only by Europeans and some Indians, was extended to adults of all races, including Indigenous Fijians, who until then had been represented by their chiefs. Fijian land rights, guaranteed by the Deed of Cession in 1874, were given constitutional protection, while Fijian chiefs received an effective veto on all important matters affecting the status of Fijians and on changes to the constitution itself. The constitution gave power to Indigenous Fijian politicians, as long as their votes remained unified. Independence was achieved on October 10, 1970, the 96th anniversary of cession.

After independence Fiji was governed by the Alliance Party, led by an Indigenous Fijian, Ratu Sir Kamisese Mara; the party pledged to follow policies of multiracialism. However in April 1987 an Indian-backed coalition, the National Federation Party, won a majority in parliament. The coalition leader, Timoci Bavadra, an Indo-Fijian, replaced Mara as prime minister. Bavadra appointed a racially balanced cabinet, but the new government, which had a majority of Indian members in the legislature, was greeted with widespread protest by Indigenous Fijians. After only a few weeks military officers led by Colonel Sitiven Rabuka deposed Bavadra in a coup, demanding greater protection for Indigenous Fijian rights and their dominance of any future government. The governor-general negotiated a compromise that would maintain civilian rule pending a constitutional revision and new elections. The compromise prompted Rabuka to lead a second coup in September and reimpose military rule. In December 1987 Rabuka declared Fiji a republic and appointed a new civilian government with Mara as prime minister. In 1990 Fiji adopted a constitution designed to ensure that political power remained with the Indigenous Fijians, but in 1997 the constitution was amended to grant political power to all races. In 1999 Mahendar Chaudhry became Fiji's first prime minister of Indian descent.

In May 2000 Fiji experienced a series of political events, beginning with the kidnapping of Prime Minister Chaudhry, who was eventually held in the parliament building for 56 days; these events have been variously interpreted and explained both inside and outside the country. The first commentaries often claimed that Indigenous Fijians, upset at the prospect of an Indian prime minister and his vague notions of land reform, were making a grab for political power. However, subsequent analyses have tied the head conspirator, George Speight, a failed businessman, to a variety of other business alliances, all of whom had engaged in some shady practices that Chaudhry's government was keen to expose. Unfortunately many Indigenous Fijians, including some sections of the military, believed the rhetoric about land reform and flocked to Speight's cause; several months of bloodshed and violence resulted. Eventually the military installed Laisania Qarase, an Indigenous Fijian,

as prime minister. Elections in 2001 retained Qarase, whose party was dominated by Indigenous Fijians, and he appointed a cabinet that excluded Chaudhry's party, which was dominated by Indo-Fijians. Qarase was reelected in 2006 and the opposition Labour Party, led by Chaudhry, accepted seven of the 17 seats in the cabinet, the first time an opposition party had been part of the cabinet.

In 2006 a fourth coup in Fiji emerged when Fiji's military commander Frank Bainimarama, the same person who had installed Qarase in 2000, overthrew the government when Qarase did not accede to the military's demands. Bainimarama granted executive powers to the country's president, Ratu Josefa Iloilovatu Uluivuda, commonly referred to as President Iloilo, and took the position of prime minister himself. Throughout 2007 he continued to hold most political power in the country after firing the Council of Chiefs and imposing a state of emergency several times. He has called for national elections in 2010, but many internal and external observers of Fijian politics are skeptical that he will give up power if a replacement is elected.

CULTURAL IDENTITY

There are two important features of Fiji's unique historical background that have contributed to the creation of today's national identity. The first and most important is the arrival of indentured Indian laborers in 1879, which created a society with two distinct, often antagonistic cultural groups: the Indigenous Fijians of Melanesian and Polynesian descent and the Indo-Fijians. The second important feature is the fact that unlike other Pacific societies, Fijians were not colonized against their will; rather, they ceded their land to Britain to end internal political strife. This independent action has meant that unlike HAWAIIANS and MAORI, for example, Fijians, or at least Fijian chiefs, have had a significant and consistent voice in the politics of their lands from before the European-dominated era through the present time. Fijians have never had to fight to retain control of their land, a central aspect of their identity as Fijians.

Since the British first began transporting Indians to Fiji as indentured laborers in the 19th century, the relationship between the Indians and the Indigenous Fijians has often been strained. The first Indians were transported to Fiji to work on sugar plantations, carrying with them the cultural and spiritual traditions of Hinduism and Islam. At the same time the

A Christian prayer service held by preachers who opposed the military takeover of Fiji in 2006. (AP/Staff)

Europeans generally ignored the traditional ethnic and cultural patterns of the indigenous people. Under colonial authority the two ethnic groups were kept broadly separate. Indigenous Fijians remained in their villages, under separate Fijian administration dominated by traditional provisional chiefs. As Indians worked off their indentures, and especially after 1920, many moved into towns and became prosperous shopkeepers or business owners.

Today Indo-Fijians continue to control much of Fiji's business and industry, a condition that has led to resentment by some Indigenous Fijians. The Indo-Fijian community also controls much of the agricultural sector and farms most of the land owned by Fijians. While the constitution provides Indigenous Fijians with landownership, the control exerted by the wealthier Indo-Fijian community continues to cause tensions in a country where land is central to identity. The nonrenewal in recent years of long-standing leases granted to the first generation of farmers to migrate from India has heightened the tensions felt on both sides of the issue of land.

While Fiji's two largest ethnic groups, Indo-Fijians and Indigenous Fijians, have continued to lead largely separate lives, with very little intermarriage, the situation may be changing. The Fijian government claims that the two groups are living more harmoniously than in the past, while keeping their own cultures and identities. Important days from all cultures are now national holidays, including Prophet Muhammad's Birthday, Diwali (the Hindu Festival of Lights), Christmas, Easter, the Queen's Birthday, and Boxing Day. It is now illegal to discriminate on the grounds of color, race, or ethnicity. The 2006 election, in which members of the opposition party agreed to be part of the cabinet of the prime minister, who was an ethnic Fijian, was believed by many Fijians to signal the beginning of a new era of reconciliation in Fiji. Unfortunately with the dissolution of this government by the military it may be many years or even decades before the two ethnic groups are able to join again to rule a democratic Fiji.

FURTHER READING

John Wesley Coulter. *The Drama of Fiji: A Contemporary History* (Melbourne: P. Flesch, 1967).

John D. Kelly and Martha Kaplan. *Represented Communities: Fiji and World Decolonization* (Chicago: University of Chicago Press, 2001).

Bruce Knapman. *Fiji's Economic History, 1874–1939: Studies of Capitalist Colonial Development* (Canberra: Australian National University, 1987).

Filipino Muslims (Moros)

The Filipino Muslim people are a community defined by religion and culture rather than language. They are members of about 10 different ethnolinguistic communities, TAUSUG, MARANAO, SAMALS, and others, all from the larger Austronesian language family. They live primarily in the south of the country in the Sulu Archipelago and the islands of Palawan and Mindanao, although increasing numbers have migrated to Manila and the country's other large cities.

GEOGRAPHY

The Sulu Archipelago, which extends southwest from Mindanao between the Sulu and Celebes Seas, is a 170-mile-long group of about 900 volcanic and coral islands. The region is classified as tropical-wet, allowing for plentiful crops of rice, coconuts, and a variety of tropical fruits; the rich seas around the islands also make fishing and pearl and pearl shell diving lucrative economic activities for some. The archipelago falls south of the Pacific typhoon belt and thus experiences less damage from these storms than the northern Philippines; however, extensive logging in the mid-20th century has left the

FILIPINO MUSLIMS

location:
The Sulu Archipelago, Palawan, and Mindanao, the Philippines; sometimes this area is called Bangsamoro

time period:
13th century to the present

ancestry:
Austronesian

language:
Various Austronesian languages and Arabic for reading the Quran

Filipino Muslims time line

B.C.E.

3000 The initial migration of the Austronesian speakers to the Philippines, including the ancestors of the Filipino Muslims.

C.E.

13th century Arab traders and sultans establish contact with Sulu and most of the rest of the Mindanao region. This marks the period of first conversion to Islam in the archipelago and the formation of the Filipino Muslim people as distinct from others.

Mid-15th century The Sulu sultanate is established by Salip (Sharif) Abu Bakkar or Sultan Shariful Hashim.

1527 The Spanish first set foot on Mindanao but in the following years establish control only over the north coast and Zamboanga.

1851 The Spanish achieve their first victory over the sultanate of Sulu and begin to incorporate the Mindanao region into the remainder of their Filipino colony.

1860 Mindanao and the surrounding islands officially become a province of the Spanish Philippines, but very few changes are felt by either Muslim lowlanders or tribal highlanders.

1899 The Spanish cede the Philippines to the United States and a local war of independence breaks out. In Mindanao these are often referred to as the Moro Wars.

1902 A U.S. civil administration replaces military rule upon the pacification of the independence fighters in the north; the fight continues in the south.

1913 The Americans defeat Muslim resistance fighters in the decisive Battle of Bud Bagsak; however, the Muslim population of the islands to this day has continued the struggle for independence.

1920 The Bureau of Non-Christian Tribes takes control of Mindanao and its surrounding islands.

1941 The Japanese occupy the Philippines during World War II.

1944 The United States retakes the Philippines.

1945 The Philippines attains independence from the United States.

1967 The Muslim National Liberation Front (MNLF) takes up the centuries-long struggle for independence from the Philippines.

1972 The Philippines declares martial law in the south after the armed uprising of the MNLF.

1976 The Tripoli Agreement, brokered by Libyan president Muammar al-Gaddafi, prompts some hope of peace, which is soon shattered.

1977 The Moro Islamic Liberation Front (MILF) breaks away from the MNLF.

1989 Abu Sayyaf, the most radical Islamic group among the Philippines' breakaway organizations, is formed by soldiers who had former military experience in Afghanistan.

1996 The Filipino government and the Moro National Liberation Front sign a peace agreement described as the final implementation of the 1976 agreement.

2001 The Filipino government and the MILF sign a separate peace agreement.

2002 The United States and the Philippines engage in joint counterterrorism training and activities against Abu Sayyaf.

2007 Abu Sayyaf continues its violent struggle for an independent Islamic state in the southern Philippines.

islands vulnerable to soil erosion, mudslides, and related disasters.

Palawan is an island province located to the east of the Visayas and north of the Malaysian province of Sabah. Unlike in much of the rest of the country, the province's rain forests have not been degraded yet to the point of collapse; it also contains mountains and is encircled by a coral reef that makes it one of the most fruitful fishing spots in the country. The climate varies by region with the northern and southern points and west coast all having six months of dry weather and six months of wet while the east coast has a short dry season but no excessive rainy season at all.

Mindanao is the second-largest island in the Philippines and is the largest island by far in the southern, Mindanao region of the country. The southern half of the island is largely mountainous with Mount Apo, the highest mountain in the country at 9,689 feet above sea level, looking down on the island's biggest city, Davao. The mountains are drained by several rivers including the Mindanao, Davao, and Tagum, which cross Cotabato and Davao Provinces. Because of its rugged terrain and combination of Muslim and tribal peoples, it is often viewed by other Filipinos as a frontier area filled with both danger and potential.

ORIGINS

The origins of the Filipino Muslims, as of all Austronesian speakers in the Philippines, are probably in south China, from which they sailed in double-outrigger dugout canoes about 5,000 years ago to Taiwan, and then later to the Philippines and Polynesia. There is no certainty as to why this population left south China; however, archaeologists have hypothesized that it was a combination of population pressure, increased commerce from the Yangtze River region of China and moving southward down the river and its tributaries, a growing demand for marine and tropical forest goods, and climate change.

Contemporary Austronesian languages can be subdivided into two distinctive groups that separate the languages of Austronesian Taiwan from those of the remainder of the family, which include all Malay and Oceanic languages. This linguistic division, in addition to several anomalies in the archaeological record, such as a lack of rice in the earliest Austronesian sites in Taiwan, indicates that the origins of the Austronesians may have been two separate exoduses from southeast China. If these did occur, the first exodus was probably from Fujian Province in China to Taiwan, which saw the rise of TA-P'EN-K'ENG CULTURE, with its distinctively marked pottery and stone tools, but without archaeological evidence of domesticated rice. The descendants of this first wave would be the contemporary speakers of Taiwan's Austronesian languages, the ABORIGINAL TAIWANESE people. The second exodus may have occurred around 3000 B.C.E., taking a second wave of Austronesian speakers from southeastern China to Taiwan and then almost immediately to Luzon in the Philippines around the same period. This second wave, with its red-slipped pottery, may also have been the ultimate source of the LAPITA CULTURE.

HISTORY

Generally when speaking of the Philippines, the year 1521 with the arrival of the Spanish is noted as a period of great cultural, political, and economic changes among the Austronesian lowlanders, which served to distinguish them greatly from the highlanders. Most lowlanders adopted Christianity fairly quickly in the colonial era as well as some other aspects of Spanish social life. The large number of Mestizos, people of mixed indigenous and Spanish descent, living in the lowlands served to hasten these changes in many areas. For the communities that did not convert the most viable option for survival was to flee into the highlands to escape the reach of the Spanish administrators and priests. In Mindanao and Sulu, however, this process was different since a colonizing Arab force had already moved through the area and established its own religion and bureaucratic structures as the dominant forces in the area. The Sulu sultanate, the first Muslim kingdom in the region, was established in the mid-15th century after several centuries of contact between the local population and both Arab and Chinese Muslim traders had seen the conversion of most tribes in the region to Islam.

Sultan Sharif ul-Hashim

Sultan Sharif ul-Hashim, or Abubakar, is remembered for anchoring Islam in the Sulu region of the Philippine Islands. Born in 1425 Abubakar arrived in Buansa from Johor in 1450 and was welcomed by Rajah Baguinda, who knew of Abubakar's claim of descent from the prophet Muhammad. Abubakar was also renowned as an authority on the Islamic faith and he promptly converted the Tausug tribes. He is also credited with giving peace and cohesion to the coastal and hill tribes. Nonetheless the hill tribes remained staunch in their adherence to their own religions and to draw them to the Islamic faith Abubakar advised the coastal tribes to offer cakes and clothing to the people of the hill. Assured of peace, the hill tribes welcomed Abubakar and were soon converted to Islam as well. Abubakar married Paramisali, the daughter of Rajah Baguinda, and assumed sovereignty over Sulu, at which point he took the title of *Sultan Sharif ul-Hashim* and promptly designated all land in which the royal gong could be heard as the rightful property of the sultan. The remaining lands were divided into five regions that were governed by rulers called Panglimas. Abubakar also established Islam as the official state religion and developed a Code of Laws based on the Quran. During his time Islamic institutions and religious instruction were emphasized as the foundation on which Sulu society could flourish, and Abubakar reigned for 30 years.

The Spanish set foot on Mindanao for the first time in 1527 but for more than 300 years were not able to consolidate their rule over the entire region. The northern coast and Zamboanga were the extent of their domain there, and the rest of the region remained in the hands of Muslim sultans until the mid-19th century. In their small holding the Spanish referred to both the Muslim or Moro peoples and the tribal highlanders as *infieles* or infidels and treated both groups with the same contempt.

The year 1851 was the time of the first Spanish victory over the sultanate of Sulu, but in the peace treaty that followed faulty translations led to considerable further conflict. In Spanish the text stated that the region was to be incorporated into the Spanish empire while in the Sulu text it called for an "agreement and union." In 1860 the Spanish made their new southern territories into a province of the larger Philippines but for the following 39 years were able to enter their province only with a military force; it has since been referred to as a "paper province." The Spanish loss of the Philippines to the United States in 1898 did not change the situation greatly in the southern part of the archipelago; the Muslim population continued its struggle for independence in the Moro Wars, which officially lasted until 1913, and their occasional allies, the highlanders, likewise resisted incorporation into the state.

After many decades of feeling unrepresented at the state level and without a voice in their own governance, Muslims in the southern Philippines once again took up arms in the 1960s. At that time the Muslim community was fairly united behind Nur Misuari's Moro National Liberation Front (MNLF), which challenged the Filipino army to such a degree that martial law was declared in 1972 to try to quell the violence. Four years later some progress was made toward a lasting peace when the government of the Philippines and MNLF signed the Tripoli Agreement, which laid out both a ceasefire agreement and provisions for Moro autonomy within the larger Filipino state. However, soon after the event the MNLF withdrew from the process when, instead of granting Moro autonomy, the Filipino government held a plebiscite about autonomy, which could not pass without MNLF support and might not have passed anyway.

In subsequent years at least two new Muslim independence movements emerged from the fractured MNLF and were divided largely along ethnic lines. The first, the Moro Islamic Liberation Front (MILF), formed in 1977 and generally attracted individuals from the Maguindanaon and Iranun communities, while the MNLF-Reformist Group is largely made up of Maranao. The MNLF, predominantly Tausug and Samals, remained the largest of these organizations and the one with which the government preferred to negotiate. These negotiations continued in 1986 after the new president, Corazon Aquino, began talks with the MNLF and Nur Misuari. By 1989 another plebiscite was held in Mindanao to decide on the formation of an Autonomous Region of Muslim Mindanao, but again without the full support of the MNLF it was doomed to failure. With the 1992 election of a new president, Fidel Ramos, the Filipino government and MNLF once again returned to the negotiation table for a further round of talks, again with the assistance of Libya, Indonesia, and a number of other Muslim countries from the Organization of the Islamic Conference (OIC). These talks led to yet another agreement between the government and MNLF, this one signed in Jakarta in 1996, which created a Special Zone of Peace and Development (SZOPAD) and a Southern Philippines Council for Peace and Development (SPCPD). The agreement was to be a "final implementation" of the one signed in Tripoli 20 years earlier but, unfortunately, did not take into consideration the significantly changed political situation among the Muslim population itself. The MILF was not included in the negotiations or in the agreement and refused to lay down its arms; nor was the newest and most violent Islamist splinter group, Abu Sayyaf, which broke free in 1989 under Abdujarak Janjalani and has engaged in bombings, kidnappings, and other acts of domestic and international terrorism ever since.

In 2001 the MILF and the Filipino government signed their own Tripoli Agreement, which finally yielded a lasting peace between these organizations. But Abu Sayyaf remained extremely active, including staging kidnappings in both Malaysia and the Philippines and car and other bombings in the Philippines. Following the September 11, 2001, terrorist attacks in the United States and the subsequent "war on terror" waged by the U.S. government in various parts of the world, the Philippines' long-running battle against Muslim independence groups became a feature of American policy as well. In 2002 650 American soldiers were deployed to the Philippines to assist in the fight against Abu Sayyaf. The counterterrorism training they implemented, called Balikatan 02-1, to distinguish it from the regular, annual Balikatan joint exercises held by the United States and the Philippines, was deemed a relative success at the time but has not quelled the use of violence by Abu Sayyaf against civilians. In August 2007 Abu Sayyaf forces killed 15 and wounded 17 Filipino soldiers in Basilan, near Mindanao, in an insurgency that does not appear to have an end in sight.

CULTURE

Filipino Muslims are in many ways similar to their Christian neighbors. They engage in agricultural work, growing rice, coconuts, and tropical fruit for both subsistence and for sale. They speak Austronesian languages brought with them on their initial migration to the islands in 3000 B.C.E., and family and community are central to each individual's identity. The only significant difference comes when discussing the two peoples' religious worldviews; although within both groups there are people who wear their religious identity lightly and others who are more literal in their interpretation of their holy books, the Bible and Quran. Some of the cultural differences that stem from these religious differences are the Filipino Muslim acceptance of polygyny, or the ability to have more than one wife, and *halal* food practices that forbid the consumption of pork and alcohol. Other important cultural attributes of Muslims generally are the belief in Allah as the one god, Moses and Jesus as important prophets of Allah but Muhammad as the final prophet, the ultimate resurrection of all human beings, and the Quran as the word of god as spoken by Muhammad. They also believe that prayer, fasting, pilgrimages to Mecca, avoiding such sins as adultery and theft, and paying a religious tax are all necessary acts in a Muslim's life. While a small number of Filipino Muslims have been engaged in acts of rebellion against the government of the Philippines and before that with the American, JAPANESE, and Spanish colonizers, the vast majority of the country's more than 4.5 million Muslims live peacefully in Sulu, Mindanao, and Palawan.

FURTHER READING

Thomas McKenna. *Muslim Rulers and Rebels: Everyday Politics and Armed Separation in the Southern Philippines* (Berkeley and Los Angeles: University of California Press, 1998).

Amina Rasul, ed. *The Road to Peace and Reconciliation: Muslim Perspective on the Mindanao Conflict* (Makati City, Philippines: Asian Institute of Management, 2003).

Marites Dañguilan Vitug and Glenda M. Gloria. *Under the Crescent Moon: Rebellion in Mindanao* (Quezon City, Philippines: Institute for Popular Democracy, 2000).

Filipinos: nationality (Pilipinos, people of the Philippines)

The Philippines are a multicultural society made up of hundreds of separate indigenous groups, mostly of Malay ancestry but with some

---

Filipinos: nationality time line

B.C.E.

c. 28,000 The Aeta cross into Luzon from China or the Andaman Islands via a land bridge that has since become submerged. What remains is now the island of Palawan. A unique ethnic group, the Aeta are characteristically short in frame (most are under five feet) and appear to be of African descent, but genetic research has revealed that they have no immediate link to African ancestry.

2500 Austronesians from Taiwan arrive in Luzon but do not blend or intermarry with the Aeta.

C.E.

1000–1200 The Filipinos engage in trading with India, China, and Arabia.

1380 Arab and Malay traders introduce Islam to the Philippine islands through Borneo, later followed by Muslim missionaries who proselytize and convert Filipinos in the southern islands.

1475 The Muslim sultanate of Maguindanao is established on Mindanao, promoting the spread of Islam throughout the Philippine Islands.

1521 Portuguese explorer Ferdinand Magellan is the first European to visit the Philippine Islands. Native warriors resistant to Spanish colonization kill Magellan and his crew at Mactan Island, under the direction of chieftain Lapu-Lapu.

(continues)

Filipinos: nationality time line *(continued)*

1543 Spanish explorer Ruy López de Villalobos arrives in the islands and names them after the young prince Philip of Spain, who later becomes King Philip II.

1565 Spanish conquistador Miguel López de Legazpi arrives in Bohol, where he and his crew obtain gold and spices after convincing the indigenous people that they are not Portuguese. Legazpi makes a blood compact of friendship with chieftain Datu Sikatuna and goes on to sack the island of Cebu and establish the first Spanish settlement.

1568–70 The Portuguese launch a series of attacks on the fledgling Spanish colony on Cebu under the claim that the Philippines are within their jurisdiction.

1571 Legazpi founds his governmental base in Manila, designating it the capital of the Philippines. He proclaims that Manila is the "distinguished and ever loyal city."

1575 Twenty-four Spanish missionaries arrive on the archipelago and convert much of the lowland population to Catholicism, making the Philippines the only Catholic nation in Asia.

1580 King Philip II inherits the Portuguese throne after the death of King Sebastian, ending the Portuguese attacks on the Philippine Islands.

The Spaniards implement forced labor for all Filipino men between the ages of 16 and 60.

1600 The Spanish government establishes the *bandala,* which is the compulsory sale of the native people's products to the government. They are paid in promissory notes.

1622–1700 A series of small and unorganized revolts occur as the natives protest forced labor, exhaustive taxation, the *bandala,* and forced tribute.

1744–1829 Spurred by a priest's refusal to give his brother a Christian burial, Francisco Dagohoy leads one of the longest and most successful revolts in Philippine history, outlasting several Spanish governor-generals.

1762 The British attack Manila and occupy the city.

1763 The Treaty of Paris ends the Seven Years' War, as well as the British occupation of Manila.

1808 Napoléon Bonaparte appoints his brother Joseph king of Spain. Under the rule of Joseph Bonaparte, the Filipino natives are granted Spanish citizenship and representation in the Spanish Cortes (Spanish parliament).

1813 Napoléon's forces are defeated at the Battle of the Nations, and the British general, Arthur Wellesley, later the duke of Wellington, forces Napoléon's troops out of Spain. Ferdinand VII, son of Charles IV, is acknowledged as the rightful king of Spain.

1816 Ferdinand VII reverses many of the changes implemented by Joseph Bonaparte, including the Filipino natives' right to representation in the Cortes.

1820 The Philippine Islands achieve a level of prosperity due to changes in economic life as well as a more efficient agricultural system in which crops are grown according to region.

1834 The Philippines open themselves to world trade.

1835 The Chamber of Commerce is established, and Francisco Rodriguez opens the first Philippine bank.

1863 Reforms are made within the educational system to improve the quality of Philippine education.

1869 The Suez Canal is opened, providing steady contact between Europe and the Philippines and thus producing a regular importation of goods to the islands.

1887 José Rizal publishes his political novel *Noli Me Tangere,* set in the Philippines. The book is published in Madrid and Barcelona.

even more ancient populations of AETA as well. Migrants from Spain, the United States, China, Japan, and elsewhere in Asia make up about a quarter of the country's population but are not differentiated in the national census.

GEOGRAPHY

Lying directly south of Taiwan and northeast of Malaysia, the Philippines consist of 7,107 islands with a total land area of 116,000 square miles. The islands are grouped into three main divisions:

1888 Filipinos in Spain establish La Solidaridad to protest the administration's abuse and oppression of the Filipino natives in the Philippine Islands. Led by José Rizal, La Solidaridad demands reforms and better representation for Filipinos in the Spanish Cortes.

1896 José Rizal is arrested and executed for treason.

A revolutionary movement is rounded up by Andres Bonifacio and later led by Emilio Aguinaldo, and the Spanish governor Ramón Blanco declares war on the provinces of Manila, Laguna, Pampanga, Tarlac, Nueva Ecija, Bulacan, Batangas, and Cavite.

1898 The United States declares war on Spain and the U.S. Navy attacks Manila.

Emilio Aguinaldo, with U.S. support, establishes a dictatorial government for the Philippines, and the Philippines is declared independent from Spain.

Spain sells the Philippines to the United States for $20 million.

1899 Revolutionaries, again led by Emilio Aguinaldo, oppose the U.S. occupation of the Philippine Islands.

1901 Emilio Aguinaldo is captured by U.S. forces and takes an oath of allegiance to the United States, formally issuing a statement to the Filipinos that freedom can be obtained only through the magnanimity of the United States.

1903 Governor Taft (later President Taft) establishes the Philippines for the Filipinos' policy, which will grant administrative control of the Philippines to the Filipinos.

1935 The Philippines becomes a commonwealth, which allows the nation more self-governance.

1941 After the bombing of Pearl Harbor, Japanese fighter planes attack the Philippines.

U.S. troops leave the Philippines and declare Manila an "open city," thereby surrendering it to the Japanese.

1942 The Japanese reform the educational system, impose martial law, and enforce the death penalty for acts such as destroying military property, sedition, robbery, and rumor mongering.

55,000 U.S. and Filipino troops are led on the Bataan Death March, on which they are denied food and water and many are bayoneted or beaten to death by Japanese guards. The survivors are imprisoned in concentration camps.

1945 U.S. troops invade Manila, and the Japanese surrender.

1946 The United States declares the independence of the Philippines.

General Masaharu Homma is tried for war crimes and executed outside Manila.

1951 The National Movement for Free Elections is created to make elections honest and uncorrupted.

1972 Unable to seek a third term, widely disliked president Ferdinand Marcos declares martial law and rules the country by decree. His presidency is renowned for its corruption and unmitigated use of force.

1986 Protests lead to an election in which Corazon Aquino is voted the new president.

Aquino's administration drafts a new constitution, but governmental reforms are impeded by national debt, coup attempts, corruption within the government, and rebel groups.

1992 Fidel Ramos is elected president and improvements are made within the economy but are later quashed by the East Asian financial crisis in 1997.

2001 Gloria Macapagal-Arroyo is elected president.

Luzon (also home to the nation's capital, Manila), Visayas, and Mindanao. The islands are all of volcanic origin, and eruptions have frequently displaced, if not devastated, whole communities. Even the Aeta people, who have traditionally maintained their privacy and cultural separation from the larger Filipino populace, were forced to move into urban areas by the massive eruption of Mount Pinatubo in 1991, which was recorded as one of the worst volcanic eruptions in history.

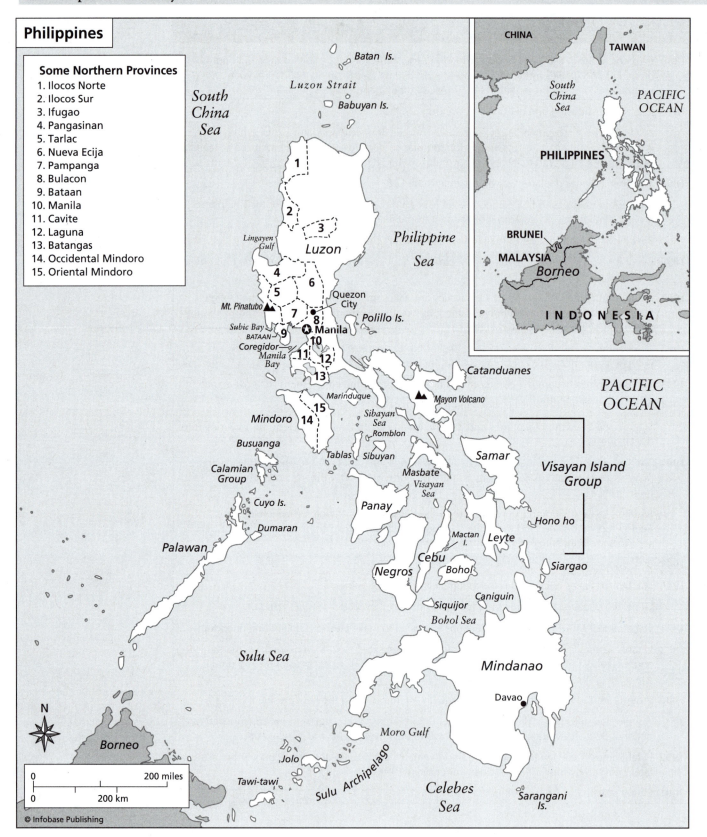

Philippines

Some Northern Provinces
1. Ilocos Norte
2. Ilocos Sur
3. Ifugao
4. Pangasinan
5. Tarlac
6. Nueva Ecija
7. Pampanga
8. Bulacon
9. Bataan
10. Manila
11. Cavite
12. Laguna
13. Batangas
14. Occidental Mindoro
15. Oriental Mindoro

© Infobase Publishing

The climate is tropical and the islands lie within the typhoon belt of the western Pacific. Much of the plant life is similar to that found on the Malay Archipelago, including the mangrove swamps. The terrain is mountainous and thickly forested primarily with pine trees;

some of the rarest orchids in the world can be found on the Philippine Islands. Animal species include the carabao (water buffaloes), pangolins (scaly anteaters), monkeys, lemurs, and the tamarau, a small species of carabao that can be found only on Mindoro. Fossil evidence has shown that elephants once roamed the islands.

INCEPTION AS A NATION

The history of the Philippines is characterized by political and social instability dating to the first European encounter in the 16th century. Since then many global powers have vied for political control of the islands, including Portugal, Spain, the United Kingdom, the United States, and Japan. Having spent nearly 500 years under foreign rule, the Philippine natives finally regained complete control over their own land in 1946, but the seeds of this independence can be most visibly traced back to the late 1880s, when various revolutionary movements began to gain influence.

As the Philippine economy began to flourish with more efficient crop production in the 19th century, many Filipino natives saw a new influx of wealth that they had previously been denied, as the natives were of the lower class and the Spanish settlers were of the ruling class. Some natives came into so much wealth that they were able to send their children to Spain to be educated, and there Philippine-born José Rizal attended medical school. In 1887 Rizal wrote and published *Noli Me Tangere,* a political novel set in the Philippines, which was meant to alert Spaniards to the injustices being perpetrated in the colony. He also became a pivotal figure in the movement La Solidaridad, which demanded reforms within the Philippine government, particularly in freedom of the press, representation in the Spanish Cortes, and legal equality for the Filipinos.

José Rizal was eventually arrested, tried, and executed as a traitor, but one of his partners in the reform movement, Andres Bonifacio, went on to found the Katipunan, an organization based in the Philippines and made up mostly of the lower and middle classes. Later the group was headed by Emilio Aguinaldo, whom the United States specifically sought out to aid them in their anti-Spanish propaganda, in exchange for helping the Philippine natives in their quest for independence. Aguinaldo agreed in 1898 and two days later the United States declared war on Spain. But after Spain sold the Philippines to the United States for $20

José Rizal (1861–96), center, can be seen on statues and monuments throughout the Philippines that commemorate his words and deeds in the fight for Filipino equality during the Spanish Colonial era. *(Shutterstock/Anthony Jay D. Villalon)*

million, the U.S. reliance on the Philippine natives faded and the United States became just another foreign ruler in the Philippines. Aguinaldo went on to become president in 1899, but after assassinating some of his opponents and openly propagating anti-American sentiments, he was captured and made to take an oath of allegiance to the United States.

Nevertheless various resistance groups continued to revolt until they were momentarily silenced when Japanese fighter pilots bombed the city of Manila in a surprise attack in 1941. The United States, unprepared for the attack, promptly surrendered and the Japanese commander in chief, General Masaharu Homma, took political control of the Philippines. Though he claimed to be giving the land back to the Philippine natives, he instituted the death penalty for acts such as sedition and destroying military property, as well as rumor mongering and looting. The education system was reformed so as to provide the Filipino people with an education of their own culture and history but also included propaganda that supported love of labor.

One of the most infamous brutalities committed by the Japanese administrators was the Bataan Death March, in which 55,000 prisoners of war were led on a three-day journey on foot, without food or water. Many were savagely killed on the way by gunshots, bayoneting, or beheading. Others were tortured, and in 1946, after the United States reclaimed the Philippines from the Japanese, General Masaharu Homma was tried for war crimes and executed outside Manila. That same year the United States proclaimed the independence of the Philippines. The Philippine nation has since signed a peace treaty with, and received reparations from, Japan.

In the postwar era the Philippines have continued to participate in the global economy in part as a neocolonial extension of the United States. The large U.S. naval base at Subic Bay was an important site during the Vietnam War, with about 30 ships visiting the port per day during all of 1967. The site was also an important rallying cry for Filipino nationalists, who decried not only the presence of the American forces but also the prostitution of Filipina women in and around the base; the base was handed back to the Filipino government in 1992.

CULTURAL IDENTITY

Having spent more than three centuries under Spanish rule, the Philippines today have a culture heavily infused with Spanish influences, particularly where religion is concerned. The majority of the country is Roman Catholic, but prior to Spanish colonization, the indigenous people practiced animism, which is the worship of nature. Rocks, shrubs, trees, and the moon were considered deities of a sort, and many different spirits were believed to be the source of both mischief and prosperity. The spirits included centaurs, giants, elves, fairies, witches that fed on unborn babies, and vampirelike children. Today many Filipinos have combined the two religious systems and are often described as Pagano-Christians.

What is considered vitally important within the Philippine culture are family and honor. For this reason many Western psychologists suggest that the Philippine culture is, in essence, an offshoot of traditional Asian culture, but some are now suggesting that it is more closely tied with Eurasian culture. Nonetheless Philippine culture places particular emphasis on honoring family and avoiding social shame, which affects not only the individual but the family as well.

One of the central features of this focus on family in Filipino culture is *kapwa*, which translates as "togetherness" and has specific mandates for the inclusion of outsiders. Though the culture is open to newcomers, *kapwa* stresses conformity and compliance. While this may seem daunting, it provides the Filipino people with a sense of unity, or *kagandahang-loob*, "shared humanity."

FURTHER READING

T. A. Agoncillo. *Nationalism in the Philippines* (Kuala Lumpur: Department of History, University of Malaya, 1968).

Sharon Delmendo. *The Star-Entangled Banner: One Hundred Years of America in the Philippines* (New Brunswick, N.J.: Rutgers University Press, 2004).

Brian McAllister Linn. *The Philippine War, 1899–1902 (Modern War Studies)* (Lawrence: University Press of Kansas, 2002).

Floro C. Quibuyen. *A Nation Aborted: Rizal, American Hegemony, and Philippine Nationalism* (Quezon City, Philippines: Ateneo de Manila University Press, 1999).

Daniel B. Schirmer and Stephen R. Shalom. *The Philippines Reader: A History of Colonialism, Neocolonialism, Dictatorship, and Resistance* (Boston: South End Press, 1987).

David Joel Steinberg. *The Philippines, a Singular and a Plural Place* (Boulder, Colo.: Westview Press, 1982).

Ben J. Wallace. *The Changing Village Environment in Southeast Asia: Applied Anthropology and Environmental Reclamation in the Northern Philippines* (New York: Routledge, 2006).

Funanese (people of Funan, people of Nokor Phnom)

Funan is the Chinese term for a kingdom located in present-day Cambodia and southern Vietnam, Thailand, and Myanmar during the first five and a half centuries of the common era. We still do not know what the people called themselves.

GEOGRAPHY

Funan encompassed much of the southern portion of the Indochinese Peninsula, including territory that is today southern Vietnam, Thailand, and Myanmar and all of Cambodia. The kingdom's capital was the city of Vyadhapura, which is believed to be the same place as Angkor Borei, Cambodia, where extensive archaeological work has been done recently. However, the most important features of the Funan kingdom were the long Mekong River and the kingdom's extensive shoreline. In a seafaring kingdom

FUNANESE

location:
Cambodia, and southern Vietnam, Thailand, and Myanmar

time period:
400–500 B.C.E. to about 550 C.E.

ancestry:
Mon-Khmer

language:
Probably a form of the Mon-Khmer language family using the Sanskrit writing system

that adopted its major cultural features from far-away India through interactions by trading ships, which also provided the kingdom's greatest source of wealth, ocean ports and the river were the keys to more than 600 years of domination in the region. The city of Oc-Eo in present-day Vietnam, about six miles inland from Rach Gia, was one of these important ports. Oc-Eo is also sometimes considered Funan's capital because of its relatively large size, 1,100 hectares, and extensive canals, walls, and buildings.

Funan's second source of greatness, its agricultural output, was also the direct result of its geographic location in the Mekong River valley. While other rivers the size of the Mekong regularly flood their banks and destroy everything in their wake, this river has a natural reservoir system, Tonle Sap, a lake connected to the Mekong by a narrow channel. During floods water rushes out of the Mekong and fills Tonle Sap, raising its level about 40 feet above its winter level. During the dry winter months the channel then drains water from Tonle Sap and back into the Mekong, keeping the flow in the delta fairly steady and conducive to wet rice agriculture throughout the year.

ORIGINS

The legendary origin myth of the Funan kingdom states that an Indian Brahmin priest, usually known as Kaundinya, dreamed of forming a kingdom in Southeast Asia. About halfway through the first century C.E. the Brahmin followed the message of his dream and set sail for Southeast Asia with a magic bow he had obtained from a Hindu temple. Upon arrival he conquered and then married Queen Soma, whose father was considered king of the cobras or *nagas*. The descendants of these two are considered the royal lineage of Bnam, which some experts believe is the old Khmer term for "mountain," though others strongly disagree. This myth establishes Funan as the legitimate ruler in the region through two different royal lineages, the Brahmin, the apex of the hierarchical Hindu cosmology, and the local cobra, which was believed to be the lord of the earth by many Southeast Asian peoples.

The actual origins of Funan are still unclear, but its language seems to indicate membership in the Mon-Khmer branch of the Austro-Asiatic language family. The Funanese are thus related to both the Mons of present-day Myanmar and the Khmers of Cambodia. Recent archaeological evidence of settlement at Angkor Borei actually points to a founding date

Funanese time line

B.C.E.

400–500 Archaeological evidence points to the initial settlement of Angkor Borei in this period. Over the subsequent 500–600 years the people of Funan gradually establish themselves as the dominant power in the region.

C.E.

205–225 Rule of Fan Shih-Man, who draws other principalities into the Funan orbit and is considered by some as the kingdom's greatest ruler.

243 Funan sends a mission to China, which pays tribute and introduces the court to Funanese music.

250 Chinese envoys use the term *Funan* for the first time to refer to the largest Southeast Asian kingdom of the time. They also document the Funanese political, economic, religious, and writing systems.

357 Funan becomes a tribute-paying state of the greater Chinese Empire. King Chandan, probably a Brahmin migrant, takes the throne of Funan.

478–514 Funan is at its geographic, political, and economic zenith under the reign of King Jayavarman.

491 Fan Tang, son of King Jayavarman, seizes the throne of the Champa kingdom after having tried to overthrow his own father.

514–539 King Rudravarman reigns in Funan as the last great king. He is a devotee of Vishnu and encourages the worship of this Hindu god throughout his kingdom.

550 Prince Bhavavarman, Rudravarman's grandson, marries a Chenla princess, becomes king of Chenla, and seizes Funan, ending to the independent Funan kingdom probably just before 600.

1944 Oc-Eo is discovered by archaeologists and contributes significantly to present-day knowledge about Funan.

1990s–2000s Excavations at Oc-Eo and Angkor Borei continue to inform us about life in the Funan kingdom.

of about 400 to 500 years before the first Chinese descriptions of Funan and preceding the gradual development of a walled, moated city of brick structures and monuments, which occupied at least 300 hectares of land. A cemetery at Vat Komnou, dated at between 200 B.C.E. and 200 C.E., which is currently undergoing extensive excavation and analysis, will provide further information about the culture of the people who created Funan.

As the occupiers of the extensive Southeast Asian coastline the people of Funan would have had contact with traders from both India and China as they plied their wares back and forth between the two important kingdoms. These foreign traders sailed with the monsoon winds, which blow east to west for half the year and then change direction for the other half. As a result they would have been forced to spend considerable time in Funan waiting for the winds to change direction. While there the traders purchased Funanese agricultural products, especially rice, and paid tribute in the form of the trade goods carried in their ships. Indian traders also introduced their religion, worldview, and writing system since all of these aspects of Funanese culture were based on the Hindu-Sanskrit systems. Funanese sailors would also have visited the ports of India and China, taking both material goods and cultural beliefs and practices home with them from a trade network that extended as far as Rome, Persia, and Greece, as evident in archaeological remains found at Oc-Eo.

HISTORY

The first known ruler of Funan was Fan Shih-Man, 205–225, who used his military might to create vassals out of all his neighboring kingdoms. The Chinese dynastic history *Liang-shu* states that Fan Shih-Man's kingdom was between 1,250 and 1,500 miles (5,000–6,000 *li*) in size. Following his death in 225, Fan Shih-Man was to be succeeded by Fan Chin-Sheng; however, the latter was killed by one of the king's nephews, Fan Chan, who declared himself king. Unfortunately nothing more is known about his reign except that trade relations and agricultural output continued to expand throughout the kingdom. Fan Chan may have been succeeded in 240 by Fan Hsun, but this remains unclear in the Chinese record. What is more clear is that in 243 Funan sent its first mission to the Chinese capital bearing both tribute and Funanese musicians to entertain the emperor; this tribute mission was repeated again under the reign of Fan Hsun in 268, and 285 through 287.

The fourth century had the first Funanese ruler bearing a distinctly Indian name, King Chandan, who ascended the throne in about 357. Chandan was probably an Indian migrant of Brahmin descent who was succeeded on the throne by another Brahmin, whose name we do not know. It may have been this period that saw the more widespread adoption of Hindu religious and political forms and the complete domination of these at the Funanese court. Nonetheless Hinduism never completely replaced what was probably the prior hegemonic religion of the region, Buddhism, because in 484 and 503 the Chinese court received Buddhist monks, Nagasena in 484 and two others in 503, from the king of Funan. The purpose for the first visit is unknown, but at least one of the monks sent in 503 worked as a translator for the Chinese emperor Wu-Ti.

The fifth century brought Funan into conflict with its powerful neighbor, Champa, the kingdom of the CHAMS of central Vietnam. In 431 the Cham king, Fan Yang Mai II, requested assistance from Funan in his fight against the Chinese governor of northern Vietnam, but he was refused. In 478 the Chams attacked a number of Funanese ships returning from a trade mission to southern China, an attack that seems to have gone unpunished. Thirteen years later in 491 the son of the Funanese king Jayavarman, Fan Tang, captured the Cham throne after having tried to stage a revolt against his father; he then succeeded in being recognized by the Chinese emperor Wu-Ti as the "commander in chief of the seashore," despite Jayavarman's request for the Chinese to punish his rebellious son. Jayavarman is also known for having reigned over Funan during the kingdom's period of greatest strength and size in the late fifth–early sixth centuries. Indeed in 502 after sending tribute to the Chinese court, including a Buddha statue made of coral, Jayavarman succeeded his son Fan Tang as "General of the Pacified South"; as general Jayavarman sent more tribute to the Chinese court in 511 and 514.

Upon Jayavarman's death in 514 he was succeeded by Rudravarman, the last great Funanese king prior to the takeover by CHENLA. He continued the trend set by his predecessor of sending regular tribute to China in an attempt to bolster Funan's regional dominance over its own vassal states. Unfortunately these actions did not produce the active Chinese alliance needed by the Funanese kings and in 527 a vassal state, P'an-p'an, sent its own tribute mission directly to China, bypassing Funan and signaling the beginning of the end of Funan's domination in the region. In 539 Funan itself was forced to pay tribute to the Khmers, whose kingdom was ruled from Laos. The end finally occurred sometime between 550 and 600, the result of Funan's Prince Bhavavarman's marriage to the Chenla princess; he inherited the Chenla throne and then seized Funan, weakened as a result of civil wars and loss of tribute.

CULTURE

The first Chinese envoys who wrote about Funan in about 250 C.E. described it as an urbanized kingdom that resembled the Chinese state rather than the region's other tribal social systems. They pointed to the structured political hierarchy and bureaucracy including a centralized judiciary system, institutionalized religion, and even libraries. In addition from the extensive archaeological work done at Oc-Eo we know that the Funanese built a very large network of canals, a city square, and many public buildings. This material supports the information in Chinese texts that it was possible to sail throughout Funan. The Funanese paid taxes to the king in the form of goods or services, and the kingdom's navy controlled most of the trade that passed by their long shoreline. They received such goods as metals and silks and traded agricultural products, wood, spices, and ivory.

The political culture of Funan and the region it dominated arose from the Indian mandala system in which concentric circles of kings who ruled a small area paid tribute to the king one step closer to the center. For much of the period of Funan's existence the central king was the Chinese emperor, to whom most Funanese kings paid some form of tribute. After the Chinese emperor the king of Funan was second in importance in all of mainland East Asia and predominant in Southeast Asia. At any given time dozens of lesser kings would have been paying tribute to Funan; the loss of much of that revenue and the peace it signaled led to the eventual replacement of Funan by Chenla as the dominant force in the mandala system of Southeast Asia.

The kinship pattern of Funan was probably cognatic descent, which resembles the Western system of recognizing mothers and fathers equally as the source of ancestors, rather than either unilineal system, matrilineal or patrilineal, which recognizes just one parent as the source of ancestors. This pattern was most common throughout all of the lowland plains of Southeast Asia and can be juxtaposed to the patrilineal systems of China and India or the matrilineal system of the Chams. With the development of agricultural-based villages in these lowland regions kinship lost much of its capacity as an organizing principle and was replaced by geography; this principle distinguishes these villages from the so-called hill tribes of Southeast Asia, which to this day have maintained very different political and social structures from their politically and economically dominant lowland neighbors.

Many aspects of Funanese society remain a mystery to contemporary scholars, from the name they used to refer to themselves to the demographic makeup of their kingdom. Chinese sources mention the existence of commoners who were black and had frizzy hair, possibly the remnants of Southeast Asia's ancient negrito population, while their language points to different origins, the proto-Mon-Khmer people. We are also unclear about exactly when Funan adopted its Sanskrit writing system, Hinduism, and other aspects of Indian society and culture. No doubt some of these features had been introduced by Indian and Funanese traders prior to the second-century emergence of the kingdom, but many sources also point to the fourth and fifth centuries as the period in which the political and economic elite became fully Indianized.

Further Reading

James C. M. Khoo, ed. *Art and Archaeology of Fu Nan: Pre-Khmer Kingdom of the Lower Mekong Valley* (Bangkok: Orchid Press, 2003).

G

Gandharan Grave culture
(Gandhara)

The Gandharan Grave culture (GGC) existed from approximately 1500 to 500 B.C.E., or perhaps as early as 1700 B.C.E. It should not be confused with the Gandharan Buddhist period in South Asian art history, which corresponds to approximately the first through third centuries C.E. Both periods take their name from the Achaemenid satrapy of Gandhara (*see* PERSIANS, ACHAEMENIDS) and the city of the same name.

Many archaeologists and historians who have worked on this region and period assume that the people of the GGC were among the earliest INDO-ARYANS who moved into south Asia from Central Asia. Horse graves and iron horse bits are evidence that the people had domesticated horses, as did the Indo-Aryans, and the similarity between GGC material culture and that of eastern Iran at the same time also points to Indo-Aryan origins. However, newer evidence and a reinterpretation of material finds from the 20th century point to the possibility that the people of the GGC were indigenous to the area and only adopted some features from outsiders. The debate continues to this day, as does the work of archaeologists from Pakistan, the United States, and elsewhere, which began in the 1950s.

Although the start and end dates of the GGC are debated, most scholars agree that the entire cultural complex can be divided into three separate phases of development ranging from the Late Bronze Age and into the Early Iron Age. The first, sometimes called the Archaic period, begins between 1700 and 1500 B.C.E. and ends about 1100 B.C.E. The second or Middle period runs until about 800 B.C.E., and the third or Late period until about 500 B.C.E., although a few nonacademic sources claim that the complex lasted until the early years of the common era. The earliest period in the GGC is usually associated with burials in rectangular pits, bronzes, terra-cotta figurines, and both red and gray pottery. The second phase was similar in material culture but instead of being buried many people were cremated with their ashes and bones interred in pottery urns; iron also began to appear in the latter years of the second period. The third period is associated with the wider use of iron; red and gray pottery continued to appear in all three periods.

In addition to their burial practices and pottery styles we know that the people of the GGC both herded animals and practiced agriculture, much as the HARAPPANS who predated them in the region by at least 1,000 years did.

Gaoshan   *See* ABORIGINAL TAIWANESE.

Gelao (Ch'i-lao, Geliao, Gelo, Jin, Kopu, Liao, Ling)

The Gelao are one of China's recognized 55 national minority groups. They live in the mountainous region of central China in Guizhou, Guangxi, Yunnan, and Sichuan Provinces.

GANDHARAN GRAVE CULTURE

location:
North-West Frontier Province, Pakistan, and possibly into Afghanistan

time period:
About 1500 to 500 B.C.E.

ancestry:
Probably Indo-Aryan but this is contested

language:
Probably an Indo-Aryan language but this is contested

They are a relatively ancient people who count the Liao people as their ancestors. Prior to the Tang dynasty in the seventh through tenth centuries they were known as the Geliao or Liao; they became known as the Gelao during the Ming dynasty in the 14th century.

The primary economic activity of the Gelao is farming. Hunting traditionally contributed most protein to their diet, but today domesticated animals serve this purpose with beef, pork, mutton, and horse being most common. Their major subsistence crops are millet, wheat, rice, and sorghum while those at higher elevations focus their efforts on corn. Opium poppies, bamboo, wine, and cork were also produced in the past for use, trade, or sale, while today's Gelao focus their cash-cropping efforts on tobacco, tung oil, palm products, and medicinal herbs. In the past most Gelao were tenant farmers who paid rent in produce and opium, although a few did own their own land; today most lease their plots from the state collective farms that were created in the 1950s and 1960s. As agriculturalists they focused much of their ritual activity on reverence toward the ox, which provided agricultural labor and transport. The Festival of the Ox King celebrates a mythic ox that saved a community by taking the people to a cave for safety during an attack.

The Gelao language, which is categorized within the Sino-Tibetan language phylum, can be subdivided into four separate dialects that are only somewhat mutually intelligible. Only about a quarter of the Gelao population today uses one of these dialects, instead relying on HAN Chinese or one of the other ethnic languages spoken in their region. Gelao is also not a written language, so all instruction, government and personal documents, and other publications have to be produced in other languages, thus contributing to a further loss of their mother tongue.

Prior to the onset of the Communist era in 1949 the Gelao were known in their region for their distinctive dress. Men wore a black turban with tassels, long scarves, and a button-down gown over the rest of their clothing. Women also wore a long scarf along with a short jacket, vest, and long pleated skirt. Much of the clothing was decorated with batik or embroidery in a variety of patterns, including stripes, fish scales, triangles, and rhombi. Today this dress has fallen by the wayside and has been replaced with standard Han clothing, except for ceremonial periods when traditional outfits and colors reemerge.

The Gelao religion can most accurately be classified as ancestor worship, although it also has many features from animism, the belief that all things have a spirit or soul. The Gelao believed that large trees, mountains, sky, earth, and some animals all had the most powerful spirits and thus engendered worship at various festivals and events. In the past all boys underwent a period of initiation into manhood when they learned the myths and rituals of their people; some groups also removed several teeth from girls to indicate they were of marriageable age. During the Communist era all religion was banned and many festivals discontinued, but in the 1980s this policy was relaxed and many rituals and events have been revived in modern forms since that time.

Geliao   *See* GELAO.

Georgians (Karts, Kartvelebi)

The Georgians are the dominant ethnic group in the independent Caucasian country of Georgia. They are the descendants of a variety of ancient tribes: Karts, LAZ, MINGRELIANS, SVAN, ABKHAZIANS, COLCHIANS, and others. As a crossroads and passageway from the Eurasian steppes their Caucasian homeland has been invaded many times throughout almost 2,000 years of history, but the Georgians have remained Orthodox Christians and have maintained their ancient language.

GEOGRAPHY

Georgia is located in the Caucasus, east of the Black Sea, south of Russia, north of Turkey and Armenia, and west of Azerbaijan. The central feature of Georgian geography is the rugged mountains that cover much of its territory. The Likhi Range runs north-south through the country, dividing the country historically between the western Colchis region and the eastern Iberian or Kartli region. The Greater Caucasus Mountain Range provides much of the border between Georgia and Russia, while the Lesser Caucasus Mountains divide Georgia from its southern neighbors. The country's highest peak is Mount Shkhara in the north at just over 17,000 feet above sea level.

In addition to glacier-covered mountains and rivers that run from the mountains to the sea, Georgia contains lowlands, swamps, and a temperate rain forest in the west and steppelike plains in the east. These varied zones and elevations also make for varied climates, ranging

GELAO

location:
Guizhou, Guangxi, Yunnan, and Sichuan Provinces, China

time period:
Around 0 C.E. to the present

ancestry:
Liao

language:
Gelao, a Sino-Tibetan language, but most speak Chinese, Hmong, Yi, or Bouyei instead

GEORGIANS

location:
Georgia, Russia, Armenia, Turkey

time period:
Unknown to the present

ancestry:
Proto-Kartvelian

language:
Georgian, a Kartvelian or South Caucasian language related to Laz, Mingrelian, and, more remotely, Svan

Historical Georgian Kingdoms

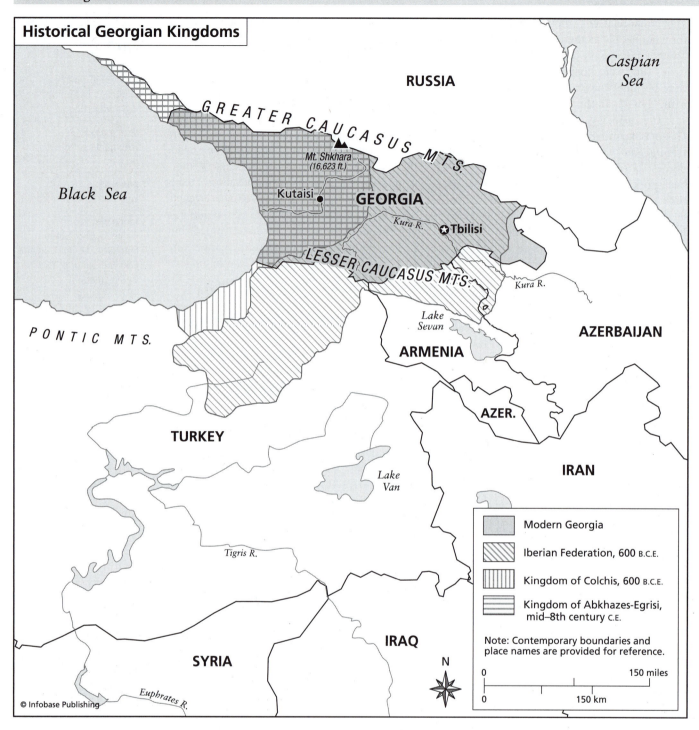

Legend:
- Modern Georgia
- Iberian Federation, 600 B.C.E.
- Kingdom of Colchis, 600 B.C.E.
- Kingdom of Abkhazes-Egrisi, mid–8th century C.E.

Note: Contemporary boundaries and place names are provided for reference.

© Infobase Publishing

from extremely cold mountaintops to subtropical beaches on the Black Sea coast.

ORIGINS

The Georgians count the ancient Colchians and Kartvelian peoples as their ancestors. Linguistically there is no doubt that the Georgians are related to all the other Kartvelian-language speakers, the Mingrelian, Laz, and Svan peoples. The connection to the Colchians is more speculative and in some ways problematic, especially given Herodotus's claim that they were black skinned and descended from Egyptian soldiers left in the Caucasus in the 19th century B.C.E. after an invasion.

There is no doubt that peoples have resided in the Caucasus since at least 50,000 years ago and perhaps as much as 100,000 years ago, but what relation those populations had to present-day Georgians is entirely speculative. The first

Georgians time line

B.C.E.

284–219 Reign of King Parnavaz I of Iberia (Kartli) when the Kartvelian peoples unite to form the Iberian federation in what is today eastern Georgia.

65 Rome conquers Iberia and then Colchis two years later.

C.E.

130s–150s Parsman II strengthens Iberia and visits Rome.

337 Mirian III establishes Christianity as the state religion of Iberia, making Georgia one of the oldest Christian states in the world.

572 Iberia expels the Persians.

645 The Arabs conquer Tbilisi and establish an emirate in the city.

Mid-eighth century Leon II unifies the western Georgian kingdoms and names it the Kingdom of Abkhazes-Egrisi.

Ninth century Unification of the eastern and western Christian churches in Georgia.

1008 The Kingdom of the Georgians absorbs the Abkhazes kingdom.

1010 Bagrat unifies all of Georgia, except Tbilisi, which is still held by the Arabs.

1068 The Seljuk Turks destroy much of Iberia.

1122 Georgians recapture Tbilisi and move their capital there from Kutaisi.

1125 David the Builder dies, leaving behind a unified, independent Georgian kingdom larger than ever before, to which subsequent rulers add even more Caucasian and Anatolian territory.

1184–1213 Apex of Georgian power under Queen Tamara.

1223 The Mongols overrun much of Georgia and kill King Giorgi Lasha.

1327 Giorgi the Brilliant expels the Ilkhanate Mongols from Georgia.

1366 The Black Death wipes out a large proportion of the Georgian populace.

1386 Weakened by the plague, Georgia is no match for Timur Leng's armies, which invade the region several times over the next 17 years until King George VII is forced to become a vassal of the Timurid empire.

16th–18th centuries Georgia is divided and repeatedly attacked in the west by the Ottoman Turks and in the east by the Persians.

1801 Most of east Georgia is annexed by Russia.

1810 Portions of central Georgia are also annexed by Russia.

1864 Serfdom is abolished in Georgia.

1918 Georgia declares independence during the chaos of the Russian Revolution.

1921 The Red Army takes Tbilisi and sets up 70 years of Soviet domination of Georgia.

1990 The South Ossetian Autonomous Oblast declares its independence from Georgia and seeks recognition from Moscow as the South Ossetian Democratic Soviet Republic, sparking civil war.

Anti-Soviet activist Zviad Gamsakhurdia is elected president of Georgia.

1991 Georgia attains independence from the disintegrating USSR.

The newly formed Georgian National Guard enters South Ossetia and wreaks havoc on the night of the Orthodox Christian Christmas, January 5.

1992 A December 1991–January 1992 coup deposes the increasingly despotic Gamsakhurdia and replaces him with Eduard Shevardnadze, who rules until 2003.

(continues)

Georgians time line *(continued)*

	A cease-fire is signed on July 14 and the Commonwealth of Independent States (CIS) begins a peacekeeping mission in South Ossetia. This is replaced with Russian peacekeepers during the 1990s.
	Following the Ossetians, the Abkhazians declare their independence from Georgia, sparking another civil war.
1994	A cease-fire is reached in the second civil war and a UN-monitored peacekeeping mission is established by the other CIS countries.
2003	The Rose Revolution, a peaceful demonstration against the corruption of the Shevardnadze government and a rigged presidential election, forces him to step down.
2004	New elections put Mikhail Saakashvili in power.
2007	The Abkhazian, Ossetian, and to a lesser degree Ajarian minority movements have yet to be worked out to anyone's satisfaction. Russian peacekeepers remain in South Ossetia and CIS peacekeepers in Abkhazia.
2008	M. Saakashvili is reelected for a second five-year presidential term.

solid evidence of proto-Kartvelian activity is the division between the Svan and the other three groups about 4,000 years ago, but where that split took place is still unknown. In the third century B.C.E. all four Kartvelian peoples emerged as the most powerful tribal federation in what is today eastern Georgia. Their federation is often labeled Iberian, sometimes Kartli, and existed alongside the dominant Kingdom of Colchis or Egrisi to the west.

HISTORY

The best date to begin the history of the Georgian people is 284 B.C.E., the start of the reign of Parnavaz I, king of Iberia or Kartli. Parnavaz is said to have united all the peoples of Iberia and expelled their enemies; he was recognized by both the Seleucids and the Colchians as the legitimate ruler of his people. Legend has it that he also created the first Georgian alphabet in the first year of his reign. Archaeological work in the last decade has confirmed that a Georgian alphabet did exist very early in Georgia's history, with the first examples being dated from the fifth century C.E. The dynasty established by Parnavaz, the Parnavazians, held the throne in eastern Georgia until the fifth century.

For the next few centuries Iberia and Colchis continued their alliance in the Georgian territories, leading some to claim that there has been a unified country there for more than 2,200 years. The Greek colonial activities in Colchis as well as the outright subjugation of the region by the Pontus GREEKS after 120 B.C.E. indicate that this is probably an exaggeration. Nonetheless the Roman conquest of Iberia in 65

B.C.E. and of Colchis two years later did lead to shared Roman domination in the region, at least until the second century C.E. At that time Iberia reemerged as a local power under the reign of Parsman II, who ruled for about 20 years until the mid-150s. Parsman II was welcomed to Rome by then-emperor Antoninus Pius and, according to Roman sources, had a statue of himself erected in the capital. Georgian histories mention this period as one in which Iberia was recognized by Rome as an ally rather than as a vassal, a position maintained for the next 300 years; however, Roman sources speak of Iberia as being under its jurisdiction.

The rule of Mirian III (284–361) saw the mass conversion of Christianity in Georgia after he made it his state religion in the 330s. Christians had lived in the region since the first century, but the religion did not completely replace the local Zoroastrian and pagan beliefs until the fourth century. By the fifth century Iberia was an ally-vassal of the Persians in political matters and a dependent of the Byzantines in church matters. At that time the Iberian king, Vakhtang Gorgasali, challenged the Persians militarily and the Byzantines religiously. He achieved independence for the Georgian Orthodox Church by withdrawing from the Catholicos of Constantinople, but he was less successful militarily, losing his life in a battle with the Persians in 502. Despite this loss Vakhtang Gorgasali I is considered a Georgian hero for having founded Tbilisi and recapturing some Georgian lands from the Persians. At this time western Georgia remained under the thumb of the Byzantine Empire.

In the last third of the sixth century the Iberians finally defeated the Persians and established a local government free of foreign oversight. This lasted for slightly more than 50 years before the year 645, when the Arabs captured Tbilisi but could not expand farther into western Georgia. Despite the small size of the Arabs' domain, they increased the trade into and out of Tbilisi and the city flourished under the local emirate. Surprisingly few Georgians seem to have converted to Islam at this time, despite Arab pressures to do so.

The middle of the eighth century introduced another movement to unify the peoples of Georgia. Leon of Abkhazia was able to defeat the Byzantines in Abkhazia and Lazica, which is what the Romans called the former Colchian lands, and declared himself king of the newly independent Egrisi-Abkhazia. He made Kutaisi in west Georgia his capital. In addition to ruling over the Abkhazian, Laz, and Mingrelian peoples, Leon also ruled over the majority of the Kartli or Georgians, as they are now known. In the ninth century this kingdom reinforced its independence as a Georgian state by withdrawing entirely from the Patriarch of Constantinople, as the Iberian church had in the fifth century. Despite the claims of a unified Georgian state for this period, some regions of the country were still held by the Arabs until David III, who ruled an Anatolian province of the Georgian kingdom in the last third of the 10th century, freed them. He also placed his adopted son, Bagrat, on the thrones of Iberia (Kartli) and Abkhazia; by 1010 Bagrat III had unified all regions of Georgia except the Arab emirate of Tbilisi. He ruled his large state from Kutaisi, the capital established by Leon several centuries earlier.

The relative peace and stability initiated by David and Bagrat were soon shattered when the Seljuk Turks invaded the Caucasus in the 1060s, destroying Iberia in 1068. The nomadic Turks did not establish a kingdom in the region, leaving politics to the Georgians, but plundered and destroyed so much property that the monarch withdrew, leaving his teenage son, David IV, to rule the kingdom. David, who became known as David the Builder, ruled from 1089 until 1125. During his three and a half decades on the throne he expelled the Turks, stopped paying tribute to them, created a regular Georgian army, and drafted 40,000 extra forces of foreign mercenaries. By 1122 David had retaken Tbilisi as well and moved the national capital there from its former home in Kutaisi. In the final days of his reign David also liberated the Armenian city of Ani from the Turks and thus expanded Georgia's boundaries farther into Anatolia. As a result of these accomplishments David is still considered one of Georgia's most successful kings (*see also* TURKIC PEOPLES).

Following David's rule Georgia experienced almost another full century of expansion until its borders stretched from the Black to the Caspian Seas and from Ossetia in the north to Mount Ararat in the south. Queen Tamara (1184–1213) ruled over the largest Georgian kingdom in its history, with large numbers of minor kingdoms and principalities paying tribute to her and thereby increasing the wealth of the royal family. Tamara's successor was preparing to lead a 90,000-man army in the Crusades when the MONGOLS arrived in 1223 and destroyed all that the Bagrationi dynasty had created in Georgia.

The century-long period of Mongol domination under the Ilkhanate divided the various Georgian principalities against one another and drained the kingdom of the wealth it had amassed in the previous era. Like the nomadic Turks, however, the Mongols were not able to sustain their sovereignty in Georgia and in the first decades of the 14th century Giorgi the Brilliant drove them out. To reestablish Georgia's economic might he also set up trade links with

---

Queen Tamara ⚜

Queen Tamara ruled Georgia from 1184 to 1213 and is credited with ushering in Georgia's golden age, proving herself such a successful ruler that she was referred to by Georgians as the "King of Kings and the Queen of Queens."

Tamara was born in 1160 to King Giorgi III and was named his heir apparent in 1178. She succeeded to the throne upon her father's death in 1184 and was titled *King Tamara,* but her right to rule was disputed by a team of nobles led by the minister of finance. A brief rebellion ensued and Tamara gracefully negotiated with the demands to quell the uprising. In 1185 a marriage to the Russian prince Yuri Bogolyubusky was arranged for Tamara, but, dissatisfied, she divorced him in 1187 and chose her second husband, Prince David Soslani from Ossetia. In 1193 Queen Tamara initiated the first of many aggressive attacks on neighboring Muslim countries, beginning with the Seljuk Turks, and she herself took part in the military campaign by leading her own army. The Georgian army met with an unprecedented number of successes and the Georgian kingdom expanded rapidly in territory and wealth. In 1201 Georgia annexed the Armenian cities of Ani and Dvin, and in 1204 Constantinople was captured by Tamara's nephew, Alexios I Komnenos, whom Tamara installed as ruler of the renamed Empire of Trebizond. In 1210 the Georgian army sacked northern Persia. Queen Tamara died in 1213 and was canonized by the Georgian Orthodox and Apostolic Church.

Byzantium, Venice, and Genoa, which saw the flow of raw materials out of Georgia and of finished products into it.

Unfortunately the second golden age for Georgia envisaged by Giorgi was not realized. The Black Death took thousands of Georgian lives in 1366 and just 20 years later was followed by a series of invasions by Timur Leng or Tamerlane. A number of Georgian monarchs tried either to appease the Timurids by converting to Islam or to defeat them in battle, but finally in 1403 George VII was forced to pledge his loyalty to Timur Leng on the condition of being allowed to retain his Christian faith and his Georgian Crown. At about the same time, the Georgians also faced invasion from the kingdom of the Black Sheep TURKMEN tribes, who had established their kingdom in Armenia and Azerbaijan in 1378. These invasions, combined with a change in trade routes caused by the Ottoman capture of Constantinople in 1453, left Georgia economically and politically weakened. The various principalities that had all joined under the Iberian kings regained their drive for independence, however, and by the early 16th century three separate kingdoms had emerged: Kakheti in the far east, Kartli or Iberia in the eastern portion of the center, and Imereti in the western portion of the center. The mid-16th century saw even further division when the Peace of Amasia divided Georgia into Ottoman and Persian spheres of influence in the west and east, respectively.

Despite the Peace of Amasia, Georgia experienced little peace in the late 16th, 17th, and 18th centuries. The Persians were especially active, invading Kakheti and Iberia again and again, even placing Muslim rulers on the Iberian throne until the mid-18th century. The Turks also tried to conquer portions of Georgia, invading the western portion of the country as far as Iberia many times during the 17th and 18th centuries. In 1762 Erekle II was able to unite Kakheti and Iberia, creating a unified east Georgia, but even this unification was not enough to repel repeated Turkish and Persian invasions. It was only the annexing of this unified kingdom by the RUSSIANS in 1801 that affected a modicum of peace in the region; this was followed in 1810 by the annexation of Imereti after much of the Georgian population was driven into Turkey. In addition to losing their political autonomy, the Georgians lost their independent Orthodox Church at this time, when the Georgian patriarch was forced to look to the Russian church as his leader.

Despite the loss of their own state and church, Georgians did not fare all badly under Russian protection. The centuries of warfare against the Turks and Persians came to a halt and economic and demographic conditions improved greatly. In 1864 serfdom was abolished in Georgia, freeing the peasants from their lifetime servitude under a single landowner, and improvements were made to the taxation and education systems that increased prosperity. With these social and economic improvements Georgians were ready in 1918 when the opportunity came to reassert national independence. In May of that year during the chaos of the Russian civil war, the national council of Georgia declared independence of Russia, which was ratified by the Soviets in a treaty two years later. The Georgian Democratic Republic lasted just under three years before the Red Army took Tbilisi in February 1921 and began the long process of "sovietization" of Georgian society. Collectivization of the land, industrialization, and a push toward the adoption of Russian language and culture were the hallmarks of 70 years of Soviet domination of Georgia.

The disintegration of the USSR in 1991 gave independence to Georgia but also many years of discord. The Georgian SSR that had existed under the USSR had been made up of several autonomous oblasts and republics occupied by significantly large minority groups. While the Mingrelians and Svan are ethnically similar to Georgians and have always considered themselves Georgian because of their shared church, Ossetians, Abkhazians, and Ajars have not. Civil wars in the early 1990s saw both the Ossetians and Abkhazians trying to free themselves from Georgian rule, and while the formal fighting ended more than a decade ago, violence and political uncertainty continue to plague both Ossetia and Abkhazia and the Georgian (and other) people living in them (*see* GEORGIANS: NATIONALITY).

CULTURE

Many Georgians continue to work in agriculture as their primary economic activity, growing grapes, hazelnuts, and citrus fruit and herding cattle, sheep, and goats. Georgians say of their fertile land that God took a break while creating the world to have a meal. He became so engrossed in eating that he tripped over the Caucasus Mountains and spilled his food onto the plains below, and the land that was blessed by God's leftovers became Georgia. The Soviet-era emphasis on industrialization also took the mining industry to Georgia, where there are pockets of manganese and copper that continue to produce income for a few Georgians. The production sector remains severely limited to the beverage industry and a few metal and chemical works.

The Georgians are one of the oldest Christian peoples in the world, having maintained their own church since about 337. Throughout history they have experienced great pressure to convert to Islam, having been conquered by Arabs, Persians, and Turks at various times, but for the most part they have maintained their adherence to their national church. A small number of Muslim Georgians, largely in the Ajar region of west Georgia, maintained their religion until the late 1920s, and today about 10 percent of the entire Georgian population consider themselves Muslim, but what proportion of that 10 percent are ethnically Georgian is difficult to surmise. In addition 70 years of religious persecution under the Soviets also affected the Christian Georgians, who became less and less religious over time. The 1970s created a bit of a revival in Georgian interest in religion when known dissidents, such as Zviad Gamsakhurdia, began using it as a nationalist rallying point. In 1988 the Soviet authorities permitted the reconsecration of disused churches, and a full-scale interest in Orthodoxy emerged along with Georgian independence in the early 1990s. By 1993 about 65 percent of the entire Georgian population were Georgian Orthodox; with ethnic Georgians making up only 70 percent of the country's population, it seems that the vast majority of Georgians consider themselves members of their national church.

FURTHER READING

Stephen K. Batalden, ed. *Seeking God: The Recovery of Religious Identity in Orthodox Russia, Ukraine, and Georgia* (DeKalb: Northern Illinois University Press, 1993).

Jonathan Cohen, ed. *A Question of Sovereignty: The Georgia-Abkhazia Peace Process* (London: Accord, 1997).

Bruno Coppieters, Ghia Nodia, and Yuri Anchabadze, eds. *Georgians and Abkhazians: The Search for a Peace Settlement* (Cologne: Bundesinstitut für Ostwissenschaftliche und Internationale Studien, 1998).

David Marshall Lang. *The Georgians* (London: Thames & Hudson, 1966).

Tim Potier. *Conflict in Nagorno-Karabakh, Abkhazia, and South Ossetia: A Legal Appraisal* (New York: Springer, 2000).

Georgians: nationality (people of Georgia)

GEOGRAPHY

Situated in the Caucasus Georgia is bordered by Azerbaijan on the southeast, by Armenia and Turkey on the south, by Russia in the north, and by the Black Sea in the west. With a land area of 43,418 square miles it is roughly the size of the state of West Virginia.

Georgia's mountainous terrain features prominently in the nation's history. The rugged Likhi Mountain range divides the country in two and accounts for the separate histories of eastern (Iberia) and western (Colchis) Georgia. The mountainous regions also served as havens for Georgians fleeing from Persian, Mongol, and Turkish invaders.

The western Georgian landscape is characterized by marshes, swamps, and rain forests, while eastern Georgia has a drier climate and plains typical of Central Asia. Approximately 40 percent of the country is forest and 10 percent is mountainous land.

INCEPTION AS A NATION

Georgia has had an indisputably vibrant history as the Georgian people were frequently invaded, by MONGOLS, Turks, Arabs, and Persians, only to arise victorious and drive out their attackers, even when impossibly outnumbered. The resulting national pride has persisted throughout Georgia's long history as a state, which frequently clashed with foreign rulers who tried to impose their own languages and ways of life.

By the mid-19th century Russian czarist rule was causing tension among the Georgian people as Georgian culture was being systematically erased. The Georgian monarchy had been dismantled and Russia had taken control of Georgian churches and monasteries. The Russian Orthodox clergy who now ran the Georgian Orthodox churches eliminated the Georgian liturgy and defaced medieval frescoes on churches throughout Georgia. Sensing the threat to Georgian culture, Prince Ilia Chavchavadze, world-renowned poet and orator, founded the Georgian Patriotic Movement and defined its goals as protecting and preserving Georgian culture. Among the movement's many endeavors were financing schools, supporting the national theater, and launching a Georgian newspaper, the *Iveria*.

Georgia experienced a short-lived independence in 1918 when the Russian Revolution

---

GEORGIANS: NATIONALITY

nation:
Georgia

derivation of name:
From the Greek word *georgios,* meaning "farmer," or from the Persian word *gurj,* meaning "wolf," for the wolf's head helmet that the Georgian king Vakhtang I Gorgasali wore when fighting the Persians

government:
Republic

capital:
Tbilisi

language:
Georgian 71 percent, Russian 9 percent, Armenian 7 percent, Azeri 6 percent, other 7 percent. In the territory of Abkhazia Abkhaz is the official language

religion:
Orthodox Christian 83.9 percent, Muslim 9.9 percent, Armenian-Georgian 3.9 percent, Catholic 0.8 percent, other 0.8 percent, none 0.7 percent

earlier inhabitants:
This region had numerous tribal groups, some of whom have been incorporated into the Georgian people; others have died out or become part of such minority groups as the Abkhazians and South Ossetians.

demographics:
Georgian 83.8 percent, Azeri 6.9 percent, Armenian 5.7 percent, Russian 1.5 percent, other 2.5 percent

Georgians: nationality time line

B.C.E.

5000   The Georgians are believed to be the first culture to produce wine.

2000–1000   Various tribes throughout Georgia frequently do battle with one another.

End of second millennium   Diaokhi and Kolkha in south and west Georgia's valleys are the first proto-Georgian states.

1200   The Kingdom of Colchis is established on the coast of the Black Sea; it later finds renown in the Greek myth of Jason and the Argonauts, who travel to Colchis to find the Golden Fleece.

800   The Kingdom of Colchis is destroyed by the northern Cimmerians, people of uncertain origin.

700   The Colchian kingdom is reestablished, and the central features of the revived society are agriculture and iron metallurgy. The Colchians also begin minting silver coins for their own market.

600   Colchis expands its trade relations with Greece and Greeks begin establishing trade colonies along the coast of the Black Sea. Greek culture significantly influences Colchian life and Greek becomes a widely spoken language in the kingdom.

300   Parnavaz I founds the Kingdom of Kartli (also known as Iberia to the ancient Greeks and Romans). Alexander the Great establishes his Macedonian empire just south of Iberia.

189   Many southern Iberian provinces are lost to invading Armenian armies.

120–63   In a campaign to expand his kingdom King Mithradates Eupator conquers Colchis and claims it for the Kingdom of Pontus, a country bordering the southern coast of the Black Sea and populated by Ionian Greeks.

65   Armenia and Pontus expand their kingdoms by claiming land belonging to Rome's eastern Mediterranean territories. Emperor Pompey attacks Iberia and Colchis because of their relationships with Armenia and Pontus, with whom Rome is at war. Pontus is consequently destroyed and incorporated into the Roman Empire, along with Colchis.

36   Iberia joins Rome in its war with Albania.

C.E.

100   Iberia obtains independence from Rome and reclaims territories formerly lost to Armenia.

200   Colchis, now renamed Lazicum, obtains full independence from Rome and establishes the Lazica-Egrisi kingdom.

327   King Mirian II of Iberia proclaims Christianity the official state religion, making Iberia one of the first states to adopt Christianity.

300–500   Iberia falls under Persian rule.

562   Western Georgia is conquered and incorporated into the Byzantine Empire.

600   Arabs conquer western Georgia.

1000   Georgia reclaims many of its territories and forms the first Georgian monarchy.

1001   Bagrat III inherits the Abkhazian throne and incorporates Iberia (now known as Tao-Klarjeti) in his kingdom.

1008–1010   Bagrat III obtains Kakheti and Ereti and becomes king of both eastern and western Georgia.

1040   Seljuk Turks invade Georgia in their campaign to expand their nomadic empire through Central Asia and Persia.

1071   The Byzantine-Armenian and Georgian armies are defeated by the Seljuk Turks at the Battle of Mantsikert.

1081   Armenia, Assyria, Anatolia, Mesopotamia, and much of Georgia have been conquered by Seljuk Turks. Georgia's more mountainous regions (Abkhazia, Svanetia, Racha, and Khevi-Khevsureti) remain beyond Seljuk control. The rest of the country is devastated by the invaders, who destroy cities and loot villages.

1089 At the age of 16 King David IV inherits the throne and organizes an army and a peasant militia to combat the Seljuk invaders.

1099 King David reclaims most of Georgia, except Tbilisi and Ereti.

1103–05 David IV invades and reclaims Ereti, as well as other Seljuk-controlled areas.

1118–20 The withdrawal of the Seljuk Turks leaves much of the Georgian land free and unsettled, and David IV welcomes the immigration and settlement of Kipchak warriors from the North Caucasus, Alans from Alania, and mercenaries from Scandinavia, Italy, and Germany.

1121 Seljuk sultan Mahmud declares jihad on Georgia. Despite outnumbering the Georgian army, the Seljuk troops are defeated, and the Georgian army goes on to conquer Tbilisi, Shirvan, and northern Armenia.

1125 King David IV dies, and he comes to be known as David Agmashenebeli, or "David the Builder."

1184 Queen Tamara, great-granddaughter of David IV, assumes the throne.

1194–1204 Tamara's armies defeat Turkish invasions from the southeast and conquer most of southern Armenia.

1204 The Byzantine Empire collapses and Tamara's troops conquer the Byzantine Lazona and Paryadria, and several other cities. The conquered lands become the Empire of Trebizond, and Tamara employs her relative, Prince Alexios Komnenos, as emperor.

1210 Georgia invades and conquers much of northern Persia, expanding the Georgian kingdom to the largest area in its history.

1215 Queen Tamara dies and comes to be known as Queen Tamara the Great. Her rule is also marked as Georgia's golden age, not only for Georgia's territorial expansion but for the development of Georgian art, science, and architecture.

1220 Mongol armies invade Georgia with marked brutality and impose high tribute on the Georgian population.

1243 Queen Rusudan of Georgia signs a peace treaty that forces her to cede many Georgian territories to the Mongols.

1259–1330 The Georgians organize numerous uprisings against the Mongol invaders without success until King George the Magnificent finally stops paying tribute to the Mongols and restores Georgia's state borders.

1386–1403 A series of Turkish and Mongol invasions nearly destroys the Georgian kingdom as cities are ruined and much of the population is killed or enslaved.

1783 Russia and eastern Georgia sign the Treaty of Georgievsk, which puts the kingdom of Kartli-Kakheti under Russian protection.

1804 Russia annexes eastern Georgia despite protests from many of the Georgian nobility.

1805 Russian troops defeat the Persian army near Zagam.

1810 Russia annexes western Georgia.

1855–1907 Prince Ilia Chavchavadse establishes the Georgian Patriotic Movement, which offers financial support for Georgian schools and the Georgian theater.

1878 Many formerly Georgian territories are incorporated in the Russian Empire.

1905 A mass peasant revolt leads to social reforms.

The Marxist Social Democratic Party becomes the primary political party in Georgia and occupies all of the Georgian seats in the Russian Duma. Well-known Bolshevik Josef Vissarionovich Djugashvili, otherwise known as Joseph Stalin, becomes the leader of the Georgian revolutionary movement.

1918–21 The Russian Revolution ends czarist rule and Georgia declares independence, renaming itself the Democratic Republic of Georgia.

(continues)

Georgians: nationality time line *(continued)*

1921 The Red Army invades and occupies Georgia. The Georgian government flees the country and the occupation is met with resistance and uprising.

Georgia becomes part of the Transcaucasian SFSR, along with Armenia and Azerbaijan. Georgia is forced to cede territories to Turkey, Azerbaijan, Armenia, and the USSR.

1921–51 50,000 Georgians are executed and 150,000 are purged.

1936 Georgia becomes a Soviet Socialist Republic.

1941 Hitler invades the USSR, but his armies do not get past Georgia in the Caucasus.

Georgians are split between the Russians and the Germans; 700,000 fight with the Red Army, but a high number also fight with the German armed forces. 350,000 Georgian soldiers are killed in battle.

1953 Stalin dies and Nikita Krushchev becomes the leader of the Soviet Union.

1956 At least 80 Georgian students are killed during a protest against Krushchev.

Georgian Communist Party leaders establish their own regional power base and Georgia's economy thrives, but blatant corruption sets in.

1964 Eduard Shevardnadze becomes Georgia's interior minister and is rumored to have organized the removal of his superior, Vasil Mzhavanadze, the corrupt first secretary of the Georgian Communist Party.

1972 Shevardnadze assumes the position of first secretary and immediately dismisses hundreds of corrupt officials.

1978 Moscow orders the revision of the constitutional status of Georgian as the official state language. Widespread protests and demonstrations force Moscow to back down.

1985 Shevardnadze is appointed Soviet foreign minister. His replacement as first secretary, Jumber Patiashvili, is considered by many to be an ineffective leader.

1989 A peaceful demonstration at a government building in Tbilisi is violently crushed by Soviet troops, resulting in the deaths of 20 demonstrators and the wounding of hundreds more.

The event spurs debate among Georgian political leaders, who ultimately conclude that they can no longer operate under Soviet rule.

1990 Georgia holds an open election in which Zviad Gamsakhurdia is elected head of the supreme council of the Republic of Georgia.

The South Ossetian Autonomous Oblast declares its independence from Georgia and seeks recognition from Moscow as the South Ossetian Democratic Soviet Republic, sparking civil war.

1991 Georgia declares independence from the Soviet Union.

Gamsakhurdia is elected president but his dictatorial behavior evokes criticism from many Georgians. Prime Minister Tengiz Sigua and two other senior ministers resign, claiming that Gamsakhurdia is a "demagogue and totalitarian."

A violent coup d'état forces Gamsakhurdia to flee to Chechnya.

threw Russia into disarray. The Democratic Republic of Georgia was run by the Menshevik group of the Social Democratic Party. However, in 1921 the Red Army invaded Georgia and occupied it, at which point Georgia became a part of the Transcaucasian SFSR. Georgia was forced to give up territory to Turkey, Azerbaijan, Armenia, and Russia and suffered mass executions and purges under Stalin's rule, despite his own Georgian origins. Between 1921 and 1924 50,000 people were executed, and from 1935 to

1951 more than 150,000 Georgian citizens were killed in Stalin's purges.

Following Stalin's death Nikita Krushchev assumed his place and launched a de-Stalinization campaign throughout the USSR and its widespread empire. GEORGIANS, who had previously taken great pride in Stalin's Georgian origins and credited him as a genius, were offended by Krushchev's program and protesters took to the streets, chanting, "Long live great Stalin." The Georgian army was called in to

1992 Eduard Shevardnadze is appointed head of the state council and Georgia later joins the United Nations.

A cease-fire is signed on July 14, and the Commonwealth of Independent States begins a peace-keeping mission in South Ossetia. This is replaced by Russian peacekeepers during the 1990s.

Following the Ossetians, the Abkhazians declare their independence from Georgia, sparking another civil war.

Georgian government forces go to Abkhazia to settle increasing separatist activity. The Abkhaz people retaliate and the violence results in the deaths of 14,000 people, with another 300,000 fleeing the country.

1993 Gamsakhurdia returns from exile and organizes a revolt against the new government.

Utilizing the government's preoccupation with ethnic violence in outlying Georgian territories, Gamsakhurdia and his followers are able to take most of western Georgia. The Russian military promptly intervenes and the uprising is quashed. Gamsakhurdia dies under mysterious circumstances.

1995 A new constitution is drawn up and Shevardnadze is reelected president.

1997 The death penalty is abolished.

1999 Georgia signs the Criminal Law Convention on Corruption and later becomes a member of the Council of Europe, an organization dedicated to the protection of human rights.

2000 Shevardnadze is reelected president, but accusations of corruption within the government, and even within Shevardnadze's own family, persist.

2001 A privately owned Rustavi-2 television station is raided by the government for its criticism of President Shevardnadze. Shevardnadze dismisses the entire cabinet.

2002 Police in the Georgian town of Zugdidi attack a local television station for its criticism of local police. Employees are beaten and equipment is destroyed.

2003 Shevardnadze's party wins the parliamentary elections, but international observers allege election rigging. Shevardnadze resigns and the election results are annulled.

2004 Mikhail Saakashvili is elected president and Zurab Zhvania is appointed prime minister. In new parliamentary elections Saakashvili's National Movement Party wins most of the seats.

2005 Prime Minister Zurab Zhvania dies of gas poisoning from a faulty heater. Finance Minister Zurab Noghaideli assumes Zhvania's post.

2006 The World Bank announces that Georgia experienced a larger reduction in corruption than any other Eastern European or former Soviet country between 2002 and 2005.

2008 Mikhail Saakashvili wins reelection in polling claimed by many Georgians to have been fraudulent. He called the election a year early in response to riots in late 2007 and a nine-day state of emergency. In reaction to an escalation in the Georgian-Ossetian conflict, Russia initiates bombing raids over several Georgian cities and sends tanks and troops across the border. Russia withdraws most of its troops and recognizes the independence of South Ossetia and Abkhazia.

handle the situation and responded to the protesters by opening fire; between 80 and 150 students were killed.

Around the same time the Georgian Communist Party took advantage of Krushchev's decentralization program and constructed its own capitalistic economy, which thrived and made Georgia one of the most successful Soviet republics. However, this economic explosion paved the way for pervasive corruption, which became so blatant that it even began to alarm officials in Moscow. First Secretary of the Georgian Communist Party Vasily Mzhavanadze was forced to resign in 1972 and was replaced by the interior minister, Eduard Shevardnadze. Shevardnadze promptly commenced a massive campaign to eliminate corruption within the Georgian government but corrupt practices persisted.

In 1985 Shevardnadze was appointed Soviet foreign minister and was replaced in Tbilisi by Jumber Patiashvili, who was ill equipped to

Even today many Georgians continue to honor the memory of Joseph Stalin, as they are doing here to commemorate the 48th anniversary of his death in 1953. *(AP/Shakh Aivazov)*

deal with the complications of glasnost and perestroika, economic- and political-reform programs put forth by Mikhail Gorbachev that culminated in the economic deterioration of the Soviet Union. Tensions mounted between the Communist Party and the Georgian Nationalist Movement and finally came to a head in 1989 when Soviet troops' response to a peaceful demonstration ended in the brutal killings of 20 people (some were killed with shovels) and the wounding of hundreds more. The violence and cruelty of the troops caused many to decide that Georgia must declare its independence from the USSR.

Georgia announced its independence in 1991 and leading dissident Zviad Gamsakhurdia was elected president. Gamsakhurdia's policies, however, proved to be authoritarian and dictatorial in nature and he was widely criticized. His prime minister and two other senior ministers resigned in protest of his totalitarian style of government, and after less than a year in office Gamsakhurdia became the target of a coup and fled the country.

In 1992 Eduard Shevardnadze was appointed president, but ethnic violence in Abkhazia and South Ossetia threw the country into turmoil, on which Zviad Gamsakhurdia capitalized. Gamsakhurdia returned from exile and rallied an uprising against the government. The fervor with which the western population of Georgia joined Gamsakhurdia's uprising alarmed many neighboring countries, and Russia sent troops to stop the uprising. The campaign collapsed and Gamsakhurdia died of a single gunshot wound to the head; whether it was self-inflicted or not has remained unclear.

Shevardnadze's presidency continued until 2003 but was riddled with conflicts over corruption. Though Shevardnadze appeared to be combating corruption within the government, it nevertheless continued. In 2001 a television station was raided for its criticism of the president, and Shevardnadze responded by dismissing the whole cabinet. The corruption, however, was not only within the government, but within Shevardnadze's own family. In 2000 a broadcast journalist who was reporting on corruption in the government claimed that members of Shevardnadze's family had threatened to kill him.

In 2003 Shevardnadze's party won the parliamentary elections, but international observers noted various irregularities that suggested election rigging. Thousands protested the election results and rose up in support of the National Movement Party. The nationwide protest, which eventually caused Shevardnadze's resignation, became known as the Rose Revolution. In January 2004 Mikhail Saakashvili was elected president, and one of his first actions while in office was to freeze Swiss bank accounts belonging to officials suspected of fraud and corruption. New parliamentary elections were held, in which the National Movement Party gained the majority of the seats and the office of prime minister was reinstated.

Saakashvili made great strides toward the reduction of corruption, which his predecessor, Shevardnadze, never did. In 2004 a new defamation law was passed, in which comments were protected from libel suits if made in parliament, in the courts, and during political debates. Furthermore the burden of proof in criminal cases was shifted from the accused to the accuser. Even education was reformed to reduce corruption. In 2005 the Ministry of Education and Science created a new entrance examination to make the academic admissions process fairer. In 2006 the World Bank reported that Georgia's reduction in corruption between 2002 and 2005 was more significant than that of any other Eastern European or former Soviet country.

CULTURAL IDENTITY

The Georgian culture dates back centuries if not millennia and Georgians have a recorded history covering 4,000 years. This may be one of the reasons that Georgians have maintained such a strong cultural identity and national pride, despite the complete collapse of the Georgian kingdom after raids and invasions from other ethnic groups, and despite the takeover by Russia.

In the contemporary period Georgian cultural identity is focused largely on the maintenance of the national homeland and the revitalization of the Georgian language and Orthodox Church after nearly 70 years of Russian domination. The importance of the national homeland can be seen in the two civil wars that Georgians have fought since 1990 to prevent South Ossetia and Abkhazia from seceding from the country. These two regions are integral to Georgian history and culture, and the homeland would be considered dismembered without them.

During the Soviet period the Georgian language was maintained in schools and other public forums because of the importance placed on it by Georgians themselves. When the central government in Moscow tried to revise this language policy in 1978, it was met with strong protests by the Georgians, who felt that to attack their language was to attack their nation. The protests caused Moscow to back down. Nonetheless just a decade later the language question was back on the agenda when the Georgian government passed a State Program for the Geor-

gian Language, which made teaching Georgian and passing a test in Georgian language and literature mandatory throughout the republic. From the Georgians' point of view this was an attempt at national unification under the banner of a common language. From many minorities' points of view, especially the ABKHAZIANS' and South OSSETIANS', this was tantamount to declaring war on them, for Georgian was not spoken by most of them.

Connected to the centrality of the Georgian language is the pride of place of the Georgian Orthodox Church as one of the oldest Christian churches in the world and a centerpiece of Georgian identity. In the 10th century Georgian nationalist poet Ioane Zosime wrote of the raising of Lazarus as a metaphor for the Georgian nation and its importance come judgment day. According to Zosime Georgian will be the language that God uses on that day, and the Georgian people's Christianity will be the basis upon which the rest of humankind will be judged. In the contemporary period Article 9 of the Georgian Constitution states, "The state recognizes the special importance of the Georgian Orthodox Church in Georgian history but simultaneously announces complete freedom in religious belief and the independence of the church from the state." When these two clauses are contradictory, the Orthodox Church's "special importance" has generally taken precedence over the concept of religious freedom.

FURTHER READING

Theodore Edward Dowling. *Sketches of Georgian Church History* (Boston: Adamant Media, 2005).

R. G. Gachechiladze. *The New Georgia: Space, Society, Politics* (College Station: Texas A&M University Press, 1995).

David M. Lang. *A Modern History of Georgia* (Oxford: RoutledgeCurzon, 2007).

Peter Nasmyth. *Georgia: In the Mountains of Poetry* (New York: St. Martin's Press, 1998).

Peter Nasmyth. *Walking in the Caucasus: Georgia* (New York: MTA, 2006).

Donald Rayfield. *The Literature of Georgia: A History* (Surrey: Curzon Press, 2000).

Jonathan Wheatley. *Georgia from National Awakening to Rose Revolution: Delayed Transition in the Former Soviet Union* (Burlington, Vt.: Ashgate, 2005).

Ghilzai (Ghaljai, Ghalji, Ghilji, Ghilzay, Gilzai, Khilji)

The Ghilzai are one of the tribal subgroups of the PASHTUNS of Afghanistan and Pakistan, who, along with the DURRANIS, make up the two largest and most important subgroups. The Ghilzai

GHILZAI

location:
Afghanistan and Pakistan with a few communities in Iran and India as well

time period:
about 500 C.E. to the present

ancestry:
Iranian

language:
Pashto, an eastern Iranian language

rose to prominence early in Pashtun history as the Lodhi dynasty, the rulers of the last phase of the Delhi sultanate, from 1451 to 1526, before being defeated by Babur, founder of the Mughal dynasty. The Ghilzai again made their mark on world history in the early 18th century when their chief, Mirwais Khan Hotak, defeated the Georgian administrator of Kandahar and then the Persian leadership of both Iran and Afghanistan. The short-lived Hotak dynasty ruled for just 22 years, 1709–31, before being defeated by the Persian king, Nadir Shah.

After these initial victories the Ghilzai took a backseat to Durrani leadership in Afghanistan in 1747, when their tribal leader, Ahmad Khan Abdali, was elected king of a united Pashtun kingdom. The Ghilzai suffered at the hands of Abdur Rahman Khan's campaign in the late 19th century to build a Durrani-based nation within Afghanistan, when many Ghilzai were displaced and had their property destroyed. In the 20th century the Ghilzai were often seen by the more urban, educated, and powerful Durrani as crude, uneducated peasants or nomads.

A turning point occurred in 1978 when the Leftist People's Democratic Party of Afghanistan (PDPA) overthrew the regime of Mohammad Daoud Khan, a Durrani, in the April Revolution. Two of the most important figures in this coup, Nur Mohammad Taraki and Hafizullah Amin, were Ghilzai Pashtuns, who, along with many of their followers, saw Marxism as a way of righting the wrongs of many generations of subjugation. Their wing of the PDPA, sometimes called Khalqis after the name of their newspaper, was opposed by a more multiethnic wing, sometimes called Parchamis for the same reason. The Parchamis were also sometimes called Royals because they were more urban, educated, and likely to cooperate with the monarch (prior to the 1973 coup) than were the Khalqis. Immediately after the 1978 coup these two rival wings tried to maintain a balance of power, with the Khalqis holding the position of prime minister while the Parchamis held deputy prime minister, defense, and interior. However, this situation did not last long; Khalqis supporters soon occupied all significant positions of power, with Taraki and Amin the two most powerful men in the country. However, their power did not last in the face of Soviet opposition to their radicalism. With the help of the Soviet Union Amin was swept from power and killed while a non-Ghilzai member of the Parchamis, Karmal, was installed. At the same time the Soviet Union began sending troops to Afghanistan to

support a puppet Communist regime in the face of thousands of mujahideen (Islamic) and other non-Communist forces that were waging war in the countryside. Many of these mujahideen forces were led by Ghilzai warlords. The most successful group, the Taliban, was a combination of Durrani and Ghilzai forces with a Ghilzai leader, Mullah Omar, perhaps the reason for their success.

In the years since the 2001 defeat of the Taliban the fate of the Ghilzai has once again been subjugation to the Durrani leadership—or at least that is the perception of many Ghilzai who have flocked back to the Taliban against the government of the U.S.-supported Durrani president, Hamid Karzai. Much of the current leadership of the Taliban, too, is Ghilzai, including Mullah Omar and Gulbuddin Hekmatyar, one of the leading mujahideen from the days of the Soviet resistance.

See also AFGHANISTANIS: NATIONALITY; AFRIDI.

Gilbertese   *See* I-KIRIBATI.

Gojoseon, people of (Dong-I, Dongyi)

In China, *Dongyi* is a general term that has been used since ancient times to refer to people living in the east; usually it carried the connotation of "barbarian of the east" as well. In Korea, however, the term is often translated into English as "eastern bowmen" and is used to refer to the people of the Gojoseon or Gochosen (Old Chosun) kingdom, the first (potentially mythological) kingdom on the Korean Peninsula. This is a misuse of the Chinese term, since it never referred to a single ethnic group, but for some it has been a useful shorthand to refer to the people of the Gojoseon period of Korean prehistory.

The founding date of the Gojoseon kingdom, 2333 B.C.E., is based on Korean mythology; that year was said to be the time that the founder of the state, Dangun, who was from the Bear clan, became king. The Korean calendar used in South Korea until 1961 also began in that year on the basis of this myth. Unfortunately no archaeological evidence has been found to support this claim. Instead most archaeologists and historians date the founding of the Gojoseon kingdom to about 500 B.C.E. and locate it in the Liao and Taedong River basins, with sovereignty over the peoples of southern Manchuria and northern Korea. The founders of this kingdom were probably members of the MUMUN CULTURE who shared

PEOPLE OF GOJOSEON

location:
Manchuria, the Korean Peninsula

time period:
Possibly 2333 to 108 B.C.E.

ancestry:
Probably Tungusic

language:
Probably an Altaic language, of which the Tungusic languages are one branch

their material assemblage of unmarked pottery, slash-and-burn agriculture, and possibly megalithic burials.

The term *Gojoseon* referring to this kingdom is a compound that includes the prefix *Go*, meaning "old," which distinguishes this period from the Joseon or Chosun period that began in 1392 C.E., and *Chosun*, which means "Land of Morning Calm." The name of the mythological founder of this kingdom, Dangun, has been assumed by many scholars to be a title rather than a given name and to be related to the Mongol term *tengri*, which was used to refer both to spiritual leaders or shamans and to political leaders. The assumption then is that the Gojoseon kingdom was led by individuals who claimed their authority from both the political and spiritual realms.

The founding of the Gojoseon period seems to have followed the introduction of bronze into Manchuria and northern Korea, and the Gojoseon kingdom seems to have been the dominant political power when the Iron Age began at the end of the fourth century B.C.E. This period also initiated the building of walled cities and fortifications, some of which were linked under a single ruler to form the kingdom. In the fourth century B.C.E. some of these walled cities fell to the Yen dynasty of northern China, one of many that ruled during the Warring States period (475–221 B.C.E.), and the Gojoseon moved the capital from Asadal to the area around contemporary Pyongyang. The Gojoseon period came to an end in about 108 B.C.E. when the kingdom was defeated after two years of warfare against the HAN Chinese. The people who were scattered by that defeat soon rose up again to form several small successor states, including Goguryeo, whose name is the basis for the modern term *Korea*.

Gond (Coetoor, Koi, Koitor, Koitur, Koytor)

The Gond are the largest tribal community in India, with about 4 million individuals. Generally their homeland is bounded by the Godavari Gorges in the south and the Vindhya Mountains in the north and is made up of the states of Madhya Pradesh, Chhattisgarh, eastern Maharashtra, northern Andhra Pradesh, and western Orissa. However, on the basis of linguistic data most experts believe that the original homeland of the Gond was farther south, in the hilly terrain between Tamil Nadu and Karnataka. There is little evidence for the

Gond timeline	
C.E.	
Ninth century	Possible date for the northern migration of the Gond into the highlands of central India.
10th century	Formation of the earliest Gond kingdoms that constituted Gondwana.
1480	Sangram Shah rises to power in the Garha-Mandla dynasty and rules from the city of Jabalpur.
1530	Sangram Shah dies and with him the zenith of Gond power in central India.
1564	Rani Durgavati, Sangram Shah's widow, dies a hero's death when trying to keep Akbar's Mughal army out of Gondwana.
1780	A Maratha Pandit kingdom annexes Garha-Mandla.
1857	The British kill the last Garha-Mandla king in his capital, Jabalpur.

time that their northern migration might have taken place, but some scholars believe the ninth century makes the most sense in view of the emergence of the Gond kingdoms a century later. Their current name was given to them during the Mughal era and means "Hill Men," while they refer to themselves as *Koitor* or any of several variations of that term; the meaning of their own name for themselves remains uncertain to this day.

Although they are listed as one of the SCHEDULED TRIBES in present-day India because most Gond do not engage in the Hindu caste system, for many centuries their kingdoms dominated much of the area of central India, known as Gondwana or Gondavana, land of the Gond. The first Gond kingdoms seem to date from about the 10th century while the last ones did not fall apart until the onslaught of the British colonial era in the 19th. The best-known dynasties during this period are the Garha-Mandla in the northern area of Gond territory around the upper Narmada valley, the Deogarh-Nagpur in the upper Wainganga Valley, and the Chanda-Sirpur in the south, where the Wainganga and Penganga Rivers join. The Gond were most powerful in the late 15th and early 16th centuries during the reign of Sangram Shah of the Garha-Mandla dynasty. His non-Gond queen was Rani Durgavati, who died in 1564 in an attempt to protect her late husband's land from the Mughals. She and the Gond armies failed and for several centuries the reigning Gond kings were forced to pay tribute to the Mughals in exchange for their relative autonomy in the country's central highlands. This autonomy was broken in

GOND

location:
Central India

time period:
Unknown to the present

ancestry:
Unknown

language:
Gondi, a Dravidian language with many dialects; many people classified as Gond also speak various Indo-Aryan languages, especially Hindi

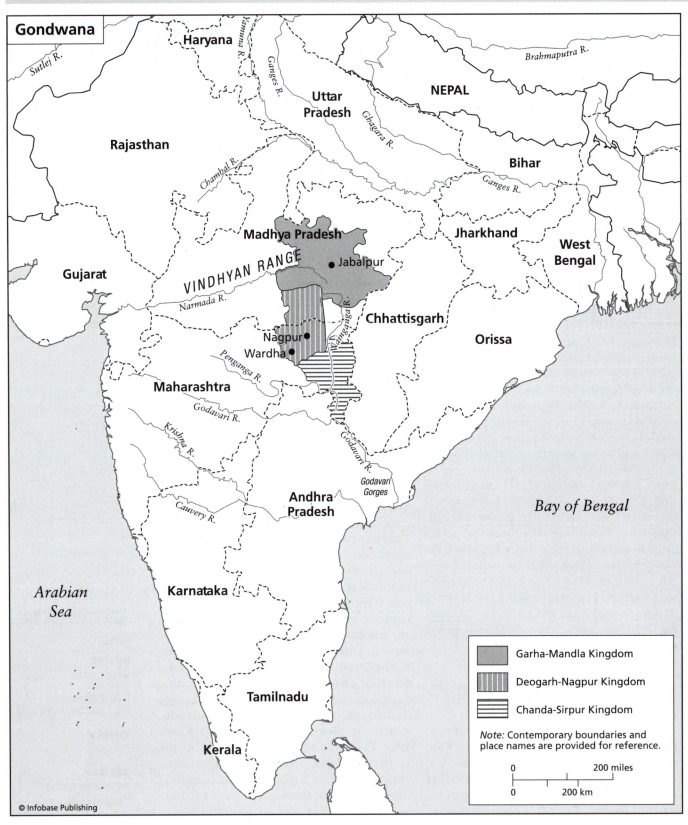

Gondwana

© Infobase Publishing

Garha-Mandla Kingdom

Deogarh-Nagpur Kingdom

Chanda-Sirpur Kingdom

Note: Contemporary boundaries and place names are provided for reference.

0   200 miles
0   200 km

the late 18th century by other, lesser known central Indian kingdoms, but the last Garha-Mandla Gond ruler died at the hands of the British in 1857; he was shot from a cannon, in front of his wife and son, in his capital city of Jabalpur.

Outside the ruling classes of the Gond most people engaged in swidden or slash-and-burn agriculture, sometimes called shifting or extensive agriculture because of the need to move onto new patches of land every year or two. The practice required that either virgin- or secondary-growth forest be cut down, allowed to dry for several months, and then burned to provide ash for fertilizer. After planting and harvesting for a season or two, depending on soil type and crops raised, each family had to move onto a new patch of forest and allow the previous one to sit fallow for a minimum of 10 to 12 years, preferably for as many as 20. In addition the Gond engaged in hunting and extensive wild-product gathering in the forests of central India; most historians assume that hunting and gathering were the primary economic activities prior to the Gond migration north before the 10th century. Today shifting agriculture has been outlawed in India because of deforestation, but most Gond continue to raise cattle and grow rice, other grains, and lentils as their most important economic activities; gathering of wild foods, wood, and honey also continues where possible.

Gond society has never existed as a single political, economic, or social unit. During the historical period of Gondwana separate dynasties and kingdoms ruled over small segments of the entire Gond population. This decentralized authority has persisted to this day; tribal solidarity does not exist beyond a generalized goodwill toward others in the same linguistic group, of which there are dozens within the larger category of the Gond people. The largest social and political unit recognized by the Gond is the tribal subsection. Some of these groups, especially those residing in the lower elevations and plains of central India, tend to have been more influenced by Hinduism and thus claim a higher status than other, less hinduized groups; however, very few have adopted any aspects of the caste system. Subsections that live in the hills and highlands have been less influenced by the surrounding Hindu culture and are less interested in the ranking system that accompanies that worldview. High rank is accorded to the descendants of the various dynastic subsections, often called Raj-Gonds today; they are generally owners of more extensive lands than are other Gond.

More important than these tribal connections are the bonds created by residence in a village or hamlet, a subsection of a village. Rather than closed geographic spaces Gond hamlets are usually spread out and incorporate many homesteads and their farmlands. In the lowlands and plains Gond hamlets and villages tend to be more compact and resemble those of their Hindu neighbors. Politically Gond villages are fairly democratic institutions with a headman elected by the male villagers. The village council, *panch,* is also representative of the community, at least of the men of the community, and includes not only the headman and religious specialists, but also a watchman and a handful of male elders. These councils traditionally settled local disputes over land, inheritance, and other matters seen as within the purview of human control; much social control, however, was meted out by the gods and spirits, especially related to breaches of exogamy laws or to internal family matters. For large and important social decision-making processes all village men engaged in discussion and participated in the final resolution.

Gond homesteads are residential units for extended or joint families, made up of a monogamous married couple and their married sons, wives, and children; polygyny, the ability to have more than one wife, is not allowed. Upon marriage women move out of their natal homes and into the homesteads of their husbands, a pattern referred to as patrilocal residence. At the time of her marriage a woman also leaves the patrilineal clan into which she was born in order to become a subordinate member of her husband's clan. These exogamous groups, which require all people to marry someone from a different clan, are made up of Gond who all believe they are related to one another through their fathers, fathers' fathers, and so on, as far back as a common, often mythological ancestor.

As is the case in many societies, kinship is extremely important among the Gond, and membership in a patrilineage and its larger unit, the clan, is perhaps the most important reference point for the Gond to locate one another in the social sphere. Marriage partners must be chosen from outside the lineage and clan, or such supernatural punishments as leprosy, worms, or other diseases will occur in both partners. During times of difficulty or conflict immediate support is received from one's closest patrilineal relatives, and if the conflict expands, then the clan may get involved as well. In the region around Mandla 18 of the Gond clans have united to form an even larger kinship unit, a phratry, which is also an exogamous unit, although some individuals have been able to marry within the phratry upon paying a fine and asking the community to accept the otherwise forbidden union.

In addition to punishing those who break the rules of clan exogamy, local spirits and gods are believed to punish adultery. Premarital sex is not a concern among most Gond, but once a couple's union is recognized by the community as a marriage, fidelity is extremely important. Adultery is believed to cause such major calamities as crop failure, widespread disease among either humans or cattle, or other natural disasters. Marriages are often negotiated between families when both partners are quite young and usually take place between cross-cousins; for example a boy may marry his mother's brother's daughter or his father's sister's daughter. Before a marriage can be seen as completed, the groom's family must pay a bride price to the bride's family; this wealth, whether in cash, cattle, land, or other objects, both reimburses the woman's family for the loss of her labor, since she is required to move out of the homestead and into her husband's family's home, and legitimates any children the couple has. The higher the status of the bride's family, the higher the bride price a man is required to pay.

There is another form of marriage among the Gond as well, usually engaged in only by poor men who do not have the ability to provide bride wealth. In these matrilocal marriages the men move into their wife's family's homestead and work their in-laws' land. It is only families without sons who choose this option for their daughter since those with sons tend to need the daughter's bridewealth in order for the son to marry; also with sons to inherit the land, a son-in-law would just be an extra mouth to feed rather than an heir.

Divorce is not an uncommon occurrence among the Gond and may be initiated by either a man or a woman. The most important and common reason for a man to seek a divorce is that his wife is unable to bear a child, although negligence in doing household work or having a bad temper can also lead a man to initiate these proceedings. Women are able to leave their husbands on the grounds of alcoholism, physical abuse, or inability to provide for the household. Both kinds of divorce must be recognized and legitimated by the village council. Gond social norms also allow young widows to remarry, usually to a close relative of her first husband; otherwise widows remain in their family home and are cared for by the youngest son, who automatically inherits the homestead.

The Gond universe is made up of a large number of gods, spirits, and ancestors, in addition to the visible world of humans and animals. The supreme god, Bhagwan or Bara Deo, is a distant being who is often invoked but rarely worshipped or engaged in ritual. Gond believe he created the earth and all the things on it, including humans, but then withdrew. More important for local rituals are the plethora of gods and goddesses connected to aspects of the natural world, such as water, rocks, trees, hills, and mountains. The earth, water, and air are the most important of these natural spirits or deities and are frequently invoked in rituals meant to improve harvests, cause rain, or ward off disasters. The spirits of Gond ancestors are likewise important in the religious system and are seen as the causes of most family problems; they also punish such familial misdeeds as breaking the rule of clan exogamy or failing to honor the ancestors through sacrifice. Finally many present-day Gond have adopted a number of gods and spirits from the Hindu pantheon, and rituals honoring Siva or Vishnu are not uncommon in Gond communities.

Many religious rituals are overseen by village priests, who inherit their positions but must be reviewed and accepted by village councils. They perform all sacrifices as well as preside over marriages, village rituals, and other events. A second category of ritual specialist is less formal and is based more on individual ability to engage the spirit world than on an ascribed position derived from kinship. These magicians or sorcerers serve as intermediaries between the human and spirit worlds, seeking information about illnesses and other misfortunes and offering compensation to the spirits for any slights or wrongs they feel they have suffered at the hands of humans. Witchcraft and the evil eye are also part of the Gond belief system and can be reversed only by these intermediaries.

FURTHER READING

Verrier Elwin. *Leaves from the Jungle: Life in a Gond Village.* 2d ed. (New York: Oxford University Press, 1958).

Stephen Fuchs. *The Gond and Bhumia of Eastern Mandla.* 2d ed. (Bombay: Asia Publishing House, 1968).

Gorontalese (Gorontalo, Holontalo, Hulontalo)

The Gorontalese are AUSTRONESIANS of northern Sulawesi, Indonesia. In the past there were six separate Gorontalic languages spoken in the region, but by the end of the 20th century only two or possibly three had survived, Gorontalo and Suwawa; Antinggola is also sometimes listed as a small, surviving Gorontalic language.

The earliest history of the Gorontalese probably resembles that of the majority of Austronesian speakers in Indonesia and the Philippines, with whom they have both a linguistic and a cultural connection. Their ancestors migrated from southern China about 5,000 years ago, down through the Philippines, and into Indonesia starting about 2500 B.C.E. Their agricultural economy allowed them to dominate any prior inhabitants and to develop larger and more complex societies throughout time. By the 16th century arrival of the Europeans on Sulawesi, which they called Celebes, the Gorontalese had been living in five separate kingdoms for about 200 years. These states were linked by a common language, culture, and political structure that favored the selection of a king or queen from among qualified candidates rather than through inheritance. According to some sources the arrival of both Islam and the Portuguese coincided with the conclusion of a long period of civil war in Gorontalo.

At about the same time as the arrival of the Portuguese in 1525 the Gorontalese began converting to Islam, which had entered the island via the sultanate of Ternate. The Portuguese, who built a number of forts in the region, including Fort Otonaha, which still exists today, were soon joined in the region by the Spanish via their own colony in the Philippines. Some remnants of that brief colonial interlude remain vital parts of Gorontalo culture today, including foods such as tomatoes, corn, and chili peppers; afternoon siestas; and horses. Following the Portuguese and Spanish in the colonial race for spices and other tropical resources were the Dutch, who landed in 1677 and finally wrested control from the Gorontalese kings in 1681. In the following century relations between the Dutch and Gorontalese were more peaceful and the latter even requested a Dutch military presence in the region in 1729 to ward off attacks from the powerful Buginese.

Gorontalese history in the 20th century is similar to that of the rest of Indonesia; they were occupied by the Japanese in 1942 and gained independence from the Dutch in 1949. The Gorontalese, however, drove the Japanese off their territory soon after occupation in 1942 and actually declared their independence in the same year, unlike other regions of Indonesia. Ridding their region of the Japanese also meant escaping the extensive bombing that took place elsewhere in the archipelago.

In the 21st century Gorontalo achieved the political status of a province when it was carved out of Sulawesi Utara in 2001. This was done to separate and give more power to the Muslim Gorontalese in relation to the largely Christian Minahasans.

The economic base of Gorontalese culture is slash-and-burn or swidden rice farming; other crops include corn, yams, millet, coconuts, tomatoes, and other vegetables and fruits. Coastal groups also fish for both subsistence and the market, while marketing has long been important at all levels of society, from spices and timber during the colonial period to handicrafts, fish, and produce today. Some Gorontalese today run "five-foot retailers," very small shops that sell a wide variety of goods as they become available locally.

Two important principles of Gorontalese society are their bilateral kinship structure, which counts mothers' and fathers' relatives as equal in the creation of larger kindred networks, and *mohuyula*, or mutual help or support. Within kin and village networks and at a wider level in linguistic communities the Gorontalese are required to provide financial and other assistance to those in their networks who need it; in turn they are also able to request assistance from others. The final important aspect of Gorontalese culture is their Islamic faith, which most sets them apart from their Minahasan neighbors, who are primarily Christian.

Greeks (Seleucid)

While European in their origins and Hellenistic in their culture, the Greek and Macedonian descendants of Alexander the Great's armies and the soldiers and leaders of the Seleucid Empire played a significant role in the history of Central Asia and northern India. Of all these figures Alexander the Great played the largest role in local legends. As late as Marco Polo (1254–1324), who claimed to visit the city of Balkh, ancient Bactra, on his travels to the East, many kings in the region boasted of descent from Alexander. Alexander's horse Bucephalus was even said to be the ancestor of a line of legendary horses from Badakhshan.

GEOGRAPHY

The territories conquered by the Greeks and Macedonians under Alexander and later consolidated by the Seleucids ranged from the middle of Anatolia or contemporary Turkey in

---

GORONTALESE

location:
Sulawesi, Indonesia

time period:
Probably about 2500 B.C.E. to the present

ancestry:
Austronesian

language:
Gorontalo and Suwawa, both Austronesian languages; four other Gorontalese dialects have become extinct

---

GREEKS

location:
Central Asia

time period:
329 to 130 B.C.E.

ancestry:
Greek and Macedonian

language:
Ancient Greek and Aramaic

Greeks time line

B.C.E.

329–327 Alexander the Great leads his army of Macedonians and Greek allies and mercenaries into Central Asia to destroy the remnants of Persian rule in the area and to secure the region. He establishes fortresses there to maintain security against Persian sympathizers and raiding nomads.

323 Alexander the Great dies at Babylon and most of the eastern portion of his empire falls into chaos. Alexander's generals take over the rule of his empire, with the Ptolemies in Egypt and Seleucids in Central Asia.

235 Greco-Bactrian kingdom established in Transoxiana by the descendants of Alexander the Great's soldiers. Diodotus II is the first Greco-Bactrian king, though his father had started the decades-long process of breaking free of Seleucid rule.

170 The Greco-Bactrian kingdom splits into eastern and western portions or the houses of Antimachos and Eukradites, respectively.

146 The Greco-Bactrian city of Ai Khanoum is sacked and destroyed by nomads.

135 The Yuezhi invasion pushes Scythians (Sakas) and Parthians into Bactria.

130 Heliocles I, the last Greek king of western Bactria, falls to nomadic invaders.

the west to the Indus River in the east, the Syr Darya River in the north, to the Persian Gulf and Indian Ocean in the south.

ORIGINS

The Central Asian and Indian settlers of Greek descent all had their origins in the armies of Alexander the Great and the later Seleucid Empire.

HISTORY

The earliest interactions between Greeks and Persians, which led eventually to the expansion of Alexander the Great's empire into Central Asia, were in the sixth century B.C.E., when Persian armies under Cyrus the Great conquered Greek-held territory in Asia Minor. The years 490 B.C.E. and 480 B.C.E. also saw significant battles between these two empires on Greek territory, with eventual Greek victories. In the fourth century B.C.E. the tables turned when Philip II of Macedon began to plan to conquer the expansive Persian Empire (*see* PERSIANS, ACHAEMENIDS). Philip himself was murdered at court, but his son, Alexander, believed that the Persians were the source of the treachery that led to his father's death.

Alexander III, king of Macedon, better known as Alexander the Great, conquered the Persian-held territories of Bactria and Sogdiana in Central Asia, the regions around the Amu Darya and Syr Darya Rivers in contemporary Afghanistan and Turkmenistan, in 329–327 B.C.E., and brought the Persian Achaemenid empire to an end. He also invaded the Punjab region of contemporary India and Pakistan and established Greek rule there around the Pakistani city of Taxila, until the Seleucids were forced to sign a treaty of alliance with the Indian Mauryans in 304 B.C.E.

While Alexander himself died in Babylon soon after these conquests, his legacy in Central Asia and the Indian subcontinent lived on for hundreds of years. In the first few decades after his death his far eastern territories fell into chaos, with the local BACTRIANS, SOGDIANS, and Persians refusing to succumb to Greek power. Finally one of his soldiers, Seleucus, was able to consolidate power and emerge as the head of a long ruling Greek dynasty in Asia, the Seleucid Empire. Under the Greek Seleucids Bactria was at least partially transformed into a seat of Hellenistic culture. From agricultural products like grapes and olives to the building of Greek theaters, mansions, and even an entirely new city of Ai Khanoum. Bactria, at least on the surface, was transformed into a Greek outpost for its Greek inhabitants.

The vast territory held by Alexander means that statues and images of him have been found throughout Europe, Asia, and the Indian subcontinent. *(Library of Congress Prints and Photographs Division)*

After less than 100 years of Seleucid building in Bactria, a local satrap or governor, Diodotus I, began accumulating power and military forces, a process that eventually led to his and his son's minting their own coins and breaking free of foreign rule. Unfortunately these events are known to us only through the coinage; written records have either disappeared entirely or not yet been found in the sands of Afghanistan. The archaeological evidence indicates that this local rule was no less Greek than that of Seleucus or his successors Antiochus I and Antiochus II. Bactria continued to trade with the rest of the Hellenistic world and to adopt artistic and building styles from the Mediterranean area. At the same time trade and relations with India that had begun earlier continued unabated during this period, at least from what we can learn from the sites that have been excavated.

The transformation from Seleucid to Greco-Bactrian kingdoms between 250 and 235 B.C.E. was relatively peaceful. It was only a generation later, between 212 and 205 B.C.E., that the Seleucid ruler Antiochus III attempted to take back this eastern portion of his empire by force. By that time the Bactrian kingdom was ruled by Euthydemus I, who was determined to hold on to the kingdom he had wrested from Diodotus II. After an early defeat the Greco-Bactrians under Euthydemus I retreated to their capital at Bactria and were trapped there for two years but without being overrun by the Seleucid armies. Eventually Antiochus III sent an emissary, who settled the grievances between the two kings and ratified the legitimacy of the rule of Euthydemus I in Bactria.

As is the case with so much Greek history of this region, very little beyond the names of some of the Greco-Bactrian kings can be read from the archaeological record. We know from the coins that a split occurred in about 170 B.C.E. between those Greco-Bactrians who continued to rule in Transoxiana, the so-called House of Eukradites, and those who ruled in the eastern portion of the kingdom on the Indian subcontinent, the so-called House of Antimachos. But what the policies of any of these kings were has been lost to history. The same is also true of the daily lives of the people in both regions. The only thing we can know with certainty is that these kings were continually under pressure from bands of nomadic soldiers and looters from the north and from the Indians to the south. Eventually it was the northern KUSHANS who overran the Greco-Bactrians or Indo-

Bactrians as they are sometimes called and established their own kingdoms in this land.

CULTURE

Hellenistic culture in this region differs somewhat from that of its European cousins, the ancient Greeks. The constant interactions among Greeks, Persians, Bactrians, Sogdians, Indians, SCYTHIANS, and other nomadic groups all contributed to developments in many cultural aspects. In the area of religion Greek gods and epic heroes were incorporated into a wide variety of other traditions, from the Zoroastrianism of the Persians and Bactrians to the Buddhism practiced in India and Pakistan. Greek architecture is evident in the Central Asian cities of Alexandria Eschate, or Alexandria the Farthest, in Sogdiana, and in numerous other Greek cities.

FURTHER READING

Frank L. Holt. *Thundering Zeus: The Making of Hellensitic Bactria* (Berkeley and Los Angeles: University of California Press, 1999).

Gujaratis (Gujars, Gujjars, Gurjars)

Gujarati is a collective term for people who speak this language as their mother tongue and can trace their ancestry to the Gujarat region of India; it is also used for people who live in the state of Gujarat, which was created along linguistic lines in 1960. Mohandas Gandhi and Mohammad Ali Jinnah are two famous Gujaratis, though only the former continued to use the language throughout his life; Jinnah advocated

---

Diodotus II

Diodotus II was a ruler of the Greco-Bactrian Kingdom from 240 to 230 B.C.E. The Greco-Bactrian kingdom consisted of the areas of Bactria and Sogdiana, today's northern Afghanistan and neighboring Tajikistan. Shortly after Alexander the Great conquered the Persians' Achaemenid empire, he died at the age of 32 and his vast empire was partitioned among his generals in the year 323 B.C.E. The generals became known as satraps, and Seleucus was satrap over Babylon and the whole of the eastern portion of the empire, including Bactria and Sogdiana. In 250 B.C.E. Diodotus I, governor of Bactria, defected from the Seleucid Empire and established the Greco-Bactrian kingdom. Other countries within the Seleucid Empire quickly followed, such as Parthia. In 240 B.C.E. Diodotus I died and was succeeded by his son, Diodotus II, who allied with the Parthian king Arsaces to unite against Seleucus II. When Seleucus II sent troops to sack Bactria and Parthia as Diodotus II and Arsaces had predicted, the Seleucid troops were defeated. Diodotus II was assassinated and his throne was usurped by Euthedymus I in 230 B.C.E.

GUJARATIS

location:
India, Bangladesh, and Pakistan, plus a large diaspora throughout the world; they also have a small presence in Afghanistan

time period:
Fifth century to the present

ancestry:
Gujar

language:
Gujarati, an Indo-Aryan language

GURKHAS

location:
Nepal and northeastern India

time period:
18th century to the present

ancestry:
Various Tibeto-Burman–speaking peoples of Nepal

language:
Nepali or Gurkhali, an Indo-Aryan language, as well as a number of Tibeto-Burman languages, such as Gurung and Magar

that Urdu become the official language of the country he founded, Pakistan. As a contemporary group the Gujaratis have very little in common other than language, as this identity is crosscut by many others, including caste, religion, class, and occupation.

Nonetheless it is useful to speak of a historical Gujarati or Gujar people who formed the foundation of this later linguistic community. The ancestors of the contemporary Gujaratis were Gujars, who seem to have entered India in approximately the fifth century, at the same time that the Huns conquered parts of the northern region of the subcontinent. As is the case with some remote Gujar communities today in Pakistan and Afghanistan, these people lived primarily as pastoralists, moving as needed to find grass and water for their herds of cattle, goats, or sheep. In the seventh century the Pratihara dynasty was established at Nandipur in northwest India, and many historians believe that this was a Gujar kingdom; others, however, contest this notion and believe the kings and their families were from other groups. In any case the majority of Gujars continued to live pastoral lives at this time.

In the 11th century north India was invaded by Arabs and other Muslim peoples, and from this period on some Gujars began to convert to Islam. This conversion also led to differences in occupation, for Islam prevents its adherents from collecting interest on money transactions, and thus among urban Gujars it was only Hindus who could serve as moneylenders and other handlers of large amounts of cash. During the native uprising in India against the British in 1857, this difference in handling money emerged as a very clear line of identification when Hindu and Muslim Gujars attacked each other. The pastoral, mostly Muslim Gujars had been under considerable pressure since the early years of the century, when the British had removed them from communally used pastures and granted their land to various agricultural castes, such as the Jats. As a result of this loss of income from herding these Gujars had experienced dual pressure from their Hindu moneylending cousins as well as from the British themselves, and when the colonial regime was weakened by other events in June 1857 they were among the first to rise up.

Today a number of descendants of these pastoral Muslim Gujars continue to live in India, Pakistan, and even as far away as Afghanistan. Those in the latter two countries tend to be nomadic, though the population in Afghanistan is known more for doing odd jobs, performing as musicians, and living as other types of itinerant workers similarly to the ROMA population of Europe. In India and Pakistan Gujar today is a caste identity, a subgroup of the larger Ksatriya or warrior *varna.*

Gujars   *See* GUJARATIS.

Gurkhas (Gorkhas)

While not technically an ethnic group, the Gurkhas are so well known in the West for their military exploits as part of both the British colonial and Indian armies in south Asia that they have come to constitute a people. Generally Gurkhas are members of several Tibeto-Burman–speaking ethnicities of Nepal and northern India, including the GURUNG, who make up the majority of Gurkhas; the MAGARS, LIMBU, and TAMANG; and others. Their name is from the Kingdom of Gorkha, which was established in the mid-16th century by a Hindu ruler, Dravya Shah, in the area around the city of Gorkha. In the mid-18th century the Gorkha king Prithvi Narayan Shah expanded the old Gorkha kingdom to encompass the Kathmandu Valley, founding the contemporary state of Nepal with its Hindu religion and castelike social divisions. Gurkhas since that period have claimed descent from the great warrior castes of India, particularly the Rajputs, and posit that their ancestors were driven from India by foreign, especially Muslim invaders.

The Gurkha military tradition began with the Shah kings' invasions and eventual conquest of the NEWAR people of Nepal's Kathmandu Valley. The first regular units of this army, however, were raised in 1763 with the creation of Sri Nath and Purano Gorakh. These units and others first became known outside Nepal in the late 18th century when, after uniting the many principalities of Nepal, they turned their war machine on both Tibet and British-controlled India. Their invasions of Tibet in 1788 and 1791 were initially successful but resulted in Chinese retaliation and occupation in the region. The Anglo-Nepalese War of 1814–16 further highlighted the Gurkhas' military prowess to the British, who, despite their victory over them, began to recruit significant numbers of their soldiers into the colonial army.

During the course of the past almost 200 years many thousands of Gurkhas have fought and died for causes that were of little or no concern to them with regard to their territory or

A Gurkha soldier with drawn *kukri* protecting the border between Hong Kong and China in 1991. *(OnAsia/Gerhard Jörén)*

identity. They fought with the British against the mutineers in the Indian Mutiny of 1857–58, the Second Afghan War in 1878–80, and the Boxer Rebellion in China in 1900. During World War I more than 200,000 Gurkhas fought on the side of the British, and thousands more, divided into 40 battalions, fought in World War II. "Ethnic" Gurkha units, actually made up of Nepalese citizens of various backgrounds, continued to serve in the British military until the end of the 20th century, primarily in Hong Kong before it reverted to Chinese ownership in 1997. Even today the Indian army recruits Nepalese citizens into its Gurkha units to serve in Kashmir and other regions of the country. Gurkha units have also served under the United Nations as peacekeepers.

As they have a variety of ethnic backgrounds it is difficult to point to a single Gurkha culture that differs from Nepal's national culture or that of its constituent ethnic groups. However, within the military tradition of the Gurkhas there is an important legend that claims that a Gurkha will never draw his sword or *kukri* without bloodshed, even if it is his own. This legend, in addition to the Gurkha war cry, *Jai Mahakali, Ayo Gorkhali,* literally, "Glory be to the Goddess of War, here come the Gorkhas!" has significantly added to their mystique as a proud, militaristic, and coura-

geous people. In Nepal today this reputation has also contributed to their social standing, where retired Gurkha soldiers hold numerous high-ranking positions in their communities, the government, and elsewhere.

Since the mid-1980s *Gurkha* has taken on a second meaning; a group of Nepali-speaking peoples from West Bengal has organized as the Gorkhaland National Liberation Front (GNLF), calling for a Gurkha state. As Nepalese speakers these people had long felt themselves to be separate from the BENGALIS of West Bengal and looked to the glories of the old Gorkha kingdom as part of their historical past. On the basis of this history and identification the governments of both India and West Bengal signed an agreement with the GNLF giving them broader autonomy as the Darjeeling Gorkha Hill Council. That has since been renamed the Gorkha Hill Council.

See also NEPALESE: NATIONALITY.

FURTHER READING

Byron Farwell. *The Gurkhas* (London: A. Lane, 1984).
C. J. Morris. *The Gurkhas, an Ethnology* (Delhi: B. R., 1985).

Gurung (Tamu)

The Gurung or Tamu as they call themselves are an indigenous people of the Himalayan region, especially Mount Annapurna and Mount Machhapuchhre in Nepal; they live in the high elevations of these mountain ranges. Their name for themselves, *Tamu,* means "horseman" in their own language and points to the importance of these animals in their culture. *Gurung* is from the Tibeto-Burman term *grong,* meaning "farmer," and has been used by outsiders since about the 18th century to refer to these people.

Gurung mythology states that their people were ruled by a king, a Ghale Raja, from ancient times until the 15th century, when the last one was overthrown by Nepali kings of the Shah family. The Gurung then became loyal soldiers and servants of their new rulers and were rewarded with high status in the new Nepali kingdom, consolidated by Prithyi Narayan Shah in 1769. With the entry of the British in south Asia the Nepali kings allowed the Gurung and others to serve the British as members of the regiments of GURKHAS, which policed the region.

As their names indicate the two most important economic activities among the Gurung are farming and pastoralism. In the past most families tended herds of sheep as their primary

GURUNG

location:
Southern Annapurna and Machhapuchhre Mountains of Nepal

time period:
Unknown to the present

ancestry:
Linguistic evidence points to Tibetan origins and some mythology indicates origins from the Central Asian Huns or Xiongnu, but they are currently considered indigenous to the Nepal region.

language:
Gurung, a Tibeto-Burman language with several dialects

activity but this diminished throughout the 20th century as a result of land degradation. Today subsistence agriculture is more important than animal husbandry, with hardy varieties of millet, wheat, and barley being the primary crops; these are supplemented with corn, soybeans, rice, and potatoes. Household gardens supply vegetables, some fruits, and herbs, and food gathering provides mushrooms, roots, and fruits. In addition some families continue to keep a few goats, buffaloes, oxen, and chickens for personal use or graze small herds of sheep or water buffaloes at altitudes too high for farming. Some Gurung men also look to the army or police force as a source of income, as they did during the colonial era in the Gurkha regiments.

Gurung society is organized according to the dual principles of kinship and residence. The kinship system is patrilineal with children inheriting membership in their father's lineage. Above the level of the lineage, which links people through about four or five generations of male ancestors, each lineage group is also a member of a patrilineal clan. Clans are larger groups of lineages with a common male, often mythological ancestor. Lineages and clans, as well as villages, are exogamous units: marriage within any of these three units is prohibited. Residence is also patrilocal, so that women must move into their husbands' family homes and villages at the time of marriage. At that point the man's nuclear family home, consisting of his parents, him, and his siblings, becomes an extended family home. At some point each son with his wife and children moves out of the family home and establishes his own household, usually in proximity to the man's father's home, and the process begins all over again.

The Gurung are Buddhists, whose practice resembles the form of that religion dominant among the TIBETANS, with a focus on monastic life and the centrality of lamas. In addition some aspects of Hinduism have been adopted by the Gurung, although not the hierarchical caste system. Local animistic beliefs and practices have also survived into the 21st century, with a belief in ancestral and natural spirits being central to this system. Most villages have their own gods and spirits as well as shamans and exorcists who oversee local rituals and festivals, engage in divination and curing ceremonies, and perform purification rituals for both personal and agricultural benefits. Brahmin priests and Buddhist lamas may also perform various rites, especially for wealthier Gurung families who can afford to hire these specialists.

H

Hakka (Haknyin, K'e-chia, Kejia, Keren, Lairen, Ngai, Xinren)

The Hakka are the descendants of northern Chinese migrants from Henan, Shanxi, and Anhui Provinces who moved into the south during five successive waves of migration; these moves started as early as the fourth century C.E. and continued through the middle of the 19th century. The term *Hakka* in CANTONESE means "guests" or "newcomers" if it is taken less literally and refers to these migrations. In the People's Republic of China the Hakka do not constitute a separate nationality from the HAN, but on Taiwan and elsewhere they are recognized as distinct.

The first wave of Hakka migration probably began in the fourth century—however, historians continue to debate this date—when the Western Jin dynasty fell and chaos drove many people from their lands. Most historians believe these early migrants left Henan, Shanxi, and Anhui Provinces and traveled as far south as Hubei, southern Henan, and central Jiangxi Provinces. The next wave of migration is less contentious among scholars and has been dated to the late ninth and early 10th centuries, coinciding with the disorder of the last years of the Tang dynasty (618–907). At this time Hakka migrants moved farther into Jiangxi Province and south into Fujian and Guangdong Provinces. The third wave of migration represents a much longer period than the first two, early 12th through mid-17th centuries, and probably resulted from the turmoil throughout China caused by the MONGOLS and the establishment of the first non-Han dynasty, the Yuan, in 1279. People from Jiangxi and Fujian Provinces were pushed even farther south at this point into Guangdong Province, and by 1368 all of the north and east of this province was dominated by the Hakka.

The fourth wave of migration began as had all the prior waves, with the chaos that marked the transition from one dynasty to the next. In the case of the mid-17th century the chaos was even greater because it coincided with the conquest of China by the northern MANCHUS and the establishment of the second non-Han dynasty in the imperial age, the Qing. Migration in this period, which lasted until the mid-19th century, moved Hakka populations into Sichuan, Guangxi, Hunan, and Guizhou Provinces; coastal Guangdong; and onto Taiwan. The fifth migratory period was caused not by a change in dynasty but by conflict between the large Hakka population and the indigenous Yue or Cantonese people, particularly the Hakka-Bendi Wars of 1854–67, and sent Hakka migrants into Hainan Island and Southeast Asia. Some scholars argue that today we are in the midst of a sixth period of Hakka migration caused by the handovers of Hong Kong and Macau to the People's Republic of China, which is carrying the Hakka people to the United States, Canada, Australia, and elsewhere. Of course as part of the large Cantonese exodus over the past centuries many Hakka already called these countries home.

HAKKA

location:
Southern China, Taiwan, and a diaspora throughout Southeast Asia and the world

time period:
About fourth century C.E. to the present

ancestry:
Han

language:
Chinese

251

Since the earliest period of migration created the Hakka ethnicity, Hakka men have left their homes and families to serve as soldiers and overseas laborers; the most famous of these men was Sun Yat-Sen, father of the Republic of China, or Taiwan. *(AP Photo)*

Throughout their history the Hakka have filled a number of economic niches in the regions and countries they have entered, from farming to various professions. Hakka farmers carried the reputation of being able to grow crops in even the most marginal of lands because prejudice and persecution meant they were forced to live and work on land rejected by the local populations. Even in these marginal fields, however, most Hakka did not own the land on which they worked but were tenants or sharecroppers of wealthy clans and lineages. Rice and vegetables were their favored crops, but sweet potatoes replaced rice as the staple food in the regions with the poorest soils or driest conditions. Even more remarkable for the populations among which they lived much of this farming work was done by Hakka women because their husbands, brothers, fathers, and sons often left their homes to seek work overseas or in the military. During every period from the Song dynasty (960–1279) through the present various Chinese armies have included large numbers of Hakka men. Women also did the majority of woodcutting, marketing, water carrying, and other domestic tasks while their men were away. Fortunately unlike for most Han women until the early 20th century, most Hakka communities did not practice foot binding so that women were freer to move about and engage in this necessary labor.

As among other Chinese peoples the Hakka kinship system is patrilineal, with membership in both lineages and clans handed down from fathers to children. Lineages, which trace descent from a common male ancestor, have always been important social units among the Hakka. In the past lineages often migrated together and took up residence in a single village or settlement, shared agricultural land and labor, and took part in common religious rites and festivals through their common lineage hall. Today lineages remain important as markers of belonging and can be used by urban Hakka to gain acceptance, alliances, and even loans when necessary. Since the 1980s ancestor worship has also reemerged as an important function maintained by lineage members. Lineages are also exogamous units that require each individual to marry someone from outside his or her own lineage. At marriage, however, Hakka women are seen ritually to join the lineage of their husbands when they move into their husbands' houses and villages in patrilocal residence and begin to worship their husbands' ancestors rather than their own. Marriages are seen as a transfer of the woman from one lineage to another rather than as a unification of two separate lineages.

Hakka religious beliefs do not differ from those of other Han, Cantonese, and other Chinese-speaking populations in China. Prior to the religious crackdown of the Communist Party the Hakka engaged with a blend of Buddhist, Taoist, Confucianist, and traditional ideas about worship and the social order. Ancestral and local spirits were important during certain festivals; at other times a Buddhist monk or Taoist priest might be consulted for certain life-cycle rituals or illnesses. In the 19th and 20th centuries a larger number of Hakka than Han or other ethnic groups converted to Christianity under the influence of French and American missionaries. Today with the relaxation in China of laws against religious practice some Hakka families and lineages have reestablished their familial and local practices while others have not. In Hong Kong, where religion was not persecuted, a smaller percentage of Hakka than Cantonese families continue to practice their local blend of religious traditions, but it has certainly not died out there either.

FURTHER READING

Nicole Constable, ed. *Guest People: Studies of Hakka Chinese Identity* (Berkeley and Los Angeles: University of California Press, 1994).

Han (Chinese, Han Chinese, Hua, Zhongguo ren)

The Han are the dominant population in the People's Republic of China, or just simply China, as well as in Taiwan and Singapore. There are also millions of overseas Chinese, many of whom are Han, living in mainland and island Southeast Asia, North America, Europe, Australia, and the Pacific. The Han take their name from a river in central China that also was the basis for the name of China's first long dynasty, the Han, 206 B.C.E.–220 C.E. They are the population usually referred to in the West as Chinese and are distinguishable from China's 55 other national minorities with regard to language and culture.

Although they are the dominant population in China, for many years of imperial China's history the large Han population was actually ruled by non-Han emperors including MANCHUS in the Qing dynasty (1644–1911), MONGOLS in the Yuan dynasty (1279–1368), and a variety of others in the periods of the Five Dynasties (907–960), Northern and Southern Dynasties (317–589), and Three Kingdoms (220–265), which immediately followed the fall of the first Han dynasty. Nonetheless, the rulers of these various non-Han dynasties all adopted most aspects of Han culture and society and became almost indistinguishable from their Han counterparts in other eras.

GEOGRAPHY

The original homeland of the Han people was the Yellow River basin of central China, and the majority of the population today remains in the region of central and eastern China. The usual borders of the contemporary Han region are listed as the Xingan Mountains in the northeast, along the Yellow River, down along the foothills between Sichuan Province and Tibet, and along Yunnan Province's northern boundary with Myanmar (Burma). The majority of the rest of China, with the exception of Xinjiang Province in the west, is also Han, but this population is interspersed with large numbers of other ethnic and national groups.

The original Han region receives plentiful rainfall and is traversed by numerous rivers to provide access to water for intensive agriculture. The core of the region has a primarily warm-temperate to subtropical climate that allows the Han's most important crop today, wet rice, to flourish, while the northern border region is colder and drier and is more favorable for wheat, barley, millet, and sorghum, which dominated the earliest phases of Han history.

Outside this central region the Han are also the dominant population on three islands. In order of when they were colonized by the Han they are Hainan, which is politically part of the People's Republic of China and was settled by the Han about 1,000 years ago; Taiwan, settled by Han about 400 years ago; and Singapore, which has been largely Chinese for about a century and a half.

ORIGINS

Although the Neolithic period began in the region of contemporary China as early as 12,000 B.C.E., the foundations of the people we know as Han are clearly distinguishable only from about 4000 B.C.E. At this time the Yellow River basin was inhabited by a farming people with domesticated animals, pottery, and other material culture that marks them as the antecedents of the Han.

Often Chinese histories list about 2200 B.C.E. as the start of imperial history, with the foundation of the Xia dynasty along the Fen River; the Xia era marked the start of the Bronze Age as well. The Xia was followed by the Shang and Zhou dynasties, on the north China plain and in the Wei River valley, respectively, which oversaw the expansion of urbanization, the first evidence of writing, and other aspects of Chinese life. Rather than dynasties, per se, however, many scholars describe these early polities as city-states, not dynastic kingdoms. Their power was extremely localized and did not reach much beyond the agricultural areas immediately adjacent to their royal cities and their courts. At the same time many features of later Chinese culture and politics emerged in the context of these city-states, including intensive agriculture and iron technology, literacy, bureaucracy, and Confucianism; Confucius or K'ung-fu-tzu lived from 551 to 479 B.C.E.

HISTORY
206 B.C.E.–580 C.E.

Han history as such is usually marked as having begun with the emergence of the Han dynasty in 206 B.C.E. The Han emerged after about a 250-year period of unrest in the Zhou

---

HAN

location:
China, Taiwan, and a diaspora throughout the world, especially in Southeast Asia

time period:
4000 B.C.E. to the present

language:
There are many languages that collectively make up the category of Chinese, all related within the larger Sino-Tibetan language family; most Chinese sources refer to them as dialects while most Western linguists categorize them as separate languages, including Mandarin, Hakka, Wu, Gan, Xiang, Yue, and Min.

Han time line

B.C.E.

4000 The early Han ancestors had already established settled agricultural communities along the Yellow (Huang) River and its major tributaries.

2200–1750 The Xia dynasty or city-state marks the transition between the Neolithic and Bronze Ages.

1750–1048 The Shang dynasty or city-state provides the first evidence of writing.

1048–221 The Zhou dynasty or city-state is established.

551 K'ung Fu Tzu or Confucius is born.

221–206 The Qin dynasty establishes the first Chinese Empire.

206 The dynasty from which the Han take their name begins its long rule in China; it is sometimes called the Western Han dynasty to distinguish it from that which is established in 25 C.E., and sometimes the First or Earlier Han dynasty.

195 The first Han emperor, Liu Bang, who took the name Gaozu, dies.

109 Sima Qian compiles China's first comprehensive history, *Records of the Historian (Shiji)*.

C.E.

2 A Chinese government census finds that more than 59 million people live in the empire, many of them Han.

9 The short-lived Xin dynasty under Wang Ming takes over from a weakened Han state, only to be overthrown itself 16 years later.

25 After a brief period without a Han ruler the Han reestablish control over China. The capital is moved to Luoyang, the former Zhou capital, inspiring the name *Eastern Han dynasty* for the period between 25 and 220.

220 The Han dynasty collapses after a protracted period of unrest; the last emperor abdicates in favor of the son of his best general.

220–65 The former Han empire is divided into three kingdoms, the Wei in the north, the Shu in the southwest, and the Wu in the southeast.

317–589 The Northern and Southern dynasties. China is broken into several empires and plagued by internal wars. Buddhism spreads on a large scale.

580–618 The Sui reunite China and the nobles begin to regain their importance, leading to a resurgence in the popularity of Confucianism.

618–907 The Tang dynasty benefits from the infrastructural developments made during the brief Sui period.

624 The Tang Code is first drawn up.

690–705 Empress Wu, China's only female emperor, calls her period the Zhou dynasty.

907 The Tang dynasty disintegrates and is replaced by 15 separate regional kingdoms of the Five Dynasties period.

939 The Chinese are defeated in northern Vietnam and lose their southern colony after about 1,000 years of domination.

955 Buddhism is officially persecuted throughout the Chinese territory.

960 The Song dynasty emerges from the chaos of the Five Dynasties and consolidates its power by conquering the south and paying tribute to the militarily powerful empires to the north.

1000 In this era wet rice replaces wheat and other dry crops as the primary subsistence food among the Han.

1125 The Jin dynasty conquers much of the territory held by the Song, driving the empire south to Linan, where it reemerges as the Southern Song dynasty.

1210 The Mongols first attack Song lands.

1279 The Han lose control of China as the invading Mongols establish the Yuan dynasty.

1368 The Yuan dynasty collapses and is replaced by a Han dynasty, the Ming.

1433 The last large Chinese sea voyage is undertaken, and after this the records of the previous voyages are destroyed and shipbuilding is limited to only very small vessels incapable of long, overseas voyages.

1644 The Han lose control of China again as the Ming are overthrown by the Manchu Qing dynasty.

1514 The Portuguese are the first Europeans to make contact with the Han since Marco Polo.

1699 The British force the opening of a trade entrepot in Canton.

1796–1804 The White Lotus Rebellion is fought by peasants over the issue of land access.

1839–42 The Opium War, as a result of which the British receive access to five Chinese ports.

1851–64 Millions die in the Taiping Rebellion, another peasant movement.

1860 The British and French occupy Beijing and receive greater access to trade.

1900 The Boxer Rebellion erupts over the number and power of foreign influences in China.

1911 Han nationalists overthrow the disintegrating Qing dynasty and install Yuan Shikai as president of the new Republic of China.

1913 The Guomindang or Nationalists under Dr. Sun Yat-sen rebel against the increasingly conservative Shikai and are defeated.

1921 The Chinese Communist Party is formed one year after the Nationalists return; neither is strong enough to take over the country and the two cooperate as allies.

1927 The alliance between Communists and Nationalists is broken when Chiang Kai-shek's army attacks Communist strongholds in Shanghai.

1928 The Nanjing Republic is formed by Chiang Kai-shek.

1931 Japan occupies Manchuria and creates the new state of Manchukuo.

1934–35 The Long March under Mao Zedong.

1937 Japan occupies Nanjing and the Chinese Communists and Nationalists briefly ally to fight off the occupier.

1946 The Nationalists and Communists go to war, which ends with the Communist victory in 1949.

1950 Chiang Kai-shek becomes president of the new Republic of China when the Nationalists flee the mainland and establish their state in Taiwan.

1958–60 The Great Leap Forward, Communist Party economic reforms, kills millions of Chinese.

1966–76 The Cultural Revolution, Communist Party social reforms, kills many thousands more.

1979 Economic reforms in the People's Republic of China transform the command economy to a system with elements of capitalism, which leads to exponential economic growth in the 1980s and beyond.

1989 Student demonstrations in Tiananmen Square result in a crackdown on political activity, indicating that the Communist Party is not going to reform its political program in conjunction with the economic reforms.

1997 China begins work on the controversial Three Gorges Dam on the Yangtze (Chang) River.

2001 Beijing is elected by the International Olympic Committee to host the 2008 summer Olympic games.

2003 China's economy outstrips Japan's to become the second-largest in the world, after that of the United States.

SARS, severe acute respiratory syndrome, breaks out in China.

2007 China hosts the women's soccer World Cup tournament; the home team loses to Norway 1-0 in the quarter finals after finishing second in Group D behind Brazil.

2008 Beijing hosts the summer Olympic games after the global torch relay initiates protests over Chinese human rights abuses, especially in Tibet.

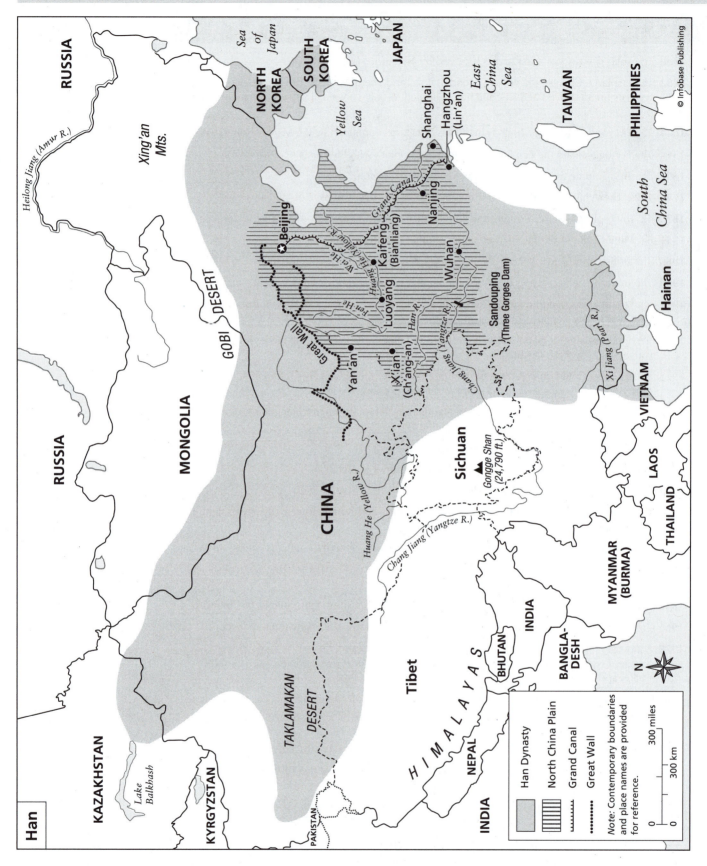

era known as the Warring States. From about 476 to 221 B.C.E. many different princes, lords, and others, engaged in both localized and major wars over who would inherit the domains of the disintegrating Zhou rulers, their vassals, and others who did not owe fealty to them. The first state to dominate fully the entire Chinese world at that time was the Qin, or Ch'in, a western city-state that was militarily superior to all of the other warring states and that conquered them in 221 B.C.E. During the short 15-year Qin period the formal title of *emperor* was adopted, the various writing systems in use at the time were standardized, a common copper currency was adopted, the Great Wall was begun, certain weights and measures were standardized, and many other aspects of a unified state were initiated. The world-famous terra-cotta army was also produced during this period to commemorate the actual army of the first Qin emperor, Shi Huangdi. Some historians believe that the Western ethnonym for the Zhongguo ren, *Chinese,* and for their country, *China,* is derived from this first unifying dynasty; however, this derivation is contested and not all historians are convinced of its accuracy.

Despite the gains made by the Qin dynasty in organizing the many lands and people over which it ruled, it could not survive the death of its first emperor in 210 B.C.E. Shi Huangdi had been unpopular with most of his people: other nobles resented his ascent, merchants and landowners chafed under his bureaucracy and taxation system, bureaucrats and scholars despised him for having burned many books that advocated political systems other than his own and having put many philosophers to death, and even peasants struggled with the high taxes of the period. His death initiated a revolt among many of the kingdom's people that the new ruler, Er Shi (Huhai), could not handle. Er Shi, who was the emperor's second son, himself took the throne under a cloud of treachery and treason when Shi Huangdi's advisers convinced his first son and rightful heir to commit suicide. Er Shi's kingdom was overthrown just four years later by Liu Bang, a prince in the Han kingdom, in a battle in the Wei River valley.

The early years of the Han dynasty were characterized by the same legalist political structure as the preceding Qin era, which allowed the state to exert direct control over its people. Over

The terra-cotta army, consisting of more than 7,000 life-sized soldiers, chariots, horses, and weapons, remained buried for more than 2,000 years until Chinese peasants near X'ian discovered pieces of pottery as they dug a new well in 1974. *(Shutterstock/Holger Mette)*

the course of the subsequent period, however, legalism began to give way in China to Confucianism. This philosophical and political system was based on a moral cohesion and structuring of society rather than a legal one. Certainly Han China maintained a legal system, but an emphasis on hierarchy and moral action within one's sphere of action soon developed, and it formed the basis of the entire society.

Han society was also characterized by a consolidation of state power over the largest territory held by a Chinese ruler up to that time. Its emperors stripped local rulers and nobility of their lands and titles and drew them into the Han sphere of influence through tribute, gift giving, and trade. Under Emperor Wudi (141–87 B.C.E.) the borders were expanded as far as central Korea, northern Vietnam, and the Gobi Desert and an estimated 2 million people were moved into these marginal Han territories as colonizers on the outskirts of the empire.

Also in this period trade, agriculture, technology, and education all expanded and improved throughout the country. Han merchants and entrepreneurs began buying and selling goods from as far away as Europe. These goods were transported along the Silk Road through Central Asia, which was actually a number of different caravan routes that traversed the mountains, deserts, and plains between China and the Caspian region. Chinese ships also plied the waters of Southeast Asia and the coasts of India in their search for exotic goods to sell on the markets of the Han capital of Ch'ang-an and other urban areas throughout the empire. Improvements in both iron and irrigation technology allowed for the expansion of the Han agricultural economy into areas in the north and west that had previously been dominated by nomadic pastoralists who moved their herds of animals as the political and ecological climate dictated. It was under the stability of the Han dynasty that Chinese inventors also led the world in the development of new technologies, including paper, new forms of ceramics, a stronger form of iron, and even the compass. Finally part of the task of any state is to consolidate its power at the grassroots level by convincing people that they are better off under that state's rule than any other and the best way of going about that is through education. The Han state used this tactic to great advantage, and during the course of its more than 400 years in power education and scholarship expanded exponentially. The first Chinese history, *Records of the Historian (Shiji)*, was written in this period as was the first Chinese encyclopedia, *The Classic of Mountains and Seas*.

In 25 C.E. after 16 years under the interregnum Xin dynasty of Wang Ming what is sometimes called the second or later Han dynasty was able to retake all Chinese territory. The new emperors moved the capital from Ch'ang-an to Luoyang, which had been the site of the ancient Zhou dynasty, and this urban area became one of the largest in the world at that time with about half a million residents. This move to the east has caused some later historians to refer to this period as the Eastern Han dynasty. This period of Han history is noted for the weakness of its emperors, in part because many of them were infants when they ascended the throne and their power was diminished by the bureaucrats, eunuchs, and relatives who oversaw their realm until they reached adulthood. In 168 groups of rival bureaucrats and eunuchs went to war for about two years, and then in 184 two more rebellions also emerged from the ranks of Taoist religious groups seeking power in their Confucian state.

Just five years before the Han dynasty disintegrated entirely its leadership had a final period of strength when General Cao Cao (also Ts'ao Ts'ao) finally put down the last of the rebellious religious groups and other factions with their sights on consolidating their own power. But this unification was short lived and by 220 the Han emperor at the time, Xiandi, could not maintain his power. Xiandi ceded his empire to the general's son, Cao Pi, and thus formally ended the Han dynasty's rule over China and initiated the start of the Wei dynasty in northern China. The Wei dynasty, however, could not maintain control over the entire region of the Han empire and two other dynasties emerged to fill the power vacuum, the Shu in the southwest and the Wu in the southeast.

Following the disintegration of the Han China was ruled by a wide variety of regional kingdoms for about 300 years. During this period Buddhism, which had been introduced from India by way of Central Asia via the Silk Road around 100 C.E., began to gain in popularity and importance throughout China. Also the sheer dominance of Han cultural and political forms became evident as most of these regional kingdoms adopted Confucian principles, Han material culture, and even the dominant form of the Han language, Mandarin Chinese.

580–1644

The first dynasty to unify the former lands of the Han dynasty was the Sui, which finally consolidated its power in 580. During its short tenure lasting through just two emperors before collapsing again, much was accomplished to set the stage for the subsequent Tang dynasty (618–906). The Grand Canal, which today runs from Beijing to Hangzhou almost 1,000 miles away, was extended to the northwest; the Great Wall was strengthened and lengthened against the so-called northern barbarians; three new cities were begun in the region of the Yellow River; grain production soared; and new storage containers were built outside most cities to hold the surplus. In addition from its weak point when Taoism and Buddhism had supplanted some of the social forms advocated by Confucian thought, Confucianism reemerged along with the class of nobles who looked to this system to justify their social position within the political and social hierarchy. Seeing themselves as the inheritors of Han greatness, the two Sui emperors, Wendi and Yangdi, also sought to expand their country's borders and tried to utilize their military toward this end. In the south they were somewhat successful and expanded as far as northern Vietnam, but in the north, particularly in Korea, they met with four separate defeats, which ultimately weakened their empire so much that it collapsed.

The Sui dynasty was followed by the Tang, which took about half a decade to consolidate its power over the various factions and regional kingdoms that had reemerged in the wake of the Sui defeats in Korea. As the Han and Sui before them had, the Tang located their capital at Ch'ang-an or what is today called Xi'an. During this period rice began to replace wheat as the dominant grain among the Han people and the major population centers moved south to accommodate the greater capacity of this region to grow this crop. Much of the infrastructure developed during the brief Sui period, especially canals and granaries, was of tremendous importance in this period as it allowed for the storage of grain surplus and its easy transportation to parts of the empire that were experiencing drought or other natural disasters. Frequently this meant a transfer of rice from the south to the poorer, drier wheat belt of the north; increased food storage facilities also allowed for the greater development of urbanization.

The Tang period introduced the first complete code of Chinese law that we can still access today; the 500-article Tang Code was drawn up in 624 and delineated the penalties for a wide variety of crimes, divided into a dozen separate categories. Tang military success pushed the boundaries of the empire into Korea, as far west as Iran, and as far north as Manchuria. As was the case throughout Han history, however, these military victories eventually led to the rulers' overextending themselves and bringing about their ultimate demise. This actually happened twice during the Tang period. The first time saw the emergence of China's only female emperor, Wu Zhao or Sacred and Divine Empress Regnant Wu Zeitan (Tse-t'ien), who took the throne in 690 and called her period the Zhou (Chou) dynasty. But the Tang nobility quickly regrouped and retook control of the empire in 705. The second time the Tang disintegrated, starting with a series of rebellions in 860 and concluding in 907, the nobles were not able to reestablish themselves and were replaced by a large number of regional kingdoms and dynasties. The period from 907 to 960 is officially called the Five dynasties but it actually saw the emergence of 15 separate kingdoms, five in the north and 10 in the south.

During the Five Dynasties period several interesting changes developed in Han culture and society. Female foot binding became popular among both rich and poor women and was adopted throughout most Han territories after 950. Starting in 955 Buddhism was officially persecuted by the Confucian nobility, who sat atop the Chinese hierarchy and did not favor a religion that preached equality and the ability of all people to gain salvation. Another undesirable aspect of Buddhism from the government's point of view was that it gave men the ability to avoid being conscripted into the military by moving into a monastery and becoming monks.

The emergence of the Song dynasty in 960 is often commented upon as a time of Han Chinese renaissance. Confucianism reemerged as the most important ideological system, underpinning both politics and society in a form often called neo-Confucianism by contemporary commentators. This new philosophy revived much of the hierarchical and educational foundation of its former guise with an expansion of the examination system, but it also took on a more metaphysical tone and emphasized the importance of abstract principles over concrete examples. The economy continued to expand under the Song as well, with a class of peasants who were freer than they had ever been to engage in trade with the urban centers, such as the capital at Bianliang, and to develop their landholdings in ways appropriate to their resources and climate.

Empress Wu Zetian ✎✎

Empress Wu (Wu Zetian or Tse-'ien) is famed as the first female ruler in Chinese history, and though her acquisition of power and status was ruthless, her reign was successful and stabilizing. Born to a noble family in 625, Wu Zetian received a comprehensive education that included literature, music, and writing. By age 13 her beauty and wit were renowned in the court of Emperor Taizong and she became one of his concubines. During her time as Taizong's concubine she also became well versed on matters of state by acting as Taizong's secretary. Upon the emperor's death Wu Zetian was sent to a Buddhist monastery along with the other concubines to become a nun. Unlike her peers Wu Zetian managed to return to the palace by becoming the favorite concubine of the new emperor, Gaozong. She gained power and status as she gave birth to sons, and to secure her place as empress, she killed her own newborn daughter and accused Gaozong's wife, Empress Wang, of committing the murder. Empress Wang was consequently removed and Gaozong married Wu Zetian, but within five years he suffered a stroke that enabled Wu Zetian to take over administrative duties. She created a secret police force that persecuted all who opposed her rule, and upon her husband's death she inhibited her eldest son from taking his rightful place as emperor and instead helped her youngest and most controllable son to claim the throne. Eventually she removed her sons from power altogether and established herself as emperor of China in 690. Her rule is distinguished by her endeavors to elevate the status of women in China through commissioning written biographies of famous women and by emphasizing the status of her mother's clan. She also established her own dynasty, the Zhou dynasty, and is said to have claimed that an ideal ruler is one who rules as a mother. Empress Wu died at 80 years of age in 705, and her third son reclaimed the throne and restored the court to the Tang dynasty.

At the same time as the Song were ruling over the territory of southern China, much of the north was under the sway of two different non-Han empires: the Liao empire of the KHITANS and the Western Xia empire of the DANGXIANG or Tanguts. The Song found it expedient to pay tribute to their northern neighbors rather than engage them militarily because for all their technological and other advancements, the Song empire had only a weak military. In part this was the result of Confucian ideas about the degradation that results from military activity; it may also have been the result of the increased emphasis on trade rather than empire building during the period. Because of these powerful northern neighbors trade relations withered in the north and flourished with China's southern neighbors in both mainland and island Southeast Asia. Additionally trade was the only way that the Song had of engaging with the south, for the chaos of the previous period combined with the Song lack of military strength allowed the VIETNAMESE to expel them from their lucrative southern colony for the first time in about 1,000 years.

Although the Song were able to hold off the Liao and Western Xia empires through the payment of tribute, the successor to the Liao, the Jin dynasty of the JURCHENS, was not so easily pacified, and in 1125 it conquered much of the territory of the Song. One of the princes of this dynasty was able to flee south, however, and for the next 154 years the Southern Song dynasty ruled from its capital of Lin'an or Hangzhou today. This new Song dynasty is often considered even greater than its predecessor for its literary, technological, and political developments. Shipbuilding was particularly important as trade with the south expanded even beyond the levels experienced previously. Agriculture, mining, and industry also expanded, making the empire very rich. With their wealth the various emperors, especially Gaozong (1127–62), were important patrons of the arts and sought to legitimate their rule through their ethnic connections to the ancient Xia, Shang, and Zhou empires; Gaozong himself is even supposed to have created a calligraphic text reminiscent of an ancient document.

Although Song China was rich and developed, it was both internally and externally weakened by a lack of focus on the military, high taxes, and corruption. In 1210 invading MONGOLS from the north first encroached on Chinese territory, and by 1279 the Han had lost control of their country entirely as the Mongol Yuan dynasty under Kublai Khan emerged in their former lands, ruling from their capital at Dadu or today's Beijing. As had happened in previous centuries, however, a foreign dynasty did not mean that a foreign culture dominated China. Instead the ruling Mongol emperors adopted many aspects of their settled, agricultural subjects, and for most of the Han people life continued as always. They raised their crops, paid their taxes, and the better educated among them focused their energies on producing works of Chinese poetry and literature; most government jobs were filled by Mongols themselves, leaving the educated Han to focus on the arts, music, literature, and other scholarship. The Mongols were excellent soldiers, but their ability to organize and run a vast empire was limited. Their incompetence in areas of trade relations, infrastructural development, and other necessities for maintaining their country led to the impoverishment of the people and weakening of Mongol legitimacy.

Finally in the mid-14th century the Mongols experienced a wave of rebellions and in 1368 a peasant, known as Hongwu or Vast Military, was able to overthrow the government and establish himself as emperor from his capital at

Nanjing. As his name implies, Hongwu placed great faith in the ability of a large and powerful army to keep him and his country safe from continual pressure by the Mongols and other outsiders. Later emperors also focused their energy on strengthening their country's seafaring capabilities as well, and between 1405 and 1433 many large ships with the capacity to carry up to 500 sailors plied the waters of Asia; Chinese ships even sailed as far as eastern Africa and took back such exotica as giraffes and zebras. In 1433, however, China's emperors changed course and turned their focus inward, limiting the size of ships and even destroying most of the records of these previous journeys. Other important developments during the Ming period were the creation of the novel as a literary form, the writing of a standard 214-character dictionary, and the final construction of the Great Wall. These positive steps, however, were also joined by significant economic problems caused by inflation when too much paper currency was printed and then again replaced by copper coins, which were often devalued through the addition of lead.

1644–today

After almost three centuries of stability these problems, in addition to the same problem that plagued the end of every Chinese dynasty, internal fighting among nobles, eunuchs, and other elite factions of society, allowed a second non-Han people to rule over the unified Chinese Empire. In 1644 the Manchu Qing dynasty supplanted the Ming and established dominance from the capital at Beijing, which from the third Ming emperor forward had also been the Ming capital. The first three Qing rulers, who reigned for a combined 133 years, enjoyed decades of peace and prosperity over their largely Han political structure, which provided significant legitimacy for their dynasty in the eyes of the Han people. So also did their powerful army and their bureaucratic structure, which saw a dual role for every position, one held by a Manchu, the other by a Han Chinese. However, the Manchus also chose to remain somewhat separate from the Han and continued to use their own language, banned intermarriage, and tried to impose Manchu styles of dress on Han men; they also tried to end foot binding among women but failed and rescinded the ban after just 22 years in power. Manchu separatism also extended to China itself, which they tried to isolate from the increasing pressures from the European powers, who wanted China to open itself to foreign trade.

The Portuguese had first made contact with China during the Ming period when they arrived on the southern coast in 1514. Limited trade and missionary activity followed and then by the early Qing period the "problem" of European outsiders was affecting the north of the country as well. In 1689 Jesuit missionaries finally assisted in negotiating a treaty between Russia and China, the Treaty of Nerchinsk, over the creation of a mutually recognized boundary between their two empires. A decade later the Qing were facing further European encroachments when the British set up their first trade mission in the southern area of Canton. This opening was enough for the British at the time, but after another century they began to push for further concessions; Lord Macartney arrived in 1793 and Lord Amherst in 1816, with tribute for the emperor to convince him to open his doors to European trade, but both failed. The British responded by flooding China with cheap opium, which eventually drove the Qing to declare war on the British. The British defeated the Qing in the Opium War (1839–42), which resulted in five Chinese ports being opened up to British traders. To mitigate the power of the British, the Qing quickly gave trade concessions to the United States and other Western countries as well. The British and French also occupied Beijing in 1860, and further concessions resulted.

Meanwhile the Qing were also facing considerable resistance within their borders as well and a number of rebellions broke out, further weakening them as they faced a barrage of external enemies. The White Lotus Rebellion (1796–1804) was fought by peasants who had been forced to relocate onto plots of relatively infertile land in central China while the Taiping Rebellion (1851–64) was a peasant revolt led by Christian Chinese that resulted in the deaths of millions. This was followed in 1900 by the Boxer Rebellion, which pitted Chinese against foreigners in an attempt to rid their country of the British, American, French, and other foreign influences.

These internal and external forces allowed a group of Han nationalists finally to overthrow the Qing dynasty in 1911 and to end the era of imperial China. However, the revolution of 1911 did not bring about two of its three stated goals: removal of the Manchus from power, democracy, and improved living standards. While the first of these goals was met as a result of the utter weakness of the dynasty, the other two could not be achieved because of the weakness of the revolutionary forces. Their own leader, a HAKKA named Dr. Sun Yat-sen, was in the United States at the time of the uprising in Wuhan in 1911, and thus leadership fell to a general from the old imperial army, Yuan Shikai. He became president of the new Republic of China, but very little changed because the nationalists were too weak to implement real policy change and Shikai was himself too steeped in Confucian and imperial tradition to envision a different kind of society.

In 1913 Sun's Han Nationalist or Guomindang Party launched a rebellion against the government it had helped to install two years earlier, and when failure was certain Sun himself escaped the country and moved to Japan. Shikai died just three years later, some say as a result of the heartbreak of being unable to establish himself as emperor. This left China essentially without any central government and opened the door to the Nationalists to reenter the country in 1920 and to the Chinese Communist Party, which formed a year later. The two parties worked in conjunction in the early years of the 1920s but when Sun died and was replaced by the military leader Chiang Kai-shek the alliance was broken. Chiang and his army attacked the Communists in Shanghai in 1927, driving many, including a young Mao Zedong, into the hills south of the Yangtze.

The war between the two sides continued for many years, even after Chiang established a second Chinese republic in 1928, called the Nanjing Republic. Mao's troops were pushed onto their Long March in 1934–35, which became part of heroic Communist mythology; 90,000 Communists departed from their base in Jiangxi Province in the south en route to Yan'an in the north. When 80,000 of these marchers died along the way, most observers in Chiang's republic were convinced they had vanquished their Communist enemies for good. In the meantime China's government lost Manchuria to the invading JAPANESE and was then fully occupied by 1937 when the Japanese took the capital at Nanjing; the episode is sometimes described as the Rape of Nanjing for the atrocities committed by the Japanese soldiers against Chinese citizens. At this time the Republicans and Communists were nominally working together to liberate China, but at the end of the war the hostilities between the two parties reemerged, and by 1946 the two sides were engaged in full-scale civil war.

After three long years Mao's armies defeated those of Chiang Kai-shek and created a government for the new People's Republic of China (PRC); Chiang's government relocated to Taiwan, where he ruled the Republic of China from 1950 until his death in 1975. There a largely Han nationalist government has ruled for more than half a century of political stability, economic growth, and, recently, democratization. Mainland China or the PRC continues to claim Taiwan as a province, an assertion that is not legally disputed throughout the world, but in essence Taiwan is an independent Chinese country where the population is about 98 percent Han Chinese.

Since 1949 Communism in the PRC has been transformed from the radical, revolutionary platform of the 1950s, 1960s, and 1970s to an increasingly capitalist economy located in a single-party political state. The two most radical programs were the Great Leap Forward of 1958–60 and the Cultural Revolution of 1966–76. The first of these focused on the economy and when failure ensued saw the death of millions of Chinese, both Han and national minority groups, while the latter emphasized purifying Chinese society of all religious, educational, and other influences from the past; this program likewise led to the deaths of hundreds of thousands of citizens. Finally in 1979 the Communist Party initiated vast economic reforms that have transformed their largely agrarian, command economy to a powerful, industrializing economy that some economists claim became the second largest in the world, after that of the United States, in 2003; others believe this event has yet to occur.

CULTURE

Over the course of the past 4,000 years or so many aspects of Chinese culture have undergone significant transformation; however, the underlying features of Chinese language, wet rice agriculture, patrilineal kinship, and Confucian ideology have dominated Han culture for much of this long period.

The Chinese language is actually 13 different sublanguages or dialects; the classification of these subgroups as separate or merely as dialects remains controversial both inside and outside China. The most important of these Chinese languages is Mandarin, while the regional variants, such as Min, Wu, Gan, CANTONESE, and Hakka, are important as well. Most of these languages are mutually unintelligible, though they all share a structure, tonality, and common writing system. The importance of this latter feature cannot be overstated, for this common system has allowed emperors and 20th-century leaders to consolidate their power over the entire region, despite other differences.

While Han power in China can in part be traced to Han control over all official documents, including laws, histories, encyclopedias, textbooks, and all other public writing of this nature, their original domination emerged in the context of the agricultural revolution. Unlike many of China's minority groups, who relied on pastoralism as their primary subsistence strategy 4,000 years ago, the Han were already intensive agriculturalists at that time. The most important crops in that period were wheat, barley, millet, and sorghum and reflect the northern center of Han civilization at the time. During the Tang dynasty (618–907) agriculture intensified beyond the subsistence level and a bit later wet rice superseded wheat as the primary commercial crop, reflecting a change in technology and the southern movement of the Han population. Individual farmers became peasants in this era, working the lands of large landowners and producing a surplus that connected them and their feudal lords to the world economy, as it was known at that time. Rather than producing all the foods and products they needed, Han peasants purchased cooking oil, condiments, alcohol, furniture, farm implements, cloth, and most of their other daily needs with the proceeds of their grain and vegetable crops. They also needed access to the cash economy to pay their taxes, which funded the imperial armies, the civil service, and all other facets of the large bureaucracy that had developed in the Han and Sui dynasties. This economic structure, where between 80 and 90 percent of the Han were peasant farmers, continued to dominate all Han society from the centuries just prior to the end of the first millennium C.E. until the last years of the 20th century. Today with the rapid expansion of the Chinese economy only about 12 percent of the Chinese people continue to work in agriculture, a proportion that reflects a tremendous change in the basis of Chinese culture for the first time since the agricultural revolution of about 1000 C.E. saw rice replace wheat as the primary staple item.

While their people have constituted at least one-quarter of the entire world's population for most of the past 4,000 years, the Han have also been important innovators in many technologies that ushered in the modern era of human history. Paper, movable type from clay (revised by Gutenberg 400 years later), gunpowder, the steam engine, the compass, and pasta are just a handful of the products first invented by the Han over the course of human history. Until imperial decree shut down the shipbuilding industry in the 15th century, the Han also led the world in that area and were superior to their European counterparts in Portugal, Spain, and Italy in exploring the world's oceans. Many historians believe that if the Chinese had focused their efforts in that period on colonizing the world, their superior technology and vast population would probably have allowed them to conquer Europe and then to expand into Africa, the Pacific, and the Americas. Instead the emperors in the latter years of the Ming dynasty (1368–1644) looked inward, stopped sending their great ships into the world's oceans, and even forbade the building of the big ships altogether. This momentary lack of focus led to the relative demise of China in relation to Europe and then the United States in terms of technological innovation and economic might. In the past two decades, however, the Chinese have made great strides toward correcting this historical mistake and by 2026 will probably have overtaken the United States as the world's largest economy.

The upper echelons of Chinese society have been dominated by patrilineal descent groups for as long as the Chinese have had writing. In the Shang and Zhou dynasties or city-states patrilineal clans, membership in which was inherited from one's father, arranged in a hierarchical pattern across each locality were the primary organizing principle of the nobility. The governments of these polities were relatively weak, and it was kinship rather than a governmental bureaucracy that held these societies together for the most part. By the end of the Zhou period these large kinship units, called *zongfa*, had diminished greatly in size and importance as the central government gained in strength and influence. Despite this relative decline in kinship, however, the concept of patrilineal values did not disappear; in fact philosophers and scholars of the period tended to highlight the importance of patrilineal principles as a way of connecting the new bureaucratic society with the kin-based social orders of the past.

The following period of the Han dynasty (206 B.C.E.–220 C.E.) placed even greater emphasis on these patrilineal values and the effects are still being felt throughout Han society today. While most aspects of a kinship-based social order could not be revived in a large, bureaucratic empire such as that maintained by the Han, those aspects that related to domestic life could. As a result much scholarship emerged during this period that affected the relative positions of women and men. Women as mothers of sons gained in importance and centrality because they allowed for the continuation of patrilineal groups while most other aspects of women's identity were devalued. For example women as daughters lost all ability to inherit family property because the patrilineal principle dictated that only sons were able to inherit and pass on the traits and property of their fathers. Other aspects of a patrilineal society that took on great significance in this era were the strict regulation of exogamy so that even marrying someone with the same surname became forbidden, and patrilocality, which required new brides to move into their husbands' family homes and thus lose the protection and comfort of being surrounded by their own families. This principle, combined with the relative importance of the mother-son bond, has made the lives of new brides in China one of the most difficult in the world.

By the period of the Song dynasty (960–1279) this patrilineal pattern had been adopted by all social classes in Han society. Whereas before this time only the rich and noble families had interest in or the ability to organize their lives around patrilineal values, by about 960 C.E. this trend had been adopted throughout Han society. In addition to affecting the relationships between women and men, patrilineal principles affected land tenure, wealth, and political power. Rather than nuclear families it was lineages that owned most agricultural land, especially in southern and eastern China, a process that allowed some lineages to grow extremely rich and powerful. With the rent collected from these holdings, some lineages were able to fund military expeditions, scholarship, and religious institutions. Very large lineages of more than 10,000 people usually subdivided into smaller sublineages that were related to each other in a hierarchical manner reminiscent of the organization of the Shang and early Zhou periods. At the same time in some localities lineages remained only marginally important in the face of other organizations based on common ethnicity, residence, or occupation.

One of the first acts of the Communist Party when it took over the governance of China in 1949 was to try to eliminate the power of these large lineal groups through a series of land reforms. Individual peasant families were granted land, and thus the economic power of these large lineages was destroyed. At the same time the religious underpinning of the patrilineal system, the veneration of male ancestors or what is sometimes called ancestor worship, was banned as feudal and replaced by the veneration of the Communist Party and its leaders. Especially during the Cultural Revolution family, village, and lineage shrines were destroyed and rituals honoring the dead were forbidden. Anybody caught trying to revive these events or salvage family altars was severely punished, sometimes with death. Despite these efforts thousand years of tradition could not be eliminated in one generation, and by the time of the economic reforms of the 1970s local lineages had reemerged as important social and even economic units. Investment and employment in the new Chinese economy are facilitated for some by lineage connections, not only in small-scale outfits in the countryside but also in the booming cities of Shanghai and Beijing.

Although patrilineal and Confucian principles are often conflated in the context of imperial China, the two sets of ideologies are not identical. Confucian thought developed in the second half of the sixth century B.C.E. around seven interrelated areas: ritual, propriety and etiquette, called *li* in Chinese; filial piety or *xiao*; honesty or *yi*; integrity or *xin*; knowledge or *zhi*; benevolence toward others or *ren*; and loyalty, especially to the state, or *zhong*. Confucius developed these ideas during the period in which patrilineal principles were diminishing at the state level but increasing in importance for scholars interested in connecting the new bureaucracy to the old kin-based societies; his ideas reflect this dominant social trend. Today just as patrilineal ideas and even groups remain important at some level of social organization, so too do the implied foci of Confucian ideology on hierarchy, family, and subservience to the state. Many scholars of modern China point out that much of Communist ideology as developed and implemented there reflects not only the writings of Marx and Lenin but also those of Confucius, especially loyalty to the state, propriety, and righteousness.

Confucianism is more of an ethical system and a political ideology than a religion, but its beliefs and practices are often pointed to when the topic of Chinese religion is raised. Prior to 1949 most Han engaged in a syncretic blend of Confucian, Taoist, and Buddhist practices that focused on their (patrilineal) ancestors, the emperor, local gods and spirits, the agricultural calendar, and, most important, harmony in all areas of social interaction. Today many of these ideas remain despite 1,000 years of cultural change and even a Communist revolution that sought to eliminate them more than half a century ago. Harmony remains central to the Chinese sensitivity and to the need to save face in all interactions, as well as in Chinese medicine, which sees balance and harmony between the body and its social and physical universe as central. Subsuming one's individual desires to those of the collective is also part of the emphasis on social harmony, but one that has diminished somewhat in recent decades with the influx of capitalist values and economic practices.

On Taiwan, Han culture has developed some differences from the pattern established on the mainland. One of the most important differences is that Taiwanese society did not crack down on traditional religious, kinship, or other beliefs and practices. Veneration of the ancestors remained important on the island during the bleakest period of repression in the PRC in the 1960s and 1970s. At the same time, Taiwanese Han society has been urban in focus since the foundation of the Republic of China in 1949, and this fact has caused some aspects of traditional Chinese culture, such as the focus on agriculture and its attendant rituals, to diminish in importance. Some of the strictest aspects of the Confucian hierarchy, especially its reliance on a family model for state authority, have also been challenged in Taiwan, where in the past decade democracy has begun to emerge as an important force in state politics specifically and in people's attitudes toward the state more generally.

FURTHER READING

Patricia Buckley Ebrey. *Chinese Civilization and Society: A Sourcebook* (New York: Free Press, 1981).

Han-yi Fêng. *The Chinese Kinship System* (Cambridge, Mass.: Harvard University Press, 1967).

Prosper Giquel. *A Journal of the Chinese Civil War, 1864*. Translated by Steven A. Leibo and Debbie Weston (Honolulu: University of Hawaii Press, 1985).

Grant Hardy and Anne Behnke Kinney. *The Establishment of the Han Empire and Imperial China* (Westport, Conn.: Greenwood Press, 2005).

Bret Hinsch. *Women in Early Imperial China* (Lanham, Md.: Rowman & Littlefield, 2002).

Huang Shu-min. *The Spiral Road: Changes in a Chinese Village through the Eyes of a Communist Party Leader* (Boulder, Colo.: Westview Press, 1989).

Alan Lawrance. *China since 1919: Revolution and Reform: A Sourcebook* (New York: Routledge, 2003).

Jonathan D. Spence. *The Search for Modern China* (New York: W. W. Norton, 1990).

Robert Weatherley. *Politics in China since 1949: Legitimizing Authoritarian Rule* (New York: Routledge, 2006).

Wang Zhongshu. *Han Civilization.* Translated by K. C. Chang and collaborators (New Haven, Conn.: Yale University Press, 1982).

Hani (Aini, Akha, Baihong, Biyue, Ha Nhi, Haoni, Haqniq, Kaduo)

The Hani have lived in southwestern China for hundreds of years, primarily farming the valleys, hills, and mountainsides. The Hani classification actually includes several smaller ethnic groups and is often conflated with the related AKHA group, many of whom live outside China in Southeast Asia. However, the Hani have a rich oral tradition that reflects their distinct identity.

According to Hani oral traditions, they descended from the YI. There is some debate as to whether the Yi and the Hani originally were from earlier groups on the Qinghai-Tibetan plateau or from groups in the Sichuan plains. Today most Hani live in southern China, between the Mekong (or Lancang) River and Red (or Yuanjiang) River. Early Chinese records and historical accounts of the neighboring Akha people describe the Hani as indigenous to the area, in contrast to DAI and other groups that arrived later.

Over their history, the Hani were both incorporated into and marginalized by incoming polities. In the eighth century C.E. Hani-populated areas were forcefully incorporated in the Nanzhao kingdom and its successors. In the 13th century Yunnan Province was overrun by Kublai Khan's armies of MONGOLS, and the Hani along with several other ethnic groups put up fierce resistance to their incorporation into the larger Chinese state. By the 14th century local kingdoms were overshadowed by the Chinese Ming dynasty and the Hani were ruled by officially designated local chieftains. The successive Qing dynasty replaced the chieftains with court officials. Qing rule was not complete, however, and in the middle of the 19th century the Hani and several other minorities rebelled in the Yunnan War of 1855–73. Between 1895 and 1935 the Hani also joined local resistance to French incursions.

Ultimately, the Hani and their neighbors were overcome by the greater power of the Chinese state and became a part of modern China. Several ethnic subgroups, including the Hani, Heni, Budu, Biyue, and Yani, were combined in the Hani category after the communist revolution in

HANI

Location:
Southwestern Chinese province of Yunnan; Lai Chau and Lao Cai Provinces of Vietnam; Laos

Time period:
Unknown to the present

Ancestry:
Sino-Tibetan

Language:
Hani, of the Tibeto-Burman family

1949 and were placed under a joint autonomous prefecture with several other officially recognized minority groups. Today there are an estimated 1.4 million Hani living in China in addition to those living in the northern regions of Thailand, Myanmar, Vietnam, and Laos.

Throughout these political changes the Hani have maintained their identity and internal cohesion, partly by emphasizing a connection with their ancestors. The Hani are sometimes described as combining the traditions of polytheism, or the belief in many gods, and animism, the belief in the power of spirits, with ancestor worship, a claim that is not necessarily accurate across all Hani communities. Traditionally the Hani have believed that the natural world is spiritual and that forests, lakes, and particular trees have their own spirits that humans must respect. Some villages still have shamans who are responsible for managing relations with spirits who can exert protective or negative influences on the weather, the harvest, and personal health. Religious figures may also be responsible for conducting community events and preserving herbal lore. Although the Hani live in a culturally diverse area where several neighboring communities adopted Buddhism centuries ago, the influence of this and other organized religions is less apparent in Hani culture.

Most Hani families have detailed knowledge of their genealogy, and some can orally name their ancestors as far back as the split with the Yi, roughly 50 generations ago. Since the Hani are patrilineal, that is, trace their kinship through the male line, this practice is facilitated in some cases by their adding the final words of a father's name to his son's. Histories, legends, and other forms of communal knowledge are also transmitted orally. Although the Yi were literate when the Hani people separated, the Hani did not retain a script of their own. Memorization of older tales is therefore an important factor in their connections with the past, and some stories are still consistent with those told by Akha communities that separated from the Hani centuries ago. Not all the stories are inherited, however, and Hani oral traditions also feature improvised songs and riddles.

Modern Hani dialects are more diverse than the language used to recite these older histories and stories. The three largest Hani dialects are Ha-Ai, Bi-Kaw, and Hao-Bai. They probably diverged from one another as individual Hani communities spread across relatively remote mountainous areas. Some Hani communities gradually moved from the valleys to the mountainsides, where they are successful farmers who use intricate terraces to convert hills and mountainsides into tea and rice fields. Others were pushed out by incoming peoples.

Hani traditional clothing often features dark blue cloth and silver ornaments. Some men may wear a black or white turban and some women may wear headdresses with coins. In some communities Hani women wear traditional long skirts while elsewhere traditional skirts are shorter and are accompanied by patterned leggings. Some unmarried women wear a braided knot on their heads to identify themselves. Children younger than the age of seven are generally dressed without gender distinction. Hani living in or near urban areas may also reserve traditional clothing for special occasions and opt for more mainstream attire on a daily basis.

The Ha Nhi residing in Vietnam are one of the smaller of that country's 54 recognized ethnic groups, with population estimates ranging from 15,000 to 30,000 or so. They live mostly in the mountainous far north of the country, on the border with China, in Lai Chau and Lao Cai Provinces, having migrated there during their general southern migration probably before the third century C.E. The Hani in the other countries of Southeast Asia have a similar pattern of migration and residence, living in the mountainous regions just outside China. As in China, Hani outside the country are agriculturalists who utilize as much of their mountainous landscape as possible through terracing and irrigation; they also retain their patrilineal descent patterns and syncretic religious beliefs and practices.

Hanunoo   (Hanunoo Mangyan)

The Hanunoo, a name that means "true" or "genuine," are a subdivision of the larger MANG-YAN group, made up of eight tribal peoples in the highlands of Mindoro Island, the Philippines. Their homeland is primarily in the eastern region of the island, in Oriental Province, and they tend to occupy lower elevations than some of their Mangyan neighbors. The Buhid often call them *Mangyan patag*, which means "Mangyan of the flatlands."

All the Mangyan tribes practice swidden or slash-and-burn agriculture in their mountain homelands to produce dry upland rice, corn, beans, and a variety of other crops. Another important marker of Mangyan identity is their traditional clothing. Even in the late 20th century some Hanunoo men continued to wear

HANUNOO

location:
Mostly in Oriental Province, Mindoro, the Philippines

time period:
3000 B.C.E. to the present, though they may have been in Mindoro only since 1200 C.E.

ancestry:
Austronesian

language:
Hanunoo, a Meso-Philippine language within the larger Austronesian language family

their traditional *ba-ag* or loincloth and *baluka* or shirt; women's clothing was a short skirt called a *ramit* and a blouse called *lambung*. Indigo was a favorite color for clothing, and embroidery in the shape of a cross, especially on the backs of shirts and blouses, was also common. When the Spanish arrived in Mindoro they were surprised to see crosses everywhere and thought that other Christians had arrived before them; however, the design seems to have entered Mindoro from India about 3,000 years ago, along with the Mangyan writing system.

Despite contemporary interactions with lowland Filipinos and in the past with Indian, Arab, Chinese, Spanish, and American traders and colonizers, the Hanunoo have largely retained their own worldview and religious system. The Hanunoo distinguish between Mangyan peoples, those who wear loincloths, and non-Mangyan, *damu-ong,* everybody else. In this worldview language is not an important marker of identity so that the IFUGAO of the Cordillera region of Luzon, who speak an unrelated Austronesian language, are considered as Mangyan as fellow Hanunoo or their linguistic relatives and nearest neighbors, the Buhid.

The Hanunoo religious system recognizes a supreme creator God named Mahal na Makaako; a benevolent caretaker of the rice spirits or *kalag paray* named Binayo and her husband, Bulungabon, who chases down souls of the wicked with his 12 dogs in order to drown them; as well as numerous evil spirits, called *labang,* that can appear as humans or animals and are feared for eating their human victims. The numerous rituals undertaken throughout the agricultural calendar to appease the rice spirits indicate the overall importance of the spirit world, called *katapusan,* in the world that is inhabited by human beings. *Katapusan* is conceptualized as the edge of the universe and as covered with thick forests and large boulders.

FURTHER READING

Harold C. Conklin. *Hanunóo Agriculture; A Report on an Integral System of Shifting Cultivation in the Philippines* (Rome: Food and Agriculture Organization of the United Nations, 1957).

Harappans (Cemetery H Culture, Indus Valley Civilization, Indus-Sarasvati Civilization, Moenjodaro Culture, Mohenjo-Daro Culture)

The Harappans are the indigenous people of the northern region of south Asia, present-day Pakistan, and the Indus Valley. These people invented agriculture, developed their own writing system, and established more than 1,000 settlements, all before 2500 B.C.E. Their civilization had disappeared entirely until the 19th century, when British military personnel discovered some ruins outside the village of Harappa in 1826 and thus labeled the civilization Harappan. Since then much has been learned of the Harappans from their archaeological remains; however, their script remains largely undeciphered, and the causes of their ultimate demise remain a matter of debate.

GEOGRAPHY

Evidence of Harappan-era settlements has been found in more than 100 different sites in an area about 1,000 miles long, running from the northwest to the southeast as far as the Arabian Sea, and 750 miles wide, encompassing much of contemporary Pakistan and the Indus Valley. This region represents the largest territorial expansion of an ancient civilization found to date, significantly larger than either the Egyptian or Mesopotamian culture areas. Because of its large size the Harappan region encompasses different ecological zones, from the high-rainfall area of the Punjabi highlands, site

HARAPPANS

location:
Indus River valley, Punjab, and Sindh in present-day Pakistan

time period:
About 3000 to 1500 B.C.E.

ancestry:
Probably indigenous South Asian

language:
Probably a proto-Dravidian language

Harappans time line	
B.C.E.	
6500	Probable period of the early cultivation of wheat and barley in this region.
5500	Extensive trade networks have developed by this time, as evident in the discovery of jewelry made of shells more than 300 miles from their source.
2300–1900	The height of Harappan civilization.
2000	Beginning of the decline of Harappan civilization, perhaps due to ecological changes.
2000–1500	According to current theory Proto-Indo-Aryans move into the territory of the Harappan civilization and, living as local elites, cause a language shift over time. This picture is sometimes contested by various scholars, who posit a more violent scenario in which the Proto-Indo-Aryans invade and forcefully assimilate the local populations.
C.E.	
1826	James Lewis, a British army deserter, discovers the first Harappan ruins outside the Punjabi village of Harappa.
1857	Many Harappan ruins are destroyed during the construction of the Lahore-Multan Railroad.
1920s	Excavations begin at a second large Harappan city, Mohenjo-daro, located in Sindh, Pakistan.

of Harappa itself, to the hot and dry deserts of Sindh, where the other famous Harappan city of Mohenjo-Daro is located. The Indus River delta and Arabian Sea coast provide yet more diversity and the possibility for development of different urban areas, such as the port city of Lothal.

ORIGINS

It is believed that the Harappan people were indigenous to their South Asian territory, with the development of an extensive urbanized territory having resulted from local advances in agriculture, animal domestication, craftsmanship, trade, political development, and urbanization. Evidence of Stone Age residence in the region dates back to about 200,000 B.C.E., with that population developing agriculture and settling into village living sometime before 6500 B.C.E. By 5500 B.C.E. the Harappans had domesticated sheep, goats, and cattle and started trading over long distances. During the subsequent 2,500 years the Harappans developed complex pottery and metalwork, and villages began to grow into larger and larger units. This period also saw increasing uniformity among these villages and protocities until about 2600 B.C.E., when true cities began to flourish.

HISTORY

Without being able to read Harappan script, much of the historical development remains unclear to present-day scholars. We know that the emergence of uniform urban settlements emerged around 2500 B.C.E., with extensive irrigation and plumbing systems, even including indoor toilets. Prior to this period the Harappans had developed advanced agricultural techniques such as irrigation and fertilizers to allow them to move beyond slash-and-burn horticulture, pottery, metalworking, and the political structure necessary to organize thousands of people and to build many uniform urban areas.

Harappan civilization maintained itself for at least 500 years as a conservative society that did not undertake significant changes during its peak. When towns and cities were damaged by floodwaters or other natural disasters, they were always rebuilt to almost the same plan. All towns and cities had a similar design, with little room for improvisation or change, indicating a society that relished stability and regularity. However, after about 500 years of constancy unknown factors contributed to a decline in this advanced civilization around 2000–1900 B.C.E. Although the causes of this decline remain a mystery, several theories have been put forth to explain it. According to the first and most widely accepted theory a proto-Indo-Aryan people from Central Asia (see INDO-ARYANS) immigrated southward into the Harappan area and settled as small elite groups who eventually brought about a language shift while leaving no genetic evidence of their presence. An older theory ascribes the changes in Harappan civilization to an invasion of the Indo-Aryans. This explanation, which draws on Indo-Aryan texts such as the Rig Veda, posits that the Harappans were driven south by the violence and destruction of the incoming population, and some archaeological evidence at Mohenjo-Daro may support this theory, although nowadays most scholars disagree with this interpretation. However, according to still another theory a gradual decline precipitated by ecological change in the region was brought about, at least in part, by Harappan irrigation practices. Salinization of the land and topsoil erosion, along with a possible change in the Indus River's pathway, could have caused the Harappans' abandonment of their settlements. This theory posits that the region was relatively empty by the time the Indo-Aryans arrived between 2000 and 1500 B.C.E.

CULTURE

Harappan society was essentially urban, with more than 100 towns and cities having developed before and during the cultural zenith. The degree of uniformity in the layouts of both the large cities, Harappa and Mohenjo-Daro, believed to have been provincial capitals, as well as the common size and shape of bricks used throughout the entire region, indicate that the Harappan civilization was probably politically unified and well regulated by some central body. It remains unclear whether these rulers were legitimated through secular or religious means, or whether they inherited, earned, or were elected to their positions. Perhaps deciphering Harappan script will increase our understanding of the political structures of their society.

Unlike Harappan politics, other aspects of their society are somewhat more interpretable from the archaeological record. For example the lack of differentiation among burial sites, the relative simplicity of these sites, and the absence of large temples, palaces, or other expansive structures indicate a low degree of social class differentiation. Harappan society

The uniformity of the structures at Mohenjo-Daro is evident in these brick remains, which have been explored by archaeologists for nearly a century. *(DeA Picture Library/Art Resource, NY / G. Nimatallah)*

was engaging in trade with societies as far away as Sumer in Mesopotamia and in what is today southern Iran. Resources including seashells, copper, gold, silver, and turquoise were acquired from trading partners in a variety of regions. The Harappans also worked with copper and bronze, some of which may have originated outside their own territory.

Another aspect of Harappan society evident in the archaeological record are the people's engineering and other technical skills. The Harappans were masters in the construction of waterworks, including earthworks to control flooding, extensive irrigation canals to carry water from the Indus to the dry soils of Sindh, and even indoor plumbing and toilets. Large baths have been found in both cities and towns; these may have served either ritual or practical bathing purposes, or perhaps both. The Harappans also domesticated a number of plants and animals, including wheat, barley, rice, peas, sesame, melons, humped cows, and elephants, which they used for their ivory. They were the first people to domesticate cotton and use it for cloth, which they dyed with colors they had created.

Harappan cities were generally built of brick. Houses were flat-roofed structures while fortified centers enclosed large halls, granaries, and other buildings. Whether these urban centers were organized for secular or religious purposes is not known, and the reason for fortified centers in cities is unclear since no other signs of militarism have been found to date. Many experts believe that the Harappans were relatively peaceful people who merely wanted to defend themselves in case of attack, while others believe that signs of military activity have not yet been found but are inevitable in such a large and wealthy society. Copper and bronze knives, spears, and arrowheads have all been discovered in Harappan sites, so that time may reveal other weapons or signs of military activity, such as artwork depicting battle scenes.

According to some archaeologists the most interesting artifacts in Harappan sites are the plethora of soapstone seals found in Mohenjo-Daro, which most people believe contain the key to deciphering the script. The seals are flat and usually square with images of humans and animals plus inscriptions believed to be either alphabetic or pictogrammatic representations of their language. If these inscriptions are deciphered, many more aspects of Harappan society and culture may become evident.

FURTHER READING

Jonathan Mark Kenoyer. *Ancient Cities of the Indus Valley Civilization* (Oxford: Oxford University Press, 1998).

HAWAIIANS

location:
The Hawaiian Islands, the northernmost tip of Polynesian expansion in the Pacific

time period:
Approximately 400 C.E. to the present, with some archaeologists arguing that the initial settlements did not occur until between 800 and 1000

ancestry:
Polynesian

language:
Today most Hawaiians speak English or Hawaiian Creole English (HCE) while the Hawaiian language, 'Olelo Hawaii, is spoken as the first language only by a very small number of people on the islands of Ni'ihau and Hawaii. It is an eastern Polynesian language.

Richard H. Meadow, ed. *Harappa Excavations, 1986–1990: A Multidisciplinary Approach to Third Millennium Urbanism* (Madison, Wis.: Prehistory Press, 1991).

Asko Parpola. *Deciphering the Indus Script* (New York: Cambridge University Press, 1994).

Gregory L. Possehl. *Indus Age: The Beginnings* (Philadelphia: University of Pennsylvania Press, 1999).

Harijans   *See* SCHEDULED CASTES.

Hawaiians (Kanaka Maoli, Kanaka 'oiwi)

The Hawaiians are the indigenous population of the 50th state of the United States, where today they constitute about 19 percent of the state's population. They are POLYNESIANS who settled the archipelago that now bears their name after having sailed north, probably from the Marquesas, in the years between 400 and 500 C.E. Some debate has occurred over whether a second group of Polynesian colonizers, from Tahiti, arrived in 1300 and conquered the original inhabitants. However, the only evidence for this theory is Hawaiian legend and is not supported by archaeological evidence of a revolutionary cultural change occurring around 1300. Probably explorers from Tahiti and elsewhere in the Polynesian triangle south of the Hawaiian Islands visited Hawaii several times over the course of more than 1,200 years of native Hawaiian history prior to the arrival of Captain James Cook in 1778.

As was the case throughout much of tropical Polynesia, the Hawaiian Islands provided the native inhabitants with a varied and plentiful diet. Seafood was used extensively to supplement the domesticated agricultural products the Polynesians took with them, including taro, which was pounded into a starchy mash known as *poi*; bananas; breadfruit; and sweet potatoes. Polynesians also carried dogs, pigs, and chickens with them from their previous island homes. The mid-19th century ended this subsistence pattern for most native Hawaiians, as imported and local commercial agricultural products replaced this native diet with one that resembled that of other industrializing people.

Native Hawaiian social structure, like that of many Eastern Polynesian peoples, was highly hierarchical, with some authors referring to the divisions between chiefly, priestly, commoner, and slave families as constituting a caste system similar to that of the Hindu caste system in India. However within these class or caste rankings, women were far less disadvantaged than in many other hierarchical systems. Women could inherit rights to land use, although this did not happen frequently, and they could also inherit their families' spiritual possessions and knowledge, as did happen frequently. Women could rise to the highest positions in the land; the final monarch in the Kingdom of Hawaii before annexation by the United States was Queen Lili'uokalani.

The islands of Hawaii, Maui, Kauai, and Oahu each had its own hierarchy, with a chief at its apex, who was related to the gods and to the chiefs of the other islands. These chiefs and their families were believed to have divine power and to be forbidden or taboo to people from outside their class or caste. The degree of forbiddenness of these chiefs varied depending on their origins. Offspring of a chiefly brother-sister bond were the most sacred and thus could not speak to others during the day, walk on the ground, or engage in other social relationships with others, while those of cousin pairings or half-siblings were less taboo and thus only required prostration or crouching from commoners and slaves. None of these chiefs, however, could marry people outside their own class.

The economic structure was similar to the feudal system in medieval Europe, in which each level of the hierarchy of commoners and slaves was able to take tribute from those below them in the form of labor or produce, with ultimate control and power resting in the chief. The chiefs and lesser chiefs also used frequent warfare to expand their spheres of control over their rivals and neighbors.

This system of rivalry and warfare continued even beyond the initial contact between the Hawaiians and Europeans in 1778, ending only in 1810 when King Kamehameha of Hawaii united the archipelago after 15 years of struggle; he joined Kauai and Ni'ihau to Hawaii and O'ahu, which he had united in 1795. He was aided by a combination of factors, including the introduction of Western diseases that killed many of his rivals, a cannon he was able to liberate from a U.S. warship, and the assistance of at least one outsider, the British soldier John Young. Having united all the islands of the archipelago, Kamehameha set about bureaucratizing the society and establishing a kingdom on the Western model. He lived only until 1819, at which time a series of weaker monarchs slowly ceded much of Hawaii's independence to outside control. The first major step in this direction occurred in 1840 when the first constitution both diminished the monarch's power in favor of an elected government and changed Hawaii's traditional collective land tenure system to a privatized, individualized system that favored outside interests and financiers. Finally less than 100 years after its founding the Kingdom of Hawaii was overthrown in 1893 by a small group of marines and businessmen from the United States. The U.S. government then annexed the archipelago in 1898 and it became the 50th state in August 1959. Despite this colonial history the royal line of the Kingdom of Hawaii continues today, and there are still small numbers of native Hawaiians who contest Hawaii's annexation and statehood.

As did most Polynesian peoples, the Hawaiians utilized a generational kinship system that classifies individuals by generation and sex, rather than by naming their specific place in the kinship structure. Since 1871 and the publication of the anthropologist Louis Henry Morgan's *Systems of Consanguinity and Affinity of the Human Family,* this kind of generational or classificatory kinship system has been referred to as Hawaiian kinship. As a simple generational system this form of kinship is the least complex of the six systems first identified by Morgan and is still in use today by anthropologists. For example instead of using separate kinship terms for mother and aunt, all females of one's mother's generation are referred to as mother, or *makuahine* in Hawaiian. The same is true for fathers and uncles, who are all referred to as father, or *makuakane.* Both sisters and female cousins are referred to as sister, or *kaikuahine,* and brothers and male cousins are referred to as brother, or *kaikua'ana.* This same pattern also holds true for the grandparents' and children's generations.

Since annexation by the United States in 1898, significant numbers of indigenous Hawaiians have contested their political and economic subordination to the mainland. Indigenous activitivism in the early 1980s focused heavily on the grave health indicators within the community, such as low birth weight, high rates of diabetes and heart disease, and low life expectancy. Since 1993 greater recognition of their plight by the U.S. government, in the form of a formal apology for the way in which their land was taken from them, has meant some movement toward self-determination. However, a U.S. Supreme Court decision in 2000 set the movement back somewhat when the nine justices could not agree that the indigenous Hawaiians constituted a tribe with its own governance structure. Today Hawaiians make up less than 20 percent of the total population on their islands; they are also among the poorest, least well educated, and least healthy.

See also POLYNESIANS.

Queen Lili'uokalani

Queen Lili'uokalani is renowned for her many accomplishments, including the composition of one of Hawaii's most famous songs, "Aloha Oe," as well as authoring the book *Hawai'i's Story by Hawai'i's Queen,* but she is best known as Hawaii's last queen and a staunch advocate for Hawaiian native rights. Born in Honolulu, Hawaii, in 1838, Lili'uokalani was educated at the Royal School, where she learned the English language and the intricacies of American society. She succeeded her brother, King Kalakaua, to the throne in 1891 and quickly entered direct conflict with the wealthy American and European sugar plantation owners when she abolished the 1887 Bayonet Constitution. The Bayonet Constitution, signed by King Kalakaua in 1887 under threat of violence, stripped the monarchy of much of its power and favored the elite sugar growers while denying many Hawaiians and Asians the right to vote on the basis of race, education, and income levels. When Lili'uokalani abrogated the Bayonet Constitution in favor of a new draft that restored voting rights to the economically disadvantaged Asians and Hawaiians, the sugar growers formed the Committee of Safety in protest. At the same time the McKinley Act removed Hawaii's status as the premier sugar producer, threatening Hawaii with not only economic collapse, but also annexation to the United States for survival. In 1893 U.S. troops arrived in Hawaii and Lili'uokalani was deposed. In 1894 the Republic of Hawaii was established under the new president, Sanford B. Dole, one of the original protesters of the queen's reign. Although Grover Cleveland's administration later investigated the queen's deposition and found the overthrow of the monarchy to be illegal, Lili'uokalani was unable to regain the throne, and she died in 1917 at age 79.

Queen Lili'uokalani of Hawaii, who was overthrown in 1893, ending 82 years of united monarchy in the archipelago. *(Library of Congress)*

FURTHER READING

Patrick Vinton Kirch and Marshall Sahlins. *Anahulu: The Anthropology of History in the Kingdom of Hawaii. Vols. 1 and 2.* (Chicago: University of Chicago Press, 1992).

HAZARAS

location:
Primarily the Hazarajat region of central Afghanistan with significant numbers in Kabul, as well as in Pakistan and Iran

time period:
Between 1229 and 1447 to the present

ancestry:
Primarily Mongol with some Iranian influences

language:
The Hazaragi and Dari dialects of Persian; as late as the 1950s two or three villages in the Herat region of Afghanistan were reputed to be speaking their original Mongol language

Hay *See* ARMENIANS.

Hazaras (Hazara Mongols)

The Hazaras are a unique people living primarily in central Afghanistan, where they make up 9 percent of the population, and in the Meshed area of Iran and in Quetta, Pakistan. They are physically unlike all other people from Afghanistan (*see* AFGHANISTANIS: NATIONALITY), with their high cheekbones, sparse facial hair, and clearly Mongol heritage. They also constitute a religious minority in Afghanistan as Shii Muslims, while the majority of their fellow citizens are Sunni. These differences have led to significant discrimination for many centuries in Afghanistan. Prior to the Soviet invasion in 1979 the Hazaras constituted a large, poor underclass within a country that by global standards was itself quite poor. Today the Hazaras claim to be Afghanistan's second-largest ethnic group but also its least recognized.

GEOGRAPHY

Hazarajat contains the highest peaks in the Hindu Kush Mountains, up to 17,000 feet in elevation, which have limited outsiders' abilities to control the region. The majority of the population lives between 8,000 and 12,000 feet. It is extremely cold in the winter and snow accumulation is significant, keeping most Hazaras in their villages all season long. The spring and summer growing seasons are fairly short but wet enough to allow grains and vegetables to survive.

ORIGINS

The origins of this people remain unclear to this day because of their unique combination of physical, linguistic, and cultural traits. They have a Mongol appearance with high cheekbones and sparse facial hair; they speak an ancient form of Persian language and practice the Shii form of the Muslim religion. The Hazaras themselves have no origin stories explaining their presence in Afghanistan that could assist historians in their task.

One hypothesis that explains their physical features is that the Hazaras are the descendants of Mongol troops who traveled through the region in the 13th century, under the leadership of either Genghis Khan or, more likely, of the troops of Genghis Khan's son, Chagatai, who occupied Transoxiana, the region north of the Amu Darya, and repeatedly attempted to occupy India. These MONGOLS failed in their Indian campaigns and some may have taken to the mountains of central Afghanistan to escape. However, both of these hypotheses fail to explain why their Persian language contains as many Turkic terms as Mongol ones.

One hypothesis that explains this linguistic mystery is that the Hazaras are a Turkic population who have been living in central Afghanistan since at least the time of the KUSHANS, when Buddhism was the dominant religion in the area. This hypothesis, however, fails to explain the group's physical features or adherence to Shiism.

In Persian territory of the 15th century *hazara*, the Persian word for 1,000, was specifically used to refer to military units and to refer to individual tribes. In Afghanistan the term was applied to mountain tribes. Therefore the 1417 reference to tribute gathered from hazara by the ruling Mongol shah Rukh may not refer to this population. By the turn of the 16th century and the invasion of Babur, founder of the Mughal dynasty in India, this reference had become more specific to the Mongol Hazaras.

HISTORY

Until the end of the 19th century, most Hazaras lived in the relatively autonomous Haz-

Hazaras time line

C.E.

1417 Reference to tribute being taken from the "hazara" by the troops of Shah Rukh.

1504 By this time the general term *hazara,* meaning "mountain tribe," is being used to refer to these people, at least in Afghanistan.

1879–81 Many Hazaras assist the British in their attempt to colonize Afghanistan; their common enemy are the dominant Pashtuns.

1880–1901 King Abdur Rahman's ethnocidal nationalizing processes drive many Hazaras into the Meshed area of Iran and British India, particularly around Quetta in present-day Pakistan. These regions continue to have significant Hazara populations today.

1978 The Afghan government targets Hazara populations as anti-Communist, sparking local rebellion.

1979 The government is successfully driven out of Hazarajat, but the Soviet invasion of Afghanistan forces many Hazaras into Iran and Pakistan as refugees.

1982–89 Infighting between two Hazara factions results in more deaths than had been caused by government or Soviet troops.

1990s Some Hazaras join the Northern Alliance and participate in the liberation of the country from the Taliban.

2004 Mohammad Karim Khalili, Hazara leader of Hezb-e Wahdat or the Islamic Unity Party, the main Shia party in Afghanistan, and member of the Northern Alliance, becomes second vice president of Afghanistan.

arajat region of central Afghanistan. In the late 19th century, however, two sets of events conspired to bring an end to this status quo. First in 1879–81 the Hazaras allied themselves with the British against their common enemy, the Pashtun government of Afghanistan. With the Pashtun victory in this Second British-Afghan War many Hazaras fled the country as refugees, some to Iran while others settled near Quetta in British India, which is today Pakistan. A number of these refugees did return to Afghanistan when they were granted land in the north of the country, but others remained in Iran and India, where their descendants continue to reside. The second event that produced great change in Hazarajat and for the Hazara people was the extensive military action carried out in the region by Abdur Rahman in the last two decades of the century in his attempts at nationalizing the country along Pashtun lines (*see* AFGHANISTANIS: NATIONALITY; FARSIWAN; PASHTUNS). Many thousands of Hazaras were killed while many others fled the country, joining their people in Iran and British India. One of Rahman's tactics in his war against the Hazaras was to frame his action in religious terms, pitting the majority Sunni against the minority Shia, a practice that set the stage for continued persecution throughout the subsequent century.

While the Hazaras had a long history of subjugation and lower-class status for most of their history, including serving as slaves to the dominant Pashtuns until as late as 1919, the 1978 coup was comparable to their most difficult period, that of the Rahman campaign against them. The Communists also targeted the numerically strong Hazaras because they had no support from them. As in Rahman's day this moved many Hazara men to participate in localized militias, often run by religious leaders. By mid-1979 the Hazaras were successful and all government troops had departed from Hazarajat.

Also as the Rahman campaigns had, these internal events, as well as the Soviet invasion in the last days of 1979, drove many Hazaras out of the country to live as refugees in Iran and Pakistan. But among those who remained the organizational remnants of the previous year's fighting and about 100 years of local religious education contributed to their ability to remain fairly autonomous under the leadership of the Shura-ye Ittifagh-e Islami (Islamic council or union). The Shura, as it is known, had formed in 1979 as an umbrella group for the many localized rebellions. Unlike most of Afghanistan Hazarajat improved somewhat during the Shura

leadership as well as under the Islamists who pushed them out a few years later. The Islamists built new roads and schools and generally modernized the region's neglected infrastructure. However, contests between traditional Hazara religious leadership, the Shura's *sayyid*, which constitutes a separate, endogamous caste believed to be descended from the Prophet himself, and Islamist sheikhs trained in the Shii religious schools of Iran and Iraq soon devolved into a kind of civil war. This infighting between the Shura and the Islamists continued until 1989 and resulted in more casualties than the Hazaras had experienced at the hands of the government and Soviets.

In 1988 a new pan-Hazara religious organization emerged, Hezb-e Wahdat, which included both Islamist and Shura factions. By 1992 and the fall of the Communist regime in Kabul this organization coordinated the efforts of many smaller Hazara organizations both inside and outside the capital. This group soon established civilian control over about half of the city of Kabul. It was continually challenged by other ethnic-based organizations, the most dominant being those of the TAJIKS, and by 1994 and the emergence of the Taliban the Hazara Wahdat group could not challenge them for the country's leadership. Hezb-e Wahdat continued to join Hazara organizations and to control some areas of Hazarajat, but it was encircled and neutralized by the Taliban until the Hazaras joined the Northern Alliance with its backing from the United States. Today Hezb-e Wahdat, as part of the Northern Alliance, plays a significant role in the government, and its leader, Mohammad Karim Khalili, is the country's second vice president; another important Wahdat member is Haji Mohammad Mohaqiq, who has also held cabinet-level positions.

CULTURE

Until the great changes wrought by the 1978 coup, the Soviet invasion, and all the subsequent fighting, the Hazaras who remained in Hazarajat were an agricultural people who lived in their tribal regions, usually bounded by valleys and mountains. They were (and continue to be) divided into several tribes, including the Besud, Yek Aulang, Timuri, Dai Zangi, and Dai Kundi. Rural Hazaras made a modest living growing wheat, barley, peas, beans, and lentils wherever there was enough water to support cultivation. This was not an inconsiderable region given the large number of springs and rivulets in the mountainous terrain. They also kept sheep,

The most reliable form of transportation in the Hazaras' rugged, war-torn landscape is often horseback. *(OnAsia/Vanessa Dougnac)*

oxen, donkeys, and horses. Oxen were used for plowing as well as for food, while sheep produced wool, meat, and milk for drinking and cheese making. Donkeys and horses were primarily used for transport, although horsemeat was not unheard of, nor mares' milk. Their houses were built out of mud and stone because almost no trees grow in their region. There were both small villages of 20–30 households and individual farmsteads located throughout Hazarajat. An administrative center at Panjao had a fort, bazaar, and government buildings, but the Hazaras did not live there. Hazaras living at the highest elevations tended to move seasonally with their flocks, while others remained in their homes throughout the year.

The majority of the population maintained this rural, agrarian lifestyle with its tribal boundaries and seasonal fluctuations, but many Hazaras moved to the cities, especially the capital, Kabul. In the cities the Hazaras lived as a kind of lower caste, doing work that other ethnic and tribal groups refused to do. The Hazaras made up the majority of porters, street sweepers, and other unskilled laborers. By the late 1970s a very few had moved into more entrepreneurial roles, running cheap hotels and teahouses, but these establishments did little to improve the national image of the Hazaras, long considered poor and backward.

Whether in Hazarajat or in the cities the Hazaras in the later half of the 20th century, despite their poverty and underclass status, had higher rates of literacy than the national average because of the efforts of local schools. These schools were largely sponsored by religious organizations in Iran and Iraq to help support the Shii Hazaras in maintaining their religion and culture. It was this backbone that contributed to the rapid organization of opposition groups in 1978 and to continued development throughout the subsequent decades of warfare.

The origins of the Hazaras' adherence to Shia Islam remain uncertain, along with so much of Hazara ancient history. One hypothesis is that conversion occurred at the hands of Iranian missionaries during the Safavid dynasty, 1501–1736. This Persian dynasty from the region of Azerbaijan ruled a vast area of the Middle East and was responsible for turning the Shia sect into a state religion; however, Safavid territory did not encompass the region of Hazarajat so this hypothesis must remain speculative. Others believe that the Hazaras have been Shia for as long as they have been Muslim, perhaps since the conversion of the Mongol leader Mahmud Ghazan in 1292. Perhaps both hypotheses have some truth to them: some Hazaras may have converted to Shia Islam in the 13th century while others were influenced by the Safavids.

FURTHER READING

Alessandro Monsutti. *War and Migration: Social Networks and Economic Strategies of the Hazaras of Afghanistan* (New York: Routledge, 2005).
Sayed Askar Mousavi. *The Hazaras of Afghanistan: An Historical, Cultural, Economic, and Political Study* (Richmond, England: Curzon Press, 1998).

Heisui   *See* MOHE.

Hephthalites (Cao, Ephthalites, Hayathelaites, Hephtal, He-ta, Hoa, Hoa-Tun, Hunas, Iranian Huns, the people of Hua, White Huns, Yeda, Ye-tai, Ye-ti-i-li-do)

The Hephthalites were a group of uncertain origin and cultural affiliation who rose to power in Central Asia and India in the fifth and sixth centuries of the common era. After just under 150 years in the spotlight they disappeared from the historical record almost as quickly as they had emerged, leaving behind a political landscape quite different from the one in which they had risen to prominence.

GEOGRAPHY

The original homeland of the Hephthalites is relatively obscure although most experts agree that they originated north of the Great Wall of China, in or near present-day Mongolia. A Chinese source from the second century states that they lived in a region of northwest China sometimes referred to as Dzungaria, a steppe area surrounded by mountain chains. At the height of their power the Hephthalites dominated most of Central Asia and northern India.

ORIGINS

As is the case with much of Hephthalite history, their origins have been obscured by the fact that they did not possess a writing system of their own, and thus most accounts about them have been written by others, who themselves were unclear about their origins. Even the Chinese, on whose borderlands the Hephthalites must have lived for hundreds of years, do not begin to write about them extensively until the fifth century.

The Byzantine writer Procopius in the early sixth century refers to them as white-bodied Huns, thus creating one of their many ethnonyms: *White Hun*. However, there is no linguistic or material evidence that they were related to the Huns or XIONGNU at all, and the name has generally been interpreted as a mistaken identity given to a nomadic people whose culture resembled that of the Huns.

HISTORY

The history of Hephthalite military domination in Central Asia and northern India is fairly brief, lasting just under 150 years. In that time, however, this nomadic group dominated most of the settled military powers of their time. In the western portion of their territory the Hephthalites conquered portions of the Persian Empire (*see* PERSIANS, SASSANIDS) and played a considerable role in placing certain rulers on the Sassanid throne. In the east the Hephthalites defeated the Guptas and ruled the Ganges basin of India for several generations. They also interacted with the Chinese as political equals, sending 13 diplomatic missions to the Northern Wei emperors between 507 and 531.

The most visible aspect of Hephthalite history in the first half of the fifth century is their military struggle against the Sassanids. Throughout most of the 420s nomadic Hephthalite raiders invaded Sassanid territories many times, plundering crops and herds as well as wreaking havoc. In 427 the Sassanid armies finally routed the invaders but only temporarily, for a generation and a half; in 454 the Hephthalites returned to avenge their earlier defeat. Their influence was so great at the end of that decade that the Sassanid Peroz or Firuz was able to take his throne in 459 only with the assistance of the Hephthalites in routing his younger brother, Hormazd II, in a two-year civil war. As a result of this assistance Peroz was supposed to pay a significant amount of tribute to the Hephthalite rulers, which drought and stubbornness prevented him from doing. The struggle that ensued finally led to Peroz's death at Hephthalite hands in 489.

At the same time as these events in Persian territory the Hephthalites were also making their military strength known in northern India. In addition to the Sassanid-held territories around Gandhara the Hephthalites conquered Gupta lands in the Ganges basin, extending their dominion eastward. They also turned their attention to Sogdiana in the northern Transoxiana region, taking those formerly Sassanid lands in the 470s and establishing one of their capitals at Pendjikent.

Despite these victories as well as their consolidation against the revived strength of the Sassanids in 484–86, the power of the Hephthalites was soon diminished. A combined army of Hindu Indian peoples took back its land in 532, just 10 years after the apex of Hephthalite power. Twenty-five years later the new Sassanid king, Khosrow I, avenged the death of his grandfather, Peroz, and retook most of the territory he had lost in his battles to retain his throne from his brother and then from the Hephthalites. He was assisted in this by the new nomadic power emerging the steppes, the western Turks. Four years after the Helphthalite defeat in 561 all mention of them disappears, leaving many scholars speculating about their later history. A few sources consider that descendants of the Hephthalites in India became the Rajputs, a caste of warriors in the Kshatriya *varna* within the Indian hierarchical caste system; however, most Rajputs themselves reject this claim. Other sources state that the descendants of the Hephthalites in the west were the Avars, a nomadic group that invaded the Carpathian Basin of present-day Hungary in the seventh century. Still others claim a link

HEPHTHALITES

location:
Origins north of the Great Wall of China but militarily successful in Afghanistan, Pakistan, India, and Persia

time period:
Fourth and fifth centuries C.E.

ancestry:
Uncertain but possibly Eastern Iranian within the larger Indo-European family for the majority. Some experts have also suggested the majority were of Turkic origins. They were certainly a mixed group who included peoples with many different origins.

language:
Probably dominated by an Eastern Iranian language, but their mixed ancestry also led to multilingualism

Hephthalites time line

C.E.

125 First textual reference to Hephthalites: a Chinese source mentions them as living in Dzungaria.

420–27 Hephthalites raid Persian Sassanid empire until they suffer defeat in 427.

454 Hephthalites avenge their previous defeat at the hands of the Sassanids.

459 Hephthalites assist Firuz (Peroz) to regain his Sassanid throne; he must pay significant tribute in return.

465–70 Hephthalites conquer Indian Gandhara.

470–80 Indo-Hephthalites wage war against the Indian Gupta dynasty; upon their victory Hephthalites claim territory in all of northern and central India.

473–79 Hephthalites conquer Sogdiana and establish a capital city at Pendjikent.

484–86 Hephthalites are militarily successful against the Persian Sassanids and turn them into a vassal state, temporarily.

522 The height of Hephthalite power.

532 Hephthalites are driven out of India by a coalition of Hindu forces.

557–61 Final victory of Khosrow I, the Sassanid king, over Hephthalite forces.

565 Almost complete disappearance of Hephthalites in the face of the emergence of the western Turks (Gokturks).

between the Hephthalites and the Pathans or PASHTUNS, the dominant ethnic group in contemporary Afghanistan.

CULTURE

The Hephthalites probably began their history as a nomadic people, moving across the Asian steppes when political, military, or social situations favored their movement. Procopius refers to them as having a favorable homeland, but no evidence of an original permanent settlement has been found. Even their capitals moved from city to city on the basis of climatic and political conditions.

As a nomadic people they would have had few belongings except their felt tents, clothing, and cooking utensils. As a result very few pieces of certainly identified Hephthalite material culture have been found. Their artistic style, for example, cannot be categorized on the basis of the very few known examples. However, a number of Hephthalite coins from the regions between Iran and India have been discovered, many of which depict a people who practiced a form of skull deformation that produced somewhat cone-shaped heads. This was probably achieved by tightly wrapping a baby's head in cloth in order to change the bone structure; why this was done remains a mystery. Some coins bear the name *Hono,* which indicates that some Hephthalites adopted the practice of referring to themselves as Huns.

As is the case with many aspects of the Hephthalite social world their religious traditions remain obscured by time. There is some evidence that Buddhism was practiced in some of the territories held by the Hephthalites; however, some contemporary authors also wrote of the persecution of Buddhists. There are references to sacred fire, which indicates at least some familiarity with Zoroastrianism. However, because Hephthalite graves have been found, not all aspects of Zoroastrianism would have been practiced, since the funerary ritual of this religion entailed leaving the body in the open to be devoured by sacred birds and dogs. As was the case with language religion was probably another area in which the Hephthalites constituted a multicultural society, with a number of faiths and belief systems being practiced at the same time.

The most interesting aspect of Hephthalite social structure, as noted in a Chinese reference to them, is the fact that they practiced the most rare marriage form on earth: fraternal polyandry. In this system a number of brothers all marry a single woman, usually with the oldest brother marrying first and younger brothers joining the marriage when they come of age. Children in this kind of marriage were either all recognized as the offspring of the first husband regardless of biological paternity or assigned to each brother in turn, with the oldest considered the father of the first child, and so on. Among the Hephthalites it was the custom for women to adorn their hats with horns, one per husband. If a man had no brothers he would often adopt another man so as to be able to marry. This marriage type, while rare, is not unique to the Hephthalites and was used into the 20th century by TIBETANS, who engaged in it in order to make sure that small family landholdings did not have to be divided among brothers. Instead all male offspring remained on their parents' land and worked it together as a single landholding. This system also limits population growth significantly since each generation produces the children of only one woman instead of offspring from the wives of all brothers. While the Tibetans who practiced this marriage form did so largely in order to preserve family farms, this was probably not the case for the nomadic Hephthalites. Instead their motivation may have been limiting the birth rate or keeping the family's herds together rather than dividing them among several brothers. There is no mention in the Chinese records of what happened to the plethora of Hephthalite women who were unable to marry because of a lack of available men.

Hezhe   *See* NANAL.

Hijras (Aruvanis, Khusras, Klibas, Muhannas, Mukhannaths)

The Hijras are communities of "demasculated" men from India, Pakistan, and Bangladesh. The term itself is usually described as derived from the Urdu word for "hermaphrodite" or "impotent one" and points to the origins of the community, although some sources indicate that the Urdu word *hich ga* meaning "nowhere" and referring to being neither male nor female is its source. Individuals can become Hijras as infants if they are born hermaphrodites or intersexed, or they can enter as boys in childhood and either be castrated or simply dress and act the part of neither man nor woman.

While no one is certain about the roots of this tradition most point to its Hindu background. Ancient Indian texts from as early as 1000 B.C.E. mention the existence of a "third sex" and the *Ramayana,* which dates from the third century B.C.E., also claims that the god Ram gave his blessing to eunuchs. Hijras worship Bahuchara Mata, a Hindu goddess of nonviolence who is also known for having castrated her husband, who preferred to live as a woman. The most sacred event for Hijras each year, when many travel to Koovagam in Tamil Nadu to participate, is a ritual marriage that acts out the marriage of Aravan, who was to be sacrificed the following day, and Lord Krishna, who took on the body of a woman for the day.

Despite these strong connections to traditional Hindu culture, many contemporary Hijras, some sources even say the majority of them, are Muslims, take on female Muslim names when they transition into Hijra society, and are buried as Muslims rather than cremated as Hindus are. Many Hijras also say that a guru or older Hijra who trains and cares for a community of younger Hijras should be a Muslim, and the most respected are those who have undertaken the hajj or pilgrimage to Mecca. There are also a number of historical precedents to Hijra society in Islamic traditions. When Muslims entered India in the 12th century they introduced with them their society of eunuchs, castrated servants, *mukhannathun,* who guarded their women. Many *mukhannathun* rose to very high political positions within the numerous Muslim kingdoms that ruled on the subcontinent until the 18th century and as a result bestowed high status on all the *mukhannathuns* who lived in such a community, including the Hindu "third sexed" individuals or *kliba* who joined their ranks.

Contemporary Hijra society has an unwritten code of conduct that requires all members to wear women's clothing, accessories, and hairstyles. Their goal is not to fool people into thinking they are biological women, although they do use the female pronoun, but rather to indicate that they are not men. Traditionally they have made their living from three different activities: threatening to curse shop owners who do not give them money to go away, bestowing fertility blessings at weddings and births, and prostitution; singing and dancing are also common in conjunction with these other activities. In Pakistan at the turn of the 21st century one study found that about 80 percent of them were illiterate, thus limiting their

HIJRAS

location:
India, Pakistan, and Bangladesh

time period:
Unknown to the present

ancestry:
Indian

language:
All the major languages of India, Pakistan, and Bangladesh can be heard in Hijra communities.

Like many Hijras, this individual lives on the outskirts of ordinary Indian society. Rather than a singer or prostitute, however, this Hijra is a *sadhu,* or ascetic mendicant. *(OnAsia / Aroon Thaewchatturat)*

Kamla Jaan

Kamla Jaan made history in 2001 as the first Hijra to be elected mayor of an Indian city, Katni in the state of Madhya Pradesh. Tired of corrupt officials the people of Katni persuaded 46-year-old Kamla Jaan to run for office as a joke because she was transgendered, illiterate, and brusque in appearance and mannerisms. Her election was a victory for transgendered communities throughout India, as Hijras have long been ostracized for their lifestyles and have often been denied the right to vote, marry, obtain health benefits, or own a passport or driver's license. While in office Jaan stunned many by taking her post seriously and dedicated herself to the task of revitalizing Katni by sinking wells, repairing drainage troughs, and renovating the bus stop. In 2003, however, Jaan was unseated because the mayoral post was reserved for a woman, as mandated by a 1993 constitutional amendment that requires a reserved quota of political seats for women and lower castes. A Hijra, the High Court claimed, did not qualify as a woman, and in February 2003 Kamla Jaan's election was struck down.

HILIGAYNON

location:
Panay and Negros, the western Visayan islands, the Philippines

time period:
3000 B.C.E. to the present

ancestry:
Austronesian

language:
Hiligaynon, a subgroup of Bisayan, a Meso-Philippine language in the Austronesian family

---

access to other forms of employment. However, in central India today some Hijras have stepped away from these traditional roles and entered politics, much as the *mukhannathun* did many centuries ago. In the town of Katni in Madhya Pradesh Kamla Jaan, a Hijra, was the first member of this community elected mayor in 1999; she was followed the next year by another in the same state. Voters in Gorakhpur in Uttar Pradesh have also elected a Hijra mayor and Madhya Pradesh elected a Hijra legislator in 2000, Shabnam Mausi. Aunt Shabnam, as she is known in English, was born a Brahmin and before entering politics worked as a singer and dancer, as is common among Hijras. Having gained a taste for politics in the state assembly, she claimed to be working on a new political party for India, one that would welcome men, women, and the third sex. Political commentary from India in the 21st century, however, indicates that she may not need to take that step for many mainstream political parties have been courting Hijras as candidates, in part because they claim their lack of children and other family ties makes them less likely to be corrupt.

Despite this new political acceptance of Hijras, at least in central India, throughout the countries in which they live they are considered dangerous because of their ritual powers; the most serious curse they have at their disposal is barrenness, and most Hijras are not reluctant to wield such a curse if they are refused money or ridiculed. There is also a social fear of Hijras due to a plethora of stories claiming that they are known to kidnap young boys, castrate them, and make them part of their communities. These stories are used by parents to keep boys in line. As a result of this dangerous image most Hijras experience significant persecution; they generally are allowed to eat only with other Hijras and are often rejected by their families of origin.

While Hijras are not a separate people in terms of their ethnicity, language, or religion, they are considered separate from all other humans because of these myriad social and ritual factors and thus constitute a special group of India, Pakistan, and Bangladesh.

FURTHER READING

Serena Nanda. *Neither Man nor Woman: The Hijras of India* (Belmont, Calif.: Wadsworth, 1990).
Gayatri Reddy. *With Respect to Sex: Negotiating Hijra Identity in South India* (Chicago: University of Chicago Press, 2005).

Hiligaynon (Ilonggo, Ilongo, Yligueyn)

The Hiligaynon or Ilongo are a subgroup of the VISAYANS, the largest ethnic group in the Philippines, who live primarily on the island of Panay and the province of Negros Occidental on the island of Negros. They are also classified as Western Visayan people.

As do other Visayan peoples, the Hiligaynon look back to their possibly mythological founder Datu Makatunaw to explain their earliest history. The story outlines the chief or *datu*'s arrival on Panay after having sailed from Borneo with eight to 10 other chiefs, their purchase of the island from the AETA chief Marikudo for the cost of a golden hat, and their subsequent establishment of an agricultural community throughout the Visayas. Actual Hiligaynon history may contain many of these elements, but it is impossible to tell from the story, which was written down for the first time in 1907, where history ends and myth begins.

Although there are some Chinese and Arabic records of trade and other interactions in the Visayas, written Hiligaynon history can best be said to have begun in 1565 when the Spanish established a colony on the island of Cebu. In 1569 as a result of harassment by Portuguese ships, the Spanish moved to Panay and settled in Capiz. The local Hiligaynon population resisted Spanish colonialism and the labor it entailed on their sugar and rice plantations and in the building industry for the construction of Spanish homes or haciendas and churches. Spanish records indicate widespread revolts in Panay and Negros in 1586 and 1663, but local weapons were no match for Spanish firearms and both revolts were put down fairly quickly. The descendants of these early revolutionaries did not forget the actions of their ancestors, however, and in 1896 many joined the fight against Spanish colonialism and later the American takeover of the archipelago. By 1901 though the newly arrived Americans had ended the resistance and the western Visayas became an integral part of the new American colony.

During the American period the people of Panay and Negros were somewhat less rebellious than they had been during the Spanish period and many took advantage of the free education that was offered to all children. The region's economic development also fared well during the period, with both rice and sugarcane providing a decent income to most workers, the former on small individual holdings and the latter on large plantations. This development came to an abrupt end in 1941 when the JAPANESE occupied the region and set off four years of guerrilla warfare between the local population and the occupiers. This lasted until 1945, when the Americans returned and ended the Japanese occupation and then granted the Philippines independence a year later. The Hiligaynon were particularly proud people at that time because one of their native sons, Manuel Roxas, became the fifth Filipino president and first postindependence president of the Republic of the Philippines.

Despite their resistance to Spanish colonialism many cultural features were adopted from the Spanish during their more than 300 years of domination. The most important is probably the widespread conversion to Roman Catholicism that took place fairly early in the colonial period. However, Catholicism in the Philippines generally, and among the Hiligaynon specifically, is more often than not a syncretic blend of both Christian and pre-Christian beliefs, such as the power of ancestral and natural spirits, the ability of witches and sorcerers to harm people guilty of social infractions, and the power of *baylans* or mediums to communicate with the spirit world. Even the traditional Catholic elements of Hiligaynon religion, such as veneration of the Baby Jesus, have been blended with local customs and beliefs, as in the common practice of bathing statues of the Baby Jesus in order to generate the rainy season through sympathetic magic.

The most important social unit among the Hiligaynon is the family, both in its nuclear form of parents and unmarried children, and in its extended form, which includes a wide range of bilateral relatives or people related through both the mother and father. Families, rather than individuals, own and control all land in the region and exert considerable power over the actions of unmarried children in such areas as their education, profession, and even marriage partners. Children in turn continue to support their family of origin well into adulthood, for example, by sending money, even from jobs held overseas. Generally Hiligaynon society can be considered a collectivist one in which individual desires, motivations, and interests must be subsumed in favor of the desires, motivations, and interests of the family. This is not to say, however, that all members of the family are equal partners in this collectivist project. Fathers are considered heads of households and must be treated with deference and respect, especially in public, when their wives and children must defer to their authority on all matters. In private this situation is often reversed, with women dominating both the financial and social lives of their family unit; many Hiligaynon men even turn over their wages to their wives for them to manage the household accounts. The centrality of the wife at home is also reflected in the residence pattern of new Hiligaynon couples, which tends to be matrilocal, either within or very near to the wife's parents' home, for at least the first year of marriage. After that year most couples establish their own, neolocal residence, which can be near one of the sets of in-laws or in a new village altogether.

Hill Tribes of Thailand (Chao Khao)

The Hill Tribes of Thailand are a population of nearly 1 million people divided into seven major ethnolinguistic groups and a number of smaller ones. Most of these groups migrated into the northern area of the country from various regions of China and Myanmar (Burma) during the latter half of the 19th century; they are the AKHA, HMONG, KAREN, LAHU, Lawa, LISU, and YAO or Mien; there are also many smaller groups, such as the T'IN. Most of these groups are subdivided further into smaller language and culture groups; for example, there are five different Karen languages, and two different Hmong, Lahu, and Lawa languages spoken in Thailand. Most of them have large populations that reside in China, Myanmar, Vietnam, or other Southeast Asian countries, but in Thailand their specific historical experience of migration and dealing with the majority Thai state government has meant that they constitute their own ethnic group. The Thai homeland of these groups is the northern highlands, especially on

HILL TRIBES OF THAILAND

location:
Thailand

time period:
Late 19th century to the present, except the Karen, who have been in Thailand since the 18th century; the phrase *Hill Tribes* came into use only in the 1950s.

language:
All tribal groups and subgroups speak their own languages from the Sino-Tibetan, Hmong-Mien, or Austro-Asiatic language families.

the western border with Myanmar and mostly higher than 3,280 feet above sea level.

The traditional economic activity of all Hill Tribes and their subgroups was usually extensive farming. This method required them to be able to move locations every few years as the land in a particular region became exhausted and had to lie fallow. Each year a family would carve out a field from the tropical forest of the region, allow the vegetation to dry out, and then burn it to provide ash fertilizer. After a growing season or two the field would then become unable to support a family and the cycle would begin again. This method requires large amounts of territory for small numbers of people and probably led to the migration of these communities out of China and Myanmar in years past. In addition to this subsistence farming, which has been discontinued in Thailand

A young woman from the long-necked Paduang, a subgroup of the Karen, one of the Hill Tribes. Her extensive necklaces push her collarbones and ribcage down and will eventually make her neck appear to be two to three times its normal length. *(Shutterstock/Alexander Gitlits)*

because of legal regulations imposed to save scarce resources, these groups hunted, fished, and gathered wild forest products. In the 20th century many individuals from these groups turned to production of opium as a major cash crop, but the work of such agencies as the Thai Royal Development Project for the Hill Tribes has provided other opportunities for joining the cash economy and opium production in the region has diminished.

In addition to their subsistence economies the Hill Tribes differ from the majority Thai people in their religious beliefs and practices, clothing, architectural styles, personal adornments, and many other aspects of material culture. Perhaps the most important difference is with regard to religion and worldview more generally. While the majority of Thai people consider themselves Buddhist, most Hill Tribes people continue to practice local animistic religions and to turn to their shamans for communication with the spirit world. While Christian missionaries have been active in the region for decades and many communities are nominally Christian, the dominant worldview remains one in which a large number of natural and ancestral spirits are seen as having control over much of the world. Prior to going out hunting, Hill Tribesmen had to seek permission from the spirits of the forest and animals, specific to each group and subgroup, to engage in the activity; upon killing an animal, further thanks had to be provided to that animal's spirit so as to prevent illness or other misfortune from the hunting party. Traditional healing ceremonies involving shamans communing with the spirit world also continue to take place throughout northern Thailand, usually in conjunction with a visit to a scientifically trained medical doctor.

The period of greatest change among the Hill Tribes began in the 1950s, when the Thai government first began to try to incorporate them into national life through the National Committee for the Hill Tribes. Several decades later in 1969–70 King Rama IX began the Royal Development Project to assist the Hill Tribes in developing cash crops to replace opium; this project also provided such infrastructure as roads and electricity to assist the integration of the Tribes into the national network. As a result today most younger Tribespeople speak, read, and write in Thai and many have become citizens of Thailand. However, for many older people the problems of lack of education and health care and access to governmental assistance continues. One of the most serious problems is statelessness. When many older Tribespeople were born, their families continued to engage in seminomadic subsistence farming, moving into and out of Thailand without the need for any kind of official documentation. Attempts to register the Hill Tribes as citizens did not begin until the 1990s; as a result many have no evidence of nationality. Statelessness means no access to government health or education programs, no assistance with land registration, and no travel inside or out of Thailand.

One of the most damaging tactics of the Thai government, which was begun in the 1950s as a way of incorporating the Hill Tribes into the Thai state and continued in the 1980s and 1990s as a way of protecting land and forest resources, is resettlement. Most of these resettlements moved communities out of the highlands and into the valleys and plains to facilitate access to schools, roads, medical facilities, and other government services. On the face of it these moves seem a good idea for they gave the Tribespeople access to services that could improve both quality and length of life. However, they also engendered significant loss of cultural identity and traditional knowledge. Luckily some resettled communities have developed new ways of accessing this old information and thus maintain vibrant highland cultures even outside their original homelands. One such program is the Mirror Art Group, which has assisted some Hill Tribal communities in putting the most endangered aspects of their traditional culture on the Internet at the Virtual Hill Tribe Museum. Other resettled communities have not been so lucky and have fallen victim to poverty, drug use, discrimination, and the psychological disorientation of being forced to integrate rapidly into the modern Thai nation-state.

See also THAILANDERS: NATIONALITY; THAIS.

FURTHER READING

Lucien M. Hanks, Jane R. Hanks, and Lauriston Sharp, eds. *Ethnographic Notes on Northern Thailand* (Ithaca, N.Y.: Southeast Asia Program, Department of Asian Studies, Cornell University, 1965).

Hindi

The Hindi people are speakers of Hindi, an Indo-Aryan language and India's official language of governance. Those with Hindi as their mother tongue make up only about 20 percent of the population of India, with smaller numbers in Nepal and Bangladesh; they are over-whelmingly Hindu. According to official Indian sources Hindi speakers constitute about 45 percent of the population, but this percentages includes those for whom Hindi is a second language.

GEOGRAPHY

The Hindi people can be found throughout India, especially in the entire northern region; however, the so-called Hindi belt or cow belt is made up of only the six northern states of Bihar, Haryana, Himachal Pradesh, Madhya Pradesh, Rajasthan, and Uttar Pradesh. This is the territory of the Ganges River, the Himalayan foothills, and the plateau of Madhya Pradesh or middle province, all of which produce the great variety in climate, landscape, and atmosphere in the Hindi belt. The climate of this region ranges from extremely hot in the months of April to June, hot and humid during the monsoon period from about July through September, with a slight cooling and drying-out period from October through December, followed by a short winter season from January through March. These dates vary slightly by region but generally are followed in the entire belt. Both summers and winters can be very dusty and dust storms, called *andhi,* are common in both seasons in the desert regions of Rajasthan, Haryana, and others.

ORIGINS

The origins of the Hindi, as for all Indo-Aryan peoples, can be arbitrarily dated to about 4500 B.C.E., with the domestication of the horse; this dating is itself contested and others claim domestication did not occur until about 2000 B.C.E. This event marks the beginning of the mobile pastoral culture that eventually led to the movements of INDO-ARYANS out of Central Asia and into northern India. The first real evidence is from about 1600 B.C.E. in Bronze Age cultures around Gandhara, in which remains of horses have been discovered. From this western entry across the Hindu Kush Mountains Indo-Aryan culture interacted with indigenous cultures. What forms this interaction took is still unknown; some argue militaristic destruction, although this theory was more favored in the past, and others argue cultural interaction. Regardless of whether the Indo-Aryans assimilated or conquered the indigenous population, or did both, once they began to dominate the northwest they moved eastward. After they became established throughout India, Indo-Aryan culture is often

HINDI

location:
India, Nepal, and Bangladesh

time period:
About 933 C.E. to the present

ancestry:
Indo-Aryan, part of the larger Indo-European peoples

language:
Hindi, an Indo-Aryan language in the Hindustani family, which includes the Pakistani languages of Urdu, Sansi, and Kabutra

Hindi time line

B.C.E.

2500–1500 The Indo-Aryans move into India from Central Asia; they are said to speak what is called Vedic Sanskrit because the Vedas are composed in this language at this time.

600 The period of classical Sanskrit and the end of the Indo-Aryan phase. Some sources date the end of the classical period as late as 250 B.C.E.

500 The Prakrits emerge as localized and colloquial versions of Sanskrit. These soon turn into literary languages of their own, especially Pali, the language of the Buddha.

C.E.

400–600 In the same way that the Prakrit languages evolved from Sanskrit, the Prakrits evolve into seven colloquial languages, commonly called the Apabhranshas. The main one is Shaurseni, which becomes a literary language in about 900.

933 Shravakachar, a Jain religious text written in Hindi, is considered the first text in this language.

1000 This date usually marks the emergence of modern Indo-Aryan languages, including Hindi. Many words and sounds are infused in Hindi from Persian, Pashto, Arabic, Turkic languages, and others.

1206 The sultanate of Delhi is established.

1526 The Delhi sultanate is absorbed by the expanding Mughal Empire.

18th century Muslims begin consciously persianizing Hindi and create the Urdu language.

1757 The British take over northern India.

19th century Urban elites in northern India begin the Hindi-Hindu revivalist movement as an anticolonial strategy.

1947 Indian independence.

1950 The Indian Constitution, making Hindi the official language of state, takes effect.

1990 Hindi becomes the second most widely spoken language in the world after Mandarin Chinese.

called Vedic civilization, named for the religious text, the Rig Veda. In the past these people were also called Aryans, taken from the Vedic term *arya,* "noble"; a similar term is also used later by the Persians and appears in the earliest Iranian ritual language, Avestan.

The language of the Vedic civilization in India was Vedic Sanskrit, which remains extant today in the texts of the Vedas. These texts were first composed about 1500 B.C.E., codified about 900 years later, and written down probably after 300 B.C.E. After about 1,000 years in which Sanskrit was the elite literary language of northern India colloquial and local versions of the language began to emerge. These languages are called Prakrits, the most famous of which was

Pali, the language of the Buddha, but there were many others as well. As did Sanskrit, many of the Prakrits also became elite literary languages, while colloquial languages of everyday life began to appear around 1,000 years after their first appearance in 500 B.C.E. These colloquial languages are often called Apabhranshas; some examples include Nagar, Magadhi, Brachad, Maharashtri, and Shaurseni. It was the last of these that became the lingua franca of northern India and the language of much literature from that region, starting in about 900 C.E.

HISTORY

Language and Politics

The break between Hindi origins and Hindi history is somewhat arbitrary but can best be placed in about 933, with the publication of the first Hindi language text, *Shravakachar,* a Jain religious text. Some sources claim that 1000 or the early 11th century is a better estimate for the start of Hindi history, but as these dates are relatively close to 933 it seems of little importance here. The script that is used to write Hindi and a variety of other Indo-Aryan languages today, Devanagari, also emerged in approximately its current form in the 11th century, having descended from the Brahmi scripts of about 500 B.C.E.

As was the case with the development of various languages in northern India prior to the 11th century, Hindi developed first as a colloquial or everyday language in the region of Delhi. It was called Hindi or Hindvi in the 11th century by Persians who moved into India and referred to the language of Hind, the territory around the Indus River. During the course of the Delhi sultanate (1206–1526), established by these Persian-speaking migrants, the language absorbed many Persian, Arabic, Turkic, and other words, concepts, and sounds. The language was also taken into southern India by the various Turkic and Afghan or Pashtun dynasties that made up the sultanate, all of whom had adopted it as their lingua franca, though Persian remained the language of state.

In 1526 the Delhi sultanate gave way in northern India to the power of the Mughal empire, when Babur, the empire's founder, defeated the last sultan of the Lodi dynasty, Ibrahim, in Panipat. The Mughals' hold over India was tenuous at best in the early years, but in 1556 a young prince named Akbar inherited the throne and eventually consolidated his power in the region through a combination of warfare, strategic marriages, and concessions to the local population. One important concession concerned religion: the religion of the Mughals, as had been true of the Delhi sultanate, was Islam, but Akbar abolished all taxes and other impediments to the flourishing of Hinduism and thus won the loyalty of many people. The language of the Mughals, including Akbar, however, was not Hindi but Persian, and the illiterate emperor spent considerable funds on translations of great Hindi texts into the language of his court.

The Mughal period in northern India came to an end only in the 18th century, first with the invasions by Nadir Shah of Persia and then with the British, who had been playing off minor rulers and nobles in the empire for many decades. The British also defeated the French, whose East India Company had first taken the initiative in India by conquering Madras in the south in 1746. During the British colonial period in northern India, which can best be dated from 1757 after Robert Clive defeated the Indians at the Battle of Plassey and retook Calcutta in West Bengal, Hindi reemerged as an important national language.

The 18th century was also the period when Urdu, the contemporary national language of Pakistan, became increasingly separate from its Hindustani parent language. Essentially Urdu is Hindi with a large number of Persian and Arabic loanwords, and it was chosen as the language of the large Muslim population in northern India for their own cultural and religious expression. Today the two languages, Hindi and Urdu, are sometimes considered different dialects of the same Hindustani language, although their political and social usages as the languages of Hindus and Muslims, respectively, have made many people consider them separate languages, despite their innate similarities.

During the English period especially the 19th century, Hindi was favored by northern Indian intellectuals as the language of the anticolonial movement. Two important anticolonial organizations, Aryo Samaj and Brahmo Samaj, both pushed for the use of Hindi to create a national community to oppose the English. Increasingly nationalistic writers used Hindi to persuade other Indians to join them in their quest for independence, and both colleges and universities began to teach Hindi and Hindi literature. At this time Hindi became standardized across regions, in both written and spoken forms, and somewhat more sanskritized than in the immediate past, largely in reaction to the conscious persianization of Urdu.

Postcolonial India has accepted its multicultural and multilingual heritage through the constitutional recognition of 15 national languages: Assamese, Bengali, Gujarati, Hindi, Kannada, Kashmiri, Malayalam, Marathi, Oriya, Panjabi, Sanskrit, Sindhi, Tamil, Telugu, and Urdu. Among these, however, Hindi is considered the official language of governance and business, with English rapidly becoming the lingua franca in both these arenas. As was the case with the rise of Urdu in postindependence Pakistan, the choice of Hindi as the official language in India has had widespread political ramifications, from riots in Madras and other Dravidian regions in reaction to the elevation of an Indic language to official status to an increase in loanwords in Hindi from English and all the national languages of the country.

Religion

The emergence of Hindi as the official language of both the anticolonial movement in India and then independent India coincided with a reform movement in the primary religion of Hindi speakers, Hinduism. Borrowing from the textual traditions of both Christianity and Islam, some reformists or revivalists in the

Akbar the Great

Akbar the Great, also known as Jalaluddin Muhammed Akbar, is considered one of the greatest rulers of India's Mughal Empire. Akbar was born in 1542 during a period of instability for his family, which was in hiding after his father, Nasiruddin Humayun, was driven from his throne by the Afghan leader, Sher Shah. Because of his family's uncertain future Akbar did not receive a thorough education and never learned how to read or write, probably as a result of dyslexia. Upon Sher Shah's death Humayun reclaimed Delhi in 1555 but died a short time later after falling down a flight of stairs. Akbar succeeded his father in 1556 at the age of 13, and the first few years of his reign were unstable as supporters of the Sher Shah dynasty attempted to usurp the throne. By the time Akbar was 15 he and his army were successful in wiping out all remaining threats to his reign, and he proved to be a wise and benevolent ruler who supported academic study and religious tolerance. The Mughal Empire comprised Muslims and Hindus; however the majority of the Mughal subjects were Hindu while the ruling class was almost entirely Muslim. To balance the distribution of power and wealth, Akbar installed many Hindus in powerful positions in his government and abolished the *jizya,* a tax placed on non-Muslims. He also promoted religious debate and even commissioned the building of a House of Worship in which Hindus, Muslims, Roman Catholics, and even atheists could debate religious views and reconcile their differences. Listening to these debates convinced Akbar that no one religion could claim to possess the truth, and in 1581 he founded the faith of Din-i-Ilahi, an unsuccessful attempt to combine tenets from all of the religions in the Mughal Empire into one faith. He died in 1605.

19th and early 20th centuries sought to provide Hindus with a set of fundamental texts to guide them in their beliefs and practices. This was a great change from Hinduism's long tradition of syncretism, preference for oral versus written authenticity, and openness to change.

The history of Hinduism as a belief system is as ancient as the Vedic texts, about 1500 B.C.E., but the form the religion had at that time was very different from today's. Between this ancient period and the contemporary period three different versions of the Hindu tradition have emerged. The first, often labeled the Vedic period, lasted until about 300 B.C.E. During this period Brahman priests were primarily responsible for bloody animal sacrifices that served as the mediating process between this world and that of the gods. In about 300 B.C.E. under the influence of Buddhism's more peaceful focus on gift giving and alms Brahman priests began working primarily as the conductors of life-cycle rituals and slowly animal sacrifice entirely died out in the religion. The priests also benefited from the Buddhist tradition of giving money, food, and land to ritual specialists and many began to accumulate land and power. The next transformation in Hinduism began in the seventh and eighth centuries, when local rulers began to erect shrines and altars for images of the gods and goddesses. Kings chose a patron god or goddess and honored him or her with what has come to be known as the Great Gift, usually consisting of a large temple with extensive lands. Vishnu and Siva were the two gods most honored in this way throughout not only northern India but also the central Deccan and southern regions as well. At the same time Brahman priests developed even greater status than they had had as officials at domestic life-cycle events; they took on the role of mediator between kings and their gods and as such were among the most powerful individuals in each kingdom.

Despite this relatively clear-cut narrative on the development of contemporary Hinduism many scholars today argue that across India there was no such "religion" as Hinduism until it was invented in the 19th century, a joint project of Indian nationalists and British colonialists. Both groups oriented their view of the world in terms of the Western notion that each group, especially a national group, had its own religion. However, late-20th-century scholars showed that despite the relatively clear time line of Hindu developments, as people lived the tradition, it differed widely from period to period and region to region. There was no overarching Hinduism to which any Indian could adhere until the 19th century, when these nationalists and revivalists wedded the Hindi language, devoid of as many Persian and Arabic influences as possible, to the Hindu religion as the essence of Indian identity. With the increasing influence of Sanskrit on the language arose a connection between contemporary religious practice and the Vedas of the ancient past. Although Vedic practice had been abandoned more than 1,000 years earlier, the linguistic connection between its texts and modern political discourse led to a strengthening of Hinduism's textual authenticity and national character, versus the oral and local character it had had for several thousand years.

Today

Hindi culture today continues to have the strong association with the Indian nation and Hinduism as a religion that it had developed in the 19th century. As the official language of state Hindi, although spoken as the mother tongue by just 20 percent of the population, is associated with governance and the country as a whole by both citizens and outsiders. In addition the vast majority of its speakers are Hindus, thus earning the swath of territory it dominates the nickname "cow belt," based on the veneration of cattle central to modern Hinduism.

CULTURE

Hindi society, as are many throughout India, Bangladesh, Sri Lanka, and Nepal that have been influenced by Hinduism, is divided into almost innumerable subunits known in English as castes. The way this term is used in English often conflates two separate concepts from the Hindu hierarchy, *varna* and *jati*. The varna or color system divides the world into four hierarchical, immutable, and discrete categories: Brahmin, Kshatriya, Vaishya, and Shudra. Outside this system entirely are the Untouchables or Dalits, today more commonly referred to as SCHEDULED CASTES. The four varnas are believed to have originated from different portions of the creator god Brahma's body and to be organized on the basis of their occupations: Brahmans are supposed to be priests or teachers; Kshatriyas military or political rulers; Vaishyas craftsmen, merchants, and sometimes farmers; and Shudras servants. The first three varnas are believed to be twice born while the fourth have been born just once.

Within each of these varnas, sometimes confusingly labeled as castes, are jatis or castes, themselves hierarchically configured within their varna. This is where the system becomes infinitely complex, however, because within each region jatis can be categorized differently, either within the same varna or even across them. For example agricultural laborers are accorded higher jati and sometimes varna status in southern India than in the north.

Regardless of these geographic and other distinctions the entire caste and varna system remains both vital and important throughout India today, especially in the cow belt, despite having been outlawed by the Indian constitution. Not every individual continues to work in the occupation of his or her jati community. There have been Dalit politicians and landowners and poor, landless Kshatriyas and Brahmins. Nonetheless it is still very important for most Hindis to marry someone from the same jati or caste, and discrimination against the Scheduled Castes or former Untouchables remains a significant social problem. The category of Untouchability emerged in the distant past from the polluting nature of certain tasks: butchery, leatherwork, dealing with human waste or the dead, and the like. The pollution of these occupations was believed to rub off onto their practitioners, making them completely outside the varna system. In addition when the Indo-Aryans and later Hindu peoples assmilated or conquered various tribal groups throughout India, these tribal members would often be incorporated into the caste system, usually at the very bottom.

As this description of the caste system illustrates, all occupations are represented within the larger Hindi community. There are farmers, lawyers, priests, politicians, barbers, washers, butchers, information-technology (IT) specialists, call-center workers, and everything else that makes the large Indian economy run today. Today the Hindi belt has both extremely rich families, mostly living in Delhi and the other major cities of the region, and extremely poor ones; in fact some analyses of the region's economy claim that it has the greatest economic disparity in the country.

FURTHER READING

Sophie Baker. *Caste: At Home in Hindu India* (London: J. Cape, 1990).

N. P. Goel. *Hindi Speaking Population in India* (New Delhi: Radha, 1990).

Ram Gopal and K. V. Paliwal. *Hindu Renaissance: Ways and Means* (New Delhi: Hindu Writers Forum, 2005).

McKim Marriott, ed. *India through Hindu Categories* (Newbury Park, Calif.: Sage, 1990).

Raja Ram Mehrotra. *Sociolinguistics in Hindi Contexts* (New York: Mouton de Gruyter, 1985).

S. S. Narula. *Hindi Language: A Scientific History* (Delhi: Oriental Publishers & Distributors, 1976).

Martha C. Nussbaum. *The Clash Within: Democracy, Religious Violence, and India's Future.* (Cambridge, Mass.: Belknap Press of Harvard University Press, 2007).

P. Kodanda Rao. *Language Issue in the Indian Constituent Assembly, 1946–1950: Rational Support for English and Non-Rational Support for Hindi* (Bombay: Distributors, International Book House, 1969).

Hindko (Hindki [pejorative], Hindkun)

The term *Hindko* as used in Pakistan refers to speakers of Indo-Aryan languages who live among the primarily Iranian PASHTUNS of the North-West Frontier Province (NWFP). The origins of the term refer merely to "Indian-speaking" rather than to any particular ethnic group. Nonetheless there are people in that region who claim Hindko identity and who trace their heritage back nearly 2,000 years to the inhabitants of the ancient city of Gandhara. These people also claim that the contemporary city of Peshawar is their ancient homeland and that this city is the heartland of their people; this claim is strongly contested by the large Pashtun population, which claims the city as their own. A further claim to the ancient roots of the Hindko is that of linguistics and those who maintain that their language is the ancient forebear of Punjabi rather than merely just one of many dialects of Punjabi.

As are the majority of Pakistan's northwestern peoples, the Hindko are largely farmers who grow wheat as well as a bit of rice and cotton. They also tend to keep goats, sheep, camels, and buffaloes, but both meat and milk production is low because of lack of fodder. They live in extended families in which the eldest male controls all the land and animals as well as the labor of younger men and all women. Women's place in society is fairly low and the patrilocal residence after marriage, which requires women to move into their new husband's family home, tends to leave younger women practically in the position of servants. Wealthy women are not much better off than the poor despite not having to work for hours in the fields because they tend to live in purdah or seclusion, away from the eyes and company of anybody outside their extended family households. Family honor is intimately connected to the control of women's bodies and sexuality, and many middle-class and wealthy households have two separate

HINDKO

location:
North-West Frontier Province, Pakistan, and the western Indian states of Punjab and Kashmir

time period:
Possibly 0 C.E. to the present

ancestry:
Indo-Aryan

language:
Hindko, an Indo-Aryan language

units, one for men in which visitors can be entertained and one for women, in the back of the house away from the rest of the world.

Rather than class or caste, kinship is the most important organizing principle among the Hindko and patrilineal clans are the most important units. These units are generally endogamous, in that most people marry within their own clan, and cousin marriages are extremely common. The clan's male elders are the political and economic leaders of the entire unit and are the face and voice of the clan to the outside world. The second most important social principle is adherence to Islam. The Hindko maintain strict interpretations of the Quran and see religious faith as central to their identity.

See also INDO-ARYANS; PUNJABIS.

Hmong (Man, Meo, Miao, Mong)

The Hmong are a collection of peoples who speak somewhat related languages, are culturally similar, and have been treated in similar ways both in their original Chinese homeland and in their adopted countries of Southeast Asia; most do not acknowledge kinship with other Hmong peoples, even those with the most similar languages and cultures. Scholars estimate that there are about 80 different subgroups of Hmong in China, Laos, Myanmar, Thailand, and Vietnam, although there are only 29 distinct Hmongic languages. There are also Hmong communities in the United States, Australia, and France, mostly those who fled Laos and Vietnam during the war there in the 1970s. In China they are considered one of the country's 55 national minority groups under the label *Miao,* which is considered derogatory by many Hmong themselves because it means "weeds" or "sprouts." In Southeast Asia they are often called *Meo* but the people themselves prefer *Hmong,* which means "free people" in their languages.

ORIGINS

Hmong origins remain a matter of conjecture today. Two possibilities have been posed by scholars, especially folklorists, but neither can claim any scientific verifiability. The first is that the Hmong descended from a population in the Yellow (Huang) River valley, also the heartland of the modern Chinese, and may even have had their own empire in China prior to the arrival of Sino-Tibetan speakers many thousands of years before the common era. Another possibility is that the Hmong were a Central Asian people who began migrating southward in about 5000 B.C.E. Evidence for the latter theory is largely from Hmong folktales that tell of snowy mountains, half-years in which darkness covered the land and half-years in light, and a Hmong girl named Mongolia.

Although there may have been a very ancient Hmong kingdom known as Jiu Li, which ruled in the region of the Yellow River basin almost 6,000 years ago, there is slightly more evidence for a later kingdom known as San Miao, which may have emerged in Sichuan Province about 2700 B.C.E. and then was defeated in 2200 B.C.E. by Yu the Great of the Xia dynasty. This kingdom may have been founded by Tao Tie and Huan Tuo after the first forced migration of Hmong people at the hands of the expanding HAN; Chinese records call its people *Ta Mung.* A third Hmong kingdom, the Chu, may have emerged in about 704 B.C.E. in what is today Yunnan Province; while there is no question that the Chu kingdom existed in this time and place, its Hmong heritage remains a matter of debate. Regardless it too was defeated by the Chinese in 223 B.C.E. just before the final unification of much of China under the Han.

HISTORY

The defeat of Chu was the final blow to Hmong unity and from that period on they have been a dispersed people throughout China and Southeast Asia. Unfortunately Chinese sources use the generic term *Miao* or sometimes *Man* to refer to all these communities, despite great differences in language and culture, so that it is difficult to tease out specific groups over time. In comparison the Chinese never referred to all the peoples within the Mon-Khmer language family by a single term, and today they recognize dozens of separate groups, such as LAHU, VA, and BLANG. The contemporary Miao or Hmong, as they prefer it, are just as different from one another as these other groups but have not gained recognition as separate peoples because of the Chinese classification system.

In about 223 B.C.E. groups of Hmong fled both northward and southward, but only those in the south were able to maintain their languages and cultures while those in the north seem to have been fully absorbed into their host societies. Everywhere they went their languages were discriminated against; their texts were burned, and the people feared for their lives. This period has been labeled genocidal by later historians, and it is certainly true that even the Chinese name for the Hmong, *Miao,*

HMONG

location:
Guizhou and Yunnan Provinces, China; Myanmar (Burma); Vietnam; Thailand; and Laos

time period:
Possibly 4000 B.C.E. to the present

ancestry:
Jiu Li tribes

language:
There are 29 Hmongic languages in the Hmong-Mien language family.

disappeared from the records in this period and was replaced by the generic term *Man* or *barbarian*. *Miao* returns much later, during the Tang or Song dynasties, 618–907 and 960–1279, respectively, although even in these periods *Man* is more common.

Throughout the following dynastic periods, Yuan, Ming, and early Qing, Hmong groups continued to migrate throughout southern China and possibly northern Southeast Asia. The Hmong in this long period, 13th through 17th centuries, tended to move into mountainous and other marginal lands ignored by the Han and other groups. They gave up their settled agricultural way of life that legend states characterized their societies along the Yellow River thousands of years earlier and took up shifting cultivation using swidden or slash-and-burn techniques to provide fertilizer in these marginal lands. Hunting, fishing, and gathering also became important economic strategies at this time.

During the Qing period (1644–1911) Hmong struggles against the centralizing Chinese state increased along with serious reprisals from the government's armies. In 1726 Chinese armies attacked about 1,000 Hmong villages in Guizhou Province, setting them on fire and destroying crops. A year later some of the affected tribes united for the first time in thousands of years to fight back against the Chinese, as they continued to do for about 200 years. Western Hunan Province saw its first Hmong rebellions in the period 1795–1806, which drove the first major bloc of Hmong out of China and into Laos, Vietnam, Myanmar, and Thailand. This was followed by a string of battles in Guizhou Province between 1854 and 1872, which sent even more Hmong from their mountain homes and into the highlands of Southeast Asia. The last major Hmong uprising took place in 1936 in Hunan Province against the Republican government's land-use policies, which required all peasants to produce crops for the state.

Throughout this long period of rebellion, government crack-downs, and migration, Chinese policy shifted many times depending on the personalities of the leaders involved, the economic and military conditions, and other factors. Sometimes the Hmong were simply pushed to assimilate to their Han neighbors' way of life: settled rice agriculture in the lowlands and plains. At other times entire villages were rounded up and "contained" in artificially created stockaded villages that acted as communal prisons; other forms of dispersal and removal were also used,

Hmong time line

B.C.E.

4000 Approximate period when the Jiu Li tribes, possible Hmong ancestors, rule the region around contemporary Beijing.

2700 The San Miao, another potential Hmong kingdom, rules parts of Sichuan Province.

2200 Period when San Miao is defeated by the expanding Chinese people of the possibly legendary Xia dynasty.

704 Founding of the Chu kingdom in Yunnan, which may be Hmong.

223 Chu is defeated by the expanding Han, who consolidate their power three years later and found the Han dynasty.

C.E.

1726 The Chinese destroy about 1,000 Hmong villages, thus uniting various Hmong tribes against them.

1790s Many Hmong begin to leave China and set up communities throughout Southeast Asia as a result of persecution at home. These migrations continue for about 150 years.

1950s Christian missionaries create the first written alphabet for the Hmong language, the romanized Popular Alphabet.

1961 The U.S. Central Intelligence Agency recruits and trains about 9,000 Hmong soldiers as part of the Vietnam War effort.

1963 The number of Hmong soldiers fighting for the United States has increased to 20,000.

1973 Many Hmong flee Laos and Vietnam for Thailand, where they take up residence in refugee camps, some of which still exist today.

1975 The first Hmong refugees arrive in the United States.

2003 15,000 Hmong refugees from Wat Tham Krabok refugee camp in Thailand receive asylum in the United States.

involving burning fields and homes and other destructive strategies. During the worst periods Chinese reprisals led to extermination of entire communities, usually justified by the fear of what they called Miao rebellion, regardless of the ethnic makeup of the people involved; not only the Hmong fought against the high taxes and other onerous government requirements. BOUYEI, DONG, HUI, Han, and many other national groups likewise participated in the southern rebellions against the Manchu-led Qing in the 18th and 19th centuries.

The position of the Hmong as well as every other citizen of the Chinese state changed significantly in 1949 when the Communists defeated the Republicans in a civil war. By 1951 Communist rule had been consolidated throughout all Chinese Hmong lands, and these people began participating in the various land-reform, collectivization, and other campaigns that swept the country as Mao Zedong and his people tried to keep the revolution alive into the 1970s. The Hmong suffered through the deprivation of the Great Leap Forward in the 1950s and in the persecutions against religion and other cultural expressions of the Cultural Revolution in the 1960s and 1970s.

Since 1979 Hmong life in China has changed again because in that year expressions of cultural and ethnic identity, religious belief, and other forms of identification separate from the state were once again allowed and even encouraged. Guizhou Province has allowed the flourishing of Hmong-language media, including radio, newspapers, books, and more recently television, and has seen a rebirth of ethnic identity within the various Hmong subgroups. To date, however, there is still little connection or identification among Hmong groups as linguistic or cultural relatives.

Groups of Hmong living throughout Southeast Asia have even less cultural contact with other Hmong-Mien speakers and thus think of themselves as even more unique than their distant Chinese relatives. In their new homes they were generally called *Meo* by their hosts, but the newcomers tried to have as little to do with their neighbors as possible. They moved into the highest mountain regions and most marginal lands in an attempt to maintain their autonomy and independent way of life.

One of the strategies for maintaining their independence taken by many Hmong in Laos and Vietnam in the 20th century was to ally with the American soldiers in Southeast Asia fighting the VIETNAMESE and LAO Communists. This process began in 1961 when General Vang Pao in Laos led an army of about 9,000 Hmong men, poorly armed and trained by the Central Intelligence Agency; their primary task was to prevent Communist supplies from entering South Vietnam from the North along the Ho Chi Minh trail. Two years later under President Kennedy the secret Hmong army in supposedly neutral Laos had grown to about 20,000 soldiers. These soldiers fought bravely for the U.S. cause in Southeast Asia, often risking the lives of 10 or more of their own soldiers to rescue just a single American airman who had been shot down over Laos. More than 100 Hmong soldiers themselves became fighter pilots after receiving training in the United States; all of them were killed in action fighting for the United States. In 1973 the United States pulled its own soldiers out of Laos and Vietnam and left their South Vietnamese, Hmong, and other allies behind. By 1975 both countries had been completely secured by the Communists and those who had fought on the other side were in grave danger. At least 100,000 Hmong crossed the borders into Thailand and settled in refugee camps while another 33,000 were killed trying. Altogether more than 100,000 Hmong died in Laos and Vietnam as a result of the war and its aftermath. Those who made it to Thailand then had to struggle for recognition of their rights as refugees and for basic provisions. In 1975 the United States slowly began to accept Hmong refugees from these camps, as did France and Australia, but even as late as 2003 there were still thousands of Hmong refugees being resettled in the United States.

CULTURE

According to Hmong legends and some Chinese records the ancient Hmong peoples were settled agriculturalists in their Yellow River basin home. It was only after being dispersed to other regions of China and Southeast Asia that many adopted more impermanent subsistence strategies such as swidden or slash-and-burn agriculture, plus hunting, gathering, and fishing; some groups also maintained small herds of domesticated animals such as goats, sheep, pigs, chickens, and dogs. Their main crops in China were barley, buckwheat, hemp, and oats plus, after the 16th century, potatoes and corn. These same crops were also suitable to the mountainous terrain inhabited by the Hmong in Southeast Asia and continued to fulfill their primary subsistence needs.

Despite these general rules there are still some Hmong communities, especially in Guizhou Province, that resemble their ancient relatives, as well as their Han neighbors, in their subsistence activities. These people use water buffaloes or bullocks to plow their permanent fields; animal, human, or chemical fertilizers to keep the land usable for many seasons; and permanent irrigation strategies. They tend to inhabit lower elevations than their upland cousins and thus are able to grow rice as well as millet, wheat, vegetables, and tobacco.

In China and probably throughout Southeast Asia as well Hmong communities tend not to be self-sufficient. They trade agricultural produce, woven and dyed cloth, embroidered items, silver jewelry, hides, bamboo products, live animals, or other products for processed consumer items including foods, bicycles, farm implements, and construction materials. Some Hmong also sell their labor as farmers, blacksmiths, carpenters, and weavers. At no period in their known history have the Hmong been large landowners. Many were tenants or sharecroppers on the land of other ethnic groups while a few clans or villages owned land communally and allowed individual families to work their own plots. In the Communist states of China, Laos, and Vietnam all land is currently owned by the state and so extensive agriculture, pastoralism, and hunting and gathering activities are all limited by the territory each village or other politically defined unit has been allocated.

It is difficult to generalize widely about Hmong kinship structures because of the vast differences among the many subgroups as well as the degree of integration of many communities into the dominant societies in which they reside. However, Hmong kinship is usually considered to be bilateral with a general preference for patrilateral or patrilineal connections over matrilateral ones; however, whether this is an adaptation to the dominant structures of China and Vietnam remains uncertain today. Regardless most groups assign clan membership to children based on their father's clan and require all individuals to marry outside their clan unit.

Like their kinship system, many other aspects of Hmong society are difficult to generalize about, given the diversity across regions and countries. Generally the higher in elevation the settlement, the smaller it is. In Guizhou, Yunnan, and Southeast Asia's higher elevations villages tend to be smaller than 20 households, while those in the lower plains and valleys can have as many as 130 families or more. Generally the ideal Hmong household consists of two generations from the same family: a married couple and the youngest son and his family. All older sons tend to move out and establish households of their own while daughters are expected to move into their husband's village and home in patrilocal residence. In the past marriages took place after groups of young men traveled from village to village to visit the young women in their "youth houses" and find marriage partners. It was not required to marry out of the village, but clan exogamy was and is still strictly observed, often requiring men to look beyond the confines of their own villages, which may have contained only two or three clans.

Hmong religious beliefs and practices vary as widely as their other cultural features. Many groups have adopted some aspects of Buddhism, Taoism, and even Christianity but which features and the degree to which they have been

Even Hmong clothing and jewelry, especially these silver coins, chains, and other decorations, are designed to protect the wearer from spirits and other supernatural forces. *(OnAsia/Stu Smucker)*

integrated into other belief systems vary widely. The traditional Hmong religious beliefs all generally concern spirits and other powerful forces that are associated with specific natural features: groves of trees, caves, mountains, large stones, and the like. Even such human-made structures as bridges and wells were sometimes believed to contain supernatural forces that could harm or assist the Hmong in their daily lives. Each village and household also had a wide array of spiritual forces believed to be active in the lives of their inhabitants, including ancestors, dragons that guarded them, and ancient culture heroes. In addition many Hmong groups recognize the existence of a single God who is more powerful than these spirits and in some ways oversees their activities. This god, Ntzi, is seen as kind and just and used to visit Earth or send his daughter to do so via a ladder that connected heaven and Earth; sadly this ladder was broken sometime in prehistory and these visitations have ceased.

Regular animal sacrifices, especially chickens, were held to propitiate and thank these beings for their efforts and, as the Chinese do, many Hmong groups burn paper money for the same purpose. All of these sacrifices as well as healing ceremonies, life-cycle rites, and calendrical rituals, usually to mark the agricultural seasons, were performed by part-time specialists, sometimes glossed as priests, diviners, or shamans. The work of these specialists straddled the tasks usually engaged in by all three of these kinds of religious specialists. For their efforts they would receive a small amount of food from the family or village that hired them, but generally they lived as farmers just as their fellow villagers did. In addition to these powerful specialists some Hmong groups also had women in their midst who served as sorcerers. They produced and controlled a poison called *gu* that could be used to curse enemies; it was not only Hmong communities that feared these women but their Chinese and other neighbors as well.

FURTHER READING

Robert D. Jenks. *Insurgency and Social Disorder in Guizhou: The "Miao" Rebellion, 1854–1873* (Honolulu: University of Hawaii Press, 1994).

Brenda Johns and David Strecker, eds. *The Hmong World* (New Haven, Conn.: Yale University Press, 1986).

Charles Johnson, ed. *Dab Neeg Hmoob: Myths, Legends, and Folktales from the Hmong of Laos* (St. Paul, Minn.: Macalester College, 1985).

Pranee Liamputtong Rice. *Hmong Women and Reproduction* (Westport, Conn.: Greenwood Press, 2000).

Bai Ziran, ed. A *Happy People: The Miaos* (Beijing: Foreign Languages Press, 1988).

Hoa (Chinese Vietnamese, ethnic Chinese in/from Vietnam, Minh-huong, Ngai, overseas Chinese, Sino-Vietnamese, Vietnamese Chinese)

The flow of migrants away from China and into Vietnam and elsewhere in Southeast Asia began in the late Ming dynasty (1368–1644) and continued throughout the Qing dynasty (1644–1911) and the years of the Republic of China (1911–49). The earliest migrants tended to call themselves *Minh-huong*, people of Ming. They were largely from Fujian and Guangdong Provinces in the south of China, especially Taishan city, and were escaping famine, overcrowding, and, at times, political unrest. The last groups, who arrived in the 1940s, were fleeing from the dangers of civil war and to a lesser extent ethnic persecution. In 1955 they were all granted VIETNAMESE citizenship and the governments of both countries agreed that integration into the Vietnamese state was the best course of action. Today they are known by the ethnonym *Hoa*, except in several small rural communities living along the Chinese border where they are sometimes referred to as *Ngai*.

The primary economic activities engaged in by the Hoa differ by region. In southern Vietnam most Hoa have been urban dwellers for many generations and have engaged in banking, trading, milling, and real estate; in the north the Hoa have been less prosperous and have engaged in shopkeeping, fishing, mining, and working on the docks. In addition small numbers of Hoa in both regions have always engaged in agriculture.

The Hoa community's active engagement in the economy has often disturbed the dominant Vietnamese community. In 1974 official South Vietnamese records note that the Hoa controlled most food, electrical, textile, chemical, and other industries; the entire wholesale trade; more than half the retail trade; and nearly 90 percent of the import-export market. The Hoa were accused of manipulating prices and remaining segregated as a "state within a state." The brutal, nationalizing South Vietnamese government of Ngo Dinh Diem had tried to limit the effects of this control as early as 1955 by forcing all Hoa to adopt Vietnamese surnames and given names but apparently with little success. By 1983 the Hanoi government of unified Vietnam claimed that nearly 60 percent of the South Vietnamese former bourgeoisie had been Hoa. While all of these claims by Vietnamese governments and organizations may be suspect, they do point to the overall economic success of the Hoa community prior to Vietnamese unification in 1976.

With their history of capitalist economic success from 1976 until the early 1980s many thousands of Hoa fled Vietnam, some moving to China, others to countries as far away as the United States and Australia. Most of those who left did so between 1978 and 1979 because of the Vietnamese government's decision to eliminate private trading activities, which was enacted in early 1978. Some estimates of this exodus put the number at 450,000; however, this seems to be exaggerated, with 250,000 probably being a more accurate figure. Of this number about 170,000 were estimated to have fled across the Chinese border in the north, despite the fact that about 1.1 million of the country's total of 1.3 million Hoa lived in the south at the time, especially in and around Saigon (Ho Chi Minh

HOA

location:
Vietnam

time period:
18th century to the present

ancestry:
Chinese

language:
Cantonese, Vietnamese

City); the remaining 80,000 escaped by boat from the south.

Today the Hoa community is Vietnam's second-largest ethnic group after the majority Vietnamese, making up about 2 percent of the population or 2.3 million people according to the 2006 census. They tend to be well assimilated with the dominant majority and are often included with them in economic and educational attainment indicators because they resemble the Vietnamese in these areas more than they resemble the other minority groups. About one-third of married Hoa have Vietnamese or other ethnic partners and most are able to speak Vietnamese as well as CANTON-ESE. On the whole the Hoa are wealthier than average, with only 8 percent living in poverty versus 36 percent of the country overall and a 5,119,000 *dong* per capita expenditure rate versus 2,751,000 overall. They also tend to live in larger households of 5.18 people versus the average of 4.71 and are comparable to the Vietnamese majority in their religious views, with about 75 percent proclaiming no religious beliefs, 22 percent Buddhist, and about 2 percent Christian.

Hoa Binh culture (Hoabinhian, Hoabinhian industry)

The Hoa Binh culture, or Hoabinhian as it is often called, refers to a culture of the prehistoric period in Southeast Asian history of about 18,000–20,000 years ago until about 7,000 years ago. At both the beginning and the end of this period, sometimes referred to as the Mesolithic or Middle Stone Age, Hoabinhian culture overlapped with other prehistoric phases; its predecessor is called Son Vi culture and its successor, Bac Son culture. The complex was first defined in 1932 at the First Congress of Prehistorians of the Far East, using the tools created in the period and the manner in which they were created: hammer stones, almond-shaped or round single-faced tools, disks, short axes, and bone tools. Despite some changes since 1932, the Hoa Binh period is still defined by its round stone tools worked on only one side, commonly called sumatraliths; its bone tools; the absence of pottery; and, somewhat controversially, perhaps the early stages of plant domestication. From 1994 the dating of the culture as Mesolithic has been abandoned in favor of late-to-terminal Pleistocene to early-to-mid Holocene, despite the awkwardness of the phrasing. The appearance of pottery in the

archaeological record along with the development of villages and farming in the plains of Southeast Asia mark the transition from Hoa Binh to Bac Son in most chronologies of the region.

The main economic activities of the Hoabinhian period were fishing, hunting, and gathering, but in the later years, about 7000 B.C.E., there is some evidence from Spirit Cave, Thailand, and from the area of Hoa Binh Province, Vietnam, that people had begun to plant peas, beans, pepper, betel, and bottle gourds. These findings, however, are still considered controversial because these plants also grew wild in the region and their remains in the sites inhabited by Hoabinhian-era people may just indicate intensive gathering activity. The people of Hoa Binh culture generally resided in caves, often located high above a valley floor for protection, and near streams; early Hoabinhian sites are also evident on the coasts of Vietnam and Sumatra. Interestingly there is almost no evidence of Hoa Binh culture in the alluvial plains of Southeast Asia, where the later Bronze Age DONG SON CULTURE thrived.

In addition to Spirit Cave, Thailand, one of the other most explored Hoa Binh sites is Con Moong Cave, located in Cuc Phuong National Park, Vietnam. Human remains were first discovered on the site only in 1974 but have continued to excite archaeologists ever since excavation began in 1976. It is the only site so far in which Son Vi-, Hoa Binh-, and Bac Son-era tools are all evident in one location. The cave marks about 8,000 years of continuous inhabitation and offers the clearest evidence that Bac Son peoples were the direct descendants of the Hoabinhians, who were themselves directly descended from the Son Vi. The earliest Southeast Asian archaeology during the French colonial era had questioned the indigenous development of pottery, agriculture, and advanced stone technology, positing instead importation from more advanced cultures from the north and/or west, but Con Moong's remains clearly show local innovation. As a marker of Con Moong's importance to human history generally in June 2006 the Vietnamese government applied to have the cave listed as a World Heritage Site by UNESCO.

Hong Kong, people of

Hong Kong today has a population of about 7 million people, one of the highest population-density areas in the world, with about 10,000

HOA BINH CULTURE

location:
Vietnam, especially Hoa Binh and Quang Tri Provinces, and in sites throughout Southeast Asia including in Thailand, Laos, Myanmar, Cambodia, and Sumatra

time period:
About 16,000 to 5000 B.C.E.

ancestry:
Son Vi culture

language:
Unknown

PEOPLE OF HONG KONG

location:
Hong Kong, including Hong Kong Island, Kowloon Peninsula, the New Territories, and 235 regional islands

time period:
1699 to the present

ancestry:
Chinese, English, other

language:
Cantonese, Mandarin Chinese, English

people per square mile. Most of this population, 95 percent, are of Chinese descent while only 5 percent have other backgrounds. The two official languages of this region are Cantonese and English. Until July 1, 1997, Hong Kong was an overseas British colony, but on that date it reverted to China after more than 150 years of British rule. Since 1997 Hong Kong has been a Special Administrative Region of the People's Republic of China with its own domestic government and economy but with ultimate sovereignty resting with China.

Hong Kong was initially settled by the Chinese in about the seventh century C.E. and the first major influx of people occurred about three centuries later. The British East India Company landed in the region in 1699 and began the international merchant-trading culture that has continued to keep Hong Kong afloat ever since. The area became an official British colony in 1842 when the Treaty of Nanking, which ended the First Opium War (1839–42), gave England sovereignty in the region. This was followed by the Convention of Beijing in 1860, which ended the Second Opium War (1856–58) and gave Britain a perpetual lease on the Kowloon Peninsula. In 1898 Britain added the New Territories to its colony for defense and security purposes and signed a 99-year lease on the land.

While Hong Kong remained an important British warehousing and distributing center in southern Asia throughout the 19th and early 20th centuries, its modern economy expanded exponentially in the wake of World War II and then the Chinese Communist revolution in 1949. At that time hundreds of thousands of Chinese escaped from the mainland and made their home in Hong Kong. The influx of labor and capital allowed for the development of the manufacturing and finance sectors while the tourist industry also grew at a high rate. In 2006 the gross domestic product (GDP) per capita was estimated by the International Monetary Fund to be more than U.S.$27,466, substantially higher than China's U.S.$7,700. In conjunction with this economic growth the health, education, and welfare systems also improved, so that today Hong Kong has a high life expectancy of 70.3 years for men and 75.7 years for women and an average literacy rate of about 94 percent, with slightly higher rates for men than women.

In July 1997 Britain's lease of the New Territories expired and through the Sino-British Joint Declaration of 1984 China regained sovereignty over the entire Hong Kong region. This Joint Declaration also stated that Hong Kong would maintain independence in the political, economic, and judicial spheres for 50 years following the 1997 reversion and that its people would enjoy their "unique way of life." In effect China's sovereignty extended to foreign affairs and defense alone. Even in the area of foreign affairs, however, Hong Kong has been allowed to maintain its separate relationships with the World Trade Organization, the Asia-Pacific Economic Cooperation (APEC) forum, and other organizations; it is known in these organizations as Hong Kong, China.

Five years after reversion to China in July 2002 Hong Kong underwent further political change with the implementation of the Principal Officials Accountability System, which added new political appointees to the governing structure, including a chief secretary, financial secretary, and justice secretary, to assist the chief executive in running public affairs. In 2004 the democratic process in Hong Kong received a setback from the Chinese National People's Congress, which decided that no significant changes to the electoral process could be implemented until at least the 2012 legislative election. At the moment the chief executive of the region is elected by an election committee, made up of about 800 residents representing a variety of groups, including labor, professionals, social services, religious interests, the business sector, and the Chinese National People's Congress. The push for democratic reform in Hong Kong continues, however, and in 2006 the Civic Party, which supports democracy, gained 134 seats in the electoral committee. This allowed Civic Party legislator Alan Leong to challenge the chief executive, Donald Tsang, in 2007. Tsang's governmental and business support gave him an easy victory with 649 votes, but Leong's 123 votes in the March 25, 2007, election indicate at least some shift toward acceptance of more widespread democracy.

FURTHER READING

Kwai-Cheung Lo. *Chinese Face/Off: The Transnational Popular Culture of Hong Kong* (Chicago: University of Illinois Press, 2005).

Werner Menski, ed., with a foreword by Laurie Fransman. *Coping with 1997: The Reaction of the Hong Kong People to the Transfer of Power* (Stoke-on-Trent, England: Trentham Books, 1995).

Wei-Bin Zhang. *Hong Kong: The Pearl Made of British Mastery and Chinese Docile-Diligence* (New York: Nova Science, 2006).

Hu (Hu barbarians, Tih, Wu hu)

Chinese chroniclers and other writers in the centuries before and after the start of the common era often did not know or care about the exact cultural or linguistic background of their neighbors and used collective terms that referred to geography instead. For non-HAN peoples to the south the term *Yue* or sometimes *BAIYUE* was used and for the northern horsemen of the Central Asian steppe the term was *Hu,* which derives from the Chinese word for "meat," *rou.* The term was first used in this way in the fourth century B.C.E. and continued until the Six Dynasties period, which began with the fall of the Han in 220 and continued through the Three Dynasties, Chin, and Northern and Southern dynasties periods, which ended in 589. During the Six Dynasties period *Hu* came to refer to a more specific group, Iranian-speaking SOGDIANS, traders who entered China along the Silk Road, having traveled from the region of contemporary Uzbekistan.

Although the Hu were not in any way a unified culture or society, a fact even acknowledged by the Chinese in their distinction between Eastern Hu or DONGHU and others, in general we can speak of them as a Bronze Age people. They used this metal to create vessels, particularly imitations of the popular Chinese styles of the time; daggers and other weaponry; armor; and a variety of other objects that have been found in sites dated to both the Xia and Shang periods, 2200–1750 B.C.E. and 1750–1040 B.C.E., respectively. These early dates, as well as many from the following Zhou period, 1040–256 B.C.E., indicate that even long before the Chinese had labeled these northerners, their culture was thriving on the fringes of China, and trade between the two peoples was frequent. The favorite artistic motifs on many of these objects included depictions of animals, especially rams, which may have indicated that these creatures were seen as sacred, ancestral, or possibly important to the Hu economy. Other depictions that have been found on bone artifacts show the Hu using horses, chariots, bows and arrows, and dogs.

While nomadic pastoralism was certainly the primary economic and subsistence activity of many descendants of the Hu, including the XIANBEI, KHITANS, and MONGOLS, artistic depictions and Chinese descriptions point to hunting as perhaps more important to the Hu. Many of the depictions of the Hu using bows and arrows as well as dogs were part of hunting scenes. The two economic strategies may very well have

existed side by side on the steppes for hundreds of years or longer, and the Hu, as a collective term, may have included groups that engaged in only one or the other of these activities.

One of the reasons the Chinese distinguished between the Eastern and other Hu groups was that in the late fourth century B.C.E., or Warring States period, a general in the Yen state of Hebei was captured by the Hu and held captive during a period of extensive warfare between the Donghu and Chinese. The general, Qin Kai, eventually escaped his captors and led his armies against them, driving them as far north as today's Inner Mongolia. His experiences with them, however, provided him with a great deal of information about their mindset and way of life, which has come down to us in various Chinese chronicles of the time.

Given the time frame and region in which the Hu lived, many experts in Chinese history assume that they were pivotal in introducing Buddhism to the Chinese people by way of India and Central Asia. It was the Hu who controlled much of the Silk Road in the centuries before and after the common era and thus the movement of PARTHIANS, Sogdians, Indians, KUSHANS, and other peoples who served as missionaries for the new faith.

While the term *Hu* came to refer more specifically to some of these western migrants, Sogdians, the Eastern Hu or Donghu are believed to have eventually become part of the large confederation of the XIONGNU, or Asian Huns.

Hui (Chinese Muslims, Dungans, Haw, Huihe, Huihui, Huijiaoren, Jiaomen, Khotan, Mumin, Muslim Yunnanese, Panthay, Tungan)

The Hui have a population of around 10 million, making them one of China's largest recognized minority groups. With their large population Hui can be found in various places in China. They also live in many of the other countries in east and Central Asia. The dominant feature that sets the Hui apart from many other Chinese peoples is their Sunni Muslim faith.

Records from the Northern Song dynasty mention the name *Hui* as the short form of the group *Huihui.* The Huihui themselves were the ancestors of today's UIGHUR, while the Hui got their name because they had similar beliefs to these Huihui ancestors of the Uighur; both were Muslims. The ancestors of the Hui are thought to be individuals from among the Arabs, Persians,

HU

location:
Northern China

time period:
Fourth century B.C.E. to sixth century C.E.

ancestry:
Non-Han northerners

language:
Unknown

HUI

location:
Most of China but primarily in Ningxia Hui Autonomous Region. Hui people also reside in some of China's surrounding countries, including Taiwan and Kazakhstan; in these places they are referred to by other names, such as *Dungan, Khotan,* and *Panthay.*

time period:
Their ancestors are ancient, but the Hui have only been recognized as a minority since the 1360s.

ancestry:
Mongols and Islamic people of Central Asia, including Arabs and Persians

language:
Chinese, Mandarin

---

and MONGOLS who entered China between the seventh and 13th centuries.

In the middle of the seventh century Arabs joined the Persians and other Central Asian peoples who had been traveling to China along the Silk Road for purposes of trade for hundreds of years. Some of these individuals remained in China and found homes in different cities including Guangzhou and Hangzhou. During the early 13th century Mongol troops were traveling to the west, mostly as conquerors. In their westward invasion the Mongols recruited individuals and entire communities from the steppes of Central Asia and ordered them east on military assignments. These civilians, some artisans, others farmers or religious leaders, became scouts and were told to settle at various places, including Gansu and Hebei, and to make a living breeding livestock while preparing for combat. As time passed, they adapted to their new forms of living and became farmers and herdsmen. These people are also considered ancestors to the Hui.

Because of their economic standing as traders and farmers, these precursors to the Hui are believed to have had a better social status during the Yuan dynasty (1279–1368) than that of the HAN. Nevertheless because of their religion and their ethnic background they also suffered from oppression by Yuan rulers. Even after traveling east as ordered, they were still controlled by Mongol officials, some even becoming house slaves to rich Mongols.

The Hui began to be thought of as an ethnic group during the Ming dynasty, in the years between 1368 and 1644. Despite dispersal throughout China as scouts, scholars, and traders, wherever they went, the Hui tended to live together in separate villages or neighborhoods, usually centering on a mosque. Therefore despite significant assimilation to Han culture, including adopting the Han language and, except for the Arabic religious language, maintaining only a few Arabic, Persian, and Mongol terms, the Hui were able to maintain an identity different from that of the dominant group.

While this difference was important to many Hui people during the years of 1856 to 1873, it was also a difficult identity to maintain. During these years thousands of Hui were massacred, and many fled to the neighboring countries of Burma (now Myanmar) and Thailand as well as to Central Asia. Cities were burned and mosques razed in Yunnan Province, beginning with a three-day massacre in the city of Kunming on May 19, 1856. This destruction of the Hui people and their homes and mosques was part of the government's brutal repression of the Hui-led multiethnic Panthay Rebellion. The rebellion itself was part of a Hui attempt to establish a separate state in Yunnan called Pingnan Guo. The rebellion was led by Du Wenxiu, an Islamic leader sometimes referred to as *sultan,* who was beheaded by Qing soldiers in 1872. The rebels captured the city of Dali and invaded Kunming many times before a final defeat and reintegration into the Chinese state.

In the 20th century life for the Hui included both improvements and grave difficulties. Capital investment in farmland and equipment, schooling for children, and increased women's rights have made life better for many Hui, especially in rural areas. However, being an ethnic and religious minority in 20th-century China was not easy. During the Communist Party's consolidation period in the 1950s, the Hui came under threat many times; even the Chinese Association for the Promotion of the Hui People's Culture, which had been established by the government early in the 1950s to assist the Hui in maintaining their Islamic faith, was eventually shut down. The government also moved many non-Muslims into the Hui-dominated regions of the country, in the northwest, in an attempt to dilute the influence of religious leaders in these regions. During the Cultural Revolution (1966–76), Islam came under fire again as being anti-Chinese and a Revolutionary Struggle Group for the Abolition of Islam was established. Nonetheless, most reports state that the Muslims actually came through this difficult period having suffered less than most people, and their position only improved over the next decades. Beginning in 2001 the U.S.-led war on terror has once again put Hui religious and ethnic differences on show, and many are beginning to feel under threat from their fellow citizens.

See also DUNGANS.

Hundred Yue   *See* BAIYUE.

Huns   *See* XIONGNU.

I

Iatmul (Nyara)

The Iatmul are a relatively large linguistic and cultural group who traditionally resided in about 20 different villages along the middle section of the Sepik River of Papua New Guinea. During the course of the 20th century German, Swiss, and American anthropologists made numerous visits to Iatmul villages. Because of the beauty and complexity of their carvings, they are also well known outside Papua New Guinea for their rich artistic tradition.

The traditional subsistence practices of the Iatmul were based on women's activities of fishing and gardening. Men's activities traditionally included clearing land for gardens, building houses and fences, carving drums and masks, and sitting around the men's house chewing betel nut and exchanging stories and ritual knowledge. One Iatmul village was also well known for producing pottery, which was women's work, while present-day men also participate in the tourist trade, especially producing carvings for sale or conveying people and goods up and down the river system. The Iatmul are part of an extensive trade network with neighboring groups, especially the CHAMBRI and Sawos, in which Iatmul women exchange fish for Sawos' sago and shell valuables and in turn pass some of these shell valuables to the Chambri for stone tools and woven bags. The Iatmul were the largest and strongest group in this network and were able to compel the others to maintain the relationship on their terms well into the 20th century.

The basic structure of Iatmul society continues to be patrilineal kin groups, groups of relatives who all trace their ancestors through men to a common male ancestor. This is also a patrilocal society, so that women move into the homes of their husbands' lineages at marriage, and a polygynous society, so that men who can afford to do so can take several wives. In addition to their lineages, individual Iatmul also inherit from their father's membership in a totemic clan and one of two marriage moieties. Both of these groups are exogamous: that is, Iatmul must marry outside their own groups. Finally Iatmul men are also members of a specific age grade, which is made up of a group of men all about the same age who undergo initiation into manhood together. Iatmul men owe special responsibilities to their age mates; these resemble the responsibilities they have toward their own biological brothers. They also participate in the initiations of younger male relatives on the basis of their age grade.

The most important aspect of traditional Iatmul religious life is ancestor worship. Both their actual ancestors as well as mythological or totemic ancestors are important in the Iatmul universe and both continue to act on the lives of the current generation. The most important mythological ancestor is the crocodile, who ritually swallows the bodies of young males, as is evident in the cicatrice or ritual scarring cut into their backs and shoulders by older males during initiation ceremonies. Once they have been swallowed and cleansed of their mother's blood

IATMUL

location:
The Middle Sepik River basin, P.N.G.

time period:
Unknown to the present

ancestry:
Melanesian

language:
Iatmul, a Papuan or non-Austronesian language

during the course of the scarification ritual, the crocodile then regurgitates the young men back into this life, where they can participate fully in Iatmul society as adult men. In addition to the crocodile every clan also has its own totemic animal or plant that is believed to be the founding ancestor of that particular group.

Finally as is the case throughout the Sepik region music is important to the Iatmul. Men have access to both the sacred music of the ancestors as played on drums and flutes and to more secular music associated with celebrations and even work; women can participate only in secular music and dance and often sing while working together.

See also MELANESIANS; NEW GUINEA SEPIK BASIN PEOPLE.

Iban (Dayaks, Dyaks, Sea Dayaks)

The Iban are an ethnic group of the island of Borneo; most reside in the Malaysian state of Sarawak on the north of the island while much smaller numbers reside in Brunei and the Indonesian region of Kalimantan, in the southern portion of the island.

As AUSTRONESIANS the Iban are probably the descendants of a population that fled southern China more than 4,000 years ago and entered the Indonesian Archipelago at about that time. With regard to the Iban most scholars assume they settled on Borneo and remained in the southwest region for thousands of years; only a few authors believe they migrated to Borneo in the past half-millennium or so. From the southwest the Iban began migrating along the Pawan, Pinoh, and Melawi Rivers into the Kapuas Lakes region. The best estimate for the period when these migrations began is about the 16th century, when Islam was introduced into the region and began changing the political landscape. In the 19th century, the Iban continued their migration from the Kapuas Lakes region in Kalimantan into Sarawak in the north; at that time this migration would have been from Dutch-held Kalimantan to British Sarawak. Pressure on land resources and a desire for virgin forest for swidden agriculture are frequently posited as the primary reasons for these Iban population movements, although relations with the European colonizers and with other indigenous peoples were also important. Some Iban subgroups were used by the British rulers of Sarawak to control other indigenous peoples or as pirates patrolling their shores and probably caused subgroups to flee from their control. All Iban participated in headhunting as

the most important source of male prestige, and that led to further migrations. In recent decades many contemporary Iban have followed in their migratory ancestors' footsteps and made the move away from the island's rural regions and into its towns and cities.

Prior to these urban migrations the most important economic activity of the Iban was rice farming, followed by other plants such as gourds, squash, cucumbers, and corn, and keeping domesticated animals such as water buffaloes, pigs, and chickens. Even toward the end of the 20th century most highland Iban used swidden or slash-and-burn methods to clear their small holdings and prepare them for planting; those in the valleys and plains practiced permanent agriculture in paddies. All villagers in a single region used the same dates to start and complete the agricultural cycle, from cutting and burning to sowing and harvesting, to share the burden of crop loss due to birds and insects. If all fields ripened at the same time, these pests spread themselves over the entire region rather than focusing on the only field with an edible crop. Each village also shared ritual responsibilities, such as divination for setting auspicious dates for cutting, burning, planting, and harvesting, thanksgiving rites, and others. Gathering wild foods, fishing, and hunting have always supplemented these agricultural foods, although in the past few decades logging in important Iban regions has greatly diminished the sustainability of these activities.

Iban society is built around the nuclear or *bilik* family group where there are no set rules determining lines of descent. At each marriage the two families negotiate over whether the children will be considered members of the husband's or wife's descent group, and Iban mobility is always taken into consideration in these negotiations. In addition to kinship groups there are reciprocal groups of kin and nonkin who work together on the agricultural cycle and even larger groups of people known as members of a "brotherhood" or "food sharing group" who participate in life-cycle rituals and other large-scale festivities.

Although the majority of Malaysians and Indonesians are Muslim, many Iban continue to practice their own indigenous religion, which combines belief in multiple spirits and gods with other supernatural beings, such as ghosts of the ancestors. Some Iban have also converted to Christianity and thus live outside both the mainstream Muslim way of life in these two countries and outside their own traditional belief system.

IBAN

location:
Sarawak, Malaysia, Brunei, and Kalimantan, Indonesia

time period:
Probably about 2000 B.C.E. to the present

ancestry:
Austronesian

language:
Iban, an Austronesian language in the Malayic-Dayak family

Ibanags (Y Bannag)

The Ibanags are a lowland tribe of northern Luzon whose traditional homeland was along the Cagayan River; their name is derived from the term *bannag* meaning "from the river." They differ from the neighboring IGOROT tribes, such as the IFUGAO, because the Ibanags at least nominally converted to Roman Catholicism during the Spanish colonial era. They reside in the valley within the Sierra Madre, Cordillera, and Caraballo Mountain chains. Over the past 200 years or so the Ibanag have dispersed from their original homeland throughout Nueva Vizcaya, Isabela, and neighboring provinces.

In their valley and other lowland homes the Ibanags are largely subsistence farmers who produce rice, corn, and vegetables in poor, overworked fields. Tobacco is an important cash crop in the region, a practice they adopted from the dominant ILOCANOS. Foreign merchants have taken advantage of the Ibanags in the past, providing substantial loans and then purchasing the tobacco at less than market prices, keeping the farmer and family in a state of perpetual debt and poverty.

Most aspects of Ibanag society, including the centrality of kinship and a desire for saving face and smooth social relationships, are very similar to those of the dominant culture in the Philippines. As with most Filipinos (*see* FILIPINOS: NATIONALITY) the most important social unit among the Ibanags is the extended family, and most would sacrifice individual comfort and gain for the good of their more extended kin networks. Many speak Ilocano or TAGALOG as a second language and the vast majority consider themselves Christian. As did most lowlanders the Ibanags quickly converted to Roman Catholicism in the early phases of the Spanish colonial period in the 16th and 17th centuries and have remained adherents of that religion, despite recent efforts of Protestants, mostly from the United States, to proselytize among them.

The reason that contemporary Protestant and even Roman Catholic missionaries have attempted to work with the Ibanags is that their own religious worldview contains numerous animistic beliefs and practices considerably outside the purview of accepted Christian doctrine. In part their syncretic belief system stems from the form of Catholicism imported to the Philippines by the Spanish more than 400 years ago. The early Spanish priests and missionaries focused heavily on the wounds of Jesus and attracted indigenous converts in part by connecting local fears of spirits and devils to the Catholic belief system; they offered Jesus and the Bible as a way of keeping these local spirits under control.

The universe as described from the Ibanag point of view is called "the whole covered region," which is then divided into such units as the Earth, sky, Sun, Moon, and stars, as well as inside the Earth and its surroundings, both of which are the abode of numerous benign and evil spirits. One of the most important features of the Earth for the Ibanags is the river, which provides not only water and fish but also rich silt deposited by floodwaters each year in which the Ibanags grow their crops. As a gift to the spirits of the river traditional Ibanag practice dictated that families must allow each newborn's placenta to be carried away by the river; it was a form of sympathetic magic whereby the placenta floating away was a metaphor for the person growing up and marrying someone who would take him or her away from the village for a more successful life elsewhere. The materials used in a healing or death rituals were also thrown into the river to purify them and carry away the cause of illness or death.

The earliest descriptions of these and many other Ibanag rituals were made by Spanish priests in 1640, and even well-educated and urban people today continue to engage in at least some of them. Ibanag mothers continue to avoid brightly colored dresses for their daughters for fear of attracting the attention of evil spirits, and eating near where a spirit is known to live requires all Ibanags to toss small bits of food to the ground as a gift to the spirit. Offending the spirits can result in either the offender's soul's being eaten by the spirit or the person's body's being possessed by it. Both of these can lead to illness, coma, fever, involuntary twitching or convulsions during sleep or wakefulness, or even death. Elaborate rituals are performed by a local spirit medium or healer after determining which spirits are involved in the illness, usually through going into trance and communicating with the spirit world.

Ifugao (Amganad, Ayangan, Gilipanes, Ifugaw, Ipugao, Kiangan, Mayaoyaw, Mayoyao, Quiangan, Tuwali Ifugao, Yfugao)

The Ifugao are a subdivision of the larger IGOROT group, which is made up of 10 groups of AUSTRONESIANS in and around the Cordillera region of central Luzon, the Philippines.

IBANAGS

location:
The Cagayan Valley of northern Luzon, the Philippines

time period:
3000 B.C.E. to the present

ancestry:
Austronesian

language:
Ibanag, a northern Luzon language within the larger Austronesian family

IFUGAO

location:
Ifugao Province, Luzon, the Philippines

time period:
3000 B.C.E. to the present

ancestry:
Austronesian

language:
There are four separate Ifugao dialects, all Northern Luzon languages within the larger Austronesian family.

The Ifugao are one of the most inland of these groups and reside in the southern region of the Cordillera region. Their name is taken from the local term *ipugo*, meaning "human beings," which they distinguish in their local cosmology from spirits or supernatural beings; *pugo* also means "hill" and probably refers to their residence in the mountains.

The Ifugao, as are many of their Igorot neighbors, are wet rice farmers who grow their staple crop on extensive terraces that their ancestors carved out of the mountains almost 2,000 years ago; new terraces are also produced regularly and today a man's status is generally determined by the size of his rice fields. Today the terraces of both the Ifugao and related BONTOC are major tourist attractions that draw substantial amounts of foreign currency into the local and national economy. In addition to wet rice the Ifugao grow a number of other irrigated crops, including beans, cabbages, cotton, peas, and radishes. In impermanent swidden fields, cut out of the forest and used for just a season or two, they also produce corn and sweet potatoes.

Ifugao settlements, called *buble*, tend to be smaller than their Bontoc cousins and consist of just eight to 12 houses, each holding three to five members of a nuclear family. Once they were old enough to take care of themselves, both boys and girls moved into special dormitories where they learned the knowledge and skills necessary to thrive as Ifugao adults. This practice has been largely lost today, but many older Ifugao adults fondly remember their time in these structures.

Ifugao hamlets are located on valley sides rather than floors or mountaintops. Both houses and granaries, the two most important structures in Ifugao society, are built on posts and have wooden walls and thatched roofs. Houses contain a hearth and in the past a shelf to hold the skulls taken by the headhunting man of the house. As among all Igorot tribes headhunting was the path to male honor and prestige prior to the pacification of the region in the early 20th century.

Even before the modern era Ifugao society was not egalitarian despite the lack of chiefs or other formal authority figures. Wealthy Ifugao families differed from their poorer neighbors by owning more cropland, water buffaloes, and even slaves. Their status in the community was symbolized by ownership of a special wooden bench, called a *habagi*, displaying their mate-

Ifugao villages are often located in valleys overlooked by hillsides covered with extensive terraces for rice production. *(Shutterstock/Jonald Morales)*

rial wealth such as Chinese jars, gold objects, and hornbill headdresses, and through hosting of parties and festivals. Wealthy families made up an endogamous class called *kadangyan,* whose members intermarried only with other members. Poorer Ifugaos with little land and significant debt were classified as *natumok* while the landless were known as *nawatwat.*

Igorot (Igorrote, Ygolot)

Igorot, which means "mountaineer" in TAGALOG, is a collective term for nine groups of AUSTRONESIANS who reside in and around the Cordillera region of Luzon, the Philippines. These nine groups are the BONTOC, Gaddang, Ibaloi, IFUGAO, ILONGOTS, Isneg, KALINGAS, Kankanay, and Tinguian.

GEOGRAPHY

The Cordillera region of the Philippines is located in the north central area of Luzon and constitutes about one-sixth of the island. It makes up one of the highest and largest mountain ranges in the country, with Mount Pulog, at 9,610 feet above sea level, being the highest in the range. The region encompasses six different provinces: Abra, Apayao, Benguet, Ifugao, Kalinga, and Mountain Provinces, as well as one city, Baguio. The Ilongot live just outside this region in Nueva Vizcaya Province, just to the south of the Cordillera region. While many regions of the Cordillera have extensive terraces for rice farming, those of the Ifugao's province are considered the most dramatic and are sometimes described as an eighth wonder of the ancient world.

The climate of the Cordillera, especially at the tops of the mountains, remains relatively cool throughout the year and is known for heavy fog and cloud cover. The mountains also contain numerous important natural resources including timber, copper, iron, and gold. The last item led to considerable Spanish interest in the region, but the local population fought throughout the entire colonial period to control this valuable resource.

ORIGINS

The origins of the Igorots, as of all Austronesian speakers in the Philippines, are probably in south China, from which they sailed in double-outrigger dugout canoes about 5,000 years ago to Taiwan, and then later the Philippines and Polynesia. There is no certainty as to why this population left south China; however, archaeologists have hypothesized that it was a combination of population pressure, increased commerce from the Yangtze River region of China and moving southward down the river and its tributaries, a growing demand for marine and tropical forest goods, and climate change.

Contemporary Austronesian languages can be subdivided into two distinctive groups that separate the languages of Austronesian Taiwan from those of the remainder of the family, which include all Malay and Oceanic languages. This linguistic division, in addition to several anomalies in the archaeological record, such as a lack of rice in the earliest Austronesian sites in Taiwan, indicates that the origins of the Austronesian people may have been two separate exoduses from southeast China. If these did occur, the first exodus was probably from Fujian Province in China to Taiwan, which saw the rise of TA-P'EN-K'ENG CULTURE, with its distinctively marked pottery and stone tools, but without archaeological evidence of domesticated rice. The descendants of this first wave would be the contemporary speakers of Taiwan's Austronesian languages, the ABORIGINAL TAIWANESE people. The second exodus may have occurred around 3000 B.C.E., taking a second wave of Austronesian speakers from southeastern China to Taiwan and then almost immediately to Luzon in the Philippines around the same period. This second wave, with its red slipped pottery, may also have been the ultimate source of the LAPITA CULTURE.

HISTORY

When they arrived in the Philippines about 3000 B.C.E. the Austronesian speakers would probably have met small bands of people who had already been residing on the islands for approximately 20,000 years. The hunting and gathering AETA peoples, as they are now called, probably lived in the most productive areas of the country, the coastlines, valleys, and lower hills, in very small, impermanent settlements. With their ability to grow their own crops the incoming Austronesians were able to maintain significantly higher population densities than the Aeta and thus to push the hunter-gatherers into the more marginal highland forests and mountaintops, where they still live today. The numerically and technologically stronger agriculturalists also seem to have lent their language to the Aeta, all of whom today speak Austronesian languages rather than the more ancient languages they would have taken with them in their much earlier migrations.

IGOROT

location:
In and around the Cordillera region of Luzon, the Philippines

time period:
3000 B.C.E. to the present

ancestry:
Austronesian

language:
Each of the 10 separate Igorot tribes speaks its own language; all are classified as northern Luzon languages within the larger Austronesian language family.

Igorot time line

B.C.E.

3000 The initial migration of the Austronesian speakers to the Philippines, including the ancestors of all 10 Igorot tribes.

C.E.

0 Approximate period when the spectacular Ifugao rice terraces are begun.

1575 The Spanish first make contact with the Igorot tribes.

1745–50 A series of Spanish military actions pushes the Igorot out of their territory at Ituy, known as Ajanas to the Igorot themselves.

1758 A change in policy direction as the Spanish declare an amnesty for Igorot who convert to Christianity; they also become exempt from having to pay tribute. Peaceful proselytizing becomes the order of the day, although few Igorot are interested in the offer.

1789 The most extensive Spanish book about the Igorot is written by Father Antolin, a priest with extensive firsthand experience of the people: *Noticias de los infieles igorrotes en lo interior de la Isla de Manila.*

1899 The Spanish cede the Philippines to the United States and a local war of independence breaks out. The Igorot side with the freedom fighters first and then switch alliance to the U.S. army.

1902 A civil U.S. administration replaces military rule upon the pacification of the independence fighters.

1941 The Japanese occupy the Philippines during World War II.

1944 The United States retakes the Philippines.

1945 The Philippines attain independence from the United States.

1969 The New People's Army (NPA) is formed as the military arm of the Communist Party of the Philippines; some Igorot join the NPA in their struggle for land and cultural recognition in their region.

1986 Corazon Aquino comes to power in the Philippines and cancels the Chico Dam project, which would have flooded significant amounts of Kalinga land.

Although the vast majority of this migration of Austronesians was to the Philippine lowlands, a number of tribes also established themselves in the mountains of Luzon and Mindanao. The Igorot are made up of nine such groups who reside in the Cordillera of Luzon.

On the basis of the information collected by the earliest Spanish colonizers the Igorot and their lowland linguistic cousins seem to have been very similar prior to the colonial era. Both groups relied on agriculture for the majority of their food and engaged in extensive trade networks with each other. The Igorot provided gold and forest products to the lowlanders and received rice and livestock in return. While the Igorot grew their own rice, their cool climate did not produce the tremendous surplus that could be grown in lower elevations with their warmer, wetter climate. As a result the two populations maintained relatively peaceful relations and the trade between them benefited both peoples in important ways.

The cultural differences and animosity that have marked the relationships between the Igorot and both lowland Filipinos and the various peoples who have colonized the region are largely the product of the early Spanish colonial period. At that time most lowland groups converted to Christianity and adopted other cultural practices from the Spanish. To distinguish between the two groups the Spanish referred to these Catholic lowlanders as *Indios* and to the "pagan" highlanders as *tribus independientes* or independent tribes. As a result of these differences the Igorot became more isolated from the lowlanders and hostile to relations with outsiders more generally.

A second reason for the animosity of the Igorot toward outsiders was the Spanish effort to gain access to the most valuable resource of the Igorot, gold; the Igorot controlled the most lucrative gold mines in the entire Philippine archipelago. Throughout the 19th century alone the Spanish sent 75 different military missions into this mountain region to try to pacify the local population and gain access to this prized resource. For the most part the Spanish failed in all their efforts and the Igorot entered the 20th century as animists rather than Christians and with access to gold, which they traded with lowlanders for other resources.

During the war between the U.S. army and the Filipinos fighting for their country's independence, 1899–1901, the Igorot initially sided with their fellow Filipinos; however, after experiencing the superior firepower of the Americans, the Igorot contingent, armed solely with spears and axes, abandoned the cause and went home to the mountains. After these events in 1899 some Igorot men became allies of the Americans and assisted them as guides and scouts against the lowland freedom fighters. This did not stop the Americans after the war from viewing the Igorot as primitive and backward nor from repeating tales of their prowess as headhunters, which continued to keep most outsiders away from their highland homes for several decades. Representations of the Igorot that were taken to the United States and displayed in various expositions and fairs, including the 1904 St. Louis World's Fair and the 1909 Alaska-Yukon Pacific Exposition, showed them eating dog and depicted them as headhunters. Both practices were seen as markers of their inhabiting the lowest rung of human social development and thus justified the U.S. colonial project as one of introducing civilization to primitive peoples.

Part of this project, as it had been for the Spanish, was to try to convert the Igorot and their fellow Filipinos to Christianity. For the vast majority of Filipinos the attempts of largely Protestant American missionaries were irrelevant since they had been Christians in the Roman Catholic Church for several centuries. For the Igorot, however, who had withstood Spanish pressure to convert for 300 years, Christianity was new. Contemporary works about the Igorot differ in their evaluation of the success of these American Protestant missionaries, with some declaring that most of these tribes have been converted and others claiming that the majority retain their own animistic beliefs. Probably the truth is somewhere between the two: some tribes have converted entirely, others have not, and the majority continue to hold and engage in some pre-Christian beliefs and practices as well as some Protestant ones.

The latter half of the 20th century carried other influences into the Cordillera as well, when land speculators, timber companies, and even the Marcos government became interested in the region's resources. The Kalinga were going to be particularly affected by a government- and World Bank–sponsored program that was to produce hydroelectric power in the region through a dam on the Chico River. For many years they withstood an onslaught by the Filipino military, including the bombing of villages, with a significant loss of life. By 1975 the World Bank had withdrawn from the project as a result of Kalinga activities and when Marcos was replaced by President Corazon Aquino in 1986 the project was abandoned altogether.

By 1986 the Aquino government was faced not only with Kalinga fighting for their homeland but an entire Cordillera People's Liberation Army (CPLA) that was fighting for the complete withdrawal of the Filipino government from the region. The CPLA was allied with the military arm of the Communist Party of the Philippines, the New People's Army (NPA), which continues to this day to struggle against government troops. The NPA is currently considered a terrorist organization by both the United States and the European Union for its activities, including bombing and other violence against civilians.

CULTURE

The Austronesian migrants to the Philippines arrived from Taiwan bearing several domesticated plants, including rice, the contemporary staple crop in Luzon; domesticated pigs, dogs, and chickens; and a lifestyle built around the agricultural calendar. For many Igorot communities rice farming required them to create enough flat land in their mountainous homeland to grow their staple crop. By the start of the common era groups like the Ifugao and Bontoc had created elaborate terraces on the mountainsides on which they could grow most of the rice necessary to feed their communities. Those built by the Ifugao people are particularly elaborate and if laid out end to end would be 10 times the length of the Great Wall of China and stretch halfway around the world.

While the Ifugao, Bontoc, Kankanay, and Ibaloi are all wet-rice farmers similar to their lowland cousins, the Kalinga and Tinguian grow a combination of wet and dry strains of this important crop. Two linguistic groups that differ from this norm are the Gaddang and Ilongot, both of whom practice shifting or slash-and-burn agriculture on temporary plots cut out of the deep Cordillera forests. Because of this difference in agricultural practice some sources do not list these two groups as members of the larger Igorot community, but their residence in the Cordillera, former headhunting practices, and antagonism toward outsiders are considered by many to be enough to classify them as Igorot.

As had all Filipino Austronesian peoples, the Igorot had their own religious traditions and practices prior to their 20th-century partial conversion to Christianity. All tribal subgroups had slightly different beliefs and practices, but in general all nine groups recognized the importance of a variety of ancestral and natural spirits; at least one important creator God, known to the Bontoc as Lumawig; and animal sacrifices. All nine of these groups also recognized the centrality of kinship in the organization of their societies, with ambilineal descent most common. This interesting kinship structure allows each individual to decide whether he or she wants to join the mother's or father's lineage; for most Igorots girls choose their mother's lineage and boys their father's. Because of this ability of every individual to choose his or her line of descent, Igorot kinship structures tend to be extremely elaborate and for an outsider to figure out who is related to whom is an arduous task.

FURTHER READING

William Henry Scott. *The Discovery of the Igorots: Spanish Contacts with the Pagans of Northern Luzon* (Quezon City, Philippines: New Day, 1974).

I-KIRIBATI

location:
Kiribati

time period:
0 to the present

ancestry:
Austronesian

language:
English is the official
language; Kiribatese,
a central Micronesian
language, predominates
away from the capital.

ILOCANOS

location:
Luzon, Mindoro, and
Mindanao islands, the
Philippines

time period:
3000 B.C.E. to the present

ancestry:
Austronesian

language:
Ilocano, a northern
Philippine language in
the Austronesian family

i-Kiribati (Gilbertese, i-Tungaru, Kiribatese)

The i-Kiribati are the indigenous people of the independent country of Kiribati, which is located in the Pacific Ocean along the equator and International Date Line. They speak a central Micronesian language and are thought to be the descendants of migrants from the Solomon Islands and Vanuatu about 2,000 years ago. Local origin myths posit Samoan origins for the i-Kiribati some 1,000 to 600 years ago, but this is not borne out by linguistic evidence.

The i-Kiribati maintain a relatively traditional lifestyle even to this day. Most housing is still made from local resources and many fishing canoes are still created from local tree trunks. Most people devote themselves to fishing and subsistence agriculture, growing taro, sweet potatoes, breadfruit, and local vegetables, although the export copra industry dominates most people's access to cash. Tourism and the civil service, both governmental and the parallel institutions maintained by the Roman Catholic and Kiribati Protestant Churches, also provide jobs for a number of i-Kiribati today. In addition to practicing one of these religions, most i-Kiribati believe in a variety of pre-Christian spirits and in the power of certain practices; for example, sorcery is still practiced in most villages and even in the capital city.

Kinship among the i-Kiribati is different from that of much of the rest of matrilineal Micronesia in tracing descent through both parents, a system known as cognatic or bilateral descent, much like that in contemporary Europe and North America. Beyond the nuclear and extended families established through cognatic descent the village is the most important social unit throughout Kiribati. However, northern and southern Kiribati have different social structures. In the north hereditary chiefs inherit positions of prestige and leadership in their villages, while other families are ranked according to their degree of relatedness to these chiefs. In the south a more democratic system developed in which collective assemblies of senior males met in *maneaba* or communal houses to discuss and organize local politics and society. Today both the northern chiefs and southern assemblies continue to participate in the political process at all levels and to have great influence over their respective populations. This influence is not formalized, having been abolished by the British colonizers, but informal and traditional through the respect granted to the older men of the villages.

The i-Kiribati differ from their fellow MICRONESIANS in the Caroline Islands (Federated States of Micronesia) and Marshall Islands in other aspects. While the people of these other island chains conducted significant interisland trade and warfare, the i-Kiribati did not conduct long-distance sea journeys for any purpose. They had the same technology and navigational skills as their fellow Micronesians but chose to limit their journeying to nearby islands and participated in very few wars, usually only between adjoining districts on the same islands.

See also: KIRIBATESE: NATIONALITY.

FURTHER READING

Batiri T. Bataua et al. *Kiribati: A Changing Atoll Culture* (Suva, Fiji: Institute for Pacific Studies, 1985).

Gerd Koch. *Material Culture of Kiribati* (Suva, Fiji: Institute for Pacific Studies, 1986).

Ernest Sabatier. *Astride the Equator: An Account of the Gilbert Islands.* Translated by Ursula Nixon (New York: Oxford University Press, 1978).

Ilocanos (Samtoy)

The Ilocanos are the dominant population in the coastal region of northern Luzon, especially their homeland provinces of Ilocos Norte and Sur, La Union, and Abra. They are a lowland Christian group whose language has become the lingua franca for many of the IGOROT tribes in the highlands of Luzon.

GEOGRAPHY

The traditional homeland of the Ilocanos was the coastal plain of northern Luzon in what are today the provinces of Ilocos Norte and Sur, La Union, and Abra, a landlocked area. Today the population has spread well beyond this area into the rest of coastal Luzon as well as many other Filipino islands, especially Mindoro and Mindanao. Indeed since the 19th century Ilocanos have been the most numerous migrant community throughout the archipelago; in the early 20th century the Ilocanos were the first Filipinos to move to the United States and many sought work in Hawaii and California on either a temporary or a permanent basis.

One of the reasons for this mass migration is the difficulty of survival in the Ilocano homeland. Just inland from the narrow coastal plains most of northern Luzon is extremely rugged and rocky. The highlands were also inhabited by somewhat hostile tribal communities who did not begin to integrate into national life until the 20th century. As the northernmost region of the island this region was also frequently buffeted by the southwest monsoon and typhoon winds, which destroyed homes and crops and made life difficult.

ORIGINS

The origins of the Ilocanos, as of all AUSTRONE-SIANS in the Philippines, are probably in south China, from which they sailed in double-outrigger dugout canoes about 5,000 years ago to Taiwan, and then later the Philippines and Polynesia. There is no certainty as to why this population left south China; however, archaeologists have hypothesized that it was a combination of population pressure, increased commerce from the Yangtze River region of China and moving southward down the river and its tributaries, a growing demand for marine and tropical forest goods, and climate change.

Contemporary Austronesian languages can be subdivided into two distinctive groups that separate the languages of Austronesian Taiwan from those of the remainder of the family, which include all Malay and Oceanic languages. This linguistic division, in addition to several anomalies in the archaeological record, such as a lack of rice in the earliest Austronesian sites in Taiwan, indicates that the origins of the Austronesian people may have been two separate exoduses from southeast China. If these did occur, the first exodus was probably from Fujian province in China to Taiwan, which saw the rise of TA-P'EN-K'ENG CULTURE, with its distinctively marked pottery and stone tools, but without archaeological evidence of domesticated rice. The descendants of this first wave would be the contemporary speakers of Taiwan's Austronesian languages, the ABORIGINAL TAIWANESE people. The second exodus may have occurred around 3000 B.C.E., taking a second wave of Austronesian speakers from southeastern China to Taiwan and then almost immediately to Luzon in the Philippines around the same period. This second wave, with its red-slipped pottery, may also have been the ultimate source of the LAPITA CULTURE.

HISTORY

When they arrived in the Philippines about 3000 B.C.E. the Austronesian speakers would probably have met small bands of people who had already been residing on the islands for approximately 20,000 years. The hunting and gathering AETA peoples, as they are now called, probably lived in the most productive areas of the country, the coastlines, valleys, and lower hills, in very small, impermanent settlements. With their ability to grow their own crops the incoming Austronesians were able to maintain significantly higher population densities than the Aeta and thus to push the hunter-gatherers into the more marginal highland forests and mountaintops, where they still live today. The

Ilocanos time line

B.C.E.

3000 The initial migration of the Austronesian speakers, including the ancestors of the Ilocanos, to the Philippines.

C.E.

1572 The Spanish explorer Juan de Salcedo first meets the Ilocanos on Luzon.

1612 Laoag's St William's Cathedral is built.

1762–63 The British occupy the city of Manila, and Diego and Gabriela Silang stage the most famous of the many Ilocanos revolts against colonialism.

1788 The Spanish impose a tobacco monopoly, which leads to an Ilocano revolt.

1807 The Spanish attempt to control the production and sale of a local wine, *basi,* made from sugar.

1814 Ilocanos in Ilocos Norte rise up in reaction to Spanish laws that treat them as second-class citizens in their own lands.

1818 Ilocos is divided into the two separate provinces of Ilocos Norte and Ilocos Sur in reaction to the bloodshed four years earlier.

1899 The Spanish cede the Philippines to the United States and a local war of independence breaks out with numerous Ilocano participants, including General Artemio Ricarte.

1901 Father Gregorio Aglipay forms a nationalist breakaway church, the Philippine Independent Church, separate from the Catholic Church.

1902 A civil U.S. administration replaces military rule upon the pacification of the independence fighters.

1917 Ferdinand Marcos is born in Ilocos Norte, the son of two schoolteachers.

1941 The Japanese occupy the Philippines during World War II.

1944 The United States retakes the Philippines.

1945 The Philippines attain independence from the United States.

1965–86 The most (in)famous Ilocano, Ferdinand Marcos, is president of the Philippines.

1969 The New People's Army is formed as the military arm of the Communist Party of the Philippines. In reaction to this and other threats Marcos declares martial law in 1971.

1983 Marcos has Benigno Aquino, his political rival, assassinated upon his return to the Philippines after a period of self-imposed exile.

1986 Ferdinand Marcos is deposed and Aquino's widow, Corazon Aquino, comes to power.

numerically and technologically stronger agriculturalists also seem to have lent their language to the Aeta, all of whom today speak Austronesian languages rather than the more ancient languages they would have taken with them in their much earlier migrations.

Prior to the arrival of the Spanish in 1572 the coastal Ilocanos were very similar culturally to the region's highlanders. All groups maintained the agricultural way of life imported with them from Taiwan and ultimately southern China, practiced animistic religions that recognized the power of a plethora of natural and ancestral spirits, and had local chiefs or headmen who dominated the political and judicial structures of local kin-based groups. The two groups traded with each other, with highlanders providing gold, wood, honey, and wild game and the Ilocanos providing rice, fish, and external trade goods obtained from the Chinese and JAPANESE, who began trading in the region before 1000 C.E. Even before the colonial era the Ilocano town of Laoag, along the Laoag River not far from its mouth, was an international port town with extensive trade relations in the Asia-Pacific region.

The first Spaniard to arrive in the Ilocano homeland was the explorer Juan de Salcedo in 1572. Almost immediately Spanish Augustinian priests and missionaries began the task of converting the local population to Roman Catholicism. They were successful and today many colonial-era churches and other buildings remain in the region as symbols of this early conversion; by 1612 they had completed St. William's Cathedral in Laoag. Many Ilocanos also collaborated with the Spanish in other ways, especially in their failed attempts to pacify and convert the region's mountain tribes.

Nonetheless the Ilocanos were not always passive collaborators with their Spanish colonial masters. As early as 1589 a number of communities rose up against the colonizers, an event that recurred a number of times until 1765. The later portion of the 18th and the early 19th centuries saw even more discord when large numbers of Ilocanos rose up repeatedly; in 1788 the troubles began with the imposition of a tobacco monopoly by the Spanish and in 1807 with the attempt by the Spanish to control the production and sale of *basi,* a local sugar-based wine. In 1814 the cosmopolitan Ilocanos of Ilocos Norte rose up again in reaction to Spanish laws that treated them as second-class citizens in their own lands; rather than accede to their demands, in 1818 the Spanish governor divided Ilocos Norte from the southern portion of the province in an attempt to divide and conquer. The final acts of rebellion among the Ilocanos occurred at the end of the Spanish period when numerous community members joined the independence fighters, first against the Spanish and then against the incoming American forces. An Ilocano, Father Gregorio Aglipay, even formed a nationalist breakaway church in this period, the Philippine Independent Church, to illustrate the desire for a complete break from the prior colonial era.

During the American colonial period numerous Ilocanos looked outward for salvation from the colonial economy and way of life and took advantage of relatively easy migration laws to move to Hawaii and California. From 1908 until immigration was cut off in 1946 thousands of Ilocanos, mostly single men, left home to work in the fields and plantations of these two American regions. In 1946 alone 7,365 Ilocano men accepted positions in Hawaii through a program sponsored by the U.S. Department of Labor. Many of these men returned home to marry or placed advertisements in newspapers and magazines at home to recruit Ilocano wives to join them in their new homes. As a result by the last quarter of the 20th century more than 70 percent of Hawaii's Filipinos had an Ilocano background.

The best-known Ilocano in history was Ferdinand Marcos, the president turned dictator who ruled the Philippines from 1965 until he was deposed by the military in 1986. Marcos

Diego and Gabriela Silang ⚔

Diego and Gabriela Silang are remembered among the Ilocano people of the Philippines as heroes of the revolution. Diego was born in 1730 in Aringay, Pangasinan (what is now modern-day Caba), and became aware of the injustices committed against the Filipino people by the Spanish government when he began working as a messenger for the local priest of Vigan, Father Cortes y Crisolo. Diego carried correspondence between Ilocos to Manila, and in his travels he witnessed the struggles of the Filipino people under heavy Spanish tribute and other abuses. He also met and married the young widow Josefa Gabriela. During this time Spain was embroiled in the Seven Years' War, having allied with France against Great Britain. Consequently British ships moved into Manila Bay in 1762 and took the city. Diego, who had already amassed a rebel group, took the opportunity to seize the city of Vigan and ally himself with the British invaders, envisioning a self-governed Ilocano nation. The British appointed him governor of Ilocos and promised him a military force that never arrived, and in 1763, Diego was assassinated by his two close friends, Miguel Vicos and Pedro Becbec. After her husband's murder Josefa Gabriela Silang continued Diego's push for independence and orchestrated a number of successful guerrilla attacks on Spanish troops until her capture. In September 1763 Gabriela Silang and 80 of her men were publically hanged.

In 1965 a young Ferdinand Marcos, left, cast his vote for president in Batac, Ilocos Norte; he went on to win that election and remained in office until the mid-1980s. *(AP Photo)*

began his long career of corruption and crime when he was just a teenager in 1935, when he shot and killed Julio Nalundasan, who had been elected to the Filipino Congress. The trial that convicted Marcos took three years and by then the defendant had nearly completed his studies to become a lawyer. From prison Marcos not only passed the bar but also wrote his own appeal, which was granted by the supreme court on the recommendation of his godfather. On the day after his appeal succeeded Marcos returned to the supreme court building to take the oath to become a lawyer. Following upon the scandal of his youth, Marcos also lied about his activities during World War II to make it appear that he had worked valiantly with the U.S. army to liberate his country; in fact he seems to have worked with both sides alternately and spent part of the period ill or in hiding. However, his reputation at home grew exponentially after the war with every story he disseminated about himself, and in 1949 he won a seat in the new house of representatives. After two reelections and the accumulation of a vast amount of personal wealth Marcos ran and was elected to the senate in 1959; there he served for six years before running for president as the candidate

from his newly created Nationalist Party. Once he won the presidency, Marcos refused to let it go. He declared martial law in 1971 in reaction to student protests and both Muslim and tribal unrest throughout the country, and when it was lifted in 1981 he held on to the extensive autocratic powers he had been granted during the previous 10 years. Although his regime lasted for another three years, the beginning of the end for Marcos was the assassination of his greatest political rival, Benigno Aquino, in 1983. Three years later after he had falsified presidential elections, the military finally marched on Marcos and installed his opposition in the election, Aquino's widow, Corazon "Cory" Aquino.

CULTURE

The primary economic activity of the Ilocanos from earliest days to the present has been agriculture; the majority today own their own small plot of land. As is the case generally among Austronesian peoples in the Philippines rice is the most important crop; poorer Ilocanos also plant corn. Tobacco and garlic are the two most important cash crops while many different kinds of fruit, onions, sugarcane, cassava, and *camote,* a form of sweet potato, are the most important secondary crops. Fish, chicken, pork, sheep, goats, and shrimp all contribute to the region's protein intake, with *bagoong,* a salty fish paste made from *ipon,* one of the unique features of the Ilocanos' diet in relation to the rest of the country. For many Ilocanos local cottage industries supplement their income from tobacco or other farm products; weaving, salt, basi wine making, pottery, and woodworking are the most important of these industries. With their extensive national and international networks through out-migration some Ilocanos also engage in petty trade, some traveling to Manila and beyond to do so.

Families, both nuclear and extended, are the heart of Ilocano society, and fear of gossip, envy, or embarrassing oneself and one's family is a strong motivator in controlling the behavior of both children and adults. Kinship generally is reckoned bilaterally with both mothers' and fathers' families contributing to one's most important social relations. Fathers are generally seen from the outside as the head of the household, but inside mothers hold a considerable amount of power and prestige. The oldest child in the household also holds a more important position in relation to his or her siblings and is seen as responsible for equitably dividing up the children's household chores on the basis of age, sex, and capabilities.

Although the Ilocanos were very early converts to Christianity, many aspects of their pre-Christian belief system have continued to be handed down to the present day. Many still believe the pre-Christian origin myth of Aran, who built the sky with its hanging Sun, Moon, and stars. Aran's companion, Angalo, used the light of Aran's inventions to see the land, on which he then built mountains, valleys, oceans, and, from his own spit, the first man and woman, the founding ancestors of the Ilocanos. Many Ilocanos also recognize the power of many natural and ancestral spirits, most of whom appear to the living as a reminder to pray, go to church, or seek forgiveness for the dead person's sins. If these tasks are not undertaken, the spirit may follow up by causing illness or other misfortune. Faith healing and spirit mediums are extremely important in Ilocano communities for assisting with these interactions.

FURTHER READING

F. Landa Jocano. *The Ilocanos: An Ethnography of Family and Community in the Ilocos Region.* (Quezon City: Asian Center, University of Philippines, 1982).

Ilonggo   *See* HILIGAYNON.

Ilongo   *See* HILIGAYNON.

Ilongots (Ibilao, Ibilaw, Ilunguts, Ilyonguts, Lingots)

The Ilongots are a marginal subdivision of the larger IGOROT group, which is made up of nine groups of AUSTRONESIANS in the Cordillera region of central Luzon, the Philippines. They live in Nueva Vizcaya Province, which is just to the south of the Cordillera region occupied by the majority of the Igorot tribes; however, cultural similarities between them and the other Igorot mean that most sources classify them in this larger tribal grouping. Their name is a TAGALOG and Spanish rendering of their name for themselves, *Quirungut,* meaning "of the forest."

Unlike the majority of Igorot peoples, the Ilongots practice extensive swidden agriculture rather than intensive irrigated farming. Each year they cut new fields from the thick forests of their region, let the vegetation dry, and then burn it off to provide fertilizer for crops of dry rice, corn, and manioc. In the following years the same fields are used for tobacco and vegetables. In their final productive years the same fields can then be used to produce sweet potatoes, sugarcane, or bananas before sitting fallow for up to a decade. To supplement their agricultural products, many Ilongot families keep domestic pigs, dogs, and chickens, the three domesticated animals that the original Austronesians took with them to the Philippines about 5,000 years ago. Ilongot men also hunt and fish and women gather such wild products as fruits, palm hearts, ferns, and rattan, to be used in making baskets, mats, and other domestic products.

Ilongot society is made up of 13 different dialect groups, averaging just fewer than 200 people per group. These groupings are made up of ambilaterally related people; that is, each individual Ilongot is usually able to decide whether to join his or her mother's or father's kinship unit. Generally men decide to join their father's and women their mother's, but there is no rule prescribing this behavior and each person is able to make his or her own decision. Once they have made their choice, however, they must abide by the marriage prohibitions, taboos, and other laws of their chosen kinship group. The only time when Ilongots are not able to make this decision for themselves is when their fathers' parents have paid the bride price, the gifts and trade goods given to a woman's family at the time of her marriage to legitimate any resulting children; in these situations all resulting children must become members of their father's lineage, or *be:rtan* in Ilongot.

Most Ilongots live in nuclear family houses built on stilts about 15 feet in height. These individual houses are often located within larger, extended family compounds, which themselves are situated in settlements of 40 to 70 people. Generally after marriage, which men and women arrange for themselves, the new couple resides for a few years in the woman's family's household, a pattern called matrilocal marriage, before establishing their own home.

Prior to the mid-20th century the Ilongots lived largely traditional lives. Men were still required to take an enemy head prior to marriage and Christian missionaries had not entered the area. Since that time Protestant missionaries have entered Ilongot territory and added their own stories and beliefs to those of the animistic Ilongots, and headhunting has largely ceased.

Indian Malaysians   *See* MALAYSIAN INDIANS.

Indians: nationality (people of India)

GEOGRAPHY

India occupies the majority of the South Asian subcontinent, with more than 1.86 million square

---

ILONGOTS

location:
Nueva Vizcaya Province, Luzon, the Philippines

time period:
3000 B.C.E. to the present

ancestry:
Austronesian

language:
Three dialects of the Ilongot language, classified as Northern Luzon within the larger Austronesian language family

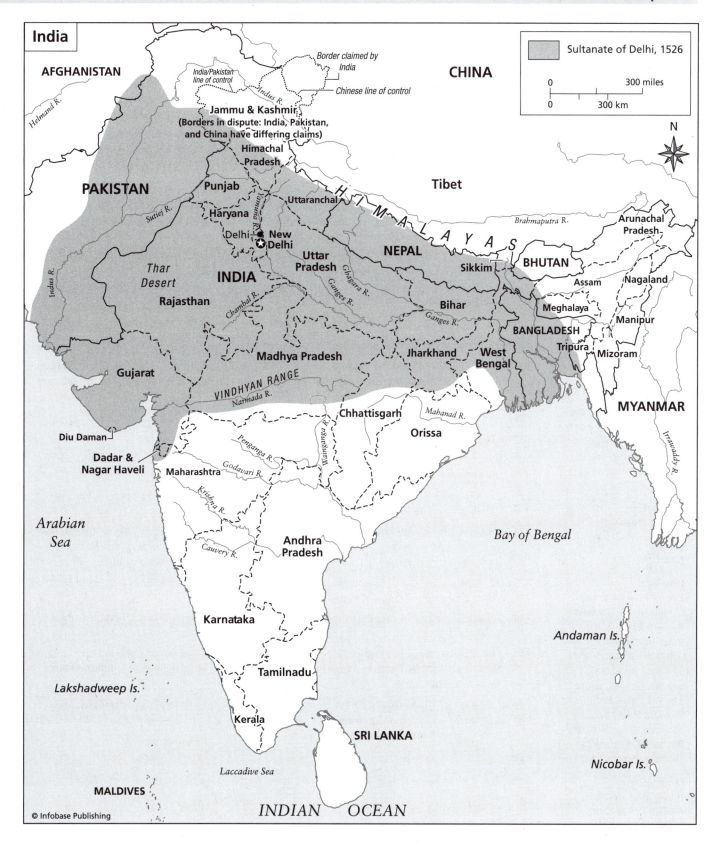

India

AFGHANISTAN

CHINA

Sultanate of Delhi, 1526

0   300 miles
0   300 km

N

Helmand R.

Indus R.

Border claimed by India

India/Pakistan line of control

Chinese line of control

Jammu & Kashmir
(Borders in dispute: India, Pakistan, and China have differing claims)

Himachal
Pradesh

PAKISTAN

Punjab

Haryana

Sutlej R.

Delhi
New
Delhi

Uttaranchal

Jamuna R.

HIMALAYAS

Tibet

Brahmaputra R.

Arunachal
Pradesh

Indus R.

Thar
Desert

INDIA

Rajasthan

Chambal R.

Uttar
Pradesh

Ghagara R.

Ganges R.

NEPAL

Sikkim

BHUTAN

Assam

Nagaland

Bihar

Ganges R.

Meghalaya

Manipur

BANGLADESH

Gujarat

Madhya Pradesh

VINDHYAN RANGE

Narmada R.

Jharkhand

West
Bengal

Tripura

Mizoram

Diu Daman

Chhattisgarh

Mahanad R.

MYANMAR

Dadar &
Nagar Haveli

Maharashtra

Penganga R.

Godavari R.

Wainganga R.

Orissa

Irrawaddy R.

Krishna R.

*Arabian
Sea*

Andhra
Pradesh

Bay of Bengal

Cauvery R.

Karnataka

Andaman Is.

Lakshadweep Is.

Tamilnadu

Kerala

SRI LANKA

Nicobar Is.

Laccadive Sea

MALDIVES

INDIAN   OCEAN

© Infobase Publishing

miles of landmass and more than 3,500 miles of coastline. India is bounded on the southwest by the Arabian Sea, on the southeast by the Bay of Bengal, and on the north by Pakistan, the Peo-ple's Republic of China, Bangladesh, Myanmar (Burma), Nepal, Bhutan, and Afghanistan. Polit-ically India is divided into 28 states, six federally administered union territories, and a national

INDIANS: NATIONALITY

nation:
Republic of India; India

derivation of name:
The name *India* originated from the Sanskrit word *Sindhu* meaning "river." The word *Sindhu* was first used by inhabitants in reference to the local river system and was later renamed *Hindu* by Persian explorers. From the Persian the Greeks renamed the subcontinent *Indos*, which later became the Latin word *Indus*. The Romans used the Latin word *Indus* to refer to the subcontinent, and it gradually changed to the word *India*. Although *India* has been used since the Romans, the name was officially adopted in 1949 as expressed in the first article of the Indian constitution.

government:
Federal republic

capital:
New Delhi

language:
The national language of India, Hindi, is spoken by more 30 percent of the population. In addition to Hindi there are 14 other official languages: Bengali, Telugu, Marathi, Tamil, Urdu, Gujarati, Malayalam, Kannada, Oriya, Punjabi, Assamese, Kashmiri, Sindhi, and Sanskrit.

religion:
Hindu 80.5 percent, Muslim 13.4 percent, Christian 2.3 percent, Sikh 1.9 percent, other 1.8 percent, unspecified 0.1 percent

Indians: nationality time line

B.C.E.

3200–1600 Cultural exchange between the Indus Valley civilization and Mesopotamia (present-day Iraq) begins and is particularly salient during this period.

1600 The Indo-Aryans move into the Indus Valley region.

1600–1000 This period reflects the Early Vedic age of Indian civilization, including the composition of the sacred texts referred to as Vedas. The Vedas eventually become the basis for classical Hindu thought.

1550 Writing disappears from India for a time with the destruction of the Indus Valley civilization. Although subject to debate, it is likely that the decline of the Indus civilization was a product of two factors: climate change and the disappearance of the Ghaggar Hakra River system due to a tectonic plate shift.

1000–500 During this period of Indian civilization, the Late Vedic period, agriculture emerges as the dominant economic activity. Because of the increased importance of land, many new kingdoms emerge. Additionally, Indo-Aryans are integrated into Indian culture and the caste system emerges.

1000 The Rig Veda, the first Vedic literature, is written.

800–600 The Brahmans, a priestly caste, begin to emerge.

800–500 During this period the Upanishads are written and the doctrines of rebirth/transmigration of souls start to appear. Consequently the Upanishads produce a significant theological transformation within Hinduism.

599 Mahavira, Jainism's final Jina, similar to a prophet, is born.

563 Gautama Siddharta Buddha, the founder of Buddhism, is born.

517–509 Darius the Great conquers the northwest region of India, making the area a province of the Persian Empire.

327–326 Alexander the Great briefly subjugates the peoples of the Indus Valley region, leaving Greek officials in the area.

323 Alexander the Great dies, providing the opportunity for an independent state to arise in northwest India. As a result Chandragupta Maurya founds the Mauryan dynasty, the first native Indian empire. The Mauryan dynasty is also responsible for the spread of Buddhism.

273–232 Asoka, grandson of Chandragupta Maurya, rules in India and institutes a series of Buddhist edicts designed to bring about moral reform.

250 A general council of Buddhist monks is held in Patna, where the canon of Buddhist scriptures is selected.

240 The Mauryan dynasty declines with the death of Asoka, and in 184 B.C.E. the Punjab region of India is invaded by Bactrians. Consequently Greek culture is revitalized south of the Hindu Kush Mountain range.

150 B.C.E.–200 C.E. The Kushan kingdom emerges after the decline of the Mauryan dynasty. The Kushan kingdom becomes recognized for its role as an intermediary in Roman-Chinese trade and also for the rising popularity of Buddhism.

C.E.

300 The Kushan kingdom collapses, resulting in the fragmentation of northern India until the emergence of the Gupta dynasty. The Guptas revive the ancient tradition of the Mauryans for close to 200 years.

500 The Gupta dynasty is overthrown.

1000–1100 Led by Mahmud of Ghazi, Arab armies infiltrate western India and sweep down the Khyber Pass. These Arab armies continue to invade India every other year for about 26 years.

1192 Muslims return to India under the control of Mohammed of Ghor or Mohd Ghori. Ghori's armies proceed to destroy the Buddhist temples of Bihar, and by 1202 the Muslims conquer the most powerful Hindu kingdoms along the Ganges.

1206 Mohammed of Ghor dies and his general, Qutb-ud-din, rules from the north. During this time the majority of southern India remains free of invaders and Arab influence.

1397 Mongols invade under Timur Lang (Tamerlane) and devastate the Delhi region, causing fragmentation of Islamic India.

1527 Founder of the Mughal Empire, Babur, comes to power. After Babur's death in 1530 his grandson Akbar extends the empire as far south as the Krishna River. Akbar tolerates local religions, establishing a tradition of cultural acceptance that contributes greatly to the success of Mughal rule.

1605 Akbar is succeeded by his son, Jahangir, who eventually passes the empire to Shah Jahan. Shah Jahan is responsible for the colossal monuments of the Mughal Empire, most notably the Taj Mahal.

1658 Aurungzebe, Jahan's son, takes control and imprisons his father, citing an increase in taxes and widespread distress. Unlike his predecessors Aurungzebe eradicates indigenous traditions, prompting resistance.

1769 Although the British have had a presence in India since 1610, it is not until this time that the British East India Company takes control of all European trade in the country. Years later the British introduce the Raj.

1784 After rumors of financial corruption, the Raj is granted half-control of the East India Company.

1858 A year-long Indian rebellion ensues against the British, ultimately resulting in the seamless British imperialism that would rule the country for around 100 years. During this time tensions heighten between Hindus and Muslims.

1885 Creation of the Indian National Congress.

1889 Hafiz Abdul Karim, a clerk from Agra, is created queen's *mumshi* (clerk); he serves as her personal attendant until her death in 1901, having replaced a previous favorite, John Brown.

1915 Mohandas Karamchand Gandhi emerges and calls for unity between Hindus and Muslims. This act of leadership eventually leads the country to independence.

1922 The first acts of civil disobedience ensue at the hands of Gandhi.

1942 The Indian National Congress leads a civil disobedience movement demanding that the British leave India (also called the Quit India movement). This act of civil disobedience is subsequently followed by rioting in Calcutta.

1947 The Raj ends at midnight on August 15, and the former colony is divided into the separate countries of India and Pakistan. In the same year the first war begins between India and Pakistan over the disputed territory of Kashmir. The United Nations orders a cease-fire two years later and grants India two-thirds control of the region.

1948 Mohandas (Mahatma) Gandhi is assassinated by Hindu radicals Nathuram Godse and Narayan Apte, who blame him for weakening India.

1952 India holds its first national elections where a turnout of more than 60 percent is recorded. The Congress Party wins an overwhelming majority and Jawaharlal Nehru begins a second term as prime minister.

1964 Jawaharlal Nehru dies and Lal Bahadur Shastri succeeds him as prime minister. A year later the Second Kashmir War begins between India and Pakistan.

1974 India tests its first nuclear weapon.

1977 Indira Gandhi calls for elections and suffers a defeat at the hands of the Janata Party. Morarji Desai becomes the first non–Congress Party prime minister of India.

(continues)

earlier inhabitants:
Indo-Aryans, Dravidians, Arabs, Turks, Europeans

demographics:
Indo-Aryan 72 percent, Dravidian 25 percent, Asian and other 3 percent

---

Indians: nationality time line *(continued)*

1984 Indira Gandhi's own Sikh bodyguards kill her and violence erupts in Delhi and parts of Punjab, causing the deaths of thousands of people.

1991 India is rocked by violence between Hindus and Muslims that eventually kills more than 10,000.

1998 India conducts underground nuclear tests that result in economic sanctions from the United States and Japan.

2004 In power since 1999 the Vajpayee administration begins to privatize and reduce taxes and deficits in efforts to increase public-works initiatives.

2008 The Indian cricket team threatens to end its summer season in Australia early in reaction to one of its players being suspended for three matches over accusations of racism. Representations of the umpires involved in the incident and several Australian cricket players are burned in effigy in several Indian cities.

---

capital territory. India's capital, New Delhi, lies in the northern region of the country almost equidistant between the borders with Pakistan and Nepal. Influenced by the Himalayas and the Thar Desert, India's climate is warmer than that in countries at similar latitudes.

INCEPTION AS A NATION

"India is the cradle of the human race, the birthplace of human speech, the mother of history, the grandmother of legend, and the great grand mother of tradition. Our most valuable and most astrictive materials in the history of man are treasured up in India only!"–Mark Twain

Before the 20th century India was dynastically ruled by foreigners for many centuries. Although India's history of subjugation ultimately led to a unique national identity, the struggle for unity and independence was difficult. India's first attempt at independence was a recent one, beginning with the Indian Rebellion against the British in 1857. Although the rebellion was a larger product of Indian mistrust, the tipping point occurred when the British forced Indian soldiers to use rifle cartridges greased with the fat of cows and pigs, an order that was religiously offensive to both Hindus and Muslims. As a result the Indian soldiers refused to use the cartridges and the British were rumored to have replaced them.

Despite the rumored replacement of cartridges Indian mistrust of the British continued. In an act of violent aggression Mangal Pandey, a soldier of the 34th Native Infantry, attacked his British sergeant and wounded an assistant. The wounded sergeant's commanding officer, General Joyce Hearsay, ordered Pandey's arrest and he was ultimately executed. The execution of Pandey birthed multiple rebellions across northern and central India, ending with the siege of Delhi and the battle at Gwalior in 1858. The siege of Delhi remains particularly important as the Indians demanded that Bahadur, the last Mughal emperor, reclaim his throne and lead the rebellion. In response to Indian revolts the British abolished the East India Company and replaced it with direct rule under the British Crown. As a result the region was partitioned into British India (known also as the British Raj) and the Princely States. Although Queen Victoria promised equal treatment of Indians under the British Crown, the rebellion of 1857 left an indelible Indian mistrust that would prove impossible to reverse.

In a renewed attempt to gain Indian trust the British instituted a series of reforms that opened government positions to Indians belonging to higher castes. Additionally the British stopped land grabs, decreed religious tolerance, and admitted Indians into civil service positions. Along with the reforms the British exiled Bahadur to Rangoon, Burma (Myanmar), where he died in 1862, bringing the Mughal dynasty to an end. After Bahadur's death Queen Victoria became the empress of India in 1877.

Despite the attempts made by the British to integrate Indians into positions of power, rebellions continued and Indians began to unite for the same cause—independence. Inspired by a suggestion made by A. O. Hume, a retired British civil servant, 73 Indian delegates met in Bombay (Mumbai) in 1885 and founded the National Indian Congress. At its inception the congress lacked a well-defined ideology and was fairly ineffective, representing only the interests of urban elites. By the early 1900s the

National Indian Congress widened its scope of representation, but Muslims felt disenchanted. Citing lack of representation and religious indifference Muslims founded the Muhammadan Anglo-Oriental College at Aligarh in an attempt to educate students about Islam. The diversity among India's Muslim population made unification impossible; thus the fighting between Muslims and Hindus continued.

Although Indian Hindus and Muslims fought against one another, both groups were concerned with the ultimate goal of independence from British control. In 1918 and 1922 the Indian movement for independence came to a head with the first series of nonviolent campaigns against the British led by Mohandas Gandhi. Ultimately Gandhi's actions helped create the unification of Indians, earning Gandhi the name "modern father of India." Unified and eager to gain independence, in 1942 the Indian National Congress led the "Quit India" movement, which consisted of additional nonviolent acts of civil disobedience. Following these acts the British Raj ended on August 15, 1947. Although the British agreed to "quit India," the price was partition and the former colony became two: India and Pakistan. Fueled by ethnic and linguistic differences, East Pakistan eventually gained its autonomy from West Pakistan in 1971 and was renamed Bangladesh (see BANGLADESHIS: NATIONALITY).

After British rule ended, the fighting among Hindus, Muslims, and SIKHS increased. Soon after the Raj relinquished power, the constituent assembly drafted the constitution and the Republic of India was officially born on January 26, 1950. The Indian constitution not only mandated secularism but officially ended the caste system. In 1952 India held its first national election and experienced more than 62 percent voter turnout.

Since the elections of 1952 India has faced many difficult issues. Internationally India and Pakistan have gone to war three times, twice over the disputed region of Kashmir and a third time during the split between East and West Pakistan. The international community continues to fear a war between both countries, particularly since the acquisition of nuclear weapons by both India and Pakistan. Domestically India remains culturally divided, with a multitude of ethnic identities, castes, and languages. Although many outsiders predicted that India's ethnic and religious heterogeneity would lead to its disintegration, the country has remained the world's largest democracy.

Mohandas Karamchand Gandhi

One of history's most universally beloved humanitarian figures, Mohandas Karamchand Gandhi, or Mahatma Gandhi, is best known for his unwavering advocacy for human rights as well as his devotion to nonviolent protest. He was born to Hindu parents in Porbandar on October 2, 1869. His mother was devoutly religious and raised him in the Jain philosophy of noninjury to other living creatures, which would later play a critical role in the development of his humanitarian campaigns. In 1883 at age 13 Gandhi was married to Kasturba Makhanji through an arrangement between their parents, and together they would have four sons. At age 18 he went to University College London to study law, and during his time in London he also studied world religions and joined the Vegetarian Society. In 1883 he accepted a contract from a firm in Natal, South Africa, and in 1887 he was attacked and nearly lynched by a white mob but remarkably chose not to press charges when given the opportunity, stating a personal principle of not seeking reparation for a personal injury. He would go on to employ this principle on a much larger scale in 1906, when the Transvaal government called for compulsory registration of the colony's Indian population. Gandhi implored his fellow Indians to protest peacefully by resisting the act and suffering persecution. After seven years of struggle the community's peaceful resistance was successful and the government negotiated a compromise with Gandhi. In 1915 he returned to India and organized nonviolent protests against heavy taxation and oppression, as well as campaigns for the poor, women, Indian independence, and religious tolerance. In 1919 he delivered an emotional speech calling for peace after the Jallianwala Bagh massacre, emphasizing the fact that all violence is evil and unjustifiable. After years of humanitarian advocacy Gandhi was shot and killed in New Delhi on January 30, 1948, by Hindu extremists.

CULTURAL IDENTITY

Since the dawn of the second millennium B.C.E. Indian civilization has played host to several migrant groups such as the INDO-ARYANS, MONGOLS, Arabs, and GREEKS. The richly diverse Indian population testifies to a history of foreign influence with more than 14 official languages and 2,000 ethnic groups. Although India's internal diversity has been the source of many cultural clashes, the country shows tolerance and acceptance of differences overall.

Rooted in the amalgamation of diverse cultures and traditions India's contemporary identity, it can be argued, is a composite of several sources. Beginning in the late medieval period India witnessed a synthesis of Hindu and Islamic civilizations, which resulted in a unique Indo-Islamic tradition. The Indo-Islamic tradition manifested itself in the form of art, architecture, music, folklore, and dress pattern. Literature from the medieval period showcases the blend of Indo-Islamic influence, made famous by the renowned poet Amir Khusro. Cultural diffusion can also be seen in the great architectural works of the Taj Mahal and Red

Fort at Delhi. The broad acceptance of Indo-Islamicism has its beginnings in Sufism, introduced to India in the 12th century. Sufism, with its teachings of brotherly love and acceptance, united Hindus, Muslims, and Sikhs alike. Today Sufi shrines can be found throughout India and continue to act as centers of integration.

In addition to cultural and religious diffusion the emergence of an Indian identity is a product of political development. Beginning with the creation of the Brahmo Samaj organization in 1828 common Indian traditions were created and disseminated throughout the country; this group also forced the British to outlaw suttee (the burning of widows). The Brahmo Samaj not only established commonality among the divided peoples of India, but laid the foundation for other secular organizations such as the Indian National Congress. In 1885 the congress was created to represent Indian interests, regardless of religion and language, against the British. After various Indian revolts and the subsequent independence of India in 1947 the Indian National Congress drafted a constitution that was inclusionary, democratic, and secular. The new constitution put an official end to the caste system and promised equal rights to all Indian citizens. The Indian independence movement and constitution were integral to the formation of nationalism as all Indians worked together to establish the same common goal.

More recently modernization and open economic practices have affected Indian identity. In 2004 the Vajpayee administration instituted a series of economic reforms that led to increased sensitivity toward domestic and international influence. As a result of heightened levels of foreign-based companies within India, cities like Bangalore and New Delhi reflect great diversity. Fast food, Western rock bands, and the resurgence of cricket all demonstrate the explosion of outside influence on Indian culture. Conversely increased trade and exposure have led to a global market for more traditional Indian forms of art. Banghra, a poplike Indian music, has made its way to the dance floors of the United Kingdom, Australia, and Southeast Asia. Similarly Bollywood films, mode by the largest movie industry in the world, have become increasingly popular internationally.

FURTHER READING

Michael Allaby. *India* (New York: Facts On File, 2005).

Leela Fernandes. *India's New Middle Class: Democratic Politics in an Era of Economic Reform* (Minneapolis: University of Minnesota Press, 2006).

M. K. Gandhi. *Non-Violent Resistance (Satyagraha)* (New York: Schocken Books, 1964).

Pranay Gupte. *India: The Challenge of Change* (London: Methuen/Mandarin, 1989).

Radhakumud Mookerji. *The Fundamental Unity of India* (New York: Longmans, Green, 1914).

B. N. Pandey. *A Book of India* (Delhi: Eastern Book Corporation, 2000).

Pavan K. Varma. *Being Indian: Inside the Real India* (Portsmouth, N.H.: Heinemann, 2005).

Indo-Aryans (Aryans, Vedic Civilization)

Proto-Indo-Aryan refers to the language spoken by the people who moved into present-day India sometime in the early second millennium B.C.E. and settled there as elite groups; this language gradually displaced the language of the native inhabitants. The people who spoke this language left little or no certain archaeological evidence of their movements and little or no genetic presence in the population of the HARAPPANS of the Indus Valley civilization and Mohenjo-Daro, who were probably early Dravidian speakers.

Almost everything about these Aryan speakers remains elusive aside from the language they brought with them. Archaeologists, linguists, historians, geneticists, and Indian nationalists have all been involved in the debate about the Aryans. Western scholars place the Indo-Aryan homeland outside India, in Central Asia, while Hindu nationalists maintain an "out of India" theory of local origins. There are also disagreements about the exact time of their appearance and the impact of their presence on the settled peoples of the region that is present-day India. Earlier writers had posited a military invasion and had interpreted archaeological remains as evidence of this, but recently scholars have pointed out that the archaeological remains can be read in any number of ways and that the presence of the Aryan language is the only firm evidence of newcomers. Aryan speakers appeared in northern Mesopotamia about the same time as they did in India, and they left no more traces of an invasion or sudden takeover there than they did in India. Thus a conservative interpretation of the little that is known about these people is preferable to imaginative reconstructions.

GEOGRAPHY

The most common hypothesis for the geography of the Indo-Aryans argues for Central

---

INDO-ARYANS

location:
Central Asian origins with migration into India

time period:
Second millennium to about 700 B.C.E.

ancestry:
Proto-Indo-European (PIE)

language:
Proto-Indo-Aryan

Asian origins with entry into India over the Hindu Kush and into the regions of Gandhara and Swat and from there toward the headwaters of the Indus and Ganges Rivers.

ORIGINS

The Indo-Aryans probably were descended from a population of Proto-Indo-European speakers who lived on the Eurasian steppes. This ancient population then divided into eastern and western branches. The western branch became the speakers of European languages, except for Basque, Hungarian, Finnish, and Estonian, which are all non-Indo-European languages, and the eastern branch became the speakers of the Iranian languages, which included Proto-Aryan and related languages. The Indo-Aryans separated from the eastern branch, perhaps around 2000 B.C.E., and migrated into northern India during the next several hundred years. There it is believed that the Indo-Aryans encountered the Harappan or Indus Valley civilization and formed elite groups whose language gradually displaced that of the original inhabitants.

HISTORY

The northern ancestors of the Aryan people had domesticated the horse sometime around 4500 B.C.E., as some claim, or 2000 B.C.E., according to others. These early horse keepers developed a mobile pastoral culture. Once the Aryans became established in India, their culture is often called Vedic civilization, named for their religious text the Rig Veda. The word *Aryan* is derived from the Vedic term *arya*, which means "noble"; a similar term is used by the Achaemenid Persians as part of the royal title. The term was erroneously used in 19th- and early-20th-century Europe to refer to the entire Proto-Indo-European language family and was adopted as a racial term most famously by Nazi Germany.

CULTURE

Most of what we know about Indo-Aryan culture is gained from analyses of their earliest religious text, the Rig Veda. We know from this text that the Aryans or their ancestors had domesticated the horse, used spoke-wheeled chariots, and lived primarily as seminomadic pastoralists practicing a little agriculture. There is some speculation that they developed agriculture only after their migration into India, probably having learned its techniques from

Indo-Aryans time line

B.C.E.

4500–4000 The horse is domesticated on the Eurasian steppes.

3500–3000 Proto-Indo-European "pit grave" culture reaches its zenith at the beginning of the Bronze Age.

2500–2000 The Indo-Iranian speakers emerge as the easternmost branch of Indo-European speakers. Scholars sometimes associate the Indo-Iranians with the Andronovo culture in Siberia and the Bactria-Margiana Archaeological Complex in Afghanistan and Turkmenistan. The Proto-Aryan-speaking people separate from the Indo-Iranians around 2000 B.C.E.

2000–1500 The spoke-wheeled chariot appears.

1800–1500 Proto-Indo-Aryan speakers move into present-day India and are thought to form elite groups in the Harappan or Indus Valley culture.

1600 The first undisputed horse remains in India.

1500–1000 The Rig Veda is written and the Vedic culture flourishes in northern India.

700 The approximate date marking the beginning of the Indian Mahajanapadas or Great Kingdoms.

the indigenous population; the same may be true of pottery as well. They lived largely on milk and milk products, grains, and vegetables. As is the case in current Hindu theology cows seem to have been extremely important, both for their economic value as the primary unit of exchange in their nonmonetary existence and as sacred beings. In the Rig Veda cows and goddesses, bulls and gods, are often compared with each other, indicating the importance of both. The other important animal is the horse, which is sometimes considered the most important feature of all Indo-European societies.

The structure of Indo-Aryan society began with the patrilineal family, in which lines of descent are passed from fathers to their children. Groups of families resided together in villages, which were grouped into ever-larger political units, including tribes of several thousand people, headed by a *rajan* or king. There is evidence that some kings may have been elected, but even those who inherited their positions could rule only with the consent and approval of their people, whose will was made known at councils of elders and experts.

Indo-Aryan society was also at least partially structured by the *varna* or caste system, which organized families according to their inherited occupations. The primary varna system then was probably similar to its structure today, with four primary varnas: Brahmin or priests and intellectuals, Kshatriya or kings and warriors, Vaishya or traders, and Sudra or workers. Brahmins and Kshatriyas constituted the upper echelons of Indo-Aryan society, with kings and warriors engaged in frequent intertribal warfare as well as cattle rustling, aided by the rituals and magic of the Brahmin priests.

The religion of the Indo-Aryans also is known to us only through the Rig Veda, which was written centuries after the Indo-Aryans reached India, and through comparing the Rig Veda with the earliest texts of the Iranian-speaking people, the *Gathas.* The elements that are similar in the two, such as the importance of sacrifice, tend to be seen as those that would have been common to the two groups prior to their separation from proto-Indo-Iranians in the third millennium B.C.E. The Rig Veda itself is largely a collection of hymns, myths, and stories, unfortunately, without an explanation of how they fit together into a religious or ideological system.

FURTHER READING

Edwin F. Bryant and Laurie L. Patton, eds. *The Indo-Aryan Controversy: Evidence and Inference in Indian History* (New York: Routledge, 2005).

George Erdosy, ed. *The Indo-Aryans of Ancient South Asia: Language, Material Culture, and Ethnicity* (New York: Walter de Gruyter, 1995).

F. B. J. Kuiper. *The Aryans in the Rigveda* (Leiden: Editions Rodopi, 1991).

Nicholas Sims-Williams, ed. *Indo-Iranian Languages and Peoples* (London: British Academy, 2003).

Indo-Fijians (Fiji Indians, Fijian Indians)

The Indo-Fijians or Fijian Indians as they are sometimes called are the descendants of indentured servants, *girmitya,* who were taken to Fiji during the British colonial period to work in the sugarcane fields and mills. The first ship bearing these servants, the *Leonidas,* arrived in Fiji in 1879 with its human cargo of Indians. Many of these early laborers had poor, landless backgrounds in India and were seeking opportunities away from the poverty of their homeland, but the population included high-caste Brahmins as well as low-caste Shudras. By 1916 the year the final ships arrived, more than 60,000 Indians had been transported to Fiji as laborers; indentured servitude, or *girmit,* was abolished in 1919.

Upon the completion of their work contracts the vast majority of Sirmitya remained in Fiji. They were unable to purchase land but could lease it; many did and began growing sugarcane, tobacco, cotton, and rice. Others opened shops or entered the service professions as public servants, clerks, or domestic workers. Later waves of migration, especially after 1930, also took Indian professionals to Fiji, including business owners, doctors, lawyers, teachers, and others seeking new opportunities to serve the growing Indo-Fijian community.

By the 1940s the Indo-Fijians outnumbered Indigenous Fijians (*See* FIJIANS, INDIGENOUS) by a small percentage and were more unified. The community had developed many religious and educational institutions to serve their families and children. As was often the case in their colonies the British tried to keep the Indo- and Indigenous Fijians fairly separate in their attempt to maintain control over the divided populace, and this policy was aided by the creation of separate educational, social, and religious organizations. In 1940 the Native Lands Trust Board was also introduced, further cementing the different treatment of the two populations when it came to land.

When Fiji attained its independence from Britain in 1970, the two separate peoples were able to work together under the Alliance Party's policy of promoting multiculturalism and multiracialism in the country. By the 1980s, however, conditions had changed in Fiji. A growing sense of indigenous nationalism had turned many against the strong Indo-Fijian community, and there were even calls for repatriation for all Indians. In response the Indo-Fijian community turned away from the traditional political parties and threw its support behind a coalition of the Fiji Labour Party and Indo-Fijian National Federation Party, which won the election in 1987. Dr. Timoci Bavadra, an Indigenous Fijian, formed a cabinet, most of whom were also Indigenous, but then was promptly overthrown by the military under Lieutenant Colonel Rabuka, an Indigenous nationalist who claimed the Bavadra government was Indo-Fijian because it had garnered significant support from that community.

In 1990 the illegitimate government under Rabuka changed the country's constitution to grant even more power to Indigenous Fijians, and two years later Rabuka was elected prime minister, legitimizing his nationalist rule. These actions spurred thousands of wealthy, professional, and skilled Indo-Fijians to leave the country, promoting international pressure on Rabuka to review the 1990 constitution. This was revised in 1997 with a much fairer document, including a bill of rights, and in 1999

INDO-FIJIANS

location:
Fiji

time period:
1879 to the present

ancestry:
Wide variety of Indian caste and ethnolinguistic groups

language:
Most speak Fiji Hindustani or Fiji Hindi; English is a common second language

new elections toppled the Rabuka government in favor of the first Indo-Fijian prime minister, Mehendra Chaudhry.

As had occurred in 1987, the perception that Chaudhry's agenda would favor Indo-Fijians and others outside the traditional Indigenous power structure led to another military coup in 2000. The 1997 constitution was proclaimed illegal and the military appointed an entirely Indigenous government. Again many Indo-Fijians with the ability to leave the country did so; others chose to remain and fight the government in court. Chandrika Prasad, an Indo-Fijian sugarcane farmer, was one of those who remained and fought for the repeal of the 1997 constitution in court. He won, setting the stage for elections in 2001. To this day the government and military in Fiji have not settled down in an appropriate separation of powers, and thousands of Indo-Fijians continue to leave the country when opportunities arise. The exodus has been so great that former prime minister Chaudhry has expressed specific concern about the drain of the most educated and prosperous sectors of the community, leaving behind the poor, less skilled sectors to fend for themselves in a situation of political and economic uncertainty.

Indonesians: nationality (people of Indonesia)

The people of Indonesia are members of hundreds of different ethnolinguistic groups, some of whom are content to be Indonesian citizens, others of whom have been fighting this inclusion off and on for more than half a century.

GEOGRAPHY

Indonesia is a Southeast Asian archipelago of about 6,000 inhabited islands and another 8,000 to 12,000 uninhabited ones, which stretch across the equator and run 3,182 miles east to west, 1,094 miles north to south. Its vast size means that the most strategic shipping lanes connecting the Indian and Pacific Oceans run through Indonesia's 2.5 million square miles of bays, straits, and open ocean. Historically this has meant that all the major civilizations of Asia have exerted great influence on the people of the region.

Of Indonesia's 6,000 or so inhabited island, there are five main ones: Sumatra, Java, Borneo, Sulawesi, and New Guinea. Two of these islands, Borneo and New Guinea, also contain territory owned by other countries. Indonesia's territory in the former is called Kalimantan and sits beside territory owned by Malaysia and Brunei, while the entire eastern half of New Guinea is the independent country of Papua New Guinea. In addition within the larger Indonesian Archipelago there are 62 other, smaller archipelagoes, including the two largest, Nusa Tenggara and Maluku, formerly known as the Moluccas.

The entire region of Indonesia sits astride two tectonic plates, Sunda and Sahel, and the action of the two bumping into each other makes the region extremely vulnerable to earthquakes and volcanic eruptions. There are about 400 volcanoes in the country, about one-quarter of those still active. In Java between 1972 and 1991, 29 separate eruptions were recorded and some of the world's most violent eruptions in recent memory have taken place

INDONESIANS: NATIONALITY

nation:
Republic of Indonesia; Indonesia

derivation of name:
Islands of the Indies

government:
Republic

capital:
Jakarta

language:
Bahasa Indonesia, a form of Malay, and hundreds of other languages; English and Dutch are also used

religion:
Muslim 86.1 percent, Protestant 5.7 percent, Roman Catholic 3 percent, Hindu 1.8 percent, other or unspecified 3.4 percent

earlier inhabitants:
Melanesians, Austronesians

demographics:
Javanese 40.6 percent, Sundanese 15 percent, Madurese 3.3 percent, Minangkabau 2.7 percent, Betawi 2.4 percent, Buginese 2.4 percent, Banten 2 percent, Banjar 1.7 percent, other or unspecified 29.9 percent

---

Indonesians: nationality time line

B.C.E.

60,000–30,000 The Melanesians arrive in New Guinea and spread out to a few neighboring islands.

7000–5000 Agriculture is invented in New Guinea.

2500–2000 The Austronesians arrive in Indonesia.

C.E.

First–12th centuries A large number of Hindu kingdoms emerge on Kalimantan (Borneo), Java, Bali, Sulawesi, and Sumatra.

700–900 Arab traders first arrive in Indonesia and begin converting various groups to Islam.

804 Perlak, the region's first Islamic kingdom, is established in Aceh.

(continues)

Indonesians: nationality time line *(continued)*

1511 The Portuguese land at Malacca and establish the first European colonial presence.

1602 The Dutch arrive and begin colonizing Indonesia.

1799 The Dutch East Indies Company is nationalized.

1811 The British East Indies Company takes over territory formerly held by the Dutch.

1815 The British return the Dutch colony after the latter frees itself from Napoleon's armies.

A volcanic eruption at Gunung Tambora kills 92,000 people.

1816 Pattimura rebels against Dutch rule in the Moluccas.

1825 Prince Diponegoro rebels against the Dutch in Java.

1873 Wars against the Dutch in Aceh and elsewhere begin to shake colonial confidence.

1883 Mount Krakatau erupts and is heard as far away as Perth, Australia, 1,930 miles distant.

1907 The Bataks also engage the Dutch in warfare in an attempt to loosen their colonial grip.

1908 King Udayana of Bali repels the Dutch from his kingdom and retains his autonomy.

1942–45 The Japanese occupy Indonesia, effectively ending the Dutch colonial era.

1949 Indonesia attains independence from the Dutch after several years of civil war.

1953 The Acehnese begin their 10-year struggle against being incorporated into Indonesia.

1961 The West Papuans begin their long struggle for independence from the Dutch and then from the Indonesian state; they continue to rebel today.

1963 Irian Jaya on eastern New Guinea becomes part of Indonesia after the Dutch withdraw from their former colony.

1967 President Sukarno is stripped of his position and military leader Suharto is appointed in his place.

1975 East Timor attains independence from Portugal only to be annexed by Indonesia; East Timor begins the long struggle for freedom that ends in independence in 1999.

1976 The Free Aceh Movement reinvigorates the Acehnese struggle for independence.

1998 President Suharto resigns after winning a seventh term in office when rampant inflation, riots, and other unrest destroy what little legitimacy he retains after decades of human rights abuses. He is replaced by Vice President Habibie.

1999 Jusuf Habibie decides not to run for president and Abdurrahman Wahid is elected.

2001 Sukarno's daughter, Megawati Sukarnoputri, is elected Indonesia's fifth president.

A bombing in a tourist center in Bali and the resulting deaths of several Australians draw Indonesia, the world's largest Muslim country, into the U.S.-led "war on terror."

2004 A tsunami with its epicenter off the coast of Sumatra kills hundreds of thousands of people across a dozen countries.

In October President Sukarnoputri is defeated in the second round of elections by a retired army general, Susilo Bambang Yudhoyono, usually known as Bambang.

2005 The Free Aceh Movement signs a peace agreement with the government and lays down its arms.

2006 Yogyakarta is hit by a 6.3 magnitude earthquake that kills nearly 6,000 people and makes 600,000 homeless.

2007 Flooding in Jakarta destroys tens of thousands of properties and makes hundreds of thousands homeless; about 55 people die.

2008 A 6.2 magnitude earthquake off the coast of West Papua injures several people and does significant damage in several communities.

Former president Suharto is hospitalized with kidney failure and other health problems; he dies not long afterward.

there, including the 1815 eruption at Gunung Tambora, which killed 92,000 people and produced "the year without a summer" throughout the world, and Krakatau's eruptions in 1883 and the 1970s. The 2004 Indian Ocean tsunami that killed hundreds of thousands along the entire perimeter of the ocean had its epicenter at an earthquake off the coast of Sumatra. The tectonic action of these plates has also created numerous mountain ranges, including the highlands of New Guinea, where Puncak Jaya, the country's highest peak at more than 16,500 feet, is located, and dozens of others at more than 10,000 feet on Bali, Java, Lombok, Seram, Sulawesi, and Sumatra.

As a result of differences in elevation above sea level, from 0 to 16,500 feet, Indonesia also experiences a wide range of climates. The coastal lowlands are all tropical, hot, and humid while the highlands range from temperate to snow capped. The majority of the country's population live in the coastal and inland plains.

INCEPTION OF NATION

Indonesia's various peoples have had widely differing histories. Some small tribal communities had no experience with centralized government until the 20th-century imposition by Dutch colonizers, while others had been organized into highly structured Hindu and then Muslim kingdoms as early as the first century C.E. The MELANESIANS of New Guinea probably migrated to that region between 60,000 and 30,000 years ago and invented agriculture between 7000 and 5000 B.C.E., while the dominant Malay-speaking peoples of the country probably arrived only between 2500 and 2000 B.C.E. as part of the greater expansion of AUSTRONESIANS into the Pacific. They carried agriculture with them from their ultimate homeland in southern China.

The contemporary era in the region can probably best be dated from 1511 and the arrival of the Portuguese in Malacca. They entered in search of exotic spices while Roman Catholic missionaries and colonial bureaucrats soon followed. After the Portuguese were the Dutch, who shared the European colonial quest, and the Dutch East Indies Company (VOC) was established in 1602 to handle the flow of spices, produce, hardwood, and other tropical products out of the region. In 1799 the VOC was nationalized and Indonesia became an official Dutch colony, with the exception of a few small Portuguese holdings in what is today East Timor. The Dutch were also unable to expand into the

western half of New Guinea, which was eventually divided between Britain and Germany. In the early 19th century the British joined in the colonial conquest of Indonesia when they built a fort in western Sumatra and then through the British East Indies Company ruled the entire archipelago while Holland was occupied by Napoleon's armies.

The Dutch returned to their Indonesian lands in 1815 but found a population that was increasingly resentful of outside colonialism. Frequent revolts erupted throughout the 19th and early 20th centuries, such as Pattimura's revolt in the Moluccas in 1816, Prince Diponegoro's in Java in 1825, the Padri and Aceh wars in Sumatra starting in 1873, the Batak war in 1907, and King Udayana's in Bali a year later. As a result of these many wars and rebellions, as well as the vast distances and cultural differences in the archipelago, the Dutch were never able to consolidate direct control over the entire region, and in 1942 the JAPANESE were able to occupy it. At first records indicate that the Indonesian people welcomed the Japanese since their rhetoric indicated that they were entering to liberate a fellow Asian population from European influences. This attitude quickly changed, however, when the Japanese turned out to be just as exploitative of the local population as the Dutch had been, and in some cases, much more so.

While the United States and Australia engaged the Japanese in battle throughout the Pacific, from western New Guinea, the Solomon Islands, Guam, Midway, and north all the way to Japan, and the British engaged them on the Malay Peninsula, most of the islands of Indonesia were left alone during the war and were reclaimed from the Japanese only at their final surrender in 1945. The Dutch returned to their former colony in 1945 to discover that two Indonesian nationalists, Sukarno and Hatta, had declared the Republic of Indonesia an independent country on August 17, 1945. The Dutch sent their military into the region to reclaim their colony and were somewhat successful in some regions. However, the war exhausted them and there was no end to the anticolonial rebellion. As a result in 1949 the Dutch withdrew from every island except western New Guinea, which they retained until 1963.

The newly independent Indonesia under its first president, Sukarno, did not have an entirely smooth transition to political and economic autonomy. Immediately following the declaration of independence Christian forces in Maluku loyal to the Dutch began fighting, first to retain the Dutch and then to attain independence from the new Indonesia. Over the course of the next half-century numerous other groups have also tried to withdraw from Indonesia, including the ACEHNESE from 1953 to 1963 and 1976 to 2005, the West Papuans from 1961 to the present, and, most famously, the East Timorese from the time of their independence from Portugal and subsequent annexation by Indonesia in 1975 to independence in 1999. In addition to these major military rebellions numerous other peoples throughout the archipelago have also used a variety of political and economic strategies to limit the centralizing effects of the largely JAVANESE government in Jakarta over their own languages, cultures, and histories.

One result of these many rebellions, plus a communist insurgency that threatened the country in the 1960s, is that the military has always been one of the most important institutions in the country. The first president relied heavily on his military leaders to quell rebellion and help create lasting legitimacy for the new country. The role of the military was solidified when Sukarno was replaced in 1967 by a top general, Suharto, who continued to rule the country with an iron grip. Human rights groups who monitored Indonesia from that year until riots and unrest drove him from power in May 1998, after having won a record seventh term in office earlier in the year, estimate that as many as 2 million Indonesians were killed during his presidency. After a handful of civilian presidents came and went, including the daughter of the first president, in 2004 another military leader was elected president on a platform of fighting terrorism and improving the economy. A book he wrote that was distributed by his presidential campaign laid out a four-part vision for Indonesia: prosperity, peace, justice, and democracy.

CULTURAL IDENTITY

The vast cultural, historic, and geographic differences that mark Indonesia's large population of about 235 million people make it almost impossible to write of a single cultural identity that incorporates all or even most of them. The country's motto, *Bhineka Tunggal Ika*, or Unity in Diversity, gives an indication of the attempts the central government has made to represent and make room for the country's hundreds of ethnic and linguistic groups. One of these efforts has been the attempt to create national identity through *pancasila*, or five principles of Indonesian national identity: belief in one God, just and civilized humanity, nationalism and unity, democracy through discussion and mutual assistance, and social justice and cultural equality. Despite these efforts, however, even citizenship is a strongly contested identity in some regions, especially West Papua and Aceh, despite the peace agreement signed in the latter region in 2005.

Nonetheless, one cultural trait that does unite about 88 percent of the population is Islam. Indonesia is the world's largest Muslim country with more than 207 million people who consider themselves members of this religion. Islam arrived in the archipelago about 13 centuries ago and in some regions quickly replaced the local animistic religion and the forms of Hinduism that had been adopted in some areas over the previous seven centuries. Islam retained its primary position throughout the colonial era, despite Portuguese and Dutch attempts at proselytizing for their respective religions, Roman Catholicism and Dutch Reformed Protestantism; the latter won converts in Maluku, where it remains an important minority religion.

Another cultural feature that has been drawn upon by the national government to try to unite its diverse peoples is the Indonesian national language, Bahasa Indonesia, which means "language of Indonesia." This language is a dialect of Malay and had been the lingua franca of the region for many centuries before being adopted by the government when it declared independence in 1945. Although spoken as a first language by only about 23 million people or about 10 percent of the population, it is a second or third language for at least another 140 million and possibly many more who have not reported it. Most Indonesians learn at least two languages, their local language and its dialect plus Bahasa Indonesia, when they go to school. Textbooks at all levels are produced primarily in this language, with the exception of some university-level books in English; television is broadcast in it, and novels, songs, and other forms of mass media likewise utilize Bahasa Indonesia almost exclusively.

FURTHER READING

Paul Alexander, ed. *Creating Indonesian Cultures* (Sydney: Oceania, 1989).

Eka Darmaputera. *Pancasila and the Search for Identity and Modernity in Indonesian Society: A Cultural and Ethical Analysis* (New York: E. J. Brill, 1988).

P. E. de Josselin de Jong, ed. *Unity in Diversity: Indonesia as a Field of Anthropological Study* (Dordrecht: Foris, 1984).

Frances Gouda. *Dutch Culture Overseas: Colonial Practice in the Netherlands Indies, 1900–1942* (Amsterdam: Amsterdam University Press, 1995).

Katharine E. McGregor. *History in Uniform: Military Ideology and the Construction of Indonesia's Past* (Singapore: NUS Press, 2007).

Leslie Palmier, ed. *Understanding Indonesia* (Brookfield, Vt.: Gower, 1985).

James L. Peacock. *Indonesia: An Anthropological Perspective* (Pacific Palisades, Calif.: Goodyear, 1973).

Jim Schiller and Barbara Martin-Schiller, eds. *Imagining Indonesia: Cultural Politics and Political Culture* (Athens: Ohio University Center for International Studies, 1997).

Indus Valley civilization *See* Harappans.

Intha

The Intha, whose name means "sons of the lake," are members of a small hill tribe residing on and alongside Inle Lake on the Shan Plateau of Myanmar. Linguistic evidence points to Tibeto-Burman ancestry, specifically the Mon people, which indicates that their distant relatives migrated south into mainland Southeast Asia from the Mongolian Plateau possibly about 2,000 years ago. Intha legend states that their more immediate ancestors were relocated to the Inle Lake region from southern Burma in 1353.

Traditional Intha subsistence is based on both fishing and agriculture. Intha men use conical nets to pull fish, especially Inle carp, from the lake's shallow waters. They are well known in Myanmar (Burma) for being able to stand up in their boats and paddle with one leg, which they wrap around the oar for maneuverability. This leaves their hands free to throw and pull in their fishing nets. Intha gardens are equally fascinating to see because they consist of large water hyacinth or bamboo baskets filled with silt, mud, and rotting vegetation drawn up from the lake floor, which float on the lake's surface. In these floating gardens the Intha produce three crops per year of potatoes, tomatoes, cucumbers, melons, cabbage, cauliflower, peas, beans, tobacco, flowers, and many other kinds of fruits and vegetables for consumption, trade, or sale in floating markets. The two most important sources of cash for the Intha are cigar rolling and their renowned weaving, both activities undertaken by women. Intha *lon-gyi*s, 6.5- by 2.5-foot cloths worn in different ways by women and men throughout India and Southeast Asia, are well known for their weft design; red, yellow, and green patterns; and bird and flower images. Some villages specialize in silk cloth and bags while others weave primarily in cotton.

INTHA

location:
Inle Lake on the Shan Plateau, Myanmar (Burma)

time period:
Possibly 1353 to the present

ancestry:
Mon

language:
Intha, a Tibeto-Burman language related to Burmese but with significant vocabulary and pronunciation differences

An Intha man paddling on Inle Lake to the perfect spot in which to use his conical fishing net. *(OnAsia/Don Gurewitz)*

As is evident from their subsistence, the Inle Lake is extremely important to Intha life generally. As do fishing and gardening, life generally takes place on and around the lake in about 20 stilted villages located along the lakeshore and islands, including Inpawkhon, famous for its weaving pattern. A few of these villages are located as far as eight miles into the middle of the lake. Moving from house to house and village to village requires the use of boats, and by very early childhood Inthas of both sexes can swim and boat with ease. Only boys and men, however, use the unique leg-paddling method described above.

As are the majority of the Burmese population, the Intha are Theravada Buddhists. They are especially connected to the Phaundaw Oo pagoda along a lakeside canal, for which they weave the lotus robe worn by the chief monk, but there are many other stilted pagodas, monasteries, and shrines located on the roughly 45-square-mile lake. The Hpaung Daw U pagoda is also very well known for its three-week festival held in September and October, as is Nga Hpe Chaung Monastery, known for its trained jumping cats; monks at Nga Hpe Chaung have trained their cats to leap through hoops held high in the air.

Ismaili Nizaris   *See* Khojas.

Ivatans (people of the Batanes)

The Ivatans are the indigenous inhabitants of the Batanes Islands, the northernmost islands of the Philippine Archipelago. As Austronesians, they have origins in Taiwan, which is actually closer to the Batanes than are the rest of the Philippines, and ultimately southern China. However, the linguistic and archaeological evidence remains unclear about whether the Ivatans settled on these islands immediately upon migrating from Taiwan or whether they traveled north from Luzon at some point after 3000 B.C.E.

The first recorded history of the islands is from 1686, when the Spanish landed there; a group of Dominican friars and priests arrived at that time but did not remain long enough to settle or begin proselytizing. Another group arrived in 1719, but the Spanish did not take formal control over the islands until June 26, 1783, when they annexed them as part of the Philippines colony; the Batanes were the last islands added to the Spanish dominion in the region.

Austronesians migrated to the Philippines thousands of years ago bearing a distinctive combination of agricultural products, domesticated animals, and pottery. The Ivatans even today continue to exhibit some traces of this ancient subsistence pattern: chickens, pigs, and goats are kept as sources of food and farming is the mainstay of most families. Rather than rice, however, the Ivatans generally rely on local root crops such as yams, taro, and sweet potatoes. Rice is an imported product from Luzon, which in recent decades has started to replace these locally grown products. As island dwellers the Ivatans consider fish extremely important; however, the two staple fish, flying fish and dolphin fish, must be caught during the short season from March to May, the only months when typhoons and other tropical storms do not make the seas nearly impossible to navigate. The difficulty in navigating around the Batanes also makes direct communication and trade with Luzon difficult for most of the year, necessitating recycling, reusing, and saving all important resources.

The most important social unit among the Ivatans is the family, especially the extended family, most members of whom live together in large multigenerational households. Beyond the extended family larger kin groupings are also important units for sharing agricultural and other subsistence tasks, especially fishing during the short season, food, and ritual obligations. Building and maintaining extensive kin ties, especially those through blood but also through marriage, are among the most important tasks of an adult Ivatan; for example, visiting close and even distant relatives is vitally important whenever an individual leaves his or her own village. In other words kin ties have to be demonstrated regularly through visitation, sharing food, and working together.

One of the characteristics the Ivatans are most known for outside their homeland is the sturdiness of their homes, built to withstand the raging typhoons that visit their islands regularly. Prior to the colonial era these houses were built from bamboo, wood, and a kind of local grass, known as *cogon*, and were set very low to the ground as protection against powerful tropical winds. They were generally located on rocky hillsides, which formed a sort of protection against the winds. In the 18th and 19th centuries the Spanish introduced stone building techniques so that today Ivatan stone houses are known as "traditional" in the area. Like their predecessors, these stone houses are extremely

IVATANS

location:
Batanes Islands, the
Philippines

time period:
3000 B.C.E. to the present

ancestry:
Austronesian

language:
Ivatan, a Northern
Philippine language
within the larger
Austronesian family

sturdy with thick cogon thatch roofs able to survive most storms unscathed; both roofs and walls are generally built about a yard thick while the floor is raised about two yards above the earth on poles. These houses are located in villages dominated by a headman or chief.

As are most Filipinos, the Ivatans are largely Roman Catholic with a significant number of pre-Christian beliefs and practices still evident among them. The most important of these pre-Christian beliefs is the strength of the *anyitus* or ancestral spirits, to whom offerings and rituals are frequently observed to make sure that their anger does not visit disaster on an individual or family group. Illness; the death of a child, healthy adult, or animal; and natural disasters are often seen as the result of an *anyitu*'s anger, which requires gifts of food or an animal sacrifice.

J

Jains (Jainist)

The Jains in India are adherents of the ancient religion of Jain Dharma or Jainism. They constitute a group of people in the country because their religious beliefs and life practices distinguish them from most of the rest of the population; the Jain reject caste, have relative gender equality, emphasize education, and maintain a general ascetic attitude toward life. There are five separate Jain groups throughout India, each one somewhat different from the others in terms of language and historical factors; these are the Jains of central, western, northern, southern, and eastern India, respectively. Altogether there about 110 separate Jain communities in India containing about 4 million people.

The exact founding date of Jain Dharma is unknown, and its earliest history is known to us only through mythology or legend. Prior to about 599 B.C.E. Jain tradition says there existed 24 Jinas or Tirthankaras, who lived in east India and freed their souls from existence through freedom from karma. According to this tradition the first Jina was a giant who lived about 8.4 million years ago while the last one, Mahavira, the Great Hero, was born in 599 B.C.E. Sometimes Mahavira is presented as the founder of the Jain community comparable to Buddha or Jesus in their own religions, but most Jains would dispute this interpretation of his role. Instead he was the last of the ancients and served as a mediator between their world and our own. Jain tradition says that in 527 B.C.E. he fasted himself to death in the ultimate ascetic sacrifice, known as *salekhana*.

According to the Jain belief system the universe, which has no beginning or end point, is made up of a series of layers categorized into seven groups. The supreme abode is where the Tirthankaras and other liberated souls live, while the upper world contains 30 heavens of the celestial beings; surrounding the upper world is universe space containing nothing but clouds. The middle world is where Earth and our own universe exist, while the netherworld contains seven layers of hell. The *nigoda* is the lowest layer containing life, while the space beyond is infinite but contains nothing: no matter, no time, no motion, no rest.

The goal of all Jains is to reach the supreme abode by freeing themselves from all karma. Unlike for Buddhism, in which only negative karma must be cleansed away or avoided, for Jains all karma, positive and negative, must be avoided. Karma is conceptualized as matter in the Jain universe, and thus any remnant of it, positive or negative, is enough to lead to reincarnation of the body back on Earth. To achieve *moksha* or liberation from reincarnation, all attachments must be abandoned through ascetic practice. The five principles that Jains believe lead to this state of nonbeing are *ahimsa* or nonviolence, *satya* or telling the truth, *asteya* or not stealing, *Brahma-charya* or chastity, and *aparigraha* or detachment from material goods,

JAINS

location:
India and a diaspora in the United States, United Kingdom, Australia, Canada, and elsewhere

time period:
Before about 599 B.C.E. to the present

ancestry:
Indian

language:
Hindi, Gujarati, Kannada, Tamil, and most of the other major languages of India

places, and even other people. As a result of these principles Jains are vegetarians and many spend time every day reading sacred texts to help them with detachment and the other four principles.

· The life course of every Jain ideally passes through four separate stages: student, family, family combined with service to the social good, and monkhood and renunciation. The last stage, that of the monk or nun, is the most difficult and is not taken up by the vast majority of Jains. Monks and nuns give up attachment to their families, all goods, other people, and, in the case of monks from one sect, all clothing. They tend to live with just a handful of fellow monks or nuns rather than in large monasteries and spend their days in prayer and learning. They accept food from laypeople in order to eat, but it must not be food prepared especially for them but rather leftovers.

The centrality of student life means that in contemporary India the Jains are the best-educated group on average with the highest literacy rates for both men and women in the country at 94 and 90 percent, respectively. Jains are also believed to be among the wealthiest groups in India, in part because many go into business rather than agriculture or the trades in the belief that these activities are less *himsic*, a term often translated as "harmful." Certainly the wealth accumulated through business makes it more difficult to engage in the fifth principle, detachment from material goods, but Jains often eschew grand displays of their wealth and prefer donating large amounts to charitable organizations, especially temple building.

As the similarities in literacy rates between Jain men and women show, the religion tends to advocate more gender equality than many other religions. This is part of the overall focus in Jainism on the equality of all sentient beings including fish, land animals, and humans. Nonetheless men and women in this group are not entirely equal, with one sect, the Digambaras, being less so than the other, the Svetambaras. Adherents of the former believe that women are inherently *himsic* and must be reborn as men before being able to achieve the ultimate liberation or *moksha* while members of the other sect disagree.

FURTHER READING

Lawrence A. Babb. *Absent Lord: Ascetics and Kings in a Jain Ritual Culture* (Berkeley and Los Angeles: University of California Press, 1995).

Mahavira

Mahavira is best remembered as a critical figure in the propagation of Jainism. He was born Prince Varhaman in 599 B.C.E., his parents were King Siddartha and Queen Trishala of the ancient Indian kingdom of Vaishali, or what is now modern-day Bihar, India. At the age of 30 Mahavira severed ties with his family and kingdom to live the life of an ascetic, an individual who practices abstinence from pleasure to purify the soul and become egoless. In his 12 years as an ascetic Mahavira renounced all forms of possession, including his own clothes, and spent much of his time meditating. By the end of his 12 years of asceticism he reportedly achieved Kevala Jnana, or "Enlightenment," the highest level of knowledge that a soul can obtain. He spent the rest of his life traveling through India, often barefoot and nearly naked in extreme weather, preaching the five main tenets of Jainism: nonviolence, truthfulness, avoidance of stealing, chastity, and nonpossession. He attracted hundreds of thousands of followers and is credited with the spread of Jainism throughout India. He is believed to have died in 527 B.C.E. at age 72.

Paul Dundas. *The Jains* (New York: Routledge, 1992).

P. S. Jaini. *Gender and Salvation: Jaina Debates on the Spiritual Liberation of Women* (Berkeley and Los Angeles: University of California Press, 1991).

Japanese (Nihonjin, Yamatonchu)

The Japanese are the dominant ethnic group in the state of Japan.

GEOGRAPHY

The Japanese Archipelago is a 1,500-mile-long group of islands bounded on the east by the Pacific Ocean and on the west by the Sea of Japan. It is located about 190 miles from Russia in the north, 110 miles from Korea in the southwest, and 480 miles from China. The archipelago is made up of more than 3,000 islands; the four main ones, from south to north, are Kyushu, Shikoku, Honshu, and Hokkaido. The northernmost portion of Honshu and all of Hokkaido, while thoroughly Japanese today, were not completely under the authority of the emperor until the 19th century, since the geography and climate limited the ability of the Japanese to displace the AINU.

The terrain of most of the islands is relatively rough; about 70 percent of the land is taken up by mountains, with the famous Mt. Fuji the tallest at 12,390 feet. The country's 60 active volcanoes and frequent earthquakes, the most famous recently being the Kobe earthquake of 1995, which destroyed most of the city of Kobe, are the result of the islands' location

Japan

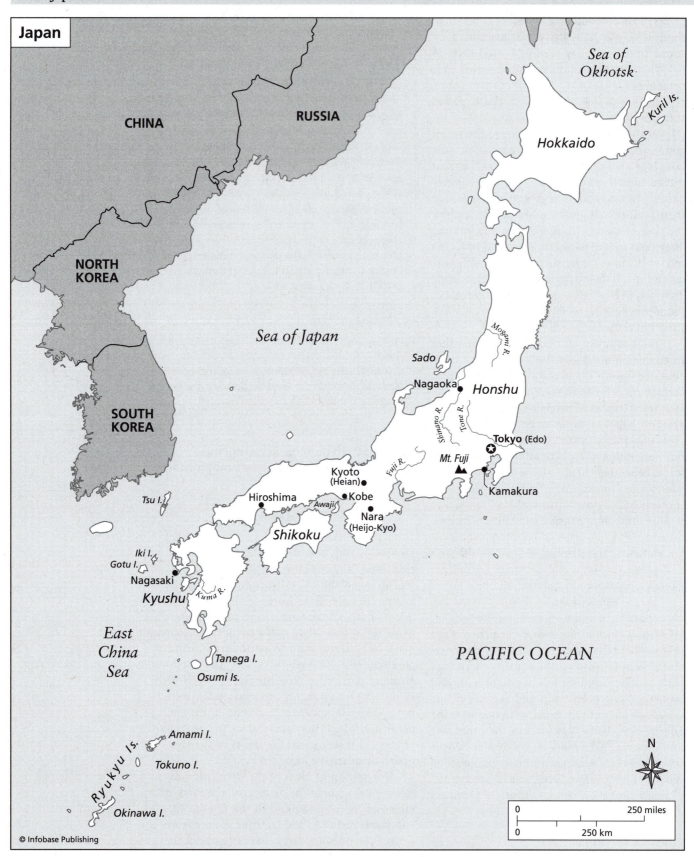

CHINA

RUSSIA

Sea of Okhotsk

NORTH KOREA

Hokkaido

Kuril Is.

Sea of Japan

SOUTH KOREA

Mogami R.

Sado

Nagaoka

Honshu

Shinano R.

Tone R.

Tokyo (Edo)

Kyoto
(Heian)

Fuji R.

Mt. Fuji

Tsu I.

Hiroshima

Awaji

Kobe

Kamakura

Nara
(Heijo-Kyo)

Shikoku

Iki I.

Gotu I.

Nagasaki

Kuma R.

Kyushu

*East
China
Sea*

Tanega I.

Osumi Is.

PACIFIC OCEAN

Ryukyu Is.

Amami I.

Tokuno I.

N

Okinawa I.

0		250 miles
0		250 km

Japanese time line

B.C.E.

10,700 The invention of pottery in Japan, the first in the world, by the Jomon people.

400 Agriculture and a plethora of other material artifacts of Korean origin appear in Japan, marking the beginning of the Yayoi period of Japanese history.

100 Class divisions begin to appear, as evident in burial sites. Warfare also increases, as seen in fortifications and military materiel in the physical remains from this era.

C.E.

300 The Kofun period of Japanese history begins with its distinctive keyhole-shaped burial mounds.

645 The Taika land reforms, which eventually diminish the power of the emperor and exalt that of the nobility.

710–94 The Nara period, named for the kingdom that established itself at Hiejo-kyo.

712 Publication of the first Japanese chronicle, which marks for many the transition from proto-Japanese to Old Japanese history, language, and culture.

794–1185 The Heian period, during which the capital is moved to Kyoto.

1068 The end of the Fujiwara family's de facto control of Japan's government, which begins at the start of the Heian period and peaks in 1016.

1185–1333 The Kamakura shogunate, with the usurpation of power by the military with its headquarters in Kamakura; the emperor remains in Kyoto as the government's figurehead.

1191 Zen Buddhism arrives in Japan from Korea and China.

1274 The Mongol invasions are repelled as they are again in 1281, but the military government is weakened by the process.

1333–1573 The Muromachi period, named for the Kyoto district that houses Shogun Ashikaga Takauji's military government.

1467–1568 The Sengoku, or Civil War, era.

1542 Portuguese traders and Christian missionaries land on Kyushu and introduce firearms and their religion, both of which are taken up more in western Japan than the east.

1573–1600 The Azuchi-Momoyama period, in which Japan is reunified by Oda Nobunaga after a long period of civil strife.

1582 Oda Nobunaga is killed, making way for Toyotomi Hideyoshi to consolidate his power over a newly reunited Japan in 1590.

1592 Toyotomi Hideyoshi invades Korea in his attempt to control both Korea and China. He fails.

1600–1868 The Tokugawa era, when the capital is moved to Edo (Tokyo) and Japan tries to remain isolated from increasing Western pressure in the region.

1853–54 U.S. Commodore Perry begins the process of opening Japan foreign trade.

1868–1912 The Meiji Restoration restores the emperor as the central authority throughout Japan; the modernization of the state is completed.

1876 The Korea-Japanese Treaty of Amity opens three Korean ports to Japanese trade and ends Korea's long-standing position as a Chinese tributary state.

1894–95 The Japanese defeat China in the Sino-Japanese War and receive Taiwan as one of the spoils of war.

1904–05 The Japanese victory over Russia in the Russo-Japanese War is the first time since the rise of Europe as a world power that an Asian country defeats a European one on the battlefield.

1910 The Japanese annex Korea and bring an end to the 518-year-old Choson dynasty.

(continues)

JAPANESE

location:
The Japanese Archipelago

time period:
400 B.C.E. to the present

ancestry:
Unknown but probably Asian immigrants from the Korean Peninsula mixed with indigenous Ainu-like Jomon peoples

language:
Japanese, a language distantly related to the Altaic language family, possibly most closely related to Korean. Some scholars also believe Japanese was related to some of the extinct languages of the Korean Peninsula, particularly those of the Koguryo Kingdom.

Japanese time line *(continued)*

1912–45 This period does not bear a formal name in Japanese history but is often referred to as the era of militarism.

1931 Japanese armies occupy Manchuria and establish the puppet state of Manchukuo.

1933 Japan withdraws from the League of Nations over criticism of its actions in China.

1937–45 Second Sino-Japanese War. The Japanese occupy much of coastal China and commit numerous atrocities in the city of Nanjing but are never able to force full capitulation by the Chinese government.

1941 The Japanese air force attacks the U.S. naval base at Pearl Harbor, pulling the United States into World War II.

1942 The Battle of Midway turns the tide against Japan and toward the Allies, although the war continues for three more years.

1945 The United States drops atomic bombs on Hiroshima and Nagasaki, forcing the complete surrender of the Japanese.

1947 Japan's new constitution, largely drawn up by the U.S. occupying forces under General Douglas MacArthur, takes effect.

1952 The U.S. occupation of Japan ends.

1956 Japan normalizes its relations with the USSR.

1964 Tokyo hosts the summer Olympics, proving to the world that Japan has cast off the militarism and devastation of the past.

1972 The U.S. occupation of Okinawa comes to an end and Japan and China normalize their relations.

1980s Japanese firms purchase companies, land, and property throughout the world, causing fear in the United States, Australia, and elsewhere, of a Japanese economic takeover that would be much more difficult to combat than Japanese militarism had been.

1990–2000s Long-term recession sets back Japanese economic growth and forces both economic and political reforms to begin to repair the damage.

1998 Nagano, Japan, hosts the winter Olympics.

2006 Japan's aging population and enormous national debt, 176 percent of gross domestic product (GDP), cause increasing concern about the country's long-term economic growth.

on the Pacific "Ring of Fire," the world's most active earthquake zone. Japan's rivers are also more dramatic than those of many comparable areas, with frequent flooding due to the large amounts of water that must be carried on steep but short riverbeds. The Mogami, the Fuji, and the Kuma Rivers are the fastest-running rivers in Japan, while the Shinano is the longest and the Tone carries the most water.

Japan's mountainous terrain, frequent flooding, and high percentage of forest cover, which at 70 percent is the greatest percentage in the developed world, mean that agricultural land has always been at a premium. Nonetheless the Japanese have tried to be self-sufficient in rice, their staple food, and their warm, wet climate has been conducive to achieving that goal in most years. Japan receives about 120 inches of rain per year, most falling during the summer growing season. This moisture, combined with rich volcanic soils and a warm climate, makes Japan extremely fertile and able to produce about 800 percent more food per square mile than is the case in Great Britain. Nonetheless only about 14 percent of Japan is currently farmland, and the Japanese import about 60 percent of their food products.

ORIGINS

The origins of the Japanese people are among the most contested scientific data in the world, in large part because many Japanese people are unwilling to learn the truth if it means disrupting their myths of uniqueness and divine origins. Before World War II it was a crime in Japan to question the divinity of the Japanese royal family and the supporting mythology. Even today many Japanese archaeologists believe that all human remains on the islands are those of Japanese people rather than an indigenous population that may have differed greatly from the present-day ethnic group.

Despite the difficulty in studying this topic, today there are at least three theories concerning the origins of the Japanese people that are accepted in different academic circles. The first of these is that the indigenous JOMON peoples, whose distinctive pottery and way of life are evident throughout Japan from about 12,700 years ago until about 400 B.C.E., adopted agriculture from Korea and ultimately became the modern Japanese people. This first theory requires its adherents to believe that the Japanese are the descendants of a population that entered the archipelago about 30,000 years ago when lowered sea levels created land bridges between Japan and the Asian mainland. According to the second theory the hunting and gathering Jomon were largely displaced by peoples from Korea who took agriculture and iron tools to the archipelago about 2,400 years ago. The third theory posits that a small wave of migrant KOREANS from the Korean Peninsula entered Japan about 2,400 years ago and combined with the indigenous Jomon to form the modern Japanese.

While the first of these theories is favored by most scholars in Japan, it is seen as the least likely possibility by physical anthropologists from the West because it presumes, uniquely in world history, that the introduction of agriculture did not mean the displacement and near-elimination of a prior hunting-and-gathering population. The lack of physical resemblance between most modern Japanese and the indigenous Jomon, who are believed to have resembled the Ainu rather than other East Asians, also suggests that the second or third theory is more likely than the first. Finally the archaeological record in Japan after 400 B.C.E. indicates the adoption of not only agriculture from Korea but also other aspects of Korean material culture including pottery types, bronze jewelry, weaving, glass beads, tools, and architectural style. All of this evidence seems to point to the large-scale replacement of the indigenous Jomon people with peoples from the Korean Peninsula.

There is a problem with this theory as well, however, because of the great disparity between the Japanese and Korean languages. The linguistic evidence alone points to a separation of at least 4,000 years between speakers of these two languages, almost twice as long as the period posited by theories two and three

but much shorter than the time assumed by theory one. Many Western linguists solve this dilemma by pointing out that modern Korean is the descendant of just one of the three dominant languages known on the peninsula at the time of the potential large-scale migration of peoples from Korea to Japan, that of the Kingdom of Shilla. In 400 B.C.E., however, Shilla did not make contact with Japan; rather, it was the Kingdom of Koguryo, which ruled in the northern half of the Korean Peninsula and into Manchuria and spoke a language that differed significantly from that of Shilla. In addition although there are very few Koguryo texts to work from, those that have been found do seem to resemble Old Japanese to a great degree. Nonetheless many scholars, especially in Japan, remain unconvinced, and with this contradictory evidence and the political ramifications of each of these theories, it will probably be several generations before the mystery of Japanese origins has been solved and accepted throughout the world.

The period of pre-Japanese history between the introduction of agriculture in 400 B.C.E. and the establishment of the Kofun culture in the fourth century C.E. is sometimes called the Yayoi period, named after the region in which distinctive pottery from this period was first found. Yayoi society was relatively egalitarian as had been the prior hunting-and-gathering Jomon society, but by around 100 B.C.E. distinct class differences became apparent. In some of the grave sites of that period have been found luxury items imported from China, such as jade and bronze pieces, while others had minimal accoutrements.

From about 300 C.E. until about 700 the burials of elite people took on even greater distinction; the tombs were covered by earth mounds in the shape of a keyhole. These burials, called *kofun,* which gives the period its name, were enormous structures of up to 1,500 feet in length and 100 feet in height. They provide evidence of significant political unity, since they are almost all the same shape, and of the ability of some individuals to control the labor of many others. At this time indigenous religious beliefs are thought to have been transformed into a state religion, Shinto; Buddhism was introduced from Paekche in Korea; and the Chinese calendar, writing system, and style of leadership emerged. In the fifth century the kings in what is today Nara Prefecture introduced the title of emperor and consolidated their power so that by 712 and the publication of the first Japanese chronicle proto-Japanese society had become truly Japanese.

HISTORY

Nara and Heian Periods

The brief Nara period, which begins about 710 C.E., marks the beginning of Old Japanese history, distinct from the proto-Japanese periods that preceded it. The period begins with the establishment of the first Japanese capital at Heijo-kyo or what is today Nara, a city built largely on a Chinese model. Many other cultural features also entered Japan from China in the Nara period, particularly the arts and those elements pertaining to the establishment of a centralized government and extensive national bureaucracy. This period also saw the explosion of interest in Buddhism in Japan with the building of many new temples in the capital and throughout the country. After just 74 years the capital was moved from Nara to Nagaoka and a decade later to Heian or Kyoto, where it remained for the next millennium. This latter move came about because Emperor Kanmu had experienced much misfortune in Nagaoka, including the deaths of both his mother and his wife, and he decided the city was bad luck for him.

The Heian period, which lasted from 794 until 1185, is notable for the increasing "japa-nization" of Chinese imports, the ramification of a change in the tax code that had occurred centuries earlier, and the rise of several noble families who challenged the emperor for centralized control. Two of the most important japanified cultural features of the Heian period were the Hiragana and Katakana Japanese alphabets. Both of these alphabets are based on Kanji, the alphabet imported to Japan from China much earlier in the common era, but transformed to enable use by Japanese women and monks, respectively. Chinese music that had been imported during the Nara period was also transformed in the Heian into Gagaku, the specifically Japanese court music of this early period. Japanese literature and artforms, including Japanese themes and motifs, also flourished, and some of the leading poets and novelists were women.

During the Heian period the Taika land reforms, which had been adopted from China in 645 and resulted in the state redistribution of all land, produced a disastrous lack of funds at the national level. The Taika reforms had given all peasants an equal amount of land in exchange for a certain percentage of crop yields. The high level of taxation forced many farmers to sell their plots to large landowners or to Buddhist temples, many of which were able to escape the taxation requirement. As a result the emperor's government was often extremely short of funds during the Heian period, allowing the emergence of a new group of power holders: land-owning aristocrats. One of these aristocratic families, the Fujiwara, had been consolidating its power for generations and dominated the political scene throughout much of the Heian period. Through strategic marriages the Fujiwara family became part of the emperor's inner circle and was able to control many important political offices throughout the country. The rise of such families was accompanied by the emergence of a new class at the top of the social hierarchy, the samurai, military men who provided security to the wealthy of Japan. In 1016 Fujiwara Michinaga was the de facto ruler of all Japan through his kinship and political ties; two nephews and three grandsons served as emperors and four daughters as empresses. Finally however, in 1068 the new emperor, Go-Sanjo, was able to overthrow the powerful Fujiwara family and rule the country himself.

The Shogunates

The period following the Heian, the Kamakura shogunate, is notable for the emergence of the samurai class as the top political actors in the country. This period also saw the introduction of the Zen sect of Buddhism in 1191 and in 1232 the Joei Shikimoku legal code, which emphasized Confucian values such as loyalty to one's superior and centralized political control. The emperor continued to have his court at Kyoto and to be considered the divine head of the Japanese people, but in fact Yoritomo Minamoto with his samurai government at Kamakura became the political head of the country in 1185. The Minamoto family had begun its ascent during the middle of the 11th century, when the family controlled the military that drew Honshu into the Japanese political sphere during the Early and Later Three Years Wars in 1050–59 and 1083–87, respectively. The Minamoto family finally consolidated its power in 1185 by defeating the rival Taira family in the five-year Gempei War; Yoritomo Minamoto became shogun, head military leader, in 1192. The family limited the power of some of the most militant of Buddhist sects, which had been fighting one another for access to political and economic power and patronage.

Yoritomo Minamoto reigned for just seven years before his death in 1199 provided an opportunity for the emperor to try to reassert his power. These maneuvers resulted in the Jokyo Disturbance in 1221 and finally in the defeat of the emperor's army at Kyoto by Kamakura samurai. This disturbance allowed the Hojo clan to emerge as the actual head of the Kamakura government, beginning with Hojo Tokimasa. The redistribution of land bought the loyalty of powerful allies throughout Japan so that in all 16 Hojo clan members served as regents between 1199 and 1333, ruling Japan from Kamakura while the divine emperors held their powerless courts in Kyoto.

The year 1274 presented a new challenge to the Japanese people and their rulers in the form of the MONGOLS, who invaded Kyushu. Fortunately for the Japanese this first attempt at conquest was thwarted by bad weather conditions, which gave them time to prepare for the Mongols' second attempt in 1281; this, too, was relatively unsuccessful because of bad weather. However, despite the Mongols' inability to conquer Japan, the extensive military preparations that the Mongol presence forced upon the Kamakura government weakened the shogunate to such a degree that in 1333 the emperor Go-Daigo overthrew the Hojo regent and reestablished himself as the country's centralized power. Samurai who had expected payment for their services from Kamakura were disappointed, for the government was unable to pay them without a victory over the Mongols. The samurai ceased being loyal to the regent and either stayed out of the fray in 1333 or sided with the emperor.

The 240-year period following the Kamakura is known in Japanese history as the Muromachi period, named after the district in Kyoto in which the ruling shogun located his government from 1378 until 1573. Although the emperor had restored his power through a challenge to the weakened Hojo clan in 1333, he was unable to maintain his position for long. By 1338 Ashikaga Takauji, a former imperial samurai, had named himself shogun and become the de facto ruler of Japan. At the same time within the royal family a schism occurred in 1336 based on a succession problem that emerged at the death of Emperor Go-Saga in 1272. Between 1336 and 1392 Japan actually had two emperors, one in the north, the other in the south, in addition to the Ashikaga regent. These two emperors and their armies fought each other many times for supremacy; several times during the 56-year period the capital at Kyoto was destroyed. The northern emperor,

The Hoshun-in Subtemple in northern Kyoto is part of the Daitokuji, built in the 14th century. Its lake and stone gardens, as well as its age, make it one of the most famous in the ancient Japanese capital. *(OnAsia/John Lander)*

Go-Komatsu, finally achieved ascendancy in 1392.

During the Muromachi period Japan's leaders sought closer connections between their country and Ming China and reformed the country's economic system to favor the development of markets and new social classes. Agricultural techniques also improved, allowing for a population increase throughout the period. In 1572 Portuguese traders and Christian missionaries arrived in Japan carrying their modern weapons and religion of salvation with them. The outsiders attracted the attention of warlords throughout western Japan, who converted to Christianity in order to gain trade advantages over their rivals. The other development for which the period is known is the rise of the *daimyo* class, a new kind of feudal lord who was able to consolidate his power over huge territories, as large as entire provinces. These daimyo engaged in almost constant battles with their rivals during the age of Civil Wars, 1467–1568. By the end of the Muromachi period the Ashikaga rulers had diminished in power and stature as a result of these incessant wars until their influence in the provinces was entirely gone. The landowning military families or *ji-samurai* with the daimyo at their heads controlled commerce, taxation, politics, and the military on a regional basis.

One of these daimyo, Oda Nobunaga, emerged from the civil war era as the single most powerful man in Japan. He captured Kyoto in 1568 and finally overthrew the last Ashikaga regent in 1573, ushering in the Azuchi-Momoyama period (1573–1600). Following these victories he continued to eliminate other rivals for power, including other warlords and several Buddhist sects that controlled land and military in certain provinces. The Takeda clan, which had been powerful in eastern Japan, was defeated in 1575 after the death of its leader, Shingen, but Nobunaga could not eliminate all of his rivals, and in 1582 he was murdered and his headquarters at Azuchi castle captured. One of his generals, Toyotomi Hideyoshi, continued the work begun by Nobunaga. He quickly retook Azuchi Castle and by 1590 had reunited Japan by destroying the infrastructure and networks established by the rival daimyo during the age of civil wars. Samurai were forced to live in castle towns rather than in the countryside, and farmers and monks were forced to give up their weapons in a campaign known as the Sword Hunt of 1588. A land survey and national census were also undertaken during this period in order to strengthen the central government through knowledge of its territorial and human resources. Hideyoshi also attempted to rid Japan of Christians and their missionaries, believing that this new religion blocked his ability to gain absolute control over his people. Not content with control over all of Japan, in 1592 Hideyoshi invaded Korea after its refusal to aid in his quest to conquer China; instead joint Korean and Chinese forces succeeded in pushing the Japanese off the peninsula in 1598, the year of Hideyoshi's death.

Hideyoshi's death opened the door for Tokugawa Ieyasu, one of Nobunaga and Hideyoshi's leading military figures, to emerge as the de facto ruler of Japan with his victory over his rivals in the Battle of Sekigahara in 1600. The period from 1600 to 1868 is named the *Tokugawa era* because shoguns from this clan dominated the government at this time. They also moved the Japanese capital from Kyoto, where it had been since the eighth century, to Edo or Tokyo, as it is known today.

At the beginning of the Tokugawa era, also sometimes called the Edo period, Japan opened some limited trade relations with the English and Dutch and continued to trade with the Portuguese, but by 1639 most contact with the outside world had been eliminated. The two exceptions to this rule were the limited commerce that continued with China and with the Dutch, but only through the port of Nagasaki. In a further attempt to limit outside influences Christianity was persecuted rather strenuously from 1614 until the end of the era, and from 1633 external travel was essentially forbidden for all Japanese, even the nobility. Internally, however, Japan flourished, with the samurai class turning to martial arts, literature, and philosophy to replace its military activities. In addition both farmers and traders increased their economic activities throughout the period. Neo-Confucianism became the most important philosophy of the day, with its stress on strict class differences, loyalty, morals, and education. Indeed class differences became so codified during this period that they developed into a castelike system in which samurai, peasants, artisans, and merchants were unable to change the class into which they were born; the fifth class, the *eta* or outcasts, considered impure and dangerous, were also unable to rise above their lowly position in Japanese society. The descendents of this group continue to reside in Japan today as the Burakumin.

The Tokugawa period saw the gradual decrease in power held by the shogun's government in Tokyo during the course of 268 years in power. One cause for this was bad luck in the form of natural disasters that led to famine, higher taxes, and riots in the countryside. Another cause was the rise in the merchant class's status in relation to that of the samurai, some of whom became dependent on wealthy merchants for patronage. Government corruption and incompetence also contributed to the general decline of the shogun's position, until finally in 1868 the emperor's status as ruler of Japan was regained in the Meiji Restoration.

Restoration

The restoration of the emperor Meiji led to significant changes throughout Japanese society. The concessions gained by U.S. commodore Matthew Perry in opening Japan up for trade, which occurred in 1854, finally came to fruition after 1868. Many other Western nations were also able to sign one-sided treaties that gave them significant economic and legal advantages over the Japanese in their own country. In reaction to this humiliation the emperor and his clique of nobles and samurai carried out drastic reforms of the country's education, legal, governance, military, and economic systems. Japan adopted Western-style technology and science, universal conscription, a European-style constitution with provisions for the elimination of class distinctions and for religious freedom and the development of a parliament, an army modeled on that of Prussia, and a navy modeled on Great Britain's. The samurai lost their special privileges and the daimyo had to return all of their land to the emperor, who restructured the country into prefectures in 1870. In exchange many Japanese were able to travel overseas to study, and powerful family businesses, called *zaibatsu,* received direct governmental support for research, development, and even production and distribution. After a brief financial crisis in the 1880s brought about by the increase in spending these reforms engendered, the Japanese currency system was also transformed and the Bank of Japan created. While these changes and Westernization meant that Japan soon outstripped its regional rivals for power, as demonstrated in 1894–95 when Japan defeated China in the Sino-Japanese War, there was also a crisis in identity for many Japanese people, who began to wonder what it meant to be Japanese in this new context. As a result conservative, nationalistic images and practices also emerged as powerful forces during the Tokugawa period, including Shintoism, Confucianism, and even emperor worship. Japanese emperors had always been seen as divine, and this cult became much more important during Meiji's reign.

In 1904–05 Japan proved itself once again to be a formidable enemy, this time defeating Russia in the Russo-Japanese War. This victory alerted not only Japan's Asian neighbors but the entire world that the Japanese army and navy were among the best. This victory also allowed Japan to annex Korea by 1910. The death of Emperor Meiji in 1912 did not interrupt the strengthening of Japan's military or the quest to join the European countries as a colonial power, though it did shift power from the weak emperor Taisho to the diet or parliament.

Japan participated with the Allied powers in World War I but only in limited ways, by liberating former German colonies in parts of the North Pacific. At first these colonies were of little use to Japan in its attempts to rebuild after the devastating Kanto earthquake in 1923 and the Great Depression of the 1930s brought their economy to a standstill. However, with the militarization of Japanese society in the 1930s and

---

Emperor Meiji

Emperor Meiji was born Prince Matsuhito on November 3, 1852, during a time when Japan was an isolated feudal country, the borders of which could not be crossed either by residents leaving or strangers entering. The son of Emperor Komei, Matsuhito was born into the Tokugawa shogunate, a clan that had governed Japan since 1603 through a system of military rule, but this rule was challenged only months after Matsuhito's birth, when Commodore Matthew Calbraith Perry led a fleet of black U.S. ships into Edo Bay and forced Japan to open its borders for trade in the Treaty of Kanagawa. The signing of the treaty was followed by a period of civil unrest as rival clans attempted to seize power, but in 1867, at the age of 15, Matsuhito took the throne and became Emperor Meiji, meaning "enlightened ruler." Little is known regarding how much authority Meiji actually wielded, as power had shifted from the Tokugawa clan to the Satsumo and Choshu clans and Meiji acted as little more than a representative. Nevertheless Japan flowered under his reign. The year following his ascension to the throne Emperor Meiji promulgated the Charter Oath, which shifted the feudal Japanese government to a modern democratic one that emphasized equality among classes, obligatory education, open discussion, and the abolition of oppressive laws and customs. His reign was also marked by a sudden nationwide move toward Westernization. Japanese officials were sent to the United States and Europe to study Western politics, economics, science, and culture, and many Japanese students were sent to Western universities and Western teachers invited to teach in Japan. Emperor Meiji personally promoted the campaign for Westernization by wearing Western style clothes. Under his rule Japan emerged from an isolated nation into a competitive world power. Though he had no children with his wife, Empress Haruko, he had 15 children by five concubines before his death in 1912.

---

the need for resources and cheap labor these colonies in the Marshall Islands and Micronesia became extremely important. They later served as bases from which the Japanese conquered much of the Pacific in World War II.

The first phase of Japanese involvement in global warfare began in 1931 when Japanese forces on the mainland occupied Manchuria. Within one year the Kwantung Army, as these Japanese forces came to be known, established the puppet state of Manchukuo, forcing the resident Chinese and other subordinate groups to learn Japanese and adopt Japanese surnames. That year, 1932, also saw Japan bomb Shanghai in order to put China on notice for allowing anti-Japanese movements to take place in the city. All of these incidents were just preludes to the Second Sino-Japanese War, fought on Chinese soil from 1937 until the end of World War II in 1945. The Japanese took the city of Nanjing and committed numerous crimes against humanity to try to force a Chinese surrender but were never able to do so.

Japan's war machine continued its roll over Asia in 1940 when it occupied France's colonies in Vietnam and Cambodia and officially joined the Axis powers of Germany and Italy. In reaction to an oil embargo set up by the United States and Britain Japan occupied the Dutch East Indies, present-day Indonesia, for its rich oil supplies. One year later the Japanese pulled the United States into the war with the surprise attack on Pearl Harbor, Hawaii. For the next four years the United States and its allies and Japan fought the Pacific war for control of the region's many islands, as well as Japan's holdings in Southeast Asia and the mainland. There were dozens of important battles during this period; the one considered the turning point in the war was the 1942 Battle of Midway. After this Allied victory Japan was forced to retreat toward its central position on the Japanese Archipelago until the United States finally forced a complete surrender on August 14, 1945, by dropping a second atomic bomb; the first had leveled the city of Hiroshima on August 6; the second and decisive bomb did the same in Nagasaki on August 9. The USSR had entered the war against Japan just one day earlier, on August 8, when it began the liberation of Manchuria.

Postwar

Japan after World War II has undergone one of the most dramatic transformations of any country in the world. In August 1945 every large city in Japan, with the exception of Kyoto, was at least severely damaged; most were utterly destroyed. The same was true of most factories, roads, ports, rail lines, and farmland. Food was in extremely short supply and even freshwater was a luxury for many urban Japanese.

The U.S. occupation, which continued until April 1952 on the main islands and 1972 in Okinawa, resulted in a new constitution in 1947, which made Japanese military aggression illegal, demoted the emperor to a symbolic figurehead, granted suffrage and human rights to all, and separated the state from the former state religion of Shinto. In addition hundreds of Japanese military figures were put on trial for war crimes, and more than 500 committed suicide before they were even tried. Within a generation Japan became a fully functioning democracy with power resting in the diet and active participation of many different political parties. The country's political relationships with the USSR were mended in 1956, although the issue of the Kuril Islands has yet to be resolved, and with China in 1972 following U.S. President Nixon's visit to that country.

Japan's economy also flourished in the postwar years, especially during and after the Korean War (1950–52). The initial stage of this development, sometimes called the Japanese economic miracle, focused on rebuilding Japan's broken infrastructure. Once this was accomplished, textiles and many other industries took off through a combination of U.S. and Japanese government investment and interventionism and the *keiretsu,* cooperative groups of manufacturers, suppliers, banks, and distributors working with the strong unions to produce high-quality goods at low prices. Japanese workers were rewarded for their loyalty and hard work with jobs for life. In the years after the 1973 global oil crisis Japan shifted away from textiles, steel, and other primary goods to the high-tech industry focused on electronics and consumer goods. Small, economical Japanese cars took over the world market in subsequent decades. Since the early 1990s the Japanese economy has not been able to sustain its spectacular postwar boom, with continuing recession finally forcing both large and small corporations to change their employment-for-life policies and other employment benefits. Nonetheless Japan remains an extremely wealthy country with a per capita gross domestic product (GDP) in 2006 estimated to be $33,100 and an overall GDP of $4.22 trillion.

CULTURE

Japanese culture is often depicted both inside and outside Japan as entirely unique, so much so that outsiders are never fully able to understand the Japanese or their particular worldview. However, while it is true that for instance the Japanese language is so remotely related to other languages as to be considered a language isolate by some experts, it is not entirely unique. Japanese is an agglutinative language as the Altaic languages are: complex words are created by combining simple root words with one another or with a number of prefixes and suffixes. In addition Japanese has been shown to be remotely related to Korean and more closely related to the ancient Korean language of Korguryo. Therefore while Japanese is unlike most other languages, it is not completely alone in the world and can be learned by diligent outsiders willing to spend many years doing so.

The same is true of many other aspects of Japanese society. As have the people of India, China, Korea, and many of the countries of Southeast Asia, the Japanese have been influenced over the past 1,500 years by a variety of forms of Buddhism; they even created several sects of their own, such as the Jodo or Pure Land sect of 1175 and the Lotus Hokke or

Nichiren sect of 1253. Interestingly, however, the Buddhist sect often most closely associated with Japan, Zen, was imported from China and Korea in 1191. Today more than 90 million Japanese people consider themselves Buddhists and while they may wear their faith more lightly than fundamentalists of other religions, most continue to visit temples for holidays, birthdays, weddings, funerals, or other significant events. Confucian beliefs, which originated in China and were transported throughout east and Southeast Asia, have also played a large part in the construction of contemporary Japanese culture. The Japanese values of education, hierarchy, filial piety, and obedience to one's superior all have their basis in Confucian philosophy and connect the Japanese to many of the people in their region of the world.

The Japanese also share some cultural traits with Westerners. The most important of these is a desire to live in a consumer-oriented society with access to the latest technological gadgets, many of them invented or at least produced in Japan since World War II, and to enjoy the privilege of participating in the electoral process. Japan's government since the enactment of the 1947 constitution has been a fairly transparent democracy with people able to choose their representatives and prime minister in regular elections. As have many Americans, many Japanese have a fervent love of baseball, which also connects them to a wider international community.

Despite these similarities between Japanese culture and many others throughout the world, it also has many unique aspects. One of these is the ideal model for all relationships, including parent-child, teacher-student, and manager-employee. This model is called *amae* in Japanese and refers to the ideal relationship between mother and child, that of indulgence toward a dependent. As a result in the same way that mothers are supposed to indulge and protect their children because of their total dependence, teachers and managers are supposed to indulge and protect their students or employees, take care of them, and encourage their dependence upon their superiors. At the same time children, students, and employees are supposed to feel their dependence and to desire it to a much greater extent than in the United States, for example, which tends to foster feelings of independence in children from very early ages.

A second unique aspect of Japanese culture is the religion that was until the end of World War II the state religion, Shinto; Buddhism was also a state religion for most of Japanese history. Shinto is an ancient religion that has been estimated to have emerged at least as early as 500 B.C.E. and perhaps even earlier. It combines beliefs and practices from nature and hero worship, shamanism, divination, and fertility cults but contains no named founder, texts or scriptures, or even laws. Even the priesthood is only a loosely organized body of practitioners at a high level rather than a hierarchical bureaucracy as in Christianity, Islam, or Buddhism. The name *shinto* comes from the Chinese term *shin tao*, "way of the gods," and the label was used in the eighth century at about the same time that the emperor was deemed to be of divine origin. This ascription was not renounced until the late 1940s when the American occupiers forced the change upon the emperor.

Another important side of Japanese culture is the degree of ritualization of various events that in other societies may be entirely practical. Two examples are the tea ceremony and ikebana or flower arranging. However, just getting dressed in premodern Japan, which meant for both men and women the wearing of a kimono, required a degree of precision that would be unfathomable to most contemporary Americans. Both the tea ceremony and ikebana are products of Buddhist tradition and thus are not entirely unique to Japanese society; nonetheless both were transformed in the Japanese context to become the highly ritualized, formal practices of today. It is often pointed out that both of these ceremonies can serve as an apt metaphor for Japanese culture more generally. Of the two ceremonies the tea ceremony is the older, from the Zen tradition first imported to Japan in the late 12th century, while ikebana was invented by a Buddhist priest in the 15th century. Both practices take decades to learn and a lifetime to perfect because of the intricacies involved in presentation, attitude, and even clothing to be worn. Both tea ceremonies and ikebana underline the importance in Japanese culture of hierarchy, since learning from a master requires total submission, formality, context, and precision. As is the case for learning to engage in these ceremonies properly, for an outsider to learn how to maneuver within the boundaries of what is considered proper in Japanese culture takes years if not a lifetime of apprenticeship and the proper attention to the Japanese rules.

Since the end of World War II and even more so in the past two or three decades, several aspects of Japanese culture have been successfully exported throughout the world. One

There are more than 100 different tea persuasions in Japan, requiring somewhat different postures, rituals, and order of events. These women are students of Sa-do, or the "way of tea," and may spend decades learning before being able to participate fully in a ceremony. *(OnAsia/John Lander)*

FURTHER READING

Harumi Befu. *Hegemony of Homogeneity: An Anthropological Analysis of Nihonjinron* (Rosanna, Australia: Trans Pacific Press, 2001).

Theodore C. Bestor, Patricia G. Steinhoff, and Victoria Lyon Bestor, eds. *Doing Fieldwork in Japan* (Honolulu: University of Hawaii Press, 2003).

Takeo Doi. *The Anatomy of Dependence: The Key Analysis of Japanese Behavior.* Translated by John Bestor. 2d ed. (Tokyo: Kodansha International, 1981).

John Hall and Toyoda Takeshi, eds. *Japan in the Muromachi Age* (Berkeley and Los Angeles: University of California Press, 1977).

Robert Harvey. *The Undefeated: The Rise, Fall and Rise of Greater Japan* (London: Macmillan, 1994).

Joe Joseph. *The Japanese: Strange but Not Strangers* (London: Viking, 1993).

Adam L. Kern. *Manga from the Floating World: Comicbook Culture and the Kibyoshi of Edo Japan* (Cambridge, Mass.: Harvard University Press, 2006).

J. Edward Kidder. *Early Buddhist Japan* (London: Thames and Hudson, 1972).

Tessa Morris-Suzuki. *Re-Inventing Japan: Time, Space, Nation* (Armonk, N.Y.: M. E. Sharpe, 1998).

Edwin O. Reischauer and Marius B. Jansen. *The Japanese Today: Change and Continuity* (Cambridge, Mass.: Belknap Press of Harvard University Press, 1995).

Roy Starrs, ed. *Japanese Cultural Nationalism: At Home and in the Asia Pacific* (Folkestone, England: Kent Global Oriental, 2004).

Paul Varley. *Japanese Culture: A Short History.* 3d ed. (Oxford, England: Premier Book Marketing, 1984).

of these is food. Restaurants selling Japanese noodles, sushi, and sashimi are now operating in most big cities in the world and even in small towns in some regions of the United States, Australia, and elsewhere. The proper way of preparing these dishes, especially sushi and sashimi, takes years of apprenticeship to master as well as a degree of precision and formality that is rarely achieved outside Japan. Other popular exports are manga and anime, comic books and animation, respectively. While neither of these was invented in Japan, when done in the Japanese style they are unique to that culture and tradition. Contemporary *manga,* which means "random or whimsical pictures," is the descendant of an art form developed in Japan in the 18th century, from the *giga* tradition of "funny pictures" of the 12th century. As a result of this traditional background, manga is much more popular in Japan than comics are anywhere else, with different forms created for children and adults, as humor, satire, and even pornography.

Japanese: nationality (Nihonjin, people of Japan)

The people of Japan are almost 99 percent ethnic JAPANESE with a very small population of KOREANS, Chinese, Brazilians, and other foreigners, mostly in the country's largest cities.

GEOGRAPHY

The Japanese Archipelago is a 1,500-mile-long group of islands with the Pacific Ocean to the east and the Sea of Japan to the west. It is located about 190 miles from Russia in the north, 110 miles from Korea in the southwest, and 480 miles from China. The archipelago is made up of more than 3,000 islands; the four main ones, from south to north, are Kyushu, Shikoku, Honshu, and Hokkaido. The terrain of most of the islands is relatively rough with about 70 percent of the land being taken up by mountains; the famous Mt. Fuji is the tallest at 12,390 feet.

Japanese: nationality timeline

B.C.E.

400 Agriculture and a plethora of other material artifacts with Korean origins appear in Japan. This marks the beginning of the Yayoi period of Japanese history.

C.E.

710–94 The Nara period, named for the kingdom that established itself at Hiejo-kyo.

712 The publication of the first Japanese chronicle, which marks for many the transition from proto-Japanese to Old Japanese history, language, and culture.

794–1185 The Heian period, during which the capital is moved to Kyoto.

1068 The end of the Fujiwara family's de facto control of Japan's government.

1185–1333 The Kamakura shogunate; the usurpation of power by the military with its headquarters in Kamakura; the emperor remains in Kyoto as the government's figurehead.

1191 Zen Buddhism arrives in Japan from Korea and China.

1274 The Mongol invasions are repelled as they are again in 1281, but the military government is weakened in the process.

1333–1573 The Muromachi period, named for the Kyoto district that houses Shogun Ashikaga Takauji's military government.

1467–1568 The Sengoku era or Civil War era.

1542 Portuguese traders and Christian missionaries land on Kyushu and introduce firearms and their religion, both of which are taken up more in the west than the east.

1573–1600 The Azuchi-Momoyama period in which Japan is reunified by Oda Nobunaga after a long period of civil strife.

1582 Oda Nobunaga is killed, making way for Toyotomi Hideyoshi to consolidate his power over a newly reunited Japan in 1590.

1592 Toyotomi Hideyoshi invades Korea in his attempt to control both Korea and China. He fails.

1600–1868 The Tokugawa era, when the capital is moved to Edo (Tokyo); Japan tries to remain isolated from increasing Western pressure in the region.

1853–54 U.S. commodore Perry begins the process of opening Japan up to foreign trade.

1868–1912 The Meiji Restoration makes the emperor the central authority throughout Japan again and finalizes the modernization of the Japanese state.

1876 The Korea-Japanese Treaty of Amity opens three Korean ports to Japanese trade and brings Korea's long-standing position as a Chinese tributary state to an end.

1894–95 The Japanese defeat China in the Sino-Japanese War and receive Taiwan as one of the spoils of war.

1904–95 The Japanese victory over Russia in the Russo-Japanese War is the first time since the rise of Europe as a world power that an Asian country defeats a European one on the battlefield.

1910 The Japanese annex Korea and bring an end to the 518-year old Choson dynasty.

1912–45 This period does not bear a formal name in Japanese history but is often referred to as the era of militarism.

1931 Japanese armies occupy Manchuria and establish the puppet state of Manchukuo.

1933 Japan withdraws from the League of Nations after criticism of its actions in China.

1937–45 Second Sino-Japanese War. The Japanese occupy much of coastal China and commit numerous atrocities in the city of Nanjing but are never able to force full capitulation by the Chinese government.

1941 The Japanese air force attacks the U.S. naval base at Pearl Harbor, pulling the United States into World War II.

(continues)

JAPANESE: NATIONALITY

nation:
Japan; Nihon-koku or Nippon-koku in Japanese

derivation of name:
Nippon means "land of the rising sun" in Japanese; the characters that indicate this are pronounced more like *jit-pan* in Chinese, which became *Japan* in most European languages.

government:
Parliamentary democracy with a constitutional monarchy

capital:
Tokyo

language:
Japanese

religion:
Shinto and Buddhist 84 percent, 0.7 percent Christian, other or none 15.3 percent

earlier inhabitants:
Ainu, Jomon people

demographics:
Japanese 99 percent; Koreans, Chinese, Brazilians, other 1 percent

Japanese: nationality timeline *(continued)*

1942 The Battle of Midway turns the tide against Japan and toward the Allies, as the war continues for three more years.

1945 The United States drops atomic bombs on Hiroshima and Nagasaki, forcing the complete surrender of Japan.

1947 Japan's new constitution, largely drawn up by the U.S. occupying forces under General Douglas MacArthur, takes effect.

1952 The U.S. occupation of Japan comes to an end.

1956 Japan normalizes its relations with the USSR.

1964 Tokyo hosts the summer Olympic games, proving to the world that Japan has cast off the militarism and devastation of the past.

1972 The U.S. occupation of Okinawa ends and Japan and China normalize their relations.

1980s Japanese firms purchase companies, land, and property throughout the world, causing fear in the United States, Australia, and elsewhere of a Japanese economic takeover that would be much more difficult to combat than Japanese militarism had been.

1990–2000s Long-term recession sets back Japanese economic growth and forces both economic and political reform to begin to repair the damage.

1998 Nagano, Japan, hosts the winter Olympics.

2006 Japan's aging population and enormous national debt, 176 percent of gross domestic product (GDP), cause increasing concern for the country's long-term economic growth.

The country's 60 active volcanoes and frequent earthquakes, the most famous recently being the Kobe earthquake of 1995 that destroyed most of the city of Kobe, are the result of the islands' location on the Pacific "Ring of Fire," the world's most active earthquake zone. Japan's rivers are also more dramatic than those of many comparable places with frequent flooding due to the large amounts of water that must be carried on steep but short riverbeds. The Mogami, Fuji, and Kuma Rivers are the fastest running rivers in Japan while the Shinano is the longest and the Tone carries the most water.

Japan's mountainous terrain, frequent flooding, and high percentage of forest cover, which at 70 percent is the greatest in the developed world, mean that agricultural land has always been at a premium. Nonetheless the Japanese have tried to be self-sufficient in rice, their staple food, and their warm, wet climate has been conducive to that goal in most years. Japan receives about 120 inches of rain per year, most falling during the summer growing season. This moisture, combined with rich, volcanic soils and a warm climate, makes Japan extremely fertile and able to produce about 800 percent more food per square mile than Britain. Nonetheless only about 14 percent of their land is currently farmland and so the Japanese import about 60 percent of their food products.

INCEPTION OF NATION

Although many Japanese sources claim unique and divine origins for their people and nation, the earliest periods of Japanese history are actually marked by significant cultural borrowing from elsewhere. Agriculture arrived in the Japanese Archipelago in about 400 B.C.E. along with migrations of people from the Korean Peninsula, known once they are in Japan as the Yayoi. The Japanese language still retains ancient connections to the languages of Korea, especially that of the Koguryo Kingdom of the north. In the centuries prior to and during the first Japanese historical period the Nara, which began in 712 with the publication of the first Japanese-language chronicle, the Japanese also borrowed heavily from their Chinese neighbors. Japan's writing system, imperial governance, urban planning, and calendar were all borrowed from Chinese originals and transformed over the following centuries to make them uniquely Japanese. In subsequent centuries the Japanese continued borrowing from the Chinese and Koreans, including two important conceptual systems, Buddhism and Confucianism.

A Japanese emperor has nominally ruled in Japan since the fifth century, but the centuries prior to the 19th were dominated by local power holders much more than by any centralized figure. In fact starting before 1016 with the rise of the Fujiwara family and for many centuries afterward, even the power of the emperor himself was surpassed by that of various powerful families or military figures. As in any feudal system, however, the power of the figure or figures at the top of the Japanese hierarchy was felt only by the nobles, landowners, and samurai on the level below them. Average Japanese peasants' understanding of the world was that they owed labor and resources to their local landowner. Even urban Japanese, of which there were many starting with the development of the first city at Heijo-kyo or what is today the city of Nara, would generally not have seen themselves as the emperor's subjects but as members of guilds, neighborhoods, and cities.

In the 16th century the Portuguese arrived as the first European power to set foot in Japan. They introduced weaponry and Christianity, both of which were used by various warlords to advance their position relative to that of others. Using these external influences, some lords emerged as the controlling force for extremely large localities; some *daimyo*, as they are called, controlled an entire province.

The period from 1600 to 1868 is named the Tokugawa era because shoguns from this clan dominated the government at this time. They also moved the Japanese capital from Kyoto, where it had been since the eighth century, to Edo or Tokyo, as it is known today. At the beginning of the Tokugawa era, also sometimes called the Edo period, Japan opened some limited trade relations with the English and Dutch and continued to trade with the Portuguese, but by 1639 most contact with the outside world had been eliminated. In a further attempt to limit outside influences Christianity was persecuted rather strenuously from 1614 until the end of the era and from 1633 external travel was essentially forbidden for all Japanese, even the nobility.

Internally, however, Japan flourished with the samurai class turning to martial arts, literature, and philosophy to replace their military activities. In addition farmers and traders increased their economic activities throughout the period, improving the local economy. Neo-Confucianism became the most important philosophy of the day, with its stress on strict class differences, loyalty, morals, and education. Indeed class differences became so codified during this period that they developed into a castelike system in which samurai, peasants, artisans, and merchants were unable to change the class into which they were born; the fifth class, the *eta* or outcasts, considered impure and dangerous, were also unable to rise above their lowly position in Japanese society. The descendants of this group continue to reside in Japan today as the Burakumin.

The Tokugawa period saw the gradual decrease in power held by the shogun government in Tokyo during the course of their 268 years in power. One cause for this was bad luck in the form of natural disasters that led to famine, higher taxes, and riots in the countryside. Another cause was the rise in the merchant class's status in relation to that of the samurai, some of whom became dependent on wealthy merchants for patronage. Government corruption and incompetence also contributed to the general decline of the shogun's position until finally in 1868 the emperor's status as ruler of Japan was restored in the Meiji Restoration.

The restoration of the Emperor Meiji opened the door for significant changes throughout Japanese society. The concessions gained by U.S. commodore Matthew Perry in opening Japan up for trade, which occurred in 1854, finally came to fruition after 1868. Many other Western nations were also able to sign one-sided treaties that gave them significant economic and legal advantages over the Japanese in their own country. In reaction to this humiliation the emperor and his clique of nobles and samurai carried out drastic reforms of the country's education, legal, governance, military, and economic systems. Japan adopted Western-style technology and science, universal conscription, a European-style constitution with provisions for the elimination of class distinctions and for religious freedom, the development of a parliament, an army modeled on that of Prussia, and a navy modeled on Britain's. The samurai lost their special privileges and the daimyo had to return all of their land to the emperor, who restructured the country into prefectures in 1870. In exchange many Japanese were able to travel overseas to study and powerful family businesses, called *zaibatsu*, received direct governmental support for research, development, and even production and distribution. After a brief financial crisis in the 1880s brought about by the increase in spending these reforms engendered, the Japanese currency system was also transformed and the Bank of Japan created.

All of this change and Westernization meant that Japan had soon outstripped all its regional rivals for power, as demonstrated in 1894–95 by the defeat of China in the Sino-Japanese War. In 1904–5 Japan proved itself once again to be a formidable enemy, this time defeating Russia in the Russo-Japanese War. This victory alerted not only Japan's Asian neighbors but other countries that the Japanese army and navy were among the best in the world. This victory also allowed Japan to annex Korea by 1910. The death of Emperor Meiji in 1912 did not interrupt the strengthening of Japan's military or the quest to join the European countries as a colonial power, though it did shift power from the weak Emperor Taisho to the diet or parliament.

Japan participated with the Allied powers in World War I but only in fairly limited ways by liberating former German colonies in parts of the North Pacific. At first these colonies were of little use to Japan in their attempts to rebuild after the devastating Kanto earthquake in 1923 and the Great Depression brought their economy to a standstill. However, with the militarization of Japanese society in the 1930s and the need for resources and cheap labor, these colonies in the Marshall Islands and Micronesia became extremely important. They also later served as bases from which the Japanese conquered much of the Pacific in World War II.

The first phase of Japanese involvement in global warfare began in 1931 when Japanese forces on the mainland occupied Manchuria. Within one year the Kwantung Army, as these Japanese forces came to be known, established the puppet state of Manchukuo, forcing the resident Chinese and other subordinate groups to learn Japanese and adopt Japanese surnames. That year, 1932, also saw Japan bomb Shanghai in order to put China on notice for allowing anti-Japanese movements to take place in the city. All of these incidents were just preludes to the Second Sino-Japanese War, fought on Chinese soil from 1937 until the end of World War II in 1945. The Japanese took the city of Nanjing and committed numerous crimes against humanity to compel a Chinese surrender but were never able to force the Chinese government into that humiliating position.

Japan's war machine continued its roll over Asia in 1940 when Japan occupied France's colonies in Vietnam and Cambodia and officially joined the Axis powers of Germany and Italy. In reaction to an oil embargo set up by the United States and Britain, Japan occupied the Dutch East Indies, contemporary Indonesia, for its rich oil supplies. One year later the Japanese pulled the United States into the war with their surprise attack on Pearl Harbor, Hawaii. For the next four years the United States and its allies fought the Pacific War against Japan for control of the region's many islands, as well as Japan's holdings in Southeast Asia and the mainland. There were dozens of important battles during this period; the one considered the turning point in the war was the 1942 Battle of Midway. After this Allied victory Japan was forced to retreat toward a central position on the Japanese Archipelago until the United States finally forced a complete surrender on August 14, 1945, by dropping a second atomic bomb; the first leveled the city of Hiroshima on August 6; this second and decisive bomb did the same in Nagasaki on August 9.

Japan since World War II has undergone one of the most dramatic transformations of any country on earth. In August 1945 every large city in Japan, with the exception of Kyoto, was at least severely damaged, and most utterly destroyed. The same was true of most factories, roads, ports, rail lines, and farmland. Food was in extremely short supply and even freshwater was a luxury for many urban Japanese. The U.S. occupation, which continued until April 1952 on the main islands and 1972 on Okinawa, resulted in a new constitution in 1947, which made military aggression illegal, demoted the emperor to a symbolic figurehead, granted suffrage and human rights to all, and separated the state from the former state religion of Shinto. In addition hundreds of Japanese military figures were charged with war crimes, and more than 500 more committed suicide before they could even be brought to trial. Within a generation Japan became a fully functioning democracy with power vested in the diet and active participation of many different political parties.

Japan's economy also flourished in the postwar years, especially during and after the Korean War (1950–52). The initial stage of this development, sometimes called the Japanese economic miracle, focused on rebuilding Japan's broken infrastructure. Once this was accomplished, the textile and many other industries took off through a combination of U.S. and Japanese government investment and interventionism and the *keiretsu*, cooperative groups of manufacturers, suppliers, banks, and distributors working with the strong unions to produce high-quality goods at low prices. Japanese workers were rewarded for their loyalty and hard work with jobs for life. In the years after the 1973 global oil crisis Japan shifted away from textiles, steel, and other primary industries to the high-tech industry of electronics and consumer goods. Small, economical Japanese cars also took over the world market in the subsequent decades. Since the early 1990s the Japanese economy has not sustained its spectacular postwar boom, with continuing recession finally forcing both large and small corporations to change their employment-for-life policies and other employment perks. Nonetheless Japan remains an extremely wealthy country with a per capita gross domestic product (GDP) in 2006 estimated to be $33,100 and an overall GDP of $4.22 trillion.

CULTURAL IDENTITY

Although the Japanese imperial state has existed since the start of the eighth century, for most of its long history the majority of its people had no shared conception of the Japanese as a distinct community or people group. During the long feudal era, in which each lord or noble controlled his own territory and people, there was no shared consensus regarding Japanese identity. A national identity or *kokka* in Japanese was created in the 19th century out of the strong links people felt to their locality in reaction to the threats posed to the country and its ways of life by outside powers, especially Europeans and North Americans. At that time many aspects of Japanese culture took on the tone of

nationalism, none more so than the emperor. The 1868 Meiji Restoration was part of a larger nationalistic project in which the emperor assumed the primary symbolic role in connecting the Japanese people to one another, to the land, and to the government. This took the concerted efforts of many Japanese intellectuals at the time and resulted in the situation in which it was illegal in pre–World War II Japan to question the divinity of the royal family.

Another aspect of Japanese national identity that was created in the 19th century was the concept of Japanese uniqueness, or *nihonjinron*. Even to the detriment of physical anthropology, archaeology, and ancient history many Japanese scholars today refuse to explore theories of Japanese origins and cultural development that posit anything but the most ancient origins on the Japanese Archipelago. Most Western scholars in these disciplines believe that the contemporary Japanese descended from migrants from the Korean Peninsula who entered the archipelago about 2,400 years ago; however, most Japanese scholars believe the modern Japanese people descend from an earlier migratory people who arrived closer to 30,000 years ago and eventually became the Jomon people. They believe the Japanese language is entirely unique and that Japanese culture is alone in the world.

Sumo wrestlers, or *rikishi,* must purify the ring before every bout by throwing salt into it. *(OnAsia/ Darren Ruane)*

JARAI

location:
The central highlands of
Vietnam, Cambodia

time period:
Unknown to the present

ancestry:
Austronesian

language:
Jarai, an Austronesian
language related to
Cham

Part of the uniqueness of Japanese culture is the way that even the most mundane features of daily life can be and are made into sacred or ritualized moments of the day. This is obvious to anyone who has seen a Japanese tea ceremony, flower arranging, or even sumo wrestling match, with its elaborate posturing and tossing of salt before each bout. Even within the sphere of international business the Japanese are able to place their work in the sphere of the larger, ancient, and unique Japanese society. For example a construction company may use a display of eighth-century Japanese building techniques to connect their work to the timeless Japanese people.

Another aspect of Japanese cultural identity concerns their place in the wider Asian world. During the 1930s Japanese reluctance to open their country to the West, which had been skillfully managed by the Japanese from about 1853 onward, was extended to their conception of the rest of Asia, at least east Asia. The Japanese publicist Kita Ikki developed and promoted the concept of "Asia for the Asians," which in Japan led to increased militarization of society and eventually Japan's participation in World War II. When Japan occupied the Philippines, Malay Peninsula, Indochina, Indonesia, China, and much of the Asia-Pacific region during the war they did so under the guise of creating a "Greater East-Asia Co-Prosperity Sphere." In reality the peoples and resources of Asia were to be used for Japanese aggrandizement and military efforts, but to the Japanese people it appeared only natural for the peoples of east Asia, under Japanese domination, to oppose the West. In the late 20th and early 21st centuries the Japanese once again see themselves as the leader of their region. Whether it is democratization or economic development, the Japanese have been very active in Asia as part of their identification as the center of the Asian world.

FURTHER READING

Jennifer L. Anderson. *An Introduction to Japanese Tea Ritual* (Albany: State University of New York Press, 1991).

Mark Caprio and Matsuda Koichiro, eds. *Japan and the Pacific, 1540–1920* (Burlington, Vt.: Ashgate/ Variorum, 2006).

Nanette Gottlieb. *Language and Society in Japan* (New York: Cambridge University Press, 2005).

Mark J. Hudson. *Ruins of Identity: Ethnogenesis in the Japanese Islands* (Honolulu: University of Hawaii Press, 1999).

Naomichi Ishige. *The History and Culture of Japanese Food* (London: Kegan Paul, 2001).

Marilyn Ivy. *Discourses of the Vanishing: Modernity, Phantasm, Japan* (Chicago: University of Chicago Press, 1995).

Peter B. Oblas. *Perspectives on Race and Culture in Japanese Society: The Mass Media and Ethnicity* (Lewiston, N.Y.: E. Mellen Press, 1995).

Lora Sharnoff. *Grand Sumo: The Living Sport and Tradition* (New York: Weatherhill, 1993).

Marie Söderberg and Ian Reader, eds. *Japanese Influences and Presences in Asia* (Richmond, England: Curzon Press, 2000).

Kiyoko Takeda. *The Dual-Image of the Japanese Emperor* (Basingstoke, England: Macmillan Education, 1988).

Haru Yamada. *Different Games Different Rules: Why Americans and Japanese Misunderstand Each Other* (New York: Oxford University Press, 2002).

Jarai (Chor, Cho-Rai, Chrai, Djarai, Gia Rai, Gio-Rai, Jorai, Mthur)

The Jarai are the largest of the many ethnic groups that reside in the mountains of central Vietnam, sometimes called as a group Montagnards or DEGA. They speak an Austronesian language related to that of the CHAMS and may have moved to the highlands from the coast during the VIETNAMESE migrations south after the 10th century. Some experts put that migration further back in time, just at the start of the common era, with the arrival of the Chamic people from Indonesia.

Like many other Dega groups the Jarai are matrilineal: that is, they trace their kinship groups through mothers, mothers' mothers, and so on. They are also matrilocal, requiring new husbands to move in with their wives' families and work their plots of land. Most inheritance passes from mothers to daughters and from mother's brothers to sister's sons. Children also take their mother's surname instead of their father's. The Jarai tend to be animists with the kings of fire, water, and wind most important spirits in the pantheon. Some Jarai have joined many RHADE people in having converted to evangelical Christianity since radio broadcasting from the Philippines in their language began after 1975.

During the 20th century Jarai life changed drastically. French colonialism initiated the earliest attempts at annexing Jarai land for use in commercial coffee and rubber plantations; the French also began missionary activity and attempts at Western styles of education. The Vietnam War introduced even greater changes as many Jarai sided with the U.S. forces who worked with them to form their own military units, ostensibly for defense against the Communists but just as often for the offensive push against the Communist forces of the National Liberation Front and the North Vietnamese. Some Jarai escaped Vietnam at the end of the war and were moved as refugees to the United States and Australia, while most stayed on in Vietnam to continue the struggle against the Vietnamization of their villages and ways of life. FULRO, the Front Unifié de Lutte des Races Opprimées or United Front for the Struggle of Oppressed Races, an umbrella organization of Vietnamese mountain peoples that worked with the U.S. and South Vietnamese armies against the National Liberation Front (*see also* Vietnamese; Vietnamese: nationality), continues its work today to resist Communism in Vietnam and the subjugation of the country's minority groups to the cultural domination of the Vietnamese.

Most Jarai social life is centered on the village with the *nha-rong,* or community house, acting as a center, specifically for men and boys. As are individual family houses, *nha-rong*s are built on stilts to help the structures survive during the frequent flooding and are oriented toward the north. In recent years many Jarai villages have suffered from the incursion of both Vietnamese villagers, moved to the highlands to help quell the ongoing struggle of the Dega people against the Vietnamese government, and corporations accessing the timber and other natural resources of the area. By 2004 private corporations had gained access to 2.7 million hectares of land in the Vietnamese central highlands, increasing the poverty and malnutrition of many indigenous people. The Jarai in Cambodia have experienced similar incursions. For example the Jarai villages of Kong Yu and Kong Thom in Cambodia have recently lost about 500 hectares of land used for subsistence agriculture to a rubber plantation owned by the Cambodian finance minister's sister, Keat Kolney, who is also the wife of Cambodia's secretary of state for the ministry of land management. The interaction was illegally pushed through with thumbprints obtained from villagers during a party given them by the company after villagers refused to sell the land legally. The case is currently being heard in Cambodia's court system.

In Vietnam many Jarai villages have been outright destroyed, with the building of dams on various highland rivers to supply electricity for the country's burgeoning industrial economy. The Yali Falls dam, built between 1993 and 1999 on a tributary of the Sesan River, forced the relocation of 2,373 Jarai villagers. They were largely slash-and-burn horticulturalists who had also adopted rice farming since interacting with ethnic Vietnamese villagers in recent decades. In addition for villagers whose land and houses were not inundated one of the most lucrative sources of cash was lost with the building of the dam: panning for gold. This activity became impossible in 1997 when the sand, silt, and other detritus from dam construction clouded the river to such a degree that panning for gold became impossible. Changes in water quality have also affected the river's fish stocks, forcing the formerly nearly self-sufficient Jarai downstream from the dam to purchase ocean fish from Vietnamese traders. The Jarai consider such fish inferior to their more familiar freshwater breeds. Finally water quality in the Sesan River watershed has also been affected, exacerbating the region's poverty with introduced diseases.

See also Austronesians.

Javanese (Orang Djawa, Orang Jawa, Tijang Djawi, Wong Djawa, Wong Jowo)

The Javanese are the largest ethnic group in Indonesia; they call themselves Wong Djawa and Tujang Djawi. Their original homeland was central Java, and today most still live in Java, particularly the provinces of Central and East Java and Yogyakarta. On their home island the Javanese are the main ethnic group living alongside such peoples as the Sundanese in West Java, the Betawis in Jakarta, and the Madurese in East Java. In addition nowadays many more Javanese are distributed on other islands such as Sumatra, Sulawesi, and the Kalimantan region of Borneo.

GEOGRAPHY

The Javanese are Indonesia's largest ethnic group and so are evident throughout the archipelago. However, the region with the greatest number and proportion of Javanese is their homeland in the provinces of East and Central Java. Java itself is one of the country's five large islands with a mixed terrain of mountains, plateaus, and coastal plains. The climate is tropical with a rainy season from September to March, dry the rest of the year. Like much of Indonesia, Java is tectonically unstable and prone to earthquakes and volcanoes. In 2006 both of these natural disasters struck the island, with increased volcanic activity at Mount Merapi and two earthquakes, one around the city of Yogyakarta and the other in West Java.

JAVANESE

location:
Central and East Java and throughout Indonesia

time period:
Approximately 2500 B.C.E. to the present

ancestry:
Austronesian

language:
Most are bilingual in Javanese and Bahasa Indonesia

Javanese time line

B.C.E.

2500 Approximate period when the first Austronesian speakers land on Java.

2000 The first definitive evidence of agriculture in Java appears.

500 Metallurgy begins to create wealth and political power differences among communities in Java.

C.E.

100 Indian chronicles mention the existence of a Hindu kingdom on Java, Jawa Dwipa.

Second century In his *Geography* Claudius Ptolemy writes about Labadius, probably from the Sanskrit name of Java, *Yavadvipa*.

680s Approximate period when the Sumatran Srivijayan Empire conquers Java.

Eighth century The first stone temples, dedicated to the Hindu god Siva, are built in Java.

770s The Sanjaya kingdom begins building one of the largest Buddhist temples in the world, Borobudur, in Java. However, it is begun as a Hindu temple.

825 Borobudur is completed as a Buddhist stupa by the Sailendra dynasty, which is usually credited with the building of the entire complex.

835 The Hindu temple complex at Prambanam is started by the Sanjaya dynasty and completed in 856.

928 Sanjaya moves its capital to east Java and abandons central Java.

1292 The Mongols invade, possibly with the assistance of Vijaya, future founder of Majapahit.

1294 Founding date of Majapahit, Indonesia's first centralized kingdom, originating in east Java, by Vijaya.

1350 Hayam Wuruk or Rajasanagara inherits the Majapahit throne at 16.

1389 Rajasanagara dies and a fight for succession begins the long disintegration of central Java's last Hindu-Buddhist kingdom.

1500 Approximate year when Majapahit falls to the sultanate of Demak.

1522 The Portuguese assist Banten in the west against the sultan of Demak.

1560 The Portuguese establish the first European post on Java, at Panarukan.

1581 Founding of Mataram.

1588 Mataram defeats the sultanate of Demak.

1596 The first Dutch expedition under de Houtman reaches the East Indies.

1601 A handful of Dutch ships defeat a 30-ship Portuguese armada in Javanese waters and begin the long Dutch colonial period.

1625 Mataram adds Surabaya in the east to its large kingdom.

1680 Mataram cedes the north central coast of Java to the Dutch East India Company (VOC).

1811–16 The British control Java.

1825–30 The Java War between the returned Dutch colonizers and guerrilla forces led by Prince Diponegoro.

1942 The Japanese occupy Java.

1949 Indonesia achieves independence from the Netherlands; the first president, Sukarno, is Javanese.

1967 Sukarno is replaced by a fellow Javanese, Suharto.

1965–66 The Indonesian military cracks down on the Communist Party by killing thousands on Java and Bali.

1998 Sukarno finally steps down and is replaced by the only non-Javanese president of the country to date, Jusuf Habibie.

2006 Java is hit by two separate earthquakes, at Yogyakarta and in west Java.

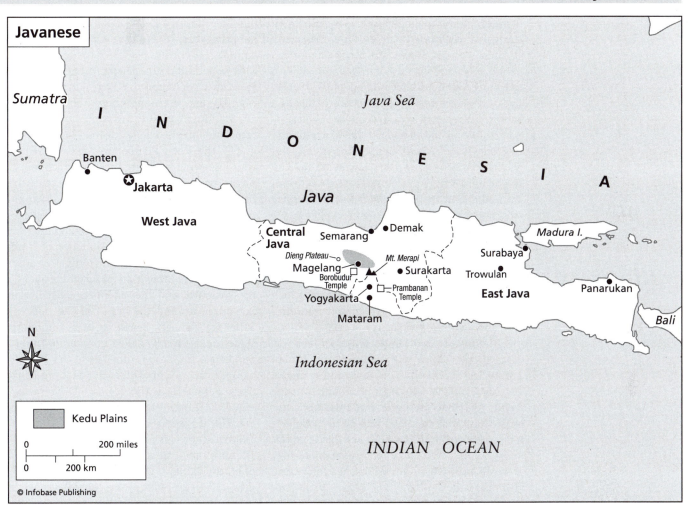

ORIGINS

The origins of the Javanese, as of all AUSTRONE-SIANS in Indonesia, are probably in south China, from which they sailed in double-outrigger dug-out canoes about 5,000 years ago to Taiwan, and then later the Philippines, Indonesia, and Polynesia. There is no certainty as to why this population left south China; however, archaeologists have hypothesized that it was a combination of population pressure, increased commerce from the Yangtze River region of China and moving southward down the river and its tributaries, a growing demand for marine and tropical forest goods, and climate change.

Contemporary Austronesian languages can be subdivided into two distinctive groups that separate the languages of Austronesian Taiwan from those of the remainder of the family, which include all Malay and Oceanic languages. This linguistic division, in addition to several anomalies in the archaeological record, such as a lack of rice in the earliest Austronesian sites in Taiwan, indicates that the origins of the Austronesian people may have been two separate exo-

duses from southeast China. If these did occur, the first exodus was probably from Fujian Province in China to Taiwan, which saw the rise of TA-P'EN-K'ENG CULTURE, with its distinctively marked pottery and stone tools, but without archaeological evidence of domesticated rice. The descendants of this first wave would be the contemporary speakers of Taiwan's Austronesian languages, the ABORIGINAL TAIWANESE. The second exodus may have occurred around 3000 B.C.E., taking a second wave of Austronesian speakers from southeastern China to Taiwan and then almost immediately to Luzon in the Philippines around the same period. They entered the various islands of Indonesia between 2500 and 2000 B.C.E. This second wave, with its red-slipped pottery, may also have been the ultimate source of the LAPITA CULTURE.

HISTORY

The Hindu-Buddhist Era

The Austronesian peoples who migrated to Java about 4,000 years ago took agricultural technology with them and thus were largely able to displace the prior populations who were living in the region. Little else is known about these early Javanese societies because the archaeological record is extremely sparse. Some examples of both red-slipped and paddle marked pottery exist, and both pollen and grain evidence points to a subsistence regimen with strong reliance on agriculture. We do not yet understand how trade and exchange more generally took place in Java, but shells and other coastal items have been found up to 620 miles inland, indicating that extensive networks did exist. By about 500 B.C.E. both bronze working and ironworking began to change the nature of Javanese society and greater centralization of political and social structures began to take place. At this time exchange and other interactions with India also introduced both religious and political ideas from the subcontinent, which in the first centuries of the common era dominated both politics and society in Java.

The first-known Hindu polity in Java was Jawa Dwipa, which was mentioned in Indian chronicles as existing on Java and Sumatra by about 100 C.E. The region remained in the hands of Hindu and later Buddhist kings for many hundreds of years, but no archaeological remains from the temples or other religious monuments of this era remain because they were all made of wood, which has long since disintegrated.

The start of a great period of building with stone began in Java in the eighth century, when a number of shrines dedicated to the Hindu god Siva were built on the Dieng Plateau of Central Java, near contemporary Yogyakarta. This is a high region, reaching almost 7,000 feet above sea level in areas and surrounded by 10 mountains; the name *Dieng* means "home of the gods." The Kedu Plains, also in Central Java, contain even greater architectural accomplishments from the eighth and ninth centuries, including the Hindu temple Prambanam and one of the world's largest Buddhist complexes, Borobudur. The latter of these complexes was begun in the 770s under the direction of Hindu rulers and their architects and religious leaders. They completed the first and second terraces of the structure and then stopped construction. Sometime around the year 790 the Buddhist Sailendra dynasty began work again on the structure eventually called *Borobudur*, "mountain of accumulation of merits of the 10 states of Bodhisattva"; an alternative reading of the name *Borobudur* is that it is from *Vihara Buddha Urh*, Sanskrit for "Buddhist Monastery on the Hill." In the 830s the giant Buddhist monument or stupa was completed but soon after was reappropriated once again by a Hindu kingdom, the Sanjaya, which had reunified central Java. However, most of the people over whom

Borobudur Temple, Java, built over the course of 60 years, during which regime changes contributed both Hindu and Buddhist features to the enormously large structure. *(Shutterstock/Morozova Tatyana)*

this kingdom ruled remained Buddhists in this period, and so extensive changes were not made to Borobudur and the local population continued to use it in the training of monks and in worship. Instead the Sanjaya kings built their own temple complex, Prambanam, from about 835 to 856. This structure contains some Buddhist elements as well since the Sanjayas were trying to attract the local population to their own religion by appealing to the traditions with which they were familiar.

The rise and fall in Java of the dynasties of Sailendra and Sanjaya are not well documented and contain significant overlaps and periods of rivalry. This history has been interpreted differently by various scholars: some believe that Sailendra and Sanjaya were actually branches of the same family and thus were part of the same kingdom, while others believe they were distinct and ruled alternately and at times in different regions of Central Java. What we do know is that stone inscriptions from Sailendra disappear from the region in about the mid-ninth century, during the most intensive period of building by the Sanjaya line. At times this kingdom is also known as Mataram, the name of its capital in Central Java. In 928 inscriptions from this kingdom also abruptly disappear as the capital was moved into East Java and Central Java was abandoned for reasons that today remain a mystery.

The other important feature to remember about this period is that whether the rulers were Hindus or Buddhists, the model of kingship that was utilized throughout was that of the Indian *devaraja,* or divine king. It was the king rather than priests or other religious elites who formed the bridge between the human population and the gods; their magnificent tombs point to the power they held because of this perceived trait. As this bridge kings also had the responsibility to ensure salvation for his people, and thus Borobudur and the other temples and monuments of the era are *yantras* or tools to promote meditation and final union with Buddha or Siva, depending on the tradition in which the monument originated.

The last Hindu-Buddhist kingdom that ruled over Central Java was the expansive Majapahit, which archaeological evidence indicates had as its capital the contemporary village of Trowulan in East Java. The founder of this kingdom, Vijaya or Wijaya, had been a prince of the eastern Javanese Singhasari kingdom who escaped when his lands were overrun by the Kadiri kingdom, also of East Java. In another version of the founding of the kingdom Vijaya was a son-in-law of the Singhasari king, who turned on him and assisted the invading MONGOLS in 1292. After the victory over Singhasari Vijaya then turned on the Mongols and defeated them and in about 1294 established his own kingdom, Majapahit. By the early 14th century this kingdom dominated most of the larger islands and trade routes between New Guinea and Sumatra, later adding territory on the Malay Peninsula as well.

Majapahit followed in the tradition established by Vijaya's family's kingdom, Singhasari, that the religious and political hierarchies were separated. As a result no large-scale or centralized religious building took place during the Majapahit era. One of the other important acts undertaken by Vijaya was to replace Java's indigenous monetary system, which had been in use for nearly half a millennium, with copper coins from China. The reason behind this change is unknown but may have to do with the expansion of trade with the Middle Kingdom in this era. These coins were in much smaller denominations than the previous gold and silver money and required containers in which to hold them. One such container was pottery in the shape of a pig, the first piggy bank, perhaps utilized because pigs at the time were considered an extremely important wealth item.

In the mid-14th century Majapahit achieved its zenith under King Hayam Wuruk and his adviser Gajah Mada, who was famous for the Palapa Oath, a proclamation that he would not eat any spices until the empire included the entire region. Hayam Wuruk, meaning "young cook," inherited his throne in 1350 at just 16 years of age, when he took the name *Rajasanagara.* Most of the territory he ruled over for 39 years had already been attached to his empire before he inherited it, but Rajasanagara consolidated power over these regions, especially those on the Malay Peninsula. Unfortunately he did not leave a clear line of succession and following his death in 1389 a son-in-law and illegitimate son waged civil war against each other for control over Majapahit. Their conflict allowed many of the outlying areas to break free of Javanese control and thus begin the long decline of the kingdom that finally collapsed around 1500 with the emergence of the first Islamic states on the island.

The Early Muslim Period and Colonial Era

Majapahit was finally conquered by the rising sultanate of Demak, which had originally been a small trading port on Java's north central coast. The exact year for this event is unknown but is sometime between 1478 and 1526 and is usually noted with the shorthand figure "around 1500." Demak believed itself to be the successor state to Majapahit, especially Central Java, and tried in the early years to consolidate its power throughout the region. By 1579 this kingdom had conquered the last vestiges of the Hindu Pajajaran kingdom in West Java, home of the Sundanese, but was not able to hold on to the lands in the central region. There the kingdom was superseded by two new Islamic states, Pajang and Mataram, located at Surakarta and Yogyakarta, respectively. Mataram was by far the more successful of these two states, defeating Pajang in 1587 and Demak a year later, and by 1625 had established its hegemony over most of the island, conquering Surabaya in that year.

From the early 17th till about the mid-19th century the Muslim Javanese kingdom of Mataram and other, smaller and more localized kingdoms focused their efforts on agricultural production rather than overseas trade and the elaboration of local customs and beliefs rather than imports from elsewhere. Java's golden age of Hindu and Buddhist kingdoms was used as a role model for the creation of an elaborate court culture with its layers of respectful language and rituals of hierarchy. Islam remained the religion of state and people, but the Hindu-Buddhist past was highlighted in all art forms, from shadow puppetry to batik. Part of the reason for this significant break with the past, when Javanese ships and traders plied the oceans of Asia and its cities had many merchants from India, Thailand, China, Cambodia, and elsewhere, was the domination by the Portuguese and then Dutch of foreign trade. The Dutch navy was larger and stronger than any of the local kingdoms', and thus in Java the leaders turned their focus inward. Indeed Mataram after the 1670s owed much of its existence to the Dutch and thus was in no position to challenge the European power for control of the seas and its lucrative trading opportunities.

The Portuguese first made contact with the Indonesian Archipelago in the early 16th century and established a trading port in Maluku. Their first action in Java was to assist the Hindu state of Banten in the west against the sultan of Demak in a battle in 1522. In 1560 the Portuguese established their first trading post on the island, at Panarukan in the east, far from the Demak center of power in the north central region. In 1596 the first Dutch expedition reached Java and while unsuccessful at first because of piracy and other mishaps along Java's north coast, set the stage for later Dutch conquest of the entire region. A second and much larger Dutch fleet arrived in Indonesia, or what they called the East Indies, in the last year of the 16th century. Within two years they defeated a much larger Portuguese fleet in Banten harbor, West Java, and began their long period of colonial domination.

Along with their domination of trade in tropical hardwoods, spices, agricultural produce, and other valuable products the Dutch participated in local political affairs, such as granting assistance to Mataram in its quest to conquer Surabaya in 1613 and sending an ambassador to Mataram the following year. In 1680 the north central coast of Java, sometimes called the *pasisir,* was ceded to the Dutch East Indies Company (VOC) in exchange for a series of debts Mataram had accumulated; for the next 100 years or so no king was able to take the throne in the kingdom's new capital of Surakarta without the blessing of the Dutch. Dutch Protestant missionaries were also active in the archipelago, with little success outside Maluku. Their presence, however, did eliminate most of the success that earlier Portuguese Roman Catholic missionaries had had in gaining converts.

The 19th century introduced significant change to the world in which the Javanese existed. In 1799 the Dutch East Indies Company dissolved and all its territories became official colonies of the Dutch government. Then just a decade later the Dutch temporarily lost their new colonies to the British while their own homeland in Europe was occupied by Napoleon's France. In 1816 however, the British ceded the lands back to their fellow Protestant country in an attempt to strengthen the Dutch against their common Catholic enemies. The Dutch returned during an era of difficulty in Java; in 1821 a cholera epidemic killed thousands of people, a failed rice crop led to famine throughout the island, and the following year a volcanic eruption at Mount Merapi did even greater damage. In 1825 the Dutch inability to assist with these catastrophes in conjunction with the imposition of further colonial rules, such as a need to obtain an expensive passport to undertake the hajj to Mecca and the abolishing of Central Java's land leases, led to rebellion.

The Java War, 1825–30, was led by Prince Pangeran Diponegoro, who had been actively resisting Dutch colonialism for several years. In raising his army against the Dutch, Diponegoro had the assistance of the religious community and numerous ulama, who raised even further support through their community networks of worshipers. Several important Javanese nobles also supported the cause of war against the Dutch and together these forces began guerrilla attacks in 1825. The war went back and forth for five years without either side's scoring the significant victory needed to end the conflict and declare the ultimate victory. By 1830, however, the Javanese nationalist forces had lost many significant leaders, including Diponegoro's uncle, and their leader agreed to peace talks, which were to take place at Magelang. Instead of negotiating the Dutch captured Diponegoro and exiled him to Manado on the island of Sulawesi and then later to Ujung Padang on the same island.

Throughout the remainder of the 19th century and the first half of the 20th the Dutch took much greater economic advantage of their colonial realm than they had done prior to their victory in the Java War. They introduced and forced the production of such items as vanilla, indigo, coffee, cola, rubber, cocoa, and, most important, sugarcane on Java and engaged in mining and other activities on their other islands. A railway line was built in Java in 1873 to ship these lucrative products to the ports for export, but little infrastructure was created for the benefit of the Javanese themselves. For much of the period these colonies provided about a third of all the state revenue for the Netherlands and funded most of the industrialization in the small country. Occasionally the Dutch were forced to deal with a small, localized rebellion, such as those in Banten in 1846 and 1888, but for the most part they were free to pillage the resources of the archipelago where and when they desired.

The early 20th century also brought about some internal changes for the Javanese, such as the attempts by several Muslim organizations to provide a new framework for their religious way of life. This move by Sarekat Islam, Budi Utomo, and other organizations was not supported by the entire population, and a conference set up by the former in 1916 saw tensions erupt between various factions over the issue of "modernization." Modernization in the Javanese and wider Indonesian context in the early 20th century, however, did not mean what it might to a contemporary Muslim, or anybody else for that matter. As a result of Java and Indonesia's long Hindu and Buddhist history when Islam was embraced after 1500 it was in a very different form from the Islam that was practiced in the Middle East, North Africa, Central Asia, or anywhere else at the time. Many local practices and customs from the Hindu-Buddhist and animist past continued to be part of people's daily practice and wider belief system; certainly most Javanese art forms reflect this more ancient past rather than the more recent adoption of Islam. Prior to the "modern" era in the mid- to late-19th century, when few people traveled outside Indonesia, there was no issue with the local, syncretic form of Islam that was so widespread in the archipelago. Once a significant number of people began to be able to travel outside the country, especially on pilgrimage to Mecca, an activity called the hajj, Indonesians became aware that their own Islam was very different from that of others and those who wished to change local practices to coincide with the more global standards were called modernizers while those who did not were called traditionalists because of their wish to maintain Java's and Indonesia's traditional beliefs and practices.

The end of the Dutch colonial era can be seen in three different ways. Some sources indicate that the real end was in 1942 when the JAPANESE began their campaign in Java by bombing Surabaya and then took the entire island. Others indicate that the period of Japanese occupation from 1941–45 was merely an interlude during the Dutch era, comparable to the British period in the early 19th century, and that colonialism ended in August 1945 when the Indonesians declared their independence upon the collapse of the Japanese regime. Still others consider Indonesian independence to have occurred at the end of the war between Indonesia and the Dutch, who returned to the archipelago in 1945 to reclaim their colony, in late 1949.

Independence

One of the first acts of the newly independent Indonesia to have wide-reaching effects on the Javanese was the policy of *transmigrasi* or resettlement, which saw the population movement of thousands of Javanese, Madurese, and BALINESE from their heavily populated homelands to the country's less populated islands. As a result of this policy by 1988 more than 6 percent of the population of all Indonesian islands was Javanese and by the mid-1990s 10 percent was. While the policy, which actually began during the Dutch era, was pursued as an economic development strategy it has often been seen by the country's other ethnic groups as one of ethnic cleansing. Java's culture has always been seen as the most Indonesian by the country's mostly Javanese leaders, and this dominance has led to fears in other regions for their languages and ways of life. In the 1960s many thousands if not millions of Javanese were also killed by their own government during a crackdown against the Communist Party of Indonesia (PKI) in 1965–66. Estimates for the deaths during this era range from half a million to 2 million, much of which took place in East Java and in Bali.

The Javanese today continue to be among the country's most successful ethnic groups in terms of political influence and economic might. Every president of independent Indonesia, except the short-serving Jusuf Habibie, has been born in Java and is part of the larger culture of the Javanese. Many of the country's most important cities, from the capital of Jakarta to the textile capital of Bandung, are located on Java. East Java is one of the most important food-producing regions of the country: sugarcane, rubber, tea, coffee, tobacco, cacao, and cinchona, the source of quinine, crops are most productively grown as plantation crops on the island.

CULTURE

Javanese culture today is a complex mixture of elements introduced during all of the region's historical eras. The language still contains hundreds of Sanskrit words borrowed during the era of the Hindu-Buddhist kingdoms prior to 1500 as well as an extremely complex system for showing respect and hierarchy also from that era; there are nine styles of speech to reflect these social distinctions.

The introduction during the Dutch era of a dual peasant and plantation economy still prevails in the Javanese countryside where many families grow rice and other subsistence foods for themselves at the same time that some family members travel to work in the rubber, cocoa, tea, or other plantations in the highlands. Nonsubsistence work has also been expanded to include mining, food processing, textiles, and other industrial production on both a large and a small scale. Fishing remains important on both subsistence and commercial levels, but most families are not able to maintain animals aside from a few fowl for lack of space. Some traditional handicrafts, such as batik, weaving, and silversmithing, also continue to provide some employment throughout rural Java, especially for the expanding tourist market.

Urban Javanese in the capital, Bandung, Yogyakarta, Surabaya, or any of the other cities and larger towns of Java are generally becoming more and more similar to their fellow urbanites throughout Asia. They have access to mobile phones and the Internet, university education at home or abroad, and work in either the public or booming private sector. At the same time most consider themselves faithful Muslims and try to adhere to the precepts of their religion, including banking at local or other Islamic institutions that do not charge interest. Many women dress modestly and some wear a headscarf, though few wear the more radical covering of the *hijab* or engage in purdah or seclusion. Boys generally undergo circumcision between ages six and 12.

Javanese kinship considers the most important unit to be the nuclear family, which is generally the primary unit of production and consumption. In rural areas a family will work a single rice paddy and eat together, occasionally with the inclusion of grandparents or other extended kin. In urban areas nuclear families are the ideal and often both the mother and father will work outside the home and, if possible, a servant or two will reside with the family to take care of their domestic needs. Descent is bilateral so both one's mother's and one's father's families are sources of ancestors and of membership in the *alur waris*, a large kinship network of people who care for the graves of their common ancestors. A second kinship group, the *golongan*, is more informal and made up of people related through blood or marriage and living in the same village; this common residence leads to common participation in many agricultural and life-cycle ceremonies and festivities.

Javanese marriage, residence, and kinship rules, while they can be generalized to a certain extent, must also take into consideration the vast differences between nobility, *prijaji* or members of the bureaucracy, and commoners. For example the nobility and *prijaji* have traditionally practiced polygyny, the ability to have more than one wife, while most other Javanese have not done so. Most commoners take up neolocal residence at marriage whereby the new couple starts its own household while the rural *prijaji* and nobility tended to move into the home of one or the other set of parents. As a result of these two principles noble and *prijaji* households tended to be much larger than those of commoners, with 20 people or more being the norm, while commoner households had an average of five or six. In the contemporary world these differences have diminished with family planning and less emphasis on traditional class differences in favor of modern class differences, but they continue to inform the Javanese way of life.

Javanese inheritance patterns differed significantly from those of many other Muslim societies in that it was daughters or granddaughters who inherited most homes after living with the parents or grandparents after marriage. Other forms of property, such as land, animals, and trees, were inherited equally among all children while sons generally inherited the major family heirlooms.

While Javanese society has been dominated by the traditional class distinctions since long before the Mataram kingdom of the 16th century, today's Javanese have embraced the notion of upward mobility through acquisition of wealth, education, and external connections. At the same time Javanese art forms and speech continue to mark the hierarchy of the past and saving face remains extremely important for most individuals. The nine separate styles of speech are practiced daily and used habitually to mark status differences in age, gender, class, and other categories. To maintain the knowledge of this cultural linguistic expression from generation to generation, the Javanese language has been included formally in the curriculum for primary and high school students in Central Java, Yogyakarta, and East Java; Sundanese West Java maintains its own educational policies. Most forms of village and private social control continue to rely on people's desire for self-control and conformity so gossip, shame, and shunning remain powerful motivating factors for most individuals, even within cities. It is still rare to find a Javanese person willing to display any kind of negative emotion, from anger and aggression to simple annoyance; criticism must be given indirectly rather than head on and in general peaceful interactions are the goal of all social intercourse.

Most Javanese consider themselves good Muslims, but in fact the form of their religion does differ somewhat from Islam in other regions. Many local spirits, from ancestral to natural ones, continue to be seen as a viable source of both good and bad fortune and many Hindu gods are believed to roam the Javanese countryside. In general the Javanese are highly spiritual and easily reconcile their desire to remain good Muslims through prayer, pilgrimage, and other activities with their belief in spirits and devotion to their ancestors and Hindu gods. Visiting the mosque and speaking to an imam about a personal problem may be followed by a visit to a *dukun* or sorcerer for a spell to end suffering without most Javanese bothering with the contradiction. A few Javanese even believe in reincarnation, a holdover from the Hindu-Buddhist past, which is condemned within orthodox Muslim teachings.

FURTHER READING

Alice G. Dewey. *Peasant Marketing in Java* (New York: Free Press of Glencoe, 1962).

Clifford Geertz. *The Religion of Java* (New York: Free Press of Glencoe, 1964).

Hildred Geertz. *The Javanese Family: A Study of Kinship and Socialization* (New York: Free Press of Glencoe, 1961).

Robert Jay. *Javanese Villagers: Social Relations in Rural Modjokuto* (Cambridge: MIT Press, 1969).

Linda B. Williams. *Development, Demography, and Family Decision Making: The Status of Women in Rural Java* (Boulder, Colo.: Westview Press, 1990).

Jewish Tats   *See* TATS AND MOUNTAIN JEWS.

Jin   *See* JURCHENS.

Jing   *See* VIETNAMESE.

Jingpo   *See* KACHIN.

Jino (Jinuo, Youle)

The Jino are one of China's recognized 55 national minority groups, although they were recognized as such only in 1979. Between 1949 and 1979 they were classified as a subgroup of the DAI, under whose rulers they lived till 1950 and the Communist takeover of their region. They are a relatively small group and almost all live in Jinoluoke Township, Jinghong County, Xinhuangbanna Dai Autonomous Prefecture, Yunnan Province. This is a mountainous region that gets plenty of rain from May to September and has a subtropical climate conducive to agriculture. For the rest of the year, when very little rain falls, the township is crossed by several rivers, including the Pani and Small Black, which allow for the cultivation of both dry highland and wet rice varieties, corn, cotton, bananas, papayas, and Pu'er tea. The region is also rich in minerals and animal life, including elephants,

JINO

location:
Jinoluoke Township, China

time period:
Unknown to the present

ancestry:
Unknown

language:
Jino, a Tibeto-Burman language

oxen, monkeys, and a plethora of birds, which have allowed hunting to continue as a viable economic activity into the present.

In addition to hunting and farming, which until 1950 was done using slash-and-burn or swidden techniques on impermanent fields and since that time on permanent fields using irrigation and additional fertilizers, Jino women gather roots, fruits, and herbs from the forest. Blacksmithing and silversmithing, furniture making in both bamboo and rattan, spinning, weaving, and the sale of produce all infuse cash in the local economy.

One of the alternative names by which the Jino have been known in the past, *Youle*, is also indicative of an important aspect of their social structure. The term means "following the maternal uncle" and indicates that this group was matrilineal in the past. Today they are considered patrilineal and trace their families through the male line only, but some scholars estimate that about 300 years ago they were matrilineal and it was the mother's family into which each child was born. Matrilineal societies are not matriarchal, that is, dominated by women. Jino women could occupy high positions in society, including as clan leaders and ritual specialists, but the society was not female dominated. Instead male children simply inherited their land, position, or titles from their maternal uncles rather than from their fathers, as is the case in patrilineal societies. Today maternal uncles retain a high position in society and their spirits are worshipped by their sisters' children as well as by their own.

In addition to being important for determining which ancestors a person must worship, the Jino lineal system helps to determine household and village structures and marriage partners. In the past all Jino households were made up of extended families of related men with their wives and children. As many as 20 people lived together, shared household and agricultural tasks, and ate together. Today nuclear families are more common, but villages continue to be made up of two or more exogamous clan groups, which require their members to marry outside the group. Membership in clans is also passed down from a father to his children, just as is membership in the lineage groups that constitute each clan.

Jomon (Joumon culture)

The Jomon were Neolithic (New Stone Age) people and among the earliest inhabitants of the Japanese Archipelago. They migrated from mainland Asia to Japan at a time when sea levels were lower than today and they became isolated from the mainland during the gradual rise of the post–ice age melt about 10,000 years ago. Earlier theories posited Southeast Asian origins for the Jomon, on the basis of material remains; however, genetic testing of Jomon remains as well as contemporary Japanese, Southeast, and northern Asian populations has pointed to more northerly origins. Interestingly a particular genetic marker carried by the Jomon is more evident in both northern and southern Japan than in the central region, indicating a greater mix of newer populations in the center.

The Jomon were a preliterate group who left no evidence of their culture save what archaeology has been able to uncover. It has been suggested that the ancient Jomon were the ancestors of the modern AINU people of Japan, and recent genetic evidence seems to support this theory. However, material remains are much less clear and the Jomon-Ainu connection continues to be a contested hypothesis among archaeologists and historians of ancient Japan.

Major evidence of Jomon settlement has been found on the Kanto plain, Chubu Prefecture (mountainous central-northern Honshu); around Matsushima Bay in northern Honshu; around Okayama City; as well as on the Kansai plain and in northern Kyushu. Relatively fewer sites have been found in the country's southwest than in these northeastern regions; however, there is evidence of Jomon settlement virtually all over Japan. The number of sites suggests a population easily in excess of 750,000 people by what has been called the middle Jomon period. It is still unclear why this middle period should have seen the greatest flourishing of Jomon culture; some scholars suggest it was related to climate change and the relative warmth of the period. It is worth mentioning that all archaeology of the Jomon period has been conducted since World War II, as before then any studies that questioned the divine heritage of the emperor and the people of Japan would have been considered seditious.

The Jomon built and lived in wooden and straw houses in villages and followed a hunter-gatherer style of subsistence in their regional territories. It remains unclear whether their settlements were year-round or whether they migrated seasonally to take advantage of resource increases and weather patterns. Their diet consisted of foods that could be found in abundance in their areas, which typically in-

JOMON

location:
Japanese Archipelago

time period:
Approximately 12,000 to 300 B.C.E.

ancestry:
Mainland Asian, probably from the northern part of the continent

language:
Unknown, with speculation about Austronesian connections; genetic evidence probably discounts this. Some also connect the Jomon language to Ainu, also without much convincing evidence

cluded taro and other tubers, grapes, chestnuts, acorns, and animals including boar and deer. The large number of shell middens from this period points to marine and river foods, especially clams and mollusks but also salmon, trout, and marine mammals such as seals and whales, as a primary source of protein. The invention of pottery in the earliest days of Jomon culture opened up many new foods to them because pottery vessels allowed for boiling and processing, especially of starchy roots and tubers. Eventually they became skilled with ceramics, probably as the first potters in the world, and their name, a modern invention, is derived from the modern Japanese words for the distinctive rope marking of much of their pottery (*jou*, rope or cord; *mon*, marked).

Jomon peoples contributed to a number of other technological innovations as well, such as bone fishhooks, harpoons, pit traps, and fish traps. Good circumstantial evidence also suggests they were able to cross open waters, though no actual watercraft have been discovered or found depicted. The normal system of storing produce seems to have used pottery, baskets, and storage pits. Evidence such as bronze and lacquer goods suggests that trade with the mainland, mainly the Korean Peninsula, also took place. One study from the 1960s

Jomon time line

B.C.E.

12,000 Approximate dating for the earliest rope-patterned Jomon pottery found in the Japanese Archipelago. Earliest evidence of Jomon culture, sometimes called the Incipient Jomon period.

10,000–6000 Rising sea levels and reduction of regional volcanic activity. The Japanese Archipelago is separated from the Eurasian mainland, isolating the Jomon peoples.

3,500–2500 Middle Jomon period, the height of the Jomon culture, with uncontested settlements on all the major islands of the Japanese Archipelago.

500 Introduction of wet rice cultivation to the Japanese Archipelago, discovered in Yayoi, Tokyo. Little change in Jomon settlement or lifestyle is immediately evident. This marks the beginning of the end of the Jomon period archaeologically.

300 Invasion of the Japanese Archipelago by what has been called the Yayoi culture. Evidence of warfare involving bronze and stone weaponry; Jomon and Yayoi settlements include fortifications.

100 Evidence of persistence of Jomon artifacts in the archaeological record comes to an end.

This stylized *dogu* figurine from the Jomon period seems to have a human body and an animal head, making it similar to many thousands that have been found throughout Japan. *(Art Resource, NY/Werner Forman)*

also posits a trade relationship between Jomon and Ecuadorian peoples of the New World, based on similarities in pottery types, but this connection has been seriously refuted by most experts ever since.

Little is known of Jomon religious life save what can be ascertained from their mortuary practices and artwork. Jomon remains appear to be buried in pits, normally with many of the material goods a person would need in the afterlife. These goods include beautiful ceramic masks and flat human-shaped ceramic talismans as well as stone rods, alternatively described as swords and phallic rods. Crescent-shaped ceramic beads, reminiscent of animal claws or more modern *shinki* beads (normally jade or crystal), are also a feature of many burials. Those who died during infancy seem to have been entombed in ceramic urns. In the middle and late Jomon periods burial pits were often lined with stone slabs, and a number of mound burials and cemeteries of this kind have been found. There is evidence of an emerging social stratification in the Jomon burial practices, which become more pronounced toward the later periods. Over time burial also became more common, perhaps as more families attained the material goods to accompany their relatives to the afterlife.

Most notable among the Jomon period religious relics are the stylized ceramic figurines, about four to 10 inches in height, found in some Jomon house sites and occasionally in burial sites. The earliest of these figurines, found in the mountainous central region, were merely animal heads akin to those dogs, cats, rabbits, and serpents, while later ones in the region have human bodies and animal-like heads. When the technology spread to the rest of Japan about 2000 B.C.E., the figurines became more human and female, although some of the wild features of these earlier animal-human combinations remain. Art historians have described the expressions and stances of many of these figures as grotesque and as representing to their creators a sense of being "not us," a combination of human, animal, and even plant features marking their absolute difference from humanity. Rather than seeking to incorporate the power of the largest animals, such as bears and boars, in their world, these figures sought to reproduce shy, sleek animals. Why this was the case remains a mystery, as does their exact meaning to the people who created them. The best guess based on the development of female figures, some of which appear pregnant, and on the number of figurines found in pits of vegetable and animal remains, is that they were fertility figurines created to encourage human, animal, and plant reproduction.

The beginning of wet rice agriculture marks the twilight of the Jomon period. Increased trade and changes in production methods indicate that as contact with the mainland became an increasing feature of Jomon life, it was soon to be interrupted by an invasion of mainland peoples. The discovery of an early rice field in Yayoi (Kanto Plain, now part of Tokyo), has given this period the name of *Yayoi*. However, later evidence suggests earlier wet rice cultivation took place on the island of Kyushu. There is considerable evidence that this invasion was a hostile one and that war was frequent. Sherds of stone and bronze weapons found in human remains and the fortification of settlements of the late Jomon period indicate that the Jomon peoples either were conquered or chose to adopt the cultural and technical innovations of the invaders.

FURTHER READING

Martin Collcutt, Marius Jansen, and Isao Kumakura. *Cultural Atlas of Japan* (Oxford: Phaidon Press, 1988).

Junko Habu. *Ancient Jomon of Japan* (New York: Cambridge University Press, 2004).

Keiji Imamura. *Prehistoric Japan: New Perspectives on Insular East Asia* (Honolulu: University of Hawaii Press, 1996).

JURCHENS

location:
Northern China and Siberia, Asian Russia

time period:
At least sixth century C.E. to 1234

ancestry:
Southern Tungusic

language:
Jurchen

Jurchens (Chin, Jin)

The Jurchens were a southern Tungusic people who lived in the region of contemporary Manchuria and to its northeast. They were the ancestors of the contemporary MANCHUS and themselves established a powerful but short-lived empire, the Jin dynasty, in 1115, when they conquered the KHITANS. This lasted until they were themselves overpowered by invading MONGOLS in 1234.

The Jurchens began their march to power in north China in the early 12th century when the rulers of the Song dynasty in China requested their assistance in conquering the Liao empire of the Khitan people. At that time the Jurchens were hunting-and-gathering forest dwellers and seemed no threat to the Song rulers, who had been in control of China since 960 C.E. The Chinese badly misread this situation, however, for after their defeat of the Khitans in 1115 the Jurchen leader, Wanyan Aguda, named himself emperor of the newly formed Jin dynasty. In 1123 Aguda was replaced by his brother, Ukimai, who led his armies against those of the Song. He occupied the Song capital at contemporary Kaifeng, Henan, then known as Bianjing, and drove the Chinese south to Hangzhou.

By 1142 under Holoma, Aguda's son and the new emperor of the Jin, the Jurchens had conquered all of northern China and signed a peace treaty with their southern Song neighbors. As had the Liao before them in the north, however, the Jurchens adopted most of the trappings and features of the Chinese governmental system and even hired Chinese civil servants to occupy most key positions in the bureaucracy. To assist in the communication between these two peoples, between 1120 and 1145 a Jurchen script was created, borrowing elements from both Khitan and Chinese writing systems. Many documents were translated from Chinese into the new script as well, facilitating translation of the Jurchen language in the present. Despite this outside assistance from Chinese technocrats the Jin dynasty fared badly; its people's tribal way of life did not facilitate the collection of taxes or other revenue and the empire was on the brink of collapse in 1214 when it had to abandon the capital at Beijing. Then in 1234 the Mongol armies swept through the rest of their northern region. The Jurchen people survived despite the loss of their empire and eventually transformed into the Manchus several centuries later, but this period was the end of this ethnic group as it was known in the 12th and early 13th centuries.

Jurchen society and culture emerged in the forests of Manchuria, where its people lived in small chieftainships dominated by both military chiefs and religious leaders or shamans. The society was organized by kinship and patrilineal groups were organized into large clans and tribes. Each of these individual units, membership in which was inherited from one's father, was loosely organized, and these groups joined only occasionally for religious rituals, military expeditions, or other communal events. Otherwise feuds between local clans and even lineages often dominated relations, and until opposition to the Liao drew the Jurchens together, the feuding prevented a single ruler from unifying the various clans and tribes.

The Jurchens lived on hunting, gathering, fishing, and some small-scale swidden agriculture. They were relatively settled in their forest homes, only migrating occasionally when military or subsistence needs forced the issue. This was different from the nomadic Mongols, who eventually conquered them, and meant that they more quickly adapted to and adopted the political structures of the agrarian Chinese they came to dominate, at least in the north.

Nonetheless the Jin dynasty was not solely a Chinese empire with a Jurchen ruler. Many aspects of Jurchen tribal society survived the transition to imperial rule and have even survived today as part of Chinese culture. The Jurchens added corporal punishment of courtiers and simplified the imperial governmental system in China to just three parts: the bureaucracy, army, and censorate. The censorate was an innovation that provided a check of all bureaucrats and was considered the eyes and ears of the emperor; it remains today in modified form as the Communist Party serves as the check on local and national bureaucrats. The Jurchens were the first rulers to establish

Wanyan Aguda

Wanyan Aguda was born in 1068 to the Jurchen chieftain Wanyan Helibo during the Khitans' Liao dynasty. When their father died, his older brother, Wanyan Wuyashu, inherited the role of chieftain and quickly embarked on a campaign to expand their clan by recruiting sick and malnourished warriors from rival Jurchen tribes. As their clan strengthened and grew, they fought and conquered other tribes, and in 1113, Wuyashu died and Aguda assumed the role of Wanyan chieftain. The following year he endeavored to unite the Jurchen tribes in rebellion against the corrupt Liao dynasty of the Khitans and only a few months later succeeded in capturing the city of Nigjiangzhou, or what is now modern-day Fuyu in Jilin Province. As the Jurchen tribes succeeded in defeating the Liao troops and capturing more territory, Aguda proclaimed himself first emperor of the new Jin dynasty. In 1119 Aguda allied himself with the Northern Song dynasty, who agreed to help in the war against the Liao troops in exchange for the return of 16 Yanyun states to the Song. By 1122 the Jurchens had captured all five Liao capitals and had succeeded in establishing a feudal government based on the Jurchen tribal system, an organized agricultural system, and a Jurchen written language. Aguda died in 1123 at age 56 and was succeeded by his younger brother, Wanyan Wuqimai, who eventually captured the Liao emperor and effectively wiped out the Liao dynasty.

a capital at Yenching or today's Beijing, and it was during their rule that Chuan-chen Taoism became an important religious movement. This form of Taoism differs from Cheng-I Taoism in that priests in the former movement live as celibate monks, having renounced family and material ties to this life; they are also vegetarians and believe that giving up these connections and comforts in this life will lead to immortality. Priests in Cheng-I Taoism have families, eat meat, and try to help others in their journey toward good fortune.

FURTHER READING

Hoyt Cleveland Tillman and Stephen H. West, eds. *China under Jurchen Rule: Essays on Chin Intellectual and Cultural History* (Albany, N.Y.: SUNY Press, 1995).

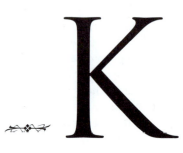

Kacharis

The Kacharis are linguistically related to the NAGAS of the highlands of northeast India and western Myanmar and to the Bodo. They also have a number of regional subdivisions, such as the Dimasa Kacharis, Mech or Boro Kacharis, and Sonowal Kacharis.

In the 13th century a powerful Kachari kingdom emerged in Assam and eventually subsumed most territory in that region under the Kachari rulers, whose capital was Hidimbapur, now called Dimapur. This city fell to the AHOM people in the 15th century, but many other Kachari city-states survived into the 19th century. In 1706 King Tamradhaja, a Kachari who ruled from Maibong on the Mahur River, likewise lost his city to the Ahom and then fled south to Khaspur, where a number of other Kachari kings ruled over the plains of Cachar, which took their name. The last Kachari king, who ruled from Haritikar, was assassinated in 1830 by fellow Indians from Manipur and did not leave an heir. As a result the British took over the former Kachari lands and ended the on-again, off-again control the Kacharis had wielded over others in the region of Assam, Manipur, and Nagaland.

The traditional Kachari economy was centered on shifting swidden agriculture with the use of a few permanent terraced fields that were fertilized and irrigated for use with wet rice. The Kacharis are patrilineal and each lineage is part of a larger exogamous clan, each named after some aspect of nature. This characteristic of the Kachari clan system led British missionaries and government commentators in the 19th and early 20th centuries to say that these clans were totemic, each claiming descent from the plant, animal, river, or bit of landscape from which they derived their name; this has been shown in subsequent years not to be the case.

The Kachari religion was traditionally a form of animism that recognized the existence of many powerful ancestral, enemy, and nature spirits. Both village and household gods were important and required extensive rituals and gifts to keep them happy; some sources also mention the existence of a supreme deity among the Dimasa subgroup, called Madai. The most important rituals took place prior to sowing and were meant to guarantee a good harvest; rituals after the harvest thanked the gods for their benevolence. The harvest Bushu festival requires large numbers of animals to be sacrificed, including chickens, pigs, buffaloes, and sheep, and the brewing of large amounts of rice beer. A village priest dedicates the offering of rice, meat, and beer to the creator gods and then the entire village or group of villages participates in the feasting, musical performances, dancing, and other festivities for one, three, or seven days, depending on the kind of Bushu.

In the past each Kachari village had a men's house, a *nohdrung*, where all adult men lived. The movement of a boy from his natal home into his village's *nohdrung* was an important rite of passage that started him on his path toward adulthood. While living in the men's house he would learn all the songs, rituals, handicrafts, dances, and other cultural knowledge needed to live as an appropriate Kachari man. Boys also learned to defend their village and started to act as guards against raids and theft by enemy villages.

Kachin (Dashan, Jinghpaw, Jingpo, Khang, Singhpo, Theinbaw)

The Kachin are a people of Myanmar (Burma) with small numbers living in China and India. The name *Kachin* is derived from the word in their language meaning "Red Earth" and refers to a valley between two branches of the upper Irrawaddy where the largest number of traditional chiefs lived in the 18th century. In China, where they are considered one of that country's 55 recognized national minorities, they are called *Jingpo*, usually written *Singhpo* in India. A number of other, small Tibeto-Burman-speaking peoples, such as the Maru, Atsi, and Lashi, are also included in the larger Kachin category.

One of the earliest references to the Kachin is from Assam in the 13th century, while in China the first mention is from Yunnan Province in the 14th or 15th century. Edmund Leach, an anthropologist who has written extensively on the Kachin, begins his history of the proto-Kachin in the eighth century, but even he must admit that information about actual historical events, rather than political principles, is nearly impossible to find and must be read between the lines of Chinese and Shan history. What we do know is that early Kachin societies paid tribute to the larger states in these regions; the people worked as blacksmiths and had chiefs who tried to imitate the status and role of larger hereditary chiefs among the SHANS and other groups.

The Kachin entered the historical record as a group of their own in the 18th and 19th centuries in connection with the Shans and other Tai-speaking peoples. At that time some Kachin communities began migrating east and south from the hilly north of Burma in conjunction with Chinese trade routes carrying opium north and Chinese material goods south. They were also participants in the Third Anglo-Burmese War in 1885 and important political actors in independent Burma, which became Myanmar in 1989. The president-elect of the country just before 1962's military coup was a Kachin chief, and ever since that period the Kachin have been central to the long-running civil war in the country. In China in 1953 the

Jingpo received their own autonomous region in southwestern Yunnan, which has housed some refugees and insurgent leaders from the war in Burma/Myanmar.

The traditional economic activity of the Kachin was farming, primarily using swidden or slash-and-burn techniques to clear fields and provide fertilizer. Rice is the most important crop, but corn, buckwheat, millet, sesame, tobacco, and a wide variety of vegetables are also grown for consumption, trade, or sale. Cotton and opium have been important cash crops over the past centuries, although the extent of the latter is often disputed. After about three years the Kachin let their burned fields lie fallow for about 12 years, but rotating fields usually does not require migration away from a village. In China wet rice in irrigated fields is more common than swidden agriculture, and terraced farming is not uncommon in the hills. To supplement these agricultural products many Kachin men fish, hunt, and breed chickens, pigs, dogs, buffaloes, and/or cattle. While dogs and sometimes horses were kept for their labor, other domestic animals were largely kept for religious sacrifices and other feast times in the past; they were not consumed on a regular basis.

Unlike the Shans, with whom the Kachin have had close relations for centuries and who do not place much emphasis on kinship, the Kachin give a great deal of weight to patrilineal descent and agnatic clan membership, which all people inherit from their fathers. Clans among the Kachin actually act independently of one another in some political situations and thus are sometimes seen as the equivalent of tribes among other groups. These clans are also organized in a hierarchical fashion with five aristocratic clans generally recognized throughout the Kachin and Jingpo areas. Clans themselves are not exogamous, but lineage segments within clans are and thus require men and women to seek marriage partners from other segments.

This importance of clans and lineages is also played out in the Kachin political system, which has been one of the most thoroughly documented in all of Southeast Asia. Interest in Kachin politics began in the 1950s when the anthropologist Edmund Leach began writing about it; many other anthropologists have followed in his wake, some agreeing with his general principles, others emphatically disagreeing. What all authors point to is an inherent contradiction between two opposite tendencies in Kachin politics: a *gumsa* system

KACHIN

location:
Kachin and Shan States, Myanmar (Burma); Yunnan Province, China; small numbers in Assam and Arunachal Pradesh, India

time period:
Possibly 13th century C.E. to the present

ancestry:
Possibly Tibetan

language:
Jingpho, a Tibeto-Burman language

KADAZAN DUSUN

location:
Sabah, Malaysia, and
Brunei

time period:
1989 to the present

ancestry:
The separate groups
of Kadazan and Dusun
were joined by the
Kadazandusun Cultural
Association into a single
ethnic group only in 1989.
Many experts agree that
the Kadazan group itself
goes back only to the
1950s or 1960s and that
the ancestors of all con-
temporary Kadazandusun
people were Dusunic
people.

language:
Kadazandusun or
Dusunic, an Austronesian
language with many
dialects

in which hereditary chiefs are able to control the labor, land, and resources of large numbers of people and essentially act as feudal kings and a *gumlao* system, which is anarchic, at least among a community of chiefs, and allows them to act only within the confines set for them by their lineage and clan members and their fellow chiefs. Leach argued that throughout Kachin history these two contrasting systems were always oscillating back and forth while others argue that the *gumlao* system is essentially a historical development of the 19th century after significant interaction between the *gumlao* Kachin and the more *gumsa* Shans. All authors argue that the Shans are the source of the *gumsa* system; their essential disagreement is based on the unclear history of Kachin society prior to the 19th century.

In addition to kinship residence is very important for determining a Kachin's relations with other Kachin. At marriage ideally the new couple moves in with the husband's family for a period of several years. However, this ideal is not always met and in cases of youngest sons, who do not inherit much property, the advantages of moving into the wife's home, farming her father's land, and taking over the farm upon the father-in-law's death often outweigh the norms of patrilocal residence. Poor men may also work for their father-in-law in lieu of or in addition to offering smaller than usual bride-wealth payments, made to the wife's family to reimburse them for the loss of her labor and to legitimate the couple's children.

Kachin villages were usually small because of the requirement for extensive landholdings to make the swidden system viable; very few had more than 100 households. Villages with important hereditary chiefs were usually larger than others, and residents in the village gained prestige from residing beside a powerful, multivillage chief. At the village level such religious-political events as merit feasts, organized by hereditary chiefs in *gumsa* villages and by whoever had enough power and influence to do so in *gumlao* villages, also create a unified community at the village level. Today many Kachin communities are Christian, but conflict between Catholic and Protestant villages continues to unite villages through common religious identity.

FURTHER READING

Edmund Leach. *Political Systems of Highland Burma* (Cambridge, Mass.: Harvard University Press, 1954).

Kadazan Dusun (Dusun, Kadazan, Kadazandusun, Kedazan)

The 30 or more subgroups of the Kadazan Dusun people account for between 20 and 33 percent of Sabah's population of 1.6 million people and are the Malaysian state's largest ethnic group; a number of Kadazan groups also reside in Brunei. Until 1989 the Kadazan and Dusun of Sabah were classified as separate ethnic groups, but a political act by the Kadazandusun Cultural Association joined the two on the basis of their common linguistic and cultural heritage. The main difference between the Kadazan and Dusun lies in their traditional geographical influences; the Kadazan originated in the valleys and deltas of Sabah's western coastal plains, which favor paddy fields, and the Dusun in the hillier inland areas of the state.

All of the Kadazan Dusun people were traditionally agriculturalists, and the name *Dusun* literally means "orchard"; their homes were usually surrounded by fruit trees. Their main crop was wet rice grown in intensively worked paddies, supplemented by dry rice, corn, sweet potatoes, and other crops grown in temporary gardens cut out of the thick forests of Sabah. During the dry season men would cut down the trees or secondary growth, burn the remains to fertilize the ground, and then plant during the wet season, a process repeated yearly on different plots. The Dusun specifically are believed to have been the first group on the island of Borneo to adopt the plow as distinct from a digging stick. Today some Kadazan Dusun continue to work in subsistence agriculture, but most have either taken up work in the region's rubber plantations or joined the market economy as laborers, bureaucrats, service providers, or even professionals.

Both the Kadazan and Dusun traditionally resided in patrilineal villages of about 150–200 people contained in 10 or so multigenerational longhouses; today only the Rungus Dusun continue to reside in longhouses while most other groups have moved into nuclear family dwellings. As patrilineal groups, descent was handed down from fathers to children. They were also patrilocal and so at their marriage to someone from outside their own patriline, required by the rules of exogamy, women had to move into the longhouses and villages of their new husbands. Their traditional religion, animism, honored a variety of local gods and spirits, specifically those related to the agricultural cycle, as well as their own ancestors. Today most Kadazan Dusun have converted to

In addition to the beauty pageant, the harvest festival provides an opportunity for men to show off their dancing skills, as this man is doing at the Kadazan Dusun Cultural Association. *(OnAsia/ Edgar Su)*

Christianity, especially Roman Catholicism, or to Islam, the dominant religion of Malaysia, but there is still some evidence of their animist past. The most significant is the harvest festival or *pesta kaamatan*. During this event priestesses perform rites to honor the rice spirits or *bambaazon* after a year's harvest. This festival takes place in May, and the two last days of the month are public holidays throughout Sabah. During the celebration the most important event is the crowning of the *unduk ngadau* or harvest queen, and girls throughout the state compete for the coveted crown. The beauty pageant is held to commemorate the spirit of Huminodon, a beautiful mythological character who gave her life in exchange for a bountiful harvest for her people.

Although today they have a reputation as a peaceful people who dislike violence and are hard-working and hospitable, in the past the Dusunic peoples were all headhunters. This past has been put on display for all to appreciate at the Monsopiad Cultural Village, which opened in 1996 in memory of a legendary Kadazan warrior and headhunter named Monsopiad. The Kadazan Dusun were one of the Austronesians or proto-Malayic peoples who migrated to Borneo from southern China sometime after about 3500 B.C.E., and this history is honored in their being classified as *bumiputra* or sons of the soil. As such they benefit from political, educational, and economic advantages not accorded to Malaysia's Indian, Chinese, and other non-Malay residents.

See also Malaysians: nationality.

Kalasha (Kafir Kalash, Kalash Kafir)

The Kalasha are a unique people living in just three valleys near Chitral, Pakistan, the capital of the North-West Frontier Province, which borders Afghanistan. Unlike their neighbors in the Hindu Kush Mountains on both the Afghani and Pakistani sides of the border the Kalasha have not converted to Islam. During the mid-20th century a few Kalasha villages in Pakistan were forcibly converted to this dominant religion, but the people fought the conversion and once official pressure was removed the vast majority continued to practice their own religion.

Their religion is a form of Hinduism that recognizes many gods and spirits and has been related to the religion of the ancient Greeks, who mythology says are the ancestors of the contemporary Kalasha. As do the Burusho, another small community in Pakistan, the Kalasha claim they are descended from a handful of Greek soldiers who remained behind when Alexander the Great moved through the region in the fourth century B.C.E. As a result of this claim many writers have been at pains to find connections between the Kalasha and the ancient Greeks and their polytheistic religion, which recognizes many gods. However, it is much more likely, given their Indo-Aryan language, that the religion of the Kalasha is much more closely aligned to the Hinduism of their Indian neighbors than to the religion of Alexander the Great and his armies.

Most Kalasha families make a living in subsistence agriculture and transhumance pastoralism, moving their herds of animals seasonally to find pasturage and water. Women are primarily responsible for agricultural work, growing wheat, corn, barley, apples, walnuts, grapes, and mulberries, while men move seasonally with their herds of cattle, sheep, and goats, the latter being most important. In winter the men reside in the lower elevations with their wives and children and then in summer

KALASHA

location:
North-West Frontier Province, Pakistan

time period:
Unknown to the present

ancestry:
Unknown

language:
Kalashamun, a Dardic language in the larger Indo-Aryan family

move to higher elevations when snows melt and leave behind rich fields of grass. Even in winter when herds and families are in the same location, the men's sacred goats must be protected from the polluting influences of women and from possession by evil spirits.

Despite this belief about the pollution inherent in women, both women and men among the Kalasha claim that the greatest feature that distinguishes them from their Muslim neighbors is that "their women are free." Kalasha woman do not wear a *hijab* or headscarf; nor are they confined to the home in purdah. Indeed this was the reason the Pakistani state tried to force conversion to Islam in the 1950s: Kalasha women were seen as immoral and tempting to Muslim men. Women have some degree of choice over their marriage partners, and running away from marriage to elope with another man is a common occurrence, though it does often spark a feud between families when negotiations over the woman's fate break down. The matrilineal kinship structure of the Kalasha also provides women with some degree of prestige since the primary cross-sex relationship is between a woman and her brother rather than a woman and her husband.

Since the 1970s significant change has entered the Kalasha valleys through the Pakistani government's efforts to link the area to the rest of the country through roads and schools. While the latter have conferred benefits, the former have largely resulted in significant inroads by timber companies with negligible benefits to the local population. In fact a landslide in the region in May 2007, which destroyed the crops of an entire village of Kalasha, is probably the most significant result of these companies' denuding the hillsides of trees.

Kalingas (Igorot, Limos, Limos-Liwan Kalingas, Linimos)

The Kalingas are indigenous inhabitants of the northern Luzon highlands in the Philippines. They speak an Austronesian language, which identifies them as among the first wave of migrants to enter this archipelago from Taiwan and ultimately from southern China approximately 5,000 years ago. They are sometimes identified as members of the collective group of the Luzon highlands known as the IGOROT; however, they refuse to be called Igorot except by their own tribespeople as the term is subject to negative connotations. Despite colonization of the Philippines by Spain, Japan, and the United States, Kalinga territory was never colonized and the Kalingas remain somewhat isolated from outsiders in the present day, especially from Westerners.

Perhaps the most important event in the history of the Kalingas occurred in the 1970s and 1980s when they successfully fought the construction of a hydroelectric dam on the Chico River. The Filipino government under Ferdinand Marcos as well as the World Bank saw the damming of this river for the production of hydroelectric power as a positive step toward further economic development in the country. For the Kalingas and their neighbors, however, the dam meant loss of both rice fields and sacred burial grounds and they refused to be moved out of the way. For many years they withstood an onslaught by the Filipino military, including the bombing of villages, with a significant loss of life. By 1975 the World Bank had withdrawn from the project as a result of the activities of the Kalingas, and when Marcos was replaced by President Corazon Aquino in 1986 the project was abandoned altogether.

The main Kalinga economic activities are wet and dry rice farming with the addition of swidden or slash-and-burn gardening for vegetables, herbs, and other subsistence products. Crops produced include sugarcane, sweet potato, taro, corn, and some bean varieties. The most important cash crop is coffee. In addition to farming the Kalingas traditionally engaged in hunting and fishing; however, the importance of these two activities has diminished as a result of deforestation and destruction of riverside-dwelling animal life by logging and mining companies. The Kalingas are expert potters and basket and loom weavers. Ceramics produced by potters are sold to generate income.

Kalinga territorial units are organized into endogamous political communities. This means marriage can occur only between members of the same tribe, and this practice is the basis of political connections. Communities are led by a select group of men known as *pangats* and each community has one or more villages in which members see themselves as being part of one distinctive group. A village is made up of competing independent families who are expected to support one another at all times. Each village entrance is guarded by a small shrine called *podayan*. At the turn of the 19th century the Kalingas were known as headhunters prone to deadly intergroup fighting, but this custom disappeared in the early 20th century.

See also AUSTRONESIANS.

KALINGAS

location:
Kalinga Province, Luzon, the Philippines

time period:
About 3000 B.C.E. to the present

ancestry:
Austronesian

language:
Kalinga, an Austronesian language

Kamboja (Ashvaka, Ashvakayana, Aspasio, Assakenoi, Kambhoj, Kamboh, Kamboj, Kamoz)

The Kamboja were an ancient tribe of Iranian-speaking people who entered Central Asia and northern India from their homeland sometime in prehistory. The earliest reference to them is that of an ancient Sanskrit author, Panini, who wrote on Sanskrit morphology in the fifth century B.C.E. He mentions the Kamboja people as members of the Kshatriya kingdoms or Janapadas of the Vedic period of Indian history (prior to the sixth century B.C.E.). Other ancient Indian texts, such as the *Manusmriti* of the second century B.C.E. and the *Mahabharata*, completed in the first century C.E., refer to the Kamboja as having once been Kshatriyas or warriors in the Indian hierarchical system but as having lost their noble status through neglect of sacred rituals. The *Edicts* of Asoka, the Mauryan king of India in the third century B.C.E., speak of the Kamboja as an independent republic within the greater empire.

In addition to these Indian references, the Kamboja of Central Asia played a significant role in that region's early history. Cyrus the Great, the ruler of the Achaemenid empire (*see* PERSIANS, ACHAEMENIDS), conquered Kamboja territory, probably around the Kabul Valley, about 530 B.C.E. The Kamboja continued to be recognized in Central Asia as a separate group when Alexander the Great's troops conquered the region in 329–327 B.C.E.

The most important cultural attribute of the Kamboja according to ancient texts, both Indian and Persian, is the centrality of horses. As a seminomadic people all the early Indo-Iranians were concerned with the breeding and training of horses (*see also* SCYTHIANS). Some of the alternate ethnonyms for the Kamboja refer to their attachment to horses, such as *Ashvaka* and *Ashvakayana* in Indian languages and *Aspasio* and *Assakenoi* in ancient Greek. In addition to their command of horses the Kamboja utilized elephants to wage war on their enemies. When they fought against Alexander the Great's men, the Kamboja were believed to have had 30,000 horse-mounted soldiers, at least 30 elephants, and 20,000 footsoldiers in the defense of their homeland.

In addition to waging war, the Kamboja were farmers and pastoralists, raising mostly cattle. A second-century C.E. Greek historian, Arrian, who summarized and documented the materials written by Alexander's armies from several hundred years earlier, wrote of the superiority of the Kamboja's 230,000 cattle.

The original religion of the Kamboja, Mazdaism, points to their Indo-Iranian roots. Even prior to Zarathustra's writing of the Gathas, the sacred texts of Zoroastrianism that describe the relationship between Ahura Mazda and humanity, the ancient Iranian people were largely believers in the one god, Ahura Mazda. During Asoka's time, the third century B.C.E., however, many Kamboja, both the Zoroastrian Kamboja of Central Asia and the Hindu Kamboja of India, seem to have converted to Buddhism, largely as a result of the work of his missionaries.

Other references to these two separate communities of Kamboja are made by Ptolemy, the Greek geographer, in his second-century C.E. work *Geography*. He states that Tambyzoi are located on the Oxus River (Amu Darya) in Bactria and have retained their Iranian culture and Zoroastrian religion. By contrast the Ambautai live on the southern side of the Hindu Kush Mountains and are largely Hindu. Both of these peoples have been identified by later scholars as Kamboja people.

Over the course of history the Central Asian Kamboja largely disappeared into the great melting pot of the Central Asian steppes. In India and Pakistan, however, about 1.5 million people today continue to identify themselves as Kamboj or Kamboh people, the former name preferred in India, the latter in Pakistan. More than 130 different Kamboj/h clans still exist, some associated with Kshatriya tradition and others with Brahmin. These modern Kamboj/h are not unified in terms of religion or culture, as Hindus, SIKHS, Muslims, Buddhists, and JAINS all claim Kamboja identity. As they did in the past, however, many modern Kamboj/h people engage in agriculture, trading, and the military, so that some aspects of their identity have continued for the past 2,500 years.

In addition to the ancient Kamboja people living in separate Central Asian and Indian communities, some sources reckon that a third Kamboja community can be traced to Southeast Asia. These sources claim the KHMERS of Cambodia believed that their own ancestors had been from the Kamboja and that they could trace their heritage back to an Achaemenid prince named Kambujiya. The legend states that ambitious Kamboja from India traveled east in the third or fourth century C.E. to engage in trade, eventually establishing a powerful empire in Southeast Asia. This connection and their ancient name that is derived from it, *Kambuja*, are the origins of the contemporary names *Kampuchea* and *Cambodia*. Other sources give no credence to this mythology and

KAMBOJA

location:
Parts of Afghanistan, Tajikistan, and northwestern India

time period:
Ancient times to the present

ancestry:
Indo-Iranian

language:
The ancient Kamboja people spoke Avestan, an Eastern Iranian language. Today the Indian Kamboj and Pakistani Kamboh people speak a number of local languages including Urdu and Punjabi.

state emphatically that there is no real connection between Central Asia and Cambodia. Instead they argue that during the Angkor period of Cambodian history, 802–1431, Indian placenames were adopted throughout Southeast Asia, probably under the influence of classical Sanskrit literature. There can be no doubt that a connection between *Kambuja* (Cambodia) and *Kamboja* exists, but whether it reflects a real relationship or merely the accident of naming will probably never be known with any certainty.

Kanak (Canaque)

The Kanak are the indigenous Melanesian settlers of the French territory of New Caledonia. Originally the term *Kanak* was from a Polynesian word for human being, *kanaka,* which was used as a derogatory term by Europeans to refer to the indigenous people of the Pacific Islands more generally. The term has been compared to the word *nigger* for its strength as a derogatory epithet. As has happened in other places, however, beginning in the 1960s, the local population in New Caledonia began to reappropriate the word from their colonizers and use it as a badge of pride to distinguish themselves from other residents of the territory, especially the local Europeans, whom they refer to as Caldoches. The Kanak also see themselves as distinct from the other peoples of New Caledonia, including Polynesians, who had been taken to the island as indentured laborers in the 19th and early 20th centuries.

The initial inhabitation of New Caledonia has been dated from around 1000 B.C.E. through the excavation and carbon-14 (^{14}C) dating of potsherds, beads, and shells that clearly delineate them as relics from the Lapita culture. Also found with the earliest Lapita pottery in New Caledonia is obsidian, a product that was transported nearly 2,000 miles from New Guinea. In addition some archaeologists claim to have found evidence of human habitation in New Caledonia dating from 3000 B.C.E., 1,500 years prior to the emergence of Lapita culture anywhere, while others claim to have found pottery that predates that of the Lapita style. These varied datings demonstrate that the origin of the Kanak people is shrouded in mystery.

Traditional Kanak society is similar to other Melanesian cultures in that the clan is generally the largest unit with which individuals identify. Clans in Kanak society are patrilineal, so that individuals inherit their membership through their father's line of descent. As it does throughout clan-based societies, kinship forms the basis for most relationships, including defining marriage partners, trading partners, and both allies and enemies. Even today the rites, rituals, and rules of social engagement defined by clanship remain important in the construction of contemporary Kanak identity; the term that politically active Kanak use for this unique indigenous culture is *la coûtume.* Other traditional cultural traits that link the Kanak to other societies throughout Melanesia are the importance of ceremonial exchange relationships, a belief that ancestral spirits affect the fortunes of the living, a great degree of separation of the sexes, and an agricultural tradition that is heavily dependent upon yam, taro, and sweet potato. To this day Kanak families often live in multigenerational patrilineal households, with men and women eating and sometimes sleeping separately from each other. Traditional subsistence patterns, however, have been disrupted to a great degree by imported and processed foods like rice and canned meats. Nonetheless one traditional food item, *bougna,* which consists of taro, yam, sweet potato, banana, and pieces of chicken, crab, or lobster wrapped in banana leaves, has attained the status of a national food for many Kanak and remains popular throughout the island. Unlike most Melanesians, but like the Trobriand Islanders, who are Melanesian but speak a Polynesian language, the Kanak recognize a degree of social hierarchy that differentiates chiefs and their families from other kin groups.

Beginning in the early 19th century the indigenous populations of New Caledonia began a long period of disruption when European explorers and missionaries arrived, carrying diseases and foreign ideas with them. The greatest disruption occurred in 1853, when France claimed the area of New Caledonia and the Loyalty Islands as colonies and then a decade later began to ship convicts to the main island, Grand Terre. From 1864 to 1896 a total of about 20,000 French convicts were transported to New Caledonia; they were joined by thousands of free French colonists as well as indentured laborers from China, Indonesia, and other regions of the Pacific. The result of this migration is that today the Kanak make up less than 50 percent of the population of their native islands. This minority status was made worse over the course of 150 years of colonial history by the fact that Kanak or indigenous culture was seen as primitive and without any value by the local elite. This disregard for indigenous culture was highlighted in the local school system, where all children were taught that their ancestors were the Gauls, the ancient ancestors of the French.

Starting in the 1960s and extending through the present time a large number of people of indigenous descent in New Caledonia began to

KANAK

location:
New Caledonia, referred to as Kanaky by the indigenous population, or Territoire des Nouvelle-Caledonie et Dépendances in French

time period:
Probably 1000 B.C.E. to the present

ancestry:
Melanesian-Polynesian mix

language:
There are around 33 different indigenous Kanak languages; French is currently the official language of the territory.

seek retribution for past wrongs against them and their land, with an eventual aim of independence from France. As part of this movement most of the 1980s in New Caledonia was a time of violence as the newly self-conscious Kanak population engaged in violent protest over their position as a colonized people and a subordinate minority in their own land. As a result of these actions in 1988 the French government and two opposing political parties in New Caledonia (one loyalist, one seeking independence) signed the Matignon Accords, which granted the local population a greater degree of autonomy than they had experienced since the 19th century. On the basis of that agreement France began to put more resources into developing the island chain beyond its capacity as an exporter of nickel, including investing in the education and training of 400 Melanesian inhabitants in the "400 Cadres" scheme, which provided greater access for a few Kanak in the local bureaucracy. The agreement also set the stage for a referendum in 1998 over independence, which did not pass; a second referendum is scheduled for 2014 within the framework of a 15- to 20-year time frame for independence.

Kandharis   *See* SERAIKIS.

Kannadigas

Kannadigas are native speakers of the Dravidian Kannada language; sometimes the term is also used to refer to residents of the Indian state of Karnataka; this entry is about the group based on language rather than residence.

Kannada is an ancient language that split off from the other Dravidian languages, such as Tamil, Telugu, and Malayalam, possibly as early as 230 B.C.E. Some sources indicate that there are a few inscriptions from that year of Asoka's Mauryan rule that are written in Kannada. The first full-length Kannada inscription, the Halmidi inscription, cannot be positively dated before about 450 C.E. The 16 lines of text on a pillar in the village of Halmidi show that at that time Kannada was used at least as a local administrative language if not a wider reaching one. About 400 years after that inscription the first extant Kannada text was written by Nripatunga, king from 815 till 877. His *Kavirajamarga* or *The Royal Road of Poets* provides the first descriptions we have of Kannada speakers, or Kannadigas, and their country. All of these works are considered part of the first phase of Kannada development, the Purva Hale Gannada or pre-Old Kannada, which dates from antiquity until about the 10th century. This was followed by the medieval period or Hale Gannada, Old Kannada, in which a large amount of Jain religious literature was produced until about the 12th century; then the Nadu Gannada or Middle Kannada period until the 15th century; then the Hosa Gannada or New Kannada period to the present (*see* JAINS).

In terms of this long history of using Kannada, or Kanarese as it is sometimes written in older British texts, Kannadigas are usually considered one of the major nationalities of India, along with the speakers of HINDI, Tamil, Telugu, and others. When India was being divided into states on the basis of first-language use in 1956, the speakers of Kannada pushed for the recognition of their nationality and were granted the state territory that is today called *Karnataka*; its prior name was *Mysore*.

Although Kannadigas today number more than 36 million, making Kannada one of the top 30 spoken languages in the world, some activists and scholars among this population are concerned about the fate of Kannada both in India and in the wider world. They accuse their fellow Kannadigas of being ashamed of their language, history, and culture and of preferring to speak Hindi or English, even with fellow Kannadigas. They are concerned that young people are no longer being educated in Kannada, that far less literature and fewer films are being produced in it, and that the state of Karnataka itself may be in jeopardy if fewer and fewer of its residents use the language as their mother tongue. While some of this rhetoric may seem out of place for such a large population, it is true that in 2006 only 66 films were released in this language and 55 of them were such major failures that they did not even recoup their expenses at the box office.

See also DRAVIDIANS; MALAYALIS; TAMILS; TELUGUS.

KANNADIGAS

location:
The Indian states of Karnataka, Andhra Pradesh, Tamil Nadu, and Maharashtra

time period:
Possibly before 230 B.C.E. to the present

ancestry:
Dravidian

language:
Kannada, a Dravidian language, the state language of Karnataka, where 9 million people speak it as their second language

One Kannada-language film that did succeed in 2006 was *Aishwarya*; the film's popularity is attributed to its catchy musical score and star, leading model Deepika Padukone, shown here with costar Upendra. *(AP Photo/Aijaz Rahi)*

KAPAMPANGANS

location:
Pampanga, Bataan, and
Tarlac Provinces, Luzon,
the Philippines

time period:
3000 B.C.E. to the present

language:
Pampangan, a northern
Philippine language in
the Austronesian family

Kapampangans (Capampangans, Pampangans, Pampanggo, Pampango, Pampanguenos)

The Kapampangans are AUSTRONESIANS who inhabit Pampanga Province and a number of towns in the surrounding provinces of Bataan and Tarlac. *Pampang* means "riverbank" in their language and refers to the flat, delta region of the Pampanga River on which they live.

GEOGRAPHY

Pampanga Province is located in the south of the Philippines' northernmost main island, Luzon. It is a low flood plain crossed by the Pampanga River and its many tributaries and bounded by Manila Bay to the south, the Zambales Range to the northwest, and Mount Arayat in the northeast. Much of the province is swampland with a rainy season between May and October and a dry season between November and April. It is a relatively urbanized area of the country with one large city, the capital of San Fernando; 21 municipalities; and 538 *barangays* or village wards. The eruption of Mount Pinatubo in 1991 destroyed a significant amount of the eastern part of the province, including much of Clark Air Base.

ORIGINS

The origins of the Kapampangans, as of most Austronesian speakers in the Philippines, are probably in south China, from which they sailed in double-outrigger dugout canoes about 5,000 years ago to Taiwan, and then later the Philippines and Polynesia. There is no certainty as to why this population left south China; however, archaeologists have hypothesized that it was a combination of population pressure, increased commerce from the Yangtze River region of China and moving southward down the river and its tributaries, a growing demand for marine and tropical forest goods, and climate change.

Contemporary Austronesian languages can be subdivided into two distinctive groups that separate the languages of Austronesian Taiwan from those of the remainder of the family, which include all Malay and Oceanic languages. This linguistic division, in addition to several anomalies in the archaeological record, such as a lack of rice in the earliest Austronesian sites in Taiwan, indicates that the origins of the Austronesian people may have been two separate exoduses from southeast China. If these did occur, the first exodus was probably from Fujian Province in China to Taiwan, which saw the rise of TA-P'EN-K'ENG CULTURE,
with its distinctively marked pottery and stone tools, but without archaeological evidence of domesticated rice. The descendants of this first wave would be the contemporary speakers of Taiwan's Austronesian languages, the ABORIGINAL TAIWANESE. The second exodus may have occurred around 3000 B.C.E., taking a second wave of Austronesian speakers from southeastern China to Taiwan and then almost immediately to Luzon in the Philippines around the same period. This second wave, with its red-slipped pottery, may also have been the ultimate source of the LAPITA CULTURE.

Despite the relative consensus of linguists and archaeologists about this version of the origins of the Kapampangans, oral traditions of the people themselves claim that they are much later migrants to the archipelago; some early Spanish chroniclers make similar claims about the Filipino lowlanders, including the Kapamapangans. These stories state that the Kapampangans are the descendants of Malay migrants who moved to their home in Luzon from the Malay Peninsula, Sumatra, and Borneo, or perhaps Java, possibly around 300 B.C.E. They also claim the Kapampangans introduced a "more civilized" culture and "more sophisticated" way of life to the Philippines than had been there before and thus probably point more to contemporary political ideologies than to ancient migration patterns. The Spanish used these stories to explain why the lowlanders adopted Christianity much more quickly and readily than the highlanders, and contemporary Kapampangans have adopted the same ideology of ethnic superiority.

HISTORY

When they arrived in the Philippines about 3000 B.C.E. the Austronesian speakers would probably have met small bands of people who had already been residing on the islands for approximately 20,000 years. The hunting and gathering AETA peoples, as they are now called, probably lived in the most productive areas of the country, the coastlines, valleys, and lower hills, in very small, impermanent settlements. With their ability to grow their own crops the incoming Austronesians were able to maintain significantly higher population densities than the Aeta and thus to push the hunter-gatherers into the more marginal highland forests and mountaintops, where they still live today. The numerically and technologically stronger agriculturalists also seem to have lent their language to the Aeta, all of whom today speak

Austronesian languages rather than the more ancient languages they would have taken with them in their much earlier migrations.

Kapampangan history as we know it began in 1571 with the arrival of the Spanish colonizers and missionaries. Prior to that year the people of the region had extensive trade contact with the Chinese and JAPANESE as well as with the Aeta and other highlanders on Luzon. Most scholars believe the Kapampangans lived similarly to most other peoples on the island, engaging in shifting agriculture and trade and practicing an animistic religion with beliefs in spirits and ghosts. The first Spaniards found a people unwilling to submit to either their sword or their religion, and Martin de Goiti, one of the first three Spanish conquistadores to arrive in the archipelago, spent a period fighting in the region before pacification. The first province the Spanish created in the region, Pampanga, was significantly larger than its namesake today and encompassed all of central Luzon. Later Bataan, Nueva Ecija, and Tarlac were carved from the original territory, thus shrinking its size and relative importance in the country.

The most important resource provided by the Kapampangans during the colonial period was food, although they also provided a significant amount of unpaid labor and lumber for building as well. As it is today, rice was the most important food grown by the people and thus it was what the Spanish used as the basis of the local economy; all Kapampangan families had to pay tribute to the colonizers in this commodity. The combination of forced unpaid labor and high tribute caused the Kapampangans to rebel against the colonizers a number of times prior to the American takeover of the archipelago in 1899. The years 1645 and 1660 were both extremely turbulent in the region, with a revolt against the tribute system led by Francisco Maniago in 1645 and an independence movement led by Andres Malong and Melchor de Vera in 1660.

At the end of the Spanish period Kapampangans again participated fully in the political and military events of the time. Pampanga was among the first Filipino provinces to participate in the revolution that began in 1896, and its main city, San Fernando, became the capital of the short-lived Philippine Republic three years later.

The American colonial period in the region produced tremendous economic, political, and social change in the region and among its people through the building of a number of military bases. Starting in 1902 the army built Fort Stotsenberg just outside Angeles City, us-

Kapampangans time line

B.C.E.

3000 The initial migration of the Austronesian speakers, including the ancestors of the Kapampangans, to the Philippines.

300 Approximate date when Kapampangan oral history and a few Spanish sources have them migrating to Luzon from Sumatra, Borneo, and possibly Java.

C.E.

1571 The Spanish create Pampanga Province.

1645 Francisco Maniago leads a revolt against the high tribute all Kapampangans have to pay to the Spanish.

1660 The Kapampangan Independence Revolt led by Andres Malong and Melchor de Vera takes place in Mexico, Pampanga Province. Defeat results in the Spanish move of the colonial capital of the region to Bacolor.

1762–63 The British occupy the city of Manila.

1899 The Spanish cede the Philippines to the United States and a local war of independence breaks out. San Fernando in Pampanga Province is the capital of the short-lived Philippine Republic before the Americans consolidate their control.

1902 A civil U.S. administration replaces military rule upon the pacification of the independence fighters in the north.

1941 The Japanese bomb Fort Stotsenberg and Clark Air Field, U.S. military installations in Pampanga Province. They go on to occupy all of the Philippines.

1944 The United States retakes the Philippines.

1945 The Philippines attains independence from the United States.

1960 Rufino Jiao Santos, a Kapampangan, becomes the Philippines' first cardinal of the Roman Catholic Church.

1961 Diosdado Pangan Macapagal the Incorruptible from Lubao, Pampanga, is elected the ninth president of the Philippines; he loses his reelection bid four years later to Ferdinand Marcos.

1969 The New People's Army is formed as the military arm of the Communist Party of the Philippines. In reaction to this and other threats Marcos declares martial law in 1971.

1973 Rufino Jiao Santos dies in Manila.

1983 Marcos has Benigno Aquino, his political rival and a Kapampangan, assassinated upon his return to the Philippines after a period of self-imposed exile.

1986 Ferdinand Marcos is deposed and Aquino's widow, Corazon Aquino, who is one-eighth Kapampangan, comes to power.

1991 Clark Air Base is abandoned by the United States when the eruption of Mount Pinatubo destroys much infrastructure.

2001 Gloria Macapagal-Arroyo, daughter of President Macapagal, takes office as the 14th president of the Philippines.

ing the labor of many local men; this was joined by Clark Field a few decades later. Clark was attacked by the Japanese at the same time as Pearl Harbor in 1941 and was occupied by the

Japanese along with the rest of the archipelago from 1941 to 1944. After the war Clark Air Base became the largest air base outside the United States, covering 156,204 acres of land carved out of the region's swampy jungles. Tens of thousands of U.S. army, navy, marines, and air force personnel passed through Clark on their way to both the Korean and Vietnam Wars; tens of thousands more local people worked on or near the base, including thousands of Kapampangan women forced by poverty into the sex trade. The United States abandoned the site in 1991 when the eruption of Mount Pinatubo destroyed much of its infrastructure. In its place the Filipino government has developed the Clark Special Economic Zone, a free-trade area with its own landing strips, hotels, tourist areas, and other infrastructure to lure international tourists and businesses to central Luzon.

CULTURE

As was the case during the Spanish period, agriculture has always been central to the lives of the Kapampangans. Wet rice and sugarcane are the most important cash crops with rice, corn, sweet potatoes, cassava, and many tropical fruits serving as both subsistence foods and secondary cash crops. Those outside the agricultural sector of the economy may work in the large fishing industry or in forestry since tropical hardwoods continue to generate revenue for the region; mining, handicrafts such as embroidery, jewelry, and woodworking are other economic sectors, and there is a large professional class.

With the proximity to Manila as well as Clark and the cities of Angeles and San Fernando, the Kapampangans had significant opportunities in the 21st century to enter the global mainstream in economic and political affairs. The country's first female president, Corazon Aquino, the widow of Benigno Aquino, one of the most famous Kapampangans in history, was herself one-eighth Kapampangan. The second female and current president of the Philippines, Gloria Arroyo, is also Kapampangan, as are a large number of Filipino actors and other public figures.

The two best-known aspects of Kapampangan culture outside the region are the cuisine and the large Christmas lanterns of San Fernando, made of a multitude of materials in towns and villages all over the province and then paraded around the capital at Christmastime for everyone to see. The people are known throughout the archipelago for their creativity in combining elements from local, Chinese, and Spanish cuisines into a unique blend of flavors and textures. Many dishes center on meat, such as *longaniza,* a kind of pork sausage, and *tapa,* dried venison or beef. *Buro* can be meat, fish, or vegetables that have been preserved or fermented in brine and then served with rice.

As is the case throughout the Philippine lowlands, the Kapampangan people are overwhelmingly Roman Catholic and have been since the early decades of the Spanish colonial period; however, theirs is a worldview that does not exclude the spirits, rituals, and beliefs of their pre-Christian ancestors. There are many beliefs about evil spirits affecting pregnant women and their unborn children that require certain acts, such as avoiding some foods and watching where they walk and sit. Capri or Cafre is a dark-skinned giant believed to inhabit the region's thick forests and to capture wayward children, tear them apart, and then eat their bodies and souls. At the time when many Kapampangan women gave birth at home instead of in hospitals all the woman's relatives and neighbors would assist in the birth by making a great deal of noise, even exploding

Corazon Aquino

Corazon Aquino is world renowned not only for being the first female president of the Philippines and Asia's first female president, but also for her advocacy work on behalf of women, democracy, and peace. Born on January 25, 1933, into an affluent family in Paniqui, Tarlac, she received a comprehensive education at St. Scholastica's College before traveling to the United States to study in Philadelphia and New York. She received her bachelor's degree in 1953 and returned to the Philippines to study law. In 1955 she met and married Benigno Aquino, Jr., or Ninoy, who, at 22, had recently been elected mayor of Concepcion and was a member of the Liberal Party Philippines. Under the regime of President Ferdinand Marcos Benigno Aquino, Jr., was arrested and exiled in 1980. Upon returning to the Philippines in 1983, Benigno Aquino, Jr., was shot and killed in the Manila International Airport. Sixteen soldiers were arrested and sentenced to *reclusion perpetua,* but no central leader or organizer was ever named. On the urging of friends and supporters Corazon Aquino assumed her husband's position as head of the Laban Party and ran for president against Ferdinand Marcos in 1986. Though she reportedly lost, the election was widely speculated to have been rigged and massive nonviolent protests and demonstrations along with foreign pressure drove Marcos into exile. Upon her inauguration Aquino immediately set to the task of reforming the government on the basis of a democratic Freedom Constitution, which was drafted and ratified in 1987. Shortly afterward congressional and local elections were held to establish a government based on democratic vote. Her campaigns for democracy garnered worldwide attention and Aquino was named *Time* magazine's Woman of the Year in 1986; she was nominated for the Nobel Prize in peace that same year but lost to Elie Wiesel. She remained in office until 1992 and continues to participate in Philippine politics to this day, despite being diagnosed with colon cancer in early 2008.

Kapampangan lanterns have made their way into the Christmas parades of the country's capital, Manila. This one was created and displayed for the holiday season in 2007. *(AP Photo/Pat Roque)*

firecrackers, which was believed to drive the infant out faster. Other supernatural beings that can cause illness or misfortune include Nunu, which live in earth mounds; Mangukukulam and Dwende, which can take on human form; and Tianaka, which live in forests and should be called out to when a human passes by their home.

Further Reading

Lino L. Dizon. *A Survey of Kapampangan Folklore* (Tarlac, Philippines: Tarlac State University, 1993).

John A. Larkin. *The Pampangans; Colonial Society in a Philippine Province* (Berkeley and Los Angeles: University of California Press, 1972).

Karakalpak (Qaraqalpaq, Qoraqalpog)

The Karakalpak are a small Turkic-speaking minority group currently residing in the Autonomous Republic of Karakalpakstan within the country of Uzbekistan. The Karakalpak population today is around 600,000, only about one-third of the population of the autonomous republic. The name means "Black Hat": *kara/* black and *kalpak/*hat refers to the traditional head covering for men.

The historical and archaeological evidence for the origins of the Karakalpak points back to the late 15th or early 16th century. At that time the KAZAKHS' Lesser Horde dominated the region of southern Kazakhstan where the Karakalpak probably emerged as a loose federation of Turkic tribes living in that area. In 1825 the Karakalpak fled their territory in southern Kazakhstan during an onslaught by the ZUNGHARS' empire. Their refugees were taken in by the UZBEKS' Khiva khanate, which gave them land on the southern shore of the Aral Sea and along the Amu Darya's delta.

Because of their early history of interaction and geographic proximity there were extensive ties between the Kazakhs and Karakalpak in the 16th–19th centuries, with some tribes from the latter federation even being ruled by chiefs and nobles from the former. Culturally the two groups are fairly similar as well, sharing a language family, aspects of their traditional material culture such as clothing, and customs such as the use of certain amulets to ward off the evil eye. However, economically the two were quite different. The Kazakhs remained nomadic sheepherders until well into the 20th century, with some continuing to live this way today, while the Karakalpak have been settled or semisettled agriculturalists for their entire history. They combined gardening with fishing and cattle breeding, activities that still occupy many rural Karakalpak. There was some seasonal movement to accommodate the need for grass and fodder in winter, but their summer and winter residences were generally as close together as possible.

The Karakalpak federation is divided into two major clan divisions, the On Tort Uriw, or 14 Tribes, and the Qon'irat; the two groups show few genetic similarities and thus suggest the mixed origins of the Karakalpak. Even today clan identity remains very important to both rural and urban Karakalpak, and clan exogamy, the practice of marrying outside one's clan, continues to be an important factor in dating and marriage practices. Marriages also tend to be patrilocal in that a young bride must move in with her new husband and his extended family. This can be a difficult transition for many rural women, who leave their villages for the first time in order to marry. The youngest daughter-in-law in the extended family also has to prove her worth by working extremely hard and being treated essentially as a servant, a practice that adds to the difficulty of early married life for many women.

KARAKALPAK

location:
About 80 percent live in the Autonomous Republic of Karakalpakstan on the lower Amu Darya, south of the Aral Sea in Uzbekistan; others live in Kazakhstan and Russia

time period:
Late 15th century to the present

ancestry:
Turkic

language:
Karakalpak, a northwestern Turkic language related to Kazakh, Bashkir, and Nogay

In addition to structuring marriage patterns the clan system points to some differences between different groups of Karakalpak. The On Tort Uriw and Qon'irat differ somewhat in their subsistence practices: the former, who live in the southern regions of the republic, focus the majority of their energy on agriculture, and the latter, northern residents, supplement agriculture with fishing and cattle breeding. In the past agricultural activities were mixed, with wheat, millet, sorghum, alfalfa, fruits, and vegetables all grown on small plots, but during the Soviet era this region was primarily dedicated to cotton and rice on heavily irrigated fields worked by large collective farms. Individual families continued to scratch out subsistence products like potatoes, vegetables, and fruits on small plots they leased from the collectives. Today rural families usually keep a few chickens, goats, or sheep to supplement their gardening activities and thus avoid the monotonous, starchy diet of potatoes, bread, pasta, and rice that plagues the urban poor.

Both during the Soviet era and today the Karakalpak have been one of the poorest ethnic groups in their region of the world. This problem has become worse since the 1960s when the building of the Kara Kum Canal and overirrigation led to ecological disasters, including the desiccation of about 80 percent of the Aral Sea and salinization of local farmland. In addition during the Soviet era this region was used to test a variety of nuclear and chemical processes, contributing to the ill health and generally bad living conditions for inhabitants of this desert region. Recently many Karakalpak and others in the republic have left the rural areas to live in cities, especially Nukus, which is Karakalpak's capital, but also the regional cities of Biruniy, Taxiyatas, and Xojeyli. There they live in large, poorly built cement apartment blocks constructed during the Soviet era and work in government services, in the oil- and gasfields, or as shopkeepers.

Most Karakalpak consider themselves Sunni Muslims but few are able to attend mosque regularly because there are so few of them in the region. Islam, and religion more generally, was heavily persecuted during the Soviet era but most Karakalpak continued to maintain Muslim traditions with regard to birth, male circumcision, marriage, and funerary rituals. In addition many pre-Islamic religious practices survived the Soviet period, especially those that either prevent the evil eye or cure its ill effects such as illness, infertility of humans or animals, and the death of a child or healthy adult. Some Karakal-

pak also engage in a form of ancestor worship in order to prevent angry spirits from striking out at them for having ignored their responsibility toward their dead relatives.

Contemporary Karakalpak life is not an easy one. In addition to the poverty and ill health that plague the region, maintaining Karakalpak identity as separate from that of the surrounding Uzbek state comes at a cost. Karakalpak face persecution and hostility from an Uzbek government that is trying to construct a national identity from largely Uzbek history, customs, and traditions. Karakalpak outside their own villages tend to keep their ethnicity to themselves and to speak Uzbek as much as possible; they also tend to claim Uzbek identity on permits or other official forms and documents, drawing on their citizenship rather than their ethnic affiliation to avoid discrimination.

See also Uzbekistanis: nationality; Turkic peoples.

Further Reading

Quatbay Utegenov. *Karakalpak Folk Tales* (Oxford: Trafford, 2005).

Karakhanids   *See* Karluks.

Kara Khitai   *See* Khitans.

Karbis   (Arleng, Mikir)

The Karbis are members of a tribal group that lives mostly in the Indian state of Assam. They are included in India's list of Scheduled Tribes as the Mikirs, but they prefer the ethnonyms *Karbi* or *Arleng*, which means "human being" in their language.

In general the original homeland of all Tibeto-Burman language speakers was western China, from which they migrated into their contemporary homes. Exactly when this migration took place remains under investigation, but there is little chance that a definitive date will be established since these early populations did not have writing and few material remains have been found to distinguish one Tibeto-Burman tribal group from another. Karbi legend states that they once lived along the Kalang and Kapili Rvers and in the region of the Kajiranga National Park, Assam, but were driven into the hills by powerful groups of Kacharis. The date for this dispersal, if it occurred in this manner, is unknown. Once the Karbis began migrating into the region of the Ahom kingdom in the 17th century there is a bit more certainty about dates and events

---

KARBIS

location:
Mostly the Karbi Anglong District, Assam, India

time period:
Unknown to the present

ancestry:
Tibeto-Burman

language:
Karbi, a Tibeto-Burman language

because of the careful records kept by these monarchs. Today there are four subgroups of Karbis that generally differ only on the basis of the region in which they live: Chinthong, Ronghang, Amri, and Dumrali.

The traditional subsistence practice of the Karbis was *jhum* or shifting horticulture, generally prepared using slash-and-burn or swidden techniques. Each year a family would have to prepare a new garden site by cutting down trees and shrubs, allowing them to dry, and then burning away the remains to provide an ash fertilizer. Once all the sites around a village had been used, entire villages would move six to 13 miles away, create a new village, and begin farming in the surrounding region. Today this kind of extensive farming is no longer viable as a result of shortages in land, and so most Karbis have adopted more intensive techniques using irrigation and artificial fertilizers. The most important innovation in the 21st century has been the introduction of spice-farming collectives in the Karbi Anglong region of Assam, which have provided significant income to some farmers willing to invest in chili, ginger, turmeric, and other spices.

Many of these new companies are operated at the village level, the traditional settlement pattern and political organization of the Karbi people. Traditionally the village council was made up of all the older men in the village and had a single headman who was chosen from the group. Today the headman or *gaonbura* is appointed by the larger Karbi Anglong Autonomous Council. Despite this change the headman remains a prestigious and locally powerful person with the ability to make economic and political decisions that affect all residents, such as whether the community will join a spice cooperative. However, in other ways, the headmen do not have the power or authority they once held since decisions about justice and conflicts tend to wind up in local or regional courts of law instead of the council or headman's office.

Karbi social structure is organized through both residence and kinship. Each individual is born into one of five Karbi patrilineal clans, which are based on the father's clan membership and his father's before him. These large clan units are also divided into subclans, which are exogamous. People from the same subclan and even clan consider themselves brothers and sisters so that marriage between them is strictly forbidden.

Today the Karbi tribe is in the midst of a regional conflict with the Dimasa and other tribes over territory, funding, and revenge over past events going back to about 1970. The violence since 2007 has included destroying homes and thus making more than 50,000 people from the two groups homeless and killing about 90. Although most of the deaths and property damage occurred among unarmed civilians, there are militarized groups on either side of the conflict: the United People's Democratic Solidarity of the Karbis and the Dimasas' Dima Halam Daogah.

Karen (Ka-Kaung, Kareang, Kariang, Kayin, Pwo, Sgaw, Yang)

The Karen are the second-largest ethnic group in Myanmar, with smaller numbers living in the highlands of Thailand; they also make up the majority of Burmese refugees in Thailand and elsewhere in Southeast Asia.

GEOGRAPHY

The traditional Karen homeland prior to the mid-18th century was the highlands of eastern Burma, a mostly forested region with north-to-south-running valleys that are watered by the Salween River system. Since that time many Karen communities have moved into western Thailand while others have moved into the lowlands. Geographers identify three different ecological niches inhabited by the Karen today: the lowlands of the Tenasserim coast and the Irrawaddy, Salween, and Sittang River deltas; the Pegu Yoma hills between the Irrawaddy and Sittang Rivers; and the highlands of Shan, Kayah, and Karen States and Tenasserim.

Generally these regions are made up of tropical rain forest with either large trees or dense jungles of bamboo and vines. The monsoon season runs from mid-May through September while the rest of the year is relatively dry. Cooler temperatures are the norm from November to February while March and April are extremely hot until the monsoon arrives and cools the temperature somewhat. Tenasserim is the wettest Karen region, receiving about 200 inches of rain per year

ORIGINS

Karen origins are still contested among anthropologists and historians, but the most common hypothesis is that they are a northern people from either Central Asia or the borderlands between China and Mongolia. The exact date of their southern migration is also unknown; the eighth century B.C.E. is often posited as a possibility. Why this migration may have occurred

---

KAREN

location:
Myanmar (Burma) and northern Thailand

time period:
Possibly eighth century B.C.E. to the present

language:
There are 21 different Karenic languages in the larger Sino-Tibetan language phylum; until recently there was no internal recognition that these subgroups were related to each other. Sgaw Karen and Pwo Karen are the two most common dialects with the former having more prestige and greater population than the latter.

Karen time line

B.C.E.

739 One estimated date for the initial migration of the Karen from northern to Southeast Asia.

C.E.

Eighth century Inscriptions mentioning the Cakraw are believed to be about the contemporary Sgaw Karen subgroup.

13th century The first written reference to the Karen as a whole, though it is spelled *Karyan*.

1826 The British annex Burma and begin proselytizing among the Karen.

1941 The Karen fight with the British against the Burmans and Japanese.

1942 The British are expelled from Burma and Karen men return to defend their villages from the Japanese and Burmans; tens of thousands are killed and tortured.

1945 The British retake Burma with significant military assistance from the Karen levies, who work under the code name *Operation Character*.

1947 Aung San is assassinated and the hopes for a multiethnic leadership in an independent Burma are extinguished.

1948 Burma becomes independent from Britain in January.

1949 The Karen begin the long military struggle for independence in Karen State, eastern Burma, which has since been renamed *Myanmar*.

1970s Burmese general Ne Win formulates and puts the Four Cuts Policy, which leads to attempts at cutting off food, money, recruits, and intelligence to the Karen rebels, into action.

1997 The State Law and Order Restoration Council, which has been fighting the Karen for decades, is renamed the *State Peace and Development Council* (SPDC); the new name does not decrease the atrocities committed by national forces.

2006 The UN High Commissioner for Refugees (UNHCR) estimates that 140,000 Karen refugees live in Thailand, with thousands more entering during the year.

remains completely hypothetical but the usual reasons, population and/or political pressure, remain the most likely scenarios.

Regardless of their migration pattern or date the Karen definitely arrived in the region of contemporary Myanmar prior to many of the region's other large ethnic groups, including the BURMANS, SHANS, and THAIS; however, the MON probably arrived somewhat earlier. Their early history in Southeast Asia remains entirely speculative and it is not until the eighth century that documents from central Myanmar mention the Cakraw, believed to refer to the modern Sgaw, the largest subgroup of Karen. Subsequently a 13th-century inscription specifically mentions the Karyan, believed to be the first reference to the group as a whole.

HISTORY

The Karen entered the historical record as we know it in the mid-18th century. By that time they had become subjugated to the larger Buddhist societies around them, including Burman, Shan, and Mon, and Europeans had begun interacting with them in their travels and in their proselytizing missions in the region. At about this time too some Karen communities began moving away from their traditional highland homes and into the valleys and lowlands, in part to escape the conflict between Burman, Thai, and Chinese kingdoms in the highlands. Unfortunately for most the move just exacerbated their subjugated position in relation to these larger, more politically organized peoples. In reaction small communities and subgroups of Karen frequently rose up against their oppressors or tried to gain greater autonomy through either political action or millenarian religious movements.

Many scholars point to the work of Christian missionaries as the starting point of a sense of larger Karen national identity, which led to these movements. Prior to the conversion of large numbers of Karen, there was no sense of larger, overarching identity based on shared language, history, or culture. But with the arrival of British and American missionaries after 1826 a class of educated Karen leaders with experience working in the British bureaucracy emerged and began pushing for autonomy and even independence. These leaders were also familiar with the Christian concepts of salvation, the return of the messiah, and the meek's inheriting the earth and used these ideas in formulating their own syncretic religious-political messages. The resulting millenarian movements prophesied that at a certain date in the not-too-distant future the messiah or an honored ancestor would return and turn the world order upside down: Karen would become the owners of land and other wealth and the rulers over their region while their tormentors would become poor servants with no power. Most of these movements disappeared soon after their prophesied end-of-days failed to come about, but all left behind a feeling of further frustration that the world order had not been reversed.

Despite the frustration of many Karen groups a few subgroups in both Burma and Thailand were able to establish a degree of self-rule. The Red Karen in Burma had three separate chiefdoms that survived the entire colonial period intact, and three other groups in Thailand established feudal kingdoms that lasted from the mid-19th century until about 1910. These small, relatively autonomous polities added to the Karen sense of nationhood, which has continued to the present day with the long military struggle for independence from Myanmar.

Another contributing factor to the Karen sense of national entitlement arose from their sometimes ambiguous relationship with the British. The two peoples shared a common goal of limiting the power of the dominant Burmans as well as their Christian religion and thus saw each other as allies. The Karen helped the British put down several Burman uprisings in the 1920s and the Saya San rebellions between 1930 and 1932, actions that helped to fuel the anger and resentment between the two Southeast Asian peoples. At the same time, however, the Karen also resented British control over them nearly as much as Burman, Shan, or Thai control, and British racial ideologies could never view the Karen as their equals. Nonetheless in the early 20th century the Karen gained a unique position within the Burmese legislative assembly, and in 1928 Dr. San C. Po made a clear call for Karen autonomy in front of this body. World War II putting the Karen and British even closer, as the two fought together against the JAPANESE and their Burman allies, resulting in significant Japanese and Burman atrocities against the Karen when the British were expelled in early 1942.

After three years of what might today be called ethnic cleansing by the Japanese and Burmans of the Karen, the British retook Burma with the assistance of their loyal Karen allies. Without the Karen Operation Character, which prevented the Japanese from moving south through the country, the British would not have been able to begin the process of retaking Burma. Nonetheless as the war ended and the country fell into greater chaos, which the British could not control, the pragmatic colonizers turned away from their long-term Karen allies and toward the strongest military and political body in the country, the Anti-Fascist People's Freedom League (AFPFL). This organization was multiethnic and its leader, Aung San, was able to hold the coalition together, even in the context of increasing Karen demands for autonomy and representation in the new government. However, Aung San himself was assassinated in 1947 and the Burman factions within the AFPFL emerged as the most viable political partners in the country. As a result the British and Burmans, former enemies, became allies and friends and the hopes of millions of Karen for autonomy or independence were sacrificed for expediency by the British.

Soon the Karen withdrew from the political process entirely and began the long military struggle for recognition of a Karen state, which has meant almost continuous civil war from 1948 until the present. However, the greatly dispersed Karen communities often reacted to the situation in different ways. Those residing in the Irrawaddy delta, far from the proposed Karen State or Kawthoolei, pushed for equality and recognition within the larger Burman state, while those in and around their eastern territories struggled for greater autonomy or independence. As a result of these differences many lowland delta Karen have today largely integrated into Burman society, converting to Buddhism and speaking Burman as their first language. Those in the highlands, however, continue to struggle as part of the insurgent group the Karen National Union based in Manorplow and its army the Karen National Liberation Army, or have left the country to live as refugees in Thailand. Since the 1980s these groups have also been joined by various other groups, including students and the National League for Democracy, led by Aung San Suu Kyi, the daughter of Aung San, Burma's father of independence, who once held the promise of a peaceful multiethnic state.

The Burmese military, which has ruled the country illegally since 1962, has been fighting many battles in the country to maintain control in the face of a multifaceted democracy movement. However, one of the most vicious of the junta's campaigns has been against the Karen and their long-term struggle for autonomy. Entire villages have been relocated or destroyed again and again, all adults pushed into labor camps or other forced labor situations, and both civilians and combatants killed by the thousands. When villages are destroyed, every single building, from homes and animal shelters to schools and churches, is burned to the ground so that nothing remains but ash and cinders. As a result the United Nations High Commissioner for Refugees (UNHCR) estimates that more than 140,000 Karen refugees are currently living in Thailand; some of them have been there for more than 20 years, while 2,000 more arrived in mid-2006.

CULTURE

One of the reasons the Karen have found it so difficult to make their claim of autonomy or independence is the complex and fluid nature of

Karen identity and culture. The various Karenic languages, while related to one another, are not mutually intelligible and the cultural differences between subgroups occupying different regions are sometimes very great. Karen identity was largely forged through opposition to Burman, Shan, and Thai identities, which often left groups foundering to find commonalities. At the same time a desire for some degree of autonomy within or outside the Burmese state has forged some links over the past century.

The traditional economic activity of the highland Karen was slash-and-burn agriculture on shifting forest plots. Small villages of Karen would carve a living from their hilly terrain using machetes and fire to develop single-use plots for dry upland rice and vegetables. Supplementing this diet would be foraged roots, berries, and herbs; meat from both domestic and hunted animals; and some fish. Those Karen who moved into the lowland delta and coastal regions tended to adopt the wet-rice agriculture of their Burman and Thai neighbors, growing rice in permanent irrigated and fertilized fields. Today these two subsistence patterns tend to exist side by side in the hills of Myanmar while lowland populations have integrated even further into Burman and Thai societies. Even in the hills of northern Thailand most swidden activity has been eliminated in favor of paddy farming by the destruction of the region's forests.

These various subsistence strategies are also reflected in the mixed relationships different groups have to the market and other trade relations. Traditional highland Karen communities have always engaged in trade with their lowland neighbors, exchanging cotton, game, domestic animals, and forest products for rice, pottery, fish paste, and salt. Today tourism also draws some income into the highland communities in Thailand, and many Karen, especially men, have spent time in towns and cities working as laborers.

Traditional Karen villages, the most important political units, were made up of 20 to 30 families, mostly living in separate households by family. However, some communities had longhouses, which accommodated many generations and segments of an extended family, with each nuclear family group adding a new room or two to the already established longhouse. Whether single or extended family, almost all houses were built on stilts or poles a few feet or more above the ground; this structure protected the dwelling from floods and provided a safe place for domestic animals to sleep.

Outside the nuclear family Karen kinship is not well understood. Some sources claim that kinship is bilateral and that children are equally related to both their mothers' and fathers' family lines while others claim that there is a matrilineal bias in which the mother's family is dominant. Certainly there are some rituals honoring ancestral spirits that require matrilineal relatives to work together among both Sgaw and Pwo subgroups; however, this does not mean that other subgroups do not have a different pattern or, perhaps, that these people are bilateral in general but that the ancestor cult recognizes a greater contribution by mothers. Unfortunately the Karen marriage system does not help to elucidate the kinship problem since close relatives from both sides are forbidden to marry. Nonetheless patrilateral parallel second cousins, or grandfather's brothers' children's children, can marry, while matrilateral relatives of that degree of closeness cannot. In addition after marriage the new couple generally resides with the wife's family for a period in matrilocal residence until the pair can establish a home, usually in the same village.

Village leadership was inherited from chief to chief, in some cases from father to son, in others from maternal uncle to nephew. Supplemental to the chief system was the council of elders, chosen from among all the male heads of household in the village. While these councils dealt solely with secular matters such as land disputes or other judicial subjects, chiefs were both religious and secular leaders, at least prior to the widespread conversion of highland Karen to Christianity and lowland Karen to Buddhism. The chief was seen as the go-between for earthly beings and both ancestral and natural spirits.

FURTHER READING

Jonathan Falla. *True Love and Bartholomew: Rebels on the Burmese Border* (Cambridge: Cambridge University Press, 1991).

James W. Hamilton. *Pwo Karen: At the Edge of Mountain and Plain.* American Ethnological Society Monographs, no. 60 (St. Paul, Minn.: West, 1976).

Charles F. Keyes, ed. *Ethnic Adaptation and Identity: The Karen on the Thai Frontier with Burma* (Philadelphia: Institute for the Study of Human Issues, 1979).

Edmund R. Leach. *Political Systems of Highland Burma* (Cambridge, Mass.: Harvard University Press, 1954).

Karluks (Qarluks, Karluqs, Qarluqs, On-ok Karluks, Uc-Karluks, Ko-lo-lu, Karluh, Halluh, Kollakhs, Geluolu)

In many ways Karluk history is intertwined with the rest of TURKIC history; the Karluks emerged from the ashes of the Gokturk khanate and were instrumental in spreading a form of the Turkic language to Central Asia. However, Karluk history is separate from that of the Seljuks, as the two were usually enemies fighting over the same Central Asian territory, and this separateness means that the Karluks played a very small role in the development of the contemporary Turkic peoples. The Karluk branch of the Turkic language has since become extinct, and the Karluks are often seen as the predecessors of contemporary KAZAKHS and UIGHUR, both Turkic peoples to be sure, but ones with separate histories.

The name *Karluk* may be derived from the Turkic term *Kara* or *Qara*, meaning "black," and the suffix *-lik*, meaning "pertaining to." Their name may also refer to hair color or tent or clothing color, or it may be an arbitrary name due to the general importance of the black-yellow dichotomy in Turkic culture. Culturally the Karluks were similar to all the other peoples of the steppes, Turkic or otherwise, in focusing their economic activity on cattle breeding and hunting. They were seminomadic and resided in felt tents that could be easily dismantled and moved to follow the herds to fresh pasture. They were shamanists and worshipped the steppe god Tengri until the 10th century, when, along with most other Turkic peoples, they embraced Sunni Islam.

The structure of Karluk society was dominated by households and patrilineal groups at the lowest level and by the larger confederation of tribal groups that bore the Karluk name at the highest level. Karluk history is often difficult to follow because sometimes some tribal groups acted together while at other times they acted separately, aligning themselves alternately with the Chinese, Uighur, Gokturks, Seljuks, Arabs, and others against each other. However, in the mid-eighth century, after helping to dismantle the Western Gokturks, the Karluks were able to act in unison to establish a state in the eastern portion of present-day Kazakhstan. Under Karluk hegemony several important Central Asian cities first emerged, such as the later Karakhanid capital at Taraz, sometimes known as Zhambyl; Isfijab, which was later renamed Sairam; and Farab, renamed Otrar.

In 751 the Karluks were the decisive factor in the historic Battle of Talas between Arab and Chinese forces over control of Central Asia. The Karluks had originally allied themselves with the Chinese but at the last moment switched their allegiance to the Arabs, leaving most of the Chinese army surrounded with no escape route. The Chinese leader was able to get away but most of his soldiers were not. This victory was the final push to rid Central Asia of Chinese domination and to replace the Chinese with a variety of Muslim khanates, many of them Turkic.

In the 10th century this first Karluk state began to disintegrate, but by the 990s at the very latest another dynasty from within the confederation had emerged as a unifying force, the Karakhanids, sometimes called Karahanlis. They were able to consolidate territory in parts of western China and the rest of the steppes as far as the Caspian Sea but were always battling with the Seljuks for ultimate control. During

KARLUKS

location:
The eastern side of the Altai Mountains

time period:
600 to 1211

ancestry:
Turkic

language:
Chagatay Turkic, an extinct branch of the Turkic language family

---

Karluks time line

C.E.

600 Tang documents list the Karluks or Ko-lo-lu as one of the branches of the Gokturk khanate.

650 The Karluks are defeated by the Chinese north of Turfan and are forcibly removed to a region north of the Tien Shan Mountains; they reside there independently of either section of the Gokturk khanate.

710 The Karluks are drawn into the second (Eastern) Gokturk khanate.

741–44 The Uighur and Karluks combine to defeat the Eastern khanate of the Gokturks.

745 The Uighur defeat the Karluks in the region of Mongolia and the latter migrate to Transoxiana in the west.

751 Battle of Talas between the Chinese and Arabs over control of Central Asia. The Chinese are defeated when the Karluks change sides mid-battle.

766 The Karluks establish a state in the region of eastern Kazakhstan with the powerful Uighur dominant in their eastern borderlands.

840 The Karluk state expands eastward with the disintegration of the Uighur state, absorbing and incorporating the fleeing Uighur into their new state, the Karakhanid.

934 The Karakhanid convert to Islam under Satuk Bughra Khan, the first Turkic khan in Central Asia to convert.

Early 12th century The Seljuks take Transoxiana from the Karakhanids, leaving them significantly weakened.

1130 The Kara-Khitai defeat a joint Seljuk-Karakhanid army on the steppe near Samarkand.

1211 The remaining Karakhanid lands are conquered by the Kwarezm.

this period the Karluks, as part of the Karakhanids along with the Uighur, Turgesh, and others, embraced Sunni Islam under the leadership of Satuk Bughra Khan. In addition the steppes began to be opened up to sedentary farmers as irrigation techniques improved with the influx of a large number of Uighur farmers fleeing the destruction of their khanate at the hands of the Kyrgyz. This allowed both economic and social change to occur, favoring settled communities over migratory nomads. Following the Karakhanids one last nomadic empire emerged on the steppes, the Mongols, in the 13th century, as a result of economic and social changes that began to take effect in the 11th and 12th centuries.

The Karakhanids were constantly struggling to maintain their sovereignty, with the more powerful Seljuks constantly pressuring their southern borderlands and the Kara-Khitan invading from the north and east. The period between 1130 and 1204 was particularly difficult, with the Kara-Khitan exacting huge tribute from the Karakhanids after their victory in 1130. The Karakhanids emerged from the Kara-Khitan yoke briefly at the beginning of the 13th century under Uthman, but he was only able to consolidate power for seven years before being defeated for good by the Khwarezmians in 1211.

Kashmiris

The Kashmiris are the people of the Indian state of Jammu and Kashmir and the adjoining Pakistani province of Azad Kashmir. The majority of the Kashmiris are Muslims, but there is also a Hindu minority, sometimes called Pandit Kashmiris or Saraswatis, who are culturally distinct from the Hindu majority in other regions of India.

The origins of the Kashmiri people remain a mystery. While they were probably migrants from the more southern regions of India, some authors posit origins from as far away as ancient Palestine and believe that they constitute one of the Lost Tribes of Israel. The evidence they present for this thesis includes a number of Kashmiri placenames that coincide with names from the Lost Tribes, such as Beit Peor, Har Nevo, and Heshubon; some cultural similarities, like the feast of Pasca each spring; and the writings of some Mughal and other Muslim historians that claim the Kashmiris were Jews until forcibly converted to Islam prior to the 12th century.

Regardless of their ancient origins the Kashmiris today are mostly Muslim, and Jammu and Kashmir constitutes India's only state with a Muslim majority. This fact has meant that the region has been extremely volatile over the past 60 years; it has even been the site of three separate wars fought between India and Pakistan. The first war began right after independence and partition in 1947 when Kashmir's Muslim majority was ruled by a Hindu prince. As the prince was making his decision to which country he should cede his territory, the newly formed Pakistan invaded in order to assist a Muslim uprising. In reaction the prince decided to join India in exchange for military assistance to quell the uprising; his decision led to war between the two new countries. The war lasted from 1947 to 1949 and ended with a UN-brokered peace agreement that granted India two-thirds of Kashmir and the vast majority of its population and Pakistan just one-third, most of which is so mountainous that it is permanently covered in glacier. China also owns a small piece of territory that was traditionally attached to Kashmir, Aksai Chin, which is similar to Pakistan's territory in being extremely high and thus under a glacier all year.

The second war between India and Pakistan in August–September 1965 was again initiated by several thousand Pakistani soldiers crossing the cease-fire line and trying to inspire the local population to rise up against Indian rule. In general this did not happen and in fact it was the local population that tipped off the Indian forces that the Pakistanis were crossing the border. The war came to an end in late September, not having accomplished much of anything in Kashmir, and the cease-fire line remained unchanged. The final war took place in 1971 and although it was not initially concerned with Kashmir but rather with the separation of Bangladesh from Pakistan, this region almost immediately became the site of some of the war's most important battles. At the end, however, just as in 1965, the original cease-fire line adjudicated by the United Nations, now called the Line of Control, was renewed and remains in place to this day.

Since 1971 India and Pakistan have technically been at peace, but since 1987 the region has been extremely volatile. In that year several Muslim political parties felt that state elections were rigged and began agitating for more representation. By 1989 some of them took up arms against the Indian government to gain their ob-

KASHMIRIS

location:
India and Pakistan

time period:
Unknown to the present

ancestry:
Unknown

language:
Kashmiri, a Dardic Indo-Aryan language, and Urdu

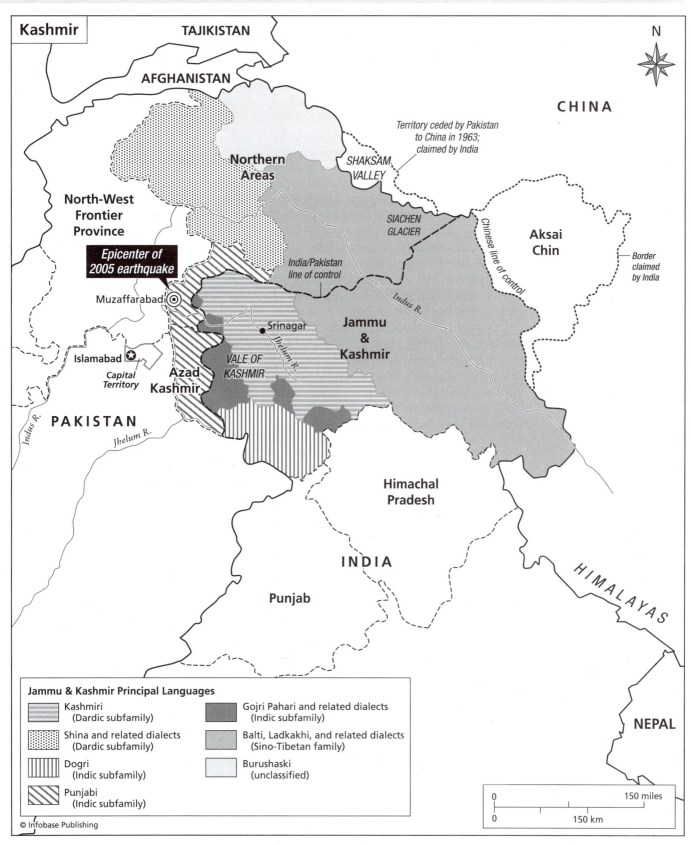

Jammu & Kashmir Principal Languages

- Kashmiri (Dardic subfamily)
- Shina and related dialects (Dardic subfamily)
- Dogri (Indic subfamily)
- Punjabi (Indic subfamily)
- Gojri Pahari and related dialects (Indic subfamily)
- Balti, Ladkakhi, and related dialects (Sino-Tibetan family)
- Burushaski (unclassified)

© Infobase Publishing

jectives, which differed: some were fighting for outright independence while others were fighting to be allowed to join Pakistan. While Paki-

stan has never outwardly supported these militant groups, they have given what the literature calls "moral and diplomatic support" to them and have consistently called for a UN-sponsored referendum on the issue. Throughout the 1990s the violence in the region continued to escalate, and several radical Islamic groups made up of former mujahideen fighters from the Afghan war in the 1980s joined in the rebellion against India, thereby turning the emphasis from nationalism and autonomy to Islam. Today India has about 600,000 military and police officers in the region to maintain peace, making it the most heavily militarized region per capita in the world.

The cultures of the Muslim and Hindu Kashmiris differ significantly and go far beyond their different religions. The Pandit Hindu Kashmiris are considered to be from the Brahmin *varna* and thus did not engage in any crafts such as pottery, weaving, or blacksmithing, or any menial or polluting labor like street cleaning or cutting hair because these were the tasks of castes below them in the Hindu hierarchy; these tasks were left to their Muslim neighbors. The many handicrafts for which Kashmir is known, including silk production and weaving, carpets, carving, metalwork, and furniture, are all the purview of Muslim Kashmiris, while Hindus are more likely to own small shops or work as teachers or doctors.

The two groups do, however, share a farming culture in which rice, wheat, barley, corn, legumes, and tobacco are the main crops along with subsistence fruit and vegetables. The fertile Kashmir valley is also well known for its fruit, almond, and walnut orchards and for its saffron. In higher elevations pastoralism is the only viable economic strategy and each family is responsible for its small herd of sheep, goats, cattle, or yaks. The Kashmir goat is the source of the fine wool known as Pashmina, which has become a luxury item known in the West for its softness and warmth.

Since 1989 economic development in the region has essentially come to a standstill and most families, Muslim and Hindu, have returned to a subsistence economy based on agriculture or handicrafts. Thousands of civilians have been killed or fled the region, and both internal and external tourism, once a major source of revenue, has all but disappeared. This situation was exacerbated in 2005 when Azad Kashmir was the epicenter of a massive earthquake that killed more than 70,000 people in Pakistan and several thousand more on India's side of the border. For a brief moment the two states reached across the divide to assist in the provision of shelter, food, and clothing, and in rebuilding efforts, but three years on the situation had become tense once again. Until India becomes willing to negotiate on the status of Kashmir and the wider world stops seeing the conflict in terms of a larger "war on terror," especially one involving radical Muslims, the condition of the Kashmiri people will continue to be plagued by violence.

Kazakhs (Qazaqs, Kazaks, Quazaqs, Hasake Zu)

The Kazakhs are a Turkic-speaking people who reside in the independent country of Kazakhstan as well as in China, Mongolia, Russia, and Uzbekistan. Unlike many other Central Asian peoples, the Kazakhs are a relatively new ethnic group, breaking off from other Turkic speakers only in the mid-15th century. From that time forward they have been at odds with the RUSSIANS over control of their political and economic destinies and have battled with other Central Asians to maintain a separate cultural identity. (*See also* TURKIC PEOPLES.)

GEOGRAPHY

Kazakhstan, where the majority of Kazakh people currently reside, has four separate climate zones: desert, semidesert, steppe, and mountainous. Most of the northern and central regions are made up of dry, undulating desert, semidesert, and steppes, while the southern and eastern regions are mountainous. The top of the highest peak, Khan Tangiri, rises to 22,950 feet above sea level.

Despite the largely dry desert and semidesert climate zone Kazakhstan is blessed with a large number of rivers and lakes, as well as the Caspian and Aral Seas, both of which are salt seas. Lake Balkhash is also half salty on the eastern side, while the western side is freshwater. The Ural, Syr Darya, Irtysh, Ishim, and Ili Rivers all provide freshwater for human and animal consumption, irrigation, industry, and other uses. During the Soviet era water resources were so mishandled that the Aral Sea shrank by about 80 percent of its original volume. Kazakhstan has been more proactive than its southern neighbor Uzbekistan in attempts to deal with this ecological crisis and has assisted in the partial recovery of the newly formed North Aral Sea, which is now separated from the Uzbek South Aral Sea by a large dam.

The region of China in which the more than 1 million Kazakhs live is largely mountainous, encouraging the continuation of their traditional nomadic way of life.

KAZAKHS

location:
Kazakhstan and Xinjiang Province of China, with smaller numbers in Mongolia, Uzbekistan, and Russia

time period:
Mid-15th century to the present

ancestry:
Turkic, Mongol, and others from the Eurasian steppes

language:
Kazakh, a Turkic language that is closely related to Kyrgyz. Until 1928 Kazakh was written using Arabic script, from 1928 to 1940 using the Latin alphabet with the addition of a few letters, and from 1940 to the present the Cyrillic script.

ORIGINS

The Turkic people were just one of many semi-nomadic groups living on the steppes northwest of China prior to the sixth century. Probably the only trait that distinguished them from the XIONGNU, XIANBEI, MONGOLS, and other steppe dwellers was their language. As these others did, they would have relied primarily on their herds for subsistence, resided in felt tents, and moved about as their herds needed grass and water. They practiced a shamanistic religion and placed great value on their horses.

The UZBEKS, from whom the Kazakhs broke free in the mid-15th century, probably entered Central Asia from their homeland farther north and east after 1000 C.E. However, they remained culturally and linguistically almost indistinguishable from other Turkic tribes in the region. In addition a great deal of intermixing of the various Turkic and Mongol tribes contributed to the development of all contemporary Central Asian Turkic peoples: Kazakhs, Uzbeks, KYRGYZ, and TURKMEN. It would be impossible to disaggregate this great cultural and genetic mixture by using the linguistic, historical, archaeological, and genetic evidence that we have.

HISTORY

As a result of their mixed origins the early history of the Turkic people who became the Kazakhs cannot be differentiated from that of the Uzbeks, Kyrgyz, or, before them, the earlier nomads of the Eurasian steppes. Even Kazakh history from the period after their separation from the Uzbeks is not always easy to tease out from that of the other Central Asian peoples. A significant problem results from consulting sources written by Russian authors during the czarist period because in Russian the Kazakhs were largely known as *Kyrgyz* to distinguish them from the Slavic Cossacks, *Kazaky* in Russian. To distinguish between the Kyrgyz-Kazakhs and the actual Kyrgyz tribes, the latter are sometimes referred to as Kara-Kyrgyz or Black Kyrgyz.

The Kazakhs emerged as a separate group, distinct from other Turkic speakers, in the mid-15th century. In about 1459 around 200,000 Uzbeks under the sultans Zhanibek and Kerei separated from their leader, Abul Khayr, and moved to a region between the Chu and Talas Rivers in the southeast of contemporary Kazakhstan, south of Lake Balkhash. They took the name *Kazakh*, which some sources say in-

Kazakhs time line

C.E.

Mid-15th century The Kazakhs begin to split from the Uzbeks to establish their own ethnic group.

1511–23 Khan Kasym unites the Kazakh tribes for the first time and the Kazakhs are recognized as a separate ethnic group. They are militarily dominant in the steppes.

16th century The Kazakhs divide themselves into three separate groups or hordes: Great, Middle, and Lesser.

1538 Haqq Nazar, the third son of Khan Kasym, reunites the three Kazakh hordes for a short time.

1681–84 The Great Horde is conquered by the Zunghars and temporarily brought under their sphere of influence.

17th century Kazakhs begin to convert to Islam, a process that continues through the 19th century.

Early 18th century The Great, Middle, and Lesser Hordes separate again.

1711–12 The Zunghars are expelled from Kazakh territory by Teuke Khan, who unifies all Kazakhs for the battle.

1723 The Zunghars attack again, resulting in the Great Disaster.

1730 The Lesser Horde requests military assistance from Russia.

1757–59 The Zunghar threat comes to an end with defeat at the hands of the Manchu Qing dynasty. Ablai Khan of the Middle Horde submits to the Qing rather than risk military defeat.

1798 The Middle Horde is conquered by Russia.

1820s The Great Horde requests military assistance from Russia.

1836 The Middle Horde under Khan Kene rebels against their Russian overlords. They do so again 11 years later.

1850 Russia begins a period of fort building in Kazakhstan, which limits the mobility of the Kazakh nomads.

1863 Russia annexes Kazakhstan and the twin processes of loss of grazing land and forced russification result in great social upheaval on the Kazakh steppes.

1916 Kazakhs rebel against forced conscription; many flee to China.

(For a continuation of this time line, *see* KAZAKHSTANIS: NATIONALITY)

dicates their independent or vagabond status. Culturally they became more and more distinct from the Uzbeks, who settled into agriculture, while the Kazakhs retained their nomadic way of life much longer, including into the present in some areas of Kazakhstan and the Ili Kazak Autonomous Prefecture of China.

Following their separation from the other Uzbek tribes, these Kazakh nomads established a large nomadic empire that ruled the steppes east of the Caspian and north of the Aral Sea as far west as the Altai Mountains. For the better part of a century starting in 1465 the Kazakhs dominated the trade routes that ran through

The tragedy of the Aral Sea is starkly clear to these Kazakhs, walking amid three stranded ships near the town of Zhalanash, west of the Aral's current shoreline. *(AP/Alexander Zemlianichenko)*

this region as well as the politics, using their fierce and fast mounted soldiers to keep their neighbors in check.

During this time Kasym Khan unified all the newly emerging Kazakh people into one protostatelike structure that is sometimes referred to as the Kazakh khanate. He was followed by his three sons, the first two of whom were less suc-

cessful than their father in holding the Kazakhs together. Under these rulers the Kazakh khanate was divided into three separate sections, called *zhuzes* in Kazakh, which is sometimes translated as "hordes." These three are alternatively known as the Elder, Middle, and Younger or Great, Middle, and Lesser. Either way these divisions were largely geographical, with the Elder or Great Horde constituting much of the eastern and southern regions of Kazakhstan, the Middle being the central and northern regions, and the Younger or Lesser being the western region. Each horde was ruled by a khan, but his authority was largely at the mercy of local chieftains, called sultans, and clan leaders, called beys or batyrs. Under Kasym Khan's youngest son, Haqq Nazar, who ruled for more than 40 years beginning in 1538, the splintering of the khanate slowed and was even reversed for a generation. However, by the first third of the 18th century the centralized Kazakh khanate had truly disintegrated in favor of these smaller sections.

Although the Kazakhs dominated the steppes both militarily and politically, during the 17th century the Russians began to enter Kazakh territory from the north in greater numbers than ever before. Russian fortifications were established in a number of places

Kasym Khan

The reign of Kasym Khan marks a turning point in the history of Kazakhstan as Kasym was responsible for uniting the Kazakh tribes into a united state for the first time. Born in 1510 Kasym was the son of Zhanybek, who had established the Kazakh khanate after organizing a successful rebellion against the Uzbek Khan. Kasym united the Kazakh tribes under his absolute sovereignty and expanded the territories of the Kazakh khanate. He even sent diplomatic missions from his new state to establish formal relations with Russia and the Crimea. In 1520, he promulgated the first Kazakh code of laws, called Kasym Khan's Light Path, shortly before his death in 1521. Despite having formalized the Kazakh khanate's internal and external relations, this essentially tribal political organization experienced significant disruption at Kasym's death. Succession problems, wars, and loss of territory weakened the state despite the efforts of three of Kasym's sons to revive the fortunes of their father's expansive kingdom. Eventually the khanate split into three separate hordes, all of which continued to battle the Oirat Mongols for control of the steppes.

on the steppes, including in what are today the cities of Uralsk and Guryev. The Little Horde even swore their allegiance to the Russians in 1730, probably as a form of protection against the more immediate military threat from the east. The Great Horde did not ally themselves with the Russians and as a result were also challenged in the east by the OIRAT federation, a Mongol force led by the ZUNGHARS. In 1681–84 the Zunghars temporarily drew the Great Horde into their sphere of influence, but in 1711–12 a unified Kazakh army under Teuke Khan invaded Zungharia. The Zunghars attacked again in 1723, with a resulting devastating loss for the Kazakhs still known as the Great Disaster, and again within 20 years of that loss. This final Zunghar invasion was much less severe, since Abul Khayr had unified the Kazakhs to withstand the onslaught. The Zunghar menace from the east finally ended when the Zunghars were conquered by the Manchu Qing dynasty in 1757–59. At that time the Kazakh Middle Horde under Ablai Khan also submitted to the Qing rather than be conquered.

The Middle Horde continued to bristle at the notion of external control in the 19th century, staging the first large-scale uprisings against the Russians in 1836 and 1847 under the leadership of Khan Kene. For his actions against Russian domination Khan Kene is still considered an important figure in the Kazakh national pantheon of heroes. Despite these efforts following the Crimean War (1854–56) Russian advances into Central Asia increased exponentially as fertile Kazakh plains were seen as a potential Russian breadbasket. Russian forts attracted farmers, who began to plow the steppes for wheat farming, while the local Kazakh nomads experienced a process the Russians labeled russification. Kazakh land and livestock were confiscated while their language and customs were pushed out of the public sphere, especially after 1863, when Russia annexed Kazakhstan.

Rather than rise up against the militarily superior Russians many Kazakhs chose migration to escape the reach of russification; thousands moved into the more mountainous or desert regions of their own country. These actions made way for the thousands of Russian peasants who migrated east to start farms of their own, on which they grew wheat, corn, and other grains, fulfilling the vision of Kazakhstan as a Russian breadbasket. While the process was disheartening for the Kazakhs, those who remained were peaceful until 1916, when the Russian czar Nicholas II sought to draft Central Asian, including Kazakh, men into the Russian army. The Kazakhs rebelled successfully for four months while the Russian army attempted to restore order; they were eventually able to do so but not before thousands of Kazakhs died and almost a million left Kazakhstan for good to start new lives in western China.

The Russian Revolution, which saw the withdrawal of Russian troops from World War I, ended the crisis in Kazakhstan caused by the potential for forced conscription; however, it did not yield peace in the region. The Kazakhs rebelled again in 1918–20 against the sovietization of their society but were eventually defeated by the Red Army. Following this pacification ethnic differences between Kyrgyz and Kazakh peoples were ignored by the Soviets in the creation of a single Kirghiz Autonomous Socialist Republic in 1920, but five years later the Kazakhs were accorded a degree of recognition when they received their own autonomous SSR, with its capital at Alma-Ata, or contemporary Almaty. This recognition, however, did not mean that the Soviet state was ready to accord the Kazakh language, culture, or way of life equal status to those of the dominant Russians. In the 1950s Kazakhstan's vast plains again became the target for the Russian government's plans for expanding its agricultural output. The Virgin Lands Project under the first secretary, Leonid Brezhnev, and his Kazakh henchman Dinmukhamad Kunayev expanded the region's wheat- and cornfields at the expense of grazing lands. The following decades saw the introduction of even more Russians and other peoples from within the Soviet Union as Kazakhstan's oil- and gasfields came under development, leaving the Kazakhs as a minority group within their own region until the exodus of Russians after the fall of the Soviet Union in 1991.

See KAZAKHSTANIS: NATIONALITY, for a continuation of Kazakh history.

CULTURE

Economy and Society

As was the case with other Turkic peoples of Central Asia, Kazakh society prior to incorporation into either the Soviet Union or China under the Communist Party was dominated by the bonds of kinship at the lineage, clan, and tribal levels. The centralized political societies formed in both the Soviet Union and China helped to weaken these traditional bonds; however, for at least a decade in the Kazakh SSR the ties of Kazakh clanship were utilized and exploited by the ruthless Kunayev to control his region. Kunayev established himself as a tribal chief and used his vast tribal network to make hiring and firing decisions for most of the major Kazakh industries and agricultural collectives. Kunayev also used traditional notions of loyalty and oaths of silence to keep word of his exploitation from the ears of his Party superiors in Moscow. He was able to maintain his position until the 1980s, when Gorbachev replaced him with a Russian; Kunayev himself went on to lead some of the first anti-Soviet riots in Central Asia in Almaty in the late 1980s.

As this example shows, the ties of *aul*, lineage, clan, and tribe did not disappear during the Soviet era. The *aul* or *awul* is a segment of a patrilineage, usually composed of people who share a father or grandfather, and who camped, moved, and herded their animals together. Bonds of mutual obligation were strong within these primary units of production and consumption and remain so for many Kazakhs, both those who have maintained a pastoral way of life and those who have settled down to farm, mine, or work in the oil- and gasfields or in more service-oriented jobs. Patrilineal clans, those in which membership is handed down from fathers to children, also retained a degree of their old importance well into the 20th century. Most Kazakhs knew which clans had been part of the more powerful Middle Horde, which ones were noble or chiefly, and which ones were considered weak or fragile. Clan leaders continued to serve as voices of authority in disputes over marriage, property, and honor, and they acted as mediators in accordance with traditional Kazakh customs and law. Many of these laws were from the original Kazakh code, composed during the rule of Teuke Khan (1680–1718), which combined tribal and Islamic laws.

The Kazakh tribes that migrated to China in the years following the 1916 rebellion were mostly members of the powerful Middle Horde, with some from the Great Horde as well. As did the Kazakhs in the Soviet Union, Chinese Kazakhs continued to honor the bonds of lineage, clan, and tribe for most of the 20th century. Indeed many Chinese Kazakhs maintain much more traditional lives than their Kazakhstani cousins because their pastoral way of life was less disrupted by the Chinese government. A few Chinese Kazakhs have settled down to farm, but most continue to live with their herds of sheep, goats, and cattle, migrating seasonally up and down the mountains of Xinjiang Province. In the spring, summer, and fall they live largely in traditional felt yurts, while in winter many have built permanent brick homes in their valley pastures. Unlike many other Chinese minority groups the Kazakhs have rejected most attempts at sinicization, that is, attempts to make them more Chinese. Most do not speak or read any form of Chinese language, and few have given up their traditional felt clothing or diet of dairy products, mutton, and wheat pastries in favor of Chinese clothing or food.

Religion and Literature

Most Kazakhs are nominally Sunni Muslims of the Hanafi school and have been since the 17th or 18th century, when they were one of the last of the Central Asian peoples to embrace Islam. However, a combination of being relatively new converts and of 70 years of official atheism in the USSR has meant that most Kazakhs in Kazakhstan practice a form of folk Islam rather than a doctrinal version of the religion. The same is true of Chinese Kazakhs as a result of the official sanctions against organized religions generally since 1949.

This folk Islam combines beliefs in god or Allah, the supernatural powers of Muslim saints, jinns, and other ancestral spirits with many pre-Islamic animistic beliefs and practices. Kazakh children often wear charms to protect them from the evil eye; others are given names that their parents hope will contribute to a long and healthy life, such as *Mynzhasar*, "to live 1,000 years," or *Toksanbai*, "to live 90 years." Other parents choose to give their child a funny name, such as *Kushikbai*, "puppy," or *Ayubai*, "bear," so that people's laughter frightens away evil spirits. Other names from this pre-Islamic belief in spirits and omens are *Tursyn*, "may he live," and *Ulbolsyn*, "may she be followed by a boy." Many Kazakh adults also leave offerings near rivers and other running water to ensure the granting of their wishes. Before lambs are slaughtered, a guest or other important community figure may be asked to gain permission from the lamb's spirit to eat it. The spirits of earth, sky, water, and fire also retain important places in the Kazakh pantheon of supernatural beings that are believed either to help or to hinder the affairs of humans, depending on whether they have been treated well.

In addition to these animistic practices Kazakhs and other Central Asians, along with Persians, AZERIS, and PASHTUNS, also celebrate Navruz as one of the most important holidays of the year. Navruz or New Year, which was originally a Zoroastrian holiday, is officially marked on March 21, the spring equinox, but unofficially continues for 13 days beyond that date as well. It is both a public holiday, with many urban and rural communities celebrating with traditional and modern festivities, and a private one in which many households plant fruit trees, do their spring cleaning, and fumigate with the smoke of the *archa* tree, a kind of juniper, to cleanse the home of evil spirits. Many people buy new clothes to mark the occasion and children receive money and verbal blessings from parents and other adults. It is a time for forgiving debts and insults as well as ending fights and sharing food.

As most other traditionally nomadic peoples do, the Kazakhs place heavy importance on their oral culture. Folklore, epic poetry, and songs were all central to the education of Kazakh children in their history and heritage and to the construction and maintenance of Kazakh identity. In the 19th century some Kazakhs, such as Abay Ibrahim Qunanbayuli, began to write down their old folktales, songs, and poems, but even well into the 20th century in rural areas the oral tradition retained its central position for many Kazakhs. Some of these 19th-century poets also composed new, nationalistic works for the first generation of Kazakhs who grew up in urban settings, to make sure this new generation did not become thoroughly russified. Among the Chinese Kazakhs, however, it was the older oral tradition that was important for helping the community to remain separate both from the HAN majority and from the other national minorities in Xinjiang Province. Within the USSR rural Kazakhs also used their long tradition of oral literature and song to undermine the Soviet state's emphasis on the Russian language, literature, and culture more generally. In the form of traditional epic poems Kazakhs could express their antipathy to the Soviet state without as much risk to their personal liberty as would have occurred if they had spoken directly.

Stages of Life

Kazakh community life is extremely important and there are several stages in a child's life in which membership in the community must be affirmed through ritual acts. The first of these occurs right after an infant's birth, when a mullah or other Islamic leader recites text from the Quran and says the baby's name into its ear three times just prior to the child's being placed into its cradle for the first time. The honor of laying the infant down in this way always goes to a village elder and mother of many children.

These acts are believed to help the baby live a long, healthy life and to have many children of his or her own. The next traditional community event marks a child's first steps into the public sphere. Once a child is ready to begin walking, his or her legs are tied with black and white thread by a female village elder, black symbolizing honesty and white symbolizing hope for the future. The child is then faced toward the mother, the threads cut, and the whole community participates in the child's first steps.

During childhood Kazakh young people undergo a variety of other periods of incorporation into the larger community. At about age five young boys are circumcised and then the entire village or community celebrates the event with large amounts of traditional foods, music, and festivity. Young girls in the past used to spend considerable time producing the wool felt textiles and embroidered pieces necessary to establish their own homes one day. Formal education has changed this practice somewhat, but the symbolic forms of animals continue to be important on yurts, rugs, saddlecloths, cradle covers, and clothing of all sorts.

At the time of marriage some rural Kazakh young people continue to practice a form of community marriage known as bride stealing, a tradition from the nomadic past of both the Kazakh and Kyrgyz cultures. Bride stealing or *ala kachuu* is illegal in Kazakhstan today and was in the USSR for most of the 20th century, but this has not stopped the practice in some remote regions. It is now done more as a symbol of the nomadic past than as an actual kidnapping, with both partners being active participants. In the past, however, the practice entailed a Kazakh man's riding into a village and carrying off the young woman of his choice. Once he had passed through the doorway of his home and his mother had tied a scarf on the young woman's head, she was considered married. The woman had no choice but to remain in her new home because running away was considered dishonorable for her and her family of origin. Her own family would more often than not reject her if she attempted to return home, in part because of the loss of honor, and in part the necessity to return the sometimes substantial bride price paid in the form of livestock, cash, and other gifts.

FURTHER READING

George Moseley. *A Sino-Soviet Cultural Frontier: The Ili Kazakh Autonomous Chou.* (Cambridge, Mass.: Harvard University Press, 1966).
Martha Brill Olcott. *The Kazakhs.* 2d ed. (Palo Alto, Calif.: Hoover Institution Press, 1995).

Martha Brill Olcott. *Kazakhstan: Unfulfilled Promise* (Washington, D.C.: Carnegie Endowment for International Peace, 2002).

Edward Schatz. *Modern Clan Politics: The Power of "Blood" in Kazakhstan and Beyond* (Seattle: University of Washington Press, 2004).

Thomas G. Winner. *The Oral Art and Literature of the Kazakhs of Russian Central Asia* (Durham, N.C.: Duke University Press, 1958).

Kazakhstanis: nationality (Kazaks, people of Kazakhstan)

GEOGRAPHY

Nestled between Russia and China Kazakhstan has a total land area of 1.05 million square miles, making it the ninth largest country in the world—equal in size to Western Europe. It borders Russia, China, Uzbekistan, Kyrgyzstan, and Turkmenistan.

As Kazakhstan is so far removed from the oceans, the climate is dry and continental. Most of the rivers are part of landlocked systems, in which they either flow into remote bodies of water or dry up in the steppes and deserts. Only 9.4 percent of the country is prairie or forest land while 33.2 percent is semidesert and 44 percent is desert; the remaining land is currently under cultivation.

Much of Kazakhstan's environment has been devastated by pollution; the most notable effects are evident in the Aral Sea. In 1950 the surface area of the Aral Sea was 41,600 square miles, and in the year 2015 the surface area is projected to be only 8,080 square miles. Irrigation procedures halted the flow of water from the sea's two feeder rivers in 1968, and heavy pollution from agricultural chemicals and increased salinity due to faulty irrigation have killed the sea life, consequently dissolving the fishing industry in that area. Furthermore as the water's edge continues to recede, it leaves behind a residue of salt and chemicals, which the wind picks up and carries into neighboring villages and farms, effectively sterilizing the soil. Some are also speculating about the effects the pollutants are having on humans, as the infant mortality rate near the former Aral Sea's edge is 10 percent, versus the national rate of 2.7 percent.

Radiation from the Soviet Union's many nuclear tests has also caused severe damage to the environment, and possible nuclear-waste contamination of the soil and groundwater is believed to pose a significant health risk to humans and animal life. In the city of Semey, or Semipalatinsk, radiation poisoning and birth defects are common today, even though nuclear testing in the region was halted in 1990.

Some efforts have been made to stem the steady rate of pollution, but governmental agencies in charge of overseeing environmental programs are typically short-funded. In 1996, however, the State Forestry Committee developed the Zailisky Alatau National Park, a 600,000-acre wildlife preserve devoted to the protection of such endangered species as the Tien Shan bear, the golden eagle, and the snow leopard.

INCEPTION AS A NATION

Although the KAZAKHS have functioned under many foreign rulers throughout their history, the most influential of them are indisputably the RUSSIANS. Having made their presence in Kazakhstan known in the 17th century, the Russians long dominated Kazakh politics and economics until the declaration of Kazakhstan's independence in 1991.

Throughout the 19th century the Russian government not only exercised its political power in Kazakhstan, but also attempted to dissolve the traditional culture and introduce Russian influence. Such endeavors included the forced use of Russian language in all schools and governmental organizations, as well as attempts to impose Russian traditions on the nomadic Kazakh lifestyle. As a result of these activities in the late 1800s Kazakh natives founded the Kazakh National Movement to protect Kazakh culture and language.

Nevertheless increasing numbers of Russian immigrants nearly outnumbered the Kazakhs, and natives often found themselves in competition with the newcomers for land and water. This competition resulted in the Basmachi Revolt in 1918. At the time Russian propaganda portrayed the organization as consisting of Islamic extremists and common thieves. The Russian word *Basmachi* translates as "bandit." The movement spread rapidly, however, and strengthened, forcing Vladimir Lenin to appease the Kazakh people through promises of food grants and tax relief. The Basmachi movement dissolved in the 1930s as a result of internal conflicts.

Following the Bolshevik revolution Kazakhstan was under Soviet rule, and in 1936 it became a Soviet constituent republic, along with neighboring Turkmenistan, Kyrgyzstan, and Uzbekistan. Of all of these republics Kazakhstan is the largest and the least ethnically homogeneous, with somewhat more than half of the population being made up of ethnic Kazakhs

KAZAKHSTANIS: NATIONALITY

nation:
Kazakhstan; the Republic of Kazakhstan

derivation of name:
Translates as "Land of the Kazakhs." There are many theories about the meaning of *Kazakh,* including "vagabond" and "independent"

government:
Republic, with an authoritarian presidential rule

capital:
Astana

language:
Kazakh (state language) 64.4 percent, Russian (official business language) 95 percent

religion:
Muslim 47 percent, Russian Orthodox 44 percent, Protestant 2 percent, other 7 percent

earlier inhabitants:
Other Turkic peoples, Mongols, Indo-Iranians, and other steppe nomads

demographics:
Kazakh 53.4 percent, Russian 30 percent, Ukrainian 3.7 percent, Uzbek 2.5 percent, German 2.4 percent, Tatar 1.7 percent, Uighur 1.4 percent, other 4.9 percent

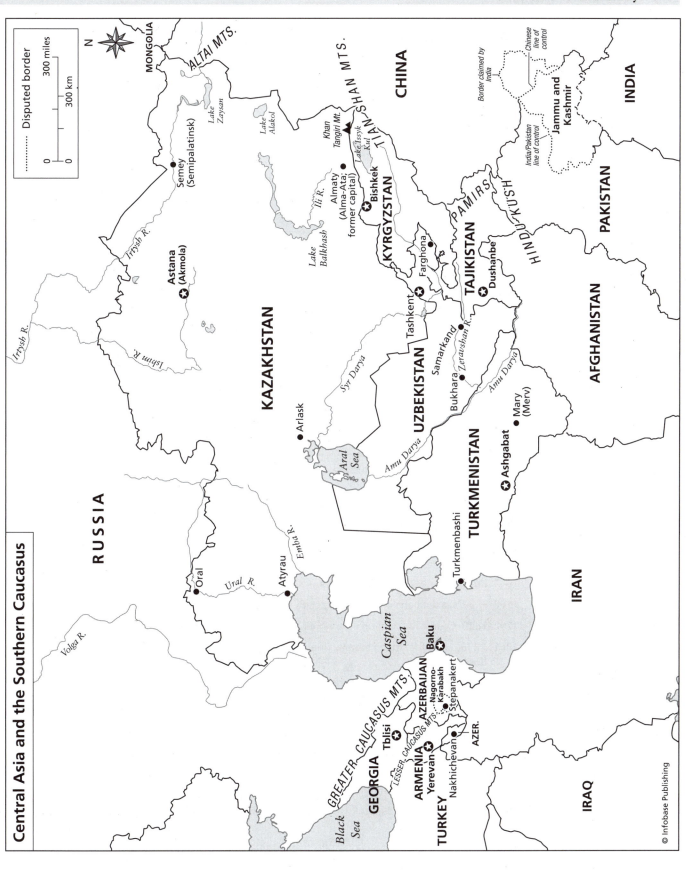

Central Asia and the Southern Caucasus

Disputed border

300 miles

300 km

N

MONGOLIA

ALTAI MTS.

Lake Zaysan

Lake Alakol

Semey (Semipalatinsk)

CHINA

Chinese line of control

Border claimed by India

India/Pakistan line of control

Jammu and Kashmir

INDIA

Khan Tangiri Mt.

TIAN SHAN MTS.

Lake Issyk Kul

Bishkek

KYRGYZSTAN

PAMIRS

HINDU-KUSH

PAKISTAN

Ili R.

Almaty (Alma-Ata; former capital)

Astana (Akmola)

Irtysh R.

Irtysh R.

Ishim R.

Lake Balkhash

KAZAKHSTAN

Farghona

Tashkent

Dushanbe

TAJIKISTAN

AFGHANISTAN

Irtysh R.

Arlask

Syr Darya

UZBEKISTAN

Samarkand

Zeravshan R.

Amu Darya

Bukhara

Mary (Merv)

Aral Sea

Amu Darya

RUSSIA

Oral

Ural R.

Atyrau

Emba R.

TURKMENISTAN

Ashgabat

Turkmenbashi

IRAN

Volga R.

Caspian Sea

Baku

GREATER CAUCASUS MTS.

Tbilisi

AZERBAIJAN

Nagorno-Karabakh

Stepanakert

AZER.

Black Sea

GEORGIA

LESSER CAUCASUS MTS.

ARMENIA

Yerevan

Nakhichevan

TURKEY

IRAQ

© Infobase Publishing

Kazakhstanis: nationality time line

B.C.E.

1500–800 The territory of present-day Kazakhstan is inhabited by the Andron and Begazy-Dandybai tribes, seminomadic people who practice animal domestication and are later recognized for their extraordinary mastery of metallurgy.

800   Nomadic Scythians live in the area of present-day Kazakhstan.

300–100 The Scythians form a state in Kazakhstan.

C.E.

546–53 Turkic peoples under the leadership of Bumin rebel against their Rouran overlords in the iron mines of the Altai Mountains and emerge as one of the most powerful groups on the Eurasian steppes, the Gokturk khanate.

565   The Gokturks defeat the Hephthalites and bring an end to that empire.

Sixth–seventh centuries Other Turkic people, living north of Transoxiana, begin to unite loosely as the Oghuz Turks.

716   The Gokturk territory west of the Altai is taken by the Oghuz, never to return to Gokturk hands.

1037 Toghril Beg I, founder of the Seljuk empire, is born.

1072 Malikshah succeeds Alp Arslan as the sultan of the Seljuks, and under his rule the empire is at its strongest and culturally most influential, including the southernmost territory of Kazakhstan.

1190–1218 The Naiman, a Mongol subgroup, are defeated by Genghis Khan in the Altai region of eastern Kazakhstan.

1258 Mongol leader Hulega Khan, grandson of Genghis Khan, invades the Near East and seizes Baghdad, overthrowing the Abbasid-Seljuk empire, which includes the Uzbeks, the Kazakhs, and the Georgians. The natives of Kazakhstan fall under Mongol rule.

1400 The Mongol empire is fragmented into smaller, individual structures known as khanates.

1470 The Kazakhs begin to split from the Uzbeks to establish their own ethnic group.

1511 Kasym Khan unites the Kazakh tribes for the first time, and the Kazakhs are recognized as a unified group.

1645 Russian trader Mikhail Guryev founds the port city of Guryev, which is later renamed Atyrau.

1700 The Kazakh khanate reaches its zenith.

1798–1820 Czarist Russian forces conquer the region of present-day Kazakhstan.

1861 Multitudes of Russian peasants immigrate to Kazakhstan with the abolition of serfdom in Russia.

1863 Russia annexes Kazakhstan and calls it the Steppe District. The Russian language is used in all Kazakh schools and governmental groups. Some Kazakhs found the Kazakh National Movement to maintain their cultural identity and nomadic way of life.

1890 Greater numbers of Russians settle in Kazakhstan to colonize the country.

1916 The Russians murder many Kazakhs during protests against forced conscription; about a million Kazakhs flee to China.

1917 The Bolshevik revolution overthrows czarist rule and establishes the Soviet state.

1918 Increasing tension due to Russian confiscation of land and resources erupts in the Basmachi Revolt.

1932–33 Joseph Stalin implements collective farming among the Kazakh people, resulting in nation-wide famine.

1936 Kazakhstan becomes the Kazak SSR, a constituent republic of the Soviet Union.

1944 Stalin orders the mass deportation of Chechens to Kazakhstan for resisting Soviet rule.

1947 The Soviets' main nuclear testing site is established near the city of Semey, or Semipalatinsk.

1949–89 A series of nuclear tests, including four major tests, performed in Kazakhstan results in the contamination of at least 500,000 people. Larger tests performed near Semipalatinsk produce high rates of birth defects and radiation poisoning in local families, including children.

1953 Joseph Stalin dies. The new Soviet leader, Nikita Khrushchev, enforces the "Virgin Lands" program, designed to utilize Kazakhstan's pastures as a major source of grain production for the Soviet Union.

1968 The Aral Sea begins shrinking when Soviet engineers introduce irrigation that diverts water from two feeder rivers.

1971 A Soviet test of weaponized smallpox at the port of Arlask in Kazakhstan results in an outbreak that infects and kills a woman and two young children.

1986 Protest demonstrations by young Kazakhs take place in Almaty to oppose Communist rule of the USSR; Soviet troops are dispatched to suppress the crowd and many demonstrators are jailed or killed.

1988 Soviet biological scientists transport hundreds of tons of anthrax bacteria in canisters to Vorrozhdeniye Island in the Aral Sea.

1990 The Aral Sea shrinks and splits into two bodies of water, separated by a patch of desert.

The USSR's constituent republics begin to assert their autonomy and sovereignty over their own lands. They refuse to pay tax revenues to the central Moscow government and refuse to recognize Soviet legislation that undermines local law. The USSR soon collapses.

1991 Kazakhstan declares its independence from Russia and elects Nursultan Nazarbayev president. Many Russian immigrants leave the country to return to Russia.

1991–2000 Kazakhstan receives $550 million in aid from the United States.

1995 Private landownership is legalized.

1997 The Kazakhstani capital is shifted from Almaty to Akmola to move it away from the Chinese border.

1998 Kazakhstan's economy sees a new influx of wealth through the utilization of oil reserves.

Efforts are made at restoring the Aral Sea through dams.

Former Kazakhstan prime minister Akezhan Kazhegeldin establishes the Republican People's Party of Kazakhstan. He is exiled in 1999 and in 2001 is sentenced to 10 years in jail for "corruption." Soon after President Nursultan Nazarbayev institutes a law stating that anyone with a criminal conviction cannot run for election. Included in the list of criminal acts is insulting the honor and dignity of the president.

1999 Kazakhstan's presidential elections are held, and Nazarbayev wins another seven-year term through alleged rigging.

Twenty-six inmates in a prison in Atyrau stab themselves in the stomach in an attempted mass suicide to protest prison conditions.

2000 Eleven thousand seals are found dead on the shores of the Caspian Sea as a result of oil-related pollutants.

A $2.5 billion oil pipeline is completed to transport 600,000 barrels a day from Kazakhstan to Russia.

Kazakhstan's parliament passes a law allowing President Nazarbayev "powers and privileges for life." Such privileges include immunity from criminal prosecution.

2005 Nursultan Nazarbayev is elected to another seven-year term, again through what many speculate to be election rigging. He wins 91.15 percent of the votes cast.

(who were less than 40 percent of the inhabitants at the time of independence in 1991). Russians and Ukrainians as well as many other Central Asian peoples all reside in the republic, making the construction of a coherent national identity separate from ethnic identities extremely difficult. In addition Stalin-era collectivization, which saw the displacement of many small-scale farmers, settlement of pastoral nomads, and, in many regions, hunger and famine, led to further divisions among ethnic groups as each turned inward and looked at the others with suspicion to survive the periods of difficulty.

The Soviet policies of glasnost and perestroika, which were initiated by Mikhail Gorbachev in the mid-1980s, created the political space in Kazakhstan and other Soviet republics for a more open airing of grievances than had occurred since the early 20th century. In both 1986 and 1989 in Alma-Ata and Novyi Uzen, respectively, some Kazakh residents took to the streets to protest Russian domination, high prices, unemployment, and suppression of the Islamic faith. Clashes also took place between different ethnic groups as high prices and inflation again saw different communities turning inward in a period of difficulty. These protests, as well as many others in the other Central Asian republics, were followed in June 1990 by the Central Asian Summit, in which many separate independence movements joined in Alma-Ata to protest Soviet domination.

Finally with the dissolution of the Soviet Union in 1991 Kazakhstan and these other constituent republics regained their independence. In 1991 the people of Kazakhstan elected their president, Nursultan Nazarbayev, and began undertaking the tasks of both nation and state building. The Kazakhs have since found a global edge in their large oil reserves, which have provided the country with rapid economic growth. In 2005 the growth rate in gross domestic product (GDP) was an impressive 9.4 percent, compared to 3.2 percent in the United States in the same year. Kazakhstan is still a lower-middle-income country, but this impressive growth should see it rise to a middle-income country within the next decade.

Development of a democratic government, however, has not been impressive since the country declared its independence. The country has no experience with, or history of, democracy and the development of a democratic civil society is a slow process. Following in the footsteps of the region's autocratic leaders of the past, Kazakhstani president Nursultan Nazarbayev has installed family and friends in positions of high authority, censored the press, blocked opposition Web sites and opponents attempting to run against him by passing a law declaring that no one who has committed the crime of insulting the president's honor and dignity can run for election. Many also allege that the last two presidential elections, in 1999 and 2005, were rigged so that Nazarbayev could retain his presidential office.

The creation of a common Kazakhstani national identity, as separate from ethnic or religious identity, is still very much a work in progress and may take many generations to succeed. The Kazakhstani advantage of strong economic growth, at least for as long as the oil reserves last, may be the one saving grace in a country in which the dominant ethnic community makes up less than 54 percent of the population, far fewer people than are necessary to base the national identity on a common ethnic heritage.

CULTURAL IDENTITY

Since the mid-1990s, when the exodus of ethnic Russians in Kazakhstan slowed, there has been some progress in blending the two largest ethnic groups in the country, and generally strong economic growth has led to an acceptance of Kazakhstani identity among many citizens. The greatest symbol of this blending is the adoption of the word *Kazakhstani* to refer to the country's citizens and government, rather than *Kazakh,* which has ethnic connotations. However, discrimination against Russians in high-level positions continues, and the Kazakhstani government has passed a law prohibiting the use of languages other than Kazakh in the public sphere after 2008. Many other cultural fault lines continue to divide the country and impede the development of a cohesive cultural identity.

The most important of these fault lines also has a geographic component; the northern portion of the country is largely Slavic, with up to 90 percent of some northern regions inhabited by Russians and Ukrainians, while the southern areas are much more Kazakh and Uzbek. In addition these ethnic differences are usually associated with religious differences as well. The northern Slavic communities tend to be Orthodox Christian or to practice no religion at all, while the southern Kazaks, Uzbeks, and other Central Asian peoples are largely Sunni Muslims, a central feature of their identity for centuries. For example anti-Islamic policies that Lenin implemented in Kazakhstan in the early 20th century became such an explosive source of conflict that he was eventually forced to reverse them to pacify the people. In addition the first anti-Soviet riots in 1986 were largely over the freedom to install Kazakh religious leaders and today Islam retains its central position in Kazakh identity.

A second difference emerges between populations that are the descendants of settled farmers, largely Slavs in the north, and those that are descendants of pastoral nomads. Because of the Kazakh people's traditional reliance on animal domestication for their livelihood, ethnic Kazakh culture is heavily infused with religious customs devoted to the protection and fertility of livestock. Traditionally it is customary for one man to ask another about the well-being of his livestock before asking after the man's health. In addition in keeping with the nomadic tradition a major symbol of Kazakh cultural identity is the yurt, a movable tent made of felt that can be assembled and disassembled in little more than half an hour. Though it is not commonly used today, the image of the yurt operates as a potent cultural symbol of Kazakh heritage.

As is the case with the Kazakhstani nation, Kazakhstani cultural identity continues to be in transition away from Soviet and Russian domination and toward something new. What this identity will be based on is still a matter of debate and contention at the highest levels of Kazakhstani politics and society.

FURTHER READING

Wayne Eastep, Alma Kunanbay, Gareth L. Steen, and William McCaffery. *The Soul of Kazakhstan* (Norwalk, Conn.: Easten Press, 2001).

Michael Furgus and Janar Jandosova. *Kazakhstan: Coming of Age* (London: Stacey International, 2004).

Martha Brill Olcott. *Kazakhstan: Unfulfilled Promise* (Washington, D.C.: Carnegie Endowment for International Peace, 2002).

Keith Rosten. *Once in Kazakhstan: The Snow Leopard Emerges* (Lincoln, Nebr.: iUniverse, 2005).

R. Charles Weller. *Rethinking Kazakh and Central Asian Nationhood: A Challenge to Prevailing Western Views* (Los Angeles: Asia Research Associates, 2006).

Khant (Hanto, Kantok, Khanty, Ostiak [until the 1930s] or Ostyak)

The Khant are one of the indigenous peoples of eastern Siberia. They are often classified with the linguistically related Mansi as Ob-Ugric peoples, and the two are the eponymous groups of the Khanty-Mansi Autonomous District, though they make up less than 2 percent of the population in that region today. While the Mansi tend to live on the western side of the Ural Mountains and are thus largely located in Europe, the Khant live on the eastern or Asian side.

HISTORY

The Khant people's original homeland was either the Irtysh River basin in the western Siberian plain or the Pechora River on the western side of the Urals; historical and linguistic experts tend to be evenly split in their opinions on these origins. Most agree that around 500 C.E. this population began migrating to the north or west, where the people settled eventually in the lower Ob River basin. Some Khant adopted reindeer herding, while the majority lived entirely on nomadic hunting and fishing, a lifestyle they maintained until the mid-20th century. The cultural and linguistic split between the Khant and the Mansi occurred in the 13th century, when the Khant moved farther east to flee the encroaching RUSSIANS.

The first references to the Ob-Ugrian peoples in Russian documents occurred in the 11th century, and at the end of the 12th century some representatives from the principality of Novgorod were killed by Ob-Ugrians who refused to pay tribute to the intruders. Throughout the 14th century Novgorod continued to claim as its own the territory of the Ob-Ugrians, called *jugra,* and military expeditions were sent to collect tribute. The Russians did the same in the 15th century, especially under Czar Ivan III (1462–1505). By the late 16th century the Russians had consolidated their power in the region by defeating the TATARS, building a number of fortress towns to aid in the collection of the fur tax and the defense of their territory, and sending out Christian missionaries. In the early 18th century the Khant were officially baptized as Christians by an Orthodox monk, Fyodor, but shamanism and animism remained central to the Khant worldview and spiritual orientation until well into the 20th century. Later the Soviets sent Khant children to boarding schools, which eliminated most traces of these indigenous belief systems.

During this initial period of Russian colonization the Khant were generally required to pay tribute or taxes in native furs to their Novgorodian and Russian overlords. The Europeans exacted a large number of workdays and products from the indigenous peoples in exchange for a few select goods, the most destructive of which was alcohol. They also stole

KHANT

location:
Northwest Siberia in the Ob-Irtysh River basins

time period:
2000 B.C.E. to the present

ancestry:
Finno-Ugric

language:
Khant, an Ugrian language most closely related to Mansi and more distantly related to Hungarian

the best land, especially territory including and adjacent to the region's many rivers, thus making it difficult for nomadic hunters and fishermen to survive without trading for food items. By the late 19th century Russian academics were claiming that the Khant would probably disappear as a separate people in the following few decades.

Fortunately this has not happened as yet. With the formation of the Soviet Union after the 1917 revolution "the small peoples of the North" began to see changes in the policy toward them. These policies, which included settling them into villages, introducing Russian education and health care systems, and eliminating the last vestiges of the indigenous religious systems, were not necessarily less destructive culturally than those of the Russian Empire, but they did allow for population expansion. In addition to "civilization" as the Russians thought of it, Soviet policy after 1928 included collectivization of hunting, fishing, and reindeer breeding to replace the subsistence activities of the Khant. In 1933 the Khant, with the assistance of the Forest NENETS, rebelled against these policies in what has been called the Kazym revolt because it centered on the "cultural base" of Kazym, set up by the Russians to serve as an administrative center for the new Khant collectives. The revolt was crushed by the Soviet army; hundreds were killed, and even distant Khant settlements were bombed. By the time oil and gas were discovered in their territories in the 1950s and 1960s the Khant could do nothing to protect themselves from the ecologically and socially destructive industrial complexes being built among them.

CULTURE

Despite the relatively limited food supplies in the frozen territory inhabited by the Khant their traditional culture included many food taboos that could not be broken without severe social and supernatural penalties. For example the Khant social system was organized around patrilineal clans, those in which membership was inherited from the father; these each bore the name of an animal such as a beaver, elk, or deer, and eating the animal of one's clan was strictly prohibited. All Khant were also prohibited from cutting elk meat with a knife or salting it, eating any white animal such as a swan or ermine, or treating bear meat with disrespect by allowing women or dogs to touch it. This last taboo says as much about the place of women in Khant society as it does about the importance of bears, which were considered

sacred as the guardians of the world order and relatives of the primordial Khant. As a result when the Soviets banned the hunting of bear after the 1933 revolt the Khant felt this as comparable to the arrest and deportation of their shamans and the destruction of their sacred groves of trees. This law was relaxed during the era of Gorbachev in the 1980s, and the Khant belief that bears that have been killed and eaten will rise from the dead as long as their bones are not broken returned with it, at least among older Khant who remembered the beliefs of their ancestors. While these animals made up about half the food resources of traditional Khant, fish made up the other half and there are a variety of taboos around the processing, cooking, and eating of fish as well. *Crucian,* as the fish of the underworld, cannot be cooked with other fish, and *burbot,* a relative of cod, must have its intact liver extracted through its mouth or it must be thrown back into the water. The portion of liver that is extracted must be cooked over a fire made from willow branches and eaten.

FURTHER READING

Marjorie Mandelstam Balzer. *The Tenacity of Ethnicity: A Siberian Saga in Global Perspective* (Princeton, N.J.: Princeton University Press, 1999).

Khasi (Cassia, Cossyah, Kasia, Kassia, Kassya, Kasya, Khasía, Khasiah, Khassia, Khassu, Khosia, Ki Khasi)

The exact origins of the Khasi of India and Bangladesh remain unknown, but linguistically they are believed to be related both to other Mon-Khmer speakers in central India and to peoples with related tongues from Southeast Asia. Their original migratory route probably took them through contemporary Myanmar (Burma), but the period remains unknown. Archaeologists have found agricultural remains, metalwork, and pottery that link the Khasi to related groups as early as the fourth century C.E., but the first written mention of this ethnonym is about 1500, in a religious tract from Assam. Not long after this first mention records from the Jaintia kingdom of Assam note that there were 25 distinct Khasi chiefdoms throughout the hill region of northeast India.

As the primary colonizing country in India the British first began interacting with the Khasi in about 1765 when they took over the local markets at Sylhet. About 30 years later the Khasi fought back against British rule and taxes, leading to a dual approach by the British: they built a series of ramparts and other militarized strongholds in the hills and then placed an embargo on Khasi products in their markets. By the mid-19th century, however, the two groups had reconciled their differences, and in 1862 the British signed several treaties with Khasi principalities freeing them from tax obligations and granting a degree of autonomy. The result of this early colonial history is that in 1972 the predominantly tribal state of Meghalaya was carved out of a once-larger Assam with Khasi as its dominant language and cultural group. The British capital of Assam, Shillong, is the contemporary capital of Meghalaya.

As British records from the 18th century indicate, the Khasi have long been a market-oriented people who have a combined economy based on agricultural labor and produce, landownership, and trade. For subsistence most families have their own gardens or family farms on which they grow both paddy and dry rice, corn, potatoes, millet, yams, legumes, sugarcane, pineapple, cotton, and a host of other crops. Many also have a few head of cattle or goats, as well as pigs, dogs, chickens, ducks, and bees, and supplement these domesticated products and animals with hunting, fishing, and wild forest products. Even in the present much of Meghalaya remains forested, allowing for substantial contributions to both household diet and economy from these items. Both slash-and-burn or *jhum* horticulture and more permanent paddies are utilized by most families, the former in the hills and dry grasslands and the latter in valleys and adjacent to rivers.

Many farming families sell their surplus products and both buy and sell labor on the market. In addition many also produce a variety of handicrafts that they sell in the local markets and in the capital. Weaving, bamboo work, tailoring, spinning, lace and silk production; jewelry, brick, and pottery making; and farm implements and many other locally made products provide the Khasi with a relatively strong familial and local economy.

Khasi social organization has developed around the kinship principle of matrilineal descent, in which all children inherit their membership in their primary kinship group from their mother; their most important male relative for purposes of inheritance is their mother's brother. Fathers tend to be indulgent of their children but cannot leave them any property or titles upon their deaths as they are primarily responsible to their own sisters' children.

The smallest kinship unit among the Khasi is the *jing* or family, made up of a grandmother, her daughters, and their children. Larger family units that share a great-grandmother consider themselves "one womb" or a subclan and are responsible to one another as strongly as to their own siblings. More extended kin groups that share a common female ancestor are made up of groups of lineages and are called clans or *shi kur*. All of these kinship groups are exogamous and require people to marry individuals from outside them or be punished for committing lineage or clan incest. Upon marriage residence depends on the status of the wife within her family of origin. If a woman is her family's primary heir, usually the youngest daughter, and will inherit the home and land, then her husband is required to move into her family's home and care for her parents in matrilocal residence; however, daughters who do not inherit land and houses are permitted to set up their own independent households at marriage, called neolocal residence. These traditional Khasi rules have not all survived into the present day, when working for wages has meant that few Khasi men are willing to move into their wife's family's home and take care of her parents in their old age.

The traditional Khasi village was an endogamous unit in which most people married and remained for their entire lives. Village solidarity was extremely important and the four to six matrilineal clans that resided in each village tended to be allies in such ventures as agriculture and irrigation, trade, and, in the past, warfare or raiding. Villages were built on hillsides with the houses located very close together as protection from wind, animals, and outsiders. Villages also had burial grounds, sacred groves of trees, wells, and public buildings, which today can include Christian churches, schools, and government offices; many also have a marketplace and shops.

The traditional political organization of the Khasi included several villages united under a single chief and executive council. These bodies acted in a number of different areas, including as a judicial system, trying individuals and groups for crimes against both property and citizens, and a religious one, performing ceremonies and rites for villages and regions. Councils and chiefs also controlled the local militias, which engaged with other Khasi groups as well as with others in warfare and raids. One area in which these bodies did not have authority was over the markets, which had their own supervisors to maintain order and equity.

KHASI

location:
Assam, Meghalaya, Manipur, West Bengal, and Tripura States of India and Bangladesh

time period:
Probably before fourth century to the present

ancestry:
Tribal speakers of Mon-Khmer languages

language:
Khasi, a Mon-Khmer language with several dialects

KHITANS

location:
Inhabited a major part of what is currently known as Manchuria and parts of north China as far south as Beijing, which the Liao made a capital city for the first time. The Kara Khitai empire ruled much of Central Asia from Balasagun in contemporary Kyrgyzstan.

time period:
300s to 1218 C.E.

ancestry:
Probably descendants of Xianbei (Proto-Mongol people)

language:
Probably a Mongolic or Turkic language. One Khitan script resembled that of the Han Chinese; the other was created roughly around 925 C.E. and resembled Uighur.

Khasi traditional religion combined a belief in a female creator goddess, U Blei Nongthaw, with belief in many minor gods, spirits, and ghosts. The gods of water, wealth, and the village received the greatest sacrifices after the creator goddess, while others would receive blessings as an occasional thank you or request for assistance. These sacrifices were carried out by priests who all were from the same priestly clan, or by village councillors with the proper ritual knowledge. A variety of other male and female specialists also participated in rituals of various sorts including marriage, birth, and funereal rites and agricultural festivals. Today, however, more than half the Khasi population has adopted Christianity as a result of the efforts of various Protestant missionaries in the 19th and early 20th centuries. This has significantly changed the ritual function of many formerly joint secular-sacred positions, including that of youngest daughters, who are no longer considered ritually responsible for performing burial rites for their parents or for performing other ancestral rituals.

FURTHER READING

Pranab Kumar Das Gupta. *Life and Culture of Matrilineal Tribe of Meghalaya* (New Delhi: Inter-India, 1984).

Khitans (Kara Khitai, Kara Khitans, Kara-Khitay, Kara Kitai, Khata, Khitai, Kitai, Liao, Qidans)

The Khitans were a Mongol or Turkic nomadic people of the Mongolian steppes whose primary economic activity was raising cattle and horses. The first reference to the Khitans as a separate ethnic group is as old as the fourth century, but they do not rise to prominence until the ninth. The Khitans adopted the Buddhist religion around the 10th century, and their leaders tended to follow this religion; however, commoners continued to believe in a combination of Confucianism, Daoism, and their own indigenous shamanistic religion. As part of the latter set of beliefs, many Khitans worshipped a white horse and a gray ox, which served as symbols of the two tribes that had been joined through marriage, the Yelu and the Xiao, to form one segment of the Khitans. The official adoption of Buddhism forced those in the Liao empire to pay taxes to both the state and the monasteries.

In 907 C.E. the Khitan tribe emerged from the Mongolian steppes to lead part of China as the Liao dynasty. This dynasty remained in power in parts of present-day Mongolia, Manchuria, and northern China for more than 200 years. The Liao leadership was frequently challenged, and their armored cavalry, more ad-

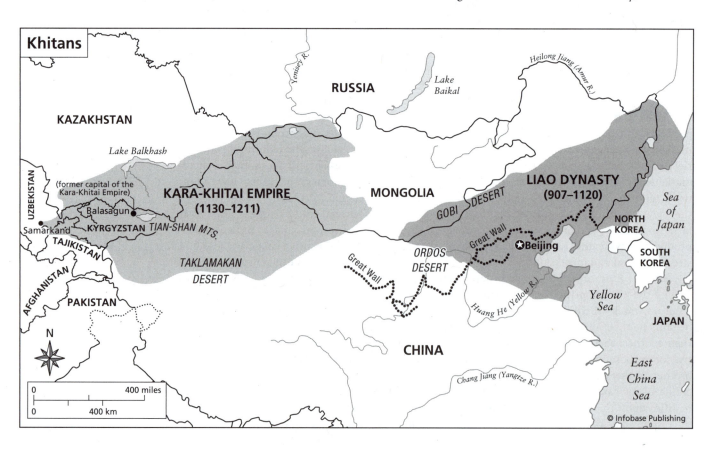

vanced than most, was frequently active. They were also noted as skilled archers. The Khitans or Liao conquered the UIGHUR in 926 and then fought with Koryo, the northern state of Korea that unified Korea's regional leaders, from 993 to 1018. By 1022 the Khitans had acknowledged defeat by the Koryo and ceded all Liao territory to them. In 1005 the HAN Chinese government offered a peace treaty in which China would pay tribute to the leaders of the northern tribes in return for peace at the frontiers. The Liao leaders agreed and eventually this treaty allowed Liao rulers to live in peace with the Chinese. The Khitans soon adapted some features of a Chinese lifestyle. They settled down and began to farm instead of preparing and strategizing for war.

In 1120 the Chinese Song empire joined with the Jurchen Jin empire to attack the Liao dynasty, which at that time was weakened with internal problems and unstable economic conditions. In 1125 the Khitans were defeated by the Jin, or Jurchen, dynasty. Some Khitans remained and served the Jin. Some, such as Yelu Dashi, the last prince of the Liao dynasty, migrated west, to the upper Yenisey River in Siberia. From there Yelu Dashi and his army, taking the name *Kara Khitai*, continued southwest into Central Asia. In 1130 these Kara Khitai defeated a joint Seljuk Turk–Karakhanid (KARLUKS) army on the steppes near Samarkand to establish themselves as one of the strongest kingdoms in Central Asia (*see* JURCHENS).

The Kara-Khitai ruled their short-lived but powerful empire from their capital in Balasagun in what is today Kyrgyzstan. Despite their leaders' settlement in this ancient city most Kara-Khitai remained largely nomadic during their century-long domination of the steppes and as a result directly held only a small amount of territory around their capital. Most of the rest of Central Asia was held through a series of vassal states nominally controlled by the KHWAREZMIANS, Karluks, and Uighur. In addition to nomadic pastoralism the Kara-Khitai increased their coffers through exacting tribute from traders who crossed their lands on journeys between the Middle East and China; some also engaged in this trade themselves. The Kara-Khitai preserved their traditional religious beliefs, a mixture of Buddhism and indigenous shamanism, while ruling Central Asia.

In 1211 the Kara-Khitai empire began to feel the winds of change when the last Khitan leader, Yelu Zhilugu, was defeated by the

Khitans time line	
C.E.	
10th century	The Khitan leaders adopt Buddhism.
907	The Liao dynasty of Khitan people emerges from the northern steppes to rule part of China.
926	The Liao defeat the Uighur and hundreds of years of relations between the two peoples begin.
993–1018	A series of wars between the Khitans and Koryo of northern Korea.
1005	Many Khitans undergo sinicization as the Han and Khitans agree to coexist in the northern borderlands.
1022	The Koryo defeat the Khitans and drive them north and west.
1120	The Chinese and Jurchens attack a weakened Liao dynasty, and five years later most of the Liao are subsumed into the Jurchen Jin dynasty.
1130	The Liao successor state, the Kara Khitai under Yelu Dashi, defeat a joint Seljuk Turk–Karluk army on the steppes outside Samarkand on its march westward.
1177	The Kara-Khitai defeat the Naiman.
1211	The Naiman ruler, Kuchlug, defeats the last Kara Khitai king, Yelu Zhilugu.
1218	Kuchlug is himself defeated by Genghis Khan, and the Kara-Khitai disappear from history.

great NAIMAN warrior Kuchlug. Prior to this uprising from 1177 until 1211 the Naiman had been merely one of the many subjugated people within the empire. They were also a Mongol people and so in the early 13th century were experiencing tremendous pressure to join Genghis Khan's larger Mongol Empire. Kuchlug refused to join peacefully and instead fled west, where his armies defeated those of Yelu Zhilugu. Most historians consider Kuchlug to have usurped the power of the greater Kara-Khitai for himself rather than replacing this empire with a Naiman one. Perhaps if he had had more time the large multiethnic Kara-Khitai empire would have become more mongolized under Naiman tutelage, but Kuchlug reigned only seven years before being overrun by the MONGOLS' invasion of Central Asia. In 1218 the remaining Kara-Khitai disappeared from history altogether after succumbing to Genghis Khan's armies.

FURTHER READING

Michal Biran. *The Empire of the Qara Khitai in Eurasian History: Between China and the Islamic World* (New York: Cambridge University Press, 2005).

KHMERS

location:
Cambodia and Vietnam with small numbers in Laos, China, and Thailand as well

time period:
Possibly 200 B.C.E. to the present

ancestry:
Mon-Khmer

language:
Khmer, an eastern Mon-Khmer language

Khmer Islam   *See* CHAMS.

Khmers   (Camarini, Coa Mein, Kambuja, Kampuch, Khmae, Khom, Kui kmi, Kumar, Mein)

The Khmers are the dominant ethnic group in Cambodia, with a second large population residing in Vietnam; smaller numbers of Khmers also live in Laos, Thailand, and China. A relatively large diaspora of Khmers who fled Cambodia during the brutal reign of the Khmer Rouge in the late 1970s and then the VIETNAMESE occupation of the People's Republic of Kampuchea in the 1980s resides in France, the United States, and elsewhere.

GEOGRAPHY

Although at one point the Khmer empire dominated most of the southern part of the Indochinese Peninsula, from the east coast of Vietnam to the border of Myanmar (Burma) in the west and from the Malay Peninsula to the capital of Laos, Vientiane, in the north, today the Khmer lands are synonymous with the country of Cambodia, located between Vietnam to the east and south, Laos and Thailand to the north, and Thailand and the Gulf of Thailand to the west. The landscape of Cambodia is generally low, with the highest peak of Phnom Aoral only 5,810 feet, and is covered in thick tropical forest. The climate is tropical, ranging from 68°F to 97°F, with monsoon rains falling from

---

Khmers time line

B.C.E.

200   The possible period in which the proto-Mon-Khmer people migrated south out of China.

C.E.

802   Jayavarman II, an ethnic Khmer, takes over the Funan empire and the Khmer empire comes into being.

850   Jayavarman II dies at his first capital of Hariharalaya and is succeeded by his son, Jayavarman III.

881   Indravarman I, Jayavarman II's nephew, builds the first Khmer royal mortuary temple at Bakong.

893   The first royal cult center at Angkor, Yasodharapara, is dedicated to Yasovarman I.

950   The Khmers attack Champa and take territory in what is today central Vietnam.

1074–80   Champa invades Cambodia and captures the stronghold of Sambor.

1112–50   Suryvarman II begins building the great temple complex of Angkor Wat.

1145–49   The Khmers attack Champa, capturing the capital of Vijaya.

1177   Champa troops sail up the Mekong River and capture Angkor.

1181–1219   Jayavarman VII converts to Theravada Buddhism, effecting great change in the Khmer cosmology, and begins building Angkor Thom. By the late 13th century most Khmers have likewise converted from Hinduism to Buddhism.

1190   Khmer king Jayavarman VII captures Vijaya again.

1191   In this year 306,372 adult Khmers from 13,500 different villages are dedicated to serving the royal Khmer temples and their cults.

1203   The Khmers invade Champa again, this time temporarily annexing Champa as part of Cambodia.

1220   A newly independent Champa becomes the Khmer ally.

1296   A Chinese embassy is welcomed by the Khmers and one of its members, Chou Ta-kuan, writes the most complete descriptions we have of the royal cult and palace life. He states that the king has 3,000–5,000 concubines and wives and 1,000–2,000 servants.

1350   The Thai kingdom of Ayutthaya is established and begins pushing the borders of the Khmer empire inward.

mid-April to October. During the rainy season the country's giant lake, Tonle Sap, expands to about four times its dry season area of 1,000 square miles to provide irrigation water and fish to the surrounding population. The Mekong River is the second most important water resource in the country as it irrigates the entire eastern lowland region and even allows for two rice crops per year in some regions. Along the coast Cambodia is dominated by mangrove swamps.

ORIGINS

The origins of the Khmer people remain unclear to this day. One hypothesis claims that the ancestors of the Mon-Khmer people migrated out of China sometime before 200 B.C.E. while others postulate Indian origins for these people. Nowadays Mon-Khmer–speaking peoples, such as the KHASI and BLANG, reside in both countries.

The origins of the Khmer state are much less obscure and lie in the development of the Indian-influenced state of Funan in about 200 C.E. The FUNANESE state encompassed much of the southern portion of the Indochinese Peninsula, including territory that is today southern Vietnam, Thailand, and Myanmar, and all of Cambodia. Through connections to India that remain somewhat unclear the Funanese practiced Hinduism, used a script adapted from Sanskrit, and utilized a god-king model of state organization similar to that of ancient

1431 Considered by many to mark the end of the Angkor period of Khmer history, the Thais sack the temple city of Angkor, which is abandoned the following year.

1620 A Vietnamese princess marries into the Khmer royal family and all Vietnamese are granted the right to settle in the eastern coastal region of the Khmer kingdom; this area today is thoroughly Vietnamese and contains Ho Chi Minh City, formerly Saigon.

1863 Khmer King Norodom signs his empire over to the French as a protectorate, in part to protect it from incursions by the Thais from the west and the Vietnamese from the east.

1887 Cambodia becomes a French colony within the French Union of Indochina.

1941 Norodom Sihanouk is installed as king by the French.

Japan occupies Cambodia but allows the French colonial structure to remain until 1945.

1945 The Japanese install an independent Cambodian government just before being defeated in the Pacific.

1946 The French colonial bureaucracy returns to Cambodia and the Khmers begin their struggle against it.

1953 Cambodia gains its independence months before France's defeat in the First Indochina War in Vietnam.

1955 King Norodom Sihanouk abdicates his throne in favor of his father to be able to join the modern political process. He becomes prime minister when his People's Socialist Party wins the first election in the country.

1960 A referendum legitimates Prince Sihanouk's position as chief of state after his father's death.

1970 Sihanouk is overthrown by General Lon Nol, who seeks to create a Khmer republic.

1975 Pol Pot's Communist Khmer Rouge overthrow the republic and begin four years of terror; around 2 million Khmer people lose their lives; hundreds of thousands of people from other ethnic groups also perish during the time of the "killing fields."

1979 A Vietnamese invasion brings down the Khmer Rouge.

1989 The Vietnamese withdraw from Cambodia, and Buddhism and private property are again legalized in the country.

1998 Pol Pot dies and the final Khmer Rouge insurgency finally disintegrates, allowing the Khmers to put the previous generation of war behind them.

2004 Norodom Sihamoni replaces Norodom Sihanouk as Khmer king of Cambodia.

India. The kingdom's capital was the city of Vyadhapura, which is believed to be Angkor Borei, Cambodia, where extensive archaeological work has been done recently. However, the most important features of the Funan kingdom were the long Mekong River and the kingdom's extensive shoreline. In a seafaring kingdom that adopted its major cultural features from far-away India, probably through interactions by trading ships that also provided the kingdom's greatest source of wealth, ocean ports and the river were the key to more than 600 years of domination in the region.

In the sixth century the Funanese began to lose control of the inland portion of their empire, and it is from that area that the subsequent power in the region, CHENLA, emerged. Chenla is first mentioned in a Chinese text as having obtained independence from Funan in about 550. From a northern base in contemporary Champassak Province, Laos, the people of Chenla had moved along the rivers and conquered most of the Mekong delta from southern Thailand to southern Vietnam and including much of Cambodia. By about 600 Chenla had conquered all of Funan and established a capital city at Isanapura, probably the contemporary city of Sambor, Cambodia. The oldest Khmer inscription, found at Angkor Borei, a former Funan stronghold south of Phnom Penh, is also from this period and is dated 611. The people of Chenla are often considered to be Khmers since they were probably speakers of the oldest form of that language, but it is more accurate to speak of them as combining features taken with them during their migra-

tions from southern China in the decades before 200 B.C.E. with Hindu and Mon-Khmer elements adopted when they overran the Funanese in about 550 C.E.

HISTORY
Precolonial

The start of Khmer history proper, as distinct from these previous indianized states in the region, is dated to the year 802. In that year Khmer King Jayavarman II expelled a short-lived JAVANESE kingdom that had gained control over Chenla in about 790 and then united the former lands of Funan and Chenla. This included territory in what is today Cambodia and southern Thailand, Myanmar, and Vietnam, all of which were ruled from Jayavarman's capital at Hariharalaya or Roluos and then from his new capital in the Kulen Hills.

Under Jayavarman II the Khmer empire adopted the institution that characterized the state and dominated the lives of all the people in it: Devaraja, the Hindu cult of the divine king. The cult of the god-king focused not only on the body and person of the king himself but also on his stone lingam, a phallic statue that was stored in the giant temples through which we have come to understand the Classic period of Khmer history, also known as the Angkor period. Many of the Khmer kings who ruled between the ninth and 14th centuries built their own temples, which housed their lingams during their lifetimes and then their ashes after their deaths. Therefore the most extensive and important remains from this period are not structures for humans to live in, which were all made of wood and have disappeared, but enormous stone funerary temples.

The first of these royal temples was built at Bakong in the royal city of Hariharalaya in 881 by Indravarman I, and the most famous of these temples is Angkor Wat, built throughout the first half of the 12th century for King Suryvarman II. Bakong, Angkor Wat, and all of the other mortuary temples of the Khmer kings were designed to reflect the structure of the mythological Mount Meru, the Hindu center of the universe and home of Brahma and other gods. Mount Meru itself was believed to be a five-leveled mountain that was surrounded by seven other mountain chains and then by the sea. Therefore all of these temple complexes contained a five-tiered temple building at the center, surrounded by seven walls, and a moat.

Between the ninth and 14th centuries the Khmer ruled much of mainland Southeast Asia

---

Jayavarman II

Jayavarman II is a critical figure in Cambodian history as he is credited as the founder of the Khmer empire, or what is now present-day Cambodia. Born around the year 770 C.E., he reportedly spent time in the court of the Sailendra dynasty in Java, although little is known about his time there, particularly whether or not he was there against his will. He was heavily influenced by Javanese culture and would later institute Javanese cultural practices in the Khmer empire. In 790 he ascended to the Javanese throne and proceeded to conquer the Kingdom of Chenla, or what would later become the Khmer empire. However, in 802 he renounced the Sailendra dynasty and declared Khmer independence, giving himself the title of *Cakravartin,* or "universal ruler." As the new ruler of the Khmer empire Jayavarman established the cult of *devaraja,* or god-king, a religious practice that he absorbed in the court of Sailendra and employed in Cambodia to deify himself and his successors. He also established several capitals throughout the Khmer empire and erected monuments to the Hindu gods. Jayavarman II died in 802, but the Khmer empire continued to flourish for another 600 years.

Angkor Wat, shown here at sunset, is the most famous of these five-tiered temple complexes, perhaps because of the mystical aura that surrounded its jungle-covered ruins until it was explored by French colonizers in the 19th century. *(Shutterstock/Luciano Mortula)*

in the name of their god-kings. Frequent wars were fought to expand the king's territory and to maintain the kingdom's hold on the territory it already had. Commoners had to turn over all surplus rice to the king and his royal ambassadors; they also had to contribute hundreds of hours of forced labor to build these extensive mortuary temples. In the year 1191 an anonymous Chinese source states that 306,372 adult Khmers from 13,500 different villages were dedicated to serving the royal temples and their cults; this is believed to be the vast majority of all adults in the kingdom. About a century later another Chinese writer, Chou Ta-kuan, wrote the most complete extant descriptions of the Khmer royal cult and palace life. According to him the king had 3,000–5,000 concubines and wives and 1,000–2,000 servants.

The end of the 12th century and beginning of the 13th introduced tremendous change in the pattern of Khmer life. After hundreds of years of almost incessant warfare against the CHAMS and other peoples in the region Jayavarman VII, who reigned 1181–1219, sought to ensure peace and justice for his people and converted to Theravada Buddhism. The king did not abandon the prolific building projects of his predecessors and actually had more complexes built than many of his royal ancestors, but his conversion led to the

eventual demise of the Khmer empire and its ruling structure. The Hindu *devaraja* model of state organization had created a strict pyramidal structure in which the god-king was the top of the pyramid, owned all land and agricultural surplus, and legitimated his power and wealth by being seen as divine. Below the king were the other nobility and the thousands of priests dedicated to the king's royal cults. At the bottom of the pyramid were the majority of Khmers, commoners who farmed, built temples, waged war, and otherwise supported the god-king's hold over them. With the adoption of Buddhism, which was quickly embraced by most Khmers, this kind of hierarchy could no longer be maintained. Buddhism's teachings about equality, salvation, and karma all led to a severe weakening of subsequent god-kings' hold over their subjects. As a result the neighboring Thai and Vietnamese kingdoms began encroaching on Khmer territory. The end of the Classic or Angkor period finally occurred in 1431 when the encroaching Thai armies sacked Angkor; the city was abandoned the following year and dense tropical jungle allowed to take it over.

Strange as it may seem, despite the survival of hundreds of thousands of Khmers, their royal city of Angkor was forgotten not long after it was abandoned. Buddhist monks who traveled into the jungles of remote eastern Cambodia often saw the ruins of the royal city but had no idea of its origins or significance. Myths and legends about a city of gods living in the jungles of Cambodia were spread throughout Southeast Asia and even into Europe after the 16th century. In 1860 a French explorer, Henry Mouhot, was the first European to see the ruins and document their existence for the Western world. In 1908 the French began a full-scale archaeological exploration and restoration project at Angkor, which has continued throughout most of the 20th century and into the 21st century, with the exception of the period of the Khmer Rouge genocide in the late 1970s and the Vietnamese occupation in the 1980s.

The period between the fall of Angkor in 1431 and the beginning of France's colonial project in the region in the 19th century was marked by the continual diminution of the size and grandeur of the Khmer kingdom. The Thai kingdom of Ayutthaya, which had been established as early as 1350, did not end its attacks on the Khmer lands after the destruction of Angkor. Former Khmer territory in the west became dominated by and then ruled over by the THAIS. From the east the Khmers were hemmed in by the powerful Vietnamese state, which had begun its march south after gaining independence from the Chinese in the 10th century. After defeating Champa in 1470, the Vietnamese continued to expand their borders southward and in 1620 finally pushed into the southernmost region around contemporary Ho Chi Minh City. Unlike most of the history of Khmer-Vietnamese interaction to that point the 1620 putsch was peaceful, the result of the marriage between a Vietnamese princess and a Khmer prince. One of the agreements that concluded the marriage arrangement allowed the Vietnamese to settle the eastern coastal region of the Khmer kingdom. From that period the Vietnamese began to dominate the region, a political state of affairs that was later legitimated by the French colonial power that ruled over all of Indochina.

This period between 1431 and the French colonial period was different from the prior centuries of Khmer history in that Buddhism created a model of state leadership that contrasted with the god-king model of the *devaraja* system. The Buddhist Khmer kings saw themselves as responsible to their people in terms of providing assistance during difficult times. They were obliged to care for the old and sick; they also began building and maintaining civil infrastructure such as roads and canals as part of their responsibility to their people. This situation differed from the pattern that had emerged earlier, in which the god-king simply used his people as servants and laborers to build structures to glorify himself and in which all wealth flowed upward to the top of the pyramid. The Buddhist kings saw themselves as father figures to their people, worthy of respect and having authority over them but also having responsibility to raise them up and care for their needs. This is not to say that all aspects of Hinduism disappeared from Khmer society, especially in art, theater, and literature, but the essence of society had changed forever.

Modern

By the early 19th century Vietnam and Thailand were constantly competing with each other to dominate the small Khmer kingdom between them. During the 1830s fighting was common throughout all of the territory that is today Cambodia and the remnants of the kingdom were close to collapse. In order to save the last of his ancestors' land and his own throne, in 1863 the Khmer king Norodom agreed to a French proposal that his kingdom become a French protectorate; outright colonialism was established with the French Union of Indochina in 1887. At that point the Khmer king became essentially a figurehead who for generations was actually chosen by the French bureaucracy. When Norodom died in 1904, the French refused to recognize his son as the rightful king and placed his brother, Sisowath, on the throne instead. The French also picked his successor, Norodom Sihanouk, who took the throne in 1941. During this French period many Cambodian institutions, such as the royal family and Buddhist monasteries, remained intact, but in addition the French established a bureaucratic civil service that paralleled their own in France and built roads, ports, and other infrastructure. The capital city of Phnom Penh, which was planned by the French and modeled on their own cities, took on the appearance of a French provincial town. Despite these changes the French actually put far less effort into their Cambodian colony than into its neighbor, Vietnam. The only real economic development in Cambodia was the establishment of a number of rubber plantations in the eastern region of the country; Cambodia also became a net food exporter at this time because of its comparatively large rice crop and small population.

Perhaps because colonialism did not disrupt most people's subsistence economy and left the Khmer royal family free to pursue its symbolic role as head of all the Khmer people, anti-French feelings did not develop to a revolutionary pitch in Cambodia. Only after World War II and the JAPANESE occupation force's creation of a nominally independent Cambodian state in 1945 did any serious push for independence emerge from within Khmer society. After the French reestablished their colonial presence in 1946, they had to deal with increasing numbers of Khmers pushing for independence. The French finally succumbed in 1949, granting Cambodia independence but within the framework of the French Union. Full independence began just four years later, in late 1953, when France, exhausted and about to be defeated in Vietnam, agreed to a split between the two regions. This was later ratified at the Geneva Accords of 1954, which marked the end of both the First Indochina War and the Korean War, when King Sihanouk was named the head of the Cambodian state.

Because of his royal position Sihanouk was largely forbidden to participate in the Cambodian political process and because of that in 1955 abdicated his throne in favor of his father. This allowed the newly titled Prince Sihanouk to control the country's politics through his position as head of the Sangkum Reastr Niyum or People's Socialist Community, the dominant political organization in the country. Because of Sihanouk's popularity as well as the harassment of opposition candidates and their supporters Sangkum won every seat in the national elections of 1955 and Sihanouk became prime minister of Cambodia. In 1960 with his father's death a national referendum made Prince Sihanouk head of state as well as head of government. During the 15 years of his reign over Cambodian politics Prince Sihanouk was popular with the majority of the Khmers, who saw his leadership as a connection to the Khmer golden age of the god-kings; he also drew significant foreign aid to the country from the United States, China, and the USSR through his policy of neutrality. However, Sihanouk and his Sangkum Party were extremely brutal to the opposition, fostering discontent in some Khmer circles.

By 1965 this policy of neutrality was withdrawn; the Khmer government ended its relationship with the United States and allowed the Communists fighting in Vietnam access to Cambodian territory for training bases. This move angered many Khmers from all sides of the political spectrum and prompted Sihanouk to realign with the United States a few years later. In 1969 the United States began bombing raids in Cambodia to try to rid the country of the Vietnamese Communist strongholds but thereby destroyed many Khmer villages and fields and radicalized some of the population. At this time Cambodia also had its own Communist Party, the Khmer Rouge under Soloth Sar, more familiarly known as Pol Pot, which was actively working to overthrow the government. Elements within Sihanouk's party also wanted to rid themselves of their long-term ruler, and finally in 1970 Lon Nol, a general in the Cambodian army, overthrew the government and established a new Cambodian republic.

As had Sangkum before it, the government of the new republic soon became extremely authoritarian and corrupt and struggled to maintain power against increasing pressure from both the Vietnamese Communists and the Khmer Rouge. The republican structure lasted just five years and was overthrown by the Khmer Rouge in 1975. The new ruling party's policies were focused on the elimination of all urban and educated Khmers and the establishment of rural agricultural communes called *Angkar* or simply *Organization*. As a result during about three and a half years at least 1 million Khmers and hundreds of thousands of Cambodia's ethnic minorities were killed or died of starvation, disease, or wounds received at the hands of the brutal government. This episode in Khmer history has been documented in the film *The Killing Fields,* which follows the plight of a Khmer journalist in the employ of the *New York Times* as the killing begins.

The period of the killing fields finally ended in 1979 when the Vietnamese government invaded Cambodia and installed a puppet Khmer regime made up of individuals who had abandoned the Khmer Rouge when their defeat seemed inevitable. The new People's Republic of Kampuchea maintained its legitimacy with the assistance of about 180,000 Vietnamese occupying forces and hundreds of other economic and political advisers. Thousands of Khmers and other Cambodians, including both Khmer Rouge soldiers and their victims, escaped from Cambodia at this time, eventually going to live in UN-organized refugee camps in Thailand. The Vietnamese occupation also led to a strange coalition government-in-exile made up of supporters of both the Khmer Rouge and Prince Sihanouk. The Vietnamese finally withdrew from Cambodia in 1989, but the Khmer Rouge did not stop its guerrilla war tactics on the ground in Cambodia until a UN-brokered peace accord was signed in 1991. Prince Sihanouk again became head of government, while the United Nations Transitional Authority in Cambodia (UNTAC), the largest UN peacekeeping force in history, did its best to maintain order, repatriate refugees, and get the country up and running again. One thing UNTAC failed to do, however, was disarm the Khmer Rouge, which withdrew its support for the coalition government in 1992 and continued its insurgency from its stronghold in the countryside. Real change finally occurred in 1998 when Pol Pot died and the remnants of his brutal army either surrendered or were integrated into the Cambodian army.

Since the late 1990s many overseas Khmers have been able to visit their old homeland, some even choosing to return after many years of exile in other countries. The country's economy has improved, assisted by membership in the Association of South-East Asian Nations or ASEAN. Many Khmers, in an attempt to evade their brutal recent history, have looked to the golden era of the Angkor period as a source of ethnic strength and revitalization. Prince Sihanouk was reinstalled as king of Cambodia in 1993 and then replaced in 2004 by his son, Norodom Sihamoni; much money and time have been spent on the restored temple sites of Angkor Wat, Angkor Thom, and others, while the temple of Ta Prohm has been preserved as it was found by the French in the 19th century, with trees and underbrush growing up through the walls and statues.

CULTURE

The earliest-known Khmer culture was a combination of indigenous proto-Mon-Khmer features, elements adopted from the indianized kingdoms of Funan and Chenla, plus other attributes that probably entered the area from India and China along the extensive trade routes connecting these countries in the ninth through 15th centuries. Some of these proto-Mon-Khmer elements even remain evident in present-day Khmer culture, such as the many supernatural beings believed to inhabit the world, from ancestral spirits to nature spirits, from demons and ghosts to those that attack only if made angry by lack of respect or inappropriate behavior. The most important of these ancient cultural features, however, was the pyramid-shaped social structure of Classic Khmer society adapted from the Hindu model of the *devaraja* or god-king. Even with

the widespread adoption of Buddhism in the late 13th century this hierarchical social model has continued to inform Khmer society to the present day, with the traditional castelike division of Khmer society into royalty, high nobility, low nobility, and commoners, in which each level has to show deference to the people above it. There are even some Khmers who refer to their king as "His Majesty with the Sacred Feet, Master of Water, of Land, and of all Existences, Master of the Inferior Arch."

While in the past Hindu priests and ritual specialists occupied hierarchical positions comparable to nobility, today Buddhist monks and ritual specialists occupy a similar exalted position within Cambodian society. Unlike in the Hindu world, however, within Cambodian Buddhism all men have an equal ability to join this exalted rank. In fact prior to the onset of the Cambodian civil war in 1970, which ushered in almost 30 years of political strife, most Khmer men spent at least a short time living as monks, usually as a rite of passage into adulthood. During the short but powerful reign of the Khmer Rouge Buddhism and its practitioners were targeted nearly as much as the urban educated elite, and only about 3,000 of 65,000 monks survived the genocide; in addition about two-thirds of the 3,369 Buddhist temples were destroyed and the rest were sacked and desecrated. Finally in 1988 just before the final Vietnamese withdrawal from Cambodia most of the restrictions on Buddhist practice were lifted, including the ban on the ordination of monks below the age of 55 and the limit on the number of monks per temple to four. By 2006 the number of monks in Cambodia had risen to about 60,000, and again serving as a monk has become an important marker of adulthood. That most men do not dedicate their entire life to Buddhist institutions has generally limited the elevation of the educational levels of the monks and made recovery from the loss of an entire generation of elders in the 1970s difficult, but the resurgence in religion does show the strength and resilience of the Buddhist way of life in Cambodia in the present day.

Another aspect of the Classic period of Khmer culture that was instrumental in its social and political development was the economic structure. For the most part Khmer commoners were subsistence farmers who grew rice in intensively used paddies irrigated by the Mekong or other rivers and the rising floodwaters of Tonle Sap; fishing on the lake, rivers, and coast was also common and continues to be important today. Though Khmer territory is not considered extremely fertile by global standards, the low population density has almost always allowed for the production of a large rice surplus throughout the country. This ability of all regions to produce their own food and the general uniformity of resources throughout the country led to a situation of minimal trade relations within the kingdom itself. Internal infrastructure such as roads, bridges, and canals was never attended to, and there was little need for ordinary Khmers from different regions to communicate with one another. Instead all interactions moved up and down the social hierarchy. Externally Khmer royalty purchased gold, silk, porcelain, lacquerware, umbrellas, and other luxury goods from China and India, in turn trading beeswax, bird feathers, rhinoceros horn, and other tropical forest products. The Khmer royalty would also have liked to import wheat and broad beans from China, but the Chinese forbade the export of these products during the Angkor period, and rice remained the mainstay of even the king's diet.

While the overarching social structure of Khmer society was and in many ways continues to be hierarchical and centralized, in their daily lives kin groups and residential patterns were more important to most Khmers than their faraway relationships with the god-king, nobility, priests, or other social superiors. The dominant Khmer kinship pattern is one that has confused outsiders for many decades. Because the Brahmin ritual office of Purohita was passed matrilineally from a man to his sister's son and much was made of this inheritance pattern, some outsiders have assumed that all Khmer kinship was based on matrilineal descent. This idea has not been borne out by research, which clearly indicates no organized kin groupings beyond the nuclear family such as exist in any lineage system; all individuals recognize both their mother's and father's relatives equally. Each individual shares rights and responsibilities with a *bong p'on* or circle of relatives gained through bilateral descent and marriage. Within this inner circle of kin there is a strong emphasis on mutual aid and harmony based on the animistic belief that conflict or discord among relatives is punished by ancestral spirits.

Marriage among the Khmers is generally monogamous today, but in the past Khmer kings were generally polygynous and took their various wives from different regions of the kingdom in an effort to unify their far-flung territories. Prior to 1975 polygyny was legal for all men in Cambodia as well but was not generally practiced because of economic constraints. The Communist Khmer Rouge government outlawed polygyny when it gained power in 1975 and the practice has remained illegal since; however, in the 1990s there were reports that some Khmer men had several informal wives in addition to their legal spouses, as a result of the relative lack of men after a generation of warfare. Khmer marriages are usually legitimated through a Buddhist ceremony as well as the payment of a bride price, money given by the groom's family to the bride's in order to decrease the financial burden caused by the elaborate ceremony. After marriage there is no hard-and-fast rule about where the new couple resides, but traditionally the pair would often spend the first few years with the wife's family, a matrilocal residence pattern. However, patrilocal residence, in which the new couple resides with the husband's family, and neolocal residence, in which the couple establishes a home away from both families, were also practiced. Some couples moved back and forth between families and their own homes as financial and other circumstances dictated.

As this variety of residence patterns indicates, Khmer households can be made up of nuclear families only, several generations of a family, or even more extended kin groupings of cousins, aunts, uncles, and other relatives. Households are the primary units of production and consumption, with families that reside together sharing work, resources, and food. Traditionally Khmer homes were rectangular structures built on stilts. Building materials differed with the economic status and caste of the family, with only royalty and nobility able to have tile roofs; others had thatch. Walls in all houses could be made of thatch or wood. Poorer homes had no internal walls but were sectioned off by cloth or wooden screens, while wealthier Khmer had more elaborate internal rooms. During and immediately after the wars of the 1970s and 1980s there were few Khmers who could afford even to build on stilts, and most simple homes were built right on the ground.

Traditional Khmer rural villages were generally made up of groups of a few hundred to more than 1,000 people. Many had their own Buddhist temple or *wat* and some had a school. Villages were sometimes located along a road or stream with all structures strung in a line along it; others had all their houses and other buildings clustered together in a circular pattern for protection; some villages were more spread out, with all homes located near the rice paddy. These same patterns generally continue to inform the building of Khmer houses and villages to this day, with the addition of some government buildings in larger villages and more schools.

As was the case during the Angkor period most Khmers today continue to work in subsistence agriculture, cultivating rice paddies for both domestic consumption and sale. People living along riverbanks may also grow more fruits and vegetables than their savannah counterparts, but even there household gardens generally fulfill the family's requirements for vegetables, spices, and fruits. Basil, pepper, beans, coconuts, mangoes, and sweet potatoes are extremely common domestic crops, as are cucumbers, bananas, and sugar palms. Fishing is also a common activity as Tonle Sap is one of the most prolific fishing grounds in the world. Even in rural areas many Khmers participate in the market economy, either selling their own labor to the French rubber plantations or to wealthier neighbors or selling fish, garden produce, rice, tobacco, or timber. Some Khmer families keep cattle, water buffaloes, ducks, chickens, or pigs.

Most of the tasks associated with the domestic economy of the Khmers are linked with either men or women. For example, men generally plow fields, build homes and furniture, and buy and sell cattle and chickens. Women plant rice, cook, and do most laundry and child care; buy and sell rice, pigs, vegetables, and all other goods besides cattle and chickens; and generally control their household's finances as well. Nonetheless this is not a strict division of labor and with the sex imbalance that prevailed in Cambodia following the Khmer Rouge period women have taken on even more household responsibilities; in addition Khmer men do not consider engaging in traditional women's tasks shameful if there is no one else to do them. Both women and men could inherit land and other private property prior to the abolishing in 1975 of private ownership, and with the reinstatement of private property laws in 1989 both are able to inherit, buy, and sell land and other property again.

Despite the emergence of the Khmer Rouge and their implementation of one of the most severe genocides of the 20th century, Khmers generally place great importance on more informal modes of social control than formalized ones. Children are raised to follow adult examples once they are old enough to understand them and, at least prior to 1975 were only rarely physically punished for misbehavior. The self-control that children are expected to learn and emulate from their elders guides social control at the village level as well. Gossip and, in more severe breaches of community etiquette, ostracism were generally enough to prevent most Khmers from violating village norms. The internalization of these community values led most adults to seek to avoid embarrassment or shame at any cost. In addition both Buddhist beliefs about attaining merit through avoiding telling lies, stealing, drinking alcohol, or killing and beliefs in supernatural retribution in the form of illness or other misfortune also kept most Khmers within the bounds of acceptable community behavior. Today such informal community sanctions have been joined by a bureaucratic police and judicial system, but among rural Khmers informal methods of social control and dealing with infractions remain more common and popular.

FURTHER READING

Lawrence Palmer Briggs. *The Ancient Khmer Empire* (Philadelphia: American Philosophical Society, 1951).

Jacques Dumarçay. *The Site of Angkor.* Translated and edited by Michael Smithies (New York: Oxford University Press, 1998).

May Ebihara. *Svay: A Khmer Village in Cambodia* (Ann Arbor, Mich: University Microfilms, 1968).

Madeleine Giteau. *The Civilization of Angkor.* Translated by Katherine Watson (New York: Rizzoli, 1976).

Ian Harris. *Cambodian Buddhism: History and Practice* (Honolulu: University of Hawaii Press, 2005).

Ben Kiernan. *The Pol Pot Regime: Race, Power, and Genocide in Cambodia under the Khmer Rouge, 1975–79.* (New Haven, Conn.: Yale University Press, 1996).

Hermann Kulke. *The Devarāja Cult.* Translated by I. W. Mabbett (Ithaca, N.Y.: Southeast Asia Program, Department of Asian Studies, Cornell University, 1978).

Ian Mabbett and David Chandler. *The Khmers* (Cambridge, Mass: Blackwell, 1995).

Leakthina Chau-Pech Ollier and Tim Winter, eds. *Expressions of Cambodia: The Politics of Tradition, Identity, and Change* (New York: Routledge, 2006).

Milton E. Osborne. *The French Presence in Cochinchina and Cambodia: Rule and Response (1859–1905)* (Bangkok: White Lotus Press, 1997).

John Tully. *France on the Mekong: A History of the Protectorate in Cambodia, 1863–1953* (Lanham, Md.: University Press of America, 2003).

Khmu (Hka Muk, Ka Hok, Kammu, Kamook, Kamoos, Kamu, Ka Mu, Kha Kmou, Kha Mou, Kha-Mouk, Khas K'kemou, Khas-Mouck, Khas-Mouk, Khmou, Kh'mouk, Kho' Mu, K'kmou, Kmhmu, Phou-qhiuong, Phu tho'ng, Thai Hai, Tsa Khmu, Xa Cau)

The Khmu are the second-largest ethnic group in Laos and are believed to be the indigenous people of this region, having inhabited it for at least many hundred years prior to the arrival of the Lao in the past millennium.

GEOGRAPHY

The Khmu live in Laos, northern Vietnam, Thailand, Cambodia, and southern China. They primarily inhabit the midranges of the region's many mountains between 1,300 and 2,625 feet above sea level, leaving the mountaintops to such groups as the Hmong and the lowlands and valley floors to the dominant Lao, Khmers, and Vietnamese. They can be found in the greatest numbers in Bolikhamxay, Luang Prabang, Oudomxay, Sayabury, Phongsali, Luang Namtha, Houaphan, and Xieng Khouang Provinces of Laos. Generally Khmu villages are located along riverbanks, which provide water, fish, frogs, algae, and other necessary subsistence resources.

ORIGINS

There is still some uncertainty about the origins of the Khmu peoples, but cultural and linguistic evidence points to a migration northward out of Indonesia sometime prior to 1000 C.E.

The Khmu themselves have an origin myth that describes how a brother and sister were saved from a great flood on the advice of a rat. When the floodwaters receded the couple realized they were the only surviving humans and so began the process of repopulating the world. Soon the woman became pregnant and gave birth to a giant gourd or pumpkin. She placed it on a smoking rack above the fire and eventually all the peoples of the Earth were delivered from inside the gourd. The Khmu emerged first, blackened by soot from the smoking rack. The Lao and Thais were next, lighter in color because they had been protected from the smoke. Finally the Vietnamese and Chinese emerged, with white skin from having been at the center of the gourd.

HISTORY

There is little historical information to document either the original migration of the Khmu into mainland Southeast Asia or the earliest interactions between the Khmu and the region's now-dominant ethnic groups, the Lao, Thais, Khmers, and Vietnamese, all of whom entered the area much later and took over the low-lying river valleys. It is also unclear how the Khmu interacted with the other indigenous and now minority groups in the region, whether hill dwellers like them, classified in contemporary Laos as Lao Thoeng, or those who live on the highest mountains, classified as Lao Sung.

During the French colonial era in the late 19th century the Khmu were among the first of the hill tribes to convert to Christianity. It is not clear why many Khmu heeded the call of the primarily Roman Catholic missionaries, but perhaps it was because they already shared a common flood myth. Another explanation that has been proposed is that conversion was seen as a way to challenge the political and social subjugation of the Khmu at the hands of the Lao, Thais, Khmers, and Vietnamese and to gain access to the superior weapons and other resources provided by the French administration. By the time of the start of the second Indochinese War, or Vietnam War as it is generally known in the United States, several thousand Khmu had become evangelical Christians. Most of them lived together in Christian villages that combined people of several ethnic groups.

Over the past several hundred years some other Khmu in Laos have also "become Lao" by converting to Buddhism, speaking Lao, and moving into low-lying villages to engage in wet-rice agriculture. In the past this was most common among Khmu men who married Lao women and took up the traditional Lao marriage residential pattern, which was matrilocal and required men to move into their wives' villages. Some men also took Buddhist vows as monks, at least temporarily, in order to learn to read and write in Lao and thus facilitate their movement into the dominant society. Today entire families may migrate away from the hills and mountain slopes and thus become Lao, although some of these families continue to speak Khmu within the family home.

During the Vietnam War some Khmu participated with other hill tribes in the region on the side of the United States and their South Vietnamese allies. A few also fought with the National Liberation Front and North Vietnam. Both sides had promised the people from the highlands that participation in the war would lead to greater autonomy, freedom,

KHMU

location:
Predominantly Laos with smaller numbers in northern Vietnam, Thailand, Cambodia, and southern China

time period:
Unknown to the present

ancestry:
The Khmu probably migrated out of Indonesia several thousand years ago.

language:
Kammu, a Mon-Khmer language

and resources for their own people. After about 1,000 years of subjugation at the hands of the dominant lowland populations many highlanders, including Khmu, wanted to believe these promises and worked very hard as scouts, runners, and soldiers. At the end of the war several thousand Khmu escaped the region and have subsequently taken up new lives in the United States, France, and Australia.

The Khmu who remained behind in Southeast Asia, today making up a population of between 500,000 and 600,000, have continued to be treated as a subordinate minority at the hands of the governments of Laos, Thailand, Cambodia, Vietnam, and China. Generally they are poorer, have lower life expectancies and literacy rates, and have higher infant mortality rates than their lowland neighbors.

CULTURE

The Khmu people have been agriculturalists for as long as they have been part of Southeast Asia's historical record. Prior to the formation of the Lao Lan Xang kingdom by Fa Ngum in the 14th century most Khmu lived in the river valleys of the Mekong and its many tributaries and engaged in wet-rice agriculture. Having been pushed onto higher ground in the 14th century, the Khmu have adapted their production system to the requirements of the hillsides. Their most important crop is rice, largely grown in extensive, swidden fields. This agricultural method requires cutting down trees, shrubs, and bamboo; allowing the vegetation to dry; and then burning it off to provide fertilizer for crops. It is called extensive agriculture because each field can be used for only a season or two before lying fallow for up to 20 years, and so each family must have access to a large or extensive amount of land. In the past 15 years was the most common length of time for a field to lie fallow. Today, however, land and population pressures mean that each field is able to rest for only three to five years; as a result it produces diminished yields of rice and vegetables each year. A small number of Khmu families do have access to irrigated fields and have changed from extensive farming to intensive forms, which require the addition of external fertilizers but allow for the same field to be used many times before lying fallow. Besides rice some families produce one or more of the following products for either family use or sale: ginger, peppers, sugarcane, sweet potatoes, taro, tea, tobacco, and other vegetables. Cash is also generated through the sale of woven baskets, mats, and other products and animal products from cattle, buffaloes, chickens, and pigs; a few families also use buffaloes and elephants in agricultural labor and hire themselves and their animals out to others. Many families also continue to hunt wild game and gather wild forest products such as honey, mushrooms, fruits, herbs, and roots as well. The Khmu are described in much of the ethnographic literature as extremely adaptive and thus accept work as farmers, laborers, soldiers, or in other areas as well when these opportunities become available.

Most agricultural activities are the responsibility of Khmu women, including planting and transplanting rice seedlings, weeding, harvesting, and then processing the rice into an edible form. Women are also responsible for all cooking, child and elder care, gathering of firewood and water, gardening, gathering of wild plants, weaving cloth, sewing, and tending small animals like pigs and chickens. It is said that a Khmu woman would be embarrassed if her household ran out of either water or firewood. Men engage in agriculture at the beginning of the process, clearing and burning the plot to prepare it for planting. They also fish and trap and hunt wild animals including frogs and rats; tend larger animals like buffaloes, cattle, and elephants; weave baskets; repair and build houses and farm implements; and engage in any trade or marketing activities taken up by the family. Khmu men are embarrassed if their household runs out of meat. Even young Khmu children participate in the family economy by tending younger siblings and caring for animals; helping with farming activities, especially by scaring birds away from the ripening crops; and helping their same-sex parent as they learn the tasks necessary to keep the household running.

As this economic system indicates, the primary subsistence or food item in the Khmu diet is rice. As is the case among the Lao, the Khmu prefer sticky or glutinous rice to other, drier varieties. Rice is consumed with every meal and is what is considered eating; if rice is not consumed then one is snacking rather than eating, regardless of how much is eaten at the time. Along with rice the Khmu eat sauces seasoned with salt and chilies as well as smoked meat from hunted game, frogs, fish, rats, and even many insects. Wild mushrooms, bamboo shoots, and a variety of domestic vegetables also contribute to their diet. Most villages also have banana, citrus, and jackfruit trees. As are these fruits, large animals, whether wild game or domesticated and killed in a sacrifice, are generally shared among many families while rice and smaller animals are usually eaten just within the household. Despite this variety of food sources many families today do not have enough to eat and many Khmu are considered malnourished by global standards.

While rice is certainly the most important staple food item among the Khmu, special black sticky rice is symbolically the most important as it represents safety to the Khmu people. This kind of rice is saved for ceremonies and is carried in a small packet whenever a Khmu person travels away from home. A variety of other taboos and beliefs also surround the cooking and eating of rice. For example rice generally must not be steamed at noon, only in the morning and evening, unless it is to be used as a sacrificial food for spirits or ancestors. Time is not measured by clocks among most Khmu but by the cooking and eating of rice. As a result if a particular day is inauspicious for the holding of a ceremony or birth of a baby, time can be sped up by the preparation of rice outside the regular time. If rice is steamed after dinner then it is symbolic of the start of a new day and the ceremony or birth can take place on this new, more auspicious day without having to wait for the sun to rise again. This method is also used to extend the length of a morning or afternoon as well. Some kinds of work are best done in the afternoon. Sometimes then it is necessary to eat lunch very early in the day so as to make for a very long afternoon and provide enough time for the work to be completed.

The Khmu live in villages on the slopes of hills and mountains, usually beside the region's many rivers. These villages can be as small as 20 families and as large as 200 families, or between 100 and 1,000 people or more. Villages are generally fenced in with fields, granaries, ponds, and other resources outside the fences. Most villages have forest land between their residential area and fields because large old trees are believed to contain spirits that protect the village and its residents from the fires used to burn off vegetation for preparing fields for planting. Most villages also contain a common house where men congregate to tell stories, sing, play music, prepare hunting materials, and engage in special men's rituals; these common houses always have a fire burning inside that is maintained by the men around the clock. In addition to these men's houses villages contain family homes, built fairly close together for protection and on stilts between three to seven feet in the air. Underneath these stilt houses is a fenced area for pigs, chickens, dogs, and other small animals.

Households are usually made up of extended patrilineal families of a senior generation and all of their sons with their wives and children. Smaller households contain just six people while larger ones can have up to 20 or more. In the past at the age of about seven most young boys left their family homes and moved into the communal men's house to learn the skills, stories, and other aspects of male Khmu life. They reentered their family homes and took their wives with them after marriage, a pattern called patrilocal marriage because the woman is required to move into her husband's family home. This pattern is less common today but continues in some very traditional Khmu villages. During the wars in Southeast Asia many young men fled their homes and villages to avoid being drafted into the army and spent time living in Thailand.

While nearly 20,000 Khmu living in Laos and Vietnam have converted to Christianity, the majority continue to engage in their traditional animistic religion, which recognizes the powers of various ancestral and natural spirits. Ritual specialists are able to go into trances in order to communicate with this spirit world and discover the causes of illness and other misfortune and to mend relations with the spirits and thus end the suffering on Earth. Some specialists are also able to practice sorcery to harm others, a fact about the Khmu that often frightens their neighbors. The shamans and sorcerers can be either male or female. Khmu villages also have another kind of ritual specialist, a priest who performs various communal rituals and inherits his position by being the oldest son of the current village priest.

FURTHER READING

Kristina Lindell, Jan-Ojvind Swahn, and Damron Tayanin. *Folk Tales from Kammu III: Pearls of Kammu Literature* (London: Curzon Press, 1983).

Kristina Lindell, Jan-Ojvind Swahn, and Damron Tayanin. *A Kammu Story-listener's Tales* (London: Curzon Press, 1977).

Kristina Lindell, Jan-Olof Svantesson, and Damron Tayanin. *The Kammu Year: Its Lore and Music* (London: Curzon Press, 1982).

Damrong Tayanin. *Being Kammu: My Village, My Life* (Ithaca, N.Y.: Cornell University, 1994).

Damrong Tayanin and Kristina Lindell. *Hunting and Fishing in a Kammu Village* (London: Curzon Press, 1991).

Khojas (Khwajahs, Mawali)

Khojas are an interesting people for the various ways in which they can be classified. In contemporary India they are considered an ethnic group that has emerged from a former caste group of traders and marketers. In Pakistan today they are considered a religious group rather than an ethnic one. In both countries Khojas are sometimes called Ismaili Nizaris or Aga Khanis for many of them are members of the Ismaili subsect of Shia Islam founded in 765 and led since 1818 by the Aga Khan. The current Aga Khan, His Highness Prince Karim Aga Khan IV, has ruled the sect since 1957, when he was anointed by his grandfather, the previous Aga Khan.

The origin of the Khojas differs somewhat depending on the region in which they live. The Punjabi Khojas were Khatri caste members, a group of merchants, prior to their conversion to Islam in the 15th century under the leadership of Hajji Saiyid Sadr al-Din, an Ismaili missionary from Persia. He attracted many Hindus to his religion by using concepts and figures from that tradition to introduce the basic tenets of his own. For example he is believed to be the author of a book, *Das-Avatar*, that describes the ways the various forms of the Hindu god Vishnu are leading his followers toward Islam. While the Punjabi Khojas were converted to Islam by an Ismaili, today their beliefs do not coincide with those of others in that faith. Instead of the Aga Khan they tend to look to the leaders of several different Sufi sects for leadership and are sometimes classified as Sunni Muslims. The Khojas from Mumbai (Bombay) and other areas south of the Punjab in India were Lohana caste members in Sind and today are Ismailis who follow the Aga Khan. Many individuals from both groups continue to identify with their caste group for social purposes of marriage compatibility if not for religious purposes.

Despite their differences the Khojas generally form an organized community as a result of their differences from other Muslim communities in the region. A colonial court in Bombay in 1847 ruled that they were to be treated separately from other Muslims in a variety of legal matters, especially concerning succession of community leadership. They also have a number of different customs from other Muslims, including marriage and divorce, funeral practice, and Chatti, a ceremony on the sixth day after birth. Each locality has its own *jama-at khana*, a structure that serves as both a mosque and a meeting house/administrative center. Officers are sometimes elected, sometimes appointed by the Aga Khan, who preside over marriages and other community events.

In general Khojas are a successful community because of their strong connections to the business community, especially in the handling of cotton, ivory, hides, mother of pearl, rice, spice, shark fins, opium, and silk. Because many Khojas have left India and Pakistan to live in the United Kingdom, Kuwait, and East Africa, those who have remained at home have a global network of merchants and traders with whom they can negotiate deals. These global connections have helped many Khojas to achieve significant wealth in the 20th and 21st centuries. Many have also moved into the medical, engineering, and legal professions.

Khom   *See* KHMERS.

Khwarezmians (Chorasmians, Huvarazmish, Kaliz, Khwarazmians, Kwarizmians, Khuvarazmish, Khwalis, Khwaris)

The people of Khwarezm were Iranian speakers who dominated the Oxus River delta, south of the Aral Sea, from antiquity until about the 11th century. For most of their history they were vassals within the empires of the Persians and Arabs, but local rulers were able to maintain semi-independence and even full independence for several periods. Despite being overrun by many different groups, including the Achaemenids (*see* PERSIANS, ACHAEMENIDS), HEPHTHALITES, KHITANS, TURKIC PEOPLES, and MONGOLS, their name continues to be associated with the region of their homeland in contemporary Uzbekistan and Turkmenistan.

GEOGRAPHY

The name *Khwarezm* points to the geography of their homeland, since the derivation of their name in the Iranian language means "lowland," from *khwar/khar*, "low," and *zam/zem*, "earth" or "land." The land around the Aral Sea, including the deltas of the Amu Darya or Oxus River and the Syr Darya or Jaxartes River, which was the Khwarezmian homeland, is the lowest area of Central Asia, with the exception of the Caspian region to the west. The entire region around the Aral Sea, incorporating sections of contemporary Kazakhstan, Uzbekistan, and Turkmenistan, is at or below 500 feet above sea level, with a few small spots lying below sea level, while much of the rest of Central Asia averages between 5,000 and 10,000 feet. Despite the existence of the Aral Sea and these two important river systems, the region is considered semiarid and even in ancient times would have seen wide fluctuations in the amount of water available from year to year. While today irrigation and industrial use of water have left an ecological disaster in the Aral region, even in ancient times irrigation contributed to rises in the Aral's salinity levels and desertification.

ORIGINS

The origins of the Khwarezmians remain shrouded in time, along with the other Iranian-speaking peoples who were to dominate portions of Central Asia at various periods during history. Two examples of the difficulty involved in accurately discussing this period will suffice. Most sources point to the original inhabitants of this region as being Hurrian speakers, who actually lived farther west in Mesopotamia and who seem not to have created an empire large enough to have incorporated the Aral Sea region. A second problem with the Hurrian hypothesis is that, according to Soviet-era writing on the region, the name *Khwarezm* is derived from *Hurri-land*, which is clearly false, given the Iranian origins of the name and its people.

A somewhat more plausible story about the origins of the Khwarezmians is from the holy texts of Zoroastrianism, the Gathas, which were written by Zarathustra himself sometime between the 14th and 10th centuries B.C.E. These claim that Zarathustra was given protection by King Hystaspes of Khwarezm, presumably because of their common Iranian language, religion, and culture. The problem with this source lies with the dates; Hystaspes is said to be the son of Aurvat-Aspa, a king of Khwarezm of the late seventh century B.C.E., who therefore could not have provided protection up to 700 years earlier.

HISTORY

As is the case with their origins, the dating of the people of Khwarezm is difficult given the large variety of peoples who conquered this region, including Persians, Arabs, Turks, and Mongols. As a result of the historical records' being incomplete and difficult to decipher, the degree of autonomy granted to Khwarezm is usually a complex issue to untangle. The choice of the beginning of the Turkic Khwarezmid dynasty in the 11th century as the end of Khwarezmian

history is relatively arbitrary given the continued use of the ethnonym *Khwarezmian* both in the dynasty and into the present day. However, it seems the most logical choice given the strong influence of Arab, Muslim, and Turkic

---

Khwarezmians time line

B.C.E.

1300 Sijavus, possibly the legendary first ruler of Khwarezm, comes to power.

Late 600s Aurvat-Aspa, another possibly legendary ruler whose name appears in historical documents.

520 Behistun inscription of Darius the Great implies that he received Khwarezm as part of his territory when he became king of the Persian Empire in 522.

Fourth century Relative independence from Achaemenid control as a separate satrapy with nearly sovereign rulers.

328 The independent Khwarezmian king Pharasmanes offers assistance to Alexander the Great. Some sources say this assistance was turned down; others say that Alexander's army included many thousands of Khwarezmian soldiers.

200–27 C.E. Khwarezm becomes a vassal state with relative independence in the Parthian empire.

Second century First Khwarezm coins are minted.

C.E.

Second century Khwarezm is taken into the sphere of influence of the Kushan empire.

276–93 Texts during the time of Bahram II, Sassanid king, note that the Khwarezmians have become vassals of this second Persian Empire. Other sources indicate that the Khwarezmians remain under Kushan vassalage until the fourth century.

305 Afrig ascends to the throne of Khwarezm, beginning a dynasty, known in the literature as the Afrigids, that is to rule until the eighth century.

Sixth–seventh centuries Khwarezm is possibly incorporated into the Western (Gok) Turkic empire; the evidence for both incorporation and independence remains vague and sketchy.

ca. 650 The last coins of Khwarezm are minted.

711–12 Arab invasion by Kutejba, who is invited in by the ruler of one of the feudal sections of Khwarezm.

973 Abu Rayhan Biruni is born of Khwarezmian parents in what is present-day Khiva, Uzbekistan. He is the best-known Khwarezmian-speaking scholar; he is also the first Muslim scholar to study Indian philosophy.

995 The last Afrigid king is killed by Mamun I Abu Ali, the governor of northern Khwarezm, who invades southern Khwarezm and establishes his own dynasty, the Mamunid, which lasts until 1017.

1048 Abu Rayhan Biruni dies.

11th century Oghuz Turks establish the Khwarezmid empire.

1218 The invading Mongols destroy the Turkic Khwarezmid empire. The name *Khwarezm* lives on in contemporary times in both Uzbekistan and Turkmenistan.

cultures after that date. With the adoption of a new language, religion, and culture the original Iranian-speaking people of Khwarezm cannot be said to have survived much beyond the end of the first millennium.

The earliest history of the Khwarezmians parallels the history of all Iranian-speaking peoples. From a nomadic population of horsemen and herders who rode out of the steppes at some undetermined date there emerged a settled agricultural population. This group spoke an Eastern Iranian language, Khwarezmian, which was most closely related to that of the SOGDIANS, and probably practiced the religions of the other Iranians, Mazdaism in the most ancient times and then Zoroastrianism after the Gathas were written.

Sometime prior to Darius the Great's seizing the throne of the Achaemenid empire, Khwarezm was either conquered by the Persians or taken under their wing in a protective relationship. In about 520 B.C.E. Darius stated in his Behistun inscription, which highlights his conquests as he consolidated his reign, that he inherited leadership in Khwarezm when he became king. At this time the Khwarezmians adopted many of the cultural traits of the dominant Persians, including the use of the Aramaic script to write their language. Despite these cultural links by the beginning of the fourth century B.C.E. Khwarezmians seem to have gained their independence or at least semi-independence from Persian rule, perhaps as a result of the remote location in relation to the central Achaemenid cities of Susa and Persepolis.

By the time of Alexander the Great's conquests in Persia in 328 B.C.E. the king of Khwarezm, Pharasmanes, was strong and independent enough to attempt to engage the great leader on equal terms. The record is unclear about the nature of their relationship. Some sources claim that Pharasmanes offered his assistance to Alexander in his war against their common enemy, the Persians, and Alexander declined the offer. Other sources claim that the two signed a treaty and that thousands of Khwarezmian soldiers marched with Alexander into Bactria, where Alexander finally defeated the Persians and brought an end to the Achaemenid empire.

Regardless of their personal relationship the fate of Khwarezm after Alexander's armies' victory was not the same as that in Bactria or Sogdiana, where the Iranian people were subjected to several hundred years of Greek rule under the Seleucids (see BACTRIANS, GREEKS,

SOGDIANS). In Khwarezm the kings remained relatively independent and failed to adopt the cultural and political trappings of Hellenistic culture, as happened farther south. Even their position as a vassal state in the empire of the PARTHIANS, 247 B.C.E.–224 C.E., which remains conjecture because of a lack of solid evidence, left the people of Khwarezm relatively free to continue developing their own independent culture. This situation seems to continue until the second century when the KUSHANS incorporated Khwarezm into their large empire. Once the Parthians were conquered by the Sassanid empire (224–642) (see PERSIANS, SASSANIDS), however, this political situation may have changed. By the time of Bahram II, who ruled from 276 to 293, Khwarezm was once again dominated by an old enemy, the Persians, in a province that contained both Khwarezm and Bactria. How long the Sassanids or Kushans were able to subjugate Khwarezm is entirely unknown at this time since the sources are unclear about the political and military developments of this faraway kingdom.

There is a bit more certainty about the internal workings of the leadership of Khwarezm during the early centuries of the common era. In the year 305 a new ruler, Afrig, ascended to the throne, beginning a dynasty known in the literature as the Afrigids, which was to rule until the eighth century. During this time the various Afrigid leaders recognized the dominant powers in their region, including the Sassanids, Hephthalites, and Turks, but generally were allowed to rule their lands in their own way. Finally, however, in 711 an internal rift within the leadership of Khwarezm divided the land and ushered in a new era of domination, this time by the Arabs. Until 995 Khwarezm was split between the capital of Kjat, which was the seat of power for the kings of Khwarezm, and Urgench, the capital for the Arab emirs who ruled after the invasion of Kutejba at the behest of the king of Khwarezm's brother Khurrazad. Although it took several generations and uprisings to do it, the Arabs were eventually able to pacify Khwarezm and begin converting the population to Islam. Finally at the end of the eighth century Khwarezmian coins began to bear Arabic inscriptions and the leaders began to have Muslim names.

The long-lasting Afrigid dynasty finally ended in 995 at the hands of a governor from the northern regions of Khwarezm, Mamun I Abu Ali, who invaded the southern region and established his own dynasty. At this time

Khwarezm was being held within the sphere of influence of a minor Persian dynasty, the Samanid, the first Iranian dynasty to displace the conquering Arabs in the Persians' traditional homeland. The Samanids lasted only 122 years before being displaced by a Turkic invasion in 999. As the ascendant power in the region the Turks only about 100 years later replaced the original leaders of Khwarezm in the region, though they borrowed the name *Khwarezmid* for their own empire and their leaders retained the Iranian title of *shah* or *king*.

Despite this turbulent history, during which Khwarezm was subject to all the powerful empires of Central Asia, the name *Khwarezm* has lived on into the present time in three separate areas. Uzbekistan's Xorazm Province is named after the historical homeland of the people of Khwarezm; the city of Khorazm in Turkmenistan is certainly named after the land of Khwarezm as well. The medieval Arab mathematician Muhammad ibn Musa al-Khwarizmi (ca. 780–ca. 850) bore a name that reflected the homeland of his ancestors. One of the greatest scientific minds in Islam, he introduced Arabic numerals and decimal calculations in an influential treatise; the English word *algorithm* is a bastardization of his name. In the early 20th century the name was even more widespread, with the Bolsheviks using the Khorezm People's Soviet Republic to designate the former territory of the khanate of Khiva, a Mongol empire in the territory of historical Khwarezm.

CULTURE

With their incorporation into the Achaemenid empire prior to 520 B.C.E. Khwarezmians seem to have undergone a distinct change in culture from a seminomadic lifestyle akin to or perhaps part of the Siberian Andronovo culture to a settled, agriculture-based one. This change led to urbanization, irrigation, and both a material culture and social structure similar to those of much of Central Asia at this time, especially the Persians. This structure recognized a distinct division of labor among nobles, soldiers, farmers, craftsmen, traders, and serfs. As it was a Zoroastrian society, there would also have been a class of religious specialists, Magi, who participated in political life as well. Zoroastrianism seems to have dominated religious and political life in Khwarezm until the Arab invasion, which resulted in eventual conversion of the population to Sunni Islam. At the end of the seventh or early eighth century there may have been Christian rulers of Khwarezm as well, because crosses ap-

pear on two rulers' ossuaries, the clay containers that hold the cleansed bones of the dead in Zoroastrian funerary practice. Today no evidence of Buddhism has been found at all despite its importance to the southeast in Afghanistan.

FURTHER READING

Shir Muḥammad Mirab Munis and Muḥammad Riza Mirab Agahi. *Firdaws al-Iqbāl: History of Khorezm.* Translated and annotated by Yuri Bregel (Boston: Brill, 1999).

Kinh   *See* VIETNAMESE.

Kiribatese: nationality (i-Kiribati, people of Kiribati)

Kiribati is a Micronesian country located in the Pacific Ocean on the equator; it lies between the Marshall Islands to the northwest; Nauru to the west; Tuvalu, Tokelau, and the Cook Islands to the south; and the Marquesas to the east. It is made up of the separate archipelagoes of the Gilbert, Phoenix, and Line Islands. In 1995 the International Date Line was moved more than 30° of longitude to the west between latitude 5° north and 12° south to accommodate these widespread island chains. The people of the largest and most dominant ethnic group in the country are called I-KIRIBATI; during the colonial period they were generally called Gilbertese.

GEOGRAPHY

Kiribati is made up of 32 coral atolls and the rock island of Banaba, which once held one of the largest phosphate reserves in the world; the reserve ran out in 1979 just as Kiribati achieved independence from Britain. The islands are divided into three separate island chains: the 17 Gilbert Islands, eight Phoenix Islands, and eight Line Islands. Only 21 of these islands are permanently inhabited, 19 in the Gilbert Islands and one each in the Phoenix and Line Island chains. Together the islands are only about 313 square miles of land spread out in 2 million square miles of ocean, so that only about 0.0001565 percent of the country's area is land.

INCEPTION AS A NATION

There seems to be some confusion about the earliest history of the residents of Kiribati, with some accounts claiming they migrated from Samoa sometime between 1000 and 1400 C.E. and others positing initial migration from the southeast Solomon Islands or Vanuatu

---

KIRIBATESE: NATIONALITY

nation:
Kiribati; Republic of Kiribati

derivation of name:
Kiribati, pronounced *Kiribas,* is a local form of the colonial name of one of the island groups, Gilbert, named for the British captain Thomas Gilbert.

government:
Republic with the president as head of state and government

capital:
Tarawa

language:
Kiribati, a central Micronesian language

religion:
Roman Catholic 52 percent, Kiribati Protestant Church 40 percent, other (includes Seventh-Day Adventist, Muslim, Baha'i, Mormons or Latter Day Saints, and Church of God) 8 percent.

earlier inhabitants:
None

demographics:
Micronesian 98.8 percent, other 1.2 percent

Kiribatese: nationality time line

C.E.

1606 Spanish explorer Pedro Fernandez de Quiros discovers Butaritari, a northern Gilbert group island, and names it *Buen Viaje* (Bon Voyage).

1788 British sea captains Thomas Gilbert and John Marshall find several islands during their journey from Sydney to China.

1820 The Gilbert Islands group is named after Thomas Gilbert.

1857 Missionaries from the American Board of Commissioners for Foreign Missions (ABCFM) arrive and introduce Protestant Christianity to the islands.

1860s "Blackbirders" kidnap hundreds of Elliceans, who never return from their forced labor in Peru, Fiji, Samoa, and Hawaii.

1870 Samoan clergy from the London Missionary Society (LMS) establish missions on several islands.

1877 The British claim the Gilbert and Ellice Islands as their own.

1888 Missionaries from the Roman Catholic Sacred Heart Mission join those from the ABCFM and LMS.

1892 The British Protectorate of the Gilbert and Ellice Islands is established.

1900 The British government annexes Ocean Island (Banaba) because of its large supply of phosphate.

1915 The protectorate becomes a full-fledged colony.

1941 The Japanese bomb Ocean Island (Banaba) and land on Tarawa and Butaritari.

1942 The Japanese occupy most of the other Gilbert Islands. The inhabitants of Ocean Island are mostly deported to Nauru and Kosrae in the Caroline Islands (Federated States of Micronesia).

1943 U.S. forces take Tarawa and most of the other Gilbert Islands, but not Ocean Island. Tarawa sees some of the fiercest fighting in the Pacific and is virtually destroyed.

1945 U.S. forces finally liberate Ocean Island. Most inhabitants choose not to return but to move to Rabi Island, Fiji, which had been purchased for them.

1945–70 Many Elliceans move to Tarawa as bureaucrats and construction workers to rebuild the destroyed capital of their joint colony, leading to significant ethnic rivalry between Polynesian Elliceans and Micronesian Gilbertese.

1974 The inhabitants of the Ellice Islands vote overwhelmingly to secede from the Gilbert Islands.

1979 Kiribati, the former Gilbert Islands, achieves independence from Britain.

The United States gives up all claims to the Phoenix and Line Island groups in a treaty of friendship with Kiribati.

Phosphate production ceases.

1989 Tarawa hosts the South Pacific Forum, at which many island nations express their concern over rising sea levels. Australian prime minister Bob Hawke establishes a monitoring project that has been studying sea levels since.

1993 Kiribati moves the International Date Line to the east so that all of the country's islands are on the same side. This is ratified internationally in 1995.

1999 Kiribati joins the United Nations.

2000 Caroline Island is renamed Millennium Island because it is the first place to usher in the new millennium on New Year's Day.

about 2,000 years ago. Linguistically the latter, Melanesian-origin theory seems to be more accurate since their central Micronesian language is far removed from the Polynesian language spoken on Samoa. Nonetheless local origin myths claim that their spirit and human ances-

Kiribatese: nationality   407

tors migrated from Samoa, so perhaps the original population was joined by Samoans several hundred years ago.

The residents of these islands saw their first European in the person of the Spanish explorer Pedro Fernandez de Quiros in 1606, but it was another 214 years before the islands were named after a British sailor, Thomas Gilbert, who had spotted some of the islands on a trip from Sydney to China in 1788. After the islands were named in 1820, the rest of the 19th century introduced significant changes to the Gilbertese people. Australian, German, and American firms began exporting coconut products at this time, while the British engaged in full-scale phosphate mining on Banaba. As was the case throughout the Pacific, the Gilbertese were heavily exploited for their labor in Peru, Fiji, Samoa, and Hawaii. The formal colonial period on the Gilbert, Phoenix, and Line Islands began in 1877, when the British raised their flag on the islands to prevent Germany or the United States from claiming them. In 1892 they were incorporated as part of the British Protectorate of the Gilbert and Ellice Islands and formally colonized in 1915.

Christianity also arrived on the various islands of the Gilbert group in the mid-19th century, first American and then British Protestants followed by Roman Catholics from the Sacred Heart Mission in 1888. These early missionaries have since been joined by representatives of many different proselytizing religions including Baha'is, Mormons, and Seventh Day Adventists. None of them has had the influence that the Roman Catholics and Congregationalist Protestants have maintained for almost 150 years.

The JAPANESE were the first of the World War II combatants to reach the Gilbert Islands in late 1941, when they bombed the British phosphate works on Banaba and occupied the colonial capital, Tarawa. The following year they took the rest of the Gilbert Islands and transferred the local Banaban population to other islands. The U.S. Navy captured most of the Japanese holdings in the Gilbert chain in 1943 after exceptionally heavy fighting, especially in Tarawa, and Banaba was retaken in 1945, but the local population chose not to return because of the environmental degradation caused by phosphate mining and war damage. Most relocated to Rabi Island, Fiji, which had been purchased by the British government from Lever's Pacific Plantations at the start of World War II.

After the war the significant postwar rebuilding projects necessary to reestablish

Tarawa as the capital of the joint colony lured many Ellice Islands residents north. This led to some fierce rivalries between the local Gilbertese population and the visiting Elliceans, enmity that lasted until the mid-1970s, when Britain began to withdraw from the islands.

The formal division between the Gilbert Islands, which became the independent country of Kiribati, and the Ellice Islands, independent Tuvalu, occurred after a referendum in the Ellice group in 1974. An overwhelming 92 percent of Ellicean voters chose secession, despite losing access to the profitable phosphate industry in Kiribati. The separation took place in 1975 with Kiribatese independence following in 1979, at the same time as the phosphate reserves on Banaba ran out.

The independent Kiribatese established a republican form of government with a president serving as both the head of state and the head of government; presidential candidates are chosen by parliament to run in general elections. Kiribati is unique in the world in that this intraparliamentary electoral system for choosing presidential candidates utilizes a little-known voting system called the Borda count, named after French political scientist Jean-Charles de Borda, who invented it in 1770. Borda argued that a first-across-the-line voting system was not the fairest way to hold elections with more than two candidates. He proposed a system in which voters rank every candidate in their order of preference so that n number of candidates are ranked by each voter in order: n, $n - 1$, $n - 2$, . . . , 1. The winning candidate is the one whose aggregate rank score is highest.

CULTURAL IDENTITY

Many Kiribatese maintain a relatively traditional identity and culture within the framework of a modern republic. With the depletion of the country's phosphate reserves just prior to independence few other employment opportunities have emerged, save for the state bureaucracy and tourism industry. Copra and fish provide some export dollars, but families primarily continue to work in subsistence agriculture, growing taro, breadfruit, sweet potatoes, and vegetables. Fish provide for the vast majority of their protein needs and local resources offer the materials for making their own homes and canoes.

A mainstay of the traditional identity that most Kiribatese cherish is their unique dance style, Te Mwaie. On the one hand Te Mwaie is seen as an embodiment of traditional beliefs

One of the largest events for Kiribatese in recent years was the start of the new millennium, which was ushered in first on Millennium Island. Naturally, the event was celebrated throughout the country with dancing.　*(AP/Katsumi Kasahara)*

in magic and spirits, intergenerational connection, and local myths and histories. On the other hand Te Mwaie is also a force for individual expression and psychological release, prestige, and even cultural change. Preparation for dance events and competitions takes a large amount of time, as well as the resources of entire families and even villages, but these efforts are seen as necessary for maintaining both individual and group identity as Kiribatese. A local proverb states, "We are known as i-Kiribati from the way we dance."

In addition to these traditional economic and cultural features Christianity provides another thread in the fabric of Kiribatese cultural identity. Roman Catholicism, with its headquarters at Teaorereke, Tarawa, has provided schooling, health services, and religious instruction for some Kiribatese since the first Sacred Heart missionaries arrived in 1888. Catholicism has been embraced more fully in the northern Gilbert Islands and continues to dominate that region today. Competing with the Roman Catholic missionaries in the 19th and early 20th centuries were the Protestants, first Hawaiian missionaries from the ABCFM and then Samoans from the LMS. By the early 20th century the HAWAIIANS had withdrawn,

leaving all Protestant activity to the Samoan and indigenous LMS converts. The current headquarters is also on Tarawa, at Tangitebu, but the schooling and religious institutions of the Kiribati Protestant Church dominate the southern Gilbert Islands.

See also MELANESIANS; MICRONESIANS; POLYNESIANS; SAMOANS: NATIONALITY; TUVALUANS; TUVALUANS: NATIONALITY.

FURTHER READING

Peter McQuarrie. *Conflict in Kiribati* (Christchurch, New Zealand: University of Canterbury, 2000).

Sister Alaima Talu. *Kiribati: Aspects of History* (Suva, Fiji: Institute of Pacific Studies, 1979).

Roniti Teiwaki. *Management of Marine Resources in Kiribati* (Suva, Fiji: Institute of Pacific Studies, 1988).

Kambati K. Uriam. *In Their Own Words: History and Society in Gilbertese Oral Tradition* (Canberra: Australian National University, 1995).

Koban culture

The Koban culture was created by a late Bronze Age people of the northern and central Caucasus, primarily in present-day Russia but also in Transcaucasia. The name is taken from the Northern OSSETIAN village of Koban, where axes, daggers, and other bronze items were found in graves in 1869. We know little about Koban culture or history since no written evidence has been discovered, but archaeological remains show that these people had strong metalworking skills in bronze and an economy based on both farming and cattle breeding. Around the end of the ninth century B.C.E. there may have been interactions between the indigenous Koban people and nomads from the Eurasian steppes. At this time horses became known in the Koban culture, evident in the bits and other horse paraphernalia found in gravesites after the ninth century B.C.E., and in depictions of horses on Koban metalwork.

Archaeological evidence gives us a little information about Koban social structure. From the number of rich burial sites accorded to women, some of whom may have been religious specialists, we can deduce high status for at least a few women. Nonetheless small bronze figures depicting humans were nude males with enlarged or emphasized genitals, believed by some archaeologists and art historians to represent abundance, fertility, or power in war. In addition bronze strips, probably belt mountings, were incised with figures of males wearing trousers and riding on, or sitting sideways on, horses, which were sometimes decorated with a human head hung about the animal's neck. Many objects, from weapons to belts and jewelry, were also decorated with images of animals, and small bronze figurines of animals were perhaps used as protective amulets. Archaeologists conjecture that wearing these amulets was thought to give the person the traits of the depicted animal, such as strength, speed, or cleverness. Some weapons found in graves, such as daggers and spearheads, resemble those of their neighbors of the northern Caucasus and Russian steppes, as do the horse bits. Other features of the weapons are similar to examples from as far away as China, such as knives and swords with handles that resemble antennae and others with ring handles. One distinctively Koban weapon is the ax, which is still used today on some versions of the South Ossetian national emblem.

See also SCYTHIANS.

Koitor   *See* GOND.

Kol

The Kol are one of the SCHEDULED TRIBES of central India, where they live in Madhya Pradesh, Orissa, and Uttar Pradesh, with a very small number of migrants in Maharashtra. In the past Kol communities were also located in Rajasthan in the west, but today these people have been integrated into other tribes or castes or have left the state. Prior to the colonial period the Kol lent their name to a large tribal classification as Kolarian peoples, which included SANTAL, MUNDAS, Ho, Kharia, and other tribes that are today recognized as culturally distinct. In medieval times *Kol* was also used as a more general term for "central Indian tribal group" and the term was used as a pejorative during the colonial era and meant "savage" or "primitive." In the early years of Indian independence many commentators on the Kol community believed that it was becoming a caste rather than a tribe, with full adoption of Hinduism and incorporation into the wider hierarchical structure of the *varna* and caste systems. However, this appears not to have occurred despite the full acceptance of Hinduism by the Kol, and today there are still a small number of people spread out over several central states who identify as a tribe and are treated as such by India's system of preferences.

Many Kol communities were traditionally *jhum* or slash-and-burn horticulturalists who were later moved into the valleys where irrigated, permanent fields could be maintained. Many refused to make this adaptation and chose to enter into waged labor instead of agricultural work; those who took up factory work or other labor are today the best off among the three strata of Kol society. Those who did not accept factory work either continued as horticulturalists or gathered wild forest products to sell in the markets of nearby towns; the most lucrative product was wood-apple, a valued ingredient in herbal medicine and natural dyes. This stratum of Kol society has generally survived at the subsistence level. A third stratum, those who live by cutting firewood or grass, is the poorest of the Kol today and lives on the margins of society.

Kol social organization contains within it a number of named, ranked subdivisions or *baenks,* parallel to the caste divisions of Hindu society. In general these groups are endogamous and thus require members to marry other members; membership is inherited from one's parents. In the past the distinctions between these groups were more strictly maintained while today there is more willingness to marry outside one's *baenk,* except for those in the Thakuria subdivision, who believe themselves to be hierarchically superior to other Kol communities.

KOBAN CULTURE

location:
Northern and central Caucasus and Transcaucasus

time period:
About 1100 to 400 B.C.E.

ancestry:
Unknown

language:
Unknown

KOL

location:
Maharashtra, Madhya Pradesh, Orissa, and Uttar Pradesh, India

time period:
Unknown to the present

ancestry:
Tribal confederation in central India

language:
Hindi and Oriya; a few speakers remain who use the Austro-Asiatic Kol language at home, especially in Orissa

Within these subdivisions kinship is bilateral in that both parents are believed to be equal contributors to one's kin group. However, unlike in English where one's mother's and father's siblings bear the same name, *aunt* and *uncle,* in Kol and related languages there is a distinction made between the two sides. There are also linguistic connections made between people of the same generation, so that the words for father, husband's father, and wife's father are very similar.

In general Kol society favors sons and men over daughters and women, with the result that most women have to leave their natal home at marriage and take up patrilocal residence in their husband's family home. Inheritance is also from father to sons, and in the past Kol men were able to marry multiple women or to keep a concubine as a status symbol. Widows were not allowed to remarry after the death of a husband but could become concubines if they were young and pretty enough.

Kond (Kandh, Khand, Khond, Kondl, Kui)

The Kond are one of the SCHEDULED TRIBES in India; they speak a Dravidian language related to that of the TAMILS, KANNADIGAS, and TELUGUS. Their homeland is the hilly region centered on the state of Orissa in the east; their ethnonym indicates their mountainous homeland and is derived from a Telugu term for hill or mountain. They use a different term for themselves, *Kui,* which is also the name of their indigenous language. Most Kond today speak Oriya, an Indo-Aryan language, as a primary language while Kui has become relegated to a ritual and "kitchen" language for private use only.

There is some evidence to indicate that the Kond were the indigenous inhabitants of the coasts of eastern India but were driven inland by the migration of INDO-ARYANS in the two millennia before the common era. In this dispersal Kond groups separated into three or more divisions, the most numerous being the Hill Kond of the central Ghat region. This group never formally gave sovereignty over them to an outside power prior to the 19th century and continued to engage in human sacrifice until 1856, when the British officers Macpherson and Campbell ended this activity. More recently, in 1994 violence again emerged between Kond and non-tribal populations in the state of Orissa, largely in areas where the Kond population does not speak much Oriya.

The traditional Kond economy is centered around crops of both wet and dry rice, grown on permanent irrigated fields and foothill *jhums* or swidden plots, prepared by using slash-and-burn techniques. In addition to rice, corn, lentils, mustard seeds, and turmeric are grown for use and for sale while most families keep a cow or two, pigs, chickens, and goats. These domesticated crops and animals are supplemented where possible by hunting and gathering, especially teak and other precious tropical products, and then used or sold to outsiders. In some regions the Kond have also subdivided along occupational lines, parallel to these distinctions in the Hindu caste system, so that basket makers, weavers, potters, ironmongers, and others, make up distinct occupational groups that tend to marry and socialize within their own groups. In other regions these subdivisions have not emerged.

Agricultural and domestic labor is divided among the Kond; women are forbidden to plow or even to touch many farm implements, and all threshing, another male task, must be ceased when there is a menstruating woman in the family. Women for their part cook, weed, raise children, care for the elderly, and assist in keeping birds and other pests out of fields of ripening rice, corn, or vegetables.

Kond social structure recognizes the primacy of the male line of descent and the creation of exogamous patrilineal clans, membership in which is inherited from one's father and within which marriage is impossible. Prior to their incorporation into wider Indian society Kond political organization was built around each clan unit, which was dominated by the most competent man, who served as a symbol of the common male ancestor who founded the entire clan. Villages also had headmen, ritual specialists, priests, and often a council of male elders who assisted in judicial and other matters of concern to the community, especially disputes over land.

Traditional Kond society also dictated that women's faces should be tattooed before marriage, a practice that has since died out. The practice arose from a myth concerning a predatory king who liked to kidnap Kond women as concubines and slaves; it was thought that tattooing made the women unattractive to him. Further beliefs posited that untattooed women turned into tigers at night and thus were unmarriageable.

See also DRAVIDIANS.

KOND

location:
India

time period:
Unknown to the present

ancestry:
Dravidian

language:
Kui, a Dravidian language that uses the writing system of Oriya

Konyak

The Konyak are the largest subgroup of the larger Naga peoples of the highlands of northeast India. From about 1913 until about 1930 the British colonial regime referred to all tribes on the Sibsagar region of Assam as Konyak NAGAS while the term is generally only self-referential for groups in the northern Mon district of Nagaland.

As for all Nagas the traditional Konyak economy was centered on shifting swidden agriculture with the use of a few permanent terraced fields that were fertilized and irrigated for wet rice. They are patrilineal and until the mid-20th century experienced significant intratribe warfare, as well as between Konyak and other Naga tribes. Their villages contained up to about 1,300 people divided into separate quarters on the basis of membership in patrilineal clans. Their religion was traditionally a form of animism that recognized the existence of many powerful spirits, including ancestral, enemy, and natural spirits. The spirit of the tiger is considered extremely powerful, and it is a concern to contemporary Konyak communities that tigers are becoming extremely rare near their highland homes.

One of the most important cultural attributes of the Konyak until about 1940 was head-hunting with all of the ceremonies that followed the taking of an enemy head. The head was fed rice beer and a spell put on it, which made the victim's relatives also fall victim to the village's hunters. Feasts afterward required that extensive food and ceremonial clothes be acquired through trade and intensive village activity to make these things, which boosted the entire region's economy. Also for a full year afterward the men and boys of the village were allowed to sing while working in fields, when otherwise they had to work silently. All men and boys who participated in the head-taking event, taking it back into the village, or the ceremonies that followed also earned the right to wear full war regalia.

It was not only the skulls of enemies taken in war, for retaliation, or for attaining personal grandeur but also the skulls of dead chiefs that were believed to hold tremendous power. The people decorated the skulls of dead chiefs by filling in the eyes and nose with white pith, adding mirrors to the eyes to represent the pupils. The tattoos exhibited by the man in life were also reproduced on the skull using an indigo dye and a bit of his hair was attached to the forehead to create a set of bangs. These skulls were stored in jars with flat stones as lids and taken out to sit on cloth-covered seats at ceremonial and feasting times, when their power was exhibited to all participating in the event.

Koreans (Chaoxian, Hangook saram, Hangookin)

The Koreans are the inhabitants of the Korean Peninsula, which is currently occupied by the two states of North and South Korea. Both North and South Korea are among the most homogeneous countries in the world, with only a few thousand Chinese and JAPANESE residents making up the sole minority groups in both countries. Koreans also reside in Japan, live in a diaspora throughout the world, and make up one of the 55 national minorities in China, where they are called Chaoxian.

GEOGRAPHY

Korea is a peninsula located in eastern Asia off the northeastern rim of China. About 600 miles long and 135 miles wide the Korean Peninsula is bordered on the north by Russia with the Tumen River and China with the Amnok (Yalu) River, the Sea of Japan to the east, and the Yellow Sea to the west. Korea was once a single country, but the end of World War II saw the peninsula split between north and south. Russia established a trustee administration north of the 38th parallel, with the United States administering the south. Tensions between the two administrators resulted in the Korean War (1950–53), which failed to reunify the country.

While the whole peninsula is mostly hills and mountains with wide coastal plains in the south and west, the mountains of North Korea are separated by deep, narrow valleys. Extending almost the entire length of the peninsula from its highest point, Paekdu Mountain (9,000 feet) in the north to the Jirisa (6,300 feet) in the south, the Baekdudaegan Mountain range, the "spine" of Korea, holds a significant place in the minds of Koreans on both sides of the border.

Korea's most important river, the Han, extends 150 miles north to south and spreads 75 miles east to west. At the mouth of the Han River sits the historically important Ganghwa Island.

Korea's position in relation to the Eurasian landmass produces a climate of extremes. Winters in the mountainous north are bitter and seacoast temperatures average 15°F in January, while

Koreans time line

B.C.E.

2333 Mythological founding of the first Korean kingdom, Gojoseon.

1500 Start of the Mumun culture, named for its unmarked pottery. Intensive agriculture arrives on the Korean Peninsula.

500–300 Founding of the Gojoseon kingdom, the first unified state on the peninsula.

108 The Han conquer Gojoseon and initiate the beginning of the Samhan or Three Han period, sometimes also called the Proto-Three Kingdoms period.

57 The founding of the state of Shilla, sometimes called Silla, one of the Three Kingdoms.

37 Founding of Koguryo, another of the Three Kingdoms.

18 Founding of the last of the Three Kingdoms, Paekche or Baekche.

C.E.

42 Founding of the small confederacy of Kaya or Gaya, which is later subsumed by Shilla.

300 The approximate date when the Three Kingdoms consolidate their power and subsume the smaller confederacies of the Three Han.

372 Koguryo adopts Buddhism as the state religion, followed by Paekche 12 years later.

433 Shilla and Paekche form a military alliance against Koguryo in the north and against other outside invasions.

528 Shilla adopts Buddhism as the state religion.

532 Shilla annexes the Kaya kingdom and finally takes this area entirely within 30 years.

612 Sui Chinese forces invade Koguryo and are soundly defeated, contributing to the disintegration of the dynasty.

660 Shilla allies with the new Tang dynasty in China to conquer Paekche.

668 Shilla and Tang armies defeat Koguryo.

676 Shilla forces drive the Tang armies off most of the peninsula.

713 Founding of the state of Parhae in Manchuria and northern Korea.

Mid-eighth century Peak of the Shilla kingdom's power and affluence.

788 A civil service examination system is adopted by Shilla to fill places in government and educational institutions.

918 Shilla falls into the hands of Wang Kon, a member of the gentry and founder of the Koryo dynasty.

926 Parhae falls to the Khitans.

935 The last king of Shilla, Kyongsun, finally abdicates, marking both the ultimate end of Shilla and the beginning of the Koryo dynasty.

---

summers are temperate. In contrast South Korea's winters are frost free and summers are warm enough to grow cotton. Summer is also typhoon season and the rains of June and July produce a stifling combination of heat and humidity.

ORIGINS

The mythological origins of the Korean people date back to 2333 B.C.E. and the founding of the state of Gojoseon by Dangun, the offspring of a heavenly father and a mother from the Bear clan. Historians and archaeologists have not been able to find evidence of this early Gojoseon state, however, and tend to put its founding sometime after 500 B.C.E. and perhaps as late as 300 B.C.E. and the fall of the MUMUN CULTURE. The people who founded Gojoseon were probably the descendants of migrants from the Altai Mountain region of China, Kazakhstan, and Mongolia, although there is still some disagreement about these origins. Even today some linguists classify the Korean lan-

956 Slaves in the Koryo kingdom are freed.

1126 An enormous fire destroys the key buildings and texts of the Koryo kingdom. With the Chinese Song dynasty under siege by the Jurchens replacement books from China are unavailable and bronze movable type is invented to print books quickly.

1145 Kim Pu-shik compiles the *History of the Three Kingdoms*.

1232 The Koryo king and his court flee and take refuge on Kanghwa (Ganghwa) Island when Mongol invasions threaten the kingdom.

Mid-13th century Iryon compiles the *Memorabilia of the Three Kingdoms* to supplement the earlier history.

1392 Fall of the Koryo dynasty and start of the Choson dynasty.

1446 The first Han-gul or Korean alphabet document is disseminated throughout the kingdom.

1592 Japan invades Korea, which receives assistance from the armies of Ming China.

1636 Qing China invades Korea in retaliation for Korean support of the outgoing Ming dynsasty, which King Injo supported in recognition of the assistance the Ming had granted Korea against Japan.

1724–76 Reign of King Yongio, who largely oversees the modernization of the Korean state and society.

1784 Catholicism is introduced into Korea from China with French missionaries leading the way.

1866 The French campaign to gain the release of captured French Catholic missionaries succeeds with a military action on Kanghwa (Ganghwa) Island.

1871 The Korean Expedition by the United States is victorious in a short military action but the Koreans continue to refuse foreign entry to their markets or territory.

1876 The Korea-Japanese Treaty of Amity opens three Korean ports to Japanese trade and brings Korea's long-standing position as a Chinese tributary state to an end.

1910 The Japanese annex Korea, ending the 518-year-old Choson dynasty.

1919 The March First Movement sees millions of Koreans in nonviolent protest against the Japanese occupation of their land and government. The movement is brutally suppressed by Japan.

1945 The Allies liberate Korea from Japan, with the Soviet Union occupying the northern half of the peninsula and the United States the southern half.

1950 On June 25 North Korea launches an attack on South Korea, starting the two-year Korean War.

1953 On July 27 an armistice is signed ending official hostilities between the two sides, although a peace treaty is never brokered, leaving the status of the two countries and their relationship with each other ambiguous.

1991 North and South Korea sign a nonaggression pact.

guage as Altaic because it shares some features with Mongolian, Turkic, and other Altaic languages, while others classify Korean as a language isolate because these similarities are few and remote enough to be questionable.

The Gojoseon state was itself conquered by the HAN Chinese in 108 B.C.E., initiating the Samhan period, or period of the Three Han. The Three Han were three tribal affiliations that ruled much of the central and southern regions of the peninsula for the period from about 100 B.C.E. to about 300 C.E., when the Three Kingdoms consolidated their power. Despite their geographic and temporal proximity the period of the Three Han does not refer to the Han people of China; *Han* is a local Korean term meaning "leader," possibly related to the Turkic word *khan*. The Three Han confederacies, Mahan, Jinhan, and Byeonhan, were later absorbed by Shilla and Paekche and their period is often considered just a subdivision of the Three Kingdoms period.

In addition to the Three Han, which ruled much of central and southern Korea, the Koguryo tribes dominated in the mountain- ous northern section, especially in the north- east. Unlike their agricultural neighbors in the south, the Koguryo continued to live primarily

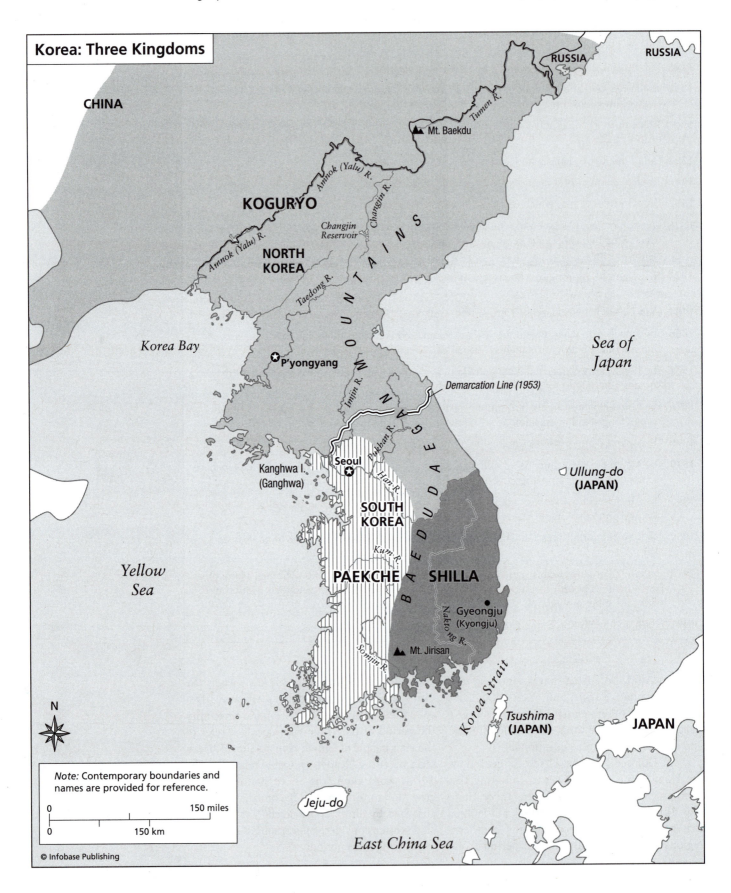

Korea: Three Kingdoms

CHINA

RUSSIA

RUSSIA

▲▲ Mt. Baekdu

Tumen R.

Amnok (Yalu) R.

KOGURYO

Changjin R.

Changjin Reservoir

Amnok (Yalu) R.

NORTH KOREA

M O U N T A I N S

Taedong R.

Korea Bay

Sea of Japan

☆ P'yongyang

Imjin R.

Demarcation Line (1953)

Pukhan R.

Kanghwa I. (Ganghwa)

☆ Seoul

▷ *Ullung-do* **(JAPAN)**

Han R.

SOUTH KOREA

B A E D U D A E G A N

Kum R.

Yellow Sea

PAEKCHE

SHILLA

Gyeongju (Kyongju) ●

Naktong R.

Sonjin R.

▲▲ Mt. Jirisan

Korea Strait

Tsushima **(JAPAN)**

JAPAN

N

Jeju-do

East China Sea

Note: Contemporary boundaries and names are provided for reference.

0   150 miles

0   150 km

© Infobase Publishing

by hunting and fishing, planting just a few crops in small-scale shifting gardens that were abandoned after just a season or two. Nonetheless military prowess and difficult terrain, which prevented invasions by outside armies, meant that the Koguryo were able to amass a significant amount of power, which they carried with them into the Three Kingdoms period.

The Three Kingdoms of Shilla and Paekche in the south and Koguryo in the north ruled over much of the Korean Peninsula from about the start of the common era until the seventh century. Some histories consider this the earliest phase of Korean history; however, this is not entirely accurate since all of these kingdoms, especially Koguryo in the north, were multiethnic in character and tribal in nature. In addition only Shilla's language seems to be the forebear of contemporary Korean, while the languages of Paekche and Koguryo were unrelated and are currently extinct. The entire period was marked by conflict among these three states plus Kaya in the south, which is sometimes included as a fourth kingdom, as well as between them and the Chinese. This period also saw the adoption of Buddhism throughout the peninsula, first in Koguryo and Paekche and later in Shilla, as well as the formation of a Confucian model of politics and society with the king at the apex of both systems.

HISTORY

Shilla and Koryo

The conflicts that had raged throughout the previous six centuries both between these kingdoms and China and among them were finally settled in about 676 when a United Shilla Kingdom finally drove the Chinese back to the Taedong River in contemporary North Korea. Prior to this event the Koguryo had been fighting the Chinese Sui dynasty off and on for hundreds of years, sometimes gaining territory in Manchuria, other times losing territory on the peninsula; throughout much of this period Shilla was in alliance with the Chinese. In 612 the Koguryo armies defeated a large Sui force and partly as a result of this defeat the Sui were swept from power in China. They were soon replaced by the Tang dynasty, however, which sought revenge against enemies in Manchuria and northern Korea by invading in 644, 648, and 655. When each of these invasions proved unsuccessful, the Tang turned to allies in the southern half of the peninsula, Shilla. Together the Tang and Shilla forces defeated Paekche and eventually Koguryo. Much to the consternation of the Shilla leaders, however, the Tang had

no intention of retreating from the peninsula and set up a Chinese military administration for much of the former Koguryo territory. In 671 Shilla began its own war against the Tang Chinese, first retaking Paekche's capital in the south and then fighting to push the Chinese farther and farther north. Finally in 676 Shilla was able to consolidate its control over all the territory south of the Taedong River, which runs through present-day Pyongyang in North Korea, and thus unified much of the Korean Peninsula under what is considered by many the first Korean state.

With these political victories the leaders of Shilla also wished to consolidate their hold over the hearts and minds of their subject populations. As part of this desire they began a voluntary military organization for young people, the Flower of Youth Corps or Hwarang, which trained the kingdom's youth in war, literature, community life, and Confucian virtues. In the early eighth century at the height of their power, the Shilla also instituted a land reform system that granted rural peasants access to arable land in exchange for a tax paid in millet, rice, barley, or wheat, depending on what crop grew best on the land. Peasants were also required to plant walnut and pine trees and mulberry trees for silkworms, and to raise cattle and horses. Shilla's leaders also wanted to make theirs an ideal Buddhist state. They sent numerous monks to China and India to study and built the 230-foot pagoda of Hwangnyongsa, the Sokkuram Grotto shrine, and the Pulguksa temple. They also sponsored the work of numerous scholars and artists, even those of the former Koguryo and Paekche Kingdoms, and the printing of numerous Buddhist texts. In 788 a new civil service examination was adopted to fill the increasing demand for bureaucrats and scholars.

Contemporaneously with the rise of the Unified Shilla kingdom remnants of the former Koguryo Kingdom along with their Tungusic allies reemerged as a powerful force in Manchuria and the northern Korean Peninsula. In 713 this state took the name *Parhae*, sometimes called *Koryoguk* or "state of Koryo" to solidify the claim to be the successor of Koguryo. By the time of this state's political apex in the ninth century Parhae controlled territory from the Amur River, which currently divides China from Russia, down to the region of Pyongyang in contemporary North Korea.

In the 10th century both Parhae and Shilla were eliminated, the former at the hands of the armies of the KHITANS from northern China,

The Pulguksa or Bulguksa Temple was built during the Shilla period more than 1,500 years ago as part of that kingdom's effort to win the hearts and minds of its people. As it is seen here today, it is a major tourist attraction in South Korea and a UNESCO World Heritage Site. *(OnAsia/Josh Kraemer)*

the latter from internal strife that lasted through the entire ninth century. Upon Parhae's disintegration many of the kingdom's nobles and scholars moved south to participate in the formation of the Koryo dynasty, the successor state to unified Shilla established by Wang Kon, a member of Shilla's noble class. The boundary established between the Khitans in Manchuria and the newly founded Koryo kingdom was the Amnok (Yalu) River, which also serves as the present-day boundary between North Korea and China.

As the Shilla leaders had before them, the early kings of Koryo emphasized the importance of Buddhism in strengthening the state; they instituted their own civil service examination system and strengthened the military border in the north against Chinese, Khitan, and other incursions. In 956 slaves who had been captured during various periods of warfare were liberated and in 982 Confucianism was enshrined as the model for developing the centralized power of the government. In the late 10th century the Khitan state of Liao invaded Koryo four times before Koryo's leading military figure, General So Hui, negotiated for peace and Koryo's territorial integrity south of the Amnok (Yalu) River. Unfortunately the peace did not last and the Liao attacked again in 1010, driving the Koryo court south from the capital in Kaesong. The harassment continued until the early 12th century, when the Liao themselves were challenged by the JURCHENS' Jin empire.

Even with the elimination of the Liao challenge from the north the 12th century was not entirely smooth for the Koryo leadership. In 1126 the king's father-in-law set fire to the palace and in the conflagration the entire palace structure and tens of thousands of books were lost. With Song China under attack from the Jin, replacement books were almost impossible to find, and in response Koryo scholars invented typography with movable bronze type to create a new royal library. As a result the 12th century saw a flowering of Korean literature. Kim Pushik compiled his *History of the Three Kingdoms* in 1145, and Iryon, a Buddhist monk, compiled his *Memorabilia of the Three Kingdoms* to supplement the earlier work in about 1250.

The 13th century presented a new military challenge to the Koryo kingdom, which had been weakened in the previous century by conflict between civilian and military leaders, in the form of invasions by the MONGOLS. The Koryo king fled his capital of Kaesong in 1232 to take refuge on Kanghwa (Ganghwa) Island, and six years later the Mongols destroyed the Shilla Buddhist pagoda of Hwangnyongsa. Nonetheless many of Koryo's subjects stood firm against the Mongol onslaught, and in the mid-14th century rebellions throughout China kept the Mongols away from the peninsula. Bureaucrats and others who supported the Mongol efforts were purged from the military and civil services from 1351 to 1374, though much land was still in the hands of pro-Mongol aristocrats. The kingdom also suffered when Confucian scholars began to agitate against the great power and wealth held by the Buddhist monasteries and when the JAPANESE were able to raid territories farther and farther inland. Finally at the end of the 14th century the various centrifugal forces pulling Koryo apart succeeded, and in 1392 the Koryo dynasty gave way to the Choson or Joseon, with General Yi Song-gye, who took the title *Taejo* of the Choson dynasty. Just two years later Taejo moved his royal capital from Kaesong to Hanseong, contemporary Seoul.

Choson and the Japanese Imperial Period

General Yi had already consolidated his command before the dynastic change through the economic power he gained from land reform, limiting the ability of the nobility or *yangban* to control parcels of land through several generations, and granting peasants the right to half of their agricultural products. The breach with the nobility was finally healed during the reign of King Sejong the Great (1418–50), a Confucian scholar, who was able to put the rebel *yangban* aristocrats and scholars under his wing. He also alleviated the peasants' tax burdens and provided relief during difficult times, earning the respect and gratitude of all levels of Korean society. Perhaps the greatest accomplishment of his reign, however, was the creation of a Korean alphabet, called *Hangul*. The country's official written language remained Chinese, just as Latin served the same purpose in Europe for more than 1,000 years, but the Korean language and alphabet, with its 11 vowels and 17 consonants, was used for ordinary documents, despite the opposition of many scholars.

The seventh Choson king, Sejo, who ruled from 1455 to 1468, also had a strong influence on the development of the political, economic, and social structures of Choson Korea generally. Under Sejo the country was divided into eight provinces and detailed maps of the entire peninsula were created to assist in the administration of these provinces as well as the kingdom. Each province and all border areas were strongly reinforced with military fortifications, and every citizen was counted in national censuses and kept track of with a national identification card system. Once these census and mapping systems gave him a clearer view of his kingdom, Sejo also began moving people into the sparsely populated regions, using a combination of carrot and stick tactics, from land grants to banishments. Perhaps Sejo's greatest contribution, however, was the creation of the *Grand Code for State Administration, Kyong-guk Taejon* in Korean, the blueprint for much of the next 500 years of dynastic administration in Korea.

Although Sejo himself had advocated a central role for both Buddhism and Taoism in Korean society, subsequent monarchs and state bureaucrats gradually undermined his efforts and put Confucianism back at the center of Korean thought and politics. The period of King Songjong's reign (1469–94), especially the early years when Korea was ruled by the dowager queen during Songjong's childhood, saw the strengthening of the Confucian scholars in relation to their Buddhist rivals and the publication of a variety of Korean histories and works of literature. At this time considerable land was also opened up for farming and large landed estates developed, with some peasants preferring bonded servitude on these large estates to freedom with its accompanying tax burden. This trend was challenged by the king, his court, and many of the country's scholars, who wanted to limit the strength of these estate owners in relation to them, but on the whole they were unsuccessful. Songjong's successor, Yonsan-gun, dispensed even harsher treatment to the Confucian scholars and their way of life, purging many from the court and banishing others to remote corners of Korea, but these actions were quickly repealed when the long-ruling King Chungjong (1506–44) reintroduced Confucian doctrine, scholarship, and leadership policies to his court.

The end of the 16th century saw a new challenge to Koreans in the form of a Japanese invasion in 1592. The Japanese had previously requested Korean assistance in attacking China, and when the Choson king refused they turned their ships and armies against the Koreans, who in turn sought and received assistance from the Ming emperor of China. After five years of failed peace talks the Japanese invaded Korea again but were once again stymied by the armies of

General Yi Seong-gye

General Yi Seong-gye was a famed military leader responsible for changing Korean history when he overthrew the Koryo dynasty and established the Choson dynasty, which would be the last imperial dynasty of Korea as well as the longest-running Confucian dynasty in the world. Born in 1335, Yi became a distinguished military general by driving the remaining Mongols off the peninsula, defending the coasts from Japanese pirates, and fending off the Chinese Red Turbans. In the late 1300s the Chinese Ming dynasty and the Mongol Yuan dynasty were locked in a struggle for control over Korea, and in 1388 General Yi Seong-gye, a Ming supporter, was sent to invade Ming territory in the Liaodong Peninsula. On his way there however, he revolted and led his army back to the capital of Gaesong, where they overwhelmed the king's forces and dethroned King U. King U was replaced by his nine-year-old son, Chang. But as monarchy loyalists protested, General Yi had both U and Chang executed and placed another member of Koryo royalty named Yo on the throne as King Gongyang. In 1392 King Gongyang was similarly dethroned and exiled to Weonju, where he and his family were executed, and General Yi took the throne, officially ending the Koryo dynasty. He became the first king of the Choson dynasty, which lasted until the Japanese annexation in 1910. General Yi abdicated the throne in 1398 amid a struggle between his sons and died in 1408.

the southern region of the country. Finally in 1598 the Japanese general who led the attack, Hideyoshi, died, and the Japanese retreated from Korea. Unfortunately for the Koreans their own General Yi was also killed in the final days of battle as Korean ships pursued the Japanese sailing away from the peninsula. Even more importantly a considerable amount of Korean land was left unable to be cultivated, thousands of artisans were killed, and thousands of government records, historical documents, books, and works of art were destroyed during the seven years of fighting. As a result of the war and its aftermath the impoverished government could not raise enough revenue through taxes and began to sell aristocratic titles, weakening the established class system and opening the way for a change in social structure in the following centuries.

This social structural change saw the rise of the merchant class over that of the traditional Confucian scholars and aristocrats and the widespread use of money, linking the rural and urban economies more closely than they had ever been. Even farming began to be commercialized with peasants selling their labor on the open market rather than indenturing themselves. The Korean government also focused more energy and resources on developing its own border, erecting shore defense systems, and reconstructing the lost infrastructure and literary and cultural artifacts.

The 17th century entailed further external involvement in Korean affairs when the Chinese Ming emperor requested Korean assistance in fighting off the Manchu invasion. The Korean king Kwanghaegun immediately responded with 10,000 soldiers, in memory of the Ming assistance granted against the Japanese, but withdrew them when it became obvious the Ming could not defeat the MANCHUS. This withdrawal led to a coup in Korea that put the pro-Ming King Injo in power and then to a Manchu invasion of the peninsula in 1627. The Manchus invaded again in 1636, this time as the Qing armies of China, and after fleeing the capital King Injo surrendered to the Qing and agreed to pay tribute to the victors. This defeat is often depicted in Korean histories as a disgraceful humiliation because the Korean armies were not given the chance to protect the homeland before the king capitulated to the "pagan" Manchus. This period also saw the development of revolutionary ideas about equality that further undermined the *yangban* or traditional Confucian aristocracy that had ruled the country for centuries.

The second half of the 17th century was also remarkable for the population increase on the peninsula, from 2.3 million in 1657 to 5 million just 12 years later. In addition the capital city's population more than doubled in that same period, from about 81,000 to more than 194,000. Both of these increases were the result of tax reform, that increased personal spending, agricultural management that increased crop output, and the increasing power of the merchants, who had been freed from onerous government tribute and taxes. The ruling class also splintered in the second half of the 17th century, making factionalism dominant in the political culture of the time.

In reaction to this factionalism King Yongio, who ruled for more than half of the 18th century (1724–76), did all he could to unify the kingdom. He left the confines of his palace walls to speak with officials, scholars, soldiers, and even peasants about what they needed and about their vision of the country. In response he revised the tax system and military service rules and increased the flow of money; he also increased the output of Korean-language books, including literary classics and practical texts on agriculture and land management. Under Yongio Confucianism was again placed at the center of the relationship between ruler and ruled, although the mercantilization of the economy continued apace throughout the following centuries regardless of the Confucian belief that such activities were lowly and unworthy of the aristocratic classes. Many of the new wealthy merchants later legitimated their rise by purchasing an aristocratic title from the government, which used this sale to raise much-needed currency throughout the 18th century.

In addition to increased mercantilism and influence from outside Korea, especially from the West and from Qing China, there was a rise in interest in what Korean identity entailed and a corresponding rise in the study of Korean history and language, geography, and literature. Artists began to look to Korean subjects to paint and write about rather than to Chinese ones. Korean history began to be written as a military history of expelling foreigners, and Dangun, the mythological founder of the first kingdom on the peninsula, was brought to light in this period. Catholicism also entered Korea from China in the 18th and 19th centuries and accorded nicely with those scholars, merchants, and artisans who were interested in the principles of equality that had been introduced from the West. While the government persecuted the new religion for its opposition to Confucian ritual and hierarchy, thousands of Koreans converted to Catholicism and began to use its principles of social justice to tend to the poor and sick. Even members of the aristocratic *yangban* class converted to Catholicism in the 19th century, especially after government persecution in 1801, 1839, and 1866 drove many Catholics into the rural areas.

The persecution of Catholics had the further effect of arousing French interest in events on the peninsula. Both the British and French had been exploring Korean waters and trading ports since the 1840s with little success, but after 1866 the French entered Choson territory on the Han-gang River and a military skirmish took place on Ganghwa (Kanghwa) Island. This was the first time Korea and a Western power engaged militarily because of the Korean government's long-standing isolationism. The two French missionaries left alive in Korea after the period of persecution were released as a result of the French action, but nine others plus countless Korean Catholics had been killed prior to the French campaign.

Although this French intervention did not succeed in opening Korea to outside trade and interactions more generally, it did begin a decade-long effort by other countries to gain access to Korean products and markets. Prior to the French events the RUSSIANS had attempted to gain access to Korea, with no success. In 1871 the U.S. Korean Expedition led to further military action on Ganghwa (Kanghwa) Island, which saw the Koreans defeated militarily but victorious politically in that they continued to refuse to open their land or waters to international expeditions or trade. Finally in 1876 the Korea-Japanese Treaty of Amity opened three Korean ports to Japanese trade and brought Korea's long-standing position as a Chinese tributary state to an end.

These events, which followed a century of strife in Korean internal politics as well, including peasant uprisings in both 1812 and 1862, left the Choson dynasty severely weakened. Throughout its long history of political domination in Korea many Choson kings had drawn upon the Confucian idea of the Mandate of Heaven, borrowed from the Chinese, to justify their leading position in society. These events of the 19th century led many Koreans to begin to see the Chosons as having lost that mandate and thus their political legitimacy.

In 1910 the Choson period ended in Korea, not through the actions of disgruntled Koreans but at the hands of the Japanese. The Japanese had proved themselves the most powerful state in the region by defeating China and Russia in two wars within the 10-year period between 1895 and 1905, giving them an almost unassailable advantage in their quest to pry open the so-called hermit kingdom of Korea. In 1905 Korea was forced to accept the status of Japanese protectorate, and five years later the peninsula was annexed with the Treaty of Annexation of Korea by Japan or, as the Koreans called it, Humiliation of the Nation in the Year of the Dog.

The Japanese imperial period of Korean history (1910–45) gave the Japanese control of most internal and external functions of the Korean government, including police, military affairs, banking, communications, foreign relations, and even the land and agricultural systems. Korean nationalists were punished or killed, especially after the March First Movement in 1919, which led millions of Koreans into the streets to protest Japanese control of their state. During the militaristic period of the Japanese empire in the 1930s and 1940s control over Korea increased to the point of outlawing the Korean language, changing Korean surnames to Japanese ones, and enslaving much of the population to work for the Japanese war effort. The most famous of these slaves were the Korean sex slaves, women kidnapped from their families and given to Japanese soldiers as "comfort women," a policy and practice for which the Japanese government apologized only in 1993. At that point the chief government spokesman made the statement of apology, which was followed in 2007 by a renewal of that apology by the Japanese prime minister.

Partition

The partition of Korea into northern and southern halves at the 38th parallel was a wartime decision of the United States and the USSR to facilitate the surrender of the Japanese on the peninsula. As the liberating armies on each side of this boundary, the United States and the USSR each supported figures who fulfilled their own ideas about proper leadership and legitimate political ideology. In the north it was Kim Il Sung, a Communist and anti-Japanese rebel leader who had fought in Manchuria during the war, who gained the support of the USSR, while in the south the United States threw its support behind Syngman Rhee, a Korean nationalist who had spent the war years in the United States. Despite the desire of the Koreans for national elections and a unified state on the peninsula, in 1947, after two years of failed negotiations, separate governments were set up on both sides of the 38th parallel. In August 1948 the United States held elections in the south and formed the Republic of Korea, while the USSR did the same a month later in the north, forming the Democratic People's Republic of Korea.

Just two years after these events in June 1950 the first salvo in what was to become the Korean War was fired by North Korea. The north claimed that the southern armies had fired first, but no evidence of this claim has ever been found. For the next two years forces from North Korea, the USSR, and China on one side fought against a large UN-sponsored force from South Korea, the United States, and 20 other countries in a back-and-forth war that ended in July 1953 having accomplished nothing but the deaths of around 2.5 million people. The armistice signed by all sides in 1953 placed the border back at the 38th parallel and established the large demilitarized zone that continues to divide the peninsula in half. A peace treaty was never signed to end the official hostilities between the north and south, although the two countries did sign a nonaggression pact in 1991.

Throughout the later half of the 20th century and into the 21st North and South Korea continued to pursue their divergent political, economic, and social goals. The North Korean state remains Communist, poor, and isolated to this day, continuing the long tradition of the Korean hermit state begun as far back as the Shilla period and maintained during much of the Choson as well. In 2002 U.S. President George W. Bush labeled North Korea part of the "axis of evil" for the country's attempts to develop nuclear weapons, and in October 2006 the country claimed to have successfully tested its first nuclear bomb. While the government has isolated itself and continues to pursue a foreign policy strategy based on that isolation, the North Korean people are believed to be among the poorest in Asia, suffering from chronic food shortages and a lack of medical supplies, trained personnel, and other basic necessities (see KOREANS, NORTH: NATIONALITY).

Conversely South Korea during the five decades since the end of the war has experienced tremendous economic growth and prosperity. The various governments that placed themselves in power from 1953 until 1987 pursued primarily an autocratic agenda, with the military playing a key role from 1960 onward. But by 1987 South Korea was beginning to democ-ratize, and in 1992 a civilian was elected president for the first time in 32 years; five years later a second civilian president was elected and the smooth transition between the two marked a historic victory for democracy in east Asia. At the same time South Korea's economy exploded after the war and for the past 30 years has been one of the strongest in Asia and the world. The South Korean people in 2005 enjoyed the 11th largest economy in the world and a per capita income of more than $16,000. They are free to travel throughout the world and enjoy strong and modern education and health care systems (see KOREANS, SOUTH: NATIONALITY).

On both sides of the 38th parallel the official goal of the governments is reunification; the same is desired by many Korean people as well. Nonetheless as the reunification of East and West Germany in 1991 has shown, this policy will not be easy. More than 60 years of divergent political, social, and economic policies, in addition to different education systems and personal lifestyles, cannot be merged for the benefit of all in a single generation.

CULTURE

With the division of Korea into two separate countries in 1945 we cannot speak of a unified Korean culture after that period. The divergent political and economic policies pursued by the two Korean states have resulted in very different material cultures, with a materialist and consumer-oriented society developing in the south and an impoverished rural culture in the north. South Koreans are also about half Christian, mostly Roman Catholic, and half Buddhist, while the Communist state in the north forbids most religious expression and practice; North Koreans' religious beliefs are largely unknown today. Nonetheless the two peoples share a common language and pre-1945 history and such traditional art forms as music, dance, and visual arts.

This shared pre-1945 history is the sum of thousands of years of interactions among cultural features adopted from Koreans' ancient nomadic and shamanistic past, Buddhism, Confucianism, Chinese influence, Japanese imperialism, and other features. For example the Korean patrilineal kinship system was largely inherited from the Chinese during the Ming dynasty (1368–1644) and exhibits the traditional Confucian values of filial piety, hierarchy, and patriarchy. However, unlike in China, Koreans required that clan records not only be written down to be legitimate but also that they had to be documented as having been passed down as an inherited written record. This practice changed somewhat in the 18th and 19th centuries, when titles and other markers of aristocratic status could be purchased, but generally it just meant that aristocratic clan records likewise were purchased along with their accompanying titles and seals.

The Korean language is another example of a cultural feature that was inherited from ancient times but changed throughout the course of history. The Korean language is probably distantly related to the Altaic languages including the Mongol, Tungusic, and Turkic language families. Nonetheless thousands of years of divergence from these other languages have meant that Korean is so remotely related as to be considered a language isolate by many linguists and historians of language. In addition the majority of words used in present-day Korean are from the long period of interaction between Koreans and Chinese, and only about 35 percent of Korean words are from the ancient Korean language.

The syncretic nature of Korean culture is perhaps most evident in the wide variety of religious and philosophical traditions that have contributed to the overall worldview of the Korean people. The original inhabitants of the Korean Peninsula were shamanists who believed in the efficacy of a wide variety of spirits from nature and in the ability of shamans, *mudang*s, who were usually women, to communicate with these spirits to ensure crop yields, human health, and other outcomes. Even into the 20th century, when many Koreans engaged in agriculture as their primary economic activity, traditional shamans continued to practice their art; the largely agricultural north may still have practicing shamans helping people to overcome the adversity of the weather and other natural conditions. In addition to shamanism Buddhism has played a large role in the development of Korean culture. Buddhist temples, texts, and beliefs continue to be held in high regard in South Korea. Two important Korean Buddhist sites located at Gyeongju, Bulguksa and Haeinsa with its Tripitaka Koreana woodblocks, have been placed on UNESCO's World Heritage list for their importance not only to Korean history but to human history more generally. The former site is a temple built in 751 and housing two pagodas and the Seokguram Grotto, while the latter is a temple built in 802 containing 81,340 wooden printing blocks of Buddhist scripture carved in the

Today the 81,340 woodblocks of the Tripitaka Koreana are stored in this library of the Haeinsa Buddhist temple, on Gaya Mountain in South Korea. *(Getty/ Linda Grove)*

13th century. As has Buddhism, Confucianism has been integral to Korean culture since the Three Kingdoms period, forming the basis of Koreans' moral precepts, legal system, and relationship between ruler and ruled, as well as that between old and young. During the entire Choson period Confucianism formed the backbone of the *yangban* class system and much of the administrative apparatus of the state, a legacy that has not been eliminated with the formation of a democratic state in the south. The legacy of the large number of Confucian schools, libraries, artisans, and artists has also not disappeared in the South's push toward consumer democracy nor the North's push toward state socialism.

FURTHER READING

Donald N. Clark. *Culture and Customs of Korea* (Westport, Conn.: Greenwood Press, 2000).

Jon Carter Covell. *Korea's Cultural Roots* (Elizabeth, N.J.: Hollym International, 1983).

Martina Deuchler. *The Confucian Transformation of Korea: A Study of Society and Ideology* (Cambridge, Mass.: Harvard University Press, 1992).

Joseph C. Goulden. *Korea: The Untold Story of the War* (New York: McGraw-Hill Book Company, 1982).

James Huntley Grayson. *Korea: A Religious History* (New York: Oxford University Press, 1989).

Tae-Hung Ha. *Guide to Korean Culture* (Seoul: Yonsei University Press, 1978).

Laurel Kendall. *Getting Married in Korea: Of Gender, Morality, and Modernity* (Berkeley and Los Angeles: University of California Press, 1996).

Chongho Kim. *Korean Shamanism: The Cultural Paradox* (Burlington, Vt.: Ashgate, 2003).

Choong Soon Kim. *One Anthropologist, Two Worlds: Three Decades of Reflexive Fieldwork in North America and Asia* (Knoxville: University of Tennessee Press, 2002).

Lee Kyong-hee. *Korean Culture, Legacies, and Lore* (Seoul: Korea Herald, 1993).

The Organizing Committee of the 29th International Geographical Congress. *Korea: The Land and People* (Seoul: Kyohaksa, 2000).

Koreans, North: nationality (people of North Korea)

Though ethnically identical to their neighbors the South Koreans, the people of North Korea have created a distinct nationality since being separated from the south in 1945.

GEOGRAPHY

North Korea occupies about 47,000 square miles on the northern section of the Korean Peninsula, a territory approximately the size of the U.S. state of Mississippi. It is bordered by China and Russia to the north, the Sea of Japan to the east, South Korea to the south, and Korea Bay to the west. The land is about 80 percent mountainous with Paektu-san, which straddles the border with China, rising to about 9,000 feet above sea level. Between the country's hills and mountains run deep, narrow valleys that have traditionally made transport and communication in the region difficult. The western coastal plain is wider than that in the east and is the home of much of the country's lagging agricultural industry. This struggling economic sector is not aided by the country's climate, which is characterized by long, cold winters and short summers that are very hot and humid.

INCEPTION AS A NATION

The process of dividing the Korean Peninsula into two separate countries began in December 1945 at a conference held in Moscow and attended by delegates from the USSR, United States, China, and the United Kingdom. The purpose of the talks was to assist Korea in recovering from the long JAPANESE occupation, which had officially begun in 1905, and to move toward independence. These talks got as far as dividing the peninsula into two trusteeships, one in the north administered by the USSR and the other in the south administered by the United States. After several more years of negotiation and attempts at reunification came to a halt as a result of the significant political, economic, and social differences between the USSR and United States, these trusteeships became separate countries in late summer 1948.

North Korea or the Democratic People's Republic of Korea (DPRK) came into existence on September 9, 1948, under the tutelage of the USSR and the political leadership of Kim Il-sung. Kim served in various posts in North Korea, including prime minister from 1948 until 1972 and president from 1972, until he died in 1994; he also served as general secretary of the Workers' Party of Korea from 1946 until 1994. North Koreans continue to refer to him as Eternal President of the Republic of North Korea and his cult of personality has certainly outlived the man himself.

In the early years both Kim and North Korea followed the USSR's Marxist-Leninist political ideology fairly closely, emphasizing heavy industry over consumer goods and trading almost exclusively with the USSR and other Communist states. However, starting in 1955 and taking center political stage about a decade later, Kim began moving North Korea away from this foreign model and toward a political concept he labeled *juche,* "subject." The main ideas underlying this concept, as elaborated in Kim's writings and speeches, are political independence, economic self-sufficiency, and self-defense. As a result North Korea moved away from its alliances with the USSR and China; even today the small country remains the most isolated in the world, as well as one of the poorest.

Very soon after the establishment of independent North and South Korea naval battles and fighting at the border by armed guerrillas became regular occurrences. In late June 1950 North Korea invaded its southern neighbor and drew an international response from UN forces led by South Korea, the United States, and 20 other allied countries; China entered the fray soon after on the side of the North Koreans. Despite the efforts of large numbers of soldiers on both sides neither was able to push the other

NORTH KOREANS: NATIONALITY

nation:
The Democratic People's Republic of Korea (DPRK); North Korea

derivation of name:
The Goryeo dynasty was visited by Persian merchants traveling the Silk Road; they referred to Goryeo as *Koryo. Goryeo* was also translated in Italian as "Cauli" in Marco Polo's time; this was then translated into English as *Corea.*

government:
Communist state; one-man dictatorship

capital:
Pyongyang

language:
Korean

religion:
Autonomous religious practice no longer exists and religious groups sponsored by the government provide only an illusion of religious freedom; traditionally Buddhist and Confucianist.

earlier inhabitants:
Some of the tribes from the Altai Mountains, who migrated to Manchuria and Siberia in about 4000 B.C.E., settled in what is now known as the Korean Peninsula

demographics:
Nearly completely homogeneous population of ethnic Koreans with a very small number of Chinese and Japanese

North Koreans: nationality time line

B.C.E.

Third–fourth centuries New pottery techniques are introduced and Koreans produce grayish blue stoneware, which later becomes common during the Three Kingdom period of Shilla, Paekche, and Koguryo.

57 Sam-han dynasty.

37–668 C.E. The Three Kingdoms era: Koguryo, Paekche, and Shilla.

C.E.

668 Start of the Unified Shilla period, which unites all Three Kingdoms.

918–1392 Koryo dynasty. During this period there is strong Buddhist influence. In the 9th century celadon porcelain spreads from China to Korea.

12th century Tal-nori, the Korean mask play, originates in the Ha-hoe village of Korea.

1231 The Mongol invasions of Korea begin.

1392–1910 Chosun period. *Bun-cheong* (brown porcelain) appears and becomes standard in the 15th century. The era ends when Korea is invaded and colonized by Japan.

1397–1450 The reign of King Sejong, who develops Korea's own unique alphabet.

1446 Hangul, the Korean alphabet, is published in *Hunmin Jeong-eum* (The proper sounds for the education of the people). King Sejong has this script developed by scholars to replace hanja (Chinese characters) so that it can be more easily learned by the uneducated and common Korean people, who are largely illiterate.

1592 Japan invades Korea and instigates more than 400 years of hatred and mistrust of the island nation among many Koreans.

1894 Hangul is adopted for the first time in official Korean documents, as a result of the Gabo Reform.

1893 Ju Sigyeo leads an academic group to standardize hangul.

1905 Japan occupies Korea following its victory in the Russo-Japanese War.

1910 Japan annexes the entire Korean Peninsula, commencing the Japanese colonial period.

1912 The term *hangul,* meaning "great script" is coined by Ju Sigyeong to define the Korean written language.

1919 The Independence Movement on March 1 is brutally suppressed by the Japanese occupation, resulting in the deaths of thousands of Koreans, the maiming and imprisonment of tens of thousands more, and the destruction of hundreds of temples, schools, and homes.

1943 The United States, Great Britain, and China promise Korea independence at the Cairo Conference during World War II.

1945 The Japanese surrender on August 15, resulting in the divided rule of the Korean Peninsula along the 38th parallel. The former USSR occupies the northern half and the United States occupies the southern half.

1946 The disputed territory of Dokdo, also known as Liancourt Rocks and Takeshima, is excluded from Japan's administrative authority.

1948 The Republic of Korea (ROK) or South Korea is established in the southern half of the Korean Peninsula. At the same time the Democratic People's Republic of Korea (DPRK) with its Communist-style government is established in the northern half.

1949 Troops from the United States and the former Soviet Union withdraw from the Korean Peninsula.

(continues)

North Koreans: nationality time line *(continued)*

1950–53 The Korean War rages between the north and south, triggered by an unexpected attack by North Korea against South Korea in June 1950. Troops from the United States and United Nations fight with ROK troops to defend South Korea from DPRK attacks, which are supported by the Communist countries of China and the Soviet Union.

1951 Armistice discussions begin between the north and south.

1953 An armistice treaty, primarily a temporary cease-fire, is signed by North and South Korea, splitting the Korean Peninsula along a two-and-a-half-mile-wide demilitarized zone at the 38th parallel of latitude. A permanent peace agreement is never signed.

1971 North and South Korean Red Cross agencies begin discussions designed to reunite families divided by the international border.

1973 Talks between the two countries break down and almost all communication ceases for another 11 years as a result of political activities in South Korea.

1980 Kim Jong-il takes over a few of the duties of president from his father, Kim Il-sung.

1994 North Korea signs an agreement with the United States to dismantle its plutonium-based weapons program.

Kim Il-sung dies and is replaced by his son, Kim Jong-il.

2002 North Korea expels International Atomic Energy Agency (IAEA) monitors from the country.

U.S. President George W. Bush refers to North Korea as one part of the "axis of evil," along with Iran and Iraq.

2003 North Korea withdraws from the Non-Proliferation Treaty and begins extracting weapons-grade plutonium from spent nuclear fuel rods.

Six-party talks among North and South Korea, China, Japan, Russia, and the United States begin to address the DPRK's nuclear programs.

2005 North Korea withdraws from the six-party talks.

2006 In October North Korea tests its first nuclear weapon. It also returns to the six-party-negotiations table.

back after the first few weeks of intense fighting and the front moved only slightly from the original border near the 38th parallel. By the time an armistice was signed by North Korea, China, and UN forces in July 1953, little had changed other than the deaths of more than 1 million Koreans, plus thousands of others from China, the United States, Australia, the United Kingdom, and many other countries. Neither South Korea nor the United States actually signed the armistice, but both parties have upheld the agreement over the past half-century; no other peace agreement between the two Koreas has ever been agreed upon.

Throughout the second half of the 20th century and the early years of the 21st North and South Korea have remained isolated from each other despite their geographic proximity and shared language, history, and traditional culture. In the early 1970s the Red Cross worked with the two governments to reunite families that had been separated by the international boundary since 1945, but the efforts fell apart just two years later and were not revived until 1984. In that year South Korea accepted assistance from the North for flood victims and the Red Cross was able to resume working with families divided by the border. Unfortunately for the families involved the Red Cross intervention lasted for just two more years before North Korea suspended all familial, trade, and political talks with its southern neighbor. A brief attempt at negotiations over cohosting the 1988 summer Olympics also ended in failure and in 1987 North Korea bombed a South Korean airplane to signal its separation from South Korea.

Despite the decades of failure on both sides neither side gave up completely and the early 1990s initiated greater cooperation between the increasingly wealthy and successful state of South Korea and its increasingly isolated and poor cousin to the north. The two countries signed a Basic Agreement on reconciliation, nonaggression, exchange, and cooperation as well as a Joint Declaration on denuclearization in December 1991. This was followed in 1992 by North Korea's signing a nuclear safeguards agreement of the International Atomic Energy Agency. Despite these agreements, however, North Korea continued to act largely on the basis of its policy of *juche,* which justified independence and autonomy, even in the area of nuclear proliferation. In 1993 IAEA inspectors were unable to gain access to several sites in the country and Kim announced that his country would withdraw from the Non-Proliferation Treaty altogether. North Korea did not do so at that time but did in 2003, one year after being referred to by U.S. president George W. Bush as a segment of the "axis of evil," and three years before testing its first nuclear weapon.

The people of the state of North Korea have grown increasingly poor during the past half-century. For the past decade or so since the death in 1994 of Kim Il-sung and his replacement by his son, Kim Jong-il, who is less dedicated to the concept of self-reliance, North Koreans have had to rely almost entirely on humanitarian aid to feed themselves. While allowing increased interventions in his country in the areas of aid and economic development, Kim the younger has not abandoned the militarism of his father's regime; his policy is known as *Songun* or "military first." As a result North Korea continues to have the third largest army in the world with more than 1 million soldiers on active duty. In addition the nuclear weapons question remains an open one, with little outside oversight of the country's weapons program even after North Korea returned to the six-party talks with the United States, China, South Korea, Russia, and Japan in December 2006.

CULTURAL IDENTITY

One of the most important aspects of North Korean cultural identity is opposition to Japan and the Japanese people and government. The two peoples have thousands of years of joint history and are probably distantly related in terms of both language and genetics; however, wars between the two states in the 16th century left Koreans languishing in poverty and destruction while the Japanese flourished. In retaliation the Koreans destroyed much of the Japanese navy a few decades later and killed about 250,000 Japanese sailors. However, these victories did not push Korea toward greater industrial or technological development, and while Japan withdrew into itself to recover and grow, an isolated Korea stagnated both economically and technologically for several centuries.

The early 20th century again saw a strong and vital Japan turn Korea into a colony and source of labor and natural resources. For 40 years Korean women were forced to engage in sexual relations with Japanese soldiers as "comfort women" while Korean men worked in labor camps, fields, and factories. The Koreans' hatred of the Japanese, begun with the Japanese invasion in 1592, gained strength and fury through this mistreatment in the first half of the 20th century. When Japan was forced to withdraw in 1945 at the end of World War II, Korea had been so weakened by the colonial period that no single state could emerge to combat the division of the peninsula into Soviet and American puppet states. At least that is how many Koreans, in both north and south, explain the division of their land and people.

As a result of this history North Korean cultural identity is fostered on two competing ideologies: self-sufficiency and revenge against Japan. The former was evident in the concept of *juche* as fostered by Kim Il-sung and, to a somewhat lesser degree, his son, Kim Jong-il. The latter can be seen in the constant militarization of the North Korean state. From maintaining an enormously large land army to testing nuclear weapons, North Korea, although extremely poor, is also highly militarized. The reason for this remains not ideology but fear of outside intervention and desire for revenge. Rather than opposition to and fear of South Korea's strong economy and emerging democracy, the North continues to look primarily to Japan as the enemy to be feared and opposed at all costs. The cost in the last five decades has been the economic prosperity of the country and health and well-being of its 23.3 million people.

While self-sufficiency and revenge are aspects of North Korean cultural identity fostered against external forces, internally the state has emphasized a unique North Korean culture that differs from the capitalist, consumerist model in the south. This identity is built on the Communist notions of mass unity, sameness, and labor as central to the development of society. The important aspects of this cultural identity can be seen every few years at the expansive Arirang Festival, held to commemorate Kim Il-sung's birthday in April. Participants in

The Arirang Festival in 2005 was particularly large because it coincided with the 60th anniversary of Korea's liberation from Japan. The centerpiece of this attraction is the five-level-high human pyramid, though hundreds of other gymnasts, dancers, flag bearers, and others participated as well. *(AP/Lee Ock-Hyun)*

the festivities train for years to perform in choreographed performances of tens of thousands of dancers, gymnasts, and contributors who carry large signs in honor of the Eternal President. Altogether more than 100,000 people participate in the Mass Games as they are called, to present a spectacle of unique North Korean politics and society.

See also KOREANS; KOREANS, SOUTH: NATIONALITY.

FURTHER READING

Michael Breen. *Kim Jong-Il: North Korea's Dear Leader* (Singapore: John Wiley, 2004).

Bruce Cumings. *North Korea: Another Country* (New York: New Press, 2004).

Paul French. *North Korea: The Paranoid Peninsula* (New York: Zed Books, 2004).

Michael Harrold. *Comrades and Strangers: Behind the Closed Doors of North Korea* (Chichester, Sussex: Wiley, 2004).

Bertil Lintner. *Great Leader, Dear Leader: Demystifying North Korea under the Kim Clan* (Chiang Mai, Thailand: Silkworm Books, 2005).

Don Oberdorfer. *The Two Koreas: A Contemporary History* (Reading, Mass.: Addison-Wesley, 1997).

Han S. Park. *North Korea: The Politics of Unconventional Wisdom* (Boulder, Colo.: Lynne Rienner Publishers, 2002).

Koreans, South: nationality
(Koreans, people of South Korea)

Though ethnically identical to their neighbors the North Koreans, the people of South Korea have created a distinct nationality since being separated from the North in 1945.

GEOGRAPHY

The Republic of Korea is situated on the southern half of the Korean Peninsula in East Asia. It borders the Sea of Japan (or East Sea to Koreans) off its eastern coast and the Yellow Sea off the western coast. It is separated from Japan by the Korea Strait to the south and southeast. Its only land boundary is with North Korea, from which it is separated by a 1,250-mile-long and two-and-a-half-mile-wide Demilitarized Zone (DMZ) at the 38th parallel of latitude.

South Korea's total area is 61,193 square miles, with 1,500 miles of coastline that includes approximately 3,400 islands in the west and south, most of which are small and uninhabited. The terrain is largely hills and mountains, culminating at the highest point of 6,400 feet at Halla-san, an extinct volcano on Jeju Island. There are three major rivers, the Han River, Geum River, and Nakdong River, which

South Koreans: nationality time line

B.C.E.

Fourth–third centuries New pottery techniques are introduced and Koreans produce grayish blue stoneware, which later becomes common during the Three Kingdom period of Shilla, Paekche, and Koguryo.

57 Sam-han dynasty.

668–37 c.e. The Three Kingdoms era: Koguryo, Paekche, and Shilla.

C.E.

668 Start of the Unified Shilla period, which unites all Three Kingdoms.

918–1392 Koryo dynasty. During this period there is strong Buddhist influence. In the 9th century celadon porcelain spreads from China to Korea.

12th century Tal-nori, the Korean mask play, originates in the Ha-hoe village of Korea.

1231 The Mongol invasions of Korea begin.

1392–1910 Chosun period. *Bun-cheong* (brown porcelain) appears and becomes standard in the 15th century. The era ends when Korea is invaded and colonized by Japan.

1397–1450 The reign of King Sejong, who developed Korea's own unique alphabet.

1446 Hangul, the Korean alphabet, is published in *Hunmin Jeong-eum* (The proper sounds for the education of the people). King Sejong has this script developed by scholars to replace *Hanja* (Chinese characters) so that it can be easily learned by the uneducated and common Korean people, who are largely illiterate.

1894 *Hangul* is adopted for the first time in official Korean documents, as a result of the Gabo Reform.

1893 Ju Sigyeo leads an academic group to standardize Hangul.

1905 Japan occupies Korea following its victory in the Russo-Japanese War.

1910 Japan annexes the entire Korean Peninsula, commencing the Japanese colonial period.

1912 The term *hangul,* meaning "great script," is coined by Ju Sigyeong to define the Korean written language.

1919 The Independence Movement on March 1 is brutally suppressed by the Japanese during their occupation, resulting in the deaths of thousands of Koreans, the maiming and imprisonment of tens of thousands, and the destruction of hundreds of temples, schools, and homes.

1943 The United States, Great Britain, and China promise Korea independence at the Cairo Conference during World War II.

1945 The Japanese surrender on August 15 and the Korean Peninsula is divided along the 38th parallel. The former USSR occupies the northern half and the United States occupies the southern half.

1946 The disputed territory of Dokdo, also known as Liancourt Rocks and Takeshima, two small, rocky islands about 134 miles east of Korea, is excluded from Japan's administrative authority.

1948 Korea gains independence. The Republic of Korea (ROK) or South Korea is established in the southern half. At the same time the Democratic People's Republic of Korea (DPRK) with its Communist-style government is established in the northern half.

Korea formally adopts hangul as its official written language.

1949 The United States and former Soviet troops withdraw from the Korean Peninsula.

1950–53 The Korean War rages between the North and South, triggered by the unexpected attack by North Korea on South Korea in June 1950. Troops from the United States and United Nations fight with ROK troops to defend South Korea from DPRK attacks, which are supported by the Communist countries of China and the Soviet Union.

(continues)

SOUTH KOREANS: NATIONALITY

nation:
Republic of Korea, also known as South Korea or Korean Republic. South Koreans refer to their country as *Han-guk, Taehan-min'guk* (or *Daehan Minguk*), or *Namhan*

derivation of name:
The Goryeo dynasty was visited by Persian merchants traveling the Silk Road and the Persians referred to Goryeo as *Koryo. Goryeo* was also translated in Italian as "Cauli" in Marco Polo's time, later translated into English as *Corea.*

government:
Democratic republic with powers shared among the president, legislature, and judiciary. The president is head of state (serving a single five-year term), and the prime minister is head of government. There is a unicameral national assembly called Kukhoe, whose members are elected for four-year terms.

capital:
Seoul

language:
Korean (*han guk*) is the official language and is spoken by most of the population. The official written script is *Hangul. Hanja* is the Korean name for Chinese characters that have been incorporated into the Korean language. English is taught widely in primary and high schools.

(continues)

SOUTH KOREANS:
NATIONALITY
(continued)

religion:
No stated religion 46 percent, Christian 26 percent (including 11 percent Catholic), Buddhist 26 percent, Confucianism 1 percent, other (for instance, Cheondogyo) 1 percent. Traditionally shamanism was the dominant religion.

earlier inhabitants:
Some of the tribes from the Altai Mountains, who had migrated to Siberia and Manchuria from about 4000 B.C.E., settled in what is now known as the Korean Peninsula.

demographics:
Predominantly Korean, with a small Chinese minority

South Koreans: nationality time line (continued)

1951 Armistice discussions begin between the North and South.

1953 An armistice treaty, primarily a temporary cease-fire, is signed by North and South Korea, splitting the Korean Peninsula along a two-and-a-half-mile-wide demilitarized zone at the 38th parallel of latitude. A permanent peace agreement is never signed.

1954 South Korea occupies Liancourt Rocks (Dokdo/Takeshima), previously occupied by Japan.

1960 Syngman Rhee is forced to resign in April. Chang Myone is elected prime minister in June.

1961 A bloodless coup overthrows the government in May. General Park Chung Hee assumes leadership.

1962 The first five-year economic development plan is launched.

1967 The second five-year economic plan (1967–71) is launched, focusing on modernizing industry and rapidly building steel, machinery, and chemical industries to substitute for major imports.

1972 South-North joint communiqué July 4, with North Korea and South Korea agreeing to work for peaceful reunification.

1977 The fourth five-year economic development plan (1977–81) fosters the development of strategic technology and intensive and skilled labor-intensive industries such as machinery, electronics, and shipbuilding, to allow South Korea to compete in the world's export markets. Heavy and chemical industries continue to develop, greatly increasing export production.

1979 Park Chung Hee is assassinated in October. Choi Kyu-hah becomes president and declares martial law amid public demonstrations.

1980 General Chun Doo Hwan becomes leader after a coup d'état.

1981 General Chun Doo Hwan is indirectly elected in March 1981 for a single seven-year term.

1982 The fifth five-year economic and social development plan (1982–86) shifts focus from heavy and chemical industries to technology-intensive industries, including electronics, precision machinery, and information, which are gaining greater demand worldwide.

1987 The prodemocracy movement leads to the restoration of a multiparty political system and the adoption of a new constitution. The first direct presidential election is held in December, with Roh Tae-Woo becoming the seventh president.

The sixth five-year economic and social development plan (1987–91) maintains the goals of the fifth plan as well as increasing research and development investment in order to enhance science and technology.

1988 The current constitution is established on February 25, launching the sixth Republic of South Korea.

1988 Seoul hosts the 26th summer Olympic games.

1988 The national pension scheme is introduced, covering all workplaces with 10 or more employees.

1989 The seventh five-year economic and social development plan (1992–96) is formulated early to prepare for development of high-technology industries, including microelectronics, fine chemicals, bioengineering, optics, and aerospace.

1991 Both the Republic of Korea and the Democratic People's Republic of Korea join the United Nations in October.

1992 Kim Young Sam defeats Kim Dae Jung to become South Korea's first civilian president, following 32 years of military rule.

1995 Three historic Korean sites are placed on the World Heritage List: Haiensa Temple Janggyeong Panjeon, the Depositories for the Tripitaka Koreana Woodblocks; the Jongmyo Shrine (The Royal Shrine); and the Seokguram Grotto and Pulguksa Temple.

1996	Korea joins the Organization for Economic Cooperation and Development (OECD).
	The first Pusan International Film Festival is held in Korea in September, showing 169 films from 31 countries to audiences of 184,071.
1997	Kim Dae Jung is elected president.
1997	The Changdeokgung Palace Complex and the Hwaseong Fortress are listed as World Heritage Sites.
1997–99	Asian financial crisis. Many of South Korea's largest conglomerates and banks are bankrupt or face severe financial strain, exposing long-standing weaknesses.
1997	The International Monetary Fund (IMF) provides a record loan package (together with the World Bank, Asian Development Bank, and Japanese government) of $60 billion to rescue South Korea from economic crisis. It is the largest amount lent to any country in a single deal. The loan leads to drastic reforms to create a more market-oriented economy.
1998	South Korea's gross domestic product (GDP) plummets by 6.9 percent.
	The tripartite commission of labor, management, and government is formed.
1999	Dokdo/Liancourt Rocks/Takeshima is designated a protected environmental area by the South Korean government.
1999	The national pension scheme is extended to cover the entire South Korean working population.
2000	The first North-South summit takes place in June between the South's president, Kim Dae Jung, and the North's leader, Kim Jong-il.
	Kim Dae Jung is awarded the Nobel Prize in peace "for his work for democracy and human rights in South Korea and East Asia in general, and for peace and reconciliation with North Korea in particular." He is the first Korean to receive a Nobel Prize.
	The Gochang, Hwasun, and Ganghwa Dolmen sites and the Gyeongju Historic Areas are listed as World Heritage Sites.
	The traditional Korean martial art, Tae Kwan Do, becomes an official Olympic sport at the Sydney Olympic games.
	The government introduces the basic livelihood guarantee system in October to provide social support and subsidies to the poor.
2001	South Korea completely pays off its IMF loans in August, three years ahead of schedule.
2002	Liberal reformer Roh Moo-hyun wins closely fought elections to become president in December.
2002	Seoul cohosts the soccer FIFA World Cup with Japan. South Korea becomes the first Asian country to reach the World Cup semifinals.
2003	Roh Moo-hyun becomes president in February, with a five-year term until 2008.
2003	The government introduces a five-day working week, reducing official working hours from 44 to 40 hours a week.
2004	President Roh Moo-hyun spends two months out of office after being impeached by parliament over election-law infractions. The constitutional court later overturns the move, saying the charges were not of a sufficiently serious nature.
2004	South Korea's GDP reaches $1 trillion, placing it firmly in the list of top world economies.
2006	Han Myeong-sook becomes prime minister in April.
	South Korea and the United States launch the Foreign Trade Agreement (KorU.S. FTA) in February, sparking controversies and protests.
2007	South Korea's ex-foreign minister, Ban Ki-moon, replaces Kofi Annan as secretary-general of the United Nations.

In 1988 South Korea's combination of a prosperous global economy and traditional artistic aesthetic was displayed for the world to see at the 24th summer Olympic games in Seoul. The official logo of the Games blends the Olympic rings with the Korean Sam Taegeuk design, representing harmony of the universe. *(AP Photo)*

provide flat fertile plans, much of which are under cultivation. Such lowlands account for only 30 percent of the total South Korean landmass.

Politically the country consists of nine provinces called *do* and seven metropolitan regions known as *gwangyoksi*, where approximately 50 percent of the population live.

INCEPTION AS A NATION

Although South Korea has been a nation in its own right only since 1948, its long history, which it shares with North Korea, includes strong traditional Buddhist and Confucian influences, JAPANESE occupation for the first four decades of the 20th century, and the welcomed cessation of Japanese rule at the end of World War II. The seeds of South Korea were sown in 1945, when, following the defeat of the Japanese on August 15, the Korean Peninsula was split by political means between the U.S. occupation in the south and the Soviet occupation in the north. On the departure of both foreign powers at Korean independence in 1948 South Korea was officially born.

Peace was not to be, however, and between 1950 and 1953 North and South Korea were embroiled in a war. In addition because of the dichotomous political beliefs of democracy and communism, this war involved the support of the United Nations and the United States for South Korea, and of China and the Soviet Union for North Korea. A temporary cease-fire was finally achieved in 1953 following more than a year of armistice discussions. The talks resulted in the creation of the Demilitarized Zone at the 38th parallel, which remains one of the most heavily fortified borders in the world. As a permanent peace agreement was never signed, South Korea and North Korea technically remain at war to this day.

The next important date in the development of the South Korean nation is 1980, when General Chun Doo Hwan assumed presidency after the head of the Korean Central Intelligence Agency assassinated President Park Chunghee, supposedly to free the country from his authoritarianism. Instead widespread protests broke out, culminating in the Gwangju massacre in May. The official death toll was reported to be 207 although there are dissident claims of a much greater carnage of between 1,000 and 2,000 victims. This incident gave greater spark to the democracy movement, which ultimately succeeded, with free elections and the introduction of civilian democratic rule in 1988 when the constitution was again revised. Since 1948 there have been five major revisions to the Korean constitution, with each heralding a new republic. The current Sixth Republic was formed on February 25, 1988, when the current constitution was signed.

Although the Korean people constitute one unified ethnic group, the distinction between North and South in many ways defines the national identity of both people. Nonetheless since the late 1990s South Korea has pursued a "Sunshine Policy" of constructive engagement with North Korea, initiated by President Kim Dae Jung. This has included resisting international calls for sanctions against North Korea and providing aid, reunions between North and South Koreans, tourism initiatives, and economic cooperation. These attempts at reconciliation led to Kim Dae Jung's being awarded the Nobel Prize in peace. The Sunshine Policy's collaborative intentions of South Korea remain today, despite some international pressure to make a stronger stance against the North.

CULTURAL IDENTITY

South Korea has a population of 48 million and is one of the most densely populated countries in Asia and, indeed, the world. Despite centuries of invasions and foreign rule Koreans have managed to retain their own cultural identity, sharing a common racial background, language, and culture. The society and culture have evolved from the long history and ancient traditions influenced greatly by both Buddhism and Confucianism.

Although South Korea shares its traditional culture with North Korea, during the last three to four decades South Korea has transformed itself from an agrarian society to a global industrial leader. Today it has the 14th largest economy in the world (in terms of GDP calculated on the basis of purchasing power parity) and the third largest economy in Asia (after India and Japan). Between 1960 and 1995 the economy grew at an average rate of more than 15 percent per year, largely as a result of the industrious nature of the Korean people, who formed a highly literate, educated, and motivated workforce for low-cost but high-quality export production. For years now South Korea has been firmly at the leading edge of the digital revolution.

The lifestyle changes that have accompanied this dramatic economic growth have prompted South Koreans to use the term *dynamic Korea* as an accurate description of their modern life instead of the traditional Korean reference to "the land of the morning calm." Koreans are extremely technology savvy and media literate with one of the world's largest percentages of the population having broadband multimedia access and mobile phone ownership, as well as reading the many national and local daily newspapers. Along with the obvious political differences it is this fast-paced, technology-dominated urban life that significantly differentiates modern South Koreans from North Koreans, who, since the political divide between communism and capitalism, have led very different lives.

Even though only a very small percentage of modern Koreans are official Confucianists, most are still greatly influenced by Confucianist values. The role of hierarchical relationships and associated duties, a strong code of conduct, and the importance of family are key components of this traditional philosophy. Koreans are extremely proud of their unique language and relatively homogeneous culture, which can be differentiated from the neighboring Japanese and Chinese cultures, which also have roots in Confucianism.

Perhaps because of their long history of invasion and foreign occupation South Koreans have emerged with great tenacity and a strong will for survival. The concept of *han* is one important key to the Korean cultural psyche and refers to oppression, isolation, lament, and injustice, especially collectively. It has been attributed to pent-up energies and frustrations stemming from historical oppression, social immobility, family vendettas, and suffering from general poverty and hardship. As a centerpiece of Korean culture *han* leads to a toughness, pragmatism, and mistrust of outsiders.

A second aspect of Korean collectivism is the importance of personal and family clan connections, as evident in their family-owned industrial conglomerates. The rapid and strong growth of these *chaebol,* such as the Hyundai and Samsung groups, contributed significantly to the transformation of South Korea into a major world economy.

See also KOREANS; KOREANS, NORTH: NATIONALITY.

FURTHER READING

Carter Eckert et al. *Korea Old and New: A History* (Cambridge, Mass.: Harvard Korea Institute, 1991).
Choong Soon Kim. *The Culture of Korean Industry: An Ethnography of Poongsan Corporation* (Tucson: University of Arizona Press, 1992).
Djun Kil Kim. *The History of Korea* (Westport, Conn.: Greenwood Press, 2005).
L. Robert Kohls. *Learning to Think Korean: A Guide to Living and Working in Korea* (Yarmouth, Maine: Intercultural Press, 2001).
James Lewis and Amadu Sesay. *Korea and Globalisation* (New York: Routledge Curzon, 2002).
Don Oberdorfer *The Two Koreas: A Contemporary History* (New York: Basic Books, 2002).

Koryak (Chavchu, Nymylan)

The Koryak are one of the indigenous peoples of Siberia and the Far East of Russia, native to the Kamchatka Peninsula and the Koryak Range to the north of the peninsula. They were first mentioned by the RUSSIANS in a travel book written by Stephan Krasheninnikov in 1755, although they are probably descendants of the first Neolithic inhabitants of the region and thus its oldest population. Their language family includes the CHUKCHIS and Itelmen people, and it is believed that the Koryak are the closest Asian relatives of the Native Americans who crossed the Bering Strait at least 10,000 years ago. Native Americans of the Pacific Northwest coast share many myths with the Koryak, including the central figure of the raven, who is believed by both peoples to have provided humans with light, the ability to hunt, drums, shamans, and a variety of chants; the Koryak also believe that the raven gave them the gift of reindeer.

Traditionally there were two separate populations of Koryak. Settled or Residential Koryak lived on the coast of the Bering Sea or the Sea of Okhotsk in permanent settlements, subsisting on sea mammals and fish in addition to gathered foods like roots and berries. Reindeer or Nomadic Koryak resided inland on the peninsula or the mountain ranges to the north and were nomadic reindeer hunters who probably adopted this mode of subsistence after interactions with the EVENS from the 11th century onward; they also fished in mountain streams and gathered wild roots and berries in summer.

The Russians first moved into the Kamchatka Peninsula in the 1690s, and for about 100 years the Koryak resisted incorporation into the Russian world both by refusing to pay taxes and by fighting against the incursions. At the end of the 18th century the Russians changed their tactics, from brute force to bribery, and were thus able to recruit local chiefs to gather their tribute for them in exchange for vodka, arms, and even local power positions. The first two Russian settlements, Penshino and Gishiga, were established in the 18th century; the 19th century introduced much

KORYAK

location:
Siberia, the Kamchatka Peninsula and adjacent mountain ranges

time period:
Unknown to the present

ancestry:
Indigenous north Asian

language:
Koryak, a Paleo-Asiatic language related to Yukagir and Chukchi

greater numbers of Russians, including traders and many Orthodox missionaries. While both groups were unscrupulous in their methods, the traders were particularly harmful, using vodka to buy furs and pelts for a pittance of cloth, salt, tobacco, or gunpowder.

The Soviet system was first established in Kamchatka in 1923, but it was the 1930s before any significant changes were felt. Inland hunters had to begin working in cooperatives that set their prices for furs, hides, and meat at artificially low levels, and those who were former nomads were settled into villages for the first time. Children from both coastal and inland villages were sent to boarding schools away from their communities, where they were compelled to learn Soviet ideology as well as disdain for their people's language and way of life. Koryak shamanism was dealt with particularly harshly by Soviet officials, who saw only primitive magic in the holistic worldview of the Koryak shaman, in which humans, animals, earth, sky, sun, and all of their spirits were considered on the same plane of existence. This "primitive" way of thinking and acting had helped the Koryak to survive for millennia in the one of the harshest environments on Earth, with average winter temperatures well below -15°F. These cultural changes have also been accompanied by dramatic physical changes, especially among the Reindeer Koryak, who continue to eat the meat of this animal regularly. Nuclear and chemical testing in Siberia has increased the levels of lead, cesium, and other heavy metals in the bones of reindeer-eating Koryak so that they measure about 100 times those of others. This population now has high rates of morbidity and mortality, including tuberculosis, high blood pressure, lung disease, and especially leukemia and cancer. Among Koryak generally the life expectancy is less than age 50, one of the lowest in Russia.

Kui (Kaa, Kha, Koy, Kuay, Lawa, Moey, Soai, Suai, Suay, Sui)

The Kui, whose ethnonym means "human being," are considered the most ancient inhabitants of the lowland regions of Thailand, where it borders Laos and Cambodia; there are also small numbers of Kui in Vietnam as well. They are Mon-Khmer speakers and were famous during the era of European colonialism for their skills with elephants as well as their penchant for rebellion against centralizing state authority, whether French or Thai. They should not be confused with the Dravidian-speaking Kui peoples of India or the Trans–New Guinea Kui-speaking Alor peoples of West Papua, Indonesia.

While Kui residence in the lowlands of central Southeast Asia goes back at least 3,500 years their history becomes clear only in the mid-19th century, when the Thai king Rama III, who ruled from 1824 to 1851, had a census taken of all the ethnic groups living in his realm. The Kui at that point became known in Thai as the *Suai,* meaning "tribute people," because they were required to pay taxes and tribute to the dominant lowland populations around them, including THAIS, LAO, and KHMERS. Generally the Kui paid their tribute with elephants, which they captured, trained, and used in agricultural labor. The names of several subgroups of Kui, the Kui Ajiang and Kui Damrei, actually mean "Elephant People" in the languages of the other lowland peoples. Even today in Surin Province, Thailand, the annual Elephant Round-up Festival draws thousands of local and international tourists to see the Kui prowess in working with these enormous creatures.

The majority of Kui families today do not own elephants, and it is only a few select men who train them to participate each year in the Round-up Festival. Nowadays the majority of their small income is derived from wet-rice farming and raising cattle and water buffaloes. There are also many Kui working in the towns and cities of Southeast Asia, some as full-time urban residents, others who move into town during the dry season to make money as unskilled laborers and then return to their farms during the wet season. When living in town many of Thailand's Kui try to hide their ethnic identity because the Thai stereotypes about the Kui are all extremely negative, characterizing them as dirty, lazy, and primitive. Nonetheless this negative image does not stop many Thai, Lao, and Khmer peoples from purchasing magic amulets, spells, and stories from Kui experts, known for their strong supernatural powers.

One of the reasons for this belief about Kui spiritual power is that they were at the center of a large millenarian movement in Southeast Asia that began in the last years of the 19th century and lasted in some regions until 1937. The Holy Men's Rebellion was one of many anticolonial movements in Southeast Asia at the time. It differed from many others, however, in having both a religious, end-of-days focus as well as an emphasis on political independence. It also differed from movements of

KUI

location:
Eastern Thailand, with smaller numbers in Vietnam, Cambodia, and Laos

time period:
Possibly 3500 B.C.E. to the present

ancestry:
Mon-Khmer

language:
Kui, a Mon-Khmer language in the larger Austroasiatic family

Here the Kui trainers at the Surin Elephant Roundup in 2003 show off their ability in front of thousands of local, national, and even international tourists. *(OnAsia/Suthep Kritsanavarin)*

Khmer, Lao, and VIETNAMESE people because the Kui were opposed to both French and local incursions onto their traditional lands. The two groups of leaders of the movement, *phumibun*, men with merit, and *phuwiset,* miracle men, predicted that the world as they knew it would come to an end on March 23, 1902, and in its place would be one where the Kui would rule over the Thais, Lao, Vietnamese, and even French. They also claimed that the Lord Righteous Ruler would turn gravel into gold nuggets and that pigs and buffaloes, especially white ones, would become man-eating demons. As a result of these prophecies many Kui gathered large piles of gravel in front of their homes and slaughtered their animals to protect themselves. The February harvest in 1902 was also left to rot in the fields or be eaten by the remaining animals since there was no point in taking in a crop when all Kui would be left with enormous amounts of gold. When the end of the world did not occur in 1902, few followers gave up hope and the movement only gradually dissipated or was put down over the next decades; the last sparks were finally squelched in Vietnam in 1937.

See also THAILANDERS: NATIONALITY.

Kuki   *See* MIZO.

Kuru

The Kuru are believed to be an association of tribes of INDO-ARYANS in post-Vedic India who ruled the region within the Himalayas to the north, the Vindhya Mountains to the south, the confluence of the Ganges and Jumna Rivers in the east, and the Sarasvati River in the west. Some scholars believe that it was the priests of the Kuru who first composed the Rig Veda in about 1500 B.C.E., but this remains a matter of conjecture. Certainly a number of Kuru chiefs and others are mentioned in these mythohistorical texts, but verification of the details remains very problematic both for historians and for archaeologists.

In the later years of the Vedic period, about 900–500 B.C.E., several Kuru tribes organized themselves into a union called the Kuru kingdom. This is often linked to another large chiefdom that emerged at about the same time, Panchala, and the two are written about as Kuru-Panchala. The Kuru kingdom, which is believed to have emerged in about the ninth century B.C.E., is also argued to be the first real state to emerge on Indian soil, where before chiefdoms and other local polities reigned supreme. The Kuru kings continued to distribute wealth, as did the Indo-Aryan chiefs, in order to maintain their balance of power; however, they also inherited their positions and were believed

KURU

location:
Northern India, especially the Ganges-Yamuna Doab

time period:
Possibly 1500 to 500 B.C.E.

ancestry:
Indo-Aryan

language:
Probably post-Rigvedic Sanskrit

to be at least semidivine, new ideas in northern India. It was under the Kuru kings that the Hindu *varna* system, usually called *caste* in English, which was described in the late Vedic texts, actually came into play in society, dividing all peoples into four discrete categories, with the Brahmins and Kshatriyas working together to dominate the rest (*see* HINDI). The kings of the latter category relied on the sacrifices and other divine rituals of the former to maintain their power and legitimacy, while the former relied on the political and military power of the latter to control land and other resources. Both groups fostered what has been called sanskritization of the language, religion, rituals, and daily life generally, both for the Indo-Aryan peoples and for those they dominated.

Along with gathering together multiple tribes under one king and using the one language, the period of the Kuru kingdom is known as part of the history of the Rig Veda as the Mantra period. At this time various versions of the oral texts were gathered together in one place, standardized, and additions made at the end of many of the verses. The rituals that these texts were meant to accompany were also standardized across the realm by the Kuru ritual priests.

The last change that marks the onset of the Kuru period in Indian history is an economic one. Both the early and late Vedic periods are notable for their heavy reliance on nomadic or seminomadic pastoralism as a way of life. Families and clans moved seasonally or as needed to provide grass and water for their cattle, horses, and other animals. Prior to the Kuru or late Vedic period the Indo-Aryans also grew some barley, as mentioned in the Rig Veda. By the Mantra period, however, the Kuru people had switched from barley to rice cultivation and rice had even become a sacrificial food, central to both humans and gods.

See also INDO-ARYANS.

Kushans (Kusana, Niuzhi, Wuzhi, Yanzhi, Yu-Chi, Yuezhi, Yuzhi)

The Kushan empire, which stretched from Afghanistan to northern India in the southeast and toward the Chinese border in the northeast in the first to third centuries C.E., had its origins in the nomadic steppe Yuezhi tribal confederation. The Kushans emerged as the strongest tribe in this group after a westward migration in the second century B.C.E. Their empire flourished for only a few hundred years before being swept away by new military powers. The Kushan people became absorbed into the local populations of all the lands they once dominated.

GEOGRAPHY

The Yuezhi tribes originated in the northern steppes bordering China and eventually dominated all of the lands between the Tarim Basin of western China and Afghanistan, including northern India and Pakistan. This is a semidesert region dominated by grassy plains that are traversed by a number of rivers and bordered by mountains, including the Tian Shan and Hindu Kush. In the second century B.C.E. agriculture would have been difficult or even impossible to sustain because of the short growing season and tough sod. This geography, however, was ideal for nomadic pastoralists, who could move their herds of sheep, goats, and horses as the weather and food and water supplies dictated.

ORIGINS

The Yuezhi were a confederation of nomadic tribes living in the regions north of China from at least the first millennium B.C.E. They are often pointed to as the easternmost speakers of an Indo-Iranian language; however, no evidence of their writing has been found and the Yuezhi are known only from the writings of Chinese authors who recorded their prowess in trade, beginning with jade and later with horses and silk. The Chinese historian Sima Qian even describes the Yuezhi as the originators of the Silk Road trade across the steppes in the third century B.C.E., especially the exchange of Chinese silk for Central Asian horses. Chinese sources also tell us that the Yuezhi were made up of five separate tribes, known in Chinese as *Guishuang, Xiumi, Shuangmi, Xidun,* and *Dumi.*

In the second century B.C.E. these people were driven westward on the steppes when the XIONGNU emerged as the strongest military force in the region. From that time they seem to have been dominated by leaders from the Guishuang or Kushan tribe and are known by that term, although Chinese records continue to refer to them as Yuezhi. As had the Iranians the Kushans conquered many of the settled agricultural peoples they encountered, beginning in Bactria (Afghanistan and Tajikistan) and continuing south into present-day Pakistan and northern India.

HISTORY

Yuezhi and Kushan history, while notoriously difficult to date with certainty, is often divided

KUSHANS

location:
The north of India, Pakistan, Afghanistan, Central Asia, and western China

time period:
First millennium B.C.E. to fourth century C.E.

ancestry:
Indo-Aryan

language:
An Indo-Aryan language, but after conquering Bactria the Kushan kings used Greek and then adopted the Bactrian language with its Greek script

into three broadly defined periods to cover the era for which we have textual references, between the second century B.C.E. and the fourth century C.E., as well as an earlier period of Yuezhi history that remains more speculative, as described earlier. The first textual period, lasting until about the first year of the common era, was characterized by the migration of the Yuezhi tribes westward from the Tarim Basin in northwest China to Bactria in present-day Afghanistan. The second period, which stretched from the first to the third centuries, was characterized by the rise and fall of the Kushan empire. The final period, which lasted just one century, was a period of disintegration, when the Kushan name was adopted by the Sassanid rulers (see PERSIANS, SASSANIDS) after they conquered the BACTRIANS. The Sassanid ruler then took the title *kushanshah*. The last of the Kushan kings was displaced by the Guptas in India, and the Kidarites conquered the remaining Kushan territories in Pakistan.

The period between the middle of the second century B.C.E. and about 30 C.E., when the Kushans established themselves as supreme within the Yuezhi confederation, was one of great change within Yuezhi-Kushan society. From a nomadic people concerned primarily with maintaining their trade links between China and the steppes, Yuezhi were transformed in this period into a sedentary agricultural society with a military. The context for this change is the military growth of another steppe-dwelling people, the Xiongnu, who drove the Yuezhi out of their homeland and westward. In their migration the Yuezhi came up against the last vestiges of the Indo-Greek kingdom in Bactria, conquering the region sometime before 129 B.C.E. This date is relatively certain since the representative of the HAN empire in China visited Bactria in 129 B.C.E. and wrote that it was ruled by the Yuezhi.

For about 150 years the Yuezhi maintained their tribal divisions within their new homeland in Bactria, but in the first decades of the common era one tribe, the Kushans, emerged as more powerful and united all six tribes into a common people. It is this date, around 30 C.E., that is usually used as the founding date of the Kushan empire. The next century is one of great military strength, with the expansion of the empire into India, Pakistan, and even back across the steppes toward the original Yuezhi homeland in the Tarim Basin of China. During this time the Kushans were primarily responsible for the spread of Hellenistic culture from their Bac-

---

Kushans time line

B.C.E.

645 Chinese economist Guan Zhong writes of the Yuezhi as suppliers of jade.

Second century The Yuezhi begin migrating west as a result of the increasing military strength of the Xiongnu.

10 The rule of Strato II, the last king of eastern Bactria, comes to an end at the hands of the Yuezhi.

C.E.

30 Kajula Kadphises unites all the tribes of the Yuezhi and becomes the first of the Kushan emperors.

64 Kushan forces conquer Taxila in contemporary Pakistan.

68 Kushan Emperor Wima Taktu uses the name *Soter Megas* (Great Savior) and conquers northern India.

80 Wima Kadphises takes the throne as the third Kushan emperor.

90 Kushans begin to encroach on the Han sphere of influence in western China.

Possibly 120s Kanishka, the fourth and best-known Kushan emperor, ascends the throne.

120 Kanishka places images of the Buddha on coins, probably the first such usage of this image.

180 Vasudeva is the first Kushan king with an Indian name.

213 The Kushan empire is divided into a western and eastern halves upon Vasudeva's death.

213 Kanishka II (or III?) becomes Kushan emperor in the eastern region of Mathura.

233 Sassanid ruler Ardashir I invades Bactria and Gandhara and installs his own king, the Kushanshah, ending the Kushans' sovereignty in the western half of their empire.

270 Kushan control of the Ganges plain in India is lost to the Guptas.

360 The last Kushan emperor, Varahran II, is defeated by the Kidarites in Pakistan.

---

trian-speaking, Greek-script-using homeland in Afghanistan. After the 120s the Kushans were more noted for their links to India and the Buddhist world than for those with Bactria and the Hellenistic one. King Kanishka, whose coronation date has been plotted as sometime between 57 B.C.E. and 230 C.E. with the mid-120s the most likely time, is one of the great names in the history of the development of Buddhism, at least outside Theravada schools of thought. He was the first to use Buddhist images on Kushan coins and is linked to the development of Mahayana Buddhism at his fourth Buddhist council.

The demise of the Kushan empire occurred over the course of about a century, beginning with the division of the empire into eastern and western regions in the early third century. From that time Kushan kings became vulnerable to the military strength of outsiders and fell victim to them. The first region to fall into outsiders' hands were the Bactrian lands once conquered by the Kushans, when in the 230s the Sassanid king Ardashir I defeated the Kushans there and established himself as Kushanshah, king of the Kushans. About 40 years later the Ganges region of India was taken by an indigenous dynasty, the Guptas. Finally in the middle of the fourth century a short-lived dynasty of the Kidarites conquered the last Kushan territory in contemporary Pakistan, subjugating the last of the Kushan leaders, Varahran II.

CULTURE

To date archaeological work in Central Asia has been relatively unsuccessful in distinguishing differences in material culture of the various nomadic peoples of that region. Other than linguistically the Yuezhi probably did not differ significantly from the SCYTHIANS, Xiongnu, or other peoples who lived primarily by herding animals across the steppes and trading with and raiding the settled communities on the periphery. As was the case with these other nomads horses were at the center of Yuezhi material and cultural life. Breeding, training, and trading these animals for necessities were the mainstay of Yuezhi economic life once they had left their Tarim Basin homeland and set off for the west.

An important aspect of Kushan culture that is undisputed is the fact that the Kushans served as important middlemen in the Silk Road trade routes that connected China, India, and Rome. As middlemen the Kushans played key roles in spreading aspects of both material and spiritual culture between east and west, north and south. For example the early centuries of the common era were a time of great proselytizing among Buddhists. As the rulers of all the routes that led out of northern India, the Kushans, whether Buddhist themselves or not, helped disseminate Buddhist ideas and practices, especially to China. Some sources even attribute the carving of the giant standing Buddha statues at Bamiyan, Afghanistan, to the Kushans in the first century; however, this date is contested by others, who believe they were carved during Sassanid rule in the sixth or seventh century.

The great Kushan ruler Kanishka is noted in Indian sources as a patron of Buddhist culture and the sponsor of the fourth Buddhist council in either Jalandhar or Kashmir, which is often cited as the founding date of Mahayana Buddhism; the council itself is not recognized by Theravadans, a competing branch of the Buddhist faith. This connection between Buddhism and a Kushan king leads some experts to describe the Kushan empire as a Buddhist principality. However, this attribution ignores the facts of a large, multicultural empire that covered many times and places. In addition to Buddhism various other religions were practiced in the Kushan-held territories. Both Zoroastrians and devotees of the Hindu god Siva left behind inscriptions showing that their religions were important under the Kushans.

As inhabitants of a crossroads in both time and place the Kushans are well known for their cultural as well as religious syncretism, or combinations of beliefs, ideas, and practices from a variety of sources. The Hellenism that was the legacy of the Greek conquerors of Bactria can be seen in the Greek titles and inscriptions on many Kushan coins, while the portraits on them are often reminiscent of the coins minted in the Roman Empire. Some art historians also point to the representations of the Buddha as a human reflecting the intersection of Hellenistic Central Asian and Buddhist Indian cultures. The Bactrian Indo-Iranian language became the primary language of the empire after the Yuezhi initial victory there and influenced not only spoken and written culture but the entire framework for thought that accompanied language. In addition to Buddhism other aspects of Indian culture that made their way into Kushan culture include some Hindu deities, as the example of Siva shows.

FURTHER READING

Kameshwar Prasad. *Cities, Crafts, and Commerce under the Kuṣāṇas* (Delhi: Agam, 1984).
John M. Rosenfield. *The Dynastic Arts of the Kushans* (Berkeley and Los Angeles: University of California Press, 1967).

Kyrgyz (Black Kyrgyz, Gia-gu, Gia-gun, Gian-gun, Jilijis, Kara-Kirgiz, Kara-Kyrgyz, Khirghiz, Kirghiz, Kirgiz, Qirjis, Xiajias, Xiajiaz)

The Kyrgyz are a Turkic-speaking people who reside in their independent country of Kyrgyzstan and in China. A small number of Kyrgyz also live in Afghanistan and the other Central Asian republics. Traditionally the Kyrgyz were nomadic, moving seasonally in their moun-

---

KYRGYZ

location:
Kyrgyzstan, China, Afghanistan, Kazakhstan, Tajikistan, Turkey, Uzbekistan, Pakistan, and Russia

time period:
Possibly 201 B.C.E. to the present

ancestry:
Turkic

language:
Kyrgyz, an eastern Turkic language most closely related to Altai

tainous homeland to provide grass, fodder, and water to their herds. Even today many Kyrgyz in both Kyrgyzstan and China continue to survive in this ancient manner, which is suitable to the high elevations in which they live.

GEOGRAPHY

The original Kyrgyz, who may or may not be the ancestors of today's Kyrgyz, resided in the upper reaches of the Yenisey River in Siberia. This region is extremely cold in winter and temperate in summer, with plenty of water in the summer provided by the area's river systems. These rivers freeze in the winter, requiring residents to melt snow and ice to acquire water.

Today the Kyrgyz occupy most regions of Kyrgyzstan, but especially the mountainous central area, as well as the Kizilsu Kirgiz Autonomous Prefecture within the Xinjiang Uighur Autonomous Region of China, which is also mountainous. In addition about 20 percent of China's Kyrgyz population live in other areas of the country. There is also a small population of Kyrgyz living in the Vakhan region of Afghanistan, the panhandle in the far northeastern corner of the country that is characterized by the rough terrain of the Pamir Mountains.

Kyrgyzstan itself is divided by the Tian Shan mountains into northern and southern regions, with about 2 million people living in each half. Temperatures in the valleys are very warm and dry in the summer, averaging more than 80°F, and cold in the winter, averaging just below 0°F in January. The mountainous region remains much cooler in summer and gets much colder in winter. Rainfall also varies by region, with the southern Ferghana Valley receiving more than 35 inches of rain per year while the eastern Tian Shan mountains stay very dry with only about seven inches of rain annually.

ORIGINS

Several theories exist to explain the origins of the Kyrgyz people. The most hotly contested theories are those that have been advocated by the first post-Communist president of Kyrgyzstan, Askar Akaev, who claims that Chinese sources describe a Kyrgyz federation or state as early as 201 B.C.E. Akaev also claims that other Chinese sources describe an independent Kyrgyz state from as early as the middle of the first century B.C.E. Most scholars, however, believe these dates are much too early to be referring to a people in any way related to the contemporary Kyrgyz.

Kyrgyz time line

B.C.E.

Fourth and third centuries The Kyrgyz may have been among the northern nomads against which the Chinese build the Great Wall.

201 Chinese sources mention that the Kyrgyz have been incorporated into a governor's territory, implying the existence of a Kyrgyz federation.

ca. 50 Chinese sources indicate the possible existence of an independent Kyrgyz state.

C.E.

618–907 Annals of the Tang dynasty describe the Kyrgyz as tall, with red hair and green eyes; they consider black hair a bad omen.

Eighth century The Orkhon inscriptions, created by the Gokturks in their runic script, list the Kyrgyz as one of the peoples residing in the Yenisey River region of northern Mongolia.

840 The Kyrgyz defeat the Uighur khanate in the Orkhon Valley region of central Mongolia.

995 Possible date for the original composition of the epic poem *Manas*.

10th–13th centuries Some Kyrgyz begin to migrate south from the Orkhon-Yenisey Rivers area in Siberia to the Tian Shan mountains.

1207 The Kyrgyz are conquered by or submit themselves to the Mongols under Genghis Khan.

13th–15th centuries The Kyrgyz are dominated by the Golden Horde and its successor khanates.

1500 Possible date of the compilation of the epic poem *Manas*.

16th century The Kyrgyz establish themselves in the region of contemporary Kyrgyzstan.

1750s Manchu forces defeat the Oirat and the region falls under Qing rule.

Early 1800s The Uzbek khanate of Kokand replaces China as the dominant ruler in Kyrgyzstan.

1876 Kyrgyzstan becomes part of the Russian Empire after Russia's defeat of the Uzbeks.

1917–20 Some Kyrgyz flee to China and Afghanistan in the wake of violence after the Russian civil war.

1920–30s Attempts at collectivization in the USSR force some Kyrgyz to settle in towns and cities; many others remain seasonally nomadic in their isolated mountainous region.

20th century Kyrgyzstan remains one of the poorest and most conservative of the USSR's Central Asian Soviet Socialist Republics.

1990 Kyrgyz-Uzbek ethnic violence takes place in Osh, in the western region of the Kyrgyz Republic; about 230 people are killed and 5,000 other crimes, from rape to looting, are reported.

1991 Kyrgyzstan achieves independence from the Soviet Union with Askar Akaev as president.

(For a continuation of this time line, *see* KYRGYZSTANIS: NATIONALITY)

Another foundation story states that the Kyrgyz originated in the region of present-day northwest Mongolia and that in the third century they migrated northward into the Yenisey River region of Siberia, where they intermarried with DINGLING and Gunn people. From their stronghold in Siberia the Kyrgyz then defeated the UIGHUR khanate in 840 and several centuries later were pushed south again into the Tian Shan mountains. However, this origin story also remains marginal in the literature on the Kyrgyz, most of which states that they originated in the Yenisey River area. Turkic records from the eighth century as well as information about the military victory over the Uighur in 840 both describe the Kyrgyz as "forest-dwelling," indicating that they probably had not formed a centralized political union more than 1,000 years earlier, as posited by Akaev and a few others.

HISTORY

The early history of the Kyrgyz is difficult to discern because they were largely nomadic and did not leave written records; their material culture as seen in the archaeological record largely resembles that of the other steppe nomads of the time. In the periods when the Kyrgyz interacted with literate peoples they emerged briefly into the historical record, usually only to recede again into nomadic obscurity shortly thereafter. Early Chinese annals describe the Kyrgyz as fighters, traders, acrobats, and jugglers, indicating that at least a few Kyrgyz entertainers must have visited the Chinese court. The Turkic Orkhon inscriptions of the eighth century also mention the Kyrgyz as a separate group from the Gokturks and Oghuz TURKIC PEOPLES. Whether any of these people are the actual ancestors of contemporary Kyrgyz remains a contentious issue among historians.

Another problem in discerning the history of the Kyrgyz as separate from their contemporary neighbors the KAZAKHS and UZBEKS is that Kyrgyz tribes were part of the constituent groups that became the Kazakh and Uzbek peoples in the 14th, 15th, and 16th centuries. The case with the Kazakhs is particularly confusing because in Russian they were largely known as *Kyrgyz* to distinguish them from the Slavic Cossacks, or *Kazaky* in Russian. To distinguish between the Kyrgyz-Kazakhs and the actual Kyrgyz tribes, the latter are sometimes referred to as *Kara-Kyrgyz* or "Black Kyrgyz," especially in sources that rely heavily on Russian records from the czarist period.

The Kyrgyz first emerged from historical obscurity in 840 C.E., when they defeated the Uighur khanate in its home in the Orkhon Valley of central Mongolia. At that time the Kyrgyz were described as forest-dwelling barbarians who spoke a Turkic language, and there is some disagreement about whether these people can be seen as the ancestors of today's Kyrgyz. This emergence into the historical record was very brief, with some historians claiming that the Kyrgyz remained in the Orkhon Valley for just a decade, dominating the trade routes of the northern steppes and gathering tribute from several other independent Turkic and Mongol tribes. Others, however, claim that the Kyrgyz did not remain in the Orkhon region at all but retreated to the north again immediately. There is some evidence that the Kyrgyz were conquered by the KHITANS in 929 on the journey westward and were driven north at that time. Probably the truth is somewhere between these two theories, with some Kyrgyz retreating from the Orkhon Valley immediately while others remained until the Khitan victory. In 982 a Persian geography text, *Hudud al-Alam,* described the Kyrgyz as living in the "uninhabited lands of the North," an indication that at least some Kyrgyz tribes began the new millennium in Siberia.

The 10th century is also posited as the earliest date in which the Kyrgyz began their final southward migration toward their present-day homes in Kyrgyzstan and elsewhere in Central Asia. However, the 15th, 16th, and 17th centuries are also put forward by various historians as the periods in which the Kyrgyz began their search for new pasturelands in the south. There is further disagreement about whether the Kyrgyz were defeated by the MONGOLS in their Yenisey River homeland or whether they surrendered to them, thus saving the lives and semiautonomy of most Kyrgyz tribespeople. Whether they were conquered or voluntarily submitted to the Mongols, we can say with relative certainty that during the two centuries between 1300 and 1500 the Kyrgyz were dominated by the Golden Horde and the successor khanates that ruled the steppes in their wake.

The Kyrgyz emerged from their contentious early history in about 1510, by which time they had completed their southern migration, regained their independence, and become the dominant group in the region of contemporary Kyrgyzstan. At this time most Kyrgyz continued to practice their indigenous shamanistic religion, having been isolated from the proselytizing efforts of the various Islamic peoples who had conquered the region prior to their arrival. The first Islamic groups to have a significant effect on the Kyrgyz people were Sufis, particularly Said Mir Jalil, Bakhaveddin Naqshbandi, and Khodja Iskhak. They not only converted many Kyrgyz to their faith but also created Kyrgyz genealogies and histories that accorded with Islamic history. For example, Mansur Al-Hallaj, a 10th-century Sufi master and teacher of the famous poet Rumi, is listed in one of these genealogies as the patriarch of all the Kyrgyz tribes.

In the 17th century the Mongol OIRAT people overran the Kyrgyz on their westward migration toward the Volga River, where they took the name *Kalmyk*. Later in 1750 the Kyrgyz lost their full independence again when the MANCHUS of the Qing dynasty conquered the region; they were followed within a century by the Uzbek khan of Kokand. However, this Uzbek dynasty never completely subjugated the Kyrgyz, some of whom turned to the RUSSIANS for protection and support during an intertribal war between 1835 and 1858. The Kyrgyz Bugu tribe allied themselves with the Russians against the Sarybagysh tribe, who sought Kokand assistance. During this period the Russians built a fort at Aksu, which currently sits on the Chinese side of the border with Kyrgyzstan, and the Kokands established Bishkek, the current capital of Kyrgyzstan.

The Kyrgyz under the Uzbek khanate rebelled at least four times against their overlords between 1845 and 1873, with little support from the Russians. However, some Russian peasants did enter Kyrgyz territory and take over much of the temperate plains areas for farming, pushing the Kyrgyz themselves farther into the mountains with their herds. By 1876 this movement of Russians saw the territory of Kyrgyzstan or Kirghizia fully incorporated into the Russian czar's empire as part of the large Central Asian territory of Russian Turkestan. The Kyrgyz were no happier being subjugated by the Russians than they had been by the Uzbeks, Qing, or Mongols, rebelling in 1916, with many fleeing to China and Afghanistan following the Russian suppression of their revolt. Finally in the 1920s the Kyrgyz people were able to achieve a small degree of recognition of their national and cultural differences from the other Central Asian peoples when their territory was granted the status of autonomous oblast and later autonomous republic. This recognition set the stage for the creation of an autonomous

Kyrgyzstan in 1991 upon the disintegration of the USSR (*see* KYRGYZSTANIS: NATIONALITY).

Life for many Kyrgyz in the Soviet Union did not change significantly from their traditional past. By the 1970s only 14.5 percent of the Kyrgyz had been urbanized, the lowest percentage in the USSR, and many continued to live as nomadic pastoralists in their mountainous homeland. The smaller numbers of Kyrgyz in the other Soviet republics were more incorporated into the urbanized industrial economy than their Kyrgyz SSR cousins, while those in China and Afghanistan remained largely seminomadic in the mountainous regions to which they had fled in the early 20th century.

CULTURE

Economy and Society

The primary economic activity of many Kyrgyz from prehistory through the present is nomadic or seminomadic pastoralism, in which herds of sheep, horses, cattle, camels, goats, asses, or yaks, depending on region and climate, provide the primary source of economic and social wealth. For example yaks were important only in the highest reaches of the Tian Shan and Pamir Mountains. In all regions, however, horses are a Kyrgyz family's prized possession, and horseback riding and other horse-based competitions are an important aspect of any communal activity. A common Kyrgyz proverb states, "If you only have one day to live, you should spend at least half of it in the saddle." In addition fermented mares' milk or *koumiss* is the most valued drink among Kyrgyz, even today.

During Soviet collectivization in the 1920s and 1930s in the Kyrgyz Autonomous Republic, at least three-quarters of all Kyrgyz livestock died or were killed for food. After this period, however, the need for meat and wool in the USSR, combined with the mountainous terrain that prevented its use for large-scale agriculture, allowed many Kyrgyz to continue living their seminomadic existence when the worst excesses of collectivization passed. Sheep continued to provide half the agricultural income of the Kyrgyz SSR in the 1970s, and in 2005 about three-quarters of Kyrgyzstan's population remained rural and tied to the rural economy. Coal mining provided another source of employment in the region; however, many of those jobs were taken by other nationalities living within Kyrgyzstan and the few Kyrgyz who did take up mining remained active in their clans and thus did not cut themselves off from their traditional social networks or structures.

These traditional social networks and structures, which were not destroyed by the Soviet government, are based at the lowest level on bonds forged through both kinship and residence in the nomadic encampment or *aul*. These encampments are made up of about 15 families who all share a common patrilineage, the connections among people who are related to one another through the male line. At a level above the encampment and lineage Kyrgyz people are also connected through the bonds of clanship, which are made up of groups of lineages that all believe themselves descended from a common ancestor. Usually this ancestor is legendary or was invented by the Sufi authors of Kyrgyz genealogies in the 16th century to connect the Kyrgyz people to the history and traditions of Islam.

Because of the continued importance of Kyrgyz *aul*s, lineages, and clans throughout the 20th century, the Kyrgyz were the least likely of all Soviet citizens to marry outside their national group: by 1989 only 6.1 percent of Kyrgyz men and 5.8 percent of Kyrgyz women had done so. In addition the strength of Kyrgyz society was such that in these few mixed marriages most of the resulting families raised their children to speak Kyrgyz and to be members of the Kyrgyz nation. In the post-Soviet world Kyrgyzstan is a multicultural nation, with at least 12 different ethnic groups, but the majority Kyrgyz population, at about 65 percent, continues to be separate from the others.

The Kyrgyz who reside in China as one of that country's 55 recognized national minorities also continue to live largely as transhumance pastoralists, seasonally moving up and down the rugged Pamir Mountains with their herds of yaks. Even as late as the 1980s many of these people would have lived in transportable felt yurts that they disassembled, moved, and reassembled in each of their seasonal encampments. Today, however, most Chinese Kyrgyz families have built permanent homes both in the valleys where they winter with their herds and on the mountaintops where they spend the short summer seasons. Some Chinese Kyrgyz have also taken up agriculture, growing wheat in the summer using ancient irrigation methods adapted to the use of plastic tubes instead of wooden ones. Despite this change the Chinese Kyrgyz remain one of the Chinese minority groups least touched by the outside world. In 1999 many were still illiterate in any language, and only a few had even heard of the independent country of Kyrgyzstan. Watches, clothing, and other consumer goods were evident in Kyrgyz encampments at that time, but such things as plastic bottles and stainless steel utensils were in short supply.

Religion

The Kyrgyz converted to Islam largely under the tutelage of a number of Sufi teachers. The appeal of this form of Islam to these shamanistic nomads has been postulated to result from two specific aspects of Sufism. First, the Sufi belief in saints and saint worship is not unfamiliar to a people who worshipped many of their ancestors for having performed miraculous deeds. Second Sufism placed music at the center of most cultural transmissions, as did the steppe nomads. So it was largely the nomadic singers and oral poets who introduced Islam to the Kyrgyz people. While most Kyrgyz today do not subscribe to any of the Sufi masters, prior to the Soviet takeover in the 1920s several Sufi brotherhoods continued to attract significant numbers of Kyrgyz men. Today the dominant religion of most Kyrgyz is Sunni Islam of the Hanafi school, which is both one of the oldest and one of the most liberal of the four separate Sunni schools of jurisprudence. This religion is more central to Kyrgyz identity in the southern regions of the country, where even the Soviet push for atheism could not separate people from their beliefs and practices, than in the north.

In addition to Islam many Kyrgyz today continue to hold a number of pre-Islamic beliefs as well, especially in the north. Kyrgyz women are rarely fully covered or, especially in the north, seen covering their hair. Women's personal independence, which was important in all nomadic steppe societies, continues to prevail over an interpretation of the tenets of Islam that prevent women from making their own decisions or controlling their own destiny. In addition shamanism and animism both continue to inform many people's religious beliefs and practices. Certain individuals seen as holy men or shamans are still consulted on a regular basis for such concerns as health, prosperity, marriage, and fighting off evil spirits. A belief that all living things, including plants and trees, animals and humans, have a spirit also persists, as do the totemic symbols of reindeer, camels, snakes, and others. A final aspect of Kyrgyz pre-Islamic religious belief that remains today is ancestor worship. Even some urban Kyrgyz in the 21st century continue to honor the spirits of their ancestors through offerings of food or recitations from the Quran to prevent misfortune at the individual, familial, or community level.

While the majority of Kyrgyz residing in contemporary Kyrgyzstan practice either Sunni Islam or this syncretic blend of Islam and pre-Islamic shamanism, animism, and ancestor worship, some Chinese Kyrgyz practice a form of Tibetan Lamaist Buddhism, which they adopted after their migration to China in the early 20th century. Others in China practice Islam or the same syncretic religious blend evident in Kyrgyzstan.

Epic Poetry

The best-known aspect of Kyrgyz culture outside Kyrgyzstan, and perhaps inside the country as well, is the long history of epic poetry recitation and singing by traveling bards called *jomokchu,* from the Kyrgyz term for "fairy tale," or sometimes the Kazakh term *akyn.* The more familiar Russian term of *manaschi* is also sometimes used to refer to these traveling bards but should be reserved only for those who limit their performances to the epic poem *Manas. Jomokchu* of both genders, though primarily men for their greater ability to move around, traveled the country from ancient times to the present telling stories, singing songs, and spreading a relatively homogeneous Kyrgyz oral culture from one end of their territory to another. It was performances such as these that helped to introduce Islam to the Kyrgyz in the 16th century, and many Sufi terms, ideas, and story lines continue to occur in both contemporary works and the performance of Kyrgyz classics. In the 18th and 19th centuries a new generation of oral poets, *zamanachi akindar* or "poets of time," also developed poems and songs to assist the Kyrgyz with the changing times created by Russian colonialism. As had the *jomokchu* of the past, however, they also sang about Sufism; nature worship; the spirits of the sun, water, and trees; and both the foibles of youth and the process of aging. Many bards accompanied themselves on a traditional Kyrgyz three-stringed instrument called a *komuz.*

The best known of the Kyrgyz epic poems is *Manas,* a trilogy that details the lives of three generations of national heroes: Manas himself, his son Semetei, and his son Seitek. Similarly to the Homeric tales of military conquest, travel, and heroism, *Manas* tells the story of the Kyrgyz struggle to maintain their independence against invaders from the east. *Manas* also shares some features with the better known

Images of Manas abound throughout Kyrgyzstan, including this one in the capital of Bishkek of the folk hero slaying a dragon. *(OnAsia/Jean Chung)*

Mongol epic poem, *The Secret History of the Mongols,* in that the heroes of both works are born holding a clot of blood, a sign portending their significant futures; also, dreams serve as important tools for prophesy in both. As is Genghis Khan in *The Secret History,* Manas is depicted as a uniter of his people in order to defeat external enemies.

Manas is different from other Kyrgyz epic poems in that it is always sung without musical accompaniment and the bard acts out the key scenes as she or he sings them. As for other epics, however, *Manas*'s original author and singer as well as the date on which it was composed have been lost to history. A particularly famous bard named Toktogul, who probably lived in about 1500, is believed to have compiled a large number of separate Manas poems, songs, and laments into the trilogy we have today, but where and when these separate pieces originated remain unknown.

In the post-Soviet world *Manas* has emerged among some Kyrgyz scholars, intellectuals, and even ordinary citizens as a key aspect in the construction of an independent cultural identity. In 1995 Kyrgyzstan and UNESCO held five days of celebrations to mark the 1,000-year anniversary of the poem. In addition contemporary maps of Kyrgyzstan note many locations that bear names from the poem, including the country's main airport, Manas.

FURTHER READING

Armin Bauer, David Green, and Kathleen Kuehnast. *Women and Gender Relations: The Kyrgyz Republic in Transition* (Manila, Philippines: Asian Development Bank, 1997).

Hu Zhen-hua and Guy Imart. *A Kirghiz Reader* (Bloomington: Indiana University, Research Institute for Inner Asian Studies, 1989).

Kathleen Kuehnast and Nora Dudwick. *Better a Hundred Friends Than a Hundred Rubles? Social Networks in Transition—the Kyrgyz Republic* (Washington, D.C.: World Bank, 2004).

Roland Michaud and Sabrina Michaud. *Caravans to Tartary* (New York: Thames & Hudson, 1985).

M. Nazif Mohib Shahrani. *The Kirghiz and Wakhi of Afghanistan: Adaptation to Closed Frontiers* (Seattle: University of Washington Press, 1979).

Andrew Wiget and Natalia Musina, eds. *Manas: The Great Campaign: Kirghiz Heroic Epos.* Translated by Walter May (Bishkek: Kyrgyz Branch of the International Centre Traditional Cultures and Environments, 1999).

Kyrgyzstanis: nationality (Kyrgyz, people of Kyrgyzstan)

GEOGRAPHY

With a total land area of 123,342 square miles Kyrgyzstan sits among China, Kazakhstan, Uzbekistan, and Tajikistan. It is roughly the size of the state of Nebraska and is dominated by the Tian Shan and Pamir Mountain ranges, which constitute 65 percent of the total land area. The sharp peaks and dramatic drops of the mountain terrain keep the country well watered, and numerous little runoff streams make the land a sharp contrast with its largely desert-bound neighbor, Kazakhstan.

Unfortunately because of faulty irrigation systems built during the Soviet era much of Kyrgyzstan's water is wasted or contaminated with metals or livestock waste runoff. Furthermore nuclear waste left over from the Soviet era has become a major source of panic within some areas of the country. In 2006 officials from the United States and China met with Kyrgyzstani officials to discuss foreign aid to help deal with problems resulting from nuclear waste contamination.

INCEPTION AS A NATION

The KYRGYZ people have spent much of their lengthy history being ruled by foreign conquerors, but contemporary Kyrgyzstan has been largely shaped by it most recent foreign occupier, the Soviet Union. The volatile relationship began in the 1860s when Russia annexed northern Kyrgyzstan and then later southern Kyrgyzstan. In 1916 Russia attempted to draft all Central Asian males into their World War I forces, but the move was met with widespread uprisings throughout the region. The revolt was brutally suppressed and many Kyrgyz people fled the country.

The Soviets that followed the czars were met with equal hostility as they approached the nation as a tool for Russian advancement. With Stalin's institution of farming collectivization much of Kyrgyzstan's arable land was converted into large state farms on which Kyrgyz peasants were not paid for their labor but rather received a small portion of the total net worth. While other countries suffered greatly under the collectivization, Kyrgyzstan's weakly patrolled borders made it easy for unsatisfied natives to leave the country and many were able to cross into China.

In 1926 Kyrgyzstan became an autonomous republic, and in 1936 it became a full Soviet republic. In the years that followed the Soviets found Kyrgyzstan to be rich with uranium deposits, and uranium mines were consequently developed. In the town of Mailuu-Suu more than 10,000 metric tons of uranium ore was processed between 1940 and 1968. However, as in its neighbor Kazakhstan, tons of uranium waste were dumped near villages, sometimes even in above-ground sites. In addition while education and literacy increased during the years of Soviet rule, Kyrgyz nationalism was quashed as Russian was enforced as the official language and atheism took the place of Islam as the national religion.

In 1990 Kyrgyzstan became the first Soviet republic to elect its own president when Askar Akaev was voted into office. However, as Akaev began asserting Kyrgyz nationalism and challenging the Soviet Communists for control over Kyrgyzstan, the Moscow Communist Party designed a coup to depose Akaev. Their coup failed and Akaev henceforth broke away from the Communist Party altogether. Subsequently Kyrgyzstan announced its independence. Shortly afterward a popular election was held to confirm Akaev's presidency and a constitution was drawn up and officially adopted.

Akaev's presidency and the political careers of his closest associates, however, were rumored to be riddled with corruption. In December

---

KYRGYZSTANIS: NATIONALITY

nation:
Kyrgyzstan; the Kyrgyz Republic

derivation of name:
Kyrg means "forty," *–yz* means "tribes," and *–stan* is the Persian word for "land." Thus Kyrgyzstan translates to "the land of forty tribes."

government:
Democratic republic

capital:
Bishkek

language:
Kyrgyz and Russian are both official languages

religion:
Muslim 75 percent, Russian Orthodox 20 percent, other 5 percent

earlier inhabitants:
Indo-Iranian tribes inhabited most of Central Asia prior to the arrival of the Turkic peoples, including the Kyrgyz.

demographics:
Kyrgyz 64.9 percent, Uzbek 13.8 percent, Russian 12.5 percent, Dungan 1.1 percent, Ukrainian 1 percent, Uygur 1 percent, other 5.7 percent

Kyrgyzstanis: nationality time line

B.C.E.

300,000–200,000 The remains of stone tools suggest the existence of early human inhabitants in the Tian Shan mountains in the area of today's Kyrgyzstan.

2000 The Chinese produce the first written records of a human society in the area known today as Kyrgyzstan.

400–300 Kyrgyz warriors from northwestern Mongolia frequently attack and raid Chinese territories and (it is rumored) are partially responsible for prompting the Chinese to build the Great Wall.

300–200 To escape Xiongnu domination, some Kyrgyz tribes travel to the Yenisey River, which, in Kyrgyz, translates to "mother-river," and to Lake Baikal, which means "rich lake."

C.E.

552 Turkic people known as Gokturks establish the first Turkic state in Central Asia.

840 The Kyrgyz defeat the Uighur khanate in the Orkhon Valley region of central Mongolia.

995 Possible date for the creation of the epic poem *Manas*. The epic survives today and takes three weeks to recite aloud.

1000 The Kyrgyz population is heavily involved in trading along the Silk Road and Islam is spreading through the region.

10th–13th centuries Some Kyrgyz begin to migrate south from the Orkhon-Yenisey Rivers area in Siberia to the Tian Shan mountains.

1207 The Kyrgyz are conquered by or submit themselves to the Mongols under Genghis Khan.

13th–15th centuries The Kyrgyz are dominated by the Golden Horde and its successor khanates. During this time numerous new peoples are introduced into the region, including Turkic, Mongol, and Tibetan nomads and traders.

1500 Possible date of the compilation of the epic poem *Manas*.

1510 The Kyrgyz people obtain freedom from their Mongol rulers and form tribal alliances, as is evident in the appearance of the same tribal names among the Kazakhs, Uzbeks, and Kyrgyz.

16th century The Kyrgyz establish themselves in the region of contemporary Kyrgyzstan.

1600 The Kyrgyz are conquered by the Oirat federation, which becomes known as the Kalmyks.

1750 The Kalmyks give way to the Manchus. The northern Kyrgyz tribes send delegations to the Russians, who have begun to take control of neighboring Kazakhstan. The Russians make no distinction between the Kyrgyz and Kazakhs, calling both *Kyrgyz*.

Southern Kyrgyzstan is conquered by the Kokand khanate of Uzbekistan. This split forever alters Kyrgyz culture.

1863 Northern Kyrgyzstan is annexed by the Russians.

1876 Russia defeats the Kokand khanate and annexes southern Kyrgyzstan.

1890 Russia begins moving Slavic farmers to the river valleys of northern Kyrgyzstan, forcing the Kyrgyz natives to move into the mountains.

1916 Russia attempts to issue a draft for Central Asian males and a revolt erupts throughout the Central Asian territory. Russia violently suppresses the uprisings, resulting in widespread deaths that deplete the northern population by 40 percent. The Kyrgyz natives are deeply shaken by Russia's destructive power, and many flee to China (Kyrgyzstan's weakly regulated borders make it easy for people to move in and out of the country at will).

1918 The Soviets come to power.

1920–40 The Kyrgyz Communist Party is established and dissenters belonging to the Kyrgyz intelligentsia are imprisoned or executed.

(continues)

Kyrgyzstanis: nationality time line *(continued)*

1924 The Kara-Kyrgyz Autonomous Oblast is created within the Russian Federation (called *Kara-Kyrgyz* to distinguish the Kyrgyz from the Kazakhs).

1926 The Kara-Kyrgyz Autonomous Oblast is upgraded to an autonomous republic.

1932–33 All arable land in Kyrgyzstan is utilized for the establishment of large state farms as Joseph Stalin institutes farming collectivization throughout the Soviet territories.

1936 Kyrgyzstan is made a constituent republic known as Kirghiz SSR.

1940–50 Soviet interest in nuclear weaponry leads to the development of uranium mines in Kyrgyzstan. Uranium waste is dumped in 36 sites around the densely populated town of Mailuu-Suu; 11 of these sites are above ground. Residents in the area complain of frequent headaches and nausea, and incidences of blood, stomach, and lung cancers continue to rise 50 years later.

1958 A total of 6,000 cubic meters of radioactive waste is washed away in Kyrgyzstan by flooding.

1968 More than 10,000 metric tons of uranium ore is extracted and processed at two refineries in Mailuu-Suu.

1990 Tension between Uzbeks and Kyrgyz erupts in a fight in Osh that leaves hundreds dead.

Kyrgyzstan becomes the first Soviet republic to elect its own leader. Askar Akaev becomes president; he makes efforts to restore Kyrgyz nationalism.

1991 Russian Communist leaders attempt to carry out a coup to remove Akaev from his presidential office and Akaev breaks all ties with the Communist Party. Kyrgyzstan declares its independence on August 31. The capital, Frunze, named for the Soviet revolutionary Mikhail Frunze, is restored to its pre-Soviet name, *Bishkek,* and Kyrgyz is announced as the official state language.

1993 A constitution is written and the country changes its name to the *Kyrgyz Republic.*

Allegations of corruption within the government result in the dismissal of many government officials, including Prime Minister Chyngynshev.

1995 Thirteen candidates compete in a presidential election. Ten are disqualified, leaving Askar Akaev, Masaliyev, and Medetken Sherimkulov. Akaev receives 72 percent of the votes.

1996 A referendum amends the constitution to give Akaev more power, including the power to dissolve parliament.

1998 An October referendum allows for private property ownership and greater freedom of speech in the media.

1993 the entire government body, except Akaev, resigned after allegations of corruption. In 1995 presidential elections were held again and 13 candidates competed for office. Ten were disqualified, leaving only Akaev and two other candidates. Akaev won with 72 percent of the votes in an election that was deemed fair and free by the international community. However, the 2000 elections were openly deemed invalid by the Organization for Security and Cooperation in Europe (OSCE) because of unfair judicial proceedings against opposition candidates as well as unequal media coverage, which openly favored the current president. As opposition members were arrested and protests were met with police brutality, a group of protesters gathered in Bishkek in 2002 to demand the president's resignation. Tension mounted in the following years, and in 2005 another presidential election was held, in which the opposition claimed only six of the 75 seats. This led to widespread protests over unfairness and corruption within the government. The uprising came to be known as the Tulip Revolution, and in March 2005 three of the 75 new members of parliament were assassinated. When the brother of one of the dead members took his place, he too was killed later in May. All four assassinated parliament members were known to be involved in major corrupt business dealings. In June of the same year protesters stormed the government building and Akaev fled to Russia, where he signed an official agreement of resignation.

A truck crashes, spilling 20 tons of cyanide into the Barskaun River, which locals in the village of Barksaun use for drinking water. Six hundred people seek medical treatment.

1999 Islamic extremists from Tajikistan invade many Kyrgyz villages, taking hostages, including a Kyrgyz general and four Japanese geologists. The hostages are freed after two months of captivity.

2000 Presidential and parliamentary elections are held in Kyrgyzstan, but an investigation by the Organization for Security and Cooperation in Europe (OSCE) deems the elections invalid by virtue of failure to comply with commitments to free and fair elections.

Four American climbers are taken hostage by Uzbek rebels in the Karasu Valley and are held for six days before they escape.

Government troops fight Islamic militants from Uzbekistan, resulting in the deaths of 95 people.

2002 Five people are killed by police during a protest over the sentencing of Azimbek Beknazarov, who was arrested for questioning the president's decision to cede territory to China.

Prime Minister Kurmanbek Bakiev resigns as a result of protests over disputes with police that left six people dead.

Protesters convene in Bishkek, demanding the resignation of President Akaev.

2004 Russia to attends meetings with foreign ministers from Kazakhstan, Tajikistan, Kyrgyzstan, and Uzbekistan in Astana, Kazakhstan.

2005 Kyrgyzstan holds parliamentary runoff elections, in which the opposition wins only six of 75 seats and claims that the election was unfair.

Crowds protest the alleged election fraud. Akaev's spokesman claims that the protests are part of a coup designed to depose President Akaev.

Protesters seize the presidential compound and President Akaev flees to Russia. One month later Akaev officially resigns, and former prime minister Kurmanbek Bakiev is elected the new president.

A top Kyrgyz official announces that Uzbeks residing in Kyrgyzstan in order to avoid violence in their own country are not considered refugees and must leave. The United Nations begins transporting hundreds of refugees to a third country, but Kyrgyz officials transport some of them back to Uzbekistan in direct violation of international treaties on refugees.

The United States and Kyrgyzstan reach an agreement to continue to allow U.S. forces to use Manas (Ganci) air base in Kyrgyzstan as a staging area for missions to Afghanistan.

Former prime minister Kurmanbek Bakiev was voted into office, but his public supporters soon began accusing him of corruption as well, as he ignored the problems of unfairness and deception within the government. He also appeared to have reneged on his promise to transfer many of his presidential powers to parliament. What is important to note, however, is that the Kyrgyzstani people recognize the corruption within their government and continue to press for reforms, exerting pressure that may lead to a more fair and honest government in the future.

CULTURAL IDENTITY

Because of the numerous foreign conquerors who have ruled Kyrgyzstan throughout its long history the country today is a cultural mosaic that has been in development for centuries. Kyrgyz origins are still widely debated, but many agree that the Kyrgyzstanis descended from the MONGOLS, with a possible mixing of SCYTHIANS and Huns. The Hun influence is visible today in the country's tradition of telling stories to the accompaniment of a three-stringed instrument, the *komuz*. "Shuundungutun Jurushu," a song that is sung today, is an elegy for Attila the Hun, reportedly composed by his loyal second in command after the famous Hun's death.

Throughout Kyrgyzstan's history many new ethnicities were introduced to the culture and today ethnic Kyrgyz constitute only 52 percent of the population. RUSSIANS make up 22 percent and UZBEKS another 14.5 percent.

In addition to the 40-rayed sun, one for each of the Kyrgyz tribes believed to have contributed to today's national group, the flag of Kyrgyzstan contains a stylized representation of a Kyrgyz yurt, the traditional tent in which the nomadic Kyrgyz lived.

There are many small communities of other ethnicities, including TATARS and Ukrainians, and even Germans. For a short time there was a community of Jews, but most fled with the collapse of the Soviet rule in Kyrgyzstan.

With Kyrgyzstan's declaration of independence, it became one of only two former Soviet republics to retain Russian as an official language (the other was Tajikistan), thereby becoming an officially bilingual state. The act of retaining the Russian language was meant to convey the sentiment that Russians living in Kyrgyzstan were welcome to stay. Though there have been efforts to promote the use of the Kyrgyz language in public and governmental institutions, Russian is still the first language of many citizens living in urban areas, such as Bishkek, while Kyrgyz is the only language known to many living in the more rural and mountainous regions.

Nonetheless despite centuries of cultural integration the Kyrgyz maintain a strong sense of national identity; this can be seen in their flag, which features a sun with 40 rays that represent the original 40 Kyrgyz tribes.

FURTHER READING

John Anderson. *Kyrgyzstan: Central Asia's Island of Democracy?* (Amsterdam: Routledge, 1999).

Claudia Antipina and Temirbek Musakeev. *Kyrgyzstan* (Milan: Skira, 2007).

Daniel E. Harmon. *The Growth and Influence of Islam in the Nations of Asia and Central Asia: Kyrgyzstan* (Broomall, Pa.: Mason Crest, 2005).

David C. King. *Cultures of the World: Kyrgyzstan* (Salt Lake City: Benchmark Books, 2006).

Erica Marat. *The Tulip Revolution: Kyrgyzstan One Year After* (Washington, D.C.: Jamestown Foundation, 2006).

Rowan Stewart and Susie Weldon. *Kyrgyz Republic* (Hong Kong: Odyssey, 2004).

L

Lahu (Co Sung, Co Xung, Guozhou, Kaixien, Kha Quy, Khu Xung, Kucong, Kwi, Laho, Lahuna, Laku, Launa, Lohei, Luohei, Mooso, Muhso, Museur, Mussar, Musso, Mussuh, Mussur, Namen)

The Lahu are a highlands tribe of Yunnan Province, China, where they make up one of that country's 55 national minorities, as well as northern Thailand and Laos, western Vietnam, and eastern Myanmar. They are subdivided into many different dialect and cultural groups, often denoted with a color term; the two most numerous subgroups are the Black Lahu and Yellow Lahu. The term *Lahu* as well as the term used by this group in Thailand, *Mussur,* refer to hunting, which is an important protein source among the Lahu even to this day.

Chinese experts on the Lahu consider them to be the descendants of the QIANG peoples who resided on the Tibetan plateau in the first centuries of the common era. Migrations during the third to fifth centuries C.E. sent the ancestors of today's Lahu into Yunnan, where they emerged as a separate ethnolinguistic group in the centuries prior to 1000 C.E. This period of consolidation was very brief, for in the subsequent centuries many Lahu groups continued their southern migration process and split into some of the subgroups evident today. Regardless of migration route, however, in the centuries following 1000 most Lahu groups were ruled by DAI leaders and then, during the Ming dynasty (1368–1644), by HAN bureaucrats. During the

Qing dynasty (1644–1911), especially between the 18th and early 20th centuries, some sections of the Lahu rebelled against the centralized power of the emperor. Their weapons were vastly inferior to those of the emperor's army and most rebellions were quickly put down, but rather than subjugation to the emperor, some groups chose migration into Southeast Asia. By the 1830s the Lahu were already well established in Burmese territory and in Laos about a generation later; migrations into Thailand began between 1870 and 1880.

The territory inhabited by most Lahu peoples today is mountainous and not exclusively Lahu; their villages tend to be interspersed with those of many other hill tribes: the AKHA, HANI, YI, and many others. In their mountainous terrain many Lahu continue to engage in swidden agriculture, using fire to burn back primary vegetation to fertilize their fields; each year a new field has to be cut from the forest, making this a difficult subsistence pattern to maintain in the face of increasing population and land pressures. They grow dry, upland rice as their major crop but also corn, vegetables, herbs, melons, pumpkins, tea, chilies, and, often in the second or third use of a field, root vegetables; cash crops among these swidden farmers include cotton, chilies, and opium. In Yunnan Province some Lahu have adopted cultural and economic traits from their Han Chinese neighbors and have given up swidden agriculture in favor of irrigated wet-rice fields and tea and fruit tree cultivation. As their name indicates,

LAHU

location:
The highlands of Yunnan Province, China; western Vietnam; eastern Myanmar (Burma); and northern Thailand and Laos

time period:
500–1000 C.E. to the present

language:
Lahu, a Tibeto-Burman language in the same family as Akha

447

hunting wild animals in addition to gathering forest products supplement the diet and income of some Lahu groups while the most important animals among the vast majority of Lahu are pigs and chickens; all traditional festivals and rituals had to be accompanied by a pork feast.

Although Lahu society is considered relatively egalitarian because it lacks ascribed class, caste, or other hierarchies, there are differences between old and young, men and women. The division of labor is based on these two pairs of distinctions. Only men are allowed to participate in hunting, and they take on the heaviest agricultural tasks such as clearing the land or, in the case of wet-rice agriculture, plowing. Women are generally responsible for the household, including cooking, cleaning, and caring for children and the elderly, but they also collect water and take care of domestic animals. Other agricultural activities, gathering firewood, and the limited trading and marketing undertaken by these groups can be done by men and women equally.

Kinship is not central to the organization of Lahu society as is the case among many other tribal peoples, but bilateral ties through one's mother and father are important for finding an appropriate marriage partner; he or she must be more distantly related than one's second cousin. A few Lahu groups have also adopted the Han practice of patrilineal clan organizations, which arrange rituals and assistance and through which members inherit their surnames. At the time of marriage the traditional residence pattern among the Lahu was that the new groom moved into his wife's family's home, matrilocal residence, and worked for his new in-laws for a period of bride service. Ultimately most couples are able to set up their own nuclear family household, usually in the woman's family's village; the exception to this pattern is the youngest child, especially the youngest daughter, who remains at home to care for aging parents even after the period of a husband's bride service has ended. Whether the household contains a nuclear or extended family, it is considered the primary unit of both production and consumption in Lahu society and is the only unit recognized by the larger village and regional political structure; individuals are seen only as members of their households.

Traditional Lahu religion includes the recognition of a wide variety of natural and ancestral spirits, both benevolent and malevolent. House building requires extensive rituals to drive away any potential evil spirits from the new structure, and established homes are all protected by white and yellow streamers flowing from their roofs. In addition to these spirits the Lahu recognize an all-powerful creator God, Gui Sha, who rules over the other minor spirits of the world. Gui Sha requires animal sacrifices, especially pigs, as well as offerings of other kinds of foods at a number of different times in the agricultural calendar, such as planting and the New Year harvest, as well as whenever a person or animal becomes sick. Today many Southeast Asian Lahu have nominally converted to Christianity through the work of foreign missionaries, but most have simply added the beliefs and practices of their new faith to those of their indigenous religion rather than having replaced them. For these groups Jesus and Mary are seen as sources of blessing equal to Gui Sha and their plethora of local spirits.

FURTHER READING

Gordon Young. *Tracks of an Intruder* (New York: Winchester Press, 1970).

Lakher   *See* MARA.

Lampungese

The Lampungese are the native inhabitants of the territory of southern Sumatra, Indonesia, which approximately coincides with Lampung Province. Today they make up a significant minority in their home region, from 10 to 20 percent, as a result of the *transmigrasi* policy of the Indonesian government, which has moved significant numbers of JAVANESE, BALINESE, SUNDANESE, MADURESE, and others into the province.

The Lampungese are a diverse group with many crosscutting subgroups based on geography, language, and community organization. The three main geographic subgroups are the Abung or highlanders of the northeast, Pubian or lowlanders in the east, and Peminggir or lowlanders on the southern coast. The Abung are probably the best known of these subgroups because when Europeans first arrived on Sumatra they were noted as fierce raiders and headhunters. The Peminggirs are also subdivided into four groups, likewise based on geography, and two subgroups based on community organization, the Pepadun and Saibatin. The former are also known as the ritual throne people because they use this honorific furniture at certain ritual events, such as weddings. Their organization is grounded in kin-based village leadership with two levels of jurisdiction, single village and groups of vil-

---

LAMPUNGESE

location:
Lampung Province, Sumatra, Indonesia

time period:
2500 B.C.E. to the present

ancestry:
Austronesian

language:
There are nine separate Lampungic languages divided into two subgroups, Pesisir with six languages and Abung with three.

lages, both of which have a leader known as a *penyimbang* who upholds traditional law. Either of these *penyimbang* can also become the leader of the clan through various rituals and events. Among the Saibatin *penyimbangs* are not able to become clan leaders because these positions are all inherited rather than earned, as is the case with villages or districts. Because of these various cultural divisions the motto for Lampung Province is "One Earth, Two Cultures."

Despite these various divisions within the larger Lampungese society there are also many similarities that allow both insiders and outsiders to consider them an ethnic group. Probably most important are their shared Lampungic languages. Although these nine Austronesian languages are not entirely mutually intelligible, especially between the Agung and Pesisir subgroups, they share many features, from vocabulary to syntax. In addition all Lampungese peoples have traditionally been horticulturalists, growing rice in newly prepared fields and then using those fields in subsequent years to grow pepper. The Abung fish in the swampy regions of their highland homes while those on the coast also fish and participate in the shipping of produce in interisland trade. Peminggirs also grow cocoa and durian, a large spiny fruit that smells like garbage when it is ripe.

Lampungese social structure is based on the dual principles of kinship and residence. Patrilineal descent, in which fathers hand down membership in their lineage and clan to their children, is the most important factor in the creation of large kin groups. At marriage women move into their husband's lineal village or neighborhood and begin to participate in his lineage and clan rituals. Village membership is also important, especially among Saibatin groups that prohibit village and clan leadership from resting on the same person.

As is the case throughout most of Indonesia the Lampungese consider themselves strict Muslims and as such do not eat pork, try to make a pilgrimage to Mecca at least once in their lifetime, and participate in the wider Islamic world. However, there are also many pre-Islamic beliefs and practices that have remained important within Lampungese communities, such as belief in ghosts and local spirits; the large and costly ritual of *pesta pepadon*, which marks the start of rice season; and *tari tigel*, a war dance that accompanies the sacrifice of a water buffalo. Many rural communities also still have an active *dukun* or shaman who is called during times of illness or misfortune to rid the person or region of demons.

See also AUSTRONESIANS.

Lao (Lao Isan, Thai Lao)

The Lao are the dominant ethnic group of Laos in Southeast Asia; however, far more Lao, called Lao Isan after the region in which they live, reside in the northeastern region of Thailand than in Laos.

GEOGRAPHY

Whether they reside in Laos or Thailand, or even Cambodia or Vietnam, the Lao live in the lowlands and river valleys, leaving the hillsides and mountains to other ethnic groups. Within Laos the government has created three broad categories of citizen: the Lao Lum include the dominant Lao and reside in the lowlands, while the Lao Thoeng and the Lao Sung live on the slopes and mountaintops, respectively. Despite the terms *Lao Thoeng* and *Lao Sung* most ethnic groups in these categories are not linguistically or culturally related to the Lao or other Lao Lum groups, who are Tai speakers; most Lao Thoeng are Mon-Khmer speakers and Lao Sung are Tibeto-Burman or HMONG-Mien speakers. As lowlanders the Lao occupy the most productive farmland in the region and usually live in clusters along the Mekong and other major rivers. In Thailand's Isan region the Lao occupy the same kind of terrain.

Generally Lao territory has a tropical monsoonal climate where it rains heavily from May

Durians are native to Indonesia and have been a staple crop there for centuries, if not longer. Recently Thailand has outstripped Indonesia as the leading exporter of the fruit, and today it is available in large cities throughout the world. But beware: Even among those peoples who eat it regularly, such as the Lampungese, the fruit's smell is considered offensive. *(Shutterstock)*

LAO

location:
Predominantly Thailand and Laos with smaller numbers in Vietnam and Cambodia; since the 1970s a Lao diaspora has lived in France, the United States, Australia, and elsewhere

time period:
0 C.E. to the present

ancestry:
Tai-Kadai speakers from Yunnan Province, China

language:
Lao, a tonal Tai-Kadai language with many borrowed words from Sanskrit and Pali

Lao time line

C.E.

0 Many Tai-speaking peoples begin migrating out of southern China and into Southeast Asia, where they settle in Thailand, Laos, Vietnam, and Cambodia.

1353 Fa Ngum founds the first Lao kingdom, Lan Xang.

1373 Oun Hueun takes over at the death of his father, Fa Ngum.

1479 The Vietnamese invade Lan Xang, interrupting more than 100 years of growth and development in the Lao kingdom.

1500 Wisunarath gains power in Lan Xang.

1520 Wisunarath dies and is succeeded by Photisarath.

1550 Photisarath dies and is succeeded by Sai Setthathirat I, who rules until 1571.

1637 After about 60 years of Lao subjugation at the hands of the Burmese Souligna Vongsa reestablishes the Lao kingdom of Lan Xang.

1694 Souligna Vongsa is succeeded by a nephew, who seizes the throne with Vietnamese assistance.

1707 Lan Xang is divided into two separate kingdoms.

1713 A third kingdom, Champassak, withdraws from Lan Xang and the kingdom ceases to exist. This begins a period of Thai domination of the Lao.

1827 King Anouvong rebels against the Thais but ultimately fails to reunify the Lao kingdoms.

1828–29 More than 100,000 Lao people are relocated as prisoners of war and Vientiane is sacked by the Thais; many significant treasures are removed to Bangkok, where they remain today.

1893 The French annex Lao territory on the east bank of the Mekong River, in what is Laos today.

1901–02 Northern Lao rise up against the French colonizers. At the same time southern Lao begin a 36-year insurgency against the French.

to October, is cooler and drier from November to February, and then is hot and dry for the last two months of the year. The Mekong River, the major waterway in Lao territory, does not often flood its banks the way other large, tropical rivers do because it contains a natural regulator in the form of Tonle Sap, a lake in central Cambodia that expands exponentially during the rainy season and then contracts during drier periods, keeping the Mekong's flow fairly consistent throughout the year.

ORIGINS

The Lao have several origin myths that explain their formation as a separate ethnic group and their location in Southeast Asia. One of these tales tells the story of Khun Burom, whose father was the creator God Thaen. Thaen sent his son to reign on earth in the area around Dien Bien Phu, Vietnam. One of Khun Burom's heroic deeds was to free the earth from the trouble caused by a giant gourd, from whose midst all the earth's people and animals sprang. Khun Burom also had two wives and seven sons, one of whom, Khun Lo, became the founder of a Lao kingdom at Luang Prabang in what is today northern Laos. Later Lao kings often looked to this tale to explain the basis of their own power by claiming descent from Khun Lo. As is the case of the Khun Burom myth other tales also speak of a giant piece of vegetation that endangers the world and must be cut back by the Lao semidivine heroes. One such story tells of a giant creeper vine that begins to choke off other plants and so the creator God Thaen sends a human couple to cut it back, both of whom die in the effort. Still other myths tell of a Toad King who kills the creeper vine by shooting an arrow into it; he too dies as a result of his actions.

The actual origins of the Lao are the migrations of the DAI-speaking peoples from the Yunnan region of China. As was the case

1930	The Communist Party of Indochina is established by Ho Chi Minh, and some Lao leaders begin to use the language of Marxist class warfare.
1946	King Sisavang Vong, a supporter of the French in Laos, is crowned.
1954	Laos attains independence from France and Royalists and Communists go to war.
1959	Sisavang Vatthana becomes king on the death of his father, Sisavang Vong.
1960s–75	Civil war between the Royalists and Communists continues in Laos, and the United States bombs Laos in an attempt to cut off Communist supply lines in the region.
1975	The Pathet Lao, or Lao Communists, win the war in Laos and establish a people's democracy or Communist state in the country: the Lao People's Democratic Republic.
1986	Following the USSR and China, the Communist government of Laos begins experimenting with private enterprise.
1989	Laos holds its first elections since the 1970s, although all candidates have to be acceptable to the Communist Party.
1990	Start of a Swiss development project in Laos that introduces new strains of rice and other new techniques to improve food production.
1994	A bridge over the Mekong River and linking Laos and Thailand is completed, bringing to fruition a security and friendship treaty signed by the two countries three years earlier.
2000	Laos celebrates 25 years as a Communist state.
2002	Parliamentary elections are held and one candidate is not a Communist Party member.
2004	Laos is the chair nation of the Association of South-East Asian Nations (ASEAN) and hosts the organization's annual conference.
	At the end of the Swiss development project rice production in Laos has increased by 1 million tons; the program contributes to rice self-sufficiency in many regions of the country.
2006	Parliamentary elections in Laos see the selection of two independent candidates and 113 candidates from the ruling Communist Party.

with the THAIS and many smaller Tai-Kadai-speaking peoples, the Lao migrated to their current Southeast Asian homes in the past millennium. The reasons for this migration remain speculative but probably include a combination of factors including population pressure, ethnic strife, warfare, and natural disasters. In the first phases of this southern migration the Lao seem not to have been distinguished from the other Tai-speaking communities that were on the move at the same time.

HISTORY

The first historical reference to the Lao people is in the 14th century when Fa Ngum established the first Lao kingdom, Lan Xang. With the assistance of the Khmer kings at Angkor Fa Ngum put all of what is today Laos and eastern Thailand under his reign. The first date we have for his activities is 1353, and for 20 years after that the Lao ruler consolidated his power and drew others into his sphere of interest. He was followed in 1373 by his son, Chao Ounhueane, who further advanced the kingdom's bureaucracy and spread the official state religion, Theravada Buddhism. One of his most important accomplishments was a complete census of his kingdom, which showed that 300,000 Lao people lived among 400,000 people from other ethnolinguistic groups. As a result of this document Ounhueane took the new name of *Samsenethai*, which means "Three Hundred Thousand Tai People." Subsequent kings similarly fostered the development of a unified Lao kingdom and Buddhist civilization. This process was interrupted in 1479 by the brief incursion of the VIETNAMESE on Lao territory, but they were soon repelled and the kingdom flourished once again.

The stability fostered by the rulers of Lan Xang allowed for the development of an indigenous literary tradition at the start of the 16th century. Under kings Wisunarath, Photisarath, and Sai Setthathirat I, who collectively ruled from 1500 until 1571, the origin tales of Khun Burom, the Toad King, and all the others were written down in a new Lao script, called *tham*, and became a part of Lao mythohistory. It was during this period that Khun Lo began to be seen not only as a mythological character but as an actual ancestor of the Lan Xang kings. The Lao kings also began to seek closer ties to the Thai rulers at Chiang Mai, or what was then known as Lanna, famous for their own literary tradition, and commissioned the writing of at least 27 unique Lao morality tales and a Lao version of the Hindu epic the *Ramayana*, known in Lao as *Pharak Pharam*.

In addition to literary sharing and developments under Photisarath the Lao engaged with their neighbors in other ways as well. During his reign Lan Xang went to war against the BURMANS of Myanmar and the Thais of Ayutthya. Photisarath's son, Setthathirath, even took over the Thai state at Lanna during his father's reign at Lan Xang, though he lost it after 1548, when he had to leave the city to return to the Lan Xang capital of Luang Prabang and take up his dead father's throne. Subsequently Setthathirath moved the capital from Luang Prabang to the current capital of Laos, Vientiane, then known as Vien Chan; he also had to deal with two separate invasions of his territory in 1565 and 1570.

Setthathirath's death in 1571 led to further invasions of his territory and even the destruction of his new capital. The Lao kingdom fell into the hands of other Southeast Asian peoples, mostly Burmans from the territory of present-day Myanmar, until 1637, when Souligna Vongsa or Suriyavongsa was able to expel the

outsiders and begin rebuilding the Lao territories. He signed treaties with both the Thais and Vietnamese to solidify his kingdom's borders and was a staunch defender of Lao literary traditions and his state religion, Buddhism. His reign, which lasted until 1690, is considered a second Lao golden age and the direct inheritor of the intellectual tradition established by Wisunarath in 1500. As his predecessor had he commissioned new courtly works, such as the *Phongsavadan Lan Xang* or Chronicle of Lan Xang of 1656, as well as numerous poems.

Souligna Vongsa was succeeded in 1694 by one of his nephews, who illegally seized the throne with the assistance of a Vietnamese military regiment. Many members of his royal family refused to succumb to the Vietnamese presence and the kingdom experienced a period of chaos before splitting into northern and southern kingdoms in 1707; the two kingdoms had their capitals at Luang Prabang and Vientiane, respectively. By 1713 the chaos had not abated with this division, and a third independent kingdom, known as Champassak, split off from the south. This event usually marks the end of Lan Xang in most chronicles of the Lao.

The 18th century saw the Lao people largely dominated by kings and princes of Thai descent. The period was feudal in nature and most Lao were landless serfs working on the farms of wealthy Thai nobles. Nonetheless several Lao histories point to the continued ethnic identity of the Lao as separate from the Thais, despite their linguistic and other cultural similarities. In 1827–28 a Lao hero, King Anouvong, led a widespread and successful rebellion against the Thai overlords, although even his forces were eventually overrun by the numerically and militarily superior Thai armies. As a result of Anouvong's actions in the following two years more than 100,000 Lao people were forcibly removed from their homes and relocated across the Mekong River. More than 6,000 Lao homes were destroyed and much of the wealth from Vientiane was carried out of the country; for example, the Emerald Buddha was taken to Bangkok, where it continues to be held today.

In Laos

The end of the 19th century in Southeast Asia was marked by increasing activity by the French; merchants, traders, colonial administrators, and Roman Catholic missionaries all became active in the region at this time. Some of the territory occupied by the Lao people in what has become Laos, mostly land on the east bank of

---

Souligna Vongsa

Souligna Vongsa was the last king of Lan Xang, or what is now Laos, and catalyzed trade with Europe. Vongsa seized the throne in 1637 after defeating competing warlords, and to secure his reign he promptly wiped out any potential rivals by banishing one of his brothers to Vietnam, the other to the priesthood, and his cousins to Siam. He is said to have been a severe ruler who lived an austere and unadorned life but nevertheless produced stability in the turbulent Lan Xang following the previous king's death. In 1641 he welcomed traders from the Dutch East India Company, who marveled at the country's riches, as well as its vast numbers of monks and monasteries. The country's economy flourished as it traded benzoin resin, which is a component of perfumes; *lac,* which is the component ingredient of shellac; and musk with the European traders. Souligna Vongsa died in 1694 without an heir, and Lan Xang consequently fractured into three smaller kingdoms: Vientiane, Luang Prabang, and the Kingdom of Champassak.

the Mekong, was annexed by the French in 1893. The west bank, however, remained in the hands of the Thais. As they had against the Thai kings who subjugated them, the Lao people continued to rebel during the French colonial period. In 1901–02 Father Kadouad led rebellions in the central area of Lao territory. Starting in the same year the people of the south rose up under the leadership of Ong Keo and Ong Komadam; their insurgency lasted for 36 years and generated continuous strife for the French colonizers. Starting in 1930, when Ho Chi Minh established the Communist Party of Indochina, some of the rebellion in the Lao territories took on the rhetoric and ideology of Marxist class struggle, though nationalism and democracy remained the central rallying cries of most leaders.

During World War II the JAPANESE occupied Southeast Asia, but for most of the period allowed the French administrators to continue their work unimpeded. It was only in 1945 just before their final surrender that the Japanese expelled the French. By 1946 after a brief period in which the Lao and other Southeast Asian peoples thought they would attain independence the French returned to the region and began to reestablish their colonial project with the export of resources for France's rebuilding effort and the convertion of souls to Catholicism. They experienced the same kind of resistance they had prior to the war and by 1950 had given nominal independence to the Lao, Cambodian, and Vietnamese peoples within the framework of a larger French Union of Indochina.

Most of the resistance to French colonialism among the Lao did not cease with the formation of the French Union. The Lao People's Liberation Army and Neo Lao Issara or Free Lao Front continued their political and military activities, including electing a prime minister and naming a minister of defense. By 1953 just before the Geneva Accords ended the first Indochinese War between France and Vietnam, the French granted both Laos and Cambodia full sovereignty. Within the newly independent country of Laos sovereignty did not end the violence of the previous decades but rather initiated a civil war between supporters of the king and his government and supporters of the Pathet Lao or Communists. As part of the worldwide struggle to contain communism the United Stated provided arms and logistical support to the Royalists. During the Vietnam War the United States continued to support the Royalist Lao government under King Sisavang Vong while the Pathet Lao allied themselves with the

The Emerald Buddha is actually carved from green jasper, although many sources mistakenly refer to it as jade. Three times a year the monks at Wat Phra Kaeo in Bangkok change the statue's clothing to be appropriate for the season; it is pictured here in its winter cloak. *(Shutterstock/Byron Busovicki)*

National Liberation Front and the North Vietnamese. As part of their war effort the United States bombed and defoliated portions of Laos that were used by the Communists as training grounds and as a trail for moving war materiel into South Vietnam from the north. According to several sources Laos during the 1960s and 1970s became the most heavily bombed country in world history per capita.

As was the case in Vietnam the Communists claimed ultimate victory in the war in Laos and established the Lao People's Democratic Republic in December 1975. To this day the Lao people in Laos are ruled by the Communist Party. They experienced a loosening of the party's economic grip on the country in 1986 when a small degree of privatization was allowed, but in the most recent parliamentary elections held in 2006 only two candidates from outside the ruling party were elected; both ran as independents.

In Thailand

While the late 19th and early 20th centuries were experienced by the Lao living in Laos as a period of European colonialism, for the Lao living in the Isan region of Thailand this period was largely a continuation of their 18th century experience. Thailand was able to remain free of European colonizers and local Lao leaders in the Isan region primarily maintained sovereignty in the northeast, providing only tribute and sworn allegiance to the Thai kings. This changed somewhat as the French consolidated their power in Southeast Asia. In reaction the Thais began replacing Lao nobles with government agents, both to show the French they had control over their own people and to prevent the Lao minority from turning to the French for assistance in overthrowing the government in Bangkok. This situation has largely continued to this day when more than 23 million Lao Isan make up a large minority in the country.

CULTURE

According to the Lao themselves there are three cultural features of all Lao people: eating sticky rice, living in houses on stilts, and listening to music made by the *khaen*, a bamboo woodwind instrument used in traditional Lao performances called *mohlam*.

The first of these features is based on the common experience of the Lao as lowland rice farmers. Upon their migrations into Southeast Asia from Yunnan Province, China, the Lao began the process of turning the low-lying regions along the Mekong and other rivers into extensive rice fields. For the Lao in Thailand this way of life is very difficult because of soil with low fertility and poor water retention. In Laos as well most Lao have been very poor farmers for most of their history. It has only been since about 2004 and the completion of a 14-year project by a Swiss development agency that the region has become self-sufficient in rice production. Both regions focus most agricultural activities on the *japonica* strain of rice, which produces a very sticky or glutinous grain, while other strains are grown as a cash crop along with kenaf, a jutelike product, and corn, cotton, peanuts, sugar, and cassava. In addition to these subsistence and cash crops the Lao Isan, especially those living on the Khorat Plateau, which is unsuitable for growing rice, also raise large numbers of cattle and buffalo.

Sticky rice, as a food item, must be soaked in water for about six hours before being steamed to make it soft enough to eat. Once it has been prepared, the Lao generally eat it with their hands, making small balls of rice that they dip into foods categorized as "with rice," usually salty or spicy sauces made from beef, fish and fish sauce, chilies, garlic, and lime. This kind of communal eating with the hands is part of the ethnic identification of people as Lao and contrasts with the style used by Thais and other local ethnic groups who tend to rely on utensils to eat less glutinous varieties of rice, especially jasmine.

As a result of their residence along the Mekong and other rivers of Laos and northeast Thailand the Lao also characterize their own people as those who live in houses raised on stilts by about one and a half yards. These houses are generally made of bamboo or wood and are roofed with thatch or, in the case of wealthier families, corrugated iron. Underneath the family's living space most households also keep their domestic animals, such as cattle, buffaloes, chickens, and pigs. Recently in the Isan region of Thailand even wealthier families have been putting most of the wealth obtained from work overseas or other participation in the cash economy into elaborate cement houses. Some of these are not built on stilts, though many are. Each village contains around 90–100 of these households, clustered together and crossed by narrow lanes to facilitate communication and movement. Villages are located along rivers about three miles apart, leaving room between them for rice paddies, ponds, forests, and, in some places, grassy plains for grazing cattle and buffalo. In Laos about 85 percent of the population still lives in these kinds of rural conditions, though the percentage of Lao may be slightly lower since they tend to dominate the government and other urban sectors of the economy. In Thailand the Isan region is the country's most densely populated region and one of the poorest; as a result, most Lao Isan continue to live this kind of rural village life.

The groups that occupy these Lao stilt houses can be either nuclear or extended families, made up of just parents and their children or several generations of the same family. Regardless of the makeup households always constitute the primary unit of production and consumption; in other words, they are made up of people who share food and work together on a single plot of land. Generally at the time of their marriages young men move into their wives' families' homes in a pattern called matrilocal marriage. Some of these newly formed couples may move into a new home later, usually after the birth of several children, but the youngest daughter and her husband usually remain to care for her elderly parents and then inherit the family home and land. Families who own enough land to support several nuclear family groups may create small homesteads in which each sister and her husband build a separate home in a compound shared by her sisters and then all the sons-in-law remain to work the large family holding.

Although residence favors women, the kinship structure generally among the Lao is more equal and can be characterized as bilateral. In this system, which most Western societies favor, both mother and father are equal sources of relatives. This kinship system tends to favor the creation of wide networks of kin and in-laws among those who are currently living rather than very deep ties to ancestors back in time. In order for a man to have his children socially recognized as his own, in other words, for them to be considered legitimate in Lao society, he and his family must pay bridewealth to the parents and relatives of his new wife. Usually this payment is made in societies that favor patrilocal marriage residence, in which women move from their natal homes into their new husbands' residences, and the payment is seen has compensating the woman's parents for the loss of her labor. In Lao communities bridewealth is seen primarily as a way of legitimating children, and upon divorce, which was quite rare prior to the onset of the Communist regime in Laos, if bridewealth had not been paid, women retained ownership of the couple's children.

The division of labor among the Lao means that both women and men must work extremely hard to provide enough food for their families. Prior to the advent of internal plumbing, which is still absent in many rural areas of Laos, women were responsible for carrying water, in addition to pounding rice for household use; tending pigs, chickens, ducks, and other small animals; caring for children and the elderly; and doing all household chores. Many women also keep a small family garden in which they grow vegetables, fruits, and herbs for household use and spend time in the evenings weaving cloth or baskets or engage in other household craft activities. Men deal with the family's larger animals, such as cattle and buffaloes, including using the latter to plow their fields. They also clear new fields, cut and carry firewood, and build and repair houses, fences, and other structures. Both women and men, in addition to children, participate in transplanting rice seedlings from their initial plot into larger rice fields and take part in the rice harvest.

Most rural Lao spend their days in rice fields such as these, located in Houamuang, northeastern Laos. *(AP/Dabid Longstreath)*

Since the earliest days of the Lan Xang kingdom in the 14th century the Lao have been ardent believers in Theravada Buddhism, which was introduced by the KHMERS from Angkor. Theravada Buddhism, or Doctrine of the Elders, is an ancient form of Buddhism that was unaffected by a reform movement within Buddhism that emerged in the first century of the common era. It is based on a canon of texts called the Tipitaka and written in Pali, an Indo-Aryan ritual language, and focuses on the achievement of nirvana through living the monastic life. Sometimes the reformed and nonreformed Buddhist schools are called Mahayana and Hinayana; however, these terms, meaning "Greater" and "Lesser Vehicle," respectively, are pejorative and judgmental and are avoided today, especially the latter. Today Theravada schools dominate in Southeast Asia, and so the sect is sometimes called Southern Buddhism, while the reform movements, which passed through Tibet and other regions of China, Japan, and Korea, are sometimes called Northern Buddhism.

As Theravadans the Lao were traditionally strong supporters of monks, nuns, and the monastic life generally. In Laos with the victory of the Communist Party and establishment of the

Lao People's Democratic Republic or Lao PDR religion was officially banned and Buddhist land and institutions taken away and closed. In recent years, however, the government of the Lao PDR has tried to foster a redevelopment of Buddhist values in an attempt both to legitimate their rule over their people and to quell the desire among many Lao to attain the lifestyle of consumption they see on Thai television.

In Isan religion has always been central to many people's lives and giving gifts to monasteries remains an important way of attaining both religious merit and social prestige. Most Lao Isan men in the past spent at least a short time around the age of 20, usually three months, living as a monk in a monastery and taking the lowest level of vows, though few remained as monks forever. This practice is not as ubiquitous as it was in the past, but it is still important for at least one son in a family to do so. Both in the past and today the monastic life was one way for very poor men to advance socially, and monasteries and nunneries remain important social mechanisms for relieving poor families of having to provide land for all their offspring.

In addition to Buddhism ancestor and village spirits are an important aspect of the Lao religious pantheon. There are also 32 different organ spirits or *kwan*s that each Lao inherits from his or her parents, 20 from the father and 12 from the mother. Each *kwan* is believed to protect a specific bodily organ, and unique ceremonies must be utilized to revitalize and thank these organ spirits at auspicious times of life such as leaving home, traveling, or just undertaking a new activity. The Lao believe that sickness is caused when these spirits leave the body and thus health and even prosperity and good luck require their proper balance and goodwill. Shamans and *paahm*s, religious specialists who can go into trance and communicate with these various spirits, can be found in all Lao Isan villages and even in many Lao villages in Laos, despite the prohibitions against religion more generally. Many villages also have exorcists, spirit mediums, and other ritual specialists who can be engaged to communicate with ancestors, village spirits, natural spirits, or other supernatural beings.

The temperament favored by Lao society is one that has been described by outsiders as "laid back"; often the region's very high temperatures and humidity have been pointed to as the reason for this temperament and its concomitant slow lifestyle. Probably more important than the climate, however, is the Lao fear of losing face through lack of control. Confrontation; displays of negative emotion, especially anger; or inability to control one's bodily movements, which results in a relative lack of hand gesturing or other body language, are all avoided as much as possible because they would bring shame upon the adult or older child who engaged in them. Touching another person's head and pointing one's feet at another person are also forbidden and can result in an immediate loss of prestige and merit. At the same time the Lao are also described as fun-loving people who work out of necessity rather than the love of work for its own sake. Joking, laughing, storytelling, and communal eating are all highly valued among the Lao as activities that make life worth living.

FURTHER READING

Helen Cordell. *Laos* (Santa Barbara, Calif.: Clio, 1991).

Grant Evans. *Lao Peasants under Socialism* (New Haven, Conn.: Yale University Press, 1990).

Grant Evans, ed. *Laos: Culture and Society* (Singapore: Institute of Southeast Asian Studies, 2000).

Grant Evans. *A Short History of Laos: The Land In Between* (Crows Nest, Australia: Allen & Unwin, 2002).

Geoffrey C. Gunn. *Rebellion in Laos: Peasant and Politics in a Colonial Backwater* (Boulder, Colo.: Westview Press, 1990).

Carol J. Ireson. *Field, Forest, and Family: Women's Work and Power in Rural Laos* (Boulder, Colo.: Westview Press, 1996).

Khamchong Luangpraseut. *Laos and the Laotians* (South El Monte, Calif.: Pacific Asia Press, 1995).

Vatthana Pholsena. *Post-war Laos: The Politics of Culture, History, and Identity* (Ithaca, N.Y.: Cornell University Press, 2006).

Stanley J. Tambiah. *Buddhism and the Spirit Cults in North-East Thailand* (London: Cambridge University Press, 1970).

Laotians: nationality (people of Laos)

GEOGRAPHY

Laos is a landlocked Southeast Asian country slightly larger than Great Britain; it shares borders with Thailand, Myanmar, China, Vietnam, and Cambodia. Thickly forested rugged mountains cover more than 70 percent of the country, with some rivers, plains, and plateaus. The Mekong River forms a large part of the western boundary with Thailand, and floodplains of the river provide the country's primary agricultural areas. Mountains form most

---

LAOTIANS: NATIONALITY

nation:
Lao People's Democratic Republic (Laos or Lao PDR)

derivation of name:
Chinese for "venerable" or "old"

government:
Communist one-party state

capital:
Vientiane

language:
Lao (official), 90 ethnic languages, French, English

religion:
Buddhist 65 percent (state religion), animist 32.9 percent, Muslim and other 0.8 percent, Christian 1.3 percent. Animism is also common among the mountain tribes; Buddhism and spirit worship coexist.

earlier inhabitants:
Various Tai peoples

demographics:
Ethnic makeup is uncertain. The government divides the people into groups according to the altitude at which they live rather than ethnic origin: lowland Lao Loum 68 percent, upland Lao Theung 22 percent, highland Lao Soung including the Hmong and the Yao 9 percent, ethnic Vietnamese/Chinese 1 percent.

Laotians time line

C.E.

1353 Ancient Lao kingdom of Lan Xang is established under King Fa Ngum.

1421 Death of Fa Ngum's son, Samsemthai; kingdom deteriorates into warring factions.

1520 King Phothisarat moves capital to Vientiane.

1637 King Suriya Vongsa begins 57-year rule, Lao's golden age.

1694 Death of King Suriya Vongsa; breakup of Lan Xang begins.

1885 Lan Xang now a number of states under Siamese or Thai control.

1893–1907 Siamese-French treaties make Laos part of French Indochina.

1896–97 Joint Chinese, British, and Siamese commissions define current Laos borders.

1907 Franco-Siamese Treaty defines the current Lao border with Thailand.

1918 The first Lao-language textbooks are published and basic Lao history books follow in the 1920s.

1945 World War II; Japan occupies Laos; French regain control.

1945–49 Increasing instability; growing resistance to French rule.

1949 Laos recognized as an "independent associate state" of France.

1950 Communist-inspired Pathet Lao (PL) government formed with Vietnamese support.

1953 Laos gains full sovereignty from France.

1957 Government of National Union, the first coalition government.

1958 Committee for the Defense of National Interests, a right-wing U.S.-backed party, takes over the government.

1960 Election alleged to have been rigged by the U.S. Central Intelligence Agency. The government is forced to resign.

1961 U.S. President Kennedy announces he will use the military to resist "Communist takeover of Laos."

1962 Geneva Convention agreement for independent, neutral Laos. Vietnamese army remains in Laos in defiance.

1964 Series of coups and countercoups between Communist and right-wing factions.

1964–73 Indochina War intensifies; the United States bombs eastern Laos.

1973 A cease-fire is negotiated and the Provisional Government of National Union (PGNU) is formed.

1975 Right-wing leaders flee Laos, the PGNU is dismantled, and the Lao People's Revolutionary Party (LPRP), a Communist party, takes control of the government and institutes a strict socialist regime.

1975–77 LPRP embarks on policy of "accelerated socialism." Practice of Buddhism is restricted and a huge exodus of Lao citizens begins.

1986 Liberalization of foreign investment laws begins a gradual return to private enterprise.

1987–88 A three-month border war with Thailand.

1991 A new constitution is adopted.

1993 National Biodiversity Conservation Areas (NBCA) set up: 21 percent of the country's land area is set aside, potentially to be developed into a national park system at some point.

1997 Laos is granted full membership in the Association of South-East Asian Nations (ASEAN).

2005 United States normalizes trade relations with Laos.

2008 Save the Children reports that 69 percent of Laotian children lack basic health care.

of the eastern border with Vietnam and most of the northern half of the country. Ethnic LAO are the traditional residents along the Mekong River and lowland areas and make up around 60 percent of the total population. In the north are located many mountain tribes known as Lao Sung (highland Lao), including HMONG, Mien, YAO, AKHA, and LAHU, all of whom migrated from Myanmar, Tibet, and southern China within the last century. Upland Lao, the Lao Theung, live on midaltitude mountain slopes, principally the KHMU, Htin, and Lamet peoples. There is a distinct rainy season from May to November, followed by a dry season from December to April.

INCEPTION AS A NATION

The Lao people are part of the Tai group of cultures. Exactly where the Tai people originated is a matter of some debate. The majority of scholars support the theory that they were from the Nanzhao kingdom, which was founded during the eighth century C.E. in present-day Yunnan Province of southwest China (see BAI). It is generally thought that the MONGOLS' defeat of Nanzhao drove a major migration of the Tai southward into the area of present-day Southeast Asia.

Two other major ethnic groups already occupied Southeast Asia in the first millennium C.E.: the Dvaravati civilization and the Angkor empire. The Dvaravati were a MON group who lived around present-day central Thailand. The dominant ethnic group in the Angkor empire were the Khom people, the ancestors of the present-day KHMERS in Cambodia. Angkor's center was located in present-day northern Cambodia.

As the Tai groups began to migrate south from China, they had contact with the Dvaravati and Angkor. Several important trade routes passed over the northeastern regions between the Dvaravati and the Khom. The Mon and Khom both used indianized forms of writing, which became the basis of the Lao and many other Tai scripts. They were also the conduit for large-scale conversion to Buddhism among the ancestors of the Lao people.

The present-day Lao developed chiefly from the Tai kingdom of Lan Xang (sometimes called Lan Chang), which moved into the region now known as Laos around the 14th century, under King Fa Ngum. *Lan Xang* is literally "Million Elephants," referring to the kingdom's great wealth and splendor. Fa Ngum was probably originally a vassal of Angkor, but his kingdom was able to develop and achieve independence mainly because of the rise of the Ayutthaya and Sukhothai kingdoms in Siam (Thailand), who posed sufficient threat to Angkor to distract the Khom armies from marching into Lan Xang and eliminating Fa Ngum.

For 300 years Lan Xang included large parts of present-day Cambodia and northeast Thailand, as well as all of what is now Laos. One of the earliest contacts with the West occurred in the form of a Dutch merchant, who arrived in Vientiane in November 1641. Contact began to increase gradually over the following hundred years. However, the Lao society of Lan Xang remained far more insular than the cosmopolitan Siamese in Ayutthaya.

From about 1695 the Kingdom of Lan Xang gradually fell apart into between three and four separate kingdoms at various times, each under a different rival leader. Bloody feuding continued until the Siamese king Taksin intervened from 1788 onward. He gradually annexed all of Laos. By 1782 the Lan Xang kingdom had all but disappeared and many Lao families had been forcibly relocated by the Siamese to Saraburi in central Siam. A large Lao community remains in the Saraburi region to this day.

In 1827 Chao Anou, the vassal king of Vientiane, led an uprising against his Siamese overlords in Bangkok. This was swiftly put down by 1828, when the Siamese captured Chao Anou and took him to Bangkok, where he soon died. Laos remained a vassal of Siam until the late 19th century. Nonetheless this incident remains a central legend in the development of a Lao nationalism, pointing to a time when the Laotians resisted the control of their Siamese cousins.

In 1893 French colonial powers forced a treaty on Siam, in which Laos and Cambodia were ceded to the French. In return the French guaranteed they would not invade the central regions at the core of Siam. Laos and Cambodia joined Vietnam to become known as French Indochina. The Franco-Siamese Treaty of 1907 defined the current Lao border with Thailand.

In the early 20th century pagoda schools began to borrow and propagate the Siamese nationalist idea of monarchy, Buddhism, and state as a means of creating a Lao national consciousness. The first Lao-language textbooks were published in 1918 and basic Lao history books followed in the 1920s. Maps and flags were also introduced as national symbols in these early schools. In the 1930s the Lao elite began to travel to Hanoi and then to France for higher education.

Several challenges during World War II pushed Laos further toward a growing national consciousness and desire for autonomy. First Siam changed its name to *Thailand* in 1939, a clear reference to the Tai forbears of numerous ethnic groups in the region. This was a clear call for a unified pan-Tai state, to which Laos had no intention of submitting. Second the Thais also fought a brief border war with the French around the Mekong region, having long been incensed at losing Lao territory to the French around the turn of the 20th century. They succeeded in regaining some of their former territory along the west side of the Mekong River, thereby reducing the size of the Lao homeland. Third to counter the Thai challenges to French rule in Laos the French drew up a plan to promote Lao nation building. They opened many new schools, published magazines praising the glories of Lao culture, and ran competitions in Lao culture, history, and poetry. At the same time the French exported a great deal of their resources from Indochina and focused on their homeland after they were forced to capitulate to Germany in 1940.

In March 1945 the JAPANESE overthrew the French, and the Lao government declared that it was once again an independent nation, albeit under Japanese occupation. After the Japanese surrender in October 1945 the Lao Issara (Lao Freedom) movement formed and began to agitate for full sovereignty. The movement forced the king to abdicate in late 1945, and in 1949 the French signed a treaty handing sovereignty back to the Lao people.

Persistent poverty fueled the growth of the Communist movement through the 1950s. Amid growing instability and successive coups in the 1960s the Communists gradually took control and Laos was thrust into the Vietnam War. Massive bombing campaigns failed to rout the Communists. In 1975 the Communist Pathet Lao took control of the government, ending a six-century-old monarchy and instituting a strict socialist regime closely aligned to Vietnam. A gradual return to private enterprise and liberalization of foreign investment laws began in 1986. Laos became a member of ASEAN in 1997.

CULTURAL IDENTITY

Although the ethnic Lao do not constitute 100 percent of the population of Laos, they are the dominant forces in the country's political and economic life. Laotian cultural identity largely derives from Lao traditions; the country's other ethnic groups must either adapt or withdraw.

That Luang temple was built originally in 1560 by King Setthathirat of Lan Xang. It has been destroyed and rebuilt several times since that period and thus has served as a powerful symbol of the nation since 1991, when the Communist hammer and sickle were dropped in favor of more local imagery. *(Shutterstock/Juha Sompinmäki)*

LAPITA CULTURE

location:
From New Guinea to
Samoa and Tonga

time period:
1500 B.C.E. to ca. 0 C.E.

ancestry:
Austronesian

language:
Probably Proto-Oceanic

In general the Lao are seen as easygoing and accepting of situations. The common saying *por pen nyang*, translated "never mind," is used in a wide variety of situations; it can also mean "we cannot do anything about it," "it will be okay," or even "it is no big deal." As well as acceptance of one's fate this idiom expresses the high value Lao people place on maintaining smooth, harmonious relationships rather than confrontation and debate. To a large extent this attitude arises from Buddhism, which is intimately interwoven into much of Lao culture. Letting go of desire and being at peace with fate is a religious ideal.

The Lao do not easily distinguish their religion from their culture. Folk Buddhist concepts pervade both Lao and Laotian culture. When the Communists gained power, they initially attempted to purge the nation of Buddhism, but by the 1980s had concluded that Buddhism was Laotian culture, not religion. The Lao have traditionally avoided the accumulation of personal wealth. Status and position are symbols of a person's having good karma, that is, being a good person. Containing emotions is socially expected. Direct requests are rare and refusals totally impolite. The golden That Luang Buddhist temple in the heart of Vientiane is a potent symbol of Lao national identity.

The Laotian economy is built on agriculture. The principal crop is a form of rice not widely known outside the region: sticky (glutinous) rice. Sticky rice is the staple in almost every meal, sweet, or savory. It distinguishes the Lao people from their Chinese, central Thai, Cambodian, and Vietnamese neighbors, who all eat fragrant rice. It is also a symbol of Laotian communal life. Planting and harvesting crops are communal affairs. Preparing and eating meals are communal so that the Laotians almost never eat alone. One could almost say that much of Laotian national identity somehow involves sticky rice. Another potent symbol of Laotian identity is the mouth organ known as the *khaen*, a musical instrument made of bamboo reeds. It remains a highly popular part of traditional and contemporary music in Laos and a symbol of what it means to be Laotian.

FURTHER READING

Arthur J. Dommen. *Laos: Keystone of Indochina* (Boulder, Colo.: Westview Press, 1985).

Grant Evans. *A Short History of Laos: The Land In Between* (Chiang Mai, Thailand: Silkworm Books, 2002).

Christopher Kremmer. *Stalking the Elephant Kings: In Search of Laos* (Chicago: Independent Publishers Group for Allen and Unwin, 1997).

Khamchong Luangpraseut. *Laos and the Laotians* (Los Angeles, Calif.: Pacific Asia Press, 1995).

Vatthana Pholsena. *Post-War Laos: The Politics of Culture, History, and Identity* (Ithaca, N.Y.: Cornell University Press, 2006).

Martin Stuart-Fox. *A History of Laos* (London: Cambridge University Press, 1999).

Lapita culture

Lapita is not the name of a group of people as they would have referred to themselves but rather a reference to an ancient Pacific culture that most archaeologists believe was the predecessor of the present-day cultures of the POLYNESIANS and MICRONESIANS. The name is derived from an archaeological excavation in New Caledonia that took place in 1952 during which a large amount of the distinctive pottery that would signify Lapita culture was found. During the dig a word in the local language meaning "to dig a hole" was misheard as *lapita* and the name stuck. In addition to pottery excavations of the Lapita culture have produced dog, pig, and chicken bones, though the people relied at least as much on fish for protein as on these domesticated animals. Thus far evidence of pottery and other artifacts has been found in an arc-shaped area of the Pacific as far east as coastal New Guinea, stretching through the Bismarck Archipelago to the Solomon Islands and Vanuatu as far south as New Caledonia and eastward through Fiji to Samoa and Tonga.

The origins of the people who developed this style of pottery and culture are probably south China and perhaps Taiwan (*see* AUSTRONESIANS; TA-P'EN-K'ENG CULTURE). However, there are some archaeologists who argue that the Lapita cultural form is merely an evolutionary advancement of cultures that were already existent on the Bismarck and Solomon Archipelagos. Regardless of the origins from the earliest recorded sites in New Guinea, the Bismarcks, and Solomons Austronesian speakers with their distinctive pottery and domesticated plants and animals traveled throughout much of the western Pacific as far as Samoa. As seafarers the people of the Lapita culture tended to remain close to the coastlines of the various islands they inhabited. In the Solomon Islands and New Guinea they may also have been restrained from settling inland or inhabiting the larger islands by the prior population of MELANESIANS. Even today artifacts can still be found in the coastal sands of many of the islands that hosted Lapita culture. In fact the first piece of what became known as Lapita pottery was found in 1909 by a Catholic priest who was walking on the beach on Watom Island in the Bismarck Archipelago.

Lapita pottery is distinctive for its designs: masses of swirls and repeated geometric patterns. Some of these patterns are in the shape of humans, faces, and animals while others are merely abstract shapes. Interestingly the farther east the pottery is found, especially at its outer limit on Samoa, the less it is covered with these distinctive shapes. The reason for this lack of design and for the absence of this pottery in the farther reaches of Polynesia is still unclear. One hypothesis is that the clay available in these eastern islands was much less suitable for making pottery because it broke easily when fired. Another theory is that pottery was simply replaced by wooden vessels because the wood that was available was easily carved. Despite a lack of Lapita-style pottery some eastern Polynesians themselves, such as some MAORI of New Zealand, point to the designs of their tattooing as evidence of a direct relationship between them and the makers of Lapita pottery.

Laz (Chan, Chanuri, Chanzan, Colchian, Colchidian, Laze, Lazepe, Lazi, Lazian, Tzan, Zan)

The Laz are a subgroup of the GEORGIANS of the central Caucasus. A large number of Laz also live in northeast Turkey, where they are called *Lazi* to distinguish them from the generic term *Laz*, which refers to the Black Sea Turks more generally.

The Laz are an ancient people probably descended from the COLCHIANS, who were described in the Greek myth of Jason and the Golden Fleece. A Byzantine historian of the sixth century, Agastias, makes the claim that the Laz and Colchians were one and the same, and thus the origins of the Laz are sometimes said to be in the eighth century B.C.E., when the Colchians were first mentioned in a text from the Urartean kingdom. The term *Laz* came into fashion, replacing *Colchians,* in the first century B.C.E., when the Laz kingdom, Lazica or Egrisi as it is also known, was founded in the wake of the fall of the Kingdom of Colchis. Egrisi became a vassal of the Romans in about 66 B.C.E., when Pompey conquered the region. Egrisi or Lazica remained within the Roman sphere of influence for hundreds of years, and the inhabitants adopted Christianity in the fourth or fifth century.

Lazica was made famous through the writings of Procopius, a sixth-century Byzantine historian who described at length the fighting between the Byzantines and Sassanids in the middle of the sixth century (*see* PERSIANS, SASSANIDS). These struggles were often called the Great Lazic War or the Great War of Egrisi, because these two large empires were fighting on and for the territory of the Lazian state in what is today western Georgia. For 20 years from 542 to 562 the Laz suffered off-again, on-again fighting until finally the Persian king Khosrow signed the Fifty Years of Peace, recognizing Byzantine sovereignty in the region.

Lazica remained a Byzantine province for the next 200 years or so until the non-Christian kingdom of Abasgia, which originated to the north of the Laz, conquered it at the end of the eighth century. Georgian sources often refer to the acts of Leon of Abasgia as having liberated Lazica from the Byzantines and having created a joint Egrisi or Lazica-Abkhazian kingdom; Leon made his capital Kutaisi in contemporary western Georgia. In the ninth century the state church of this kingdom withdrew from the authority of the Patriarch of Constantinople and joined with the East Georgian Church, and thus the independent history of Lazica came to an end with the beginning of a unified Georgian national history (*see* GEORGIANS: NATIONALITY).

The Laz today on both sides of the Turkey-Georgia border are no longer Christian but Sunni Muslim, the heritage of conquests of the Turks at various times in the 15th, 16th, and 17th centuries. In rural regions they produce tea, hazelnuts, corn, collard greens, and beans. They are also keen pastoralists, and both meat and milk products contribute greatly to the Laz economy. In Turkey, where they constitute a large but unrecognized minority, the Laz are frequently the butt of ethnic jokes and their language is not taught in schools, published, or broadcast legally. The fewer Laz who live in Georgia are often combined with the related MINGRELIANS because of their linguistic and cultural similarities.

Lazi   *See* LAZ.

Lepcha (Mutanchi, Rong, Rongpa, Ronke)

The Lepcha are a small ethnic group residing in Bhutan, Nepal, Sikkim, and a few other states of India. Their homeland, which they call "hidden paradise" or "land of eternal purity," is the area of central Sikkim, where they are considered

LAZ

location:
Southwest Georgia and northeast Turkey

time period:
Eighth century B.C.E. to present

ancestry:
Possibly Colchian

language:
Lazuri, a South Caucasian or Kartvelian language, related to but mutually unintelligible with Svan and Georgian; it is more closely related to Mingrelian

LEPCHA

location:
Bhutan, Nepal, and the Indian states of Sikkim and West Bengal

time period:
Unknown to the present

ancestry:
They are usually referred to as the aboriginal population of Sikkim; however, there is some linguistic evidence of a migration from Tibet in prehistory.

language:
Lepcha, Rong-aring, or Rongring, a Tibeto-Burman language

indigenous. Today they make up a relatively small minority in that state and live primarily in the north. The name *Lepcha* is derived from a derogatory nickname given to them by the Nepalese, *Lap-che*, meaning "inarticulate speech"; however, today the name is in general use and does not bear this negative connotation.

Lepcha history prior to the 17th century remains a mystery to this day. Their own mythology states that their homeland was Mayel, a kingdom on Khangchendzonga, the world's third-highest mountain, and that upon their entry into Sikkim they absorbed the region's aboriginal peoples, the Naong, Chang, and MON. Linguists and physical anthropologists believe they may have originated in Tibet, Myanmar (Burma), or even Mongolia. By the time the BHUTIA migrated into Bhutan and Sikkim in the early 17th century, the Lepcha were the sole inhabitants of the region, having either assimilated or pushed out any prior inhabitants, if there were any. The migrating Bhutia found them living as subsistence farmers who supplemented their garden foods with hunting and gathering. They lived primarily in canyons and their names for themselves, *Rong pa,* meaning "people of the ravine," and *Mutanchi,* meaning "Mother Earth's people," point to their way of life.

Starting in the 17th century the Lepcha began a period of significant change. The migration of the Bhutia, who sought residence in the high Himalayas, drove the Lepcha into the valleys and plains at lower elevations. The Bhutia also introduced their own version of Red Hat Buddhism, which many Lepcha combined with their own religious beliefs and practices. This century also saw the invention of an indigenous script for the Lepcha language, one of the few tribal languages in the world to have an indigenous script. Legend states that it was invented by Thikung Mensalong, a Lepcha intellectual who had been strongly influenced by Buddhist monks, although the story that the script was a gift to the Lepcha from Mother Earth, Itbu-moo, is also prevalent in some Lepcha communities. Contemporary scholars tend to credit the third Bhutia king of Sikkim, Chador Namgyal, with the script's invention; that attribution would date it to the 18th century rather than the 17th.

Today the main economic activities engaged in by the Lepcha are farming cardamom and oranges for sale on the market and subsistence agriculture; growing wet and dry strains of rice, corn, buckwheat, millet, which is fermented for the local alcoholic beverage rather than eaten, and tomatoes, chili peppers, and other vegetables. Gathering and hunting continue where possible but fish remain marginal to their diet. Some wealthier Lepcha are able to maintain herds of dairy cattle and goats, which are sacrificed and eaten rather than milked, and pigs are commonly kept by Lepchas of all economic classes.

The most common religion among the Lepcha is Buddhism, legacy of the Bhutia efforts at proselytizing in the 17th century and beyond, but some Lepchas in recent decades have converted to Christianity. In addition most Lepcha continue to practice at least some aspects of their own indigenous belief system, Mun. Mun is an animistic religion that recognizes the centrality of both familial and nature spirits and gods, especially those of the mountains, rivers, and forests. One of the most important gods is Yeti, god of the hunt, known as the abominable snowman in English, who is believed to own all wild animals. Central to this religion is animal sacrifice, especially of goats and pigs, and this practice has continued into the 21st century despite the prohibition against animal sacrifice in the Buddhist faith. The Lepcha seem to be able to live with this contradiction as easily as most Western Christians are able to reconcile moneylending and the accumulation of wealth with their own faith, which prohibits both practices. The Lepcha also engage the services of shamans, who are ritual specialists with the ability to communicate with the spirit world to learn the causes of illness and other problems and to discover what sacrifices or other means are necessary to end the misfortunes.

The Lepcha kinship system is patrilineal: everyone inherits membership in his or her lineage and clan from the father, father's father, and so on. However, the matrilateral relatives, those on their mother's side, are also important and generally speaking the same kinship terms are used for close relatives from both sides; the only exception are mother's brothers, who have their own term. Matrilateral kin are counted back as far as four generations while on the father's side it is nine generations. Sexual relations and marriage with anybody within these degrees of relatedness are absolutely prohibited as incestuous; therefore every Lepcha must be extremely knowledgeable about his or her most extensive kinship ties on both mother's and father's side.

Prior to the modern era most Lepcha married very early, prior to age 14 for girls and 16 for boys, in unions that were organized by the young people's families. While most people are marrying somewhat later these days, the groom's family continues to give at least nominal bridewealth gifts to the bride's to thank them for raising their daughter and to compensate them for the loss of her household labor, for at marriage she is generally required to move into her husband's home, called patrilocal residence. Families with more resources often allow the new couple to set up a new household in a pattern called neolocal residence. Intermarriage with the Nepalese and Bhutia is also much more common today than it was in the past.

Within Lepcha families there is a gendered division of labor for only a small number of activities; for example women are absolutely forbidden to kill animals. For most activities, however, including working in the fields, women and men work together. It is more common for women to spin yarn and men to weave baskets and mats, but there is no taboo against these activities for the opposite sex and both sexes tend to be able to engage in these activities equally well. With increasing intermarriage with the Nepalese this pattern has tended to break down in recent decades and men's and women's activities have tended to become more segregated.

In mid-2007 the Lepcha of Dzongu, northern Sikkim, have burst onto the global scene because several of their leaders have been engaged in an indefinite hunger strike in protest over the planned hydroelectric dam project on the Teesta River. A number of leaders of Affected Citizens of Teesta (ACT), Concerned Lepchas of Sikkim (CLOS), and the Buddhist Sangha of Dzongu began their strike in June 2007 to call attention to the thousands of people who will be displaced from homes, villages, and farmland if the dam projects are undertaken. It remains to be seen whether the 22 separate projects slated for the Teesta River, which drains the Himalayas and runs into the Brahmaputra River in Bangladesh, will commence or not.

Lhoba (Luoba)

The Lhoba are the smallest of China's 55 recognized national minorities with between 2,000 and 3,000 members; they were recognized as such only in 1965. Some sources indicate that the ADI people of India are a subgroup of Lhoba, while others claim that there are closer to 200,000 Lhoba in China, but there seems to be no consensus on these matters. This entry will be limited to the small number of recognized Lhoba in China.

The Lhoba do not use this ethnonym but refer to themselves with clan or geographic terms. The name *Lhoba* means "southerners" in Tibetan and points to the long relationship they have had with this larger, more dominant population in their region. Lhoba is not a written language so instruction and all other documents are in Tibetan or HAN Chinese. The Chinese state considered the Lhoba to be oppressed in their relationship with the TIBETANS, and it is true that Tibetans did not intermarry with them or allow them to live in certain areas. At the same time, however, the Lhoba did not encourage intermarriage either, and there were castelike relations between different segments of the Lhoba community for which intermarriage was forbidden. The *maide* and *nieba* castes remained quite separate, with the former allowed to own slaves from either the latter group or outside the Lhoba people entirely. The name *nieba* even means "those who cannot lift their heads casually" and thus refers to their inferior position in society.

Traditionally the Lhoba were both farmers and hunters who traded wild animal products, including hides, musk, and paws, for wool, salt, grain, tea, and farm implements. All Lhoba families also kept domesticated animals such as goats, sheep, and, most important, chickens, and women gathered many wild forest foods from fruits and tubers to medicinal herbs. Weaving and working with bamboo have always provided some access to cash, despite depictions in some Chinese sources of the Lhoba as isolated and primitive until they were recognized as a national minority in the mid-1960s. One of the reasons for this depiction is that the Lhoba generally eschew the wearing of shoes. Another reason is that their local religion was largely animistic, recognizing the spirits of the sun, moon, animals, mountains, rocks, trees, fire, water, and their dead ancestors. They also used animal sacrifice as an offering to these various spirits, and haruspication, which is a form of divination that uses animal entrails to discover information about the future. In the case of the Lhoba they examined rooster livers to discern whether good or bad luck was in the future. These two religious rituals involving animals required the work of two separate ritual specialists: *myigyi* killed roosters and divined information from their livers, while *nyiubo* sacrificed other animals as a form of exorcism to cure illnesses or bad luck. Some sources indicate that these practices have gone by the wayside, while others claim that although the Chinese state has

---

LHOBA

location:
Southern Tibet, China, and possibly Arunachal Pradesh, India

time period:
Unknown to the present

ancestry:
Tibeto-Burman

language:
Lhoba has two dialects, Yidu and Bogar, and is a Tibeto-Burman language

LHOTSHAMPA

location:
Bhutan

time period:
Nineteenth century to the present

ancestry:
A variety of ethnic groups all with Nepalese origins

language:
Nepali

tried to eliminate them, they have continued to be important to rural Lhoba life.

Lhotshampa (Bhutanese Nepali, southern Bhutanese)

The Lhotshampa people are Nepalese migrants who began moving to Bhutan in the late 19th and early 20th centuries; legal immigration ceased in 1959 when the Bhutanese government forbade it. In Nepal they were members of a variety of different ethnic groups but all spoke Nepalese and most were Hindus. They settled largely in the southern part of the country, as their collective name in the language spoken by the dominant BHUTIA indicates; it means "people of the southern border" in Dzongkha.

Politically and socially the Lhotshampa have experienced significant discrimination in their adopted homeland almost since their arrival. This came to a head after the enactment of Bhutan's Citizenship Act of 1985, which required, among numerous other things, that in order to become a citizen individuals had to "be able to speak, read and write Dzongkha proficiently" and "have good knowledge of the culture, customs, traditions, and history of Bhutan." The Lhotshampa also claimed that the 1988 census did not accurately count their numbers and that many other government policies discriminated against them, such as the necessity of wearing traditional Bhutia clothing in public offices and temples. Perhaps most worrying to these people is the change in language policy in 1988; among the three official languages recognized until that time, Dzongkha, English, and Nepali, only Dzongkha was to receive that status in the future.

Starting in the early 1990s protests in southern Bhutan were broken up by police and the military and many activists were jailed or exiled. Between 1988 and 1994 but mostly during 1991 large numbers of Nepali-speaking people fled Bhutan and entered eastern Nepal. More than 100,000 people were housed in United Nations High Commissioner for Refugees (UNHCR) camps and remain there to this day. A verification process jointly sponsored by Bhutan and Nepal for determining actual refugee status began in 1994 but was able to make little headway; the entire process was disrupted in 2003 when the Bhutanese members of the verification teams were attacked by frustrated camp residents, and there is no indication that the process will be resumed. Within Bhutan the relatives of people considered activists, either for their actions within the country or for having fled to Nepal, have been "retired" from the civil service. This does not affect only Lhotshampa; a number of Bhutia and SHARCHOPS have also been involved in prodemocracy movements in the country, but the majority of "retirees" are from the Lhotshampa, making such actions appear to be part of a wider strategy of ethnic cleansing within Bhutan.

As for most people in Bhutan, the traditional economic activity of the Lhotshampa was agriculture. Most were sedentary farmers with only a few engaging in swidden or slash-and-burn agriculture, which predominates among other Bhutanese groups.

Li

The Li people are one of China's recognized 55 national minority groups with a name taken from the local term for "mountains." They have lived on Hainan Island off the southern coast of China for about 3,000 years. It is believed they migrated from the Chinese mainland, perhaps to escape either population or political pressure. The HAN people arrived from the mainland about 800 years after the Li and have been in control of the region for many centuries. As a result most Li communities migrated away from the coastal plains of Hainan and into the Wuzhi Mountains. Today many Li can both speak and read Chinese and have adopted other aspects of the dominant culture, but at the same time, Li identity remains important to most people.

Hainan, which is approximately the size of Taiwan, is located at about the same latitude as Hawaii and thus has a tropical climate with copious rainfall. As a result the agricultural Li can harvest their subsistence and cash crops three times in good years. Their staples are wet rice, corn, and sweet potatoes while cash crops include coconuts, cocoa, coffee, cashews, cassava, betel nut, and a wide variety of tropical fruit, including pineapples, bananas, and mangoes. Bamboo is an important product for construction and furniture and both kapok and sisal are also grown for use and trade.

Li communities are generally made up of people who are related by blood or marriage and work together on communal lands. Households consist of nuclear families, but it is these larger settlement units that are the primary productive units. As it is among the Han, Li women move into their husbands' family home in patrilocal residence; however, rather than at marriage this move does not occur until the woman becomes

LI

location:
Hainan Province, China

time period:
1000 B.C.E. to the present

ancestry:
Southern Chinese

language:
Li, a Zhuang-Dong language in the Sino-Tibetan phylum; most also speak Chinese

pregnant. Li husbands also have to pay bride-wealth to their wife's parents to compensate them for the loss of her labor, or, in the case of poor men, they must go to work on their in-laws' land for a period of bride service.

Many other aspects of Li culture differ from that of the Han. For example their week is 12 days long with each day bearing the name of an animal. In addition one of the most powerful individuals in each community is the shaman, who is able to communicate with the spirit world of dead ancestors, the natural world, and a variety of gods. Shamans both request favors from the spirits and thank them for their kindness. In the case of illness or bad luck a shaman will go into trance to discover the spiritual source of the misfortune and to find out what must be done to propitiate the spirit and thus bring about a cure or an end to the bad luck. Usually illness is the result of an individual or family's ignoring duties to provide gifts and food to their ancestors or disobeying an important social norm. In the past headhunting was

Li women prior to the mid-20th century received tattoos as part of their coming-of-age rituals, when their lineage and other social identifying features were marked upon them to prevent kidnapping. Tattoos received later in life indicated marital status, residence, and other social markers, as do this woman's marks on her face, wrist, and ankles. *(OnAsia/Luke Duggleby)*

an important way of providing gifts to these spirits, as was animal sacrifice, while today the Chinese government claims that blood sacrifice has been eliminated.

Another important cultural trait that has gone by the wayside is tattooing. While Li men usually had just three blue rings tattooed on their wrists, women received tattoos on their necks, faces, and throats as part of their coming-of-age rituals. Throughout their lives women usually also received tattoos on their legs and arms as well. According to early Western sources on these practices the Li could identify a woman's family, lineage, village, social position, and identity through her tattoos.

Liao   *See* Gelao; Khitans.

Limbu

The Limbu are a tribal group living in eastern Nepal, from the Arun River to the Sikkim border. Until the 18th century they lived in small tribal communities away from the dominant events that were contributing to the political, economic, and social landscape of south Asia. In the 18th century some of their lands and villages were ruled by the kingdom of Bijayapur, which was itself swallowed up by the dominant Shah family in the late 18th century. At that time many Limbu lost their clan and lineage landholdings to more powerful Hindu migrants, who had the support of the king, leaving many families with only the subsistence lands they were currently working. Even to this day many Limbu clans are still struggling with the social system, which favors the literate and well-educated Hindus in land claims over their own informal land-tenure system that had prevailed prior to the consolidation of Nepal as a kingdom in 1769 (*see* Nepalese: nationality).

Most Limbu today continue to rely on subsistence agriculture as their primary economic activity. Wheat, rice, and corn are their primary crops for both personal use and trade or sale, while household gardens provide vegetables, fruits, and herbs. Agricultural work entails a fairly strict division of labor with men engaging in plowing and women in planting; both sexes as well as children assist at harvest time. Children may also help with weeding and keeping birds away from the ripening crops. Some Limbu men have turned to the Indian and Nepalese armies as an external source of cash as well as respect and honor within their own communities.

LIMBU

location:
Eastern Nepal

time period:
Unknown to the present

ancestry:
The Kiranti, a Mongol people who have been subdivided into Limbu and Rai groups

language:
Limbu, a Tibeto-Burman language with four separate dialects

In addition to the control of land in the past the Limbu kinship system is an important social marker that dictates marriage, association, and assistance. The most important kinship principle is patrilineal descent. Groups of people related through common male ancestors are considered to be "related by the bone" and must not marry each other and must go to the assistance of others within the group. Both patrilineages, made up of people related to a common male ancestor about four or five generations back, and clans, made up of groups of lineages and founded by a common male ancestor, usually mythological, are important groups within this system and contribute to each individual's social identity. The death of a member of one of these groups, but especially within one's own lineage, pollutes all members of the group and leads to a number of food taboos, such as avoiding salt and oil, and other prohibitions. Women, who must marry men from outside their own lineage but become honorary members of their husbands' lineages, also become "impure" at the death of a husband's lineal relative.

The main religion within Nepal is Hinduism, which is dominated by ideologies and practitioners from the Brahmin caste. For the Limbu, however, Hinduism provides only one part of their religious outlook. The most important indigenous religious practice is blood sacrifice, which requires the ritual killing of an animal and its offering to local gods and spirits. Ancestral, forest, and other spirits also inhabit the Limbu cosmology and require attention through rituals overseen by indigenous religious specialists.

LISU

location:
Western Yunnan Province, China; eastern Myanmar (Burma); and northern India and Thailand

time period:
Unknown to the present

ancestry:
Tibeto-Burman

language:
Lisu, a Tibeto-Burman language

Lisu (Anung, Che-nung, Khae Lisaw, Khae Liso, Lasaw, Lashi, Lasi, Le Shu O-op'a, Lesuo, Leur Seur, Li, Lihsaw, Lip'a, Lipo, Lip'o, Lisaw, Li-shaw, Lishu, Liso, Loisu, Lusu, Lu-tzu, Shisham, Yaoyen, Yawyen, Yawyin, Yeh-jen)

The Lisu are a highland people of Yunnan Province, China, where they are one of that country's 55 recognized minority groups; northern India; Thailand; and Myanmar. They probably originated in the eastern region of the Tibetan plateau and migrated into Yunnan Province prior to the start of the common era about 2,000 years ago. Once settled in Yunnan the Lisu had a mixed relationship with the dominant HAN majority. The two peoples could live side by side for generations without any conflict; they engaged in cultural- and material-exchange relationships and even intermarried. However, in some locations and at some points in time the two peoples engaged in raids, kidnapping, warfare, slavery, and the mutually reinforcing political behavior of suppression and rebellion. These two patterns existed simultaneously until the Chinese Communist revolution in 1949 transformed the way of life for everybody in China. By 1956 indentured servitude and slavery were abolished, all debts to landlords and others had been canceled, and the state had begun the long process of land reform.

During the 19th century land and political pressures in Yunnan led some Lisu individuals, families, and even communities to move south into India and Southeast Asia; the first Lisu groups arrived in what was then called Burma just after the turn of the 20th century. For the most part Lisu communities established themselves in the high elevations of their new homes, between 4,265 and 9,845 feet, although there are a few Lisu villages interspersed among Han, THAIS, and others in the lowland valleys. As a result of these migrations the Lisu inhabit an expansive territory that also contains many other highland ethnic groups such as the AKHA, HMONG, and KAREN. One internal consequence of this residence pattern is that no large group recognizes itself as the Lisu; instead each village is its own relatively autonomous political unit with few ties to any other unit, Lisu or otherwise.

These Lisu villages generally contain about 25 houses, although they can be as small as five houses and as large as 150. At least one house must be built and maintained by the village for the village spirit, preferably on the highest slope in the area. Villages are controlled by a group of the oldest males in residence, from whom they elect a single representative to serve as the village headman. Election requirements vary but generally include superior leadership ability, experience, a large number of allies, and wealth. Among a small number of Lisu subgroups, such as the Black Lisu of Yunnan, the position of headman was hereditary rather than elected, and among all Lisu, class position, whether aristocrat, commoner, or slave, dictated who could and could not participate in leadership positions.

Wherever they live the Lisu are known as swidden farmers, who use fire to clear forest land for agriculture. Traditionally their most important crops were dry, upland rice for subsistence; corn to feed their pigs; and opium poppies for the market. This last item was eliminated by the Communist government of China starting in the early 1950s and has in recent decades been limited somewhat in Thailand as well, where several royal initiatives have targeted the production and consumption of drugs and replaced them with other economic and social activities. In addition in China the government has abolished the practice of swidden or slash-and-burn agriculture in favor of the irrigated fields and wet-rice agriculture of the Han.

In addition to village residence the other marker of social and political identity that matters in managing Lisu identity is membership in a patrilineal clan group or *zo*. These groups, membership in which is inherited from one's father, are exogamous and thus require every individual to marry outside his or her own clan. Each clan also has its own set of ancestral and other important spirits, religious rituals and beliefs, and clan names, usually derived from plants and animals, such as bees, hemp, fish, and bears. These clan names are now used as surnames. Although today these clans never act as a group, in the past the potential for interclan warfare and feuding was always present and occasionally realized. Accusations of witchcraft from a rival clan were also quite common and have not disappeared entirely from the Lisu experience of the world. As was the case in the past, clan members are considered the most trustworthy and reliable allies, neighbors, and friends, and relations between members are supposed to be marked by reciprocity and assistance.

Despite the preference for clan members' acting together, the rules of exogamy and residence generally mean that these are dispersed groups that never join in any corporate action. Immediately after marriage many Lisu couples move into the wife's father's home, a pattern called matrilocal residence, and work in his fields and homestead. In lieu of this work some men pay substantial bridewealth to their fathers-in-law, which allows the couple either to move in with the husband's parents or to establish a new, neolocal residence. After the period of bride service or working in his father-in-law's fields a man generally moves his young family into his own father's home or into a new home in the same village.

Whether it is made up of a couple and unmarried children or is an extended group of grandparents, parents, children, aunts, uncles, and other relatives, it is the household that forms the basic unit of production and consumption among Lisu generally. Taxation, contributions to collective labor projects such as digging wells and ponds, and ritual activities all draw upon household members and resources rather than on those of an individual. The oldest male generally represents his household to these larger units although today sometimes exceptions are made when younger men contribute far more wealth to the household economy.

Longshan culture

The Longshan culture is a Neolithic culture that was located along the Yellow (Huang) River in what are today Shandong, Henan, Shanxi, Shaanxi, and Inner Mongolia Provinces, China. Its approximate period of existence was 3000–1900 B.C.E., although the slightly shorter period of 2900–2000 B.C.E. has also been suggested by some archaeologists. The longer period can be divided into Early, 3000–2500 B.C.E.; Middle, 2500–2400 B.C.E.; and Late, 2400–1900 B.C.E., Longshan periods, with evidence of the three being found at Dinggong, Chengziya, and Taosi, respectively. Longshan culture has been described by many as the cultural inheritor of both the DAWENKOU CULTURE of the lower Yellow River basin and the YANGSHAO CULTURE of the region slightly to the west of Dawenkou.

The shift from Dawenkou to Longshan is marked by a number of cultural changes, the most important of which was a population move from small, scattered villages to walled towns; the first walled settlement in China was built as early as 4000 B.C.E. but it took about 1,000 years for that pattern to become the norm. Some of the towns that developed during the Longshan period were quite large, including Shijiahe, which is estimated to have had a population of between 15,000 and 50,000 people. All of these towns were built in a rectangular pattern with drainage systems to prevent flooding and buildings made from mud bricks. Sites like Shijiahe were at the top of a four-tiered system in which they administered smaller units below them, and so on, down to the smallest village. Yaowangcheng and Liangchengzhen, two very large Longshan settlements, would also have been at the top of this administrative tier, possibly even representing separate polities that saw each other as rivals and enemies.

It is not at all out of the realm of possibility that Yaowangchange, Liangchengzhen, Shijiahe, and the other Longshan towns and cities were enemies at the time of their zenith. All

Longshan walled settlements exhibit fortifications with rammed-earth walls and a great increase in the number of weapons left behind in relation to Dawenkou and Yangshao cultures. This evidence combined with several mass burials of people who died at the hands of others has led archaeologists to assume that the Longshan period was a fairly violent period of Chinese history.

In addition to an increase in violence Longshan culture differed from its predecessors in a number of other ways, but in general these differences were a matter of degree rather than of kind. For example while prior cultural periods had pottery, agriculture, and emerging class distinctions, these features all became more developed and widespread during the Longshan. Some of the wheel-produced pottery from this period is remarkable for its thin walls, some as thin as eggshells; black was the preferred color for pottery in this period. As had the pottery, other handicrafts of the period had reached a much higher state of professionalism than previously, including silk weaving, ivory and jade carving, and tool production. This last saw the introduction in this period of copper and, according to one source, early bronzework, both of which were used for decorations and jewelry as well as for tools.

In agriculture Longshan culture differed from Dawenkou culture in the improvements in techniques and seed types. Both broomcorn and foxtail millet were extremely important crops, supplemented by paddy rice, rape, hemp, and Chinese cabbage. Domesticated dogs, pigs, sheep, and cattle were also present during the Longshan period, with special emphasis on pigs. With these advancements in agriculture the roles of men and women in Longshan society are believed to differ from those of previous periods, where there was greater equality based on a shared workload. During the Longshan period men began to play a greater role in agriculture and tool production, leading to their higher social status compared to women's. This differentiation is parallel to the development of different social classes, which had begun during the Dawenkou period but expanded during the Longshan, when more consumer goods of high quality became available to those with the resources to make or acquire them. Grave sites show a marked increase in the difference between tombs of rich and poor, which would have developed out of the increasingly complex division of labor and possibly even private ownership of productive land.

While the exact religious beliefs of the people who created Longshan culture may never be known to us, their material remains do provide some insights into their religious practices. A large number of augury bones have been found from sheep, pigs, deer, and cattle; these indicate that divination, or discovering information from the supernatural world through a toss of the bones, was a common practice. That both domesticated and wild animals provided bones for this activity may indicate that each was used for a different purpose or was used by different kinds of diviners. Jade animal masks have also been found; these may point to an extensive system of beliefs concerning the supernatural power of animals, either in spirit or live form, to affect people's lives. Finally archaeologists have found a form of writing on sherds of pottery, known as ostraca, which may have been used as divination bones were to discover information from the spirits or other supernatural beings.

Lumad

Lumad, a Visayan word meaning "grown from the place" or native, is a collective term for 18 different tribal groups from the Filipino island of Mindanao. The term was adopted only in 1986 by representatives from the first 15 groups recognized as Lumad: Bagobo, Banwaon, Blaan, Dibabawon, Higaonon, MANDAYAS, Manguangan, MANOBOS, Mansaka, Subanen, Tagakaolo, Talaandig, Tboli, TIRURAYS, and Ubo peoples. Since that time the Ata, Mamanwa, and Tasaday have also been added to this list. Sometimes the term *Bukidnon* is also used to refer to the tribal peoples of that province and they are included in the umbrella category of Lumad.

GEOGRAPHY

Mindanao is the second-largest island in the Philippines and is the largest island by far in the southern, Mindanao region of the country. The southern half of the island is largely mountainous, with Mount Apo, the highest mountain in the country at 9,689 feet above sea level, looking down on the island's biggest city, Davao. The mountains are drained by several rivers including the Mindanao, Davao, and Tagum, which cross Cotabato and Davao Provinces. Because of its rugged terrain and combination of Muslim and tribal peoples it is often viewed by other Filipinos as a frontier area filled both with danger and potential.

LUMAD

location:
The highlands of Mindanao, the Philippines

time period:
3000 B.C.E. to the present, though the term was only officially adopted in 1986

ancestry:
Austronesian

language:
Each of the 18 subgroups speaks its own Austronesian language.

ORIGINS

The origins of the Lumad, as of all AUSTRO-NESIANS in the Philippines, are probably in south China, from which they sailed in double-outrigger dugout canoes about 5,000 years ago to Taiwan, and then later the Philippines and Polynesia. There is no certainty as to why this population left south China; however, archaeologists have hypothesized that it was a combination of population pressure, increased commerce from the Yangtze (Chang) River region of China and moving southward down the river and its tributaries, a growing demand for marine and tropical forest goods, and climate change.

Contemporary Austronesian languages can be subdivided into two distinct groups that separate the languages of Austronesian Taiwan from those of the remainder of the family, which include all Malay and Oceanic languages. This linguistic division, in addition to several anomalies in the archaeological record, such as a lack of rice in the earliest Austronesian sites in Taiwan, indicates that the origins of the Austronesian people may have been two separate exoduses from southeast China. If these did occur, the first exodus was probably from Fujian Province in China to Taiwan, which saw the rise of TA-P'EN-K'ENG CULTURE, with its distinctively marked pottery and stone tools, but without archaeological evidence of domesticated rice. The descendants of this first wave would be the contemporary speakers of Taiwan's Austronesian languages, the ABORIGINAL TAIWANESE people. The second exodus may have occurred around 3000 B.C.E., taking a second wave of Austronesian speakers from southeastern China to Taiwan and then almost immediately to Luzon in the Philippines around the same period. This second wave, with its red-slipped pottery, may also have been the ultimate source of the LAPITA CULTURE.

HISTORY

When they arrived in the Philippines about 3000 B.C.E. the Austronesian speakers would probably have met small bands of people who had already been residing on the islands for approximately 20,000 years. The hunting and gathering AETA peoples, as they are now called, probably lived in the most productive areas of the country, the coastlines, valleys, and lower hills, in very small, impermanent settlements. With their ability to grow their own crops the incoming Austronesians were able to maintain significantly higher population densities than the Aeta and thus to push the hunter-gatherers

---

Lumad time line

B.C.E.

3000 The initial migration of the Austronesian speakers, including the ancestors of the Lumad, to the Philippines.

C.E.

13th century Arab and Chinese Muslim traders establish contact with Sulu and most of the rest of the Mindanao region.

1527 The Spanish first set foot on Mindanao but in the following years establish control only over the north coast and Zamboanga.

1851 The Spanish achieve their first victory over the Sultanate of Sulu and begin to incorporate the Mindanao region into the remainder of their Filipino colony. They do not complete this project prior to losing the colony to the United States.

1860 Mindanao and the surrounding islands officially become a province of the Spanish Philippines but very few changes are felt by either Muslim lowlanders or tribal highlanders.

1899 The Spanish cede the Philippines to the United States and local wars of independence break out. In Mindanao these are often referred to as the Moro Wars.

1902 A civil U.S. administration replaces military rule upon the pacification of the independence fighters in the north.

1906 Davao's governor Bolton is murdered by the Bagobos, and the larger Tungud movement led by struggling Lumad peoples of Davao spreads to other provinces.

1913 The Americans defeat Muslim resistance fighters in the decisive Battle of Bud Bagsak; however, the Muslim population of the islands to this day has continued the struggle for independence.

1920 The Bureau of Non-Christian Tribes takes over control of Mindanao and its surrounding islands.

1926–27 The Subanen Lumad tribe rises up against the Americans.

1941 The Japanese occupy the Philippines during World War II and many Lumad groups continue their struggle for independence from outside control.

1944 The United States retakes the Philippines.

1945 The Philippines attain independence from the United States.

1967 The Muslim National Liberation Front, founded by Nur Misuari, takes up the centuries-long struggle for independence from the Philippines. It later splits into a variety of subgroups that continue the fight into the present.

1986 The term *Lumad* is adopted by 15 tribal communities from Mindanao and made official by Republic Act 6734, signed by new Filipino president, Corazon Aquino.

---

into the more marginal highland forests and mountaintops, where they still live today. The numerically and technologically stronger agriculturalists also seem to have lent their language to the Aeta, all of whom today speak Austronesian languages rather than the more ancient languages they would have taken with them in their much earlier migrations.

Although they lived on swidden agriculture, many groups of Austronesians followed the Aeta into the highlands of both Luzon and Mindanao, where they lived in ways very similar to those of their lowland linguistic cousins. Prior to the Spanish colonial era all Austronesians practiced the same kind of animistic religions and intercommunity trade and lived in small tribal communities with a chief or elder as the main authority figure. Many of these communities, especially in the mountains, shifted every few years when all of the land around them had been used for rice and other produce and needed to lie fallow for a period before being cut, burned, and planted again.

Generally when speaking of the Philippines the year 1521 with the arrival of the Spanish is noted as a period of great cultural, political, and economic changes among the Austronesian lowlanders that served to distinguish them greatly from the highlanders. Most lowlanders adopted Christianity fairly quickly in the colonial era as well as some other aspects of Spanish social life. The large number of Mestizos, people of mixed indigenous and Spanish descent, living in the lowlands served to hasten these changes in many areas. For the communities that did not convert the most viable option for survival was to flee into the highlands to escape the reach of the Spanish administrators and priests. In Mindanao, however, this process was somewhat different since a colonizing Arab force had already moved through the area and driven some of the nonconverts into the highlands. Today it is difficult to say which Lumad peoples are highlanders because they fled from the Arabs and Spanish in the 13th through 17th centuries and which were there before that period, and in many ways it is not important. What is important is that it was in these centuries and those that followed that Lumad and other highlander cultures began to take shape as distinct from those in the rest of the archipelago.

Another important difference between Mindanao and the rest of the Philippines is the difficulty the Spanish encountered when faced with large numbers of lowlanders who had previously converted to Islam and pledged their loyalty to the sultans of the area. The Spanish set foot on the island for the first time in 1527 but for more than 300 years were not able to consolidate their rule over the entire region. The northern coast and Zamboanga were the extent of their domain there, and the rest of the region remained essentially independent until the mid-19th century. In their smallholding the Spanish referred to both the FILIPINO MUSLIMS or Moro peoples and the tribal highlanders as *infieles* or infidels and treated both groups with contempt.

The year 1851 marked the first Spanish victory over the sultanate of Sulu, but in the peace treaty that followed faulty translations led to considerable further conflict. In Spanish the text stated that the region was to be incorporated into the Spanish Empire while in the Sulu text it called for an "agreement and union." In 1860 the Spanish made their new southern territories into a province of the larger Philippines but for the following 39 years were able to enter their province only with a military force; it has since been referred to as a "paper province." The Spanish loss of the Philippines to the United States in 1898 did not change the situation greatly in the southern part of the archipelago; the Muslim population continued to struggle for independence in the Moro Wars, which officially lasted until 1912, and the highlanders likewise resisted incorporation into the state. Small-scale rebellions in the region, such as the murder of the governor of Davao in 1906 by the Lumad Bagobo tribe, meant that the regular American colonial apparatus of the Department of Mindanao and Sulu was unable to handle the situation and the United States turned it over to the Bureau of Non-Christian Tribes. As the Spanish before them the Americans saw the Muslims and the highlanders as equivalent because both refused to submit to a plantation economy, American-style education, or Christianization.

Filipino independence following World War II caused widespread Christian immigration to Mindanao, which saw the percentage of people in the region of Muslim or Lumad descent fall dramatically with the overall population increase of more than 700 percent from 1950 to 1980. Indigenous property rights in the highlands have been one of the most important losses experienced by the Lumad when the central government opened their land to migration by the central and western VISAYANS, a process actually begun during the American era when both Dole and Del Monte plantations had displaced some Blaan, Higaonon, Talaandig, and Banwaon communities. Since 1950 logging companies have been the greatest threat to Lumad communities, especially in the Pulangi watershed, home to Bukidnons, Talaandigs, Manobos, and a number of other Lumad peoples. Both the removal of more than 90 percent of old-growth forests and the resulting degradation of both land and water sources have meant that there is very little space available for these communities to maintain their way of life. Many have had to adopt a lowland agricultural pattern or to work as unskilled labor for the many companies operating in the area.

CULTURE

All Lumad peoples were traditionally swidden agriculturalists who burned secondary forest growth and used the resulting ash as their only fertilizer. This form of agriculture is also called slash-and-burn or extensive, for the extensive amount of land it requires for a relatively small population. Each Lumad community collectively held its land and other resources, making them available to families as needed. Land and nature more generally were considered sacred, and both farming and hunting required extensive religious rituals to request permission from the spirits and ancestors to use their resources and to thank them in return. Kinship and residence were the primary organizing principles of the Lumad prior to the modern era, although each group had its own kinship system and pattern of residence. Most Lumad were led by a local chief or *datu;* however, there were exceptions to this rule, as among the Mandayas, who were led by a military or warrior figure called a *bagani.*

Since the start of the Spanish colonial era in the 16th century some Lumad groups have been involved in the struggle for independence in the region in some form. Both Moro militias and the New People's Army, the military wing of the Communist Party of the Philippines, have had some success in recruiting among some Lumad peoples with the promise of land rights to territory considered by the Lumad as their ancestral domains.

FURTHER READING

William C. Hall. *Aspects of Western Subanon Formal Speech* (Arlington: University of Texas at Arlington, 1987).

Lynda Angelica N. Reyes. *The Textiles of Southern Philippines: The Textile Traditions of the Bagobo, Mandaya and Bilaan from Their Beginnings to the 1900s* (Quezon City: University of the Philippines Press, 1992).

Lushai   *See* MIZO.